# THE
# OUTLINE HISTORY
# OF THE WORLD

.SUBLIME EMBODIMENT OF WHAT AUGUSTUS MEANT FOR THE ROMAN WORLD

Peace was what the Roman world above all longed for, and the success of Octavian and his system is best explained by this one fact—that he gave it peace. This splendid statue embodies the feelings of his subjects towards him; he stands, majestic, already 'Augustus' in name and fact, wearing a cuirass on which the Earth is shown rejoicing in the blessings of peace, though a Parthian victory symbolises his frontier successes.   (See Chapter 10.)

*Vatican Museum ; photo, Anderson*

# THE
# OUTLINE HISTORY
# OF THE WORLD

A Record of World Events
from the Earliest Historical
Times to the Present Day

Edited by
## SIR J. A. HAMMERTON
Editor of The Universal History of the World

*Illustrated with nearly*
*ONE THOUSAND HISTORICAL DOCUMENTS*
*AND MAPS*

LONDON
THE AMALGAMATED PRESS LTD

Printed in Great Britain by The Amalgamated Press, Ltd., London.

# PREFACE

THE continuous story of world events, the pageant of history, rather than the study of the inwardness of these events or the slow unfolding of cultural processes in the lives of races, is the aim of this work. Hence one should emphasize the fact that it is offered to the public as an *outline* of WORLD history. Indeed, the double emphasis is needed to remind the reader, in the first instance, that he must not expect any amplification of detail in what is offered as an Outline, and in the second, that an effort has been made to chronicle all the epoch-making events and briefly to sketch the dominating personalities throughout the six thousand years of recorded history.

THUS anyone desirous of following in detail the history of the British Isles, for example, is by implication warned to look elsewhere. And yet I am prepared to assert that, scanty though British history may appear in these pages, it is not too meagre for the rôle which our country has so far played in world history. Not even the critical reader will find, in a close examination of our text, that any matter of true world importance has been neglected, although I am ready to hear that someone has looked in vain for the names of certain kings of Scotland and England and of other European countries, for catastrophes and " battles long ago." That these are missing may be taken as an indication of how little they affected the course of the history of the world.

FOR I would impress upon my readers that a considerable and uncommon task has been attempted here. I am not aware of any single volume published in recent years wherein any writer or group of writers has tried to cover so much ground. The reading public is here offered a work that, without treating as drama what must at best remain the raw material of drama, deals in chronological order with all the vital facts which historians are agreed upon as providing the basis of world history. Not indeed to record these in the dull and lifeless manner of the annalist, but with as much liveliness and interesting detail as can be contrived within certain limits of space. What measure of success has been attained the reader must be left to judge.

BY dividing our record of world events into ten eras, following upon a brief sketch of the prehistoric world, I may be held to have given at least the semblance of dramatic form to what is inchoate and lacking in unity. But in order to present any shapely statement of historic facts some sort of order must be imposed upon the facts and it seemed to me, after a careful examination of world history, that some such division into sections and sub-sections—for that, in effect, is what my arrangement of eras and chapters amounts to—was desirable in order to make comprehensible to the reader in a relatively brief narrative so large a subject as universal history.

I AM not anxious that these ten eras should have general acceptance as the best and most natural divisions of historical time. They are merely one editor's idea of how the events and the facts of history present themselves to him, and as such they are as useful for the purpose in hand as any other series of divisions that could be suggested. No more than that is claimed for them.

BUT I do not think that any reader who wishes to acquire a useful general knowledge of the main events in the recorded history of the world will turn unsatisfied from our pages, although he may well wish to amplify his knowledge of the past by studying the manifestations of human thought, energy and aspiration which every age of the world has presented, but which can be surveyed only in a work of approximately eight to ten times the dimension of the present one : such a work as I have already carried out with the assistance of some 150 collaborators in " The Universal History of the World."

I NEED scarcely draw the reader's attention to the extensive series of synchronised tables of dates which accompany the different chapters. It will be obvious to anyone that an immense amount of careful research and compilation has gone to their preparation. Hardly any event of historic importance can have escaped the vigilance of the compilers, and these very useful tables form a valuable addition to our narrative in enabling the reader not only to " date " any important event or personality but to " place " either of these in relationship to contemporary events and persons.

THE illustrating of our " Outline History of the World " called for much con-sideration and, as its pages will testify, a vast amount of research. If there is another single volume of history that contains a thousand illustrations, each one an authentic historical document and not merely the invention of an illustrator, I am not aware of it. The value of these illustrations, which appear here in their order of time and in close association with the text to which they refer, is certainly not less, and perhaps it may even be more than that of the narrative itself, despite all the care and learning with which that has been prepared.

To be placed in possession of authentic pictures which illustrate historical details, the personalities of kings and conquerors, of great statesmen and empire builders, of contemporary scenes and of ancient monuments, is to have the mind vivified with truthful impressions of the periods and personalities under discussion and in this way, even if our narrative should lack the glamour of a Gibbon's, it gains from association with these pictorial documents something more graphic than the written word can supply, even when it is written by the hand of genius, something that brings the reader more intimately in touch with the event or the personality. The numerous original maps introduced into the text should also be of great use to the reader in aiding him to visualize the topographical background of the events described. In some cases they offer, almost at a glance, as much information as would call for many pages of text adequately to convey.

J. A. H.

# CONTENTS

# THE OUTLINE HISTORY OF THE WORLD

## Introductory Sketch

## BEFORE HISTORY BEGAN

HISTORIANS approaching the task of compiling a world history may do so with equal propriety and success in any one of a dozen different ways. A favourite study of our time is Economics, and by limiting his enquiry to the economic condition of the earth and its inhabitants throughout all the known ages of their existence a competent economist—provided that he stated his facts in an effective manner—might write a history of absorbing interest, from which nothing that was vital to our knowledge of the world need be excluded. Indeed, by concentrating upon some well-defined line of enquiry and following it faithfully through all times and countries a true universality of treatment is most easily attained. The story of man's sheltering places, from the cave dwelling of prehistory to the luxury hotel of today, would be true " world history " as distinct from any, and even the most voluminous, history of the purely national and political kind. The history of religion, of any one human institution, let it be kingship or slavery, the history of art, of the chase, of literature, of anything common to all peoples, implies in each case a world interest and if adequately presented should create in the mind of the reader a large and impressive concept of humanity.

How men and events react and interact is a theme that offers of itself a wide field for investigation, the result of which could do no more than elucidate but one branch of historical study. Although a study so specialised does not enter into our present scheme, events and men will chiefly engage us, for our purpose is to present in one continuous and orderly narrative all the events of world importance since the first " syllable of recorded time " ; to produce, as it were, a pageant of history which shall have all the world for its stage and for its players the men and women whose names are evocative of great events of the past.

But even to attempt in outline a sequential story of historical events demands at least a preliminary peep into the mysterious unrecorded past of our planet : a realm of fascinating investigation which is shared today by the astronomer, the mathematician, the geologist and the archaeologist, of whose continuous and surprising discoveries the historian must content himself with being recorder. Such a glimpse of the prehistoric world this chapter is designed to supply as briefly as may be, so that our proper business of recording and illustrating the known events of history may proceed.

IN the days, not so far distant, when one single act of creation was held to have brought man and the Universe simultaneously into existence much as we see them now, it was possible to write an apparently reasonable history of man and his world that took no account of the other 'histories,' of natural history or astronomy or geology, or of that still more recent science called anthropology.

Today our whole outlook on these matters is profoundly altered. We now know that for millions of millions of years this universe of matter, a mere handful of whose brighter bodies star the sky at night, was evolving before our tiny world was born—an event of yesterday in stellar history ; that our Sun is just a small star among the stars ; that even compared with the Earth's brief story the life of Man upon it is like the last few seconds of a long day ; and that only during about

1

a fiftieth part of his existence has Man been leaving conscious records.

## Mysterious Beginning of Things

No limit can be set to the age of the Universe. It is impossible to imagine a distribution of matter and energy that might not have had an antecedent stage of development. But such marvellous strides have been made by astronomy that today it is possible to suggest a round number of years during which the oldest star visible to us can have existed as a star. The figure is 200 million million ; and on this scale our Sun would be between 7 and 8 million million years old.

Before the longer period, it seems, every star that we know must have been part of a nebula. Thousands of these clouds of tenuous gas may still be observed, scattered through the heavens at all stages of what appears to be a slow but progressive and universal development, and the comparison of one with another so patiently, so ingeniously made by our modern astronomers, leads to the conclusion that they are shrinking, rotating and condensing, and that a colony of stars is the ultimate product of each.

Are planets, such as our Earth, born from stars in the same manner ? So it was once thought, but physical facts do not support the view. According to the theory of Sir J. H. Jeans, a star acquires a family of planets, not slowly and inevitably, but by what is probably a rare and sudden accident—the near approach of another heavenly body which, by its gravitational pull, drags the planets out of the body of their parent. Such a catastrophe once happened to our Sun.

How long ago this event took place it is impossible to say with exactitude ; but as radioactivity demands at least 1,500 million years since the solidification of the Earth's crust, and as there is reason to think that this process did not take long (on an astronomical time-scale), perhaps an estimate of 2,000 million years would not be far wrong.

## Life's First Emergence on Earth

Vast figures like these convey little by themselves ; let it be said then that, compared with the age of the Sun given above, the age of the Earth is as the length of the last brick in the last house in a street more than half a mile long. Even to realize this, it is necessary to think consciously of a familiar street and then gaze at a brick wall.

From the moment of the appearance of life on the Earth we can trace its evolution with some approach to certainty ; how it appeared is still a matter for conjecture. But a surprising number of most interesting facts bearing on the question has been accumulated by chemist and biologist, and the geologist of today can trace the history of the Earth through the great epochs of its development with an approximation to accuracy that was almost unthinkable fifty years ago.

The divisions of geological time are grouped into four eras, for which varying names have found acceptance. As considerable confusion often results, the two schemes of nomenclature most commonly in use may be set side by side, with the meaning of the second in a third column :

|  |  | Era of : |
|---|---|---|
| Archaean .. | Pampalaeozoic.. | Primeval Life |
|  | (or Eozoic) |  |
| Primary .. | Palaeozoic .. | Ancient ,, |
| Secondary .. | Mesozoic .. | Middle ,, |
| Tertiary } Quaternary } | Cainozoic .. | Recent ,, |

## Epochs of Geological History

THE first set of terms applies more specially to the types of rock, the second to the living species that characterise each Era ; but they are interchangeable, and indeed there is little valid distinction between them because of the number of rocks that owe their origin to organic agencies. These agencies have usually been lowly forms of types that still provide by far the greatest quantity of living matter in the world today, though they were the first of all to evolve ; but with the emergence of backboned animals in the Palaeozoic Era the story of that progressive minority, the higher forms of life, begins to unfold itself and to fascinate the modern student.

In the meantime, however, while species were multiplying, growing, flourishing and dying out, or else evolving into more complex varieties, the great processes of earth-building were still going on. The crust was shrinking and folding, mountains were being upraised and planed down again by water and wind and ice, continents rising and sinking. The fact that in that immensely remote age of the Earth's development those minerals were formed which were eventually to prove of inestimable use to Man when he appeared on the face of the globe need not be held to involve the question of a design in nature, which, at any rate, is outside the scope of this History.

### The Upward Urge of Life

IN rocks of the Palaeozoic Era the earliest fossils are encountered. First they are of low, shell-fish forms that had adopted a stony armour to protect them against carnivorous foes, then of horny-coated crustacea, the trilobites. Next on the upward ladder came the fish, with a backbone and internal skeleton. It was one group of these which, forced from the shrinking lakes during a long epoch of drought, developed lungs and limbs and so evolved into the amphibian inhabitants of the great Coal Forests.

The same climatic change that blotted out the rank vegetation of these forests probably stimulated certain amphibia to take the momentous step of severing their dependence on water and becoming completely terrestrial. At any rate there were reptiles on the Earth before the close of the Era of Ancient Life, though their great age of ascendancy was the Era of Middle Life when monsters of all shapes and sizes were undisputed masters of every element. In the same way mammalian forms had actually evolved at the beginning of this middle era, though they were of little account until the reptiles vanished with the dawn of the Era of Recent Life.

The world now began to assume a vaguely familiar appearance. The outlines of the present continents took shape, though there were many land-bridges where today is sea. Indeed the degree of resemblance to modern conditions has provided the names for the periods into which this Era is divided, so that we speak of the Eocene, Oligocene, Miocene and Pliocene periods, implying the "dawn" of modern conditions, little modern, not very modern and more modern ; while the Pleistocene, meaning most modern, is regarded by anthropologists as the first period of a new Era called the Quaternary, whose second period, the Holocene or entirely modern, includes today.

QUITE early in the Era of Recent Life there emerged a group of little creatures in which we take a pardonably exclusive interest, for they were probably the ancestors of some hitherto undiscovered ape that in its turn gave rise to the modern anthropoids and to Man himself. They are known as the Tarsioids. Their living representatives are the tarsiers.

The intermediate ape has so far yielded no certainly identified fossils. Not so primitive man. We now have remains—crania, thighbones, teeth—dating back to the late Pliocene and early Pleistocene, and belonging to creatures that walked erect and had a brain capacity far larger than that of any known ape. Whether mankind today, admitted to form a single species (Homo sapiens), is directly descended from these early types is highly doubtful.

### Human Species now Extinct

WITH a later group the question of species, however, becomes more acute. Between these earliest bones and the first men who dwelt in caves, and whose remains are therefore preserved in fair numbers, there stretch aeons of time represented by strata that yield flint implements of primitive manufacture. Their makers dwelt on the drifts beside river margins. But when we come to the cave men we have to deal with creatures whose humanity is undoubted and whose intelligence must have been of a very high order. It is nevertheless stated that they were a collateral, now extinct, offshoot from the human stem, constituting a separate species called Homo neanderthalensis, from the Neander Valley near Düsseldorf where they were first found.

But before taking up the story of Homo sapiens it were well to glance back at two separate questions hitherto ignored because of the difficulty of giving anything like positive answers. What time-relation do our four geological eras bear to the 1,500 million years postulated for the age of the solid Earth, and how long ago did Man evolve ? Secondly, can any reason be given for his intellectual climb out of the ruck of the other mammals ?

Arguing from the thickness of strata geologists are inclined to say that the Primeval Era must have lasted four times as long as the other three put together, the Palaeozoic half as long again as the other two, and the Mesozoic more than three times as long as the Cainozoic. If we allow 30 million years for the Cainozoic, this just accounts for our 1,500 million ; but it must be admitted that some scientists, more especially the zoologists, are only prepared to give the Cainozoic two million—which is the sort of discrepancy that must be expected in the present state of our knowledge.

Sir Arthur Keith, our greatest anthropologist, adopts the lower figure ; so that

as the oldest discovered human remains are referred to late Pliocene times, Man is on this basis *at least* 300,000 years old. Moreover, as this only takes us back a short way into the Cainozoic, the estimate would serve almost as well on the longer reckoning.

Now the Earth towards the end of Pliocene times underwent what is known as a glacial epoch. The ice-caps spread outwards from the poles, the mountain ranges were laden with snow and great glaciers ground their way down the valleys to cover the plains with ice. Much

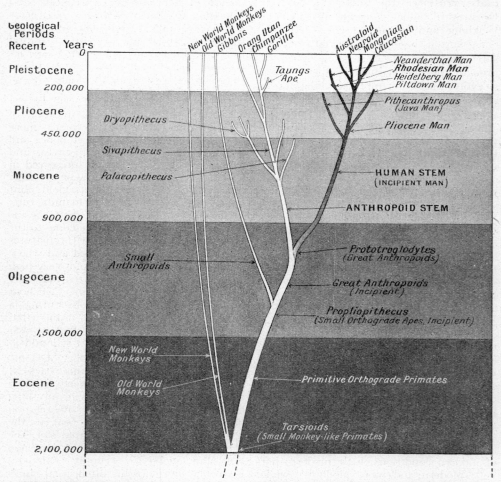

**THE COMMON GENEALOGICAL TREE OF MANKIND, ANTHROPOIDS AND MONKEYS**

This diagram, prepared by Sir Arthur Keith, gives us an idea of the ages during which Man has been evolving and of his lowly origin. It will be seen how early the branches of the apes and the monkeys, springing from a common trunk, became differentiated, and how the former in turn split into the anthropoid and the human stems. The way in which some species of Man, such as the Java, Piltdown and Neanderthal, have become extinct is also clearly indicated.

of Europe then experienced Arctic conditions and Pliocene man vanished.

## When Mankind Lived in Caves

THE Ice Age, however, was not a homogeneous phenomenon. Several times throughout the Pleistocene · the ice advanced and retreated, with quite clement conditions in the intervals. The first long warm interval was the great age of the drift-dwellers, as we can tell from their flint implements ; but during a subsequent glaciation we find a group spreading into Europe along the borders of the ice and apparently acclimatised to cold conditions—the Neanderthalers already mentioned. They were presumably drift-dwellers who had learnt to combat the rigours of the cold by taking to caves and making fire. May it not be that the Ice Age, with its stimulus to invention and adaptation, is responsible for the great intellectual advance of which the Neanderthalers are the earliest example ?

Of course, these changes of climatic environment must have had suitable material to work upon. No other mammal was thereby stimulated to a progress comparable with that of Man, who for ages had used stone weapons, and could probably already speak.

It was in a warmer period, after the worst of the Glacial Epoch was spent, that modern men first came upon the European stage and so enter our ken. They probably spread in successive waves from North Africa and south-western Asia, districts that are now largely desert but received sufficient rain to make them habitable grasslands when the ice was over Europe. Neanderthal man retreated northward with the colder climate to which he was accustomed, or perhaps was exterminated.

## First Advent of Modern Men

EUROPE, though no longer Arctic, was still fairly cold steppe-land, with the rigours of a continental climate unmodified by extensive forests ; and these new men were cave-dwellers like their predecessors. But they had great intellectual potentialities, and towards the end of their period there was a tremendous outburst of art. Bows and arrows appear, and probably also clothing and artificial dwellings of wood or skins.

Society was probably organized by these early food-gatherers on family lines, for man seems to have inherited the idea of the family-society from his ancestors the apes, and the older theory of a primitive horde is now no longer held.

THE phrase " food-gatherers " brings us to the next event in human evolution. Somewhere near the Euphrates and the Nile the discovery was made that food could be produced as well as gathered ; in other words, cultivation of crops began. It used to be thought that this was preceded by a pastoral and nomadic stage, but more probably pastoralism was in most cases a secondary accompaniment of agriculture.

Agriculture brought in its train a whole host of other inventions. The arts of weaving and of pottery were elaborated. Stones were ground instead of chipped, and so flint was no longer used exclusively. This interest in other minerals led to the discovery of copper and of its alloy bronze. The necessity of tending the crops made for more permanent settlements. Villages and finally cities arose, and the advantage of organized work—irrigation, especially—led to the establishment of kingship.

Religion we may also regard as having begun at this stage. Of course, it is largely a question of nomenclature, for there is plenty of evidence for supernatural beliefs among the food-gatherers. But the four elements that seem to make up religion—magic, fear, ethics and a learned priesthood—had not before now been fused.

## How Religion First Came to Be

THE primitive hunters believed that Nature could be influenced by imitation—that prey, for instance, could be ensured by representing a successful hunt in make-believe. Hence magic. Misfortune was apt to be connected with anything unusual—thunder, a strange rock—and the weapon of magic used to avert it. But causation implies an idea of will and personality. Hence gods. At this stage magicians and witch-doctors might arise, but scarcely priests. There is reason to think that divinity was only attributed to the more regular manifestations of Nature, such as heavenly bodies, with the introduction of agriculture, and that the gods did not receive human form without the analogy of the kingship or of deified ancestral heroes. Finally, religion was born when the tribal god was made guardian and sponsor of the tribal ethics, which are still completely separable from religion in certain backward races, and no less strict on that account.

### When Agriculture was Invented

THE date to which we must assign the invention of agriculture has been one of the most vexed questions among anthropologists. It was once the fashion to throw it back into a remote past ; but while modern research has greatly extended the antiquity of Man, it tends to bring agriculture down to comparatively recent times, say 7,000-10,000 years ago.

Meanwhile modern man, still in the food-gathering stage, had occupied the rest of the habitable globe, including the New World. Among his communities there slowly spread the ' invention-complex ' of the food-producers, in ever widening circles from the original centres in south-western Asia and Egypt, favoured in her possession of the annually flooded Nile ; but communications were bad and Man conservative, and at first there penetrated little more than scraps and shreds.

The spread of the forests, for instance, had caused a period of misfortune to overtake the old homeland of the European hunter-artists. Their cultural descendants still eked out a miserable life on the shores of the North Sea with a diet of shell-fish, while agricultural folk, whether newcomers or not, made way in the clearer zones. But the equipment of these latter did not include the knowledge of metal, only the improved treatment of stone ; so that we speak of a Neolithic or New Stone Age, though the term should be used with great reserve except when applied to Europe.

This word, Neolithic, is used in contradistinction to the previous Palaeolithic or Old Stone Age ; both are archaeological terms referring to methods of flint-working. As we have seen, a more significant division for historical purposes is into drift-dwellers and cave-dwellers (both food-gathering), and settlement-dwellers (food-producing) ; yet a proper insight into the successive styles of stone-working is of immense importance, for it is almost entirely on these more durable specimens of his handiwork that we base our knowledge of pre-record man.

### Beginning of Recorded History

IT was in Egypt and Mesopotamia less than 6,000 years ago that Man first began to leave conscious records, and ' prehistory ' came to an end. But there are areas today where in all essentials the native inhabitants are still pre-record men. Moreover, in the remotest of these areas they are still food-gatherers, even if possessing stray elements of a higher culture ; and indeed so primitive that they may be used to illustrate the prehistory of more advanced races.

However, as we are concerned in this Outline History mainly with the marshalling and recording of the known facts in the development of the nations of the world, their flourishing and decay, rather than with the data and speculations of anthropology, we shall follow the stream of history proper, from the headwater at which we have arrived, and content ourselves with this very cursory glance at the prehistoric world.

# First Era

## EARLY CIVILIZATIONS

### 4000 B.C.–550 B.C.

---

Chapter 1
TWILIGHT, 4000—1580 B.C.

Chapter 2
DAWN, 1580—900 B.C.

Chapter 3
DAYLIGHT, 900—550 B.C.

---

THIS division of our work comprises the First Era of record history ; it narrates the growth and collapse of the ancient empires down to the first flowering of Hellenism and the entry of Persia on to the world's stage, thus preparing it for the epic contest between these two rival cultures. As for dates, all that lie before 1580 B.C.— the concern of Chapter 1—are the merest approximations ; thereafter, world chronology, within a year or two, gives rise to no serious disputes.

# First Era: 4000-550 B.C.

# SYNCHRONISED TABLE OF DATES

| *Egypt and the West* | Chapter 1. 4000—1580 B.C. | *Mesopotamia and the East* |

| B.C. | Egypt and the West | Mesopotamia and the East | B.C. |
|---|---|---|---|
| 4241 | Invention of Solar Calendar in Egypt? | Sumerians established in Babylonia. | c. 4000 |
|  | Predynastic period: Upper and Lower Kingdoms. | Semitic Dynasties recorded at Kish. |  |
| c. 3800 | Brick cemeteries in Egypt. Copper in use. | Sumerian Dynasties recorded at Erech, Ur, etc. |  |
|  | Early Minoan Period I in Crete: Bronze in use. |  |  |
| 3400 | First Egyptian Dynasty; Narmer (Menes?) combines Upper and Lower Kingdoms. Memphis refounded. | Ur-Nina, priest-prince of Lagash. | c. 3000 |
| 2980- 2900 | Third Egyptian Dynasty (Khasekhemui). Memphis made capital. First Stone Pyramid (Zeser). | Eannatum of Lagash. | c. 2925 |
|  | Sneferu conquers Sinaitic Peninsula. | Lagash at war with Umma. Stele of Vultures. |  |
| 2900- 2750 | Great Pyramid Age in Egypt (Khufu and Khafra—Fourth Dynasty). | First contemporary records. |  |
|  | Crete: Early Minoan II. | Entemena of Lagash. | c. 2350 |
| c. 2870 | First City of Troy. |  |  |
|  |  | Urukagina of Lagash. | 2781 |
|  |  | Conquests of Lugal-zaggisi. | 2775 |
| 2750 | Fifth Dynasty. Pharaohs thenceforth deified. | Sargon founds Agade; Semitic Empire. | 2750 |
|  |  | Pamba, Hittite king ruling at Hattusas. | c. 2670 |
|  |  | Stele of Naram-Sin. |  |
|  |  | Inroad of Gutians into Babylonia; period of anarchy. | 2542- 2416 |
|  |  | Gudea of Lagash. | c. 2450 |
| 2430 | End of 'Old Kingdom' in Egypt; first interregnum of anarchy. | Aryan migrations in progress; dates uncertain. |  |
|  |  | Independent kings of Assyria: Ushpia and Kikia. | c. 2400 |
|  | Heracleopolitan usurpers; invasion of Asiatics. | Sumerian Empire under Ur-Engur at Ur. | 2409 |
|  | Crete: Early Minoan III. | First Babylonian Dynasty (Semitic). | 2225 |
| 2160 | 'Middle Kingdom' begins with Eleventh Dynasty. Thebes the capital. Bronze now common. | Hammurabi at Babylon. (Code, 2090). | 2123- 2030 |
|  | Crete: Middle Minoan I. | Kassite raid. | 2072 |
|  |  | Dynasty of 'Sea Country' Kings; hostilities with Babylon. | 2070 |
| 2000 | Twelfth dynasty. Great revival of Egyptian Art. | Expansion of Hittites under Hattusil I. | 2000 |
|  | Crete: Middle Minoan II. | Hittite raid on Babylon under Mursil I. | 1926 |
| 1788 | Succession of weak dynasties in Egypt; second interregnum of anarchy. |  |  |
|  | Middle Minoan III in Crete. | Kassite conquest of Babylon, and Dynasty. | 1746 |
|  | Hyksos conquest of Egypt—two dynasties; introduction of war-chariot. | Establishment of Mitannian kingdom on Upper Euphrates (now or earlier). | 1700 |
| 1600 | Egyptian war of liberation; Seventeenth Dynasty ruling at Thebes. | Assyria independent and overlord of Middle Euphrates. |  |
| 1580 | Expulsion of Hyksos by Thebans. Aahmes founds 'New Kingdom.' Crete: Late Minoan I. |  |  |

| *Egypt and the West* | Chapter 2. 1580—900 B.C. | *Mesopotamia and the East* |

| B.C. | Egypt and the West | Mesopotamia and the East | B.C. |
|---|---|---|---|
| 1580 | 'New Kingdom' of Egypt. First Empire. | Kassite Dynasty still reigning in Babylon. |  |
| 1543 | Thothmes I marches to Euphrates |  | 1543 |
| 1501- 1479 | Reigns of Thothmes II, Queen Hatshepsut and Thothmes III. Expedition to Punt. |  |  |
| 1479 | Battle of Megiddo. |  | 1479 |
| 1474 | Thothmes III reconquers Syria and crosses Euphrates. |  | 1474 |
| 1412-1360 | Development of diplomatic relations between Egypt, Babylon, Mitanni, Hittites, Assyria. |  | 1412-1360 |
|  |  | Growth of Hittite power under Subbiluliuma. | 1395- 1350 |
| 1375- 1358 | Religious reforms of Akhnaton. | Ashur-uballit; Assyrian activity begins. | 1381 |
|  | Akhetaton founded at Tell-el-Amarna |  |  |
|  | Crete: Late Minoan II and III. |  |  |
|  | Period of the Amarna Letters |  |  |
| 1358 | Tutankhamen. |  |  |
|  | Disruption of Egyptian possessions in Syria; End of First Empire. |  |  |
|  | Crete: Sea Power of 'King Minos'? |  |  |
| 1350- 1321 | Internal reforms of Harmhab. | Accession of Mursil III to Hittite throne | 1345 |
|  |  | Accession of Mutallis | 1320 |
| 1321 | Second Empire: Rameses I. Hittite and Egyptian contests in Syria. | Adad-nirari I of Assyria; defeats Kassites. | 1315 |
| 1296 | Battle of Kadesh between Rameses II and Mutallis. |  | 1296 |
| 1280 | An 'uti possidetis' peace between Hittites and Egyptians. |  | 1280 |
|  |  | Shalmaneser I; conquests in Asia Minor. | 1276 |
|  | Iron in use in Egypt. | Tukulti-Ninurta of Assyria; wars with Hittites; defeats Kassites. | 1256 |
| 1225 | Merneptah: reputed Pharaoh of Exodus. | Great migrations of northern peoples; Philistine invasion and settlement. | c.1200 |
| 1221 | First Raid on Egypt by 'Peoples of the Sea.' | Extinction of Hittite power. |  |
| 1190 | Second Raid by 'Peoples of the Sea'; Philistines defeated in sea battle. | Ashur-dan of Assyria breaks Kassite power. | 1174 |
|  | Achaean expansion. Fall of Troy. | Babylonian raid on Assyria; Assyrian relapse. | 1107 |
| 1090 | End of Egyptian Empire; disruption. |  |  |
|  | Dorian expansion. | Hebrew kingdom: Saul. | c.1025 |
|  |  | Aryan domination in Northern India. |  |
| 947 | Shashank (Shishak) founds Twenty-second Dynasty and reunites Egypt; Bubastis the capital. | Disruption of Hebrew kingdom. | 945 |
|  | Nubia independent. |  |  |
| 930 | Shashank invades Palestine and captures Jerusalem | and captures Jerusalem | 930 |
|  |  | Adad-nirari II; revival of Assyria. | 911 |

| Egypt and the West | Mesopotamia and the East |
|---|---|
| **B.C.** | **B.C.** |
| c. 900 Etruscan and Latin penetration of Italy ? | |
| Homeric poems. | Assyrian chronological record begins. 893 |
| Development of Greek city states. | Tukulti-Ninurta II ; wars with Urartu (Armenia) ; 889– |
| | recovery of Assyrian power. 884 |
| 884 Laws of Lycurgus, Sparta (traditional). | Ashur-nasir-pal II marches to Mediterranean. 876 |
| 860 Thebes and the Delta under independent rule. | |
| | Syrian confederation headed by Ben-Hadad ; alliance 853 |
| | with Ahab of Israel ; battle with Shalmaneser |
| | III at Karkar. |
| 800 Carthage founded (traditional). | Civil wars in Assyria. 827 |
| 776 First Olympiad ; Greek Chronology. | Order restored in Assyria. 821 |
| 753 Rome founded (traditional). | |
| 745 Complete disruption of Central Authority in Egypt ; | Tiglath-Pileser III. 745– |
| Kashta the Nubian holds Thebes. | 727 |
| 734 Syracuse founded. | |
| 722 Piankhi the Nubian invades Egypt. | Supremacy of Assyria ; Sargon II. 722 |
| 720 Defeat of Egyptians by Sargon at Raphia. | 720 |
| | End of Kingdom of Israel. Rise of Mushki (Phrygia). |
| 705 Tarentum founded. | Sennacherib. 705– |
| | 681 |
| 700 Defeat of Egyptians by Sennacherib at Eltekeh | 700 |
| Sparta predominant in Peloponnese. | Rise of Media and Lydia. |
| | Babylon taken and sacked. 690 |
| 689 Taharka (Tirhaka) the Nubian king in Egypt. | |
| 683 Annual archons at Athens. | |
| | Esarhaddon. 681– |
| | 669 |
| 671 Egypt subdued by Esarhaddon of Assyria. | 671 |
| 669–626 Ashurbanipal (Sardanapalus) establishes Assyrian overlordship in Egypt. | 669–626 |
| 663 Psammetichus I founds Twenty-sixth Egyptian | |
| Dynasty ; revival of art and power. | |
| 625 Periander ' tyrant ' of Corinth. | |
| | Alliance against Assyria of Cyaxares the Mede and 620 |
| | Nabopolassar the Chaldaean. |
| | Destruction of Nineveh by Medes and Babylonians. 612 |
| | Neo-Babylonian Empire founded by Nabopolassar. |
| 605 Final defeat of Assyrians and Egyptians under Necho by Nebuchadrezzar at Carchemish. 605 | |
| 600 Thales of Miletus. | |
| Etruscan (Tarquin) Dynasty at Rome. | |
| 594 Solon's legislation at Athens. | |
| | End of Kingdom of Judah : Babylonish captivity. 586 |
| 570 Servian reforms at Rome (traditional). | |
| 569– Aahmes II (Amasis) king of Egypt ; relations with | |
| 526 Greeks. | Croesus King of Lydia ; conflicts with Medes. 565 |
| 560 Peisistratus tyrant of Athens. | Birth of the Buddha. c. 560 |
| | Birth of Confucius. 551 |
| | Rise of Cyrus the Persian. 550 |

# KINGS & DYNASTIES OF EGYPT

Many variants of Egyptian names are in use. The commonest Egyptian forms of the kings' personal names are given here, with different readings, time-hallowed erroneous forms or well known Greek or Biblical versions in brackets. For some of the earliest only the throne-name or ' Horus name' is known ; sometimes both personal and Horus names appear, if each has obtained currency. Both this and the subsequent Mesopotamian list, for the sake of completeness, go beyond the closing date of our First Era. All dates before 1580 B.C. are tentative.

### Predynastic Kings
Before the first dynasty there were two kingdoms ; a few names of kings of the North and kings of the South have been deciphered from the ' Palermo Stele ' (Fifth Dynasty) and others:

Ro (South)
Tiu (North)
Thesh ,,
Hsekiu ,,
Uaznar ,,

### 1st Dynasty
Circa 3400–3200 B.C.
Southern conquerors of the North and unifiers of Egypt. Memphis founded.

The ' Scorpion,' Ip
Narmer
Aha Men. Menes ?
Zer Atoti (Khent)
Za (Zet, Ata)
Den Semti
Enzib Merpeba
Semerkhet Hui (Shemsu)
Ka Sen

### 2nd Dynasty
Circa 3200–2980 B.C.
Perhaps a family of northern origin.

Hotep-sekhemui
Raneb Kakau
Neneter
Perenmaat
Peribsen
Senedi
Neferka-ra
Neferka-sokari
Huzefa

### 3rd Dynasty
Circa 2980–2900 B.C.
New conquerors from the South. Memphis made capital.

Khasekhemui Besh (Bebi)
Zeser (Tcheser, Zoser)
Sanekht
Zeserteti
Sezes
Neterka Huni
Sneferu

### 4th Dynasty
The great pyramid builders ; zenith of the ' Old Kingdom ' in power and art.

| | | B.C. |
|---|---|---|
| Sharu (?) | .. | .. c. 2900–2898 |
| Khufu (Cheops) | .. | .. 2898–2875 |
| Razedef.. | .. | .. 2875–2867 |
| Khafra (Chephren) | .. | .. 2867–2811 |
| Menkaura (Mycerinus) | .. | 2811–2788 |
| Shepsekaf (and perhaps others) | .. | 2788–2755 |
| (Thamphthis ?) | .. | .. 2755–2750 |

### 5th Dynasty
Northern kings from Heracleopolis ; prominence of Ra-worship.

| | | B.C. |
|---|---|---|
| Userkaf | .. | .. c. 2750–2743 |
| Sahu-ra | .. | .. 2743–2731 |
| Neferirika-ra | .. | .. 2731–2730 |
| Shepseska-ra | .. | .. 2730–2723 |
| Khanefer-ra .. | .. | .. 2723–2722 |
| Ne-user-ra (User-en-ra) | .. | 2722–2691 |
| Menkau-heru | .. | .. 2691–2683 |
| Dedka-ra Isesi | .. | .. 2683–2655 |
| Unis .. | .. | .. 2655–2625 |

## 6th Dynasty

Central power of the Pharaoh steadily waning.

|  |  | B.C. |
|---|---|---|
| Teti | .. | c. 2625– ? |
| Userka-ra Ati | .. | ? –2595 |
| Pepi I | .. | 2595–2542 |
| Meren-ra I | .. | 2542–2538 |
| Pepi II | .. | 2538–2444 |
| Meren-ra II | .. | 2444–2443 |
| Neterka-ra | .. | 2443– ? |
| Menka-ra | .. | ? 2431 |

## 7th, 8th, 9th, 10th Dynasties

### Circa 2431–2160 B.C.

Here follows the first period of anarchy; invasion of Asiatics. Two dynasties ruling at Heracleopolis appear to be the most important, but how far they were contemporaneous with other princes ruling elsewhere whose names are recorded is uncertain. The country was split up and when centralised power (the 'Middle Kingdom') reappears with the eleventh dynasty, Thebes in the south is its seat.

## 11th Dynasty

From Thebes. Intef I was the first to assume the royal title; Mentuhotep III to conquer all Egypt.

|  |  | B.C. |
|---|---|---|
| Intef I | .. | c. 2160– ? |
| Intef II | .. | ? |
| Mentuhotep I | .. | ? |
| Mentuhotep II | .. | ? –2078 |
| Mentuhotep III Nebha-petra | .. | 2078–2030 |
| Mentuhotep IV | .. | 2030–2000 |

## 12th Dynasty

Dates are given from the death of the father, although the son in this dynasty was usually admitted as co-regent.

|  |  | B.C. |
|---|---|---|
| Amenemhet I | .. | c. 2000–1970 |
| Senusret (Usertsen, Sesostris) I | .. | 1970–1935 |
| Amenemhet II | .. | 1935–1903 |
| Senusret II | .. | 1903–1887 |
| Senusret III | .. | 1887–1849 |
| Amenemhet III | .. | 1849–1801 |
| Amenemhet IV | .. | 1801–1792 |
| Sebekneferu-ra (Queen) | | 1792–1788 |

## 13th, 14th, 15th, 16th Dynasties

### Circa 1788–1580 B.C.

Here follows the second anarchical period, with Thebes losing power and invaders coming from the east. Finally two dynasties of foreign Hyksos or 'Shepherd' kings rule practically all Egypt.

## 17th Dynasty

Contemporary with the last of the Hyksos, a line of Theban rulers were independent. The final struggle broke out under Sekenenra III.

|  |  | B.C. |
|---|---|---|
| Sekenenra I | .. | 1635–1615 |
| Sekenenra II | .. | 1615–1605 |
| Sekenenra III | .. | 1605–1591 |
| Uazkheperra Kamose | .. | 1591–1581 |
| Senekhtenra | .. | 1581–1580 |

## 18th Dynasty

Hyksos expelled by Aahmes, who founds the 'New Kingdom' or 'Empire.' Thebes the seat of power; climax of Egyptian greatness; Amen-worship pre-eminent.

|  | B.C. |
|---|---|
| Aahmes (Ahmose, Amasis) | 1580–1557 |
| Amenhotep (Amenophis) I | 1557–1541 |
| Thothmes (Thutmose) I | 1540–1501 |

|  |  | B.C. |
|---|---|---|
| Thothmes II | | |
| Hatshepsut (Queen) | .. | 1501–1479 |
| Thothmes III | | |
| Thothmes III | .. | 1479–1447 |
| Amenhotep II | .. | 1447–1420 |
| Thothmes IV | .. | 1420–1411 |
| Amenhotep III | .. | 1411–1375 |
| Akhnaton (Amenhotep IV) | | 1375–1358 |
| Smenkhkara (Sakere) | | 1358 |
| Tutankhamen | .. | 1358–1353 |
| Ay (Ai) | .. | 1353–1350 |

## 19th Dynasty

A fresh period of power after the temporary confusion occasioned by Akhnaton and his heresies.

|  |  | B.C. |
|---|---|---|
| Horemheb (Harmhab) | .. | 1350–1321 |
| Rameses I | .. | 1321–1320 |
| Seti (Sethos) I | .. | 1320–1300 |
| Rameses II | .. | 1300–1225 |
| Merneptah | .. | 1225–1215 |
| Amenmeses | .. | 1215 |
| Sa-ptah | .. | 1215–1209 |
| Seti II | .. | 1209–1205 |

## 20th Dynasty

After a short period of anarchy, during which Arsu, a Syrian usurper, reigned for some years, order was restored by Setnekht, of the family of Rameses II. Loss of Egyptian Empire in Syria.

|  |  | B.C. |
|---|---|---|
| Setnekht | .. | 1200–1198 |
| Rameses III | .. | 1198–1167 |
| Rameses IV | .. | 1167–1161 |
| Rameses V | .. | 1161–1157 |
| Rameses VI | .. | 1157–1154 |
| Rameses VII | .. | 1154–1152 |
| Rameses VIII | .. | 1152–1150 |
| Rameses IX | .. | 1150–1130 |
| Rameses X | .. | 1130–1124 |
| Rameses XI | .. | 1124–1094 |

## 21st Dynasty

### 1094–947 B.C.

The last few kings of the Twentieth Dynasty were mere nonentities in the hands of the priests of Amen ; and on the death of Rameses XI, Her-Heru, the high priest, seized the power, founding the line of Priest Kings. In the meantime, however, a prince of Tanis in the Delta assumed independent royalty—Nesu-ba-neb-tet, the Smendes of Manetho ; and during this period sometimes a Tanite king practically ruled the whole land, generally Thebes maintained a precarious independence, and on one occasion at least a high priest obtained the Tanite throne by marriage.

## 22nd Dynasty

The old order is definitely at an end ; the founder of this dynasty was a descendant of Libyan mercenaries who had made themselves powerful in Heracleopolis. Bubastis was chosen as the capital, Egypt united and some measure of foreign power regained.

|  |  | B.C. |
|---|---|---|
| Shashank (Shishak) I | .. | 947–925 |
| Osorkon I | .. | 925–889 |
| Takeleth (Takeloti) I | .. | 889–865 |
| Osorkon II (co-regent, 880) | | 865–850 |
| Shashank II | .. | 850–825 |
| Iuput | .. | 825–821 |
| Shashank III | .. | 821–769 |
| Pamai | .. | 769–763 |
| Shashank IV | .. | 763–725 |
| Osorkon IV | .. | 725–720 |

## 23rd Dynasty

A younger branch of the Libyan family had been installed in the high-priesthood of Amen at Thebes, and in

the reign of Osorkon II declared its independence, passing as the Twenty-third Dynasty. But by the end of these two contemporaneous dynasties almost every town had a petty chief.

|  |  | B.C. |
|---|---|---|
| Harsiesi | .. | 860–838 |
| Pedubaste (Peta-bast) | .. | 838–815 |
| Takeleth II | .. | 815–780 |
| Osorkon III | .. | 780–750 |
| Takeleth III (co-regent 757) | | 750–745 |
| Rudamen (co-regent 750) | | 745–742 |

## 24th Dynasty

From 726 the real power in the north belonged to Tafnekht, prince of Sais, whereas in about 745 Thebes had passed to a Nubian king, Kashta, and his son Piankhi, who in 722 attacked and defeated the Saite. Owing to a defeat of the Nubian arms in Palestine by the Assyrians, Tafnekht resumed sway.

|  |  | B.C. |
|---|---|---|
| Tafnekht | .. | 720–718 |
| Uahkere Bokenranef (Bocchoris) | .. | 718–712 |

## 25th Dynasty

Shabaka, who had been associated with Piankhi from about 715, now descended upon Egypt and recovered the Nubian ascendancy, founding the 'Ethiopian' Dynasty.

|  |  | B.C. |
|---|---|---|
| Shabaka | .. | 712–700 |
| Shabataka | .. | 700–689 |
| Taharka (Tirhakah) | .. | 689–664 |
| Tanutamen | .. | 664–650? |

## 26th Dynasty

In the reign of Taharka Egypt was subdued by Esarhaddon and Ashurbanipal, successive kings of Assyria. Taharka and his successor made sporadic re-descents upon Egypt from Nubia or Thebes, but after some revolts and disturbances Ashurbanipal established Psammetichus at Sais. During this dynasty there was a brilliant revival of art and a last flash of military energy.

|  |  | B.C. |
|---|---|---|
| Psamtek (Psammetichus) I | | 663–609 |
| Necho | .. | 609–593 |
| Psamtek II | .. | 593–588 |
| Uahibra (Hophra, Apries) | | 588–569 |
| Aahmes (Amasis) II | .. | 569–526 |
| Psamtek III | .. | 526–525 |

## 27th Dynasty

### 525–420 B.C.

Egypt conquered by Cambyses and ruled by Persian kings who assumed the old titles (see list of Persian kings in opposite page).

## 28th, 29th, 30th, 31st Dynasties

### 420–332 B.C.

Evanescent princes who succeeded in regaining some independence from time to time ; Nectanebos, of the Thirtieth Dynasty, was Egypt's last native king. Finally the Persians regained complete control of the country in about 340 B.C., Darius III counting as the Thirty-first Dynasty.

## The Ptolemies

### 305–30 B.C.

In 332 B.C. Alexander the Great wrested Egypt from Darius III ; and his successors, Philip Arrhidaeus, Alexander II and the Ptolemies, among whom was Cleopatra (51–30 B.C.), ruled from Alexandria for some 300 years. Finally, in 30 B.C. Egypt became a Roman province.

# KINGS & DYNASTIES OF MESOPOTAMIA

## Traditional

Dynasties of kings, grading insensibly from mythical to actual, recorded at Kish (Semitic) and Erech, Ur, Awan, Khamazi and Adab (Sumerian). Several kings are proved to be historical personages by discoveries of statues, mace-heads, etc. The overlordship shifts from town to town and dynasties are often contemporary. Kish usually predominant.

### Dynasties at :

| | | B.C. |
|---|---|---|
| Maer .. | .. | c. 3103–2967 |
| Akshak | .. | c. 2967–2868 |
| Kish (3rd) | .. | c. 2967–2775 |

All three probably Semitic; last two probably contemporaneous.

## Lagash

Contemporary with the above, the Sumerian ' patesis ' (priest-princes) of Lagash were often independent enough to style themselves kings ; from them come our first contemporary records.

| | | B.C. |
|---|---|---|
| Enkhegal | .. | ? |
| Ur-Nina | .. | c. 3000 |
| Akurgal | .. | c. 2950 |
| Eannatum | | |
| Enannatum I | | |
| Entemena | .. | c. 2925–2795 |
| Enannatum II | | |
| Enetarzi | | |
| Enlitarzi | .. | c. 2795–2790 |
| Lugalanda | .. | c. 2790–2781 |
| Urukagina | .. | c. 2781–2775 |

## Erech–3rd

A prince of Umma now crushes Lagash and Kish, makes Erech his capital, and founds an empire over all Mesopotamia as far as the Mediterranean.

Lugal-zaggisi .. c. 2775–2750 B.C.

## Agade

Sargon the Semite deposes Lugalzaggisi and founds new capital at Agade. Ur-Bau (c. 2620) patesi at Lagash.

| | | B.C. |
|---|---|---|
| Sargon (Sharrukin) I | .. | c. 2750–2695 |
| Rimush | .. | 2695–2686 |
| Manishtusu | .. | 2686–2679 |
| Naram-Sin | .. | 2678–2641 |
| Shargalisharri | .. | 2641–2616 |
| Six more kings | .. | 2616–2577 |

## Erech–4th

Circa 2571–2542 B.C.

The last kings of Agade were feeble, and a dynasty of five kings now rules from Erech.

## Gutium

Circa 2542–2416 B.C.

Anarchic rule of Gutian invaders, during latter part of which Gudea and Ur-Ningirsu are patesis of Lagash.

## Erech–5th

A prince of Erech crushes last of the Gutians.

Utukhegal .. c. 2416–2409 B.C.

## Ur–3rd

Last great Sumerian revival, and empire.

| | | B.C. |
|---|---|---|
| Ur-Engur (Ur-Nammu) | .. | c. 2409–2391 |
| Dungi (Shulgi) | .. | 2391–2345 |
| Bur-Sin | .. | 2345–2336 |
| Gimil-Sin | .. | 2336– ? |
| Ibi-Sin | .. | ? –2328 |

## Isin and Larsa

In 2357 B.C. Ishbi-Girra, a Semite from Maer, made himself master of Isin and in 2328, in alliance with Elam, crushed the Ur dynasty. At about the same time a rival Semitic dynasty arose in Larsa. Principal kings :

| | | B.C. |
|---|---|---|
| Ishbi-Girra (Isin) | .. | 2357–2325 |
| Idin-Dagan ,, | .. | 2315–2294 |
| Ishme-Dagan ,, | .. | 2294–2274 |
| Lipit-Ishtar ,, | .. | 2274–2263 |
| Gungunum (Larsa) | .. | 2264–2237 |
| Ur-Ninurta (Sumerian usurper, Isin) | .. | 2263–2235 |
| Bur-Sin ,, | .. | 2235–2214 |
| Sumu-ilu (Larsa) | .. | 2226–2197 |
| Sin-idinnam ,, | .. | 2181–2175 |
| Warad-Sin (Elamite conqueror, Larsa) | .. | 2167–2155 |
| Rim-Sin ,, | .. | 2155–2094 |

## 1st Babylonian Dynasty

In 2125 Rim-Sin, the Elamite king of Larsa, captured Isin ; but in the meantime a Semitic Dynasty had arisen in Babylon and in 2094 its sixth king, Hammurabi, crushed Rim-Sin and ruled the whole country.

| | | B.C. |
|---|---|---|
| Sumu-abum .. | .. | 2225–2211 |
| Sumu-la-ilu .. | .. | 2211–2175 |
| Zabium .. | .. | 2175–2161 |
| Abil-Sin .. | .. | 2161–2143 |
| Sin-muballit .. | .. | 2143–2123 |
| Hammurabi .. | .. | 2123–2080 |
| Samsu-iluna .. | .. | 2080–2042 |
| Abeshu .. | .. | 2042–2014 |
| Ammi-ditana .. | .. | 2014–1977 |
| Ammi-zaduga .. | .. | 1977–1956 |
| Samsu-ditana .. | .. | 1956–1926 |

## Kings of the Sea Country

2070–1703 B.C.

In the reign of Samsu-iluna, Ilumailu founded the dynasty of the ' Sea Country ' round the mouths of the Tigris and gradually absorbed large portions of the Babylonian domains. The Babylonian dynasty was brought to an end by the Hittite raid in 1926, after which follows an obscure period filled only by names of Sea Country kings.

## Kassite Dynasty

1746–1169 B.C.

Kassite barbarians invaded the country and founded a dynasty at Babylon under Gandash in 1746. Their rival is now the growing power of Assyria in the north. Period of diplomatic relations with Egypt.

## Assyrian Kings

Kings of Assyria can be traced back perhaps to 2400 B.C. ; the two earliest, Ushpia and Kikia, being possibly Mitannians. Hitherto tributary to the empires of Ur or Babylon ; but at this period they divide Mesopotamia with the Kassites. The first to make real headway against the latter was Shalmaneser.

| | | B.C. |
|---|---|---|
| Adad-nirari I | .. | 1305–1276 |
| Shalmaneser I | .. | 1276–1256 |
| Tukulti-Ninurta I | .. | 1256–1232 |
| Ashur-nadin-apli | .. | 1232–1213 |
| Ashur-nirari III | .. | 1213–1207 |
| Enlil-kudur-usur | .. | 1207–1202 |
| Ninurta-apal-Ekur I .. | .. | 1202–1177 |
| Ashur-dan I .. | .. | 1175–1140 |
| Ninurta-tukulti-Ashur | .. | 1140–1137 |
| Mutakkil-Nusku | .. | 1137–1127 |
| Ashur-resh-ishi | .. | 1127–1115 |
| Tiglath-pileser I | .. | 1115–1102 |

## Isin Dynasty of Babylon

1169–1039 B.C.

Under Ashur-dan the last of the Kassites had been suppressed, but a new dynasty from Isin arose in Babylon. Only the first few kings are important.

| | | B.C. |
|---|---|---|
| Marduk-shapik-zeri | .. | 1169–1152 |
| Ninurta-nadin-shum | .. | 1152–1146 |
| Nebuchadrezzar I | .. | 1146–1122 |
| Enlil-nadin-apli .. | .. | 1122–1116 |
| Marduk-nadin-akhe | .. | 1116–1100 |

A period of confusion follows ; on the death of Tiglath-pileser Assyria relapses under pressure from Aramaean tribes, Babylonia from Chaldaeans. A second line of Sea Country kings arises ; and to end of Assyrian dominance Babylonia is ruled by a succession of powerless dynasties, Elamite or Chaldaean usurpers, Assyrian kings or Assyrian nominees.

## Assyrian Empire

Under Adad-nirari II Assyrian power begins to revive.

| | | B.C. |
|---|---|---|
| Adad-nirari II | .. | 911–889 |
| Tukulti-Ninurta II | .. | 889–884 |
| Ashur-nasir-pal II | .. | 884–859 |
| Shalmaneser III | .. | 859–824 |
| Shamshi-Adad V | .. | 824–811 |
| Adad-nirari III | .. | 811–782 |
| Shalmaneser IV | .. | 782–772 |
| Ashur-dan III | .. | 772–754 |
| Ashur-nirari V | .. | 754–745 |
| Tiglath-pileser III | .. | 745–727 |
| Shalmaneser V | .. | 727–722 |
| Sargon II .. | .. | 722–705 |
| Sennacherib | .. | 705–681 |
| Esarhaddon | .. | 681–669 |
| Ashurbanipal (Sardanapalus) | | 669–626 |
| Ashur-etil-ilani | .. | 626–621 |
| Sin-shum-lishir | .. | 621 |
| Sin-shar-ishkun | .. | 621–612 |

## Chaldaean Empire

Nabopolassar the Chaldaean made himself master of Babylon in 625, allied himself with Cyaxares the Mede, and in 612 participated in the sack of Nineveh, thereafter dividing the Assyrian Empire with Cyaxares.

| | | B.C. |
|---|---|---|
| Nabopolassar .. | .. | 625–605 |
| Nebuchadrezzar II | .. | 605–562 |
| Amel-Marduk (Evil Merodach) .. | .. | 562–560 |
| Nergal-shar-usur (Neriglissar) .. | .. | 560–556 |
| Labashi-Marduk | .. | 556 |
| Nabu-naid (Nabonidus) | .. | 556–539 |

## Persian Empire

Astyages, the Median king, had wedded his daughter to Cambyses I, the Persian, then ruling in Elam. Their son, Cyrus II, defeated Astyages in 550, took Babylon in 539, and inaugurated the Persian Empire.

| | | B.C. |
|---|---|---|
| Cyrus II, ' the Great ' | .. | 558–529 |
| Cambyses II | .. | 529–522 |
| Darius I .. | .. | 522–486 |
| Xerxes I .. | .. | 486–465 |
| Artaxerxes I | .. | 465–425 |
| Xerxes II .. | .. | 425–424 |
| Darius II, Nothus | .. | 424–404 |
| Artaxerxes II | .. | 404–359 |
| Artaxerxes III, Ochus | .. | 359–338 |
| Arses .. | .. | 338–336 |
| Darius III | .. | 336–330 |

## Seleucidae and Parthians

Alexander conquered the Persian Empire in 331 ; on his death it went to pieces, Seleucus, governor of Babylonia from 319, emerging as king of the eastern portions of his domains. This line lasted to 65 B.C., when its lands were annexed by Rome. But by that time most of Mesopotamia east of the Euphrates had fallen to the Parthians (Mithridates I, 170–138 B.C.), who maintained their line with varying fortunes in opposition to Rome until the rise of the Sassanians under Ardashir I (Artaxerxes), a native Persian, in A.D. 212.

11

Ip, 'the Scorpion' (left), would seem to be the earliest king of the First Dynasty in Egypt (c. 3400–3200 B.C.), and his successor, Narmer (middle), was a warrior who is known to have subdued the Libyans of the western Delta. It was probably these two rulers, together with King Aha Men, who brought about the fusion of Upper and Lower Egypt and gave rise to the traditional personality of 'Menes.' Semerkhet, later in the same dynasty, subdued the unruly tribes of Sinai.

*From J. E. Quibell, 'Hierakonpolis' and Sir Flinders Petrie, 'Researches in Sinai'*

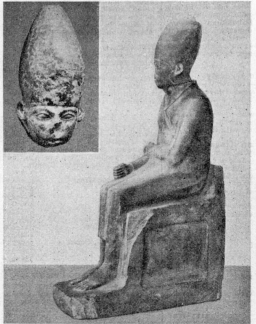

As the founder of a line of powerful kings—the Third Dynasty (c. 2980–2900 B.C.)—Khasekhemui (left) is a figure of considerable importance ; his carven portrait, damaged though it be, suggests a resolute man of keen intelligence. His son Zeser, who succeeded him, firmly established his house on the throne of Egypt, and seems to have governed with a strong hand and to have extended the frontiers. An index of Zeser's importance is his pyramid at Sakkara, the first built.

## MONARCHS WHO LAID THE FOUNDATIONS OF EGYPT'S GREATNESS

*Statue of Khasekhemui from J. E. Quibell, 'Hierakonpolis'*

### CHAPTER 1

# TWILIGHT: 4000—1580 B.C.

THE basins of two great rivers, the Nile and the Euphrates, were the cradles of civilization ; not of mankind, but of civil institutions. It was here, so far as we know, that men first organized societies on a large scale, and first consciously created for the admiration and instruction of posterity lasting records of their own activities.

Organization in the Nile valley was already far advanced and covered a very large area when the first recognizable records were made. They begin at the point where the kingdoms of the North and South, that is Lower and Upper Egypt, or the Nile Delta and the Nile between the Delta and the cataracts, were united under a single Pharaoh ; the point where the First Dynasty emerges.

The latest date to which this event can be assigned is 3400 B.C., but dates as untenably high as 5000 B.C. are still sometimes quoted ; and though it breaks the ordered sequence of our narrative, a brief explanation of such an apparently huge discrepancy is necessary at this stage.

## Dating the Dawn of Egyptian History

THE stream of Egyptian history falls into three periods of organized central control, complete with monuments and records, divided from each other by two periods of internal disruption and foreign invasion. It may be likened to a mountain brook with still pools, that reveal a teeming aquatic life through their limpid surface, separated by confused rapids and waterfalls. The last ' pool,' which debouches into the main river of world record, began in 1580 B.C., the earliest fixed date in Egyptian history and the closing date of this chapter.

Now we know a considerable amount about the two previous organized periods, enabling us to fix their total duration and the length of the kings' reigns ; but they are cut off from each other and from world-history by the two anarchical periods, of which little has been recorded except confused lists of dynasties that may have been consecutive but were more often, no doubt, contemporaneous, the kingdom having been split up. Almost the only other thing that can guide us in estimating their duration is the comparison of art-forms immediately before and after. The problem is therefore highly speculative ; and according to the length assigned to them, so the date adopted for the First Dynasty must vary.

### Earliest Records from the Nile Valley

HERE, in the belief that the balance of probability inclines to the shorter estimate, 3400 B.C. is the date assigned to the dawn of Egyptian history. In the Euphratic, or Mesopotamian area, although traditions that can often be verified tell of dynasties to which we may assign dates that go back to a period as early as 3500 B.C., the first contemporary records can hardly be dated before 3000 B.C.

In this sense, at any rate, it is in the Nile valley that the chronicle of civilized mankind begins. It is here that we first get statements made for the information of posterity, at the time when the events took place, decipherable in this twentieth century of our era. Earlier records may indeed be found and deciphered, but we do not yet know of them. Traditions containing a very substantial element of truth may go back to a much earlier day, but we have no contemporary evidence by which to test them. In this region, contemporary evidence of events and persons certainly not less than five thousand years ago has been discovered and deciphered, and the volume of it increases year by year, as fresh monuments are disentombed and the science of interpretation advances.

From this evidence we can draw with confidence certain conclusions as to the preceding centuries, the ' predynastic ' period, supplementing these by remains which do not amount to actual records, and by traditions in which we can recognize elements of truth plentifully wrapped up with fiction.

For predynastic Egypt only one approximately fixed date has been suggested. In reconstructing its story we must go back to a dim ' once upon a time '—say 2,000 years or so before the dynastic era. Lower and Upper Egypt, the Delta area and the Nile basin between the Delta and the cataracts, had both been long occupied by people in no sense primitive, when the conquering people who ultimately made Egypt broke in upon them.

### Makers of the Dynastic Civilization

THE newcomers possibly came from Punt, the modern Eritrea and Somaliland, having racial affinities with the modern Somalis, not with the negro or negroid Nubians—perhaps we must seek for their ultimate origin in the East, on the farther side of the Red Sea. Without, however, abandoning the view that Egypt may have suffered incursions from the East in the predynastic period, we must give weight to the latest evidence which seems to show that these ' dynastic' invaders penetrated in a southerly direction from the Delta. Their leader was by later generations called Horus, identified as the sky god whose symbol is the hawk. His great figure looms dim and tremendous through mists of confused legend and of countless years. We may, if we please, regard him as the inventor and originator of the idea and the institution of monarchy, the organized control of an obedient people by one man, accepted as wielding a divine authority; though more probably his personality is wholly mythical.

Although later traditions elaborated the Victories of Horus, no reliance can be placed upon them ; they are too much mixed up with what is obviously mythological, and entangled with reminiscences of later wars. We can hardly even guess plausibly how many decades or generations or centuries passed before the followers of Horus were masters of all Upper Egypt. But we can be sure that two distinct kingdoms, the North and the South, were definitely established some centuries before the dynastic era began.

At about this stage we come upon what may be reckoned as the definite date mentioned above. These early Egyptians, in the Delta, had carried their study of the heavenly bodies so far that they adopted a calendar which gave the year 365 days ; and this invention may perhaps have been made in 4241 B.C.

They reckoned twelve months of thirty days with five holidays over. But they did not put in a leap year to correct the error of a quarter of a day ; so that new year's day in the calendar shifted one day from the astronomical date in four years, and the two did not coincide again till 365 leap years —1,460 years—had been missed. In the year A.D. 139 one such period, or ' Sothic cycle,' came to an end ; and if we assume that the calendar had been in use for three cycles, this takes us back to the year named ; though two cycles is as likely. Many centuries elapsed before the most advanced peoples adopted this early calendar, only correcting it by introducing the leap year.

### Kings of Upper and Lower Egypt

IT is probable that each of the two kingdoms of the North and of the South was a fusion of several minor kingdoms. Of persons and events we know next to nothing. We do know that their handicrafts belonged to the Age of Stone and were of an amazingly fine quality. Metal— copper—was only beginning to come into use ; the tradition that the followers of Horus owed their victory to their metal-tipped weapons is probably a later fiction.

Centuries afterwards, under the Fifth Dynasty, lists of early kings were compiled, presumably from records of some sort ; but they are names and nothing more. We are told nothing of what they did ; nor do we learn more of them from the predynastic cemeteries which have been excavated. But we do know that the first king of the South, who joined the two kingdoms under his single sway not later than 3400 B.C., was officially and traditionally the descendant and the representative on earth of the divine or deified Horus.

Until the ancient monuments began to yield their records to the research and interpretation of modern Egyptology, our knowledge of ancient Egypt was derived

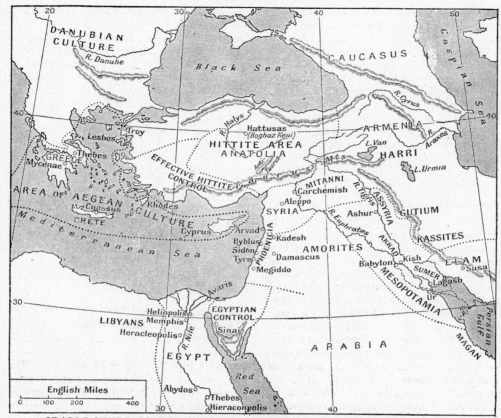

**CRADLE LANDS OF THE WORLD'S EARLIEST ORGANIZED CIVILIZATIONS**

It was in the valleys of the Nile and the Euphrates that advanced political societies first arose. This map gives the names and boundaries necessary for the understanding of their history down to 1580 B.C., but does not illustrate any single moment of that period. The nomadic Gutians and Kassites, for instance, were not pressing down into Babylonia from the indicated regions at the same time.

from the Hebrew scriptures, the traditions collected by the Greek inquirer, Herodotus of Halicarnassus, in the fifth century B.C. and the compilations of the Egyptian Manetho in the third century B.C., of which only fragments survive. That such information must diverge widely from the actual historical facts is a matter of course. What surprises the modern student is the extent to which it has been confirmed by the real contemporary monuments.

The king named Menes, who according to Manetho established the First Dynasty, was in actual fact one of the first of the long line of the Pharaohs; probably his legendary exploits are a combination of the historical accomplishments of the first three kings : the 'Scorpion,' Narmer and Aha Men (Menes), of whom we know

from the early lists or from contemporary remains. It is not always that individual kings on Manetho's dynastic list can as yet be identified; but the many identifications are a valuable endorsement of the traditions as a whole.

The northern kingdom was subjected not to the southern kingdom but to the southern king, who added the attributes of the northern king to his own and became Lord of the Two Kingdoms. He—or one of his immediate successors—refounded an ancient city, 'of the White Wall,' on the border, as a centre from which he could rule over both, though it was probably not until the Third Dynasty that it actually became the royal seat, and not until the Sixth that it was called the Egyptian equivalent of Memphis.

The North does not seem to have acquiesced in the change tamely. Two more at least of the First Dynasty pharaohs record triumphs over the northerners, or easterners of the Sinaitic peninsula : Den Semti, and Semerkhet. The vanquished are portrayed as of a Semitic type markedly distinguishable from the Egyptian conquerors. War was also waged far to the south against the Nubians. The founding of Memphis is claimed anew for Enzib Merpeba. The appearance of the Second Dynasty a little later points to the passing of power to a northern family.

### Organized Government 5,000 years ago

THE first two dynasties ruled for approximately 400 years. The second records no memorable doings, and ends with a fresh conquest from the South. The victor, Khasekhem, altered his name to Khasekhemui, married the heiress to the throne and became the progenitor of the Third Dynasty—the first Pharaoh of what is known as the Old Kingdom.

With Khasekhemui, provisionally dated about 2980 B.C., begins a series of mighty monarchs. His own statue has been found in his tomb in Upper Egypt at Hieraconpolis, the Hawk City, the centre of the Horus cult. Already an enormous interest attached to the burial place of the king, an interest presently responsible for the development of pyramid building.

The tomb of Khasekhemui is the first one to contain a complete chamber of hewn stone ; his son Zeser, or Zoser, raised his entirely of stone, layer on layer, each layer smaller than the last, forming what is known as the first or 'step' pyramid. Sneferu, or Senefru, following Zeser after four reigns, filled up most of the terraces of his tomb at Medum, thus making a sloped instead of a terraced surface, though he did not add the completing cap. This is alternatively known as the first pyramid. After Sneferu came the great pyramid builders of the Fourth Dynasty.

The Egypt of which we have been speaking, Egypt before the third millennium, was a populous nation in an advanced stage of civilization. Of this the great tombs of the period at Abydos and elsewhere in central Egypt would be sufficient proof. Though we have to be satisfied with carven

monuments, Egyptian scribes were already writing their records on papyrus also. Great progress was evidently made in the four centuries of Menes and his successors and this must be largely attributed to the intelligent activity of the centralised government.

The government itself was highly organized. The southern kings introduced in the north the system of government by districts, 'nomes,' which had long prevailed in the south—relics probably of the early division into small kingdoms. The Pharaoh was the centre of all. Around him were the nobles, his personal friends and advisers. If he lived in magnificence and was laid in a magnificent tomb when he died, his life itself was strenuous enough. We see him leading his soldiers in battle, smiting the foe with his mace, cutting the first sod of a new canal, in his leisure time hunting game big and small.

### The Pharaoh and his Duties

HE is an active administrator. He has been trained from his youth to take a responsible part in his father's rule—probably has been his chief minister. His accession to the throne has been celebrated with pomp and ceremony, and in his thirtieth year he will hold a kind of jubilee coronation, the 'Sed' festival. It may be that originally actual abdication or something still more drastic took place when a king had reigned thirty years, but this is at best doubtful.

His nobles are buried in mortuary chambers under a mass of brickery, the 'mastabas' from which the Third and Fourth Dynasties perhaps developed the pyramids. More than 5,000 years ago the virtues for which the dead had desired to be remembered by future generations were recorded in epitaphs which show a lively sense of the responsibilities of greatness, and indicate a high standard of public spirit.

Zeser set to his successors the example of building himself two tombs, though in this he may not have been original. Like his father he was a warrior ; he subjugated the Nubians, to some distance above the First Cataract. He also built temples of stone, but discoveries seem to show these had a stone-building technique behind them, and to bear out the tradition that Neneter of the Second Dynasty was the first to use limestone for temple construction. The wealth of Egypt under Zeser is demonstrated by the immense amount of man power that could be absorbed in unremunerative labour without producing exhaustion ; that exhaustion did not result is proved by the vast expenditure of his successors.

THE dynasty attained its zenith with its last monarch Sneferu. As a witness to his power he built at Dahshur, south of Sakkara, a second and nobler pyramid on a larger scale than his first— a complete one. He smote the Nubians. He brought the Sinaitic peninsula enduringly under the sway of the Pharaohs. He developed its copper mines, as Zeser had done before him. He created a flotilla of great Nile boats and sent ships to Phoenicia to bring back cedar-wood from Lebanon. The nobles of his day built their mastabas not of brick but of stone; and he left a name which was held in high honour centuries after his death.

SNEFERU left no son. Unless an ephemeral Sharu intervened, his successor was Khufu, the founder of the Fourth Dynasty, from Middle Egypt. Why he came to the throne we do not know ; presumably his title was by marriage. Of his deeds, and those of his son Khafra and his grandson Menkaura, we know for certain only that they built the three great pyramids at Gizeh, and almost certainly the Great Sphinx. They are familiar to us by the names of Cheops, Chephren and Mycerinus, from the pages of Herodotus, who gathered traditions about them which contain more fable than history ; though they reigned for twenty-three and fifty-six years respectively, he makes Khafra the brother of Khufu. The priests, who were his informants, had no good to say of either, though they lavished praises on Menkaura : they were tyrants and contemners of the gods.

From this we can fairly conclude that the priesthood and the monarchy were at odds in their day, but that under Menkaura there was a reconciliation ; and it

**EGYPTIAN RULERS WHO HAVE LEFT PROOFS OF THEIR WEALTH AND POWER**
Very little is known of these two kings of the Fourth Dynasty, Khufu (2898–2875 B.C.) and Khafra (2867–2811 B.C.) ; yet the magnificence of their tombs demonstrates clearly that under them Egypt was at peace and extremely prosperous, and that the monarchy was absolute. For Khufu was the builder of the Great Pyramid at Gizeh, and Khafra of the larger of its two neighbours : works that could not even have been begun without an army of workers and vast resources.
*Photos, Egypt Exploration Society and Mansell*

is scarcely conceivable that the Great Pyramids should have been built without the exercise of a grinding tyranny. The biggest, the pyramid of Khufu, covers 13 acres; it is computed to consist of 6,000,000 tons of stone, in 2½-ton blocks hewn to shape with an extraordinary exactitude of angle and surface.

THAT it took—as Herodotus says— 100,000 men 20 years to build it is probable enough. Those huge blocks had to be hewn in the quarries beyond the Nile, brought over the river and dragged up an inclined plane to the site of the pyramid. The enormity of the toil is almost unimaginable. The strain, both economic and physical, must have been terrific. On the other hand, the organization which controlled such a vast mass of labour must have been amazingly efficient.

Khafra's pyramid was somewhat smaller than the other, with more apparent haste and less perfection in the workmanship. For both, the latest date is the twenty-ninth century. It is not surprising that, according to tradition, the land groaned under the burden, and the memory of the pyramid builders was held in abhorrence. The much smaller size of Menkaura's pyramid is evidence either of exhaustion or of the milder spirit of the Pharaoh.

The accession of the Fifth Dynasty would seem to mark the victory of priestly influence, and the supersession of the southern sky god Horus by the northern sun god Ra, or Re. Apparently the pharaonic theory of actual divine parentage was transferred to the offspring (according to the flesh) of Ra's high priest at On; the connexion at least is obvious in the personal names and the monumental buildings of the new dynasty.

Possibly something may be suspected of a phenomenon familiar in later ages, a blending of aristocratic and sacerdotal interests; for another departure from past custom is apparent. The great offices of state are no longer appropriated to the royal family; they become hereditary in the families of magnates. The germs of something analogous to medieval feudalism are beginning to appear.

**THIRD GREAT PYRAMID BUILDER**

While tradition makes Menkaura, whom we see here with his wife, a great king, the smallness of his pyramid—the latest of the three at Gizeh—suggests that during his reign the resources of the realm were becoming exhausted.

*From Boston Fine Arts Museum*

USERKAF and Sahu-ra developed fleets on the Mediterranean and Red Seas, which sailed to Phoenicia and to Punt (Somaliland), and brought home the products of those regions—including slaves. Expeditions were sent to Nubia, and started the series of inscriptions above the First Cataract. The dynasty went on building pyramids, though by no means on the old scale. It could not afford to magnify itself after the old fashion, but was actively in search of new sources of wealth from commerce; while its dependence on the forces that had set it on the throne was raising the personal prestige of the nobility at the expense of that of the Pharaoh.

The policy of the Fifth Dynasty was carried out most effectively in the Sixth,

in the fifty-three years' reign of Pepi I—
if he actually reigned so long. He may
have been a sort of Mayor of the Palace
to his immediate predecessors, a powerful
feudatory who succeeded to the throne
unopposed. At any rate, he proved so
adequate a ruler that two very young
sons followed him, the second of whom,
Pepi II, is credited with a reign of ninety-
four years, the longest on record.

Pepi II began his reign as a child and
ended it a centenarian, without having
done anything in the interval to re-
establish the royal authority. At his
death we are probably in the twenty-fifth
century. After it came the first of our
two periods of anarchy. The ' nomarchs,'
lords of the nomes, the dukes and counts
of the Old Kingdom, became so many
petty princes, defying the nominal kings
of two very shadowy dynasties ; till a
Ninth Dynasty followed by a Tenth—
perhaps contemporaneous with the Eighth
at Memphis—was set up at Heracleopolis
in Central Egypt by a group of nobles,
who restored some local order at least, but
only after irremediable damage had already
been wrought. And the confusion was
accentuated by an invasion of Asiatics
from Syria.

### Rise of Thebes & the Middle Kingdom

THE South, however, renounced allegiance to the Heracleopolitans ; and
after fierce wars a Theban house established the Eleventh Dynasty, the
Middle Kingdom and the supremacy
of Thebes—hitherto an unknown town,
capital of a petty dukedom. Though the
royal residence was for long at Itht-Toui
for the sake of a better strategical position, and though later it was temporarily
interrupted by the Hyksos, this supremacy
was to continue for more than a thousand
years. We date the first of the line—all
the Eleventh Dynasty pharaohs were
Intefs or Mentuhoteps—at the middle of
the twenty-second century.

Two Intefs and four Mentuhoteps ruled
for a century and a half. The great
families would seem to have ruled very
much on their own responsibility in their
own provinces, while the royal authority
preserved the public peace, revived the
policy of internal development, and in the

**ABLE RULER OF SIXTH DYNASTY**
While probably not of royal birth, Pepi I (2595–
2542 B.C.) proved a far-seeing and capable
monarch. He carried out a wise domestic policy
and a vigorous and successful foreign policy, which
together ensured a century of peace in Egypt.
*From J. E. Quibell, Hierakonpolis*

time of Mentuhotep III warred against
Libyans on the west, Nubians on the
south and Sinaitic Semites. One noble
was official Lord of the Marches in the
south. Another was the Pharaoh's hereditary first minister ; his house succeeded
to the throne, probably not without
opposition, on the death of Mentuhotep IV,
inaugurating the Twelfth Dynasty of
Amenemhets and Senusrets—of which the
Greek form Sesostris is more familiar.

This dynasty ruled in power and
splendour from about 2000 to 1788 B.C.,
if we accept the latest possible dates.
Amenemhet I survived sundry conspiracies—presumably the work of jealous
aristocratic factions—against his own life,
and in his thirty years' reign fully established, not at first the old-time despotism, but the very effective supremacy
of the crown, so long as it was worn by a
strong and capable ruler.

EGYPT then, under the Twelfth Dynasty,
enjoyed two centuries of prosperity.
The succession was secured, with one
exception, by the association of the
crown prince with his father formally
as joint king, during the father's life.
The climax of power was attained under
Senusret III, and of splendour under

Amenemhet III. The southern border was definitely carried beyond the Second Cataract. Egyptian armies raided Syria, though the tradition of a conquest is mythical. The prestige of the throne was raised when a Senusret fought victoriously at the head of his troops as in the ancient days.

GREATER, however, than the renowned achievements of Senusret III in war were those of his son Amenemhet III in peace ; for it was he who developed the regulation and distribution of the waters of the Nile in upper Egypt, and practically created a new highly productive province by transforming Lake Moeris in the Fayum into a vast reservoir for irrigation purposes. Indeed, not a single one of the Twelfth Dynasty rulers neglected the development of the wealth and resources of Egypt ; but no other accomplished so much.

The great dynasty had succeeded in once more centralising the sovereignty, and reducing the personal power of the nobles, replacing it with the administrative authority of crown officials ; so that government could carry on peacefully and automatically unless subjected to a strain which called for exceptional capacity in its head. But the line ended—strangely enough for Egypt, with a queen—a few years after the death of the great Amenemhet. The new dynasty and its successor lacked the capacity of that which had passed ; the second interregnum of anarchy began, with the kingship split into rival houses at Thebes and Itht-toui ; and the whole system went to wreck with the Hyksos invasion, early in the eighteenth century.

WE have now followed the course of events in Egypt for sixteen hundred years, a period equal to that which has elapsed since the Romans were in Britain. Yet if we cast our eyes over the rest of the world to glean material for historical narrative, black darkness still meets us everywhere—with one exception. It is true that the archaeologist has recovered the material evidence of considerable cultures from sites all round the Mediterranean, especially in Crete and the Aegean, and has equated their development with Egyptian chronology ; but

**WARRIOR-KINGS WHO REVIVED THE POWER OF EGYPT**

After three centuries of disruption (2430-2160 B.C.) Egypt recovered cohesion under a series of strong and beneficent rulers. It was Mentuhotep III (left ; circa 2078 B.C.) who really united the country and made it strong within. Senusret I (1970-1935 B.C.) greatly enlarged his dominions by conquest in the upper Nile valley ; and Senusret III (1887-1849 B.C.) was even more successful in his wars, as his victorious armies not only subjugated neighbouring tribes but penetrated into Syria.

*Photos, R. B. Fleming, Sir Flinders Petrie and W. F. Mansell*

of records that the historian can chronicle there is nothing. The progress of our narrative does not admit of any detailed interpretation of the very considerable remains that have been discovered in these Mediterranean areas.

As for the Hittites, that mysterious people of Asia Minor whose power has only lately been revealed, their entry into world history is more properly a subject for the following chapter, in which references will be found to their existence and activities. But one or two definite events that may be referred to this period emerge from a study of their archives discovered at Boghaz Keui, and from the records of neighbouring powers. Thus the first king of whom we find mention—Pamba—lived about 2750 B.C., but he seems only to have ruled a petty state. It was not until about 2000 B.C. that Hattusil I made Hattusas the capital of a considerable kingdom with its boundaries on the Mediterranean, while the sack of Babylon by the Hittites may be regarded as having taken place at about 1926 B.C. (see below).

## Dawn of History in Mesopotamia

FOR the civilizations of India and China a high antiquity has been claimed, but research does not support the claim. China was, no doubt, ahead of her neighbours in material culture, and something of the main lines of progress can be inferred from later knowledge ; but the bulk of India, save for culture stations of Sumerian affinities, such as Mohenjo-Daro and Harappa in the far north-west, does not seem to have been above the general level.

Probably the first wave of Aryan immigration began some time during our period. America we can safely assume to have been still in the hunting stage of barbarism, in spite of exaggerated estimates of the age of Inca and Maya civilizations that have at one time and another acquired a certain amount of credence.

The one exception of which the historian can take advantage is Mesopotamia. Here, during all these centuries, a civilization was developing, and records

**BUILDER OF EGYPT'S PROSPERITY**

One of the most enlightened of Egyptian rulers was Amenemhet III (1849–1801 B.C.). His strong, centralised government maintained peace, while his brilliantly conceived public works led to an increase in wealth.

*Courtesy of Sir Flinders Petrie*

being made in an elaborate script, without any contact with Egypt other than cultural through the medium of trade ; for chronology will not support a theory that an early king (Naram-Sin) met Menes in battle. It is possible, however, that some of the early predynastic invaders of Egypt may have originated in this area.

As in the Nile basin, the beginning of recorded history can hardly be dated earlier than the second half of the fourth millennuim B.C., probably about its close ; but from known conditions when the records begin, from earlier relics and from traditions, something of the preceding two thousand years may be inferred, though little can be positively affirmed.

The name Mesopotamia applies generally to the whole district lying between the rivers Tigris and Euphrates. The land about the two rivers between the modern Bagdad and the Persian Gulf may be distinguished as Babylonia ; in those ancient days the rivers entered the gulf by separate mouths, the sea having

**BABYLONIA'S FIRST WELL KNOWN KING**

Ur-Nina, king of Lagash, is the first real
personality to emerge in Babylonian history.
He stands here wearing the Sumerian flounced
'kaunakes' imitating a sheep's fleece, with
his butler, Anita, and a group of his sons.

*From the Louvre*

probably since then receded some two
hundred miles. Beyond the Tigris rose
the mountains of Elam. West and south
of the Euphrates spread the Syrian desert.
West of the desert and the upper waters
of the Euphrates plain came what were
known later as Syria and Phoenicia ; and
beyond the mountains of the Taurus and
Anti-Taurus, on the north and north-west,
the highlands of Anatolia and Armenia.

OUR beginnings, then, are in a Babylonia
where as yet there is no Babylon. In
the dim twilight centuries we discern
the presence of Semitic peoples and—
whether later comers we do not know—
Sumerians, a folk akin, it may
be, to the Dravidians of
India. Sumerians predomi-
nated always in the southern
portion, Sumer ; Semites
generally in the northern,
Akkad. They were city
dwellers and tillers of the
soil ; they exchanged produce ; they had begun at least
to work copper and make
tools of copper ; the Sumerians
at least had developed a script
on lines of their own.

Their cities make war on
each other ; one is now predominant, now another ; tradition tells of dynasties at

Kish in the centre, Akshak in the far
north, Ur and Erech in the south, to say
nothing of mythical predecessors. Their
chiefs claim a dubious kingship over the
rest. Most commonly the ascendancy
rests with Kish and its apparently Semitic
dynasties, so that the very word 'kish'
came to mean Universal Dominion, until
a century or so before or after 3000 B.C.,
when the historical contemporary records
of the Sumerian city of Lagash begin with
its king Ur-Nina.

BEFORE this date there are indeed inscribed remains that enable us to
grope through the centuries, such as those
of A-anni-padda of the First Dynasty of
Ur—prehistory grades into history much
more gradually here than in Egypt ; but
at Lagash occur the first long inscriptions
from which we can reconstruct anything
like a narrative of events. It seldom
seems to have been a city of first-rate
importance, but its intellectual influence
was great and by chance it is the one
about which we know most at this stage.

The first monument we have, that known
as the Stele of the Vultures, belongs to the
reign of Ur-Nina's grandson Eannatum
(about 2900 B.C.). Primarily, it commemorates the victory of Lagash over
its neighbour Umma, but this warrior
claimed also to have waged successful
wars with other cities, Ur and Erech, to
have smitten the Elamites—a people of
ancient culture on the east—and to have
vanquished Kish. The most distinguished

**EANNATUM OF LAGASH IN CONQUERING GUISE**

A fragment of the so-called 'Stele of Vultures' gives us a
picture of Eannatum, grandson of Ur-Nina, leading a phalanx
of heavy-armed Sumerian spearmen in one of the perennial
feuds between Lagash and Umma. Lagash was victorious ;
and Eannatum claims to have vanquished Kish as well.

*From the Louvre*

of his successors at Lagash were Entemena and, after an interval, Urukagina, who was remarkable as an economic reformer. With him, however, the independence of Lagash ended. He was overthrown by the conqueror Lugal-zaggisi of Umma, who transferred his capital to Erech and claimed to have carried victorious arms from the lower sea (the Persian Gulf) to the upper (the Mediterranean).

THEN he in his turn was overthrown by Sargon of Agade, who, followed by his sons, set up a Semitic empire, traditionally dated in the twenty-ninth and twenty-eighth centuries. The Assyrians of later ages looked back upon Sargon as their first national hero.

As happened with so many other national heroes, legends gathered about the birth, youth and upbringing of Sharrukin or Sargon. Obviously he was not a king's son. Having achieved kingship, he reigned for fifty-five years, conquering all lands 'from the rising to the setting of the sun.' He crossed the eastern sea and smote the Elamites from the south. He marched to the western sea, subduing the Amorites (i.e. 'westerners'). He crossed that sea, though whether this means that he visited Cyprus we cannot be sure.

He had begun his career of victory by overthrowing the mighty Lugal-zaggisi ; he ended it with half of his empire more or less in revolt, but still unable to make head against him successfully. The traditions concerning him were very early, and very firmly established, and his own inscriptions mention expeditions to the 'silver mountains' which can only mean the Taurus and its silver mines, and to the cedar forests, certainly Lebanon.

**NARAM-SIN**

For Naram-Sin of Agade we have a portrait from the stele set up to commemorate his victory over the mountaineers in the lands beyond Tigris.

*From the Louvre*

Two sons, Rimush and Manishtusu, followed Sargon and maintained his empire, not without much fighting against rebellious chiefs. The next, the illustrious Naram-Sin, passed into tradition as a third son, but as he reigned at least thirty-eight years this scarcely seems likely ; and indeed the latest discovered king-list makes him the son of Manishtusu.

The most valuable contemporary monument of Naram-Sin is that known as the Stele of Victory, which commemorates his triumph over Lulubu (trans-Tigris). It would seem that at an early period he overthrew nine armies and carried captive three kings, in chains ; that he conquered Magan, probably on the Arabian shore of the Persian gulf ; that Kish, forgetting that she owed her liberation from the Sumerian overlordship to Sargon, ungratefully headed a rebel confederacy against Naram-Sin, and paid the penalty for so doing. Naram-Sin also reasserted his authority in the west, where it can never have been very firmly established, and very possibly carried his arms through the passes of the Taurus and Anti-Taurus into Anatolia and Armenia.

Some predecessors in what may be called the high-kingship had adopted the swelling title of King of Universal Dominion ; for which Naram-Sin substituted King of the Four Quarters of the World, subsequently appropriated by the Babylonian monarchs whose city had not hitherto attained a general supremacy.

### The Coming of the Gutians

NEXT came Shargalisharri, once thought to be a grandson but probably a son of Naram-Sin. The records of his reign are meagre, but he seems to have been troubled by the same sorts of revolt as his predecessors. At any rate, he too smote Elam on the east and the Amorites in the west.

We find him moreover at war with Gutium in the north-eastern mountains, whence a barbarian flood was presently to inundate Babylonia, though for the time it was held back. Probably the torrent overwhelmed Shargalisharri's successors for the dynasty flickered out with a brief series of names and nothing more, and the kingship melted away among the ' hosts of Guti which had no king,' as the dynastic lists put it.

The Gutian invasion and domination were very destructive of monuments and records, as of other things. In fact they had kings, but they probably left the local administration to run very much as it had run before under the local princes, who combined the functions of priest and ruler and bore the same title of ' patesi ' which in the past they had borne except when the extended domination of a particular city, Kish, Ur or Erech, had entitled its patesi to claim the higher kingly title now appropriated by the Gutians.

### Herald of a Sumerian Revival

BUT like other barbaric hordes the Gutians were not organizers of empire. The older culture was temporarily submerged but not destroyed ; and presently there appears the distinguished figure of Gudea, patesi of Lagash—still a vassal of Gutium—under whose beneficent rule justice, prosperity, religion and the general concomitants of a wise government once more prevailed.

Our dates are very doubtful ; but if we place Shargalisharri in the second half of the twenty-seventh century B.C., Gudea will come in the middle of the twenty-fifth. He prepared the way for Sumerian revival. Shortly after his time the Gutians were ejected from Babylonia, by a prince ruling at Erech ; and then the ancient city of Ur once more becomes an imperial capital.

In the course of a long reign Dungi of Ur, whose father Ur-Engur (or Ur-Nammu) had established his supremacy in Sumer and Akkad, conquered Elam, extended his sway over upper Mesopotamia, and probably attached the flourishing Babylonian colony in Cappadocia to his empire. Yet the power of the dynasty hardly survived Dungi ; it was overthrown by a disastrous Elamite raid ; and the somewhat feeble sceptre passed for just two hundred years to an undistinguished dynasty at Isin, until Semitic conquerors, newcomers to the Two Rivers, set up the first ascendancy of Babylon.

Probably we must assume a prolonged and persistent penetration, rather than a conquest, by ' Amorites '—that is, Semites from the trans-Euphrates, west of Mesopotamia. At any rate at the close of the Isin dynasty we find its most prominent rivals at Larsa, whose lords bear Semitic names, and in the rising power of Babylon under foreign Semite rulers ; complicated by the secular feuds and occasional alliances with Elam.

The Babylonian dynasty was established by Sumu-abum, in the days of Bur-Sin of Isin and Sumu-ilu of Larsa, probably about 2225 B.C. Half a century later, the Larsa dynasty was overthrown by the king of Elam ; and some years afterwards, with the accession of his second son Rim-Sin—an Elamite though he bore a Semitic name—the struggle for supremacy was inaugurated by that ambitious chief. In the course of twenty years Rim-Sin gradually absorbed his neighbours' territories till he had conquered Isin itself, though once he suffered a reverse at the hands of Sin-muballit of Babylon. And then he met his match in Sin-muballit's son, the great Hammurabi.

### Hammurabi and his Triumphs

IN his first years Hammurabi dealt firmly with Rim-Sin, who had to surrender most of his acquisitions to that Babylonian Alfred the Great. In the forty-two years of his reign he established a vast and well-ordered empire ; but his greatness lies in the fact that his aim was not expansion by military exploits so much as unification by peaceful organization.

After he had defeated and bridled the elderly aggressor of Larsa, we hear little of war and battle for many years ; but we have indications that his authority was accepted all over Mesopotamia and that only small bodies of troops were needed for its enforcement. At the close of his reign or near it he had to suppress Rim-Sin finally and thoroughly, and to send expeditions to Elam. He must have been involved in other military activities, of which perhaps we have a glimpse in the biblical story of Abraham—if, as seems not unlikely, Amraphel of Shinar stands for Hammurabi.

His grand work, however, was in the system of administration which culminated in the famous Code. The laws of Hammurabi were not his own invention ; they are a codification, shaping into one harmonious whole a multitude of laws and customs already in existence, and no doubt modifying them. But the codification is an epoch in the science of government.

A SLOW disintegration set in after Hammurabi was dead. No one of his line, progenitor or descendant, approaches this greatest known personality among the rulers of the oldest civilizations. None of this dynasty seems to have been a fighting man by choice ; but no oriental empire had ever preserved a prolonged sway without periods of energetic militarism.

**HAMMURABI THE LAWGIVER**

Hammurabi is separated from Gudea by the short-lived empire built up by the kings of Ur, Sumerian in name at least but largely Semitised. He is here seen on a stele set up by one of his officials as a dedication to a goddess.

*From the British Museum*

The dynasty of Hammurabi lost grip. Among the marshes that were steadily encroaching on the head of the Persian Gulf there grew up a 'Kingdom of the Sea Country' which was in frequent conflict with the successors of the great king. It lay on the lower Tigris, since the Babylonians tried to flood it out by damming that river ; but one of its kings, Iluma-ilu, came near to obtaining control of the whole country. The mountains on the east were full of tribesmen who were more than ready to take advantage of any signs of military weakness among the plain-dwellers—in 2072 B.C. there was a Kassite raid that caused five years of confusion. Behind the mountains of the west were surging the hordes of the Hatti or Hittites—a menace to upper Mesopotamia, where it can never have been easy to maintain a firm control from a centre in Babylonia.

Some century and a half after Hammurabi's decease, the dissolution of the dynasty was brought about by the devastating Hittite raid already mentioned, which left the power of Babylon shattered and helpless. The actual course of events is extremely uncertain ; but the next

**GUDEA THE BENEFACTOR**

Gudea was a prince and benefactor of Sumerian Lagash during the Gutian domination. He represents the end of the old order in Mesopotamia, just as the great lawgiver Hammurabi, sixth king of the Semitic First Babylonian Dynasty, typifies the new.

*From the Louvre*

apparently indisputable fact is the establishment of a Kassite dynasty at Babylon by the conqueror Gandash, who assumed the old title of King of the Four Quarters of the World, about the middle of the eighteenth century—a date not far removed from the latest assigned to the Hyksos invasion of Egypt, in the earlier half of that century.

### Dark Age in Egypt and Babylonia

THERE would seem to have been an interval of nearly two hundred years, according to Assyrian documents, between the fall of the Babylonian dynasty and the Kassite conquest ; an interval filled in only by the names of rulers in the Sea Country, and at Ashur (in Assyria), but without any record of events. On this basis the accepted date for Hammurabi is 2123-2080 B.C. Some authorities, however, mistrusting the Assyrian evidence, will admit no gap, and date Hammurabi 1944-1901, the date 1746 B.C. for Gandash being practically fixed. Almost certainly this is too low, but recent evidence seems to date the beginning of the Babylonian dynasty to 2169 B.C.—which would place Hammurabi's accession in about 2067. Until further confirmation, however, it is safer to follow the accepted chronology.

For some centuries following the close of the Twelfth Dynasty in Egypt and of the Hammurabi Dynasty in Babylon, the chronicle of both regions is involved in obscurity. The records we have are of later date, and are not easily reconcilable. The mists will rise again in Egypt at a date of which we are assured within a year or two—1580 B.C.—with the expulsion of the Hyksos and the founding of the Egyptian Empire ; in the Euphratic region they are hardly dispersing till about a century later.

In both regions the obscurity is in part the outcome of the incursion of a foreign element which breaks up the existing political system, but passes away without leaving any other permanent mark of its own. In both regions the date of the actual catastrophe is uncertain ; but we can at least be fairly confident that in the eighteenth century—probably during the first half—Semitic rulers from Syria,

known as the Hyksos, established themselves in the Nile Delta ; and that in the middle of the same century a dynasty known as the Kassites established itself at Babylon.

The Kassite conquerors were rude barbarians from the eastern mountains. Though their royal family ruled for nearly six hundred years, bearing names which were not Semitic nor Sumerian, but sometimes apparently Indo-European, their tribes never formed more than a fraction of the population into which they were absorbed. Under their rule, Babylon by slow degrees recovered something of her old ascendancy and claimed the old high-sounding titles.

The Kingdom of the Sea Country faded out and was absorbed ; Ashur (Assyria), on the upper Tigris, paid homage to Babylon which was little more than formal. In upper Mesopotamia the independent power of Mitanni appears firmly established when the mists rise ; its sway never extended over the Amorites, the trans-Euphrates Syrians and Phoenicians of the west. The Hittites had not followed up the devastating incursion which shattered the old Babylonian dynasty ; it was in the coming centuries that they were to make their bid for rank among the civilized powers of the ancient world.

### Egypt invaded by Foreigners

FOR the Nile Region the later Egyptian compilers enumerate five dynasties between the Twelfth and the Eighteenth, which founded the Empire : three legitimate and two foreign, the latter being counted as the Fifteenth and Sixteenth. On the latest-date calculation, they are crowded into 208 years. The two Hyksos dynasties must be regarded as contemporary with two of the other three ; but we must still assume a large proportion of very short reigns and a rule divided between simultaneous claimants to the pharaonic dignity, if we have to compress the three Egyptian dynasties into barely two centuries.

The points which seem clear are these. The weak pharaohs of the thirteenth dynasty were ejected from the Delta by foreign invaders ; but they and their successors were permitted to maintain at least a show of authority in Upper Egypt, though they eventually became tributaries of the Hyksos.

The Hyksos were certainly of Semitic speech ; presumably they were a horde or confederation of pastoral nomads from Syria, of whom the Israelites or Hebrews may just possibly have been a section that either before or after the invasion settled in the Delta, but was retained in its settlement at the time of the expulsion. The one novelty that Egypt owed to the invaders—for future use—was the war-horse and the war-chariot. Their domination was wholly destructive, though their later monarchs found themselves unable to resist the immemorial influences of the country. Tradition, of course, denounced them as infidels, brutal tyrants and oppressors.

The much later Jewish identification of the Hyksos as a whole with the Hebrew tribes is untenable, though we may recognize an intimate legendary connexion between the sojourn in Egypt and the Hyksos occupation. Uncertain also is the theory that the name is to be translated 'shepherd kings,' which is appropriate enough if they were a horde of pastoral nomads, but may very possibly be only an ingenious etymological error. 'Princes of the Deserts'—in other words, Beduins—is a more probable interpretation. A name easily identified as the Semitic Yakub (Jacob) is found among the Hyksos king lists, but it obviously has no connexion with the Hebrew patriarch.

### The Hyksos and their alien Rule

THE Hyksos formed a great armed camp, garrison or fortress at Avaris —a position on the east of the Delta which cannot be exactly identified— so that they might dominate Egypt from it and at the same time control their Syrian empire or confederacy, concerning which we have no further information. Their mightiest ruler was Khian, who took the title which means 'Embracer of Territories,' besides a regular pharaonic throne name. Under him and his successors there was probably

no independent Egypt in the south. Relics of him are found as far afield as Crete and Babylonia, though of a kind which suggests that they may very well have been merely spoils carried off thither at a much later date.

Towards the close of the seventeenth century, the Seventeenth Dynasty was reigning in Upper Egypt at Thebes, which had probably regained a measure of independence under Sekenenra I, but was still vassal to the Hyksos over-lord Apopi III in the Delta. Apopi, says tradition, sent word that he was annoyed by the roaring of the hippopotami in the realms of the king Sekenenra III. No doubt the envoy spake a parable. Sekenenra took alarm ; he revolted, and the revolt developed into a war of liberation.

### Egypt's War of Liberation

PATRIOTISM rallied to the daring rebel, and when he himself fell fighting— as testified by the wounds on the dead man's skull, which is preserved—it did not desert his young sons. Though tradition describes the war as a long one, its conclusion was achieved within twenty years by the third and youngest of them, the still youthful Aahmes. In the final stage, Memphis had been captured and the foreigners were besieged for three years in Avaris.

It is significant of the difficulties under which the patriots laboured that, during the prolonged siege, the Nubians in the south revolted in conjunction with some Egyptian nobles. So grave was the peril that the young king left the siege in person to lead an expedition against the rebels. His success was swift and complete ; he returned to the siege with all a victor's prestige ; and Avaris fell. The Hyksos army was driven over the border or cut to pieces, and the Hyksos vanished from the land they had plagued so long.

Egypt was once more free, and with the establishment of the Eighteenth Dynasty a new era commences. In Mesopotamia, however, the Kassites were still ruling ; obscurity besets the records on every hand, and Assyria had not yet felt her power.

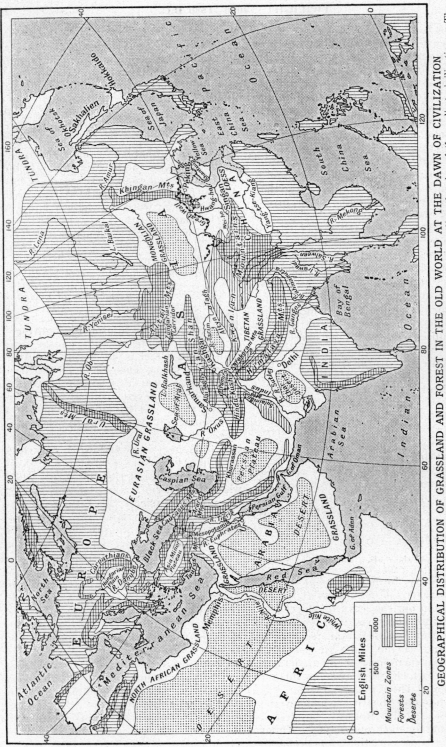

GEOGRAPHICAL DISTRIBUTION OF GRASSLAND AND FOREST IN THE OLD WORLD AT THE DAWN OF CIVILIZATION

An attempt is here made to show, from a purely human point of view, the geographical conditions attending the rise of the earliest civilizations. The important features for the history of Man were open country (grassland with parkland fringes); difficult country (forests and deserts); and impassable barriers (forested mountains). Forests are shown cloaking many regions whence they have subsequently been cleared; and in those far-off days the climate was damper, so that grass covered much that is now desert and most mountains were forest-clad. Only those mountains are given that were significant for human movements, irrespective of height; notice also the coast-line alterations of North China and the Persian Gulf.

### CHAPTER 2

# DAWN: 1580—900 B.C.

A T the beginning of the sixteenth century B.C. a blight of anarchy was passing away; but the world, the 'known world,' was not what it had been when the blight descended upon the old civilizations of Senusret and Hammurabi. Those old civilizations were not dead; but they re-emerged with a difference.

Egypt, it is true, rose again with a phoenix-like recuperation of power, but the unification of Mesopotamia had broken down under the disintegrating influence of barbarian invaders, and these had not yet learnt to organize new empires. While the Kassite conquerors turned themselves into Babylonians, upper Mesopotamia was not merged into Babylonia, but was dominated by the new half-alien power of Mitanni, in the bend of the Euphrates north-west and west of Assyria; between these nether and upper millstones lay Assyria, not crushed but not yet terrible, and probably with an independence but recently won from Mitannian overlordship. And on the north-western hills still lowered the Hittite storm-cloud.

## Syria a Bridge between the Powers

N o less conspicuous was the change which had taken place in the great Syrian area which intervened between the northern powers and Egypt. In the old days the shifting tribes of Semites who populated that region had never constituted a power, until the confederacy was formed of which the Hyksos monarchy in Egypt was presumably an off-shoot, perhaps the head. The Hyksos had gone, but the confederacy remained, however loosely knit together. What a powerful Beduin league had done in the past, Syria united under strong leadership might accomplish again, with the added incentive of vengeance for the Semitic débâcle in Egypt.

Moreover, Syria had now become not a barrier but a link, not a gulf but a bridge, between north and south; all the powers had an interest in the Syrian problem,

but immediately and most obviously Egypt. And it was Egypt's solution of the problem that brought her at last into direct political contact with the northern peoples, which during the earlier stages remained for the most part inactive.

When in 1580 B.C. Aahmes the Liberator flung the foreign tyrants in rout over the Egyptian border, unconsciously inaugurating a new era, not alone for Egypt, but for the civilized world, he was only at the beginning of his work. He had to consolidate a kingdom, and he had first to secure it against a renewal of the Semite aggression. Across the border the Semite power was far from being broken.

## Military Regeneration in Egypt

A CCORDINGLY, immediately after the expulsion, we find Aahmes engaged in a strenuous campaign in southern Palestine, where he laid stubborn siege to the fortress of Sharuhen, probably in what was later Judea. Sharuhen held out for three years before it fell: evidence that the campaign was no mere raid like that of Senusret, but had a serious purpose, and was waged against a still powerful foe. Moreover, we again find his armies battling successfully in north Palestine and Phoenicia. The probable object of these campaigns was not an imperial expansion but the security and consolidation of the restored kingdom of Egypt. The Syrian wars of Aahmes were no more than the completion of the war of liberation.

The menace from Asia being thoroughly curbed, Aahmes and his immediate successor Amenhotep I (1557–1541 B.C.) had a sufficiently heavy task before them in the reorganization of the state and the recovery of the upper Nile. In the nature of things, it was only through a new military system that the new monarchy could be established, and a new art of war was developed when the Egyptians learnt to appreciate on Syrian soil the possibilities of the war-chariot.

Aahmes must have shaped the organization. He had loyal supporters, but there was a serious disloyal element ready to take advantage of his embarrassments, especially in the south. When his successor Amenhotep found it necessary to march into Nubia, rebels rose in his rear with whom his officers dealt faithfully ; but the fact shows how hard it was to restore the central authority after two centuries of disintegration. At this point, however, our records become less complete, having hitherto been derived from the autobiographical memoirs of a notable servant of these two kings, Aahmes the son of Ebana, who took an active part in most of the campaigning, but soon after this disappears from the stage.

The power of the dynasty was fully established by the time of the accession of Thothmes I as husband of Amenhotep's daughter (also named Aahmes), some forty years after the liberation. The Nubians, however, between the Second and Fourth Cataracts were still incompletely subdued, and almost the last record of the old Aahmes, son of Ebana, tells of their subjugation at the beginning of the new reign.

Thothmes looked upon Syria as part of his dominion, though his predecessors must have had little enough hold on it and it ignored his sovereignty. He set about a conquest, but only in the old style ; that is to say, conquest was not accompanied or followed by the organization of effective control. He marched as far north as

SCENE OF THE EARLIEST IMPERIAL EXPANSIONS THAT HISTORY RECORDS

As far as possible this map shows the political situations in the Near East during the eventful period between 1580 and 900 B.C., which saw the rise and fall of Egyptian and Hittite empires, the first rumblings of the Assyrian volcano and the appearance of those new peoples to whom the history of the future belonged. Arrows show important racial movements, but they must not be taken to indicate the exact routes that were followed.

Naharin, the region lying between the Orontes and the Euphrates, meeting generally with little resistance but winning a great victory ; and he set up a stele beside the great river. Then he returned home proclaiming that he had made the ' circuit of the sun ' the boundary of Egypt.

Back in Egypt, he set himself to the restoration of past splendours. But the annals at the close of his reign (about 1501 B.C.) are complicated by an unsolved puzzle about the succession.

### Queen Hatshepsut's Golden Days

THOTHMES had a daughter by his queen Aahmes, who represented the line of Aahmes the liberator. This daughter, Hatshepsut, he had recognized as the legitimate successor to the throne which he himself occupied because he was her mother's husband. By inferior wives he had also two sons—or just possibly a son and a grandson—both named Thothmes. Presumably in order to keep the succession in the royal family, Hatshepsut was married to the younger.

Now it is certain that the elder was Pharaoh, as Thothmes II, with or without a co-regent, for two or three years. It is certain that Hatshepsut reigned for several years as independent sovereign, and was able in spite of her sex to ignore her young husband's title, which only attached to him through her. It is certain, too, that both she and her husband Thothmes III, who ruled gloriously for many years after her death, dated their reigns from 1501. But whether the brief reign of Thothmes II preceded their accession, in opposition to the wishes of the old Thothmes I, or was a revolutionary episode in Hatshepsut's first years, is an undecided question.

That Thothmes III resented intensely the treatment he suffered at her hands, and afterwards did his best to obliterate her memory, is not to be denied. It is to his deliberate defacement of her monuments that we owe this tangle of obscurity.

But the surprising fact remains that for some twenty years a queen not only reigned but ruled in Egypt, relegating her exceptionally able spouse to the position of a mere consort, though there was no precedent for such a happening. Indeed,

**THE ' NAPOLEON OF EGYPT '**

A brilliant general with a comparatively scientific understanding of warfare, and the vitality required for active campaigning, Thothmes III by force of arms and bellicose display greatly extended Egyptian influence in Syria and Nubia.

*Cairo Museum*

so ingrained were the conventions attached to a male ruler that on her monuments Hatshepsut is actually represented with a beard and in male attire ; certainly in her rule she displayed a masculine energy.

WAR not being her province, since she could not lead armies in the field, she indulged in no foreign excursions of a military order. The country was not threatened on any side ; and to give Thothmes the chance of outshining her by winning the military honours for which his soul craved would by no means have suited her. But under her rule Egypt flourished exceedingly, if the splendours of her temple building and temple restorations are any criterion of the national wealth and prosperity.

The most remarkable of her efforts, however, was a grand expedition by land and water to Punt, where no Egyptian had been seen for untold years—an entirely friendly expedition with no thought of war. It returned most richly laden with the products of that region, and is magnificently commemorated on the walls of the splendid queen's splendid temple at Deir el-Bahri, opposite Thebes.

With her death, in 1480–79 B.C., the energies of Thothmes III were released from the shackles she had imposed on them. We have come to the reign of the man who is perhaps entitled to be called the prototype of constructive empire builders ; a conqueror, but no mere captain of victorious armies ; a statesman even more than a warrior, though a warrior of genius.

In 1479—that is, at the earliest possible moment after the death of Hatshepsut— Thothmes set out on his first Asiatic campaign. It was more than time, if the work of his predecessors was to be pre- served. Since Thothmes I had planted his boundary stone on the bank of the Euphrates, the only expedition into Syria had been a raid led by Thothmes II during his brief reign. The Syrians, once the masters of Egypt, had no mind to remain the subjects of the Pharaoh, and a great confederation was in arms in the north.

The headquarters of the confederates lay at Kadesh on the Orontes, whose king was no doubt the moving spirit of the league. All Syria would seem to have joined it, except the chiefs of southern Palestine, on whom the first onslaught would fall. Thothmes kept a systematic account of his operations ; those written records have not survived, but from them were extracted the monumental records which enter into great detail. For the first time in the world's history we have revealed to us a captain of the highest rank not only as a fighting man but also as a strategist and a military organizer.

In April, 1479, Thothmes had assembled his army on the frontier of Egypt proper. Nine days later he was at Gaza, on the twenty-second anniversary of his formal accession. He did not pause to celebrate it, but was on the march again next morning. The confederates, rebels from his point of view, had gathered in force with their base at Megiddo on the other side of the ridge of Mount Carmel, to bar the route by which an invading force from the south must enter Syria. No resistance was to be looked for in the south ; in ten days he was at the eastern foothills of Carmel.

Megiddo lay at the far mouth of a very narrow pass. Apart from this, he might follow the main route, skirting the south of Carmel, or turn the enemy's position by way of a broader pass on the north. Through the Megiddo

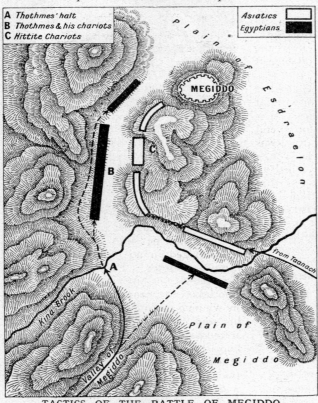

**TACTICS OF THE BATTLE OF MEGIDDO**

Megiddo, with three roads converging thereon, blocked the route to North Syria. The Syrians were guarding the obvious open road by Taanach ; Thothmes III flung his army through the narrow central pass and gave successful battle to the hurriedly recalled enemy beneath the walls of the town.

pass his army would have to move often in single file ; as his council of war pointed out, it might very well be trapped and cut to pieces. But the king's calculated audacity overruled the counsels of caution. Others were free to take what route they chose ; he was going through the pass at the head of those who dared to follow.

### First of the many Battles of Megiddo

AUDACITY succeeded. The whole army of course followed the intrepid king ; no preparation had been made on the other side for a move so unexpected, no resistance of consequence was met with, and the troops were able to form up on the comparatively open ground at the mouth of the pass, while the surprised enemy, who seem to have been at Taanach guarding the southern route, hastily threw themselves between Thothmes and the town. The chariots must have found the pass rough going ; but the whole force had been carried through and re-formed in less than twelve hours—a fair proof of the smallness of the expeditionary army.

It was too late in the day to deliver battle. Troops were flung out to right and left to cut off the enemy's retreat and, in case of defeat, to cover a line of retirement. When battle was joined next morning, the king, leading the charge of his troops, broke the enemy's centre, and the Syrians were soon flying in headlong rout to the walls of Megiddo, which closed its gates, but let down sheets whereby the fugitive princes, including the kings of Kadesh and Megiddo, were hauled over the battlements. But to the exceeding wrath of Thothmes the victorious troops, instead of completing their work, fell on the camp wherein was vast booty ; consequently the king of Kadesh was able to escape before the exits could be blocked.

The first battle on the field of Armageddon ('Har-Megiddo '—the Mountain of Megiddo) had been fought and won, but by no means the last. The town was closely invested, and gradually starved into surrender while the besiegers lived on the country. Meantime, from far and near the chiefs who had not been with the defeated army came in to make their submission to Thothmes. After some weeks,

the despairing princes within the beleaguered city threw themselves on the mercy of the conqueror, who entered its gates in triumph. Immense spoils were carried off, and the harvest of the plain of Esdraelon was commandeered ; but no vindictiveness was displayed towards the vanquished. Thothmes contented himself with the very substantial indemnities provided mainly by the treasures in Megiddo.

The campaign was completed by a rapid march to the foot of the Lebanons, where further submissions were received and a fortress was planted and garrisoned. The chiefs who had been in arms were probably dispossessed and others whose loyalty might be relied upon put in their places. As a further security, both immediate and for the future, their sons were sent to Egypt to receive an imperial education, to imbibe Egyptian ideas and in due time to return to the government of their own people imbued with a spirit of intelligent loyalty. Six months after leaving the Egyptian frontier the conqueror was back at Thebes, endowing the supreme god Amen with the unexampled fruits of his victories.

### Consolidating Egypt's Syrian Empire

IN each of the three following years Thothmes conducted a bloodless ' campaign' through the territories which he had restored to Egypt ; confirming his authority, but postponing further military adventures till all should be thoroughly secured. On one of these progresses he had the satisfaction of receiving a gift-bearing embassy from distant Ashur, then the chief town of Assyria, proving the wide renown of his achievements.

Then fell an interval during which he was laying far-sighted plans for future campaigns. To reach the distant and still defiant Kadesh, he needed a new base ; and he conceived the idea, brilliant for his days, of turning the Syrian position by sea, at the same time avoiding the difficult terrain of Palestine. Thus in the seventh year a great fleet transported him to northern Phoenicia, which on the fall of Arvad made ready submission and for many years afforded Egypt a secure naval base in the north. The next year's

B*

campaign saw the fall of Kadesh, hitherto the stubborn centre of Syrian hostility. The policy followed in southern Syria was repeated in the north, though another by no means bloodless campaign was needed before all resistance was quelled in the maritime cities.

### Napoleonic Genius of Thothmes III

𝕭EYOND Kadesh, however, was Naharin, and behind Naharin again was the powerful state of Mitanni—the first probably Aryan-speaking power to appear on the scene, since Babylon retained its indigenous character in spite of its Kassite dynasty ; and at most the Aryan character of the Kassites is doubtful. That the Mitannian ruling family spoke an Aryan tongue and worshipped Aryan gods is certain, but whether they were of the same blood and speech as their subjects we cannot be sure.

Mitanni must have been anxious to preserve the Naharin barrier between herself and the aggressive warrior of Egypt. The eighth expedition was directed from Phoenicia upon Naharin ; her cities fell before Thothmes, who smote a Mitannian force at Carchemish, reached the Euphrates and crossed it, and planted his boundary-stone on its farther side. But, true to his principle, he halted to organize before carrying his arms farther.

In fact, when Thothmes reached the Euphrates, the limit beyond which his predecessors had at no time claimed dominion, he abandoned, if he had ever entertained, the idea of further expansion. He crossed the Euphrates merely by way of a demonstration that he had done something which no one before him had succeeded in accomplishing.

Such was the fear inspired by his invincible prowess—unwontedly free though it was from what we have learnt to call frightfulness—that even from the land of Hatti, which lay beyond the Taurus, the Hittites thought it politic to send the complimentary gifts which by him were naturally styled tribute ; nor was it long before he received similar compliments from Cyprus over the sea—if Alashiya is to be identified with Cyprus, and not with a district on the southern coast of Asia Minor. Taurus and Euphrates were natural physical boundaries beyond which it would never be practicable to exercise efficient control, and only one more campaign was needed to round off the empire by subjugating what was still unsubdued on this side of Taurus.

𝕱OR nine more years, however, the regular military demonstrations or progresses were annually repeated, usually from Phoenicia. Sometimes they were real campaigns, when rebellion attempted to make head in the north, or, as once, in the south. But for the last ten years of the reign even demonstrations ceased to be necessary. Peace was unbroken from the Euphrates to the Nile.

### DEFEATED AND HUMBLED BY THE WARRIOR PHARAOH

An epitome of the far-reaching conquests of Thothmes III, this throne painting represents a group of supplicants containing representatives of peoples vanquished by him. Of the fair-skinned men, one—he on the left with a shawl draped over his shoulders—may be a Mitannian, while the other is a Semite from Syria. The negroes with the typical insignia of African warriors—ostrich feathers stuck in the hair and leopard tails attached to their loin-cloths—are Nubians.

*From Wrezinski, Altägyptischen Kulturgeschichte*

Some six months of nearly every year, for twenty years after the death of Hatshepsut, had been passed by Thothmes in Asia. In his absences, the administration of Egypt itself was the care of trusty viziers—in medieval England they would have been called justiciars. But whenever he was at home, Thothmes was immensely energetic in every department of government, as well as in the execution of innumerable public works. Incidentally, he found time for campaigns in Nubia, which brought the Nile country under complete control at least as far as the Third Cataract ; and the oases on the west of the river were placed in direct charge of an officer of state.

By personal tours of inspection and supervision he ensured the sound administration of justice together with the honest and equitable collection of revenue. It is evident that all the productive resources of the country were actively developed, and the products of foreign climes poured into Egypt, from without the empire as well as from within it.

The organization of the Asiatic empire of Thothmes presents remarkable features, though our knowledge of details is small. We can discern in it what might almost be called suggestions of the relations to-day between the Supreme Government in India and the 'Protected Princes.' Native princes continued to rule in the subject principalities, conditionally on their good behaviour, including the regular payment of the recognized tribute. In some instances they were attended by an imperial officer who discharged the functions of a British Resident. Egyptian garrisons were stationed in fortresses at strategic points. The north was under the general supervision of a military governor.

**POWERFUL RULER**

Celebrated for his warlike valour, Amenhotep II successfully reaffirmed the conquests of his father, Thothmes III, and gave Egypt twenty years of peace.
*Cairo Museum*

Every effort was made to bring the native rulers into sympathy with Egyptian and imperial ideas, especially by educating them in the princes' college at Thebes. There was no interference with native religious or other customs. The rule was a foreign rule, established at the sword's point, and was felt and resented as such ; but it was a rule beneficent and irresistible, which gave to the weak a secure protection against their stronger neighbours.

Thothmes died a month before the completion of the fifty-fourth year of his nominal and thirty-third of his unfettered reign. His successor was his son, Amenhotep II (1447-1420 B.C.), whom he had associated with himself on the throne a year or two earlier.

It was long since the secretly hostile princes of Syria had ventured to attempt rebellion. The death of the old king was the opportunity for which they had been waiting, and they promptly rose to arms. The new king was no less prompt. Within a month from his father's death he was on the march from Egypt. Before another month was past he had routed the advance force of the enemy in northern Palestine, performing mighty deeds of personal prowess at the head of his troops—he was a big man, of whom it was said that none in his army was strong enough to draw his bow. Before the swift rush of his march resistance crumpled up. As he swung up to the Euphrates, a cowering embassy from Mitanni came to implore grace. The rebellion collapsed utterly and never again ventured to raise its head during the life of this Egyptian Coeur-de-Lion.

Amenhotep returned to Egypt in triumph after his brief tornado-like campaign. He sailed up to Thebes with seven captive kings hanging alive head downward from his prow ; six of them he slew in the temple of Amen, as an acceptable sacrifice to the god. The victory in the north was followed up by a campaign in Nubia, which carried his southern frontier to the Fourth Cataract, where the seventh of the northern princes was hung up on the walls of Napata as a grim warning to rebels.

The statesmanship of Thothmes made him a lenient conqueror ; Amenhotep could certainly be a thoroughgoing barbarian when it suited him. Once was enough, however ; the need—or the opportunity—never recurred. But there is no warrant for reproaching the cruelty of Amenhotep. The methods of Samuel and David were no less drastic ; every campaign was attended by the deportation of slaves by the hundred, and human sacrifices were a matter of course.

Amenhotep had proved himself a mighty man of his hands, and a commander in the field who was no unworthy son of the great Thothmes. Nevertheless, he was not moved to any further military exploits in the remaining twenty years or more of his reign. There is no record of later campaigns. The irresistible strength of the government had been decisively demonstrated, and Egypt enjoyed apparently unbroken peace and prosperity.

It was a matter of course, however, that his death (c. 1420) should be the signal for risings in the remote provinces of the empire. At any rate, his son Thothmes IV had to undertake a campaign in Naharin, from which he returned with spoils and slaves. It was also made the occasion for the opening of friendly diplomatic relations with Mitanni. Probably the far northern power was growing fearful of the aggression of its Anatolian neighbours, the Hittites ; who were the more dangerous because the Taurus barrier practically secured them from attack. Naharin and Phoenicia were similarly exposed to the Hittites, whom Mitanni and Egypt had a common interest in checking.

### First Royal Marriage for Reasons of State

WE may assume that the overtures had come from Mitanni, which had been thoroughly taught to fear the power of the southern empire. Having failed to preserve a buffer in Naharin, policy required friendly relations. Babylonia, always pacific, also offered amity. The result was an unprecedented departure from Egyptian practice ; Thothmes IV invited a Mitannian princess to become his queen—the first instance of a political alliance cemented by a royal marriage. In due time Mutemuya (to give her her Egyptian name) became, it is said, the mother of the next emperor, Amenhotep III—though this is difficult to believe, since the reign of Thothmes seems hardly to have exceeded ten years, so that the child would scarcely have been eight at his accession. Perhaps the Mitannian was not Mutemuya but her successor as ' chief wife.'

A campaign at the southern as well as the northern extremity of the empire was almost a matter of course. But the might of Egypt was too well es-

#### MOST SPLENDID OF THE PHARAOHS
When Amenhotep III succeeded to the throne, Egypt was flourishing and at peace ; his government was able enough to maintain these conditions and to command respect. Free from political anxieties, the king devoted himself to artistic magnificence—the cast above (right) is probably his actual death-mask.
*Photo, left, Mansell ; right, Berlin Museum*

tablished for such operations to be regarded as anything more than punitive expeditions into the outskirts of the empire, reminders that the arm of the supreme government was a long one and its power not to be disputed with impunity. There were no clouds on the imperial horizon when Amenhotep III ascended the throne of the Pharaohs in 1411.

During the thirty-six years of his reign Amenhotep III seems once and only once to have taken part in even the semblance of a military expedition. This was into Nubia, in his fourth year (no more than thirteen years after his father married the Mitannian princess, who can therefore hardly have been his mother). For the rest of the reign, the imperial peace seems to have been unbroken.

### Egypt at the Zenith of her Magnificence

IN the reign of Amenhotep III Egypt was at the height of her power, the zenith of her magnificence. Of all her rulers he was the most splendid. Wealth poured into his treasury, to be poured out in a correspondingly lavish expenditure on every form of art. He had no political or military anxieties to vex him. With all the Mesopotamian powers on the best of terms, there seemed to be no danger of external attack, and the organization of the empire created by his forebears had reached such perfection that no internal disturbance was to be feared. With the wealth that lay to his hand, he need stint himself in nothing of his desires, and his desires were all in the direction of artistic magnificence. In all this, the reign of Amenhotep III was the golden age of Egypt. He was her ' Roi Soleil.'

The contemporary historical documents, apart from the monuments, are particularly illuminating. For his reign and that of his son we have the singular mass of diplomatic correspondence, known from the place where they were discovered as the Tell el-Amarna letters.

Since the Kassite conquest in Babylonia, our narrative has carried us across the Euphrates only at the moment when a Thothmes or an Amenhotep thought fit to set up a boundary-stone on its farther bank in celebration of victory won on the hither side. The meagre chronicles of the Mesopotamian regions give us no events to record. In Babylonia a foreign dynasty reigned, but with little about it that was foreign save the names of its princes. Elam had long been inactive; the Sea Country as a separate state had passed away; no new invaders later than the Kassites had burst in from the mountains. Babylon, as the sacred city and the seat of the monarchy, enjoyed a dignified prestige, but was placidly unaggressive. Her pretensions to sovereignty were unchallenged, perhaps because they were practically ineffectual. Ashur acknowledged her authority as a polite convention.

At some not clearly distinguishable stage the state of Mitanni, under its Aryan rulers, had developed in upper Mesopotamia : a distant forerunner of the Medes and Persians, an advance guard of the Aryan migration, but content to abide in her settlements without further extension of conquest. With Assyrians on the east, Syrians—now under the sway of Egypt, since their confederation had failed to transform itself into an empire—on the south-west, and the Hittite storm-cloud on the Taurus, her interest was certainly peace. For each and all of the Mesopotamian states it had become a matter of primary importance to conciliate the mighty empire of the south.

### Amicable Relations with Mitanni and Babylon

MITANNI had been taught her lesson once for all by Thothmes III ; she had humbled herself before Amenhotep II ; she had definitely made her peace with Thothmes IV when he honoured her by receiving her king's daughter as his wife. It is difficult, as has been remarked, to believe that Amenhotep III was that lady's son ; but he received a niece of hers into his harem, though not as his chief wife (a position already occupied), and later a great-niece to be the chief wife of his heir. He also wedded a daughter of Babylon, and married a daughter of his own either to the king of Babylon himself or to his heir. The kings address each other as ' My Brother,' but there is an obvious suggestion that the Egyptian brother was the bigger.

Yet amidst all this splendour might have been detected warnings of trouble to be guarded against ; they remained unheeded. Where there were any signs of defection, it was so easily suppressed that the Pharaoh no longer saw need for the progresses through Asia which none of his predecessors had neglected. From the far north came warnings of Hittite raids, but a Hittite attack on Mitanni had been heavily defeated by its king, Dushratta. Amenhotep declined to regard as serious the appeals of his provincial governors for more active measures ; and the empire paid the penalty in the reign (1375–1358 B.C.) of his son Amenhotep IV, better known as Akhnaton.

### The Cost of Unpractical Idealism

IN many respects Akhnaton was a very remarkable man. He was a reforming enthusiast and idealist in art, morals and religion, a seeker after truth who attempted to impose his own spiritual conceptions on an age and a people very far from spiritual. Instances are not wanting of great idealists having also been great practical rulers and statesmen, but Akhnaton was not of these. As a king, he was a failure. Absorbed in his religious revolution, he neglected entirely the practical tasks of government.

The machinery broke down and rapid disintegration of the empire set in.

Although at the close of the reign of Amenhotep III the loyal princes in the north were painfully aware of the disloyal element and of the Hittite menace, they had failed to convince the Pharaoh of the danger. No sudden storm burst immediately on his son's accession. The Hittite king was anxious to lull suspicions, and among the Syrian princes the arch-traitor Aziru the Amorite was an adept in the art of giving a plausible colour of loyalty to his most disloyal operations. In spite of urgent appeals, the loyalists were not reinforced, while city after city was falling into the hands of Aziru or his Hittite ally, and Dushratta of Mitanni and Burra-Buriash of Babylon were clamouring for the gold that Egypt could so easily supply.

EVIDENTLY the Egyptian governors and residents appointed in the latter years were not of the calibre required in an emergency, and paralysed the loyalists instead of helping them. Farther south, Palestine was in chaos, overrun by the Khabiru—desert tribes, suspected by some of being the 'Hebrew' conquerors of Canaan, and almost certainly not unconnected with them in some way. And Amenhotep at home was too busy replacing the worship of Amen by that of the Aton, and changing his own name to 'Akhn-Aton,' to give attention to the needs of his Asiatic subjects ; though incidentally he was lending his countenance to Assyria and recognizing her independence, despite the remonstrances of both Babylon and Mitanni, each of which claimed to be her suzerain.

The paralysis of Egypt continued till the middle of the century. The revolutionary king was probably no more than thirty when he died ; of his three immediate successors, two, Sakere and Tutankhamen, were his sons-in-law, while the third, Ay, was a figurehead,

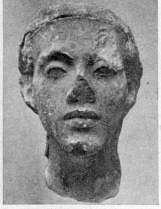

**HERETIC KING WHO LOST THE EMPIRE**
Preoccupied with his religious reforms and his philosophy, Akhnaton was content to let the Egyptian dependencies in Palestine and Syria slip from his possession. Intelligent as he appears in these portraits (that on the right is a contemporary cast), he yet seems to have lacked all practical ability.
*The Louvre and Berlin Museum*

perhaps placed on the throne by Horemheb, or Harmhab, who may be reckoned as either the last of the Eighteenth or first of the Nineteenth Dynasty. Tutankh-Amen, by the changing of his name from Tutankh-Aton, marks the collapse of Akhnaton's idealist 'heresy' and the recovery of power by the priesthood of Amen. An attempt was made in his reign to reassert the imperial authority in Asia, but it was already too late. The empire created by the genius of Thothmes III had passed away.

Under a government efficiently controlled and directed, by a competent head and competent viceroys, the disruptive movement in Syria

**HEIRS TO A DIMINISHED INHERITANCE**

Second of the three insignificant successors of Akhnaton, Tutankhamen (left) was incapable of repairing the damage caused by the reformer but did attempt to renew Egyptian authority in Palestine. He was succeeded by Ay, who was Pharaoh from 1353 to 1350 B.C. This cast (right), probably a life-mask, has been thought to represent him.

*From Carter and Mace, ' The Tomb of Tutankhamen,' and the Berlin Museum*

would have met with no more success than those that had preceded it during the past century. As matters stood, it was the craft of the very able Hittite king, Subbiluliuma (1395–1350 B.C.), that fostered the movement and turned it to full account. Cunning as Aziru was, he was, in fact, only the cat's-paw of the Hittite; if he shook off the yoke of Egypt, it was but to find himself the vassal of Hatti.

**Asia in the Melting-pot**

UNWITTINGLY, Akhnaton's religious revolution was responsible for a revolution in the international system. When Horemheb, having probably been for some time the saving power behind the throne, himself assumed the responsibility of the crown, Asia had been passing through the melting-pot. Subbiluliuma had absorbed Naharin and the coastlands, from the Euphrates to the Mediterranean, and Mitanni, too, had disappeared into the Hittite maw, or partly into that of Assyria; while Babylon was rather dependent on Assyria than Assyria on Babylon.

The Hittite power and Assyria had adopted similar methods; they had not conquered Mitanni and Babylon, but had

intervened in dynastic revolutions. In Mitanni at least the established prince was merely Subbiluliuma's puppet; we hear no more of her as an independent power; while in Syria Aziru had preferred submission to challenging destruction.

Horemheb was an Egyptian noble apparently unconnected with the royal family. He had discharged numerous administrative functions with efficiency, evidently retaining the confidence of Akhnaton himself and his successors in spite of his adherence to the old religion. Finally, his influence and authority with the Amen party, joined with loyalty to the throne, had led to his endowment with official powers practically amounting to a dictatorship. On the death of Ay (c. 1350) there was no one with a clear title to the succession; he was obviously the necessary man of the hour; the army was in his hands, there were no rivals, and the divine oracles were prompt to give their sanction. He provided himself with a formal title by marrying the sister of Akhnaton's queen, and ascended the throne of the Pharaohs.

His business was a conservative reconstruction. Ambitious imperial schemes were out of the question until a sound

**NOBLE WHO BECAME KING**

Commander of Tutankhamen's armies—he is here represented with his baton in his hand—and dictator during the reign of Ay, Horemheb succeeded the latter as Pharaoh, when he inaugurated a policy of vigorous reconstruction.

*Cairo Museum*

system of domestic administration had been restored and brought into thorough working order. Corruption, peculation, official oppression, evasion of the law, downright lawlessness, were rife. The cleansing of the Augean stable required infinite courage, tenacity and patience, a ruler of character rather than of genius. Egypt had found one who could make it his sole boast that he had wholeheartedly sought the welfare of Egypt. The stable was cleansed, and was kept clean. Horemheb was an old and tired man before his reign was ended (1321 B.C.); but during that reign he had done a king's work for the people over whom he ruled.

Rameses I, the man whom Horemheb had chosen to be his own successor, was presumably of the old blood-royal. He survived for a year or two years only; but he had already associated with himself on the throne his son Seti I (1320-1300 B.C.), a prince well fitted to carry on the task of revival.

Even through the period of disintegration, Egypt had kept a hold on Nubia, and to some extent on southern Palestine or Canaan; there, however, it can have amounted to little more than a somewhat uncertain collection of tribute. The Beduins who were overrunning the land—whether they were Hebrews or not—would no doubt pay under mild pressure, while the restoration of order in Palestine must perforce await the restoration of order in Egypt. With the exception of one expedition, probably under Tutankhamen, no considerable Egyptian force had been in the country for the better part of a century. On the other hand, its 'milk and honey' had not been a bait sufficient to bring down the Hittites or Amorites.

### Asiatic Adventures of Seti I

SETI as crown prince had conducted a little frontier war with Nubia as a necessary display of authority, with the customary complement of spoils and captives. Evidently he had decided that the time had come to restore in what was left of the outlying portions of the old empire the order which Horemheb had re-established in the Nile valley.

The first move was a march on Palestine. An attack by the desert tribes of Edom was scattered. Seti marched by the usual coast route through southern Palestine unresisted, entered Megiddo, and pushed north as far as the Lebanon and Tyre, receiving the submission of the princes. The march had been more a demonstration than a campaign, but it had served its purpose of bringing the country and the coast under control as far as the districts now claimed by the Hittite king or his Amorite vassals. With them there was no collision, such as in the time of Thothmes III would have been inevitable. Conditions had changed.

Seti returned to Egypt in triumph. The Libyans on the west had been making experimental raids on the Delta and required a lesson before he made his second and last Asiatic expedition to confirm the effects of the first. On this occasion there was an engagement with Hittite forces in which the latter were routed; but no attempt was made to extend conquest. In effect it was tacitly admitted that what Hatti had taken during the period of Egyptian disruption, she had taken.

The conquests of Thothmes III had been won not from the grasp of a consolidated state, but by a systematised series of campaigns against a confederation of small principalities with no common head, each conquest having been organized before he proceeded to the next. Subbiluliuma of Hatti had in his turn engorged the Syrian artichoke leaf by leaf, never colliding with a great power, while Egypt was out of action. Mursil, a successor of Subbiluliuma, was in possession now (1345-1320 B.C.), and to evict him would perhaps have been a task too hard even for a Thothmes.

Seti did not attempt it. There was no likelihood of counter-aggression on the part of the Hittite, and the two powers came to an agreement satisfactory to both, each re-cognizing t h e rights of the o t h e r in the territory where its sovereignty w a s actually established. If S e t i returned

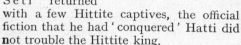

with a few Hittite captives, the official fiction that he had 'conquered' Hatti did not trouble the Hittite king.

Though Seti reigned for twenty years he attempted no further conquest of Asia. He carried out public works on a great scale of magnificence, but also others which were or ought to be of direct benefit, notably the sinking and protection of wells—not always with success. Before his death he secured the succession of his eldest son; but he was hardly in his grave when his second son Rameses II (1300-1225 B.C.) supplanted his elder brother, who not only disappeared himself but was forthwith effaced from the monuments on which, as crown prince, he had been portrayed.

Rameses II never hesitated to efface anyone whose honours he could thereby more easily appropriate to himself, and achieve a spurious glory in addition to that to which his own deeds entitled him. The obliteration of a portrait of his brother as crown prince, for which his own was substituted, is still traceable.

Endowed with an enormous self-confidence and unsurpassed egotism, Rameses resolved to recover all the imperial glories of the past in his own person. The fourth year of his reign saw him, in imitation of the great Thothmes, establishing his hold on the northern coastland; early in the fifth (1296), he was on the march against Mutallis, the Hittite king, who, in preparation for the attack, had gathered a great army and occupied the commanding strategic position at Kadesh.

Advancing from the coast with his force in four divisions named after the four great gods—Amen, Ra, Ptah and Sutekh—Rameses was skilfully drawn into a trap which all but wrought his ruin.

**RESTORER OF IMPERIAL GREATNESS**
With Egypt again consolidated within, Seti I recovered for her the effective control of much of Palestine and Syria. Here we may compare, side by side, his mummified head, and a bas-relief of him at Abydos.
*Photos, Mansell and Sebah*

Deceived into believing that the enemy had fallen back, he flung himself on Kadesh with the Amen division, leaving the others far in the rear. The Hittites and their allies, ambushed behind the town, suddenly launched their chariots upon the Ra division as it straggled up, cut it in two, broke into Amen's encampment, routing most of the unprepared occupants, and would have annihilated the King and his personal bodyguard but for the desperate valour with which he headed chariot charge after charge against them.

Meanwhile, news of the disaster reached the tardy Ptah division, which arrived on the scene just in time to fall on the rear of the enemy and turn the tables on them. The Hittite chariots were driven into the river, some of them making the farther bank, where the infantry was standing ; but to attempt a renewal of the battle was hopeless.

**GUIDED BY VAST AMBITIONS**

In attempting grandiose conquests in Asia, Rameses II was actuated by hunger for glory and empire rather than by statesmanship. This statue and even the head of his mummy convey a clear impression of his great pride and vitality.

*Photos, Mansell*

The enemy fled, according to the Egyptian account, and sent envoys to implore for peace, which was granted by the magnanimous victor. Rameses withdrew in triumph, and returned to Egypt to celebrate his glories. As a matter of fact, he had by his personal valour retrieved the disastrous blunder for which he had been personally responsible, but at a cost that made it impossible to follow up the victory, such as it was. Kadesh itself remained, as it seems, uncaptured. A Hittite version would be interesting !

### Treaty that Ended the Hittite War

ACTUALLY, Rameses was so far from having broken the Hittite power that he was very soon engaged on a campaign to make good his position in southern Palestine, where the Hittites were making common cause with the foes of Egypt. It took some three years before that region was sufficiently subdued to enable him to proceed with his efforts at reconquest farther north in Naharin. The course of these wars cannot be traced with any accuracy. He is found campaigning considerably beyond Kadesh, which may imply that he captured it ; on one occasion he was surprised, and was forced to fight without having time to put on his armour. He captured cities year after year, but capturing did not always mean retaining.

It all ended in Peace with Honour. Mutallis was killed—perhaps assassinated —in 1295 and his brother Hattusil, who succeeded to a probably precarious throne, proffered terms, by no means in the character of a vanquished suppliant. Peace and amity were better than an interminable war between rivals, neither of whom seemed in the least likely to achieve decisive victory. That was all. Hatti and Egypt were on an equal footing—and Egypt was quite ready.

The treaty struck in the twenty-first year of Rameses II is the first instrument of the kind preserved for posterity, possibly the first to which the name ' treaty ' can be applied definitely, though a treaty so called had certainly been made between Seti and Mursil, the father of Mutallis, to which, and to a previous treaty (with Horemheb), reference is made in this instrument. Here, however, we have a formal diplomatic document—copied on the walls of Egyptian temples—of which parts, in an earlier draft, have been found in cuneiform at the Hittite capital ; a regular treaty of alliance and brotherhood for ever ; pledging the two potentates to abstain from aggression against each other, to make common cause against foreign aggressors and internal rebels, and mutually to hand over political offenders. And that treaty was at any rate so far faithfully observed that Hatti and Egypt were never again in arms against each other (1280 B.C.).

Some years later, Rameses took a daughter of Hattusil to wife. He had evidently had his fill of fighting, for we never hear of him on campaign again after the treaty, though he lived till 1225. His wars won him a posthumous glory out of all proportion to his military achievements, though his personal prowess is not to be questioned. With all his campaigning, the ' conqueror of the Hittites' does not appear to have won a foot of territory from them. For the peace he made with them, however, he almost deserves to be called a great man ; though even for that the credit belongs more to Hattusil than to Rameses. But his unrivalled genius for advertisement is attested by his posthumous reputation. He successfully attached to his own name the honours belonging to the most distinguished of his predecessors.

### Magnificence Cloaks the Empire's Decay

𝔚HEN the lust of battle and adventure had departed from him, Rameses left the empire to sink into decay while its outward splendour hid the process. Long before the end—for he lived to about ninety —he had probably sunk into senile decay himself. The eldest survivor of his multitudinous offspring, Merneptah (who was formerly identified with the ' Pharaoh of

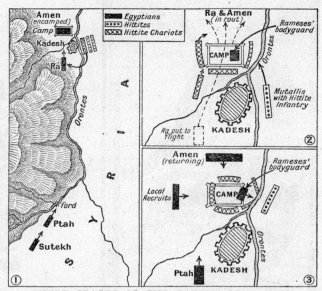

THREE STAGES OF THE BATTLE OF KADESH

Rameses II, with the four divisions of his army strung apart in column of route, fell into a Hittite trap (1) and had his second division cut up. Most of his own division, encamped, was carried away in the panic (2), and only his personal bodyguard sustained the battle until the arrival of the third division (3).

the Exodus'), though already an old man, made a creditable attempt at recovery, crushed revolts in Palestine, and inflicted a shattering defeat on the forces of Libyan raiders reinforced by the ominously multiplying bands of sea-rovers (1221). But on his death (c. 1215) there ensued a period of anarchy, pretender after pretender seizing the throne of the Pharaohs ; until the last of Egypt's warrior kings, Rameses III of the Twentieth Dynasty, came to the throne after the vigorous but very brief rule of his father, Setnekht, in 1198.

In the latter half of the fourteenth century Mitanni had disappeared, swallowed up by Hatti. Babylon, under a young ruler, Kurigalzu, who had been established on the throne by the intervention of Ashur-uballit of Assyria, was for a time virtually a dependency of that power. But Kurigalzu proved vigorous.; Ashur-uballit's successors were inactive, and Babylon recovered her independence. Neither was disposed to challenge Hatti, which was too occupied with the problem of absorbing the Syrian territories of the Egyptian Empire to turn her ambitions eastward.

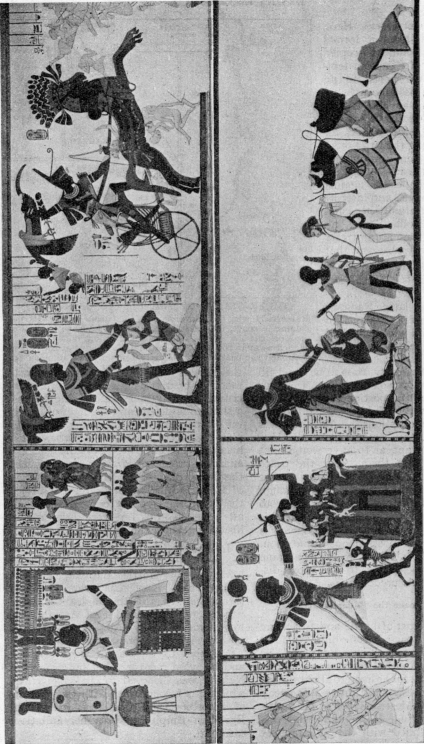

VIGOROUS REPRESENTATION OF INCIDENTS IN THE CAMPAIGNS OF THE VAINGLORIOUS RAMESES II.

In fact an indifferent general, though apparently possessing plenty of impetuous courage, Rameses II took an inordinate delight in commemorating, pictorially and otherwise, the details of his conquests. Although his successes do not appear to have been considerable, the records usually take the form of scenes of victory such as are included in this mural decoration (the two strips form a continuous band in a Nubian temple). Rameses is shown seated upon his throne while Asiatic prisoners are haled before him; next are representations of him slaying a Libyan, and charging Syrian foes in his chariot. Below, he is seen capturing a Syrian fortress, and receiving more prisoners—Libyans on this occasion.

*Photos, Mansell*

44

When Rameses II and Mutallis were in the grip of their fifteen years' struggle, Shalmaneser I of Assyria (1276–1256 B.C.) had hopes of profiting at the expense of Hatti, but still refrained from an open challenge. Any projects of aggression were dashed by the great peace. Hattusil, however, became most friendly with Babylon, which was most unfriendly with Assyria, though there was evidently a strong pro-Assyrian, anti-Hittite party there as well, while both powers were intriguing for the ascendancy. The general result was that about the middle of the century (1256) Shalmaneser's son Tukulti-Ninurta ejected the pro-Hittite king of Babylon, Kadashman-Buriash, made himself king and ruled for seven years, while the Hittite—Hattusil had died not long before—made no attempt to defend his ally.

The Hittite power was already dissolving ; before the century was over it had passed away. Babylon revolted against Tukulti-Ninurta, recovered her freedom, and under her kings Meli-shipak II and Marduk-apal-iddin I is found once more holding Assyria apparently in vassalage. But after this comes chaos for a time.

**PHARAOH ENGAGES HIS FOE**

Rameses II's personal prowess is beyond dispute, and the active part that he played in battle is shown by this spirited relief at Abu Simbel, representing him in the act of smiting a Libyan soldier with (apparently) his lance.

The old Kassite line perishes in an Assyrian revolt early in the twelfth century ; not Kassites, but a genuine native dynasty from Isin reigns in Babylon, with no sort of distinction for its first twenty-five years, while Assyria, though independent, lies under a cloud.

𝖂HEN the twelfth century opened, the old powers which still survived were in decline, and new forces hardly yet recognizable were coming into play ; forces whose movements we can only now begin to chronicle.

For centuries past a high civilization had existed among the islanders of the eastern Mediterranean, having its principal centre in Crete ; it is conveniently known as Minoan. There had been much commercial intercourse with Egypt, but no definite political relations, and the annals of this maritime power cannot as yet be traced out.

It had extended its penetration to the coasts of the Aegean, till its primacy had passed from Cnossus to its offshoot Mycenae on the Greek mainland ; but at the end of the thirteenth century it was being, or had already been, absorbed by the advance of Hellenic peoples, who spread through Greece and the islands, and presently penetrated the coastlands of Asia Minor. These folk we know under the name of the Achaeans from

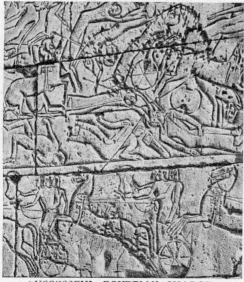

**SUCCESSFUL EGYPTIAN CHARGE**

An expression of the pride taken by Rameses II in the means by which he won the battle of Kadesh—repeated chariot charges led by himself—these reliefs in the Ramesseum show Egyptian chariots breaking the Hittite ranks.
*Courtesy of Sir Flinders Petrie*

the Homeric sagas, the Iliad and the Odyssey ; and their advent as conquerors or dynasty founders from the north, or at least from the north of Greece, now seems unquestionable. Whether they were the first 'Greeks' in Greece—indeed, whether they themselves were by origin 'Greeks' at all—is another question ; but it is on the whole probable that the bulk of the people over whom the Minoan dynasts had ruled were already Hellenic in speech. In any case, rigid uniformity of opinion on such an open question is neither possible nor desirable, and the different authorities will be found to exhibit a wide range of argument and conjecture.

Kindred but not actually Hellenic peoples, inclusively known as Phrygians, had already entered Asia Minor from the west, crossing the Hellespont. The undoubtedly historical siege of the city of Troy, probably about the beginning of the twelfth century, marks a stage in the contest between the expanding (Hellenic) Achaeans and the already established Phrygians, using the latter term in its widest sense.

This Greek or Hellenic expansion in the Aegean, and the Phrygian pressure in

Asia Minor, forced upon the earlier dwellers in those regions movements which from this time bring them more and more into collision with the peoples that have hitherto monopolised the stage.

Such a movement was now taking place on a large scale. These peoples of Asia

HARD-FOUGHT NAVAL BATTLE THAT RESULTED IN AN EGYPTIAN VICTORY

The onslaughts of the so-called 'Peoples of the Sea,' among whom were the Achaeans, the Danaans and the Philistines, were met and repulsed by the last great warrior-Pharaoh, Rameses III. He defeated them on land and sea, and carvings at Medinet Habu record one of his triumphs, constituting the earliest historic representation of a naval engagement known. The drawing (bottom) shows the minute details of part of this remarkable historical record and above is a photograph of the rectangular portion of the carving marked in the drawing.

*Photo, Mansell*

Minor, the 'Northmen' of the ancient world, had already for generations been sending out rover bands which vexed the coasts of Egypt, but also provided the Egyptian armies with mercenary troops of professional fighting-men, the Shirdanu, who had become a regular part of the military establishment. A bigger movement had been heralded when a great pirate host joined with the Libyans, to be heavily repulsed by Merneptah (see above). Migratory bands from the west had probably much to do with the rapid decay of the Hittite power. These things were the precursors of the great Irruption of the Northerners.

**ROYAL HOMAGE TO DIVINITY**

Meli-shipak II maintained the independence of Babylon after its revolt from the Assyrian domination imposed by Tukulti-Ninurta. On this boundary stone he is shown with his daughter before the goddess Nana.

*From J. de Morgan, 'Délégation en Perse'*

Rameses III delivered Egypt from the barbarian onslaught; but, gallant and skilful soldier though he was, he could not save her from herself. It was her last hour of glory. She was freed from foreign attack, but the rule of the land had passed into the hands of an organized priesthood of the most ruinous type. Rameses followed Rameses on the throne, each vying with his predecessor in the lavishness of his temple endowments, careless of aught else ; till, in about 1094 B.C., Her-Heru or Hrihor, the high priest of Amen, assumed the title of Pharaoh, and the monarchy (Twenty-first Dynasty) became little more than a name.

Rameses III (1198–1167 B.C.) was king of Egypt when the storm broke. A great confederate host of the 'Peoples of the Sea,' among whom, besides the Shirdanu, who would have to fight their own kinsmen in the Egyptian armies, and the Pulasati (Philistines), we can now detect the names of Achaeans and Danaans as well, swooped upon the Delta, the Libyans joining them. Rameses met them in 1190 and smote them in a great fight by land and sea ; but the peril was not yet over. The defeated fleet was only an advance force. The migrant hordes were even now streaming into Syria.

### Last Hour of Glory of the Fading Empire

**R**AMESES was equal to the emergency. Somewhere on the Palestine coast he again caught and smote them by land and sea—a blow so shattering that Egypt was never again molested by them. The wars of Rameses III against the Peoples of the Sea have given us our first historic picture of a naval battle. Once more he had to draw the sword, and with decisive effect ; but it was against a western enemy, the Meshwesh, Berber tribes from beyond Libya who dreamed of an Egyptian conquest, but were utterly put to rout.

To this period of the Ramesids belongs the development of a practice familiar in the histories of later Oriental (especially Mahomedan) dynasties, but ascribed by the Hebrew story of the Exodus to a much earlier period : the practice of bestowing the highest offices of the state, the court and the army on slaves. Joseph's 'chief butler' has a Ramesid office and title, probably imported into the tradition in later days.

In Asia the Egyptian sovereignty hardly survived even in name. The great victory of Rameses III did not prevent the Philistines from settling upon and mastering at least the plains of southern Palestine, where we find them at perpetual feud with the 'judges' of Israel, whose principal foes after the conquest had been the still active Syrian Amorites and Midianites. Even in her palmiest days Egypt had exercised little enough control over the tribal feuds of her Asiatic subjects, so long as they did not interfere with the payment of tribute. Under the Ramesids there was no control at all, and in Phoenicia Egyptian commissioners found their authority politely but uncompromisingly repudiated.

Syria then—using that term in its widest signification as covering the region from the Euphrates to the peninsula of Sinai—now recognized no power as exercising sovereign authority. Beyond the Euphrates the sovereignty was divided between Assyria and Babylon, which collided whenever there arose in either a more than usually aggressive monarch ; while Babylon, as of old, was subjected to occasional attacks from Elam.

The third ruler of the Isin dynasty, Nebuchadrezzar I (1146-1122 B.C.), was the first who displayed any marked energy. He inflicted severe chastisement on Elam, but suffered defeat in a conflict with the Assyrian Ashur-resh-ishi, who was probably the aggressor. Both powers were perhaps laying claim to Amorite territory once subject to the Hittites, as the battle was fought in this region (c. 1125).

The son of Ashur-resh-ishi, Tiglath-pileser I, then embarked on a career of conquest. Twice he entered Babylon itself, now ruled by Marduk-nadin-akhe (d. 1100), the last Isin king of any vigour ; he assumed the old title of ' king of Sumer and Akkad ' ; he seized all the western territories claimed by Babylon, and as much as still remained of the old Hittite dominion ; he even penetrated the Taurus and hammered the former land of Hatti itself, claiming to have carried his conquest as far as the shores of the Black Sea ; he asserted his sovereignty, which was promptly acknowledged, over the Phoenician cities.

Babylon and Elam, which had snatched at the opportunity for attack while he was engaged in the west, next felt the weight of his hand before his brief but exceedingly vigorous thirteen years' reign ended in 1102. But he was not the founder of an Assyrian empire. For more than the next hundred years incompetent and lethargic monarchs or dynasties ruled or did not rule obscurely in Assyria and Babylonia.

**KING OF BABYLON**

Profiting perhaps by the absence of its ruler, Tiglath-pileser I, on a campaign, King Marduk-nadin-akhe of Babylon raided Assyria.

*British Museum*

Nor did Egypt fare any better under the nominal government of sacerdotal Pharaohs, while a Libyan ' peaceful penetration ' dominated the Delta, Nubians dominated the south and the troops for the most part consisted of foreign, especially Libyan, mercenaries.

### Upheavals in the Syrian Area

DURING this paralysis of Egypt and Mesopotamia states were rising and falling in the great Syrian area, now set free from their long domination. The maritime cities of Phoenicia waxed in wealth, each under her own king, not seeking dominion but gathering commercial spoils from distant shores. There was no prospect of a Syrian empire arising, because the utmost unity attainable was that of a league between independent cities and tribes ; and though such leagues might be formed readily enough for defensive purposes in the face of a common danger, aggressive combinations inevitably dissolved as soon as the individual members found their special interests clashing or saw any one among them acquiring predominance, or suffered any disastrous defeat.

The Philistine league, however, had established itself as a union of city states on the plain of southern Palestine, to which they gave their own name, Pulasati, permanently ; subjecting the Canaanites, or driving the most unsubduable of them, the tribes of Israel, into the hills. Presently they set about a serious attempt to conquer the hill-men, whose tribes scarcely possessed a common organization, though they had a bond of union in their unique religion and their tribal traditions.

Realization of the imperative need for a unity, attainable only through a supreme military chief, led the Hebrew clans to elect the Benjamite Saul as king ; Saul led them to battle and won a great victory at Michmash, which drove the oppressor back to his own cities. The new war-chief was able to turn on the Amalekites, southern tribes with which Israel had been at constant feud, and crush them.

The Philistines, however, were not minded to retire after one rebuff. The war was renewed ; Saul had not established national unity ; the king was alarmed by the popularity of his most brilliant lieutenant, David, whose loyalty he repaid by treating him as a rebel. Deprived of his aid, Saul met his death in a heavy defeat at the hands of the Philistines at Mount Gilboa. But Israel rallied to David as the one possible saviour, though the succession was disputed by a rival faction ; and under David's leadership the supremacy of the Hebrew kingdom was decisively established, the Philistine power was shattered and the hostile encircling tribes were forced to become David's tributaries (C. 1000 B.C.). The reconstruction of these early historical events from the Biblical narrative is accompanied by very considerable difficulty.

Less than half a century of constant warfare had welded the Hebrew tribes together and made Israel into the greatest territorial power in the Syrian area. David's son Solomon, like his Phoenician neighbours, with whom he was on the best of terms, sought not imperial expansion but material wealth ; and the wealth accumulated under his long rule has become proverbial.

## Disintegration of the Hebrew Kingdom

𝕴N the third generation, however (c. 935), the Hebrew kingdom broke up. The royal house of the south, closely associated as it was with the theocratic idea, had never commanded the unqualified allegiance of the north ; it broke away from the feeble Rehoboam under the leadership of Jeroboam, a military chief who assumed the crown of Israel. The south, however, remained loyal to the house of David as the kingdom of Judah ; less powerful but less exposed to aggression and to external decadent influences than the northern kingdom, and consequently destined to a longer independence and a less hopelessly disastrous ultimate downfall.

Meanwhile, something like a recovery took place in Egypt, where the Libyan Shashank (Shishak) established his supremacy and in 947 inaugurated the Twenty-second Dynasty ; making his authority felt with such effect that on the disruption of Israel he was able to assert his nominal sovereignty so far as to invade Palestine and carry off considerable spoils ; though there was little prospect of Egypt reappearing as an imperial power.

Much more ominous were the signs that Assyria was on the point of throwing off her long lethargy with the accession of Adad-nirari II in 911 B.C. ; a definite date which marks for the historians a new era by the Assyrian institution of an official chronicle in which events were recorded year by year, so that from this time it is possible to speak with unwonted precision.

### Movements of the New Peoples

𝕱INALLY, we must glance at the new ingredients in the melting-pot. No exact chronicles can be given of the movements of those northern peoples who are beginning to come within our ken, but something may be recorded.

By the eleventh century the Hellenic expansion had mastered the islands of the Aegean, and was making ' Aeolic ' settlements on the coast of Asia Minor. In the century that followed there came from the north the migration or invasion of the last great group of Hellenes, the Dorians ; as yet comparatively barbarous, but armed with the iron weapons which placed them at an advantage in conflicts with their bronze-bearing precursors. They were thus enabled to secure their supremacy in the Peloponnese and in Crete, and to penetrate Asia Minor ; where they did not so much displace the native populations as provide the states with dynasts of Dorian ancestry.

The eastward movement in Asia Minor corresponding to the pressure from the west was gradually consolidating in the centre a Phrygian power, soon to be known in the east as Mushki. Beyond the mountains, whence in an earlier day had issued Gutians and Kassites, Iranians were massing in Media. The new peoples were not yet known as powers, but they had entered the stage.

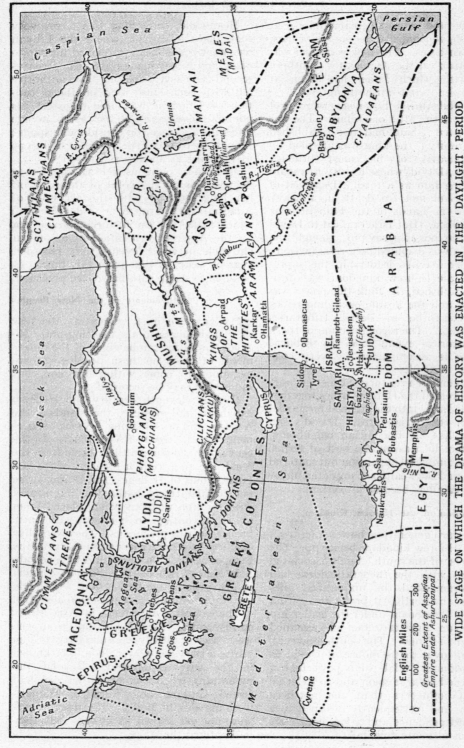

**WIDE STAGE ON WHICH THE DRAMA OF HISTORY WAS ENACTED IN THE 'DAYLIGHT' PERIOD**

In the three and a half centuries with which Chapter 3 is concerned, the principal interest of Man's history was transferred from Egypt and Babylonia to the more widely extended area shown above. For the first half of the period human action was mostly concerned with Assyria's struggle for supremacy over, first, Babylonia and then over the various peoples to the west of the river system of Mesopotamia. Simultaneously, however, the colonial expansion of Greece began, while the Medes, the Scythians, the Cimmerians and the Treres were preparing to appear on the stage.

50

# DAYLIGHT: 900—550 B.C.

**W**HEN we reach the ninth century B.C., our chronicle-horizon has already widened and our materials become fuller and less disputable.

To the Euphratic, Nilotic and intervening areas, to which the purview was at first restricted, the Aegean area has been definitely added ; in touch, but as yet only just in touch, with the East (in a political sense), and barely beginning to provide a conscious record of itself.

Eastward the great Aryan migrations have attained completion. In the course of many centuries the Iranian branch has populated the unknown lands beyond the trans-Tigris hills which we now know as Persia ; but it has not yet shaped itself into organized kingdoms. Another branch, passing across Afghanistan and through the mountains of the Hindu Kush, has penetrated into the Punjab and thence down the Ganges basin ; subjugating but rarely exterminating the earlier Dravidian and Mongolian populations and everywhere establishing its own supremacy, but not always preserving the purity of race ; expanding southwards also over the whole peninsula, but by way of infiltration rather than conquest. India, however, still remains, as concerns the outer world, a realm of magic and fable, behind a veil raised only for fleeting moments.

### Ebb and Flow in East and West

**W**ESTWARD, other Aryan races have displaced or dominated the earlier peoples. Phrygians are penetrating Anatolia from the West, Hellenes are masters of the Aegean lands and sea, Latins and Oscans are streaming into Italy, there to clash with another host of non-Aryan invaders from over sea, the Tyrrhenians or Etruscans. A Celtic tide is following a more northerly course, eastward and westward, through Europe, perhaps already crossing the Channel into the British Isles and the Pyrenees into Spain.

In this general ebb and flow of peoples of the east and of the west mention may be made of the Indians, and also of other, still nomadic, tribes from the lands about the Caspian and the Black Seas : the Scythians and the Cimmerians, who had at least a strong Aryan tincture. The Iranian and western developments will play a prominent part in our story, but it still centres in the region of the ancient empires, and primarily in Assyria.

Through the eleventh and the first half of the tenth centuries, the Mesopotamian and Syrian areas had been without any state that was or that threatened to be definitely predominant. For Babylonia, as for Phoenicia, commercial interests were the controlling factor ; political ascendancy was of value mainly for the preservation of open trade routes with the west ; at no period of her history had she seriously, or at least continuously, aimed at winning empire by force of arms. In Assyria, no king since Tiglath-pileser I had shown either inclination or capacity for active aggression. Both powers, moreover, were kept constantly on the defensive against the encroaching attacks of the hill-folk beyond the Tigris.

Their weakness facilitated the movement of the Aramaean Semites from the south, primarily Beduin in character, who displaced, absorbed or combined with the Amorite or Hittite principalities on the upper Euphrates and in the old Naharin, as far south as the Lebanons and Damascus, or pushed down the Euphrates and up the Tigris, curtailing the effective if not the nominal dominion of Assyria and Babylon.

### Reawakening of Assyria

**B**ETWEEN the Euphrates and the Mediterranean, on the other hand, no state or principality had arisen capable of holding its neighbours in more than a temporary subjection, or of welding them together in a corporate state. The Hebrews, led by such a war-lord as David, did in the tenth century set up a wide dominion ; but it could not long survive the decadence in the majority of the tribes of Israel which set in with the reign of Solomon. By the end of the century the premier position among the Syrians had passed to the vigorous chiefs of Damascus. Egypt had again relapsed after the signs of a possible revival under Shashank.

But there was reality in the revival that had been taking place in Assyria since the middle of the century. When Adad-nirari II became king in 911 B.C., he found a machinery which had been restored to working order by his recent predecessors, and he set himself, not as yet to expansion, but to careful consolidation —that is, to bringing under effective control the trans-Tigris regions, the northern border and the Syrianised western border along the Euph-rates and the Khabur.

In this process the most persistent of the campaigns were called for in the north. The subjugation was finished off in the traditional Assyrian fashion by the deportation of what re-mained of the popula-tion to distant territory. After this, Adad-nirari's campaigns in Mesopo-tamia, designed not for the annexation of new dominions but to im-press his nominal sub-jects with the reality of his supremacy, were in the nature of demon-strations. Twice, how-ever, Adad-nirari found himself in conflict with Babylon over disputed territories ; on both occasions the Babylon-ian was defeated. The second victory was fol-lowed by a boundary treaty which left the Assyrian the acknow-ledged lord of Mesopot-amia, to the Khabur

on the west, the Euphrates on the south and the neighbourhood of the modern Bagdad on the south-east.

The process of actual expansion was barely begun in the six years' reign of Tukulti-Ninurta II (889–4), who was in search of a scientific frontier on the north, involving successful campaigns and annexations. Aggressive Assyria definitely revealed herself under Ashur-nasir-pal II. The state organization had reached the necessary standard.

**RUTHLESSNESS INCARNATE**
Succeeding to the throne in 884 B.C., Ashur-nasir-pal II inaugurated a policy of conquest which, prosecuted with merciless ferocity, resulted in a greatly extended Assyrian Empire.
*British Museum*

Ashur-nasir-pal was indebted to his pre-decessors for a highly organized army trained to hill warfare, well supplied with artillery and horses and very efficiently armed. The policy of conquest on which he embarked may have been either his own, or merely the develop-ment which those pre-decessors had in view in reorganizing their king-dom on a militarist basis. With foes on all her borders who would take prompt advantage of any weakness, Assyria must make herself feared, and attack be-fore she could be attacked ; and the sup-pression of each foe would extend her bor-ders to march with those of a new potential enemy, to whom she would have to apply the same treatment. It was a programme of un-limited but organized conquest, not merely of victorious campaigns.

The main objective was Syria, partly be-cause it had once owned the sovereignty of an Assyrian conqueror, Tiglath-pileser I, partly because it commanded

Dismounted from his chariot and shaded by the umbrella of state, the victorious Ashur-nasir-pal receives the submission of his enemies. One stands before him apparently offering fealty, while another lies prostrate at his feet, hoping perhaps, by such abject humiliation, to escape the ferocious vengeance usually inflicted by the terrible Assyrian upon those who defied him.

Chariots and horses formed an important part of Ashur-nasir-pal's forces, as they did of all oriental armies ; but the long invincibility of the Assyrians was largely due to their combination of archers and heavy infantry, who also figure in this spirited representation of one of the many battles in which the redoubtable Ashur-nasir-pal was personally engaged.

Vast tribute and innumerable captives fell to Ashur-nasir-pal as the fruit of his victories. Among other uses to which he put them was the rebuilding of Calah, where he erected a luxurious palace, for he was a great builder as well as a great conqueror. Art was greatly developed during his reign, as is shown by these wall sculptures from his palace illustrating his career.

### ENDURING RECORDS OF THE TRIUMPHS OF A GREAT ASSYRIAN KING

*British Museum*

the western trade routes ; but before an attack on Syria, the possibility of an attack in the rear must be precluded.

The name of 'the Terrible' might deservedly have been bestowed upon Ashur-nasir-pal, for his methods were appalling in their ruthlessness. In his own person he set the extreme example of that merciless ferocity, only occasionally tempered by policy, which became characteristic of the Assyrian Empire, of which he may be regarded as the founder. It was his regular practice to flay alive the chiefs who headed revolts ; when cities defied him and offered stubborn resistance to his arms, the inhabitants were massacred with every circumstance of savagery ; the populations of conquered districts were deported, in part or in bulk. Where he had once passed with his invincible troops, it was not likely that resistance would again arise.

In the opening campaigns of his reign the Assyrian thoroughly terrorised the hill-folk on the left bank of the Tigris, northward up to the district called Nairi, the borderland of Armenia, where the river has its source. Thence he swooped upon rebellious Aramaeans between the Khabur and Euphrates, rapidly reducing them to humble submission for the moment. The harshness of the new regime generated a new revolt, countenanced by the alarmed king of Babylon who sent a strong contingent to the aid of the insurgents ; they were nevertheless crushed in a decisive two days' battle by the archers and the heavy infantry of the Assyrians, who were proving their superiority over the chariots

**CONSOLIDATOR OF ASSYRIA**

Son of Ashur-nasir-pal II, whom he succeeded in 859 B.C., Shalmaneser III continued his father's policy of Assyrian expansion. This stele was found at Kurkh on the Tigris.

*British Museum*

and horses on which oriental armies were wont to place their reliance.

The battle practically completed the subjugation of all Mesopotamia above the Babylonian kingdom. When Ashur-nasir-pal crossed the Euphrates, it was not to conquer the principalities between the river and the coast of the Mediterranean, but to receive their submission. For the remaining fifteen years of his reign, the conqueror sought no more extension of territory. In 859 B.C. he was succeeded by his son Shalmaneser III.

Ashur-nasir-pal had refrained from challenging the great trans-Euphrates power, the loose confederacy of Syrian states of which the hegemony lay with Ben-Hadad of Damascus—too disunited to form an aggressive empire, but capable of gathering a formidable combination for defence, as Shalmaneser was soon to learn when he renewed the policy of Assyrian expansion. Damascus remained the bulwark of the south against Assyrian aggression for some generations; though when she was not in the throes of an Assyrian war she was generally fighting with Israel or with other tribal principalities, which might nevertheless reconcile their jealousies in face of the menace from the north.

Such a quarrel, in which King Ahab of Israel had gained substantial success, had just taken place when Shalmaneser turned his arms against Syria in the seventh year of his reign, 853 B.C. Yet Ahab and a host of minor princes joined Ben-Hadad, and there was a great fight at Karkar. The Assyrian recorded it as a great victory ; but though the Syrian army dispersed,

Shalmaneser had suffered so heavily that it was five years before he attempted again to conquer his stubborn foe.

Ahab, on the other hand, seized the apparent opportunity to ' go up to Ramoth-Gilead ' against Ben-Hadad, actually to his own death. A few years later his house, ' the house of Omri,' was extirpated by Jehu. Ben-Hadad's energies, however, were absorbed in beating off the renewed attacks of Shalmaneser in three successive years. Each onslaught failed, though in the last Shalmaneser brought into the field a force of unprecedented magnitude, computed at no less than 120,000 men. Ben-Hadad must have been a first-rate fighter, though Assyrians and Hebrews alike ignored his greatness.

The murder of Ben-Hadad by Hazael who succeeded him, and the fall of the house of Omri in Israel, gave Shalmaneser another opportunity. In 842 he inflicted a heavy defeat on Hazael, but still failed to crush Damascus, though her power and influence were seriously diminished. The task of establishing the Assyrian sovereignty over all the region north of Damascus between the Euphrates and the sea was greatly simplified.

Of no less importance for the consolidation of the Assyrian empire was Shalmaneser's intervention in a contest for the throne of Babylon between two brothers; which had the natural result that the brother who owed him his crown became his tributary. The Babylonians in general were well content to pay the price for the trade security they enjoyed under the Assyrian supremacy, while it paid Assyria to foster her tributary's wealth.

At intervals throughout his reign, Shalmaneser III came into conflict with the highland people of Ararat (Urartu), then consolidating themselves as a power—also called the Vannic kingdom, from Lake Van—that later expanded and formed an alliance with the Medes. This strip depicts the Vannites coming down from the mountains to engage in battle with the Assyrians.

In this strip, a continuation of the one above, the Assyrians are seen besieging Arsashu, one of the many cities of Ararat that were captured, plundered and destroyed by Shalmaneser. The city is shown with flames soaring above its battlements, and Assyrian frightfulness is represented in the corpse already decapitated, although the battle is still raging.

Yet another strip records the capture and destruction of the cities of Pargâ, Adâ and Karkar. In the portion of it reproduced here the victorious Shalmaneser is depicted seated on a throne receiving spoil, including horses, from the men of Karkar. These bronze bands adorned the gates set up by Shalmaneser III to record his conquests, and are superb examples of the Assyrians' skill in metal work.

**BRONZE PLATES FROM SHALMANESER'S GATES OF HONOUR**
*British Museum*

At intervals, from the beginning of his reign till his death in 824, Shalmaneser's troops had been in collision with a power which was consolidating itself in the northern hills—the 'Vannic' kingdom (named from Lake Van), also called Urartu (Ararat)—which first came under the casual notice of Assyria in the days of Ashur-nasir-pal. The Vannites, though Aryanised as to language at a later date, seemingly had at this period no Aryan affinities. The collisions at the time were not of serious moment, but they foreshadowed trouble.

The power of Shalmaneser in his last years was diminished by the revolt of his eldest son, Ashur-danin-pal, whose claim to the succession was set aside in favour of the younger, Shamshi-Adad V : a revolt which was not finally suppressed till the latter (824–811 B.C.) had been nominally reigning for three years. Consequently Shamshi-Adad's remaining years were mainly occupied, not with the extension of the empire, but in re-establishing within it the authority which had been shaken by the prolonged civil strife. Revolt in northern Syria had to be suppressed. In Babylonia the anti-Assyrian party had recovered ascendancy with the weakness of Assyria, and it was not till 813 that the decisive battle was fought. Two years later Shamshi-Adad was dead, and Adad-nirari III, his son, reigned in his place ; though from 811 to 808 the government was controlled by the queen-mother, Sammu-ramat, original of the famous Semiramis.

This Adad-nirari was the last efficient ruler of his line. He lost no territory, he established his authority throughout his

On the east side of the monolith, these panels represent (above) payment of tribute of elephants and apes by the people of the land of Musri (in Syria ?), and (below) tribute of ivory and rare woods from Marduk-apal-usur of the land of the Sukhu (Aramaeans).

### THE BLACK OBELISK FROM SHALMANESER'S PALACE AT CALAH

In his central palace at Calah (Nimrud) Shalmaneser III set up a black alabaster monolith inscribed on the four sides with an account of his campaigns in the thirty-one years of his reign and with twenty panels in relief illustrating the text. Among the vanquished princes is Jehu the Israelite, from whom Shalmaneser received tribute in the course of his expedition against Hazael of Damascus in 842 B.C.

*British Museum*

dominions and he exacted tribute from the hitherto unconquered princes of Syria even to the southernmost region of Edom. Many of the new tribu-
taries probably looked on the Assyrian rather in the light of a liberator from the yoke of Dam-ascus ; a ready homage brought no worse evil with it than the pay-ment to him of tribute which they had not been able to withhold from Hazael and his son Ben-Hadad III. Jealousy of the powerful state close at hand was a more urgent motive than fear of the distant power, whose fiercest attacks Damascus had hitherto been able to repel.

Adad-nirari could com-fortably boast himself the sovereign of many peoples who had never owned the sway of his prede-cessors ; and Damascus, still stubborn though de-serted if not actually attacked by her former confederates, was the only formidable foe with whom he had to deal in the south ; it surrendered in 802. In northern Syria, Phoenicia and Mesopotamia, including Babylonia, he had only to confirm what had been accomplished by Shamshi-Adad.

**KING SHAMSHI-ADAD V**
Younger son of Shalmaneser III, whom he succeeded in 824 B.C., Shamshi-Adad V spent most of his reign in suppressing civil strife engendered by the revolt of his elder brother.
*British Museum*

More. credit probably ought to attach to his more difficult but more obscure opera-tions on the northern and eastern marches where the power of Urartu, the Vannic kingdom, was expanding and allying itself with the Medes on the east and with the Mannai, who may have been at least in part a sort of Median advance guard. It is claimed that Adad-nirari penetrated to the shores of the Caspian, but, though he had to do hard fighting, and his hand fell heavily on many Median townships, he occupied no new territory.

After his death in 782, Assyria again fell from its high estate, under the three successors whose rule covered the next thirty-seven years. In their wars these mon-archs were habitually unsuccessful. In the highland debatable land Sarduris and Argistis of Urartu firmly established themselves, and the Assyrians had to fall back. Babylonia, long quiescent, revolted and recovered her independence. Princes in north Syria rebelled and defeated punitive ex-peditions. In the farther south, since the crippling of Damascus, the kings of Israel were extending their power, at the ex-pense of their old rival.

The incompetence of the monarchy plunged Assyria herself into re-volts and civil war, kindled perhaps by the superstitious excitement caused by an eclipse in 763. The great kingdom fell into a state of an-archy which ended only when, in 745, an able captain named Pul (ac-cording to the generally received view) extermi-nated the royal family and seized the crown him-self, under the style of Tiglath-pileser III, a name recalling ancient glories.

𝕭EFORE proceeding with the chronicle of the second phase of the Assyrian Empire, we should remind ourselves of that once great southern power which had been so long in eclipse ; and of the nation-making that was in progress outside the area to which detailed and connected record has hitherto been for the most part confined. For the new streams and the old are now nearing their confluence.

We left Egypt at the close of the tenth century, when she had been showing signs, not destined to fulfilment, of a revived vigour under Shashank I (the Shishak of Scripture), a Libyan founder of what is known as the Bubastite dynasty (947 B.C.), the royal seat being at Bubastis in the western Delta.   Her momentary energy had, however, waned ; though Philistia, to secure herself from Hebrew hostility, had declared allegiance to her, she had made no military appearance in Asia since the raid of 930, in which Shashank carried off his spoils from Jerusalem. The Bubastites did no more than rule lethargically in a lethargic land, while princes of the house that Shashank had dispossessed reigned over an independent Nubian kingdom in the far south at Napata, and Egyptian nobles paid little enough heed to Pharaoh.

In 860, Upper and Lower Egypt were again parted by the setting up of a companion dynasty at Thebes.   About a hundred years later, at the moment when Tiglath-pileser was seizing the Assyrian crown, a partly Nubian or Ethiopian king of Napata, Kashta, whose wife was daughter   of   the   Bubastite Pharaoh, secured for himself the throne of Thebes.

In the hills on the other side of the lower Tigris, the vigorous state of Elam played an active part in the early chronicles of

**ASSYRIA'S MAN OF DESTINY**

A great soldier, Pul, as he is named in the Old Testament, seized the throne of Assyria in 745 B.C. as Tiglath-pileser III, conquered Babylonia and Syria, and before his death in 727 extended his empire to the confines of Egypt.

*British Museum*

Babylonia, but for many centuries her appearance had been only occasional. Never able to dominate Babylonia for any prolonged period, she had more than enough to do in maintaining herself against the pressure of the Iranian tribes which had been pushing through the hinterland for a thousand years.   But she was still discharging her office as a bulwark against their advance, although the time was approaching when, broken by Assyria, she would be absorbed by the Persians ; and she still provided occasional aid and an occasional asylum for revolting pretenders to the Babylonian crown.

### Advent of the Medes and Persians

THE Iranians, the Medes and Persians, had not yet developed an organized state, but they occupied the country to the rear of Elam, and were in possession of the mountain ranges from which in times long past the hordes of the Gutians and Kassites had descended upon Mesopotamia.   The Persians are not yet specifically in evidence, but the Medes, ' Madai,' have come definitely on the stage in the northern wars of Adad-nirari III. Through the Mannai, they are now linking up with what has developed into the organized Armenian state of Urartu. The Vannic kingdom is not mighty enough to quit its mountain fastnesses and try conclusions with Assyria on the plains of Mesopotamia, but is already a dangerous menace on her rear whenever she turns her face to the south and west.

Since the break-up of the old power of the Hittites no other so formidable has developed in Anatolia ; but on the ruins of Hatti there has arisen a Phrygian ascendancy, the ' Mushki ' of the Assyrians, an aftermath of that penetration from the west which had set in motion the forces that had been bridled by Rameses III.   We can only conjecture the story of the development of this ascendancy on the theory familiar to students of the Aryan expansion.   No migrating hosts had conquered Anatolia, dispossessing its ancient inhabitants ; but the Phrygian immigrants had   gradually   established   aristocratic families so that in the west whence they had come their name was given to the country in which they settled and ruled. The mass of the population in what was known to the Greeks as Phrygia was certainly not of the stock known to the Homeric bards as Phrygian, but there is every probability that their princes were of Phrygian descent.

In the eighth century B.C. most of Anatolia behind the coast-lands was dominated by the Phrygian kingdom whose capital was at Gordium, and whose princes always seem to have borne the name of either Gordius or Midas, both familiar to Greek legend in later days. In Assyrian annals the Phrygian king appears as ' Mita of Mushki.'

**ASSYRIAN ARTILLERY IN ACTION**
Methods of warfare stereotyped by the terrible Ashur-nasir-pal II were employed by Tiglath-pileser III more than a hundred years later; witness this marble slab from his palace at Calah, depicting impaled prisoners from a town under siege by Assyrians with archers and battering rams.
*British Museum*

To the Mesopotamians, with a historical tradition and a continuous culture of at least two thousand years behind them, Medes and Vannites and Phrygians were all barbarians on a lower plane than themselves ; but beyond them lay the outer barbarians of the north, from Thrace on the west to the Caspian Sea on the east, who were on a still lower plane, barbarians in the view of Medes and Vannites and Phrygians, nomad hordes roughly divided as yet into Scythians and Cimmerians, who were destined before very long to be a disturbing factor in the affairs of the civilized world. And in the west were the peoples, as yet all but unknown in the east, who had already left the barbarian stage behind them, though they had not yet learnt to regard the immemorial East as no better than barbarian in comparison with the Hellenic race. The world was not yet divided for them into Barbarians and Hellenes.

### Developments in the Hellenic World

**B**Y the tenth century Hellas had come into full being. What we all think of as 'Greece' in Europe, with all the isles and most of the remaining northern and eastern coast-lands of the Aegean, was occupied by Hellenic communities. The north-western coasts of Asia Minor had been settled under the name of Aeolis. The Dorian migration had run its course. Under its pressure Ionia in the middle regions of the coast of Asia Minor had been colonised, while the Dorians themselves occupied the south. Broadly speaking, every community took the form of a city state (though the state was not necessarily confined to one city), ruled by a hereditary king with a council of nobles. But gradually, state after state following a similar course with minor variations, the king dropped to the level of the nobles, and the old monarchy passed into an aristocracy of birth.

With few exceptions this change had attained completion in all the cities of Hellas before the middle of the eighth century. The most notable exception is Sparta (Lacedaemon), whose unique institution of the dual kingship survived for centuries ; and kings were still reigning in the great rival Peloponnesian city of Argos. And in the wilder mountainous regions of the north and west, such as Macedonia and Epirus, the city organization had not yet developed, the king remaining rather as the high chief among a number of clan chieftains.

**CHALDAEAN KING OF BABYLON**

King of Babylonia from 721 to 709 B.C.,
Merodach-baladan was Chaldaean by origin.
On this stele he is confirming a grant of land
to Bel-akhe-iriba (right), a Babylonian magnate.
*Berlin Museum*

Elsewhere the city-state system had
long been thoroughly established. Every
one of the great cities which was to play
a prominent part, continuously or tran-
siently, in the developments of the next
four hundred years—Sparta, Corinth,
Athens, Thebes and the rest—had been a
recognized sovereign state for centuries
already ; and as yet the most advanced of
them were those on the Asiatic coast.
But the westward Mediterranean expansion of Greater Hellas had not yet begun.

Hellas, however, was not so much a concrete fact as an idea. The great aggre-
gate of Hellenic states was without
political unity. There was unity of sentiment, a sense of common kinship and common superiority to other races, resting
upon common traditions, common religious
conceptions, a common pantheon, a common language and a common literature.
But ordinarily the crowd of independent
states was linked together solely by this
thread of sentiment, of which, politically

speaking, the unifying force was much less
than the disintegrating force of rival
interests and rival ambitions.

But now for the first time we must for
a moment turn our eyes to the western
horizon. For in the first half of the eighth
century two cities were founded, one on the
African coast and one in Italy, whose
development was big with fate. About
800 B.C. the Phoenicians of Tyre planted a
commercial colony at Carthage ; and in
753 B.C., according to the traditional
chronology, Rome was born.

### Assyria's Man of Destiny

THE might of Assyria, which had been
weakened, not by organic decay but
by the incapacity of the last kings of the
old line, was restored, as we have seen,
and more than restored after 745 B.C. by
the very able usurper Tiglath-pileser, the
third of that name, though often styled
the fourth.

During the last disastrous years, Assyria
herself had been torn by civil strife. She
had lost her grip on Syria ; she had
allowed Urartu to consolidate her power
on the north and north-east highland
marches ; and on the south and south-east
Babylonia, practically a protectorate for
half a century, had recovered her independence but not her power. In the
eighteen years of his reign Tiglath-pileser
ruled undisputed over the homeland,
restored the Assyrian domination over
Syria, drove back Urartu, strengthening
his own frontier, again took the Babylonian
Nabonassar under his protection and,
finally, annexed the crown of Babylon
himself. Evidently the Assyrian armies
under capable leadership were as irresistible as ever.

On his accession the most immediately
pressing task of statesmanship lay in
Babylonia and on the lower Tigris, owing
to the feebleness of the central government,
which could not control the communities
of Chaldaeans, who, like the Aramaeans,
were a fresh Beduin infiltration into the
land. Tiglath-pileser's first campaign was
directed to securing a peaceful Babylonia
by the establishment of Assyrian authority
as the power behind the king Nabonassar,
through whom it continued to be exercised

when the Assyrian withdrew. There followed after a short interval, spent in the hill country east of the Tigris, an attack on a north Syrian confederacy fostered if not organized by Sarduris of Urartu. The confederates were routed, and Sarduris, who was present, had to flee ignominiously from the field. After two more years of campaigning Tiglath-pileser was once more master of all northern Syria, including Damascus.

## Climax of Tiglath-pileser's Glory

OPERATIONS against Urartu were interrupted or delayed by another Syrian revolt in 739, for which the old king of Judah, Uzziah, may have been responsible, the advance of Israel having been brought to a sudden stop by a series of revolutions. Then came the main attack on Urartu, which was effectively crippled for some time to come though all attempts to capture the capital failed. The next three years were passed in Syrian campaigns, in the course of which Philistia was reduced to submission, Damascus was finally crushed and practically all Syria paid service and tribute to Assyria.

Meanwhile disorder had again broken out on the south in Babylonia, various claimants with or without plausible titles snatching at the crown on the death of Nabonassar in 734. Among the Chaldaean princes, Marduk-apal-iddin II, the Merodach-baladan of the Bible, makes his first but by no means last appearance. Tiglath - pileser took matters in hand in summary fashion, smote all insurgents impartially—probably to the general satisfaction of the citizens of Babylon, who took no interest in the broils—and deported to distant regions more than 100,000 of the provincial populations. For a time he left Babylon kingless under Assyrian governors ; but in 728 he assumed under his own name, Pul, the crown and titles of the Babylonian kingdom. A year afterwards he died.

The reign of his successor Shalmaneser V (727–722 B.C.), was brief. Israel revolted under her last king, Hoshea, and the siege of Samaria was in progress when, in his fifth year, Shalmaneser died—the victim perhaps of the conspiracy that gave Sargon II undisputed possession of the Assyrian throne in 722.

Tiglath-pileser presumably had no better title to the throne that he seized than the fact that he was the man of destiny who had come forward and saved the commonwealth. Sargon, on the other hand, claimed to be the representative of the ancient royal stock. His name, like that of Tiglath-pileser, may have been assumed to remind Assyrians of past glories associated with Sargon of Agade. His accession seems to have been accepted without demur. But from the outset he found hostile forces active.

One army was actually engaged in crushing the obstinate king of Israel. In Babylonia the Chaldaeans were again in arms, and the diplomacy of Merodach-baladan, who had escaped in the last insurrection, had reinforced them with the more efficient troops of Elam. Rusas, the successor of Sarduris in Urartu, was concerting alliances with the Medes on one

**KING SARGON AND HIS GRAND VIZIER**
Next to the monarch, the highest place in the Assyrian social organization was held by a kind of grand vizier, the Tartan or commander-in-chief of the royal armies. He is usually shown facing the king in a dignified and respectful attitude.
*The Louvre*

side and on the other with Mita of Mushki (otherwise Midas of Phrygia), who in his turn was fostering disaffection in what we may henceforth call Cilicia. And Egypt was on the point of making once more at least a display of intervention in Asiatic affairs. Already Hoshea had counted, vainly enough, on Egyptian aid, when he refused tribute to Shalmaneser.

### Egypt incites Syria to Revolt

WHEN Kashta the Ethiopian established himself at Thebes in 745, the Bubastite dynasty was ingloriously flickering out in the Delta, mere nominal overlords of a number of baronial kinglets. Presently the most powerful of these, Tafnekht of Sais, was bidding for recognition as Pharaoh. By the appeals of a recalcitrant baron, Kashta's successor Piankhi was easily induced to intervene. Dissatisfied with the result of the first expedition dispatched, he took the field in person, reduced the northern barons to submission, was universally recognized as Pharaoh (722) and then withdrew himself to Nubia, leaving a viceroy in the north—probably the Shabaka who followed him on the throne.

The Assyrian generals before Samaria captured the city and deposed the rebel Hoshea immediately after the death of Shalmaneser. Sargon himself was first occupied in an attempt to suppress Merodach-baladan and his Elamite allies; but he met with a repulse at the hands of the latter which caused his withdrawal from Babylonia, and the Chaldaean was triumphantly seated on the throne.

Sargon postponed further interference, finding other problems more pressing. The Egyptian revolution excited fresh hopes in Syria; from south to north, from Gaza to Hamath and Arpad, revolt broke out. Leaving Babylon to its own devices, Sargon swept south. The Egyptian viceroy marched to the aid of the Philistines, and was ignominiously and overwhelmingly routed at Raphia (720). Ignoring Egypt, Sargon exacted the customary penalty from the rebels—a redistribution of the populations, including that of the northern Hebrew kingdom, on whose soil a mixed multitude of folk was planted, the ' lost

tribes' vanishing out of ken. Thenceforth Israel was not; but Judah had not taken part in the revolt.

For some years to come Sargon had no time to spare from preoccupation with the northern menace which centred in Urartu. Doubtless incited by Rusas, tributary princes or chiefs east of Van attacked those who were loyal to Assyria, and several hard campaigns had to be fought before the rebels were reduced to subjection. Among them appears the name of a Median, Daiukku, who was carried captive to Hamath, and is very doubtfully identified with the Deioces who was the traditional founder of the Median monarchy. Sargon's methods varied; for whereas one rebel chief was flayed alive, another was pardoned and reinstated as a local prince.

Mita of Mushki pursued a course similar to that of Rusas, inciting revolts in Cilicia, but himself keeping out of reach of Sargon's arm. As a consequence of these disturbances, Sargon developed the practice, departing from that of his predecessors, of placing Assyrian officers in charge instead of leaving the administration of the provinces in the hands of the native princes. To the competence of the new type of governor the strength of Assyria may be largely attributed.

### Troublous Times in Egypt

IT was probably in consequence of the Egyptian disaster at Raphia that Tafnekht recovered a brief supremacy in Lower Egypt, where he was succeeded by Bokenranef, the Bocchoris of the Greeks; but in spite of a high reputation for wisdom the latter was overthrown in 712 by Shabaka, who had now succeeded Piankhi and proceeded to recover the mastery of all Egypt. If he was the commander whom Sargon routed at Raphia, he may have been meditating an anti-Assyrian policy already, but he did not venture to move as long as Sargon was living. An abortive insurrection in Philistia in 715 had merely been a warning that Assyria was not to be trifled with.

Twelve years after his defeat by the Elamites, Sargon again turned his attention to Babylon. This time Elam did not come to the rescue; Merodach-baladan was deposed without difficulty, but curiously enough was allowed to retain a tribal principality ; while Sargon resumed the crown without the full royal titles.

Another movement, however, was imminent beyond the northern frontier. In 707 Argistis of Urartu found himself facing an irruption of the Cimmerian hordes, and met with a great defeat. In 705 Sargon himself fell, probably in battle with the same horde, and was succeeded by his son Sennacherib. But the campaign must have been victorious; for the Cimmerians turned to the west and flooded Anatolia, submerging Mita of Mushki in the end and immediately paralysing him for any intrigues against Assyria.

The death of Sargon encouraged the irrepressible Merodach-baladan to seize once more the crown of Babylon, since Sennacherib did not immediately assert his own title. He again drew to his side the king of Elam. At the same time he incited Judah and Philistia to a revolt, which, however, was delayed. But the city of Babylon always preferred the

Assyrian to the Chaldee. In 703 Sennacherib routed the Elamites and ejected Merodach-baladan, but left another Babylonian, Bel-ibni, as king. Then, too late for Merodach-baladan, but encouraged by hopes of Egyptian aid, south Syria, joined by Sidon, revolted.

THE campaign which followed was entirely successful. The king of Sidon fled on the approach of Sennacherib, who swept south, over-ran Philistia, shattered at Eltekeh the forces sent by Shabaka of Egypt to help the rebels, and subjugated all Palestine except the almost impregnable city of Jerusalem ; whose king Hezekiah nevertheless made full submission when Sennacherib retired to the north, for reasons not specified. This was in 700 ; and according to the Assyrian record he never had cause in the remaining fifteen years of his reign to revisit the south.

We are forced, however, to doubt the completeness of the official story. From two separate sources we have it reported that at some time or other a great disaster

**SENNACHERIB AT THE HEAD OF HIS GLEAMING COHORTS**

Desire to transmit the remembrance of their exploits to posterity was a distinguishing characteristic of the Assyrians, and their kings employed sculptors primarily to commemorate every act of their life, especially as conquerors. It is as commander-in-chief that Sennacherib is here represented at the head of his army. The long documentary series of bas-reliefs that cover the walls of the royal palace are the illustrations to a history of which the cuneiform inscriptions are the text.

*British Museum*

befell Sennacherib's army near the Egyptian border, attributed in both reports to direct Divine interposition. More than two centuries later the Egyptians told Herodotus that Sennacherib advanced against Pelusium, but the gods sent an army of field-mice which destroyed the bow-strings and other equipment of the Assyrians so that they were easily cut to pieces. The Hebrew historian, in his very dramatic account, says that Sennacherib was laying siege to Libnah when the Angel of the Lord passed by night over his army, and 'when they arose early in the morning, behold, they were all dead corpses' (2 Kings 19, 35).

These variants may be reconciled on the theory of an outbreak of plague introduced in the Assyrian army by mice, which are notorious carriers. As a matter of fact, an outbreak of plague might very well have decided Sennacherib against the contemplated extension of a campaign of which the primary objects had already been thoroughly secured; and it would account for the apparently hasty withdrawal of his main force from the south. On the other hand the Egyptian story was only a tradition, and the Hebrew account is chronologically confused. The Assyrian invasion is apparently placed in the eighth year after the fall of Samaria, at the beginning of the reign of Sargon, and is immediately followed by the assassination of Sennacherib, who reigned for twenty-five years after Sargon's death; moreover the Egyptian is 'Tirhakah king of Ethiopia' instead of the reigning Pharaoh Shabaka, of the same dynasty.

**ESARHADDON THE ASSYRIAN**
Set up at Shamal (the modern Senjerli) in North Syria, this stele with his portrait in relief details Esarhaddon's conquest of Egypt in 671 B.C.
*Berlin Museum*

It was apparently Sennacherib's original intention to preserve Babylon as a separate but dependent kingdom. But the fugitive Merodach-baladan persisted in his intrigues; Bel-ibni was incompetent; and so after an expedition a younger son of Sennacherib—not his presumptive heir—was installed. Elam still sheltered the rebels. An expedition was sent in 694 to make a flank attack on its south, which Elam countered by invading Babylon and carrying off her Assyrian king and leaving a Babylonian in his place, who in turn was ejected by the Assyrians; after which constant confusion reigned, until in 690 Sennacherib fell on Babylon itself, sacked it and laid it in ruins. Esarhaddon, the son whom Sennacherib destined to succeed him, was made not king but viceroy of Babylonia.

The rest of the records of Sennacherib's reign are obscure. In 681 he was assassinated by two elder sons, who probably resented the selection of Esarhaddon as his heir; but the assassins were very promptly and thoroughly crushed by the new king. In Babylonia Esarhaddon had already inaugurated a policy of pacification, conciliation and restoration; since the grand ambition of his life was the conquest of Egypt.

Some years in fact passed before Esarhaddon could give effect to this project. Elam was disturbed, though its troubles did not actually involve serious war. Tribal movements in the eastern hills called for military expeditions, which were mainly demonstrations. In the north Scythians were pushing on the track of the Cimmerians, who were over-running Anatolia and incidentally raiding therefrom through the Taurus passes. The Medes were pressing westward, and Urartu would not long be able to serve the function, latterly forced upon it by circumstances, of a buffer between the barbarians and Assyria. Esarhaddon struck no crushing blow ; he did no more than was enough to give pause to immediate aggression and suppress the local revolts which inevitably accompanied pressure on the frontier, while he prepared for the invasion of Egypt, where Taharka (' Tirhakah the Ethiopian ') was now reigning.

The conquest itself presented no very great difficulties. The Assyrian army met with a check on its first campaign in 675 owing to a storm, an event with which it is just possible to identify that divine destruction of Sennacherib's army, of which there is no Assyrian record. But next year Assyrian forces were in the Delta; and in 671 these experimental campaigns

were followed up by an invasion in force. Taharka's army was scattered in rout, Memphis fell a fortnight later, and Esarhaddon was master of Lower Egypt. Assyrian officers or Egyptian nobles, supported by Assyrian garrisons, were appointed governors of the nomes or districts. Among them was Niku (Necho) of Sais. Esarhaddon then withdrew. He was hardly gone when Taharka, who had been left at large in the south, raised the standard of revolt ; and Esarhaddon, returning in wrath to crush him, died while on the march (669).

He had willed that his elder son Shamash-shum-ukin should rule as king in Babylonia, but as vassal of his younger brother Ashurbanipal, the heir to the throne of Assyria. Ashurbanipal, known to the Greeks as Sardanapalus, made haste to crush the Egyptian revolt ; with no undue severity. Taharka was again defeated, and Memphis, which had

**KING ASHURBANIPAL IN THE HUNTING FIELD**

Cruel in war and tireless in the chase, Ashurbanipal was also a patron of literature and the arts, establishing in his palace at Kouyunjik a library that is now invaluable to Assyriologists and enriching the building with many superb bas-reliefs. In his reign Assyrian art aimed higher than ever before, and the pictures describing his campaign against the Elamites and his hunting exploits are triumphant representations of energy—especially in the case of the animals.

*British Museum*

C*

**DOOM OF THE CITY OF KHAMANU IN ELAM**

Crudity of drawing notwithstanding, the flames issuing from the turrets, the stones and timbers sent crashing to the ground by the picks of the demolition party, and the men issuing from a postern laden with booty, make a vivid picture of the destruction of Khamanu by Ashurbanipal about 640 B.C.

*British Museum*

opened its gates to him, was reoccupied. But the Assyrian's back was no sooner turned than Taharka returned to the Delta and started intrigues with Necho and other governors, Assyrian as well as Egyptian. This conspiracy, however, was nipped in the bud, Taharka was driven back to Napata and Necho taken in chains to Nineveh. Curiously enough, however, on arrival he was not only pardoned, but reinstated at Sais.

Five years later (663) Taharka's nephew Tanutamen again broke out, and was welcomed in Thebes ; Necho, who remained loyal, was slain, but this time Ashurbanipal took summary vengeance. Thebes was sacked and devastated ; as a city it ceased to exist. Psamtek (Psammetichus), the son of Necho, was made viceroy of all Egypt and allowed to assume the pharaonic titles—to prove in after years a much more dangerous because a much more crafty

foe of Assyria than the Ethiopian. The might of Assyria, however, seemed at the time to have been more convincingly established than ever.

WHILE the Assyrian kings were expanding their empire, the Cimmerians and their kinsmen the Treres, who had probably entered Asia Minor from Thrace, had annihilated the power of Phrygia ; but they had not prevented the rise of a new power, the Mermnad dynasty of Lydia, in the west. Gyges of Lydia, now engaged in a desperate struggle with the barbarians, appealed to Assyria for help, which was given either not at all or very half-heartedly ; consequently Ashurbanipal missed the chance of an alliance which might have proved invaluable when the Cimmerians had been finally driven out of Anatolia by Ardys, son of Gyges.

For some fifteen years longer, Ashurbanipal could flatter himself that the power of Assyria was ever advancing. Assyrian armies rarely met actual defeat in the field. Revolt within the empire was invariably suppressed with alternate displays of magnanimity and brutality. Psammetichus in Egypt, without open display of disloyalty, quietly made himself completely independent, but the Assyrian merely ignored his action. Expeditions beyond the border were officially successful in attaining their objects. An incursion in the west, of the Cimmerians retreating before the advance of Lydia, was repelled by the Assyrians on the spot.

But the great triumph of Ashurbanipal, the overthrow of Elam, was probably a grave factor in the approaching downfall of the military empire ; since hitherto Elam had served to bridle the Iranian tribes on her rear, and Assyria had reached the point where extension of dominion meant not added strength but weakness.

In this fateful war Elam had herself been the aggressor. Her king Te-umman seized the opportunity of the last expedition to Egypt for an invasion. He was defeated and beheaded, some Elamite territory was annexed, and a vassal king was installed. The next stage was the insurrection of Shamash-shum-ukin, king of Babylon, Ashurbanipal's brother, who was joined by Chaldaeans and by the king of Elam

**A WILY PHARAOH**

Appointed viceroy of Egypt by Ashurbanipal with the title of Pharaoh, Psammetichus I managed in 651 to free himself from Assyria.

*British Museum*

(652). But the allies were themselves rent by factions. Ashurbanipal came down on them in 648. The Chaldaeans were driven off to Elam ; Shamash-shum-ukin was blockaded in Babylon, where he set fire to his own palace and perished in the flames. The Assyrians advanced on Elam, they stormed and destroyed its capital Susa (unwisely, as it turned out), and Elam as an independent state disappeared for ever.

In 642 Ashurbanipal held in Nineveh a great triumph to celebrate the glories of his reign, a triumph in which four captive kings were harnessed to his chariot. The Assyrian chroniclers tell us of no more achievements. We are aware only that at the close of his reign a Scythian tornado swept through and laid waste the western and coastland provinces of the empire, practically unresisted. Already that empire was tottering in the year of his death, 626. Fourteen years later it was mercifully obliterated.

THE connecting link between the ancient East and the rising West lay in Anatolia or Asia Minor, the lands between the Taurus Mountains and the western sea. In the centre and east of this region, Phrygia, still known to the East as Mushki, had entered on the inheritance of the Hittites and was certainly dominant for a century before the great Cimmerian irruption which had begun about the time of Sargon's death. In that deluge Phrygia, left unaided to her fate, had gone under ; the last Midas perished, if tradition be true, by his own hand, overcome by despair, while Esarhaddon was planning the conquest of Egypt. The task of holding up the nomad hordes in the west thus fell upon the rising principality of Lydia, whose crown had been torn, according to Greek legend, from the old Heraclid dynasty by Gyges.

We have seen Gyges appealing in his struggle for aid from Assyria. With or without aid, he inflicted defeat on the Cimmerians, but only in his turn to be defeated and slain. The struggle was main-

**FATE OF KING TE-UMMAN OF ELAM**

Almost immediately after his accession to the throne of Elam, King Te-umman provoked a quarrel with Ashurbanipal. In the battle that took place Te-umman was seized and decapitated, with his eldest son. This relief shows him kneeling and wounded while the son defends him.

*British Museum*

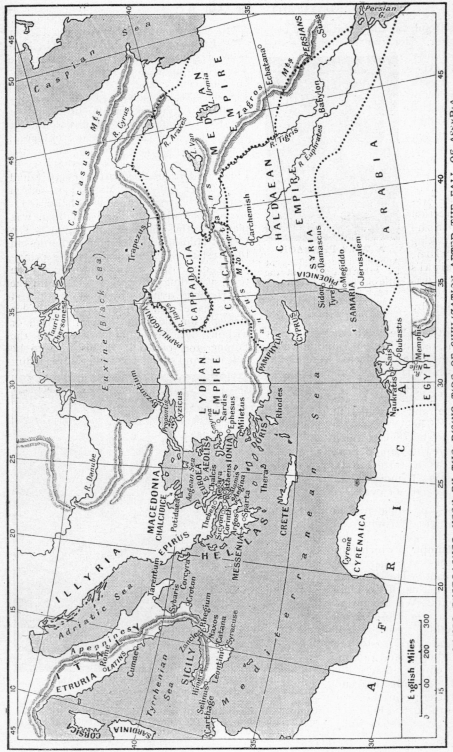

LANDS ENCROACHED UPON BY THE RISING TIDE OF CIVILIZATION AFTER THE FALL OF ASSYRIA

After the extinction of the Assyrian Empire, the western half of its territory was absorbed by the Chaldaean Empire, with its capital at Babylon, the Median Empire taking possession of the eastern portion. Egypt virtually disappears from the arena and the interest of the human drama shifts steadily westward to peninsular Europe, where Greek colonial expansion attains its maximum and the Etruscans and Latins appear in Italy. In the East Lydia was at the height of its power, exercising dominion over the coastal Greek cities, while Cilicia was independent. Persian tribes held Elam.

tained by his son Ardys, who ultimately succeeded, with help from the Ionian cities, in beating off and driving back the barbarians ; who finally evacuated Anatolia altogether, leaving Lydia the most powerful state in Asia Minor.

Although Ionian cities made common cause with Ardys in battling with the common danger which threatened them as well as Lydia, they were themselves

which were to bring her a unique military prestige, and from which she emerged with her equally unique political constitution—ascribed to a legendary lawgiver, Lycurgus—in full play.

The next period witnesses the expansion of Greater Hellas, the establishment of colonies in Italy and Sicily and on the shores of the Euxine sea, the Propontis (the sea of Marmora), and the as yet un-

**CUMAE, THE MOST ANCIENT GREEK SETTLEMENT IN ITALY**
Notable as the first deliberate colony founded by Hellenes in Italy, Cumae was planted from Aeolian Cyme fourteen miles to the westward of Naples, of which, with Puteoli and other port towns, it later became the founder. Cumae was thus one of the sources of Greek civilization in Italy. The Acropolis rock is honeycombed with caves, from one of which, according to the legend, the Cumaean Sibyl brought the Sibylline books to Rome. These ruins are of Roman date.

the object of Lydian attacks both before the Cimmerian onslaught and after its final repulse ; for the successors of Ardys (who died about the same date as Ashurbanipal), and probably that monarch himself, definitely aimed at the lordship of all Asia Minor.

We have seen that by the middle of the eighth century the city states had already long been established over all Hellas proper, and the whole Aegean area, Asiatic as well as European ; and that almost throughout it the old monarchy of the heroic age, the ' god-descended kings,' was giving place to the rule of aristocracies. At this time the wealthiest and most prosperous among them were to be found mainly in Aeolis and Ionia. Sparta had not yet fought the Messenian wars

Hellenised Thracian and Macedonian coast on the north of the Aegean ; as well as the fuller political development of the several Hellenic states.

The planting of a colony was the enterprise of the single state (or more rarely the combination of two or three states) which planted it. The colony was itself an independent city state, often bound to the mother city by a strong tie of sentiment but no longer under its jurisdiction.

The cities of the island of Euboea, but more especially Chalcis, were the pioneers of colonisation. At some date unknown, two of them combined with Cyme in Aeolis to plant Cumae far away on the coast of Campania—perhaps not the first appearance of Hellenes in Italy, but certainly the first organized colony.

**MERCHANT ADVENTURER OF CYRENE**

Dating from the second quarter of the sixth century B.C., this scene inside a Laconian cup illustrates the oversea commerce then being carried on by Greek colonists. It depicts Arcesilaus of Cyrene seated on the deck of a ship watching the weighing of merchandise in a balance hung from the yard.

*Cabinet des Médailles, Paris*

Sicily; of which the most western were Selinus and Himera. Achaeans and Locrians from the shores of the Corinthian gulf founded Sybaris—that type of effeminate luxury—on the gulf of Tarentum, and Croton and other less famous cities on the south and west coasts of Italy; and Tarentum or Taras itself was founded from Sparta, her one colonial effort, about 708. It was not perhaps till the end of the seventh century that Aeolian Phocaea, hard pressed at home by Lydia, founded Massalia, far away on the shores of Gaul, whence colonies were presently to be planted even on the Iberian Peninsula.

But in Sicily the Hellenes had other maritime rivals to compete with; for the Phoenicians from their great outpost at Carthage had already established trading stations in the west of the island. Moreover, long before the Hellenes, those Shirdanu and Tursha whom we met with in the story of Egypt had sought new homes on the western Mediterranean, and had not lost their piratical instincts. We incline to find in them the origins of the Sardinians and of that Etruscan people who were becoming or had already become the dominant group in Italy, though challenged and ultimately to be mastered by the Aryan Latins and Sabellians.

Why these settlers came to be known to the Italians as Graii (modified into Graeci) we cannot tell; they were presumably responsible for teaching the Latins to identify their own deities with those of the Hellenic pantheon. The curious influence they exercised is shown by the Roman legend of the Cumaean Sibyl and the Sibylline books. The real era of activity began in the second half of the eighth century.

Chalcis led the way in the western expansion by founding the first colony in Sicily, Naxos, on the east coast almost facing the extreme toe of Italy, in 735; Catana and Leontini, Zancle (better known as Messana) and Rhegium on the Italian side of the strait following before the century closed. Corinth followed suit with Corcyra (on the island of Corfu) and Syracuse in 734, if the traditional dates be correct; in the course of the next century more colonies were planted—some the daughters of those already there—along the south and also the north coast of

THE cities of Aeolis and Ionia turned their colonising energies mainly to the Euxine and the Propontis, with a view to commerce, almost monopolising that region, though it was Megara on the isthmus of Corinth that founded Byzantium. The Euboeans added to the western enterprises of Chalcis the colonisation of the north, and especially of the triple promontory which became known as Chalcidice; though here Corinth also thrust in and planted Potidaea. In the second half of the seventh century, Cyrene was planted on the Libyan coast from Thera, one of the most southern isles of the Cyclades. Naukratis, on the Canopic mouth of the Nile, started about the same time merely as a trade depot of Miletus, but grew into a market for Greeks generally.

On the mainland of Greece there were three cities which may be distinguished as gaining during the eighth and seventh centuries the status of territorial powers. Sparta became lord of half the Peloponnese, Attica was united with Athens, and Thebes dominated Boeotia. The Spartans were lords of a subjugated population ; the minor states of Attica were voluntarily incorporated with Athens and their citizens became citizens of Athens ; the Boeotian states were theoretically independent, but could not stand out of the Boeotian confederacy in which Thebes was practically dictator.

Sparta had long been supreme in Laconia. Spartan citizenship was confined to the few who were of the Spartiate tribes. The rest of the population was free but politically subject to Sparta—these were the 'perioeci,' the 'dwellers round'—and there was also a very large slave population, the Helots, the pre-Dorians who had been conquered and enslaved.

**FLOWER OF THE SPARTAN ARMY**

It was to the efficiency of her infantry armed with heavy spears that Sparta largely owed her growing predominance on the mainland. This painting inside a cup shows two such 'hoplites' carrying a slain warrior on their shoulders.

*Berlin Museum*

**ARMED TYPES OF THE ASIATIC GREEKS**

Huge vessels containing calcined bones have been unearthed at Sparta. Details of the armour and of the Homeric battle in the moulded reliefs on these fragments show that the urn was copied from an Ionic original.

*British School at Athens Annual*

In the eighth century Sparta was only one of several powerful states—Argos, Sicyon, Corinth—to any one or to none of which it was still possible that definite leadership might fall. The development of the Spartan military system in the Messenian wars of that eighth century gave the ascendancy or 'hegemony' definitely to her in the course of the century following. Only Messenia, however, was added to her subject territory ; the independence of the northern states was unaffected, and their rivalry was still a possibility. The whole organization of the Spartan state was directed to military efficiency, so that the Spartan discipline has become a proverb.

In this connexion, it may be remarked that Sparta owed her military ascendancy in part at least to the high state of perfection to which she raised the heavy-armed infantry, the mail-clad spearmen called 'hoplites' by the Greeks, who were to give them repeated victory in the coming conflicts with oriental forces.

The unification of Attica was the basis of the power which Athens was on the way to attain. Unlike Sparta, she was a sea-going state, but at this period she was only one among several of equal rank, enjoying no special predominance. She had immediate rivals in Aegina, Megara and the cities of Euboea, whose mutual feuds were destined to lose for them that supremacy which at one time seemed likely to be theirs. The direct conflict with Aegina was deferred ; but two wars with Megara for the possession of the island of Salamis, in the last quarter of the seventh and the second quarter of the sixth centuries, beginning with the defeat and ending with the victory of Athens, gave her the definite ascendancy over that competitor, though she was still far from being a naval power.

Corinth, planted on and commanding the isthmus that joins or severs northern and southern Greece, and difficult to approach by land, in a position equally adapted for eastern and western maritime expansion but virtually isolated north-wards and southwards, was not to enter into competition for political hegemony. North of Boeotia and the Maliac gulf there were no cities of equal prominence with these ; there were only loose leagues or confederacies. Beyond Thessaly the hill-tribes of Macedon acknowledged a king who claimed to be a Hellene, but ruled over what could hardly be called an organized kingdom.

On the east of the Aegean we have no such detailed knowledge of the develop-ment of the great cities of Aeolis, Ionia and Doris as of their western contem-poraries. What we do know is that both intellectually and materially they were rather in advance of the states of Greece itself than behind them. They held their cities against Cimmerian onslaughts. Their ' wise men ' and their poets were famed all over Hellas. But they were as incapable of close union as their European kinsmen. Failing to recognize a common menace when they were individually attacked by an alien power, they were forced one by one to submit to the far from exacting overlordship of Lydia under the successors of Ardys—Sadyattes, Alyattes and finally Croesus, the monarch whose sway, in the second quarter of the sixth century, extended all over Asia Minor as far as the river Halys.

A class dominant in the government of any state always tends to subordinate the interest of other classes to its own. The aristocracies of birth which were ruling in nearly all the Hellenic states in the middle of the eighth century were no exception to the rule. The subordinate classes demanded release from the

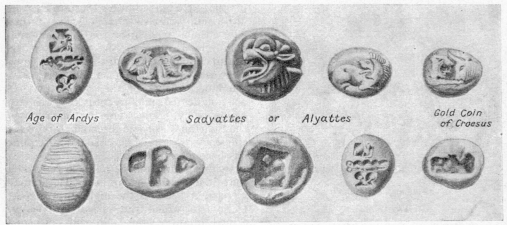

Age of Ardys          Sadyattes    or    Alyattes          Gold Coin of Croesus

**RELICS OF THE DAYS WHEN LYDIA DOMINATED THE ASIATIC GREEKS**

Memorials of the Lydian Empire that loomed so large behind the Asiatic Greeks are few, principally through lack of archaeological excavation. Most interesting are the coins, because they seem to have been the earliest struck ; the system of weights is Babylonian, but the idea of minting these weights in figured medallions may be specifically Lydian. The occurrence of lions' and bulls' heads in the Hittite manner among the devices is interesting as a survival. The material of these examples is electrum.
*British Museum*

economic burdens imposed on them, and political power. In state after state a struggle developed. Sometimes the aristocracies simply held their own ; sometimes wealth succeeded in superseding birth ; sometimes aristocratic statesmen carried through reforms out of which democracy was in time evolved, such as those introduced in Athens by the most famous of ' wise men,' Solon, in 592, or the little less famous Pittacus in Mitylene at about the same period. The study of these social and political changes still engages students of history ; but we cannot enter upon it here.

A very common stage in the struggle was the appearance of what the Greeks called the Tyrannis, a despotism seized generally by a popular leader who had overthrown the aristocrats as a champion of democracy and maintained himself in power by troops of mercenaries. The Tyrannis produced many rulers whose oppression gave a very sinister meaning to the name of ' tyrant ' ; some who in fact were very brilliant princes, such as Periander of Corinth, Cleisthenes of Sicyon and Peisistratus who made himself Tyrant of Athens in 561. Several tyrants had established themselves in the cities of Ionia and Aeolis at the close of our period, and the Tyrannis was generally supported by the Lydian overlord.

### Developments in the Far West

TURNING again to the far west, we have seen that Italy was brought into touch with the Hellenic world by the expansion into Magna Graecia. But apart from the Hellenic colonies, the centre of Italy's development is in the lands lying between the Apennines and the western sea, the lowlands of Etruria and Latium to which the nearest approach was made by the colony of Cumae. Etruria, however, and Latium are now themselves within our ken, though not yet in the full light.

We know little enough of the earlier inhabitants of the peninsula, who were doubtless the basic stock of the Italian people. The progressive peoples were the later invaders, the Etruscans who came over the sea probably from the east, but in any case non-Aryans, and the Aryans

who came in through the Alpine passes or round the head of the Adriatic. The lowlands are divided in two by the river Tiber, flowing due south from the hills to the sea. When dawn breaks in the eighth century, we find the western region, Etruria, occupied by the Etruscans or Tuscans, the eastern, the plain of Latium, by the Aryan Latins ; behind and past whom are pressing southward through the mountains a second Aryan group of Oscans or Sabellians (a name which also appears as Sabines, or later as Samnites). Etruscans and Latins have both developed the city-state system, and are in hot competition, while both are holding back the pressure of the still migrant Oscans in the mountains.

The date traditionally fixed for the entrance of Rome on the scene is 753. Planted on the Tiber, the city strategically commanded the gate between Etruria and Latium, and the possession of it was a constant bone of contention between Latins, Sabines and Etruscans. It remained predominantly Latin, but with substantial Sabine and Etruscan elements. The story of the monarchy in Rome is mainly legendary ; but in the sixth century the reigning dynasty, there certainly and perhaps in some other Latin cities, was Etruscan, while her nobles and her commons were of all the three races. Owing to her position, her state organization was necessarily directed to military efficiency. It was not till the close of the sixth century that she shook off her monarchy and established an aristocratic republic.

### Decline and Fall of Assyrian Empire

THE closing years of Ashurbanipal were troubled by disease and by family discords. Though Herodotus says that a great attack by the Medes was utterly routed, no Assyrian record of it remains ; and Ashurbanipal was certainly unable to check the Scythian irruption. The old native Assyrian fighting force had been depleted by endless wars, and the levies from subject peoples provided much less efficient troops. Egypt was free of control under Psammetichus, and after the Scythian incursion the cities of Syria and

Phoenicia no longer acknowledged the Assyrian overlordship.

The successors of Ashurbanipal had but a precarious hold even on the Assyrian crown. He was hardly dead when Babylon revolted and set up a Chaldaean king, Nabopolassar, against whom the new

**AN UNPOPULAR PHARAOH**

King of Egypt from 588 to 569 B.C., Apries rashly fostered a revolt against Nebuchadrezzar, as the result of which Judah and Tyre suffered heavily. This stele, showing Apries offering vases of wine to a god, came from Abydos.

*British Museum*

Assyrian monarch could take no action. A powerful Median kingdom had meanwhile been consolidated—by Deioces and Phraortes, according to Herodotus, by Arbaces according to Ctesias. Medes and Babylonians were alike waiting eagerly to enter upon the inheritance of Assyria, whose only (very doubtful) allies were among the Scythians. When fear as a motive was removed, loyalty in the subjects of that most grievous empire was not to be looked for.

In 612, not 606, as is proved by recently discovered evidence, Nabopolassar and Cyaxares the Mede united to destroy Assyria, and her last king, Sin-sharishkun, perished helpless in the flames of Nineveh, as Shamash-shum-ukin had perished in the flames of Babylon thirty-six years before—if the Greek legend that so describes the end of Sardanapalus is accurate save for the confusion of names. Save for a remnant that fled to Harran and maintained itself there for a few years, Assyria the Terrible, the eternal type of bestial force, of ruthlessness systematised, was utterly blotted out ; and the world breathed more freely.

### Empires of Media and Babylonia

THE empire was parted between Nabopolassar and Cyaxares ; the Babylonian taking Mesopotamia and Syria, the Mede all that lay east and north of the Tigris.

In 608 the successor of Psammetichus, Pharaoh Necho, nominally as champion of an Assyrian pretender, occupied northern Syria, where the new authority was by no means securely established ; and perhaps smiting Josiah king of Judah at a second battle of Megiddo. The events are obscure ; but in 605 Necho was overwhelmingly defeated at Carchemish by Nebuchadrezzar, Nabopolassar's heir, and was pursued to the borders of Egypt, whence Nebuchadrezzar was recalled to the north by the news of his father's death. Necho made no further demonstration against the new empire, nor, probably, was there any later attack on Egypt.

The Median power pushing westward under Cyaxares and the Lydian pushing eastward under Alyattes came into collision in eastern Anatolia. The war ended in 585. A great battle was actually in progress, but was interrupted by a solar eclipse (foretold by Thales of Miletus, another of the Grecian ' wise men '), which so perturbed the combatants on both sides that a truce was called on the spot. The rivals agreed to invite the mediation of the kings of Babylon and Cilicia, and a formal treaty established the river Halys as the boundary between the two kingdoms. Media had already absorbed Urartu. The new alliance was cemented by the marriage of Astyages, the Median heir-apparent, to the daughter of Alyattes.

Lydia overlapped Hellas on the west and was now in close association with Media, the rising power in the east. The clash between Hellenism and Orientalism was bound to come ere long.

### Nebuchadrezzar's Napoleonic Qualities

**N**EBUCHADREZZAR (Nabu-kudur-usur) of Babylon, the Nebuchadnezzar of the Bible, was a great captain (an unusual phenomenon among the Chaldaeans), an able administrator, a great architect and engineer ; but as a matter of course he followed the methods which had been the established practice of Assyria almost from time immemorial. When Judah revolted in 596, he suppressed the revolt and deported part of the Jewish population. When she was mad enough, in 587, to revolt a second time (in conjunction with Tyre and Sidon), in spite of the warnings of Jeremiah, he slew the king's sons before his eyes in cold blood, blinded him and carried off most of the population into a cruel captivity, while the remnant for the most part found an asylum in Egypt. But he established throughout his dominion an order which was not that of pure terrorism, and his ' hanging gardens ' in the magnificent city he made of Babylon were among the ' wonders ' of the world.

There was no collision with Media, nor with Egypt while Necho and Psammetichus II after him were ruling there ; but the latter's successor Uahibra, the Hophra of the Bible and the Apries of the Greeks, brought trouble, stirring up the (second) revolt of Judah, and that of Tyre, by promises of assistance which was not forthcoming. That Tyre was reduced at all, though only after a siege of more than two years, is proof of Nebuchadrezzar's military skill ; her situation gave her an unequalled power of defying siege operations.

Hophra had started the revolt by an invasion of Phoenicia, but had retired incontinently when Nebuchadrezzar moved. The prevalent idea that the Babylonian at a later date marched into Egypt and effected a temporary conquest rests upon insufficient and doubtful evidence. Hophra was extremely unpopular, owing

partly to the favour he showed to the Ionian and Carian mercenary troops who were actually the core of the Egyptian armies. Hence a popular but low-born general, Aahmes, known to the Greeks as Amasis, had no difficulty in deposing him and making himself Pharaoh in 569. Nevertheless as Pharaoh Amasis continued the policy of favouring the western aliens. It was at this time that Naukratis was established, as a privileged Greek trading station and factory for Greek wares rather than a colony in the proper sense.

Nebuchadrezzar died in 562. His Chaldaean dynasty rested on no more secure foundation than his own personality. Six years later it was deposed, and the Babylonians set on their throne the amiable archaeologist Nabonidus, who soon seems to have become unpopular with the priesthood.

### The End of the Old Order

**A**SSYRIA was stone dead. The virility if not the vitality was gone out of Egypt. The life went out of the new Babylon with Nebuchadrezzar. But Hellas was young, Lydia was young, Media was young. With them, to a discerning eye, lay the future. And behind the Medes were the kindred tribes of the Persians—as near akin as Scots to Englishmen, differing in little except the fact that they led harder lives in a sterner country. To them it had fallen to absorb the once turbulent but now ruined Elam, and to make its old capital, Susa, their own principal city, though they were not city-dwellers. Moreover, within the last century, they had organized a kingdom with a double royal line, descending from the two sons of Teïspes or Chispis the son of Achaemenes (to use the Greek renderings of his name).

Cyrus, of whom tradition affirms that his mother was a daughter of Astyages the Mede, became the fourth king of Anshan (Elam), of the elder line, about 552. In 550 with his Persians behind him he claimed and seized the crown of Astyages, and the Medes accepted the dynastic revolution apparently without demur. That event was the death-blow of the Old Order.

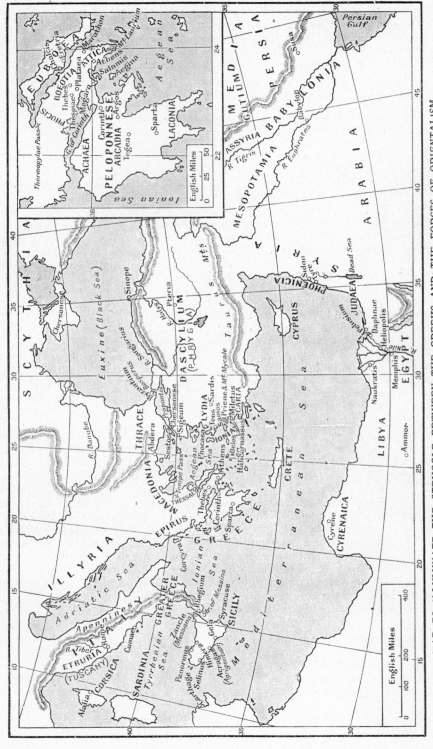

**MAP TO ILLUMINATE THE STRUGGLE BETWEEN THE GREEKS AND THE FORCES OF ORIENTALISM**

Century by century as communications developed and territorial ambitions increased, the collision of the Oriental empires with the growing civilization of the West became imminent. In the sixth century B.C. the Persians were to reach the Aegean and establish their dominion over the Ionian cities; the Greeks had gone west to Sicily; Carthage had in its turn pioneered a western policy and all the Aegean communities were restless. Here then is the stage set for the great Persian invasion of Greece in the early years of the fifth century, and the contemporary struggle between Greeks and Carthaginians in Sicily.

# Second Era

## THE HELLENIC AGE

### 550–201 B.C.

---

Chapter 4
PERSIA AND GREECE IN COLLISION, 550—478 B.C.

Chapter 5
THE RIVAL CITIES, 478—360 B.C.

Chapter 6
THE HELLENISTIC AGE, 360—280 B.C.

Chapter 7
THE BEGINNINGS OF ROMAN POWER, 280—201 B.C.

---

THE shortness of this Era compared with those before and after it emphasises the amazing rapidity with which the Greek peoples brought their genius to fruition, playing out in a bare three hundred years a microcosm of the whole historical and intellectual drama of the human race. History for the first time gives the impression of gathering speed, but the surrounding peoples have not yet caught the fire and still seem to move from event to event with the ponderous momentum of the preceding Era.

Hence the narrative of this Era may appear unduly concerned with purely Greek affairs ; Chapter 4, it is true, having much to tell about the rise of the Persian Empire and its clash with Hellas, but Chapter 5 being almost entirely devoted to that Peloponnesian War from which Thucydides drew such profound lessons for posterity. During the latter period Persia yields to the political historian little more than the names of its successive kings, while Egypt, as a mere province of the great Empire, remains sunk in an obscurity only brightened by sporadic revolts.

In Chapter 6, however, we see Alexander cutting clean across the established order of things, bringing East and West into new relationships and inaugurating an era that was to last till the rise of Islam. In Chapter 7 Rome takes the field.

It will be observed that our earlier Chronological Table covered the Chapters of an entire Era. The Table that follows applies to Chapter 4 only, and henceforward each chapter will be accompanied by a separate Table, either in a single sequence of dates as here, or in parallel synchronised columns as required.

The last date exceeds the nominal limit of the Chapter by four years, both in order to link on with the succeeding Chapter and to round off one aspect of the events dealt with—the Greek and Etruscan rivalry in the West. The breaks in our historical narrative must of necessity be arbitrary, and it is impossible to select a date that shall be equally appropriate for all contemporary movements ; so that the device will often be adopted hereafter.

# TABLE OF DATES FOR CHAPTER 4

# PERSIA AND GREECE IN COLLISION: 550—478 B.C.

FROM the middle of the sixth century B.C. to the end of the first quarter of the fifth, the supreme, but by no means the sole, interest lies in the rise of the new Persian Empire and its collision with the Greeks, the first armed conflict between East and West.

For East and West have at last come into full contact. Hitherto they have been developing almost though not completely apart. Now they meet, each of them at a height of its own specific development which has in some respects never been surpassed, except, perhaps, in the hundred years immediately following. And because they meet in hostility, the conflict is one of the most momentous in the world's history.

But we are in face of something more than this Oriental reorganization and its clash with the younger world of the West. Our horizon has already widened, bringing a farther East and a farther West into our purview. Carthage as well as Greater Greece is in contact with the farther West, which as yet means, in effect, Italy. Persia, eastward, is coming in contact with India, and a remote China may now be described as at least recognizable.

The farthest East, however, will not for some time to come demand the close attention of the chronicler

From Japanese legend the most we can infer is that the Japanese race was making its way into the great eastern islands before or during the sixth century B.C.

## First Glimpses of the Farther East

BUT in the period of which we have now to speak the history of China emerges out of legendary obscurity. For the life of the most famous of Chinamen, K'ung Fu-tze, whom the West knows as Confucius, exactly coincides with it ; and the records compiled by him remain a Chinese classic. Something in the nature of a Chinese state and an advanced civilization had been in existence for two thousand years or more.

When Confucius was born in 551 B.C., the third of the three 'ancient' dynasties, the house of Chou, had already held the imperial throne for nearly six hundred years, and was to retain it for nearly three hundred more. But the vast territory, isolated from the rest of the world by geographical barriers, neither influenced it nor was influenced by it ; not touching it at all save in relations with India, itself only a degree less isolated.

### Rise of Cyrus the Persian

ABOUT the year 550 B.C., Cyrus the Persian, king of Anshan, of the house of Achaemenes which had ruled among the Persians for four generations, seized the crown of Media from his reputed kinsman Astyages, and united the kindred peoples of the Medes and Persians under his sway. There was no conquest of the Medes by the Persians, who had recognized the over-lordship of the Median dynasty ; but a Persian dynasty took the place of the Median. To the western world, Mede and Persian became equivalent terms, except in respect of the specifically Persian troops, which enjoyed a high reputation.

Assyria had perished some sixty years before. From its ashes had arisen the new Babylonian Empire of Nebuchadrezzar, but that empire's vitality departed with his death ; its sceptre was now in the hands of Nabonidus, a scholar, a dilettante, who left the business of government mainly to his far from competent son Belshazzar, while his antiquarian unorthodoxy vexed the souls of the Babylonians. In all Syria no prince had arisen to undertake the part once played so efficiently by Ben-Hadad of Damascus and afterwards so inefficiently by the kings of Israel or Judah, all of whose kingdoms had been wiped out.

Egypt as a military power was effete ; dependent for fighting purposes mainly on troops of foreign mercenaries, whose valour could be more relied upon than the fidelity of their officers. Long ago she had been contemptuously described as a broken reed which would only pierce the hand of him who leaned on it for support; and she had fully justified that gibe at every opportunity.

On the other hand, to the west of Media, herself little more than half a century old as an effective power, another power had grown up during the same period on the ruins of Phrygia, separated from Media by the agreed boundary of the river Halys, overlapping and considerably influenced by the Hellenic world beyond. But the capacities of Lydia were still untested. And the Hellenic world was as yet known to the East, with which it was now linked by Lydia, mainly as a nursery of mercenary soldiers for the armies of Egypt.

Such was the world upon which Cyrus the Achaemenid looked, when he made himself the first ' King of the Medes and Persians,' the ' Great King.' The old empires would never revive ; who, if anyone, was to enter on their inheritance ? It was a world that for its own part viewed the new northern monarchy with acute suspicion.

It is manifest that the personality of Cyrus made a tremendous impression on his contemporaries. Bred in the remote obscurity of the Persian highlands, legends gathered about his birth and upbringing. He was the child of destiny, miraculously preserved at birth from the doom his grandfather Astyages had prepared for the expected babe, and reared in obscurity till his identity was revealed. The tradition of his training was idealised a century and a half later by Xenophon, the soldier

**CYRUS THE GREAT**
Military genius and humanity were his attributes ; but this winged figure on a bas-relief from Pasargadae, with head-dress of goats' horns and solar disks, show him in his divine capacity.
*From Dieulafoy, ' L'Art antique en Perse '*

pupil of Socrates ; and in all the legend of Cyrus the humanity of the man is a conspicuous feature. We may credit as much or as little of such tales as we please ; but the fact of his humanity is convincingly attested by his statesmanship, in noble contrast to the old Assyrian ruthlessness, which the last Babylonian empire had by no means discarded.

When Cyrus dethroned Astyages, he spared the old king's life. In effecting the revolution, he undoubtedly had the support of a substantial body of Median nobles, though it may well be that for the next two years he did not feel his authority fully established. At any rate, it was not from him that the first aggressive movement came.

Croesus of Lydia perceived a menace. His father had fought, but finally concluded a treaty of peace and alliance, with the father of Astyages ; their friendly relations had been maintained, and the royal houses were closely connected by marriage. Could those relations be continued with the supplanter of Astyages ? Since the Median war the power of Lydia had increased materially ; if another fight with Media was imminent, it would be better to strike before the new kingdom was consolidated. He tried to awaken Nabonidus and Amasis of Egypt to the common menace, and procured an anti-Persian alliance with them and with Sparta. But before his allies were ready to move, Croesus, beguiled by a rather obviously ambiguous oracle, flung down the challenge to Cyrus by crossing the Halys early in 546 and seizing Pteria.

Cyrus took the field. An indecisive battle, followed by no active move on the part of Cyrus, induced Croesus to withdraw to his western capital at Sardis and send an urgent summons to his allies for a spring campaign. But the Persian gave him no time. He swooped on Sardis, captured it, and took the king prisoner. Greek tradition says that he treated his captive generously after a divinely frustrated attempt to burn him alive ; another, that he put him to death. In either case he turned Lydia into a Persian province. The Ionian cities which had submitted to the suzerainty of the half-Hellenised Croesus were disposed to resist the conqueror, but were soon induced by force or by diplomacy to bow to the inevitable. Spartan envoys forbade the Great King to interfere with the Hellenes as ' they would not permit it,' but Sparta took no further action and Cyrus took no further notice. Egypt and Babylon sat still.

### Babylon becomes a Persian City

AGAIN there was a pause. Probably Cyrus found or foresaw troubles on his eastern border from the ferment among the nomads of those regions ; we hear of him in conflict with the Sacae and Bactrians. Then in 540 he turned on Babylon. The government of Nabonidus was not popular in Babylonia ; it was well understood that the conquest of Lydia had brought upon the conquered nothing worse than a change of masters, since the populations had been subjected to none of the accustomed penalties. For the Babylonian dynasty no Daniel was needed to interpret the writing on the wall. When Cyrus swept down on Babylon, half the population looked on him not as an enemy but as a liberator ; Gobryas, the Babylonian governor of Gutium, captured the great city for him before his arrival in person, and put Belshazzar to death, though Nabonidus himself was spared. There may or may not be truth in the legend that the city was taken by diverting the waters of the great river that flowed through it so that the army marched in waist-deep on the bed of it.

However that may be, in 539, after a very brief compaign, to the new empire of Persia, Media and Lydia Cyrus had added all the Asiatic territories over which the mightiest of the ancient empires had ever held sway. Of all those who had boasted themselves lords of the world, not one, from the half-mythical Sargon of Agade to Nebuchadrezzar, had held effective rule beyond the mountains of the Taurus on one side and the Zagros on the other. Cyrus was master of all from the shores of the Aegean to the Caspian, and from the Euxine to the deserts of Arabia. Twelve years before, he had been only the obscure king of Anshan.

It was a tremendous achievement, though it had no doubt been made

**LYDIAN MOUNTED SOLDIERS SUCH AS WERE DEFEATED BY CYRUS**

Lydian armies in the sixth century were dominating Anatolia. The three soldiers here depicted are well seated on stout horses, carry a spear and, on the back, perhaps a quiver. It is uncertain whether they are wearing helmets, because of the mutilated condition of the heads. Nevertheless, the evidence of this marble bas-relief, part of a frieze from Sardis, warrants the conclusion that, in these warriors, Cyrus met no unworthy foe when he came into conflict with Croesus of Lydia.

*British Museum*

**CROESUS THE LAST LYDIAN KING**

A red-figured amphora of Attic work, c. 500 B.C., in the Louvre, shows Croesus on the burning pyre after his defeat. Herodotus adorns the tale and points the moral of unstable fortune.

*From Furtwängler-Reichhold. ' Griechische Vasenmalerei,'*

comparatively easy by the factions which had given him their support and welcome in the conquered states ; but Cyrus was more than a great conqueror—he was a great king. The new regime was not merely accepted ; it was welcomed. In the ten years that remained to Cyrus after he became King of Babylon, no revolt was raised throughout his vast dominion. No doubt his subjects had a wholesome fear of his power, but they had no reason to dread his cruelty. There were no flayings, no massacres, no deportations. On the contrary, the populations deported by Assyrians or Babylonians were, so far as practicable, restored to their old homes. The gods whom previous conquerors had been wont to carry off were returned to their old shrines. Everywhere the renewal of the ancient rites was permitted. A universal clemency and toleration took the place of the old universal terror.

Cyrus made no move against Egypt. For the last ten years of his life he was concerned not with further expansion but

with the security of his eastern border against the incursions of the wild nomad tribes ; and it was during the campaign against them that he met his death in 529 B.C., in some way that is not known.

He left two sons : Cambyses, his heir, and Smerdis, the latter of whom, with or without excuse, was secretly put to death by his elder brother.

For Cambyses, the immediate object of ambition was the conquest of Egypt. But the accession of a new ruler in such circumstances was bound to be attended by the possibility at least of disturbances, demanding vigilance, and the frontier trouble was made the more pressing by the death of Cyrus. Four years passed before the Persian picked a quarrel with Aahmes (Amasis), who died himself while Cambyses was preparing for the campaign.

### Cambyses becomes Pharaoh

Now Egypt had enjoyed material prosperity under his long reign of forty-four years, but its fundamental weakness had been rather intensified. The mercenaries were still its effective army, and they were still—mercenaries. Their good will was precarious, and the favour shown to them by the court was resented by the Egyptians. One of their captains—Phanes of Halicarnassus—deserted, and offered

**TOMB OF CYRUS AT PASARGADAE**

Diverse opinions as to the purpose of this limestone monument in the old Persian capital are held. Some have thought that it was a fire-temple ; but most probably it is the Great King's tomb. Ionian influence in the architecture is also suspected from certain structural details, but the claim is ill founded.

*From Dieulafoy, ' L'Art antique en Perse'*

his services, which his knowledge of the conditions rendered invaluable, to Cambyses. Amasis had hoped to ensure command of the sea, in the inevitable conflict with Persia, through his old ally Polycrates, the tyrant of Samos ; but the new pharaoh (Psammetichus III) found that Polycrates had transferred his friendship to Persia.

Advised by Phanes, Cambyses procured from the local chiefs the provision of an adequate water-supply for the march through the southern desert. When his army reached the frontier fort of Pelusium, a single sanguinary battle sufficed to decide the fate of Egypt, though the fortresses at Memphis and Heliopolis offered a stubborn but brief resistance. In the spring of 525 Egypt was annexed to the Persian empire.

Cyrus, when he conquered Babylon, had assumed the ancient crown with the religious rites of the ancient kingdom, untroubled by the fact that that religion was not his own. Cambyses in Egypt followed the example, and was proclaimed Pharaoh as though he had been an orthodox worshipper of Amen, without

**TOMB OF KING CAMBYSES**

Solid below, this tower at Pasargadae stood 23 feet square and 39 feet high. The upper part contained a chamber placed 16 feet from the ground and reached by a flight of steps.

*From Dieulafoy, ' L'Art antique en Perse '*

any idea of disloyalty to his own Zoroastrian faith ; a course which no Assyrian had dreamed of adopting, but one to which in fact the Persian dynasty owed much of its stability.

All at first seemed to go well, then came disappointment and disaster. Carthage was the next objective ; but the Phoenician sailors flatly refused to sail against their kinsmen, and the project in consequence had to be abandoned. Cambyses desired to possess himself of the Oasis of Ammon ; a great expedition was dispatched thither, but was totally obliterated by desert sandstorms and was never seen or heard of again. He led a greater expedition in person to crush the Nubian kingdom of Napata, but his convoys were cut off and a starving army had to struggle back through the foodless region of the upper cataracts. Then, says the Greek historian, Cambyses went mad, and committed frenzied outrages against the religion he had at first sought to conciliate and its devil-deities, as no doubt they now seemed to him.

### Death of King Cambyses

ON the top of all this came news of a Persian revolt, engineered by the adherents of the old Magian religion in antagonism to the Zoroastrianism of the Achaemenids. They had proclaimed a sham Smerdis king. Persian authority was thoroughly established in Egypt—thirty years passed before it was again challenged—and Cambyses started for the north with a portion of his army and some leading nobles, among whom was his distant cousin, the Achaemenid Darius the son of Hystaspes, to crush the pretender. On the way, somewhere in Syria, the king died suddenly. The army went on, taking the dead body with them. The impostor retired from Susa to Media, where the Magians were stronger than in Persia. Thither he was pursued, surprised and run to earth by Darius, with six companions, all Persians, who slew him.

Of the house of Cyrus there was none left. But Darius and his now aged father Hystaspes, who was reigning as sub-king in Khorassan, the cradle of Zoroastrianism, were the representatives of the junior branch of the house of Achaemenes ; and the crown of Cyrus was set on the head of Darius (522 B.C.).

THE creation of the vast Persian empire had been the work of a single man. It combined under a single ruler many peoples and kingdoms never before united. His son had added Egypt to a dominion already of unprecedented magnitude, and died within eight years, leaving no heir with a clear title to the succession ; Darius could at best claim no more than to be the nearest of kin, with a vigorous Persian backing. If in such circumstances he had merely succeeded in preventing the disruption of the empire it would have been a notable achievement ; but he did very much more. He gave it an organization which enabled it to endure undiminished for two hundred years.

In two years Darius established himself so firmly on the imperial throne that no serious revolt occurred till another twenty years had passed. In those first two years he had many revolts on his hands. Medes revolted, hoping to recover Median ascendancy over the Persians. Persians revolted, in the belief that a grandson of the great Cyrus was still alive. Babylonians and Armenians both revolted, dreaming of recovering their independence. There were signs that officers of the empire itself, the satraps of Egypt and Lydia, had ambitious thoughts of setting up independent kingdoms. The only troops on which the new king could place implicit reliance were the Persians, led by those Persian

**CYLINDER SEAL OF DARIUS**
The king hunts lions among palm trees. His name is inscribed in Persian, Susian and Babylonian. Above appears the symbol of Ahuramazda, the national god, in a winged disk.
*British Museum*

**KING DARIUS WITH CROWN**
Merciless to those who defied authority, Darius yet combined the qualities of humanity with wise statesmanship. To him were due the reform of the satrapies, a postal system, a uniform coinage and Persia's naval prestige.
*By permission of Trustees of British Museum*

nobles whose loyalty was never in doubt— forces that sometimes had to be distributed to deal with enemies in quarters far apart. But in two years he had disposed of all the overt rebels ; between whom, fortunately, there was no concerted action.

In the course of the next three years Oroites, the too independent satrap at Sardis, was suppressed and executed. The same fate befell Aryandes, the satrap of Egypt. At the same time Darius took measures to conciliate the Egyptian sentiment outraged by Cambyses in the days of his fury, assuming the pharaonic titles and dignity with all due religious ceremony, reinstating despoiled temples and raising new shrines.

By 517 Darius was the accepted and unchallenged lord of the entire civilized world in Asia and Africa, except that Carthage was beyond his range. His attempts at wider conquest were merely experimental, and were not followed up. He was in face of the eternal problem that presents itself to every civilized state with predatory and uncivilized peoples on its border, whose attacks must be held in check. Were they to be forcibly annexed, or was the frontier to be merely policed ?

THERE was certainly at some time an easterly expedition, probably a prolonged one ; since the mountain barrier of India was penetrated and the Persian claimed to have conquered ' India.' That, however, probably meant no more than that princes on the right bank of the Indus paid a tribute. The Aryan Hindus had by this date long established their dominion over all northern India, as well as a fairly complete religious and political ascendancy in the south. Hindu kingdoms covered the Punjab and the Ganges basin ; and it was probably in this century—the dates are very uncertain—that an Indian prince

resigned his crown to be the founder of Buddhism (see Chap. 40).

But of all this the western records tell us nothing, and of a Persian conquest the Indian records tell us nothing. It is in fact clear only that Darius did touch the fringe of India, but no more. Nor did he take personal part in the expedition.

His other experiment was unfortunate. In 514 he led an army into Europe across a bridge of boats thrown over the Bosporus. But the Greeks were not his immediate objective. Ionian cities on the European side were already the vassals of Persia as the heir of Lydia. He marched through

**DARIUS CELEBRATES HIS TRIUMPH OVER TEN REBEL CHIEFS**

The king, right hand raised, with two attendants (one shown), gives thanks to the god Ahura-mazda for victory, after two years of revolt, over Gaumata—prostrate underfoot—and the nine satraps roped together : Atrina of Susa ; Nidintu-Bêl, of Babylon ; Phraortes of Media ; Martiza of Susa ; Citrantakhama of Sagartia ; Vahyazdata, second pseudo-Smerdis ; Arakha of Babylon ; Frada of Margiana ; and Skunkha the Scythian. The sculptures are on the Rock of Behistun.

Thrace to the Danube and crossed it into Scythian territory. There he suffered what all armies have suffered in attempting to penetrate Russia. An extremely mobile enemy kept out of reach but cut off all his supplies. He could only struggle back to the Danube with little more than the wreck of an army.

The Ionian contingent had been left in charge of the bridge, but had not adopted the suggestion claimed for Miltiades — tyrant of the Chersonese, but an Athenian noble—that they should quit their post ; which would have involved the total annihilation of Darius and his force. So Darius escaped, unconscious of the contemplated treason. He left a force in Thrace, however, under Megabazus, to convince the regional chiefs that all peoples must own allegiance to the Great King.

These are the features of the enterprise as related from a Greek point of view. But the presumption is that the subjugation of Thrace, which was actually effected, was the main object in view, while investigation rather than conquest—like Caesar's invasion of Britain—was the purpose of the excursion that was made across the Danube.

**SCYTHIAN REBEL**

Skunkha was a Scythian chief who revolted against Darius on his accession but, with the other rebel satraps, was defeated and taken prisoner.

*British Museum*

THERE were no more such experiments. Conquest engaged the attention of Darius less than the vast imperial system, which he developed no doubt from the organization created by Cyrus. The next stage in the story of the Persian Empire is the staying of its expansion at the hands of the Greeks.

One portion of the Hellenic world lay actually within the confines of the Persian empire. All the ' Ionic ' cities—Dorian and Aeolian as well as Ionians proper—in Asia Minor and on the Propontis, with the exception of Miletus which retained its independence by treaty, had submitted to the Lydian overlordship under which their self-government —generally in the form of a ' tyrannis '—had not been interfered with. When Croesus was overthrown by Cyrus, they had striven to recover their independence ; but as they persistently acted individually instead of concertedly, Harpagus, the lieutenant of Cyrus, had no serious difficulty in reducing them, while Miletus came in of its own accord.

The people of Phocaea and Teos abandoned their homes rather than remain as the slaves of the barbarian, the Phocaeans sailing away to the west (see page 89) while the Teans planted themselves at Abdera on the Thracian coast. Bias, the sage of Priene, urged that Ionia should migrate en masse to Sardinia ; Thales, the sage of Miletus, who had foretold the eclipse of 585, proposed union under one central government ; but the wisdom of neither prevailed.

So Ionia was absorbed and subjected to tribute and military service, but remained as Ionic as before. The major part of it was included in the satrapy of Lydia or Sardis, and the more northerly in that of Phrygia or Dascylium. The several Ionian despots or tyrants secured their own authority by making friends with their respective satraps, who naturally preferred dealing with autocrats rather than democracies or oligarchical groups. Thus when, as related above, Miltiades proposed the liberation of Ionia by cutting Darius off in Scythia, the plan was rejected at the instance of Histiaeus, the tyrant of Miletus, who, not unnaturally, preferred the security of his tyranny to the ' liberation of Hellas '

The island of Samos suffered a peculiar fate. It was never subject to Lydia, and under its tyrant Polycrates was a formidable sea power. Polycrates deserted his old alliance with the Egyptian Amasis, and offered his friendly services to Cambyses, but was soon after treacherously trapped and murdered by the ambitious satrap Oroites when Darius was fighting for his crown. Samos detested the able but ruthless tyranny under which it had prospered and suffered ; the dead man's brother Syloson was expelled. But when Oroites was put to death, Syloson appealed to Darius, and was reinstated as the vassal of the Great King, though only after the population had been almost exterminated. At the time when Polycrates ' Medised ' and associated himself with Cambyses Sparta had been persuaded to send an unaccustomed naval expedition to ' overthrow the tyranny ' ; but its mismanagement and failure confirmed in her a permanent distaste for the naval operations which were not in conformity with her peculiar military system.

The despot system was convenient for the Persian government and was therefore upheld by it ; but nearly every state would have welcomed the chance of ridding itself of its tyrant—and the Persian government was in general the supreme though not the only obstacle. The Persian government stood for the tyrannies. It was that fact which provided the tinder when the disappointed ambitions of a despot led him to kindle the flame of the Ionian revolt that opened the secular struggle between East and West.

## Political Events in Mainland Greece

IN the Greek peninsula Sparta, before the star of Cyrus rose, had already achieved a military pre-eminence which caused Croesus of Lydia to seek her alliance as the premier state of Hellas. That pre-eminence was confirmed by a war with Tegea, in Arcadia, which left the victory with Sparta after a severe struggle. Tegea (c. 560–550) became a vassal state, bound to render Sparta military service without losing her individuality.

The seal was set upon the Spartan ascendancy by a final conflict with and victory over her constant rival in the Peloponnese, Argos, at the beginning of the next decade. Actual territorial annexation was not, after the Messenian wars, a part of the Lacedaemonian policy ; Sparta's aim was not empire but ' hegemony '—to be the acknowledged captain of the Hellenes, not the direct ruler of Hellas. Incidentally, a captain is apt to assume the rôle of a dictator, though in theory as the champion of public right.

It was in this character that Sparta intervened in other states to aid in the suppression of tyrants ; it might be unsuccessfully, as in the case of Polycrates of Samos, or with the credit of a liberator where the tyrant's position was already precarious. But the effective hegemony was established by the gradual growth of the system of alliances known as the Peloponnesian League.

### Objects of the Peloponnesian League

ONE state after another in the Peloponnese or even outside it became, not in the strict sense a member of the league, but an ally of ' the Lacedaemonians,' the two parties being mutually bound to make no attack on each other and to render each other aid when attacked. The states of the group were not in form allied together, but were all the allies of Sparta. The effective predominance of the position thus secured to Sparta is obvious. When the league took action, it was as ' the Lacedaemonians and their allies.' If its troops took the field, they were under Spartan command and no member of the league would act against them. Within the Peloponnese, Achaea, the non-Dorian strip on the south shore of the gulf of Corinth, was left out because Sparta had no need of her ; and Argos stood apart in jealous isolation.

The two states on the Isthmus, Corinth and Megara, were both in the league ; and we shall find even Athens herself becoming a member for a time. She had not yet risen to such power as to make her Sparta's rival for the hegemony ; the neighbouring island of Aegina was the ally of Sparta's enemy Argos, and was also the commercial rival of Corinth and the age-long foe of Athens ; so that policy encouraged friendly relations between those two states and Sparta.

Athens as yet was only one among several cities that had equal claim to recognition as being in the first rank, the pre-eminence of Sparta being admitted. Though a commercial and maritime state, she had not yet realized that the sea was to be the base of her power. Her democratic development—and she was far from having arrived at pure democracy—is of special interest, because, politically speaking, Athens was not the city but all Attica, so that there were regional diversities of interest to be accommodated as well as those which were common to other cities.

Here we must recall three leading features of the history of Athens in the first half of the sixth century : the movement towards a democratic instead of an aristocratic constitution inaugurated by the reforms of Solon ; the annexation to Athens of the island of Salamis, as the outcome of a victorious war with Megara ; and the success of Peisistratus, the hero of the war, in establishing himself as tyrant.

### Aristocracy versus Democracy

𝔄 COMBINATION of the aristocratic party of ' the Plain ' with one of the two democratic parties, ' the Coast ,' which was led by Megacles the Alcmaeonid, head of a leading but turbulent family, expelled Peisistratus after five years ; five years later a reconciliation with Megacles effected a brief restoration ; a fresh quarrel brought a second exile for ten years. But the third faction, ' the Mountain ', which had originally brought him into power, still adhered to him ; and when, in 540, he reappeared in Attica with a force of mercenaries supplied by the friends abroad whom he had been assiduously cultivating, his second restoration was effected without difficulty. The Alcmaeonids were exiled with their adherents. The tyranny was thoroughly established. Peisistratus himself reigned for another twelve years, and eighteen more passed before the expulsion of his son Hippias.

Peisistratus was a despot who ruled under the forms and through the machinery of the Solonian constitution, and in popular as against aristocratic interests. Abroad he was a skilful diplomatist who was able to maintain friendly relations with both Argos and Sparta. He was a notable patron of art and literature. But perhaps his most important contribution to the power of Athens lay in his securing for her a dominant position on the Propontis ; where the Athenian noble Miltiades—the father of the Miltiades whom we have met—became ' tyrant ' of the Chersonese by invitation of the local Thracian tribe, the Dolonci—the tyrant being accompanied by a band of Athenian colonists. Sigeum on the Asiatic side had been already secured by the energy of Peisistratus.

Much misplaced sentiment has been lavished on the story of the expulsion of the Peisistratids. Hippias ruled as a despot, but by no means tyrannically, for some fourteen years. An entirely personal quarrel, wholly discreditable to all the persons concerned, arose between the tyrant's brother Hipparchus and two of his associates, Harmodius and Aristogeiton, who resolved to assassinate the brothers, of course in the name of Liberty, at the Panathenaic festival. They only succeeded in killing Hipparchus, and turning Hippias into a frightened and therefore a cruel tyrant ; whereby he sealed the doom of tyranny in Athens. Four years later the Athenians, with the aid of the Spartan king Cleomenes, drove the tyrant and his family into exile, to find an asylum within the realms of the Great King (510 B.C.).

### Athens Won for Democracy

ℭLEOMENES had intervened mainly at the instance of the Delphic Oracle, doubtless influenced by the exiled Alcmaeonids, for whose return the expulsion of their enemies the Peisistratids opened the way. For a time Athens became a member of the Peloponnesian league. Cleisthenes, the son of Megacles, returned to lead the Alcmaeonid party ; the party conflicts, repressed under the tyranny, revived. Despite the ill-advised intervention of the Spartan king, with support from both Thebes and Chalcis, in the domestic

**ATHENIAN POLITICAL MURDERERS**

Hipparchus, brother of Hippias the Tyrant, was slain in 514 B.C. by Harmodius (sword raised) and Aristogeiton, and the Athenians erected the group, of which this is a copy, as a political memorial to the 'Liberators.'

*After the restoration by Michaelis at Strasbourg*

affairs of an allied state, the victory fell to Cleisthenes, who effected the important constitutional reforms which resulted in the Athenian state becoming the type of democracy (c. 506). Sparta herein displayed the bias which was always to be dominant in her policy, as in that of Thebes, of supporting aristocratic against democratic factions.

The outcome of the Theban intervention was the separation of the little city of Plataea, by the help of Athens, whose devoted ally she remained thenceforth, from the Boeotian confederacy headed by Thebes, of which she had been a most reluctant member. The whole episode was somewhat humiliating for Sparta, and did not tend, as at first had seemed likely, to increase the cordiality of her relations with the rising state.

In Italy and Sicily the cities, no less than in the east, tended to fall into the control of tyrants; among whom Phalaris of Acragas (Agrigentum) achieved a proverbial reputation for barbarous cruelty, about the middle of the century. There were the usual rivalries among the cities but no marked ascendancy until, at the beginning of the fifth century, Gelon established himself as tyrant of Syracuse, which from that time outshone its neighbours and played the leading part in the impending struggle with Carthage.

This Phoenician power materially strengthened its position in the western quarter of Sicily during the third quarter of the sixth century; whereas the colonising adventures of Greeks—of Dorieus, the half brother of the Spartan king Cleomenes, in particular—in the Carthaginian sphere of influence have an interest which is merely romantic. The most notable events of the half century, however, took place farther afield even than Sicily.

The sea power of Carthaginians and Etruscans combined to thrust out the intrusion of the Greeks. The Phocaeans of Ionia, who had already planted a colony at Alalia in Corsica, emigrated in a body to escape subjection to Persia, hoping to make of Corsica a new Phocaea; but a desperate sea fight with the combined navies of the Etruscans and Carthaginians off Alalia proved so costly that they were obliged to abandon Corsica, of which the Etruscans took possession (535), while the Phocaeans moved on to found Massalia (Marseilles). The Carthaginians annexed Sardinia.

THE other event of primary importance was in Italy itself. In 510, the Roman aristocrats expelled the reigning dynasty of the Tarquins, which was Etruscan, and established an aristocratic commonwealth or republic—the year that Athens expelled the Peisistratids. The picturesque legends concerning the expulsion, which became a part of the creed of every Roman and of the literature of the world, probably contained a quite substantial element of truth. Rome under able if unamiable kings was perhaps the most powerful of the states in the Latin league, which were to a great extent dominated, like Rome, by Tuscan or Tuscanising dynasties. The Roman revolution was a heavy set-back for the Etruscan ascendancy ; though undoubtedly Rome had to fight hard for many years before she was secure in the liberty she had won. But the ' Regifugium,' the expulsion of the kings, dealt a fatal blow to the threatened domination of Italy by the non-Aryan power. Nevertheless, historical details are still too obscure for any definite record of the Roman state which is still in an age that is half mythical.

### Outbreak of the Ionian Revolt

AT the end of the sixth century Darius, King of Kings, was undisputed lord of the vast empire he had won as the heir of Cambyses the son of Cyrus ; an empire enormously wider than any the world had known before. Within its bounds, save on the remote barbaric frontiers, there seemed to be no possibility of dangerous revolt. It must have appeared that in course of time it was inevitably destined to absorb the world ; though the only expansion the king himself had sought was the mastery of the Thracian tribes whence, almost within the memory of living men, invading hordes had wrought devastation within what were now the Great King's dominions. Nevertheless, revolt was near.

The revolt was contrived by a tyrant, fomented by the unpopularity of tyranny, and backed by the Hellenes' ingrained passion for political independence.

The ambitions of the tyrant Histiaeus of Miletus aroused the suspicions of a Persian governor ; consequently he was inveigled to the court at Susa, the far-away Persian capital, where he was politely detained. His place at Miletus was taken by his son-in-law Aristagoras, who

devised for his own advancement in court favour a scheme for annexing the islands of the Aegean, which he submitted to Artaphernes the satrap at Sardis, who took it up. But the plan miscarried, and in such fashion that all hopes of court favour disappeared. Disappointment suggested a desperate remedy—organized rebellion, with an organized expulsion of tyrants as its preliminary, and a diplomatic campaign in Greece proper to procure armed aid in liberating Hellenes from the ' barbarian ' yoke.

The tyrants were duly expelled, Aristagoras resigning his own tyranny. Sparta proved cold or cautious ; Athens and Eretria sent squadrons to help the rebellion ; the insurgents marched on Sardis (498) and captured the town but not the citadel ; and the former Lydian capital was burnt down by a fire accidentally started. The insurgents with their allies went off to the coast, fighting an unsuccessful engagement with some Persian troops on the way ; and the Athenians and Eretrians sailed for

**ROMAN LEGEND IN AN ETRUSCAN TOMB**
This fourth-century fresco in an Etruscan tomb depicts an episode in the half mythical history of Etruria and Rome. Cneve Tarchu Rumach (upper), that is Gnaeus Tarquinius Romanus, may be Tarquinius Priscus, the first Etruscan king of Rome ; another figure (Macstrna), his successor Servius Tullius.
*From Rostovtzeff, ' The Ancient World : Rome,' Oxford University Press*

PLAIN OF MARATHON WHERE THE GREEKS ROUTED THE PERSIANS

Early in the fifth century, a Persian army invaded Greece and was met by an Athenian force under Callimachus and Miltiades. The Persians encamped on the coastal plain of Marathon, and the Athenians, outnumbered by three to two at least, faced them from the mouth of a pass. Most of the fighting was on the flanks and eventually the invaders were driven back to their ships with heavy loss ; but they were to return in greater strength ten years later.

home. Histiaeus, who had been allowed to escape to safe quarters across the sea, later claimed credit as the originator of the whole movement—probably an afterthought on his part. However, as he took to piracy, he was caught and crucified by Artaphernes.

### First Persian Invasion of Greece

THE revolt, which had spread to Caria and Cyprus, was suppressed, not without difficulty. Cyprus was reduced by the Phoenician fleet, which also defeated the fleet of the Ionians at Lade. Miletus, the arch-offender, was heavily smitten after a hard siege. A number of the islands were reduced. The rebels were treated with leniency on the whole.

There conceivably the matter might have ended, but for the original intervention of Athens and Eretria. That was a piece of pure impertinence which the Great King could not pardon. ' Who then are these Athenians ? ' he asked, as Cyrus had once asked, ' Who then are these Lacedaemonians ? ' And the exiled Hippias, seeking the countenance of Artaphernes at Sardis, could answer the question.

Darius, says the picturesque tradition, vowed vengeance. Meanwhile, he abolished one of the grievances of the Ionians. The rebellion had been kindled by tyrants, and in place of the tyrannies they were allowed democratic constitutions.

In fact, however, the support given to Greeks who were Persian subjects by Greeks who were not suggested, if it did not impose, the incorporation of Hellas in the Empire. Thrace had seized the opportunity to break away, and the Scythians across the Danube were breaking in. The first step was to re-establish mastery in Thrace and Macedon.

When the last embers of the revolt had been quenched, Darius sent a great expedition to Thrace by land and sea under Mardonius to accomplish this object (492); owing, however, to the destruction of the fleet by storms, it was only in part effected, and Darius decided no longer to defer an expedition against Eretria and Athens.

The punitive force was dispatched straight across the Aegean, preceded by a demand for ' earth and water,' the token of submission, from the free islands and states. The islands that refused were

**THE TRIUMPH OF EUROPE OVER ASIA SYMBOLISED**

Upon a beautiful fourth-century Italiote-Greek wine-vessel found at Canusium and preserved at Naples, Darius, the central figure, is seen in this decorative design in consultation with his nobles on the question of preparations for his expedition to Greece. Below, the treasurer collects the war-tax. In the upper row (left) the divine protectors of Greece are shown; to the right sits the personification of Asia led to war by 'Apate,' goddess of Deceit.

*From Furtwängler-Reichhold, ' Griechische Vasenmalerei,' Bruckmann A.G.*

reduced en route by the fleet. The commanders, Datis and Artaphernes, were accompanied by the old ex-tyrant Hippias, who was to be reinstalled in a humiliated Athens. On reaching Euboea the Persians laid siege to Eretria, which resisted stubbornly. Then, by the advice of Hippias, they landed part of their forces under Datis on the northern part of the plain of Marathon in the north-eastern corner of Attica, in order to prevent the Athenians coming to the aid of Eretria.

Sparta had promised Athens her aid— after the full moon; so Athens took the field alone, save that she was joined by a gallant contingent from little Plataea, heroically loyal to her benefactress.

The quickest way from Athens to Euboea cuts across the Attic peninsula to the ferry at Chalcis. The Athenian force, which was presumably marching by this road, suddenly discovered that a Persian army, perhaps outnumbering them by five to one (though modern computation has reduced the odds to three to two) had occupied the plain of Marathon, whence an easy coast road leads to Athens. Consequently they swung aside to the right and came down on Marathon by a hill path, occupying an impregnable pass overlooking the plain; and the position was stale-mate. The Persians, content in that they had kept the Athenians out of Euboea, and denuded Athens of its defenders, would not attack, but awaited the fall of Eretria; the Athenians were not to be enticed from their position, since every day brought nearer the promised reinforcement from Sparta; and neither side could move without exposing rear or flank to the enemy.

At last news came of the fall of Eretria and the embarkation of Artaphernes for Athens. The Athenians must attack now or never, with or without the Spartans.

Their spearmen, whose strength had been deliberately or accidentally thrown into the wings, coming to close quarters, charged. Their weakened centre was pushed back, but the wings shattered the Persian line and drove it into the sea. The rest of the Persian army hastily embarked, the ships picking up as many fugitives as could reach them, but leaving more than 6,000 slain on the shore. The Athenian loss was less than two hundred.

The fleet of Artaphernes, joined by Datis, sailed round the promontory of Sunium, perhaps hoping to find the city undefended; but the victors, marching on the day of the battle, were there before them. The Persians, not caring to attempt a landing in the circumstances, and possibly warned of the belated approach of the Lacedaemonians, gave up the whole adventure and returned to Asia.

The resolution of the Athenians had doubtless been strengthened by the return of Miltiades, the persistent foe of Persia, who, having been at least associated with the Ionic revolt, had abandoned the Chersonese. To him the successful and brilliant strategy and tactics adopted at Marathon were attributed, though probably no less credit was due to the polemarch, the official commander-in-chief, Callimachus.

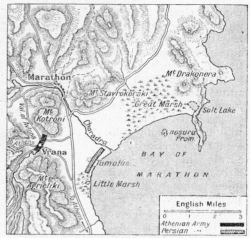

PLAN OF MARATHON

The Athenians camped at Vrana : the Persians were drawn up in the plain. Both armies closed a road to Athens. When the Greeks attacked their centre gave but their flanks conquered; the tumulus covers their heroic dead.

Marathon could be looked upon as no more than an initial defeat for the Persians which would inevitably be followed by an attack on a much greater scale. But it was in actual fact very much more. It was a revelation. Single-handed, the city of Athens had utterly routed a force larger than her own of the picked Persian troops hitherto reputed invincible. The arma-

TUMULUS ON THE PLAIN OF MARATHON COVERING THE HEROIC DEAD

On the south-east side of the battle-ground near the shore rises the mound wherein lie the remains of 192 Athenians killed in the famous struggle with the Persians. The topographical position may well mark the strategic one where the Athenian centre, thinned by over-extension of the line, broke, but the victorious flanks, instead of plundering the ships, turned inwards and overwhelmed the Persians who were pursuing their comrades inland towards Vrana.

*Photo, Mansell*

ment of Greek hoplites had decisively proved its vast superiority to anything the Persians could put in the field. The fact had never been put to the proof before. And it was Athens, not Sparta, that had dared the hazard unaided, and vindicated the superiority of the Hellene over the Barbarian. By that feat Athens acquired a prestige undreamed of hitherto. However honest were the religious scruples that had delayed the Spartans, the fact remained that they arrived only when the foe was already in full flight, and they could only compliment the Athenians on their prowess and go home.

There could be no doubt, then, in the minds of the Greeks after Marathon, that Persia would ere long set about the punishment of Athens for the reverse she had dared to inflict upon Persian prestige, or that the subjugation of Hellas would be included in her programme, to prevent the repetition of such incidents. Hellas would certainly be absorbed piecemeal, unless by a great co-ordinated effort she could inflict a permanently decisive defeat on the empire which commanded all the resources of Asia. Yet Hellas, a great congeries of small states full of mutual jealousies and clashing interests, each one determined to surrender no fraction of its individual independence, had never shown any disposition and possessed no effective machinery for concerted action on a large scale.

Persia, however, was unable to act at once, trouble having arisen in Egypt which required to be dealt with before the undertaking of a task so serious as the subjugation of Hellas now seemed likely to prove. Her action was further postponed by the death of her great ruler Darius

**GREEK EQUIPMENT**

The Greeks owed their victory at Marathon largely to the superior equipment of their heavy-armed soldiers. This bronze statuette from Dodona shows just such a ' hoplite' armed with breastplate, greaves and Boeotian shield.

*Berlin Museum (cast)*

(486 B.C.) while Egypt was still unsettled; and the task of subduing Hellas was left to his son Xerxes.

The delay made possible an invaluable development at Athens. In the interval she transformed herself from a second-class into a first-class sea power; a development which she owed to the acutest and most brilliant intellect that ever dominated her politics — Themistocles. It was he who realized that in her rivalry with her neighbours the means to ascendancy must be found in a supreme fleet and that the possession of a superior fleet was essential to the defeat of Persia. The fleet that had brought the Persians to Marathon came unopposed and departed unmolested; that was not to happen again. A windfall—the discovery of a rich vein of silver at Laurium —brought a large sum to the treasury, which instead of being distributed was appropriated to shipbuilding; there was a large sea-going population; and in the ten years after Marathon the actual primacy of the Athenian fleet was admitted.

THE invasion which by this time Xerxes had made ready was on lines no doubt laid down by Darius. A vast army—the error of under-rating the fighting power of the Greeks was not to be repeated—was to march through Thrace, attended by a great fleet. The actual facts were of course exaggerated and most picturesquely adorned by Greek imagination; half a million men summoned from all parts of the great empire, including India—onetenth of the estimate of Herodotus—is not perhaps an excessive estimate of the total numbers, though again a modern computation has reduced it to 180,000 effectives.

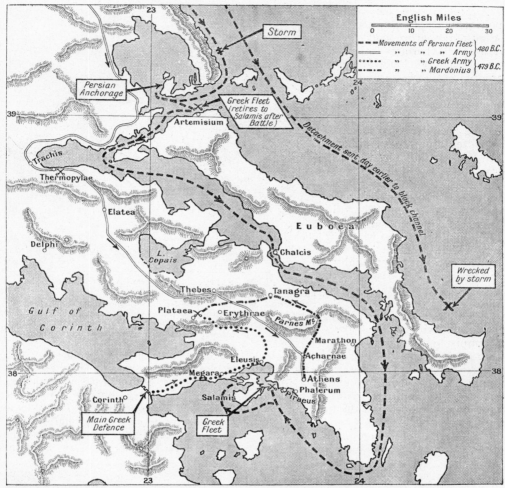

**PLAN OF THE MEMORABLE CAMPAIGN THAT DECIDED THE FATE OF EUROPE**

The Peloponnese being impregnable by land but completely vulnerable by sea, the Greek plan was to defeat the Persian fleet in the narrow waters to the north of Euboea, while holding up the army at Thermopylae. The naval engagement at Artemisium, however, was inconclusive while Thermopylae proved a minor disaster, so Central Greece had to be abandoned ; the Greek fleet, pursued by the Persians, retired to Salamis, there to repeat its tactics with complete success (480 B.C.). The following year, after Mardonius had reoccupied Athens, saw the decisive Greek victory at Plataea.

Most of the Hellenic free states rejected the preliminary demand for earth and water. A congress of the states, called by Sparta and Athens, conferred on Sparta the command by land and sea, Athens waiving her obvious claim to naval control in the interest of unity. Some thirty states which took part in the congress pledged themselves to the defence of Hellas, Athens and Aegina burying their old feud. Argos remained apart, and in Thebes there was certainly a Medising faction.

The princes of Thessaly, on which the first onslaught would fall, made the common protection of their frontier a condition of their adherence ; but when it was found that the pass of Tempe on the northern border could be turned, Thessaly had to be abandoned, and the 'pass' of Thermopylae, between the mountains and the Maliac gulf, was substituted as the next gateway that could be held. If that went, everything north of the isthmus of Corinth would go.

Xerxes crossed the Hellespont in the spring of 480 ; in August the army had rolled down to Thermopylae. The force, mainly Peloponnesian troops, sent forward under the Spartan king Leonidas to hold the pass, was only 6,000 strong, the contingent of Phocians having been detached to guard an alternative path inland through the hills by which it was possible to gain the south via Phocis. The Athenians were on the fleet, whose business it was to prevent the Persian fleet from supporting the army, a business which in fact it accomplished not brilliantly but still successfully ; but truth and legend can hardly be disentangled in the story as we have it.

Of this much we can be sure. On two successive days attempts were made to storm the fortified position in the pass by frontal attacks, without making any impression. Then the existence of a mountain track to the rear of the Spartan position, diverging from the path guarded by the Phocians, was betrayed to the Persians ; a picked column was sent to carry it, and the Phocians, thinking that

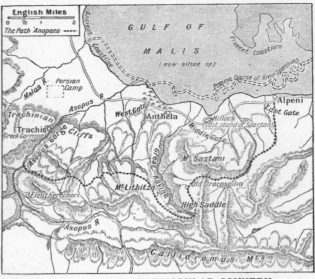

PLAN OF THE THERMOPYLAE COUNTRY

Leonidas held Thermopylae, but Trachis must have been garrisoned to guard the equally important Asopus pass. After desultory fighting the path Anopaea was betrayed, and a picked body of Persian ' Immortals,' slipping past Trachis at night, came down behind the Spartans at daybreak.

their homeland was threatened, retreated. The rear being in danger, Leonidas sent away some two-thirds of his force, or less, retaining his three hundred Spartans, a thousand Laconians, the very loyal Thespians and the very half-hearted Thebans ; probably in the hope that the others would be able to secure his rear.

HOW TIME .CAN ALTER THE FEATURES OF HISTORIC TERRAIN

Leonidas can only have hoped to hold up the Persians in the narrow strip between mountain and sea called ' The Gates,' or Thermopylae, while the fleets were fighting out the more important issue at Artemisium. As the Persian fleet was not destroyed, his position would have been hopeless even had the path Anopaea remained unbetrayed. To-day his whole task would have been impossible, for the retreat of the sea has turned Thermopylae into a plain where many armies might deploy.

But they, coming into collision with the Persian turning column, were driven off.

Whether retreat was or was not possible, the pass could no longer be held ; surrender was not to be thought of, and Leonidas with his three hundred, leaving the fortified position, charged down on the vast Persian host, and fought shoulder to shoulder till every man was slain. The Thebans were later reputed to have surrendered ignominiously, since the city ' Medised ' ; the rest fought behind the defences to the last. No doubt there was a tremendous slaughter of the barbarians. No doubt, too, the last stand was, strategically speaking, a futile waste of life. But the name of Thermopylae still rings across the ages, an inspiration to heroic self-sacrifice.

### Greek Naval Victory at Salamis

THE force which held Thermopylae and had now been wiped out was only an advance guard whose supports had tarried ; but the gate having been forced the Peloponnesians would not attempt to defend the country north of the Isthmus. It submitted perforce to the Persians, who found, however, that the Athenians had taken to their ships and had transferred non-combatants and, so far as was possible, property, to Aegina and Salamis. The fleet, of which the Athenians formed more than half, had fallen back when Thermopylae was lost, to cover the Isthmus, though a garrison that refused to leave the Acropolis of Athens—or was deliberately left there— held the Persians at bay for a fortnight.

The Isthmus might be impenetrable, fortified as it was ; but unless the great Persian fleet met with a heavy defeat, it might land a host on the shores of the Peloponnese. For its defeat it must be inveigled into fighting a decisive battle in the narrows about Salamis, so that its overwhelming numbers could not come into play. Yet all the persuasive powers of Themistocles would have failed to convince the Peloponnesians of the necessity, if the Persians themselves had not played into his hands—beguiled, it was said, by an apparently treasonable message from the wily Athenian himself—by block-ing the exit through which the Greeks purposed withdrawing, and themselves delivering battle in the narrows.

The victory won by the Greeks was complete and decisive. The Ionian squadron, compelled to serve in the Great King's navy, fought instead for the freeing of Hellas. The ships were too crowded for manoeuvring, and the Greeks proved more expert in ramming and boarding than their adversaries. The Persian fleet was not annihilated, but it was broken up and demoralised past hope. Among the Greeks the palm of valour was awarded to the men of Aegina, but the glory of the victory belonged without possibility of question to Athens. And for Hellas the splendid disaster of Thermopylae was more than avenged.

Salamis was a victory not merely brilliant, but as concerned maritime ascendancy decisive. Of the war as a whole, however, it was no more decisive than a Trafalgar, and no less. The great undefeated army of Persia was in occupation of the major part of Greece, though, unsupported by a fleet, the maintenance of supplies for so large a force became a serious problem. A reverse so conspicuous as that of Salamis would encourage revolts all over the Empire. For both reasons, a reduction of the expeditionary force was immediately desirable, but as yet there was no sufficient ground for abandoning the scheme of conquest.

### Cunning Tactics of Mardonius

THE divisions in the counsels of the Greeks were notorious, and the blindness of the Peloponnesians to the need of protecting anything outside the Peloponnese itself was conspicuous. The quality of the Lacedaemonian soldiery was above praise, as Thermopylae had proved, but the Spartan command was terribly weakened by the incurable habit of postponing necessary movement in deference to religious scruples. Moreover, however excellent the Greek hoplites might be, the Greek armies were practically without cavalry, since Thessaly, the land of horsemen, was in the hands of the Persians.

After Salamis, then, Xerxes withdrew a portion of his army to Asia by way

D*

of the Hellespont, since the Greeks, in spite of the urgency of Themistocles, made no effort by sea to cut off the passage. Mardonius, left in command of a still huge force, fell back to Thebes and Thessaly for the winter, on account of supplies. To Athens he made extremely attractive overtures to detach her from her allies, which she loyally rejected ; nevertheless when Mardonius reoccupied Attica in the spring of 479, it was only by her threat of withdrawal that Sparta was induced to bring up the Peloponnesian forces for the defence of Attica, Megaris and Plataea, under the command of Pausanias, the kinsman and guardian of the actual king, the young heir of Leonidas. The whole Greek force may have numbered from 70,000 to 100,000, the Persian total from 150,000 to 300,000.

The Athenians had hitherto refrained from urging active naval operations, lest another decisive victory at sea should satisfy the Peloponnesians that they had no need of protection by the Athenian fleet, and could therefore abandon the defence of Attica. Now, however, the activity of the fleet was renewed, and the actual share of Athens in the land campaign was a minor one. It is quite clear, despite the misrepresentations to which Athenian influences have given permanent currency, that the finally decisive triumph of the Greek arms at the battle of Plataea was won by the generalship of Pausanias and the valour and discipline of the Lacedaemonians and their comrades in arms from Tegea.

### Persians Shattered at Plataea

IN the manoeuvring which preceded the battle both the Persian and the Spartan showed high ability. Each strove to entice the other into delivering the attack upon ground where his own troops—the cavalry of one, the heavy infantry of the other—would have the advantage ; neither wished to open the attack. Both knew that delay was in favour of the Persians, because of the dissensions and jealousies among the Greeks, though these were not absent among the Persians. Mardonius was the more successful in manoeuvring

the adversary out of skilfully chosen positions ; and when Mardonius did actually make the attack, it was because, in consequence of orders being either misunderstood or disobeyed, the Lacedaemonians, with the Tegeans, were isolated, and the movement of the Greek forces which was in progress was in confusion.

But practically single-handed the Lacedaemonians routed the attack and drove their way into the Persian camp, the already delayed reinforcements being again held up for a time by those Greek troops which had Medised. A panic ensued when Mardonius himself fell. Artabazus, the second in command, who had kept a large division out of action, withdrew it in good order, but attempted nothing more than to draw together what he could of the scattered remnants of the once mighty host, and hurry it back to Asia. Persia had put forth all her powers, and she had failed ; failed so utterly and so disastrously that the attempt was never renewed.

### Fleet Operations in the Aegean

THE finishing touches were given by the fleet operations. Persian forces were mustered at Mycale in Asia Minor facing the island of Samos to overawe the Ionians, their fleet being beached. Thither, in answer to an appeal from Samos, moved the Greek fleet from its station at Delos, found a suitable spot for disembarking, and thence marched its force on the encampment at Mycale, which was duly stormed and carried, the Ionians, of course, for the most part joining their brethren. It was generally believed that the battles of Mycale and Plataea were fought and won on the same day (August 27, 479), but such coincidences were dear to the Hellenic imagination.

Mycale, however, had the effect of kindling a fresh Ionian revolt that brought further prestige to Athens. Sparta, now that the Peloponnese was safe, had no mind to oversea ventures ; but Athens threw herself into the cause with zeal and profit. The capture of Sestus, in effect by the Athenians, gave them the control of the Hellespont (479-8). In another respect it marked a turning-point. From that time the hegemony of the maritime states, abdicated by Sparta, passed, de facto if not de jure, to the great democracy. The freedom of Ionia was won by the energy and under the leadership not of Sparta, but of Athens.

### Carthage and Etruria assert themselves

PRECISELY at the moment of the great Perso-Hellenic struggle, a corresponding contest between Orientalism and what we may perhaps call Europeanism—between Aryan and non-Aryan, rather—was taking place in the west. Carthage struck for the lordship of Sicily ; the Etruscans were battling for the lordship of Italy. That there was collusion we may guess, but we can only guess ; there was no effectual combination. The movement, if it may be called a movement, was independent of the Persian attack upon Hellas ; but in that attack Carthage may well have seen her opportunity. The Etruscans were fighting not to win a new domination but to retain a tottering ascendancy.

The north of the island of Sicily as far west as Himera was under Greek domination, the south as far as Selinus ; the western end was the Phoenician sphere, which had now become definitely the Carthaginian. When the fifth century opened there was no immediate expectation of the collision which sooner or later was inevitable.

The Greek states were more conscious of their own mutual rivalries than of the common rival. Tyrannies were established, at Rhegium on the Italian side of the strait of Messina by Anaxilas in 493, and by Cleander, followed by his brother Hippocrates in 492, at Gela on the south coast of Sicily. Each had the idea of absorbing other states under his own sovereignty as vassals or dependents. Of the two, Hippocrates was the more successful. He managed to plant in Zancle, not yet known as Messana, a tyrant who was his own instrument, just when Anaxilas thought he had secured his own influence there. He would also have brought Syracuse under his sway—as champion of one of the parties in that state—but for the intervention of the mother city Corinth in very unwonted

conjunction with another daughter state, Corcyra. Anaxilas watched and waited.

About 485 Hippocrates died, and a very distinguished officer, Gelon, manoeuvred himself into the succession to the tyrannis. Following the methods of Hippocrates, he succeeded, where his predecessor had been frustrated by outside intervention, in capturing for himself the tyrannis of Syracuse ; making that city his capital, and handing over Gela to his brother Hieron as his lieutenant or viceroy. Obviously he aimed at making himself overlord of the whole island, excepting such states as Acragas on whose loyal friendship he could rely. Syracuse was thenceforth the leading power in Sicily.

Meanwhile, however—precisely how and when is not known—Zancle had passed into the hands of Anaxilas, whose son-in-law Terillus was tyrant of Himera. Syracuse was the insuperable obstacle in the way of his ambitions, and he made a secret alliance with Carthage, perhaps with a view to a partition of the island. Selinus was drawn in, because she felt herself threatened by Theron of Acragas, the friend and ally of Gelon. Theron expelled Terillus from Himera, as being a friend of Carthage ; and in collusion with Anaxilas Carthage launched a great expedition to Sicily under Hamilcar—a name very prominent in Carthaginian history.

### Carthaginian Disaster in Sicily

GELON had only just declined to send forces to aid Hellas against the impending Persian invasion, unless claims put forward by himself to the leadership were admitted ; though it appears that at the moment he did not intend his refusal to be final, nor base it on the peril that threatened Sicily. By the time that he knew of the passage of the Hellespont by the army of Xerxes, which took place immediately afterwards, the peril was upon him. Evidently Carthage had been extremely skilful in concealing the forwardness of her preparations, and was only awaiting the signal from Anaxilas.

Anaxilas took no active part in the campaign, though we may well suppose that it was fear of what he might do that kept the Syracusan fleet from meeting the Carthaginians on the seas. The expedition, though it met with heavy losses from storms, reached its western port, Panormus, otherwise unmolested. Thence by land and sea it advanced on Himera, where Theron was in possession. The fall of Himera seemed imminent before Gelon was satisfied that he could strike decisively; but when he did arrive, just in time, the blow he dealt was crushing. The expeditionary force was virtually annihilated, no second blow was needed, and nearly a century passed before the Sicilian Greeks again felt themselves in danger from Carthage. But the Carthaginians were left in their settlements and there was no thought of a counter-invasion of Africa. The policy of Gelon was marked by his admitting to alliance both Selinus and Anaxilas. Two years later he died, and was succeeded in his supremacy by his brother Hieron.

The whole episode was roughly speaking contemporary with the campaign which opened with Thermopylae and ended with Salamis. Tradition declared that Himera and Salamis were fought on the same day, just as it did of Plataea and Mycale.

### Events in Etruria and Latium

THE Etruscans who, as we saw (page 89), joined forces with the Phoenician power to exclude the intruding Greeks from the islands of Corsica and Sardinia, took no part in the Sicilian affair, though six years later their fleet was to suffer disaster at the hands of Hieron of Syracuse, intervening on the part of the mainland city of Cumae. Corsica was near at hand and available for appropriation; in Sicily they could have nothing to gain. Rome with her grip on the Tiber, and her affinities with both Latins and Sabines, was the power that threatened the Tuscan domination. Rome, which had succeeded in freeing itself from its Etruscan rulers, became the natural centre of resistance when all prospect of a Tarquin restoration had disappeared, about the first decade of the fifth century.

The popular traditions of later years are the sole but uncertain authority for the actual events of Roman history at this period. Quite certainly the monarchy was displaced by an aristocracy of birth, ruling by the unique system of double magistracies, to which appointment was made at first exclusively from among the aristocrats, the ' patrician ' houses; elected annually by the votes of the free citizens, but in practice responsible to the Senate—a patrician body composed mainly of officials and ex-officials. Legislation, initiated only by the magistrates, had to be submitted to the assembly of citizens known as the Comitia Centuriata.

The commons or ' plebs,' however, had been active in the revolt against the Tarquins; Brutus, the hero of the tradition, was not of patrician family; at a very early stage, the commons began to claim political rights monopolised by the patricians.

### Party Rivalry in Rome

THE struggle between the ' Orders ' was a long one; but the first definite victory of the plebs is dated as early as 494. The citizen-soldiery returning from a victorious campaign threatened to leave Rome in a body unless reforms were granted; and the result of their secession to the ' Sacred Mount ' was the concession to the plebs of officers of their own called Tribunes, with powers of intervention to veto legislation and curb arbitrary action to the injury of plebeians on the part of the patrician magistrates.

The traditions regarding the time are also full of more or less legendary tales of the wars of the Romans with rival Tuscan or Sabellian states, with Veii, the Aequi or the Volscians; of which perhaps the most famous is the story of Coriolanus.

To the fifth century we should probably attribute the early stages of the Celtic or Gallic immigration which we shall presently find in occupation of all north Italy between the Alps and Apennines, the region soon to be known as Cisalpine Gaul; an overflow perhaps from Farther Gaul. But the pressure from them was not felt in central Italy for another half-century.

Orientalism has met with its first decisive defeat in the west, and the stage is cleared for Hellenism : for its intellectual glory and for its political failure—the main theme of our next chapter.

## FORCING-HOUSE OF CIVIC EXPERIMENTS : GREECE AND ITS CITY STATES

The dotted lines on this map, demarcating the areas attached to the city states, emphasise the complicated political structure of Ancient Greece, divided as it was into tiny cantons each with an intense and fervently independent civic life of its own. Certain backward territories, such as Thessaly, Aetolia, Elis, Arcadia, were larger ; of the rest, the only areas of any size were Laconia, through Spartan conquest, Boeotia, through partial federation of the constituent cities, and Attica, through identification of rural interests with the policy of Athens.

# TABLE OF DATES FOR CHAPTER 5

*Unless otherwise stated in Italics, dates refer to events in the Greek world*

B.C.

479 Athenians and Ionians capture Sestus. Spartan hegemony in Greece, Athenian maritime hegemony.

478 Athens refortified (Themistocles).
Hieron succeeds Gelon as Tyrant of Syracuse.
*China :* Death of Confucius.

477-6 Intrigues of Pausanias.

477 Delian Confederation framed (Aristides).

474 *Italy :* Etruscan sea power crushed by Hieron at Cumae. Forty years' peace between Rome and Veii (Etruscan).

471 Themistocles exiled.
*Rome :* Volscian and Aequian wars.

470 Secession of Naxos from Delian League.

468 Suppression of Naxos and of right of secession.
Birth of Socrates.

467 Cimon's victory by land and sea at the Eurymedon.

466 End of tyrannis at Syracuse. Democracy set up.

465 *Persia :* accession of Artaxerxes I.

464 Messenian (Helot) revolt against Sparta ; Siege of Ithome.

462 Democratic reforms of Ephialtes and Pericles at Athens. Spartans dismiss Cimon from Ithome.

461 Ostracism of Cimon. Ascendancy of Pericles at Athens. Ephialtes assassinated.

460 *Egypt :* Inarus, in revolt against Persia, appeals to Athens for help.

459 Megara joins Athens. War with Corinth and Aegina.
Fall of Ithome. Messenians settled at Naupactus by Athenians.
*Egypt :* Athenian expedition captures Memphis.

457 Long Walls complete fortification of Athens.
Athenians conquer Boeotia though defeated at Tanagra by Spartans, who retire.
Athenians conquer Aegina.

455 *Egypt :* Persians under Megabazus reconquer Egypt.

454 Disastrous end of Egyptian expedition.
Transfer of Delian League Treasury to Athens.

451 Five years' truce between Athens and Sparta.
Cimon at Athens. Birth of Alcibiades.
*Rome :* First Decemvirate ; the Ten Tables.

450 Death of Cimon. Battle of (Cypriote) Salamis.
*Rome :* The Ten Tables expanded to Twelve.

449 *Rome :* Fall of Decemvirate. Legend of Virginia.
Second secession of the Plebs ; Valerio-Horatian Laws strengthen Plebeian Assembly.

448 Peloponnesians reject Athenian proposal of a Pan-Hellenic Congress for restoring Temples.

447 Battle of Coronea. Athens loses Boeotia.
Peace (of Callias) with Persia ends Persian War ?

446 Revolt of Megara and Euboea ; Euboea reduced.

445 Thirty Years Peace : Athens loses her mainland conquests.
Aristophanes born.
*Rome :* Canuleian Law sanctions marriage between patricians and plebeians.

443 Mixed colony of Thurii (Pericles).
Ostracism of Thucydides, son of Melesias.
*Rome :* Institution of Censorship.

441 Revolt of Samos.

439 Reduction of Samos.

438 The Parthenon. Pheidias floruit.
*Rome :* End of Etruscan truce. War with Veii.

437 Athenian colony at Amphipolis.

435 War between Corinth and Corcyra.

433 Alliance of Athens and Corcyra. Battle of Sybota.

432 Revolt of Potidaea from Athens. Megarian decree of Pericles.
Peloponnesian congress.

431 Theban attack on Plataea.
Spartan invasion of Attica. Peloponnesian War.
First (annual) Athenian invasion of Megarid.
*Rome :* Defeat of Volsci and Aequi at Mount Algidus.

430 Second Spartan invasion ; plague at Athens ; attacks on Pericles. Phormio at Naupactus. Surrender of Potidaea. Plato born ?

429 Death of Pericles. Cleon leader of war-party.
Siege of Plataea by Lacedaemonians.

428 Revolt of Mitylene.

427 Fall of Mitylene and Plataea. Corcyrean civil war.
Ineffective expedition of Laches to Sicily.

426 Demosthenes in Aetolia.
*Rome :* Pressure of Gauls on Etruria. Etruscan truce with Rome after defeat of Veii and Fidenae.

425 Massacre of the Oligarchs in Corcyra. Demosthenes at Pylos. Surrender of Spartans in Sphacteria.
*Persia :* Death of Artaxerxes I ; Xerxes II, followed by Darius II.

424 Athenian invasion of Boeotia and defeat at Delium ;
Socrates saves life of Alcibiades.
Brasidas in Thrace. Revolt of Amphipolis.
Congress at Gela, led by Hermocrates, rejects Sicilian interference by or with mainland states.
*Italy :* Samnites invading Campania seize Capua.

422 Brasidas and Cleon killed before Amphipolis.

421 Peace of Nicias between Athens and Sparta, whose allies repudiate the terms.

420 Athenian alliance with Argos (at war with Sparta).

418 Argive defeat at Mantinea, and revolution.

416 Melian expedition ; seizure of Melos by Athens.

415 Segestan embassy to Athens, against Selinus.
Desecration of the Hermae. Sicilian Expedition sails under Nicias, Alcibiades and Lamachus.
Alcibiades, recalled, intrigues against Athens.

414 Siege of Syracuse. Arrival of Gylippus ; death of Lamachus.

413 Sparta declares war and occupies Decelea. Demosthenes at Syracuse. Athenian force annihilated.
Sparta builds a fleet.
Growth of Macedonian power under Archelaus.
*India :* Nanda Dynasty in Magadha.

412 Revolts of Athenian subject-allies in succession.
Sparta intrigues with Persian satraps.
Advanced democracy in Syracuse ; Diocles.

411 Oligarchic revolution at Athens ; the fleet at Samos, loyal to democracy, recalls Alcibiades.

410 Battle of Cyzicus. Athenian democracy restored.
Banishment of Hermocrates from Syracuse.

409 Carthaginian advance in Sicily. Hermocrates at Selinus.

408 Death of Hermocrates.
Lysander in Asia ; relations with Cyrus.

406 Athenian victory at Arginusae.
Carthaginian advance against Syracuse.
*Rome :* Renewal of Etruscan war ; siege of Veii.

405 Dionysius, tyrant of Syracuse ; makes peace with Carthage.
Athenian fleet destroyed at Aegospotami.

404 Fall of Athens ; the Thirty Tyrants.
End of Peloponnesian War. Spartan supremacy.
*Persia :* Accession of Artaxerxes II.

403 Thrasybulus restores Athenian Democracy.

401 *Persia :* Revolt of Cyrus ; battle of Cunaxa. Retreat of the Ten Thousand Greeks, led by Xenophon.

400 Extending power of Dionysius in Sicily.

399 Sparta at war with Elis and with Persian Satraps.
Death of Socrates.

398 First Carthaginian war of Dionysius in Sicily.

397 Siege of Syracuse by Himilco. Peace made.

396 Agesilaus in Phrygia.
*Rome :* Capture of Veii by Camillus.

395 Recovery of Athens.

394 Conon in command of Persian fleet ; Cnidus.
Corinthian war. Spartan victories at Nemea and Coronea.

393 Conon at Athens with Pharnabazus.

392 Athenian successes. Iphicrates and his peltasts.
Successes of Dionysius against Carthaginians.

390 Dionysius in Italy ; fails before Rhegium.
Alliance of Dionysius with Lucanians.
*Rome :* Battle of Allia ; Gauls sack Rome.

389 Battle of Elleporus ; Italiote cities join Dionysius.

387 Dionysius takes Rhegium.

386 Sparta and Persia negotiate and impose the King's Peace or Peace of Antalcidas.

384 Birth of Aristotle.

383 Second Carthaginian war of Dionysius.

382 Spartans garrison Acropolis of Thebes.
Chalcidian League. Olynthian war begins.

379 Liberation of Thebes. Chalcidian League crushed.

378 War of Sparta and Thebes. Athens joins Thebes.

376 Spartan fleet defeated at Naxos.
Power of Thessaly under Jason of Pherae.

375 Spartans defeated at Orchomenus by Pelopidas.

374 New Athenian League.

371 Victory of Epaminondas at Leuctra. Theban supremacy. Arcadian League.

370 Thebans invade Peloponnese. Messene founded.

369 Megalopolis founded. Alexander of Pherae.

367 Dionysius II succeeds Dionysius I at Syracuse.
*Rome :* Licinian Laws passed ; political equality of the orders established.

366 Rivalry of Athenian and Theban influence in Macedon and Thessaly.

364 Death of Pelopidas.

362 Victory and death of Epaminondas at Mantinea.

### CHAPTER 5

# THE RIVAL CITIES: 478—360 B.C.

THE great struggle recorded in our last chapter was a critical stage in the history of progress. It was decisive of the question whether the system of the great Oriental empire should be extended over Europe, or Europe should develop on its own lines. The East put forth its great effort, and was defeated. Presently we shall find the most advanced division of Europe putting forth its counter-effort to bring the East under its own domination.

What we have immediately before us, however, is the interval of western development which led up to the second conflict. The West has proved itself capable of such a degree, but only just such a degree, of unification as to enable it to defeat the attempt at absorption. It has set a bound to the world empire of Persia. Can it attain such a unity as will bring world empire within the scope of its own powers? In other words, is Hellas capable of political consolidation? The genius of Cyrus and Darius has achieved a quite amazing unification of the East; but that has already reached its limit, and there are in it the seeds of disintegration. Should such imperial development take place in Hellas, there is little enough prospect of a corresponding and counteracting political development in the Oriental empire.

## Aftermath in West and East

THE battles of Salamis and Plataea together decided the war, and the decision was confirmed by the victory at Mycale and the capture of Sestus. The battle of Himera was decisive of the war between the Sicilian Greeks or Siceliotes and the Carthaginians—so decisive that it needed no confirmation. But of both wars there was an aftermath, with which it is convenient to deal first before turning to internal Greek affairs.

Syracuse had defeated Carthage, but without driving her off the seas; and another power still claimed predominance in the Tyrrhenian waters. The Etruscans, checked in Latium and conscious of danger threatening from the prosperous Greek communities of the south, turned predatory eyes on their most northerly city, Cumae, and attacked it. Cumae appealed to Syracuse for aid against the barbarian. Hieron, now reigning there in succession to his brother Gelon, answered the call; and Etruria's fleet was shattered and her sea power broken at the naval battle of Cyme or Cumae in 474. The blow struck by the Syracusan also probably decided another struggle with which she did not concern herself, the struggle for supremacy on the mainland between Etruscan and Latin.

## Continuation of the Persian War

IN the east the Persian war, viewed as a war of Persian expansion, ended with the battle about Mount Cithaeron which has always borne the name of the neighbouring city of Plataea. Viewed, however, as a war for the liberation of Hellenes from barbarian domination, it would not be over till the cities and islands of Ionia were in full possession of independence; and that was not yet secured, though a great step had been taken in that direction, even when the fleet captured Sestus.

The part played by the Ionians in the struggle gave them a strong moral claim on the aid of their kinsmen in Europe, a claim which Sparta as the recognized leader of the Greeks could not entirely ignore; but her recognition of it was of so perfunctory a character—of all the Peloponnesians not one was disposed to any further effort after their own safety was secured—that she could offer no opposition when the Ionians placed themselves under the willing leadership of Athens, whose primacy among the maritime states was indisputable. A war for the liberation of Ionia must necessarily be, primarily at least, a maritime war.

As head of the new 'Delian Confederation,' Athens at once became, in fact if not

## THE GREEK WORLD IN WHICH ATHENS SOUGHT TO BUILD HER EMPIRE

Civilized Europe after the Persian war was divided into very many small city states, but there were only three powers, all Greek, of any magnitude : Syracuse, Sparta, Athens. The Sicilian Greeks, under Syracusan leadership, had defeated Carthage and shattered the Etruscan navy ; the league of which Sparta was the centre was the supreme military power in Greece ; while Athens, as head of the Delian Confederation with its navy, was mistress of the Aegean Sea.

in name, the rival of Sparta in the hegemony of Hellas. Broadly speaking, the result was that the Hellenic world found itself drawn into one or the other of two groups, a maritime confederacy dominated by Athens and a continental confederacy dominated by Sparta. At the same time most of the states in the one group were or supposed themselves to be Dorian, in the other Ionian ; and states which felt a special jealousy for individual reasons towards Athens or towards Sparta also affected the grouping.

Moreover, in almost every Greek state there was a democratic faction and an oligarchic faction ; Sparta always encouraged where she could not impose oligarchies, Athens democracies ; and a transfer of allegiance from one group to the other was the almost inevitable

accompaniment of an oligarchic victory in a democratic state, or of a democratic victory in an oligarchic state. Thus the internal dissensions in the several states always threatened to be a disintegrating factor ; while in any league whatsoever every individual member was ready to resent any curtailment of its own unfettered freedom of action at the bidding of any external authority.

In its immediate intention, however, the new maritime confederation was simply a league for carrying on the Persian war until all Hellas should be free, to which end it was necessary that an Hellenic navy should be mistress of the Aegean waters ;  for every city or island on the eastern Aegean the thing was vital. The work was practically completed in 467, by Cimon the son of Miltiades. Xerxes apparently contemplated a great effort for the recovery of maritime supremacy, the northern Aegean having by now been wholly lost. Cimon, however, at the head of a large fleet sailed the southern waters, brought the cities of the south as well as of the west coast of Asia Minor—of Caria, Lycia and (Dorian) Pamphylia—into the Confederation, and in the neighbourhood of the river Eurymedon shattered on land the Persian forces and on the sea annihilated a Phoenician fleet of two hundred sail.

But the need of maintaining the Greek navy under the direction of Athens was, of course, in no wise diminished by Cimon's victory. For practical purposes the navy of the Confederation by this time had almost become the navy of Athens.

The transformation did not spring from a conscious project of empire on the part of Athens, though that project may well have been in the mind of Themistocles, whose genius created the Athenian fleet

and taught Athens that her future was on the seas. The scheme may have been inspired by Themistocles ; but the organization of the Confederation was the work of Aristides, and its operations were conducted by Cimon the son of Miltiades— the one a man whom all men trusted, the other a most loyal Athenian patriot, but also a most loyal friend and admirer of Sparta. For both of these the Confederation was what it professed to be, a league for the liberation of Hellas from the power of the common foe, the Barbarian ; unconsciously they made it an instrument for the aggrandisement of Athens.

The explanation scarcely presents difficulty. Lack of unity had all but wrought disaster ; for a new campaign there must be unity not merely of aim but of method. A single high command, a common war-chest and a regulated standard for contribution in ships, men and money were essential to success. The treasury was

**HEADQUARTERS OF THE CONFEDERATION THAT BECAME THE ATHENIAN EMPIRE**
The league of Greek cities known as the Delian Confederation had its name from the island of Delos, where its treasury was established. In the temple of Apollo, to whom the island was sacred, the synod of the Confederation met to transact its business under the presidency of Athens. Here we look from the central heights of Delos towards the strait that separates it from Rheneia ; in the foreground are the ruins of the semicircular theatre and adjacent buildings.
*From ' Picturesque Greece,' Fisher Unwin, Ltd.*

deposited at Delos, which gave its name to the Confederation ; questions were settled by the representatives of the member-states in council, under Athenian presidency, each state, large or small, having one vote. The bigger states contributed ships, the smaller states ship-money ; larger states that pre- ferred to follow the second course were allowed to do so ; the apportionment of the contributions was entrusted by uni- versal consent to Aristides ; and, since the ships representing the ship-money were provided by Athens and remained an integral part of the Athenian navy, the practical effect was that the Confederation paid Athens to enlarge her own fleet.

Pressure, again, was inevitably brought to bear on all the islanders to join and take their share in maintaining the Confed- eration, to whose activities they owed their security. Those that joined under pressure were always on the paying and not the ship-providing list. The federal principle, denying the right of secession, was soon laid down and enforced. The paying states, to which in the first instance at least Athens appeared in the character of a protector, were in fact her clients or dependents from the beginning ; and thus she was able always to control a majority of the votes on the council.

### Delian Confederation subordinate to Athens

THE complete subordination of the Con- federation to Athens became obvious some years later when (in 454) the treasury was removed from Delos to Athens and placed under her sole control. By that time the Athenian confederacy embraced the whole of Asiatic Hellas, most of the ports on the north coast of the Aegean and all the islands, including at last Aegina. Lesbos, Chios and Samos alone· enjoyed comparative independence, not having commuted their contribution of ships for payment of money. States which had been coerced into joining or remaining in the Confederation had for the most part been deprived of the autonomy which all had enjoyed at the outset. Officially the Confederation was still an alliance ; actually it was an Athenian Empire.

The specific purpose for which the Delian Confederation had been created was achieved at the battle of the Eurymedon. Though after the battle the war with Persia remained in being, it languished until the growing power of Athens tempted her into a daring act of direct aggression against the Barbarian empire which was too ambitious for her strength, since she was at the same time engaged heavily elsewhere. The murder of Xerxes and the succession of his son Artaxerxes (Ahasuerus) in 465 was, as usual, an encouragement to revolts in the Persian em- pire. In 460, at the invitation of the Libyan Inarus, a great Athenian fleet sailed to take part in the liberation of Egypt.

The expedition went so far that in 459 it captured the city but not the fortress of Memphis. There, however, it was locked up ; no reinforcements could be sent ; three years later a Persian army expelled it from Memphis. Finally, after a long blockade on the island of Prosopitis, it was reduced to surrender, the fleet having been burnt, but was allowed to make its way to Cyrene, and so home. The Egyptian revolt was completely crushed.

The Athenian expedition was a disaster, not indeed on a small scale, though also not without honour ; and the failure was driven home soon afterwards by the annihilation of an Athenian squadron at the hands of the Phoenician fleet. Yet even after this Cimon was able to lead another expedition for the freeing of Cyprus, which missed success only because of the great captain's death, though it was followed by a naval victory over the Phoenicians (449). But Athenian zeal for continuing the Persian war passed with the passing of Cimon ; and hostilities with Persia ceased (possibly with an under- standing rather than a formal treaty, the Peace of Callias) in 447. No renewed attack upon any portion of Hellas was now to be feared from Persia, though Cyprus remained under her power.

### Retrospect of Internal Developments

FOR internal Greek affairs we must retrace our steps to the days when the Delian Confederation was yet un- created and Cimon still alive. When the battle of Plataea had been fought, and won practically by the Lacedaemonians, the part

## THE CITY STATES AND ISLANDS WHOSE BITTER RIVALRIES DIVIDED GREECE

Local patriotism, ever an effective check upon Greek strivings after national unification, had been temporarily overcome by the menace of Persian conquest, but quickly revived after Plataea. Sparta's interests were solely in the Peloponnese, where she enjoyed an unchallenged primacy, so that the Greek cities outside her sphere of influence and the islands looked to Athens for guidance in their struggle against Persia. Thus there arose two parties—the Spartan and Athenian groups of states.

played in the war by Athens brought to her a new prestige, making her second only to Sparta, but still second. The Spartan hegemony was still undisputed ; it belonged to her in right of the admirable military virtues of her soldiery and the unmatched excellence, despite limitations, of her military machine. But from the pan-Hellenic point of view her exclusively Peloponnesian outlook had been extremely marked, in contrast to that of Athens. Pan-Hellenism demanded an active maritime war in which Peloponnesians had no direct interest and Sparta had no inclination to participate, whereas Athens was obviously marked out for the leadership ; and by the mere fact of that leadership she had been projected upon the path of imperialism, along which, from about 460 onwards, she was guided by the most famous of her statesmen, Pericles.

Sparta had unwittingly abdicated her primacy. The states which were passing under Athenian hegemony were outside her sphere, and there was no immediate development of open jealousy, at least on that score. But her prestige was weakened by the misconduct of Pausanias, the victor of Plataea ; who, not content with his position in Sparta, plunged into ambitious projects of personal aggrandisement, intrigued with Persia, and ended his life as a condemned traitor—miserably starved to death in the precincts of a shrine where he sought asylum from the emissaries of justice.

Only less disastrous was the end of Themistocles, to whom even more than to Pausanias Greece owed her freedom, to whose brilliant guidance throughout the great crisis Athens owed almost her existence. Rightly or wrongly, against

**PRIZE WON BY ATHENS' ALLIES**
With the intention of reducing Spartan predom-
inance, Athens and Argos joined in operations
against Corinth, Sparta's friend.  A victory of the
Argives is commemorated by this captured
Corinthian helmet, dedicated to Zeus.
*British Museum*

him, too, was brought the charge of
' Medising.'  But, more fortunate than
Pausanias, he eluded his pursuers and died
in wealth and ease, a pensionary of the
Great King and an exile execrated by his
own countrymen.

Friendly relations were maintained between Athens and Sparta for some
time, owing to the influence of the popular
soldier Cimon, too honest to be an
intriguer, too simple-minded to be a statesman, but with a genius for winning
victories inherited from his father, the
victor of Marathon.  Admiration for
Sparta, hostility to Persia and loyalty to
Athens were his guiding principles.  His
influence, however, was ended by an act
of sheer stupidity on the part of Sparta.

In 463 she was in difficulties over a
serious revolt of the helots of Messenia,
who had occupied the fortress of Ithome,
where they defied all her efforts to reduce
them.  Sparta was driven to appeal for
aid to her allies, including Athens.  Cimon,
in spite of the active democratic opposition
led by Ephialtes and Pericles, prevailed on
the Athenians to send an expedition under
his own command to their help ; he failed
to carry the fortress, and was promptly
informed that Sparta had no further use
for the services of Athens.  Meanwhile, the
democrats had introduced some highly
popular reforms by which their hands were
strengthened ; Athens smarted under the
insult of Ithome ; Cimon returned to find
that his popularity had vanished ; and a
year later he was banished by the form
of vote known as ostracism—the common
expression of a sharp popular revulsion.

The democratic anti-Laconian imperialists were carried into power ; Ephialtes
was slain by an unknown assassin (461) ;
and thenceforth for thirty years, with
scarcely an interval, the policy of Athens
was the policy of Pericles.  Thenceforth,
also, friendship between Sparta and Athens
was at best a hollow pretence.  The
Messenian insurgents were eventually suppressed, but Athens provided them with a
refuge and a settlement at Naupactus,
her recently established outpost on the
north shore of the Corinthian Gulf.

The influence of Cimon and his personal
popularity had deferred the breach between Athens and Sparta, which was
hastened by his ostracism.  Athens allied
herself with Sparta's inveterate Peloponnesian rival, Argos, and was very soon
involved in a war, not at first with Sparta,
but with her Dorian and at the same time
maritime allies, Corinth and Aegina, whom
the Athenian maritime development was
threatening to throttle ; a foretaste of the
Peloponnesian war.

### Foretaste of the Peloponnesian War

The quarrel broke out when Megara, at
the north end of the Isthmus, sought
and obtained the protection of Athens
against the domination of her powerful
neighbour Corinth.  Megara from the
Peloponnesian point of view was the gate
of Attica, whose ' wooden walls ' were
impenetrable.  With Megara in her hands,
Athens could be attacked only on her
northern flank through Boeotia, dominated
by Thebes.  Corinth attacked Megara ;
Athens came to the rescue ; Aegina joined
Corinth ; but so successful were the
Athenian arms that not only was Megara
held but Aegina was reduced to complete

submission and forced to enter the Delian Confederation as a tributary ally of Athens before two years were over (457). Yet at the very moment when the struggle began, Athens was embarking on that Egyptian adventure, the story of which has been told above. With her great expedition locked up in Egypt while her main energies were engaged in the conflict nearer home, she could not exert her full strength in neither field—and Cimon, her great captain, was in exile. Her achievement in the circumstances was sufficiently astonishing.

Then in 457 Sparta took the field ; not at the first avowedly, but still unmistakably, as the enemy of Athens. She found an excuse for dispatching a strong force to Boeotia, really to reorganize the Theban League. The return march involved an invasion of Attic territory, a battle at Tanagra in which the adherents of Cimon —whose personal services were offered to and rejected by the city which always commanded his utter loyalty—fought as patriots with the bravest, and a technical victory, which was a practical defeat, for the Peloponnesians. It is disputed whether Pericles procured the recall of Cimon at this point, who negotiated a truce with Sparta ; certainly Athens proceeded to force Boeotia, Thebes excepted, into the Delian Confederation.

ᛒETWEEN 456 and 448 Athens was apparently at the height of her power. The coasts on both sides of the Gulf of Corinth were dominated by her ; she was mistress of Megara and of most of Boeotia ; the treasury of the Delian Confederation had been transferred from Delos to Athens ; Cimon was now back, in the double character of pacificator in relation to Sparta and

**VOTE TO BANISH THEMISTOCLES**

Notwithstanding his great services to Athens, in 472 B.C. the requisite 6,000 citizens voted that Themistocles should be ostracised. Here we see the potsherd (ostrakon) inscribed with his name by which one vote for his ostracism was cast.

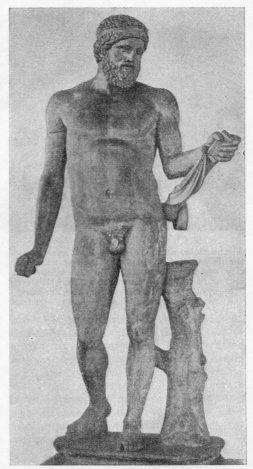

**GREAT ATHENIAN IMPERIALIST**

After his ostracism Themistocles fled first to Argos and then ‚to the Persians. Found at Magnesia in Asia Minor, where he was allowed to settle by the Great King, and now in Munich, this statue has lately been identified as the man who laid the foundations of Athenian greatness.

*From Percy Gardner, ‘ New Chapters in Greek Art ’*

incomparable commander of fleets and armies, and bearing no malice to either Sparta or his own countrymen. When he died, as recounted above, the long strain of the Persian war was over.

At this auspicious moment, then, in 448, Pericles made the proposal which (if it was genuine) displays the pan-Hellenic idealism underlying his Athenian imperialism. Hitherto Hellas had acted in something like unison only under stress of a manifest necessity for common defence against an overwhelming common

**TO PRESERVE ATHENS AGAINST ATTACK**

At the close of the Persian war, Themistocles so strengthened the defences of Athens as to make it a fortress in itself. The city was surrounded by a high, carefully constructed wall, a section of which is shown here ; and the fortifications of the Acropolis, partly destroyed by the Persians, were restored.

*Photo, Deutsches Archaeologisches Institut*

menace. Now, in time of assured peace, so far as the Barbarian was concerned, he invited all Hellas to join in a sort of imperial conference with a view to joint action for common ends in which all Hellas was interested ; primarily the restoration of the temples, revered by all alike, in territory that had been ravaged by the Barbarians, and the suppression of the piracy from which the commerce of all Hellas suffered.

Such a conference would have held in it immeasurable possibilities of future pan-Hellenic development. But unmistakably it would also have involved Athenian hegemony—moreover, the Peloponnese had not been ravaged by the Persians. The proposal did not appeal to Sparta nor to the rest of the Peloponnesians ; they declined it ; and Pericles was free to fall back on Athenian imperialism. And against the imperialism of the great maritime democracy was inevitably arrayed the whole force of oligarchic militarism under Spartan hegemony—not of Spartan imperialism ; for the Spartan state was too slow and too politically timid, for all the valour of her soldiers, to contemplate the responsibilities of empire.

Meanwhile Athens itself, the actual ' city of the violet crown,' had become

much better able to defy military attack than she had been in the past. In the old days Peisistratus had for his own ends dismantled the old city wall ; when the Persians came to Marathon, and ten years later to Thermopylae, Athens was unfortified. The actual citadel, the Acropolis, was the only position that could be held for a week. When the war was over and the Athenians returned to the city, Themistocles, in spite of the benevolent remonstrances of Sparta, raised a new wall and fortified the great port of the Piraeus, from which the city itself, four miles away, was however still liable to be cut off. It was only under the rule of Pericles that the harbour fortifications were completed and the famous Long Walls were carried from the city to the port, so that the whole was from the military point of view one great fortified town.

But the years immediately following the Peace of Callias brought the lesson that extension of dominion by land was a mistake for the power whose strength lay in her navy. Revolt followed revolt, usually the outcome of oligarchical plots. Boeotia broke away, Thebes recovering her ascendancy. Euboea broke away, but here the revolt was stamped out. Megara broke away, massacred its Athenian garrison and joined the Peloponnesian League ; Attica was once more open to invasion along the whole of her land frontier, though little Plataea held indomitably to her alliance. Encompassed with dangers, Athens in 445 concluded a thirty years peace with the allied Peloponnesians, surrendering almost all her recent acquisitions on the mainland of Greece.

THE precise status of Athens at this stage is not altogether easy to grasp. It had no precedent. It was not, like the hegemony of Sparta, a universally recognized pre-eminence resting on acknowledged military prestige ; Sparta claimed no right of applying compulsion to her allies as arising from her hege-mony. But the Delian Confeder-ation had at a very early stage claimed the right of compelling maritime states to join it and, having joined, to remain in it ; and the voice of the Confedera-tion from the outset was in effect the voice of Athens. Save for the contingents from three islands, the fleet was her fleet ; whenever compulsion was ap-plied, Athens applied it ; virtu-ally if not formally she fixed the contributions, and unequi-vocally she alone controlled the expenditure. Wherever she applied compulsion it was attended by some curtailment of autonomy, a definite loss of independence, formally ac-knowledged by treaty ; in effect she was not the president of a league of equal states, but the mistress of a number of dependent states whose tribute maintained the Athenian navy.

Moreover, beyond this Pericles deve-loped a new system of colonisation, planting on the lands of the allies settle-ments of Athenian citizens who remained Athenian citizens under Athenian juris-diction, and served in effect as a sort of Athenian garrison. The land was not stolen—it was paid for generally by some

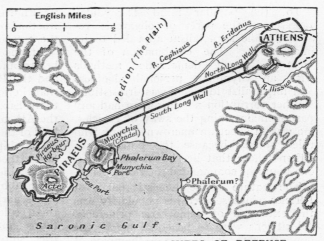

**WELL PLANNED MEASURES OF DEFENCE**

While Athens was adequately protected against attack by the battlements raised at Themistocles' instigation, her safety was not really ensured until Pericles had her connected with the Piraeus by the Long Walls. These strongly fortified lines made communication between Athens and her port practically secure.

reduction of the tribute. The system was popular at Athens ; it made provision at a convenient distance for surplus popu-lation, practically without cost to the exchequer, and it helped to extend com-merce. It was not equally popular with the allies, but it tended to keep them under control. The bonds that attached them to Athens were scarcely silken.

THE magnetic power exercised by Pericles over the people of Athens was shaken but not broken by the reverses which brought about the comparative humiliation of the Thirty Years Peace. His triumph was a triumph of personality, since he rejected entirely the vulgar arts of the demagogue, holding himself aloof from the crowd. He maintained his rule because he compelled confidence even in the face of failure and of an opposition, mainly factious, no doubt, but headed by a leader of distinguished integrity, Thu-cydides (not the historian), the son of Melesias, who was actuated partly by mistrust of his popular innovations and still more by dislike of his domineering treatment of the allies. But when, three years after the peace, Thucydides chal-lenged a direct trial of strength, it was he himself, not Pericles, who was ostracised.

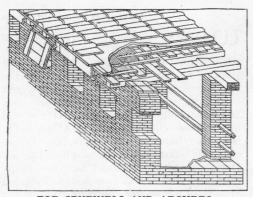

**FOR SENTINELS AND ARCHERS**

The Long Walls at Athens were solidly con-structed of stone, and were surmounted by a crenellated gallery of brick, roofed with tiles—as seen in this reconstruction—which would afford perfect protection to the garrison.

*From Weller, 'Athens and its Monuments'.*

To the popular mind Thucydides represented the party of oligarchic reaction, while imperialism appealed to its imagination. The combination of the most advanced democratic methods with an Olympian personal aloofness and imperialist idealism was irresistible. Neither corruption nor terrorism had any part in maintaining the sway of Pericles. He was in effect an uncrowned king who ruled simply because the populace of Athens chose that he should rule as the one man who commanded their confidence.

The feature in the domestic policy of Pericles which secured his popularity was the extension of democratic principles. All citizens were to be equal before the law. He came into power as champion of the curtailment of the privileges exercised by the Areopagus (an ancient and time-honoured body from the membership of which the great bulk of the citizens were by its constitution permanently excluded), and of the transfer of its functions to a body admission to which was open to all.

## Democratic Policy of Pericles

ONCE in power, he systematically extended the principle of payment for the discharge of all minor public services for which the average citizen could not otherwise have afforded to spare the time, and he made the discharge of those functions an integral part of the citizen's duty to the state. There was no political office which any citizen might not aspire to attain by election or by lot. He eased the economic burden of the surplus population by turning his imperialism to account and planting them out on those settlements or ' cleruchies ' already described, thereby also increasing the popularity of imperialism—at Athens.

Not the least of the means by which he acquired his ascendancy was the magnificence which flattered the Athenian's pride in his city and in himself. Greece at large refused, as we have seen, to aid in that restoration of the ruined temples which was a sacred obligation upon all Hellenes. The work was left to Athens, and what under the guidance of Pericles she wrought is the immortal heritage of mankind. If Athens was wealthy she gave of her wealth freely; for but an infinitesimal fraction of the cost was defrayed from the treasury of her tributaries.

Athens through her own outposts or her tributaries controlled the Dardanelles and the Bosporus; it is tolerably certain that Pericles had dreams that extended to the Euxine—he very much strengthened the Athenian hold on the northern coastland of the Aegean, though later his colony of Amphipolis became a source of weakness rather than strength. In the west she commanded the entry to the Gulf of Corinth by the possession of Naupactus on its north shore. Corcyra was a Corinthian colony, but always on such bad terms with her mother city that her friendship could almost be reckoned upon.

In Italy and Sicily the Dorian element was immensely preponderant. But even here Pericles sought to introduce an Athenian penetration through the establishment of pan-Hellenic colonies—first a ' New Sybaris,' then Thurii—under Athenian influence; though with only limited success.

The weakness from which such a dominion as that of Athens is always liable to suffer was illustrated by the revolt of both Samos, one of the three ship-contributing states, and Byzantium, though both revolts were ended (439) without Peloponnesian intervention, Samos becoming a subject state.

### Mutterings before the Storm

WHATEVER jealousy Sparta may have felt towards Athens, she was too self-centred, too inert, too ready to rest stolidly in her own strength to make the first move against her rival until the spur to action was supplied by someone else. She was wholly devoid of the enterprise and initiative so characteristic of Athens. On the other hand it was hardly less certain that the spur would be applied by the Dorian state which found her own maritime and commercial ambitions thwarted at every turn by her energetic rival.

Athenian fleets dominated the Saronic Gulf and the Gulf of Corinth; they were invading Corinth's preserves in the west; in Chalcidice the Corinthian colony of Potidaea had been absorbed into the

Athenian League. If Corinth should see a chance of arousing the lethargic wrath of Sparta against Athens to the point of action, she would certainly make the most of it. And then the scale would be weighted with the entire force of the Peloponnesian League ; and Sparta, feeling her hegemony bound up in the struggle, would be doubly dangerous. On that head Pericles can have had no illusion.

A series of disconnected incidents produced the opportunity. First, in 435, Corinth and her colony Corcyra fell out about the Corcyrean colony of Epidamnus, and Corcyra won a naval victory over her parent city. Corinth, having the Peloponnesian League behind her, prepared to punish Corcyra, who, having no one behind her, sought the alliance of Athens, whom Corinth pressed to remain neutral. The alliance might precipitate a Peloponnesian war, but in that event the Corcyrean fleet would be useful. Athens agreed to help Corcyra, but only if Corinth attacked her. In a sea-fight at Sybota a small Athenian squadron saved the Corcyrean fleet from a grave disaster (433). Corinth had an arguable case for charging Athens with a breach of the Thirty Years Peace.

Next year Potidaea revolted, refusing to dismiss her Corinthian magistrates and to raze her own walls at the bidding of Athens. Half the Chalcidian peninsula followed suit, incited thereto by the Macedonian king Perdiccas, who had a private personal grievance against Athens. In 432 an Athenian force defeated the Corinthian commander of the Potidaeans and laid siege to the city. Corinth appealed to Sparta ; Pericles retorted with a decree forbidding entry to any Megarian at any port under Athenian control—Megara having aided Corinth at Sybota—which meant commercial ruin for Megara.

### How the War at last broke out

SPARTA found the Corinthian appeal convincing, backed as it was by other Peloponnesian states. But, as always, she wanted time to get into movement. She gained some delay by raising irrelevant points which were brushed aside as a matter of course. Then came the ultimatum. If Athens did not free the

**UNCROWNED KING OF ATHENS**

Secure in the unwavering confidence of the Athenian democracy, Pericles never had recourse to dubious political expedients. At home he realized democratic principles, but in foreign affairs was an uncompromising imperialist.

*British Museum*

Hellenes whom she held in subjection, there would be war. Athens responded that if Sparta would set the example in her own dominion she would follow it. This being the last thing that Sparta would dream of doing, it meant that Athens had confidently taken up the gage which Sparta had hesitatingly thrown down.

The war which opened in the spring of 431 was a struggle for domination between a maritime empire and a mistress of continental armies, with this qualification, that Attica had a long and indefensible land frontier, while she had on the continent no more effective friend than the small state of Plataea, though her fleets included those of Chios and Lesbos.

In the eyes of its great historian Thucydides, the war was by far the most important in the history of Man. Some moderns, on the other hand, are apt to scoff at it as no more than a paltry squabble between petty states. In fact, its one indisputable result was the disappearance of any possibility that may have previously existed of Hellenic unification, which, just conceivably, might have been the outcome of an unqualified Athenian victory. A politically consolidated Hellas was possibly a Periclean dream ; but the war in actual fact brought it no nearer to achievement and was, therefore, a sheer waste. Unification was incompatible with the conception of state individualism ingrained in the Greek mind. But the history of the war was written by Thucydides, and whether we overrate or underrate its significance, the record is one of the masterpieces of the world's literature.

**FIRST SCIENTIFIC HISTORIAN**

Our knowledge of the Peloponnesian war is largely derived from Thucydides, whose account and interpretation of events are unbiassed, although he was an Athenian. This bust, in Holkham Hall, Norfolk, is one of the best extant.

*From Poulsen, ' Greek and Roman Portraits '*

PERICLES from the outset realized the fundamental fact that on land the hostile forces were overwhelmingly superior, and that Attica, as distinguished from the city of Athens with its ports, was indefensible. Year by year the Peloponnesian armies ravaged Attica, practically unopposed. In the second year (430), Athens was brought almost to her knees by the outbreak within the city—over-crowded by the rural population gathered behind its wall—of bubonic plague, which destroyed a quarter of the people but extended no farther than the city itself.

The anti-democratic and the ultra-imperialist parties seized the opportunity for an attack upon Pericles, who had found it hard enough to induce the Athenians to watch the devastation of their property outside the city walls. Yet his ascendancy, though seriously shaken, was not lost. But in the following year (429) he died, and the leadership of the democratic imperialists passed into other hands.

The war policy of Pericles rested on the conviction that nothing could be gained and much might be lost by attempting to meet the main Peloponnesian armies on land. The reply to the attacks upon Attica must be the throttling of the Peloponnesian states by an irresistible sea power, killing their commerce and incidentally threatening their coasts with harassing raids. To this end the command of the western sea was vital, that of the Aegean being already secure.

The policy was implicit in the decree against Megara which immediately preceded the war ; and Pericles had promptly accepted overtures for alliance from Sicilian Leontini as a check on the connexion between Corinth and Syracuse. Immediately this led to little ; but during these first years Athens strengthened her position in the western islands and on the Acarnanian coast, and some brilliant victories were won over superior squadrons by the able commander Phormio, whose career however was somewhat unaccountably brief. On the Chalcidian peninsula the siege of Potidaea was carried to the finish, the Potidaeans were expelled and the place was occupied by the Athenians. Aegina was completely Atticised in the first year by the total expulsion of the Aeginetans, who were planted by the Spartans on Laconian soil.

No marked progress on either side is to be observed in the years immediately following the death of Pericles. But to this period belong three episodes which have been made famous by the vivid narrative of Thucydides.

THE opening incident of the war had been an attempt of the Thebans to get possession of Plataea by a trick. The trick was foiled in circumstances which could fairly be called a breach of faith on the part of the Plataeans, who appealed to Athens. She withdrew the non-combatant inhabitants, leaving a garrison of 400 Plataeans and eighty Athenians. In spite of promises, no more was done for Plataea, to which in the third year the Peloponnesians laid siege, since the garrison stoutly refused to surrender. In the fifth year the place was so closely invested, and in such force, that though all attempts to carry the defences were foiled by the ingenuity and dauntless resolution of the besieged the place was on the verge of reduction by starvation. Half the garrison cut its way out and escaped to Athens; the other half then surrendered at discretion and were all put to death because 'they had done nothing to help the Lacedaemonians and their allies.'

The second episode is the revolt from the Athenian League of the free island of Lesbos (with the exception of loyal Methymna) headed by Mitylene. This time it was the Peloponnesians who promised aid but sent none. Mitylene was forced to surrender, submitting its fate to the judgement of Athens. So fierce was the wrath of the democracy at the revolt, which could not in this case be attributed to Athenian tyranny, that the Assembly, now led by the notorious or famous Cleon, condemned the entire population to death or slavery. A ship was dispatched with the order; happily it went on its awful errand with no great haste, but it had arrived and the order was on the point of execution when a second trireme swept into the harbour bearing a reprieve. A second specially summoned meeting of the Assembly had reversed the fatal sentence, and the oarsmen, racing without a

moment's relaxation as if their own lives were at stake, arrived barely in time, with a start of twenty-four hours to make up. A strong interest attaches to the debate in the assembly as reported by Thucydides; for in it the question of humanity is entirely ignored, and the decision turns wholly on the political danger of putting in execution a sentence in itself regarded as obviously just and legitimate.

This was in the fourth and fifth years; in the fifth also began the episode of the Corcyrean revolution, which the Greek historian makes the text for profound generalisations on the effects of revolutionary frenzy. With the obvious variations in the staging of the tragedy, Corcyra was very much like Paris in the days of the Terror. The oligarchic pro-Corinthian party attempted a ' coup d'état,' and paid the penalty of failure in full. An Athenian fleet which was on its way to Sicily played a sorry part in the closing scene of the struggle, some two years after its beginning.

THE pan-Hellenic idealism which we are warranted in attributing to Pericles disappears with his death. If we have read him aright, his conception was that of a united Hellas wherein Athens should be queen in virtue of her moral and intellectual ascendancy. Athens was to be to Hellas what Pericles was to Athens; not a tyrant ruling by force in her own interest, but a sovereign because the incarnation of all that was best in Hellas. She was so

ON BOARD AN ATHENIAN TRIREME

The type of battleship generally used in the Peloponnesian war was the trireme, a heavy but swift vessel propelled by oars arranged in three banks. Archaeological discussion, based very largely on this Athenian relief, has not succeeded in deciding exactly how the banks were arranged.

*From a cast in the British Museum*

because her people enjoyed a personal freedom without parallel elsewhere. That her leadership might win recognition she must have power, but the power was the means to the fulfilment of an ideal.

THERE was no second Pericles in whom the democracy could place its trust; the men who took his place were democrats and imperialists, but their democracy was hostility to the class which owed its influence to birth and wealth, and their imperialism was the lust of rule. All the pictures of them that we possess were painted by their enemies, who would allow them no virtues; charges of dishonesty and blank incapacity count for little; but it is not easy to find signs of real statesmanship either in them or in their antagonists, the ' gentlemen '—a term which perhaps more nearly than any other expresses the meaning of the epithet they applied to themselves. There were no longer any grand issues at stake; the war party wanted only to extend the dominion of Athens, the peace party only to thwart the war party, while the Peloponnesians mainly desired to humiliate the ' tyrant of the seas.'

Politics apart, there appeared, one on either side, two military leaders endowed with some originality and initiative, the Athenian Demosthenes and the Spartan Brasidas. These were qualities which the Spartan system tended to suppress entirely in the Spartan armies, but it may be remarked that they were not infrequently displayed by the Spartan in foreign service.

Demosthenes dealt the most effective blow on the part of Athens. While with the fleet, weather-bound off the Messenian coast, he seized and fortified Pylos on the modern Bay of Navarino. The Peloponnesians tried to eject him, but only succeeded in landing a small Spartan force on the island of Sphacteria; which in turn was reduced to such straits that surrender or death was the only possible choice. The Spartans surrendered, much to the surprise of their neighbours, though no one else would have hesitated for a moment; and so long as they remained captive the Lacedaemonians ceased their annual devastation of Attica.

PERICLES, when the thirty years truce was made, had learnt, and never afterwards forgot, that attempted conquests on land were bad policy. Yet the democrats twice tried—and failed—to master Boeotia. The second attempt was accompanied by a grave military disaster at the battle of Delium, where the life of the young Alcibiades was saved by the sturdy philosopher Socrates. In the same year (424) Brasidas with a small body of irregular troops was sent by Sparta to help the malcontents of the Thracian coast and Chalcidice, which broke into general revolt against Athens.

By this time there was a strong peace party in both Athens and Sparta, and in 423 a truce was actually formulated; but it broke down. Brasidas, now playing brilliantly for his own hand in the north, and Cleon at Athens, meant the war to go on; and

**YOUNG SOLDIER BOUND FOR THE WARS**
The strength of Greek armies lay in heavy infantry, ' hoplites,' of which Sparta possessed the most efficient force. In battle the typical hoplite was equipped with cuirass, greaves and sword, in addition to a tunic, vizored helmet, spear and emblazoned shield such as we see in this drawing of about 450 B.C.
*From a tomb lekythos in the National Museum, Athens, after Pfuhl*

it was only when both of them were killed in a battle before Amphipolis (422) that the peace parties carried the day and the first stage of the war was concluded by the Peace of Nicias, the Athenian high priest of Respectability. For the time it satisfied Sparta and Athens; but it left Corinth, Megara and Boeotia raging. It had in it no element of durability.

THE terms of the peace involved the restoration on both sides of sundry conquests. They were rejected by Sparta's allies; she was unable to enforce them; Athens consequently refused to carry out her part of the bargain. War parties and peace parties predominated alternately in various states; local hostilities broke out in various quarters; kaleidoscopic combinations and dissolutions and recombinations followed in bewildering succession; until in 415 emerges the determination of Athens to embark on the great venture which was to prove her ruin, the Sicilian expedition.

Ostensibly it was in answer to an appeal from Sicilian allies—from Segesta for aid against Selinus, and from Leontini for deliverance from Syracuse. Actually the intention was to absorb Sicily into the Athenian empire. The great advocate was the brilliant, erratic and utterly unprincipled Alcibiades, an aristocrat who when it suited him posed as a democratic leader; the opposition was led by Nicias. The Athenians enthusiastically adopted the proposal in spite of the huge expenditure and the enormous risks it involved, and then appointed to the command Nicias and Alcibiades, the one as timid and half-hearted as the other was eager and reckless, between whom zealous co-operation was inconceivable; a quite impossible combination. With them was associated the capable soldier Lamachus, who made no pretence to be a politician and possessed no other influence.

ARMS AND ARMOUR OF GREEK WARRIORS

Although this painting (c. 460 B.C.) has a mythological subject —the slaughter of Amazons—the details enable us to visualise the gear of a contemporary soldier. While each of these heroes is only partially armed they have all the accoutrements of the ordinary hoplite apportioned between them.

*From Pfuhl, 'Masterpieces of Greek Painting,' Chatto & Windus*

HITHERTO Sicily and Italy had stood outside the conflict in eastern Hellas. The tyrannies had given place generally to democracies before the middle of the century, soon after the death of Hierôn in 467, and there had been a long period of general prosperity, while Syracuse continued to maintain a dominant position. Pericles had sought nothing more than some extension of Athenian influence in the west; Ionian cities in those regions had rather incited Athenian intervention through jealousy of the Syracusan ascendancy; but when the Peloponnesian war was in full swing, a congress of the Sicilian states, under the persuasive influence of the Syracusan Hermocrates, made it tolerably evident that Sicily generally meant to keep itself clear of that complication, and that outside intervention in Sicilian affairs would be resented.

But Athenian imperialism in its most aggressive and wanton form was at fever heat, owing to the successful and utterly inexcusable conquest and annexation of the island of Melos in 416, just when the opportunity for aggressive action in Sicily presented itself. Athens snatched at the chance, and paid the penalty.

The expedition which sailed from Athens in 415 was on a scale without precedent. Its departure was immediately preceded by an outrage which can only have been intended to prevent its sailing—the midnight mutilation of the sacred images known as Hermae. Popular rumour, sedulously fostered, fixed the guilt of the sacrilege upon the notoriously reckless and profane Alcibiades, who immediately challenged trial. As this would have involved delaying the expedition, inquiry was postponed.

### Athenian Expedition to Sicily

THE generals reached Sicily, to find that the promises of financial and military support on which Athens had acted had no material basis. Lamachus, as a plain soldier, urged an immediate attack on Syracuse, which would probably have been successful. Nicias favoured a demonstration, to be followed by retirement. Alcibiades wanted diplomacy to precede the fighting. The schemes of Lamachus being over-ridden, he gave his support to Alcibiades. The military opportunity was lost, and then the whole scheme of diplomacy was wrecked by a summons for Alcibiades to return to Athens and stand his trial—a manifest conspiracy of his enemies at home, working on popular superstition.

Lamachus and Nicias were left, while he started on his return journey ; but, seeing no prospect of a fair trial, he made his escape on the way home, was condemned to death and forfeiture in his absence, and became for the time the most vindictive and virulent enemy of the Athenian democracy which had wronged him. In his new character he found no difficulty in persuading Sparta that it was her duty to throw her weight once more into the scale against Athens ; which was more determined than ever to carry on the Sicilian adventure.

That adventure might still have been successful but for the pathetic confidence of the Athenians in the generalship of the pious but incompetent Nicias, in spite of his own desire to relinquish the command. Diplomacy having broken down, the Athenians laid siege to Syracuse. Their fleet was able completely to blockade the harbour, and there was only a small gap remaining in the siege lines which cut off the city from the interior, when Lamachus, to whom the chief credit so far was due, was killed. That gap Nicias omitted to close ; with disastrous results. For it enabled Gylippus—almost but not quite another Brasidas—who had been sent from Sparta to help the Syracusans, to effect an entry ; and with his arrival the whole situation changed. Nicias in his dispatches was forced to declare that, so far from victory being in sight, the whole affair would have to be abandoned unless a second expedition on as large a scale as the first could be sent from Athens.

She was beset now by the whole of the old Peloponnesian alliance. Sparta, urged by Alcibiades, had seized and garrisoned Deceleia, on Attic soil, whence she could conduct raids at any moment. But Athens would not admit defeat ; nor did she permit Nicias to resign. But as colleagues she sent in command of a new great force Demosthenes and Eurymedon.

### The Disaster before Syracuse

THE second expedition, arriving in the late summer (413), found an already desperate situation, the Athenian forces thoroughly demoralised by failures and defeats, the Syracusans full of confidence, brilliantly led and dominating not only the Great Harbour but the siege lines as well. Desperate endeavours to retrieve the position on land and on sea were disastrously defeated. The Athenian fleet after a severe struggle was cooped up in the harbour, the mouth of which was blocked. A last frantic effort to break out was hopelessly crushed. Retreat inland to friendly territory while there was yet time was the only chance ; but before it could begin every line of escape was ambushed or blocked.

Never have the ' pity and terror ' which are the essence of tragedy been more movingly presented than in the wonderful pages wherein Thucydides tells the story of those last days. Out of those once proud Athenian hosts, all who survived the slaughters and the agonies of that despairing retreat passed what was left to them of life in exiled slavery.

The annihilation of the Sicilian Expedition was the end of the Athenian Empire.

It was not indeed immediately evident that the empire was at an end. Athens maintained the struggle for nine years more. But she had no reserve left to fall back on, no trusted leader who could command steady confidence and carry on a consistent policy. The one man, Alcibiades, who perhaps had the necessary ability, was wholly lacking in the character which was still more necessary. Faction after faction at home snatched an incomplete and precarious control for a time ; treason, it can hardly be doubted, was perpetually at work ; experimental reconstructions of the constitution followed one after another in rapid succession ; but the resolution to fight on to the last gasp never wavered, though the odds had become almost overwhelming.

A YEAR after the Sicilian disaster, all Ionia was in revolt against the 'tyrant' state, not realizing that subjection to Persia was still the inevitable alternative to the tyranny ; only Samos remained loyal. The Persian satraps of the west, Tissaphernes at Sardis and Pharnabazus at Dascylium, were fully alive to the situation, though each had his own game to play. Sparta had never troubled about Ionia, and was quite ready to bargain with the satraps for the downfall of Athens at the price of Ionia, and in particular for the money necessary to keep a fleet in commission. Presently, too, she found in Lysander a soldier and statesman who could ignore tradition, seize occasion when it offered, act on his own responsibility, and—very unlike most Spartans—was not to be bribed.

**POLITICAL DOCUMENT CARVED IN STONE**

After the disaster of Aegospotami in 405, Athens had no friend but the democracy of Samos, which offered to help her to continue the war with Sparta. The treaty arranged between the two states was engraved on this marble block, decorated with their patron goddesses, Athena and Hera, on the Acropolis.

*Acropolis Museum, Athens*

ALCIBIADES, having fallen out with the Spartans, and possibly aiming to make himself tyrant, was intriguing at Athens for his own restoration as a chief of the democrats ; the satraps intrigued against each other with Alcibiades or Lysander. The one constant factor is the association of Sparta with one or both of the Persian governors, who intended through her to recover effective dominion in Ionia ; and the most surprising feature is the extent to which Athens went on holding her own, in spite of her endless domestic dissensions, for close upon eight years, gaining one notable victory at Arginusae (406).

Unconquered she remained, maimed and weakened though she was, until the almost incredible carelessness of her naval commander in the Hellespont gave Lysander the chance which he was not the man to let slip, and practically her whole fleet was captured while the crews were on shore at Aegospotami in 405.

Athens without an effective fleet was helpless. By land and sea she was completely blockaded, and in 404 was reduced to unconditional surrender by starvation. It was only one of Sparta's rare momentary flashes of generosity that saved her from the utter obliteration to which the vindictive wrath of her Peloponnesian rivals would have condemned her. Sparta could afford to be generous when generosity did not endanger her political hegemony; she could afford to remember that Hellas owed much to Athens, now that the Athenian Empire was gone beyond recall. The Long Walls were pulled down; but Athens, humiliated, exhausted and shorn of her dependencies, still survived as an independent state, with an inherent power of recuperation which ere long enabled her to resume her position among the leaders of Hellas.

### Persian Interference in Greek Affairs

THE interest of Persia in Hellenic affairs, which had slumbered since the Peace of Callias, in 447, was revived by the disastrous end of the Sicilian expedition. With the Aegean closed to her by the sea power of Athens she had been content to leave her turbulent neighbours to their own devices. Since the suppression of that Egyptian revolt in which Athens had played an unfortunate part, peace had reigned throughout the vast empire under the mild rule of Artaxerxes I. In 424, after his death and the assassination of his son Xerxes II, Darius (II) Nothus succeeded. Tentative suggestions for alliance were made to him by both sides in the Hellenic war, but he was not tempted to intervene. Athens was still mistress of the seas.

In 412, however, the situation, as we have seen, was changed. The possibility was opened to the Peloponnesians of challenging Athens on her own element. The satraps, though responsible to the Great King, enjoyed almost unrestricted liberty of independent action. The government reasserted the claim, long in abeyance, to tribute from the Ionian cities, and entered upon willing negotiations with the complaisant Spartans who, for the overthrow of Athens, were quite

ready to betray the pan-Hellenic cause; and it was largely through the financial and political co-operation of the satraps that Lysander was able in 405 to crush the stubborn resistance of Athens at the price of Ionian freedom.

On the fall of Athens, Sparta set up a tyranny (in the modern sense) of her own in the states which had formed the Athenian Empire, on lines devised and organized by Lysander. The effective government was put in the hands of Spartan officers ('harmosts') who ruled with a rod of iron, infinitely more oppressive than the 'slavery' she was professedly abolishing, and resting solely on the irresistible force at her command. She was possessed now with a lust of empire, though the whole system upon which her prestige had been built up was incompatible with the extension of her dominion beyond the Peloponnese.

Precisely at this moment occurred a remarkable crisis in the history of the Persian empire.

Darius Nothus had two sons. The elder, Artaxerxes (known as 'Longimanus'), was his destined successor on the throne, to which however the younger, Cyrus, also aspired. Darius, seeing the obvious dissensions and jealousy between the satraps Tissaphernes and Pharnabazus, had sent his younger son, a prince of brilliant ability, to the West to watch and really to supersede both.

### The March of the Ten Thousand

CYRUS had been quick to grasp the immense superiority of the Greek soldiery over the best of Oriental levies. He had established close personal relations with Lysander, whom he had even left as his lieutenant in his own province during a temporary absence. And he had probably already resolved to seize the throne by the aid of his Greek friends, when his father died in 404 and Artaxerxes II became king at a moment when the hill-men in the remote interior were causing trouble. Cyrus, in collusion with Sparta, collected a strong force of Greek soldiers of fortune, of whom large numbers were available owing to the termination of the war, ostensibly for the suppression of the insurgents in Pisidia (once a centre of Hittite power) ; with these he marched inland, and then made known to them his real purpose. This was the famous Anabasis, the ' Going up ' to Susa, the immortal tale whereof was recorded in the matter-of-fact prose of one of the chief actors in the adventure, the Athenian Xenophon.

The adventure failed only because, on the way to Babylon, in the very moment of what should have been decisive victory at Cunaxa, won by the prowess and discipline of the Greeks over immensely superior numbers, Cyrus himself, in hot pursuit of his brother, was cut down and slain on the field. When Cyrus fell there was nothing more to fight for. If he had won, Persia would have been carried out of her lethargy by a king of such enterprising ability as she had not known since the death of Darius the Great. There is no limit to speculation on the possible results.

But Cyrus was slain, and the Ten Thousand Greeks, whom the Persians dared not attack directly, elected Xenophon to command them, and made their perilous and famous retreat, having learnt the lesson to which seventy years later Alexander was to give such tremendous effect—that Persia was penetrable, and that eastern armies stood no chance against the disciplined spearmen of the West.

**KNIGHT WHO SERVED AGAINST SPARTA**

The presence of Athenian contingents in the Corinthian army operating against Sparta in 394 is commemorated by this cenotaph erected at Athens as a tribute to Dexileos, who was killed at the battle of Corinth, a Spartan victory. He was one of five knights—the others are anonymous—celebrated for their heroism.

*From Percy Gardner, ' Sculptured Tombs of Hellas '*

ON the fall of Cyrus the satraps of Dascylium and Sardis again dominated the West. Sparta, implicated in the great adventure, had broken with both of them. But in Hellas she had set out to establish in practice her own despotic authority, not only in her own dominions proper and in those which had been transferred to her from the Athenian Empire, but—in fact if not in form—among her own allies. Her ambitions soon drew her into war, not so much with Persia as with the satraps. The conduct of that war passed in 396 into the hands of a new king, Agesilaus, who had dreams of a conquest, though he had neither the means nor the ability to set about it on a great scale.

Conon, the able Athenian admiral who had saved a remnant of the Athenian fleet from the disaster of Aegospotami, had taken refuge in Cyprus with Evagoras, tyrant of Salamis by grace of the Great King. He was now placed in command of the Persian fleet, having nothing so much at heart as the humiliation of Sparta ; who could no longer retain her very recent and unaccustomed rôle as mistress of the Aegean. Athens was rapidly recovering, owing largely to the moderation and freedom from party spirit of the leaders of the restored democracy. Corinth and Thebes, Sparta's old allies, were now seething with indignation at her.

ℑN 395 open war broke out between Thebes and Sparta ; next year she found herself faced by a coalition of Thebes, Athens, Corinth, Argos and other states, and was penned in the Peloponnesus. The Persian fleet under its Athenian commander won a decisive victory at Cnidus ; and Conon, accompanied by Pharnabazus, paid a visit to Athens, whose recovery was thereupon celebrated and confirmed by the restoration of the Long Walls. Corinth succeeded in holding the barrier of the Isthmus, largely owing to the skill with which Iphicrates, an Athenian soldier of original genius, reorganized and re-armed the light troops, known as ' pel-tasts,' hitherto a merely subsidiary force, as a new and highly efficient military arm.

Incidentally the inherent weakness of the Persian system had been revealed not only by the march of the Ten Thousand but by the successful breaking away of Egypt, always restive under foreign rule. This probably took place about the time of the death of Darius II, with which it was doubtless connected. It is evident that the successive kings at Susa neither exercised sufficient control over the great satraps nor gave them sufficient support when the authority of the government was at stake. The Greeks, however, were so divided among themselves that they failed to take advantage of the position, and were each and all ready for an alliance with the Persian by which their own individual interests might be furthered.

### Effects of the ' Persian Peace '

Ⓐ CCORDINGLY we now find Sparta, hard pressed by the new confederacy, changing her anti-Persian policy, and, in her own interest, bringing in the Great King as arbiter in the Greek quarrel—and the confederates bowing to his dictation. The diplomacy of the Spartan Antalcidas brought about, in 386, the peace which bears his name, the ' Peace sent down by the King.' Artaxerxes claimed for Persia all the cities and lands in Asia, with Cyprus. Of the islands, Lemnos, Imbros and Scyros were appropriated to Athens ; the rest were to enjoy autonomy, as were all other Greek states—which involved the overthrow of the Theban supremacy in Boeotia. The treaty involved also the desertion by Athens of her ally Evagoras of Cyprus, who was waging a valiant struggle for independence. Sparta's pre-war subjects were still her subjects.

Practically the peace meant that Sparta had a free hand for the establishment of ' autonomy ' ; and that, as interpreted by her, meant the suppression of all leagues, and of democracies. She used her power —for to the Great King she was now his trusted agent—to suppress the Olynthian or Chalcidian League, which might otherwise have become an invaluable barrier to the aggression of the rising power of Macedon. Incidentally, by an act of gross treachery in collusion with a party in Thebes, she used it to establish her own friends in power, with a Lacedaemonian garrison in the Theban citadel, the Cadmeia, to keep them there, while most of the prominent patriots escaped to Athens, which refused to surrender them.

It was a fatal blunder. In 379-8 a very daring plot was

**EMBLEM OF ATHENS' REVIVED STRENGTH**

The fortifications of the Piraeus were largely demolished at the end of the Peloponnesian war, but were restored after the triumphant return of Conon from his victory over Sparta at Cnidus. The stonework of this section of the walls indicates how thoroughly Conon's masons carried out their work.

*From Weller, 'Athens and its Monuments'*

**MASSIVE COAST DEFENCES**

The heights of the peninsula of Acte overlooked two harbours of the Piraeus, and were
accordingly fortified with a wall, some 12 feet
high by 26 feet thick, and nearly sixty towers—
equally strong, as this ruined example shows.

*From Weller, ' Athens and its Monuments '*

organized by the exiled Pelopidas. The
oligarchs were assassinated, the city rallied
to the conspirators, and the great Spartan
garrison was only allowed to withdraw.
For a brief and glorious hour sluggard
Thebes displays in herself, or at least in the
person of her greatest citizen Epaminondas,
the quintessence of the finest qualities of
the Hellenic race. A fervent patriot,
he yet never set the interests of Thebes
above the welfare of Hellas ; neither
party spirit nor personal ambition ever
moved him ; we seem in him suddenly to
come upon that rare being, the man of
genius and the perfect knight in one.
From his military genius young
Philip of Macedon learnt lessons in the art of war which his
own wit and the still greater
genius of his son were to turn
to full account.

To Epaminondas, acting
politically with his warmest
friend Pelopidas, and as the
head of the Theban armies in
the field, it was given to overthrow the Spartan tyranny,
and to raise Thebes to the
hegemony of Hellas, as the
result of his victory at Leuctra
in 371. But he fell in the very
moment of another decisive
victory on the field of
Mantinea in 362, two years
after the death of Pelopidas

on the field of Cynoscephalae ; and the
loss of those two great men left Thebes
unfitted for the position she had won. The
future lay with none of the cities of
Greece, not with Thebes or Sparta or
Athens, for all had been found wanting
in something, but with the state which
all had hitherto held in contempt as semi-
barbaric or doubtfully Hellenic despite the
pretensions of her dynasts—Macedon.

While the prospects of union in Greece
were growing ever more remote, and
Greek states were vying with one another
in seeking support from Persia, which was
itself moving less palpably but not less
surely on the path of disintegration, the
activity of the Graeco-Phoenician struggle
revived in the west ; and Syracuse was
attaining such an ascendancy that intelligent anticipation might more readily
have fixed upon her than on Macedon as
destined to dominate the Hellenic world.

SYRACUSE, led by Hermocrates, the
champion of the doctrine of Sicilian
aloofness from the rivalries and from the
intervention of Greece proper, had broken
the power of Athens with the aid of the
Spartan Gylippus. But the struggle had
exhausted her. Carthage found her opportunity in an appeal from Segesta against
Selinus, the Athenian intervention in that
quarrel having come to nothing. She
swooped suddenly upon Selinus and then

**WHERE STOOD AN IMPORTANT GATEWAY**

From the land side, the Piraeus could only be entered by gates
set in the engirdling wall ; the most important was the Asty
Gate, through which passed the main road from Athens. Here
we see the fragmentary remains of one of the twin flanking
towers that guarded each gate in case of attack.

*Photo, Deutsches Archaeologisches Institut*

on Himera.    Aid from Syracuse, whence
Hermocrates had been ejected by the
extreme democrats, arrived too late, and
both cities were ruined.

Hermocrates, still excluded from Syracuse, raised what might be called a ' free
company ' of Sicilian patriots, occupied
the ruins of Selinus, and waged war on the
Carthaginians on his own account ;   but
he was killed in attempting to return to
Syracuse by force in 408.   The partisan
war he had carried on from Selinus gave
the Carthaginians   excuse   for   another
invasion ;    and they captured Acragas
after a stubborn defence, in which no very
creditable part was played by Syracuse.
Incidentally, we find a band of Italian
mercenaries from Campania in the service
of Acragas, which was now apparently
destined to be the base for a Carthaginian
conquest of Sicily.

### Rise and Policy of Dionysius

THE   misconduct   of   the   Syracusan
generals provided an opportunity for
Dionysius, a former partisan of the slain
Hermocrates, who had distinguished himself in the fighting at Acragas. By attacking
the generals, he procured for himself the
supreme   military   command,   which   he
used to establish himself as tyrant, though
his unscrupulous despotism was exercised
without abrogation of constitutional forms.
Actually his first move was to make a
treaty with the Carthaginian Himilco,
which   in   effect   surrendered   half   the
island to him, but in return for a Carthaginian guarantee of his own position as
lord of Syracuse.   This however was only
a preliminary step.    He must be secure
master of Syracuse before he could do anything more.   But the mastery of Syracuse
was only a beginning.

For some years Dionysius was the very
good friend of Carthage—while he was
defeating   domestic   conspiracies   against
his own power and bringing eastern Sicily
into his grip.   Then he dropped the mask,
and renewed the conflict with the Punic
power.   In Sicily the attitude to military
despotism that prevailed all over Hellas
was modified by the plain fact that the
last liberator from the Carthaginian menace
had been Gelon, the tyrant of Syracuse ;

only a soldier wielding despotic powers
could again deliver Sicily from that menace,
and the abilities of Dionysius were equal
to the task.    To his genius was due a
quite unprecedented development of engineering operations in the conduct of war,
coupled with a systematic avoidance of
pitched battles ;    though when occasion
demanded a direct encounter he could
display high tactical skill.

In his first Carthaginian war (398 to
392), he pinned the Carthaginians into the
western corner of the island, though he
deliberately refrained from crushing them
completely.   It suited him to make Syracuse and Sicily feel that the enemy was
there, and that so long as she was there
they dare not dispense with him, that his
dictatorship was necessary to their security.   And he was politic enough to abstain
from any personal vindictiveness or wanton maltreatment of enemies or subjects ;
not out of magnanimity, but because he
recognized that it was good business.

### The Dominions of Syracuse

HAVING made his settlement satisfactorily with Carthage, Dionysius set
about the extension of his dominion over
Hellenic states on the mainland.   The gate
of Italy was Rhegium, which fell to him
after a long siege.    Against other cities
he allied himself with Italian tribes of
Lucania, and many of them he won over
by an act of calculated magnanimity.
Having trapped a large force, he compelled
it to surrender unconditionally, and then
allowed it to go free without ransom.   He
went on to plant outposts which were at
once garrisons and trading stations on the
Adriatic coast of Italy, with a shrewd eye
to commercial development.    When he
died in 367 he was a potentate far more
powerful than any other Greek state.

At its greatest extent, the dominion of
Dionysius included almost all Sicily, outside the reach of the Carthaginian strongholds in the west, and of them he destroyed Motya, one of the older cities, so
completely that the enemy had to replace
it by the more famous fortress of Lily-
baeum, across the bay.   It extended along
the south coast of Italy to include Tarentum, all the ' heel,' the Adriatic coast as

far as the spur of Mount Garganus and, beyond this, the principal ports, Ancona and Hadria. East of the Adriatic he held strong ports around Issa, and had a working agreement with the Molossians between Corcyra and Thessaly. Some of these regions—for the most part the nearer—were governed by Syracuse or its ruler directly ; others, free internally, had their foreign policy controlled ; others again were occupied by communities of veteran mercenaries, which in some respects resemble the Roman colonies.

From the great fortress of Syracuse this empire was ruled and defended with large mercenary forces, an efficient fleet of new-model ships and every kind of military device, more especially the first batteries of stone-throwing machines. The expenses were enormous, taxation heavy and other financial devices unscrupulous : base coinage, raids on temple treasures and the like. The paramount necessity of conserving his own position at the head of affairs made Dionysius regardless of Greek interests or aspirations which crossed his own, and he did little in detail for the spread of Greek influence or ideas. His service to the Greeks was more elementary,

and at the same time more indispensable ; for at all events he kept the Carthaginians at bay for more than a generation, and he created for Syracuse a position, and—what was more—a prestige, which made it possible for more than one of its later rulers to repeat, in a measure, his unification of Greek interests and resources, and give the western cities a consciousness of a common destiny which was to lighten eventually the task of Rome.

### Contemporary Events in Italy

BUT his empire was the child of his personality. His dynasty and his system had no roots in the past. His heir, Dionysius II, would have had great possibilities before him, had he not been of another calibre. But he lacked his father's qualities ; and between his incapacity and the idealism of Dion, the minister left him by the great tyrant, the tyrant's empire went to pieces in a few years.

Meanwhile, the city on the Tiber, Rome, was moving along the path which was to carry her step by step to a goal undreamed of as yet by her. She was not consciously seeking dominion. Probably dominion would have come to her much

### MASTERPIECE OF FORTIFICATION BY SYRACUSAN ENGINEERS

To secure his military power Dionysius made the ramparts of Syracuse extraordinarily formidable, while the key fortress of Epipolae, planned by the great Archimedes, was unique in its strength. Built on a rocky height, its walls were massive enough to resist heavy missiles, while its war-engines were the most efficient then known. Above, a sally port in one of the three fosses cut in the solid rock to guard the way of approach ; in the background are piers that supported a drawbridge.

more rapidly, though in other guise perhaps, if she had not broken free from her Etruscan despots.

Her revolt had made her the champion of Latinism against both Etruscans and Sabellian or Oscan hill-men, of whom the most prominent were at this time Aequians on the north and Volscians on the south-east of the plain of Latium, where the Latin cities were her natural but jealous allies. Consequently she is perpetually at war, attacked by or attacking her Etruscan neighbour Veii, or the Volscians or Aequians, or an occasional Latin foe; while the Hernicans, wedged between Aequians and Volscians, and, like the Latins, threatened by both, prefer her alliance.

When the Etruscan sea power was shattered by Hieron of Syracuse at Cumae the menace from Etruria was so much weakened that for nearly forty years there was no war with Veii. The Aequian and Volscian powers were broken; in all the wars of the fifth century the balance of victory is with Rome and her allies. Usually this involved a cession of territory to the victors, the lion's share going in effect to Rome, whose strength constantly increased relatively to the other cities of Latium; the relation of the cities of the Latin League to Rome being not unlike those of the sixth-century Peloponnesian League to Sparta —they are not each other's allies but hers, and the command of the allied forces passes into her hands. She becomes in fact all but mistress of Latium before the fifth century is ended; the cities remain autonomous, but they are subject to her suzerainty.

**GREEK-ARMED SAMNITE RAIDER**

Naturally bold and determined fighters, the Samnites, Sabellian hill-men, became a serious danger to the Latin cities when they adopted Greek arms.

*The Louvre*

A final war with Veii ended with definite conquest (396) which added a great area on the west of the Tiber to Roman territory. The decisive victory was in part due to the pressure on Etruria of a new enemy, the Gauls, who by this time had completely overrun the basin of the Po and were now penetrating through the Apennines into Etruria itself. The Etruscans had also been driven out of their possessions in Campania, south-east of Latium, by the Samnites descending from the hills; of whom this first group, having made themselves masters of the Campanian plains, presently lost the sterner qualities of their mountain kinsmen, until their chief city of Capua became a byword for softness and luxury.

When Veii fell, Etruria was already being submerged by the Celtic flood. Six years later (390) it burst into Rome itself. Legends afterwards accumulated about that invasion; of the barbarians who broke into the Senate House and were awe-stricken by the sublime dignity of the silent seated senators; of the attempt to surprise the Capitol, frustrated by the startled cackling of the sacred geese; of the huge ransom that was being weighed out when the Gallic chief Brennus tossed his sword into the scale with the words 'Vae victis,' Woe to the vanquished; of the sensational deliverance wrought by the hero Camillus, the conqueror of Veii. The definite fact which survives is that the Gauls, having swept devastatingly over Etruria, poured into Rome, sacked it, and then rolled back to the north.

Etruria never recovered from the blow ; Rome reeled under it. Aequians and Volscians, joined even by some of the dependent allies, seized the moment to make a last desperate stroke for the breaking of the Roman ascendancy, only to be themselves finally broken by her indomitable tenacity (389). The Latin League was reorganized in a form which made it even more dependent on Rome than before ; its chief city, Tusculum, was absorbed, while her people received full Roman citizenship (380). Rome was queen of all Latium from the hills to the Mediterranean, from the borders of Campania to the Tiber, and had finally brought under her sway a substantial section of Etruria. And it was precisely at this moment that the long struggle between Patricians and Plebeians, the Old Aristocracy of birth and the free Commons, was definitely decided in favour of the plebs by the abolition of the privileges which restricted administrative offices to men of patrician birth.

## Political Development of Rome

WE have already noted that when Rome expelled her kings her government was in the hands of a close aristocracy, who alone held the executive offices or magistracies and exercised priestly functions. They alone had the power of initiating legislation in the Popular Assembly, the Comitia Centuriata, which passed it ; the voting therein being so arranged that its decisions were practically under patrician control. The patricians had so far misused their power that the plebs had been driven to wring from them the appointment of Tribunes, who, without being magistrates, had powers of intervention to prevent arbitrary action by magistrates—meant only as a defensive step. The tribunate was a clumsy enough device, especially as its intervention could be called into play capriciously.

Moreover, the patricians not only administered the law ; the magistrates themselves were the only authority who could declare what the law was. The next demand was for a published written code. In 451 a commission of ten, the Decemviri, was appointed as an interim government charged with the drawing up of the code, which was afterwards known as the Twelve Tables. The decemvirate was renewed, attempted to establish itself as a permanent oligarchy, and was overthrown in the popular revolt to which tradition attached the tragic legend of Virginia.

### The Battle of the Orders

NOW the battle of the orders was two-fold. The wealthier influential commoners resented the social and political privileges of the patrician families and their own corresponding disabilities ; the poorer felt only that the law was being consistently wrested to their detriment for the convenience of patricians, especially the laws under which lands owned or acquired by the state, the ' ager publicus,' were distributed. The plebs united to demand reform in both directions, but had no machinery to give effect to its wishes except the clumsy tribunate and the emphasising of popular sentiment in the formal resolutions—which had no force except as mere expressions of opinion—of its own assemblies.

The patricians found it at least politic to make occasional concessions—often indeed such that their expected effect could be practically evaded. As early as 445 they were obliged to legalise marriage between patrician and plebeian ; but they fought to the last against admitting plebeians to the magistracies. In fact, it was only when the old warrior Camillus, the hero of aristocratic conservatism, realized that it was no use to keep up the struggle against the inevitable, that the measure known as the Licinian Rogations, combining the agrarian and constitutional demands of the plebs, was passed in 367. The agrarian part of it was too easily evaded to be effective in the long run : but the enactment that thenceforth one of the consuls must be a plebeian was the death-blow to the privileges of the old aristocracy.

It was in the same year, as we have seen, that the great tyrant of Syracuse died, leaving to his son the empire which at the moment seemed destined to dominate Italy, a more mighty power than the expanding Republic on the Tiber. But the future lay with the Republic.

| B.C. | *Rome and the West* | *Greece and the East* | B.C. |
|---|---|---|---|
| | | Death of the Thracian King Cotys. | 360 |
| | | *Persia:* Artaxerxes III Ochus succeeds Artaxerxes II. | |
| | | Philip II usurps Macedonian crown. | 358 |
| 357 | Dionysius expelled from Syracuse. | Philip captures Amphipolis. | 357 |
| | | Revolts of Athenian allies. The Social War. | |
| 356 | Five years' war between Rome and Etruscans begins. | Phocians seize Delphi. Sacred War begins. | 356 |
| | | Philip takes Potidaea. Birth of Alexander the Great. | 355 |
| 354 | Roman alliance with the Samnites. | End of Social War. | 354 |
| 353 | Hipparinus tyrant at Syracuse. | | |
| 351 | Forty years' truce with Etruscans. | *Persia:* Revolt of Phoenicia and Cyprus. | 351 |
| 350 | Gallic war with Rome. | Philip takes Chalcidice. Athens and Olynthus allied. | 349 |
| 348 | Second (?) Treaty of Rome and Carthage. | Capture of Olynthus by Philip. | 348 |
| | | First Athenian embassy to Philip. | 347 |
| | | Death of Plato. | |
| 346 | Dionysius returns to Syracuse. | Peace of Philocrates. Philip crushes the Phocians. | 346 |
| 344 | Timoleon arrives in Sicily. Battle of Hadranum. | *Persia:* Artaxerxes recovers Egypt. | 345 |
| | Archidamus of Sparta in South Italy. | | |
| 343 | Dionysius finally leaves Syracuse. | | |
| 343-1 | First Roman-Samnite War. | Conquest of Thrace by Philip. | 342 |
| 341 | Peace and alliance with Samnites. | | |
| 340 | Beginning of the Great Latin War. | Naval reconstruction at Athens. | 340 |
| 339 | Timoleon defeats Carthaginians on the Crimesus. | Sacred War against Amphissa. | 339 |
| | Publilian Laws confirm powers of Roman Plebs. | | |
| 338 | Dissolution of the Latin League. | Chaeronea. Congress of Corinth names Philip General. | 338 |
| | Death of Archidamus in Italy. | *Persia:* Death of Artaxerxes Ochus; Arses the usurper. | |
| 337 | Death of Timoleon. | Assassination of Philip. | 336 |
| | | Accession of Alexander, and of Darius III. | |
| | | Alexander destroys Thebes. | 335 |
| | | Aristotle at Athens. | |
| 334 | Alexander the Molossian (of Epirus) in South Italy. | Alexander invades Persia: Battle of the Granicus. | 334 |
| | | Battle of Issus; rout of Darius. | 333 |
| | | Siege and capture of Tyre. Alexander in Egypt. | 332 |
| | | Alexandria founded. Persian campaign renewed. | 331 |
| | | Battle of Gaugamela (Oct.). Fall of Susa (Dec.). | |
| | | Alexander at Ecbatana (Mar.). Darius killed (June). | 330 |
| | | Alexander conquers Arachosia. | 329 |
| 329 | Death of Alexander the Molossian. | Conquest of Bactria and Sogdiana. | 328 |
| | | Alexander marries Roxana. The Chitral campaign. | 327 |
| 327 | Second or Great Samnite War begins (to 304). | Invasion of the Punjab and defeat of Porus. | 326 |
| | | Capture of Multan. Voyage of Nearchus. | 325 |
| | | Alexander at Ecbatana. Harpalus at Athens. | 324 |
| | | Death of Alexander at Babylon (June). | 323 |
| | | Greek revolt (Lamian War) against Antipater. | |
| | | Lamian War ended by battle of Crannon. | 322 |
| | | Deaths of Demosthenes and Aristotle. | |
| | | *India:* Chandragupta (Sandracottys) expels the Macedonians and founds Maurya empire. | |
| | | Death of Perdiccas. Antipater (Macedon) becomes Imperial Regent; Asia to Antigonus and Seleucus; Egypt to Ptolemy Soter. | 321 |
| 321 | Samnites trap Roman army at Caudine Forks. Rome renounces the capitulation; war rages doubtfully for seven years. | Polysperchon succeeds Antipater as Regent. | 318 |
| | | Cassander, son of Antipater, raises war against Polysperchon. Deaths of Phocion and Philip Arrhidaeus. Athens submits to Cassander. | 317 |
| 317 | Agathocles tyrant of Syracuse. | | |
| | | Cassander takes Pydna and kills Olympias. | 316 |
| | | Coalition against Antigonus. Five years war. | 315 |
| 314 | Tide begins to set against Samnites. | The Diadochi come to terms; war suspended. | 311 |
| 311 | Etruscans join Samnites. | War renewed between Ptolemy and Antigonus. | 310 |
| 310 | Agathocles, defeated in Sicily, invades Africa. Romans defeat Etruscans at Lake Vadimo. | | |
| 309 | Roman successes against Samnites and Etruscans. | Demetrius Poliorcetes, son of Antigonus, at Athens. | 307 |
| 307 | Agathocles returns to Sicily. | Demetrius defeats Ptolemy's fleet off Cyprus. | 306 |
| 306 | Treaties of Rome with Carthage and Rhodes. Hernicans join the Samnites. | Epicurus and Zeno (Stoic) at Athens. Demetrius attacks Rhodes. | 305 |
| 305 | Capture of Bovianum (Samnite capital). | *India:* Unsuccessful invasion by Seleucus. | |
| 304 | Samnites accept an honourable peace. | Antigonus killed at Battle of Ipsus. | 301 |
| | | *India:* Embassy of Megasthenes to Chandragupta. | 302 |
| 299 | Designs of Agathocles on S. Italy. | Bindusara succeeds Chandragupta. | 298 |
| 298 | Third Samnite (and Etruscan) War (to 290). | Death of Cassander. | 297 |
| | | Independent kingdom of Bithynia (Ziprites). | |
| 295 | Roman victory at Sentinum. | Demetrius king of Macedon. | 294 |
| 294 | Samnite war; Etruscans withdraw. | | |
| 292 | Defeat and death of the Samnite Pontius. | | |
| 290 | Treaty of peace between Rome and Samnites. | | |
| 289 | Rome aids Thurii against Lucanians. | | |
| | Death of Agathocles. | | |
| 287 | Hortensian Law at Rome finally confirms the legislative powers of the Plebeian Assembly. | Demetrius expelled from Macedon by Pyrrhus and Lysimachus, who then expels Pyrrhus. | 287 |
| | | Demetrius gives himself up to Seleucus. | 286 |
| | | Ptolemy II Philadelphus joint king of Egypt. | 285 |
| 285 | War with Gauls and Etruscans. | | |
| 284 | Roman disaster at Arretium. | Deaths of Ptolemy I and Demetrius. | 283 |
| 283 | Roman victory over Boii at Lake Vadimo. | | |
| 282 | Peace with Boii for forty-five years. | | |
| | Breach between Rome and Tarentum. | Seleucus overthrows Lysimachus at Corupedium. | 281 |
| 281 | War declared with Tarentum, which calls in Pyrrhus. | Ptolemy Ceraunus murders Seleucus, and seizes the Macedonian crown. Antiochus I king of Syria. | 280 |
| 280 | Pyrrhus in S. Italy. | Gauls invade Thrace. Death of Ptol. Ceraunus. | |
| | | Achaean League inaugurated. | |

# THE HELLENISTIC AGE:
## 360–280 B.C.

**F**OR a hundred years since the rise of Pericles to power at Athens, about 460, the struggle between Europe and Asia had been in abeyance, when Artaxerxes II (Mnemon) died (359 B.C.). Throughout that period the great empire organized by Darius the Great was tending slowly but surely to disruption. But Hellas was no nearer to unity than she had been a century before.

The dream of Pericles—if indeed we are right in thinking that he had dreamed it—of a mighty Hellas united through the moral and intellectual ascendancy of the city he idealised, had been dissolved by the internecine rivalries of the Greek states, and by the subordination of the pan-Hellenic idea to the individualist imperialism of Athens or Sparta or, finally, Thebes. In the west a great Hellenic power had arisen, but its might depended wholly on the genius of the man who had created it, Dionysius of Syracuse, and it hardly outlived his death. Hellenism was to permeate the world, not to conquer it.

Yet a conquest altogether unsuspected was near at hand, which was to be a mighty instrument for that permeation. Before another generation had passed, Europe was hurling herself upon Asia under the leadership of a power which posed at least as the champion of Hellenism, though itself, in the eyes of Hellas, scarcely half Hellenic. It shattered the old Persian Empire for ever. It carried Hellenism into the heart of Orientalism. It created a new empire vast beyond all previous vision, though one whose unity scarcely survived its creator, because he left no heir; and it changed the political order of the world.

This amazing achievement was the work of two men, Philip of Macedon and the son by whom his fame has been eclipsed, Alexander the Great.

Hitherto Macedon has made no more than an occasional appearance on the fringe of the story of Hellas. It lay beyond the northern border of Thessaly—the limit of continental Hellas, though Hellenic colonies fringed the north coast of the Aegean. The Thracians, east of the Chalcidian promontories and the river Strymon, and the Illyrians of the western highlands, ranked definitely as barbarians, not Hellenes. The Macedonians proper, though of Hellenic stock, were unacknowledged; but their dynasty, the antiquity of which was unquestionable, claimed Heraclid descent, and had been recognized as legitimate competitors in the pan-Hellenic Games. On the other hand, while the Macedonian king ruled his Macedonian subjects with the absolute authority of a clan chieftain, his kingship extended over Illyrian clans, among whose chieftains he was merely the high chief. Macedonia's political development had therefore hardly passed out of the tribal stage; her organization remained primitive, though her territory was far greater than that of any Hellenic state; but her people provided admirable material for a great military organizer.

### Awaiting the Man of Destiny

**S**UCH an organizer had not hitherto appeared; nor had Macedon been admitted to the comity of Hellas. When Xerxes poured his hosts into Greece her king Alexander had been among his vassals, though he had used his position to supply useful information to the Greeks. In the first stage of the Peloponnesian war we have seen another king, Perdiccas, fomenting troubles in the Chalcidian colonies in order to turn them to his own advantage. A successor had played his part first in fostering and then in wrecking the Chalcidian (Olynthian) League. But always the mainspring of Macedonia's activities had been not her Hellenic sympathies, but the pressure on her of the hill tribes of Paeonia on the north and Illyria on the west.

E*

Now in 368 when Thebes was advancing to the hegemony of Greece, a disputed succession and northern frontier troubles in Macedonia had enabled the rising power to force on Macedon an alliance, guaranteed by the presence in Thebes, actually though not nominally as hostages, of several youthful members of the Macedonian nobility, including Philip (382–336), the younger brother of the young king Perdiccas. For three or four years the boy dwelt in Thebes, learning everything that was to be learnt of statecraft and military craft in the city of Epaminondas and Pelopidas. Then he was allowed to return to his own country.

Four years later (359), Perdiccas was slain in battle with the Paeonians, leaving a child, Amyntas, on the throne, with his uncle Philip, who was then twenty-three,

as guardian or regent. The hour and the man had arrived.

Philip was endowed by nature with a frame of iron, a clear head, a cool and calculating brain, boundless ambition, dauntless resolution and—in full measure —those moral virtues which can always reconcile themselves to the dictates of expediency. He was an astute diplomatist, and his natural military genius had been trained in the school of Epaminondas, the greatest captain and organizer yet seen in Hellas. Thus equipped, he set himself forthwith to work out step by step the task his ambition had marked out for him. Macedon was a minor power ; she should be the greatest power in Hellas. Hellas had no leader, nor any state competent to lead her ; Macedon should be that state. And then—Persia should go down

MACEDONIAN SPHERE OF INFLUENCE IN EUROPE BEFORE ALEXANDER

It was by military conquest that Philip incorporated Illyria, Paeonia, Thrace and, last, Chalcidice in the kingdom of Macedonia. Diplomacy attached Epirus and Thessaly to his cause, and by his victory at Chaeronea he secured the hegemony of Hellas. After Philip's death Alexander crushed all Hellenic opposition and crossing the Hellespont proceeded with the conquest of Asia Minor.

before Hellas. Stage by stage Philip marched toward his goal ; the first stage being the making of Macedon.

Pretenders to the throne which he had not yet seized himself had to be removed ; a matter easily effected by cajoling their foreign supporters, including Athens, with illusory promises. Next, the Illyrians and Paeonians were to be dealt with ; Philip spent the winter in training a Macedonian force, with which next year he shattered both in pitched battles. He employed the tactical principles he had learnt from Epaminondas, but with a modification of his own, never practised by the Greeks, the use of heavy cavalry in shock tactics on the wings ; while his phalanx of spearmen was an improvement on the ordinary hoplite formation. The second victory gave him control of the Illyrian passes.

### Stages in Philip's Policy

**M**ONEY was the next necessity, for Macedonia was poor, her commerce being insignificant. But on the Thracian border there were unexploited mines. Again mainly by diplomatic cajolery, Philip possessed himself of those mines, from which he derived a larger revenue than any Greek state could boast ; though it involved the absorption of Amphipolis in defiance of Athenian resentment. Athens was defeated simply by his superior skill in the game of diplomatic trickery, while he was also cajoling Olynthus into acquiescence. This stage of his work he completed by quietly deposing his infant nephew and ward (who afterwards married one of his daughters) and assuming the crown ; and by organizing what might be called standing territorial regiments from his Illyrian highlanders—a material step towards producing a common national sentiment among his heterogeneous subjects.

The next stage was opened by an experimental intervention in the ' sacred war ' of Phocis, by way of asserting his Hellenic position. Phocis, hitherto a somewhat insignificant state, but always jealous of her powerful neighbour Thebes, had suddenly asserted and enforced a traditional but unrecognized claim to Delphi and the guardianship of its shrine. This claim made by Phocis was opposed by

## COIN OF AN EMPIRE BUILDER

Born 382 B.C., Philip II usurped the crown of Macedon in 359 and devoted his genius to the creation of a Macedonian army which should establish his supremacy in Greece and shatter the power of Persia. He was assassinated in 336 B.C.
*British Museum*

Thebes and by the Thessalians, but supported by Athens and Sparta, while her enemies charged her with sacrilege for turning to her own use the treasures of Apollo. Phocis bought over the powerful but unpopular tyrant of the Thessalian state of Pherae ; the rest of Thessaly appealed to Philip, who marched against Pherae with a small force, as the champion of the outraged deity.

The Phocians marched to aid their ally in superior force, defeated Philip, and compelled him to withdraw. He returned with a larger army and put them to rout ; but they were in possession of the pass of Thermopylae ; Athenians and Spartans came to their help, and Philip again retired. His hour had not yet come, and for some ⸱time he again devoted himself to extending and consolidating his power in the northern regions where the intention of his operations was less immediately conspicuous ; though they were alarming enough to those who suspected him of a desire to ' enslave ' Hellas.

Philip did not wish to enslave Hellas even to such an extent as the democratic imperialists of Athens or the Lacedaemonians at the height of their power. But he did want in the first place to make his own kingdom an irresistible power ; and whereas it had hitherto stood practically outside Hellas, he was determined that it should now be recognized not only as an integral part of Hellas, but as its leader and accepted champion. He seems to have had the same kind of sentimental reverence for Hellas, and especially for Athens, as in a later age was felt towards

Rome by the barbarian princes who deliberately elected to act as Lieutenants of the Empire instead of as conquerors. But it was only as the acknowledged head of Hellas that he could lead her to the great adventure to which not Athens nor Sparta nor Thebes was capable of leading her—the overthrow of Persia. To that end he must have the co-operation of Hellas, but no rivals.

Above all, he wanted the willing co-operation of Athens and her fleet ; and it would have been sound policy for Athens to have accepted the rôle of his honoured coadjutor, since she had proved herself incapable of holding the position of accepted leader. Unfortunately, there was in Athens a patriot party which dreamed impossibly of a Periclean revival and, seeing that its own aspirations were incompatible with Philip's, made a point of thwarting him, and convinced itself that his concealed aim was the ruin of Athens—actually the last thing he desired. This

party was led by an orator of extraordinary power, Demosthenes, in whose eyes the Macedonian menace was infinitely more important than Persian policy, and his impassioned rhetoric has done much to discredit very unduly the character and aims of the great Macedonian, whose actual treatment of Athens was always more than generous.

Philip now rapidly effected a partial conquest of Thrace—an apparent threat to the Chersonese and the Athenian command of the Propontis ; a serious matter for Athens, as she was largely dependent on corn supplies imported from those regions. But Philip did not attack the Chersonese ; his next objective was the Chalcidian peninsula. In 348 he captured Olynthus, Athens being prevented from effectively interfering by the revolt of Euboea.

### Philip Secures Hellenic Status

PEACE negotiations were then opened between Athens and Philip, who meant to carry out his programme of suppressing the sacrilegious Phocis and taking her place in the Amphictyonic Council, which might be called the official religious synod of Hellas. He was not at all afraid of Athens, but he was prepared to make large concessions to her to secure her good will and support. The terms of the Peace of Philocrates (346) were duly arranged, but before completion Demosthenes succeeded in breaking relations. Philip went on his way, pending the acceptance by Athens of a modified treaty ; but she could not make up her mind on a policy ; consequently Philip effected his object without her, suppressed Phocis, and became not only a member but president of the Amphictyonic Council. His Hellenic status was thus established. Athens was reduced to a sulky acquiescence (346).

Hellas, however, was still a long way from being reconciled to a Macedonian hegemony, and though Philip had shown unmistakable proofs of his power, and incidentally of his moderation, it was still not sufficiently consolidated to enable him to undertake the grand project of his ambitions. The incorporation of a loyal Thrace with his own kingdom was a necessary precaution. Internal dissen-

**PERFERVID ATHENIAN PATRIOT**

This portrait bust of the great Athenian orator and statesman Demosthenes (c. 385-322 B.C.) gives a clear impression of the dynamic personality which made him so formidable an obstacle in the way of Macedonian expansion.

*Ny Carlsberg Museum, Copenhagen*

sions in that region gave him his chance in 342, though the conquest, of the details of which we have no knowledge (except that Philip lost an eye in battle), must have put both his military and diplomatic powers to a severe test. In 341 Thrace became a part of the Macedonian kingdom. Within Hellas the Thessalian league had named him its president, and on the west of Thessaly his influence was supreme in the almost barbarian kingdom of Epirus, where he had established on the throne the brother of his Epirote wife Olympias.

Meanwhile, however, Demosthenes had been exerting his powers to the utmost to rouse animosity against him, not in Athens only, and in Athens against all politicians who inclined to the Macedonian alliance. The fever of suspicion was generally rife. In 340, Philip was reluctantly goaded into war.

Athens could not be threatened by sea, but her sea power could not work effective injury to Macedon, as to her Peloponnesian foes in the days of Pericles ; on the other hand, against Macedon in alliance with Thebes, Attica was by land entirely defenceless. Philip was in no haste to strike ; but the development of a sacred war on Amphissa, the ally of Thebes, by the Amphictyonic Council which called for Philip's support, brought him down to Boeotia with an army in 338, and simultaneously threw Thebes into the arms of Athens. The result was that he met the combined armies on the field of Chaeronea and put them completely to rout, the picked troops of Thebes alone remaining on the ground and fighting to the last.

YET the magnanimity of the victor shows how groundless were the denunciations of Demosthenes. Chaeronea gave the hegemony of Hellas to Macedon as indisputably as Leuctra had given it to Thebes. Philip was manifestly irresistible, but he did not proceed to the enslavement of Hellas ; he dealt with Thebes no more harshly than Sparta had dealt with her in the past, and Demosthenes himself admitted that his treatment of Athens was generous. But the situation differed from any that had existed before ; because Macedon was not a state with an Hellenic

**THE LION OF CHAERONEA**

On August 2, 338 B.C., Philip of Macedon routed the combined armies of Thebes and Athens at Chaeronea in Boeotia and destroyed the independence of Greece. This colossal lion, restored in 1902, marks the burial place of the Theban dead.

*Photo, E.N.A.*

tradition behind it, and was not a city state at all, but a great territorial despotic monarchy without parallel in Hellas.

Thebes, which had elected to desert the Macedonian alliance, was not unreasonably penalised. The Boeotian league was broken up and the independence of the cities restored. A Macedonian garrison occupied the Cadmeia, the citadel of Thebes, and the party that favoured Philip was installed in power. Sparta, which sulkily refused to join the Hellenic league designed by Philip for the overthrow of Persia, suffered the overrunning of Laconia and the transfer of some of her territory to former foes or subjects. From Athens Philip required no more than the Chersonese, the dissolution of what remained of her maritime league, and her entry into the new League of Hellas ; the Athenian prisoners taken at Chaeronea were restored without ransom.

At last the way was clear. Philip summoned a pan-Hellenic congress at Corinth ; all the states except the still sulky Sparta were represented. At the congress in 337 he declared his great project—the pan-Hellenic war, which had been impracticable for a divided Hellas, upon the Asiatic empire which had sought and would still seek to enslave Hellenes. The congress assented—it could hardly do otherwise—and settled upon ways and means with no great enthusiasm ; but it was enough for the man who would have the whole direction of the adventure, the grand ambition of his life, in his own hands.

### Assassination of Philip of Macedon

As a military organizer, as a strategist, as a commander in the field, Greece had never produced the superior of Philip, unless it were his unconscious master Epaminondas. As a matter of course he was made captain-general of the Hellenic forces with practically unlimited powers. For twelve months after the congress he was engaged in organization ; the fleet of Athens, though latterly her admirals had displayed no distinguished ability, commanded the Aegean. In the spring of 336 he dispatched the man whom he called his only general, Parmenio, to secure the passage of his armies into the north-western corner of Asia Minor ; in the summer he was on the very point of following with his main force when he was struck down by the hand of an assassin, probably the emissary or agent of his wronged and repudiated wife Olympias, the mother of his mighty son. For a moment the great expedition was deferred.

To the victor of Chaeronea unwilling Hellas had bowed the knee perforce ; more sore at being dominated by one imperious will than eager to do battle with the ancient foe at his bidding. Philip fell when he was in the plentitude of his powers, but no more than forty-six years old. His heir was a lad of twenty, who no doubt had shown his mettle at Chaeronea ; but everywhere Philip had

subjects, dependents or positive enemies who were ready enough to rise up against an untried youth whose title even to his own throne it was possible to dispute. In Athens and elsewhere the murder of Philip was hailed with premature acclamations. There were Thracian tribes eager to revolt, Illyrian tribes whom the fear of the dead man had curbed. Had there been even the briefest delay Alexander would have found himself in the centre of a general conflagration.

But the delay was not given. Before his enemies could combine, though not before they were in open revolt, he had swung his Macedonians down to the Thessalian border, outflanked the pass of Tempe, carved a road through the mounrains, and swept into the plain. Thessaly submitted without a blow. Athens made repentant overtures which were accepted without demur. The League made haste to appoint him captain-general in succession to his father.

### Destruction of Thebes by Alexander

The Thracian insurgents were dealt with in a swift campaign in the early summer of 335 ; but meanwhile the Illyrians were gathering to attack Macedonia. For a few weeks Alexander vanished in the Illyrian mountains. The rumour spread that he had been slain in Thrace ; an eye-witness of his fall was produced. Thebes gave the lead in revolting ; half Hellas was preparing to follow. But by movements of unparalleled audacity and swiftness Alexander and his Macedonians had in fact shattered the Illyrians, and even while Thebes still believed that he was dead, he appeared at her gates and summoned her to surrender. A hot-headed Macedonian captain seized an opportunity to break into the town without waiting for orders ; Alexander threw in supports ; the Thebans fought stubbornly but vainly, and the city suffered the common fate of cities carried by storm, although ' The great Emathian conqueror bade spare the house of Pindarus,' the famed poet of old. But the destruction of Thebes was the work of her age-long foes in Locris and Boeotia far more than of the Macedonians.

The smiting of Thebes sufficed. Every one else made prompt submission, and Alexander exacted no penalties. In spite of all, he chose to trust that magnanimity would be answered by loyalty. But it was fear, not loyalty, that held Hellenic jealousies in check. Fear, however, was so thoroughly established that in the next year, 334, Alexander could turn his back on Europe, and was over the Hellespont with the army of conquest. The great adventure of his adventurous career had begun.

The attack was fully expected in Persia. But the Great King's government had sunk back to its normal ineptitude under the amiable but futile Darius III Codomannus. For twenty years, while Philip was building up the Macedonian power, Artaxerxes III Ochus had ruled forcefully, reconquered Egypt, kept his satraps in awe, and permitted rather than maintained the general peace and prosperity of his empire.

Greek states had, indeed, seldom been ashamed to seek Persian aid in their private quarrels, and appeals were, of course, made to him against Macedon, but he did not care to precipitate a rupture with Philip, though it suited him well enough to have Greeks in his pay. In 338, however, he was slain by an assassin, like Philip, two years later ; Darius had secured the succession only in 336 and was, as we have seen, quite unfitted to save the empire.

## Opening of the Persian Campaign

ONEY had been sent to Greece ; but the defence of the west was left to the western satraps in joint and jealous association with an able Greek adventurer, Memnon of Rhodes. Alexander's task would have been made much harder if Memnon had been in supreme command. Alexander met and routed the army of the satraps on the river Granicus. The battle in its result had the effect of leaving Asia Minor open to conquest.

The mastery of Syria and Phoenicia was the next step. Having made Asia Minor sufficiently secure, Alexander struck through the ' Cilician gates,' the passage of the Taurus barrier, and spent some months in reducing Cilicia. Then he moved south. Meanwhile Darius had taken the field in person with a vast army, and was on the borders of Cilicia expecting his attack. At Issus (332) the Persian was decisively defeated and fled for his life behind the shelter of the river Euphrates.

## Alexander Advances to Babylon

NSTEAD of immediate pursuit Alexander went forward with the conquest she had immediately in view. When Tyre was won the whole navy of Persia was in his hands. Egypt in turn welcomed him as a deliverer. Not until 331, however, did he turn to complete the overthrow of Persia.

The battle of Gaugamela, some miles from the old Nineveh, was overwhelmingly decisive. Though again Darius escaped from the field with his life, for the little that remained of it he was no better than a fugitive hunted from one place to another.

The conqueror marched on to Babylon, which opened its gates to him. But Persia and Media, whence the empire of Cyrus had arisen, were still unsubdued, and Darius was still at large in his ancestral lands. It was in Alexander's view imperative to seize the royal residences, Susa and Ecbatana, and the political capital, Persepolis, which meant an advance by way of difficult and dangerous mountain passes.

Of such operations Alexander's early experiences in Illyria had made him a past master. Susa had already been occupied by an advance column, and in a winter campaign (331–30) he captured Persepolis and Pasargadae, the first home of the great Cyrus, together with vast treasures, including spoils which Xerxes had carried off from Athens and which were now by this happy stroke restored to her.

Even now he gave Darius and the Persian loyalists time to offer submission before advancing on Ecbatana. But they were determined to offer a final resistance. When the blow could no longer be delayed, he struck with his wonted swiftness ; but when he reached Ecbatana, the heart of Darius had failed him, and he was already in full flight. Alexander was soon in hot pursuit ; but before he could overtake the fugitive, treachery was at work, and the fallen monarch was murdered by Bessus, satrap of Bactria (July, 330).

### Achaemenid Empire Overthrown

THE Macedonian, or as he himself would have said the Hellene, had taken the place so long held by the Persian. Politically he followed, though with a difference, the precedents established by the great Cyrus and Darius, not by a Tiglath-pileser or a Nebuchadrezzar ; he conquered not to enslave but to incorporate and develop ; fostering and even reviving, local traditions and customs, and installing native administrators wherever it was reasonably safe to do so, never penalising loyalty to his defeated antagonist, however sternly he might deal with Hellenic renegades. His foundation of Alexandria in Egypt was only the most distinguished example of a definite and statesmanlike policy, and his selection of its site as the world's central mart was in itself a mark of genius.

But there was more to be done besides the overthrow of the Achaemenid, whose ineffective rule over the wilder regions east and south-east must be made effective. The conquest of Persia, Persia proper, had begotten new imaginations. The very dissolution of the immemorial barriers between Hellene and Barbarian, the actual amalgamation of East and West, would seem to have become from this time more and more an integral part of Alexander's incredible dream.

Persia was won, but the eastern provinces or—what came to the same thing— their satraps, who had conspired to murder Darius, were in revolt. Their intention had been to set Bessus, who called himself Artaxerxes, in the place of their victim. Alexander started on his far eastern campaigns with the double object of establishing his sway over the whole empire and avenging the murder of his royal predecessor. On his march, which was in the nature of an armed exploration in regions of which little was known, there were risky adventures, astonishing marching feats, and brilliant exploits ; but there

was no foe who could make a stand against his army. He penetrated Afghanistan, struck north through the Hindu Kush into Turkistan, captured Bessus, who died the death of an oriental traitor (crucifixion, preceded by mutilation), and thrust beyond the bounds of the empire across the Oxus (Amu Daria) to Samarkand. On the way new Alexandrias arose, meant to be the centres of a new civilization ; Herat, Kandahar and Kabul are among the probable sites. He planted his extreme outpost, Alexandria Eschatê, ' Farthest Alexandria,' on the banks of the Jaxartes (at Khojend). Before he had completed the subjugation, he captured the Scythian chief Oxyartes, with his daughter, the famous Roxana, whom Alexander wedded according to the Scythian rite : the most conspicuous method possible of illustrating in his own person the cosmopolitan theories he was so anxious to impress upon the Macedonians.

### Alexander's Conquest of the Punjab

THERE still remained unvisited and unsubdued one dim region, ' India,' over which the Achaemenids from Darius I to Darius III had claimed sovereignty ; to which the conqueror now turned (327). Afghanistan was already secured, and the winter was passed in subjugating the hill tribes of what we know as the Northwest Frontier. That is to say, the war-worn veterans fought their way through the unexplored passes till in the spring of 326 they came down to the Indus, crossed it, and routed the hosts of the confederate princes of the Punjab in the great battle of Hydaspes —the river Jhelum as it is called today. Not until the battle had been lost beyond hope of redemption did Porus, the indomitable chief of the confederacy, surrender himself to Alexander, who treated him with well-deserved royal honours, appointing him sub-king of the major part of the Punjab, under the aegis of himself, the Great King.

But the Punjab was to be the limit of Alexander's conquest ; very much against his own will. For when the advancing army reached the Hyphasis (the Beas), which flows into the Sutlej, the last of the

Five Rivers that give its name to the Punjab, not even its hero Alexander could persuade it to move a step farther. He had no choice but to turn back.

But Alexander was an explorer at heart ; and before returning he had already resolved on an expedition down the Indus, to be followed up by the navigation of the Indian ocean—the latter task to be entrusted to Nearchus. The southern tribes resisted the advance ; and it was where Multan s t a n d s to-day that in the assault on the citadel Alexander, first as usual up the scaling ladder, went near to meeting his death.

When the Indus mouth was reached, the fleet of Nearchus was fitted out and he was dispatched on the voyage of exploration westwards. The main army made its way back to Afghanistan by the Bolan pass ; the rest of the force, led by the king, plunged into the almost uninhabited Gedrosia, or southern Baluchistan, and struggled through in little more than half its original strength, after cruel sufferings which the king shared with his soldiers.

**MACEDONIAN RULER OF ASIA**

Seleucus Nicator, one of Alexander's generals, made himself king of Syria in 301 ; and thereafter ruled most of the Asiatic provinces once included in Alexander's empire.

*From Delbrück, 'Antike Porträts'*

THIS expedition was in 325. Meanwhile Nearchus had explored the coasts from Karachi to the Persian Gulf, Craterus had suppressed the revolts, and before the end of the year both had joined Alexander in Carmania (Kirman), the rendezvous, on the east of Persia. Already the king had been long enough away for satraps and officials, Macedonian and Persian, to take advantage of an absence which might be permanent, and misuse their powers. On all such his hand now fell with stern justice, even-handed and unsparing. His treasurer Harpalus saved himself, not empty-handed, by fleeing.

The career of conquest was suspended. In 324 Alexander, already wedded to Roxana, took also to wife Statira, the daughter of Darius ; and many Macedonians, following his example, also married Persian women. Alexander further emphasised his theory of cancelling racial barriers by organizing not only regiments of Orientals trained in the Greek discipline and commanded by Persians, but also regiments in which easterns and westerns were combined. He was even now planning maritime adventures and expansion on the newly discovered ocean, and the annexation of Arabia over which the Persian conquest had never extended ; and early in 323 the preparations were well advanced. He had made Babylon his headquarters, when in June a fever seized him. Within a fortnight he died, leaving no man capable of building the structure he had designed on the foundations he had laid.

The fatal fact in the situation brought about by Alexander's sudden death was that there was no heir with an indisputable title to the succession, though a child by Roxana was expected, and there was a feeble son of the great Philip, Alexander's half-brother, known to the world as Philip Arrhidaeus.

A council of the generals decided to recognize Philip, with whom Roxana's son, if (as actually happened) a son should be born, was to be associated. They were to be under the guardianship of Perdiccas, a general high in Alexander's confidence, whom the dead king may have intended to designate as his heir. In the meantime the empire was to be distributed among the leading Macedonians in governorships over-riding the satrapies. Antipater was to retain the regency of Macedonia and Greece which Alexander had left in his charge eleven years ago ; Egypt was to go to Ptolemy, the satrapy of

Babylon to Seleucus, who already held it, Thrace and part of Asia Minor to Lysimachus, most of western Asia to Antigonus, and the rest to Leonnatus and Eumenes ; while the guardianship of Philip and of the baby Alexander, together with an independent military command, placed Perdiccas in a position at least of equality with the rest.

This, or something like this, was the only possible way of dealing with an unprecedented situation. It could not last because it provided no dominant central authority, the nearest thing to such an authority being that of Perdiccas. Even so supreme a personality as Alexander's could not have maintained the system long. The much smaller satrapies of the Persian empire, under a dynasty whose authority had been established for a century and a half, had been a constant menace to the unity of that empire. This emergency system was possible only so long as the several generals stood loyally by each other ; it was inevitable that sooner or later personal ambitions and rivalries would undermine loyalty ; and so in fact it befell in a very short time.

The half century following Alexander's death in 323 rings with the clash of strife between the Diadochi, the ' Successors,'

**VICTORY COINAGE OF DEMETRIUS**

Demetrius Poliorcetes commemorated his naval victories on several coins, using as the design the statue of Victory which he dedicated in 305 B.C. It was this coin that led to the identification of the statue shown in the opposite page.

*From G. F. Hill, ' Select Greek Coins,' G. Van Oest*

**BESIEGER OF CITIES**

Son of Antigonus who became king of Asia on Alexander's death, Demetrius gained his surname, Poliorcetes (the Besieger), from the machines constructed by him to break down the defence of Rhodes in 304 B.C. He died in 283 B.C.

*From G. F. Hill, ' Select Greek Coins '*

Macedonians who were seeking to obtain the lion's share in the partition of the vast dominion, and setting up dynasties of their own, each battling to overshadow his neighbour's power. Only by 280 (to sum up in anticipation) was something like a final settlement emerging, with the house of Seleucus (who was murdered in that year) established in Syria, Babylonia and part of Asia Minor, the Ptolemies reigning in Egypt, and the house of Antigonus not yet finally secured in their positions as kings of Macedon and sovereigns over Greece. Native or minor Macedonian dynasties were in the meantime shaping kingdoms over the greater part of Anatolia. In Cappadocia Ariarathes, a Persian or a native, was king ; in Pontus on the shore of the Euxine, Mithradates, the grandson of the Persian satrap Ariobarzanes ; in Bithynia a native, Nicomedes ; and Pergamum, held by the Macedonian Philetaerus, first in fief to Lysimachus and then independently, was soon to become a kingdom under his nephew Attalus.

Of the generals named in the first partition, Ptolemy, Lysimachus and Seleucus were active almost through the whole period, dying respectively in 283, 281 and 280 ; Antipater and Antigonus, older men, died in 319 and 301 ; all five, however, at about eighty years of age. The two last were represented after their deaths by their sons Cassander and Demetrius Poliorcetes the 'Besieger'; the death of Cassander's three sons gave Macedon to their Antigonid rival. When Lysimachus fell in battle with Seleucus, he left no heir to his claims. Perdiccas and Eumenes had been eliminated two years after Alexander's death ; and Leonnatus, who had saved Alexander's life in Multan, was killed in battle still earlier (see below). Neither he nor Craterus entered into the rivalries.

While Alexander was conquering Asia, Hellas had remained for the most part quiescent, suffering under a sense of subjection (though its liberties were not touched in fact), because it knew that it enjoyed those liberties only by grace of the Macedonian. The Spartan king Agis did indeed try to incite a

war of liberation, but he found no support, even from Demosthenes, outside the Peloponnese, and was easily suppressed by the regent Antipater. Athens, with still expanding commerce and her finances under very able direction, was particularly prosperous, while the great orator was wise enough not to play the fire-brand. Even when Harpalus, Alexander's rapacious ex-treasurer, fleeing from his master's righteous wrath, appeared on the scene with much treasure, hoping to stir up a revolt by bribery, the counsels of prudence prevailed ; though the failure of Demosthenes to take

### NIKE OF SAMOTHRACE : AN EARLY HELLENISTIC MASTERPIECE

Early Hellenistic art created nothing more beautiful than this Victory statue found in Samothrace. It commemorates a naval victory—possibly of Antigonus Gonatas of Macedonia—and was carved by a third century Rhodian sculptor in imitation of the earlier statue set up by Demetrius Poliorcetes as stated opposite. The goddess Nike stands half flying on the prow of a warship ; as shown in the reconstruction (left) she probably bore a wreath in her right hand and a standard in her left.

*Left, after Falize and Cordonnier : right, the Louvre*

proper charge of the money sequestered from the rebel, which was entrusted to his care, caused his banishment (324).

An immediate change, however, was wrought by the death of Alexander. In Athens the patriot party at once became dominant, and assumed that rôle of leader in a war of liberation in which Agis had failed. This time it was the Peloponnesians who held aloof. The aged Antipater came down to suppress Athens and her allies in Thessaly, but was defeated and shut up in Lamia, which gave its name to the ' Lamian ' war. Leonnatus came to his aid from the Propontis, but was defeated and slain. Triumphant, Athens recalled Demosthenes. But the triumph was brief. Craterus appeared on the scene, and at Crannon (322) routed the allies, who had lost their ablest leader, the Athenian Leosthenes. The resistance collapsed, and Antipater was able to dictate his own terms to the allies, not as a league but individually.

### Tragic End of Demosthenes

THE Athenian democracy was restricted by a narrow franchise, a Macedonian garrison was placed in the port of Munychia, and the surrender of Demosthenes was demanded. The great orator, the life-long foe of Macedon, took sanctuary in the temple of Poseidon at Calaurea, where he swallowed poison, so escaping the vengeance of his enemies.

Demosthenes was the most brilliant of orators and the most fervent of Athenian patriots. All through his life the policy he urged on his countrymen was based on his ineradicable conviction that Macedon was the enemy of Athens, in spite of the unfailing magnanimity with which she was always treated by both Philip and Alexander. He was the incarnation of that attitude of the Greek mind which made the unification of Hellas impossible, because no Greek state was willing, except in extreme emergency, to accept the control of a common federal authority or the hegemony of any state other than itself. But so great was his rhetorical genius, so vigorous his conviction that he was right, and that all men who opposed him were traitors, that his eloquence has

often persuaded posterity almost as thoroughly as the Athenian juries, not seldom in defiance of sober evidence.

Little more than a year had passed since the death of Alexander, but the incompatible ambitions of the generals were already manifesting themselves. The obvious intention of Perdiccas, as guardian of the feeble-minded Philip and the baby Alexander, and ally of the old queen Olympias and the young queen Roxana, to secure the supreme authority for himself, led four of the other Diadochi— Antipater, Antigonus, Ptolemy and Seleucus—to form a league against him. In 321 Perdiccas marched against Ptolemy in Egypt, but was assassinated. Antipater was nominated regent, but the old man died in 318, his death causing a fresh complication, since he named as his successor not his own aspiring son Cassander, but another old general, Polysperchon ; between whom and Cassander there was war, with Macedon and Greece as a battle-ground. While Seleucus was busying himself in the far eastern provinces, more intent on carrying out Alexander's policy than on fighting for Alexander's crown, Antigonus was making himself more and more supreme in Asia.

### Dissensions Among the Diadochi

BY 316, Philip and his valorous and energetic wife, Eurydice, had been done away with by fierce old Olympias ; she herself had been put to death by Cassander ; Polysperchon's career was ended ; and Cassander was dominant in Europe. In the course of this struggle another notable Athenian, Phocion, ended a long and honourable but not a successful career. A man of ability, but not of brilliant talents, he was one of those whose character at once compels respect and admiration and forbids popularity ; who was always by preference on the unpopular side, and most doubted his own wisdom when it was most applauded ; who never pandered to popular sentiment ; always just but always unsympathetic. He disliked because he mistrusted the democracy which rarely listened to his sensible but uninspiring advice, which habitually aimed at amicable relations with Macedon. At the age of eighty-five he was condemned to death for treason after the travesty of a trial by his political enemies, and drank his hemlock with the serenity of Socrates. Characteristically, the Athenians raised a statue to his memory.

From 315 to 307, war was going on with little intermission between Antigonus, now the most powerful of the Diadochi, and his rivals. In 307 his son Demetrius, who had not yet earned his nickname (Poliorcetes), entered the field in his support, invading Greece, which was in the hands of Cassander and his ally Ptolemy, in the character of liberator. Roxana and the boy Alexander had been murdered some years before by Cassander, so that there was now no one with any pretence to a title to the imperial throne. In 306, Antigonus assumed for himself and Demetrius the title of king, an example promptly followed by Lysimachus, Ptolemy, Seleucus. Demetrius set about the siege of Rhodes where his novel but unsuccessful operations won him his name of Poliorcetes. The war went on with varying fortunes, till in 301 the old Antigonus was slain at the battle of Ipsus in Phrygia, and a fresh compromise was reached, under which Asia was practically divided between Lysimachus and Seleucus, while Demetrius and Cassander were left to fight out their rivalry in Europe, with the leaderless Greek states as pawns in their game.

Still the welter of wars and murders continued. Cassander died; his eldest son, known as Philip IV, died; the two younger sons disputed the succession, and

**A VICTIM OF INGRATITUDE**

Phocion (402–317 B.C.) was a good soldier and a sincere patriot. Yet despite his fine military career and high integrity he became suspect in Athens and, like Socrates, drank the hemlock.

*The Vatican, Rome*

the younger, Alexander, called in to his aid a new ally, Pyrrhus (318-272), the famous king of Epirus, whose grandfather had been the brother of Olympias. Meanwhile Demetrius had attacked Athens, once his ally, then the ally of Cassander, and captured the city when it had been starved out at last after a long siege. He, too, went ostensibly to the aid of Alexander, between whom and his brother Pyrrhus had already divided Macedon; but Demetrius assassinated his ally and seized the throne himself (294).

'The Besieger,' however, aimed at the recovery of his father's dominion, which was now shared between Lysimachus and Seleucus. He was on friendly enough terms with the latter, who quite recently, though past sixty, had married Demetrius' young daughter Stratonice, being himself some twenty years older than his father-in-law. But the effect of Demetrius' obvious preparations for war was to bring down on him in 287 both Lysimachus and Pyrrhus, who was immensely popular with the Macedonian soldiery. Demetrius had to fly to Asia, where he fell into the hands of Seleucus, who held him in honourable and opulent captivity till his death in 283. His claims descended to his son Antigonus Gonatas; but Pyrrhus seized the throne, only to be ejected again after a seven months' reign by Lysimachus. We shall find Pyrrhus on his next appearance in our following chapter engaged on an adventure in quite another quarter.

Old Ptolemy Soter died in 283, having abdicated two years before in favour of

**PTOLEMY II AND QUEEN ARSINOE**

Ptolemy II Philadelphus (309–246 B.C.) succeeded to the throne of Egypt on his father's abdication in 285 B.C. Although they were Greeks the early Ptolemies adopted all the habits of the Egyptian Pharaohs, and were represented by the Egyptian sculptors in the conventional pharaonic style, as on this bas-relief.

*British Museum*

his younger son Ptolemy II, called Philadelphus, to the wrath of the elder half-brother, Ptolemy Ceraunus. Only Seleucus and Lysimachus were left of the original Diadochi. They were very soon fighting each other ; but Lysimachus was killed at the battle of Corupedum (281). Seleucus was master of the situation and proposed to end his days in Macedon where he had not set foot for fifty years, leaving the East to his son Antiochus Soter and reserving Thrace for the grandchildren of Lysimachus ; but while he was passing through Thrace he was murdered by Ceraunus ; who was hailed as king by the army (280)—to be driven out again two years later by Antigonus Gonatas.

Seleucus passed through all the wars of the Diadochi with cleaner hands than any of the rest, except Antipater, whose age saved him from being involved in any but the first contest with Perdiccas. As a young man he was said to have performed the Herculean feat of wrestling with an enraged bull and throwing it ; he was a soldier of distinguished courage and capacity. But more than this, he was the one man among Alexander's generals who seriously strove to carry out Alexander's ideals, stood by his engagements, and took what was his due and no more in the various settlements. He had no hand in any of the assassinations unless perhaps that of Perdiccas. To his share had fallen little but the most remote and least coveted eastern provinces, till the fall of Antigonus at Ipsus gave him Syria, from which the kingdom of the Seleucids took its name. He sowed Hellenism in the East, founding over seventy cities or settlements with that intent, the most important being Antioch, which he made his capital. But he had to abandon the attempt to retain India within the bounds of the empire, and to be content to establish friendly if distant diplomatic relations with the mighty Maurya kingdom of Magadha, to whose story we now pass.

Ɜɴ the fourth century B.C., as from the days of the first Darius, the Achaemenids had claimed a shadowy sovereignty in India, which perhaps meant that beyond the Indus, the probable boundary of the official satrapy, there were princes or communities in the Punjab that paid occasional tribute and sent occasional contingents to serve in the armies of the Great King. All over the basins of the Indus and the Ganges there were innumerable groups, principalities or federations, with boundaries expanding or contracting according to the aggressive vigour of their rulers, more or less subject to the sovereignty of any neighbouring power or dynasty strong enough to enforce tribute. In the time of Alexander, the Nanda dynasty of Magadha (Bihar) held such rule over the Ganges area ; and with that power Alexander would have come into collision had he crossed the Sutlej. Brahmanism or Hinduism was everywhere dominant ; but the reformed or reforming religions—Jainism and Buddhism—were spreading over a wide area, diminishing the influence of caste ; both the Nandas and their subverter Chandragupta, whom the Greeks called Sandracottys, have been claimed as Jains, though the mild ethics of Jainism are not easily recognizable in the life of Chandragupta, whose guide and minister was Chanakya, the Brahman prototype of that astute Florentine, Machiavelli.

## Macedonia's Hold on India Lost

**A**LEXANDER had doubtless hoped to make the Punjab a base from which to extend his conquest ; but on the news of his death, young Chandragupta, probably a junior prince of the royal house, attacked and expelled the Macedonian garrisons in the Punjab, and, immediately before or after this exploit, exterminated his Nanda kinsmen and made himself king of Magadha —the first of the Maurya dynasty—reigning from 322 to 298. Ten years later Seleucus planned a reconquest ; but by this time the king's power was consolidated. Seleucus realized the impracticability of his project, and Chandragupta was amicably recognized as independent monarch of India with Afghanistan and Baluchistan ; while by way of compensation he presented Seleucus with five hundred elephants. Alexander's name (Iskander) survived in Indian memory ; Megasthenes, on a mission from Seleucus, visited the Maurya court ; Greeks appear from time to time in the north-west region ; but there was no later attempt at conquest, and the influence of Hellenism in India was small though there are indications of Indian origins in some aspects of the later western religions.

Chandragupta established a great empire extending from Herat to Bengal and to the river Narbada, ruling as an absolute despot according to the maxims of Chanakya which exalt force and cunning

above all moral principles in state-craft. In 298 he abdicated and was succeeded by his son Bindusara (d. 273), the father of the great Asoka, whom we shall meet in the next chapter.

Western Hellas took no part in the adventure of Alexander or the rivalries of the Diadochi. Within a few years after the death of Dionysius I of Syracuse, his empire was in dissolution ; Syracuse and Sicily generally became an arena in which tyrants and would-be tyrants struggled for the mastery. Carthage was on the point of turning the situation to her own advantage, when Corinth sent the noblest of her sons, Timoleon, to the deliverance of her daughter city.

Timoleon's character and abilities were of the highest ; but he had retired from public life because his exalted sense of duty had compelled him to sanction the death of his own brother, who had sought to make himself tyrant at Corinth. Now he accepted the charge laid upon him (344), and achieved splendid success. He set Syracuse free, finally expelling Dionysius II. With a force of twelve thousand men he attacked and shattered on the Crimesus (339) a Carthaginian army of invasion, of six times his numbers,

### SAVIOUR OF HIS COUNTRY

Seleucus Nicator's son, Antiochus, was called Soter (Saviour) from his repulse of the Gauls who invaded Asia Minor in 278 B.C. He died in 262 B.C., after a reign troubled by wars with Syria, Egypt and Pergamum.

*From G. F. Hill, ' Select Greek Coins,' G. Van Oest.*

**IDEALIST AND MAN OF ACTION**

Possessed of an imagination that knew no
limits, Alexander had also great intellectual
power, a genius for practical affairs and the gift
of command—a complex nature suggested in
this portrait, usually considered reliable.

*The Louvre ; photo, Alinari*

removing that danger almost for another
generation ; he cleared the cities of Sicily
of their tyrants ; and when his work was
finished in 338 he claimed no reward,
but simply laid down the powers he had
so admirably exercised ; though for the
year or two of life that remained to him
his counsels were eagerly sought, freely
given and zealously obeyed.

Nevertheless, the political instability
of Sicilian Hellas was incurable. In 317
another tyrant arose in Syracuse, Agathocles. The ' master' of Syracuse—for his
self-chosen title is that used later by Greek
historians to translate the Roman terms
' dictator ' and ' imperator '—had been
born a Carthaginian subject, at the
' Baths of Himera,' but had been brought
young to Syracuse, and turned a potter's
skill to the moulding of an empire.

Personally attractive, a typical soldier of
fortune, he married a rich widow, raised a
free company, tricked the Syracusans
into accepting his help, as they had
accepted that of Dionysius, established
himself in their city by treachery and
soon had Greek Sicily at his feet.

His power was a renewal of the challenge to Carthage, which was not politically
affected by the conquests of Alexander
or the disputes of his successors. She
again threatened to overrun Sicily, and
inflicted heavy defeat on Agathocles at
Himera in 310 ; but he dared to counter
the blow by himself invading Africa,
where he won brilliant successes on Carthaginian soil. But his absence was the
signal for revolt ; in 307 he left his army
in Africa to its fate and sped back to
make peace with Carthage and recover
his own despotism ; an object which he
accomplished by methods which have
made his name a by-word. A domestic
feud wrecked his plans for restoring the
south Italian dominion of Dionysius.
With his death in 289 at the age of
seventy-two—tradition says that he was
poisoned by his own grandson—ended
the last attempt, except the adventure
of Pyrrhus ten years later, to set up in
Sicily a Hellenic power united enough to
hold the Punic power at bay, or check its
maritime ascendancy. But Agathocles
had shown for the first time that Carthage
was vulnerable in Africa itself.

### Final Eclipse of Syracusan Power

ON the Italian mainland the Syracusan
ascendancy melted away on the death
of Dionysius I even more rapidly than in
Sicily. The great tyrant had made use
of the Lucanians and other Italians to
bring the Greek cities under his sway ;
when he died the Italians combined and
formed the Bruttian league against the
divided Greeks, pressing them so hard
that Tarentum appealed for aid against
the barbarian to its mother city Sparta
(343). Sparta responded ; for in Greece,
already dominated by Philip, there was
no outlet for her military ambitions.
King Archidamus headed an expedition,
his troops being for the most part hired
from Phocis whose brief hour of distinction

was over. The expedition failed, and the king was killed in battle with the Lucanians in 338, the year of Chaeronea.

Greece had no spare energies to expend on Magna Graecia; but in 334, when Alexander of Macedon was starting on the great eastern venture, his uncle Alexander ' the Molossian ' of Epirus answered the call of the western Hellenes, perhaps with an imperial dream of his own which descended to his nephew Pyrrhus. His success was rapid, but in 330 his career was cut short by the dagger of an assassin before he could consolidate his power in Italy. When he fell he had already formed an alliance with the advancing Roman state whose foes in the south were also his foes; but he left no successor to carry on his projects—Pyrrhus was not yet born.

At the moment when the magistracies, the great administrative offices of the Roman state, ceased in 367 to be the monopoly of the old aristocracy. Rome was more

ITALY AND SICILY IN THE HELLENISTIC AGE

Western Hellas stood aloof from Alexander's eastern adventures. Domestic feuds and conflict with Carthage prevented Syracuse from securing ascendancy in Sicily, and on the Italian mainland Rome, as yet dominant only in Latium, was drawn into conflict with the Samnites and Carthaginians.

powerful than any other single state. Notwithstanding this, the area of her supremacy was still limited to Latium and a portion of Etruria, and even within that area her domination was liable to be challenged. And now we find her faced by a new and formidable foe, whom perhaps we ought rather to call an old foe in a new guise, the Samnite confederacy. The leading feature in the advance of Rome during this period to an Italian supremacy is to be found in the series of Samnite wars beginning in 343 and ending in 290; with the honours divided as concerns the two principals, but a great concurrent increase in the power of Rome.

But before the struggle with the Samnites opened, the ascendancy which Rome had been able to establish after the great Gallic irruption was seriously threatened. It was perhaps only because the neighbours who feared her feared still

more the Gallic menace from which they had already suffered so severely, that she was able to do something more than hold her own. There were, moreover, Latin cities which even allied with the Gauls against her, thereby forcing the rest of the Latins, however reluctantly, to throw themselves in effect under the protection of Rome, in spite of the subordination to her involved. The Latin League was renewed on terms more definitely emphasising the superior status of Rome (358), and the second Gallic tide was rolled back in 354. Etruscan cities seized the opportunity to attack Rome in the hour of her embarrassment; she suffered some defeats; but by 351 the Etruscans were forced to accept a peace for forty years.

In that year and the next the Gauls renewed hostilities for the third time, only to be decisively beaten by the son of the great Camillus who had beaten them off forty years before. The Latins were held well in hand, and Etruria was bound to peace for many years to come.

At this stage, then, Carthage recognized Rome as the coming great power, and made with her the very important treaty of 348—in the view of some authorities, the first between the two states ; while others regard it as a renewal with modifications of one which, according to Polybius (c. 150 B.C.), had been made in 509, the first year of the Republic.

In the supposed original treaty Carthage had undertaken to respect all Latin territory and coast towns as a Roman sphere of influence, and granted to Roman traders admission to the ports of Carthage itself, of Africa and Sardinia, and of the parts of Sicily which it then ruled ; the Romans undertaking not to sail beyond the Fair Cape (C. Blanco), and to withdraw promptly if driven south of it by stress of weather, and recognizing the Carthaginian claim to regulate trade in the other districts mentioned.

### Treaties between Rome and Carthage

THE second treaty was an adjustment of the situation in the west to political changes elsewhere. In general, it amplified the terms of the first, defining more precisely the limits of Roman seafaring, the use of Carthaginian harbours by Roman ships operating against third parties, and Carthaginian freedom of action in Italy ; but it excluded Roman settlers from Sardinia and Africa, while admitting merchants to Carthage itself and its possessions in Sicily. Carthaginians were to have similar access to Rome.

To appreciate the inclusion of Tyre and Utica as well as Carthage in this treaty we must remember that after long loyalty to Persia since the days of Cyrus, and tolerance of growing misgovernment, the cities of Phoenicia had revolted openly in 351 ; that this revolt was part of what seemed at the moment to be a general break-up of the western half of the Persian Empire, which was only stayed by the ruthless efficiency of a new king, Artaxerxes III ; and that in the suppression of the Phoenician revolt Persia had received Greek help.

Though Greeks are not mentioned, the effect of this treaty was to bind Rome, through commercial concessions, not to interfere with Carthaginian attacks on the Greek cities of the south ; and a significant distinction was drawn between the protectorate of Rome and those cities which were merely allied with the Romans by treaty. In particular, if Carthaginians should sack a town in Latium which was not under Roman protection, though captives and loot might be taken away, the site was to revert to Rome ; a lurid glimpse of what had been going on, out of reach of Dionysius' warships.

Five years after the conclusion of the treaty with Carthage, Rome was at war with the Samnites. For centuries the Sabellian highlanders of the Apennines had struggled to force their way into the plains between the hills and the Mediterranean ; but Tuscans and Latins had held them in check, and for the past hundred years the direction of their expansion had been not on Latium but east and south-east. We have seen that they had begun to stream into Campania where they had been seduced from their old characteristic hardiness, and the Campanians were now a soft folk, ill fitted to cope with their kinsmen of the hills. The most powerful group of the highlanders, the confederated Samnites, were now, in the middle of the fourth century, swarming down upon their degenerate precursors in Campania, as, farther east and south, Lucanians and Bruttians were pressing upon the degenerate Hellenic colonies ; the semi-civilized were hammering the over-civilized. The Greeks were appealing to Hellas and were ere long to appeal to semi-Hellenic Epirus ; the Campanians appealed to Rome, and Rome went to their rescue.

### Beginning of the Samnite Wars

THE first Samnite war (343–341) was brief. It was marked by Roman victories in the field and by a mutiny on the part of the soldiery, which was suppressed by the sympathetic common sense of the distinguished dictator, Marcus Valerius Corvus, who as a youth had vanquished a Gallic Goliath in single combat. The war was ended by a hasty peace, owing to the revolt of Rome's Latin allies ('socii') who resented their dependence on the dominant city.

In effect the Romans deserted the Campanians, in face of an immediate menace to their own position. They had forced the members of the Latin League into the Samnite war without consulting them. The Latins demanded only that they as a group should stand on an equality with Rome ; she rejected the insolent proposal, and in two years' campaigning asserted her supremacy (340–338) in the Latin War, in which tradition recorded two picturesque episodes illustrative of the Roman character.

The consul Manlius Torquatus had won the torque or collar that gave him his name as a young man, by vanquishing a Gaulish champion in single combat, in accord with time-honoured custom. But as consul, for the sake of discipline, he issued an order that all such challenges were to be refused. Nevertheless his son, eager to prove himself worthy of his parent, ignored the order, fought a Latin champion, and slew him. Death was the penalty laid down for disobedience, and the father's unbending justice would yield to no prayers. His own son should not be spared, lest any man might say that another than the consul's son would have suffered the full penalty. By the father's order the son was doomed for his breach of discipline.

### Roman Consul's Roman Virtue

THE colleague of Manlius in the consulship was the plebeian Decius Mus. On the eve of a decisive battle both were warned in dreams that victory would fall to the army whose leader was slain on the field. When Decius saw that the wing he commanded was giving ground, he solemnly dedicated himself and the opposing army to the gods of the underworld, dashed headlong and alone into the ranks of enemy, and was slain. But 'behind

**SAMNITE WARRIORS' INDOMITABLE COURAGE**

The stubbornness of the Samnites in their conflict with Rome is suggested in this mural painting from a Samnite grave at Capua. It depicts two Samnite warriors in tunics, greaves and helmets, engaged in gladiatorial combat and fighting on although one is pierced by a spear and both stream with blood.

*From Jahrbuch des deutschen archaeol. Institut*

him Rome's long battle came rolling on the foe,' and the victory was won.

The effect of the Latin War was to tighten Rome's grip upon Latium and to provide her with more lands upon which to settle her ever-increasing agricultural population. The Latin League was finally dissolved (338). Some of the cities were incorporated with Rome ; others were admitted to the civil but not the political rights of Roman citizenship ; all were at the military service of Rome ; all were debarred from forming separate alliances or combinations in any shape with each other or with any external state.

The next few years witnessed the beginning and the end of the successes of the Epirote Alexander in southern Italy ; and in 327–6 the Samnite confederacy directly challenged Rome to fight for the mastership of Italy, since their conflicting claims could be decided only by the arbitrament of arms.

The second Samnite war lasted twenty years ; and it was not decisive. At first the Roman arms were so successful that in 321 the Samnites sued for peace ; but the terms offered were so stringent that they were rejected and the war went on. In the same year the two consuls, leading an invading force into Samnium, were trapped in a mountain pass known as the Caudine Forks where they could neither advance nor retire, and after a desperate struggle would have been annihilated if they had not submitted to the ignominious terms imposed by the Samnite victor Pontius. The troops were disarmed and compelled to pass ' under the yoke,' man by man, as a foe vanquished and disgraced, while the consuls pledged themselves to a treaty on the most favourable terms for the Samnites. But the Roman Senate refused to ratify the terms, and again the war went on.

### Conclusion of the Samnite Wars

FOR six years, till 314, success seemed to flow with the Samnites ; Campania was on the verge of deserting Rome. Then the tide turned. But the Roman victory was delayed by the intervention of the Etruscans in 311 when the forty years' peace reached its term. It was only postponed, however. After the first shock the Romans continuously defeated both their enemies. In 308 the Etruscans sued for peace, which was granted to their cities severally ; and in 304 the Samnites obtained peace on terms probably severe but certainly not crushing.

For in 298 the Samnites renewed the war. Enemies were stirred up against Rome—Etruscans, Gauls, Umbrians, Sabines—on every side. But they lacked cohesion, and a shattering victory was won over their combined forces at Sentinum in Umbria in 295, when one of the consuls, the son of Decius Mus the hero of the Latin war, repeated his father's act of heroic devotion. Nevertheless, the stubborn Samnites fought on till a final defeat in 291 made further resistance hopeless, and in the following year peace was made on more favourable terms for the Samnites than Rome was wont to accord to any less dogged foe.

The Campanian cities, Italian or Greek, through which Rome had been involved in the Samnite wars, Capua and others, were now the allies of Rome, with variations in the degree of independence— never really complete—which they severally enjoyed ; and Roman military colonies were settled in Campania as well as on the eastern outskirts of Samnium at Luceria and Venusia (290).

Since the passing of the Licinian Law in 367, the old contest between the Orders had dwindled into nothing more than an occasional attempt on the part of a patrician faction either to evade the law or to recover some fraction of exclusive privilege by indirect methods. In effect the old charmed circle had become extended so as to include a number of plebeian families of influence, wealth or distinction, to whom office was in practice restricted hardly less rigidly than it had been by law to the purely patrician families of old. Technically, however, the disappearance of plebeian disabilities was now finally confirmed by the Hortensian Law (287), which recognized the Assembly of the plebs voting by tribes as a constitutional legislative body.

### Menace to Rome from Southern Italy

MEANWHILE beyond the effective reach of Rome's arm, the Greek cities, since the death of Alexander of Epirus, had been suffering continuously from the pressure of Lucanians and Bruttians. In 302 Sparta made another effort to aid Tarentum ; Tarentum, by a selfish disregard for the interests of her allies, strengthened her own position relatively, but lost the confidence of other Greeks. The Samnite wars brought them into a closer contact with Rome, to whose protection many of them were inclining to turn like their fellow-Greeks of Campania ; while to Tarentum, which had entered upon a maritime treaty with Rome as early as 302, the new colonies at Venusia and Luceria seemed an intrusion menacing her own influence and commerce. The embroilment of Rome in the affairs of southern Italy could not long be postponed. From 285 to 282 she was engaged in a short and sharp war with the Gallic Boii and Senones in the north, which destroyed the latter and bridled the former for forty years to come ; but even before that war was finished, she was drawn in to the southern complication. The story of the new conflict against Pyrrhus will be told in the next chapter.

# SYNCHRONISED TABLE OF DATES: CHAPTER 7

| B.C. | Rome and the West | Greece and the East | B.C. |
|---|---|---|---|
| 280 | Pyrrhus in Italy ; Roman defeat at Heraclea. | Philetaerus at Pergamum. | 280 |
| 279 | Pyrrhus defeats Romans at Asculum. | Gallic invasion of Greece repulsed at Delphi. | 279 |
| 278 | Rome-Carthage alliance. Pyrrhus goes to Sicily. | Antigonus Gonatas becomes king of Macedon. | 278 |
| 277 | Pyrrhus campaigning in Sicily. | Gauls invade Asia Minor. | 277 |
| 276 | Pyrrhus returns to Tarentum. | Gauls defeated by Antiochus. | 276 |
| 275 | Pyrrhus, defeated at Beneventum, quits Italy. | War between Pyrrhus and Antigonus. | 274 |
| 273 | First treaty between | Rome and Egypt. | 273 |
|  |  | *India :* Asoka succeeds to the Maurya kingdom. |  |
| 272 | Surrender of Tarentum ; end of Samnite war. | Death of Pyrrhus at Argos ends war. | 272 |
| 271 | Hiero of Syracuse besieges Mamertines in Messina. |  |  |
| 268 | Military colonies at Ariminum and Beneventum. |  |  |
| 264 | Mamertines appeal to Rome. Beginning of the First Punic War, 264–241. |  |  |
| 263 | Hiero makes peace and alliance with Rome. |  |  |
| 262 | Romans capture Agrigentum (Acragas). | Eumenes of Pergamum defeats Antiochus I. | 262 |
|  |  | Antiochus I killed in battle with Gauls (Galatians). | 261 |
| 260 | Rome builds fleet. Naval victory of Mylae. | *India :* Asoka's Kalinga War. |  |
|  |  | *India :* Asoka's conversion to Buddhism. | 259 |
| 256 | Romans invade Africa ; Carthage hard pressed. | *India :* ' Kalinga ' and ' Rock ' edicts of Asoka. | 257 |
| 255 | Xanthippus at Carthage. Defeat of Regulus. | Bactria under Diodotus revolts against Antiochus II. | 255 |
| 254 | Romans capture Panormus. |  |  |
| 253 | Great Roman fleet lost in a storm. |  |  |
|  |  | Aratus of Sicyon joins and heads the Achaean League. | 251 |
| 250 | Romans reject Carthaginian offer of peace. | Rise of Parthians led by Arsaces. | 250 |
|  |  | *India :* Asoka's Buddhist mission to Ceylon. |  |
| 249 | Naval defeat of Romans at Drepanum. | *China :* End of Chou Dynasty. | 249 |
|  |  | Tiridates (to 211) chief of Parthians. | 248 |
| 247 | Hamilcar Barca in Sicily. Birth of Hannibal. | Accession of Ptolemy III Euergetes in Egypt. | 247 |
|  |  | Accession of Seleucus II Callinicus in Syria. | 246 |
|  |  | Syrian war of Ptolemy and Seleucus. | 245 |
|  |  | Liberation of Corinth by Aratus. | 243 |
| 242 | Naval defeat of Hanno at Aegatian Islands. | *India :* ' Pillar ' edicts of Asoka. | 242 |
| 241 | Sicily, except Syracuse, becomes a Roman Province. | Attalus I succeeds Eumenes at Pergamum. | 241 |
|  | Insurrection of Carthaginian mercenaries. | Great defeat of Galatians by Attalus. | 240 |
| 239 | Birth of Ennius. | Death of Antigonus Gonatas of Macedon. | 239 |
| 238 | War with Boii renewed (after forty-five years). Carthage surrenders Sardinia to Rome. End of Carthaginian Mercenary war. |  |  |
| 236 | Rome makes peace with the Boii. | Cleomenes III king of Sparta. | 236 |
|  | Hamilcar founds Carthaginian empire in Spain. |  |  |
| 231 | Sardinia and Corsica made one province. | *India :* Death of Asoka ; Maurya empire divided. | 232 |
| 230 | Rome declares war on | Illyrian pirate states. | 230 |
| 229 | Death of Hamilcar ; Hasdrubal in his place. | Accession of Antigonus Doson in Macedon. | 229 |
|  | Illyrian war ; Corcyra, etc., come into Roman alliance ; | Demetrius of Pharos left in control of Dalmatian coast. |  |
| 228 | Rome admitted to the Isthmian | Games. Negotiations with Greek states. | 228 |
|  | Boundary agreement with Hasdrubal in Spain. New Carthage founded. | War of Cleomenes and Achaean League. | 227 |
| 226 | Italy threatened by a general Gallic rising. |  |  |
| 225 | Roman victory over Gauls at Telamon. | Reforms of Cleomenes at Sparta. | 225 |
| 224 | Submission of Boii. | Aratus calls in Antigonus Doson. | 224 |
|  |  | Accession of Antiochus III the Great in Syria. | 223 |
| 222 | Submission of Cisalpine Gaul to Rome. | Accession of Ptolemy IV Philopator in Egypt. | 222 |
| 221 | Death of Hasdrubal ; Hannibal acclaimed by army. | Battle of Sellasia ; fall of Cleomenes. | 221 |
|  |  | *China :* Shih Hwang Ti creates New Empire. |  |
|  |  | Accession of Philip V in Macedon ; alliance with Achaean against Aetolian League. | 220 |
|  |  | *China :* Building of the Great Wall by Shih Hwang Ti. |  |
| 219 | Rome expels Demetrius of | Pharos, who goes to Philip. | 219 |
|  | Hannibal attacks Saguntum. |  |  |
| 218 | Declaration of (Second Punic) War, 218–201. Fall of Saguntum. Hannibal evades Scipio in Gaul, and crosses the Alps. Battle of Trebia. |  |  |
| 217 | Scipios in Spain. Battle of Lake Trasimene. Q. Fabius Maximus made Dictator. | End of the war of the Leagues. Ptolemy defeats Antiochus at Raphia. | 217 |
| 216 | Death of Hiero of Syracuse. Battle of Cannae ; Hannibal occupies Capua. |  |  |
| 215 | Treaty between Hannibal | and Philip V. | 215 |
|  | Hannibal in S. Italy, Romans in Spain and Sicily. |  |  |
| 214 | First Macedonian war. | Antiochus recovers most of Asia Minor. | 214 |
| 213 | Scipios in Spain negotiate with Syphax of Numidia ; Masinissa joins Carthaginians. | Death of Aratus. *China :* Burning of the Books by Shih Hwang Ti. | 213 |
| 212 | Destruction of Roman armies in Spain. Hannibal seizes Tarentum ; Romans invest Capua. |  |  |
| 211 | Young Scipio sent to Spain. Fall of Capua. | Macedonian war ; Romans ally with Aetolians and a Greek coalition against Philip and Achaeans. | 211 |
| 210 | Successes of Scipio, who takes New Carthage. | *China :* Death of Shih Hwang Ti. | 210 |
|  | Egypt renews alliance | with Rome. |  |
| 209 | Hasdrubal, brother of Hannibal, evades Scipio. | Eastern campaigns of Antiochus III | 209–5 |
| 208 | Hasdrubal escapes into Gaul. | Philopoemen commands Achaean League. | 208 |
| 207 | Hasdrubal crosses the Alps, but is crushed and killed by Claudius Nero at the Metaurus. | Philopoemen's victory at Mantinea. | 207 |
|  |  | Antiochus recognizes Euthydemus of Bactria. | 206 |
|  |  | *China :* Western Han Dynasty begins. |  |
| 205 | Scipio in Sicily. | Accession of Ptolemy V Epiphanes, who is made a ward of the Roman People. | 205 |
|  |  | Philip and Antiochus conspire against Ptolemy |  |
| 204 | Scipio invades Africa ; Masinissa joins him. |  |  |
| 203 | Syphax overthrown by Scipio and Masinissa. Hannibal recalled to Carthage. |  |  |
| 202 | Siege of Carthage. Battle of Zama. |  |  |
| 201 | Carthage submits to peace terms dictated by Scipio. |  |  |

**149**

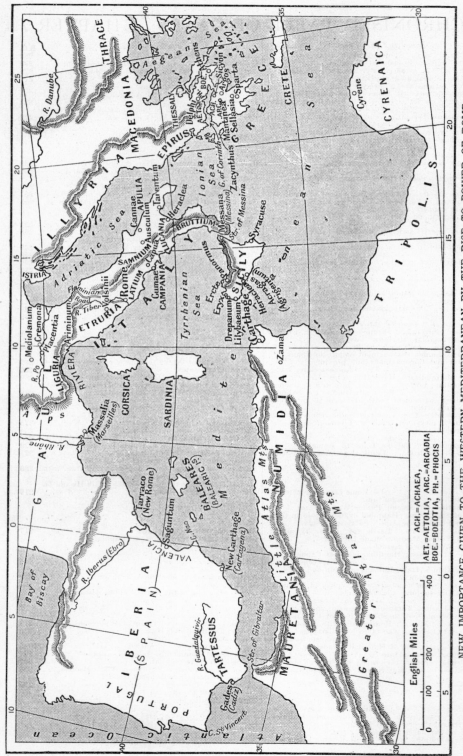

NEW IMPORTANCE GIVEN TO THE WESTERN MEDITERRANEAN BY THE RISE TO POWER OF ROME

Before the third century B.C. the eastern Mediterranean was all-important; west of Greece no capital power had as yet arisen. But the wars of the Succession States after the death of Alexander the Great plunged western Asia and Greece into confusion, while in Italy a new force was coming into being, Rome. Her defeat of Pyrrhus consolidated her predominance in Italy; and by 275 B.C. she had only one rival, Carthage, which she crippled in the First Punic War and totally destroyed in the Third. Rome was left supreme in the Mediterranean, and thereafter that expansion of her power which resulted in universal dominion.

### CHAPTER 7

# THE BEGINNINGS OF ROMAN POWER: 280—202 B.C.

THE central feature of the last chapter was the revolution wrought by the brief but tremendous career of Alexander the Great ; which shattered the old Asiatic power and carried Hellenism into the heart of Asia, but failed to create a new Hellenic power of equal magnitude in place of that which it destroyed, or to Europeanise the Orient. The central feature of the period now before us is the consolidation of a power in the West, emerging victoriously from a struggle that threatened its very existence, and prepared at last to effect the political conquest of both the Hellene and the Oriental, with neither of whom had it hitherto been brought into direct collision.

We shall, however, also see how Hellenic and Oriental disintegration was preparing the way for, and practically inviting, the coming Roman expansion ; and incidentally we shall turn our attention to far eastern realms, to which Rome never penetrated and of which Alexander himself had touched only the fringe. For a long reign as ordinary human lives count, but for a brief span in the passing of the centuries, a vast Indian empire enjoyed perhaps the most enlightened rule known in the history of mankind, under the sway of Asoka—a prince whose very name never reached the West till he had been dead for more than two thousand years.

### Rome the dominant Power in Italy

THE end of the Samnite wars left Rome incomparably the greatest power in Italy, but neither the north nor the south yet owned her as mistress. She had not yet actively intervened in the quarrels of Greeks and Italians in the south nor come into conflict with Sicily, where Agathocles at the age of seventy was contemplating a revival of the south Italian empire of Dionysius. But the death of Agathocles in 289, a year after the Samnite treaty, removed the practicability of Syracusan intervention ; the campaigns of 285-2 bridled the Gauls in the north ; Samnites and Etruscans were in no mood for a renewal of the exhausting and unprofitable struggle ; and the Lucanians, no longer useful to Rome as a check on the Samnites, were renewing their attacks on the Greek cities. Distrusting Tarentum, the most powerful and prosperous among them, the rest in 283 appealed for protection not to her but to Rome.

The Romans sent help promptly and effectively. The wiser heads in Tarentum saw no reason to object ; but the popular party was furious, and began again to look eastwards for someone to fight their battles for them. The arrival at this moment of a small Roman squadron in forbidden waters was probably excusable as a war measure in defence of Greek allies ; but it was a formal breach of the treaty of 302 B.C. ; the populace of Tarentum lost its head, insulted the Roman mission of apology, made trouble among the other Greek cities, and prepared to avenge a nominal grievance by war.

### Adventures of King Pyrrhus in the West

ONCE again sudden help came to Tarentum from beyond the Adriatic. Pyrrhus, king of Epirus, was nephew and successor of that Alexander who had brought help before. He had also married a daughter of Agathocles, and seems to have regarded himself as his predestined successor, a part for which he was in many ways well suited. Sicily rather than Italy, which was to serve as a stepping-stone, was probably his real objective from the beginning. He had the reputation of a fire-brand among the ' Successor States,' whose kings seem to have sent him considerable forces (which they could now well spare), on the understanding that he did not employ them near home. Hence, for example, his elephant corps, a weapon new to the West, though the

Carthaginians were to use it before long. What Alexander had done in the Persian Empire, Pyrrhus evidently thought was possible also in the West, and Tarentum seemed the necessary base for such conquests.

This was not quite what the populace of Tarentum had intended, and the declaration of martial law by the advance guard which garrisoned their city in 280 B.C. cooled their love for Pyrrhus, who unlike previous adventurers had evidently come to stay. The other Greek cities had not asked for him, and the Romans had no intention of resigning her protectorate to a nominee of Tarentum.

Pyrrhus evidently had not heard much about the Romans ; what he heard now evoked his respect ; still more, what he saw, with a soldier's eye, in hard fighting

**SYRACUSAN IMPERIALIST**

An able soldier, Agathocles, tyrant of Syracuse, made himself king of Sicily and was establishing his power in southern Italy when he died in 289 B.C.

*National Museum, Naples*

at Heraclea and at Ausculum. Italian dominion was clearly not for him ; he had come too late, and if Carthage was the enemy, as he had learned from Agathocles, there was nothing to be gained by quarrelling with Rome too. Carthage naturally thought otherwise, and sent a squadron up to the Tiber mouth to offer help against Pyrrhus. The terms of the 'third Treaty' now concluded between Rome and Carthage are instructive. If either state should ally itself with Pyrrhus against a third party (which could only be Greek) it was not only to reserve its own neutrality if Pyrrhus should attack the other, but to bind itself to resist him, and in this event Carthage undertook to supply all naval transport. The effect was to limit Pyrrhus's career in the West to aggression against the Greek

**RECORDS OF THE FIRST ELEPHANT CORPS USED IN ITALIAN WARFARE**

In the army that Pyrrhus led against the Romans in 280 B.C. was a force of which the Italians had no experience whatsoever—war-elephants. One of these, bearing a howdah occupied by Greek soldiers, is represented in a contemporary South Italian platter (left). The legend that at Asculum (279) the corps was stampeded by the grunting of swine is perpetuated by the Capuan bronze 'brick' in the British Museum (right) which has an elephant on the obverse, a sow on the reverse.

*Museo Villa Giulia, Rome (photo Alinari), and Hill, ' Historical Roman Coins'*

states which he had nominally come to protect against either Rome or Carthage, or both ; for it prevented him from making use of either of the contracting parties against the other.

Old soldiers of Aga-thocles, settled now at Messana, offered their help too ; but Campania and most of the south gave Pyrrhus, at best, no encouragement. Only Etruria thought the tide had turned against Rome, and quickly discovered its mistake. After two campaigns, in which, though he always won battles, Pyrrhus was losing more men than he could afford, he moved on into Sicily (278), and the Romans had little difficulty in dealing with his friends and his rearguards.

**COINS OF A WEALTHY CITY**

Tarentum, the prosperous Greek colony in Calabria which invited Pyrrhus into Italy, surrendered to Rome in 272 B.C. Above, two of its staters minted during the Pyrrhic war.

*From John Ward, ' Greek Coins ' (Murray)*

The Carthaginians had not waited to be attacked. When Pyrrhus sailed for Sicily, they were besieging Syracuse, his necessary base, and looking for him with their fleet. He evaded their ships, however, and drove off their field army, captured Panormus and Eryx, and refused their offer to surrender everything in Sicily except Lily-baeum, which they really needed if they were to keep their hold on Sardinia. He seems to have hoped to reach Africa as Agathocles had done ; but his losses had been heavy, and reinforcements were few. Tarentum was hard pressed by the Romans, and between them and the Carthaginian fleet he might find himself interned in Sicily. So he returned into Italy, fought one more campaign with the Romans, lost it, because the Romans had learned meanwhile how to deal with his spear-men and his elephants, and so returned home, to die ingloriously three years later. His parting words were memorable : ' What a battlefield I am leaving for Carthage and Rome ! '

In the year of his death (272 B.C.) Tarentum was surrendered to the Romans ; Greek cities and Bruttian tribes, with their valuable forest-country, surrendered like-wise, undertaking to supply Rome with ships and crews in future ; and the main lines of communication between Campania and Magna Graecia were secured by Roman ' colonies.' In the north, where the last free Etruscan city, Volsinii, revolted and was des-troyed in 264 B.C., similar precautions were taken ; so that all Italy now, from the Strait of Messina to the Apen-nine frontier towards the Gauls, became a single political whole, including indeed self-governed Greek colonies ' in alliance with the Roman people,' and Italian townships man-aging their own local affairs. But the whole was dominated by the ' Senate and People ' of Rome, and gar-risoned by substantial detachments of citizens domiciled in the great ' colonies ' on the lands of those tribes which had given most trouble, or held the strongest natural positions. The place attained by Rome in the eyes of the world was attested by an embassy of amity in 273 from the Macedonian king of Egypt, Ptolemy Philadelphus ; the first recognition of the kind she had received.

ЂERE things might have rested for a while, and the West might have had the chance of settling down, after a century and a half of disturbance following upon the defeat of the Athenian armada, if it had not been for the legacy of trouble which remained from the schemes of Agathocles. He, like Dionysius, had planned to weld Italian and Sicilian cities, Lucanians and Sicilians alike, into a Syra-cusan empire, and had made large use of free companies of highland irregulars from the mainland. Between Italy and Sicily there was, in any case, but a mile or two of water, and, on the Sicilian shore, Messana had fallen at Agathocles' death into the

hands of one of these free companies—
the Mamertini or 'Sons of Mars'—who
made themselves a nuisance to their
neighbours on both coasts, and to all
who used the straits, that is to say, to
Greek traders from all parts.

They had recently been in league with
a company of their Campanian countrymen, who, being in the Roman service,
had mutinied, seized Rhegium, and held
it against the Romans for ten years. The
revolt had been suppressed in 270 by the
aid of the commander of the Syracusan
forces, who bore the historic name of Hieron
(or Hiero as the Romans called him), and
immediately afterwards had made himself
master and ' king ' of Syracuse (270–216) ;
much as Agathocles and Dionysius had
done, but with a more modest programme.

In 265 B.C. Hiero thought it time to
make an end of the Mamertine pirates ;
and, so far as their own merits went, no
one was likely to be aggrieved. But if he
did, what was to happen to Messana and
who had something to gain by using the
Mamertines to obtain a footing there, or
to prevent Hiero from gaining one ? The
Mamertines were not Greeks, and could
make themselves very useful to Carthage,
the traditional enemy of all things Greek.
On the other hand, they were of Italian
origin, and Rome now stood as the conscious and very efficient protector of all
Italian interests. The Mamertines offered
themselves and their Sicilian city to the
Romans ;  and thereby brought Rome
itself to the cross-roads of destiny.

### Rome's Decision at the Cross-roads

IF the Romans helped the Mamertines,
who were (as we have seen) evil
breakers of the peace, they must offend
Hiero, their friend and well wisher, and
their own Greek allies, who had suffered
worst from Mamertine ravages. They
would probably also offend Carthage, and
Carthage could put much trouble in their
way. The Mamertines, while they were of
Italian origin, were being threatened by the
city which had shown most capacity for
managing Greek interests on a large scale.
If Rome refused help, would not Carthage
herself step in ?  And what were the
prospects of legitimate Italian trade,

with Carthage in control of the Strait ?
Left to itself, the Senate might have
abandoned the Mamertines to their fate,
and Carthage, evidently expecting this, and
encouraged by another faction in Messana,
sent their required help. This settled the
matter ;  popular clamour and business
interests combined to force the Senate's
hand.  An advance force was sent to
Messana, made touch with the partisans
of Rome in the city, and ejected the Carthaginians, whose government, with characteristic abruptness, executed their own
general, made alliance with Syracuse,
reconciled Hiero with the Mamertines, and
sent over a fresh force to support both
against the Romans. By the end of the
year, however, they had been expelled
from the neighbourhood of Messana, and
Hiero was shut up in Syracuse.

But the main issue was now clear :
whether Rome or Carthage was to guide
the fortunes of Sicily.  Hiero saw this
clearly, and for the representative of
Greek interests there was but one course
of action possible. For nearly five hundred
years Greek and Phoenician had worked
and plotted and fought for this central
region of the West.  To co-operate with
Carthage now, against the new power
which had delivered the Greeks of Italy

**CARTHAGE'S GREATEST SON**

Hannibal (c. 246-183 B.C.), son of Hamilcar Barca,
devoted his life to wreaking vengeance on Rome
for her implacable hostility to Carthage.  As a
military genius he ranks with Alexander the
Great, Julius Caesar and Napoleon.
*Naples Museum; photo, Alinari*

from Etruscan, Samnite and Lucanian, repelled the Gauls and wrecked the designs of Pyrrhus for an Empire of Epirus, would be folly and treason unimaginable. Under Roman protectorate, Syracuse and all western Greeks would be safe ; with Greek subsidies, ships and crews Rome could be trusted to win ; and Roman victory meant the expulsion of Phoenicians from Sicily. Hiero accordingly offered the Romans the possession of Messana and a subsidy of one hundred talents annually for fifteen years if they would guarantee his ' kingship ' of Syracuse. It was a small price to pay for security unattainable otherwise ; and for the Romans, too, the bargain was a good one (263).

The ' First Punic War,' accidentally begun but directed to a clear issue by the statesmanship of Hiero, lasted twenty years, and ended with the total defeat of Carthage. But it was a hard struggle, and the result was long doubtful.

### Events of the First Punic War

Jn the first three years (264-261 B.C.) the Romans captured the great fortress of Acragas, which they called Agrigentum, still the next city of Sicily after Syracuse, and confined the Carthaginian forces to the rugged western districts around their own ports. But by resigning territory Carthage simplified the problems of defence on land, and was able to raid not only the Greek coast cities, but also the long Roman lines of communication, which were mostly within reach of the sea. For this state of things there was but one remedy : ' a sea power, with its arsenal overseas, can only be vanquished on the sea, and by superior sea power.'

If Rome was to win, Rome must have a fleet ; and in the second stage of the war (260-253) not only was this accomplished, with liberal help from Greek ' naval allies ' organized on a grand scale, but in spite of early defeats, and other disasters due to Roman inexperience, the traditional seamanship of the Carthaginians was foiled by mechanical devices for bringing their ships to a standstill, and so ' fighting a land battle on the water.' In 256 the destruction of the Carthaginian ' grand fleet ' off Heraclea on the south coast of Sicily

by a Roman squadron, encumbered though it was with a convoy of transports, laid open the way to Africa. Here the natives rose against their masters, as they had risen for Agathocles, and the Roman force advanced within sight of Carthage. At this point peace might have been made ; but the Roman commander, Regulus, demanded too much ; the Carthaginians found in the Lacedaemonian adventurer Xanthippus a soldier of genius to reorganize and lead their forces ; Regulus was defeated and captured, and the survivors of his army were wrecked on their homeward journey. The Roman ' blow at the heart ' had failed (255).

Carthage, however, had suffered severely in prestige as well as equipment, and might have suffered worse had not the next year's Roman fleet been wrecked on its way to Africa (253), with the result that for a while only coast defence squadrons were in commission, and Roman commanders concentrated their resources on the reduction of enemy fortresses in Sicily. By 250 B.C. only Lilybaeum and a new naval base at Drepanum remained untaken, and it became clear once more that these remote ports might hold out indefinitely, if the Romans could not blockade them also by sea. Again Carthage tried to compromise, but her overtures were flatly rejected.

### The Romantic Story of Regulus

The established Roman tradition affirms that the rejection was due to the action of the captive consul Regulus, and the story, whether true or not, has set him among the heroic figures of the world. For five years he had been held a prisoner by the Carthaginians. Now they sent him with their embassy to Rome, under parole ; never doubting that all his powerful influence would be exerted in favour of the peace which would restore him to liberty. Nevertheless, so runs the tale, with no illusions as to the cruel fate which awaited him, he set aside all thought of self, bade the Romans to take no thought of him, and urged them to refuse the offered terms. He might easily have broken his parole and remained at Rome a free man, but his high sense of honour forbade him to do so, and he returned to Carthage with the disappointed and angry ambassadors, there to suffer a barbarous death at the hands of his vindictive captors. But at Rome the memory of him was cherished and revered, as the supreme exemplar of the qualities Pietas and Gravitas, to which above all else Rome loved to think that she owed her greatness.

So Rome resolved to see the war to a satisfactory end and began building ships again, and training admirals in the rude school of naval disasters. At this stage it was a serious disappointment that in renewing their treaty with Hiero in 248 B.C. they had to forgo the Syracusan tribute. Sicily was, indeed, well nigh ruined by the long war, and in particular by the cost of great sieges at the distant west end. Henceforward the cost of these operations and of the renewal of their fleets fell principally on the Romans themselves, while any trade they had had was paralysed by Carthaginian cruisers, which ranged as far north as the home district of Latium.

A fourth stage of the war opens in 247 B.C. with the appearance of a Carthaginian commander, Hamilcar Barca, worthy of the honourably descriptive name (Barca, or Barak, means 'lightning') that he bore. By vigorous privateering—for Carthage, too, was running short of state-owned ships—and by establishing fresh raiding ports at Ercte and Eryx, whence he could devastate the Romans' communications with their own siege works, he prolonged the desperate resistance of the blockaded fortresses, and all but exhausted the resources and the determination of the besiegers.

### Carthage brought to her Knees

FINALLY, in 242 B.C., the perilous experiment of naval action was adopted once more by the Senate. The new fleet was built with private subscriptions, but it was well found, and at last efficiently handled. Its sole commission was to cut off

**WALLED ERYX**

The ramparts of Eryx, where Hamilcar established himself in 244 B.C., and its temple are represented in this coin.

*British Museum*

supplies from the Sicilian fortresses, and in this it not only succeeded, but had the good luck to intercept and destroy the last ill escorted convoy that Carthage was able to send. The Carthaginian government could do no more; there were native revolts in Africa; and mercenaries will not fight long without pay. Hamilcar was prepared to persist, but was induced at last to conduct the negotiations himself.

The Roman terms were severe : Carthage was to evacuate Sicily and surrender it to Rome, with all adjacent islands ; to restore prisoners and deserters ; to pay an immense indemnity spread over ten years ; and to promise not to make war in future on Hiero or his allies. Hiero's territory was enlarged, and his independence as an ally of Rome guaranteed. Messana and a few other cities were received likewise into 'free' and equal alliance ; but the rest of Sicily remained in Roman hands as conquered territory, administered by a resident governor and chief justice, sent annually from Rome, and paying to Rome a tithe on all produce, and harbour dues on all imports and exports (241).

This was a fresh departure in Roman foreign policy, due partly to the circumstances of annexation after ruinous war, partly to an unfortunate imitation of Carthaginian methods. For in Italy all districts which were not either the territory of a 'free and allied' city and consequently self-governed, or depopulated and therefore assignable as war booty to Roman citizens or for public use as grazing grounds, had been retained by their original inhabitants, under separate treaty in each district, and on the understanding that those inhabitants should help Rome in time of need, and meanwhile enjoy some or all of the civil rights of the Romans themselves. The more favoured peoples were even admitted to Roman citizenship ; they were qualified, that is, to serve in the legionary army, even if they had neither desire nor facilities for exercising their political franchise in one of the numerous ' rural tribes ' which were added to the voting list from time to time. The best reason for the new distinction between ' Italians ' and ' provincials ' was that the civilization of the Sicilians was fundamentally Greek ; their laws, customs, and beliefs were Greek. It seemed, therefore, to be the more considerate course to leave them in enjoyment of the culture and rights that they had, with only a Roman appeal court to see that local customs were observed, and so prevent private grievances from breeding political discontent, and with a Roman commissioner to organize local resistance in case of attack, until the home government could intervene.

But it was one thing to make local taxation balance the expenses of administration, and quite another to impose a permanent tribute for the use of the ' Senate and People of Rome,' even if for the immediate future it might be fair to supplement the huge Carthaginian indemnity by a subsidy, to restore Rome itself to solvency. Worse still, the mismanagement of the ' public lands ' (confiscated as already described from the more obstinate of the conquered peoples), which had long been a public scandal in Italy, was greatly aggravated when it occurred on the very large scale, which seems to have been allowed in Sicily, and with only the quite inadequate supervision of an annually appointed governor, without opportunity for inspection, or even experience of the system. And the reckless and oppressive exploitation which the Carthaginians seem to have practised in all their dominions set a disastrous example to the Roman speculators and absentee landlords, who alone had the private wealth to undertake the management of what were nominally ' estates of the Roman People.'

### Aftermath of the Exhausting Struggle

If Rome had suffered heavily in the war, Carthage was almost ruined ; and the peace brought worse disasters still. First, the vast mercenary forces which had been levied, but not yet transported to Sicily, mutinied for arrears of pay ; and for three years the Carthaginians carried their lives in their hands, while the ' truceless war ' raged till Hamilcar's strategy and personal influence outmatched the blunders of the government and the blind fury of the rebels, and exterminated the survivors of the army he had hoped to command. Though Rome refused to take advantage of this African mutiny, it was another matter when Hamilcar was at last able to set sail for Sardinia to deal with a similar rebellion there. This the Roman Senate chose to regard as a breach of the peace treaty, and by way of compensation extorted not only an additional indemnity, but the surrender of Sardinia itself, and Corsica also. Probably the mere knowledge that Hamilcar was at sea at all bred panic, and cruel injustice ; but whatever the motive, the possession of these imperfectly civilized islands gave Rome frequent anxiety thereafter ; and, worst of all, provoked Hamilcar to the vast project of reprisals in Spain, which occupied the remainder of his life. Sardinia, in due course, became a Roman ' province ' on the same model as Sicily ; Corsica merely derelict territory at the disposal of the Senate and any Roman speculator who cared to venture thither for timber or minerals.

### Causes and Effects of the War

The First Punic War was probably inevitable. It was the outcome of centuries of well matched rivalry between Greek and Phoenician on Sicilian soil, and of the complications oversea, as far distant as Etruria, Corsica and Epirus, which that rivalry provoked. Now, after almost as long a preparation, the quite separate feud between highland and lowland peoples in Italy had been settled wholly in favour of the latter ; and the lowland interests of Italy, with the sole exception of Etruria, were intimately connected with those of the Greek cities on the coasts. In the course of that struggle for supremacy in Italy the other question, whether Etruria was to retain its early mastery, had been settled in Campania by the Samnite invasion, and farther north by Rome and its Latin allies. Finally the blunders of Tarentum and its Spartan and Epirote helpers had convinced all Greek cities in turn, from Cumae to Syracuse, that the West fared best when it looked after itself ; that their sole alternative to hereditary feuds and divided counsels was general but separate agreement to co-operate with Rome. Historically, Sicily had been unified with Magna Graecia, and Magna Graecia with Campania, by the Greek colonisation of all three ; and, in view of the past, Greek Sicily could not feel itself safe as long as Carthage held even one defensible port on its coast. And if Greek freedom of intercourse with Phocaean Massalia (called by the Romans Massilia, modern Marseilles) was to be assured, Corsica, at least, and even Sardinia, must be in friendly control ; for Massalia too had had its own troubles with Carthage, and in due course became a 'free and equal ally of the Roman People,' like its sister cities in South Italy.

Africa, on the other hand, and western Libya were a separate affair. Between Greek Cyrene and the Phoenician Tripolis there was no-man's-land enough behind the Quicksands ; west of Sicily there had never been Greek colonies ; and the old Phocaean connexion with Tartessus seems to have lapsed early. Daughter cities of Massalia, indeed, existed as far afield as Tarraco near the mouth of the Ebro ; and Roman politicians argued from the look of its name that Saguntum (in the rich coast plain of Valencia) had been once a colony from Greek Zacynthus. But with these exceptions Spain, like Africa, was unexplored by Greeks, and there is little reason to believe that even Phoenicians had seriously tapped the wealth of the land, except around Gades (Cadiz).

### Two Courses open to Carthage

THE Carthaginians, therefore, had not lost everything, though they had been driven out of waters where they necessarily collided with Greeks, and increasingly with Italian traders also, as their commercial treaties with the Romans show. There were two distinct careers still open to them : their original exploitation of Africa, both the mountainous north

and the oases and caravan routes towards the Niger basin, in the first place ; and the development of trade in the farther west of the Mediterranean, above described. Conservative managers were prepared to be content with Africa, relying on mutually advantageous trade with their late enemies, to make good their losses of oversea territory. Hamilcar Barca on the other hand was for the bolder plan of forestalling Greek and Roman alike in Spain, while that was still possible ; like Canning, but in a more literal sense, he would ' call a new world into existence to redress the balance of the old.' It was in the long run the inability of Carthage to choose definitely between these two policies, and also to keep family feuds out of public life, that forfeited the fruits of both.

### A New Carthage founded in Spain

THE ' new world ' of Spain, to which Hamilcar now (238) turned, with the sceptical and lukewarm concurrence of the home government, was a continent rather than a country. Around its great central plateau lie to the north-west the distant, rugged, barbarous, but metal-yielding highlands, to the north-east the wide trough of the Iberus (Ebro) valley, which gives its ancient name to the whole ' Iberian ' peninsula. South-east, a continuation of the Atlas range curves round from the Strait, parallel with the Mediterranean coast, and sinks seaward to form the chain of the Balearic islands ; like the north-west, this highland is very rich in copper and other ores. Behind this, and between it and the south edge of the plateau, lies the Guadalquivir basin, like another Ebro, and of almost tropical fertility. Beyond, the range which reaches the sea at Cape St. Vincent is another mining district, and then come the coastal plains of Portugal, intersected by the great rivers which drain the central plateau. Smaller frontage plains, on the Mediterranean littoral, extend some way both north and south from Cape Nao opposite the Balearic islands.

Whereas former explorers, both Phoenician and Greek, had made Gades and the Tartessian country, beyond the

Strait, their headquarters, Hamilcar's wider designs required a more accessible and also a more defensible base. This he found in a detached spur of the south-eastern range, midway in the more southerly of the frontage plains already noted. At its seaward end it is the south horn of a deep bay, which has caused a long bar of shingle to form across its mouth and enclose a lagoon, while river-silt has accumulated landward, in a very fertile plain. The situation is in essentials a duplicate of that of Carthage itself: defensible promontory, safe harbour, flanking lagoon, adjacent garden ground, with arable and pasture beyond and good valley routes through the mountains towards the plateau and the headwaters of the Guadalquivir.

Here then ' New Carthage ' was set out; and modern Cartagena preserves its name. How it flourished, and what success Hamilcar had in conciliating native peoples and exploiting natural wealth, is evident from the treaty which was drafted after Hamilcar's death in 228 B.C. between his son-in-law Hasdrubal and the Romans, by which the Ebro river was to be recognized as defining the spheres of influence of Rome and Carthage respectively. As Rome, though busy enough since the First Punic War along her northern frontiers, had no footing yet beyond the Apennines, this Ebro frontier clearly represented only the reasonable claims of Massalia and other old Phocaean settlements. But it illustrates the indifference with which responsible people in Carthage regarded Hamilcar's doings, that this agreement seems to have been neither rejected nor ratified; and certainly the Romans made no secret, a few years later, of their alliance with Saguntum, which lay nearly a hundred miles south of the Ebro, and moreover was the key to the rich coast plain of Valencia. The date of this alliance is unknown, but whether it was earlier or later than Hasdrubal's agreement, the distinction between Roman dominion and Roman alliance was quite

**ROMAN REMAINS IN A SPANISH TOWN THAT WAS ONCE INDEPENDENT**
The indifference of Carthage with regard to Spain in the decade following Hamilcar's death is illustrated by the fact that Saguntum could openly ally itself with Rome, although in the Carthaginian sphere of influence according to the treaty made in 228 B.C. A native Spanish city (erroneously believed by the Romans to have been a Greek colony), Saguntum was a wealthy commercial centre; it later became a Roman colony, when the theatre whose ruins are shown above was built.

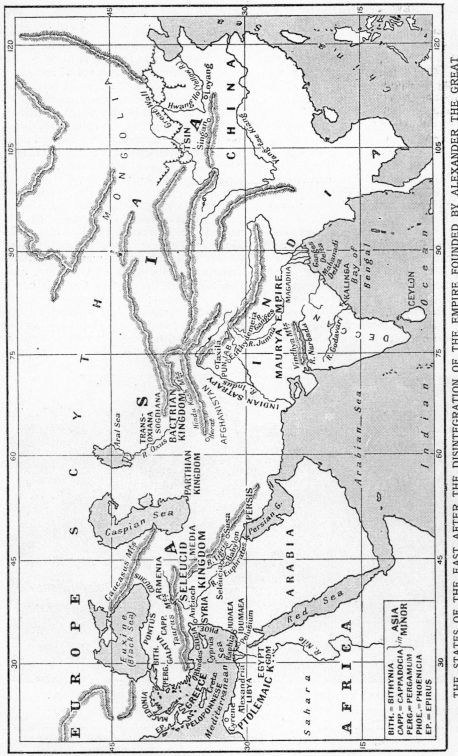

THE STATES OF THE EAST AFTER THE DISINTEGRATION OF THE EMPIRE FOUNDED BY ALEXANDER THE GREAT

Three kingdoms ruled by dynasties established by Macedonian generals emerged from the wreck of Alexander's empire. Under the Ptomelies Egypt entered upon a period of renewed prosperity; the Seleucid kings of Syria secured most of the Asiatic territories conquered by Alexander; and Macedonia was ruled by the descendants of Antigonus. Parthia, however, revolted from the Syrian kingdom, and eventually became a powerful independent empire; India quickly recovered from the Macedonian conquest, and prospered under a line of great emperors, including the saintly Asoka. In China Shih Hwang Ti made himself supreme, and welded the feudal provinces into a centralised empire. These conditions endured until Rome's invasion of Asia.

**MILITARY HIGHWAY BUILT TO SECURE ROME'S NORTHERN MARCHES**

To make his victories over the Gauls in Italy permanent, the censor Gaius Flaminius had the old military road that connected Rome with Spoletium extended to Ariminum (see map in page 149). Named the Flaminian Road after him, it now ran across the main ridge of the Apennines to Cales, and thereafter followed the pass of Intercisa (modern Furlo), where it is seen above. At Forum Fortunae it touched the Adriatic coast, which it skirted until Ariminum was reached.

*Photo, Alinari*

well recognized; for example in the Carthaginian treaty of 348 B.C.

In eight years more, by 220 B.C., all the native peoples up to the Ebro line had been brought into formal subjection to Carthage; only Saguntum remained not only independent but positively allied with Rome. Hasdrubal was dead (he had been assassinated in 221), and it was on his successor Hannibal that the responsibility lay for what followed. Hannibal was the son of Hamilcar Barca; he had been consecrated from boyhood to avenge his father's expulsion from Sicily, and was a man of amazing energy and resource, one of the great personal leaders of all time. Wise heads in Carthage had done what they could to prevent his succession to the Spanish viceroyalty; but his father's army worshipped him, and would have no other; so the government accepted him. The Spanish venture had been throughout a personal enterprise of his family; there was no obligation to support him, and in case of trouble he could be disowned. It seems certain that Carthage itself did not want another war with Rome.

Nor did the Romans want it. Since the treaty with Hasdrubal they had been forced to undertake heavy work by a fresh raid of Gauls from beyond the Alps; they had been obliged to occupy Gaulish territory as far as the Po, to found colonies at Placentia and Cremona, for the defence of the passage of this river, and to raid beyond it as far as Mediolanum (Milan). The great Flaminian Road had just been carried forward to the Adriatic coast to ensure communication with their new conquests. They had had little wars in Liguria and also in Istria, and in 221 B.C. their whole field force was in Illyria across the Adriatic, destroying the league of pirates which had been harrying the east coast of Italy.

The significance of the Illyrian affair is not to be overlooked. Piracy had long been rife in the Adriatic, with which until recently Rome had scarcely been concerned; but the Punic war had left her mistress of its Italian shore as Dionysius of Syracuse had once been for a short time; and her orderly instincts gave her a corresponding sense of responsibility. In suppressing the Illyrian buccaneering power, she appeared as the protector primarily of Greek commerce, a champion of Hellenic interests against the barbarian ; and by so doing she was preparing the states of Greece to turn to her as protector against Macedon.

All these operations tended to consolidate the Roman power in Italy ; if the Roman domination restricted political liberties, it at least gave as compensation an unwonted security. But for Rome they had been costly and exhausting ; and the last thing she desired was to be forced into a war likely to prove still more costly and still more exhausting, of which the issue would be extremely doubtful.

Accordingly, when the news reached Rome that Hannibal was attacking Saguntum, the Romans sent him only a formal protest ; and when this was ignored, took up the affair with the responsible government of Carthage. Here opinion was divided : one party wished to surrender Hannibal and compensate Rome, but Hannibal's friends prevailed. They appealed to the treaty of 228 B.C.—which had not been ratified—and laid the blame for the collision on Saguntum, thus gaining time till Hannibal had destroyed it. Then, when Roman envoys arrived again, they tried too late to repudiate the draft treaty, and all responsibility for Hannibal's acts : did the Romans wish to pick a quarrel or not ? 'Peace or war, as you shall choose,' was the reply ; and as peace was broken, war it was—the 'Hannibalic war' of the next seventeen years.

### The World East of the Adriatic

THE critical struggle in the West (218-202) involved the first entanglement of Macedonian affairs with those of Rome ; so that before proceeding to the story of the Second Punic War, we must follow the developments that had been taking place in the world lying east of the Adriatic Sea since Pyrrhus planned his great adventure in the west in 280.

In that year Ptolemy Ceraunus stabbed his benefactor Seleucus in the back while engaged in a religious ceremony, and was somewhat incomprehensibly hailed as king by the army. Lysimachus and Poliorcetes were dead ; the son of the latter, Antigonus Gonatas, and the son

of Seleucus, Antiochus I of Syria, were not immediately ready to challenge the assassin and usurper. His career, however, was cut short by a new and unlooked-for enemy. He was slain in the same year, in battle with the Gauls.

There is no earlier record of a recognizable Celtic incursion in the east. When the first Celtic tide flowed westwards, it had not struck the lower waters of the Danube. But now in the early third century B.C., swarms of Gauls—whether they were a back-flow, as seems more probable, or a belated horde—flooded into Thrace. The crown was hardly on Ptolemy's head when he had to march against them, to his own doom. In 279 they poured down through Thessaly into Phocis ; but at Delphi the god—so runs the legend—guarded his own against the sacrilegious barbarian with earthquakes and portents ; and the demoralised Gauls were put to utter rout by the hastily gathered levies of the Greek cities. They rolled back into Thrace, where for some time to come they remained in possession.

### Dynasties of the Diadochi

IN the turmoil which followed the death of Ceraunus, Antigonus Gonatas won the Macedonian crown, but had to fight hard for it. For Pyrrhus on his return from the west advanced a rival claim ; the cities of Greece were tumbled into the fray ; and it was only brought to an ignominious end when Pyrrhus was killed by a tile, flung by a woman's hand from a house-top, as he was fighting his way through the streets of Argos (272).

Pyrrhus left no efficient successor. As a soldier, Hannibal rated him as second only to Alexander ; but, being a soldier for the love of soldiering, and nothing more, he achieved a magnificent reputation, and accomplished nothing at all.

Just over half a century, then, after the death of Alexander, the dynasties of three of his generals were established in three parts of the vast dominion of which he had made himself lord. The grandson of Antigonus ruled in Europe, the son of Seleucus in Asia, the son of Ptolemy in Egypt. But in Europe Thrace was no longer a part of the Macedonian kingdom ;

in Asia the effective Seleucid dominion or empire corresponded in extent to the old Assyrian empire, with Media and Persia— all that lay to the east of that had gone or was on the point of going. As in the ancient days, Egypt disputed the sovereignty in a great part of Syria ; and, again as in the ancient days, most of what lay west and north of the Taurus barrier was broken up into independent and ill-defined kingdoms, or states whose rulers had not yet assumed the royal title.

· Antigonus Gonatas was secured in Macedon by the fall of his brilliant and dangerous rival, in 272. Theoretically, the states of Greece were still independent ; but the old states were as incapable as ever of effective combination, and individually there was not now any one of them strong enough to impose active co-operation on others, or by itself to challenge the supremacy, which in actual fact meant the dictation, of the king of Macedon. The support given to Pyrrhus by several Peloponnesian cities and by Athens now afforded Gonatas an excuse for reducing them to subjection, and establishing in most of them tyrants who were at his service.

### The Achaean and Aetolian Leagues

**W**ITHIN the next few years, however, two leagues were coming into prominence, the Achaean and the Aetolian. Achaea is that strip of the Peloponnese which lies on the shore of the Gulf of Corinth. Hitherto it had played no conspicuous part in history. The league in which its cities had united themselves practically formed a neutral state amid the general commotions. But it had felt the heavy hand of Antigonus, and in 251 it was joined by Sicyon under the guidance of Aratus, who had effected the expulsion of the tyrants who ruled there by favour of Macedon. Aratus at once became the moving spirit of the Achaean League, which within a few years was joined by city after city within and

**AN ARMED GAUL**
This Roman badge of pewter represents a Gaulish warrior of the period of the Celtic invasions of Thrace.
*British Museum*

without the Peloponnese, Sparta as usual holding aloof.

The Aetolian League was a long-standing confederation of the politically undeveloped highland tribes in the west, on the north side of the Corinthian Gulf. In the past, Aetolia had stood clear of Greek political complications, though the Athenian general Demosthenes had tried— and failed—to make it a base for attacking Boeotia. Latterly, however, it had been absorbing wider territories, and after the death of Gonatas in 239 the Aetolians were even succeeding in bringing considerable portions of the Peloponnese under their sway.

Antigonus Gonatas was succeeded by his son Demetrius II, who died in 229, leaving an heir (afterwards Philip V), who was as yet too young to succeed. For nine years the throne was occupied by his cousin and guardian Antigonus Doson, on whose death in 220 Philip, being then only seventeen, became king, Antigonus having regarded himself as regent on behalf of the boy.

In the last years of Gonatas a pathetic attempt was made by the young Spartan king Agis IV to revive the old heroic ideals of Sparta, which cost him his life. His chief opponent was the other king, Leonidas ; and, curiously enough, it was on Cleomenes, son of Leonidas, that the mantle of Agis fell. The result appeared in a revival of military vigour while Demetrius and Antigonus Doson (Antigonus the ' Man of Promises ') were reigning in Macedon. But a Spartan recovery meant collision with the new Peloponnesian power, the Achaean League (227- 221) ; Aratus was compelled to invite the intervention of Antigonus ; and the rising Spartan power was shattered at the battle of Sellasia. The death of Antigonus next year (220) made young Philip king of Macedon—just when Rome was completing her operations against the troublesome pirates of the Illyrian coast.

**FORTRESS THAT DOMINATED THE WEALTHY CITY OF PERGAMUM**

The citadel of Pergamum was renowned as an inviolate stronghold in the Hellenistic age, and here Lysimachus, king of Thrace and later of Macedon also, kept his treasures. They were entrusted to the care of Philetaerus, a eunuch in his service, who appropriated them when he revolted to Seleucus. On the death of this monarch he declared himself independent, and by his political genius laid securely the foundations of the Pergamene kingdom that he bequeathed to his nephew Eumenes.

*From 'Altertümer von Pergamum IV'*

The blow to Sparta, however, encouraged the Aetolians to develop their aggressive activities in the Peloponnese and brought them into direct conflict with the Achaean League, which again appealed to Macedon. Philip sent aid, but deserted Aratus in 217. For Hannibal was in Italy and Demetrius of Pharos, one of the pirate chiefs, appealed for aid against Rome. Philip's eyes were turned to the West, and from this time Greek affairs are intertwined with the story of Rome. Philip made alliance with Hannibal ; as he was the friend of the Achaeans, the Aetolians sought and obtained alliance with Rome ; but both to Rome and to Macedon, though both intervened, the affairs of Greece were a secondary matter. The conflict was in 205 closed for the time by a decisive victory won over the Aetolians and Lacedaemonians by the great Arcadian captain of the Achaean League, Philopoemen (c. 243–183), at Mantinea.

When Seleucus was murdered by Ptolemy Ceraunus he had actually become lord of all that had once been the Persian empire except Egypt and the Indian satrapy, with the addition of Alexander's farthest eastern conquest, Sogdiana ; but in Asia Minor his authority was merely nominal. In the sixty years following his death, his successors, Antiochus I (280–261), Antiochus II Theos (261–246), Seleucus II (246–226) and Seleucus III (226–223), were wholly ousted from Asia Minor, lost all the territories east of Persis proper and Media, where new powers were rising, and lost to Egypt Phoenicia and a substantial part of Syria, though the Syrian or Seleucid power revived under Antiochus III, called ' the Great ' (223–187).

In Asia Minor the native kingdoms of Cappadocia, Pontus and Bithynia were already established. Philetaerus and his nephew Eumenes were founding a principality of their own at Pergamum. In 277 the Gauls from Thrace, first coming at the invitation of Nicomedes of Bithynia, poured into the country, and though Antiochus inflicted a severe defeat on them, he could not prevent them from conquering a great area in the centre, where their confederacy became known as Galatia. The Gallic menace was not in fact quelled till Attalus I of Pergamum (241–197), the successor of Eumenes, refused to pay the

**FOUNDER OF A DYNASTY**

Philetaerus, the first ruler of Pergamum, achieved his position by skilful political intrigue, having originally governed that city for Lysimachus of Thrace. He is here represented on a Pergamene tetradrachm, with Athena on the reverse.

*From John Ward, ' Greek Coins ' (Murray)*

accustomed blackmail demanded by the brigand power, and by a decisive victory delivered the neighbouring lands from their aggressions—incidentally winning thereby grateful recognition as King of Pergamum, and a large accession of territory.

The reigns of Antiochus I and II were much occupied with a series of ' Syrian ' wars with Ptolemy Philadelphus (285–246), the effect of which was to place most of the south coast of Asia Minor as well as Phoenicia in Ptolemy's control. Antiochus II was still reigning when, in 250, Diodotus the governor of Bactria declared his independence, and two enterprising nomad chiefs, Arsaces and Tiridates, ejected the governor of Parthia and founded the Arsacid Dynasty of what was to be ere long the Parthian empire.

Seleucus II, who almost throughout his twenty years' reign was at war with his brother Antiochus Hierax, failed to recover what had already been lost, and lost more of Asia Minor to Attalus. During this reign, Ptolemy III Euergetes (247–222), a celebrated patron of literature and the arts, as his father had also been, carried conquering arms as far as Susa and bore back to Egypt vast spoils, but did not seek to retain his fresh acquisitions. A year after the accession of Antiochus III, Ptolemy IV Philopator (222–205) succeeded Euergetes in Egypt.

The young king of northern Syria—for at the beginning of his reign Antiochus was hardly more—showed energy and capacity. He crushed a revolt in Media and Persis, and recovered Phoenicia ;

but when he attempted a direct attack on Egypt he met with a crushing defeat at Raphia (217) which compelled him to relinquish this conquest, though Ptolemy made no further use of the victory. But in the course of the next few years Antiochus carried his arms into Parthia, where Arsaces III was forced to acknowledge his suzerainty, and into Bactria, where Euthydemus, the successor of Diodotus, only saved his independence by threatening to call in the Scythians, which would have meant the disappearance of that Hellenism of which the house of Seleucus boasted itself to be traditional champion. Before the Bactrian expedition, he had recovered lost provinces in Asia Minor from Pergamum. Thus when the Punic war in the west was drawing to its close, Antiochus ' the Great ' was the most powerful potentate east of the Adriatic and west of the Hindu Kush.

### Developments in the Farther East

IN India, however, the great Maurya empire, founded by Chandragupta, had in the meantime been glorified by the

**AN ABLE AND SUCCESSFUL DESPOT**

After crushing the Gauls in Asia Minor, Attalus I of Pergamum (who is almost certainly portrayed in this bust) took the title of king. A capable ruler, he enlarged his dominions, and encouraged learning and the arts.

*Berlin Museum ; from Delbrück, 'Antike Porträts '*

reign of Asoka ; and far away in unknown China important events were happening.

China was in effect a vast empire of the order commonly called feudal ; that is, the whole was an aggregation of principalities or baronies, large and small, which professed allegiance to one emperor whose actual authority was of the slightest. Since about the twelfth century B.C. the Chou dynasty had been reigning. But while common institutions prevailed, there

**BRILLIANT RULERS OF HELLENIC EGYPT**
Ptomely II Philadelphus (left) and Ptolemy III Euergetes (right) both increased the wealth and power of Egypt ; and by their assiduous patronage of learning made Alexandria the greatest contemporary centre of Greek culture. Ptolemy II married his sister—the famous Arsinoë (middle).
*From Delbruck, ' Antike Porträts,' and John Ward, ' Greek Coins '*

was no effective central control ; princes and barons ruled as seemed good to them according to their power in their own provinces ; the defence of the empire against the incursions of the central Asian nomad hordes was left to the barons of the marches. Towards the middle of the third century a group of confederate barons headed by the prince of T'sin, on the western march, overturned the Chous without setting up a new emperor. The obvious necessity, however, was the establishment of a central authority ; and in 220 the young and exceedingly vigorous prince who had recently succeeded in T'sin, the most powerful of the principalities, boldly declared himself sole emperor by the name of Shih Hwang Ti and proceeded to make good his position.

In the ten years of his reign (220–210) he built the Great Wall of China, a solid rampart 1,200 miles in length, against the nomads, from T'sin in the west to the

north-eastern sea—the labour involved must have been terrific—and he deliberately destroyed nearly all the books and records, in particular the works of Confucius, to which Chinese conservatism could appeal in support of the system which he was engaged in obliterating. The books which were not burned in the holocaust were saved and secreted at the peril of the lives of their saviours, of whom some five hundred were actually buried alive ; while thousands, probably, were sent to labour on the building of the Wall. While Shih Hwang Ti reigned, there was no doubt about the power of the central authority. He did not live long enough to found a dynasty ; but that was done a few years after his death by a soldier of peasant origin, known to history as Kao-ti or Kao-Tsu (206–193), who became the first ruler of the great dynasty of Han.

Ɜɴ India Chandragupta had so extended the Magadha dominion that when he abdicated in 298 he was recognized sovereign from Herat to the Narbada and the Ganges Delta. When his son and successor, Bindusara, died, after a reign of twenty-five years, in 273, the empire had been carried across the Narbada and embraced a great part of the Deccan or what is now the Nizam's Dominion. There was, apparently, some dispute over the succession, for the accession of his son, Asoka, to the throne, was in 269.

After the normal manner of Indian princes, Asoka started on a career of

**FIRST KING OF PARTHIA**
Arsaces, having headed a successful revolt of the Parthians against Antiochus II of Syria (250 B.C.), founded the Parthian Kingdom. He is depicted on the obverse (left) of this tetradrachm struck a century later by Mithradates I.
*British Museum*

conquest, and subjugated Kalinga, the eastern territory lying between the rivers Mahanadi and Godavari. He conquered no more ; and it was not that he lacked either the means or the ability, but simply because his campaigning experience made the miseries and iniquities of war utterly detestable to him. He had undergone conversion. What is fundamental in the story, if it can be called a story, of his reign, which ended in 232, we know from his own ' pillar edicts ' and ' rock edicts,' which constitute an autobiography ; the later fictions of Buddhist monks may be ignored. Conversion with him meant that he embraced the doctrines of Buddhism with conviction, and on the moral side not only practised them himself but required his ministers to make them the basis of their administration.

His vast realm was governed on the principles of an intelligent humani-tarianism, which relied upon moral force but was under no illusions as to the need for efficient physical force behind it. Significantly, his subjects are bidden to turn from evil ways ' lest they be chastised,' and doubtless he was puritanically severe in compelling them to abandon practices enjoined by long religious usage but incompatible with Buddhist teaching. But the unique fact in his regime was his constant insistence upon truth, justice, reverence and compassion, but above all compassion, in public administration no less than in private conduct.

Nor does it seem possible to doubt that so long as he lived the enlightened experiment was amazingly successful. After the victorious war which made Asoka loathe war, the reign was one of unbroken peace ; a peace, moreover, which was extended beyond the borders of the empire, because independent poten-

**RAMPART TO PREVENT THE INCURSIONS OF BARBARIANS INTO CHINA**
The strength of the central government in China under the Emperor Shih Hwang Ti is indicated by the fact that he could undertake so ambitious a work as the building of the Great Wall, although, indeed, it was not completed by him. Forced labour alone was employed, but the cost of operations must have been immense. Here we see the section that crosses the hills above the Nankow Pass.

*Photo, Underwood*

tates in their quarrels learnt to seek in the arbitration of the great king a better solution than in the arbitrament of battle.

When Asoka came to the throne of Magadha, Buddhism was but a minor sect. His own conversion to it inspired him with a missionary zeal which transformed it into one of the great religions of the world, though in India itself it fell back to a less than secondary position. Among the misssionaries were Asoka's younger brother and sister, who carried it into Ceylon.

The peaceful and prosperous rule of Asoka favoured the high artistic development of the period ; but we must not forget that it was powerful as well as peaceful. He held friendly communication not only with Antiochus I and II, whose territories were in contact with his own, but with Ptolemy, and with an Alexander who may have been the successor of Pyrrhus in Epirus.

Such an empire, however, as that of Asoka needs a succession of Asokas to weld it into permanence. Of what befell after his death in 232 we have the scantiest knowledge.

It would seem that the great dominion was parted between two of his grandsons, and within fifty years the last of the Mauryas was dead. For centuries to come, Indian history is illuminated only by occasional sidelights ; and we must now revert to the history of the West, and the decisive struggle which in its result left the great Italian Republic the foremost world power.

## Outbreak of the Second Punic War

THE Second Punic War, like the first, falls into distinct stages, which we summarise. The Roman plan of attack was to invade Africa at once with the first army, and at least disorganize Carthaginian mobilisation. The second army was sent to Massalia, in case Hannibal should interfere with friends of Rome north of the Ebro. A third force was obviously required to garrison the Gaulish territories between Apennines and Po, which had only surrendered three years before, and were known to have been visited by agents of Hannibal, and to have promised him free passage if he should try to reach Italy by land.

Some of the Gauls indeed revolted at once, and delayed the departure of the northern force for Massalia, till it was too late to stop Hannibal even at the Rhône. For this was his master stroke, to circumvent both Roman sea power and Rome's Greek allies between Ebro and Alps, and establish an enemy base in the heart of the Roman dominion. He certainly counted on such measure of support from his friends in Carthage as would deplete the Roman garrisons in Italy, for the defence of Sicily and the south ; with good fortune the Roman first army might be shut up in Africa, and destroyed there like that of Regulus.

### Hannibal's Adventures in Italy

FORTUNATELY, all the Roman commanders acted with true perspicacity. The southern army was diverted just as it was sailing for Africa, and brought round by sea to the Adriatic flank of the northern front, where the new military road gave it direct reinforcement from Rome. Consequently when Hannibal after unprecedented hardships descended on the Italian side of the Alps, he found a Roman field army strongly posted under shelter of the new garrison colonies on the Po.

More happily still, the force that was too late to intercept Hannibal at Massalia was led at once into Spain, to disorganize his only sure source of reinforcements, and undo the empire-building of his father and himself.

Hannibal's tactics and leadership, however, were as brilliant as his strategy. His first Italian campaign in 218 broke Roman resistance north of the Apennines at the fords of Trebia and Ticinus. His next destroyed their whole army (217) at Lake Trasimene in Etruria, and seemed to open the straight road to Rome. But the third year found him not at the gates of Rome, but far to the southward, now in Apulia, now in Campania ; and even the victory in which he destroyed yet another whole army at Cannae (216), brought him no nearer to his object than when he abandoned Etruria.

There were several reasons for this. A flying column such as his necessarily consisted largely of cavalry, and for horse-pasture Italy has no large plains except in the far south. The greater corn-lands also are all remote from Rome ; no nearer indeed than Campania. If Rome itself, therefore, did not fall at the first assault, it was necessary to find some such Italian base, and await reinforcements from Carthage or from Spain. And so far from taking Rome by assault, Hannibal did not come even within sight of its walls till after Cannae ; for the great citizen-colonies along all lines of communication with the city blocked approach, resisted attack from light forces such as his, and threatened his rear if he left them unblockaded.

### Roman Allies stand firm

So long as these outposts stood, the countryside dared not rise even if it wished to do so ; and it was the worst disillusionment of Hannibal, that the peoples of Italy, and even what was left of the Etruscans, gave almost no sign of disaffection. Hannibal could remember the ' Truceless War ' between Carthage and her mercenaries, and the African campaign of Regulus was only ten years before his birth ; but this was quite another situation. The subjects of Carthage had been ready enough to make common cause with her enemies ; but Rome's bold experiment of clemency after surrender, and progressive incorporation of old enemies in her own commonwealth, had succeeded too completely for panic or desertion to be possible.

Hannibal's first stroke then had failed. But he had established himself in southern Italy, where Pyrrhus had fought, and he had secured possession of Capua, the key to Campania ; it was another thirteen years before he left Italy by his own choice. He had, however, no sea-port, and, what was worse, no assurance of help from Carthage, which seems to have taken little further part in the war, except for a raid on Sardinia in 215 B.C., when it ought to have been sending men to Hannibal, and the landing of a small force in southern Italy in the following year.

Two strokes of ill luck, however, befell the Romans in this middle period of the war. Hiero of Syracuse died in 216 B.C., a very old man ; ancient feuds broke out there at once, and the popular party seized the chance to revive old dreams of Syracusan empire. These were encouraged by Hannibal, and also by the Carthaginian government, which profited by the Sicilian revolt to reoccupy a large part of the island ; and it was only after two years' blockade that Syracuse was recovered and Hiero's hoarded wealth made available for the conduct of the war. Even so, Carthaginian forces were not completely expelled from the province until 210.

The other misfortune was the dislike of Rome inspired by Illyrian refugees in Philip V of Macedon, and the help consequently rendered by him to Hannibal from oversea, until the Romans managed to capture his Adriatic ports, and distract his attention by encouraging a coalition of Greek cities against him, and accepting the overtures of the Aetolian League, with the significant consequence that while Philip was not able to be of much use to Hannibal, and still less to Carthage, Rome succeeded at very small cost in confirming the reputation she had long enjoyed for sympathy with Greek cities.

### Success of Rome's Fabian Tactics

Meanwhile, Hannibal's situation in Italy became steadily worse. Capua, which had fallen into his hands after his victory at Cannae, was besieged in 212 B.C. and destroyed utterly in the following year, in revenge for its treachery to Rome. Tarentum, which deserted to Hannibal in 212 B.C. and should have been invaluable, had Carthage used this direct means of communication to send him reinforcements, was retaken in 209 B.C. ; and the long-expected risings in Etruria and in a few Latin towns, when they did at last take place, were half-hearted, and easily suppressed. The ' Fabian tactics ' adopted by Q. Fabius Cunctator, of remaining on the defensive and refusing battle, had now been mastered by the Romans and gave the enemy little chance to gain spectacular successes like those of the first three campaigns ; the whole country was sick of the war; the invader had outstayed his welcome, and a veteran army ages rapidly without reinforcements.

Hannibal had left in Spain his brother Hasdrubal, with instructions to follow with another flying column like the first. But the wise concurrence of the Senate in the strategy of the two Scipios, who had occupied first Massalia and then Tarraco near the mouth of the Ebro, in the first year of the war, quite deranged this plan. Their ' New Rome ' at Tarraco was a serviceable counter-stroke to ' New Carthage,' and their personal qualities and diplomatic skill shook the allegiance of native leaders in Spain, and even in Numidia. There was a reaction, however, about 212 B.C., for the Spanish tribes found that they had only made a change of masters, and attempted to free themselves from the new ones. But the young and brilliant son of the consul of 218 volunteered for the Spanish command, and succeeded in 210 in capturing ' New Carthage,' and therewith much treasure, a serviceable fleet and, best of all, Hasdrubal's Spanish hostages.

### Brilliant Victory on the Metaurus

**B**Y this time, however, Hasdrubal was ready; he slipped past Scipio's forces, spent the winter of 208 quietly in the central highlands of Gaul, and entered Italy unopposed in 207 B.C. Only the skilful co-operation of the two consular armies prevented his junction with Hannibal, which seemed inevitable. Leaving in the south only a portion of his army, which effectively masked his movement, C. Claudius Nero raced north with a picked force, joined his colleague Livius, surprised, defeated and killed Hasdrubal at the Metaurus river, east of the Apennines, and was back in the south before Hannibal discovered that only a skeleton force had been facing him. The battle of the Metaurus destroyed his last hope of receiving reinforcements.

Meanwhile Scipio had expelled the remaining Carthaginian forces from Spain, defeated their counter-attack in 206, and persuaded Masinissa, a leading chief of the Numidians, to exchange the Carthaginian for a Roman alliance. Having returned to Rome, he was then allowed (with grave misgiving among the older men) to raise a fresh army largely composed of Italian volunteers, for a blow at the heart of Carthaginian rule in Africa. Here, his old friendship with Masinissa enabled him to distract and eventually to capture Syphax, the chief Numidian ally of the Carthaginians, and to cut off at the source their supply of cavalry. Hannibal was paralysed; Rome had been relieved of the Macedonian complication in 205, and was able now to concentrate upon the war in Africa.

### Hannibal's last stand at Zama

**B**Y 202 B.C. the condition of the Carthaginian home territory was desperate. Hannibal, and his other brother, Mago, who had escaped from Spain and landed on the Riviera coast of Italy, were recalled to defend Carthage itself, and attempts were made to obtain peace before the situation became more serious. But Scipio and Masinissa, each for his own reasons, persisted; they defeated the last field army that Carthage could rake together at Zama, and were able to impose their own terms.

Carthage formally surrendered Spain, and all other dependencies outside the home district of Africa. Even within these narrow limits, no war was to be declared without Roman permission. All ships but ten were surrendered, all elephants, and prisoners of war; and the enormous indemnity that was imposed—ten thousand talents spread over fifty years—made the Carthaginians practically tributaries of their conqueror. Masinissa received the whole of Numidia and Roman citizenship, as the ' friend and ally ' of the Roman people, so that he could invoke Roman intervention in Africa, whenever it was convenient. Hannibal was allowed to remain in Carthage, and did what he could to restore public confidence and credit. But his old political enemies were too strong for him, and in 196 B.C. he was banished, and spent the rest of his life at the courts of Greek kings in Syria and in Asia Minor, always looking out for occasions to damage Rome, and build up new combinations against her.

# *Third Era*

## THE WORLD STATE

### 201 B.C.–A.D. 476

---

---

WHAT we saw Alexander the Great attempting in Chapter 6 it fell to the lot of Rome to achieve. Alexander, it is true, penetrated farther to the eastward than Roman sway ever extended, but the underlying ambition of his campaigns (which would undoubtedly have included the West had his life been spared) was by stilling its internecine quarrels to liberate Hellenism for the task of civilizing the world. His death cut short his schemes ; but Rome, after absorbing Greek culture, and by her own native genius for organization, created the ' World State ' in microcosm through which Hellenism was transmitted to posterity.

In this Era we trace the fortunes and the social significance of that Empire, through the two distracted centuries of its formation under the Republic, the two centuries of its splendour under the first Caesars, and its more than two centuries of slow decline down to the deposition of the last emperor—a period of some six hundred years that no other empire has exceeded (since only at intervals has China been an empire, properly so called), and that had a continuation at Byzantium for a further thousand years.

# TABLE OF DATES FOR CHAPTER 8

*Unless otherwise stated in italics, dates refer to events in the Graeco-Roman world*

B.C.

201 Rome annexes Spanish dominion of Carthage.
Numidia an independent ally under Masinissa.
Philip of Macedon, in association with Antiochus of Syria, invades Ionia; checked by Attalus of Pergamum, he retires.

200 Philip attacks Attica. As champion of Greek independence, Rome declares (Second Macedonian) War. Athens relieved by Roman fleet.
Rising of Boii and Insubres in Cisalpine Gaul.

199 Indecisive campaigning.

198 Flamininus in Thessaly. Achaean League joins the Roman alliance.
Antiochus recovers Coele-Syria from Egypt.

197 Decisive Roman victory at Cynoscephalae.
Gauls defeated in Italy.
Rome organizes the four provincial governments, Sicily, Sardinia, and the two Spains.

196 Peace terms granted to Insubres (Trans-Po); the Boii remain in arms.
Peace terms with Philip as a dependent ally.
Flamininus proclaims the Freedom of Greece at the Isthmian Games.

195 Hannibal, exiled from Carthage, joins Antiochus, hoping to form a great coalition against Rome.
M. Porcius Cato in Spain.
Birth of Terentius Afer (Terence). Plautus fl.

193 Ptolemy V marries Cleopatra, d. of Antiochus.

192 Antiochus III crosses to Greece. Beginning of Syrian War. Philip sides with Rome. Roman fleet, in conjunction with Rhodes, Pergamum, etc., commands the Aegean.

191 Antiochus routed at Thermopylae; he retreats to Asia Minor.
Final subjugation of the Boii in Italy.

190 L. Scipio (Asiaticus), in command against Antiochus; whose fleet is shattered at Myonnesus, and his army at Magnesia.
Manlius Vulso, of his own authority, conducts a victorious campaign in Galatia, for which he is awarded a triumph.

189 Antiochus is deprived of Asia Minor and of his fleet, and Armenia is made an independent kingdom.
Roman colony planted at Bononia (Bologna).
Final subjugation of the Aetolians.

188 Northern extension of Flaminian and Aemilian Ways.

187 Death of Antiochus III. Seleucus IV king.

185 Ligurian highlanders in N. Italy maintain war for twenty years.
Scipio Africanus retires from public life.
*India:* Bridhatratha, the last Maurya, killed by Pushyamitra who founds the Sunga dynasty of Magadha. Brahman reaction against Buddhism.

184 Roman colony of Aquileia, at the head of the Adriatic.
Censorship of M. Portius Cato 'the Censor.'

183 Death of Scipio Africanus.
Death of Hannibal in Bithynia.
Death of Philopoemen.

181 Romans in Spain. Great defeat of the Celtiberians by Fulvius Flaccus.
Accession of Ptolemy VI Philometor. His mother Cleopatra regent till 173.

180 Ligurians almost crushed by Aemilius Paullus.
*Asia:* Demetrius of Bactria 'king of the Indians.'

179 Pacification of Spain by policy of Tiberius Sempronius Gracchus (father of the Gracchi).

178 Macedon; death of Philip V and accession of Perseus.

175 Gracchus in Sardinia.
Accession of Antiochus IV Epiphanes.
*India:* Repulse of a Greek conqueror (Menander ?) by Pushyamitra of Magadha.

173 Death of Cleopatra; quarrel of the government with Antiochus IV over rights in Coele-Syria.

172 Attempted assassination of Eumenes of Pergamum attributed to Perseus of Macedon.

171 Third Macedonian War begins.

170 Antiochus takes Pelusium and retires.
*China:* Wen Ti emperor till 157; period of revival of learning and humanitarian legislation.

169 Philometor shares the crown of Egypt with his brother Ptolemy Physcon. Second invasion by Antiochus.

168 Intervention of Roman envoys in Egypt; the 'circle of Popillius'; Antiochus retires, and sacks Jerusalem. Revolt of the Hasmonaeans (Maccabees) led by Mattathias.
Macedonian war: Perseus crushed at Pynda by Aemilius Paullus.

167 End of Macedonian monarchy. Macedon divided into four dependent republics.
Aemilius Paullus deals mercilessly with Epirus.
A thousand Achaean hostages, Polybius being one, are taken to Italy.

166 Massalia appeals to Rome for aid against Gauls.
*Syria:* Judas Maccabaeus, son of Mattathias, leads the Jewish insurgents.

165 Judas Maccabaeus takes and holds Jerusalem.

164 Death of Antiochus Epiphanes; the Syrian monarchy in dissolution.
Ptolemy Philometor, appealing to Rome, is reinstated as sole king.

161 Roman treaty with Judas Maccabaeus.
Death of Judas. He is succeeded by his brother Jonathan.

160 *India:* Menander reigns at Kabul till c. 140.

154 Ligurians, raiding Gaul, defeated by Opimius.

153 Revolts of Celtiberians and Lusitanians in Spain, owing to misrule of Roman governors.

151 Lucullus in Spain breaks faith with the Spaniards.
Treacherous massacre of Lusitanians by Galba.
Remnant of Achaean hostages repatriated; they stir up hostility to Rome.

149 War declared against Carthage (Third Punic War).
Death of Masinissa, and partition of Numidia.
Revolt of Andriscus (Pseudo-Philippus) in Macedon. Fourth Macedonian War.

148 Andriscus crushed by Metellus Macedonicus. Macedon made a Roman Province.

147 Achaean League attacks Sparta. Rome intervenes.
Scipio (Africanus Minor) sent to command in Africa.

146 Siege and fall of Carthage, which is obliterated, and its site solemnly cursed.
Roman Province of Africa constituted.
Corinth taken and sacked by Mummius.
Greece constituted Roman Province of Achaea.
Ptolemy VII Physcon succeeds Philometor.

143 Viriathus heads Lusitanian insurgents (S. Spain); Numantia revolts in the north.

142 Hasmonaean dynasty in Judaea established, under Simon, last of the brothers.

141 Senate ratifies peace with Viriathus.

140 Viriathus assassinated. War renewed.

139 *Asia:* Yueh-chi (Scythians) on the Oxus.
*China:* Mission of Chang Ch'ien to Yueh-chi.

138 Lusitanians subdued by Decimus Brutus.

137 Numantians compel Mancinus and Roman army to capitulate; terms negotiated by Tib. Gracchus repudiated by Senate. War continues.

136 Decimus Brutus in Galicia.

135 Outbreak of great slave revolt in Sicily.

134 Numantian war; Scipio sent to command.

133 Surrender of Numantia, which is obliterated.
Death of Attalus III of Pergamum, who bequeaths his kingdom to the Roman People. First territorial possession of Rome in Asia.
Tiberius Gracchus elected Tribune of the Plebs.

### CHAPTER 8

# THE NEW AGE OF ROMAN CONQUEST: 201—133 B.C.

THE Persian Achaemenids at the opening of the fifth century B.C. had come very near to the creation of a world state. Had the outcome of the three great battles of 480 and 479, Salamis, Plataea and Himera, been reversed, the greater part of Hellas would have been absorbed into the Persian empire immediately, and the rest of it into a Carthaginian empire which, presumably, would presently have followed the same course. Whether that world state would have broken up is an interesting study in the might-have-beens ; but the Hellenes prevented it decisively from ever coming into being. When a century and a half had elapsed, Alexander had come very near to the creation of a world state centring in Macedon instead of Persia ; but his death decisively prevented its actual realization. When another hundred years had passed, no one could have dreamed of a universal empire for any one of the five Great Powers— Macedon, Syria, Egypt, Carthage and Rome—which among them dominated the whole civilized world (except the Indian and Chinese empires, which might be called a separate world or worlds).

## Changed Aspect of the Ancient World

TWENTY years later all was changed ; for Hannibal had failed in his Titanic effort, directed not so much to the creation of a vast, all-embracing Carthaginian empire, which would have been impossible, as to the destruction of Rome. He had only succeeded in ruining Carthage and welding Rome into a supremely powerful state for which world empire was no impracticable dream. For centuries to come, the history of the world is the story of the expansion of the Italian power into the world state, whose bounds were the bounds of the known civilized world, beyond which lay not states but tribes still migrant and unsettled.

When Zama had been lost and won, and Carthage had accepted the terms dictated by the victorious Scipio, Rome was without even a potential rival to her power on land or sea west of the Adriatic. Her supremacy over all Italy south of the Po was consolidated ; she was undisputed mistress of Sicily ; Carthage was disarmed, and all her dependencies in Africa or in Spain were dependencies of Rome ; the only native potentate in Africa who could bring a strong force into the field, Masinissa of Numidia, was a friend and ally whose dominion she had herself helped to extend. The Cisalpine Gauls of North Italy, the Transalpine Gauls of what is now France, the semi-Gallic Celtiberian tribes of Spain, owed her no allegiance ; but none of them had passed beyond the stage of tribal confederation to the institution of a definite polity. Their gradual subjection to the organized power was merely a question of time—though actually of a longer time than might reasonably have been anticipated at the conclusion of the second Punic War.

## Division of Power in the East

TURNING to the East : three Great Powers were masters of what had been for a brief moment the empire of Alexander— Macedon in its European part, and Syria (the Seleucids) in Asia, the third power being Egypt under the Macedonian dynasty of the Ptolemies, still dominant in Coele-Syria and parts of the Asiatic coast. Rome had already been brought into hostile contact with the first, and friendly contact with the third ; for the Ptolemies looked to her as a counterpoise to the Antigonids and Seleucids. Not only had Ptolemy IV Philopator renewed with Rome in 210 the treaty of amity made by his grandfather in 273, but on his death in 205 the guardianship of his five-year-old son and heir, Ptolemy V Epiphanes, had been offered by the regency to the Roman Senate, and accepted ; while Philip V of Macedon and Antiochus III of Syria were coming to a private agreement for the sharing of the infant's dominions between Macedon and Syria. Virtually, though not technically, Egypt had already become a Roman protectorate.

Carthage was no longer a power in east or west ; she might with perfect safety be neglected. Any notable recrudescence of her fighting power would merely provide Rome with an excuse for blotting her out altogether, as eventually happened clearly enough. She herself, not Rome, drove Hannibal into exile, and there was not even a return from Elba for her Napoleon. Though while he lived his personal influence was exerted to stir up enemies against Rome and his unequalled military genius was at their service if they had had the wit to make use of it, Carthage repudiated her mighty son, and concentrated upon commercial revival—though as we shall presently see she did not thereby escape her doom.

Sixty years after the battle of Zama Carthage had been levelled with the ground ; the kingdom of Egypt was nominally the ally, actually the dependency, of Rome ; Macedon and Greece were Roman provinces administered by Roman governors ; and the Seleucids had been cleared out of Asia Minor for good and all. For every step Rome could persuade herself that more than sufficient justification had been provided by the victims, but the victims were not of the same opinion.

Two years had not elapsed since the battle of Zama when war was for the second time declared between Rome and Macedon. The peace of 205 had never been more than an armed truce ; though the war preceding it had never assumed large proportions, since on the part of Rome it had been simply a diversion to prevent Philip from giving Hannibal active support in Italy. Just as Philip had been seduced into seeking an aggressive alliance with Hannibal by the crushing victory of the Carthaginians at Lake Trasimene in 217, the Roman victory on the Metaurus in 207 had soon convinced him that nothing was to be gained by continuing active hostilities, though he sent a contingent to the help of the Carthaginians in their last hopeless struggle. But no Roman government, however pacifically

**STONE THAT IMMORTALISES A PTOLEMY**
Set up at Memphis to commemorate the coronation of Ptolemy V Epiphanes, the Rosetta stone is inscribed with a decree in Greek and Egyptian. It was from this bilingual record, which is set down in three scripts—Greek, hieroglyphic and demotic—that modern archaeologists learnt to read the Egyptian hieroglyphs.

*British Museum*

disposed, could have shut its eyes to the fact of his hostility to Rome ; and a government not pacifically disposed was quite certain to make the most of any activities on the part of Philip which could bear a suspicious interpretation. If Philip did not intend to invite war, he certainly provided ample excuse for such suspicions. For the policy to which he committed himself was palpably aggressive, and was directed against friends and allies of Rome if not immediately against Rome herself.

Philip's purpose of consolidating and extending his despotic rule over the nominally free cities of Greece, the Aegean and the coasts of Asia Minor, was scarcely disguised. In 201 he carried troops across the Hellespont and set about the conquest of Caria, where after some successes he was shut up for a time by the united efforts of the Rhodian fleet and Attalus, king of Pergamum. Thence he escaped, to find Athens and other Greek cities breaking away (200) and appealing to Rome, to whose remonstrances he replied in defiant terms. The Roman people had had its fill of fighting, and refused to declare war until bluntly warned by the Senate that the real choice before them was not between war and peace but between war in Macedon or in Italy. In the character of liberator, Rome declared war.

### Decisive Roman Interference in Greece

$\mathfrak{J}$T was tolerably clear that the Greeks could not throw off the yoke of Macedon without the help of Rome, and that if they did not throw it off it would weigh them down with a merciless oppression. Whether in ridding themselves of the Macedonian bear they would merely be falling into the maw of the Roman wolf was a question not so easily answered. Those who were in the most immediate danger from Philip made their choice without hesitation ; others were doubtful ; others were fast in the grip of Philip's creatures. But to understand the political confusion in Greece during this period calls for specialized study.

The campaigning in 200 and 199 was ineffective. In 198 the command of the Roman and allied army was taken by Titus Quinctius Flamininus ; and no one

save the great Scipio was so well qualified for the task. He succeeded in winning over the Achaean League, which had been reluctant to join hands with the rival Aetolian League, the allies of Rome

**WARD OF THE ROMAN REPUBLIC**
Rome became the guardian of Ptolemy V (left) on the death of his father (205 B.C.). Its attitude towards Egypt is suggested in the denarius (right) showing a Roman ' tutor,' Lepidus, crowning Ptolemy—probably a fictitious event.
*From J. Ward, ' Greek Coins,' and G. F. Hill, ' Historical Roman Coins '*

from the beginning. Negotiations with the king proved fruitless, since the demands of the Roman on behalf of the allies would have practically deprived Philip of all control in Greece. But in 197 Flamininus was able to bring Philip to a decisive engagement at Cynoscephalae in Thessaly, where the Macedonian phalanx was thrown into disorder in attempting an advance over broken ground, the Roman seized the momentary advantage, and Philip's army was annihilated.

After Cynoscephalae Flamininus could dictate his own terms—to his Greek allies no less securely than to the vanquished foe, whom he chose to treat with a generosity by no means to the liking of more vindictive enemies. Philip was to remain king of Macedon and to pay a heavy indemnity, leaving his son Demetrius and other hostages in Rome ; he was to withdraw his garrisons from the three towns which he himself named ' the Fetters of Greece '—Chalcis, Corinth and Demetrias in Boeotia. They passed into the occupation of Roman troops.

The full terms, however, were not immediately known ; they could be laid down finally only by the Roman Senate, and all Greece waited anxiously to hear what measure of freedom would be granted; for it had known no real freedom since the days of Philip II. The celebration of the

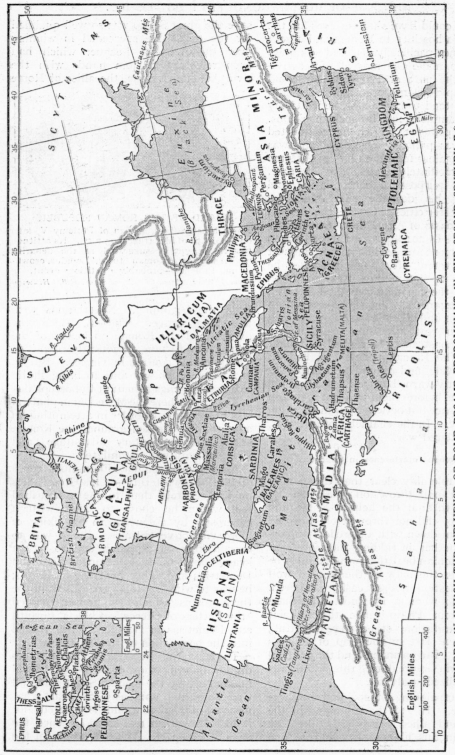

SPHERE IN WHICH THE INFLUENCE OF ROME BECAME PREDOMINANT IN THE SECOND CENTURY B.C.

At the beginning of the short period of barely seventy years dealt with in this chapter Rome had become one of the great powers, and the Mediter-ranean rang with her defeat of Carthage : but the Greek and the Roman worlds were still separate, standing back to back on opposite sides of a line running down the Dalmatian coast and so to Africa. At the end of the period Rome was the only great Mediterranean power, and Hellenistic monarchs were bowing to the mere word of her envoys. It should be noticed that the map above covers both this and the following chapters.

common Hellenic festival of the Isthmian Games at Corinth in 196 was the scene and hour chosen ; when the ringing voice of the herald proclaimed, to the amazed delight of the assembled multitude, the independence and freedom of all the Greek states that had been subject to Macedon.

But to proclaim freedom was one thing ; to establish peace with freedom was another, owing to the jealousies and hatreds that divided city from city, state from state—causes of dissension that gave endless trouble. Two more years elapsed before Flamininus could leave Greece in the belief that his task was accomplished, withdrawing the Roman garrisons even from the Fetters of Greece. And even then the freedom he left behind him was an illusion.

### Schemes of Hannibal and Antiochus

THE Aetolians, the most bitter and the most ambitious of Philip's enemies, had been treated with scant regard by Flamininus and were now angrily hostile towards Rome, though powerless to act against her ; they and others who shared their sentiments found a new ally in the ambitious king of Syria, who had hoped to make his own profit out of the Macedonian war by annexing the eastern territories over which either Philip or the child Ptolemy had claimed or held sway. After Cynoscephalae the Romans had sternly to warn him off an invasion of Thrace, following upon the seizure of cities in Asia which Philip had been forced to evacuate. Hannibal's attempt to reorganize Carthage after her humiliation had been frustrated, and the great captain, driven into exile but still relentlessly bent on the overthrow of Rome, made his way to Antiochus, at Ephesus, seeking to build up a new coalition against his lifelong foe. From the Aetolians came a mission with the same object, though there was no hope of support from Philip, who was no friend either of Antiochus or the Aetolians, and little enough from the Achaean League.

Antiochus viewed the scheme with favour ; under Hannibal's direction, it would have been very formidable. His plan was that he should carry a powerful force to Carthage, bring Carthage herself into the war, and invade Italy in force while the Greeks rose, supported by an overwhelming force from Asia. Even so, the success of it turned on Hannibal's old mistaken assumption that Rome's subjects and allies would spring to arms and hail with joy their liberators from the yoke of the tyrant state. But it was ruined from the outset by the blundering impetuosity of the Aetolians and the arrogant folly of Antiochus.

Encouraged by the favourable attitude of the king of Syria, the Aetolians and their ally Nabis, the unspeakable tyrant who had long been established in Sparta, where he was thoroughly hated, struck at once (192) ; but they only succeeded in capturing Demetrias (one of the three ' Fetters ') and driving the Achaean League into active opposition under the still effective leadership of Philopoemen. With equal recklessness Antiochus threw overboard the large scheme of the Carthaginian, and, all unready as he was, flung himself into Greece with a wholly insufficient force, ignoring Hannibal altogether, and heedless of the fact that Athens and the Achaeans were unshaken in their loyalty to Rome.

### Asia feels the Hand of Rome

THE end was not long in coming. Early in the next year (191) Roman armies, Philip co-operating, were entering Thessaly. To protect the south Antiochus occupied the historic pass of Thermopylae. As in the old days, the position, otherwise almost impregnable, was turned by a column which forced a way over the hills, and the defending army, taken in rear, broke and was cut to pieces ; the hero of the day being Marcus Porcius Cato, type of the Roman equivalent of Puritanism. Antiochus escaped with a remnant only of his force to Chalcis, and thence to Asia.

Thither he was followed next year (190) by a Roman army under the command of Lucius Scipio, the less distinguished elder brother of Africanus ; the Phoenician fleet having in the meantime been swept off the Aegean by the combined Roman and Rhodian squadrons, at the battle of Myonnesus. Near Magnesia, the huge but very miscellaneous host he had managed to collect was annihilated in a battle in which

The Altar of Zeus, built by Eumenes II, was the crowning glory of Pergamum. Here shown reconstructed, it stood on a huge base, surrounded on three sides by colonnades and approached on the fourth by a staircase. A frieze over 150 yards long, brilliantly executed and superb in effect, ran round the base.

*State Museum, Berlin*

the Roman losses were computed at four hundred, and those of Antiochus at 53,000. Again the monarch escaped with his life ; but now he could only sue for peace on such terms as the victors might be pleased to grant. Those terms left him his kingdom of Syria ; but in addition to the payment of a heavy indemnity he was required to surrender for ever his fleet, his elephants and all his possessions north and west of the Taurus mountains. Thus was the last power shattered which might, under other guidance, still have remained a possibly formidable rival to Rome. Hannibal escaped to Prusias, king of Bithynia, and not long afterwards (183) ended his own life, since Prusias was on the point of surrendering him to the Romans.

### BUILT WHEN PERGAMUM WAS AT THE ZENITH OF HER MAGNIFICENCE

As the friend and ally of Rome Pergamum gained vast accessions of territory in Asia Minor, and became one of the greatest centres of Hellenistic culture under Eumenes II, who reigned from 197 to 159 B.C. Very much wealthier than his predecessors, he was able to make Pergamum a city of majestic splendour, adorned with noble buildings and works of art. Above we see the Greek theatre, whose steepness and height make it the most impressive ruin of its kind.

*From ' Altertumer von Pergamon IV '*

The expulsion of Antiochus from Asia Minor was followed by an episode not without future significance. Lucius Scipio withdrew to Rome to receive a triumph and the hardly deserved title of Asiaticus, as his brother's great achievement had won for him that of Africanus. The eastern command devolved upon the new consul, Manlius Vulso, who, thirsting for military honours, discovered that the Galatians had fought in the armies of Antiochus—conduct obviously requiring punishment, the infliction of which incidentally offered promise of much booty accumulated by them in the course of half a century of brigandage. Accordingly Manlius declared war on his own responsibility, a

**WARRING GODDESSES AND GIANTS DEPICTED ON THE ALTAR OF ZEUS**

Noble in conception and execution, the frieze on the Altar of Zeus at Pergamum represents the Battle of Gods and Giants—a subject emblematic of the city's struggles against the Gauls. In these sections, typical in their animation, we see a goddess in the act of hurling a snake-wreathed jar (upper) ; and Victory crowning Athena who, assisted by an enormous serpent, drags a giant to the ground ; his mother, the goddess Rhea, rises from the earth to plead for his life.

*State Museum, Berlin*

ARCHITECTURAL GLORIES OF PERGAMUM IN THE HELLENISTIC AGE : THE ACROPOLIS AFTER IT WAS BEAUTIFIED BY EUMENES II

Described by the Romans as ' pre-eminent above all towns of Asia,' Pergamum in the reign of Eumenes II was the most beautiful of Hellenistic capitals. The principal buildings are here reconstructed. The Altar of Zeus is in the foreground ; on the terrace behind it Attalus I had erected statues of his Gaulish enemies. Beyond these are the formidable walls of the ancient fortress. The square above contains the ancient temple of Athena ; near it is the library, whose collection of books was second only to that of Alexandria. On the summit of the Acropolis is the much later Roman temple of Trajan.

*From Thiersch & Blum, 'Pergamon'*

course of action for which there was no precedent, smote the Celts in a vigorous campaign, carried off plentiful spoils, and was rewarded with a triumph, despite the protests of those who condemned his action as flagrantly unconstitutional. The official sanction thus given to independent action on the part of a Roman general commanding Roman armies abroad was fraught with danger for the future.

Rome, as conqueror of the aggressive king of Syria, exercised the right of distributing the territories from which she had ejected him. She did not, however, as yet claim for herself any Asiatic soil ; but the bulk of what Antiochus had held in Asia Minor was handed over to Eumenes of Pergamum, the successor of Attalus. He, like his father, had held fast by the Roman alliance and rendered good service in the recent war, as Attalus had done against Macedon. The result was the creation of a brilliant kingdom that figures little in contemporary narrative owing to its wise policy of friendship to Rome, but in all other respects now takes equal rank with the other 'successor states.' Pergamum itself rivalled Alexandria as a seat of learning and the arts.

Caria and Lycia, however, which had been stolen from Egypt, were transferred to the Rhodians as a reward for the services rendered by their fleet, instead of being restored to Ptolemy Epiphanes, that young king having been so injudicious as to marry a daughter of Antiochus.

## Settlement of Greek Affairs

MEANWHILE there had been no change in the ostensible policy of Rome in Greece. Flamininus had once more been called upon to conduct the settlement of affairs when Antiochus was flung back into Asia. The war had been forced upon Rome, and she could claim to have entered upon it as much in the interests of the Greeks who had invited her to intervene as in her own ; but having intervened, she could not escape responsibility for the establishment of a just settlement among the jealous and vindictive states that had taken part in the war. It would have been strange indeed if she had allowed the finality of her decisions to be challenged.

What Philip as an ally had taken from the confederates in Thessaly he was permitted to retain ; but just as after Cynoscephalae the Aetolians had not been allowed to wreak their vengeance on Philip, so now they were saved from the vengeance of their most vindictive foes. Like Philip they were given another chance. Cities which had hitherto held aloof from the Achaean League were compelled to join it, but the League itself was somewhat grimly warned that its sphere of action was confined to the Peloponnese, ' since a tortoise is safe just so long as it keeps its head within the shell.' There was no interference with autonomy, but the governments of the various states were palpably dependent on the good will of the Roman authority. Rome was in actual fact not less mistress of Greece than the great Philip had been master.

### Roman Policy in Gaul and Spain

NOR was it only in the East that she was preparing the way for imperial expansion during these years. During the decade after Zama the perpetually insurgent Gauls between the Alps and the Apennines were finally subjugated ; though another decade passed before the Ligurian highlanders—a folk who until this time had not developed aggressive activities, but now began to issue in raiding swarms from their mountain fastnesses—were suppressed and scattered ; and soon Roman roads and Roman military colonies were rendering the north of Italy as secure as any part of the peninsula. Before long the whole of what had been the Gallic and Ligurian area, independent of Roman authority, was transformed into the Roman province of Gallia Cisalpina, which, when once peace had been permanently established, became extremely flourishing.

In Farther Gaul, modern France, between Alps and Pyrenees, Rome had as yet no footing ; but the Punic War had planted her in Spain with no rivals other than the native tribal communities. The Carthaginian dominion founded there south of the Ebro by Hannibal's father Hamilcar had passed into her possession, as well as her own former sphere of influence north of that river. She was therefore mistress of its whole Mediterranean coast, with an undefined amount of the hinterland, but with the government of this territory still to be organized ; the authority she enjoyed, however, was at the best dubious, the natives being warlike and by no means amenable to control, while in two-thirds of the peninsula it was non-existent.

Nevertheless, by 197 she had set up the first official machinery of a provincial government, dividing the dominion into a Nearer (the northern) and a Farther (the southern) Province ; whereof the immediate result was a general rising of the tribesmen who had the customary objection to anything like an organized foreign domination. The subjugation of the insurgents was entrusted to Cato, consul in 195, who four years later distinguished himself, as we have already seen, at Thermopylae. After subjecting his troops to a severe training, in which he did not spare himself, he inflicted a great defeat on the insurgents, and by the severity of his measures and the rapidity of his movements soon brought the whole of the northern province into subjection for the time being ; though the Spaniards, resentful of his tyrannical measures, were in arms again as soon as his back was turned. There followed years of constant fighting, which was only at last ended in 179 by the unwontedly conciliatory and sympathetic policy of the praetor, Tiberius Sempronius Gracchus, the chosen son-in-law of Scipio and, later, the father of two still more famous sons.

### The Campaign against Perseus

FOR several years after the settlement of Asia Minor, Rome was involved in no foreign wars except the military operations against the Ligurians and in Spain. But the uneasiness of the dependent populations under her shadow grew. Philip plotted and schemed, but dared not show open hostility. In 179 he died, and was succeeded by his son Perseus, who was watched with jealous suspicion by Eumenes of Pergamum, always the faithful henchman of the power which had enlarged his kingdom. The policy of Perseus was directed to winning popularity and support from Greek states, now more fearful of Roman than of Macedonian oppression, since many of them were suffering from tyrants or oligarchical governments that were the creatures of Rome. In 172 Eumenes laid before the Roman Senate charges against the king of Macedon. The verdict of the Senate was a foregone conclusion. When an attempt was made to murder Eumenes on his way home, it was assumed that Perseus was the instigator. In 171 Rome declared war.

Careful and unostentatious reorganization had made Macedon much better prepared for war than she had been at any time since Cynoscephalae. Rome met with no speedy success. In 171 and 170 her consular armies under Crassus and Mancinus were defeated. But in 168 the command was given to an old and tried chief, Aemilius Paullus, the brother-in-law of Africanus and father of the boy whom the son of Africanus adopted. He reorganized the forces and at Pydna won a victory as overwhelming as that of Cynoscephalae. A few weeks later the unhappy Perseus, deserted and betrayed by his followers, came into the camp of the victor and surrendered.

### Final Crushing of Macedon

AS a power, Macedon was eliminated. The country was divided into four 'republics,' vassals of Rome, debarred from any political or commercial relations with each other, deprived of all leaders, and thus left to conduct their own administration as best they could under a code of laws formulated by the conqueror. Epirus, which had thrown in its lot with Perseus, was mercilessly punished ; no fewer than seventy towns were required to deliver up all the gold and silver they contained, their walls were levelled with the ground and their inhabitants to the number of 150,000 were sold into slavery. Monstrous as such treatment sounds to modern ears, it did not in the least shock the civilized world two thousand years ago ; Hannibal had offered almost identical terms to Saguntum when he summoned it to surrender ; and the selling of conquered populations into slavery was almost the normal sequel when cities were taken by storm. The more enlightened might deplore such methods, but they excited no denunciation.

## Ominous Change in Roman Temper

IN the twenty-nine years that passed between Cynoscephalae and Pydna the Roman attitude had been undergoing change. Flamininus honestly regarded himself and was regarded by the Roman people as a Liberator, assuming temporarily and with reluctance an authority which he desired to lay down at the earliest moment compatible with the general security. But the possession of power begets the lust of exercising and extending it, easily cloaked under pleas of necessity ; even Flamininus was not the same after Thermopylae as after Cynoscephalae, and Paullus after Pydna was many degrees removed from Flamininus, though probably quite unconscious of the fact. There was less excuse for the abolition of the Macedonian monarchy in 168 than there would have been in 197, apart from the fact that Rome was now deliberately aiming at dominion. The new Macedonian republics were not independent or even dependent states ; to all intents they were subject to Rome. And it must be added that Rome showed no sense of responsibility for the welfare of the new subjects brought under her sway, provided that they were held well in hand and were not too much impoverished to be economically useful.

The overthrow of Macedon was followed by another interval during which active expansion was suspended, though just before Pydna Rome had in very significant fashion asserted her effective power in another quarter. Antiochus IV Epiphanes was engaged in a war with Ptolemy VI Philometor of Egypt (page 189). Rome regarded Egypt as being in some sort under her protection ; and the envoy, Popillius Laenas, who had been sent there to warn Antiochus off, peremptorily ordered him to leave the country. When the king asked for time to consider, the envoy traced a circle round him, and then replied that his answer must be given before he crossed that line.

Antiochus bowed to the inevitable, and asserted no more claims in Egypt.

Rome, in plain terms, had, since the great days when she was fighting against Carthage with her back to the wall, degenerated into an irresistibly powerful bully. Governorships—confined to the scions of wealthy and powerful senatorial families—over remote provincials whom it was in no one's direct interest to protect from their rapacity, offered demoralising temptation too strong to be resisted, and sapped the moral sense of the governing class. The loot of the campaigns in Asia had begotten a new lust for wealth that might be had for the grasping, and for vicious luxuries unknown and unsought in the days when Rome was battling for existence rather than dominion. There was scarcely a pretence of consideration for justice in the Senate's high-handed treatment of nominal allies, or the exploitation by praetors of the subject peoples over whom they were sent to rule during a term of office which was comparatively brief.

### Men who stood for the Older Virtues

THERE were men who preserved the old Roman virtue in its best sense—as the younger Scipio (185–129), the son of Aemilius Paullus ; or in its most rigidly narrow sense—as Cato (234–149), who was in fact of the older generation The doctrines of the Stoic philosophy (derived from contact with the Greeks) tended to preserve and even to elevate the old spirit where they found acceptance ; but, on the other hand, the more popular forms of the rival Epicurean teaching fostered the new spirit of moral laxity generated by irresponsible power ; and the degradation of the moral standards of life, whether public or private, is the most markedly conspicuous feature of the era of expansion.

The new temper was manifested towards Greece as well as Macedon. The Achaean League had been very lukewarm latterly. Philopoemen, its greatest statesman, had been dead for some years. At the instance of the ambitious intriguer Callicrates, who had sold himself to the Romans, a thousand of the leading

Achaeans were carried off to Rome in 167, nominally to stand trial on the charge of complicity with Perseus, actually to be detained as prisoners till the Romans chose to liberate the remnant still surviving in 151. The League itself was left in the hands of Callicrates, while in almost every city reigned a tyrant in the service of Rome.

### Roman Misgovernment of Spain

DESPITE the wise measures which had pacified Spain during the governorship of Gracchus, the Roman administration in that land of tribes intolerant of any limitation of their freedom was conducted after his departure on the lines of the new tyranny. Before long, the whole country was seething with hatred of its new masters, and praetors or consuls who could barely hold their own in the field against the hardy tribesmen did not hesitate to save their authority by acts of the grossest treachery which the degenerate Senate did not fail to endorse ; though not without vigorous protest from old Cato and men of like mind, who were as honest as they were pitiless. The evil seed was to bear bitter enough fruit in due season.

But now the hour was at hand for the playing of the last act in the tragedy of Greece and the tragedy of Carthage.

In the years that followed the fall of Perseus, Macedon and Greece had sunk into a sad welter of misrule. Whether intentionally or not, the effect of the Roman methods was almost the disappearance of the very semblance of ordered government. In 149 there appeared in Macedon a claimant to the throne, calling himself Philip and pretending to be the grandson of Philip V. As a matter of course he found supporters, and as a matter of course he was suppressed as soon as Rome took the affair seriously.

But, before she did so, the pretender had been allowed to achieve some rather humiliating successes, which encouraged the latest intriguer who had captured an ascendancy in the now miserably disorganized Achaean League to take action against Sparta without referring the cause of quarrel to Rome, to whom Sparta, more cautious, appealed. While she was

finishing off the Pseudo-Philippus, as the Macedonian pretender was called, Rome dispatched commissioners to the League council assembled at Corinth, to signify her pleasure—and her displeasure. Sparta, Corinth and Argos were to be released from the League's jurisdiction.

The council lost its head and insulted the commissioners. Rome still gave them another chance of making submission to a second commission (147) ; but the leaders, too deeply committed to hope for pardon themselves, attempted to stir up a necessarily futile war of liberation (146). The Roman army from Macedon marched down to Corinth, dispersing resistance on its way. There the command was taken over by the new consul Mummius. The League commander Diaeus offered battle before the walls of Corinth, but his troops broke and fled at the first onset ; and Mummius, learning that a garrison still occupied the Acropolis, entered the city and gave it to sack as if it had been carried by storm.

### Last Act in the Tragedy of Greece

THE men were massacred ; the women and children were sold into slavery ; the art treasures were seized for the state, save where the boorishness of the consul prevented him from recognizing their value —for Mummius achieved for himself a permanent niche in the temple of Stupidity by giving out that if any work of art were damaged the careless workmen would have to replace it with an equivalent ; the loot was lavishly distributed ; and when nothing removable was left, the beautiful city was given to the flames. It would be unfair to think of Mummius as a general type. The average Roman of the day conceived himself to be a man of superior culture and had a genuine if debased appreciation of things intellectual and artistic ; but the callous brutality of the man was typical, and even in his stupidity he was by no means unique.

The fiction of independence was over. The precise year in which the formal changes were made is doubtful ; but Macedonia (probably) first, and then Greece under the name of Achaea, were very shortly after the destruction of

Corinth converted into provinces of the Roman dominion under Roman governors.

In the same year as that in which Corinth perished, Carthage was levelled with the ground, and what was left of her empire became the Province of Africa.

The smiting of Carthage was a measure prompted rather by a vindictive jealousy than by any real political necessity. While Hannibal was still in the city, there was always the possibility that his genius would again render her formidable ; when he was an exile intriguing at the court of a still undefeated Antiochus, that possibility still survived. But when the eastern power had been swept out of existence at Magnesia, and Hannibal could find no safer asylum than with Prusias of Bithynia, and could only save himself from the Romans by taking his own life in 183, there was left no possibility that Carthage with or without allies would become once more a menace to the Roman state. But by a strict attention to business, the commerce of Carthage revived ; humbled and crippled as she had been, she ventured to resist the encroachments of Masinissa, who was as ready at ninety to take the field in person as he had been at forty ; the octogenarian Cato proclaimed in the Senate, in and out of season, that ' Carthage must be blotted out.' And blotted out she was.

### Revival of Carthaginian Trade

THE recuperation of Carthage after Zama had given amazing proof of her vitality. With Hannibal in exile, it may be assumed that his political opponents were in power, and the policy alternative to his was to gain Roman friendship if possible, and develop those resources, namely, the overland trade with the south and the carrying trade of Numidia, which in any case were beyond Roman reach, and little likely to compete with the produce or industries of Italy.

But Roman friendship was hard to gain. All Italy, as well as Rome itself, had suffered irreparably in the long war ; agriculture in particular had been disorganized, and the fact that grain was one of the principal exports of Africa benefited only the cities, and spoiled the market for farm produce in Italy. The continual drain on the Italian peasantry of Rome's eastern wars, which had begun against Philip of Macedon long before the Hannibalic War was over, led to the replacement of free labour by slaves, acquired easily in the course of those wars, or from the pirates whom it was impossible to check as long as no single power was supreme at sea and could assume responsibility. Most irremediable of all, Roman merchants had been obliged by war needs to trade on an even larger scale, and had acquired and created business connexions abroad, which they had no mind to neglect in peace time ; and they had sufficient influence with their own government to put the worst construction on any complaint that came concerning the behaviour of Carthage.

### Friction between Carthage and Numidia

NOW such complaints could hardly fail to come where there was a ready ear for them. In particular, Masinissa had been established as head of an independent Numidian state, ' free and allied,' with no natural frontier between his country and the home district of Carthage, and with an ambiguous clause in the peace treaty granting him ' all that he or his ancestors had ever possessed,' which, strictly interpreted, gave him the ground on which Carthage itself was built. It was almost inevitable that there should be border troubles, and that the blame for these should be always on the city which was prohibited by treaty from ' making war in Africa ' without the consent of Rome. Gradually the home district, on which Carthage depended for its food, passed into Numidian hands ; only once, in the crisis of the last war with Macedon, was it thought prudent even to be considerate to Carthage ; and with these territorial gains the moment came ever nearer when Masinissa's horsemen, deliberately unruly, would be within striking distance of the southward caravan routes, the only commercial monopoly which Carthage still held. Hence the persistent claims of Masinissa to the possession of the Libyan Tripolis, with its grassland moors, its rich coast plain, and its alternative routes to the south, from Leptis.

G

Then came for the Romans local troubles in Spain, where Masinissa could, if he tried, be a very dangerous neighbour; and therewith fresh complaints of the wily old Numidian against Carthage. A Roman commission of inquiry and arbitration was sent to Africa in 150, with Marcus Cato at its head, old-fashioned, narrow-minded, unscrupulous; incapable of realizing that the world had changed in the last half-century; firmly convinced that the figs he saw in the market at Carthage proved the necessity for protecting Italian agriculturists by the elimination of their African competitor. On the point immediately at issue, the award was, of course, in favour of Masinissa; the result, further encroachment; and then, what Cato and his friends most desired, reprisals by Carthage and the inevitable Roman intervention. The old man, however, did not live to see the actual fulfilment of his craving.

### ' Delenda est Carthago '

THERE was, it is true, a 'popular party' in Carthage which had lost patience, and thought that Rome's momentary embarrassment with her Greek allies, and a futile revolt in Macedon, gave a desperate chance of resistance. Wiser heads probably realized that in Africa as in Macedon Roman foreign policy was shifting on to a new basis; that the day of 'free and equal allies' was over. Everything short of the worst was offered by the Carthaginian government in mitigation of sentence, and offered in vain. The Roman commanders had their orders; Carthage was to be destroyed, and its inhabitants interned where they pleased, so long as they were out of reach of the sea.

The effect of this order might have been foreseen. The desperate war party took control of the city; moderate men, who had tried to save what was not already lost, were massacred with the Italian residents, who were by this time numerous; levies were made among those towns and tribes of the neighbourhood who felt their own fate inseparable from that of Carthage, and preparations were made for a siege. The Romans made matters worse by allowing time for such measures;

then realized their mistake, and closed in on the city, suffering more severely from the marshes, where they made their camp, than from the enemy. It was not until after two years of mismanagement that the younger Scipio Aemilianus, who had already shown unusual ability, was elected, before his time, to be consul and commander-in-chief in Africa (147).

The northern suburbs of Carthage were soon occupied without difficulty, but the shorter lines of defence were stronger and easier to hold; and supplies still came by sea through the Roman blockade. It was only when Scipio had carried out the huge engineering works necessary to close the harbour entrance by a broad embankment, and also defeated the squadron which emerged through a newly dug channel beyond it, that the city was restricted to its own resources. Yet another winter passed before the moment came for an assault, on the merchants' quarter between the citadel and the port. It succeeded, and then from house to house the Romans cut their way up the slope for six days and nights, the ruined town being burnt and levelled behind them.

Fifty thousand Carthaginians surrendered before the end, and were spared; but the citadel, with the small remnant of heroes and deserters who held it, was burned. The whole site was devastated, solemnly cursed and ploughed over, and the smaller cities of Africa likewise. Only Utica, which had surrendered early, remained to be the capital of the new 'province of Africa.' Numidia remained 'free and allied'; but Masinissa was dead at last, and his three sons held separate baronies, and quarrelled with each other. The Libyan Tripolis, too, was kept separate from the African province, under direct Roman administration.

### Mercantile Outlook of Roman State

IF the fate of Carthage had been completely detached from any policy or movement in contemporary history it would have been tragic enough, and attributable only to the profound animosity of leading Romans, and perhaps also of Italian peoples generally, against the city which had bred Hannibal and shown such amazing tenacity of purpose in spite of Roman persecution. But it was more than this : it was an expression of the same new outlook, mercantile rather than statesmanlike, of responsible people in Rome, which wrecked and despoiled Corinth in the same year as it obliterated Carthage, and remained a constant danger in all dealings with Greek leagues and succession kingdoms. Senators, it had been long realized, could not be trusted to govern business communities fairly, if they themselves had business interests ; on the other hand, business men had their own ways of influencing senatorial government, without sharing its responsibility. The shortcomings of the Roman provincial system in the next hundred years, as well as the worst disorder of Rome's republican decline, are mainly due to this conflict of principles, and it was only an accident— the fact that the domestic disorders came to a head before provincial grievances became intolerable—that made it possible for the Principate to be established without loss of Empire.

On the other hand, Carthage had failed to learn the lesson of the Sicilian and Hannibalic Wars. To have ruled in Africa for centuries without acquiring the political experience which could conciliate the Sicilians or Sardinians, or even after a longer period the Spanish peoples which furnished such good citizens to Rome, and without admitting the population even of the home territory to share in the privileges or the responsibilities of government, was a lapse which would have been conspicuous even if there had been only the loosely knit empire of the Persians to contrast with it ; compared with the Greek successor kingdoms, still more with the Roman dominion in Italy, it was a failure and a disgrace. And it was the partial adoption of Carthaginian methods of estate management, in the generation which followed the fall of Carthage, that led to the one serious mistake of the Romans, for which they paid so dearly in the next, through the revolt of their Italian ' allies.' The Greek city states had for the most part failed or succeeded politically according as they remained exclusive corporations, based on hereditary privilege or accumulated wealth, or accepted the ' desirable alien ' and measured men's deserts by their abilities. Carthage, like

### HEADQUARTERS OF A ROMAN LEGION BESIEGING A SPANISH CITY

Scipio Africanus the younger was appointed in 134 B.C. to the command of the Roman armies operating against the Celtiberians of northern Spain. Their resistance centred in the wealthy city of Numantia, which Scipio accordingly proceeded to reduce. Strong camps, well supplied with war engines, were built at strategical points, and Numantia blockaded into surrender. Here we see the remains of the tribunes' quarters in the first of these camps, situated at Peña Redonda.

*From Schulten, ' Numantia,' Bruckmann A.G.*

**INGLORIOUS KINGS OF SYRIA**
Succeeding to a kingdom diminished by war,
Seleucus IV (top) reigned feebly, and was assassinated in 175. His successor, Antiochus IV,
was an unbalanced ruler who drove the Jews to
revolt; he died, mad, while warring in Persia.
*From J. Ward, ' Greek Coins ' (John Murray)*

its Etruscan friends, remained ' exclusive ';
it acquired unexampled monopolies ; and
reserving them jealously for its own enjoyment, perished apparently unregretted.

While Macedon and Carthage were
receiving their coup de grâce, the Spaniards
maintained their attitude of stubborn
defiance, in spite of the cruel blows dealt
them by the perfidy of the consuls Lucullus
and Galba in 151 and 150. In the south
the Lusitanians found a brilliant guerrilla captain in Viriathus, who in 142
manoeuvred the Roman consul Servilianus
into a trap, and was able to dictate terms
so reasonable in point of fact that they
were ratified by the Senate, which even
recognized Viriathus as ' friend and ally '
of the Roman People. Nevertheless, two
years later a new consul, Caepio, not only
attacked the friend and ally, with the
assent of the Senate, but procured his
assassination, a blow from which the
Lusitanians did not recover, though they
were not further penalised.

No less stubborn was the resistance
offered in the north by the Celtiberians,
whose principal fortress or city was
Numantia, on the borderland of what
had been the vague Roman sphere of influence before the Hannibalic War. Here

the fighting, temporarily suppressed by
Lucullus, broke out again in 143 when
Viriathus' campaign was being carried
through with most effect. One Roman
general, Metellus, the same who had
finished off the last Macedonian war but
had been superseded in the east by
Mummius, held the Spanish command for
two years (143–2), and met with much
success, but was withdrawn before he
could complete the task of pacification.
This labour continued to prove too much
for one after another of his successors ;
until in 137 the consul Mancinus was
reduced to what was, in fact, a capitulation,
the terms of which were negotiated by his
quaestor Tiberius Gracchus (c. 1691–33) ;
in whom the Spaniards did not hesitate
to trust, since he was the son of that
Tiberius Gracchus who had made the
generous but ill-kept settlement of 179.
The Senate, however, with strict legality
but doubtful honour, declined to ratify
the treaty ; and the war was renewed, to
the indignation of Gracchus.

Against a foe so indomitable, it was
obviously useless to continue the ordinary
routine method of appointment to the
military command. Rome in 134 turned
to her greatest citizen and soldier, the
conqueror of Carthage, the second Scipio
Africanus. Although he was not a candidate for the consulship and was in fact
legally disqualified from standing, his
election was carried by the unanimous
vote of the Assembly of Tribes, and the
legal technicalities were set aside in the
face of such an expression of public opinion.

EVEN for Scipio the task was no easy
one. It was not till he had restored
by hard training the long-relaxed discipline
of the demoralised troops that, in 133, he
set about the Numantian campaign, and
laid siege to Numantia itself. Like Carthage the doomed fortress held out grimly to
the last moment. When there was nothing
left to eat but human flesh, it surrendered ;
and it was then, like Carthage, obliterated ;
so completely that its very site was forgotten. The work of reorganizing the
Spanish provinces was left for others.

In 134, the year of Scipio's unprecedented election to the consulship, his

colleague, Fulvius Flaccus, was called upon to deal with a terrifying insurrection of the widespread slave population in Sicily, the outcome of the huge development of the slave system in the constant wars of the last hundred, and more particularly the last seventy, years—wars which had flooded the market with slaves of every conceivable nationality. Of this first slave war and of others we shall hear more in the following chapter. The disastrous effect of the increase of slave labour on the agricultural population in Italy is a vital subject to all students of sociology.

### Retrospect of Eastern Affairs

**H**ITHERTO the affairs of the East since the time when Antiochus III, by his campaigns in Parthia, Bactria and Asia Minor, had acquired the title of ' the Great '—when Rome was still in the grip of the Second Punic War—have demanded attention only as they were directly related to the Roman expansion. We have seen Antiochus intervening in Europe and paying the penalty for his presumption by total expulsion from Asia Minor in 190 ; and we have seen his second son, Antiochus IV Epiphanes, obeying a per- emptory order from Rome to remove himself from Egypt in 168. We have seen, also, that down to 133, Rome had not sought to annex any Asiatic territory, and had not even been involved in any military operations in Asia since the Galatian campaign of 189–8. But we have still to observe how during this period the course of events, without Roman intervention, was at the same time preparing the way for Rome's Asiatic expansion during the hundred years following, and setting bounds for it which it never effectively crossed.

The Seleucidae were, in effect, the re- presentatives of the old Persian Empire, with a Macedonian, instead of a Persian Achaemenid, on the throne of the Great King. At the moment when Antiochus III so rashly flung down his challenge to Rome, his title Megas, the Great, was not a palpable misnomer. He had recovered sovereignty, lost or en- dangered, westward in Asia Minor and eastward to Trans-Oxiana ; and he had

forced Egypt to admit his sovereig:·ty, often claimed as her own, in Coele-Syria ; though in order to ensure at least her neutrality in the coming struggle, he had just married his daughter Cleopatra to the young Ptolemy V Epiphanes, giving certain revenues drawn from Coele-Syria as a part of her dower. An incidental consequence of this has already been noticed. When Rome chastised the arrogance of the Great King, she handed over to Rhodes or Pergamum the districts in Asia Minor which Egypt had been wont to claim.

Antiochus III died soon afterwards, in 187. The troubled reign of his elder son, Seleucus IV, was ended by his murder in 175, when he was succeeded by his brother Antiochus IV Epiphanes, known by the gibing nickname of Epimanes (the Mad- man). He quarrelled with the Egyptian government of Ptolemy VI Philometor (181–146), because it still claimed the Coele-Syrian revenues though the king's

### TO PAGANISE THE JEWS

In his endeavour to suppress the Jewish religion, Antiochus IV decreed that a pagan altar should be erected in every village throughout Judaea. This example, found at Gezer, is dedicated to Heracles, but bears also the name of Jehovah.

*From R. A. S. Macalister, ' Bible Sidelights from Gezer '*

mother, Cleopatra, was dead. The conquest of Egypt seemed imminent, when the Roman envoy Popillius interposed his veto.

Epiphanes died, actually and completely mad, as it is said, in 164. The most familiar event in the reign of Antiochus Epiphanes is the revolt of the Jews under the leadership of Judas Maccabaeus and his kinsmen, a revolt which ultimately won independence from their Syrian, or rather Macedonian, overlord. The Maccabaean wars no doubt played their part in completing the disintegration of the Seleucid power ; which, however, could have been saved, if at all, only by a ruler of first rate political and military genius. The fundamental importance of this struggle lies in the fact that if its issue had been different the Jews as a nation with a local habitation and a name would have been blotted out two centuries before this fate actually befell them. For the essential object of the wars was to secure that unique type of nationalism which differentiated the Hebrews from all other peoples.

The Jews of the southern kingdom, deported by Nebuchadrezzar to Babylon in accordance with the policy so fully developed by the Assyrians, had been reinstated by the humane and liberal policy of the early Achaemenids. Unlike their northern kinsmen, they had adhered rigidly to the Mosaic Law ; and the Persian system not only permitted but actually encouraged them to restore the old religious structure of their society. Alexander inherited and even extended the Persian policy of fostering local and national customs, which in this case made the Chosen Race a people apart from and in some sense hostile to the entire Gentile world. But among the Jews there was always an unorthodox element, attracted by pagan learning and pagan laxity.

Now Judaea and Jerusalem, the centre of Judaism, lay in that debatable land which had at all times been a bone of contention between the Euphratic and the Egyptian empires and continued to

**WALLS OF A CASTLE ONCE HELD BY POWERFUL JEWISH PRINCES**

In 142 B.C. Simon Maccabaeus succeeded his brother Jonathan as leader of the Jews, and shortly afterwards advanced against the Syrian garrison in Gezer (Gazara). Having captured the city, he established himself in it, as is related in the Apocrypha. Here we see the ruins of the castle, refortified and occupied by him, and later held by his son, John Hyrcanus. On the extreme left are the remains of the gateway, and in the foreground the foundations of the walls of Gezer.

*From R. A. S. Macalister, ' Bible Sidelights from The Mound of Gezer '*

be a bone of contention between Seleucidae and Ptolemies, while commonly finding itself compelled to acknowledge the Seleucid sovereignty. There was a large Jewish colony in Egypt which was patronised by the Ptolemies ; consequently the intensely nationalist puritan party among the Jews tended to look to Egypt—to be, in fact, an Egyptian party. The unorthodox, on the other hand, sought and found favour and support from their actual overlord, the Hellenising Seleucid, against whom the nationalists were the more embittered by the heavy financial demands made on them for the indemnity claimed by Rome from Antiochus after his overthrow at Magnesia.

Religious persecution as such was quite alien to Hellenic ideas ; but evidently Antiochus IV, when on the Egyptian expedition, the object of which was so rudely frustrated by Popillius, acquired the conviction that the Jewish puritans were a political danger. On his return in 168 he vented his wrath and disappointment on Jerusalem, which was ruthlessly sacked, and set about the suppression of the religion which appeared to be at once the motive and the binding force of Jewish disaffection. For the Jewish puritans, religious zeal and the fervour of patriotism were welded into one passion.

### The Maccabees in Palestine

INSPIRED and led by the old Mattathias, of the Hasmonaean house, the puritans took to the hills and waged a fierce guerrilla warfare against the officers of the persecutor. Mattathias died and the struggle was carried on by his son Judas, surnamed Maccabaeus, and his brethren. Antiochus died, and the Syrian crown was tossed from head to head among claimants, some of the blood royal and some mere adventurers. Judas recovered Jerusalem but was slain in battle in 161. He was followed by his brothers Jonathan and (in 142) Simon, and before the latter was murdered in 135, to be succeeded by his son John Hyrcanus, the Hasmonaean dynasty may be regarded as established. The dynasty, however, was of minor importance, the essential point was that Judaism had been saved.

**AMBITIOUS RULER OF MACEDON**

Philip V consistently endeavoured to restore Macedon to the predominant position that she had formerly held. An able politician and soldier, he was successful against Greek opponents, but was decisively beaten by Rome in 197 B.C.

*From G. F. Hill, ' Select Greek Coins,' G. Van Oest, Paris*

When Antiochus Megas was expelled from Asia Minor, his sovereignty was still acknowledged not only by the satraps in Media and Persia, but by the native princes who had set up kingdoms in Armenia and Parthia. To Bactria he had conceded independence only because as an independent state it was a buffer between Hellenism and the Scythian barbarians, with whom its Greek rulers threatened to make common cause rather than submit to the Seleucid. The position continued substantially unchanged during the reign of Epiphanes, though he found it necessary to march armies into both Armenia and Persia.

Demetrius I, nephew of Epiphanes and son of Seleucus IV, who became king in 162, gained the title of Soter (saviour) by crushing in 160 a dangerous revolt in Media, whose satrap had assumed the royal title. Very soon after this, however, Demetrius found himself forced to fight for his crown, and in the period of dynastic chaos that ensued Armenia dropped away, and the Parthian Arsacids not only recovered independence but absorbed Media and Persia into their own dominion, of which the Euphrates became in effect the boundary. In 138 Demetrius II. the son of Demetrius I who had been killed in 150, attempted to recover the lost territory, but was defeated and himself taken captive by the Parthians. The Parthian Empire, which was to prove an endless and unsubduable source of trouble for Rome, had thus definitely come into being only a few years before Rome's first actual acquisition of Asiatic territory.

The same Parthian king who captured Demetrius penetrated into India and apparently claimed to have added the old Persian satrapy of India to his dominions, but the brief conquest—so called—did not survive his death in 136. In this direction the kings of Bactria had preceded those of Parthia. Demetrius of Bactria, son and successor of that Euthydemus whom Antiochus III had reluctantly confirmed in the Bactrian kingdom, actually made himself king in Afghanistan and a considerable part of the Punjab ; and, though he lost his crown about 175, various Graeco-Bactrian principalities seem to have achieved an ephemeral existence in this region during the next forty years. The most notable of these invaders was Menander, who about 175 carried victorious arms as far as the mouth of the Indus in one direction and the Jumna in another. Here however he was held up and driven back by the Sunga king, who in 185 had snatched the crown from the last of the Mauryas. But Bactria itself was crumbling under the pressure of the central Asian nomads.

No Bactrian dominion was established in India ; Hellenism in its far eastern outpost was submerged and wiped out, leaving only a dim memory of itself here and there among the peoples of the East. The mainly Mongolian nomads, held off from the west by the Parthian barricade, now filtered and now flooded southwards, sometimes conquering, commonly destroying, never constructing, never organizing, always melting indistinguishably away after a brief apparition. At this stage their movement may be at least in part attributed to the impediment imposed on their penetration eastward by the recent construction of the Great Wall of China recorded in Chapter 7, and to the progressive organization of the Chinese Empire begun under Shih Hwang Ti and continued under the Han dynasty (c. 205 B.C. A.D. 225), whose princes were now actually endeavouring to learn something of the world beyond the mountains which encircled their realm. India fades out of our vision. Little can be with confidence affirmed concerning it, save that the brief ascendancy of Buddhism passed with the Maurya dynasty, and Brahmanism recovered its sway. Virtually for centuries world history is the history of Rome.

**VIVID AND DELICATE CARVING BY AN ANCIENT CHINESE ARTIST**

Culture progressed rapidly in China under the Han monarchs ; there was a great increase of wealth and art flourished. On this slab of stone, cut during the Han period (c. 205 B.C.–A.D. 225), two separate episodes are represented. In the upper panel is seen a two-storeyed pavilion in which the Taoist goddess, Hsi Wang Mu, receives the ancient emperor Mu Wang. In the lower an official procession is depicted—a mandarin in his state chariot (extreme right) preceded by officials and soldiers.

*From Chavannes, ' Les sculptures chinoises sur pierre '*

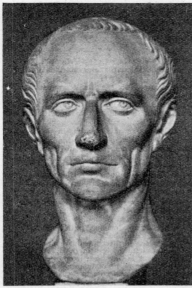

Busts and portrait statues equally testify·to the commanding intellect and character of Julius Caesar, who furnishes an example of greatness as orator, man of letters, soldier and statesman unexcelled in history.

*British Museum ; photo, Fleming*

Gaius Julius Caesar was born in Rome, July 12, 102 B.C., of patrician rank.  Allying himself with the democratic party he became quaestor in Spain, praetor and, in 59, consul.  His military triumphs while governor of Gaul provoked enmity at home, which resulted in the Civil War.  After routing Pompey at Pharsalus in August, 48, Caesar attained supreme power, ended by his assassination March 15, 44 B.C.   The statue (right) admirably portrays him as one of the world's greatest captains.

## HOW ROMAN SCULPTORS EXPRESSED THE GREATNESS OF JULIUS CAESAR
*Naples Museum and Capitoline Museum, Rome ; photos, Alinari and Anderson*

G*

# TABLE OF DATES FOR CHAPTER 9

B.C.
133 Tribunate and death of Tiberius Gracchus.
    Fall of Numantia. Acquisition of Pergamum.
132 Suppression of Sicilian slave-revolt.
    *The East:* end of the Bactrian kingdom.
129 Death of Africanus.
    Organization of the Province of Asia (Pergamum).
126 C. Gracchus quaestor in Sardinia.
125 Flaccus, proposing reforms, is sent to Gaul.
    Revolt and punishment of Fregellae.
123 First Tribunate of C. Gracchus. Sempronian Laws.
    New status of the Equites; distribution of cheap
    corn; new colonies.
122 Gracchus, Flaccus, and Livius Drusus (senatorial
    candidate) tribunes. Drusus outbids Gracchus
    who fails for re-election. Opimius consul.
    War continues in S. Gaul.
121 Death of Gracchus; slaughter of the Gracchans.
    Victories in S. Gaul. Gallia Narbonensis (Narbonne)
    founded.
120 Accession of Mithradates VI in Pontus.
118 Partition of Numidia between Jugurtha and the
    sons of Micipsa.
116 Commission of Opimius for settlement of Numidia.
113 Teutonic incursion and Roman defeat in Istria.
112 Jugurtha murders Adherbal. Rome declares war.
111 War suspended. Jugurtha, summoned to Rome,
    murders Massiva there.
110 War renewed. Albinus in Africa.
109 Metellus takes command in Africa.
108 Metellus drives Jugurtha into Mauretania.
107 Marius, elected consul, supersedes Metellus.
    Gaul: disaster to Roman force under Cassius, at
    the hands of the Helvetii.
106 Bocchus of Mauretania surrenders Jugurtha to
    Sulla. End of Jugurthine war; death of
    Jugurtha. Birth of Cicero and Pompey.
105 Cimbri destroy a Roman force in the Rhône
    valley, but move on Spain instead of Italy.
104 Marius consul (2); army reforms.
103 Marius cons. (3). Second Sicilian slave-war.
    Cimbri concert invasion with Teutones.
102 Marius cons. (4) shatters Teutones at Aquae
    Sextiae.
101 Marius cons. (5) with Catulus shatters Cimbri at
    Vercellae (Campi Raudii) in Cisalpine Gaul.
    Saturninus and Glaucia at Rome.
100 Marius cons. (6) unites with Saturninus; exile of
    Metellus Numidicus. Marius breaks with
    Saturninus, who is killed. Victory of Senate.
99 Recall of Metellus. Ten years' ascendancy of the
   Moderates. End of the Servile war.
92 Sulla, praetor in Cilicia, restores Ariobarzanes
   (expelled by Mithradates) in Cappadocia.
91 Tribunate and death of Livius Drusus Minor.
   Aggressions of Tigranes of Armenia, incited by
   Mithradates.
   Union of Marsi and other dissatisfied Socii; beginning of Social or Marsian war.
90 Roman commanders fail to press their successes;
   concessions to Italians. Samnites over-run
   Campania.
89 Successes of Pompeius Strabo and Sulla; general
   submission of Italians, except in Campania.
   Mithradates incites and supports Greek revolt.
   Beginning of First Mithradatic war.
88 Sulla consul. The tribune Sulpicius Rufus procures
   transfer of the eastern command to Marius
   from Sulla, who marches on Rome and restores
   the constitution. Marius escapes to Africa.
   Cinna, elected consul, swears to keep the
   constitution, and Sulla takes up the command
   in Greece.
87 Cinna's revolution; return of Marius; the Marian
   massacres.
86 Marius consul (7) dies. Sulla takes Athens and
   defeats Archelaus at Chaeronea.
85 Sulla wins battle of Orchomenus.
84 Sulla makes peace with Mithradates and crushes
   Fimbria. Cinna cons. (4) killed in mutiny.
83 Sulla with troops lands in Italy. Sertorius goes to
   Spain as praetor.
82 Sulla destroys Marian and Samnite forces at the
   Colline Gate.
   Sulla Dictator. Proscription of Marians.
81 Cornelian Laws or Sullan Constitution, designed
   to make the Senate supreme.

B.C.
81 Sulla allows Pompey (aged 25) a Triumph.
80 Sertorius heads Spaniards and Marians in Spain.
79 Sulla resigns.
   Sertorius leagues with the Mediterranean pirates.
78 Death of Sulla. Insurrection of Lepidus.
77 Fall of Lepidus. Pompey goes to Spain.
75 Sertorius, undefeated, makes treaty with Mithradates.
74 Second Mithradatic war. Lucullus in command.
73 Cilician (pirate) war of Marcus Antonius.
72 Lucullus drives Mithradates back to Pontus.
   Lucullus drives Mithradates from Pontus, and
   reorganizes the province of Asia.
   Murder of Sertorius. Pompey settles Spain.
   Gladiators' revolt under Spartacus in Italy.
71 Revolt broken by Crassus; arrival of Pompey.
70 Consulate of Crassus and Pompey; hostile to the
   Senate. Birth of Vergil.
69 Advance of Lucullus in Armenia.
68 Lucullus checked by insubordination of troops.
67 Lucullus forced to fall back.
   Pompey clears the Mediterranean of pirates.
66 Pompey, granted full powers in the East (Manilian
   Law), drives Mithradates from Pontus.
   Rise of Julius Caesar as a democratic leader.
65 Pompey settles Asia and goes to Syria.
64 Democratic extremists led by Catiline at Rome.
   Pompey takes Jerusalem; Syria a Roman Province.
63 Cicero consul. Defeat of Catiline's conspiracy.
   Pompey completes his settlement of the East.
62 Death of Catiline. Pompey returns to Italy, but
   disbands his forces.
61 Caesar praetor in Spain.
60 Caesar returns to Italy. Informal coalition of Caesar,
   Pompey and Crassus (' First Triumvirate ').
59 Caesar consul; popular measures. Caesar given five
   years' proconsulship in the Gauls.
58 Caesar in Gaul; defeats Helvetii and Ariovistus.
   Tribunate of Clodius; Cicero exiled.
57 Caesar in Gaul; conquest of Belgae and Nervii.
   Return of Cicero.
56 Conference of Triumvirs at Lucca. Caesar's campaign against Veneti (Brittany).
55 Pompey given five years' command in Spain,
   Crassus in Syria, Caesar (extension) in Gaul.
   Caesar's first expedition to Britain.
54 Crassus goes to the East. Strained relations of
   Caesar and Pompey. Second British expedition.
53 Crassus defeated and killed by Parthians at Carrhae.
   Caesar's trans-Rhine campaign.
52 Disorders at Rome. Clodius killed by Milo. Pompey
   made sole consul.
   Gallic revolt of Vercingetorix.
51 Conquest of Gaul completed.
   Ptolemy Auletes succeeded by Ptolemy XII.
50 Intrigues against Caesar.
49 Caesar crosses the Rubicon. Pompey abandons
   Italy. Caesar secures Spain and returns to
   Italy.
48 Battle of Pharsalus. Pompey's flight and death.
47 Caesar in the East. 'I came, I saw, I conquered.'
46 Caesar's African campaign. Thapsus.
45 Caesar's Spanish campaign. Munda.
44 Murder of Caesar (March). Arrival of Octavian.
   Republican leaders withdraw to their provinces. Antony attacks D. Brutus at Mutina.
43 Octavian unites with Antony and Lepidus. They
   are appointed Triumvirs with full powers, for
   five years. Proscription of Republicans.
   Death of Cicero.
42 Campaign and battles of Philippi.
41 Antony goes to the East and meets Cleopatra.
   Perusian war in Italy.
40 Parthian invasion of Syria and Asia.
   Reconciliation of Octavian and Antony, who
   marries Octavia.
39 Ventidius Bassus expels Parthians from Asia.
37 Triumvirate renewed. Sextus Pompeius commands
   the seas.
36 Agrippa defeats Sextus. Lepidus deposed.
36-4 Failure of Antony's Eastern campaigns.
33 Breach between Antony and Octavian.
32 Antony repudiates Octavia. War declared.
31 Antony decisively defeated at Actium.
30 Death of Antony and Cleopatra.

### CHAPTER 9

# ROME'S EXPANSION AND HER RIVAL GENERALS: 133—31 B.C.

THE year 133 B.C. is a conspicuous landmark in the world's history ; since in that year Rome for the first time became not merely a dominant political influence but an actual territorial power in Asia ; and in that year Tiberius Gracchus, all unconsciously, inaugurated the Roman Revolution. Another century had barely passed when the victory of Octavian's lieutenant Agrippa at Actium set the seal upon both the revolution and the expansion, making one man the master of the civilized world.

When the year 133 opened, even western Europe was far from being subjugated. Scipio was still engaged on the campaign which crushed the defiance of the far west. Transalpine Gaul was untouched. The heirs of Masinissa were disputing among themselves for the ascendancy in Africa, west of what had been the Carthaginian homeland and was now the Roman province of Africa. Egypt and all Asia were theoretically independent.

## Rome secures a Footing in the East

AN accident gave Rome the footing she had not chosen to claim before on the eastern continent. The king of Pergamum, Attalus III, died, leaving no son. The dynasty had been studiously—and profitably—loyal to Rome through all the shifting policies of the last seventy years ; and Attalus, dying, bequeathed his very flourishing kingdom to the Roman People. The Senate accepted the inheritance ; and though the inevitable pretender appeared and gave some trouble for a year or two, the Roman title was established without serious difficulty, though not without force.

Thus Rome became direct mistress of that half of Asia Minor (henceforth the Province of Asia) which roughly corresponded to the old-time kingdom of Lydia at its widest extent in the days of Croesus ; but Bithynia, Pontus (the realm of the house of Mithradates), Cappadocia and Galatia still lay outside its bounds. Beyond them on the north-east was the kingdom of Armenia ; while the Parthian empire of the Arsacids had extended its borders westward as far as the river Tigris. The kingdom of the Seleucidae was going rapidly to pieces, the crown, like that of the Ptolemies in Egypt (after the death in 146 of the last creditable ruler of that name, Philometor) being not uncommonly worn as the precarious reward for the murder of the reigning king's predecessor.

### Organization of the Provinces

THE expansion of the Roman power outside the Italian peninsula, except for the annexation of a part of the island of Sicily at the close of the First Punic War in 241, had been effected entirely during the last hundred years. The whole of this extra-Italian territory was now not in alliance with but subject to Rome, divided into provinces each under the rule of a Roman governor, a praetor, propraetor or proconsul (that is, a praetor or consul to whom at the end of his year of office his powers were extended for a further period, but only to be exercised within the province then assigned to him), whose imperium gave him command of the troops, irrespective of his military experience. Such extensions, it may be remarked, had first been instituted for consuls on foreign military service whose active command it had been felt advisable to prolong. Within Italy Cisalpine Gaul had been added to the number of the Provinces.

The rest of Italy was on a different footing. All the Italian communities had either been admitted to full Roman citizenship, with their members enrolled in the Roman Tribes ; or they were individually ' socii,' not Romans but allies, enjoying only treaty rights and subject to treaty obligations. Rome had been infinitely indebted to their services and their loyalty in the tremendous crisis of the Hannibalic

War as well as in numerous later campaigns, and there was among them a widespread sense of dissatisfaction at the inadequate recognition of her debt to them.

When Tiberius Gracchus procured election to the tribunate and started the revolution, he had probably no thought of subverting the constitution. His aim was economic. Long before, the plebeians who wanted office and social recognition had made common cause with their humbler brethren who merely wanted land. The political object had been achieved ; the agrarian laws had soon become a dead letter, but the land-hunger had been satisfied by centuries of conquest, at the expense of the conquered. Now, however, the old trouble had once more become acute. The land did not support the peasantry ; while the men of wealth had accumulated vast estates, especially in the more recently conquered territories, which they ran by slave labour. It was at least a tenable proposition that those estates had been acquired in actual violation of law, according to which the peasantry should have shared in them, and that the state had the right of resumption. Pasturage under slave labour paid the owners better than tillage under free labour, and the hideous-

**ASIA MINOR WHEN ROME FIRST ENTERED IT**

When in 133 B.C. Attalus III left his domains to Rome, by whom they were organized as the Province of Asia, the rest of Asia Minor was split up into this tangle of independent kingdoms. Mithradates I of Parthia (d. 138) had extended the Parthian Empire to the Tigris, and shortly afterwards it reached the Euphrates. For the rest of the Roman world, see map in p. 176.

ness of slave labour as recently developed was just being very vividly illustrated in 133 by the terrible Servile War in Sicily, the slave rising which was threatening to give the island new masters.

Tiberius Gracchus (163–133 B.C.) had returned from Spain, indignant at the senatorial betrayal of Rome's honour by the repudiation of the Spanish treaty of Marcinus. For projects of reform which would touch their own wealth or power there was nothing to be hoped from the nobles, least of all for such a project as the resumption and redistribution of the lands in which they had acquired a prescriptive right, wherein he saw the remedy for the worst of the evils from which the state was suffering. But if the government was by constitutional practice in the hands of the Senate, the elected tribunes possessed by law powers intended to be exercised only on emergency by which they could force the hand of the government. Tiberius stood for the tribunate, and opened his campaign in 133.

**BEST OF THE PTOLEMIES**

Ptolemy VI Philometor (181–145 B.C.) was an intelligent prince and a brave soldier. His reign was disturbed by constant rivalry with his brother and successor, Ptolemy VII Euergetes, each of them in turn supported by Rome.

*British Museum*

He had prepared a bill to lay before the popular or tribal assembly, for resumption and redistribution, which his opponents denounced as sheer confiscation, though the technical right of resumption was confirmed by the most eminent legal authorities, including the consul, Mucius Scaevola, in Rome—Scipio was in Spain. But when the bill was brought in, another tribune, Octavius, interposed his veto. Gracchus replied by applying his veto to every sort of administrative action, revising his bill so as to make it more drastic than before, and again introducing it at the next assembly. There was no sort of doubt that it would pass, but again Octavius vetoed it. At the next assembly Gracchus moved that Octavius should be deposed from the tribunate. There was no precedent, but the motion was carried by the unanimous vote of the tribes. The agrarian law was then again introduced and, being similarly carried, became law.

But the deposition of Octavius was an act as palpably revolutionary as ' Pride's purge ' or Cromwell's ejection of the Rump. As long as the popularity of the tribune ensured the support of the Assembly of tribes, he could carry any legislation he liked. But men began to discover that they might under the new law be deprived of land which they imagined themselves to

hold by an indefeasible title, and they took fright. It was becoming evident that Tiberius himself would be in danger the moment that he ceased to be protected from attack by the immunity conferred by his office, the person of a tribune being sacrosanct. He must procure re-election— and he might fail ; there was no precedent for re-election without an interval. The proceedings were stayed over the day on which his office expired. On the following morning a party of hostile senators, led by his cousin Scipio Nasica, came down to the Assembly ; a riot arose, and Tiberius was struck down and murdered. The murderers claimed that they had acted only as loyal citizens must act in the face of revolution. So it seemed even to Scipio Aemilianus, away in Spain—no lover of the existing order, but an unqualified opponent of revolutionary methods. And young Gaius Gracchus (153-121 B.C.), who was serving under him, held his peace ; a silence more ominous than any hasty utterance.

NASICA had to flee the country and died at Pergamum ; on the other hand, the party of law and order punished some of the supporters of Gracchus by methods which were in fact positively illegal. Constitutionalists turned to Scipio, on his return from Numantia, as the man who

### STRIKING A BARGAIN IN THE SLAVE MARKET

In the second century B.C. the conditions of the slave population under Roman mastery grew steadily more deplorable until discontent culminated in the Servile War. The specific traffic in human flesh is illustrated in this bas-relief on a funeral stele from Capua ; it depicts a naked man standing on a stone pedestal between a Greek slave-dealer and a togaed Roman who is purchasing him. It represents an actual incident in the life of one Satur, who happily rose from slavery to honourable freedom.

*Museo Campano, Capua ; from Rostovtzeff, ' History of Ancient World : Rome,' Clarendon Press*

must save the state. No man could be more utterly relied upon to do what he conceived to be his duty without fear or favour ; his instincts were intensely conservative ; he was by no means blind to justly felt grievances ; probably he was in sympathy with the real aims of Tiberius Gracchus, while detesting his methods. But the task needed a man of larger imagination and less rigid scrupulosity. One morning he was found dead in his bed, and the world believed that he had been murdered by the demagogues (129).

### Political Programme of the Gracchi

THE agrarian law was being applied in a manner which created a fresh grievance among the allies ; to counterbalance it, the Gracchans proposed to grant them the franchise, a measure distasteful alike to the already enrolled tribes and to the reactionaries. To be rid of Flaccus, the close personal friend and supporter of the murdered Tiberius, who proposed the measure, the Senate sent him off as consul to Transalpine Gaul to protect their allies of Massilia who had appealed for aid against the aggressive Celtic tribes. The result of his operations was conquest, annexation and the establishment of the Province of Gallia Narbonensis, which still bears the name of Provence ; seventy years later it became the base of Julius Caesar's operations. While Flaccus was absent, Gaius Gracchus, who had been serving latterly as quaestor in Sardinia, returned to Rome to take the place and avenge the death of his brother ; being now some thirty years of age. He was elected at once to the tribunate (123). Flaccus also now returned and celebrated a triumph for his Gallic victories.

The programme initiated by the younger Gracchus was wider in scope and much more far-reaching than that of his brother. The new Sempronian laws extended the operation of the agrarian law and supplemented it by planting new colonies : one was for the first time to be over sea, on the desolate and forbidden site of Carthage. A dangerous precedent was set by a measure for providing the city population with corn at half price, the first of a series of more or less open bribes

to the city voters. The next measures struck full at the power of the Senate. In the courts instituted for the trial of charges against provincial governors, the juries were composed of senators who even if honest were likely, and if dishonest were quite certain, to give judgement for the officials, members of their own order. For the Senate the law of Gracchus substituted members of the equestrian order, the wealthy commoners who were outside the senatorial body, and were virtually excluded from holding such appointments.

Gracchus did not, probably he could not legally, stand again for the tribunate ; but the number of candidates being short, the tribes exercised their power, unquestionably legal in the circumstances, of re-electing him, together with his most prominent supporter Flaccus. But the nobles had put up a candidate of their own, Drusus, to outbid Gracchus in bribes for popular support. Drusus may have been honest enough himself, but the whole matter was an obvious political trick. He offered so much more than Gracchus that the tribune's popularity began to wane. Nor was his next measure calculated to restore it—a large extension of the franchise to the Italians, the scheme which had been held up by dispatching Flaccus to Gaul. Whatever the original intention may have been, the purpose was now clearly a unification of Italy much desired by the Italians, but not at all by most of the full Roman citizens. Drusus vetoed the bill, and added to his own popularity.

### Gracchus' Fall from Power and Death

THEN the Senate, as before they had removed Flaccus by dispatching him to Gaul, removed both Flaccus and Gracchus by sending them to superintend the colonising of Carthage. By the time they were able to return their popularity had been completely undermined. Their bitterest enemy, Opimius, was elected consul, and both were rejected for the tribunate. Without the tribunician power they were helpless. Religious sentiment was excited by the portents reported from Carthage, profanely revived by them in spite of the solemn curse that had been laid on the site only twenty-five years since. It became obvious that the fate of Tiberius was to be their fate also. The mob had turned against them, and respectable public opinion in panic was convinced that they were subverters of the state. Flaccus raised a handful of armed supporters ; the forces of law and order, led by the consul Opimius, marched against them, and cut them to pieces. Gracchus died by the hand of a faithful slave, who slew himself on his loved master's corpse.

For some twenty years after the fall of Gaius the revolution was in abeyance. The moderates, who predominated, shook their heads over the prevailing corruption, but were too politically timid to be active reformers. Reform slept, but before long the state was involved in wars which brought the need of some change for the better into glaring relief.

### Outbreak of the Jugurthine War

$\mathfrak{I}$N 118 the king of Numidia, Micipsa, last of the sons of Masinissa, died, leaving the crown to his two young sons Hiempsal and Adherbal, jointly with a much older bastard nephew, Jugurtha, who was an experienced soldier, able and ambitious. He procured the assassination of Hiempsal ; Adherbal fled for his life, and appealed to the Senate. Jugurtha had no case, but he had gold, with which his agents reached Rome before Adherbal, whose appeal was received by the Senate with a strange coldness. A commission, however, was sent, with Opimius, the enemy of Gracchus, at its head, to divide the kingdom between the two claimants. It awarded the major and wealthy part of it to Jugurtha, and Opimius returned a richer man. Then Jugurtha murdered Adherbal.

Political morality was not dead in Rome. Hither Jugurtha was summoned and charged with his crimes before the Senate. The proceedings were stopped by the interposition of a tribune. So effective were Jugurtha's methods that even while he was in Rome he had another cousin murdered in the city. This was too much, but as he had come under safe-conduct he was only ordered to depart. 'A city for sale ! ' he sneered as he left.

**A GREAT GENERAL**

Gaius Marius, though born of humble parentage, achieved the unique distinction of being elected consul seven times. He rendered distinguished service in the Jugurthine and Social Wars, and further created the professional Roman army.

*Vatican Museum ; photo, Alinari*

The Jugurthine war had already been declared in the previous year (111) ; it was not ended till 106. It was so ill managed that a commission of inquiry was held, which elicited such revelations that three ex-consuls, one being Opimius, retired into exile, and the incorruptible Quintus Metellus, one of several distinguished sons of Macedonicus, was sent out, with the low-born but equally incorruptible Gaius Marius (157–86), who had risen by sheer merit, as second in command, in 109.

$\mathfrak{I}$UGURTHA was a past-master in the arts of guerrilla warfare. Metellus was a good soldier who conducted his campaigns with skill and vigour, but Jugurtha held out. Marius, a better soldier than Metellus, returned to Rome to stand for the consulship, claiming that if the command were given to him the war would be ended at once. In fact, by the time he returned to Africa as consul to supersede Metellus, it appeared that Jugurtha was beaten. Metellus went home bitterly disappointed at having had his laurels snatched from him ; but Jugurtha was not finished yet. Marius could not catch him, and he found a dubious ally or protector in his neighbour Bocchus, king of Mauretania. Finally it was the supreme audacity and diplomatic skill of the quaestor Lucius Cornelius Sulla (138–78) that induced Bocchus to betray his protégé to the Romans and to a miserable death at Rome. But the conquest was credited to Marius.

Before the conqueror of Numidia was back in Rome (104) he was re-elected to the consulship for the ensuing year, though the law as it then stood forbade re-election and required the candidates to be present in Rome. He was the soldier of the hour, and the hour demanded a first-rate soldier commanding universal confidence. For during the Numidian war a tremendous menace had been gathering head on the northern frontiers of Italy. The Teutonic or German-speaking tribes were making their first appearance on the stage of definitely recorded history.

The advance hordes of the migrants, collectively known as Teutones and Cimbri (who were not, as we might be tempted to suppose, Celtic Cymri), threatened but were checked on the northeastern frontier of Italy in 113 ; rolling west , past the Swiss mountains they poured into Gaul, flooding down the valley of the Saône and Rhône and also setting in motion the Helvetic (Swiss) Celts. They defeated one Roman consul, Silanus, in 109 ; and in 107 another, Cassius, was trapped by the Helvetii and lost his army and his life. In 105 the forces of the proconsul Caepio and the consul Mallius were severally annihilated by the Cimbri, with the loss of more than 100,000 men. Then for no obvious reason the tide for a moment surged off elsewhere.

Rome, then, turned to account the breathing-space allowed her, by placing the control and reorganization of her armies in the hands of her one general,

**SOLDIER AND STATESMAN TOO**
Lucius Cornelius Sulla (138–78 B.C.) proved his brilliant military qualities in the Jugurthine, Teutonic, Social and Mithradatic Wars. He was appointed dictator in 82 B.C.
*Chiaramonti Museum, Rome*

making him consul year after year, regardless of rules framed not with military efficiency but with political stability in view. By new methods of recruiting and promotion and of rewarding service, Marius created a thing hitherto unknown in Italy—a professional army. By rigid training and discipline he brought it up to the highest standard of efficiency.

He was only just in time. In 103 the Germans were again massing on the Saône, with the intention of carrying out a double invasion of Italy—the plan which they developed next year —by way of the Maritime Alps on the west and of the north-eastern Alps ; the Teutones taking the west and the Cimbri the east. In 102 Marius, consul for the fourth time, annihilated the Teutones at Aquae Sextiae in Transalpine Gaul, while his colleague, the aristocrat Catulus, kept guard in the Cisalpine province. In 101, when the Cimbri poured through the passes into the plain of the Po, they were in turn annihilated by Marius and Catulus at Campi Raudii near Vercellae. Sulla, who was present, recorded his opinion that the greater credit was due to Catulus, with whom Marius shared the triumph ; popular opinion gave the whole of it to the man of the people, and elected Marius to his sixth consulship.

**Marius crushes Teuton invaders**

Marius the consul had himself insisted that Catulus the proconsul should share the triumph ; but he was proud and the masses were proud of his humble origin. He was no politician, but he was inveigled easily enough by the demagogues, who saw a simple tool in the blunt old warrior, into serving their ends. His sixth consulship, not justified, like those preceding it, by any public emergency, was their work. The leaders, Saturninus and Glaucia, set about violent measures directed against the senatorial party; measures popular among the Italians, who reckoned Marius as one of themselves, but unpopular in the city.

Marius found himself losing credit; the violent partisans on each side got the upper hand, while he wavered between them. Prominent men were or were believed to have been murdered by the other party; finally the city mob slew Saturninus and Glaucia, who had been among the most violent; and then in the reaction against violence it appeared for a time that the moderates would be in the ascendant. But the root causes of the unrest were untouched, since they lay in the corruption of society—of the high-born, of the wealth-seeking Equites and of the city mob—and in the real grievances of the allies; the former being repeatedly illustrated by the gross miscarriages of justice in the law-courts.

### Festering sore of Slavery

THE general brutalising of moral stand-ards had been further illustrated also by a second slave revolt in Sicily. The first had been accompanied by savage atrocities on the part of the insurgents, and its suppression the year after the murder of Tiberius Gracchus had been marked by wholesale atrocities on the part of the government, when in one locality there were no fewer than twenty thousand crucifixions. Yet in 103 the slaves dared to revolt again—a sufficient demonstration of the hideous conditions under which they must have been living. It is not surprising that they fought so stubbornly that the revolt was only stamped out after a three years' struggle—during which, it is true, the resources of the state were being severely taxed by the Cimbrian war.

Then for nearly a decade after the sixth consulship of Marius, from 99 to 91, there was a lull, followed by another decade of strife; the story of which is complicated by events in the East and then in the West which withdrew from or brought back to Italy at critical moments leading actors in the revolutionary drama, as actors also in the imperial expansion. The pivot of the Eastern affairs was Mithradates VI, king of Pontus (to be distinguished from the Parthian kings bearing the same name), a monarch of great abilities and yet greater ambitions, whose activities called for the intervention of Roman arms and Roman diplomacy; but the further account of the Mithradatic wars themselves must be postponed until after the narrative of the troubles in Italy.

THE two matters which mainly occupied the minds of politicians were the en-franchisement of the allies, and the friction occasioned by the rival desires of senators and equites, or knights, to dominate the political courts of justice; while to carry out any policy whatever it had become necessary to secure the suffrages of the voters in the Assembly of Tribes, who resented all attempts to admit the much more numerous allies to anything like an equal share in their privileges. In 91 the senatorial moderates allied themselves with Livius Drusus, the son of that Drusus who had been brought forward by the same party to outbid Gaius Gracchus for popular favour in 122. If the honesty of the father is open to doubt, that of the

### END OF THE JUGURTHINE WAR

References to recent history are frequent on coins of the Re-publican mint. Thus this coin, struck by Faustus Sulla, son of the Dictator, shows on the reverse the surrender of Jugurtha, the able but unscrupulous king of Numidia, to Sulla by Bocchus in 102 B.C. The obverse bears a head of Diana.

*British Museum*

son is not. As tribune he proposed to add to the Senate an equal number of the knights, to extend the franchise to the Italians, and to reward the humbler citizens for their assent by new schemes for colonisation and a further cheapening of corn for their benefit at the expense of the state. The populace, the senators and the knights each felt that they would be conceding too much and getting too little—and Drusus was assassinated.

### Outbreak of the Social War

THE moderates had stood by Drusus loyally enough ; but the opposition tribune now carried a bill declaring that to have supported franchise extension was treason. The excitement among the allies rose to fever heat ; a Roman official was killed by an enraged mob at Asculum, the chief city of the Piceni, in central Italy ; and from north to south the socii broke into open revolt, Marsi and Paeligni, Samnites,. Lucanians, Apulians — eight nations in all. A federation was hastily formed with an emergency constitution ; the Roman Senate declined to negotiate until compensation had been made for the outrage at Asculum ; and the Social War (90–88) began.

Ill organized as they necessarily were, since the outbreak was unpremeditated, the socii put up a very valiant fight. A number of towns fell into their hands at the outset, and they cut up a consular army. Marius, taking the field again, defeated them, but—perhaps deliberately —made no effort to crush them.

They had a strong party of sympathisers in the Senate, who in 89 were able to win over waverers among the allies by the Julian law, granting the franchise to all who had not joined the insurrection. But the die-hards, especially the Samnites, only fought the harder, and on the other hand the death of one consul gave Sulla, who had been his lieutenant, the chance of showing his brilliant powers in the Samnite country ; while the second consul, Pompeius Strabo, the father of a more famous son, conducted successful operations among the Piceni. By the end of the year resistance was maintained only in a few Samnite

and Lucanian strongholds ; and the Senate, though Asculum and other places had been dealt with hardly, supplemented the Julian law of the previous year with the Lex Plautia-Papiria, which granted the franchise to all who laid down arms within sixty days. But the question as to whether the new citizens were to be enrolled as new additional tribes or distributed among the existing tribes remained unsettled.

At the beginning of 88, then, the Social War was ended, save for the garrisons which were still holding out ; but the immediate dispatch of an army to the East was made necessary by the activities of Mithradates. Sulla, as consul elect, and as the man who had won the Social War, expected the command ; but Marius wanted it. He found an ally in the eloquent tribune Sulpicius, who proposed that the new Italian citizens, who were quite certain to vote for Marius (always their friend), should be distributed among the tribes, whereby the Roman vote for Sulla would be swamped. The Marians organized a coup de main, appearing at the Assembly with concealed arms, and carried their point, not without bloodshed.

### Sulla's sudden Coup de Main

BUT Sulla sped straight from the scene in Rome to his still undisbanded troops before Nola in Campania, where Samnites were still holding out, and appealed to them to follow him. The officers hesitated ; the men did not ; and the consul marched on Rome at the head of six Roman legions. He was joined by his colleague Pompeius Rufus ; they seized the city gates, marched in, and routed the force collected by Marius. Marius and Sulpicius fled ; the Senate, overawed, at the bidding of the consuls issued a decree of outlawry against the fugitives and ten of their followers, none protesting save a distinguished lawyer and leader of the moderates, Mucius Scaevola.

Sulpicius alone was betrayed by one of his slaves and slain. The old bulldog Marius—he was in his seventieth year— made a most adventurous escape from Sulla's bloodhounds to Africa and thence to Corsica. Sulla annulled the legislation of Sulpicius, but could not prevent the election of Lucius Cornelius Cinna to the consulship in succession to Pompeius Rufus, who was murdered by the soldiery with the connivance of Pompeius Strabo, whom he had superseded ; and then Sulla, threatened with a charge of treason for having led an army into the sacred precincts of the city, departed for the East with his troops, leaving Rome in the hands of Cinna, his declared enemy (87).

Four years (87–83) passed before Sulla thought fit to return from his extremely efficient campaigning and diplomatising in the East. During those years the revolution was rampant. Cinna revived the legislation and the methods of Sulpicius as champion of the Italians, and when his violence in the city was defeated by violence on the other side, he appealed as consul to the troops that had remained in Italy, and practically revived the Social War. Marius returned and joined him, more intent on vengeance than anything else. The senatorial commanders were inefficient or remained inactive of set purpose ; the city had to open its gates to Marius and Cinna ; and, in the week's reign of terror which followed, Marius wreaked his revenge on his enemies and on all whom he chose to reckon as enemies.

### Sulla reappears in Italy

AFTER the brief but hideous orgy of blood-lust which alarmed Cinna and disgusted the very notable Sabine Sertorius (c. 125–72), who had joined the anti-senatorial party, Marius seized his seventh consulship without election, but died a fortnight later (Jan., 87). Cinna remained master of Rome, and was continuously consul till he was killed in the course of a mutiny early in 84. But he made no notable use of his power, and Sulla was only waiting to put the finishing touches to his triumphant career in the East before returning to deal with the Italian situation after his own fashion as champion of the 'optimates' (as the oligarchic or senatorial party called themselves) against the 'populares' or democrats. In the spring of 83 Sulla landed in Italy with the army he had so often led to victory behind him. The forces at the disposal

of the government were far larger ; but Sertorius was ere long on his way to Spain as praetor, and every day adherents flocked to the standard of the avenger.

Sulla as he marched through the country held his troops well in hand. He had not the smallest objection to shedding blood, except where policy suggested a meticulous clemency. He had come avowedly to punish the crimes of the Marians ; and he was technically a rebel in arms at the head of rebel legions against the legally constituted government. The real tug-of-war came in 82, when the Samnites flung themselves whole-heartedly into what was now the struggle of the popular revolution against the reactionary revolution of Sulla. But the prolonged and desperate battle of the Colline Gate (Aug., 82) was decisive. It made Sulla the master of the Roman world.

### Sulla supreme as Dictator

FIFTY thousand men, dead or dying, were left on the field ; eight thousand who were taken prisoners were three days later massacred in cold blood by Sulla's order. In Italy at least no further resistance was possible. The champion of the constitution was appointed dictator for so long as he might think fit to retain the office, in order that he might ensure the restoration of order. To that end he issued a series of proscriptions— lists of persons who had forfeited their property and their lives, including any one who was or might be obnoxious to himself or to any friend who had a grudge to be satisfied. If he chose to spare, he spared ; and one of those whom he suffered to escape was a dissolute young patrician of eighteen, whose father's sister had been the wife of Marius, and who was himself the husband of Cinna's daughter—Gaius Julius Caesar.

Then he set the constitution in order ; in such wise that the whole power of the state would be in the hands of the senators if they had the wit to use it. The tribunate and the Assembly of Tribes had been the instruments used by the democrats for the overthrow of the senate ; tribunes were to be barred from all further office, and the Assembly was deprived of

the power of initiating legislation. The senatorial control
of the courts was restored at
the expense of the knights.

There were to be no more
repeated consulships, like those
of Marius and Cinna. Consuls
were not to hold military commands till, after their year of
office, they went abroad as
proconsuls, when their powers
could be exercised only in the
particular province assigned to
them. Such were the main
features of the Sullan constitution of 81. Then in 79 the
dictator discarded his powers and devoted
the remaining months of his life to the
debaucheries which carried him off in 78.

**MITHRADATES VI**

Mithradates VI, king of
Pontus, 120–63 B.C.,
waged three separate
wars with Rome, ended
only by his suicide after
his defeat by Pompey.
*From Ward, ' Greek Coins'*

### Affairs in the East : Mithradates of Pontus

Ｗ E must turn now to survey the affairs
of the East during this half-century.
Since the acquisition of Pergamum and
its conversion into the Roman Province of
Asia, the Empire in the East had been
ruled by governors both of the best and of
the worst type ; but even the best could
not prevent, though they might now and
then succeed in punishing, the gross oppression to which the provincials were
subjected by the system which farmed the
taxes to wealthy Roman knights. When
the knights and the governors leagued
together the oppression was intensified,
since the oppressors could secure the ear
of the Roman court of appeal, whether it
was composed of senators or knights or
both. In such case the provincials had
no redress and no means of resistance ;
and the sense of helpless resentment grew,
while it could not take active form.

But outside the bounds of the Empire
Mithradates VI (132–63), who had succeeded to the kingdom of Pontus in 120
at the age of twelve, set about the expansion and consolidation of his dominions,
which he extended over the eastern litt-
toral of the Euxine, known as Colchis, and
to which he sought to add the semi-independent kingdoms of Cappadocia and
Bithynia. In 99 he had withdrawn these
pretensions at the bidding of Rome, just
released from the Teutonic menace ; he

renewed them and again withdrew them in 92 at the bidding
of Sulla, who had been sent as
governor to Cilicia. When the
Social War broke out, however,
Sulla was back in Italy, and
Rome was very fully occupied,
so Mithradates invaded the
Roman Province of Asia, which
welcomed a deliverer from the
Roman tyranny. He successfully overran it, captured and
put to death its detested governor Aquillus, and ordered a
general massacre of Italians, to
the number of 80,000. Half
Achaea, Athens taking the lead, followed
the example of Asia, and rose against its
Roman rulers, supported by the king and
troops of the king of Pontus. Such was
the situation when in 87 Sulla carried his
army from Italy to Greece, leaving Rome
in the hands of Cinna.

Athens was the centre of resistance in
Greece. Its fortifications, and those of
the Piraeus against which Sulla directed
his main attack, defied all the efforts of
his engineers, while his lieutenant Lucius
Lucullus was raising a fleet to deprive
Mithradates of his command of the
Aegean. Early in 86, however, Athens
was starved out, and the port soon afterwards surrendered. Both paid a heavy
penalty. But Archelaus, the ablest officer
of Mithradates, had now assembled a large
army in Thessaly. Sulla, with no more
than a sixth of his numbers, shattered his
force on the old battlefield of Chaeronea.

A Roman consul, Valerius Flaccus, with
his lieutenant Fimbria and fresh forces,
was in Epirus, on the way to supersede
Sulla, who had no intention of being superseded. While he was on his way north
to deal with Flaccus, huge reinforcements
arrived from Asia for Archelaus. Sulla
promptly wheeled southward, and repeated
at Orchomenus the triumph of Chaeronea.
Meanwhile Flaccus, avoiding a conflict with
Sulla, was hastening to the Hellespont to
fight Mithradates in Asia; but Fimbria,
with schemes of his own, made away with
his chief, assumed the command himself,
and crossing the strait started operations
on his own account.

Sulla opened negotiations with the defeated Archelaus, who was disposed to peace on the terms of a return to the pre-war position, the more because Lucullus was now master of the sea. A conference was arranged between Sulla and the king, and a treaty was struck by which Mithradates was to surrender his conquests, to hand over seventy ships and to pay an indemnity (85).

It remained to settle with Fimbria, who committed suicide when he found himself deserted by his troops on Sulla's approach ; and thus in 84 Sulla was able to return to Italy to carry through the revolution already described, leaving the settlement of the East in the very competent hands of Lucullus, who dealt with the sorely pressed provincials as gently as his instructions permitted. The command, however, passed on to another of Sulla's lieutenants, Murena, who before the dictator's resignation attacked Mithradates again, and was allowed a triumph ; though the war was promptly stopped by orders from Rome.

Two men had risen to prominence as supporters of Sulla. One was Publius Licinius Crassus (117–53), to whom the victory of the Colline Gate was largely due ; the other, Gnaeus Pompeius (106–48)— Pompey—the young son of Pompeius Strabo. Youthful though he was, Pompey had shown remarkable m i l i t a r y talents, which induced Sulla to entrust him with the suppression of the M a r i a n s in Africa ; whereby he won from the dictator the complimentary title of Magnus, ' the Great.' Crassus had no little ability, but he chose to concentrate it on the acquisition of wealth, with power as a subsidiary aim.

Sulla was hardly dead when the inevitable attempt to overturn his constitution was made by the consul Lepidus, posing as champion of the popular party. When he took up arms, however, he was easily crushed (77).

IN one quarter, the Marians had not been suppressed. Sertorius, as we saw, retreated to Spain when Sulla returned to Italy, and there he was making himself a formidable power, partly as the real representative of Rome—that is, of the old government—partly by rallying the Spaniards to his own standard as their leader. He was very much more than a match for the Roman forces sent to deal with him. Pompey, charged with the business in 77, fared not much better than his predecessors ; and presently Mithradates—resentful of Murena's attack and no longer in awe of Sulla—was negotiating with Sertorius, with the intention of renewing the war in 74. The alliance in fact came to naught, because Sertorius was assassinated in 72—not with any connivance on the part of Pompey, though very conveniently for him ; since when the great leader was gone, the suppression of what remained of Marianism in Spain presented no serious difficulties. He returned to Italy to claim and receive credit, scarcely deserved, for having succeeded where others had failed.

By this time the Third or Great Mithradatic war was already in full swing in the East, and a third slave-rising, this time in Italy itself, was receiving its death-blow. Slaves were trained as gladiators ; and in 73 such a one, a Thracian named Spartacus, broke away with seventy comrades from the ' school ' at Capua and took refuge in the hills. The numbers of his band swelled rapidly ; for months he kept his men well in hand under strict discipline, and routed two com-

**POMPEY THE GREAT**

Gnaeus Pompeius, known as Pompey (106–48 B.C.), won glory in Africa, Spain, and in the East. Thereafter his influence declined and he was defeated by Caesar at Pharsalus.

*Ny Carlsberg Museum, Copenhagen*

**TIGRANES THE GREAT**

Tigranes I, king of Armenia 95–55 B.C., greatly
extended his dominions, annexing Syria among
other regions. This fact explains the Genius
of Antioch with Orontes at her feet (see also
page 144) on the reverse of this silver coin.
*From Ward, ' Greek Coins,' John Murray*

manders who were sent to take him. In 72
he had so formidable a host at his back
that two consular armies were sent against
him, and he routed them both.

Pompey was away in the West, Lucullus
in the East. It was Crassus who at the head
of six legions at last brought Spartacus
to bay, shattered his army, and slew him
on the field (71). Five thousand of the
gladiatorial soldiery cut their way through,
but only to be blotted out by the forces
of Pompey, just back from Spain. To his
Spanish laurels Pompey added those which
were justly due to Crassus. Crassus, seeing
that the popular soldier might be useful
to him, did not quarrel : Pompey and he
together could clearly do what they chose.

THEY chose, in fact, to undermine the
foundations of the Sullan constitution. Both by its terms were barred from
standing for the consulship, Pompey by
his youth, Crassus because the law required
an interval between the consulship and the
praetorship which he then held ; but both
stood and were elected. As consuls, during
70, they procured the annulment of the
disabilities imposed on the tribunate by
the Cornelian laws, thereby restoring also
the lost legislative powers of the Tribal
Assembly ; and another law gave a new
constitution to the Courts—which became
one-third equestrian and one-third senatorial, while the remaining third was
selected by certain elected officers. They
had won the first point because the Senate
dared not refuse the demand, however unconstitutional, of two successful generals,
each with an army behind him.

Meanwhile, the developments in the East
had produced a situation for dealing with
which some quite unprecedented step was
becoming imperative. In this situation
there were two factors, the war with
Mithradates and the Cilician pirate fleets
which infested the Mediterranean.

When Sulla the invincible disappeared
from the stage, Mithradates was on the
alert for a chance of reviving his project of
an Asiatic empire. The opportunity came
in 74, when Nicomedes of Bithynia died
and, like Attalus, left his kingdom to the
Roman people. Mithradates put up a
pretender on whose behalf he invaded
Bithynia. The consul Cotta could make
no head against the king ; but Lucius
Lucullus, formerly the very able lieutenant
of Sulla in the East, where he had won the
good will of the Asiatics, was dispatched
to be governor of Cilicia and to deal
with Mithradates.

### Fluctuating Progress of the War

THOUGH provided only with a comparatively small and undisciplined force,
Lucullus conducted his operations with
such skill that within the year he had
broken up the army of Mithradates without
having had to fight a pitched battle, and
driven the king into his own territory. By
a series of campaigns during the following years Mithradates was compelled to flee
to Tigranes of Armenia. Lucullus, having
subjugated Pontus, proceeded to a general
settlement of Asia Minor, to the great
satisfaction of the population and the
corresponding annoyance of the soldiery
and the tax-farmers, whose depredations
he firmly repressed. In 69 he advanced
against Tigranes, who had scornfully
refused his demand for the surrender of
Mithradates, captured his capital, Tigrano-
certa, and in the next year routed his
forces. But then Lucullus found himself
paralysed by the mutinous spirit of his
own troops, and was forced (67) to withdraw to Pontus, where Mithradates had
reappeared ; there Lucullus learnt that
he himself was to be superseded.

While Lucullus was pursuing his victorious career, the Cilician pirates were
successfully defying the naval power of
Rome. Matters came to something like

a climax in 74. In that year Marcus Antonius, son of a famous orator and father of the still more famous Mark Antony, was given a special commission for their suppression and failed disgracefully. After his death, indeed, matters were improved, when the consul Quintus Metellus was sent out in 69 ; but Pompey had now decided that the task was eminently suitable for himself. In 67 a measure proposed by the tribune Gabinius in the teeth of senatorial opposition, but supported by Caesar, who was now making himself the rising hope of the old Marians, gave Pompey an almost unlimited command in the Mediterranean.

A commander with a perfectly free hand and control of unrestricted resources was what the situation required. In three months Pompey accomplished what no half-hearted measures could have effected. He spread his fleets across the Mediterranean and swept it clean from end to end. The pirates were destroyed.

Not so Mithradates or his ally Tigranes : the generalship and the statesmanship of Lucullus were fully equal to the task, but they were foiled by a mutinous soldiery and the hostility of the Roman moneyed interest. By popular acclamation Pompey, fresh from his brilliant triumph over the pirates, was given supreme and unlimited authority over the whole East, to be retained until he himself should be satisfied with the completeness of the settlement he might effect. Such powers had never before been bestowed on any man save Sulla. Senatorial constitutionalists might shake anxious heads, but the tide of Pompey's popularity was irresistible. From 66 to 62 the East absorbed him.

### Pompey takes Command in the East

IN his first campaign Pompey forced Mithradates to fight him, and routed him on the eastern border of Pontus, whence the king, refused an asylum by Tigranes, escaped to the northern shores of the Black Sea. There, out of reach of the Roman, he busied himself with a grand scheme of invading Italy at the head of the barbarian tribes of eastern Europe. That project, however, was brought to naught by the revolt of his son Pharnaces,

and in 63, broken at last in his old age, Mithradates died by his own hand.

Pompey, on defeating Mithradates, left the fugitive king to his own devices while he secured the conquered territory from external attack. In this there was little difficulty. Tigranes had already suffered so severely at the hands of Lucullus that he had withdrawn his countenance from Mithradates and his troops from Syria, to which he had recently extended his sovereignty. When Pompey marched into Armenia, the king made haste to offer abject submission. The Roman graciously confirmed him in the possession of his kingdom—limited however to Armenia proper—and accepted friendly overtures from Phraates of Parthia, who had now assumed the old title King of Kings.

### Reorganization of Asia Minor and Syria

RETURNING to Pontus, Pompey saw that nothing was to be gained by attempting to hunt down Mithradates beyond the Caucasus, and so ended his first triumphant year devoted to the organization of Asia Minor. Pontus was transformed into a Roman province, with Bithynia, and the province of Cilicia was enlarged. The minor principalities on the border, Cappadocia, Galatia and Commagene, were recognized as being under Roman protection. The second year was spent in bringing this work to completion, and in 64 Pompey turned his attention to Syria.

During the last sixty years the once mighty kingdom of the Seleucids had gone utterly to wreck. Parthia had already absorbed Media and Persia. A Jewish kingdom was established under the Levitical Hasmonaean dynasty, with an Idumean (Edomite) kingdom to the south of it, in the north-west of Arabia. Claimants, legitimate or otherwise, to the crown of the Seleucids wrangled and deposed and assassinated each other in lurid succession till in 84 Tigranes of Armenia fell upon the distracted land and annexed it. A few years later the Roman menace to his own land made him retire from it again. Syria lay at the feet of the conqueror of Mithradates and Tigranes.

Syria had everything to gain and nothing to lose from the setting up of an efficient authority. When in 64 Pompey descended from Cappadocia upon the ancient Land of the Amorites, he only needed, so far as the whole northern region was concerned, to assume the sovereignty on behalf of Rome, and to give it the organization of a Roman province. On the other hand, the Hasmonaean princes of Judaea had been admitted to the alliance and occasional protection of Rome for

**ARISTOBULUS IN DEFEAT**

'Bacchius the Jew,' named on the reverse of this coin, is Aristobulus, the prince of Judaea, who in 63 B.C. resisted Pompey's arbitration in favour of his brother Hyrcanus. He is represented making submission to Pompey.

*British Museum*

half a century, and there was no immediate warrant for annexation. The Jews themselves provided the justification.

As always, there were two parties among the Jews ; the rigidly orthodox and the latitudinarians, who leaned to the learning and the customs of the gentiles. The Maccabees had been the heroic champions of the former ; but since they had become princes as well as priests, political rather than religious considerations had guided the various rival members of the family in seeking the support of one party or the other. The government was generally in the hands of those who stood for puritanism and isolation, while the other side was commonly the more popular.

At this time (63) the supremacy was in dispute between two brothers, Hyrcanus and Aristobulus, and appeal was made to Pompey to arbitrate between them. Pompey's award was in favour of Hyrcanus, and the puritans ; but the followers of Aristobulus in Jerusalem rejected alien dictation. Consequently, Jerusalem underwent a stubbornly contested siege ; and when at last the conqueror entered it, he left Hyrcanus in possession, but as a tributary of Rome. Judaea was

made a division of the province of Syria. Pompey had in effect extended the empire of the Roman Republic to the Euphrates. He passed the time between the fall of Jerusalem and his slow return to Italy late in the next year (62) in completing the organization of the new provinces—without consulting the Senate. Mithradates being dead, Pharnaces his son was left to reign in his stead in the European realm north of the Euxine.

During the five years of Pompey's absence in the East the government at Rome had passed through a grave crisis. Caesar, the nephew of Marius and the son-in-law of Cinna, was systematically and even audaciously courting popularity, while he was far too cool-headed to commit himself to any of the schemes of subversive violence that might be developed by the hot-heads of the anti-senatorial party. Among these hot-heads was Lucius Sergius Catilina (Catiline—c. 106–62) a profligate patrician, who was reputed at least to have no scruples in such matters as assassination, but was undoubtedly possessed of the virtues of courage and loyalty to his associates.

### Cicero champions the Senatorial Party

ON the other hand the ranks of the senatorial party were joined by the most brilliant orator of the day, Marcus Tullius Cicero (106–43), a 'new man' to whom the exclusive optimates were by no means eager to extend a welcome. He had distinguished himself, too, by his attack on Verres, who as praetor in Sicily had been guilty of many enormities, and by his panegyric on Pompey—no favourite with the senatorial class—when the Manilian law gave him his Eastern command. But democracy frightened him, and his panacea for the diseases of the state was alliance between the optimates and the knights, the body from which he as well as Pompey derived, as the forces of law and order against veiled or open revolutionaries. Both groups had at least a common interest in the preservation of stable government and the rights of property. And these were threatened by Catiline, who in 64 was a candidate for the consulship of the ensuing year, having just been barely acquitted on a charge of treasonable conspiracy. To save so dangerous a situation, the optimates adopted the popular orator as their candidate, and Catiline was defeated.

Then, if not before, Catiline definitely planned revolution ; while Caesar occupied himself with measures certain to enhance his own popularity, whether they were carried or not, and to diminish that of the consul who, having now definitely attached himself to the optimates, was bound to oppose them. Caesar's unwelcome success was demonstrated by his election to the dignified office of Pontifex Maximus over the heads of the most eminent senatorial candidates.

### Defeat of the Catiline Conspiracy

BUT the great event of the year (63) was Catiline's conspiracy and its defeat. The intrigue was afoot, but on the one hand Catiline did not mean to move until he had attained the consulship, and on the other Cicero had unsuspected confederates in the conspirators' camp. Neither, in fact, felt ready to strike till, near the end of the year, the information in Cicero's hands warranted him in laying a statement before the Senate. Catiline, again defeated in the consular election, slipped away to the north to head the intended insurrection in the provinces, leaving his accomplices to carry out the programme arranged for the city.

A treasonable correspondence between him and the Gallic tribe of the Allobroges fell into the hands of the consul, who was endowed with emergency powers ; the principal conspirators were surprised and arrested ; and from some of them confession of their sanguinary intentions was extracted. The prisoners were condemned to death by decree, without trial—on the legal plea that they were not citizens whom it was illegal to put to death without sanction of the Tribal Assembly, but public enemies. Cicero told the whole story to the multitude gathered in the Forum amid frantic applause, and ever after regarded himself as the acknowledged saviour of Rome.

There, in fact, the insurrection had been throttled at birth ; but in the country

Catiline and his principal lieutenant fell fighting indomitably at the head of the troops they had succeeded in raising. For the moment at least the spectre of revolution was laid. Caesar as the constitutional leader of the democrats denounced the unconstitutional execution of the prisoners, but it was quite impossible to bring home to him any charge of complicity in the conspiracy, while his popularity with the mob and the senatorial mistrust of him were increased.

Catiline fell early in 62. Pompey was on the point of returning with his laurels and his legions from the East. No one knew what he intended to do, and every man knew that he could do whatever he chose ; but he gave no sign. Both Caesar and Cicero wanted his alliance ; but Caesar knew how to wait and turn events to his own account. At present Crassus

### ROME'S GREATEST ORATOR

Famous as a pleader in the law courts, Marcus Tullius Cicero (106–43 B.C.) was successively quaestor, aedile, praetor and, in 63 B.C., consul. He abjured politics after Pompey's defeat at Pharsalus and devoted himself to literature.

*Apsley House Collection, permission of Duke of Wellington*

with his gold was more important than Pompey with his men ; the money of Crassus enabled Caesar to take up the pro-praetorship in Spain, soon after Pompey's landing at Brundusium.

The anxiety caused by Pompey's approach was intensified by the proposal of one of his partisans that he should be invested with the supreme command in Italy because of the disturbed state of the country ; actually this was vetoed, but not till Caesar had taken the opportunity to commend it.  Constitutionalists, however, took comfort when the returned general instead of remaining in arms dismissed his troops.  He was not minded to play the part of a Sulla or a Marius ; but what part he did mean to play was, and remained, an open question.  Caesar having left the field clear, the optimates should have been able to secure Pompey ; but Cicero's combination of irrepressible vanity with ostentatious devotion annoyed him ;  the Senate withheld ratification of the arrangements he had made in the East without consulting them ; and the opportunity was lost.

In 60 Caesar returned from Spain, enriched by the spoils of successful campaigns against insurgent tribes, to stand for the consulship.  The temper in which he found Pompey made it easy for him by an exercise of his diplomatic astuteness to secure the alliance of the general and to reconcile him with the useful Crassus.  The partnership was to be sealed next year by the marriage of Pompey to Caesar's daughter Julia.  With Pompey and Crassus supporting him, Caesar was triumphantly elected consul.

### First Consulate of Julius Caesar

**H**E used his year of office (59) to establish his position.  An agrarian law, obstinately opposed in the Senate, but openly supported by Pompey and Crassus, was carried in the Assembly.  The knights, whom Cicero thirsted to unite with the optimates, were detached by the relaxation —opposed by the latter—of the terms of their contract for the farming of taxes in Asia.  The acts of Pompey in the East were ratified.  And finally Caesar procured for himself, for the unprecedented term of

five years, the proconsulship of Cisalpine Gaul and Illyricum ; to which the Senate, hoping to be well rid of him, added Transalpine Gaul, where serious trouble was threatening.

Before departing for his province in 58 Caesar arranged to leave the optimates without a leader, by dispatching the austere and uncompromising Cato ' of Utica ' (95–46) to effect the annexation of Cyprus, and by enabling the profligate Publius Claudius, better known as Clodius, who had a violent grudge against Cicero, to obtain the tribunate.  The orator, attacked for the illegal execution of Roman citizens in his consulate, was obliged to go into exile in Greece.

### Disorder in the Capital

**F**OR a time Clodius exercised his powers unchecked, since neither Pompey nor Crassus chose to interfere ; among his measures was one that ensured the distribution of corn not even at half price but gratis to the populace.  But the reckless violence of his conduct lost him the countenance of Pompey, who next year (57) showed his displeasure by procuring the recall of Cicero ; a measure which Clodius and his associates opposed by riotous force, which was met and defeated by the equally lawless violence of the senatorial tribune Milo Cicero, who on his return found himself surprisingly popular, had nothing better to propose than that Pompey should be invested with dictatorial powers for the restoration of order ; which might have been useful had Pompey had any clear idea as to what he should do with them, or if the senatorial reactionaries had been better disposed towards Pompey himself, his backer Crassus, and his absent associate Caesar.  The full powers were not conveyed to him, and of those he did receive he made no effective use.

Clodius was indeed held in check, but, beyond that, a senatorial reaction was clearly threatening ; very dangerous to the interests of Caesar, who in the intervals of his Gallic campaigns was keeping keen watch on affairs at the capital.  In 56, when he was in Cisalpine Gaul, he held a conference with his two allies at Lucca ; the result of which was that Pompey and

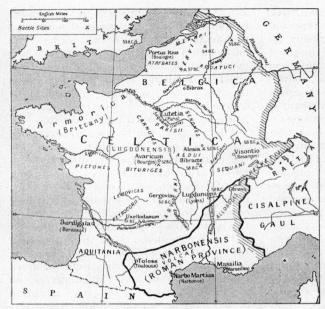

**EXPLOITS OF CAESAR IN THE 'THREE GAULS'**

Caesar's military energy can be gauged by the number of his battles in Gaul. His division of Transalpine Gaul, other than Narbonensis, into three parts—Aquitania, Celtica and Belgica—was recognized by Augustus when, with some alterations of boundaries, he made of it three provinces.

But in the ensuing years Caesar was kept at a distance by the Gallic campaigns which demanded all his energies. In 54 Pompey's young wife died and with her death disappeared the personal link that had bound him so closely to his father-in-law. Crassus started for the East ; but only to meet his death next year (53) at the hands of a foe whom Rome was destined never to subdue, in the terrible military disaster of Carrhae in north. Mesopotamia, where the Roman army was almost destroyed by the Parthians. And Pompey, remaining in or near Rome, did nothing. Only he watched with growing jealousy the successive triumphs of Caesar in Gaul. Even the ordinary routine of government was thrown out of gear by the tribunes of either party, who vied with each other in suspending elections to the magistracies.

In 52 matters seemed to have come to a head. Clodius, still the leader of the popular extremists, was killed in an affray with the followers of Milo, the leader of the senatorial extremists. Cicero wished but did not dare to defend Milo publicly ; Pompey did not choose to protect him, and he had to take flight. Pompey, commissioned to restore order and elected sole consul, was virtually dictator ; but his official dictatorship might have involved an immediate collision with Caesar. What he actually did made a hardly less definite breach between them. While he procured a five years' extension of his own Spanish proconsulship, he had a law passed under which Caesar's successor might take his place nearly a year earlier, in March, 49, instead of January, 48, according to the previous arrangement, and consular candidates must be present at their election ; though a special decree exempted Caesar from this latter condition. For the moment Caesar was paralysed by a sudden revolt in Gaul on a very large scale.

Crassus stood for the consulship against a senatorial candidate, and were elected mainly because the son of Crassus, who had been serving brilliantly under Caesar, was at no great distance from Rome with a returning legion.

It did not suit Caesar to return to Rome at this stage. To secure the control of the situation for himself and his associates, Pompey procured the extension of Caesar's proconsulship for a further term of five years (till the end of 49) ; Crassus received the Eastern command against the Parthians, who were pushing across the Euphrates into Roman territory, since he wanted military honours to counterbalance those which Pompey had won and Caesar was winning ; and for himself Pompey obtained the proconsulship of Spain, though he intended to discharge the duties of that office by deputy, while he himself remained at Rome in effective control. These also were appointments for five years. The powers of these three colleagues, unofficially known as the First Triumvirate, were irresistible.

We must now turn to Caesar's own career during these years of his Gallic command.

In the first year of his governorship, 58, Caesar's powers had been put to the proof. Hitherto, though his youth had not been without military experience, his abilities as a general had been tested only in Spain. His presence was now urgently required in Gaul—Transalpine Gaul—because of the movement among the Teutonic tribes on the east of the Rhine and their pressure on the Helvetic (Swiss) Celts. It was doubtless in consequence of this pressure that the Helvetii determined to migrate eastwards in a vast body and establish themselves in new pastures. That would mean a general upheaval in Gaul, and a serious threat to the Roman province. The year 58 was therefore at first occupied with a campaign in which the invaders were split in two and their forces so heavily defeated that they had to retire to their own mountains.

But this only brought into relief the German menace which had been scotched by the great victories of Marius at Aquae Sextiae and Campi Raudii between forty and fifty years earlier. German tribes (Suevi, Swabians) were over the Rhine, threatening to subjugate the Aedui, the Gallic allies of Rome on the northern borders of the Province ; their chief, Ariovistus, having in mind a partition of Gaul between himself and the Romans. Caesar led his legions to the help of the Aedui, inspired with his own audacity the men who were on the verge of panic, since the German warriors had a terrifying reputation, and utterly routed Ariovistus, who barely escaped across the Rhine with a remnant of his forces.

### Victory over the Nervii

THE Germans were driven back, but the victory aroused all over Gaul the fear that a general conquest was impending. The Roman approach was especially resented by the Nervii, the leading tribes of the warlike Belgae of the north-east, who had hitherto refused intercourse with the southern people. Caesar, warned by friendly Gauls that an attack was to be expected, struck first, invading Nervian territory in 57. The Nervii fought heroic-

ally ; there was a moment in the decisive battle when only the personal leadership of Caesar saved the Roman army from annihilation ; but the actual victory was overwhelming, and was followed by a general submission of the tribes between the Aisne and the Rhine. ' The day he overcame the Nervii ' was celebrated in Rome by a prolonged public festival.

The alarm of the Belgae, however, had been thoroughly warranted ; for during the next year, 56, Caesar, after his conference at Lucca with Pompey and Crassus, reduced the whole of Gaul to submission in the course of three campaigns—justified, of course, by aggressive movements among the barbarians—conducted either by himself or his lieutenants in the north-east, the south-west and Armorica (Brittany).

The two following years were occupied with expeditions and campaigns of an experimental kind. In 55 a fresh irruption of Germans across the middle Rhine was completely shattered in the neighbourhood of the modern Coblenz—a pretext having been found for detaining their chiefs, who had been invited to a conference—and the victory was followed by a great raid over the river into German territory, which made Caesar decide that the Rhine should remain the boundary.

### Caesar invades Britain

AN enemy of the Romans acting as Caesar had done would have been denounced for treachery, and in Rome Cato did not hesitate to denounce the proconsul ; though without effect, as there had as yet been no breach between Caesar and Pompey. Afterwards, Caesar made his first exploring expedition to Britain, a land hitherto known only by report of mercantile travellers. In 54, when Crassus was on his way to the East, Caesar made the second British expedition, and reduced the south-east of the island to submission, but decided that a real conquest was not worth undertaking, for the present at least.

In that winter and in 53, the year of the disaster of Carrhae, Caesar was occupied with the suppression of ominous insurrections in north-eastern Gaul ; and then, in 52, just when Pompey's jealousy was at its height, a great war of liberation was

**TRIUMPHAL ARCH AT ORANGE**

One of the earliest examples of the Roman triumphal arch, this splendid structure was erected at Orange, not far from Avignon, about 46 B.C. to commemorate Caesar's conquest of Massilia and the reduction of Gaul to submission.

*Photo, Mansell*

organized in the very heart of Gaul by the heroic Arvernian chief Vercingetorix.

So stubborn and so able was the Gallic chief that all Caesar's energies were required for the campaign before the centre of resistance was broken and Vercingetorix himself captured ; and the whole of 51 was fully occupied with the military organization and the establishment of the garrisons needed for the effective reten-

tion of Caesar's conquests, which were said to have been accomplished at the cost of more than a million Gallic and German lives. Meanwhile the party in Rome most hostile to him was straining itself to the utmost to effect his destruction between the termination of his present appointment and his entry upon new powers.

Caesar would be secure from attack if he passed straight from his proconsulship to a new consulship, to which he was secure of election, but on which he could not enter till 48. If he could be deprived of his troops before that date, he would be indicted for his questionable proceedings in Gaul, and his fate would be sealed, while Pompey with his prolonged command would still have the disposal of his own troops. Pompey's jealous fears forced him at last into definite alliance with the optimates. In 51 Caesar's agents in Rome delayed a decree which would have displaced him in March, 49, but the proposal was only deferred, and meanwhile two legions were detached from him, but retained in Italy, to be ready for service against the Parthians in the East.

In the spring of 50 the question of redistributing the provinces—authorised by the legislation of 52—came up again for settlement. Caesar's agents in Rome proposed compromises : that he and Pompey should resign simultaneously, or that he should retain one only of his three

**SHOCK OF BATTLE BETWEEN ROMAN AND GAUL**

The bas-reliefs on the triumphal arch at Orange furnish much detailed information as to the armour, including large oblong shields and horned helmets, and the weapons used by the Gauls in Provence in the first century B.C. On the north and south fronts are animated pictures of the Romans and Barbarians in the shock of conflict, from which we learn that the Gauls fought naked except for the 'sagum,' a coarse woollen blanket worn plaid-wise over the shoulder.

*From Caristie, ' Monuments antiques à Orange '*

provinces. Pompey refused, but proposed that Caesar should not resign till November, 49 ; which would still leave two months for his prosecution and overthrow. Caesar refused ; and, having completed the settlement of Farther Gaul, he was now in Cisapline Gaul with one veteran legion. Pompey, commissioned by the Senate, left Rome to raise more troops in Italy. In January, 49, Caesar repeated his offer of a joint resignation ; the Senate again rejected it, and replied with a decree giving a free hand ' for the defence of the Republic ' to the consuls for the current year, both senatorials.

Caesar was still in his province, of which the boundary was the river Rubicon, with his veterans behind him. The momentous choice was before him ; he must submit and suffer his enemies utterly to destroy him, or strike for empire. He made his choice. At the head of his one legion, on the night of January 6, 49, he crossed the Rubicon—an act of open rebellion against the government.

### Rupture between Pompey and Caesar

POMPEY was not prepared for the sudden swiftness of his adversary. Without waiting for the reinforcements which he forthwith summoned from Farther Gaul, Caesar swooped on Umbria and Picenum, which were not prepared to resist. Town after town yielded, and having yielded was won over to his side by his politic clemency and the firm control under which he kept his soldiery. In six weeks he was before Corfinium, where he was joined by another legion from Gaul ; Corfinium was surrendered by the soldiery and he sped south in pursuit of Pompey. For the legions that Pompey had ready were those which had been led to victory after victory in Gaul by Caesar himself. Pompey had, therefore, already made up his mind to abandon Italy and raise in the East the forces which were to overwhelm the rebel, and he with all his troops embarked at Brundusium, which he had reached before Caesar could come up with him.

Caesar, thus baulked, was back in Rome, with no foe to fight in Italy, within three months of the crossing of the Rubicon, and with all the ordinary machinery of

government suspended. He secured the sinews of war by seizing the treasury, and before setting out in pursuit of Pompey turned west, to deal with Spain and put the Pompeian legions there out of action. Not so much by fighting as by skilful manoeuvring, in which however Caesar was once by his own admission outgeneralled, the Spanish campaign was

### TROPHIES FROM GAUL

Caesar returned to Rome in 49 B.C. and the trophy on the reverse of this coin denotes his victories in Gaul. The figures LII (52) on the obverse may indicate his age and his eligibility for a second consulate.

*British Museum*

brought to a successful issue in six months, most of the troops joining his standard.

Returning to Rome, Caesar assumed the dictatorship in order to hold a consular election ; as consul he passed some popular laws, and then prepared for the decisive contest in the East, where a large force was now collecting under Pompey and the senatorial leaders. The Pompeians held the seas, and it was with difficulty that he succeeded in crossing with his first army to Epirus, where he was shut up within his own lines by the much larger army of Pompey in November. With even more difficulty his lieutenant, Mark Antony, joined him with the second army in the spring of 48.

Some months of manoeuvring followed. Pompey, though his forces outnumbered Caesar's, knew that his eastern levies were not to be matched with Caesar's veterans, and wished to avoid a pitched battle ; so did Cato, alone among the senatorials, because he wished to avoid bloodshed. The rest, detesting Pompey only less than Caesar, scoffed at his pusillanimity, and clamoured for battle ; till at last, at midsummer, Pompey was goaded into delivering an attack, on the plain of Pharsalus in Thessaly. The fight hung long in the balance, but ended in the complete rout of Pompey's army, with immense slaughter. Caesar's promises of clemency, faithfully kept, induced most of the Romans to surrender when the field was definitely lost, though that clemency was afterwards ill requited. Pompey himself escaped to the coast, took ship with a few loyal comrades, and made his way by slow degrees to Egypt, where on landing he found awaiting him not the asylum he looked for but the dagger of a Roman assassin, commissioned by the Egyptian government.

Until the battle of Pharsalus (or Pharsalia) had been lost and won, the odds on paper were all against Caesar. The Roman legions with Pompey numbered more men than those with Caesar, and Pompey had the resources of the East to draw upon. If Caesar had the treasury at Rome in his hands, Pompey had the wealth of Asia. Judged by military critics, Pompey was the sounder general. But half the men in Pompey's legions would have fought twice as enthusiastically under Caesar, while Caesar's were devoted to their leader. The orientals were no match for the westerns, and Greeks had long ceased to be good soldiers. And Pompey's hand was forced by the senatorial chiefs.

Even after the great defeat, all was not lost. Asia no doubt was off the board, but Egypt might be brought on to it. The Pompeians were in complete command of the sea. Africa was in their hands, and Juba of Numidia was with them. Caesar was not yet master.

### JUBA I OF NUMIDIA

Cicero comments on Juba's fine head of hair and Suetonius relates that in 62 B.C. Caesar once pulled him by the beard. Thus this coin, inscribed in Punic on the reverse, bears a characteristic portrait. Juba was king of Numidia, 60–46 B.C.
*British Museum*

### JUBA KING OF MAURETANIA

Juba II was taken as a child captive to Rome by Caesar to grace his triumph in 46 B.C. He married the daughter of Antony and Cleopatra, and in 25 B.C. was recognized King of Mauretania where he reigned until about 18 B.C.
*British Museum*

Therefore, at the first possible moment, he set out with a small force after Pompey and, evading the enemy fleets, tracked him to Egypt, where the government's envoys met him not with his living rival but with the dead man's head. For months to come, however, Caesar with his troops was locked up in Egypt. For the government, nominally that of the young king, Ptolemy Dionysus, was actually in the hands of a powerful minister, an ambitious adventurer named Achillas, who had no more intention of falling under Caesar's domination than Pompey's ; while he was playing off against each other Ptolemy and his fascinating sister Cleopatra. Meanwhile the Pompeians were taking heart to renew the contest in Africa, and their fleets prevented reinforcements from reaching Caesar in Egypt, where in the intervals of critical fighting he was amusing himself with Cleopatra's charms.

It was not till the turn of the year that Caesar was able to inflict a crushing defeat on Achillas in which both the minister and Ptolemy lost their lives ; and Caesar set Cleopatra on the throne of Egypt, where he continued to dally till May (47).

Pharnaces, the son of Mithradates, had seized the opportunity to recover power in Pontus. The legions in Spain were in mutiny against their Caesarian commander. Italy was uneasy. The Pompeians, among them two of Pompey's sons, Gnaeus and Sextus, were making head in Africa. In a lightning campaign, Caesar shattered the power of Pharnaces—the occasion of his famous dispatch, 'I came, I saw, I conquered '—and in July he was back in

Rome, formally appointed dictator for the second time.

He found the legions in Campania mutinous, demanding their discharge. What they wanted was not discharge but more pay. Caesar coolly, but with stinging words of contemptuous reproach, discharged them ; whereupon they implored him with tears to reinstate them on any terms, and he granted the petition. It was a triumph of personality.

Then he carried a force to Africa, but was unable to strike a decisive blow until in February (46) he shattered the senatorial forces at Thapsus. Cato, in charge at Utica, had declined all command in the civil war ; but when he knew that the senatorial cause was lost, he committed suicide.

The sons of Pompey and some of the leaders who escaped fled to Spain ; others, like Cato, slew themselves. In friendly but mortal single combat Petreius—who in 49 had all but entrapped Caesar in Spain— was killed by the bold king of Numidia, Juba ; who then by his own order was slain by one of his own slaves. Numidia was annexed and made a new province. At the end of May Caesar returned to Rome to celebrate a series of triumphs, not over Roman citizens but over the Gauls, Egypt, Pharnacés and Juba. For four months he was occupied, as dictator for the third time, in reorganizing the imperial system, in legislating and in planning and starting public works.

Then he was called again to Spain, where the Pompeys were once more trying to make head ; both were sons born to Pompey before his marriage to Caesar's daughter. In Spain sickness kept him

CLEOPATRA QUEEN OF EGYPT : LAST OF THE PTOLEMAIC DYNASTY

Cleopatra, daughter of Ptolemy XIII Auletes, was born in 69 B.C. and became Queen of Egypt at the age of seventeen. Her personal fascination captivated Julius Caesar, by whom she had a son, Caesarion. All three are represented on the relief (left) on the temple of Hathor at Dendera. After Caesar's assassination Cleopatra returned to Egypt, became the mistress of Mark Antony, and after his defeat by Octavian at Actium fled to Alexandria, where she committed suicide, August 29, 30 B.C.

*Photos, Donald McLeish and Mansell*

inactive till the end of the year. Then he moved on the Pompeians, and in March, 45, crushed them finally at Munda, the most desperately fought of all his battles. Sextus Pompeius escaped to the hills ; Gnaeus and the other leaders fell. Six months more were occupied with the settlement of Spain ; in October Caesar was once more in Rome.

Caesar did not promulgate a new constitution by legislation. Almost the only piece of legislation in that kind was the enlargement of the Senate which added to that body an immense number of nominees, including even provincials. Another—but more in appearance than in fact—was the extension of full Roman citizenship to all the Italian communities ; for, since no system of representation had been devised, the right to vote did not in effect convey true political power. It was

however, a definite expression of Italian national unity.

But the scheme of a new constitution was implicit in his methods, which concentrated permanently in the hands of one man what had hitherto been emergency powers given only for a limited period. To Caesar they were conveyed in the form of a perpetual dictatorship over-riding the powers of the ordinary magistrates, but not dispensing with them.

Into the few months of his regime he compressed a surprising amount of social and economic legislation, intended at least to palliate chronic evils from which the community suffered. Incidentally, he reformed the calendar and placed it on the sound astronomical base which, with one small subsequent modification, is in use at the present day. It must also be remarked that on his return to

**AUTHENTIC SITE OF JULIUS CAESAR'S FUNERAL PYRE**

On the spot in the Forum where Julius Caesar was cremated an altar was erected and a marble pillar inscribed 'Parenti Patriae.' Augustus later built a temple, the Aedes Divi Julii, on the site, and above is shown all that remains of that structure—blocks of tufa once coated with marble to which the beaks of the warships captured at Actium were affixed at the time. The actual spot where Caesar was incinerated is marked by the round core of an altar built of concrete with chips of the original pillar.

*From Rudolfo Lanciani, 'The Roman Forum'*

H

Rome in 46 Caesar astonished the world by setting aside all precedent and declaring a complete amnesty; taking no sort of revenge on any of his past enemies, public or private, and extending to many of them favours which almost any other man would have reserved for his personal friends or partisans. Yet that magnanimity failed to conciliate either their jealousy or their abstract devotion to republican theory.

A monarchy, a tyrannis, was in fact established, under the republican title of dictatorship, while the ancient title of kingship remained as intolerable as ever to the Roman mind. That fact was made obvious when Caesar's lieutenant Antony offered him a kingly crown at the festival of the Lupercalia in February, 44, an offer which he rejected with dramatic effect but with obvious reluctance. On that fact his enemies, former adherents of Pompey for the most part, counted, but counted too confidently. To effect his overthrow by any legal methods was manifestly impossible, but Caesar was aiming at making himself king, and tradition extolled tyrannicide. A conspiracy was formed by a group which included several men who were designated for the highest offices, some of them his personal friends. He never took precautions for his personal safety; and at a meeting of the Senate on the Ides (15th) of March, they gathered round him on the pretext of urging a petition, and stabbed him to death.

### Mark Antony and Octavian

FOR the moment Caesar's fall produced sheer paralysis. The conspirators imagined that they were going to restore the senatorial republic amid general acclamation; when, actually, none save politicians of their own party were ready to acclaim them. Among them there were prominent and able men, but no individual of dominating capacity or personality. The enemy they had most to fear was Mark Antony, consul designate, a favourite lieutenant of the murdered dictator, a notorious profligate, a man of brilliant but erratic abilities, boundless ambition, no moral scruples and a whole-hearted devotion to his dead chief. There would

**MEMORIALS OF TRAGIC LOVERS**

The upper copper tetradrachm of Mark Antony bears a bust of his wife Octavia on the reverse above a mystic cista set between coiled serpents. On the Phoenician tetradrachm below Mark Antony appears with her supplanter, Cleopatra.

*From Ward, 'Greek Coins,' John Murray*

almost certainly be a duel between the conspirators' party and Antony. Neither of them took count of a lad of eighteen away in Macedon, whom the childless Caesar had adopted, his great-nephew Octavius; now to be known as Caesar Octavianus, though the adoption had not been made in form.

THE duel did not open at once; there was a hollow reconciliation. Antony, however, secured Caesar's papers and obtained from a hesitating Senate formal ratification of Caesar's acts, and a public funeral; at which the consul's speech and the reading of Caesar's will produced a violent revulsion of popular sentiment against the self-styled 'Liberators.' The assassins withdrew hastily from Rome, where Antony, who could produce authority for everything he chose to do from Caesar's papers, genuine or forged, was master of the situation. The ablest soldier among the conspirators, Decimus Brutus, took possession of Cisalpine Gaul, which Caesar had assigned to him; the military position was extremely uncertain, and negotiations continued to pass between the republican chiefs and Antony.

Young Octavian appeared on the scene, self-contained and inscrutable, but of an adamantine resolution, claiming to be his dead uncle's representative, and as his heir discharging faithfully all the provisions of the will ; ready to make terms, but only his own terms, with either party, holding the balance in his own hands. Antony began to fear an active rival, the liberators a remorseless enemy, while the young man would commit himself to neither. The legions that were in Italy seemed likely to transfer their allegiance to the young Octavian.

Decimus Brutus was in possession of his province. Lepidus, a most ineffective person, was in possession of the old Transalpine Province. The dictator had assigned Macedon and Syria to two of the most prominent among the conspirators, Marcus Brutus (85–42) and Gaius Cassius ; who left Italy to take possession and raise troops for the coming contest, in the autumn. Antony claimed the three provinces for himself, his brother and his fellow consul Dolabella, whom he had bought.

In the autumn, then, Antony was trying to vanquish Decimus Brutus, whom he besieged in Mutina. Cicero, who had known nothing of the conspiracy but approved it as an accomplished fact, was left to lead the party of opposition to Antony ; he conceived his own influence to be supreme with Octavian, and he now attacked Antony in the famous series of orations known as the Philippics. Antony was declared a public enemy ; Octavian joined the new consuls, Hirtius and Pansa, old officers of his uncle, and now the official commanders of the government

**AN IRRECONCILABLE REPUBLICAN**

Marcus Junius Brutus (85–42 B.C.) took the side of Pompey in the Civil War. Although after Pharsalus Caesar showed him clemency, Brutus was one of the Dictator's murderers. He committed suicide after his defeat at Philippi.

*Museo Capitolino, Rome ; photo, Brogi*

forces. In the early months of 43 Antony was driven out of Cisalpine into Transalpine Gaul. But both the consuls were killed in the fighting ; Antony persuaded Lepidus and his legions to join him, and the pair came to terms secretly with Octavian.

Octavian with his legions marched to Rome and at the age of twenty claimed the consulship; having none to say him nay. Then he summoned the assassins of Caesar to stand trial. They were, of course, condemned to death by default. While the governors of Spain and Farther Gaul were at last declaring themselves supporters, Antony, Octavian and Lepidus met at Bononia (Bologna) and constituted themselves (officially by decree of the Senate) Triumvirs for the establishment of the Republic, the term which always stood for the Roman state. A part of their programme was a proscription, for the thoroughness of which Sulla had set the precedent, with no mercy and more malice than policy in it. The most distinguished of their victims— whom Octavian did not think it worth

**A CRIME IN LIBERTY'S NAME**

A cardinal event in history is commemorated in this coin with its portrait of Brutus and, on the reverse, the famous Cap of Liberty, set between daggers above the date the Ides of March, when Caesar fell.

*British Museum*

while to protect from the venomous, if natural, hatred of Antony—was Cicero. Then the triumvirs appropriated their respective shares of the West, though with very little regard for Lepidus, and prepared for the decisive struggle in the East.

No heavy engagements took place before the two battles on the plain near Philippi in Macedonia, fought with an interval of some three weeks in the late autumn of 42. In the first the actual success was with Brutus, but Cassius, under the mistaken impression that the day was lost, was by his own order slain by a slave. In the second Brutus was defeated ; his men refused to renew the battle next day, and he died by the reluctant hand of a friend.

The victors, Antony and Octavian, parted the empire between them, for Lepidus did not count. In effect Antony took the East and Octavian the West, though in fact they did find an unexpected rival in Sextus Pompeius, who, having held a command in the enemy's fleet, acquired naval supremacy in the Mediterranean. For nearly ten years there was no

**FUTURE MASTER OF THE WORLD**
Octavian was eighteen, studying at Apollonia, when he learnt of the death of Julius Caesar ; and the immature, studious-looking features of this bust show how little the Roman world can have recognized its future master.
*Uffizi Gallery, Florence ; photo, Brogi*

open collision between Antony and the young Caesar, though there was much friction and actual war was more than once averted with difficulty.

While Octavian returned to Italy, Antony proceeded through Greece and Asia Minor, mainly for the purpose of extorting money from the provincials. At Tarsus in Cilicia, about the midsummer of 41, he met the queen of Egypt, Cleopatra, and from that time was utterly enslaved by her fascinations.

The East, in fact, demanded vigour ; for a Roman officer, Labienus, joined the Parthian king Pacorus ; already in 41 Pacorus was overrunning Syria and Labienus Asia Minor. Antony roused himself, but was diverted by dissensions with Octavian in the West, leagued himself with Sextus Pompeius against his rival, and would have plunged into open war had not the death of his wife Fulvia provided an opportunity for a hollow reconciliation at Brundusium, when he married Octavian's sister Octavia. The deserted Sextus demonstrated his effective power by a naval blockade of Italy, now mainly dependent on imports for its corn supplies, whereby he forced the triumvirs to admit him to partnership,

**A SPLENDID VICTIM OF AMBITION**
Marcus Antonius (83–30 B.C.) was one of the triumvirs who at Philippi avenged Julius Caesar's murder. Thereafter he shared the Roman world with Octavian until in 31 B.C. East and West joined battle, and at Actium he met defeat.
*Vatican Museum ; photo, Anderson*

receiving as his share Sardinia, Sicily and Achaea (39).

Antony lingered at Athens with his new wife before returning to Cleopatra. The Parthian war had been entrusted to a soldier whose abilities had raised him from the ranks, Ventidius Bassus. In this year (39) he routed and captured Labienus, and drove the Parthian forces over the Euphrates, and in 38 repeated his success against Pacorus, who fell in the battle.

Octavian was preparing for a struggle with Sextus ; but in 37 his relations with his brother-in-law were still amicable,

**THIRD OF THE TRIUMVIRS**
At the time of Caesar's death M. Aemilius Lepidus was commanding a proconsular army, which, more than his own character, obtained for him the position of triumvir with Octavian and Antony.
*Vatican ; photo, Anderson*

and the triumvirate was renewed without other authority than that of the triumvirs themselves. Now, however, Antony tired of Octavia and returned to his Egyptian mistress, who never again lost her fatal hold on him. In 36 he flung himself into a new Parthian campaign to recover the standards lost seventeen years before at Carrhae ; but instead of achieving a triumph narrowly escaped destruction by a hasty retreat. Antony consoled himself, however, by a military demonstration in Armenia, on the strength of which he celebrated a triumph on his return to Alexandria. Incidentally, of his own authority he redistributed the crowns of

**REBEL SON OF POMPEY**
Defeated at Thapsus in Africa, Sextus Pompeius joined his elder brother in Spain, but escaped from the defeat at Munda and, after Caesar's death, raised a fleet that dominated the Mediterranean until defeated by Agrippa at Naulochus.
*British Museum*

minor vassal kingdoms, handing over Judaea to Herod of Idumaea; while his behaviour in Egypt warranted the growing belief that he was dreaming of making himself King of the World, with Cleopatra as his consort.

On his return to Rome after Philippi, Octavian had been forced to satisfy his veterans by great confiscations of land wherewith to reward them, according to promise. Advantage of the intense and justifiable resentment thus aroused in Italy was taken by Antony's brother Lucius ; as consul he attempted to overthrow Octavian by armed force, but was compelled, mainly by the abilities of Agrippa (63 B.C.—A.D. 12), formerly the comrade and now the right-hand man of Octavian, to abandon the contest in 40 and retire from Italy. This was the occasion of the breach between the triumvirs, ended by the pact of Brundusium in 39 ; which set Octavian comparatively free for the task of reorganizing the West.

But Sextus, master of the seas, was an embarrassment, and the first attempts to challenge his power failed completely. The invaluable Agrippa came to the rescue. Only in 36, when he had organized and trained new fleets, was the naval campaign inaugurated. Sextus, after a defeat by Agrippa and a victory over Octavian, was crushed by the former at Naulochus, and, falling later into the hands of lieutenants of Antony, who had held aloof, was put to death. The third triumvir, Lepidus, then tried to assert himself, but submitted when his troops deserted to Octavian, was deposed from the triumvirate, and was relegated to a dignified obscurity as Pontifex Maximus.

Friction, complaints and counter-complaints, popular uneasiness and suspicion of Antony's designs grew rapidly, and reached a climax in 32, when Antony insulted Caesar by openly repudiating his marriage with the blameless Octavia, who had borne with his flagrant infidelity and done her best to smooth matters between her husband and her brother. Octavian's time had come. Rome declared war on Egypt—it had not even been necessary to wait for the formal repudiation.

At last Antony roused himself, and repaired to Greece, of which he had retained possession. But his design of invading Italy was rendered futile by Agrippa's fleet. Octavian landed with troops in Epirus, but he knew that as a general he was no match for Antony, and through the winter both sides played a waiting game which was all in the favour of Octavian. Antony could trust neither his officers nor his men, who were being seduced from their allegiance.

He had, however, collected a great fleet ; and at midsummer (31) he decided to abandon his army and retreat with his ships. Having made all his preparations secretly, he embarked with Cleopatra at the end of August, and the whole fleet sailed away ; but it was overtaken by Agrippa and forced to engage off Actium on September 2. Antony's fleet was much the heavier, and the issue was still doubtful, when Cleopatra with sixty ships broke away in full flight for Egypt. Antony deserted the battle and followed the magnet. The rest of the fleet fought on desperately, till every ship was burnt, sunk or captured. The army which had been left behind went over en masse to Octavian.

The battle of Actium was decisive. There was no need for Octavian to hasten in pursuit of the fugitives in their ignominious flight. Antony, from the moment when he yielded to that mad impulse at Actium, was a beaten man. He shut himself up in Pharos, facing Alexandria. Cleopatra, for whose sake he had flung himself away, had been the mistress of Julius and the mistress of Antony ; now she was, or seemed to be, ready to become the mistress of the new master of East and West.

But when in July (30 B.C.) Octavian appeared before Pelusium with his fleet, she too secluded herself in Alexandria. Pelusium promptly surrendered. Antony made one despairing effort : at the head of a body of horse he fell upon and routed a body of his enemy's troops. But the whole fleet at Alexandria went over ; resistance was an obvious absurdity ; the false rumour had been circulated that Cleopatra was dead, so Antony committed suicide, surviving only long enough to die in the arms of the repentant queen. From Octavian she soon learnt that she had nothing to hope but shame ; and his emissaries only found, as he had feared, that she had followed her lover to death, not without a characteristic regard for dramatic effect.

Octavian stood alone, without possible rival, undisputed and indisputable lord of the civilized world.

**OCTAVIAN'S MOST TRUSTED MINISTER**

Born of undistinguished parentage, M. Vipsanius Agrippa was a student friend of Octavian and afterwards became his right-hand man, equally successful as general, admiral, foreign administrator and director of public works. This bust conveys an excellent impression of his stern, blunt character.

*Uffizi Gallery, Florence ; photo, Alinari*

# TABLE OF DATES FOR CHAPTER 10

**B.C.**

**31** Battle of Actium. Flight of Antony and Cleopatra to Egypt.

**30** Octavian follows to Egypt. Death of Antony and Cleopatra. Annexation of Egypt, which becomes the appanage of Octavian.

**29** Octavian returns to Italy, where Maecenas has been left in charge. Confirmation of the Acts of Octavian. Temple of Janus closed, the Republic being at peace. Moesia made a Province.

**28** Official restoration of Senate. Octavian assumes the obsolete title of Princeps Senatus. Reversal of all illegal Acts since 43 B.C.

**27** Octavian formally resigns emergency powers but receives Proconsular 'Imperium' for ten years, with the title of Augustus.
Distribution of Provinces as Senatorial or Imperial. The latter are held by Augustus with proconsular powers, and administered by the governors he appoints, legates, prefects, etc.
Formal reinstatement of the Republic ; actual institution of an autocratic Principate.
Augustus goes to Gaul.

**26** Augustus in Spain.

**25** Julia, daughter of Augustus, marries Marcellus.

**24** Augustus returns to Rome.

**23** Augustus retires from the consulship, which he has hitherto held annually ; but receives the Tribunician Power which he holds permanently.
Death of Marcellus.

**21** Marriage of Julia to Agrippa.

**20** Augustus in Asia.
Parthians restore standards taken at Carrhae.

**19** Agrippa in Spain. Settlement of Spain.
Death of Vergil.

**18** Five years' extension of Proconsular Imperium.
Augustus confers Imperium and Tribunician Power on Agrippa.

**17** Augustus adopts his grandsons, Gaius and Lucius, the infant sons of Agrippa and Julia.

**16** Frontier wars. Gallic disaster of Lollius.

**15** Campaigns of Tiberius and Drusus, the stepsons of Augustus, in Rhaetia. Rhaetia and Noricum are made Provinces.
Birth of Germanicus (son of Drusus).

**14** Agrippa in the East.

**13** Agrippa sent to Pannonia.
Five years' extension of Proconsular Imperium.

**12** Death of Agrippa. Birth of Agrippa Postumus.
Campaigns of Tiberius in Pannonia and Drusus in Germany.

**11** Continued campaigns of Tiberius and Drusus.
Tiberius compelled to marry Julia.

**10** Continued campaigns of Tiberius and Drusus.
Birth of Claudius (younger son of Drusus).

**9** Death of Drusus. Fourth Pannonian campaign of Tiberius.

**8** German campaign of Tiberius.
Death of Maecenas and of Horace.
Ten years' extension of Proconsular Imperium.

**6** Tiberius goes into retirement, in Rhodes.

**4** Death of Herod 'the Great.' Birth of Christ.

**2** Disgrace and banishment of Julia.

**1** Gaius Caesar sent to the East.

**A.D.**

**2** Tiberius summoned from Rhodes. Lucius Caesar dies.

**3** Ten years' extension of Proconsular Imperium.

**4** On the death of Gaius Caesar, Augustus adopts both Tiberius and Agrippa Postumus. Tiberius adopts his nephew, Germanicus.
Third German campaign of Tiberius.

**5** Tiberius reaches the Elbe.

**6-9** Pannonian wars of Tiberius.

**9** End of Pannonian War.
Germans led by Arminius annihilate Varus and his legions in the Saltus Teutoburgiensis.

**10** Tiberius with Germanicus in Germany.

**12** Birth of Gaius Caesar, son of Germanicus.

**13** Tiberius confirmed in Imperium and Tribunician Power, practically ensuring his succession.
Germanicus remains in command on the Rhine.

**14** Death of Augustus. Tiberius Claudius Nero, emperor.

**15** Germanicus defeats Arminius.

**17** Germanicus recalled and sent to the East. Policy of imperial expansion definitely abandoned.

**A.D.**

**19** Death of Germanicus. Suspicion falls on Piso and Tiberius.

**20** Death of Piso.
Extension of the Law of Majesty (Treason) ; growth of the delatores (informers).
Rise of Sejanus, the praetorian prefect.

**23** Death of Drusus (Minor), son of Tiberius.
*China:* End of the First Han Dynasty.

**26** Tiberius withdraws permanently from Rome to Capreae. Sejanus supreme in Rome.
Pontius Pilate made procurator of Judaea.

**29** Death of Livia Drusilla Augusta, mother of Tiberius and widow of Augustus.

**31** Fall of Sejanus and extirpation of his family.

**37** Death of Tiberius.
Accession of Gaius Claudius Caesar (Caligula), son of Germanicus.

**38** Birth of Lucius Domitius Ahenobarbus (Nero, son of Caligula's sister Agrippina the Younger).

**39** Caligula's Gallic and 'Britannic' expeditions.

**40** *Asia:* Approximate date of Kadphises I, Indo-Scythian king, the centre of whose power was established at Kabul.

**41** Assassination of Caligula. His uncle Tiberius Claudius Nero, brother of Germanicus, is made emperor by the Praetorians.

**42** Birth of Britannicus, son of Claudius.

**43** Invasion of Britain and conquest of the south-east by Aulus Plautius. Province of Britain created.

**44** Death of Herod Agrippa.

**47** Ostorius succeeds Plautius in Britain.

**47-49** Caractacus maintains the British struggle in the west against the Romans.

**48** Death of Messalina. Development of government through the emperor's secretariat.

**49** Claudius marries his niece, Agrippina, and adopts her son, who thus takes the name of Nero.

**50** Caractacus betrayed to Ostorius by the Brigantes.

**54** Death of Claudius. Undisputed accession of Nero.

**54-59** The 'Quinquennium Neronis' ; five years of quiet government under Seneca and Burrhus.

**55** Britannicus dies ; suspicions of poison.

**59** Nero murders his mother. End of Quinquennium.
Suetonius Paulinus governor of Britain.

**61** Welsh campaign of Paulinus.
Revolt of the Iceni under Boadicea ; massacre of Roman colonists ; revolt crushed by Paulinus.

**62** Festus procurator of Judaea.

**63** S. Paul at Rome.

**64** Great Fire of Rome, attributed to the Christians.
The Neronic Persecution.

**65** Death of Seneca.

**66** Great revolt of the Jews. Conduct of the Jewish war entrusted to Vespasian.

**67** Nero in Greece. Roman sentiment scandalised.
Servius Sulpicius Galba plans revolt in Spain.

**68** Galba marches on Rome. Flight and death of Nero (June). Galba emperor.

**69** (Jan.) The legions on the Rhine proclaim Vitellius. The legions at Rome mutiny, murder Galba, and proclaim M. Salvius Otho. The troops of Vitellius invade Italy (April) ; defeat and death of Otho. Aulus Vitellius emperor. (July) The troops at Alexandria proclaim Vespasian. Defeat and death of Vitellius (December).

**70** Titus Flavius Vespasianus emperor.
Revolt and suppression of Civilis in Gaul.
Siege, sack, and destruction of Jerusalem by Titus, elder son of Vespasian.
Vespasian's ten years' (70-79) rule of peace, retrenchment and reform inaugurated.

**77** *India:* Kadphises II extends the Indo-Scythian power over the Ganges basin.

**78-85** Cn. Julius Agricola, governor of Britain, organizes the province, and carries the Roman arms over the Forth and the Tay.

**79** Titus Flavius Vespasianus emperor.
Herculaneum and Pompeii buried by the eruption of Mount Vesuvius.

**81** T. Flavius Domitianus emperor.

**83** Futile German expedition of Domitian.

**86** Disastrous expedition of Domitian against Dacia.

**c. 90** Severe persecution of the Christians.

**96** Murder of Domitian. The Senate elect M. Cocceius Nerva emperor.

**97** Nerva adopts Trajan, as colleague and successor.

**98** Death of Nerva. M. Ulpius Trajanus sole emperor.

### CHAPTER 10

# THE SHAPING OF THE ROMAN EMPIRE: 31 B.C.—A.D. 98

HE battle of Actium was one of the decisive moments in the world's history. It closed a struggle which, if the issue of the fight had been different, might have been indefinitely prolonged. As it was, the re-organization of the world empire was now in the hands of one man who still had five-and-forty years of life before him in which to carry out that tremendous task.

The triumvirate powers had not been renewed for a third term, but Caesar Octavian at Rome had been endowed afresh with extraordinary powers for an indefinite period, the equivalent of his uncle's official dictatorship, though that title had been abolished during Antony's ascendancy. This was the authority on which he now continued to act. He passed nearly a year after Actium in touring Greece and Asia and visiting Italy, before turning to Egypt, where the seal was set on his victory by the suicide of Antony and Cleopatra.

The first step following was the annexa-tion of Egypt, which Octavian took per-manently into his own hands, giving it no senatorial officials, but placing it under the administration of a prefect directly responsible to himself. The last indepen-dent kingdom west of the Euphrates, the granary of Italy, became Caesar's appan-age; and the entire Mediterranean littoral from end to end, with the exception only of Mauretania, which as against Rome was powerless, was now under Roman rule.

For nearly a year Octavian remained in the East, leaving the West in the compe-tent hands of the diplomatic Maecenas. The Senate had duly ratified his acts before his return to Rome in August, 29 B.C., when he celebrated several triumphs and signalised the restoration throughout the Empire of a peace long unknown by closing the temple of Janus. In the same year Moesia, between Thrace and the Danube, was officially added to the provinces

of the Empire. Again in 28 Octavian's rôle as pacificator was emphasised by the reversal of the illegalities for which he and his colleagues had been responsible during the long period of arbitrary authority, and a revision of the senatorial lists seemed at least to restore the tradi-tional dignity of that body, somewhat besmirched in recent years; Octavian himself assuming the dignified functions of its Princeps (president).

The time, then, had at last arrived for Octavian to give convincing proof that public spirit, not ambition, was the motive of his life. In 27 he laid down his extraordinary powers. No one, of course, knew better than he that his retirement was impossible; he resigned his powers only that he might resume them in slightly different guise in constitutional form, in response to the urgent prayer of the Roman people, not of his own will as the master of legions.

### Caesar a Constitutional Emperor

HE titles conferred upon him were such as to concentrate attention not on his power and its bases but on his dignity, on the reverence he commanded from a grateful world. The Imperator is veiled in the Pater Patriae, father of his country, Princeps, its first citizen, Caesar Augustus —almost, but not as yet, divine. Hence-forth we speak of him as Augustus.

Great as were the powers thus conveyed to Augustus, they were masked by a republican terminology and were war-ranted, moreover, by appeal to republi-can precedents. The weakness of the imperial position—not in that of Augustus personally—lay in the absence of any law of succession to the imperial authority. Had fortune granted him sons of his own he would doubtless have succeeded in making the succession hereditary, but the sole immediate heir of his body was a daughter, Julia, and all but one of Julia's sons died before Augustus.

In spite of the closing of the Temple of Janus in 29 B.C., the Pax Romana, the Roman Peace, was not yet in fact established throughout the Empire ; for the whole vast frontier line was constantly liable to attack from the miscellaneous barbarians surging upon it in Europe, and from the Parthians on the Euphrates ; further, in remote parts of Spain and Gaul there were still tribes unreconciled to the Roman lordship. Aquitania, however, was brought to final submission in 27 B.C., the year from which the Principate of Augustus is dated. In the north-west of Spain the Asturians and Cantabrians maintained a gallant but vain struggle for freedom for many years, in the course of which Augustus took the field against them in person with no remarkable success. It was only when the task of subjugation and pacification had been entrusted to Agrippa the unfailing that the stubborn tribes made an honourable and permanent submission in 19 B.C. Otherwise the wars of Augustus in which Roman legions were engaged were all on or beyond the confines of the Empire, and were waged against not subjects but foreign foes.

The East gave no serious trouble. The small dependent kingdoms still surviving in eastern Asia Minor and in Syria were pacifically and gradually absorbed into the Roman provincial system. Parthia under Phraates had no desire to challenge a military struggle with Rome. The unavenged disaster of Carrhae in 53 B.C., however, had always rankled in the

SCENES OF EGYPTIAN PLENTY FROM A MOSAIC FOUND IN ITALY

Octavian, with the burden of the legions on his shoulders, recognized that Egypt was potentially the richest province of the Empire, and retained it as his personal appanage, instead of assigning it to the Senate. Its prosperity had woefully declined under the later Ptolemies, but he inaugurated a wise policy of economic reform ; and the famous ' Palestrina ' (Praeneste) mosaic suggests the prosperity of the land in early Imperial times. Above, a scene in the Delta during flood time.

*Palazzo Baronale, Palestrina ; photo, Alinari*

H*

**OCTAVIAN AS VICTOR**

A fine bust of Octavian in the Glyptothek at Munich shows us a younger man than the 'Augustus' statue in the preceding page. The head is crowned with oak leaves, in reference to the award of the Civic Crown.

*Munich Glyptothek, courtesy of Dr. F. Stödtner*

Roman mind; so when in 20 B.C. a demand was made, and emphasised by a military demonstration in force, for the restitution of the captives and the standards which had been carried off from that fatal field, Phraates displayed his political wisdom by a ready acquiescence and perhaps even by an illusory form of submission which Roman poets were not slow to turn to account for the glorification of the Father of his Country.

On or beyond the European frontier, however, there were many campaigns. A German incursion across the Rhine defeated a Roman commander, Lollius, in 16 B.C., and called for the temporary presence of Augustus at the front, where he left the command in the hands of his stepson Drusus (38–9 B.C.), who was permitted to engage in an attempt to carry the Roman frontier up to the Weser or the Elbe. Drusus and his elder brother, Tiberius (42 B.C.–A.D. 37), had already been campaigning in Raetia, and the subjugation of the whole border belt on the south of the Danube had become a necessity. Drusus did in fact reach the Elbe before his premature death in 9 B.C., while Tiberius was establishing the Roman supremacy in Noricum and Pannonia, a task which occupied him for two years more. To Drusus had been accorded the complimentary title of Germanicus, which descended to the youthful son who is always known by that name.

Agrippa had been marked by his achievements as the man to whom the control of the empire would naturally pass if he outlived Augustus, at whose

**MEMBERS OF THE ILL-FATED FAMILY OF AUGUSTUS**

Livia Drusilla (left), first the wife of Tiberius Claudius Nero, by whom she had the future emperor Tiberius, married Augustus in 38 B.C. His daughter Julia (by Scribonia) proved profligate and unbalanced, and died in exile, A.D. 14. Agrippina the Elder, wife of Germanicus and grand-daughter of Augustus, also died in exile quite unmerited. The family life of Tiberius—we see him here as a young man—was marked by his unfeeling treatment of Agrippina and his mother Livia.

*From Poulsen, 'Greek and Roman Portraits' (Clarendon Press), Ny Carlsberg and British Museum*

bidding he had married the daughter of the latter, Julia, in 21 B.C. But he died in 12 B.C., leaving by that marriage two daughters, Agrippina, who was later married to Germanicus, and Julia, who followed her mother's profligate example, and two sons, Gaius and Lucius Caesar. A third son, Agrippa Postumus, was born just after his death. Of these three grandsons of Augustus, only the last survived him.

On the other hand, Tiberius (Claudius Nero) and Drusus (Claudius Nero) were, as has been remarked, the stepsons of Augustus, the offspring of his very able and ambitious wife, Livia Drusilla, by her former husband, Tiberius Claudius Nero ; though Drusus had actually been born after her marriage to Augustus in 37 B.C. The explanation of these family complications is somewhat wearisome, but is necessary to an understanding of the course actually taken by the imperial succession. The three next emperors were all in fact Claudii, though only the third is known as Claudius, Caesars (like Augustus himself) only by adoption.

### Stabilisation of the New Order

AGRIPPA had done more than any other man to create and to stabilise the New Order ; yet the stabilisation owed hardly less to the very different work of the second of the great ministers of Augustus, Gaius Cilnius Maecenas, who followed his colleague to the grave in 8 B.C. He rendered his services not as a state official but as a personal counsellor and a social influence, guiding Augustus in the way he should go. He was supple, skilful and conciliatory ; by his discriminating but munificent patronage of art and letters attracting to the support of the new regime all that was best as well as all that was cleverest in the intellectual society of the capital.

Such was the outcome of twenty years of the Principate in 7 B.C., when Augustus stood alone and both of his great ministers were dead. Alone he was to stand for twenty-one years more. For, young children excepted, his nearest relative was his step-son Tiberius, whom neither he nor probably any other man ever

**MAECENAS, PATRON OF THE ARTS**

As Agrippa was Augustus' most trusted minister for the more active kinds of government, so Maecenas (died 8 B.C.) managed internal affairs for him. It is interesting to note that he was of Etruscan parentage on both sides.

*Palazzo dei Conservatori, Rome ; photo, Alinari*

loved or could love ; a man, it would seem, of an unswerving loyalty, a general of tried capacity, but always morose and repellent ; he was son-in-law now as well as step-son, since he had been compelled to marry Julia the Shameless on the death of Agrippa. But the principate was an established fact ; none but a few doctrinaires could dream of a return to the old order, at least during the life-time of Augustus, though he was still in theory only a republican magistrate whose resignation or refusal of the functions imposed on him the Republic could not afford to accept.

The Christian world in a later age adopted a chronological system which reckons the years and centuries backwards and forwards from a supreme moment in the reign of Augustus, the humble birth of a Babe in Bethlehem of Judaea. The actual date was incorrectly assigned ; for at the time Herod, curiously entitled the ' Great,' was still the dependent king of Judaea ; the year which we call 4 B.C. ought to have been named A.D. I.

On the death of Drusus, the principal command of the frontier fell to Tiberius, whose campaigns had in 8 B.C. nominally completed the subjugation of Germany as far as the Elbe, and also of Pannonia. Very shortly, however, he went into retirement in the island of Rhodes. The hopes of Augustus for the founding of a dynasty seemed to centre in his two elder grand-sons ; both were introduced to public life at the earliest possible moment ; but both died young (A.D. 2 and A.D. 4). He thereupon adopted the third brother, Agrippa Postumus—though the boy had shown no signs of either character or capacity—and also Tiberius, while dis-playing in a marked manner his personal dislike for both. At the same time Tiberius was compelled to adopt Germanicus, the elder son of his dead brother Drusus.

For some years Tiberius was employed on campaigns, in which his nephew was at times associated with him, for the most part either in south Germany against the Marcomanni or in the turbulent province of Pannonia : campaigns in which he admittedly showed very high military ability in extremely difficult conditions, receiving only the most perfunctory recog-nition of his services. But while he was thus engaged in the south, there befell in north Germany the heaviest reverse to the Roman arms since the disaster of Carrhae. Three Roman legions under Quintilius Varus were entangled in the Teutobergerwald (Saltus Teutoburgiensis) between the Ems and the Weser—the pre-cise position is uncertain—and annihilated by the Cherusci under the brilliant warrior known to the Romans as Arminius (A.D. 9).

For the Germans had learnt the lesson, as Tiberius knew well by weary experience,

**AUGUSTUS THRONED AS GOD BUT PATHETIC IN THE LONELINESS OF AGE**

During his latter years Augustus stood alone, his direct descendants dead before him, save for one weak-minded youth. He was forced to turn to Tiberius, son of his wife Livia by an earlier marriage, whom he disliked personally but who was unquestionably able. This famous sardonyx cameo shows Augustus throned as a god beside ' Roma,' while Tiberius, on the left, steps from a triumphal car in reference to his Pannonian victories. At the head of his horses stands the young Germanicus.

*Vienna Museum ; photo, Giraudon*

**'GIVE ME BACK MY LEGIONS'**

P. Quintilius Varus was in command of that part of Germany which had been subdued by Drusus when there occurred the terrible disaster of the Saltus Teutoburgiensis, three legions and three cavalry squadrons being wiped out by Arminius.

that it was to their advantage not to hurl themselves upon the drilled legions in the open, but to trap them. The victory of Arminius was a turning point. The meaning of it was that the Roman Empire would never succeed in effectually establishing itself on the farther side of the Rhine and the Danube. Tiberius might— in fact he did—march through Germany as he had marched before, without meeting a serious check ; but to subdue it and hold it was beyond the power of Rome at her mightiest.

Tiberius was presently recalled from his task of restoring the prestige of the Roman arms in Germany, where the command was left in the hands of young Germanicus, who was as popular as his uncle was the reverse. Had Germanicus been afflicted with political ambitions he might have been a dangerous rival, but his heart was in the camp. The young Agrippa was impossible—probably quite incapable. And the disadvantages in the position of Tiberius were counterbalanced by the fact that he already shared, though as a subordinate to Augustus, a large part of the exceptional powers bestowed upon the Princeps.

Therefore when at last the old man died in A.D. 14 it was a matter of course that the Senate, still the nominal governing body, should petition Tiberius to accept the succession, and that he should do so, though with a show of reluctance not wholly fictitious. The soldiery had already sworn allegiance to him as imperator ; the representatives of the old great families were men without administrative experience or military position— Augustus had seen to that ; Germanicus was far away ; Agrippa Postumus, who could never have been more than a figurehead for plots, died—so conveniently that men whispered of assassination.

Tiberius reigned for twenty-three years. The picture of that reign irresistibly impressed on our minds by the great Roman historian Tacitus, who was born some twenty years after it ended, is lurid and repulsive ; nor can it be doubted that in certain of its aspects the reign was lurid and repulsive in actual fact. Nevertheless it assuredly had another side.

As under Augustus, the Empire at large enjoyed peace and prosperity, showing no signs of general disaffection. The

**YOUNG LEADER OF GREAT PROMISE**

Drusus the Elder was the younger brother of Tiberius and the most promising of all the family of Augustus ; but predeceased him in A.D. 9 after winning the complimentary title of Germanicus that descended to his son.

*Naples Museum ; photo, Brogi*

**TIBERIUS ON A FAMOUS CAMEO**

If the morose Tiberius on his accession (A.D. 14–37) proved a suspicious tyrant to the upper-class Romans, he was an admirable ruler of the Empire as a whole. And doubtless the stories of his debauches at Capreae, which we owe to his political enemies, have been much exaggerated. Above, Tiberius and his family ; in the heavens, the deified Augustus.

*Bibliothèque Nationale, Paris ; photo, Giraudon*

the madness of Caligula, the feebleness of Claudius and the crimes of Nero.

But though no little ability, insight and resolution were needed to face imperial problems as Tiberius faced them, agitators, vested interests and upholders of the aristocratic tradition united in denouncing the man who in the eyes of the moralists was an epitome of evil, a well-spring of social corruption.

Apart from hard drinking, however, we hear nothing of the emperor's addiction to animal vices till after his retirement to Capreae in the twelfth year of his rule (A.D. 26), when he was nearing seventy ; it is at least easy to suspect that by that time his brain had become not unhinged but diseased. Nor were the other despicable qualities fully developed in the early years. That he trusted no one was clear enough, until he fell under the malign influence of Aelius Sejanus, the ambitious and utterly unscrupulous Prefect of the Praetorians, in whom he did repose for many years a confidence as blind as it was undeserved. But the charges brought against him by the voice of popular scandal of plotting and procuring the deaths of prominent persons whose ambitions he chose to suspect were never substantiated and were sometimes in themselves improbable.

Yet even from the outset such charges were readily believed and as difficult to disprove as to prove ; the more so because of the rapid extension of the law of treason and the detestable practice of ' delation ' which accompanied it, and which grew into perhaps the most hateful feature of Roman social life. Not merely overt acts of treason against the state, as hitherto, but words which could be construed as reflections on the Caesar were brought within the meaning of the law, and ' delators,' informers who brought forward charges or evidence which led to condem-

provincial system worked under Tiberius, as it had worked under his predecessor, very much better than the old senatorial system ; governors who were continued in office during good behaviour were more disposed to do their duty by the governed than men who held for a year a post out of which they had every temptation to extract the utmost possible profit in the shortest possible time with a minimum of risk ; Tiberius was deaf to the beguilements of vested interests, popular agitation, or family influences. Therefore, in so far as the Empire was concerned, the reign of Tiberius confirmed and made permanent the work of Augustus. The organization was brought into such a sound condition that it survived the blighting influences of Tiberius himself, nation—as in such circumstances they generally did—were handsomely rewarded. No viler machinery of demoralisation could have been devised. Delation became a trade, and no man was safe from it.

Despite the development in the body politic of this particular disease, which, at least in his early years, Tiberius treated rather with sombre acquiescence than encouragement, there was undeniable statesmanship in his conduct of the affairs of the Empire outside Italy. He maintained on the whole a respectable standard in the provincial governments; and his own personal experience beyond the borders of the Empire had taught him the soundness of the testamentary advice of Augustus that those borders should not be extended.

In domestic affairs, the establishment of the personal supremacy of the monarch was the fundamental necessity. Like all monarchs similarly situated, whose personal prestige was insufficient to secure the needful authority, he made it his definite policy to repress the nobles and such of his own kin as were potentially dangerous, and to conduct the administration through creatures of his own; while even the semblance of political power was withdrawn from the 'people' in general, who had already come to mean no more than the populace of the capital. Even in this field he did in the main achieve his object; but it was at the cost of his reputation both for justice and for insight; and he paid the penalty in leaving behind him a name universally execrated.

As a result, the greater part of the history of the reign seems to resolve itself into a record of personal scandals. In its first pages, something of the halo of romance attaches to the young Germanicus, the darling of the legions in the

**THE YOUNG GERMANICUS**
Germanicus, a brilliant leader and very popular with his troops, might have succeeded Augustus if his loyalty to his adoptive father Tiberius had not prevailed.
*Lateran Museum*

north, who would have tried to set him in the place of Tiberius if they could have won his own consent. But his heart was vainly set on the conquest of Germany, where he succeeded in retrieving the prestige of the Roman arms and inflicting a heavy defeat on Arminius. But his military career was cut short by his recall, in A.D. 17, when he was dispatched to the East—through jealousy of his reputation and popularity, men said, but probably also because Tiberius had made up his mind that the Rhine, not the Elbe, was to be the northern boundary. While in the East he died in circumstances which gave some slight colour to the popular belief that his death had been designed, or at best connived at, by Tiberius, and his memory was cherished as a victim of the emperor's jealousy.

On the other hand, Aelius Sejanus is the accepted type of the vaulting ambition which o'erleaps itself. Succeeding to his father's position as Prefect of the Praetorian Guards, the 'household troops' stationed in Italy, he wormed himself at a very early stage into the confidence of Tiberius, procured the concentration of the Guard, whose units had heretofore been scattered, in a permanent camp close to the capital under his own command, and established in the mind of Tiberius a firm conviction that in the Guards and their trusty prefect lay the sole security of the Princeps against the machinations of hydra-headed treason. By craft, by intrigue, by the fascination he had for women, he removed one after another of the human impediments to his ambition. For further security he induced Tiberius, in A.D. 26, to bury himself in the isle of Capreae (Capri) surrounded by the instruments of debauchery, leaving Rome and the exercise of the imperial functions in the hands of the unscrupulous favourite; while decent folk could find safety only in obscurity, or escape from the nightmare by suicide.

Undoubtedly the aim of Sejanus was to make himself secure, murder Tiberius, and seize the imperial authority, relying on the Praetorians. But in spite of his precautions the old man's suspicions were at last aroused. He gave, however, no open sign. In A.D. 31 a messenger, Macro, came from Capreae to the Senate, ostensibly to heap new honours on Sejanus, but with a secret commission which transferred to him from Sejanus the command of the Praetorians. The doomed man was completely hoodwinked. All unsuspected, Macro took over the command of the soldiers and made his dispositions. The Senate was assembled; the long preamble of the letters was read; the blow was reserved for the conclusion. Sejanus was to be deprived of all his offices and arrested for treason. The selected guards were at the doors; the mask was dropped; every man turned on the fallen favourite; the

**CALIGULA THE MADMAN**

Tiberius was succeeded by the young son of Germanicus, Gaius nicknamed Caligula. His reign (37–41) opened with such promise that it is only reasonable to attribute his later excesses to madness, following a severe illness.

*The Louvre*

mob clamoured for his blood and flung down his statues in the streets as he passed to his prison on the way to death. With him his kith and kin were exterminated, even to his eight-year-old daughter.

For the last eleven years of the life of Tiberius, the years during which he was sunk in the iniquities of Capreae, Pontius Pilate was procurator or lieutenant-governor of Judaea, while Herod Antipas (the slayer of John the Baptist), one of the brood of Herod the Great, reigned in the north. This is all that may be fitly said in this place of the Crucifixion; an event whose significance was wholly unsuspected for so long that Tacitus after seventy years was content to say of it no more than that 'Chrestus' was the originator of a most pernicious superstition among the Jews, and had suffered the extreme penalty of the law under 'one of our procurators,' Pontius Pilate.

### Assassination of Tiberius

THE fall of Sejanus served only to relieve the nightmare, not to dissipate it. For six more years Tiberius remained at Capreae; at the last he was murdered (A.D. 37) by that Macro who had been his instrument in the fall of Sejanus. So at least it was affirmed by common rumour, which later associated with him in the crime the young prince whom Tiberius had adopted as his personal heir, and whose succession to the principate was assured—Gaius Caesar, whom all men call by his childhood's nickname Caligula.

Gaius was the third son of Germanicus. His two elder brothers and his mother, the elder Agrippina, were all dead. His sister, the younger Agrippina, was the wife of a noble, Domitius Ahenobarbus, and became about this time the mother of the future emperor Nero. Gaius, now twenty-four, had in his earliest childhood been the pet of his father's legionaries, who gave him his never-forgotten nickname from the imitation military boots which he was accustomed to wear. As the son of Germanicus he was certain of the support of the soldiery and the populace; there was no rival to set up against him, for his uncle Claudius, the younger brother of Germanicus, was without ambition and was reputed to be feeble-minded, while Gaius was credited with all his father's virtues. He was forthwith acclaimed Princeps. Augustus on his death had been accorded divine honours ; Caligula was applauded for refusing them to the dead Tiberius.

For the moment it seemed that better days were in store. Much was to be hoped from a prince who was young, popular and generous ; who began his reign by liberating prisoners, recalling exiles, publicly burning incriminating documents, and flinging himself zealously into the unaccustomed business of administration. But after a few months Caligula fell ill, and he rose from his sickness in effect a madman ; bereft of all moral sense but not of that distorted but occasionally acute intelligence which accompanies some forms of mania. The new nightmare was more terrible than that which had passed.

Caligula was possessed with the idea of his own divinity. He slew, it might be with some definite reason, it might be merely because he had the fancy to slay, whether from blood-lust or as a mere demonstration of power. A sister died ; none might mourn her death, for she was a goddess, but none might therefore rejoice, for she was dead. He inaugurated magnificent public works, and forgot them when the fancy passed. He resolved to conquer Britain, gathered his army of invasion at Boulogne, and then set the men to gather shells on the shore, and these he sent to Rome as the spoils of the conquered Ocean. He returned to Rome threatening slaughter because the Senate had not been sufficiently zealous in preparing for him a magnificent triumph— and there Cassius Chaerea, an officer of the praetorians at whom he had gibed, summoned up courage to assassinate him,

**EMPEROR IN SPITE OF HIMSELF**

Germanicus had a brother, Claudius, who was regarded as a witless recluse. After the murder of Caligula he was dragged forth by the soldiers and hailed as Caesar ; and, though weak, proved a better emperor (41-54) than might have been expected.

*Vatican Museum ; photo, Anderson*

with the aid of a few companions, in the fifth year of his crazed reign (A.D. 41).

For the moment the assassins escaped. As the news spread, the Senate gathered in haste ; several of them were ready to press their own claims to the succession, to which none had any title ; others urged that the moment had come for restoring the Republic. While they debated, the Guards took matters into their own hands. A company of them, tramping about the deserted palace, dragged a new Caesar from behind a curtain where he was hiding, carried him off to the camp, where he was promptly hailed as Imperator, and marched back to the Senate, who had no choice but to obey their mandate. Thus was greatness thrust upon the alarmed and reluctant Claudius, the almost forgotten brother of Germanicus, who all his life had passed for a half-witted but harmless student.

The soldiers had chosen better than they knew. Claudius was at least extremely conscientious ; his intentions were excellent, and his political theory, if derived wholly from books, was intelligent. The phrase applied to James I of England, whom in many respects he resembled closely, seems to fit him admirably : he was ' the wisest fool ' in Rome, but he kept his wisdom for the state, while his domestic follies and foibles made him a figure contemptible to his contemporaries and ridiculous to posterity.

## Conquest of Britain by Claudius

CLAUDIUS was already fifty years old when he began his reign (A.D. 41–A.D. 54). Throughout the period the Empire enjoyed general prosperity and there were few complaints from the provinces. Save in one important particular, Claudius held firmly to the principle that the existing border was to be maintained but not extended ; yet the military expeditions conducted against the aggressive north-German tribes of the Chauci and Catti— who had probably absorbed the Cherusci— were completely successful, though not followed by any attempt at annexation. Within the Empire the practice of extending full Roman citizenship to favoured communities was actively developed. But the signal achievement of the reign was the organized conquest of south Britain and its conversion into a Roman Province.

In A.D. 43, 97 years after the second expedition of Julius Caesar, a fully appointed and efficiently organized army of conquest landed in Kent under the command of Aulus Plautius. The country from the Channel to the Tyne was at this time divided among a score or more of tribal kingdoms or confederacies, some of which acknowledged a queen as their head. Most of them certainly belonged to the Brythonic group of Celts, while the latest

comers in the south-east were Belgic Brythons modified by a German element. On the other hand, Ireland and the greater part of Scotland were Goidelic (Gaels). A general supremacy over the sub-kings of the south-east had long been held by the Catuvellaunian Cunobellinus (Cymbeline), who had recently been succeeded by his son Caradoc, more familiarly known to us as Caractacus or Caratacus, the Roman version of his name.

Much had been learnt concerning the geography, the resources and the internal politics of the island, through the penetration of traders and the intercourse between Gaul and Britain, in the century that had passed since the strictly experimental and investigatory campaigns of Julius. It was not, however, without hard fighting that Plautius drove the Britons over the Thames and forced the passage of the river ; after which he waited for Claudius himself with some reinforcements to take the field and claim the honours of the inevitable victory which secured the Roman supremacy and the formal submission of most of the chiefs of the south-east. Roman military headquarters were presently established at Camulodunum (Colchester).

### Stubborn Resistance by Caractacus

CARACTACUS, however, escaped to the west, roused the tribes on the Welsh border, and maintained so stubborn a resistance that his forces were only shattered finally in a great engagement in A.D. 50 by Ostorius, who had succeeded Plautius. Meanwhile an officer of great ability but of humble birth, Titus Flavius Vespasianus, (A.D. 9–A.D. 79), who was destined himself to wear the purple, had subjugated the south, westward as far as the Exe and the Severn, and a Roman frontier had been established from the Severn to the Wash.

Even now the valiant spirit of Caractacus had not been broken, though his wife and children had been captured. He escaped again, to the north. But he failed to win over the Brigantes, whose cautious queen preferred to seize him and hand him over in chains to the Romans in 51. It is, however, to the credit of Claudius that when the brave captive was sent to

Rome he was granted an honourable liberty, though he never returned to his native land.

The emperor's honest zeal for good government was displayed by an active attention to the law courts which the regular lawyers found embarrassing. But unhappily the feature of the reign most conspicuous to the public eye, and at the same time most offensive to public sentiment, was the influence exercised over him by the freedmen, for the most part Greeks, who won his confidence, and by the successive wives who plotted against his honour and his authority while they fooled him as they pleased.

Of the freedmen, the most notorious were, perhaps, Narcissus, Pallas and Felix, the brother of Pallas, who became governor of Judaea. Their rivalry did not prevent them from working in concert to their common advantage ; they battened upon the secret—almost the public—sale of honours and privileges ; but they were men of ability, who rendered useful service when it was in their own interest to do so, forming a sort of imperial secretariat quite untrammelled by class interests or social prejudices, which affected them personally not at all. But the fact in itself made them the more odious and their master or puppet the more contemptible in the common view.

### Agrippina's Evil Influence

**R**OMAN society was mainly divided between profligates and puritans ; but the profligacy of Messalina, the wife of Claudius when he became emperor, disgusted even that society, while it gibed at the besotted blindness of her husband until matters reached such a pass that even his eyes were opened, and she met the death she deserved in A.D. 48. The place she vacated was secured by the emperor's ambitious niece—Agrippina the younger—sister of Caligula, widow of Domitius Ahenobarbus, the mother of the young Nero, for whom she was determined to capture the succession.

Claudius was the putative father of a son who had been named Britannicus, born to Messalina in 42, so the first step was to make him adopt Nero, who was

**MOTHER OF THE TYRANT NERO**

Agrippina the Younger, unlike her mother, was cruel and licentious. After marrying Claudius she secured the succession for her son by Cn. Domitius Ahenobarbus—Nero ; for whom she was virtually regent until A.D. 59.

*Ny Carlsberg Museum, Copenhagen*

three years the elder. Agrippina was a very clever woman who pursued her ends with a perfect tenacity and an entire absence of scruple. In the training of her son she sowed the wind—and she reaped the whirlwind. At first her husband was brought completely under her influence ; she had gained her position in alliance with the favourite Pallas ; for a time all seemed to go well with her plans. Then other influences began to predominate ; there were signs that the old man was inclining to Britannicus rather than Nero. Agrippina took counsel with one Locusta, a woman who bore an evil reputation as an expert in poisons ; and Claudius died suddenly. Nero, not Britannicus, was hailed emperor (A.D. 54).

The new emperor, a Domitius by birth, had received the name by which he is known and execrated, one borne generally by the Claudii, on his adoption by Claudius. He was now sixteen ; of his character little was known ; he had been highly educated, and his tutor was a famous philosopher and writer, Lucius

**ROME'S WORST EMPEROR**

Nero was one of the few emperors who seem to have completely deserved their evil reputation. Born in A.D. 37, he was only seventeen when he succeeded ; and his descent from the profligate, unbalanced Julia must also be borne in mind.

*Uffizi Gallery, Florence ; photo, Alinari*

succession, which finally fell to the plebeian but very capable Vespasian, whose services in the subjugation of southern Britain have already been noted ; three other emperors having risen and fallen again during this year and a half. Thus was revealed the fundamental weakness from which the Roman Empire could never completely escape. So long as the troops held to their allegiance their Imperator was an irresistible autocrat ; while he lived, there was no one to whom

**NERO'S EVIL GENIUS**

Poppaea Sabina was one of the worst influences in Nero's life. It was at her instance that he had his mother, Agrippina, put to death and divorced his wife Octavia. She died, after marrying the emperor, from his brutality.

*Olympia Museum ; photo, Alinari*

Annaeus Seneca (c. 5 B.C.–A.D. 65) ; but his mother was Agrippina. For five years the government was directed by Seneca and Burrhus, the prefect of the Praetorians, whose support had ensured the accession of Nero ; five years in bright contrast to those which followed.

The young emperor did not interfere with the business of government ; he left honest, competent and generally respected ministers a free hand, and his own official appearances were creditable. Britannicus died in circumstances sufficiently suspicious to give colour to the usual rumours, but that was all. A breach, however, widened between the ministers and Agrippina, who found her influence with her son slipping away, and tried to recover it by methods which only made the young man resent it the more. He became infatuated by a mistress, Poppaea Sabina, who hated Agrippina, and in 59 Nero murdered his mother.

For nine years Nero reigned as an unqualified tyrant, and then for eighteen months generals from Spain, from Gaul and from Syria fought for the imperial they could transfer their allegiance except their immediate commander if he chose to accept it ; once an emperor was firmly established with general consent he needed not to fear revolt unless he made himself wantonly intolerable ; but the settlement of the succession lay with the soldiery and primarily with the Praetorians, in their camp near the capital.

The reign of Nero saw the confirmation of the Roman dominion in Britain from the Channel to the Dee and the Wash, by the campaigns of Suetonius Paulinus in Wales, and by the crushing of the great revolt of the Iceni in the eastern area under their queen Boadicea. Still more familiar is the story of the Great Fire of A.D. 64, when half Rome was burnt to the ground while Nero, as men said, gave himself up to the emotional joys of the thrilling dramatic moment, and then sought to recover his popularity with the mob by illuminating his gardens with a public display of burning Christians ; on the pretence that those incomprehensible and therefore formidable Jewish fanatics had set fire to Rome. All Roman senti-

**TITUS THE MAGNIFICENT**

Elder son of Vespasian, Titus (79–81), in spite of his short reign, was one of the most popular of the emperors. He united clemency and moderation with almost Oriental magnificence, in contrast with the parsimony of his father.

*National Museum, Naples ; photo, Anderson*

ment was especially scandalised when the emperor gloried in taking a personal part in public competitions which to Roman eyes were fit only for Greeks, or freedmen, as well as by the shamelessness of his vices, and his extravagances. No man was safe, whose character was a reproach to the emperor or whose wealth excited his rapacity. At length the cup brimmed over, and the old soldier Servius Sulpicius Galba (5 B.C. - A.D. 68) 'whom all men counted fit to rule—had he not ruled,' raised the standard of revolt in his province of Hither Spain in 67–8.

Galba, a rigid old warrior, marched on Italy. Nero found himself deserted on all sides, and sought refuge in an ignominious death barely in time to escape capture. Galba was hailed emperor, but displayed an injudicious niggardliness to the soldiery, who in consequence transferred their allegiance to Marcus Salvius Otho, once the complaisant spouse of Poppaea, and Galba was slain (January, 69) after a reign of six months. But the legions of the Rhine preferred their own commander Vitellius, for no better reason than the fact that he was their

**BLUNT SOLDIER-EMPEROR**

The accession of Vespasian (70–79) marks a turning point in the history of the Principate. After the confusion of the conflict between Otho and Vitellius, he was elected emperor, not in Rome, but in the East, and by the army.

*Ny Carlsberg Museum, Copenhagen*

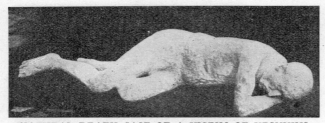

**NATURAL DEATH CAST OF A VICTIM OF VESUVIUS**

Many of those who met their death at Pompeii left a perfect mould of their contours in the mud and scoriac dust that formed their shroud : and it has been found possible to take plaster casts, gruesome and pathetic, of bodies that mouldered away more than eighteen hundred years ago.

committed suicide. Vitellius entered Rome and assumed the purple while Vespasian was being proclaimed in Egypt and Syria. The troops in Illyricum sided with the latter, whose lieutenant Antonius Primus with his first army defeated the forces of Vitellius in the second battle at Bedriacum and marched on Rome. The final scenes are somewhat nauseous. In the end, Vitellius, whose most marked characteristic was a repulsive gluttony, found himself deserted, was dragged from hiding and was hacked or beaten to death (December, A.D. 69). Vespasian himself arrived in Italy in the following year ; but in the meanwhile he was represented by his younger son Domitian (51–96) : his

commander ; and carrying him with them they marched on Italy. Meanwhile in the East Vespasian and his senior officer Mucianus, with their troops, decided that Vespasian himself should rule.

The lieutenants of Vitellius defeated Otho's troops at Bedriacum ; Otho duly

**POMPEII DISENTOMBED FROM THE DUST THAT OVERWHELMED IT IN A.D. 79**

The reign of Titus is made memorable by one appalling disaster—the destruction of the flourishing town of Pompeii on the bay of Naples by an eruption of Mount Vesuvius in A.D. 79. Titus exerted himself nobly to relieve the suffering. But, however terrible the event, it was of great value to posterity, for the town was not blotted out by lava so much as entombed in volcanic dust, thus preserving priceless information about contemporary life. Above, Vesuvius seen from the Forum.

*Photo, E.N.A.*

lieutenants were loyal ; there was no rival or possible rival on the scene ; Rome only craved for the anarchy to end ; and his full and formal recognition as emperor was a foregone conclusion.

Vespasian was the practical man of the hour. Like Marius, he was of the people, and in no wise ashamed of the fact. He had no ideals and no illusions. Like the founder of the Tudor dynasty, he looked upon the running of the Empire as a business proposition which had been badly mismanaged and wanted a new manager who would attend to business, repair the machinery, reorganize the staff, and make the concern flourish. He had been fighting, commanding troops, organizing, administrating for thirty years ; he was a shrewd judge of character ; he knew the system thoroughly by personal experience ; he had served among orientals and hyperboreans, and knew the empire from end to end ; and so he took over control.

### Vespasian's practical Qualities

THE vices and extravagances of Roman society had no attraction for the economical soul of Vespasian ; in his own household he set an example of simplicity or parsimony which reacted upon society at large, so that simplicity came into fashion. He scoffed at the intellectual refinements and affectations of his sons ; but he knew quite well that they had a social value. He could chuckle over his own shortcomings and the shams which surrounded him. Titus, his heir, reproved him for an unseemly interest in a paying drainage scheme. ' That doesn't stink,' said the Emperor, pulling out a coin ; and ' I'm turning into a God, I take it,' as he lay on his deathbed.

His hard-headed shrewdness was the best possible antidote to the corruption of the times, and a most salutary if occasionally vulgar contrast to the prevalent levity and recklessness ; it made decency more fashionable than indecency.

Vespasian indulged in no proscriptions and no violence. His business was to restore law and public confidence, to conciliate all classes without pandering to any, and to hold the control firmly in his own hands. He was well served by the men he appointed ; his public works were directed to the dignity of the state and the welfare of the people ; and his expenditure was economical not in the sense that it was parsimonious, but that it eschewed wastefulness and merely wanton display. He was not picturesque, but he was effective, and he gave the Empire, and above all Italy, the heart of the Empire, that peace and order which had been so rudely shaken by the clash of civil strife ; he restored the sense of personal security which had been perishing under the latter emperors ; and he gave a new stability to the imperial system.

### Civilis' Mutiny on the Rhine

TWO episodes at the beginning of Vespasian's ten years' reign (A.D. 69–79) demand attention. When he resolved to make his bid for empire, he was engaged in suppressing a great rebellion of the Jews. Consequently, when he moved from the East he left the completion of the task in the hands of his elder son, Titus. Here, then, it is enough to say that Jerusalem fell after a prolonged defence in September, A.D. 70. The Jewish people was depatriated and dispersed, and the event was commemorated in Rome by erecting the Arch of Titus.

The second event was the revolt or mutiny of Civilis on the Rhine. Civilis himself was a Batavian Gaul, but like multitudes of the Gauls a full Roman citizen and a legionary officer. The legions were made up of Roman citizens, but were by this time mainly recruited not from Italy, but from the provincial citizens of the region where they were quartered, and the frontier armies were supplemented by the cohorts raised from the subject peoples who were not citizens. For the most part these ' auxilia ' did not serve among their own kin but in some distant quarter of the Empire. The Rhine frontier, however, was exceptional. When Civilis saw the legions making and unmaking emperors, he saw also his opportunity for setting up an independent Gallic empire by means of the armies on the Rhine. The attempt failed, mainly because the Gaulish legionaries remained loyal to Rome and the general population stood inert ; but it met with sufficient initial success to call for its suppression by Mucianus (accompanied by the emperor's younger son, Domitian), a subsequent rectification of the strategic frontier, and the substitution of foreign for native auxilia on the Rhine.

Titus had been for some years formally associated with his father as imperator, and succeeded him as a matter of course in A.D. 79. He reigned for only two years, long enough to win a lasting reputation, hardly expected at the time of his accession, for clemency and generosity. He was emperor at the time of an appalling calamity for which there had been no precedent, the utter obliteration of the cities of Herculaneum and Pompeii by an eruption of Vesuvius in A.D. 79.

Leaving no son, he was succeeded by his brother Domitian (A.D. 81–96), who left to posterity a reputation as foul as that of Titus was fair. The satires of Juvenal and the epigrams of Martial give a most unsavoury impression of the Rome of that day, but the satirist can seldom paint a picture that is wholly true, since he necessarily concentrates on the evil and ignores the good that he sees. From the known characters of eminent men of the time—Agricola, Tacitus, Pliny—we know that it had become entirely possible to be neither profligate nor puritan without being in the least singular.

But there were plenty of survivals of the Neronic days, and Domitian himself seemed to make Nero his model when he was not posing as the champion of religion and reformer of degenerate morals. The combination of personal depravity with superstitious fanaticism is not uncommon, and in him was emphatically marked. It

**DOMITIAN THE OPPRESSOR**
Unsuccessful in war, of the most doubtful personal morals, cruel and oppressive towards the end of his reign, Domitian (81–96), brother of Titus, yet showed himself a not incapable ruler.
*Museo Communale, Rome ; photo, Alinari*

drew him into the encouragement of vile parasites, the revival of delation and other black features of Nero's reign ; oddly accompanied by sumptuary and social legislation of a puritanical kind.

At the outset Domitian coveted martial glory, but his participation in frontier campaigns on the Danube abated his ardour. Mucianus, when he marched against Civilis, had realized the incapacity of his princely colleague and carefully kept him away from the front. The most creditable feature of the reign was the Britannic governorship of Gnaeus Julius Agricola (A.D. 37–93), for which Domitian was not responsible, though his jealousy terminated it prematurely in 85. Agricola, appointed to Britain in 78 by Vespasian, not only advanced the permanent effective frontier to the line from Solway to Tyne, but partly subjugated the lowlands of Caledonia, planted forts from Forth to Clyde, penetrated into the Highlands, and inflicted a heavy defeat on the northern clans. His administration of the province, moreover, gives him high rank amongst the best of Roman provincial governors.

Domitian excited less terror but hardly less disgust in his latter years than Nero. Rome endured him with growing anxiety and displeasure, but only one revolt was attempted. Lucius Antonius Saturninus, a distinguished officer in command of two legions on the Rhine, tried to follow the example of Galba, and had the warm support of his men, but in 91 was promptly overthrown by a loyalist officer. The only effect of the rebellion was to increase the suspicions and fears of the emperor and intensify the worst traits in his character. Bad as he was, no one wanted a renewal of armed contests for the position of emperor. But, as in the case of Caligula, the third and last ruler of the Flavian house was slain (A.D. 96) by an assassin who had no political object in view, a freedman of his own household.

An Octavius, three Claudii and a Domitius had achieved or successively acquired the Principate on the basis of a legal fiction that they were Caesars. Even of such fictitious Caesars the last had disappeared with Nero. Four emperors had followed, with no other title than the allegiance of the legions under their command ; but to all four the name of Caesar was given. Flavius Vespasianus, grandson of a small Sabine farmer or farm-labourer, had a fictitious descent from heroic ancestry concocted for him and, like him, his two sons bore the name of Caesar. That title, as well as the complimentary 'Augustus,' had become permanently appropriated to the Principate. When Domitian was murdered there was not even a Flavius, much less a Caesar, to succeed him. But the time had passed when the most fervent of theoretical republicans could dream of a return to the republican system.

T HEORETICALLY the prerogatives of a new emperor were accorded to him constitutionally by the Senate, though the Senate had repeatedly found itself reduced to endorsing the dictate of the soldiery. But now there was no ambitious general at the gates, and the Senate could and did assert its constitutional authority without let. It proceeded immediately to the appointment of a new Caesar, and, to assert the civil as opposed to the military character of the authority the more emphatically, it chose a purely civilian member of its own body, Marcus Cocceius Nerva (A.D. 32–98), of an old Roman family which for some generations had been established in Crete ; a Roman of the old Roman blood, but a provincial Roman. It was a new departure, significant of the new imperial idea.

Nerva was not a born ruler of men, but he was a man of lofty character, wise and courageous. There was an immediate end of the grievances that had been growing up under Domitian. But

he also faced facts and realized the fundamental weaknesses of the situation. An old man, he had no heir, and the power of the Principate rested on the army. In the choice of his successor lay Rome's destiny. Instead of leaving it to chance, faction or intrigue, Nerva took it upon himself to nominate his successor.

The very able general now commanding on the Rhine was Marcus Ulpius Trajanus (A.D. 52–117), like Nerva himself a provincial Roman whose family had long been settled in Spain. In 97 the emperor adopted Trajan as his heir, and associated the general with himself in the full imperial authority. The choice was made acceptable by Trajan's already high reputation ; it gave immediate promise of security, since he was in the full vigour of manhood ; it ensured the loyalty of the soldiery, and it was more than justified by the event. The nomination was Nerva's legacy to the Empire, and in the next year, A.D. 98, he died.

**PREDECESSOR OF TRAJAN**

A man of middling capacities, the Emperor Nerva (96–98) was yet one of the foremost benefactors of the Roman State; for recognizing his own shortcomings he appointed the great Trajan his colleague and successor.

*Italian Dept. of Antiquities, Professor Halbherr*

# TABLE OF DATES FOR CHAPTER 11

A.D.

**98** Death of Nerva.

Trajan (Marcus Ulpius Trajanus) emperor, having been already associated with Nerva as Caesar. Trajan completes military organization on the Rhine, and returns to Rome.

Revival of the policy of expansion.

**101** Trajan's first campaign on the Danube.

**102** Trajan forces the 'Iron Gates' and penetrates Dacia.

**103** Pliny pro-praetor in Pontus. Correspondence with Trajan about the attitude he is to adopt towards the Christians.

**104** Conquest of Dacia and death of the Dacian king Decebalus.

**106** Erection of the Forum and Column of Trajan in Rome.

Colonisation of Dacia.

**114** Trajan advances against Parthia.

**115** Desolating earthquake at Antioch.

Trajan crosses the Tigris.

**116** Trajan captures Ctesiphon; but insurrections on his rear compel him to retire.

**117** Trajan dies at Selinus in Cilicia.

Hadrian (Marcus Aelius Hadrianus) emperor.

Hadrian reverts to the policy of non-expansion, and makes peace with Parthia.

**118** Partial withdrawal from Dacia.

Hadrian returns to Rome, and makes preparation for his 'peregrination' of the Empire. (The dates of the itinerary are uncertain.)

**120** Hadrian in Britain. Construction of Hadrian's Wall from the Solway to the Tyne.

*India:* Probable date of the Kushan monarch Kanishka, 120–162.

**121** Hadrian in Gaul. In the next ten years he visits in succession Spain, Africa, Syria, Asia (Minor), Greece, where he makes a long stay at Athens; returns to Rome; again visits Carthage, Athens and Antioch, and in the East confirms the Parthian Peace.

**131** Hadrian at Alexandria.

**133** Last organized revolt of the Jews, and their final dispersion.

**134** Hadrian at Rome.

**135** Hadrian nominates his worthless favourite Verus as his successor.

**137** Verus dies, leaving a child, Lucius Verus.

**138** Hadrian adopts a distinguished Senator, Titus Aurelius Antoninus (Pius), aged fifty-two. Antoninus adopts his own nephew, Marcus Annius Verus (Marcus Aurelius Antoninus) and Lucius Verus.

Death of Hadrian.

Antoninus Pius emperor.

**138–161** Reign of Antoninus Pius. An era of wholly uneventful tranquillity and prosperity; but it encouraged barbarians on the borders to believe that the Empire was losing virility.

Ptolemy (astronomer and geographer) and Arrian the historian of Alexander the Great flor.

**161** Death of Antoninus Pius.

Marcus Aurelius, emperor, makes Lucius Verus his colleague.

**162** *India:* Huvishka succeeds Kanishka as Kushan king.

**165** Parthian incursions.

**165** Verus takes official command in the East, but the work is done by Avidius Cassius and other competent officers, Verus taking to himself the credit, and the title of Parthicus.

**166** Unrest on the upper and middle Danube frontiers, where Quadi and Marcomanni are in movement.

Outbreak of plague. Religious revival, and severe persecution of Christians.

**167** Marcus and Verus march against the Quadi, who seek and obtain peace.

**168** Death of Verus; Marcus sole emperor.

**169–179** Repeated campaigns of Marcus in Pannonia.

**175** Revolt of Avidius Cassius, the successful commander of the Parthian war. He is put to death by his own followers.

**177–180** Sarmatian war. Commodus the son and heir of Marcus is with the army.

**180** Death of Marcus Aurelius.

Accession of Commodus.

Commodus makes an ignominious peace with the Sarmatians and returns to Rome.

**180–183** Commodus leaves the government to his father's ministers and plunges into private dissipation.

**182** *India:* Vasudeva, Kushan emperor (to 220).

**183** Plot to kill Commodus discovered. Henceforth he acts as a panic-stricken tyrant. Power of the favourite Perennis.

**186** Fall of Perennis. Power of Cleander.

**189** Fall of Cleander.

**192** Assassination of Commodus.

Pertinax made emperor by the Praetorians (first of the 'praetorian emperors').

**193** Pertinax murdered by the Praetorians, who offer the throne to the highest bidder, and force the Senate to accept the purchaser, Didius Julianus.

Pescennius Niger commanding in Syria, Clodius Albinus in Britain and Septimius Severus in Illyria declare against the usurper. While Pescennius is in arms in the East, Severus marches on Rome as the avenger of Pertinax, crushes Julianus, and is proclaimed emperor, but makes large concessions to his own troops. Severus, emperor, disbands the Praetorians,

**194** Severus recognizes Albinus as Caesar, but marches against Pescennius.

Defeat and death of Pescennius. His followers hold out for two years at Byzantium.

**197** Contest of Severus and Albinus, who is defeated and slain at the sanguinary battle of Lugdunum (Lyons).

**198** Severus organizes a new Praetorian Guard under his own command, whose prefect is in fact, the civilian First Minister. The administration is directed by the prefect Plautianus, an eminent legist.

**201** Parthian campaign of Severus.

**203** Fall and execution of Plautianus; who is succeeded as prefect by the lawyer Papinian. Development of the legal doctrine of Autocracy.

**209** Severus in Britain. Costly campaigns in Caledonia. Building of the Wall of Severus.

**210** Bassianus and Geta, sons of Severus, with the army in Britain.

**211** Death of Severus. Joint succession of his sons Caracalla (Bassianus) and Geta. They return to Rome.

### CHAPTER 11

# THE EMPIRE IN ITS GRANDEUR:
## A.D. 98—211

THE majesty of the Roman Empire was at its zenith under the four rulers who followed Nerva, from A.D. 98 to 180: Trajan the embodiment of clear-eyed strength and justice; Hadrian the man of genius; Antoninus Pius the peace-lover; Marcus Aurelius Antoninus, who may dispute with Asoka the claim to represent the Platonic ideal of the philosopher sovereign. Of the four, only the first yielded to the temptation of conquest, though the last found himself compelled to engage, not over successfully, in heavy frontier warfare. All devoted themselves primarily to the development of the welfare of the Empire as a whole, and the era, commonly known as the 'Age of the Antonines,' is justly accounted the golden age of the Roman Empire.

### First of the Antonine Emperors

TRAJAN—Marcus Ulpius Trajanus—A.D. 98–117, was chosen by Nerva as his successor because in the circumstances it was essential that Caesar should command the confidence and the obedience of the army from the outset, and in Trajan he saw a man of sterling character and high ability who had spent half his life in military service and enjoyed the trust of all who knew him.

Trajan made no haste to celebrate his accession. His work on the Rhine frontier had first to be completed, a work not of conquest but of strategic fortification. He was, besides, more at home in the camp than in the city. His letters to the Senate, however, were of good augury, promising that in his reign no senator should be put to death arbitrarily, and flatly declining for himself the divine honours proffered during his life.

When in due time he left his legions and came to Rome, the good impression was fully confirmed and he achieved immediate popularity by the frank simplicity and sincerity of his manners, and his fearless confidence in the loyalty of those who surrounded him: a confidence which, so far as his personal safety was concerned, he did not hesitate to carry to what seemed to be the extreme of rashness. The atmosphere of suspicion was allayed, the more when Trajan's judgement was justified by the event, and the tongues of delators and scandalmongers were silenced instead of being encouraged. Nor was there in Trajan's simplicity any such failure of dignity as had in some degree marred the character of Vespasian.

### Reorganization of the Finances

THOUGH he found the finances of the state in very bad order, he entirely declined to replenish the treasury and the privy purse either by heavy taxation or by the familiar expedients of arbitrary confiscations and fines. The need for economy was met by the curtailment of extravagances, not only in the imperial household but in public departments, the stopping of leakages, the development of a graded civil service in which advancement was the reward of efficiency and dishonesty did not pay. Economists might be alarmed when the emperor refused the 'voluntary' contributions which it had been customary to accord, not from good will but from policy—a variant of the 'benevolences' whose exaction became so serious a grievance at one period of English history. Interests might clamour over the suppression of monopolies which brought money into the treasury; but the abolition of these things removed burdens that checked the development of trade and therefore of the sources of revenue, and the revenue itself increased instead of diminishing.

With increased revenue came an expenditure on public works, especially on means of communication, roads and ports,

**TRAJAN, ROMAN EMPEROR**

Marcus Ulpius Trajanus, born at Ithica, near
Seville, c. A.D. 52, succeeded Nerva in A.D. 98.
His high character and military talents were
matched by his administrative ability, and the
Empire was admirably governed by him.

*The Louvre ; photo, Alinari*

which again increased trade and revenue.
The result of all of which was that in the
long run no reign left more splendid and
convincing monuments of public wealth
and prosperity than that of Trajan, paid
for without any undue pressure of taxation
either in Italy or in the provinces.

Trajan, moreover, imbued the provincial government with his own spirit.
He chose for governors men of the best
type, who were almost too anxious to
seek his sympathetic counsel, which he
was ready to give whenever it was asked,
counsel always directed to the welfare of

the governed. The correspondence which
passed between the emperor and his
fervent admirer, the younger Pliny, whom
he had sent as governor to Bithynia in
103, is typical of the kind of relations that
subsisted between the emperor and his
subordinates.

Great as were the services rendered to
the Empire by Trajan as an administrator, he probably set more store by his
renown as a conqueror, since he was a
soldier by instinct and a ruler by force
of circumstance. Yet by common consent
his military achievements were of no lasting advantage and were far from being an
unqualified success. That is no reproach
to his great qualities as a soldier, but it
does mark the defect in his statesmanship,
the adoption of an aggressive policy of
expansion for the Empire.

In pursuance of that policy, he carried
the Roman arms across the Danube in
the campaigns of 101–106, and over the
Euphrates in those of 114–117, discarding
the principle recommended by Augustus
from which the only departure during the
last century had been the conquest of
Britain under Claudius. The event may
be taken as proving that Augustus was
right and Trajan was wrong ; the more
confidently because that was emphatically the verdict of Trajan's successor
Hadrian, the most brilliant in the whole
line of Roman emperors unless we include
the mighty Julius in the list.

### 'Forward Policy' in Dacia

YET so far at least as Dacia is concerned,
Trajan was not without warrant in
his calculation that the policy was sound
when he embarked upon it. It corresponded very closely to what was known
two generations ago as the 'forward
policy' on the British-Afghan frontier in
India. The mass, if not perhaps the weight,
of military opinion, conscious of menace
from incalculable powers at a distance,
called for farther-flung outposts of the
Empire, the alternative being a buffer state
which might prove to be not a buffer
but an enemy advance-guard.

The population of Dacia (which corresponded roughly to modern Hungary and
Rumania) in Trajan's time was doubtless

heterogeneous, probably mainly Slavonic. Six centuries earlier, the great Darius had plunged into those wild regions, and barely succeeded in extricating himself and a remnant of his army from the wilderness. The Illyrian hills and the Balkans were a permanent barrier which held back the Mediterranean peoples even from the Danube, till the Romans in the time of Augustus set about the reduction of Moesia and Pannonia. But now 'within the last twenty years the Dacian chief Decebalus had been welding the trans-Danube tribes into some sort of unity, had crossed the Danube and raided Roman territory, and had so dealt with the punitive legions of Domitian that the Roman prestige in those quarters had fallen to a very low ebb.

$\mathfrak{I}$T is scarcely surprising, then, that a soldier, conscious of his powers, should have deemed that the time had come for discarding the prudent policy of Augustus in favour of that which would certainly have been adopted by Julius. Something more was wanted here than the organization of the forces and the fortresses on the Rhine and Rhine-to-Danube frontier, the work, admirably accomplished, on which Trajan had been engaged when called upon to assume the principate.

From the moral point of view there was justification enough for bringing the Dacian monarch severely to book ; his activities, encouraged by his experience of Domitian, were emphatically provocative. In 101, therefore, Trajan organized his first Dacian expedition, on which he was accompanied by the young kinsman Publius Aelius Hadrianus (A.D. 76-138), whom he chose later to be his imperial successor. The campaign taxed heavily the strategic powers of Trajan and the discipline of his troops ; the more because Decebalus was an astute prince who understood how to gain time by diplomacy, and also had a thorough knowledge,

GLORIFICATION OF TRAJAN AS PUBLIC BENEFACTOR

Two of Trajan's popular benefactions to the state are commemorated in these reliefs on the balustrades in the forum that bears his name. In the upper relief he is depicted in the curule chair with Italia, a child in her arms, thanking him for the institution of the ' alimenta,' state charities expected to arrest the depopulation of Italy. On the other balustrade he is shown witnessing the fulfilment of his order for the burning of the records of arrears of taxes owing by the provincials.

*Photos, Anderson*

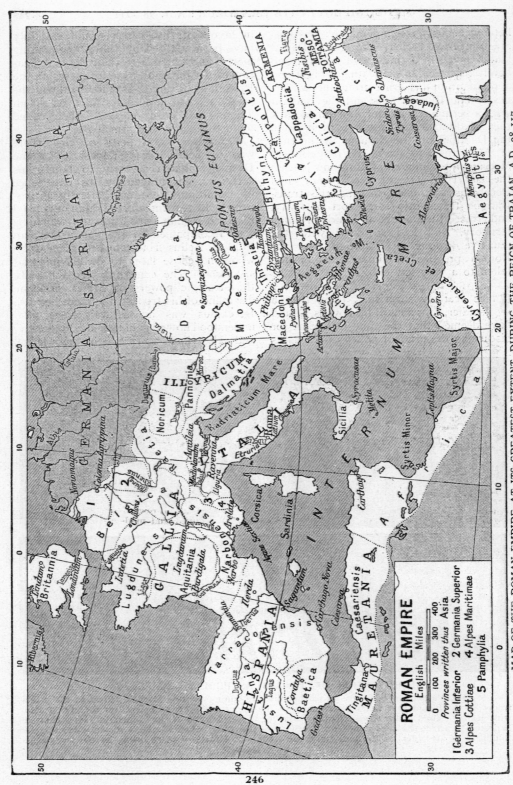

MAP OF THE ROMAN EMPIRE AT ITS GREATEST EXTENT, DURING THE REIGN OF TRAJAN, A.D. 98-117

**ROMAN EMPIRE**

English Miles

0 100 200 300 400

*Provinces written thus* Asia

1 Germania Inferior  2 Germania Superior
3 Alpes Cottiae   4 Alpes Maritimae
5 Pamphylia

which the Roman had not, of the extremely difficult country in which the campaign must be fought. But when, after very hard fighting, Trajan had forced the pass still known as the Iron Gates, the ultimate victory of the Romans was assured. When his capital was captured, Decebalus made humble terms of submission (102) ; but Trajan's back was

in his forum the mighty monument known as Trajan's Column, and to abide in peace till in 113 affairs in the East again awakened his military ambitions.

The Euphrates had long been the vaguely acknowledged boundary between the Roman and Parthian dominions, but both empires claimed the northern kingdom of Armenia as a dependency. The

**DEATH OF DECEBALUS ON THE FIELD OF BATTLE**

As shown in the relief opposite Decebalus made humble submission to Trajan at the end of the first Dacian War ; but he soon resumed hostilities and Trajan again took the field. He crossed the Danube at the modern Turnu Severin, forced the passes, occupied Sarmizegetusa, the Dacian capital, and completely defeated Decebalus who, despairing but defiant to the last, threw himself from his horse and took his own life. After his death Dacia was completely subdued and made a Roman province.

*From Cichorius, ' Die Traianssäule,' G. Reimer, Berlin*

hardly turned before his diplomacy was at work, raising a fresh confederacy.

So in 103 Trajan again took the field, bent this time not merely on asserting the power of the Empire but on crushing the Dacian once and for all time. The Danube was spanned by a mighty bridge, of which probable remnants may be traced to this day ; at three different points the passes were forced ; and the kingdom of Decebalus was destroyed in 104. Roman legionaries were planted as colonists in the depopulated region of Transylvania, and in 106 the conqueror returned to Rome, after completing the settlement, to raise

Arsacid dynasty was in decline, but had not abated its claims, and here Trajan found his excuse for what was in fact a project of conquering expansion ; for the Parthian monarch Chosroes presumed to set a kinsman of his own on the throne of Armenia. So in 113 Trajan set his armies in motion and proceeded to the East to take the command in person.

On the way he was met by ambassadors praying for peace. Chosroes had taken alarm, set up a new prince, Parthamasiris, in Armenia, and offered his protégé's homage. This was not enough. Trajan advanced, meeting no resistance, till he reached the borders of Armenia. Then Parthamasiris humiliated himself and came in person to the emperor, but only to be told that Armenia was no longer a kingdom but a Roman province, and he had leave to depart. The circumstances in which he was slain almost immediately afterwards are obscure, but certainly could not reflect credit on Trajan.

Armenia with Mesopotamia was secured, but Parthia was the emperor's real objective. Operations, however, were delayed till 116 owing to the need for creating some organization, and then to the havoc wrought by a terrific earthquake at Antioch, in which Trajan himself barely escaped with his life. Then came a great campaign over the Tigris, the passage of which in the face of an active foe was no easy task, and the advance to Susa, the last triumphant achievement.

For in rear of the victorious armies revolt broke out in all the annexed territories. Trajan was obliged to retreat by the enemy behind him, not in front of him—and his own health, of which he was unsparing at sixty-four as at forty, had at last broken down. He was indeed only checked, not defeated ; but he saw at least that his dream of emulating Alexander could never be accomplished, and even the widespread revolts were still unquelled when he turned his face homeward and died on the way in Cilicia (117).

Trajan had found, and named (though only on his death-bed), his fit successor, in Hadrian, the cousin, now commanding in Syria, whose capacities he had gauged in spite of the most marked contrasts between their characters. Scandal, wholly without foundation, whispered that the new emperor owed his selection to the favour in which he had always stood with Trajan's empress Plotina, who sent the dead man's instructions to the Senate.

HADRIAN (Publius Aelius Hadrianus) was now forty years of age. His family, of north-Italian origin, had long been settled, like that of Trajan, in Spain. His father had been a near cousin of Trajan, who had constituted himself the boy's guardian. He was brilliantly clever and amazingly versatile ; and had accom-

TRAJAN'S COLUMN IN ITS ORIGINAL SETTING AND AS IT IS TO-DAY

The Column of Trajan was set up in the open space contained between the façade of the Basilica Ulpia and the wings of the library facing the Temple of Trajan. The column, including the base, is 127 feet high and is encircled by spiral reliefs forming a continuous narrative of the Dacian wars. The column still stands, amid fragments of the surrounding colonnades (right), but Trajan's statue on the summit was replaced in the sixteenth century by one of S. Peter.

**TRAJAN'S CONSORT PLOTINA**

Pompeia Plotina, wife of the Emperor Trajan, had no children, and willingly communicated to the Senate her husband's deathbed nomination of Hadrian as his successor. After her death Hadrian built a temple in her honour.

*Capitoline Museum, Rome*

Hadrian was as complex as Trajan was simple, of a type more readily associated with the Greek than with the Roman, suggestive perhaps of a Celtic element in his ancestry. Endowed with an immensely wider intellectual range than Trajan, he was eager in the pursuit of beauty, still more eager in the pursuit of knowledge, and possessed all the imagination which Trajan lacked, while himself lacking the intensity of Trajan's moral conviction ; yet he held ideals of empire not perhaps more noble but more penetrating and less conventional, or at least less traditional. His military talents were probably not small, and apparently he had shown marked courage in the field, but he was not, as Trajan was, a born soldier called to be a statesman, but a statesman who could on occasion prove himself an able soldier ; and conquest for the sake of conquest had no attraction for him.

The statesman in Hadrian was swift to realize that for the Roman Empire conquest was not statesmanship. With a frontier which could hold any attack at bay, nothing was to be feared from

panied the emperor on his campaigns, sometimes holding high command, in which he had acquitted himself with credit. He had just been placed in charge of Syria, and no one can have been surprised when at the last Trajan nominated him to the succession.

Trajan was a man of a grand simplicity, who set before himself and acted upon a noble conception of his high duties and responsibilities. He might be said to have been almost the perfect type of the traditional Roman character at its best ; devoted to the service of the state of which he was lord ; magnanimous, self-reliant, clear-eyed, just, fearless, entirely practical ; a little too contemptuous of intellectual subtleties, a little lacking in imagination, too prone to assume the point of view of the professional soldier.

**HADRIAN, ROMAN EMPEROR**

Publius Aelius Hadrianus was born at Rome A.D. 76, and was brought up by his kinsman Trajan, whose great-niece, Julia, he married. Hadrian's reign, A.D. 117–138 was one of the happiest periods in Roman history.

*Vatican ; photo, Anderson*

I

barbarians only half organized at their best ; nothing was to be gained by routing them in the field or occupying their territory. With the old boundaries the Empire was large enough to tax the organizing abilities of any government to the utmost. Hadrian discarded all designs of expansion, and deliberately abandoned the recent conquests beyond the Euphrates. Chosroes of Parthia, in whose place Trajan had set up a puppet of his own, was reinstated.

In 118 Hadrian returned to Rome. His reversal of Trajan's policy was of course resented by the advocates of aggressive imperialism, and posterity accused him of abandoning Dacia as well as Trans-Euphrates ; but this seems to be sufficiently disproved by the permanence of the Latin or Roman element in Tran-

**HADRIAN AS ARCHITECT AND PONTIFF**

Hadrian had so practical a knowledge of architecture that he himself designed the double temple of Venus and Roma erected by him north of the Sacra Via. This fragment of one of the pediments shows the emperor attended by lictors passing before the temple on his way to its dedication.
*Lateran Museum, Rome ; photo, Anderson*

sylvania. The broad fact stands that he preferred a consolidated frontier to indefinite expansion.

Hadrian reigned for twenty-one years (117–138) and a very large proportion of that time was occupied in peregrinations of the Empire, every part of which he visited in person at one time or other, becoming thoroughly acquainted with the prevailing conditions and local diversities, and making his hand felt in organization and government. In Britain, ' Hadrian's Wall ' from Solway to Tyne confirmed the permanent effective military frontier of the Roman province, while the northern line of forts served as a screen to hold the Picts of the Caledonian Highlands in check, the main wall being practically one extended fortress.

The visit to Britain was the first of Hadrian's expeditions to the remote provinces after his return from Dacia, which had demanded his immediate attention. The special characteristics of the island in its relation to the Empire apart, as concerns Britain in its special relation to Hadrian its treatment may be regarded as a typical instance of his methods. The province proper was to be thoroughly organized and controlled ; its frontiers were to be made impregnably secure by a fortress-barrier which could neither be penetrated nor outflanked ; the country beyond was not to be subjugated

**HADRIAN AMONG HIS PEOPLE**

This relief is one of a pair that decorated an arch that spanned the Via Lata, south of the Ara Pacis. It shows Hadrian (head wrongly restored) making a proclamation to the Roman people, represented by males of varying ages.
*Palazzo dei Conservatori ; photo, Alinari*

and occupied, but sufficiently garrisoned to discourage tribal concentrations.

Within the province, the army of occupation consisted of the legions of Roman citizens recruited from the provinces (only the praetorians being recruited in Italy) with their complements of auxiliary cohorts from Dacia or other distant parts of the Empire. But the tendency was for both legions and cohorts to remain continuously, for the men to take native wives, and for their sons to follow the father's profession, while there was nothing to prevent the cohorts from being locally recruited. The intention had been to prevent the recurrence of such military insurrections as that of Civilis on Vespasian's accession ; but in actual practice it can hardly be doubted that a generation or two sufficed to convert what had been and still was nominally a foreign into a native cohort. And the result of this was that the army in each province tended to develop a sort of provincial patriotism, and jealousy of the armies of other provinces ; while the common and distinctive Roman citizenship of the legionaries preserved in all the armies a sense of imperial unity

without distinction of race. The danger of provincial patriotism lay no longer in the old desire to break away from Rome's alien rule, but in a new ambition to be a dominating force within the Empire.

This, however, was not yet to manifest itself. Unification and consolidation were at the root of Hadrian's conception ; they would not be forwarded by war and expansion, but security was necessary, and military efficiency was necessary to security ; therefore Hadrian the man of peace was as zealous as Trajan himself to maintain his armies at the highest pitch of efficiency. There was no depreciation of the majesty of Rome, but to him Rome meant the whole Empire, not, as to those before him, the imperial city.

### Hadrian's Energy and Ability

SPAIN, Africa, Syria, Egypt, were all visited in turn, and no little time was spent by Hadrian in Greece and especially at Athens, the academic home of his spiritual affinities. The histories have no events of consequence to record ; but evidently the Roman world was immensely impressed by an amazing activity which

**CASTEL SANT' ANGELO, HADRIAN'S WAR-SCARRED MAUSOLEUM**

About the year A.D. 130 Hadrian built a mausoleum beside the Tiber to contain the ashes of himself and his descendants. The reconstruction (left) shows that it consisted of two diminishing circular structures surrounded by pillars, set on a square base and surmounted by a conical roof. In the seventh century the church of S. Angelus Inter Nubes was built upon its summit and later it became a papal fortress, the history of which would be an epitome of the history of medieval Rome.

it did not understand, but which conveyed at every turn unexpected originality as well as a versatility rare indeed among Romans ; in fact, Romans of the old tradition probably found their emperor rather alarmingly clever and unconventional. But as concerned the business of government, his cleverness was convincingly practical. Probably it was Hadrian himself who incited the eminent jurist Salvius Julianus to make that codification of legal decisions, known as Hadrian's Perpetual Edict, which practically amounted to a much needed code of Equity. We cannot but regret that we have not a more complete knowledge of a character and a genius so brilliant and so complex.

Only in the last years of his strenuous and exhausting life — he was sixty-two when he died —did his powers and his self-mastery show signs of failing ; he began to display an unhappy vindictiveness, and his first choice of a successor was Aelius Verus, a youth who had no particular qualifications other than a handsome person. Happily he soon died, and Hadrian adopted in his place a senator of mature years and distinguished character, Titus Aurelius Antoninus, of whose virtues the Senate expressed its appreciation by giving him the title Pius. By some curious caprice, Hadrian also required Antoninus to adopt a youth of the highest promise, Marcus Annius Verus (121–180), whom the world remembers as Marcus Aurelius, and at the same time Lucius, the very young son of Aelius Verus.

Hadrian was the victim of a mortal disease, which may at least help to account for the capricious cruelty he displayed at the close, and only at the close, of his life. A year after the adoption he was dead, and Antoninus Pius was emperor (138-161).

ANTONINUS PIUS

Titus Aurelius Antoninus (A.D. 86–165) was adopted by Hadrian, whom he succeeded in A.D. 138 with the official style of Antoninus Pius. Equity and justice flourished under his sway.

*Vatican ; photo, Alinari*

The twenty-three years of the reign of Antoninus are almost recordless. On barbarian frontiers occasional military movements were inevitable, but even there Antoninus preferred conciliation to coercion. His was a reign of peace still more complete than that of his predecessor. If a nation is happiest when it has least history, and has least history when it is happiest, the Roman world was assuredly never happier than in the days of Antoninus Pius, who in 161 ended a blameless life with an honoured death.

More troubled was the reign of his successor Marcus Aurelius, a born student, called unwillingly by his overpowering sense of duty to be a man of action. If fate had been kinder to him, his reign would have been a repetition of that of Antoninus. Obeying the call not of inclination but of duty, he had been constant in the practice of public functions whilst his heart was in the pursuit of abstract truth ; he had in full measure the moral qualities demanded in an ideal ruler ; but the special problems he had to face needed perhaps a keener insight than his, and his difficulties were increased by one defect—his blindness to the deficiencies in those whom he loved and unwisely trusted. To say that he was a failure would be a gross injustice ; but he made mistakes which in the long run had most unhappy consequences.

Marcus Aurelius (161–180) on his accession—a highly popular event, for he was already justly credited with all the virtues of Antoninus—of his own choice shared the imperial authority with his younger adoptive brother, Lucius Verus, whose principal merit was his ready deference to and respect for Marcus. The troops had known the vigour of Hadrian but had never felt the hand of the mild Antoninus, and the legions in distant Britain were eager to raise their own chief, Stat us Priscus to the purple, but he was too stoutly loyal to be tempted. The mutiny collapsed ; but it was not without ill omen for the future, and even at the moment was a symptom of general uneasiness on the frontiers. The peace of Antoninus had been purchased at some cost to the discipline of the armies, and to the fear those armies had been wont to inspire beyond the frontiers.

### Outbreak of War with Parthia

THE fact was already being exemplified in the East. Parthia once more asserted her claim to Armenia ; Parthian forces poured over the border and threatened Syria, a region always destructive to the discipline of the troops quartered there unless under officers of the school of Vespasian and Trajan. Hadrian had everywhere maintained very strict army discipline ; Antoninus had no doubt neglected it, being himself no soldier. In Syria it was now very indifferently enforced. For two centuries and more it might be said that only Ventidius Bassus and Trajan had been able to win laurels in conflict with the Parthians—at any rate to give decisive proof of the superiority of the Roman over the Parthian arms. Now Roman prestige in the East was so threatened as to call for the emperor's presence.

Marcus had no craving for the laurels of the conqueror. Officially the supreme command for the Parthian war was taken by Verus, who remained for the most part ingloriously at Antioch, the most cosmopolitan, the most luxurious, and the most depraved of the cities of the Empire. The work of organizing and campaigning was carried out by the subordinates who had been chosen for their efficiency, Priscus, who was summoned from Britain, and Cassius Avidius, sternest of disciplinarians and an able soldier to boot. But some five years of hard campaigning were needed before Parthia would submit to the terms by which she surrendered her title in Mesopotamia and Armenia. Verus claimed the credit, and the name of Parthicus, for what not he but the

generals had done ; but he had the grace to insist that the reluctant Marcus must share his honours.

But the Parthian war (161–165) was only a prelude. On the upper Danube the German Quadi and Marcomanni were threatening, and the return of Verus with the troops from the East was attended by a tremendous outbreak of the plague in Italy which delayed the necessary operations. Marcus, disciple of Epictetus and the Stoics as he was, was not free from the conviction that the thing was a visitation, a punishment sent by the gods for some flaw of sacrilege in the state ; and to this superstition may well be attributed the severe persecution of the Christians, who had enjoyed almost complete immunity under Hadrian and Antoninus, which he set on foot ; for Stoicism was punctilious in its regard for religious observances.

In 167 Marcus took the field in company with Verus. The demonstration, however, sufficed to bring the Quadi to terms without fighting. In 168 the emperors were able to return in peace ; but Marcus was relieved of one embarrassment by the

**THE PHILOSOPHER KING**

Marcus Aurelius (A.D. 121–180), who succeeded Antoninus Pius in A.D. 161, represents the Platonic ideal philosopher king and the highest pre-Christian conception of character. His Meditations are his imperishable monument

*British Museum*

**MARCUS AURELIUS IMPERATOR**

This bold and spirited piece of sculpture is one of the very few ancient equestrian statues in bronze still extant, its preservation being largely due to a mistaken idea in the Middle Ages that it was a statue of Constantine. Traces of gold on the horse's head show that originally it was gilt.

*Capitol, Rome*

were only preserved by a timely deluge of rain from perishing of thirst. Disaster, indeed, was escaped, and when the enemy could be brought to an engagement they were defeated ; but the mobility of the barbarians made all such campaigning harassing, hazardous and inconclusive.

Marcus was on his way to the East in 175 to suppress a revolt headed by Cassius Avidius, when news came that the rising was over ; the rebel had been slain by his own soldiers. With a rare magnanimity the emperor forbade all punishment of his family or his adherents, and destroyed unread all incriminating documents. Before returning to Rome he passed through his eastern dominion ; and when he did return it was no long time before he was again called to the Danube frontier. On this occasion his arms proved more unequivocally successful ; but the campaign was not yet finished when he was struck down by sickness, and died, worn out by his labours, in the sixtieth year of his age (A.D. 180).

death of his colleague, and henceforth he reigned alone.

The pacification, however, was illusory. The trans-Danubian peoples were in ferment, not on the upper Danube only. Year after year was occupied with conscientious campaigning which the emperor would not shirk, however uncongenial he found it, since it fell within the range of his responsibilities as he conceived them ; though he was under no illusion as to his own very mediocre abilities as a general, and trusted more in the military judgement of his officers than in his own. Once—it is piously recorded on his Column at Rome—he and his troops, cut off in the passes from their supplies,

All men united in praising the emperor, whose one aim had always been the welfare of his people, and who had constantly sacrificed all his own natural inclinations and predilections to toil unremittingly at the task which had been laid upon him. The worst that could be said of him was that the sternness he should have shown towards defaulters was too exclusively reserved for himself ; that for others he was too ready, even too anxious, to find excuse and to shut his eyes to their failings. Under him, as under Antoninus, the standard of civil administration was admirable. And in a corrupt society the personal example that these two emperors set was above praise.

But Marcus did not deal successfully with the growing problem of frontier defence, since he was naturally incapable of the vigorous measures necessary. That is the sum of the failure of the philosopher sovereign, save that he also failed in that he nominated his son Commodus as his successor, and that he misread Christianity.

Commodus (180–192) had been born in the year of his father's accession. Now, at twenty, he was an ill-conditioned youth whose education had been excellent in theory and ineffective in practice. He was accepted with anxiety, no doubt, but without opposition. He had been on the last campaign and was left in active command; but fighting under difficulties was not to his taste, and instead of carrying the war through he promptly made an ignominious peace—which confirmed the conviction of the hostile tribes that the day of Roman supremacy was past—and returned to give himself up to private dissipations while he left the uncongenial business of the administration in the hands of his tutors.

**LARGESS TO THE POPULACE**

Seated on a raised platform Marcus Aurelius is here depicted assisting at the distribution of the 'congiarium' or largess to the Roman people—represented by four figures below—after his return from the trans-Danubian campaign.

*Attic of Arch of Constantine*

**TRIUMPH OF MARCUS AURELIUS OVER THE GERMANS AND SARMATIANS**

These are two of a number of panels that adorned a public monument in honour of Marcus Aurelius. Most of the series were afterwards incorporated in the Arch of Constantine, whose head, as in the top panel, was substituted for the original. Here, the reliefs in their unaltered state give contemporary portraits of Marcus Aurelius : on the left, riding among his guards and acknowledging the submission of barbarian chieftains, and, right, as 'triumphator' before the temple of Jupiter Capitolinus.

*Palazzo dei Conservatori, Rome ; photos, Anderson*

Then the fundamental weakness of the position developed. The personal character of the last two emperors compelled a respect and admiration which safeguarded them in spite of a gentleness which amounted to weakness. The young emperor had neither force nor elevation of character nor intelligence. Plots were formed against him ; they were discovered and suppressed ; but he took alarm, and panic transformed him from a fainéant debauchee into a tyrant who alternated between raising worthless favourites to power and surrendering them to the enemies they excited. His tyranny was directed against persons, not his subjects generally, while he kept the city mob in good humour by a degrading participation in the public contests of the arena conducted on a lavish scale, though always with due regard for his personal safety.

For such a reign, the inevitable end was assassination at the hands of alarmed members of the tyrant's own disreputable household. In 192 Commodus was duly murdered, with the connivance of the prefect of the praetorians, Laetus, who was ready with an eminently respectable candidate for the purple, a senator named Pertinax ; whose nomination, thus supported, was accepted by the Senate.

PERTINAX opens the series of Caesars known as the Praetorian Emperors, who were raised to the purple by the praetorians or by the legions under their own command in the provinces, most of whom ruled only till ejected and killed by another soldier who seized the succession ; men of every variety of nationality and birth— Moor, Illyrian, Gaul, Syrian, Arabian, even Roman. Now and then an emperor was

**VICTORIOUS ROMAN SOLDIERS CARRYING OFF PRISONERS AND BOOTY**
In A.D. 174 the Senate and Roman People erected a column to Marcus Aurelius which still stands in the Piazza Colonna. It is a repetition in Carrara marble of Trajan's column, 100 feet in height and surrounded by a continuous spiral band of reliefs representing the events of the Marcomannic Wars. The reliefs are wonderfully animated and have contributed greatly to modern knowledge of the conduct of military operations under the Empire.
*Photo, Anderson*

strong enough or his adherents were strong enough to pass on the immediate succession to a son. But at the death of Commodus we have only a foretaste of the chaos ; because a strong man arose, Lucius Septimius Severus, who held the reins in his masterful grip from 193 to 211.

Pertinax, an old soldier, was made emperor by favour of the praetorians and their prefect. He lost that favour because, in a conscientious effort to rectify the misdeeds of Commodus and the evils which had sprung up during his rule, he tried to tighten discipline instead of relaxing it. Before Commodus had been three months dead, the praetorians mutinied, broke into the palace, murdered Pertinax, paraded his head through the streets on a pike, and offered the imperial throne to the highest bidder. The precarious prize fell to a wealthy senator, Didius Julianus.

At Rome the Guards could dictate at ease to the civilians, but the provincial armies had a preference for a chief of their own selection. The legions in Britain and on the Rhine chose Clodius Albinus, the army in Syria proclaimed Pescennius Niger, the troops on the Danube hailed Septimius Severus.

Rome was the necessary objective. Albinus was a sluggard, a glutton ; Pescennius was popular in the East, but the army stationed in the East had the least experience of fighting, and its discipline habitually went to pieces unless it was under command of a martinet like Cassius Avidius. Severus was a hard soldier at the head of hardened troops, and he was nearest to Rome. Neither Albinus nor Pescennius was ready to strike ; but Severus struck straight. He marched on Rome. Didius passed from empty fulminations

**WHOLESALE DECAPITATION OF CONQUERED GERMAN CHIEFTAINS**
As compared with the work of the Trajanic sculptors the reliefs on the column of Marcus Aurelius are more sympathetic in their interpretation of the tragedy of war. This is due to the disposition of the philosopher emperor, who acquiesced in the brutalities of conquest only from a sense of duty. The representation of a German acting as executioner of his own defeated kinsmen recalls the fact that in the Marcomannic Wars Marcus employed an unprecedented number of German auxiliaries.
*Photo, Anderson*

I*

**A DEGENERATE PRINCE**

Lucius Commodus (A.D. 161–192) succeeded his father, Marcus Aurelius, in A.D. 180. Dissipated and lacking in intelligence, he degenerated into a capricious and merciless tyrant, incurring general hatred that led to his assassination.

*Capitoline Museum*

and furiously contested battle, the issue of which was at one time extremely doubtful, at Lugdunum (Lyons), that Severus in 197 could feel himself the undisputed master of the Roman world, though his reign dates from 193.

All the previous Caesars or Augusti— the latter title was the higher, as it had always been reserved exclusively for the emperor himself, whereas the former was habitually bestowed on an emperor designate—had been of Roman or at least Italian descent, even when of families long settled in far-away provinces. Severus was the first of many who had no pretence to Roman ancestry. He was an African who might properly be called a Moor, a race which has given birth to not a few very able soldiers. He did not regard his position as fully established till he had

to equally vain offers of compromise. Severus ignored both. As he drew near, the praetorians, inexperienced in war, realized the uses of discretion and deserted to the veteran leader of hard-bitten veterans, who was quite ready to save time and trouble by making promises which he had no intention of keeping. No resistance was offered, Didius Julianus was executed, and the Senate declared Severus emperor. The praetorians were disgraced, and the force was reorganized as a vast bodyguard, fifty thousand strong, under the emperor's direct control (193).

Pescennius was described as the best of the three candidates ; but as soldier he was no match for Severus, who elected to deal with him next, crushed him and killed him in a campaign in Asia Minor (194), and then returned to the west to dispose of the pretensions of Albinus. But to beat the better trained and hardier troops of the north was a more difficult matter ; and it was only after a heavy

**WEAKNESS MASKED AS STRENGTH**

Commodus with the attributes of Hercules, whose reincarnation he pretended to be—lion's skin, club and apples of the Hesperides. It is a tribute to Roman art that we can still recognize the weak youth (top) in the bearded man.

*Palazzo dei Conservatori, Rome ; photo, Alinari*

inspired a wholesome fear in the minds of the possibly disaffected by dooming several senators to death ; since the rude soldier chosen by soldiers as a soldier was accepted with reluctance by a body which still looked upon itself as the supreme constitutional authority. Moreover, to the man of the camp the mildness of the Antonines would have seemed an encouragement to treason.

The one lesson was enough. No more armed legions and no assassins' daggers were turned against Severus, nor did he play the tyrant. The domestic administration he left to competent and trustworthy officials, spending his own time among the armies

**VICTIMS OF VAULTING AMBITION**

This sardonyx cameo probably bears the heads of Didius Julianus, to whom the Empire was sold by auction after the murder of Pertinax, and his consort, Manlia Scantilla. On the arrival of Septimius Severus, whom the troops on the Danube had proclaimed emperor, Didius was executed, June 1, 193.

*British Museum*

on one or another frontier. Frontier policy was his chief concern, and the policy he followed was that of Hadrian.

In the years immediately before his accession he had held command on the most dangerous of all the Roman marches, the banks of the Danube, and had learnt that the Empire's need was defence, not aggression, but that the aggressively-minded barbarian must be kept in healthy awe of the Roman power. He was not far from being a barbarian himself. Grim, hard, and unscrupulous, with no touch of magnanimity, he was yet free from wanton cruelty or mere vindictiveness, and he ruled his empire as he ruled his troops. The method was effective so long as the man was there ; it was the culmination of military autocracy ; but it broke down when the man was gone, as it was bound to do unless he left in actual control an equally efficient successor.

Severus spent the last years of his life in Britain, where he completed the system of frontier fortification. The last password issued by the dying Antoninus fifty years before was ' Equanimity ' ; the last password of Severus was ' Work ' (laboremus). Each was singularly expressive of the character of him who chose it, and of the quality of his rule. By unremitting

**EMPEROR FOR THREE MONTHS**

Publius Helvius Pertinax was the first of the ' Praetorian ' emperors, raised to the throne by their legions. He incurred disfavour by his disciplinary reforms and was murdered March 28. A.D. 193, after reigning barely three months.

*British Museum*

**SEPTIMIUS SEVERUS**

Lucius Septimius Severus (A.D. 146–211) was proclaimed emperor by his legions in Pannonia in A.D. 193. He was a born soldier—of African stock—and established himself on the throne as a military autocrat. Severus died at York.

*The Louvre*

that the Senate was the sovereign body which had delegated its powers to the princeps. Severus hardly pretended to maintain the fiction, and the very eminent lawyers of his reign, Papinian and Ulpian, made a fundamental legal doctrine of the emperor's personal sovereignty. The constitutional theory of the Empire had in effect ceased to be tenable.

In our last three chapters, since the establishment of the Western Han dynasty in China and the fall of the Maurya empire in India about the beginning of the second century B.C., we have given no records of the Far East and central Asia beyond the Parthian area, owing to the scantiness of the material and the uncertainty of dates. We must now take up the tale again, in spite of its meagreness, omitting for the moment any detailed reference to China.

hard work Severus restored and increased the security and prestige of the Empire, which were being sapped in the days of Commodus. But the desire to found a dynasty led him at the last to the very blunder into which Marcus Aurelius had been drawn away by a very different motive, and the succession passed (211) to his infamous son Bassianus, better known as Caracalla.

Vespasian, the Sabine soldier, had become emperor by very much the same process as Severus, the African soldier— as the successful captain among candidates whose rival claims could be decided only by the sword. But excepting the sons who followed him as a matter of course, the succeeding emperors previous to Pertinax had owed their elevation not to the army but to the Senate, nor had any of the line departed from the formal tradition

**SEVERUS AND HIS CONSORT JULIA DOMNA**

Septimius Severus was still in private station when he married Julia Domna, daughter of Bassianus of Emesa. A beautiful and able woman, she had great influence over her husband, by whom she was the mother of Caracalla.

*From Bernoulli, ' Römische Ikonographie '*

We saw Shih Hwang Ti building the Great Wall for the defence of the new Chinese empire against the incursions of the central Asian nomad hordes, the Hsiung-nu Mongols and the semi-Iranian Yueh-chih. The latter were then pushed westward to the Oxus and appear to have established themselves precariously among Sacae and other Scythians in this region, overrunning the Graeco-Bactrian kingdoms in the second century B.C. From them or from their princes emerges, somewhere in the first century A.D., the Kushan dominion, monarchy, or empire, which begins with Kadphises I, provisionally dated circa A.D. 40. For the last two centuries India had had no recoverable history. Kadphises, pushing down from Bactria through the Hindu Kush, apparently made himself master of Afghanistan and the Punjab. We find his son, Kadphises II, extending his dominions and at war with China under the Eastern Hans. The great figure of the dynasty is Kanishka, whose date, on which all the other dates turn, is much disputed ; but (probably in the second quarter of the second century A.D.) his sovereignty, with Peshawar or Kabul as its centre, was acknowledged over the north-west of India, Kashmir, Afghanistan and Chinese Turkistan. Remembering always that the dates are provisional and uncertain, it is presumed that the dynasty and the dominion came to an end somewhere about A.D. 220, when the Han dynasty ended in China and Parthia was passing from the outworn Arsacids to the vigorously aggressive sway of the Persian Sassanids. Of the rest of India we know little more than that powerful independent kingdoms had by this time grown up, notably the Kshaharata 'satraps' in the West (Gujarat), and the Andhras in the farther south.

**DIMINISHED GLORY OF THE ARCH OF SEPTIMIUS SEVERUS**
The Arch of Severus was dedicated in A.D. 213 in memory of his victories in the Parthian campaign in A.D. 198–202 On the face towards the Forum, shown in detail above, are representations of Severus haranguing his troops, a defeat of the Parthians and a capture of a town by the Romans
*Above, from Reinach, ' Répertoire des reliefs romains '*

# TABLE OF DATES FOR CHAPTER 12

A.D.

**212** Caracalla murders Geta ; becomes sole emperor.
Decree extending Roman citizenship to all free subjects of the Empire.

**213** Execution of Papinian for refusing to defend the murder of Geta.
Caracalla leaves Rome. His whole reign, which is passed in the provinces, is an orgy of bloodshed. Excessive privileges and indiscipline of the army.

**217** Caracalla assassinated in Syria by agents of the prefect Macrinus, who assumes the purple.

**218** Macrinus defeated and killed by the troops of Bassianus (Elagabalus), the thirteen-year-old priest of the Syrian sun god at Emesa, a great nephew of Severus. Elagabalus emperor.

**220** *India:* Break up of the Kushan empire.

**222** Elagabalus murdered. Alexander Severus emperor.
*China:* End of Han dynasty. Three Kingdoms, to 265.

**223** Ulpian, minister till his murder in 228.

**226** *Persia:* The Sassanid Artaxerxes (Ardashir) overthrows the Arsacid dynasty of Parthia and founds the new Persian Empire.

**233-4** Artaxerxes challenges the Roman Empire. Doubtful successes of Alexander ; services of Chosroes, Arsacid king of Armenia.

**235** Alexander murdered while campaigning on the Danube. The mutineers make the Thracian Maximinus emperor.

**237** The Gordians in Africa revolt against the usurper. They are slain, but the Senate proclaims Maximus and Balbinus.

**238** Maximinus killed at Aquileia by mutineers.
Maximus and Balbinus killed by the soldiery, who proclaim the boy Gordian.

**239** The prefect Misitheus rules in Gordian's name.

**240** *Persia:* Sapor I succeeds Artaxerxes.

**243** Sapor invades Syria. Syrian campaign of Gordian and Misitheus. Death of Misitheus.

**244** Gordian assassinated. The prefect Philip ' the Arabian ' usurps the purple.

**248** Celebration of the thousandth year from the traditional foundation of Rome in 753 B.C.
Appearance of Goths on the lower Danube.

**249** Revolt of Decius. Philip killed at Verona.
Decius emperor. He inaugurates reformation in morals and religion, revives the censorship, and persecutes the Christians.

**250** Decius campaigns against Goths on the Danube.

**251** Decius killed in great defeat at Forum Trebonii. Peace made with the Goths by the new emperor Gallus (appointed by the Senate).

**253** Aemilianus in Illyria defeats Goths ; revolts and kills Gallus, but is crushed by Valerian.
Valerian emperor ; associating his son Gallienus.

**256-258** Successes of Gallienus and Postumus against Alemanni and Franks on Gallic border.

**258** *Persia:* Sapor subjugates Armenia, expelling the infant Tiridates.

**259** Goths on Black Sea overrun Asia Minor. Destruction of the temple of Diana at Ephesus.

**260** Goths capture Cyzicus and raid Aegean coasts.
Sapor invades Mesopotamia. Persian War.
Defeat and capture of Valerian by Sapor at Edessa. Gallienus sole emperor.
Sapor surprises and sacks Antioch, but his attack on Syria is checked by Odenathus of Palmyra.

**261-268** Decree of Gallienus excluding senators from military service. During this period, some score of local commanders assume the purple—they are known as the Thirty Tyrants—but are crushed, except in Gaul. Gallienus, however, recognizes Odenathus at Palmyra as associate Augustus in the East.

**265** *China:* End of the Three Kingdoms ; union under the Western Ts'in (Chin) dynasty.

**266** Assassination of Odenathus ; who is succeeded by his widow Zenobia.

**268** Gallienus killed in quelling a revolt.
Claudius II emperor. For two centuries the emperors with few exceptions are of Illyrian stock.

**269** Gothic war. Great victory of Claudius at Naissus.

**270** Claudius dies of plague. Aurelian emperor.
Treaty establishing Goths as allies in Dacia.

A.D.

**271** War with Alemanni who break into Italy.

**272** Aurelian repulses the Alemanni, and surrounds Rome with a new military wall.
Suppression of Tetricus, the Gallic ' Augustus.'

**273** Capture of Zenobia and fall of Palmyra.

**274** *Persia:* Death of Sapor ; acc. of Varanes (Bahram) I.
Aurelian prepares a Persian expedition.

**275** Aurelian assassinated. No emperor for eight months. The Senate then appoints Marcus Claudius Tacitus.

**276** Tacitus dies on Persian campaign. His brother Florian usurps the purple, but is put down by Probus, who is formally accepted as emperor. Persian campaign abandoned.

**277-281** Probus conducts a series of successful transRhine campaigns.

**279** Suppression of unwilling revolt of Saturninus.

**282** Probus murdered in a mutiny. Carus emperor.

**283** Persian campaign of Carus. He is killed by lightning in trans-Tigris. Roman retreat.
Carinus in West, Numerianus in East, sons of Carus, respectively proclaimed emperor.

**284** Death of Numerian ; military election of Diocletian, who marches against Carinus ; on the assassination of Carinus, Diocletian emperor.

**285** Diocletian associates Maximian, as Augustus for the West. The centre of the supreme imperial authority shifts from Italy to the East. In Italy Milan displaces Rome as headquarters.

**286** Carausius dominates the Channel.

**287** Carausius recognized as Britannic Augustus.

**290** Tiridates recovers the Armenian crown.

**292** Quadruple partition of the Empire ; Diocletian Augustus in the East (capital Nicaea), with Galerius Caesar on the Danube (cap. Sirmium) ; Maximian Augustus at Milan, with Constantius Chlorus Caesar at Trèves.

**293** Carausius assassinated by usurper Allectus.

**296** Constantius recovers Britain ; fall of Allectus.

**297** Narses of Persia recovers Armenia. Persian War.

**298** Defeat and victories of Galerius.

**299** Forty years' peace with Persia. Tiridates restored in Armenia.

**303** Edict for suppression of Christianity, which Constantius declines to enforce. The last or Diocletian persecution.

**305** Diocletian abdicates : also Maximian.
Galerius and Constantius, Augusti ; Maximin (Daza) and Flavius Severus, Caesars.

**306** Death of Constantius. His son Constantine becomes Caesar, Severus becomes Western Augustus.

**307** Revolt of Maxentius and Maximian, who are both proclaimed Augusti ; death of Severus. They also proclaim Constantine Augustus.

**308** Galerius relinquishes invasion of the West, but makes Licinius Caesar on the Danube and concedes title of Augustus to Maximin. Maximian is deposed but continues intrigues.

**310** *Persia:* Birth and accession of Sapor II Postumus.

**311** Fall of Maximian and death of Galerius. Licinius becomes fourth Augustus. Intrigues of Maxentius and Maximin.

**312** Constantine invades Italy ; tradition of his Vision. Maxentius crushed and killed at battle of the Milvian Bridge.

**313** Constantine comes to terms with Licinius, who crushes Maximin. Two Augusti only.
Constantine issues the Milan Edict of Toleration.

**314** Constantine arbitrates at Council of Arles.

**314-322** Campaigns on and across the Danube ; and reorganization of the West.

**317** *China:* Eastern Ts'in dynasty.

**320** *India:* Rise of Gupta empire under Chandragupta II.

**323** Final duel between Constantine and Licinius as Pagan champion. Licinius crushed. Constantine sole emperor, with no rival.

**324** Edict of Toleration throughout the Empire.

**325** General Council of the Church at Nicaea, under Constantine's presidency ; Arianism condemned.

**326** Athanasius Patriarch of Alexandria.
Dedication of Constantinople which takes the place of Rome as the centre of the Empire, still called Roman.

**330** *India:* Accession of Samudragupta.

262

### CHAPTER 12

# THE EMPIRE IN DECLINE:
## A.D. 211—330

THE expansion of the Roman Empire had practically ceased with Julius Caesar, save that the annexation of Britain, which he had postponed in order to give his attention to other more immediately important considerations, had been carried out a hundred years after his death by Claudius and the Flavians. Augustus and Tiberius, after experimental campaigns, had realized that Germany— the Trans-Rhine and Trans-Danube—was not to be subjugated. Trajan had yielded to the temptation of conquest, and succeeded in organizing a precarious colonisation of Dacia, but had failed to make good in his adventure across the Tigris. In that region, the Parthian power was indeed in decay, but was on the point of being resuscitated under a Persian dynasty.

To hold the Rhine-Danube-Euphrates frontier imposed a tremendous strain on the military resources of the Empire; beyond that frontier the imperial armies might wage victorious campaigns, but to follow up victories by attempting permanent occupation would have involved an enormous increase in the permanent military establishment for garrisoning the annexed territory. And now the movements among the migratory barbarians were making the problem of maintaining the existing frontier increasingly difficult. After Severus, the Empire is fighting not so much to roll back the barbarian tide as to hold its own against the rising flood.

### Oriental Menace to the State

DURING a period covering some three centuries, Europe west of the Adriatic and the Rhine had become so thoroughly Latinised that its peoples have never lost their Latinity, though preserving their several racial characteristics. Greece, on the other hand, had remained essentially Greek, Asia and Africa essentially Oriental though tempered with Hellenism, while the great belt along the south bank of the Danube from Illyria to the Black Sea had never been either Latinised or Hellenised; and the Latinising of Britain had been superficial. Beyond the border of the Roman Empire in the East, the exotic Hellenism planted by the Macedonians had altogether died out. Across the Euphrates and the Arabian desert, all was unequivocally Oriental. Could Rome prevent her eastern empire from being reabsorbed by its native Orientalism ?

Beyond the Rhine-Danube border lay the New Peoples, tribes bred to arms : Germans, Dacians, ' Scythians ' ; behind them Scandinavians, ' northmen.' Would the Latinised or the Hellenised Empire be able to escape submersion ? The Empire had on its side the supreme advantage of a vast organization, under a single central control—if that control were adequate— and of a sense of unity despite its diversity.

### Universal Citizenship decreed

THE diversity was sufficiently marked when an emperor, who was himself an African with a Syrian wife, died at York in Celtic Britain in A.D. 211, having been raised to the purple eighteen years before by the legions and cohorts serving in Illyria and on the Danube, in defiance of the only legions whose recruiting ground was in Italy, the Praetorians. The succession to Septimius Severus was shared at first by the two degenerate sons who were serving with the army in Britain, Bassianus, known always by his nickname Caracalla, and Geta. The theoretical unity at least was formally emphasised by the first public act of Caracalla, the extension of Roman citizenship in A.D. 212 to all freemen in the Empire.

Caracalla at one swoop did away with the surviving distinction between provincials and citizens. Conceivably, however, when citizenship ceased to be a privilege it also lost some of its sentimental value to those who enjoyed it.

Severus had restored the military power and prestige of the Empire, which had suffered grievously under Commodus ; ruling as an autocrat with hardly veiled disregard of constitutional forms, he had more than maintained the authority of the principate. The succession of his sons was undisputed, but neither meant to share the power with his brother for long. The two young men made no pretence of concealing their mutual hostility which their mother, Julia Domna, the long and deservedly trusted consort of Severus, did her best to allay. Yet she could not even save Geta from being murdered in her very arms by Caracalla, who claimed that he had been forced to slay his brother in self-defence.

The assassin's bestial savagery was at once displayed. The prefect Papinian, to whose wisdom Severus had for the most part left the civil administration, refused to provide an official defence of the murder, and paid the penalty for the refusal with his life. A host of Geta's real or suspected partisans were put to death by Caracalla's order. The decree of universal citizenship was issued doubtless as a bid for popularity in the provinces, whither Caracalla, now sole emperor, soon betook himself lest the capital should be too hot to hold him ; leaving a fellow-countryman, Macrinus, in the office formerly held by Papinian.

In the provinces Caracalla continued his career of savagery, shifting from place to place. At Alexandria, having suffered some insult to his dignity, he had some thousands of the population massacred. These things were endured because he bought the good will of the soldiery by relaxation of discipline and lavish donations and increase of pay, both at the expense of the civil population as well as of military efficiency. The terror was ended in 217, the sixth year of his reign, because the prefect Macrinus discovered that his own life was threatened, and suborned an assassin to do away with the tyrant, who was then in Syria, before the blow should fall. Yet the death of Caracalla only plunged the Empire a fraction deeper into the abyss of degradation.

Macrinus, whose guilt was at first unsuspected, procured his own elevation to the imperial dignity, since there was no obvious rival. But he was no soldier, and lacked both the abilities and the character to maintain the position at which his ambition had snatched. When a rival was produced his fate was sealed. There were no descendants of Severus, but there were surviving his wife's sister Maesa, her two daughters Soaemias and Mamaea, and their two young sons Bassianus and Alexander.

**CARACALLA AND GETA, DEGENERATE SONS OF SEPTIMIUS SEVERUS**

Caracalla (left), to give Bassianus his historic nickname, and Geta, his younger brother, were with their father, Septimius Severus, in Britain when he died at York in A.D. 211, and they immediately returned to Rome as joint heirs to the purple. Almost immediately Caracalla, then only twenty-three years of age, murdered Geta, actually in the arms of his mother, Julia Domna (right), and so embarked on a six years' reign of terror that was terminated by his own assassination.

*Berlin Museum (left) and The Louvre*

## PRESENTATION OF CARACALLA TO THE SENATE

With the blood of his brother Geta still wet upon his hands, Caracalla appeared before the Senate to demand and receive their recognition of his assumption of the imperial purple and power. Ratification by the Senate of the appointment of each new emperor was a matter of constitutional procedure, but it became purely formal and was not even invited when Carus was proclaimed. The outstanding event of Caracalla's reign was his extension of Roman citizenship to all freemen in the Empire.

*Palazzo Sacchetti ; courtesy of Dr. Thomas Ashby*

These Syrian women were ambitious. The elder of the boys had been made high-priest of the Syrian sun god Elagabalus at Emesa. To win over the soldiery, his mother and grandmother did not scruple to spread the story that Caracalla was his father. The actual responsibility of Macrinus for the death of Caracalla was becoming known, and the soldiery were full of suspicions that he intended to curtail the privileges and the licence they had enjoyed under Caracalla. The bulk of the troops in Syria were incited to rise in the name of Caracalla's son ; Macrinus was overthrown in a battle some miles from Antioch, and the young high priest of Elagabalus became Augustus Caesar (218), the Senate in Rome assenting as a matter of course. History knows him by the name of his sun god, often twisted into the form of Heliogabalus. He dated his reign, actually of nearly four years, from the death of Caracalla (217–222).

The reign was one vast orgy of the most extravagant and monstrous luxury and unspeakable vices ; the only redeeming feature in it was the comparative absence of sheer blood-lust. In Rome the obscene rites of Oriental deities superseded those of the western pantheon. After making every allowance for the exaggerations of shocked moralists and the inventive capacity of gloating prurience, what remains leaves the figure of Elagabalus the most contemptibly nauseating in the history of civilization. The one mitigating circumstance is the emperor's youth ; for when at last the exasperated Praetorians slew him and flung his dead body into the Tiber, he cannot have been more than one-and-twenty.

Such a career as his was doomed from the first to be brief. Maesa, no doubt, very soon realized that if her hopes were to be fulfilled it must be through her second grandson, whose upbringing was very different ; for Alexander's mother, Mamaea, was a shrewd and able as well as an ambitious woman. The younger boy was of an amiable nature, intelligent and free from the inordinate sensuality of the elder ; and virtuous influences were brought to bear on his training. He was, so to speak, everything that Elagabalus was not, though it may be doubted whether he had real strength of character.

welcomed a prince who was, at any rate, mild and virtuous. If he was young and inexperienced, there were plenty of men who had been trained to administration under Septimius Severus and Papinian to aid him in the task of government.

SYRIAN PRINCES, BAD AND GOOD, WHO WORE THE IMPERIAL PURPLE

Almost unimaginable moral degeneracy stigmatised Varius Avitus Bassianus, who became emperor in A.D. 218 under the name of Elagabalus. Very different both in character and by training was his first cousin, Alexander Severus (centre), son of Julia Mamaea (right), whom he adopted in 221, and by whom he was succeeded in the following year. These young men were grandsons of Julia Maesa, who had used her influence as sister of Julia Domna to secure their ultimate succession.

*Capitoline Museum, Rome ; Archaeological Museum, Florence ; and the Vatican*

Pains were taken to make him personally popular with the soldiery, who were sickened at the unmanliness of the emperor ; and it was finally their disgusted conviction that Elagabalus, in panic jealousy of his cousin, was determined to do away with him, that drove the Praetorians to invade the palace, slay Elagabalus, and proclaim Alexander Severus (A.D. 222–235) emperor, while yet in his seventeenth year.

Another nightmare had passed. The chroniclers are unanimous in their praises of the virtues displayed by the young emperor, the restoration of tranquillity, the revival of the prosperity which had suffered grievously from the merciless and capricious taxation imposed to meet the extravagances of the two last reigns. Probably the moving spirit of the government for some years was Mamaea, who exercised a supreme influence over the son she had judiciously trained and guided. The empire had suffered from a surfeit of the fruits of degeneracy, and

Alexander, in his all too brief reign, would seem to have taken Antoninus and Marcus Aurelius as his models. In the civil administration he was guided by a carefully selected council of state, in which during his first years the leading minister was Ulpian, a pupil of Papinian ; holding, like his master in the days of Severus, the curious composite office of praetorian prefect, which had in effect become a judicial rather than a military appointment. But the problem of effective control was rendered for him more difficult than it had ever been for the Antonines, through the failure of military discipline and the insubordination of the rank and file of the soldiery for which Caracalla was mainly responsible.

Alexander owed his throne, probably his life, to the Praetorians, and neither he nor they could forget it. Attempts on the part of their own protégé to curtail military licence were the more angrily resented by them, though at first they were content to attribute them to their own prefect

**FOUNDER OF A PERSIAN DYNASTY**

In 226 Ardashir, grandson of a Persian chief named Sassan, established himself upon the throne of Persia and assumed the ancient title ' King of Kings.' The Sassanid dynasty thus founded by him endured until 637.

*From Sarre, ' Die Kunst des Alten Persiens '*

Ulpian, whom, rising in mutiny, they slew in the very presence of the emperor, who strove in vain to shield him from their fury.

Alexander in person led Roman armies on at least one great campaign against the Eastern power which now again bore the Persian instead of the Parthian name. Trajan at the beginning, and Cassius Avidius in the second half, of the second century A.D. had struck heavy blows at the long formidable Arsacid power ; Severus also had conducted a vigorous campaign against the Parthians. But now the Arsacids had been swept away by a Persian chief, the founder of the Sassanid dynasty, who assumed the old Persian name Ardashir (Artaxerxes) and was bent on nothing less than the recovery of the old empire of the Great King. He deliberately .challenged Rome and bade her depart out of Asia; and Alexander took up the challenge.

The emperor returned from the campaign to render to the Senate a grandiloquent report of great victories won against immense odds. It seems clear however that the honours on the whole rested with the Persian who, though he suffered heavy defeats at the hands of the Romans and their dependent ally, Chosroes of Armenia, did not in fact lose any territory; while it would appear that the personal prestige of Ardashir was

enhanced. Alexander, hitherto untried, had no military reputation to lose, but achieved none with the soldiery ; and since they were already more than sufficiently disposed to mutiny and insubordination, the failure was fatal to the emperor.

Alexander had scarcely returned to Rome when he was summoned to the northern frontier where the pressure from the German and other barbarian hordes was never-ceasing. There he met his fate. The story is obscure. The soldiery mutinied, murdered Alexander in his tent, and proclaimed emperor the willing captain of their own choice.

The new master of the world, the elect of the fighting frontiersmen who now formed the bulk of the Roman armies, was the Thracian Maximinus (235–238), a giant whose vast strength and almost incredible powers of endurance had attracted the attention of Severus thirty years before. Such a man easily becomes a hero in the eyes of men whose highest ideal is found in sheer physical prowess. Moreover, this barbarian of mighty thews had sufficient intelligence to win and to justify his promotion, not indeed to the highest military command but to positions of responsibility. The soldiers believed

**EMPERORS DURING THE ARMY'S PLEASURE**

Brute strength was the dominant characteristic of the Thracian Maximinus, whose three years' reign was a nightmare of oppression and cruelty. It ended with his murder in 238—in which year four other emperors met a violent death—and then under Gordian III (right) the Empire had comparative quiet.

*Capitoline and National Museums, Rome; photos, Alinari and Anderson*

**PHILIP THE ARABIAN**

Marcus Julius Philippus I—his bust is a splendid portrait—was yet another who waded to the throne through blood and perished by the sword. During his reign (244–49) the millenary of the foundation of Rome was celebrated.

*Vatican ; photo, Anderson*

that they had found to lead them a soldier of their own kind, of the only kind to whose discipline they were ready to submit.

Maximinus was more than willing, but his crude intelligence was not commensurate with his highly developed muscles. For the moment, however, the sheer brute force of the man was irresistible ; the more because the murder of a prince generally esteemed (as Alexander had been) was wholly unexpected. For three years, remaining himself with the army on the Rhine or the Danube, Maximinus ruled the Empire ; which meant mainly that he avenged himself on every one whose ambition, character or abilities he feared, or by whom he conceived himself to have been slighted in the past ; while all over the Empire he robbed the cities of their public funds and stripped temples of their treasures, stamping out resistance by ruthless massacre.

The general wrath and terror came to a head in the province of Africa. The people slaughtered an imperial official charged with the business of executing an imperial robbery, and forced Gordian,

their own octogenarian prefect, in whose veins ran the blood of the Scipios, to assume the purple, very much against his own will, associating with him his scarcely less reluctant son (A.D. 237).

The Gordians made haste to report these proceedings to the Senate, submitting themselves to its decision as the constitutional authority. The Senate responded by confirming their election and declaring Maximinus a public enemy. But meanwhile the commander in Mauretania fell upon the Gordians and slew them. On receiving this alarming news the senators, who could hope for no mercy from Maximinus, elected two of their own number jointly, Balbinus and Maximus, to the principate (238) ; though forced by the city mob to associate with them as Caesar a very youthful Gordian. Maximinus, however, had to be reckoned with ; for after some delay he was now moving down from the northern frontier upon Italy, and the armies which could there be mustered had little prospect of being able to meet him successfully in the field.

Maximinus, passing the Alps, found before him a denuded country, and a strongly defended fortress in Aquileia. He sat down before it and his troops began to starve ; starving, they became mutinous, and murdered their chief in his tent. They had, of course, no alternative but to profess loyalty to the constitutional authority. The senatorial revolution was apparently complete. The joint emperors set about an honest attempt to place the government on an orderly basis and restore the discipline of the army, which very soon mutinied again, cut them in pieces, and declared the thirteen-year-old Gordian sole emperor. Five emperors—the two elder Gordians, Maximinus, Maximus and Balbinus—had all been slain within a period of twelve months (237–8).

### Millenary of Rome's Foundation

THEN there was a respite, since there was no reformer bold enough to exasperate the soldiers again. The civil administration fell at first into the hands of a group of venal intriguers, and then into the worthier control of the young emperor's tutor Misitheus, who, during his brief rule, accompanied and directed Gordian on a successful campaign across the Euphrates. But Misitheus died, and his place as praetorian prefect was taken by a soldier, Philip the Arabian ; who lost no time in supplanting and slaying Gordian, having first won the favour of the soldiery, who hailed him emperor on the banks of the Euphrates (A.D. 244).

Tradition affirms that Philip was by birth an Arabian and had been by profession a brigand before entering the military service, his rise in which marks him as a man of some capacity. Also tradition claims him as a Christian. The most notable event in his five years' tenure of power was the magnificent celebration in 248 of the thousandth anniversary (according to the accepted popular chronology) of the foundation of the City of Rome in the legendary days of Romulus. A few months later news came to Rome that the legions on the lower Danube were in revolt and had proclaimed one Marinus emperor.

### Decius' Worthy Use of Power

THE next report was that the soldiers had turned on their own nominee and murdered him ; but the position was sufficiently serious to demand the sending of an able commander, Decius—no Asiatic nor barbarian from the north, but of a famous old Roman family—to control the troops in that barbarian region. They, however, were not to be controlled ; and offered their new chief the choice between empire and present death. He chose empire, and marched with his troops upon Italy ; Philip met him with numerically superior forces near the border ; but the victory lay decisively with the war-hardened veterans of Moesia. Philip was slain either in or after the battle. The Senate made haste to ratify the election of Decius (249), who professed, perhaps with truth, to have accepted the decision of his soldiers against his will.

He would seem to have been a man of ability and character who was genuinely resolved to make a worthy use of the power which had been thrust on him. He proposed to restore the state by a revival of the old Roman virtues ; the first steps

to that end being the appointment of an honoured and distinguished senator, Valerian, to the long obsolete office of censor, and a zealous return to the pristine worship of the ancient gods of Rome ; which brought about a sharp but short persecution of the Christians, who had been undisturbed since the days of Marcus Aurelius. But action of another kind was immediately necessary. The menace on the middle and lower Danube was greater than it had ever been before.

We have been familiar with Germans under various tribal names on the Rhine and the upper Danube, since the first appearance of the Cimbri and Teutones in the time of Marius, down to the Quadi and Marcomanni who vexed the emperor Marcus. The southern group was now coming to be known collectively as the Alemanni ; those of the north were later to acquire the general title of Franks. The tribes in Dacia and on the lower Danube who challenged Trajan were of a different

**DECIUS, ROMAN EMPEROR**

Integrity of purpose as well as ability and a high courage distinguished Decius, who reluctantly accepted the purple after his defeat of his predecessor, Philip, at Verona in 249. He fell in battle against the Goths in 251.

*Capitoline Museum*

**VAINGLORIOUS VERSION OF A VICTORY**

Persian pride in the triumphs over Roman arms found expression in many reliefs on rocks and gems. This sardonyx seal depicts the Persian king Sapor I (distinguished by the grooved globes attached to his helm and shoulders) personally pulling the Roman emperor Valerian from his horse—an imaginary incident, since Valerian was trapped by treachery.

*Bibliothèque Nationale, Paris ; photo, Giraudon*

stock, Sarmatians and others, to whom Romans and Greeks applied the very indefinite name of Scythian.

But a new movement was now working among the more northern peoples who occupied both shores of the southern Baltic. The first of these to make themselves felt were the Goths, who now emerge in the place of the Sarmatians on the Danube. In 250 Decius was summoned to the Balkans by the news that a vast Gothic host, supplemented by the fighting men of various non-Gothic tribes, had swarmed over the Danube and was ravaging the Roman province of Moesia.

He found them engaged in besieging the fortress of Nicopolis. On his approach they left it to attack the much more important stronghold of Philippopolis, farther south. Decius marched in pursuit ; the Goths turned, surprised his army, put it to rout, and rolled on to Philippopolis, which fell after a stubborn resistance —since the Roman forces, demoralised by defeat, could not be hurried to its relief— yielding a great booty and many prisoners of high station. Decius, however, reorganized his army. blocked the passes, cut the Goths' communications with the Trans-Danube, and threatened them with destruction. He was bent on dealing

them nothing short of an annihilating blow and when at last he had brought them to bay he very nearly succeeded. Both sides knew that the stake was all or nothing. In the great battle of Forum Trebonii, the emperor's gallant son was slain before his eyes, but the first line of Goths was shattered, and the second. But the front of the third was covered by a bog in which the imperial legions, pushing on to complete the victory, became hopelessly entangled, so that they were cut to pieces in the endeavour to extricate themselves, the emperor perishing with the rest (A.D. 251).

The disaster was terrific, but not without precedent ; its sequel, however, was even more ominous. Decius had realized that the Goths were foes who for the safety of the Empire must be broken utterly and at all costs. Gallus, the successor chosen by the Senate—for the legions made no move—was of another mould. The defeat was of a character which by no means proved that the Goths were invincible by the Roman arms, but Gallus would take no more such risks. In return for retirement with all their booty and their prisoners, and a pledge not again to invade the Roman territory, he offered them a heavy annual subsidy. They accepted the terms with alacrity, and as a matter of course broke them as soon as it suited them to do so.

Within a few months, the Goths or their allies were pouring into Illyria. Aemilianus, commanding Pannonia, flung himself upon them and routed them. Having redeemed the honour of the Roman name, he, with the enthusiastic support of his legions, claimed the majesty so unworthily enjoyed by Gallus. He invaded Italy ; the troops of Gallus, who marched against him, deserted to the rebel ; Gallus was slain at Spoletium (A.D. 253). The Senate had barely time to ratify the title of the victor before he was in turn overthrown, four months after his victory.

Valerian, nominated three years before to the honourable office of censor by Decius, had been sent to command the armies on the Rhine. Gallus had been a constitutionally appointed emperor; Aemilianus was a usurper. Valerian marched against him; the fickle soldiery turned against Aemilianus and murdered him; and Valerian began a seven years' reign (A.D. 253–260) which brought fresh disaster. With himself he associated his son Gallienus, who reigned for eight years longer.

**SAPOR, ' KING OF KINGS '**

Sapor I succeeded his father Ardashir (Artaxerxes) on the Sassanian throne in 241 and carried on the conflict with Rome. He died in 272.

*Berlin Museum*

Valerian was already not less than sixty when public acclamation set him on the throne of the Caesars. Despite his virtues,

the event did not justify the selection. The guardianship of the German frontiers was placed in the hands of his son and colleague, together with the able soldier Postumus, who achieved what were claimed as glorious victories over the Franks and the Alemanni; but the actual fact appears to be that the north-Germans flooded across the lower Rhine into and through Gaul, even penetrating the Pyrenees; while the Alemanni were not so much curbed by the Roman arms as conciliated by Gallienus' marriage to the daughter of their most powerful prince, upon whom estates were bestowed in Pannonia.

**ABJECT SUBMISSION OF ROMAN EMPEROR TO PERSIAN KING**

Under the tombs of the Achaemenids at Naksh-i-Rustam, near Persepolis, are a number of rock carvings. Very notable is this representation of the proudest moment in the career of Sapor I, when, mounted on horseback and wearing the royal crown and armour, he received the surrender of the Roman emperor, Valerian, who knelt before him suing for grace. This event occurred in 260, and thenceforward until his death the captive emperor suffered every humiliation at his conqueror's hands.

*From Friedrich Sarre, ' Die Kunst des Alten Persien '*

While Gallienus was engaged in the West, his father Valerian was plunging into disaster in the Farther East. The great Ardashir was dead ; he had held his own and a little more against Alexander, but at too great cost to be able himself to prosecute the ambitions he bequeathed to his son Sapor, or Shapur. Sapor's aggression was the cause of the campaign on which the young emperor Gordian was engaged when Philip usurped the purple in 244. Sapor, though checked for the moment, soon gathered strength.

Chosroes of Armenia, himself one of the old Arsacid stock which Ardashir had ousted from the Parthian monarchy, had always successfully defied the Persian, and had in fact achieved the most notable victories against him in the war of Alexander Severus, as the ally of Rome. Sapor turned his arms against Armenia, having first taken the precaution of procuring the assassination of Chosroes, whose young heir, Tiridates, was unable to make head against the invader. Armenia fell an easy prey to Sapor, who captured the Roman fortresses of Carrhae—the scene of the Parthian triumph over Crassus three hundred years before—and Nisibis.

There was more than enough military employment already for the younger of the two emperors, on the German front. Valerian, old though he was, assumed the command in the East. Near Edessa his army, by the treachery of the praetorian prefect Macrianus, was led into a trap. The legions failed in a desperate attempt to cut their way out ; Valerian entering Sapor's camp to hold a conference with him was treacherously seized, and the Roman force surrendered (A.D. 260).

The tale of the insults and degradations to which his imperial captive was subjected—

**AN IGNOBLE EMPEROR**
Gallienus succeeded his father Valerian (taken captive by the Persians) in 260 and reigned until 268, when he was murdered by his troops. His profligate reign was one record of disaster.
*Museo delle Terme ; photo, Alinari*

Sapor is said to have set his foot on the kneeling Valerian's neck whenever he mounted his horse—is doubtless more or less mythical, but certainly the old man did not long survive. The conqueror swept devastatingly over Syria, gathering spoils and captives, but without thought of setting up an organized dominion ; only from Palmyra, on the border of the Syrian desert, came horsemen under their gallant leader Odenathus, who evaded battle, cut Sapor's communications and harassed his retreat over the Euphrates.

Gallienus, the unworthy son of an estimable though far from great father, was now sole emperor, save for the fact that an unfailing crop of claimants to the title was raised up in the provinces, at intervals of a few months, throughout his reign ; though only nineteen of them can be counted, and most of them were tyrants only in the sense that they snatched at power by rebellion, tradition has labelled them the Thirty Tyrants. Enumeration would be superfluous. Gallienus was a tyrant rather of the Neronic type, since he regarded himself as an intellectual.

The 'Thirty' were for the most part forced into rebellion by the soldiery and removed by assassination. Only on Odenathus at Palmyra was the title of Augustus, with practically independent powers, bestowed by a grateful Senate and by Gallienus himself—a title which on his death Odenathus passed on to his admirable and famous wife Zenobia. The whole wretched picture of the period is made the more ghastly by the fact that throughout it famine and plague raged from end to end of the anarchical Empire.

The end came when a general, Aureolus, invaded Italy at the head of the legions from the Rhine. Gallienus, who, like King John, was capable of occasional outbursts of startling energy, roused himself from the round of vicious indulgence to march against him, and shut him up in desperate plight in Milan. But the cup was full; a conspiracy was formed; Gallienus was enticed from his cups and slain. With his last words he nominated as his successor the very man whom the conspirators themselves had selected, the low-born but able Illyrian soldier Claudius (268).

The choice, ratified by the Senate and accepted by the legions, was justified by the event. Claudius would make no terms with the rebel in Milan save his unconditional surrender, nor did he interfere when the Senate condemned Aureolus to death ; but he soon gained a reputation for clemency by issuing a general indemnity. His business was to save the Empire from the Goths, who had assembled a vast force computed at 320,000 men, carried on a vast fleet in the Black Sea, and were pouring into Macedon and Thrace. The great campaign against them involved heavy fighting and fierce battles ; very definitely it was the supreme skill of the emperor's dispositions that finally won the decisive victory of Naissus and earned for him the title of Gothicus. In the next year (A.D. 270) the victor died of the prevailing pestilence, but he had named as his successor the best of his officers, a man probably of his own race, and of peasant birth like himself, Aurelian.

### Aurelian crushes the Alemanni

THE defeat of the Goths was only a first step in the saving of the Empire, and even their defeat by Claudius was not final. His death gave them fresh hopes, and it needed a fresh conflict with Aurelian to bring about a conclusive treaty to which both parties loyally adhered. The Goths engaged to supply the Roman armies with a contingent, and withdrew over the Danube ; but they were allowed to settle in Dacia, while the Dacian colonists were either transplanted to new lands in Moesia

**AURELIAN, ' RESTORER OF THE WORLD '**

Lucius Domitius Aurelianus was born about 213 of Pannonian peasant stock and became one of the chief officers of Claudius, whom he succeeded in 270. An autocratic but statesmanlike ruler and a brilliant soldier, he crushed all the enemies of Rome and restored the integrity of the Empire before his assassination.
*British Museum*

or remained under Gothic dominion if they so elected ; which many of them did.

With the Goths Aurelian had effected a genuine pacification, but even while he was doing so the Alemanni were on the move again in great raiding contingents, pouring through the Raetian Alps into the plain of the Po. By a swift march up the Danube Aurelian caught the raiders as they were returning, and crushed their van on the north of the river while the rear was still on the south bank. The second body was enveloped ; but, threatened with annihilation and unable to advance, it burst through to the south again. The Germans had the advantage in mobility, and it was only after a severe campaign and at least one defeat on Italian soil that Aurelian finally crushed them on the banks of the Metaurus ; where nearly five centuries before Claudius Nero had fought and won the decisive battle of the Hannibalian war. Never in all those centuries had a foreign foe thrust so near to the heart of Italy ; and there is a real significance in the fact that Aurelian was moved to raise a new wall of defence encircling Rome.

The overthrow of the Alemanni, following the Gothic pacification, seemed to promise a long period of security on the Rhine-Danube frontier. There remained beyond the borders of the Empire the insolent Persian, still unpunished for the devastation he had wrought and the humiliation he had inflicted. But before that matter could be taken in hand there

**AURELIAN'S WALL, NEAR THE PORTA S. PAOLO**

Aurelian began his new walls to defend Rome in 271 and they were completed under Probus in 280. They were more than twelve miles in circuit, were 60 feet high externally, were built of brick-faced concrete and had massive towers at intervals of about fifteen yards. Much of the wall still exists.

*Photo, Anderson*

was still the task of reconsolidating the Empire itself, which had fallen asunder in the days of Gallienus.

One general, Postumus, had set up a practically independent dominion in Gaul ; his fourth successor, Tetricus, was now ruling in the West. In the East Zenobia, following Odenathus, not only claimed for herself the imperial title which had been legitimately bestowed on him, but was in fact recognized throughout the East and in Egypt, which owed to Palmyra their preservation from the Persians. The abilities first of Odenathus and then of Zenobia, aided by the wisdom of the philosopher Longinus, had given protection and restored no small degree of order and prosperity, without aid from the emperors recognized in the West, to whose pretensions Zenobia was by no means willing to yield. When, however, such a captain as Aurelian asserted himself, Zenobia, with all her very unusual abilities, her courage, her virtues and her beauty, could stand no chance against him. But Tetricus and Gaul took precedence.

In truth this self-styled emperor in Gaul and the West was only anxious to be relieved from a situation where he was anything but master. It would have cost him his life at the hands of the soldiery to make

submission to Aurelian ; but while making a show of defiance he was engaged in betraying the troops who were driving him on, with the result that Aurelian won a crushing victory near Châlons, and established his authority.

Then it was the turn of Zenobia. Dispatching his lieutenant Probus (afterwards emperor) to Egypt, which acknowledged Zenobia's sovereignty, Aurelian led the imperial troops against Palmyra. Zenobia and Zenobia's army offered a valiant but vain resistance. Palmyra itself was besieged. At last Zenobia's defiant courage broke down, and she was overtaken and captured in an attempted flight. Along with Tetricus the captive queen was displayed in the magnificent triumph which celebrated the victories of Aurelian and the restoration of the Empire in its completeness from the Euphrates to the Atlantic. The pride of Rome and of Aurelian being satisfied, the emperor displayed his magnanimity by receiving both the fallen monarchs into favour and endowing them liberally.

It remained to deal with Persia ; and ere long a great expedition organized to that end was well on its way when the emperor fell a victim to a vile conspiracy. He was struck down (in A.D. 275) still in the fifth year of a reign which had been a succession of triumphs, not in a rebellion, but because a few guilty persons feared detection and exemplary punishment.

### Probus' too brief Imperial Career

So well had Claudius and Aurelian restored discipline that the legions loyally awaited the Senate's dilatory choice of a new emperor. In character and capacity Tacitus, the successor eventually chosen, was no unworthy selection ; but he was an old man, and he died on a campaign in Asia for which he was physically unfitted when he had reigned six months. Notwithstanding the pretensions of Florianus, Tacitus' brother, the claim of Probus—another Illyrian—to the Empire was formally submitted to, and confirmed by, the Senate (A.D. 276).

Sapor was dead and the Persian expedition was abandoned. If the Goths were quieted, the Germans and the Vandals and other Scandinavian peoples were growing increasingly active on the Rhine and the Raetian border, to say nothing of miscellaneous 'Scythians.' Probus, a most distinguished soldier, spent the six years of his reign in vigorous and successful campaigns, carried far across the Rhine, enlisting from the barbarians themselves large bodies of auxiliary troops in the service of Rome. But no series of successes could disguise the fundamental dangers of the situation. While Caesar Augustus was constantly engaged personally on campaigns on one frontier, he could not give his personal attention to the other regions of the great Empire, where the most apparently trusty of lieutenants might prove a broken reed.

So it was now with Saturninus in the East. His legions forced him into a revolt, in which he neither expected nor desired to be successful. It collapsed before the advance of the imperial forces, as did one or two others still more futile. The trouble was that such performances were possible even when the emperor was a soldier so brilliant and a statesman so clement as Probus. Still more ominous was it that one so universally applauded by soldiers and civilians alike was slain in a sudden hare-brained mutiny which had no better excuse than a rumour that the army was to be reduced (A.D. 281). With returning sanity the mutineers gave their allegiance to the praetorian prefect Carus.

Probus had emphasised his loyalty to the constitution by his deference to the Senate. He had not, in form at least, usurped the principate ; like Valerian and Claudius, he had taken the field as a champion of the constitution against a usurper, and, when acclaimed emperor by his troops, had submitted his title, for free acceptance or rejection, to the sovereign choice of the Senate at Rome ; as emperor he had treated the senatorial authority with even exaggerated respect. But with his death, all this was at an end. The Praetorians proclaimed Carus ; even the formal acquiescence of the Senate was hardly invited ; its authority, always dependent on the

### A ROMANCE OF HISTORY AND ITS HEROINE

The Syrian city of Palmyra reached its apogee under Odenathus. After his death, however, his widow, Zenobia (above), claiming independent sovereignty, was defeated and captured by Aurelian, and Palmyra fell. Splendid ruins, including this triple-gated triumphal arch, testify to its former greatness.

*Coin from Bernoulli ; photo, F. M. Good*

**REORGANIZER OF THE EMPIRE**

Diocletian (b. 245) was proclaimed emperor by the troops in 284. A brilliant soldier and an able administrator, he virtually refounded the Roman Empire before his abdication in 305. He died in retirement at Salona in 313.

*Capitoline Museum ; photo, Anderson*

imperial recognition, flickered out and was never again revived.

Carus, though advanced in years, was an able and experienced soldier. Leaving his elder son Carinus in the West with the title of Caesar, he himself again took up the project of the Persian war. On the way eastward, marching through Illyricum, he inflicted a heavy defeat on a horde of Sarmatians, continued during the winter his advance through Thrace and Asia Minor, and in 283 conducted a triumphant campaign in Mesopotamia and even beyond the Tigris. There, being seized with sickness, his tent was struck by lightning during a terrific thunderstorm ; but whether it was the lightning or the illness or merely mortal agency that slew him, Carus perished in that storm. Though he would seem to have been not undeservedly popular, superstition elected to attribute his fate to the wrath of the gods of Persia ; and the troops compelled his second son

Numerian (on whom, as on Carinus, the title of Caesar had been bestowed) to abandon the expedition, on which he had accompanied his father.

The title of the two young Caesars to the succession as joint emperors was not disputed, though Carus was said to have intended to adopt a worthier heir in the person of Constantius, great-nephew of Claudius and governor of Dalmatia ; for Carinus had begun to display traits of character intolerable to his father. Now he gave his vicious propensities free rein and indulged in extravagances paralleled only by the worst of his predecessors.

Numerian in the East was credited with both character and ability ; but his health had broken down under the hardships of the Persian campaign. Though he accompanied his army in its withdrawal westward, he was constantly confined to a sick-bed, where he was rarely seen by anyone save Arrius Aper, the praetorian prefect, through whom passed all business, and indeed all communication with the outside world. At length the general suspicions became uncontrollable ; soldiers forced their way into his pavilion, and found not a sick man but a corpse.

That Aper, whose daughter Numerian had married, was intriguing for the succession to the dying emperor there was no manner of doubt ; whether he had deliberately compassed his son-in-law's death is another question on which the enraged soldiery, whose affections the dead prince had won, entertained no doubt. In a formal and orderly assembly of the army, the self-constituted council of the officers announced that they had chosen the captain of the bodyguard, Diocletian, to succeed and avenge Numerian. Aper was forthwith brought in chains before the new emperor who, there and then, calling the gods to witness the act of justice, slew him with his own hand.

A few months later the tyrant Carinus was slain, by the dagger of a man whose wife he had seduced. Yet another Illyrian, of birth still humbler than were Claudius or Aurelian or Probus—for the parents of Diocletian were slaves—was on the throne of the Caesars (A.D. 285). The first three in their brief reigns had served the Roman

Empire well. The fourth, who reigned for twenty-one years, might be called its second founder.

Diocletian reconstructed the imperial system. In some respects his reconstruction was adapted for meeting an existing emergency, but not for permanence, and so far it broke down when he himself resigned the helm ; but, in other respects, he was the founder of the system which enabled the Byzantine Empire to survive his death for more than eleven centuries.

Claudius, Aurelian, Probus, in the course of the last sixteen years (A.D. 268–283) had fully vindicated the majesty and might of Rome after more than half a century of repeated disasters and degradations. By their personal qualities, as soldiers mainly, they had broken the onslaughts of the barbarians on every frontier, had saved the Empire from impending disruption, and had restored discipline in the armies. What they did could only have been done by men who were primarily great soldiers with a military outlook. But they certainly had not the opportunity, and perhaps none of them had the outlook needed, to set about the political reorganization required to secure the Empire from dissolution ; this was the achievement of Diocletian, who was fortunate in having twenty years during which to effect it.

### Diocletian refounds the Empire

THIS Illyrian 'ranker,' who had been chosen deliberately by the officers of the army in the East in solemn conclave assembled, not because he was their acting chief, but on his merits, must have been a man of the most impressive and individual personality. He had risen from the humblest position with no advantages of education, simply by character and ability, and he continued to exercise a complete mastery over men by no means inclined to recognize a master. He was entirely unfettered by precedents and conventions, though he made no war upon them as such. He opened his career as emperor by publicly slaying a criminal with his own hand ; he ended it, as no man before him save Sulla had done, simply because he was tired of it. He shed the ingrained

tradition of a thousand years, and practically ignored the city of Rome, a thing that no man not of a remarkable original genius would have dreamed of doing, because his genius taught him that the centre of gravity was not in Italy, but in the East. And, from beginning to end, after the fall of Carinus, his authority was undisputed, even when he seemed to be voluntarily sharing it with others.

The most conspicuous of his acts, that which most appeals to the imagination and is most generally remembered in connexion with his name, was precisely this sharing of the imperial authority, first with one colleague who bore like himself the supreme title of Augustus, and then six years later with two more subordinate colleagues with the title of Caesar, commonly bestowed on a designated heir.

### Partition of the Empire

IN 286 he had already made up his mind that the East and the West must be under separate military command and have separate Imperators, without splitting East and West into two rival dominions. The dominion was to remain one, but under two emperors, the second of whom would never think of himself as a rival of the first, as would be only too likely if he were officially a satrap or viceroy ; he must therefore be a colleague. The man for the place was Maximianus, a mighty warrior but Diocletian's devoted admirer, and, almost inevitably, an Illyrian or Pannonian, who would certainly defer to his colleague's judgement on any doubtful question. The partition into East and West was a personal arrangement, and if one of the emperors died there could be no question of a disputed succession. Meanwhile, Maximian should have charge of the West, the senior emperor that of the East, with a general supervision of the whole.

The scheme worked well ; for the fancy names the two chose to assume, Jovius and Herculius, were expressive ; Hercules was the heroic instrument of Jove the omnipotent. The harmony was complete. It worked so well that in 292 the principle was extended. Each of the emperors took a subordinate colleague ; the Augustus would in each case be ultimately succeeded by his Caesar, who, meanwhile, was Imperator in half of his half of the Empire. For the western Caesar was chosen that Constantius whom Carus was said to have determined to appoint his own successor; for the eastern, Diocletian's able but brutal son-in-law Galerius. Maximian had Italy and Africa, Constantius had Gaul, Britain and probably Spain, Galerius the Balkans, and Diocletian Asia with Egypt. The arrangement remained in force, and continued to work well, till A.D. 305, when Diocletian himself chose to abdicate and to compel the reluctant Maximian to do the same. Then began the rivalries inevitable sooner or later under such a system.

This experiment collapsed when it had served its turn; as it was bound to do. But other features of Diocletian's system were enduring. He made Asia the pivotal centre of the Empire instead of Italy (where Maximian made Milan instead of Rome his capital), preparing the way for Constantine to plant its headquarters at Byzantium. He obliterated the fiction that the Empire was a modification of the old Republic, or indeed was anything other than an unqualified despotism. He gave the imperial court an Oriental character foreign to all tradition. The functions of the Senate, even as a deliberative body concerned with the affairs of the commonwealth, disappeared.

### Reforms in the Administrative System

THE most complete change, however, was in the development of the administrative system, severing the military and the civil functions. The first Claudius had indeed laid the foundations of a bureaucratic system which had done much towards preserving the routine of government; but it was insignificant in comparison with the network of officialdom which grew up under the new order, when civil and military functions ceased to be discharged by the same officers. The continuous uninterrupted working of the civil machinery which resulted was one of the most material forces in preserving the Empire from dissolution.

If Diocletian's partition of the Empire was in the nature of things not destined to last, it served its immediate purpose of carrying on the work of the Illyrian emperors. (We may remark, incidentally, that all Diocletian's colleagues were also of Illyrian stock.) That had been the defence of the frontier and the unification of the Empire, which was in danger of breaking up into Roman, Gallic and Syrian states. The western Augustus had hardly entered on office and signalised his authority by crushing a widespread insurrection of the downtrodden peasantry in Gaul, when Britain declared its independence; and for seven years the two Augusti found themselves compelled to recognize a third in the person of the Batavian or Belgian adventurer Carausius.

### Carausius' adventure in Britain

IT was a curious episode, not without significance. For some years the north Germans had been developing piratical fleets in the harbours and estuaries of the North Sea, whence they raided the Roman provinces of Gaul and Britain. Those fleets were successfully checked only when Maximian placed in command of a defence squadron Carausius, a daring sailor, probably of the Belgae. He held up the pirates, but was charged with appropriating the recovered booty to his own ends; whereupon, instead of meeting the charge, he crossed the Channel and was hailed with acclamation when he proclaimed himself emperor of Britain. Holding the seas he could defy invasion and threaten to raise insurrection in Gaul. For the time it was worth while for the Roman emperors to accept the accomplished fact and come to an agreement with him, acknowledging him as a partner; for Africa and Egypt demanded their active attention.

Carausius ruled with vigour and success. But by 292 Maximian had overcome the tribesmen of Mauretania and Diocletian had restored order in Egypt. They appointed the Caesars Constantius and Galerius, and resolved to remove their unwelcome colleague in the north; but they failed, because they could by no means cross the Channel. Their work was done for them, however, when Carausius was assassinated by his ambitious

**CONSTANTIUS ENTERS LONDON**

In 296 Britain was in the power of the usurper Allectus when Constantius Chlorus, father of Constantine, sent an army to crush him, and later himself took over the administration of the island. This gold medallion, the only known Roman representation of London, shows him welcomed by the genius of the city.

*Arras Museum*

but incompetent lieutenant Allectus in 293. In 296 the lieutenant of Constantius evaded the fleet of Allectus, effected a landing in Britain, and easily crushed the usurper ; a tyrant who depended not, like Carausius, on loyal subjects, but on bands of hired Frankish adventurers. No reconquest was called for ; the whole province welcomed Constantius on his arrival, and continued to prosper under his able and enlightened rule till his death in A.D. 306.

Diocletian, however, found another Persian war forced upon him. For Tiridates, the son of that Chosroes of Armenia who was the ally of Alexander Severus, had recovered the kingdom from which he had been ejected when an infant by the Persian Sapor, but was now again driven out by Narses, a descendant of Sapor. Rome could not be deaf to the appeal of her ally and protégé. In 297 Galerius was summoned from the Danube to take the field as Diocletian's lieutenant on the Euphrates. Over-rashness brought on him a heavy defeat at Carrhae, from which he barely escaped with his life. He was, however, allowed to redeem the disaster by another campaign, in which he won a

decisive victory, enabling Diocletian to dictate a treaty which the Persian could accept without humiliation, followed by a peace which endured for forty years.

It was perhaps the sense that the Christian Church was an organization apart from the state, and demanding from its members an obedience which might be inconsistent with obedience to the state, that caused Diocletian to let loose the severest persecution to which that body, for some time almost immune, had yet been subjected.

In this persecution there is no doubt that he was urged on by his half-barbarian colleagues Maximian and Galerius ; Constantius, a man of cultivation and superior birth and breeding, would have nothing to do with it in his quarter of the Empire.

The persecution was in full swing when Diocletian, at the height of his power and prestige, resigned the imperial diadem which Aurelian had been the first to

**NORTH GATE OF AUGUSTA TREVIRORUM**

Made the capital of Gaul by Diocletian, and the administrative centre of the western provinces, Augusta Trevirorum—the modern Trèves—was the favourite residence of Constantine, during whose reign this noble gateway, the Porta Nigra, was probably built. There are many other Roman relics in the city.

*Photo, E.N.A.*

assume, and retired to cultivate his garden unencumbered by cares of state (A.D. 305). Maximian, overborne by his colleague's stronger will, resigned at the same time. Galerius and Constantius automatically became Augusti, and two new Caesars took their places. Ignoring the claims of Constantine the son of Constantius, and Maxentius the son of Maximian, Diocletian, by his last public act, confirmed the selection made by Galerius of his nephew Daza, better known as Maximin, and an undistinguished adherent, Severus.

### Struggle for the Supremacy

CONSTANTIUS retained the western division, his headquarters being at Augusta Trevirorum, the modern Trèves or Trier. Galerius took the Danube and Asia Minor. Severus was sent to Milan, Maximin to the East. Constantine, who was now thirty-three and had already distinguished himself in the Eastern wars, hastened to join his father, whose health was very precarious. Fifteen months later, in 306, Constantius died at York, and Constantine was able to inform Galerius that he had been compelled by the legions to accept the succession without waiting for formal appointment. Galerius dared only to ratify his accession as the junior Caesar, while Severus became the second Augustus.

Constantine, however, was not the only person dissatisfied. Maximian was thirsting to resume the honours he had so unwillingly resigned. The Roman Senate wanted to reassert itself, and, incited no doubt by the ex-emperor, proclaimed his son Maxentius Augustus. Maximian emerged from his retirement to support his son with his own military ability and prestige. Severus, marching hot-foot from Milan, found that Rome was already lost, and fled to Ravenna, but was tricked by Maximian into surrender, and was then required to end his own life. Maximian then himself resumed the title he had resigned, and, to win from Constantine the support he could hardly afford not to give, offered him his daughter Fausta in marriage, and the title of Augustus. Constantine accepted both offers, but without committing himself too deeply.

Maximian prepared to defend Italy against the impending invasion of Galerius.

Galerius with his legions from Illyricum, came, saw, and—retreated. All Italy was against him, and could only be won by a long series of sieges, which was out of the question. Returning to the East, he handed over the command in Illyria to his countryman and friend Licinius, nominating him Augustus in the room of Severus. Thereupon Maximin demanded and extorted from him the higher title instead of that of Caesar ; so that there were now six claimants to the name of Augustus.

Then in 308 Maximian and his son quarrelled, the soldiery declared for Maxentius, and for two years Maximian, refused an asylum by Galerius but harboured by Constantine, intrigued to recover power, till his repeated treacheries drove his son-in-law to require him to die as Severus had died. In the following year (311) Galerius too died of a loathsome disease, having retained his supremacy in the East undisputed to the end. His last act, whether dictated by remorse or by superstition, was the repeal of the persecuting decree against the Christians.

### Constantine's Victory over Maxentius

OF the four surviving Augusti three had no present desire to challenge a struggle for supremacy. But when it became obvious that Maxentius was preparing to attack Constantine, the iniquities of the rule of the former in Africa and Italy warranted his rival in anticipating the blow and striking first, in the character of liberator. In 312 he swooped through the Alps, shattered two opposing armies at Turin and Verona, and finally wiped out Maxentius under the walls of Rome at the decisive battle of the Mulvian Bridge.

Tradition, resting on statements made by Constantine himself, affirms that he had seen a vision of the Cross displayed in the sky, with the inscription, 'by this standard thou shalt conquer.' Whether he saw, imagined, or invented the vision none knows nor ever shall know. The two fundamental facts remain · that Constantine made himself the champion not of the Christian creed, but of the Christian body, and that he did not become a member of the Christian body by the rite of baptism till twenty-five years had passed. He accepted and retained the official dignity of Pontifex Maximus, high priest of the immemorial religion of Rome, and he sanctioned his own deification ; but he placed Christianity in the category of religions sanctioned and no longer proscribed officially ; and once that was done the magnificent organization of the Church, a brotherhood spread over the whole Empire, ensured that it should have no rival. No other religion had that element of brotherhood.

The West hailed the victory of Constantine joyfully. To the Roman Senate he spoke comfortable words which meant nothing, and they responded by the pronouncement, which also meant nothing, that he was the supreme Augustus. Licinius had viewed the overthrow of Maxentius with entire good will, though he gave no direct assistance ; whatever the Roman Senate might be pleased to say was of no account to him ; and when in 313 Constantine issued from Milan the decree which was the charter of Christianity, Licinius published it on his own account with perfect equanimity, and with some advantage to himself in the contest now rashly forced upon him by the third (and in actual fact the senior) Augustus. Maximin, utterly crushed in a swift campaign, died by his own hand. The families of Maxentius and Maximin alike were obliterated by the two victors. After the year 313 there were only two emperors, one in the East and one in the West.

**Final Triumph of Constantine**

TEN years later there was only one emperor. As early as 314 Constantine found reason or excuse for attacking Licinius, but the forces of the rivals were so evenly matched that after one indecisive campaign, somewhat in Constantine's favour, they came to terms, fixing a boundary which left Licinius no more than a corner of Europe. For the next nine years Constantine was administering the West, completing the reorganization of the governmental machinery and of the army, and preparing for the final contest with Licinius. While Constantine was

**CONSTANTINE THE GREAT**
Constantine I began his reign in the West in 306, and by his defeat of Licinius in 323 became sole master of the Empire, when he transferred the seat of empire to Byzantium (Constantinople, dedicated in 330). He died May 22, 337.
*Conservatori, Rome ; photo, Brogi*

welding his subjects together and winning their confidence, Licinius was alienating the forces which were in the ascendant but were already in his eyes engaged on the side of his adversary. When the crash came he made it a battle between Christianity and the old paganism, of which he posed as the champion in spite of his record in 313—and the fight, though stubborn, was fought and finished in the course of the single year 323. The fallen emperor shared the fate of Maximian and Severus. Never had any man enjoyed power so vast and at the same time so utterly undisputed as Constantine during the fourteen years of life that remained to him.

In the nine years when Constantine was undisputed master in the West, but only in Europe and Africa (in which we must remember that Roman terminology did not include Egypt), besides elaborating civil administration and reforming the army, he and his son Crispus had waged victorious wars against Germans and Goths, whose aggressions had been renewed. Not less vitally important, however, was the fact that an entirely new relation was established or inaugurated between the monarchy and the hitherto

K

officially unrecognized or actually proscribed Christian Church. The state had not concerned itself with creeds except where they led or were supposed to lead to anti-social or politically seditious activities ; though it had required occasional conformity to ceremonial observances which had acquired a political significance, making exception only in favour of the Jews. The ground on which it had chosen Christianity for repression was precisely that the Church was a morally dangerous organization claiming for itself an authority higher than that of the state.

Constantius had realized that there were no more law-abiding subjects than the Christians ; Constantine had discovered that the support of the Church was politically valuable. The result was a sort of informal concordat, the Church cementing its association with an emperor who was almost persuaded to be a Christian by appealing to him as arbiter on certain pressing questions of Church discipline on which it was divided ; with the further effect that on the one hand what had been a purely religious brotherhood acquired a great and increasing political influence, while on the other the state invested itself with powers of ecclesiastical legislation.

### Official Recognition of Christianity

THE seal was placed on the new order when in A.D. 324 Constantine confirmed and extended the edict of Milan by a final edict of toleration, and in the following year presided over the General Council of the Church at Nicaea, which repudiated though it could not crush the Arian doctrine—henceforth condemned as ' heresy '—concerning the Mystery of the Holy Trinity which continued to divide the Christian world for centuries to come.

Constantine reigned for twelve more years, till his death in 337, giving completeness to the system of which Diocletian had laid the foundations ; but A.D. 330 has been taken as the terminal year of this Chronicle, as the moment when Rome yielded place to Constantinople as capital of the Empire, which remained in being for eleven centuries more. Rome indeed had

lost her primacy when Diocletian took up his own headquarters in the East, at Nicomedia. Constantine recognized the essential fact. But in his final struggle with Licinius he had learnt the enormous strategical value of Byzantium on the strait separating Asia from Europe ; its commercial value was already conspicuous, though it was only one of the minor cities of the Empire.

He resolved to make it the Imperial City ; for five years he planned and builded ; he gave it his own name, the City of Constantine. In 330 the work was completed, with a lavish magnificence, and from that time, though lip-service continued to be rendered to the dignity of the city on the Tiber, the city on the Bosporus was in fact the New Rome.

### The East : Gupta Dynasty in India

BRIEFLY we must turn to the obscure annals of the farther East. Our materials provide us with no more than a note. In India the Scythian (Turkish ?) dominion of Kushan is presumed to have broken up into satrapies early in the third century A.D., and it was while Constantine was reigning in the West that a new and powerful native dynasty, the Gupta, was founded in Oudh and Magadha by a second Chandragupta, whose first regnal year is dated 320.

While Alexander Severus was reigning in the West and Ardashir was transforming the Parthian into the Persian dominion, the Han dynasty in China was wiped out and the empire was divided (220–265) for the period of the ' Three Kingdoms '— North, South and West—after which it was more or less reunited under the western Chin dynasty (265–317), which in turn gave place to the eastern Chins. In central Asia the nondescript Scythian tribes of diverse races, mainly perhaps Mongol, owned no masters for long, but warred promiscuously with each other or with their neighbours to south, east, or west ; by turns acknowledging or repudiating the sovereignty of the Chinese or the Persian overlord. The great westward eruption of the Huns was to come in the fifth century.

# TABLE OF DATES FOR CHAPTER 13

# THE SUNDERING EMPIRE:
## A.D. 330—476

𝔍 N the days of Constantine the Great, one vast political organization covered every part of the civilized world that was recognized as civilized by the citizens of the Roman Empire. The Empire held its marches against the barbarians of the north and the Persians in the east ; but upon them it could make no effective counter-impression. And their pressure westward and southward increased continually because in the west and the south lay wealth for the winning, but also because from the farther north, and now from the farther east as well, they were themselves subjected to pressure by migrant hordes. For the nomads from central Asia, whom the Chinese called Hsiung-nu and the Europeans Huns, were streaming into Europe past the Caspian.

### Organization of Constantine's Empire

𝕿 HE fact which the third century had proved past dispute was that the Empire was too large for control by one man. Constantine did not share his authority as Diocletian had done ; but he retained Diocletian's quadruple partition, with a civil governor—a prefect in entire charge of justice and finance, but with no military authority—in each governorship or prefecture, directly responsible to the emperor but to no one else. The two capitals also, Rome and Constantinople, had each a separate prefect. The areas corresponded to the divisions made by Diocletian. The whole was subdivided into twelve ' dioceses,' each under a ' vicar ' or vice-prefect, immediately responsible to the prefect, and these again into one hundred and sixteen presidencies or provinces correspondingly subordinated.

Necessarily there was a host of minor, but well paid, officials, and each of the higher officials was provided with a huge secretarial staff ; the expense was enormous and bore very heavily on the taxpayers. Whether the machinery worked ill or worked well at a given time in a given place, it had at least the advantage that automatically it always remained working.

On the military side, now completely severed from the civil, the same principle was adopted. The armies in each of the four territorial divisions were under two general officers, ' magistri,' masters, of the horse and foot respectively ; under the eight generals were thirty-five ' duces,' dukes, of whom some ten enjoyed the superior title of ' comites,' companions or counts. In both services each grade had its own title of dignity, corresponding to the ' excellency,' ' most noble,' ' honourable,' and so on, of modern high officialdom. And in both the subordinate, immediately responsible to his immediate superior, was ultimately responsible to the emperor.

Nevertheless, we shall see that before thirty years had passed after the death of Constantine a reversion to the system as at first inaugurated by Diocletian was so far imposed by circumstances that the Empire was again parted into East and West, and was never effectively reunited ; and further that the Christian Church, closely associated with the state, as we have seen in page 282, by the action of Constantine, was similarly parting into Eastern or Greek and Western or Latin.

### Death and Successors of Constantine

𝕬 T the close of his long reign Constantine was summoned east by the activities of the most dangerous of all the Persian kings, Sapor II (310–381), sometimes called the Great. It would seem that he was at least contemplating a campaign when he fell ill and died at Nicomedia (Diocletian's eastern capital) in A.D. 337 at the age of sixty-four, in the fourteenth year of his reign as sole emperor, and the thirty-first since his accession as Caesar. Almost at the last he had been baptised ; nevertheless the customary divine honours were bestowed on the departed Augustus.

Constantine had destined three sons and two nephews to the succession. Two of his sons, Constans and Constantine, the youngest and the eldest, were absent. With the consent of the third, Constantius, the other members of the imperial family except two young cousins were slaughtered by the soldiery. The Empire was by agreement parted between the three sons, Constantine taking the west, Constans the centre and Constantius the east. The eldest of the three new emperors was one and twenty ; their two cousins, Gallus and Julian, nephews of the great Constantine, were in 337 aged twelve and six respectively.

### Renewed Conflict with Persia

JFROM the outset Constantius was very thoroughly occupied in coping with the activities of the Persian Sapor ; but in a short time the two other brothers were quarrelling and then actually fighting over the possession of Illyria. The elder, Constantine, was slain in an ambush near Aquileia (340), and the younger, Constans, was recognized throughout the western dominion. Ten years later his reign, too, was brought to a violent end.

Meanwhile Constantius was fighting with Sapor, a much more interesting personality than any of the sons of Constantine. Born in 310, he was already a crowned king when he first saw the light, the ceremony having been performed after his father's death during his mother's pregnancy. Following the peace of Diocletian, won by the arms of Galerius, more than thirty years had passed without actual collision between the Roman and Persian empires, though a clash was impending at the moment of the death of Constantine, when Sapor was twenty-seven. For Sapor II, like Ardashir and Sapor I, conceived that all Asia, with Egypt, belonged of right to the Persian Empire. In the long years of his minority nothing of note had befallen ; but as soon as he came to man's estate he showed vigour, smiting the Arab enemies who had taken advantage of his youth, yet dealing so temperately with their tribesmen that he was accounted a protector rather than a conqueror.

The opportunity of challenging Rome was provided by the condition of Armenia, following the death of the old king Tiridates, who had been reinstated by the peace of Diocletian. That monarch had become a Christian. His zeal for the faith did not find favour with the Armenian nobles, though the personal prestige of Tiridates kept them quiet during his lifetime ; but on his death a conspiracy ejected his youthful heir Chosroes. A persecution was set on foot ; the rebels appealed to Sapor and the Christians appealed to Constantius. The full extent of Sapor's ambitions was not yet apparent ; but he was resolved at least to recover those provinces on the Persian side of the Tigris which had been ceded to Diocletian, and the suzerainty of Armenia, so often a bone of contention between the two great powers. His forces poured into Mesopotamia.

Roman troops—troops, that is, of the imperial army in the East—marched into Armenia, and restored Chosroes to his throne, but with little advantage ; for that prince desired only to live in undisturbed luxury, purchased by submission to the energetic Sapor. Armenia was finally absorbed into the Persian Empire, though the old Arsacid dynasty remained on the throne for nearly a century more.

### Exhausting War in Mesopotamia

CHE real seat of the struggle, however, was in Mesopotamia, where the war raged for some years without any decisive result. Both sides called into action hosts of Arab horsemen, who raided and wrought havoc far and wide ; nine pitched battles were enumerated, in which, by admission of the Roman historians, the advantage generally lay with the Persians. Constantius himself was twice present ; but it is safe to assume that his officers, not he, were responsible for the military direction. A most notable feature was the stubborn defence of the main frontier fortress of Nisibis, on the capture of which Sapor three times concentrated huge forces, to be three times repulsed after sieges of from two to three months' duration. Even after the third repulse the attack would have been renewed ; but simultaneously there came an urgent call to the west upon the Roman emperor, and to the east upon the Persian ; and each could regard with relief a suspension of the exhausting hostilities in the Mesopotamian debatable land.

Nearly nine centuries previously Cyrus, the original founder of the Persian Empire, had fallen in battle with the Massagetae, the Scythians beyond the Oxus. The same name is given to the Scythian tribes whose irruption now summoned the remote heir of Cyrus to the defence of Persia on her eastern instead of her western frontier ; a part, no doubt, of that general ferment among the nomads of central Asia which was about to flagellate Europe with the scourge of the Huns.

THE West summoned Constantius, be-cause Constans was dead and a new emperor had assumed the purple. The proceedings so familiar in the history of the Roman Empire had been repeated. Constans after his brother's death conducted

himself as an irresponsible tyrant. He forfeited the loyalty which was at first given to him because he was his father's son ; what remained of it was undermined by the scheming general at his own headquarters in Gaul ; and when Magnentius was acclaimed by the legions while the emperor was away hunting, Constans could only flee for his life, to be overtaken and slain on the Spanish coast. Of the three prefectures of the Empire which had acknowledged Constans, two, the Gallic and the Italian, did not hesitate to acknowledge Magnentius (350). In the third, the Illyrian, the soldiery set up their own general, Vetranio. The two new emperors made haste to come to terms and to proffer their equal amity to the surviving son of Constantine in the East.

Constantius, opportunely relieved on the side of Persia, dealt not unskilfully with the situation. Reconciliation with his brother's murderer was out of the question ; it was no less impossible to fight Magnentius and Vetranio at once.

**SUCCESSORS OF CONSTANTINE UPON THE IMPERIAL THRONE**

All the sons of Constantine the Great by his second wife, Fausta, are featured on the three medallions on the left, Constantine II and Constantius II above, and Constans below ; on the reverse of the lower medallion the three brothers are presented together, each holding the sceptre that devolved upon him on his father's death in 337. The upper medallion on the right bears the bust of Magnentius, to whose disloyalty Constans owed his death, and below is the portrait of Valentinian I.

*British Museum and (bottom right) Bernoulli, ' Römische Ikonographie '*

While he refused to treat with Magnentius, he succeeded not merely in detaching Vetranio, but in persuading him to return to his allegiance. With the army of Illyria now at his back, he could proceed to the critical conflict with Magnentius, which was decided in the sanguinary battle of Mursa in Pannonia, where more than 50,000 of the best troops of the imperial armies were left on the field of slaughter, or drowned in the Drave river. Mursa was not the end ; Magnentius still strove to make head, but his troops gradually deserted him ; and when those that were yet left with him were on the point of delivering him

conciliatory terms, to meet him in the West. When the meeting took place, in Pannonia, short was his shrift. He died ignominiously by the sword of the executioner (354). Save Constantius himself, the only surviving male descendant of the father of Constantine the Great was Julian, the younger brother of Gallus.

Constantius remained in the West for three years more. Julian, now twenty-three, a youth of high promise but wholly without practical experience, was withdrawn from his seclusion in the east and was permitted to pursue at Athens the literary and philosophic studies to which he was devoted ; until Constantius was

GUERRILLA WARFARE WITH SCYTHIAN RAIDERS IN THE CRIMEA

Wherever they dwelt, whether as nomads or as more or less settled agriculturists, the Scythians were troublesome neighbours. This tomb painting from Kertch—the ancient Panticapaeum on the Cimmerian Bosporus—depicts a frequent incident : a Panticapaean landowner fighting a troop of Scythian raiders from the Crimean lowlands. The landowner is supported by a well-equipped little army of friends and serfs, and one of the invaders already lies with his horse dead upon the field.

*From Rostovtzeff, 'Ancient Decorative Paintings'*

to his rival, he chose rather to die by his own hand (353).

Before marching to the West, Constantius had liberated Gallus, the elder of his two young cousins, from what had practically been captivity, to assume the position of Caesar in the East. As prince of the East in the absence of Constantius, he displayed all the familiar vices of an irresponsible tyrant. The reprimands which reached him from the emperor only goaded him into reckless and unpardonable violence to the emissaries, who themselves addressed him with intolerable and calculated insolence ; he was certainly planning treason on the customary lines ; but he did not dare to resist a summons from the victorious Constantius, couched though it was in smooth and

persuaded, very much against Julian's will, to raise him to the dignity of Caesar and the sovereignty of transalpine Europe, while he himself returned to the East, where the emperor's presence was becoming necessary. The fact that the Empire was too large to be managed without viceroys was once more proving itself ; especially since Sapor, having dealt successfully with the Massagetae, was back on the borders with ambitions renewed. The barbarians, moreover, were again swarming over the upper Danube.

So Constantius occupied himself with successful campaigns in that region while his lieutenants in Asia were intriguing with Sapor ; who imagined that the time had come for him to assert his claims to the whole empire of Asia. It was impossible not to take up the challenge he issued. Nevertheless, in 359 the Persians would have swept Mesopotamia, if Sapor had not been piqued into pausing to reduce the fortress city of Amida on the upper Tigris, where his army was depleted by the stubborn valour of the besieged. Amida fell at last, and its inhabitants were duly massacred or enslaved ; but Mesopotamia was saved and Sapor's field force was withdrawn.

Meanwhile the student Julian had been proving himself a capable and valiant man of action in Gaul and on the Gallic frontier. The two boys, Gallus and his brother, had been cut off from all natural companionships and had been allowed only a very restricted liberty, but their education had by no means been neglected. On Gallus it had little enough effect ; but Julian imbibed a passion for learning and an enthusiasm for the great writers of antiquity which filled his soul with lofty ideals and with a repulsion for Christianity as it was presented to him by his Christian preceptors.

A strong man was needed in Gaul ; for in the recent civil war Magnentius had called to his aid hosts of the Franks and Alemanni, who promptly assumed the rôle not of auxiliaries but of conquerors. Despite his inexperience and his academic predilections, Julian proved himself equal to the emergency, winning battles against heavy odds with distinguished personal valour, and restoring law and order in the devastated districts ; till the reputation he was winning aroused jealousy

**JULIAN THE APOSTATE**

Owing to his declared paganism Julian (331–363) has been much misrepresented. Actually he was a moral and intellectual man and a brilliant writer. The ascription of this statue to him is supported by the coin above.

*The Louvre and British Museum*

in Constantius, whose own credit was being not at all enhanced by his operations in the East, either as soldier or as ruler. Jealousy rapidly developed into suspicion and probably into secret designs against the life of the younger man. Constantius ordered the immediate dispatch of the best of the legions of Julian to the Mesopotamian front ; and the legions responded by calling upon Julian to save the Empire by assuming the purple as Augustus.

For some time Julian held out loyally, but the soldiery would take no denial till he yielded, at last convinced that loyalty to the Empire was above loyalty to the emperor. Though he professed to demand only his own recognition as Western Augustus, Constantius naturally refused to look on him as anything but a rebel. When this was made clear to Julian and his legions there remained no alternative but civil war ; and suddenly Julian with no more than three thousand men at his back vanished into the forests and mountains of south Germany to reappear on the lower Danube. Constantius, returning from his inglorious campaign in the East to meet the attack from the West, was taken ill in Cilicia, and died (A.D. 361). There was no civil war.

Julian the Apostate reigned for no more than two years. He bears that name because he renounced the Christianity of his earlier years and proclaimed himself the champion of the ancient gods. Less than half a century had elapsed since Christianity had ceased to be a proscribed religion. Constantine had countenanced it, favoured it, all but established it as the official religion of the Empire. It had not sought to avenge the old-time persecutions by retaliation on paganism ; but in a tolerationist state it had forthwith become the religion of respectability, and was much less occupied in combating its effete opponent than with the profusion of sectarian divisions, ' heresies,' springing up within its own fold.

### Julian a conscientious Apostate

DESPITE the pronouncement of Nicaea in A.D. 325, the Arians were in higher favour with Constantine himself, and still more with Constantius, than the orthodox ; and Christians levelled their fiercest denunciations at the other Christians to whom they denied the name. The teachings of the Master were too often obscured or forgotten or set at nought in the virulent dissensions of His disciples. The fruits of Christianity were not conspicuous in the lives of the rulers, orthodox or Arian, of the Christian state.

Julian, to whom in his boyhood the conventional Christianity had not been presented in an attractive light, felt nothing but repugnance for its fundamental doctrine of the Divine Logos incarnate in a Galilean carpenter's son who suffered crucifixion at the hands of the law. His philosophical studies had taught him to graft the ethical conceptions of Stoicism upon an attractively mystic interpretation of the old mythology. His method, however, of suppressing the religion he discarded was not that of persecution in the ordinary sense. He went no further than to exclude Christian teaching and teachers from the schools ; while the paganism still fashionable in society gave no zealous support to a paganism founded on the rigid morality of Stoicism. His reformation collapsed of inanition with his death, two years after he initiated it.

When Constantius died in A.D. 361, Julian crossed over to Asia—his title was undisputed—and never returned to Europe. The close of his brief life—he was only thirty-two when he died—was occupied with the Persian war. A victorious campaign, in which he penetrated beyond the Tigris, ended in disaster. The army, advancing under the direction of rashly trusted guides whose aim was to lead it to destruction, was almost overwhelmed by the myriads of foes with which it suddenly found itself surrounded. Valour and skill broke every onslaught, but in the pursuit which followed the last repulse, Julian was wounded by a javelin, and was carried back to camp only to die (A.D. 363).

There was no surviving male scion of the imperial house, and Julian had named no successor. The army chose an old soldier, Jovian, who lived long enough to patch up an ignominious peace with Persia and withdraw the exhausted troops behind the Tigris. Six months after his accession Jovian too died. Again the choice of a successor lay with the soldiery, and lighted on a soldier of barbarian (Pannonian) stock and mean descent but proved capacity, Valentinian I (A.D 364).

### Accession of Valentinian I

BY his first act, the new emperor recognized the practical necessity for partition ; no one man could successfully hold in his own hands for long the responsibility for both East and West. Valentinian chose for himself his native West, and made his brother Valens Augustus of the East. This time the division was permanent, though the Empire still remained nominally one.

For twelve years Valentinian ruled the West with vigour and, apart from the savage mercilessness he was wont to display towards all opposition to his will, with conspicuous justice and moderation. He had been open enough in his own opposition to the pagan zeal of Julian, but for others to emulate his own example was to court death. Nevertheless, despite his own orthodoxy, he was rigid in his insistence on equal treatment for all religions and all sects, pagans, Arians and orthodox Christians. He held the Gallic

K*

frontiers with a strong hand against the swarming Franks and Alemanni whom he smote in successful campaigns beyond the Rhine, though he was never able to inflict a thoroughly crushing defeat on them. It was on a campaign against the Quadi on the upper Danube that one of those outbursts of ungovernable rage which marred his character wrought his own undoing—so men said, at least—by inducing an apoplexy which killed him.

Perhaps, however, the most significant event of Valentinian's reign is to be found in the struggle for the succession to the bishopric of Rome, the Papacy, which set Damasus in the chair of S. Peter in 366. Rival candidates were supported by rival mobs in the streets and by rival dames in Roman society in a singularly unseemly contest for the spiritual headship, in the West at least, of the now dominant faith ; and the victory of Damasus over Ursicinus was the victory not of principle nor of character, but of intrigue and partisanship and successful violence ; as it would have been no less had the vanquished been the victor. It meant that the highest office in the Church was the prize of ambition and the reward of intrigue.

On Valentinian's death, his elder son Gratian was at once recognized as his successor, though the emperor had discarded the mother in favour of a wife who bore him a son (Valentinian II), a four-year-old child whom Gratian associated with himself as emperor. Hitherto, all the Augusti had bestowed an official sanction on paganism by allowing themselves to be formally invested as its high priest, ' Pontifex Maximus '; Gratian was the first who found himself unable to reconcile acceptance of the office with the profession of Christianity. Privileges had been bestowed on the Church, but without official curtailment of the current privileges attaching to what had been the state religion. The time had come when those privileges began to be withdrawn, though as yet there was no departure from the official principle of toleration. In consequence polite paganism grew restive, while the Church was becoming increasingly intolerant towards paganism.

THE reign of Valens in the East was as conspicuously feeble as that of his brother in the West was strong. In the great theological question which divided the Church, he made himself the tool rather than the partisan of the Arian party, while the defects in his character reflected those of Valentinian, as his virtues unhappily did not. The gravest mistake Valentinian made was in his appointment of the emperor of the East. The worst faults of Valens, however, were feebleness and indecision, not brutality ; and to these it was due that Sapor in his old age was able to recover a complete if detested mastery over Armenia. The great disaster of the reign of Valens did not befall till after the death of Valentinian.

ILL-FATED MEMBERS OF THE HOUSE OF VALENTINIAN

Valens (left) was appointed emperor of the East by his brother Valentinian I immediately upon the latter's accession in 364. A weak man and a feeble ruler, he was responsible for the admission of the Goths into the countries south of the Danube and lost his life in the war with them which forthwith ensued. Gratian (centre) and Valentinian II (right), sons of Valentinian I, divided the Western Empire after their father's death in 375. Both brothers came to a violent and untimely end.

*British Museum and (right) Bernoulli, Römische Ikonographie'*

**THEODOSIUS THE GREAT**

Nominated emperor of the East in 379, Theodosius dealt effectually with the Gothic menace and showed considerable diplomatic as well as military ability. His reign is memorable for the complete triumph of Christianity.

*S. Sepolero, Barletta ; photo, Alinari*

About the middle of the century the widespread Gothic confederation had been extending and consolidating its sway between the Baltic in the north and the Danube and the Black Sea in the south, under the leadership of Hermanaric the Amal, whom all their tribes recognized as king. But during the same period a new and formidable foe was pouring from Asiatic into European Scythia, the flood of the terrible Huns. Now it rolled down on the Goths. Officially at least the Goths were now the friends and allies of Rome. Reeling under the shock, the Visigoths sought the aid of Valens, whose succour took the form of granting them wide lands for settlement on the hither

side of the Danube barrier. Their vast swarms, only in part disarmed, were ferried across the river by hundreds of thousands, in numbers which had been utterly under-estimated ; the conditions to which they were subjected were wholly intolerable ; and the host of suppliants became forthwith a massed enemy. Valens had in effect sown the dragon's teeth, and the harvest was to reap.

War then raged in the Balkans, a war so critical that Valens called upon Gratian to come to his aid. But Gratian had hardly less serious embarrassments of his own, for the Alemanni were upon him. It was not till he had won a decisively crushing victory over them that he could report himself as on the march to effect a junction with the army of the East. But Valens would not wait. In the neighbourhood of Adrianople he flung himself upon the Goths ; and in the battle that followed his army was annihilated, he himself perished, and the triumph of the Goths was complete (A.D. 378).

### New Hope for the Empire in Theodosius

THE battle of Adrianople stopped the advance of Gratian. Tremendous though the disaster had been, Adrianople and the greater capital on the Bosporus could defy the onslaughts of the Goths, who were no experts in siege warfare ; but, for the young emperor, to march on the Goths would have been to court certain disaster both in the West and in the East. The Alemanni had been disposed of only for the moment. By his own or his counsellors' wisdom he made haste to appoint a new emperor in the East to take in hand the Gothic problem ; and his magnanimous choice fell upon Theodosius, the son of a great captain and servant of the state on whom in Gratian's first year the intrigues of traitors had brought the undeserved penalty of treason. The son, who had already had time to show capacity, had been suffered to retire into private life ; and was now raised to the purple at the age of thirty-three.

Theodosius took up his hard task with admirable skill and prudence, but no lack of courage. Hermanaric had fallen before the Gothic war began. The able successor who had led the united Goths to victory died, and with his death their unity departed. Theodosius made no ambitious attempt to retrieve the position by staking the fate of the Empire on a pitched battle. He risked no great engagements ; but while he struck minor blows against their divided forces he encouraged their internal divisions ; his diplomacy attached some of their leaders to the Empire, for which they had an almost superstitious reverence ; and in little more than four years a comparatively enduring if precarious peace was established.

Gratian meanwhile was losing the high reputation he had won. Of his courage and his private virtues there could be no question, but the appearance of high capacity may have been due to his early submission to wise direction. He abandoned the cares of state for amusements not in themselves pernicious, but undignified, which brought him into contempt with the soldiery.

Theodosius had hardly set the seal on his own reputation in 382 by his much applauded treaty with the Goths, when the army in Britain, as in the days of Carausius, renounced its allegiance to Gratian and proclaimed an emperor of its own choice, the Spaniard Maximus, who, reluctantly by his own account, accepted the dangerous honour. In 383 Maximus crossed the Channel with a great force which depleted the garrison of the island, and marched upon Lutetia (Paris), where Gratian was residing. The soldiery in Gaul refused to move. Gratian fled, but was overtaken at Lyons, where he was treacherously assassinated with or without the connivance of the British emperor.

The successful usurper had nothing to fear from the boy Valentinian II—or rather from his mother Justina—reigning at Milan. But he hastened to send an embassy to Theodosius, repudiating and condemning the murder which had been so hastily committed in his name, but justifying his own assumption of the purple and inviting the friendly alliance of the Eastern emperor. Theodosius may well have felt that the pacification he had just effected was too precarious to warrant him in plunging the Empire into a civil war, whose result would be doubtful, though justice and honour demanded the punishment of Gratian's murderer. He contented himself with recognizing the title of Maximus in the Gauls and Britain as a third Augustus, provided that the sovereignty of Valentinian in Italy, Africa and western Illyria were unquestioned ; and to those terms Maximus agreed.

But the excessive ambition of Maximus wrought his fall. Justina was unpopular because she was an Arian heretic and the West was fanatically orthodox. Maximus broke treaty and invaded Italy. Justina fled to Theodosius with Valentinian and her daughter ; the emperor fell in love with the daughter and married her. The

**THE ' SHIELD OF THEODOSIUS '**

Theodosius is depicted at the zenith of his power on this fine piece of silver plate at Madrid. He sits enthroned, with his son Arcadius upon one hand and on the other Valentinian II, whose cause he championed against Maximus in 388 and whom he restored to authority as emperor of the West.

*From 'Annales archéologiques'*

cautious policy which had at first seemed likely to prevail with him was blown to the winds, Maximus was promptly wiped out, and Valentinian was restored to the Empire of the West ; where on his mother's death he fell completely under the influence of the orthodox party (A.D. 388).

His reign was brief although he had barely emerged from boyhood. The supreme command in Gaul was conferred on the pagan Frank, Arbogast, an able captain who had stood loyal to Gratian and had taken service with Theodosius instead of with Maximus. The Frank now gave way to aspirations of his own. After a quarrel with Arbogast, Valentinian committed suicide or was murdered, and Arbogast set up in his place his own puppet, Eugenius, in 392. In 394 Theodosius disposed of the usurper, and divided the succession in East and West between his own sons Arcadius (382–408) and Honorius (384–423). The latter at once became Western emperor. and on the death of Theodosius in A.D. 395 Arcadius succeeded him at Constantinople.

**AN INGLORIOUS EMPEROR**

Flavius Honorius became emperor of the West in 394 when ten years old, and reigned ineffectually 29 years. This ivory diptych at Aosta, made for the consul Probus, is significant because of its early Christian interest.

*Photo. Moscioni*

For more than half a century after Constantine's official recognition of Christianity by the Milan decree, religious toleration was the guiding rule of the Empire. The pagan rites had remained by the side of the Christian rites, Arianism beside orthodoxy. That phase ended with Theodosius, who received baptism on his accession, attached himself strenuously to the orthodox party in the Church, not hitherto favoured at Constantinople, and pronounced that paganism and Christianity could not live side by side. Pagan temple revenues were sequestrated, the images of the gods and their shrines were broken up, pagan rites were sternly prohibited, Arianism was proscribed both in the East and in the West. Paganism yielded a reluctant conformity without challenging martyrdom ; but Arianism had taken too strong a hold, especially among the Gothic and other barbarian converts, to be altogether suppressed, and continued for some time to be a political force. The destruction of Arbogast and Eugenius was probably facilitated by the fact that they constituted themselves the champions of the moribund cause of paganism.

The young heirs of the powerful Theodosius were feeble and incompetent. From the death of Theodosius to the disappearance of the Western Empire, mighty figures stalked across a tragic stage, but they were those not of Roman or Byzantine emperors but of barbarians : Vandal, Visigoth, Ostrogoth, Frank ; or Hun, more terrible than all the rest. For the dykes had burst, the Western Empire was falling asunder, and the East was barely holding its own.

Theodosius had named as the guardian of his sons and chief of the armies of the West a soldier of approved ability and worth, the Vandal Stilicho. He discharged his office with more loyalty than Arbogast the Frank. Virtually the rule of the West was in his hands. While he was engaged in crushing the dangerous independence of a Moorish prince and tyrant, Gildo, in Africa, the misrule of the prefect Rufinus at Constantinople brought on a great rebellion of the Visigoths—that branch of the Gothic race which Theodosius had settled in Moesia and Illyria, the Ostrogoths remaining beyond the Danube—led by Alaric the Balt (of the family, that is, which among the Goths stood second to the Amals, who were Ostrogoths).

The Goths overran Greece practically unchecked, and wrought much destruction, till the appearance of Stilicho, his work in Africa accomplished, stayed their conquering career. Alaric was in danger of being enveloped, but escaped with great skill; and in fact frightened the court at Constantinople into buying him off by appointing him to the command in Illyria as an imperial officer.

The Goth accepted the position, but as a stepping-stone. Italy was the objective on which he had fixed his ambitions; the very miscellaneous and for the most part barbarian troops now at his disposal were ready to follow him; and in A.D. 403 Honorius and Italy were terrified by an apparently wholly unexpected invasion. The genius of Stilicho, who with amazing energy gathered together troops from every possible quarter, saved the situation. In the duel between the two great captains Alaric met with a heavy defeat at Pollentia, and the caution of the Gothic chiefs compelled him for the time to abandon the contest. The withdrawal of Alaric only left the way open for a fresh flood of mixed barbarians—worshippers for the most part, as the Goths had been before they elected to call themselves Christians, of Odin and Thor —to pour into Italy in 406, under their chief

Radagaisus. They swept over the plain of the Po, over the Apennines into Tuscany on their way to wipe out Rome; but while they delayed to besiege Florence, Stilicho again gathered troops in the north, spread them round the besieging hosts, cut off the supplies of the barbarians and reduced them by sheer starvation. Radagaisus with a third of his forces was compelled to capitulate; he himself was slain; the rest of the miscellaneous horde, Vandals, Sueves, Burgundians, Ostrogoths, Huns, Alans, were deliberately allowed to retreat unmolested across the Alps, and their various bands were soon spoiling and looting in Gaul on their way to Spain—doubtless with reinforcements from their respective homelands (A.D. 406).

Thus, it was only Italy that was quit of the invaders, who in 407 were harrying Gaul; and the harrying of Gaul was the warrant for the army in Britain to proclaim its own Augustus. Constantine III, probably a native Briton, was raised to the purple and betook himself to Gaul to save it from the Germans and add it to his own empire; taking with him not the whole imperial garrison, but a very substantial part of it. The Vandals, Sueves and Alans, however, did not seek to remain permanently in Gaul to dispute possession with Constantine, but took their devastating way through the south and the west to Spain; where they established themselves. On the middle Rhine the Burgundians appear to have remained in effective possession. Constantine pushed on to Spain, established his dominion in Aragon, and succeeded in extorting from Honorius his own recognition as a third Augustus.

**FLAVIUS STILICHO**

Stilicho (c. 359–408) saved the Western Empire by his military abilities and under Honorius was its virtual ruler. He fell a victim to intrigue and was put to death at Ravenna.

*From a diptych at Monza*

His movement to Gaul in 407 is commonly referred to as the Roman evacuation of Britain.

What of Stilicho meanwhile ? His ambitions evidently centred in the relations between the Eastern and Western Empires, in both of which he sought to be the power behind the throne, as he already was in the West ; the key to this position was the possession of the whole of Illyria, and he meant Alaric to be his agent. The Eastern court had no inclination to be dominated by him, and the relations between Byzantium and Ravenna (where for greater security Honorius had fixed his residence) were strained. He could not afford wholly to neglect the rebellion of Constantine, but left him to Alaric, with whom he had made his own bargain, and Alaric only made so much show of action as he considered sufficient.

Early in 408 Arcadius died, leaving the diadem to the six-years-old Theodosius II. Men believed on all hands that Stilicho, who had married the feeble Honorius to his own daughter, meant to make himself emperor. His enemies formed a plot and gained ascendancy over the mind of Honorius ; in the height of his apparent power he was suddenly arrested, condemned without trial as a brigand and an enemy of the ' republic,' and executed. But no evidence of any treasonable designs on his part was ever forthcoming. Among those most active in his downfall was Heraclian, who was rewarded by being made count of Africa. Of him we shall hear again.

### Sack of Rome by Alaric

STILICHO's fall opened the way on the one hand to friendly relations with Constantinople, and on the other to the ambitions of Alaric. It was, in fact, the expression of the simmering hostility

**GALLA PLACIDIA**

Daughter of Theodosius I, Placidia by her second marriage to Constantius became the mother of Valentinian III, during whose minority she was regent of the Western Empire.

*Bibliothèque Nationale ; photo, Giraudon*

of Italy towards men of barbarian blood, and it was followed by the massacre of many of the foreigners in the country, which gave the Gothic king more than adequate warrant for swooping on Italy before the year was out.

Alaric marched straight on Rome, ignoring Honorius at Ravenna. The city was rapidly reduced to starvation, and plague broke out. He demanded all the treasure within it and all the barbarian slaves. ' But what will you leave us ? ' asked the envoys. ' Your lives,' he answered. He was, however, persuaded to some contemptuous abatement of the terms, to which the unhappy Honorius had to send his sanction. But in the next year the emperor's evasions irritated the Goth into setting up the prefect Attalus as puppet emperor. Honorius, however, was made safe in Ravenna by the arrival of forces from the East ; Attalus declined to be altogether a puppet, and was deposed ; further negotiations with Honorius broke down ; Alaric lost patience, and on August 24, A.D. 410, he loosed his Goths and other followers on Rome, which suffered a three days' sack.

He did not, however, make himself emperor. He ravaged southward, and was planning an invasion of Africa, the granary of Italy, when at the end of the year he died. The Goths accepted as their king his brother-in-law, Athaulf. For another year they remained in Italy, though of their doings during that time we have no record. Clearly, however, Athaulf abandoned the design of invading Africa, perhaps because of naval difficulties ; he had not made up his mind to turn the Roman into a Gothic empire ; and in 412 the Visigoths crossed the Alps into Gaul.

While Athaulf was still lingering in Italy, the empire of Constantine III was collapsing. It extended, we have remarked, from Britain to Aragon. It broke down, partly owing to the revolt of one of his officers in Spain, Gerontius, and partly because, in 411, the place once held by Stilicho was to some extent filled by another able soldier, Constantius. Gerontius was besieging Constantine at Arles, when Constantius intervened on the hypothesis that both were rebels. Gerontius retreated to Spain, where he was murdered ; Constantius captured Arles, and with it Constantine, who was executed.

No sooner had Constantius returned to Italy, which Athaulf was evacuating, than a new emperor, Jovinus, was proclaimed in Gaul. Athaulf and Jovinus might make

common cause, or more probably fall to fighting each other, especially as the Burgundians on the Rhine were supporting Jovinus ; and then arose a new complication. Heraclian, the count of Africa, proclaimed himself emperor early in 413, and having already collected a great fleet sailed for Italy. Heraclian's rebellion proved an utter fiasco ; he was taken and executed by midsummer ; but meanwhile it had not been possible for Constantius and Honorius to take direct action in Gaul. Instead, they had bargained with Athaulf, who crushed Jovinus.

Now a hitherto unexploited figure of romance comes upon our stage—the princess Galla Placidia, sister of the very

unromantic Honorius. When Alaric sacked Rome, the princess was one of the captives he carried off and kept for bargaining purposes. She left at the imperial court a devoted admirer whose passion she did not return, in the person of Constantius. Honorius wanted her back ; so did Constantius. It was part of their bargain with Athaulf that she should be sent back, and also that they should supply his troops with corn ; but unfortunately Heraclian's rebellion cut off the corn supply. Consequently Athaulf, instead of returning the princess, married her himself in 414 ; apparently with her own willing consent, but without that of her brother. There can be no doubt that her shrewd wits and (in a perfectly legitimate manner) her personal attractions exercised on the Gothic chiefs an exceedingly valuable influence.

The marriage did not draw Athaulf closer to the imperial court ; and, not obtaining from it what he wanted, he carried his Goths and his bride into Spain. There he was murdered (415), and his successor Wallia bargained to make war on the

MAUSOLEUM OF A ROMANTIC EMPRESS

Carried off captive by Alaric and married—not unwillingly—to the Gothic king Athaulf, Galla Placidia later became the wife of Constantius, and was virtually empress after his death. She died about 450 and was buried in this mausoleum at Ravenna, brilliant with splendid mosaics.

*Photos, Alinari*

other barbarians in Spain. Placidia was at last sent back to Ravenna, where she reluctantly accepted the hand of the faithful Constantius. The Vandals, Alans and Sueves in Spain hastened to seek peace with the Empire, which they obtained ; and Wallia with his Visigoths were settled in Aquitania instead, as ' federates.' This meant that they occupied most of the soil upon condition of

embarrassing affection for her, and retreated with her small children to Constantinople. Honorius, after a reign of twenty-nine years, during which nothing whatever is recorded to his credit, died at the age of forty (423). On the hypothesis of hereditary succession, the obvious heir was Placidia's child Valentinian ; but a usurper named John, a rival of no particular merit, had to be suppressed before Placidia could effectively take up the regency in 425.

**CHRISTIANITY AND PAGANISM BLENT**

The silver toilet casket of Projecta, member of a noble fourth-century family at Rome, illustrates the tolerant Christianity of the period. Projecta appears on the side in an architectural setting between pillars ; the inscription contains the monogram of Christ ; and Venus sports with Nereids on the lid.

*British Museum*

military service to the Empire, under their own king. A similar settlement was made with the Burgundians on the Rhine. In 417 Wallia was succeeded by Theodoric I, probably a grandson of Alaric.

The position in Britain at this time is by no means clear. Constantine had not left the island denuded of troops but only depleted. The Roman magistrates and the Roman government did not disappear, but they had to make the best they could of the situation out of their own resources ; and the situation was difficult, as the raids of the unsubdued Picts and Scots on the north, Irish Celts on the west coast and Saxon rovers on the east and south coasts increased in intensity and frequency with the increasing weakness of the garrison and the neglect of the Roman channel fleet. But many years were still to pass before the raiders established a permanent footing.

In 421 Constantius was associated with Honorius as Western emperor, but died after a few months. Placidia quarrelled with her brother, who had developed an

The leading figure in the West, however, for nearly thirty years to come was Aetius (395–454), a native of Moesia but of Italian descent. He had Gothic connexions, his wife being of a noble Gothic house, and Hun connexions because he had passed a long time as a hostage among the Huns. When John the usurper was overthrown, Aetius had been engaged in bringing a Hun force to his aid, but on John's fall made his peace with the reluctant Placidia, and was entrusted with Gaul, where he checked the expansive disposition of the Burgundian Gunther in the east and the Goth Theodoric in the west and south, as well as of the Salian Franks on the Scheldt.

ᴮUT the most notable movement during Placidia's regency was that of the Vandal-Alan group which had taken possession of southern Spain—whence its modern name Andalusia. In 428 Boniface the, count of Africa had broken with the imperial government, and invited the help of the Vandals in his own ambitious projects. Africa offered a more promising field than Spain ; the Vandals in a body, led by their crafty and able king Geiseric, crossed to Africa and proceeded to ravage Mauretania in a merciless fashion.

This was not what Boniface had intended. He returned to his allegiance, but when he fought the Vandals he was so heavily defeated that he threw up the contest and retired to Italy, where his rivalry with Aetius brought about an armed conflict in which he was killed (432), while all Africa—the province, not the continent—was at the mercy of Geiseric. The position in Gaul was too critical to permit a reconquest of Africa ; but Geiseric was quite ready to make peace (435) on terms which left him practically master of Mauretania and part of Numidia.

In his conflict with Boniface, Aetius was in actual rebellion ; but his rival's fall restored his ascendancy, which became a virtual supremacy when Placidia had to surrender the regency on the marriage of Valentinian, at eighteen, to his cousin Licinia Eudoxia at Constantinople (437).

The treaty had no sooner been made with the Vandals than Aetius found himself forced to curb first the Burgundians and then the Visigoths. The former he broke by calling in aid from the Huns, with whose king Rugila he had always been on the most friendly terms ; but the remnant were resettled in Savoy. The Visigoths, who aimed at establishing themselves on the Mediterranean seaboard, were pushed back into Aquitania ; but Aetius could not spare the energy or the forces simultaneously to hold in check the continued aggressions of the Vandals in Africa. Gaul kept him very thoroughly occupied.

### Vandals Established in Carthage

GEISERIC, then, a man of commanding personality, established over his own people so powerful a sway that, alone among the Teutonic communities, the Vandal kingdom became an absolute hereditary monarchy, in which the king's unfettered will was law. He was the tyrant of the Vandals, because he made the Vandals tyrants over the subject populations. In spite of the treaty of 435, he extended his African dominion till he won Carthage. Then, satisfied of the weakness of Italy, he collected a fleet and, as a preliminary, attacked Sicily.

The menace brought the Eastern Empire to the rescue of the West, and he was held up by the arrival of a Byzantine fleet on the scene. His own resources were obviously limited—the numbers of the whole Vandal nation in Africa are given as no more than 80,000—and Theodosius II

wanted not war but peace, being threatened by the Huns ; so Geiseric was persuaded to withdraw for the time, retaining possession of Carthage. But the ancient Carthaginian menace to the Empire was again in being, with the Vandal substituted for the Phoenician (442).

### The Huns and the Eastern Empire

NOW, however, the storm was gathering in a fresh quarter. We saw the Gothic movement accentuated at the close of the fourth century by the Hun inundation. The Visigoths had placed the Danube between themselves and the Asiatic torrent, but the Huns had brought under their own sway the trans-Danube Ostrogoths, Sarmatians and other barbarians ; they had occupied Hungary, and they had extorted blackmail, an annual subsidy or tribute from Constantinople, as the price of peace. Their forces were united under the khan Rugila, who had been the friend of Aetius ; and Hun troops appear generally as allies or auxiliaries of the imperial armies, as for instance against the Burgundians, till some time after the death of Rugila (c. 434). Rugila was succeeded by two nephews, one of whom does not concern us. The other nephew was Attila, the self-styled Scourge of God.

The dominion of which the Huns were lords extended eastwards indefinitely, and Attila's first years were probably given to consolidating his power in that direction ; but in 441 he opened his attack on the Eastern Empire, to which we have been making only incidental references since noticing the accession of Arcadius in 395.

The East, in fact, had not been subjected to the need of constant struggles with the barbarians. Persia had ceased from aggression westwards, having always the Scythian menace on her eastern frontier, and Arcadius had not been long on the throne before Alaric and the Visigoths transferred their attentions from the Balkan to the Italian peninsula. The independent Arab tribes, now beginning to be known as Saracens, might worry Romans and Persians alternately, having their own retreat secured by the wastes of the Arabian desert, but they constituted

### PULCHERIA AND MARCIAN

Pulcheria, daughter of Arcadius, was born A.D.
399. In 414 she became guardian of Theodosius,
was declared empress, and was virtual ruler until
his death in 450. She then married Marcian,
reigning with him until she died in 453.

*British Museum*

a menace to neither of the great powers.
The Hun advance was engaged with the
subjugation of trans-Danube barbarians,
and eased instead of increasing the Gothic
pressure after the Visigoths had passed
within the borders of the Empire.

No pretenders arose to challenge the
legitimate monarchy at Constantinople.
Stilicho's policy made constant friction
between Constantinople and Ravenna ; but
that phase passed when both Arcadius and
Stilicho died in 408. And the general
administrative machinery worked almost
automatically. Some friction recurred
between East and West, but without
serious consequences, and for the most
part friendly relations were preserved.

Theodosius II, succeeding when a child
of seven, reigned but did very little ruling
—that was left to more competent hands
—for forty-two years, till his death in 450,
in tranquil respectability ; and the Empire
enjoyed a placid prosperity instead of
breaking up as might well have been
anticipated. Able and judicious ministers
were in charge from the outset ; practically
the place of Theodosius was presently
taken by his rather older and much abler
sister Pulcheria, under whose pious regime
the court almost became a nunnery, while
the emperor devoted himself mainly to
literary, theological and scientific pur-
suits. The coming strife between the civil
and the ecclesiastical authorities was fore-
shadowed by the strife between the
patriarch Cyril and the semi-pagan prefect
Orestes at Alexandria, from which Cyril
emerged victorious in spite of his responsibility for one of the most inexcusable

crimes of which religious fanaticism has
been guilty, the murder of the famous
and blameless but pagan Hypatia.

On the death of Honorius, it was to
Theodosius that the child Valentinian III
owed the Western throne ; it was the
daughter of Theodosius whom he married
in 437 ; and we have seen how the intervention of Theodosius prevailed on
Geiseric to withdraw from Sicily in 441,
at the moment of Attila's threatening
approach to the Danube.

The popular impression concerning
Attila and his Huns is somewhat misleading, the more so because the connected
terms Mongol and Mongolian are confused
and confusing, since the peoples who fall
under the general, linguistic rather than
ethnic, appellation of Mongolians include
very distinct types, among whom the
Mongols proper are one. The Huns were
Mongols proper, pastoral tribes of central
Asia ; who had been propelled westward
in a great and comparatively rapid
migratory movement. The Alans whom
we have met in Europe were Mongolians
in the inclusive sense, but not Mongols.
So were the Avars, Magyars, Bulgars and
Turks, whom we shall meet hereafter.
But after the disappearance of the Huns,
Europe is untouched by the Mongols
proper till the thirteenth century.

### Attila's boundless Ambition

ATTILA intended to be universal emperor,
overlord of all other rulers ; and the
first step was to make the emperor at
Constantinople submit to his lordship.
The pretext was that Hun deserters were
harboured in the Empire, in breach of the
existing treaty. In 441 and 442 he overran a great part of the Balkan peninsula,
capturing cities and devastating ; but he
did not attempt Constantinople, which
was virtually impregnable. In 443 Theodosius came to terms ; his subsidy or
tribute was to be doubled, and a great belt
of territory on the south of the Danube
was to be left a waste, a no-man's-land,
between the two empires. From Attila's
point of view, Theodosius had acknowledged himself his tributary. The Hun
was still dissatisfied, however, and again
overran the peninsula in 447 ; but he

contented himself with a confirmation of the treaty in 449, and, like Alaric, turned his attention to the West.

In 450 Theodosius II died. The most notable achievements of his reign had been the issue of a great codification of the laws, known as the Theodosian code, and the establishment of a university at Athens. He had named as his successor an able officer, Marcian, with whom Pulcheria consented to go through the form of marriage in order to bring him into the imperial family circle. His brief and prosperous reign—he died early in 457—was distinguished by very judicious financial reforms, and by his repudiation of the Hun tribute ; which would undoubtedly have brought Attila down on him but for the lure of the West.

A curious episode had perhaps determined Attila's course. The court at Ravenna proposed to marry Valentinian's sister Honoria to a safe and distinguished but elderly husband ; she objected, and sent secretly to the mighty Hun, inviting him to rescue her. Attila accepted the message as a betrothal, and claimed his bride with half of her brother's empire for dowry (450). Valentinian raged and rejected the demand ; and Attila marched on Gaul. He told Ravenna that he was coming to save the Romans from the Goths and the Goths that he was coming to take their part against the Romans ; but the diplomacy of Aetius, exercised through his lieutenant Avitus, and the intelligence of Theodoric, sufficed to combine Romans and Visigoths against the Hun as being in fact their common enemy.

### Defeat of Attila at Châlons

ATTILA swept, devastating, over the Gallic frontier, with Orléans (the city of Aurelian) as his objective. Theodoric, aroused to the peril, effected a junction with Aetius ; Attila began to retreat, turned to bay near Châlons, and suffered a crushing defeat, while Theodoric himself was killed. His son hastened home to secure the succession, and Aetius, following the example so often set by Stilicho, allowed Attila to retire over the border. The power of Attila was not in fact wrecked by the battle, though it was a heavy check to him, and Gaul was delivered from his devastations.

Châlons (451) had been won by the temporary concert of the imperial government with the Visigoths. Even in the next year Attila threw himself on Italy to enforce his demand for Honoria's hand. Aetius could not risk a pitched battle ; so that Attila destroyed Aquileia and marched on Rome. Tradition says that he was overawed by the Pope Leo ; another story says that plague broke out in his camp ; at any rate he did withdraw without attacking the city or being himself attacked, and certainly with no intention of resigning his claims. But in 453 he died or was murdered, and the whole terrifying if flimsy fabric of his empire dissolved. The Huns were helpless without a head : Ostrogoths, Gepids, Rugians, Herulians, rose and overwhelmed them at the battle of the Nedao in Pannonia (454) ; and the Huns are heard of no more as a power to be reckoned with. The service they had rendered to the Empire in Rugila's day, in checking the Teutons, outweighed the devastations wrought by Attila.

### Extinction of the House of Theodosius

AETIUS, the 'last of the Romans,' met with the same reward as Stilicho the Vandal. The mind of the emperor was poisoned against him by the wealthy and ambitious Maximus and the chamberlain Heraclius. Valentinian charged the unsuspecting man with treason at the council table, and slew him with his own hand, but the great general was soon afterwards avenged by two of his servants, who slew Valentinian and the chamberlain (455). Two years later Marcian, the emperor of the East, died, and neither in East nor West was there a son of the house of Theodosius to succeed, nor any successor nominated by the deceased emperor.

At Constantinople the choice was dictated by the powerful soldier and minister Aspar, an Alan by race and an Arian by creed, who nominated Leo, a Thracian. Leo reigned, not at all as the puppet of the man to whom he owed his elevation, from 457-474. He countered the Teutonising tendencies of Aspar by recruiting his armies and his ministers from his own people. He secured the succession to his son-in-law Zeno, an Isaurian, whose reign belongs to the next chapter.

The twenty years between 455 and 476 saw the establishment of the Teutonic ascendancy in the West and the disappearance of the separate Western Empire, or rather emperor. The Roman Empire, to which the West still owed allegiance, still existed, but its seat was Constantinople, and there was no Augustus of the West.

### Chaos and Disintegration in the West

WHEN Valentinian was murdered Maximus bought the crown, and forced the widowed Eudoxia to marry him. Geiseric the Vandal—summoned to her aid, as some say, by Eudoxia—arrived two months later with a fleet. The mob tore Maximus limb from limb, which did not prevent Geiseric from occupying Rome, sacking it with methodical and conscientious thoroughness, and retiring with a host of captives, including Eudoxia and her two daughters, the younger of whom he married to his son Hunseric.

A few weeks later a new emperor was proclaimed by the Goths at Tolosa (Toulouse), Avitus, the lieutenant of Aetius, who had been mainly instrumental in bringing the Goths up to the Châlons campaign. Marcian in the East and Avitus in the West both threatened Geiseric, who defied them both. Avitus put his armies under control of Ricimer, a Sueve, but also grandson of the Visigoth Wallia, and Ricimer won a naval victory over the Vandals.

Meanwhile Theodoric II, posing as imperial champion, attacked the Sueves in Spain, breaking but not destroying their power. Avitus was bound closely to the Goths, while Italy detested them, and did not want their championship; Ricimer was a Sueve. Avitus had to beat a hasty retreat from Italy; Ricimer joined in setting up the Roman Majorian, an officer of distinction, as emperor, and the deposed Avitus was consoled with a bishopric (457). Majorian before his death had bestowed on Ricimer the title of Patrician—in effect, first minister—which had been borne by Stilicho, Constantius and Aetius before him. Four years later Ricimer deposed

Majorian, and set up a puppet, Libius Severus. Majorian had declined to be puppet, but the fleet he collected against the Vandals met with disaster, a sufficient excuse for his removal. Severus died, and for a time there was no emperor save Leo at Constantinople, till in 467 Leo appointed, as Western Augustus, the Greek Anthemius, son-in-law of Marcian. Ricimer was placated by receiving the new emperor's daughter to wife. Then East and West combined to crush the Vandals, who were masters of the Mediterranean. They seemed on the point of doing so when the craft of Geiseric, aided by fortune, turned the tables on them, and it was the imperial fleet, commanded by Basiliscus, that met with overwhelming disaster (468).

The Vandal held the commerce of the Mediterranean at his mercy; when the Empire tried to attack him, the stars in their courses fought against it. The Visigoths under the ablest of their kings, Euric, were bringing southern Gaul, from the Loire to the Rhône, under their sway. Britain had slipped her cables; and Jutes and Saxons had at last fastened their grip on her eastern and south-eastern shores, though they had not yet penetrated far inland. Northern Gaul was drifting after Britain. To the east of Gaul the Burgundian kingdom was waxing so strong that the Gallo-Romans were looking to it as a counterpoise to the Goths. In Italy, half the soldiers and most of the officers, with Ricimer at the top, were Teutons; while Ricimer himself was still clinging to the theory of a dual Roman Empire and quarrelling with his father-in-law, who scorned him as a barbarian and whom he despised as a ' Greekling.'

### Deposition of the last Western Emperor

IN 472 Ricimer resolved to depose Anthemius, against whom he advanced, having proclaimed in his room Olybrius, the husband of the elder daughter of Valentinian. Anthemius was taken and put to death, but within a few weeks Ricimer died. For a time his place was taken by his Burgundian nephew Gundobad. Olybrius died, and after some delay Gundobad set up a puppet, Glycerius (473), whom Leo at Constantinople declined to recognize. Gundobad returned to Burgundy, and Leo proclaimed Julius Nepos ; while Glycerius exchanged his diadem for a mitre (474). Next year Julius was a fugitive from Rome, ejected by his master of the soldiers, Orestes, who made his own son, contemptuously known as Romulus Augustulus, emperor. At the same time Zeno, the successor of Leo, was a fugitive from Constantinople, ejected by that Basiliscus whose fleet had been annihilated by Geiseric. Both the usurpers fell in 476. In the East Zeno was restored ; but in the West the power was seized by the Scirian Odoacer. And Odoacer chose neither to be Augustus himself nor to serve another Western Augustus, but to be the viceroy of the one Roman Emperor at Constantinople.

### Events in China and India

$J$N the far East during this period China was in a state of political disintegration. A Chin or Ts'in dynasty was more or less predominant, with its capital at Nanking, when Constantine the Great was transforming Byzantium into the capital of the Roman Empire. Buddhism was in considerable favour, and some of our information about India, where that creed still survived in some strength, is derived from the Chinese Buddhist Fa-Hien (or Fa-Hsien), who paid it a prolonged visit in the first decade of the fifth century.

Before that time was reached, China (c. 384) split into two main empires, of the North and South ; the Toba dynasty reigning in the north, while in 420 the Tsins in the south were displaced by the Sungs. The dynasty founded by Toba is better known as that of the Northern Wei. Both the Sungs and the Wei had to deal with subordinate or insubordinate kings, besides occasionally fighting each other. And their monarchs died at frequent intervals, usually by violence.

In India, on the other hand, the period was one of prosperity. The ' Indo-Scythian ' Kushan monarchs still reigned at Peshawar, though their greater dominion had broken up when Chandragupta (to be distinguished from the Maurya ; see page 282) inaugurated the Gupta kingdom or empire in Magadha, about 320. A succession of powerful monarchs, each ruling for many years, gave to it a sway as wide as that of the Mauryas. Samudragupta (c. 330-375), the second of the dynasty, made himself lord of the whole Ganges basin, penetrated far into the Deccan, established relations with Ceylon and claimed that the eastern princes, even to Assam, were his tributaries. His son Chandragupta II Vikramaditya (c. 375-413) subdued the rulers of Malwa (Ujjain) and the Maratha country, who still bore the title of satraps inherited from the days when they were feudatories of the Kushans who yet ruled the Punjab from Peshawar.

It was while Chandragupta II was reigning that the Chinese Fa-Hien made his pious pilgrimage, incidentally noting the personal freedom and the prosperity enjoyed by the subjects of the great king whose name he never mentions. Kumaragupta (413-455) was the monarch in whose reign flourished the greatest, perhaps, of Indian poets, Kalidasa, the author of Sakuntala. Through Kumaragupta's rule and that of his successor, Skandagupta (455-480), the majesty of the Gupta empire continued undiminished ; for the latter drove back triumphantly the new hordes pouring into India through the north-west passes, by way of which came the similar invaders who in the next generation broke through the defences.

### Prosperity and Culture in India

$T$HE arts flourished greatly in the Gupta period. Samudragupta was poet and musician as well as warrior and statesman ; the name of Kalidasa speaks for poetry. In spite of the destruction wrought in later ages, enough of temple building and sculpture survives to show that the work of the period was of the very highest quality.

But the wreckers were coming ; for at the time when the Huns who had migrated to Europe were rising to the height of their power and falling plumb to the depths again, their kindred in central Asia were hammering the eastern borders of Persia and beginning to advance southwards. It was a Hun invasion that was stemmed by Skandagupta—not the last of the Guptas, but the last of their great emperors.

# Fourth Era

# THE BYZANTINE AGE

## 476–1073

---

---

WITH the final break-up of the Roman Empire—the 'world state' that had given a certain homogeneity to history in the West for more than half a thousand years—a period of confusion set in, of destruction and reconstruction, of the stirring of new forces. It is often known as the Dark Ages, but the obscurity is due not so much to any lack of historical material as to the difficulty of finding connecting threads amid the tangle of warring purposes. In western Europe the outstanding movements are the consolidation of the Teutonic invaders into nationalities on the wreckage of the old Roman provinces, the rise of the Papacy, the birth of the Holy Roman Empire under Charlemagne and its re-birth under Otto the Great, and the endless struggle of the two partners to the theory, temporal and spiritual; in the East the appearance of Islam and its conquering advance outweigh all other events. But there is one element of continuity that provides a double link, between past and future, between East and West, and has accordingly been chosen to name our Fourth Era: the Byzantine Empire, heir of the Roman traditions and Europe's bulwark against Islam.

# TABLE OF DATES FOR CHAPTER 14

476 End of the Western Roman Empire.
477 Restoration of Zeno; fall of Basiliscus.
  Recognition of Odoacer as patrician in Italy.
  Hunneric Vandal king; Gundobad Burgundian king.
478 War of Zeno with Ostrogoths, under King Theodoric the Amal and Theodoric Strabo; to 482.
481 Clovis (Chlodwig) the Merwing becomes king of the Salian Franks, and begins the subjugation of north and central Gaul.
482 Zeno's Henoticon; breach with Roman Church.
483 Theodoric recognized as master of the soldiers.
484 Revolt of Leontius in Syria.
486 Clovis subjects Ripuarian Franks and extirpates other branches of the Merwing family.
488 Accession of Kobad in Persia. Ten years of dynastic conflict.
489 Theodoric invades Italy to supplant Odoacer.
491 Odoacer, defeated, holds out at Ravenna.
  Anastasius succeeds Zeno (to 518).
  Landing of Aella in Sussex (trad.).
493 Odoacer capitulates and is assassinated.
  Theodoric king of Italy, nominally viceroy.
  Clovis, a pagan, marries the orthodox Christian princess, Clothilda of Burgundy.
495 Landing of Cerdic and West Saxons (trad.).
496 Franks adopt orthodox, not Arian, Christianity.
  Clovis overthrows the Alemanni.
498 Burgundian war of Clovis.
  Kobad restores monarchical power in Persia.
c. 500 *India*: White Huns invade Punjab. Break up of Gupta Empire. Starting point of Rajput clan-traditions.
502 Persian war of Anastasius.
507 Clovis in alliance with Burgundy attacks Visigoths in Aquitaine. Their king, Alaric II, killed.
508–510 Theodoric intervenes, checks Clovis, drives back Burgundy, establishes Amalric as Visigothic king in Spain and western Provence under guardianship of Theudis; places a Roman prefect (Liberius) at Arles; but leaves Clovis in possession of Aquitaine.
511 Clovis dies. Quadruple division of Frank dominion between his sons. Eastward expansion and development of Austrasian kingdom under Theuderich, to 533, and Theudebert to 548.
518 Justin I succeeds Anastasius at Constantinople. Henoticon withdrawn: reconciliation with Rome.
520 English checked in Britain at Mt. Badon.
524 Death of the philosopher Boethius.
526 Theodoric dies. Athalaric king, under guardianship of his mother Amalaswintha.
527 Accession and marriage of Justinian.
529 Justinian's Code, First Edition.
530 Persian incursions. Victory of Belisarius at Daras.
531 Amalric dies; Theudis elected king of Visigoths.
532 Nika Riots; suppressed by Belisarius.
  Peace with Persia.
  Burgundy annexed by the sons of Clovis.
533 Belisarius obliterates the Vandal kingdom.
  Justinian's Pandects (Digest) and Institutes.
534 Justinian's revised Code.
  Athalaric dies. Amalaswintha makes Theodahad king.
535 Amalaswintha murdered by Theodahad.
  Belisarius in Sicily.
536 Theodahad deposed and killed; Wittiges elected.
  Belisarius captures and holds Rome.
537 Wittiges besieges Rome; Franks invade N. Italy.
538 Wittiges buys off Franks by ceding Roman Provence.
539 Belisarius besieges Wittiges in Ravenna.
540 Fall of Ravenna. Belisarius leaves Italy.
541 Chosroes invades Syria and sacks Antioch.
  Goths led by Totila begin reconquest of Italy.
  Chosroes transfers the Persian war to Colchis.
542 General paralysis caused by the Great Plague.
544 Belisarius sent with feeble force to Italy.
545 Five years' truce with Persia.
546 Totila captures and evacuates Rome.
547 Belisarius reoccupies Rome.
548 Belisarius recalled. Totila dominates Italy.
  Theudis killed in Spain; rival Visigoth kings.
549 Landing of Ida in Northumbria (trad.).
550 Justinian's troops occupy Andalusia.
  Third Persian war.
552 Narses sent to recover Italy. Fall of Totila at battle of Taginae.
  Introduction of silk-worms from China.

553 Last stand and annihilation of the Ostrogoths.
554 Narses shatters a Frank invasion.
555 Narses rules Italy from Ravenna.
558 Chlothar (last surviving son of Clovis), king of all the Franks.
561 End of Persian war.
  Frank kingdom divided between Chlothar's four sons.
565 Deaths of Justinian and Belisarius.
  Justin II emperor.
566 Avars and Lombards on the Danube.
  Marriage of the Visigoth sisters Brunhild and Galswintha to Sigibert and Chilperic.
567 Chilperic murders Galswintha and marries Fredegonde; seventeen years of civil war.
568 The Lombards under Alboin invade Italy.
569 Birth of Mahomet.
571 Leovigild king of Visigoths till 586. He drives the Romans to the coast and practically subjugates all Spain, defeats a Frank attack, and masters the nobles.
572 Persian war renewed.
573 Lombards, masters of North Italy and of provinces in the south, are kingless till 584.
575 Death of Sigibert; ascendancy of Chilperic.
577 English reach Bristol channel. B. of Deorham.
578 Emperor Tiberius succeeds Justin II.
582 Emperor Maurice succeeds Tiberius.
584 Authari elected Lombard king.
  Chilperic killed; Guntram of Burgundy dominant.
586 Reccared king of Visigoths. He abandons Arianism for Orthodox Christianity; Arianism dies out, leading to development of ecclesiastical ascendancy, and rivalry of the churchmen and nobles.
590 Gregory the Great, pope; to 604.
  Agilulf Lombard king.
591 Accession of Chosroes II in Persia, by help of Emperor Maurice. End of Persian war.
593 Death of Guntram. Brunhild in Austrasia to 614.
595 Wars of Maurice with Avars and others on Danube.
596 Kent Christianised by mission of Augustine.
602 Mutiny and usurpation of Phocas; Maurice killed.
604 Death of Gregory the Great.
606 Chosroes II invades Syria as avenger of Maurice. Continuous expansion of Persian power.
  *India*: Rise of Empire of Kanauj under Harsha.
609 Revolt of Heraclius the elder in Africa.
610 Phocas is overthrown by the younger Heraclius, who is proclaimed emperor at Constantinople.
  Mahomet's Vision and Call as Prophet of Allah.
613 Mahomet's first converts at Mecca.
  Northumbrian English reach west coast (Chester). Wales severed from north and south Britons.
614 Chlothar II king of all the Franks. Rise of the Austrasian, Neustrian and Burgundian mayors of the palace.
  Chosroes completes conquest of Syria by taking Jerusalem and carrying off the True Cross.
616 Persian conquest of Egypt.
617 Supremacy of Northumbria and adoption of Christianity under Edwin.
620 Persians overrun Asia Minor.
621 The Eastern Empire devotes itself to a Holy War headed by Heraclius in person against Persia.
622 Mahomet and his Companions withdraw from hostile Mecca to Medina; the 'Hijra' (Hejira) dating the Year One of the Mahomedan Era.
  First Persian campaign of Heraclius, who drives a wedge between the Persian forces in Asia Minor and Syria.
623 Mahomet resolves to propagate Islam by the sword.
  First battle (Bedr) between Medina and Mecca.
623–627 Victorious campaigns of Heraclius in and beyond Mesopotamia.
623–628 Arnulf of Metz and Pepin the Old, mayor of the palace; Dagobert king, in Austrasia.
626 Persians and Avars besieging Constantinople are completely repulsed.
627 Decisive victory of Heraclius at Nineveh.
  Mahomet's letter to Heraclius.
628 Mahomet comes to terms with Mecca.
  Fall of Chosroes; end of Persian War; all Roman possessions restored.
630 Final submission of Mecca.
631 Mahomet designs the conquest of Syria.
632 Death of Mahomet. Accession of Abu Bekr as first khalif.

304

### CHAPTER 14

# EAST AND WEST IN FERMENT: 476—632

᠎N A.D. 476 ended the twelve months'
nominal reign of the last phantom
emperor of the Western Roman
Empire, when Romulus Augustulus was
deposed by the Herulian or Scirian
Odoacer, disappearing into a peaceful
obscurity. Technically, no change had
occurred in the imperial constitution;
actually, the date marks a stage in the
disintegration of a great world empire.
' Patrician ' was the official title claimed
by Odoacer as an imperial officer from the
emperor Zeno. It was not a title which
carried with it specific functions; but
practically it meant that the Augustus
who conferred it conferred with it vice-
regal powers; in the case of Odoacer, the
vice-royalty of Italy and Noricum. The
title of king which Odoacer also used was
derived not from the emperor but from
Odoacer's election to this dignity by
his miscellaneous Teutonic host.

### Zeno recognizes Odoacer's claim

᠎T the moment when Odoacer deposed
Romulus, the emperor Zeno was fighting for his crown with the usurper Basiliscus.
That revolt had been crushed when in the
following year, 477, the deputation arrived
from Rome; not to inform him of the
election of a new Augustus, but to desire
his ratification of the election of Flavius
Odoacer as his own lieutenant in the West,
a second Augustus being superfluous.
Zeno promptly acceded. He was in no
position to refuse recognition to the de
facto ruler; the West must take care of
itself; and it could at any rate do no
harm if the ruler chose to call himself the
subordinate instead of the colleague of the
Augustus at Constantinople.

In that same year, 477, died Geiseric.
He was succeeded by his son Hunneric,
who was his peer in iniquity, but not in
ability. Under him and his successors
the Vandal kingdom survived the death
of its founder for 57 years, to be obliterated as it deserved in A.D. 533.

When Basiliscus in 475 ejected Zeno and
snatched the diadem, he did it by the
aid of Teutonic mercenaries, whose commander was the Ostrogothic soldier of
fortune Theodoric, called Strabo—the
wall-eyed or one-eyed. When Zeno came
back with his Isaurians and suppressed
the futile Basiliscus in 477, Theodoric
Strabo retired with his troops into the
Balkan mountains, and invited Zeno to
make him his master of the soldiers or
take the consequences.

### The Fortunes of the Ostrogoths

᠎HE Ostrogoths have hitherto played
only a fleeting part in our story. They
had fallen under the sway of Attila. But
on Attila's death in 453 they recovered
their independence, like the rest of his
Teutonic dependents. They had come
down to the Danube, and then, on the
Visigothic precedent, they had been admitted to settle within the borders of the
Empire, en masse, in Moesia. The Visigoths had to content themselves with a
king of the house of the Balts; the Amals,
god-descended, still reigned among the
Ostrogoths; and at this critical hour their
king was the youthful but already famous
warrior, Theodoric the Amal. To him,
since a rival Ostrogothic leader could
hardly be to his taste, Zeno turned for aid
in the suppression of Theodoric Strabo.

It was a risky game. The old fox very
soon persuaded the young lion that their
business was to unite, not to fight each
other, which would be playing into the
hands of the crafty Zeno. They combined
and marched on Constantinople. But
unless the port could be blockaded, the
capital could laugh besiegers to scorn,
though they might ravage the peninsula.
Zeno tried, and failed, to detach the Amal
from Strabo, but when he reversed the
process he succeeded. Strabo went over;
but what was now the war between the
Ostrogoths and the Empire went on for
four years (479-483), with all the honours

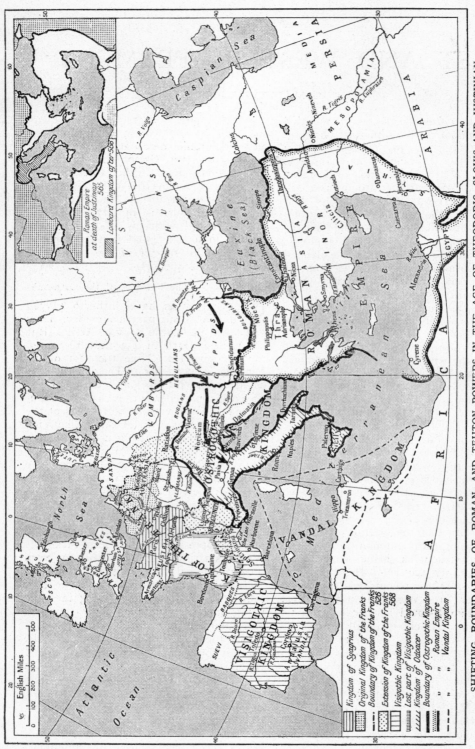

**SHIFTING BOUNDARIES OF ROMAN AND TEUTON POWERS IN THE AGE OF THEODORIC, CLOVIS AND JUSTINIAN**

The resounding exploits of the confused period covered in the present chapter were the establishment of the Ostrogothic kingdom of Theodoric the Amal in Italy (488–91); the destruction of the Vandal kingdom by Belisarius in 533; the eviction of the Ostrogoths from Italy by him and his successor Narses, with the resulting brilliant but hollow expansion of the Eastern Roman Empire; and the intermittent hostilities between the Empire and Persia. Far more important, however, though less spectacular, was the Frank advance under Clovis.

**EMPEROR ZENO AND ODOACER**

Zeno was ruling at Constantinople when Odoacer deposed Romulus Augustulus. That Odoacer regarded himself as a lieutenant of the emperor is shown by coins that he struck bearing Zeno's image (left), though others (right) bore his own.
*British Museum*

and this could only be done at the expense of the native Italians who, at least since the days of Stilicho, had resented the domination of a barbarian soldiery, and had more than once or twice, when a convenient opportunity offered, displayed their resentment by massacres.

With Gaul and Spain Odoacer did not greatly concern himself. In fact, he was content to maintain friendly relations with Euric and his successor Alaric II, the kings of the Visigoths, and Gundobad,

on the side of Theodoric the Amal. The other died, and the emperor was troubled with conspiracies and the fear of conspiracies. So Zeno and Theodoric came to terms, the Ostrogoth being made master of the soldiers, and receiving fresh grants of land for his followers.

Then came the revolt of a certain Leontius in Syria, who appealed for aid to the Persian king Balas, and to Odoacer. Before the aid which was promised could arrive, Zeno had crushed the rebellion by the help of Theodoric. But such a helper was dangerous ; the attitude of Odoacer was menacing. All might be well if the two could be embroiled.

In 488 Zeno matured his plan. Like Alaric, Theodoric was more than ready to exchange Moesia for Italy. The emperor dismissed his disloyal lieutenant in the West, and appointed the trusty king of the Ostrogoths in his place.

Odoacer had been ruling Italy for a dozen years with an unquestioned sway, when his authority was denounced by the same emperor from whom he had demanded and received it. He was a strong man and a wise man, who did what he had to do and attempted nothing beyond the reasonable range of achievement. What he had to do was to establish peace and order in Italy, where ten different emperors had been pulled down and set up in the course of twenty-one years ; and to secure the north and north-eastern Alpine frontiers, Raetia, Noricum and—as belonging to Italy—western Dalmatia. To this end he had to preserve the loyalty of the miscellaneous host which had elected him king ;

**PRUDENT RULER OF THE EAST**

This ivory diptych commemorates the consulship of Anastasius, a court official of wide experience and high character who later, on the death of Zeno without heir, was appointed his successor and ruled the Eastern Empire from 491 to 518.
*British Museum (cast)*

king of the Burgundians. Euric had already extended his effective dominion over the greater part of Spain as well as Aquitaine. Gundobad had established himself on the Saône and the upper Rhône ; and Odoacer had no compunction in ceding to Euric the seaboard of the Gulf of the Lion. A Roman, Syagrius, was still holding together central Gaul, but the northwest had gone, and the north-east was already passing under the domination of the Salian Franks, whose habitat was between the Scheldt and the Somme.

In Raetia, however, the Rugians, after the scattering of the Huns, had established themselves with aggressive designs. Against them Odoacer sent a force which shattered their power but evacuated the territory, bringing back the inhabitants—by their own desire—to be settled in less disturbed quarters on Italian soil. Odoacer wanted to recover western Dalmatia, but the ex-emperor Julius Nepos was established there by the authority of Leo I and of Zeno; it was not till Nepos was assassinated in 480 that the Patrician was able to annex it to his dominion.

### Theodoric wrests Italy from Odoacer

ODOACER had no thought of acquiescing in his deposition. In fact, when Theodoric marched against him he offered a magnificent resistance. The odds were all in favour of the younger man, who was an ideal leader, at the head of an armed nation, with a tradition of national kingship and the precedent of Alaric to urge it on. Italy, apart from the army, had no love for Odoacer, and owed allegiance not to him but to the emperor whom he was defying. His own men were for the most part loyal, but the Goths among them could only be half-hearted. Thrice his forces were beaten in the field in 489 ; yet he held out in the almost impregnable Ravenna for a year and a half after he

**THEODORIC THE OSTROGOTH**
Zeno's diplomacy turned the energies of Theodoric the Ostrogoth from the Balkans to Italy, where, crushing Odoacer, he set up a brilliant Ostrogothic kingdom (491).
*British Museum*

was finally driven behind its walls in 491. The end came when the place was starved out, and Theodoric committed the one act of treachery which stained his fame. Odoacer capitulated on the offer of generous terms, and was assassinated immediately after his surrender.

A year before the fall of Ravenna, Zeno died. During his reign the Balkan peninsula had been devastated and very largely depopulated first by the Ostrogothic war, and then by the departure of the Ostrogoths ; but it offered no very tempting bait to the Slavs and non-Aryan tribes from the region of the Volga—the Bulgarians —who were swarming down to the Danube again. When the Goths were gone, there was probably a considerable and continuous infiltration of the former, and an occasional raid by the latter, but no serious invasion for some time to come. The peace of Asia Minor and Syria had been disturbed by the insurrections of Basiliscus and Leontius, but there was no threat of a permanent disruption of the Empire in the East such as was taking place in the West.

Zeno was not a person who commands much respect, but he had some astuteness ; he had no disposition to play the tyrant ; he was cautious to the verge of pusillanimity ; and he was a lover of compromises —qualities which, if not altogether admirable, tended to tranquillity and security. But the act by which he is best remembered was a well-intentioned attempt to establish a religious compromise which was a pathetic failure. He promulgated the Henoticon, the Instrument of Union which sought to provide a common formula that could be accepted both by the Orthodox and the Monophysites, the two intensely hostile parties into which the Church in the East was now divided. The result, however, was that both parties impartially denounced the emperor and each raged against the other more furiously than before. Constantinople from top to bottom was divided between the supporters of the rival clubs (primarily the sporting ' clubs ' of the Hippodrome), the Monophysite 'greens' and the Orthodox ' blues,' who were the champions of either ecclesiastical faction.

Zeno died leaving no obvious heir, and without having appointed a successor. An eminently wise choice, mainly influenced by Zeno's widow, Ariadne, bestowed the diadem on Anastasius, an experienced official of the highest character, and

Gaul had begun his aggressive advance. Clovis is the name by which everyone knows Chlodwig (Ludwig, Lewis) the Merovingian (Merwing), the first king of France. The clans drew their chiefs or kings from the royal family of Merwings. In 481, Clovis succeeded his father Childeric in one of these kingships on the river Scheldt ; when the mighty Visigothic king Euric was at the height of his power. In 485, Euric died and was succeeded by his young son Alaric II. Euric would probably have made short work of

Clovis, who, in conjunction with his kinsmen, took the opportunity of starting on a career of aggression, being one and twenty.

The Franks fell upon Syagrius, patrician of central Gaul. The Visigoths under existing circumstances were not disposed to come to the rescue. In the next four or five years, Clovis conquered most of northern Gaul, and proceeded to consolidate his personal position by the wholesale suppression of the Merovingian kings of the other clans. The next step

universally and deservedly respected. He was already fifty-three on his accession (491) ; but he lived and reigned, to the great benefit of the empire, till 518.

Theodoric (A.D. 455–526) was thirty-eight years old when the death of Odoacer left him undisputed king of Italy—the title which he assumed—in 493. His reign of thirty-three years places him among the great rulers of men ; though most of his work perished after his death, since there was no second Theodoric to bring it to completion.

By this time the king of the Salian Franks on the northeastern frontier of what had already ceased to be Roman

REMINDERS OF THEODORIC AT RAVENNA

The most tangible relic of Theodoric's splendid reign that still exists at his capital, Ravenna, is his mausoleum (top), a rotunda with a monolithic roof weighing some 300 tons. The ruins called ' Theodoric's Palace ' (lower) were more probably an addition made by a Byzantine exarch in Lombard times.

*Photos, Alinari*

was to make himself king of the other group of Franks on the Rhine, to harry the Alemanni out of the neighbouring territory, and to make friends with the Burgundian Gundobad, whom he did not as yet wish to challenge.

Instead, he married Gundobad's niece, who, curiously, happened to be not an Arian but an orthodox Christian ; with the natural consequence that in 476 the heathen Clovis and his Franks were baptised into the orthodox Faith. All the other Christian German kings were Arians, not orthodox Christians.

By dint of embracing Catholic orthodoxy, Clovis enlisted on the side of the Franks—as against the Arian Goths and Burgundians—all the Latin populations and all the influence of the Church which looked to the pope, the bishop of Rome, as its head.

Clovis now thought himself strong enough to attack Gundobad ; but after the first surprise got soundly beaten and hastened to obtain a reconciliation. For his eyes were turning to Alaric and the Visigothic kingdom, on which, after an experimental move in 504, frustrated by the king of Italy, he opened his attack in 507, in conjunction with Gundobad.

### Theodoric's Policy of Consolidation

ℍITHERTO Theodoric had been mainly concerned with the organization and development of his Italian kingdom. He desired only friendly relations with his fellow kings, with each of whom he sought matrimonial alliance ; at a very early stage he married his two daughters to Alaric and the heir of Gundobad, and himself married the sister of Clovis ; he even gave his own sister to the Vandal king Thrasamund, Hunneric's nephew. None of these kings could attack another without risk of finding the mightiest of them all ranged on the side of his adversary. When Clovis attacked Gundobad, Theodoric would have intervened, if the Burgundian had not very soon made intervention superfluous. He had stopped Clovis in 504, and would have stopped him in 507, if he had not at the moment been engaged in a difference with Anastasius over the Illyrian boundary—a dispute

which encouraged the emperor to bestow patrician honours on the Frank. Evidently it was Theodoric's aim not only to keep the peace himself but to prevent others from breaking it.

When Clovis did attack Alaric, his excuse—in spite of his alliance with Gundobad—was the Arian Alaric's persecution of his Catholic subjects. Clovis marched on Aquitaine, Gundobad on Provence. Clovis defeated and killed Alaric ; the succession of Alaric's legitimate son Amalric—Theodoric's grandson—was disputed by an elder but illegitimate son Gesalic, who held his ground in Provence while the loyalists were driven out of Aquitaine into Spain. Clovis was master of Aquitaine— in fact, of all Gaul except the old ' Province ' in the south-east. In 508, however, Theodoric intervened, though his quarrel with Anastasius was not yet settled, routed Franks and Burgundians before Arles, suppressed Gesalic, confirmed Amalric as king of the Visigoths in Spain under his own guardianship, established a Roman prefect at Arles, and left Aquitaine to Clovis. Clovis died in 511, when the Frank inheritance was divided between his four sons ; but he had founded the French monarchy.

Theodoric reigned in Italy, and as guardian of the Visigothic kingdom, with undiminished power till his death in 526 ; this dominion including the seaboard of the Gulf of the Lion. No one ventured to attack or to challenge him, and aggression was not his business. The rest of Gaul he left to itself. As king of Italy, he was king of the Goths and other Germans, and at the same time king of the Italians. The recognition of this dualism, coupled with an unqualified even-handedness in the treatment of all his subjects, was the basis of his statesmanship ; but the dualism could not yet yield to unification.

### Internal Conditions in Italy

ⓄN his accession, Theodoric satisfied his Ostrogoths mainly if not entirely with the land vacant by the fall of so many of Odoacer's followers. The Ostrogoths and other Germans, planted on the soil, lived under their own Germanic laws ; the Italians under the Roman law adminis-

**MOST POWERFUL EMPEROR OF THE EAST**

Justinian, in whose reign the Eastern Empire was at its height, is commemorated by mosaics at Ravenna. This (an old photograph taken before recent wholesale restorations) is in the Basilica of S. Apollinare Nuovo. Another, in S. Vitale, shows Justinian with his wife Theodora.

*Photo. Alinari*

tered by Italian officials, as under the old system ; mixed tribunals adjudicated upon cases in which the parties were mixed. He allowed neither race nor creed to stand in the way of any man's advancement ; he sent the Roman Liberius to Arles, because he was the best man ; Italians as wells as Goths had places on his councils.

Theodoric was, of course, an Arian, but the Orthodox had nothing to complain of except that Arians were not repressed. He protected the unpopular Jews as sternly as the Christians ; he repudiated persecution on the ground that no man can be compelled really to believe what he is told to say he believes. His financial organization materially relieved the burden of taxation and, at the same time, filled the treasury. He was the ablest soldier of the day, but after his accession he waged no war which was not almost forced upon him. He inaugurated his reign in Italy by a crime ; at the close of his long

life he became suspicious and stained his name by acts of cruel tyranny ; but not by these aberrations must he be judged.

Theodoric was past seventy when he died. The son-in-law whom he had chosen to be his successor died before him, and his heirs—for he had no son—were his daughter, Amalaswintha, and her young son, Athalaric. The fabric of which Theodoric had laid the foundations was doomed never to be builded. His rule over the Italians, however able and just, was the rule of an alien who was also a heretic ; and the Ostrogoths were too turbulent to be ruled by any hand less firm than that of the great king now dead.

Anastasius died, an old man, after a highly creditable reign, eight years before Theodoric, in 518. His rule had been that of a sound and experienced administrator, and he had done his best to calm the theological animosities which were reproduced in the civil factions of the Eastern capital. He concerned himself with the West only when Theodoric's

**ACTRESS CONSORT OF JUSTINIAN**

The mosaic of which this forms a part is in the Basilica of S. Vitale, Ravenna, and shows Theodora, the plaything of all Constantinople, the actress and courtesan, who rose to be the empress of Justinian

*Photo. Alinari*

ONE OF THE FORTRESSES THROUGH WHICH CONSTANTINOPLE RULED AFRICA

After Belisarius had reconquered Africa from the Vandals and restored it to the Roman Empire—the Eastern Empire, that is—it was ruled by a succession of officers appointed from Constantinople. There were the Prefects of the Praefecture of Africa on the civil side, and the Magistri Militum (' masters of the soldiery ') later replaced by exarchs (591) : corrupt incompetents, many of them, whose only duty was to squeeze as much taxation as possible out of the land for Justinian's depleted treasury. This is a reconstruction of the Byzantine fortress at Haidra on the borders of the modern Tunisia and Algeria.

*From Diehl, 'L'Afrique byzantine'*

312

activities in Illyria involved him in a boundary dispute with his powerful lieutenant. Thrace and Moesia were vexed by Bulgarian raids from across the Danube, and Anastasius built a great defensive wall fifty miles long to hold the raiders in check. The Isaurian troops, who had made themselves so unpopular in the capital, were disbanded, returned home to their accustomed occupation as brigands, and were not suppressed without some difficulty.

There had been no serious collision with Persia for a century. The Sassanid kings of Persia had for some generations been losing control over the nobles ; and the tribes known as the White Huns or Ephthalites—a people quite distinct from the Huns proper—had been hammering the East and developing a very considerable power in the region of the Oxus. The Sassanid Empire was waning. But a revival of the monarchy was now taking place under Kobad (Kavad), who succeeded in 488 to the throne, on which he had not established himself securely till 499. In 502 he revived a treaty claim on the Empire for certain payments for frontier defences which had long been dropped ; and, meeting refusal, he invaded Mesopotamia. He captured Amida— Nisibis he held already—but in 505 the Ephthalites again gave trouble, the imperial arms met with some successes, and peace was restored on the pre-war basis.

THE wars of Anastasius were merely disturbing episodes, significant only as warnings of possible troubles in the future ; they neither added to nor materially detracted from the general credit of his reign. Like Theodoric, he left a well-filled treasury.

He left no heir, and the diadem was unexpectedly secured by an elderly Illyrian officer, Justin, the respectable uncle of a very remarkable nephew, Justinian, who succeeded him in 527, the year after

**VANDAL RULER OF ROMAN AFRICA**

A mosaic found at Carthage shows a horseman quitting his villa for the hunt. His features and dress are markedly different from those in the earlier African mosaics ; and it is not unjustifiable to regard him as one of the Vandalic invaders or, less probably, of the Byzantines who ousted them.

*British Museum*

Theodoric's death. Justin continued the safe policy of his predecessor. He was the first of the emperors since the extinction of the line of Theodosius who thoroughly satisfied the Catholic party ; and he would have persecuted the Arians, but for a threat from Theodoric of reprisals against the orthodox in the West. Zeno's Henoticon had caused a schism between the Eastern and Western churches, which was healed when Justin withdrew it.

Justin was an old soldier who had served in the imperial armies for some fifty years. At the end of his nine years' rule he associated with himself on the throne his nephew Justinian (A.D. 527–565), who was then between thirty-five and forty, and had been practically his colleague throughout the reign. Justinian on his accession was already thoroughly conversant with the whole system of administration. He had just scandalised society by marrying a lowly-born dancer, Theodora, whose reputation was notorious ; but her loyalty to her spouse after the marriage never wavered, nor did her influence over him wane ; and once at least it was her unfaltering courage that saved him from disaster at a dangerous crisis.

L

Justinian's permanent legacy to the world was his great codification of Roman law, which became the basis of almost all the legal systems in Europe. But this was only, from his point of view, a part of his vast scheme for raising the Roman Empire to an unprecedented height of power and magnificence; a scheme which involved an expenditure on war and on splendour, especially on building, which wrecked the financial resources of the Empire; a consummation materially advanced by the great pestilence of A.D. 542, which was as disastrous as the Black Death eight centuries later.

The vast sums expended on building by Justinian do not demand detailed attention. The trouble was that the Empire could not afford them out of normal revenue, and they had to be raised by abnormal taxation which crippled trade and industry of every kind, at the same time that a very heavy war-taxation was demanded by the revived imperialism of the emperor's policy. The contrast with Theodoric's methods in Italy is notable, for the Goth observed a wholesome ratio between public works of great economic value and expenditure which was merely impressive; while warrant was found for the latter in the fact that the burden of taxation was reduced. Theodoric left a full treasury at the end of a reign little shorter than Justinian's, who left the Empire exhausted and the treasury drained dry. Justinian's predecessors had not been men of genius, but they had succeeded in holding the Empire in the East together largely by

**BRAVE DAUGHTER OF THEODORIC**
It is almost certain that the figure on this panel of an ivory diptych is Amalaswintha, the valiant daughter of Theodoric, who attempted to continue his policy in Italy after his death.
*British Museum (cast)*

leaving the West to take care of itself as best it could, and abstaining from all schemes of aggrandisement. Justinian could scarcely perhaps have avoided his Persian wars; his suppression of the Vandal kingdom was more than justified, though in any case it could hardly have survived much longer; but his reconquest of Italy benefited neither the East nor the West.

The first Persian war was forced upon Justinian in the year following his accession, 528. It brought into prominence Belisarius (505-565), the brilliant soldier to whom the emperor was mainly indebted for the military glories of his reign. Kobad, as we saw, had revived the power of the Sassanid dynasty in Persia, and had fought a drawn battle with Anastasius. Now, after twenty years of peace, he renewed his aggression and invaded Mesopotamia. Nothing of a decisive character occurred till 530. Belisarius, the very young officer in command of the forces on the frontier, had previously only been able to stand on guard; but in that year he routed a much larger Persian force, in what resolved itself into a great cavalry engagement, by tactics which recall the battle of Marathon, where there was no cavalry, and the tactics of Hannibal at Cannae. Kobad died next year, and his son Chosroes (Khusru), as yet insecurely seated on the throne, made peace.

The Vandals in Africa, even when Geiseric's power was at its height, had never been more than an armed garrison in the midst of a wide and intensely hostile, if defenceless, country. Since

Geiseric's death their enemies had been gathering strength, though they still held their domination by sheer brute force, and the usurper, Geilamir, who seized the crown in 530, had replied with singular insolence to the protest of Justinian. There was warrant enough for drastic action.

The emperor, however, was at the moment not yet free from the Persian entanglement ; and just then the capital broke out in what is known in history as the Nika insurrection. The rebellion was utterly crushed ; the unlucky figurehead was himself beheaded with his brother ; a truce with Persia followed the death of Kobad ; and in 533 Belisarius surprised the unexpectant Vandals by landing in Africa— though his force numbered only fifteen thousand men. The Vandal force on the spot was routed before Carthage, which joyfully hailed the victor as a deliverer. Geilamir retreated to the West and gathered the forces which there had not been time to collect at first, while every city was flinging open its gates to Belisarius. The decisive battle was fought in December at Tricameron, where the Vandals were virtually annihilated ; and though Geilamir escaped he soon realized that a further struggle was hopeless, and surrendered himself—to be relegated to an easy retirement in Phrygia. But the Vandal kingdom was wiped off the face of the earth. Belisarius with fifteen thousand men had succeeded where the vast armaments of Leo I had failed ignominiously. He returned in triumph to Constantinople, to make ready for a fresh task.

## Exploits of Belisarius in Italy

FOR eight years after Theodoric's death, his daughter Amalaswintha strove valiantly to carry on Theodoric's work in her son's name ; a thing beyond the power of any woman—or any man not of heroic mould. In 534 the boy died ; and Amalaswintha procured the succession for Theodoric's nephew Theodahad (in con-

**COIN OF THEODAHAD**

Theodahad, who had murdered Amalaswintha, Theodoric's daughter, was ruling the Ostrogoths in Italy when Belisarius, fresh from his victories in Africa, began his campaigns against them.

*British Museum*

junction with herself), an Amal, clever in his way, but a poltroon who was both worthless and ambitious. The queen had many enemies ; Theodahad conspired with them, captured her and had her murdered, giving Justinian the warrant for intervention. The Goths were ready to fight against any intervention ; and in 535 Belisarius with a small force landed in Sicily.

Theodoric had given the Italians admirably just and firm government, but they had never been able to reconcile themselves to the fact that the power was in the hands of aliens and Arians. The Goths were said to have 100,000 fighting men in the country, but the entire Italian population was on the side of the imperialist invaders, while the Goths themselves were paralysed by the inaction of their king. In Sicily Belisarius was welcomed instead of being opposed. In the next spring he advanced through South Italy with seven thousand men, meeting no resistance till he reached Naples, while fifty thousand Goths lay about Rome. Then the Gothic army in despair deposed Theodahad, who was promptly murdered by a private enemy ; and, as there was no Amal left, they elected as king Witiges, a valiant but stupid old warrior who had forgotten anything of generalship that he may once have known.

Instead of marching to overwhelm Belisarius, who had captured Naples, Witiges carried almost his entire army north to deal with a force of Franks who had seized the opportunity to pour through the Alps. Belisarius with his small force pounced on Rome, which the garrison evacuated in a panic as he entered it. Witiges made composition with the Franks, ceding Roman Provence to them, returned with the whole Gothic army, and laid siege to Rome, but never made the blockade complete, so that at first supplies and later reinforcements continually dribbled into the city. In spite of the huge circumvallation which had to be held by only five thousand men, all attacks were repelled with heavy loss. After a year sufficient reinforcements from the East had arrived to enable Belisarius to take the offensive (538).

After two more years of campaigning, Witiges, shut up in Ravenna, would have accepted the generous terms offered by Justinian. The Goths would not have it, and actually offered the crown to Belisarius, who, without accepting it, beguiled them into opening the gates to him ; whereupon he took possession in the name of Justinian. When Ravenna fell it seemed an easy matter to complete the conquest ; and Belisarius was recalled to take up the command against the Persians, with whom a second war had broken out.

**W**ITIGES had, in fact, thought too late of creating a diversion by inciting the Persian to make an attack. Ravenna was on the point of falling when Chosroes in 540 flung himself on northern Syria, where he was not expected, and captured Antioch, whence he carried off great spoils. In the spring of 541, Witiges was a captive and Belisarius was in Mesopotamia ; but Chosroes was far away, more profitably employed in overrunning the trans-Caucasian province of Colchis than in giving battle to Belisarius, who was awaiting an attack that was not delivered. Next year both armies were paralysed by an abnormally severe outbreak of the plague. In 543 Belisarius was recalled from the East to take up once more the western command from which he had been transferred ; his successor met with reverses, and in 545 a five-years' truce was patched up with Chosroes.

The fall of Ravenna had not disposed of the Goth problem. The stubborn garrison at Pavia held out and proclaimed a new king, Hildebad. Half

a dozen imperial generals had been left in Italy, each with an independent command ; they could not or would not co-operate, and the Goths rallied to the capable Hildebad, who recovered the plain of the Po. He was assassinated in 541, but a fresh champion arose—his nephew Baduila, better known as Totila, first of the knights of the Middle Ages, one of the rare heroes on whose name no stain has ever fastened ; one who was more than worthy to be the successor of Theodoric.

The Italians might anathematise the Goths, but would not fight them. By the end of 542 Totila had routed the imperial armies in the field wherever he met them, had driven them all into a few fortified towns—Rome, Ravenna and some others —and was in effect master of Italy once more from north to south. He held his men in hand as resolutely as a Henry V or a Louis IX, protecting the population from all violence, and treating the garrisons that resisted him with a magnanimity of which the Plantagenet never dreamed. Belisarius had fallen woefully out of favour with Justinian and Theodora, but he was needed to cope with Totila. So in 543, as we have seen, he was sent again to Italy. But he was never given a fair chance by his master. Instead of his devoted veterans he was allowed only a meagre force of raw recruits with which to fight the Goths, whose shaken moral had been thoroughly restored by a leader of brilliant ability and inspiring personality. Belisarius could gain no decisive advantage. In 545 Totila laid siege to Rome ; Belisarius vainly attempted to relieve it, and it fell in 546. Totila removed the population and dismantled the defences. Justinian would send neither the men nor the money needed. Two years later the great captain was recalled at his own request, and

**BELISARIUS THE WARLIKE**
Next to Justinian on the observer's right, in a mosaic in S. Vitale, may be seen a figure whose features are here enlarged. It has been suggested that it represents Belisarius.
*Photo Alinari*

it seemed that Totila's ultimate triumph was all but certain. Belisarius had reoccupied and refortified Rome before his departure ; but when he was gone Totila took it again.

Justinian was now at war with Persia for the third time. Nevertheless in 552 he made a great effort in the West which was crowned with unexpected success. He gave the Italian command to his chamberlain, the eunuch Narses, to whom he supplied the troops he had persistently withheld from Belisarius. The long struggle had depleted the Gothic army. Marching on Rome with a somewhat superior force, Narses brought Totila to a decisive engagement at Taginae. Belisarius and the Goths alike had relied almost wholly on cavalry, the arm which generally predominated in the Middle Ages. Narses won at Taginae as Bruce won at Bannockburn and Edward III at Crecy, by turning part of his cavalry into pikemen, against whom the Gothic horse, charging under a storm of arrows from the flanks, hurled themselves with desperate but useless valour.

Totila and his brother were slain and the Gothic army was all but annihilated. The Ostrogothic power was no more. Narses was still called upon to deal with a destructive Frankish incursion in North Italy, where he completely wiped out the whole invading force. But the ceaseless struggle which had been waged for twenty years had destroyed what might have become a regenerating force, and had left Italy depopulated and desolated ; and the ruin was in no wise compensated by the re-establishment of the shadow of an imperial government under an ' exarch ' at Ravenna. There was no effective attempt at rehabilitation.

Incidentally, Justinian sought to restore the imperial authority in Spain, where some cities were secured, occupied and garrisoned with imperial troops. The third Persian war was exclusively a struggle to recover Colchis, which the Persians had retained at the truce. Finally the peace of 555 restored it, in return for a substantial indemnity.

Justinian and Belisarius died in the same year, 565. The story that the old

### TOTILA THE OSTROGOTH

Witiges the Ostrogoth was followed by Hildebad, Hildebad in 541 by Baduila or Totila, who found it easy enough to cope with the meagre levies allowed to Belisarius ; until Narses, with an adequate army, defeated and slew him at Taginae.
*British Museum*

general was reduced to a pitiful beggary in his last days is happily mythical. The imperial succession passed undisputed to Justinian's nephew, Justin II.

The great emperor had concerned himself with the farther West only in his late years, when the fortunes of the Visigothic kingdom gave him the opportunity for recovering in Spain an imperial foothold, though it amounted to no more. When Theodoric intervened in 508 to secure the Visigoths from the joint onslaught of Burgundians and Franks, he allowed Clovis to retain Aquitaine, but established his own grandson Amalric in the Visigothic kingdom of Spain, to which a substantial portion of Provence was still attached. Amalric being a child, he entrusted the regency to Theudis, a capable soldier, who discharged his trust faithfully during the minority of Amalric, retained the administration till Amalric's death in 533, and was then elected to the kingship, since there was neither a Balt nor an Amal to succeed.

### Events among the Franks and Visigoths

WHILE Theodoric lived, no one ventured to attack his grandson, though the sons of Clovis hammered Burgundy almost out of existence. When Theodoric was gone, they fell upon Amalric, who was slain ; but Theudis held his own till his death, at a great age, in 548. The Merovingians had shared Burgundy between themselves in 532, and in 538 Witiges bought off their attack on Italy by ceding to them the Ostrogothic or Roman half of Provence ; but the other half, Septimania, remained under the Visigoths for a long time to come.

Theudis was himself assassinated. Eighteen months later his successor, Theudigisel, was assassinated. Then there was a struggle between Agila and Athanagild for the succession ; the latter invited Justinian to intervene. In 555 Agila was assassinated, and Athanagild found that he could not rid himself of the interveners. Before his death in 568 he had married his daughters Galswintha and Brunhild to the Merovingian kings Sigibert and Chilperic—with tragic consequences. The disruption of the Visigothic kingdom was arrested under his successors Leovigild (568–586) and Reccared (586–601).

Leovigild, a very capable soldier, thoroughly established his personal ascendancy over the nobles, smote the minor Suevic kingdoms, and recovered Andalusia, which had been occupied by Justinian's officers. He dealt successfully, as only a strong man could deal, with one of the two great stumbling-blocks which prevented the development of a strong kingdom, the independence of the nobles. But he only accentuated the other, the impossibility of reconciling the Catholic clergy and the Catholic population to the traditional Arianism of the dominant people. The Arianism of the Goths was bound up with their pride of race, and the religious intensified the racial antagonism.

### Religious Troubles in Visigothic Spain

LEOVIGILD'S son Reccared during his father's life gave no hint of the revolutionary project which he inaugurated immediately after the old king's death. Leovigild's hostility to Catholicism had been fierce ; Reccared, without showing any hostility to Arianism, announced his own acceptance of the Catholic creed, and induced many of the nobles to follow his example. Like Theodoric in Italy, he made no distinction between Catholic and Arian, and in the course of a generation Arianism practically disappeared. His success was no doubt largely due to the good fortune which attended his arms whenever he had to resort to fighting.

But in removing one stumbling-block he had raised up another, all unconsciously. The grateful clergy were a useful counterpoise to the turbulent nobles.

When he consulted the national council, much the larger part of it consisted not of the great Gothic nobles but of the bishops. With the bishops at his back the king's authority was greatly strengthened. But when a smaller man than Reccared was king, he soon became the tool of the bishops ; and the age-long curse of Spain, the subservience of the crown to the churchmen, came into being. The Gothic monarchy became priest-ridden. The constitutional struggle became one between nobles and churchmen.

### Blood-stained Annals of the House of Clovis

A DIFFERENT course was followed in the Frank dominion set up by Clovis. There was no religious antagonism to accentuate racial antagonism, and there was a royal house to whose title the nobles were unswervingly loyal ; though partition of the inheritance among the sons was the destructive custom of the Frankish race. Clovis at his death in 511 left his dominion so divided between four sons, while Burgundy lay between the active Frankish hammer and the solid anvil of Provence.

The annals of the house of the Merwings reek with blood from the outset. Clovis had killed off all the members of the royal house except his own sons, to clear the field for himself. By a strict adherence to their father's fundamental principle that treachery, audacity and ruthlessness are the basis of statecraft, the four brothers made themselves masters of all Gaul except the fragment which remained to the Visigoths ; while the eldest, Theuderic, and after his death in 533 his son Theudebert, extended their supremacy over the German tribes beyond the Rhine. It was Theudebert who was responsible for the first of the two invasions of Italy which have already been recorded.

Chlothar (Lothaire), the youngest and worst of the brood, survived his brothers, took the surest means of surviving their offspring, and died sole king of the Franks in 561, fifty years after his father. Incidentally he had fired the house over the head of his own eldest and rebellious son, who perished in the flames with his wife and children. The kingdom was once again divided in four between Chlothar's surviving sons. The eldest dying in 567, Guntram took the centre (Burgundy), Chilperic the north and west (Neustria), and Sigibert the Rhenish and trans-Rhenish territory (known as Austrasia).

A blazing quarrel broke out between Sigibert and Chilperic. Guntram managed to effect a brief reconciliation while the Franks made common cause against a new danger. The Langobards, to whom we shall return, had just entered the stage, poured into Italy, and were threatening Provence. In 573 the invaders were driven over the Alps, and the contest between the brothers was renewed.

They had married the Visigothic princesses Brunhild and Galswintha respectively. Then Chilperic murdered Galswintha and married his mistress Fredegonde. Brunhild was set on revenge. Guntram had succeeded in composing matters for the time by awarding ' blood-money ' according to common German custom— some cities in Aquitaine ; but Brunhild wanted blood. Chilperic and Sigibert each devastated the other's territories ; Sigibert was winning when Chilperic or Fredegonde had him murdered. The Austrasian nobles crowned the infant heir Childebert. Brunhild had been taken, but her captor, Chilperic's son, fell in love with her and married instead of killing her. Fredegonde procured his murder, but Brunhild escaped to Austrasia. The Austrasian nobles held by the child, but would not submit to his mother, and the ceaseless strife between Brunhild and the nobles, during his minority, wrecked the power of the crown among the Austrasians.

Guntram too stood by Chilperic ; war raged all over Gaul, Chilperic having the upper hand, while his evil queen Fredegonde indulged in innumerable crimes. But he was murdered when hunting. His infant heir Chlothar fell with Fredegonde into Guntram's hands (584) and the welter of blood was stayed for a time.

### Decline of the Merwing Dynasty

IN 593 Guntram, the one tolerably respectable Merwing, died ; Childebert, son of Sigibert, succeeded to his dominions as well as Austrasia. The fighting started again. Childebert died leaving two infants ·

in charge of his untamable mother. For twelve years practically there had been no grown up king among the Franks ; the nobles had been under no control ; and from this time there was only one of the Merovingian kings of the Franks who can be said to have exercised regal authority.

There is no need to follow in detail the monotonous record of murder and fratricide. Fredegonde died in her bed ; the indomitable Brunhild in her old age fell into the hands of Fredegonde's son Chlothar and was torn to death by wild horses. There was not a little of the tigress in her, but she had the makings of a great queen. Her great-grandchildren were murdered at the same time (614) ; the Austrasian nobles had deserted her ; and once more Chlothar was sole king of the Franks.

### Mayors of the Frankish Palace

BUT their king was not their master. He was king because Austrasians and Burgundians had offered to acknowledge him on terms that limited the royal prerogatives and conceded to the nobles prerogatives which in effect transferred the supreme authority to their hands. The acting heads of their governments, the ' mayors of the palace,' were made irremovable. A generation later that office became hereditary. When the first noble in the state held the office for life and passed it on to his son, the minister was bound to dominate the sovereign. Thenceforward, too, the royal decrees were issued as having the approval of the king's counsellors, lay and ecclesiastical.

Apart from the savage revenge taken on Brunhild the reign of Chlothar (613–628) was not particularly sanguinary. In 623 he made his son Dagobert king of Austrasia—broadly speaking, Neustria was that portion of the Frankish dominion which had been under Roman government, Austrasia the non-Romanised German portion. Dagobert had the advantage of two very able and loyal counsellors, his mayor of the palace Pepin (the Old) of Heristhal, and Bishop Arnulf of Metz, the joint progenitors of the house of the Arnulfings, later known as the Karlings or Carolingians. Dagobert became sole king of the Franks in 628, nominally transferred Austrasia to his son Sigibert in 632, and died in 638, the last of the Merovingians whose authority was more than a shadow. Both his great counsellors survived him. The Neustrian and Burgundian mayors of the palace had been of no particular distinction.

### First Advent of the Lombards

IN Italy Justinian obliterated the Ostrogoths and set up his exarch at Ravenna, but the East could spare neither the money from its empty exchequer, nor the men from its oriental population, nor the energy which had more than enough calls upon it elsewhere to rehabilitate the exhausted country, defend it from vigorous foes, or reorganize a supreme government. In 568, fifteen years after the Gothic wars, a new barbarian group was overrunning the peninsula.

The Langobards (long-axes ?), or, to adopt at once the more familiar form of their name, the Lombards, were a backward division of those various tribes associated with the Gothic name. They had never come prominently into collision with the Empire ; but about the close of the fifth century they had pushed their way to the middle Danube. Towards the middle of the sixth century they broke the domination of the Heruli and the Gepidae, in alliance with the Avars, a Mongolian race who had pushed into Hungary ; they provided Narses with mercenary troops for his campaigns against the Ostrogoths ; like Alaric and Theodoric, the attraction of Italy appealed to their king Alboin ; and when the emperor Justin II dismissed Narses from the Italian exarchate in 567, they left their Danubian lands to their allies the Avars, and poured through the Alps to take the place vacated by the Ostrogoths.

Apart from the stubborn defence of a few fortified cities, notably Pavia, no resistance was offered to their conquest

**DAGOBERT THE FRANK**

Dagobert I (623–632) was the last Frankish king who was anything but a puppet. His mayor of the palace was Pepin the Old, who inaugurated the greatness of the Carolingian line.

*British Museum*

and settlement in the much depopulated ‘ Lombard plain.’ Alboin was the last of the Lethings, the family recognized as royal. When in 572 he was murdered by his wife—he had forced her to drink from a cup which was made of the skull of her father, the king of the Gepidae whom he had slain in battle after their marriage—the chiefs or dukes of the various clans regarded a new king as a superfluity, and for several years ranged over Italy, establishing themselves as dukes at their own convenience. From Ravenna, Perugia and Rome imperial officers ruled over considerable and almost contiguous territories ; the ‘ foot ’ of Italy could remain defiant ; but otherwise almost the whole peninsula passed under Lombard dominion — the dominion of a variety of Lombard dukes who owned no central authority.

In the south the Lombards were few, and did not materially affect the character of the population or the traditional organization. In the north, where they were at least comparatively numerous, they made Lombardy something distinct from the rest of Italy. There, after a brief interval, they set up a new elective monarchy ; with all the instability incidental to the elective system.

They had arrived as pagans, but adopted Catholic (not Arian) Christianity under the influence of the Christian queen Theodelinda, who married successively the kings Authari (583–590) and Agilulf (590–615). The latter did a good deal towards consolidating the kingdom in the north, but did not otherwise extend it, though he called himself king of all Italy. There are no records of note regarding the reigns of his two immediate successors.

The other feature of the time is the papacy of Gregory I the Great (590–604), who made the pope not only the acknowledged spiritual head of western Christendom, but also in effect the temporal ruler of Rome, and may be said to have inaugurated that conception of the supreme authority of the Papacy which was to play so large a part in medieval history. His responsibility for a series of rather deplorable puns, and for sending the lesser Augustine to plant the Latin Church in England, have made his name familiar to British children.

### Saxon Settlement in Britain

**B**RITAIN had, so to speak, loosed her moorings to the Continent, while the English were already beginning to settle on her shores, before Odoacer deposed Romulus Augustulus. The Roman unity had broken up under pressure of raiding Picts and Scots—Irish clans who had established themselves in Argyll—on the north, Irish raiders on the west, Jutish and Saxon rovers on the south. Legend and historical fact are too inextricably mingled to be disentangled with any confidence, but in the course of a hundred years 'between the (reputed) landing of Aella in Sussex (477) and the victory of the West-Saxon Ceawlin at Deorham in the west country (577) successive groups of pagan Saxons or Angles conquered and established their domination in about half of so much of the island as lies south of the Forth ; and when Aethelfrith, of Northumbria, won the battle of Chester in 613 the half had become two-thirds or three-quarters. How far the Britons were exterminated, enslaved, or amalgamated with the conquerors, is vehemently disputed. Everything east of a line drawn roughly from Edinburgh through Gloucester to the Channel was under English domination, all to the west of it was Celtic ; but those two battles, Deorham and Chester, severed the Britons of Wales from the south and north Britons respectively, carrying the Saxons in the south and the Angles in the north to the west coast, which they had not reached before.

The Britons were broken up into chieftainships or principalities, with Celtic institutions modified by four centuries of Roman supremacy ; and they retained their Christianity. The Celts beyond the old Roman frontier in the north were being Christianised during the second half of the sixth century—the five-hundreds —by the missionary zeal of S. Columba and his Irish followers, since Ireland had been independently Christianised (the Romans never having gone there) more than a century earlier.

In the last quarter, then, of the sixth century all the English were pagans, and there is no trace of Christianity surviving in the conquered districts. We can distinguish certain kingdoms : most definitely the Jute kingdom of Kent, the earliest settled conquest ; the Saxon kingdom of Wessex ; the Angle kingdoms of Deira and Bernicia ; less definitely, of the East Angles and East Saxons, and of South Saxons wedged between Kent and the West Saxons ; and in the midlands the Middle Angles established in Mercia, on the March of the Welsh Britons, contiguous in the south with the West Saxon kingdom of Hwicce ; British kingdoms survived in Elmet, Cornwall and Cumbria (see map in page 344).

### Augustine's Introduction of Christianity

**K**ENT, for obvious reasons, was the gateway to the Continent, and was naturally the part of the island most open to European influence. The marriage of Ethelbert of Kent to the Merovingian princess Bertha no doubt encouraged Pope Gregory to carry out his long-projected design of sending a mission to England. Augustine and his company were favourably received (597) ; with the result that before sixty years had passed Christianity was the established religion over the whole island, though the antagonisms between the ' Latin ' practices adopted by the English and the ' Celtic ' practices which continued to hold their own in the rest of the island and in Ireland effactually counteracted what might have been expected to prove a unifying influence.

As yet there was political unity neither in the English nor in the Celtic regions. There was no king of the English and no king of the Britons. Unification could be accomplished only by force of arms. The foundations of Northumbrian ascendancy were laid by Edwin of Northumbria (617 – 633) ; but that

L*

Christian monarch was slain in battle by the last champion of paganism, Penda of Mercia. But neither the Northumbrian nor the Mercian power was destined to effect the unification of England.

**W**E have traced the dissolution of what had been the united Roman Empire in the West, and the preservation of its unity in the East down to the death of Justinian; we have followed the fortunes of the West for nearly seventy years more. We have now to revert to the East, its continued struggle against disintegrating forces, and the unsuspected prelude to the Great Eruption.

The last years of Justinian had been inglorious. Save that Athanagild had enabled him to recover a temporary footing in Spain, there was no extension of the imperial authority, nor was its grip upon what had already been won effective. Exhaustion had set in, and the emperor himself in his old age was obsessed by the idea that he was a great theologian. Absorbed in theological controversy, he neglected the problems of state.

His successor, Justin II (565–578), was ambitious, but lacked both the capacity and the means to achieve his imperial ambitions. By this time the Slavs or Slovenians were rather flooding than infiltrating the Balkan peninsula in an inexhaustible stream. The Avars in conjunction with the Lombards had just obliterated their trans-Danubian enemies, the Herulians and Gepidae, and, when the Lombards departed to take possession of Italy, were ready to expand southward. The financial and military resources of the Empire were reduced to a very low ebb.

Justinian had kept the Avars quiet by a subsidy. Justin invited their attack by withdrawing the subsidy, and they responded by raiding with ever increasing intensity. Then in 571 he refused to continue the payments to the Persians, under the agreement which had been made when they evacuated Colchis. Thus began a prolonged Persian war (572–591), which was a steady drain on the resources of the Empire, bringing no counterbalancing gains; though, on the whole, the Persians had the worse in the fighting. Then Justin went mad, recovered sufficiently to nominate Tiberius Constantius as his colleague —the wisest act of his life—and relapsed again. For a time the power remained in the hands of his own empress. On his death, Tiberius II, of whom much was expected, became really emperor ; but with the best intentions could accomplish nothing, save an untrustworthy agreement with the Avars, before his premature death in 582.

**THE TYRANT PHOCAS**

Phocas, who had deposed and slain Maurice in 602, met a like fate eight years later at the hands of Heraclius. It is thought that this bronze steelyard weight preserves his lineaments.

*British Museum*

Tiberius nominated as his successor Maurice I (582–602), who had been doing good service in command of the eastern army. He was a good soldier, but custom forbade the emperor to command the armies in the field, and he did not understand army administration. The one truth he realized was the need for economy, and his economies ruined the discipline of the forces. Still, the war was ended by a Persian revolution. The king Hormisdas was killed and the crown was usurped by Varahnes. The legitimate heir Chosroes fled to the Romans ; Maurice gave him help which enabled him to carry out a counter-revolution and recover the throne. In such circumstances it was not difficult to negotiate a peace much needed by both sides, on the basis of a return to the pre-war conditions.

Meanwhile the Avars had broken the peace which Tiberius had induced them to accept. Also the Slavonic flood was rising. In 599 the economical emperor refused to ransom some thousands of prisoners who had fallen into the hands of the Avars ; whereon the khan of the Avars had them massacred. Public opinion laid the blame on Maurice. Then in 601, again for the sake of economy, the troops at the front were ordered not to return to winter quarters. The soldiers mutinied, chose Phocas, one of their own number, as their leader, marched on Constantinople, murdered Maurice, and proclaimed Phocas emperor (602).

Chaos followed, for Phocas was nothing but a brutal savage. Chosroes, as the avenger of his old protector Maurice, set about the conquest of the East, while Avars and Slavs ranged practically unresisted over the Balkan peninsula, and Phocas occupied himself in hunting out conspiracies and killing conspirators real or only suspected. Year by year the Persian raiding columns carried their incursions farther and farther west over Mesopotamia, northern Syria, eastern, central and at last even western Asia Minor; only south Syria, Africa and Egypt were immune.

In 609 Heraclius the elder, who had governed Africa long and well, organized revolt. In 610 his son, Heraclius the younger, arrived at the Dardanelles with a fleet. The tyrant found himself utterly deserted. He was seized and handed over in chains to young Heraclius, who forthwith sent him to the death he merited. Then Constantinople proclaimed the deliverer emperor.

The task before him was incredibly difficult. Experienced officers, disciplined troops, money above all, were wanting. Disaster followed disaster. The Persians turned on Syria ; in 514 the pagan host captured Jerusalem, sacked it, and carried off what had been for centuries treasured as the True Cross on which the Saviour had been crucified. Two years later they invaded Egypt, which offered no resistance at all. In 617 they took and garrisoned Chalcedon, facing Constantinople across the Bosporus. The end seemed at hand.

Despair wrought almost a miracle. High and low rallied to the cause ; the Church leading, they brought in by voluntary effort all their treasures, and troops were raised. Heraclius proclaimed his resolve to break through tradition and take the field in person—to stake all on the last desperate effort to save the Empire and Christianity. But first the Avars and Slavs had to be bound over. It was not till 622 that Heraclius was at last free to launch his attack.

He had one vital asset, the command of the sea, and he used it. While he had it, Constantinople was safe, and he used it to fling his whole force on the Persian centre in Cilicia, cleaving Asia Minor from Syria, and compelling the Persians to withdraw from the West. Next year he drove straight at Media. Year after year success followed success. He penetrated victoriously farther into the heart of Persia than any Roman commander before him.

CHOSROES THE CONQUERING PERSIAN

This Persian figure in relief, taken from a splendid silver cup, is probably that of Chosroes II, Parviz (591–628). Nominally to avenge the death of his ally Maurice, he invaded the Empire, and had possessed himself of Asia Minor, Syria, Palestine and Egypt when Heraclius turned the tables on him.

*Bibliothèque Nationale, Paris ; photo, Giraudon*

When the Avars broke treaty again, he dared to risk leaving the capital to the strength of its own defences, and the siege was broken up in 626. In 627 he shattered the last of the Persian armies near Nineveh. The Nemesis of overweening success at last overtook Chosroes ; the very army deposed him, and his successor was prompt to sue for peace, which Heraclius was willing enough to grant on generous terms. The Persian threat to the Empire was finally nullified. The idol of the army and the people, Heraclius returned in 628 to Constantinople, unconscious of the rise, in remote Arabia, of a menace far more terrific than that which he had so gloriously broken—the world-shaking menace of Islam. For the Prophet had arisen on the occasion of whose death four years later the flood-gates would be opened.

### World Events in the Distant East

WE left China parted between the Wei dynasty of the north and the Sung in the south. The Ch'i displaced the Sung in 479, to be succeeded by the Liang in 502, and the Ch'ên in 557. About the last date the Wei separated the eastern and western provinces of its dominions ; and then in 581 a successful usurper, Yang Chien of Sui, made himself emperor of both north and south. The Sui dynasty was short-lived. In 618 it was displaced by Li Yüan, the founder of the T'ang dynasty, whose rule is counted as another Golden Age, when Chinese literature was at its zenith. Li Yüan was given the name of Kao Tsu ; his son and successor Tai Tsung (627–649) was, like his father, a patron of art and literature, but also a law-giver and a conqueror, who extended the empire to the Caspian Sea and encouraged intercourse with foreign powers. His reign, however, had barely begun at the point where our chapter closes.

Towards the close of the fifth century, the last of the great Guptas beat back the invasion of India by the White Huns. Skandagupta's successors were less successful ; though the dynasty was not destroyed the empire was broken up. During the sixth century the invaders, who were akin to the Turks rather than the Mongols proper, established themselves all over northern India, their chiefs forming a new nobility, which preferred to associate itself with the old governing class rather than to destroy it. Hence there is at least plausible ground for the view that the later Rajputs whom Hindu law identifies with the old Kshatriya caste are in fact much more White Hun than genuine Hindu. Throughout the century, however, the records are meagre.

### Chinese Descriptions of India

BUT in the first half of the seventh century there is more light. In 606 the young prince Harsha-vardhana succeeded to the throne of a rising kingdom on the Jumna, and in the course of forty years developed it into an empire which covered the whole of northern India, except the Punjab, between the Himalayas and the Narbada. Very full description of that great kingdom was recorded by a Chinese traveller (as usual), Yuan Chwang, a Buddhist pilgrim. Kanauj on the Ganges, due east of Agra, was Harsha's capital ; and his tributaries included the kings of Gujarat in the west and Assam in the east. Both Brahmanism as represented by countless temples and Buddhism by many monasteries flourished exceedingly under the monarch, who was Brahman by birth but Buddhist by inclination. After the not very prolonged wars which established his empire in 612, Harsha would seem to have tried to emulate Asoka rather than Chandragupta ; justice and humanity pervaded the administration, though less completely than in the days of the great Buddhist emperor. The king himself not only patronised but practised literature with some distinction ; he was the Indian counterpart of his Chinese contemporaries Kao Tsu and Tai Tsung.

With the departure of Yuan Chwang a few years before Harsha's death, obscurity again descends upon the Indian records.

# TABLE OF DATES FOR CHAPTER 15

632 Abu Bekr first khalif. First Syrian expedition.
633 Suppression of pretenders in Arabia. Khalid in Irak.
634 Roman defeat on Yermak. Omar khalif, to 644. Mothanna in Irak ; battle of Boweib.
635 Fall of Damascus.
Yezdigird IV k. of Persia. Battle of Kadesia.
636 Fall of Antioch. Heraclius evacuates Syria.
Rothari Lombard king.
637 Fall of Jerusalem and of Ctesiphon. Founding of Kufa and Basra.
638 Dagobert k. of Franks dies. 'Rois fainéants' from this time. Sigibert k. in Austrasia.
639 Pepin the Old dies. Grimoald claims mayoralty. Moawiya (Ommiad) governor of Syria.
640 Amru invades Egypt.
641 Heraclius dies. Constans II emperor.
Amru takes Alexandria. Fostat (Cairo) founded. Chindaswinth k. of Visigoths to 652.
642 Persian Empire ended at battle of Nehavend.
Grimoald son of Pepin mayor, to 656.
643 Rothari's Lombard Code.
644 Omar assassinated ; Othman khalif.
646 Alexandria recovered and lost again.
647 Amru in Egypt superseded by Abu Sarh.
India : Harsha dies ; Kanauj Empire breaks up.
649 Beginning of Saracen fleet on the Mediterranean.
'Typus' of Constans ; denounced by Pope Martin.
651 Moawiya begins invasions of Asia Minor.
Othman's recension of the Koran.
652 Naval victory of Abu Sarh off Alexandria.
655 Naval victory over Constans at Phoenix.
Captivity and death of Pope Martin.
Penda killed ; Northumbrian supremacy in England.
656 Othman murdered. Ali khalif to 660. Revolt of Zobeir and Talha. Battle 'of the Camel.'
Fall of the mayor Grimoald ; Neustria dominant.
657 Moawiya and Ali in conflict ; battle of Siffin.
658 The 'Arbitration.' Rise of the Kharejites.
Constans campaigns against Slavs ; settlement.
659 Truce between Moawiya and Constans.
660 Ali killed. Moawiya khalif, Hasan resigning. Ommiad Khalifate to 750.
Ebroin mayor of Neustria.
662 Lombard crown usurped by Grimoald of Benevento.
Constans invades Italy.
663 Constans retires from Italy to Syracuse.
664 Constans organizes campaigns in Africa.
668 Constans killed ; Constantine Pogonatus emperor.
Renewal of war with Moawiya ; Saracen successes in Asia Minor.
671 Berthari Lombard king to 680.
673 Second siege of Constantinople ; Saracens repulsed.
673-677 Defeats of Saracens by Constantine.
676 Moawiya has his son Yezid elected as successor.
678 Moawiya forced to make peace with Constantine.
Ebroin's supremacy over Franks established.
679 Bulgar kingdom established in Moesia.
680 Decline of Visigoth monarchy.
Yezid I succeeds Moawiya. Fall of Husein, son of Ali, at Kerbela.
681 Abdallah Ibn Zobeir claims Khalifate at Mecca.
(Church) Council of Constantinople condemns the Monothelite heresy. Rome reconciled.
Ebroin killed. Seven years of civil war.
683 Yezid's army takes and sacks Medina. Mecca saved by Yezid's death. Moawiya II, then Merwan, khalif at Damascus, Abdallah at Mecca.
685 Abdallah's lieutenants overcome Shiahs and Kharejites at Kufa and Basra.
English invasion broken by Scots ; Nechtansmere.
Constantine dies. Justinian II emperor.
686 Merwan killed. Abd el-Malik Ommiad khalif.
687 Pepin the Young, grandson of Pepin the Old, wins battle of Testry over Neustrians.
687-714 Pepin rules the Franks as mayor of east and west ; recovers lost authority over Germans on the east, West Frisia, Thuringia, Swabia ; develops Christian missions among German pagans ; establishes central control.
688 Cunibert Lombard king to 700.
689 Hajjaj for Abd el-Malik wrests Irak from Abdallah.
690 S. Willibrord 'apostle of Frisia,' to 639.
691 Abd el-Malik's troops besiege Abdallah in Mecca.
Justinian's successful campaign in Bulgaria.

692 Fall of Abdallah. Abd el-Malik sole khalif.
693 Justinian's campaign in Cilicia ; Sebastopolis.
695 Justinian deposed and exiled. Leontius emperor.
698 Saracens finally capture Carthage. Continuous progress of Musa in Mauretania.
Leontius deposed. Tiberius III emperor.
701 Aribert (to 711) usurps Lombard crown.
705 Return and restoration of Justinian II. Reign of terror to 711.
Walid succeeds Abd el-Malik ; to 715.
709 Koteiba captures Bokhara.
710 Roderic, last Visigothic king of Spain.
711 Philippicus kills Justinian and usurps crown.
Saracens under Tarik invade Spain and annihilate Spanish-Gothic army on the Guadalete. End of Visigothic dominion. Saracens overrun all Spain ; resistance maintained only in N.W.
Saracen fleet takes possession of Sardinia.
Saracens under Kasim subjugate Sindh.
Saracen armies invade Asia Minor, which they overrun in the next four years.
712 Koteiba takes Samarkand.
Liutprand Lombard k. ; he consolidates the realm.
713 Fall of Philippicus. Anastasius II emperor.
China : Accession of Lung Chi, to 763. Forty years of prosperity.
715 Walid dies ; Suleiman khalif.
Fall of Anastasius ; Theodosius III emperor.
Austrasian mayoralty disputed on Pepin's death.
Gregory II pope to 731.
716 Neustrians attack Austrasians, who find a leader in Charles Martel, son of Pepin. Four years of civil war.
Suleiman prepares grand attack on the Empire.
Revolt of Leo the Isaurian.
717 Theodosius abdicates in favour of Leo III.
Moslemah, brother of Suleiman, besieges Constantinople by sea and land. Leo defeats fleet.
Omar II succeeds Suleiman.
718 Saracens reinforced. Leo shatters their fleet, crosses Bosporus, and cuts communications. Bulgarians advance and defeat a Saracen army. Moslemah withdraws his remnants over the Dardanelles and cuts his way to Cilicia. Remnant of grand fleet destroyed in a storm.
East Europe delivered from the Saracen menace.
719 Campaigns to expel Saracens from Asia Minor.
Charles Martel, after victories of Vincy and Soissons, mayor of east and west to 741. Ascendancy of Austrasia. Charles retains a Merwing puppet king.
720 Yezid II succeeds Omar II. Depravity of the Ommiad court and rivalry of factions.
720-730 Charles restores authority in Trans-Rhenish dominions, lost during the civil wars.
721 Saracens, having mastered Spain, invade Aquitaine but are routed by Duke Eudo at Toulouse.
723 Boniface (Winfrith) 'apostle of Germany' made bishop for Germany by Gregory II, under protection of Charles Martel.
724 Hisham succeeds Yezid II (to 743). Yemenite and Syrian factions, and Shiahs, and a secret Abbasid propaganda.
725 Saracens overrun Septimania but league with Eudo.
726 Leo III ('Iconoclast') prohibits image worship. His officers cannot enforce edict in Italy ; violent breach with Pope Gregory.
727 Saracen defeat at Nicaea drives them from Asia Minor.
Charles Martel subjugates Bavaria.
729 Exarch Eutychius marches on Rome, while Liutprand is enforcing obedience in the south.
730 Liutprand imposes pacification of Italy, which leaves Gregory virtually independent.
Revolt of Swabia stamped out by Charles Martel.
731 Othman in Septimania revolts against Abd er-Rahman in Spain, Eudo against Charles. Othman is crushed ; Eudo submits.
732 Gregory III pope. Leo's fleet for subjugation of Italy destroyed by storms.
Abd er-Rahman invades and conquers Aquitaine, routing Eudo ; but he is killed and his host shattered by Charles Martel at decisive battle of Poitiers (or Tours).
West Europe delivered from the Saracen menace.

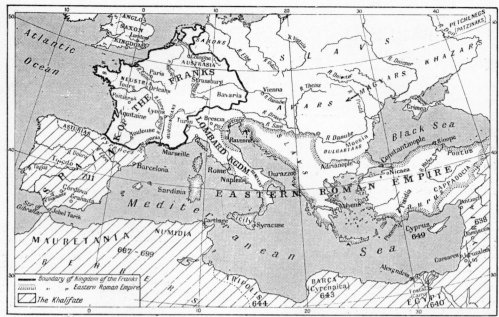

From Egypt the Saracens spread in a westward direction over the whole of the North African littoral, securing control of the Mediterranean. In 711 a Saracen host crossed the Strait of Gibraltar and, after a stubbornly contested battle on the Guadalete, overran the whole of the Iberian Peninsula. Their further advance over Europe was finally stayed in Aquitaine in 732 by Charles Martel, 'mayor of the palace' to the Frankish king, who drove them back across the Pyrenees.

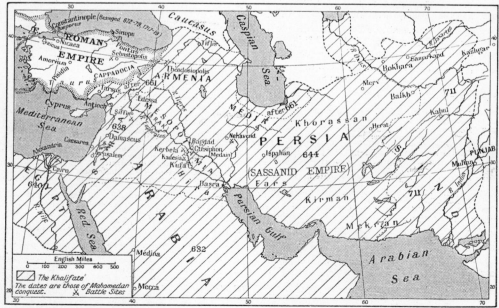

How rapidly and over how large an area Mahomet's dream of world-conquest was carried into effect in the century following his death is shown graphically in these two maps. Restricted to Arabia in 632, Islam absorbed first Syria and then Egypt and, later, Armenia to the Caucasus. By their victory at Nehavend in 642 the Saracens won the whole of Persia, and thereafter extended their dominion eastward and north-eastward to the Indus and the Jaxartes.

## ISLAM'S CONQUESTS IN EUROPE AND ASIA IN THE SEVENTH CENTURY

### CHAPTER 15

# ISLAM'S GREAT CENTURY OF CONQUEST: 632–732

THE dominating feature of the hundred years whose story is recorded in this chapter is the sudden and unprecedented expansion in the East of a newly organized and semi-barbaric but militant religious community into a conquering world power. In Europe, on the other hand, we have to watch the continuation of the process that was dominant in our last chapter, the disintegration of the old order and the emerging of the bases of a new order.

Among the followers of the Prophet there was none whom he trusted more completely or more deservedly than Abu Bekr and Omar. He had not, however, definitely nominated any successor. He left no heir of his body; but, if the headship of the Faithful was to go by heredity, Ali, his daughter Fatima's husband, was the obvious and, in fact, the only claimant. Practically the decision lay with the chiefs who were present at Medina when the Prophet died; they ignored the theory of heredity and chose the man whose record and character carried the most weight, Abu Bekr, the father of Mahomet's youngest and favourite wife, Ayesha.

## Abu Bekr Secures the Khalifate

THERE was no lack of pretenders to the succession which had been fixed by the arbitrary action of one group among many. By the skill of Abu Bekr's lieutenants and by the khalif's own tact the tribal jealousies were all rapidly suppressed; the more readily, perhaps, because he did not allow them to interfere with the immediate execution of Mahomet's project of conquest. One army was dispatched to Syria, another to the lower Euphrates—Mesopotamia or Irak—where the population was largely Arabic and had no love for its Persian rulers; tiny forces indeed to launch against the might of Persia and the might of Rome simultaneously, at a moment when it was at least doubtful whether Arabia was to hold together or break in fragments.

But the revolts were suppressed, not without ruthlessness, but also not without generosity; and in 633 reinforcements were dispatched to both fronts, under Abu Obeida to Syria, and under Khalid, surnamed 'The Sword of Allah,' to Irak.

Persia was rent by dynastic turmoils; but the satrap Hormuz could bring into the field a force much larger than Khalid's 20,000. Nevertheless the Persians were routed in three successive engagements in March, April and May. The story runs that in the third battle, of Allis, and the pursuit, seventy thousand prisoners were collected and then massacred in cold blood in the dry bed of a canal, known thenceforth as the River of Blood. Khalid then proceeded to reduce the Hira province on the west of the Euphrates.

### Syria abandoned to the Saracens

THE armies in Syria were meeting with no such brilliant successes. The Roman forces were mustering and the Arab or Saracen captains were not so enterprising as Khalid. The opposing battalions lay so long facing each other and doing nothing more, on an extended front, the Romans of course being much the more numerous, that Khalid with half his men was transferred in 634, with his work in Irak uncompleted, to Syria. The veterans who took part in the great Persian campaigns of Heraclius, not ten years earlier, had been for the most part disbanded; the new levies were of poor quality; the presence of Khalid was an inspiration; and in the late summer the Saracens won a crushing victory on the Yermak.

Next year Damascus fell. Heraclius once more took the field in person, but he had become hopelessly enfeebled by disease; the supreme and magnificent effort of the Persian war had been followed by reaction, besides leaving the Empire desperately crippled ; and in 636 the emperor abandoned Syria, emphasising the completeness of the defeat by carrying with him to Constantinople the True Cross, which, after his triumph over the Persians, had been once more enshrined at Jerusalem. Antioch and Jerusalem itself fell in 637, and the capture of the great port of Caesarea in 640 completed the conquest of Syria.

Equally decisive were the operations against Persia. Mothanna, the very able commander, left by the withdrawal of Khalid with a very small force, could only maintain himself with extreme difficulty, and was barely able to extricate a remnant of the troops from a disaster brought upon them by a captain who had been sent to supersede him. For Mothanna was only a Beduin chief, under whom neither the Companions of the Prophet nor the great families of Medina would condescend to serve.

Perhaps because he was a Beduin, Mothanna made his appeal not to the religion but to the patriotism, the sense of common nationality, of the Beduins of the Mesopotamian region. On that score he was able to add to his little force Christian tribes who refused to renounce their faith, by whose aid he won a brilliant victory at Boweib. Shortly after, however, he died, just as a new commander, Zaid, was arriving with new levies.

It was Zaid who directed the campaign of 635, in which was fought the decisive three-days' action of Kadesia, an overwhelming victory, though almost until the close of the third day the issue was extremely doubtful. The Persian field army was shattered, and the way was open for the conquest of Mesopotamia. In the summer of 636 Zaid was able to advance on Medain (Ctesiphon), the Persian capital, lying on both sides of the Tigris. Early in 637 Ctesiphon fell, and the Persian king and empire were driven behind the mountain barrier on the east of the great river.

**CONQUEROR OF CHOSROES**
East Roman emperor from 610 to 641, Heraclius' reign, troubled by war and theological dissension, ended with the Empire menaced by the rising flood of Islam.
*British Museum*

The khalif Omar, who had succeeded Abu Bekr some two and a half years before, was minded to organize the conquests that had been made rather than to push farther afield. The subjugation of northern Syria and of upper Mesopotamia, completed during the next three years, was only giving the necessary finish to what had been done when the capture of Ctesiphon in the east balanced the capture of Jerusalem in the west. The Taurus on one side and the Perso-Median mountains on the other would be the natural bounds between the Saracen Empire and the empires of Persia and Rome.

By 640 those bounds had been attained ; the Saracen dominion covered all that had ever owned the sway of Babylon or Assyria, save Egypt. But circumstances were too strong for the khalif's policy. Egypt was a bait too valuable to be resisted, and Persian rather than Arab aggression forced his hand in the east. Both Egypt and Persia had been annexed before his death in 644.

The conquest of Egypt in fact presented no very serious difficulty. The population of the Nile basin, as distinct from the cosmopolitan city of Alexandria, had no affection for the Empire, being strongly addicted to the Monophysite heresy, which orthodox Byzantium sought to repress. Moreover, since it was mainly from Egypt that the Empire obtained its central corn-supply, the Egyptian cultivator was systematically exploited for the requirements of the imperial government. An Arab conquest would merely mean a change of task-masters. On the other hand, the possession of Egypt would be invaluable, both as an immediate source of wealth and as crippling the Empire.

In 640, when Caesarea had fallen, and Syria, under its governor, the Ommiad Moawiya (Muavia), no longer offered promise of distinction, one of the commanders, Amru, obtained a somewhat reluctant permission from Omar to invade

Egypt. A force of sixteen thousand men proved sufficient to effect the conquest, finishing with the capitulation of Alexandria, in 641, with little serious fighting, the dying Heraclius making no effort for its relief.

So when the news came in 641 that the Persian king, Yezdigird, was mustering from every province of his empire a vast army of invasion, Omar took up the challenge, and was hardly restrained from himself assuming the command of the force he raised to smite the Persian. In 642 at the battle of Nehavend thirty thousand Mahomedans shattered and scattered a Persian army of five times their numbers. Even then Yezdigird the Unlucky refused to come to terms, and, though driven perpetually from pillar to post, maintained the hopeless struggle for nearly ten years, until his death in 651. But Nehavend had decided the issue. Persia had been won for Islam. Yezdigird was the last of her Sassanid kings.

The great Omar fell in 644 beneath the dagger of an assassin who then slew himself—the victim of a purely personal vindictiveness. The policy of expansion to which he committed himself only in his last years was continued under his successors in the Khalifate. While Othman ruled at Medina (644–656), the conquest and incorporation of Persia were carried to the Oxus. Amru, the conqueror of Egypt, annexed the Cyrenaica, or Barca and Tripolis, pushing along the Mediterranean littoral. The regency at Constantinople (the emperor at the time being a young boy) put forth a great effort soon after Omar's death, and recaptured Alexandria, which Amru was only able to recover after a year's siege (646). Six years later the attempt was repeated ; but this time it was defeated by the Saracen fleet which had been created in the interval by Amru's successor, Abu Sarh.

Moawiya in Syria had long ago urged on Omar the necessity of a fleet ; but to him the idea had seemed a tempting of Providence. Othman, however, proved more amenable. A fleet was built, manned by Syrian and Egyptian sailors and Arab

PIECE OF THE TRUE CROSS RECOVERED BY HERACLIUS FROM THE PERSIANS

After the defeat, deposition and assassination of Chosroes in 628, Heraclius signed a treaty of peace with the Persian Siroes, including in its terms the restitution of the true wood of the Holy Cross. In the following year Heraclius made a personal pilgrimage to Jerusalem, and the relic was restored to the Holy Sepulchre. A fragment of the true cross, brought probably from Constantinople about 1155, is enshrined in this enamelled gold triptych now in the Metropolitan Museum of New York.

*From 'Archaeologia,' by permission of the Society of Antiquaries and the Pierpoint-Morgan Library*

warriors. In 649 it effected the capture of Cyprus, Abu Sarh being one of the commanders ; again under his command it won the victory which drove the imperial fleet from Alexandria in 652 ; and in 655 it crowned its successes by inflicting a decisive defeat on the Byzantine fleet off Phoenix on the Lycian coast, in the heaviest sea-fight since Actium.

The revival of Byzantine activity under the regency was not confined to the effort at Alexandria. In 646 a Byzantine force invaded Syria from Asia Minor. Omar's embargo on aggressive movement beyond the borders was no longer operative, and Moawiya not only repelled the attack but carried the war into the enemy's country. Troops from Syria raided farther and farther into Asia Minor in successive years, pushing nearer and nearer to the western limit of Asia, while the security of Europe itself was threatened by the passing of the command of the eastern Mediterranean into the hands of the Saracen fleet.

Thus much had been or was being achieved on the western side when, in 656, the murder of Othman and the acceptance of the Khalifate by Ali the twice disappointed brought to a head the family jealousies and tribal rivalries which threatened Islam with disruption, and immediately developed into a war of contending factions. Moawiya, who was to be one of the leading figures in the fight, made haste to arrange a truce with the Eastern emperor, to whom a respite from the Saracen war was more than welcome. For a time the expansion of Islam was suspended by civil war.

### Dissension in the Ranks of Islam

THE initial strength of Islam lay in the unity created by Mahomet, and with difficulty preserved by the great qualities of the first two khalifs. But no satisfactory scheme of appointment to the Khalifate, on which the whole system of Islam centred, had been devised. Personal prestige had carried the day for Abu Bekr and Omar, to whose fidelity, moderation and organizing ability Islam was deeply indebted. But on Omar's death and the flat refusal of the successor on whom his own choice had fallen, the committee of selection had chosen the least competent of their number, the septuagenarian Othman, whose strongest recommendation was that he was Mahomet's son-in-law.

Othman was of the Ommiad family, to which also belonged Moawiya, the governor of Syria ; a house whose favour was deeply resented by many, since it had for many years headed the Meccan hostility to Mahomet, though itself of the Koreish tribe to which the Prophet himself belonged. Disaffection, then, spread among the old Companions of the Prophet on the one hand and on the other among the Beduin chiefs who always resented the priority of the Koreish.

### War between Ali and Moawiya

THE head and front of Othman's offending was the unpopularity and the arrogance of his governors at Kufa, at Basra and in Egypt ; but additional ground for complaint was found in his issuing a revision of the Koran, and additional encouragement to disaffection in his obvious weakness in dealing with the disloyal elements. The most prominent of the Companions at Medina, Ali, Zobeir and Talha, flattered themselves that they were loyal, but when the crisis came in 656 their display of loyalty was of a most perfunctory character. They offered no effective resistance to a long-prepared insurrection at Medina, in which the aged khalif was cruelly done to death ; and the insurgents, before they left the city, compelled Ali to assume the Khalifate. The immediate result was civil war.

The insurrection had been jointly organized from Kufa, Basra and Egypt, but each had chosen a different candidate. Ali was the choice of the Egyptian group who carried the affair through. Zobeir and Talha, old Companions both, gave their allegiance to Ali ; but were soon in open rebellion urged on by Ayesha, Mahomet's widow, who detested Ali. The pretext was Ali's failure to punish Othman's murderers, which Moawiya in Syria too made a ground for refusing allegiance. Apart from Syria there were four factions, Basra, Kufa, the regicides who had actually made Ali khalif, and those who adhered to Ali as loyalists. Kufa came over to Ali, but none of the parties could really be reconciled with the regicides, who broke up attempted negotiations lest they should find all the rest making common cause against them. Near Basra they forced a fierce engagement, known as the ' battle of the camel,' because the camel and litter of Ayesha were the centre of the hottest fighting, between Ali and the rebels. The khalif was victorious ; both Talha and Zobeir were killed ; but it was the victory not of

**EMPERORS WHO STAYED THE MARCH OF ISLAM**
Constans II (left), emperor 642–68, and his son and successor Constantine IV, were both capable rulers. The former checked the Arab advance in Africa, the latter repelled the Saracens' successive assaults upon Constantinople. The beard which gave him his sobriquet ' Pogonatus ' is well shown in this coin.
*British Museum*

order represented by the khalif himself but of his allies, the regicides and the ever-turbulent Kufa.

Moawiya then was the one positive rival. The supreme authority of the khalif was essential to Islam, but Ali had been raised to the Khalifate by the murderers of the legitimate khalif Othman. He could not be recognized till he dissociated himself from and crushed the forces of anarchy, to which the victory of Basra had in effect only attached him the more closely. Moawiya was strong in having at his side Amru, the conqueror of Egypt. Ali, the least vindictive of men, desired not war but peace, but he could not simply acquiesce in Moawiya's defiance.

He marched against Moawiya. Negotiations were opened while skirmishes went on ; then a severe but indecisive battle was fought at Siffin. Then both sides agreed to refer the question to the authority of the Koran, with Amru and Musa, the governor of Kufa, as judges. Amru

overreached Musa, so that the judgement which should have deposed both Ali and Moawiya actually deposed only the former, six months after the suspension of hostilities—and the conflict remained in suspense. Moawiya had a colourable pretext for claiming that he was khalif, but it was not his policy to attack his rival directly ; while Ali not only viewed civil war with reluctance, but was also hampered by the development among his former followers of a fanatically puritan sect called the Kharejites, who wished to abolish the Khalifate and set up an impossible theocracy.

Their number was small, but though they were temporarily crushed at Nehrwan they were not extirpated. The result was that three of the zealots resolved to assassinate both the khalifs (who had come to an agreement) and Amru, lest the last should succeed to the Khalifate. Amru escaped altogether ; Moawiya survived the attack and recovered ; but Ali's wound was mortal (560).

His elder son Hasan, a feeble creature, succeeded him, but very soon abdicated in favour of Moawiya, who thus became sole khalif and founder of the Ommiad dynasty (661).

Formal unity having been restored, Moawiya reigned unchallenged till his death in 680. It was his ambition to make the Khalifate hereditary in his own family ; and to that end, four years before he died, he procured the nomination of his son Yezid as his successor.

IT has been noted that at the beginning of the troubles Moawiya arranged a truce with the Empire. The pacification set him free to renew the policy of expansion. This was at first directed to the African littoral. In 663 the Saracen advance captured Carthage but was driven back again to Tripolis. But Moawiya's forces were soon operating in Asia Minor, the emperor Constans II being fully occupied in the west till he was assassinated in 668. The new emperor Constantine IV

Pogonatus was only eighteen, and for some time Moawiya's arms met with success. In 673 he was in possession of the Asiatic shore of the Sea of Marmora and laid siege to Constantinople itself. Then the tide turned. The Byzantine fleet, armed with a new weapon, presumably some kind of explosive, known as Greek fire, recovered the mastery of the sea and drove off the Saracens. In 678 Moawiya had to sue for peace, and the hostilities were again suspended for several years. If conquest had been checked in the West after some striking successes, in the East the power of the Saracens had made itself felt both in Khorassan and on the borders of India. But the accession of Yezid (680–683) inaugurated a fresh period of civil discord which continued for five and twenty years.

### Troublous Reign of Yezid I

YEZID'S reign began with tragedy. There was no precedent for the manner of his appointment. A strong backing was to be expected for the claims of Husain, the second of Ali's sons and Mahomet's grandsons, and also for Abdallah the son of Zobeir. Both were at Mecca. Unhappily, Husain was induced by the expectation of support from Kufa to march thither with his family and a very small group of adherents. The Beduins who joined him on the way deserted as soon as they learnt that no help was forthcoming from Kufa, which was in the iron grip of its governor, Obeidullah. An overwhelming force was sent out to arrest Husain. To fight was madness, but a madness which he preferred to the unconditional surrender demanded of him. He and his little band sold their lives dearly ; but they were all cut to pieces, among them two of his sons, two sons of Hasan, and six brothers. The women were treated with honour, and the youngest son was spared. But seventy heads were carried in to Obeidullah.

The slaughter was quite unnecessary, for Husain had offered to surrender on condition that he should be sent to Yezid at Damascus, the residence of the Syrian khalifs. Yezid denounced Obeidullah and repudiated his action. But the thing was done. The seed of the Prophet had been all but extirpated at Kerbela on the tenth day of the month Moharram, and the Ommiad khalif was responsible for the deed his minister had perpetrated. A shudder ran through the whole Mahomedan world, and of Husain's martyrdom a creed was born, the creed of the divine right of the seed of the Prophet to the Khalifate ; the creed which was to split Islam in twain between the Shiah party who adhered to it and the Sunnis who rejected it.

Medina and Mecca, the nursery and the sanctuary of Islam, refused to recognize Yezid ; Mecca proclaimed Abdallah. In 683 Yezid's army stormed and sacked Medina ruthlessly, and Mecca was on the verge of suffering the same fate when Yezid died. The Syrian army retired when Abdallah rejected the overtures of its chief, whose share in the sack of Medina the men of the old school would not forgive. Kufa acknowledged Abdallah, while Syria sought out a new Ommiad, Merwan. Broadly speaking, the main cleavage was between Syria and Irak ; but of the two Irakian centres Basra was rent by the remnant of the Kharejite zealots and Kufa by the new Shiah sect, which would acknowledge no khalif save one of the seed of the Prophet. At the same time, what was left of the old believers betook themselves to Africa, where the advance had again become active since the death of Constantine Pogonatus in 685. The absorption of Numidia and Mauretania prepared the way for a further geographical cleavage of Islam.

### The Ommiad Dynasty restored

ABDALLAH IBN ZOBEIR maintained himself at Mecca till 691. In Syria Merwan was murdered in 685, but he had already secured the succession of his son Abd el-Malik (685–705), who turned on Irak, and in a very short time crushed or won over the supporters of Abdallah. Then his famous general Hajjaj in 691 renewed the attack on Abdallah at Mecca which had been broken off by the death of Yezid eight years before. Mecca was again besieged, but was saved from impending destruction when Abdallah, in a desperate sally, was siain (692) at the head of his small band. With the fall of Abdallah, resistance ended.

Once more there was a single Ommiad khalif, Abd el-Malik, the inventor of the capitation tax upon Christians throughout the Khalifate. But though order and control were gradually restored, insurrections were constant. On the other hand, marked progress was made in the African advance. Carthage was finally taken in 698, and as the Arabs slowly gained the mastery over the Berbers, Numidians and Moors, these tribesmen became foremost in their Mahomedan zeal. When Abd el-Malik died in 705, Islam was already casting greedy glances towards the shore of Spain. But before carrying further the story of Islam, we must again take up the tale of the West.

### Fortunes of the Heraclian House

**W**HEN Heraclius died in 641, he was succeeded by two sons, Heraclius Constantinus and Heracleonas. The elder died almost immediately ; his ten-year-old son, variously known as Constans II or Constantine IV, was associated with Heracleonas as emperor ; in 642 Heracleonas died, and the boy Constans became sole emperor. During his minority the government was conducted by the Senate. The truce between Moawiya and Constans, brought about by the death of Othman, enabled the emperor to devote himself to the affairs of Italy, on which he was mainly engaged till his death in 668.

Before departing for the West, however, the young emperor reorganized the governments in Asia Minor. He had already attempted to enforce a compromise, known as ' the Type,' in the Monothelite controversy, but this proceeding met with the usual ill-success of such efforts, embittered the parties, and caused a violent breach with the Roman Pope Martin, who had in consequence been in effect kidnapped and carried off into exile in the Crimea, where he died. Rome on this question was in agreement with the Orthodox in the East ; but the affair intensified the antagonism between the pretensions of Rome to spiritual supremacy and the claims of the imperial patriarchate at the Eastern capital.

Constans apparently had the design of restoring the imperial supremacy in Italy, now dominated by the Lombard kingdom in the north and the Lombard dukes in the south. Rothari, duke of Brescia, had succeeded to the Lombard crown in 636. He had completed the subjugation of the north and narrowed the boundaries of the imperial exarchate at Ravenna, and he reduced the laws and customs of the Lombards to a written code. His reign (636–652) gave promise of consolidation which was wrecked by his death. Ten years later the crown was seized by Grimoald, duke of Benevento, who set his son Romoald in control of the south ; and it was in these circumstances that Constans set out on his Italian expedition in 662.

In the campaign of 663 Constans overran South Italy and visited Rome ; but then, without attacking the northern kingdom, he retired unmolested through the south and took up his headquarters at Syracuse.

**HAVOC LEFT BY CONQUERING ISLAM**
These ruins of a Byzantine basilica are a memorial of the Carthage that was a stronghold of early Christianity in Africa. Belisarius in 533 recovered the city to the Byzantine Empire from its Vandal conquerors, but in 647 the Arabs swept into North Africa and in 698 burned Carthage to the ground.
*Photo, G. R. Ballance*

From that base he directed the African campaigns which recovered the recently captured Carthage from the Saracens and drove them back to Tripoli. But his merciless exactions from the Sicilians and south Italians for the expenses of the war alienated the populations.

In 668 Constans was murdered at Syracuse by a slave who was probably the instrument of a conspiracy. He was succeeded by his son Constantine IV (668–685), as yet a beardless youth, though he soon acquired on campaign a beard which won him the nickname Pogonatus, ' the bearded.' After suppressing a usurper at Syracuse who had tried to make his own profit out of the murder of Constans, the young emperor plunged into the war which Moawiya, now sole and undisputed khalif, had recently renewed in Asia Minor. His armies were at first so far unsuccessful that in 673 the Saracens opened the siege of Constantinople. At that point, however, the tide turned. The Saracens were forced to retire to Cyzicus on the Asiatic shore of the Sea of Marmora, their fleets were constantly beaten off, and in 678 Constantine imposed a peace which established his high reputation.

At about the same time, however, Bulgaria came into being as a kingdom. The Slavs had long been in occupation of Moesia. To expel them had proved impossible, and Constans had made terms with them which practically left them independent. The Bulgars had then crossed the Danube in force, dominated the Slavs, and were now rapidly amalgamating with them. Constantine recognized the Bulgarian kingdom in 679.

In the next year a general council of the churches, Eastern and Western, was held at Constantinople, which finally banned the Monothelite heresy.

**A**FTER the death of Constantine the Bearded in 685, the Empire fell on evil days. The young emperor, Justinian II, who was deposed in 695, restored in 705

LAST OF THE HERACLIAN DYNASTY

Justinian II was born in 669 and came to the throne in 685. A brilliant but tempestuous and vindictive man, he was deposed and banished to the Crimea in 695, but recovered his throne in 705 and thereafter indulged in an orgy of cruelty, ended by his own murder in 711.

*British Museum*

and killed in 711, was not unlike the English King John ; for he had brilliant abilities which he exercised spasmodically, but was too completely the slave of his own passions, vindictiveness in particular, to be able to preserve what he won.

A successful campaign against the Bulgarians in 690 excited his military ambitions, and in 693 he picked a quarrel with Abd el-Malik, whose rival Abdallah Ibn Zobeir had been slain a year before. Justinian invaded Syria through the Taurus, only to meet with an overwhelming defeat at Sebastopolis ; where he was deserted by a number of his forced levies, for whose defection he took a strange revenge by slaughtering their comrades who had remained loyal. Meanwhile his ministers at Constantinople had been extorting monstrous taxes by monstrous methods ; and he himself had been dealing so drastically with generals who met with reverses that one who had hitherto been successful, Leontius, revolted in 695, seized his person, slit his nose—an ingenious method of disfigurement that had recently come into vogue—and sent him off to imprisonment in the Crimea.

Leontius was deposed in 698 by officers returning from Africa, who were afraid of paying the penalty for the loss of Carthage, just captured by the Saracens. They slit his nose, shut him up in a monastery, and made Tiberius III emperor (698–705). He fought some successful campaigns against the Saracens and penetrated into northern

Syria. But in 705 Justinian escaped from the Crimea, got help from the king of Bulgaria, was received into Constantinople by traitors, seized the palace, resumed the diadem, and put to death both Leontius and Tiberius, after treading on their necks as they lay bound and prostrate before him. He then indulged in an orgy of undiscriminating cruelty, which was only ended by a military insurrection headed by the general, Philippicus, and his own death at the hands of the soldiery in 711. So ended the house of Heraclius.

𝕴N Italy Grimoald usurped the Lombard crown, as we have seen, in 662, expelling the young heir, Berthari. His rule was vigorous ; he checked the threatened attack of Constans in the north ; he repelled invasions of the Avars and Franks ; he maintained friendly relations with the Papacy. On his death in 672 the Lombards recalled Berthari, a mild and religious prince, who reigned peaceably and benevolently till his death. His son Cunibert (688–700) had much trouble with rebellious dukes. When he died the crown was snatched from his young son by his cousin Aribert of Turin (701–711), who in his turn was overthrown by the adherents of the old royal family, so that in 712 the Lombard crown fell to Liutprand (712–743), probably the ablest of all the Lombard kings.

In the Frankish kingdom the power had in the meantime passed for ever from the royal house of the Merwings ; though a succession of phantoms continued to occupy the throne, crowned usually when children, and surviving only long enough to beget a boy or two to keep up the phantom line of the ' rois fainéants,' the ' do-nothing kings.' Sigibert, the first of the fainéants, succeeded Dagobert, the last effective Merwing, in 638. Next year died Pepin the Old, whose son Grimoald claimed to succeed him as mayor of the palace, and made good his claim by force of arms. But when, on Sigibert's death in 656, he tried to set his own son on the Austrasian throne, the Franks would not displace the old dynasty. It was the Neustrian mayor of the palace, Ebroin, who secured the supremacy, and ruled tyranically till 670, when he was overthrown and thrust into a monastery by a coalition of Austrasian and Neustrian nobles and bishops. But he broke out again some years later when the reigning king, Childeric, died, got his own Merwing nominee, Theuderic, on to the throne, and again ruled as a tyrant till he was murdered in 671. Then after seven years of constant strife, Pepin the Younger, nephew of Grimoald and grandson both of Pepin the Old and Arnulf of Metz, established himself as mayor of the palace for both Austrasia and Neustria, while he still left Theuderic III titular king of all the Franks. The king did not count.

On Pepin's death the succession to the mayoralty was secured after a four years' struggle by his (illegitimate) son Charles Martel (the Hammer), who reigned from 719 to 741, and thoroughly established the Arnulfing dynasty, though it was only in the reign of his son that it assumed the regal title and the name Carolingian, by which it is known.

Meanwhile the Visigothic kingdom was making the way easy for the power which was preparing to supersede it. Two only of the many kings who reigned between 631 and 711 were men of capacity and vigour. The first was Chindaswinth (641–652), who was verg-

**THE IRON CROWN OF LOMBARDY**

Made for Agilulf, king of the Lombards, in 591, this iron crown was used in the coronation of all Lombard kings and all Holy Roman Emperors who were also kings of Lombardy. The interior is said to be hammered from a nail of the true cross. The jewelled exterior was added about 1100.

*Photo, Alinari*

ing on eighty when he was elected, but displayed all the energy of a ripe middle age in reducing the turbulent nobles to obedience, and enabled his son to rule peaceably for twenty years after his death. The election then fell upon Wamba (672-680), who was again forced to smite the rebellious nobles with a heavy hand in the first year of his reign, but was thereafter able to rule in peace. With these two exceptions every one of the kings, both before and after them, was more occupied with conciliating the clergy than with the governance of the land. The last of the series was Roderic, elected in 710, who lost his life in the cataclysm of 711.

GREAT was the glory of Islam in the days of the khalif Walid (705-715), and evil were those days in the history of the Christian Empire. For in the year of Walid's accession Justinian II recovered his crown, and when he had regained power used it only to play the tyrant. In 711 Philippicus slew him and made himself emperor after the evil precedent set by the mutineers who had made Phocas emperor a century earlier. In that same year the Saracens destroyed the Visigothic kingdom and laid the foundation of the Moorish dominion in Spain, not to be eliminated till all but eight centuries had gone by. Also in that year their fleets descended on Sardinia and tore from the Empire the most westerly province which still acknowledged its sovereignty.

Two years later another conspiracy set Anastasius II in the place of Philippicus; after two years more, in 715, the year in which Walid died, Anastasius fell and Theodosius III was made emperor. Collapse seemed imminent, but at that critical moment the Khalifate passed into feebler hands, and two years later Theodosius anticipated his own deposition

**VISIGOTHIC VOTIVE CROWNS OF GOLD**

After the reign of Reccared (586–601) when Catholicism was made the state religion, the Visigothic kingdom of Spain grew gradually weaker under a succession of priest-dominated kings. These votive crowns of gem-encrusted gold, found at Guarrazar, point to the deference paid by the state to the church

*Photo, Giraudon*

by a judicious abdication in favour of the man who would otherwise have forcibly ejected him, Leo III the Isaurian.

Walid succeeded at what might fairly be reckoned a fortunate moment. There were no dangerous pretenders to the Khalifate. He had in his service the mighty and merciless Hajjaj, who had crushed by degrees the perpetual sporadic resistance in Irak and Persia to the rule of Abd el-Malik. In Abd el-Malik's latter years the Byzantines had been finally ejected from Africa, and the khalif's lieutenant, Musa, had carried the Saracen dominion to the Pillars of Hercules. The time was ripe for advance.

Walid, or Walid's officers, did advance, and without delay. In Transoxiana Koteiba waged successful war, subjugating or enrolling the Turkish nomads; in 709 he captured Bokhara after a hard siege; in 712 Samarkand fell to his arms. He was on the way to Kashgar when the campaign was suspended in 715 by the death of Walid and the accession of his son Suleiman (715–717).

During the reign of Abd el-Malik, Kabul had been made tributary. In 711 Hajjaj at Basra found occasion to quarrel with Dahir, the Rajput raja of Sindh and the southern Punjab, thus for the first time bringing India into direct contact with the Mahomedan power. Hajjaj sent his son Kasim to deal with the Indian prince; and though a stubborn resistance was offered by Multan

**LEO THE ISAURIAN**

Leo III (717–741), founder of the Isaurian Dynasty, saved Constantinople from the Saracens in 717, routed them at Nicaea in 727 and finally removed the menace by his victory at Acroinon in 740.

*British Museum*

and other towns, Sindh was subjugated, and remained under Arab sway till the fall of the Ommiad dynasty.

The greatest triumph, however, of the Mahomedan arms was in the West. In 711, which Islam might well have reckoned as its 'year of victories,' the bolt fell upon Spain. Musa, now master of the whole north African littoral, dispatched a great force across the Strait of Gibraltar (Jebel Tarik), named after Tarik, the leader of the expedition. The Saracen host landed unopposed; Roderic gathered all the troops that he could muster, and on the banks of the Guadalete fought a seven days' battle with the invaders. His

**GREAT MOSQUE AT DAMASCUS BUILT BY THE EARLY OMMIADS**

Damascus became the seat of the Khalifate on the establishment of the Ommiad dynasty in 661, but it was not until the reign of Walid (705–715), a great patron of architecture, that the Moslems erected a mosque there. The Great Mosque was then built in its present form. It comprises a vast open court, measuring 430 feet by 125 feet, surrounded by stone arcades, that on the south side opening into the mosque proper, the dome-crowned inner sanctuary.

*From Briggs, ' Muhammadan Architecture' : Oxford University Press*

army was virtually annihilated. Roderic was never seen again, and a mere remnant escaped to the hills. The Saracens swept irresistibly over the peninsula, subduing the whole of it before two years were passed ; only in the fastnesses of the far north-west a stubborn few, who doubtless seemed not to be worth the trouble of subduing, still upheld a precarious freedom.

While Tarik was obliterating the Visigoths in Spain, the Saracen fleet was annexing the island of Sardinia, as another naval base for the lordship of the Mediterranean. This was also the moment when Philippicus was appropriating the imperial crown, which he was quite unfit to wear. It is not surprising, therefore, that in this same year Walid's armies renewed the long-suspended attack on Asia Minor, raided through the Taurus, and wrought havoc in Cappadocia. Before Walid was dead they had mastered Pisidia and Pontus ; but it was left to Walid's successor, Suleiman, to concentrate on the second great attack on Constantinople, where the third revolution in the course of four years, the sixth in eighteen, had just crowned the unwilling Theodosius III.

### Suleiman's disastrous Reign

THE glories of Walid had been due not to his own genius or vigour, but to his wisdom in choosing ministers whom he trusted, who knew that he trusted them, and who repaid his trust. Suleiman, like Philip II of Spain, trusted no man, dreaded everyone who had shown distinguished capacity, and, whenever he could, killed everyone whom he dreaded. As a natural consequence, his two years' reign was disastrous. From the time of his accession the Ommiad dynasty hastened to its inglorious end.

Hajjaj, happily for himself, was already dead. Musa was promptly disgraced. Koteiba, the conqueror of Transoxiana, sought to prevent the evil day by revolting, but his troops remained loyal, and he was slain ; the eastern advance, however, was stayed.

At the moment everything seemed auspicious for the great blow at the Empire. A mighty armament was made ready by sea and land under the command of the khalif's brother Moslemah for the siege of Constantinople. At Amorium, in the heart of Asia Minor, the Empire had a stout defender in its commander Leo the Isaurian, who held the Saracens at bay ; but Leo chose to make a truce with the foreign foe, and to march on the capital proclaiming himself emperor in the place of the latest incompetent occupant of the imperial throne. A struggle for the crown seemed likely to make the fall of Constantinople only the more certain.

### Constantinople saved by Leo

BUT Constantinople did not fall. Not for the first nor for the last time that city of factions, when it seemed to be past redemption, showed an amazing power of recuperation. A century ago it had risen to the call of Heraclius ; now it rose to the call of the Isaurian to whom the relieved Theodosius handed over the diadem to which he preferred for himself the cowl of a monk. The hosts of Arab and Persian warriors poured for the first time across the Hellespont, but the walls of the city were impregnable. Their fleets swarmed up to the Bosporus, but the fleet which issued from the port of Byzantium spread panic among them by sending down fire-ships, and completed their defeat by the new and terrible artillery of the Greek fire, an explosive of which the composition was a rigorously guarded state secret. Its first use would seem to have been by Constantine the Bearded. The Saracen fleet fell back, and with the Black Sea open to them the Byzantines were in no lack of supplies.

Suleiman died. In the spring the new khalif, Omar II (717-719), sent great reinforcements by land and sea. Again the fleet sailed up the Bosporus ; and this time practically the whole of it was sunk or taken and carried to the harbour of Byzantium, partly by a repetition of the previous tactics, partly because many of the crews deserted to the other side. Leo followed up the naval victory by landing a force on the Asiatic shore which dispersed the Saracen force there, and cut the communications between Asia and the European force under Moslemah, who had the utmost difficulty in keeping his army

**ICONOCLASTS DEFACING A GRAVEN IMAGE**
This illustration from a Byzantine eleventh century psalter depicts a company of image breakers defacing an icon. The iconoclastic controversy was brought to a head by the edict of Leo III in 726, forbidding the worship of images and relics, and rent the Church for a hundred years.
*British Museum, Add. MSS.* 19352

from starvation. Then came the news that the Bulgar king was mobilising a great force against the Saracens. Moslemah raised the siege, and cut his way back through Asia Minor to Syria with what was left of the Grand Army. What was left of the Grand Fleet was shattered in a storm off the Lycian coast (718). Leo had decisively saved the Eastern Empire from the Arab menace. Centuries passed before Asia Minor was again invaded in force by Saracen armies.

Omar, a most virtuous and pious prince, was succeeded by Yezid II (720–724). Revolt was again raised in Irak, and in Africa, which was on its way to separation. Yezid was followed by Hisham (724–743), who was mainly occupied in accumulating wealth and maintaining a balance between the Irakian and Syrian factions, while the Abbasids, a second branch of the Hashimites, the kinsmen of Mahomet, were unostentatiously propagating their own claim to be the true representatives of the Prophet, which propaganda was presently to bear fruit.

**The Iconoclastic Controversy**

THE reign of Leo III (717–740) opened with the triumphant conflict with the Khalifate, the issue of which was confirmed in 727, when a victory over the Saracens at Nicaea finally drove them beyond the Taurus, though it did not completely terminate their incursions. But his rule is only less important in another field ; for he is perhaps more

familiarly recognized as Leo the Iconoclast than as Leo the Isaurian, the name under which we think of him as the saviour of Europe.

As a political factor, the Monothelite controversy pales in comparison with the iconoclastic controversy. Orthodoxy had not long won the decisive victory which finally banned Monothelitism in the Eastern as well as the Western church, when the ecclesiastical world was rent by a fresh contention. The age in which theological subtleties, the correct formulae for expressing especially the Godhead and Manhood at once of the Second Person of the Holy Trinity, most absorbed the acutest intellects of the doctors of the Church, and excited the most violent animosities among those who were not doctors at all, was also the age in which unreasoning credulity was most rife ; when unaccustomed natural events were habitually attributed to supernatural agency, when miraculous legends became accepted history, and when the power of working miracles was commonly believed to reside not only in saints departed or still in the flesh, but also in relics and in carven or painted representations of Christ, of His Mother, and of the saints.

Inconoclasm was the revolt against such doctrine and its expression in the worship of such images, a worship almost universally encouraged by the clergy, but denounced by the iconoclasts (that is, image breakers) as idolatry. Judaism, and Mahomedanism basing itself on the Hebrew tradition, condemned the ' graven image ' altogether, precisely because its existence was an encouragement to the worship of that which, so long as it was regarded as a symbol and nothing more, was harmless ; Mahomedanism took credit to itself for the destruction of idols and pointed the finger of scorn at the Christian idolators.

Leo, then, resolved to do away with this reproach to Christendom, and in 726 he issued a rescript forbidding the worship of images, and ordering the removal or painting out of sacred statues and pictures, an example which was to be followed in England nine centuries later, in the days of the Puritan domination. The Cross as a symbol he retained ; the Crucifix bearing the image of the Saviour he banned. A mass of intelligent lay opinion was with him ; the clergy, headed by Pope Gregory II at Rome, were solidly against him, and with them were the uninstructed masses to whom the images had become fetishes.

In Italy it was impossible to enforce the edict, while Gregory not only defended the principle of image worship, but denounced the sacrilegious emperor in person with surprising freedom of abuse. Elsewhere the execution of the rescript was attended by furious riots. The antagonism between the papal and the imperial authority reached an unprecedented bitterness, so that Leo prepared once more to appeal to the sword in 732 ; but the elements fought against him and wrecked his fleet before it could reach Italy. So ended, almost before it began, the last attempt of Byzantium to make good its theoretical sovereignty in the West. But in the East the battle between iconoclasts and iconodules was only inaugurated.

### Drastic Interference by Lombardy

THE collision between Gregory and Leo had given the Lombard king Liutprand occasion for aggressive action. The Ravenna exarchate was a wedge between the northern kingdom and the southern duchies. He attacked the exarchate, and before the end of 727 the whole of it was in his hands, with very little fighting. The exarch Eutychius, however, escaped to Venice, now rising to prominence in the security of her lagoons, and in 729 recovered Ravenna by a surprise attack in Liutprand's absence. He then marched on Rome to bring Gregory to reason. Liutprand, who had been engaged (successfully) in similarly bringing the southern dukes to reason, was able to impose a pacification on all the parties, which left the exarch in possession only of Ravenna, and Gregory virtually independent. It was this that caused Leo, two years later, when Gregory III—an equally resolute

opponent—had succeeded Gregory II in the Papacy, to prepare the great but futile expedition of 732.

Meanwhile, Charles the Hammer, firmly established since 720 as mayor of the palace both in Austrasia and Neustria, with Theuderic IV as puppet-king of the whole realm, had been making good the losses that had befallen in the years of anarchy which followed the death of Pepin. Aquitaine, which under its duke Eudo had made itself in effect independent, was left for the time to its own devices ; Charles, as an Austrasian, was more immediately interested in the subjugation of the outlying German provinces on the east. In the course of ten years the Saxons beyond the border had felt the weight of his hand and the reach of his arm ; the Frisian duke was co-operating in the Christianisation of his subjects ; Bavaria was again brought to submission as a vassal state by a series of hard-fought campaigns ; and Charles extended his powerful protection to the English missionary Winfrith or Boniface, whose work among the remoter pagans won him the name of ' the Apostle of Germany.'

By this time, however, a far more dangerous foe was menacing the south. But the story of Charles Martel's culminating triumph must be reserved for the close of this chronicle.

### Contemporary Events in England

ENGLAND during these hundred years of change elsewhere was developing in isolation, save for her contact with the Scots kingdom on the north. The period of invasions was passed. The independent Britons were confined to their own borders in the south-west, in Wales and in the Cumbrian hills ; but neither among them nor among the English was there any tendency to unification other than that of the ascendancy of one or another kingdom or principality over its neighbours. The lead taken by Northumbria, which stretched from Forth to Humber, was lost at Heathfield, recovered on the death in 655 of Penda, the last great heathen, and was again being threatened by the midland kingdom of Mercia as the eighth century advanced ;

while the southern kingdom of Wessex was making marked progress. An attempt to conquer the Scots by the Northumbrian Ecgfrith was decisively shattered in 685 at Nechtansmere.

Paganism disappeared with Penda. The whole island was Christianised, the Celtic portions holding, like the Irish, to the Celtic church, while Northumbria decided (at the Synod of Whitby in 664), like the rest of the English, in favour of the Latin or Roman branch. The organization of the Church in England was carried out mainly by the great archbishop (669–690) Theodore of Tarsus ; the English monasteries, of which the most famous was perhaps Jarrow, enjoyed a high reputation both for learning and piety, and in the eighth century could claim in the Venerable Bede (673–735) the finest scholar and perhaps the most attractive personality in Europe, and the most famous of missionaries in Winfrith or Boniface (680–755) and his predecessor Willibrord (657–738), the apostle of the Frisians.

### TOMB OF THE VENERABLE BEDE
Bede, born c. 673, died at Jarrow, May 26, 735, and was buried in the Benedictine monastery church there. In 1022 his bones were removed to Durham Cathedral and, in 1155, placed in a sumptuous shrine. This was destroyed under Henry VIII, and Bede's bones now rest in this tomb in the Galilee chapel.

*Photo, John R. Edis*

INDIA we have seen brought into temporary contact with the main stream of history by the Arab invasion of Sindh in 711. Harsha's Kanauj empire broke up on his death in 647, but no new empire took its place. It is from this period that most of the great Rajput clans date their records ; a fact which lends force to the theory that their true origin is to be found in the ' Hun ' invaders, who had chosen to merge themselves in the old Kshatriya aristocracy of the Hindus, the royal and warrior caste of Hindu tradition.

China in 632 was under the single sway of Li Shih-min (T'ai Tsung), the second great ruler of the T'ang dynasty. In his reign (627–649) and that of his son Kao Tsung (649–683) Korea was added to the Chinese empire, and its tributary states included Kashmir and Kashgar, the latter of which soon after passed into the possession of Turkish tribes. From the early years of Kao Tsung till the accession of Lung Chi (713–763) the government was controlled by ladies more distinguished for masterful-ness than virtue. A temporary relief, and attendant prosperity, came with the early years of Lung Chi, who improved the administration of justice by insisting on a properly qualified magistracy, and encouraged economy by rigidly cutting down the extravagance of the court. But he, too, in the latter part of his long reign, which extended far beyond the limits of the present chapter, relapsed under sinister female influences.

Here, then, we turn back to the last decisive episode of our period, in the conflict between the Mahomedan and the Christian powers.

### Saracen Irruption into Aquitaine

WE have seen that, before the death of Pepin the Younger of Heristhal, the Saracens—the term applied throughout the Middle Ages to Mahomedans, of whatever race, when in contact or conflict with Europeans—were already masters of Spain and the Visigothic province of Septimania in what was later known as Languedoc. There, however, and in Africa they were torn by the same dissensions and disaffections as in the East. Thus their further advance was checked.

Nevertheless, in 720 they broke over the Pyrenees into Aquitaine and laid siege to Toulouse. They were driven out again by Duke Eudo, who, having professed formal allegiance to the king of the Franks, received aid from the neighbouring Frankish governors; but they still kept their hold on Narbonne, in what had been the Visigothic province of Septimania. In 724 they raided over Burgundy. Internal dissensions kept them quiet for some time; Eudo took the opportunity to make alliance with Othman the governor of Septimania and throw off his own allegiance to Theuderich, while Othman revolted against Abd er-Rahman, the governor of Spain. Othman was promptly crushed, and Eudo made haste to return to his allegiance (731), but in 732 Abd er-Rahman swept into Aquitaine with a vast army and drove Eudo in complete rout over the Loire. The fugitive duke betook himself straightway to Charles to implore his aid.

Fourteen years before, Leo had saved eastern Europe. If in that critical year Moslemah had captured Constantinople, the Saracens would undoubtedly have overrun the Balkan peninsula, and the Eastern Empire, which was still to be the bulwark of Christendom for more than seven centuries, would have gone down. Abd er-Rahman's advance from Spain was probably in fact much less momentous. The conquest of the West would not necessarily have resulted from even the most overwhelming of victories, for there could be no sort of comparison between the Frank power of resistance and recuperation and that of the Visigoths, which crumbled like a pack of cards on the first impact. Nor was there in the West any strategic position which dominated the whole situation as did Constantinople in the East. Moreover, if Islam in the West had not already reached something very near the limit of its capacity for expansion, a single defeat, however overwhelming, would not have driven it, as actually befell, once for all behind the Pyrenees. But a Saracen victory would have brought a Saracen conquest within the range of practical possibilities, and the victory of Charles did at a blow save the West from a prolonged and exhausting struggle with a very uncertain issue.

### Charles the Hammer's final Blow

CHARLES, a master of swift movement, rapidly drew in a great force from every quarter, with which Abd er-Rahman suddenly found himself faced in the neighbourhood of Poitiers—though Tours has given the battle the name by which it is most commonly known. For six days the armies lay opposite each other, manoeuvring and skirmishing. On the morning of the seventh day Abd er-Rahman attacked. Through the day a furious battle raged; vast numbers, including the Saracen chief himself, were slain. The Franks believed that the battle would be renewed the next day, but when the morning broke the enemy were in full flight for the south and their camp was deserted. Charles at Poitiers had repeated, no less decisively, the work of Leo at Byzantium. In Europe it was only in the Spanish peninsula that Islam had made good its footing. Never again did it penetrate beyond the Pyrenees.

# TABLE OF DATES FOR CHAPTER 16

732 Western advance of Saracens broken at Poitiers.
737 Theuderich dies ; no ' King of the Franks.'
741 Charles Martel succeeded by Pepin and Carloman. Emperor Leo III succeeded by Constantine V (Copronymus). Zacharias pope (to 752).
742 Childeric, last Merwing, made titular king. Birth of Charles the Great (Charlemagne).
744 Accession of Merwan II, last Ommiad khalif.
747 Carloman abdicates. Pepin sole duke of Franks.
750 Ommiad Khalifate ended by battle of the Zab. First Abbasid khalif, Abdallah (Al-Saffah). Massacre of Ommiads ; Abd er-Rahman escapes. India : Sindh revolts and expels the Arabs.
752 Pepin first Carolingian king of the Franks. Aistulf of Lombardy takes Ravenna.
753 Iconoclast Council of Constantinople.
754 Pepin's first Lombard campaign ; Aistulf submits. Mansur second Abbasid khalif. Capital transferred from Damascus to Bagdad. Institution of wazirate and mercenary bodyguard.
755 First Bulgar War of Constantine Copronymus. Offa king of Mercia, to 797.
755-6 Pepin's second Lombard campaign. Aistulf compelled to cede Ravenna exarchate to Papacy.
756 Abd er-Rahman (Ommiad) established as independent emir at Cordova (see 750).
759 Pepin expels Saracens from Narbonne and drives them permanently behind the Pyrenees.
761 Constantine begins persecution of the monks.
764 Second Bulgar War of Constantine.
768 Pepin dies. Charles (Charlemagne) and Carloman joint kings of the Franks.
769 Aquitaine finally subjected to the crown.
771 Carloman dies. Charlemagne sole king of Franks.
772 First expedition to Saxony. Pope Stephen appeals to Charlemagne against Desiderius of Lombardy.
773 Lombard campaign of Charlemagne.
774 Submission of Desiderius. Charlemagne annexes the Lombard crown.
775 Leo IV succeeds Constantine Copronymus. Mahdi succeeds Mansur at Bagdad. Charlemagne's first Saxon campaign.
776 Charlemagne's second Saxon campaign.
777 Charlemagne celebrates subjugation of Saxony at the Diet of Paderborn.
778 Charlemagne, invited by Moorish rebels, invades Spain and retires. Fall of Roland at Roncesvalles.
779 Saxon revolt ; third Saxon campaign.
780 Constantine VI succeeds Leo IV. Iconodule reaction under regency of Irene.
782 Fourth Saxon campaign. Massacre of prisoners.
783-5 Conquest and submission of Saxony.
784 Saracens extort tribute from Irene.
785 Advance of Franks in N.E. Spain (Catalonia).
786 Haroun al-Raschid khalif.
787 First Danish raid on English coast.
788 Dukedom of Bavaria broken up and incorporated. Cordova : Hisham succeeds Abd er-Rahman as emir.
789 Charlemagne subjugates northern Slavs.
790 Charlemagne's Avar campaign. Constantine seizes control by a coup d'état.
795 Progress of Frank arms in Catalonia ; appointment of a margrave of the Spanish March. Leo III pope, to 816.
796 Victories of Pepin over the Avars.
797 Irene deposes and blinds Constantine, and herself reigns as empress till 802.
799 First Danish raid on coast of Aquitaine.
800 Pope Leo at the Christmas-day service in S. Peter's crowns Charlemagne Roman emperor. Inauguration of the Holy Roman Empire (to 1806).
801 Barcelona taken from the Spanish Moors.
802 Irene deposed ; Nicephorus Eastern emperor. Egbert king of Wessex (to 839).
803 Haroun destroys the Barmecide family.
805 Tunis independent under the Aglabid dynasty. Submission of the Avars. They are not incorporated, but left dependent and tributary.
807 Hakim emir at Cordova.
808 Godred the Dane harries Frisia.
809 Haroun al-Raschid dies. Emin khalif.

810 Godred killed. Truce with the Danes.
811 Capture of Tortosa by the Franks. Nicephorus killed on Bulgar campaign.
812 Accession of Michael I (Rhangabe) ; he recognizes the Western Empire. Hakim cedes conquests between the Pyrenees and the Ebro ; Moors evacuate Catalonia.
813 Michael I deposed by Leo V (the Armenian). Death of Emin ; Mamun khalif.
814 Death of Charlemagne. His only surviving son, Louis the Pious, emperor
817 Partition of Aachen : Lothair co-emperor and king of Italy, Pepin king of Aquitaine, Lewis (the German) king of Bavaria.
818 Revolt and death of Bernard of Italy.
820 Leo V assassinated ; accession of the Amorian Michael II (the Stammerer).
821 Abd er-Rahman II succeeds Hakim at Cordova.
822 Danish attacks on Frisia renewed. Birth of Charles (the Bald)—the source of many partitions and consequent civil wars.
823 Battle of Ellandune transfers ascendancy in England from Mercia to Wessex. Crete captured by Saracen corsairs.
827 Saracens of Tunis, incited by the traitor Euphemius, invade Sicily and begin the conquest.
829 Egbert acknowledged as over-king in England. Theophilus succeeds Michael II. Louis proposes to provide a kingdom for the child Charles at the expense of his brothers. Beginning of civil wars.
831 Mamun invades Cappadocia. Beginning of a prolonged war between Empire and Khalifate. Slow but continuous progress of the Aglabid conquest of Sicily (till 859).
833 Mutassem succeeds Mamun at Bagdad. War of Louis with his sons. The Lügenfeld. Deposition and restoration of Louis.
835 Danes sack Utrecht.
839 Ethelwulf succeeds Egbert as over-king.
840 Death of Louis the Pious. Lothair emperor. Rival dukes of Benevento invite Saracen aid from Sicily and Crete.
841 Defeat of Lothair at Fontenay by Lewis the German and Charles the Bald. Danes plunder Rouen. Mutassem dies ; Wathek khalif.
842 The bi-lingual Oath of Strasburg. Saracens in Sicily capture Messina. Michael III (the Drunkard), aged four, succeeds Theophilus. Fourteen years' regency of Theodora.
843 Western Empire : Partition of Verdun. Lothair (emperor) takes Middle Kingdom, with Italy ; Lewis (first German king) the Trans-Rhenish territories ; Charles the Bald (first king of France) the West.
844 Pictish and Scots kingdoms united under Kenneth McAlpine. The name of Pict disappears slowly.
845 Lewis, son of Lothair, king of Italy. Danes plunder Paris and are bought off.
847 Danes capture and occupy Bordeaux. Leo IV pope, to 855. Mutawakkil succeeds Wathek as khalif.
849 Pope Leo's victory over Saracens (Ostia). Alfred the Great born.
852 Mahommed succeeds Abd er-Rahman II at Cordova.
855 Lothair dies. His son Lewis II emperor ; he remains in Italy ; Trans-Alpine Middle Kingdom divided between his brothers Lothair and Charles. Danes winter in Sheppey. Michael III takes control at Constantinople.
857 Michael deposes Ignatius and makes Photius patriarch ; denounced by Pope Benedict III.
858 Nicholas I pope.
859 Fall of Enna completes Saracen conquest of Sicily.
860 Ethelbert king of England. Many Danish raids.
861 Conversion of Bulgars to Christianity.
863 Nicholas excommunicates the patriarch Photius.
866 Ethelred k. of England. Danish invasion begins. Synod of Constantinople condemns the Heresies of the Latin church. Permanent severance of the Greek and Latin churches.
867 Murder of Michael. Basil the Macedonian first emperor of the Macedonian dynasty (to 1056).

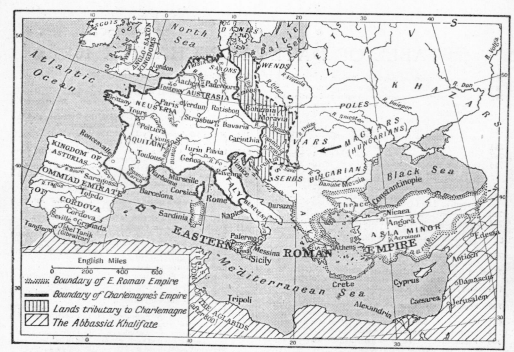

In the eighth–ninth century the supreme historical event in Europe is the substitution of the Holy Roman for the Eastern Roman Empire as the predominant power; as established by Charlemagne it comprised Gallo-Latin Neustria, Teutonic Austrasia and Lombard Italy. In the Iberian Peninsula the Ommiad emirate was set up by Abd-er-Rahman. In the Near East, Bulgarian and Serbian kingdoms were coming into existence. Islam controlled Africa and western Asia, except Asia Minor.

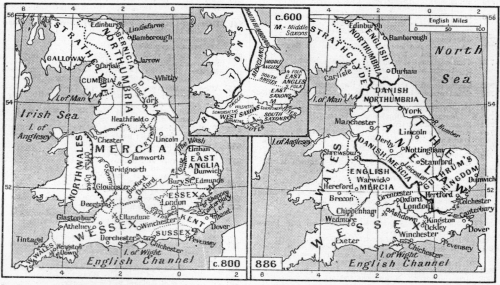

In England the salient facts are the restriction of the Britons within an ever more limited area in the West, and the transference of supremacy from Northumbria to Mercia and, after 800, to Wessex under Egbert. The period of peace inaugurated by his success was broken by incursions of the Danes resulting, after the treaty of Wedmore in 878, in the establishment of the Danelaw as an independent region. In 886, by the 'peace of Guthrum,' its boundaries were altered in Alfred's favour.

STAGES IN THE MAKING OF MODERN EUROPE AND OF ENGLAND

### CHAPTER 16

# EMERGING OF THE NATIONS: 732–867

IN the year A.D. 732 Charles Martel's great victory at Poitiers set the seal upon Leo's achievement fourteen years earlier at Constantinople. Leo and Charles between them had fixed the limit to the westward expansion of Islam for more than six centuries to come, just one hundred years after the death of the Prophet. Europe belonged to the West, Asia and Africa to the East ; but the West still kept its hold on Asia Minor, while the East had laid its grip on the most western peninsula of Europe.

The year, however, is significant also for another reason. It marked the collapse of the last attempt of the Eastern Roman Empire to assert its authority in the West by force of arms. The hour was drawing near for a new Holy Roman Empire to arise, again claiming the Eternal City itself as its centre, the abode of its spiritual head. It will be useful, then, to start with as clear an idea as may be of the powers which dominated or were about to dominate Europe.

## Dominion remaining to the Caesars

CONSTANTINOPLE still enjoyed the prestige of the empire of the Caesars ; for the oriental, the City of Constantine was ' Rome ' ; but its face was turned not to the West but to the East. Asia Minor formed the larger part of its dominion. In Europe the Danube had long ceased to be its northern boundary ; the interior of the Balkan peninsula had passed into the occupation of the tribes which had flooded over the Danube since the departure of the Goths, mixed Bulgars and Slavs in Moesia and Slavs on the middle Danube. A Bulgarian kingdom with only the most shadowy subordination to the Empire was already established, and a Serbian kingdom was shaping. In Italy there was still an imperial exarch at Ravenna ; there were imperial governors in Sicily and Calabria ; and at the head

of the Adriatic Venice chose to own the imperial overlordship mainly because it involved her in no inconvenient obligations. The Papacy made a certain profession of loyalty to the Empire, as a protection to itself from Lombard aggression ; but would make no abatement of claims to spiritual pre-eminence wholly incompatible with those of Constantinople, while, on the great controversy of the day—image worship—its views and those of the imperial government were irreconcilable.

Italy was, in fact, ruled by the Lombards ; but it was only in the Lombard Plain that they formed a substantial portion of the population. And the Lombard kings, unless like Liutprand they happened to be men of exceptional ability, could exercise very little control over the Lombard dukes.

In Spain the Visigothic dominion had just been wiped out and its place taken by the Saracens or Moors. The Peninsula had passed under Moslem sway, though a stubborn remnant of Goths and Spaniards in the north-west were even now girding themselves to a struggle which was to be waged for seven and a half centuries.

## Territories under Frank Dominion

THE rest of what had been the Roman Empire on the European continent, together with much that had never been included therein, was now absorbed in the Frank dominion, of which the eastern limit was not the Rhine but the Elbe, save for the northern Frisian and Saxon districts, still unconquered, between the Weser and the Elbe. The east and the west of the dominion were of different cultures—Teutonic and Gallo-Latin—and were destined to split apart ; though between them from the North Sea to the Mediterranean lay a broad mixed belt.

East and north of the German dominion of the Franks, other non-German peoples had come or were coming into ken. The

Northmen of Denmark, Sweden and Norway were on the point of taking to the sea as piratical rovers, and of repeating the excursions of the Goths towards the Black Sea, overland. Letts and Wends and non-Aryans of Finnish stock occupied the southern and eastern shores of the Baltic, and were pushing southward through the multitudinous Slavonic tribes; the khan of the Avars was still lord of what we now call Hungary. All these peoples were exercising a westward pressure upon the Germans; but east of the Frank dominion there was no community which had attained to such a degree of political organization as would entitle it to be called a state.

### Dynastic Struggles in Islam

A T the stage we have now reached in the story of Islam, a crisis was at hand in the Mahomedan world. A century had passed since Mahomet had given to the Arabs an Arab religion, and through that and his own unique personality had given them also an unprecedented unity. That unity was in immediate danger when the Prophet's death necessitated the choice of a successor; Abu Bekr and Omar had, however, preserved it by strenuous effort and by their personal character. Under Othman it was dissolving. Its semblance was restored, but not its substance, under Moawiya, and no more than its semblance was preserved under the dynasty he founded. The Arabs themselves were never in accord in their submission to the Ommiads; and Islam now included vast populations positively hostile to the Ommiad title.

Hisham, the khalif who was reigning in 732, had the skill to play off the discordant elements against each other, postponing the evil day; though before his death in 743 Africa was in revolt, and in Spain the factions were in almost ceaseless conflict. A severance between eastern and western Islam was, in any case, made all but inevitable by geographical conditions; when it did come, it had the curious effect of restoring the Ommiad in the west because he had been dethroned in the east. The stage of the true crisis was in the east.

A year after Hisham's death, his son Walid II was deposed by Yezid ibn Mohallab. Next year Yezid III was removed by Merwan II, acting in the name of Walid's young son. Persia was already in revolt on behalf of the house of Ali. But for years past the crafty brothers of the house of Abbas had been intriguing secretly on the hypothesis that they were the true representatives of the Prophet's family, since in Arab practice the brother succeeded, not the daughter; and it was in the name of the Abbasids that Abu Muslim in 747 revolted in Khorassan and drove out the Ommiad governor. The Abbasids pushed aside the Fatimids; in 750, in a fierce battle on the Zab, they routed the Ommiad army. Merwan escaped to Egypt, where he was killed. Incidentally, the dynastic struggle enabled the Hindus of Sindh permanently to expel their Mahomedan rulers and garrisons.

### Foundation of the Abbasid Dynasty

A BDALLAH ABUL-ABBAS, the first khalif of the Abbasid dynasty, which was not extinguished till many centuries had passed, enjoyed a reign of four years (750–754), in which he thoroughly justified the name by which he was popularly —to his own gratification—known, al-Saffah, 'the butcher.' He removed such members of the house of Ali and such of their supporters as seemed likely to be troublesome; by a treacherous device he extirpated the entire Ommiad family, with the exception of one, Abd er-Rahman, who escaped to find his way to the far west after many adventures; and when the adherents of either of the rival houses, the Ommiads or the family of Ali, broke into rebellion, they were repressed with appropriate mercilessness.

The Abbasids owed their throne to Abu Muslim, the governor of Khorassan. When al-Saffah died, his brothers fought each other for the succession. In that contest Mansur owed his success to the decisive intervention of Abu Muslim, who, fanatically devoted to the common cause of the Hashimites, the house of the Prophet, had hesitated between the Abbas and the Ali branches. Abu Muslim was loyal; but the king-maker was distrusted by the king, and Mansur was no sooner firmly established than Abu Muslim was assassinated. The new khalif was as merciless and as treacherous as his brother had been. He found those qualities useful.

The establishment of the Abbasids meant much more than a mere change of dynasty. The centre of the forces which had effected the dynastic revolution was in the east, and to the east Mansur transferred its political centre. The seat of the Khalifate was removed by him from Damascus to Bagdad, the dominating influence in Asiatic Mahomedanism becoming no longer Arabic but Persian.

## Mansur's Reforms and Achievements

FOR two other features of the new order Mansur was personally responsible; the creations of a mercenary bodyguard, and of the wazirate—of troops whose allegiance was directly to the person of the khalif, drawn from sources untouched by Arab factions, and of a minister in complete charge of the details of administration but directly responsible to the khalif. The wazir of a strong khalif was very really his servant; a weak khalif's wazir was not unlikely to be no less really his master.

When Abd er-Rahman escaped from the massacre of the Ommiads, al-Saffah gave the western rebels a leader who could claim to stand for the legitimate line against a usurper. The west had revolted not against Islam, nor against Ommiads or Abbasids in particular, but against the temporal sovereignty of a distant khalif whoever he might be. Abd er-Rahman was able in a short time to rally the rebels to his own standard as no one who had risen as a faction leader could do; two years after Mansur became khalif he was reigning as emir at Cordova (756–787), and declared the political independence of Africa and Spain without as yet assuming a separate religious headship.

When Mansur died in 775 he had consolidated the power of the Bagdad Khalifate; but it was a task which had absorbed all his energies, and there had been no practical extension of dominion. Mansur's brother attempted unsuccessfully to contest the succession with his son Mahdi (775–785), a mild and tolerant prince; whose reign was nevertheless disturbed by many insurrections, notably that of Mokanna, the ' veiled prophet of Khorassan.' Under the influence of the Persian temperament there was a rapid development of speculative activity in the intellectual and religious fields which was quite alien to the Arab, and sects or schools multiplied correspondingly ; at the same time commercial enterprise was greatly stimulated ; and Bagdad became a centre of wealth, luxury and intellectual activity far in advance, for a time at least, of any city of the Europeans. Mahdi was followed in 785 by his elder son Hadi, who was assassinated a year later and was succeeded by his younger brother, hero of numberless fascinating fables, in whose day the Khalifate was at its zenith, Haroun al-Raschid (786–809).

## Haroun al-Raschid's glorious Reign

THE court of Haroun, the ' Just ' or the ' Orthodox,' was no doubt a brilliant centre of culture and enlightenment, and his title was fairly earned by the general administration, which was left entirely in the hands of the Barmecide family, the famous wazir Jafar and his brothers, to whose father, Yahya, Haroun was largely indebted for the peacefulness of his own accession. The vast wealth at the khalif's disposal made it easy for him to display a lavish and not always discriminating liberality which was highly popular. Haroun, when his will was not crossed or his suspicions aroused, was the incarnation of careless benevolence ; but he was equally capable on occasion of cold-blooded cruelty and treachery ; as was exemplified in his slaughter of the entire Barmecide family, against whom his mind had become poisoned, in 803.

The temporary disappearance of the wazirate led to a grievous falling off in the administration ; and it was doubtless in view of the increasing signs of disruption that Haroun at his death parted his dominion among his sons, while appropriating the Khalifate proper, with its religious supremacy, to the eldest, Emin (809). Already, some years before Haroun's death, Ibrahim ibn Aglabi had established another independent principality ruled by the Aglabid dynasty at Tunis. Even in that reign of splendour the area of the khalif's effective authority was contracted. Haroun made successful campaigns in Asia Minor, but they were no more than raids.

LEO III at Constantinople was an administrator of high ability; after 732 he recognized that Italy was out of reach, but in the East he was able to enforce his iconoclastic principles on reluctant Europeans and approving Asiatics; the more because the best of the imperial troops were recruited from his own Anatolian hill-men, who inclined even fanatically to his own way of thinking. Prosperity revived, and prestige was strengthened by a victory, won under his personal command, at Acroïnon, over a large invading army which Hisham sent over the Taurus in 739. Two years later he died and was succeeded by his son Constantine V.

**EMPRESS IRENE**

Throughout her regency for her son and her own reign (797–803) Irene was an ardent anti-iconoclast. The Empire suffered under her misrule.
*British Museum*

opprobriously nicknamed Copronymus by his detractors (741–775).

Constantine's rule was vigorous and active; judged by results it was successful. The prolonged conflicts attending the fall of the Ommiads and the establishment of the Abbasids gave him many opportunities for campaigns in Armenia or beyond the Taurus, by which some territory was recovered. He fortified the passes of the Balkan range, curbing Bulgarian and Serbian aggression; and when Bulgar kings replied by attacks he smote them, and was only prevented from crushing them by a disaster to his fleet and transports for which not the enemy but the winds and waves were responsible. He cleared the country of the brigands by which it was infested, so that merchants and merchandise travelled in security, to the marked increase of trade.

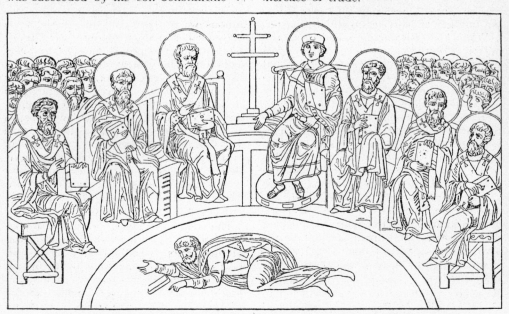

**SESSION OF THE COUNCIL OF NICAEA WHICH RESTORED IMAGE WORSHIP**

Consequences disastrous to the peaceful government of the Eastern Empire attended the controversy that raged in the eighth century concerning the worship of images. The Council of Constantinople definitely forbade image worship, but in 787 Irene, while regent during the minority of her son Constantine VI, adopted the opposite policy and summoned the Council of Nicaea, represented in this drawing from a ninth century Greek Testament, which reversed the decisions of the earlier one.

NICEPHORUS I AND MICHAEL I
By a coup d'état in 802 Nicephorus (left) secured
the removal of the empress Irene and reigned
until 811, when he was succeeded by his son-in-
law, Michael Rhangabe.   The latter was an undistinguished, ineffective ruler.
*British Museum*

But he left an ill name and an ugly
nickname because where his father had
been a puritan he was a zealot.   Not
satisfied with imposing public conformity,
he searched out and penalised those who
continued to practise 'image worship' in
private, instituted a harsh religious persecution, basing it on the decisions of a
general council at Constantinople (753)
which was repudiated before its session
began by the patriarchs of Jerusalem and
Alexandria as well as by the entire Church
in the West, and then embarked on a
campaign against monks and monasticism
which was shocking to all but the
extremists of his own party.

The same policy, though with a degree
less of brutality and intolerance, was
pursued by his son Leo IV (775–780), who
also in the course of his brief reign fought
two successful campaigns with the khalif
Mahdi.   But when he died, leaving a ten-
year-old son, Constantine VI, the power
passed into the hands of his widow, the
empress Irene, an ambitious woman who
had hitherto concealed the fact that she
was herself a zealous 'iconodule.'

For ten years the dowager empress
reigned in her son's name.   Beginning
by relaxing the measures against image
worshippers, she went on to dismiss
iconoclast officials civil and ecclesiastic,
and to set iconodules in their places.   She
called a fresh council, which in effect
reversed the decrees of the last.   A plot
was formed against her in favour of one
of the late emperor's brothers, but it was
discovered, and its only effect was that
all the young emperor's uncles were

forced to enter religion.   The imperial
guard mutinied, but was suppressed.

But while Irene was carrying through
her reversal of ecclesiastical policy the
Slavs broke out in Thrace and the khalif's
armies raided Asia Minor from end to end
with impunity, so that they had to be
ignominiously bought off.   So in 790
Constantine, chafing at being still kept in
tutelage, effected a coup d'état, took the
reins into his own hands, and began to
display signs of salutary vigour.   But he
again allowed his mother a freedom and a
degree of authority of which she took
advantage to effect another coup d'état on
her own account (797), seize her son,
depose him, put out his eyes, shut him up
in a monastery and—a thing for which
there was no precedent—herself assume
the imperial diadem.

FOR five unhappy years (797–802) Irene
was empress, presumably because
there was no one ready to take upon himself
the risk and responsibility of deposing her.
They were years of disaster, for Haroun's
raiders, checked for a time by Constantine,
again overran Asia Minor and again had
to be bought off by the promise of a heavy
tribute.   The domestic government was in
the hands of pernicious favourites whose
scandalous misrule was diversified only by
the scandal of their private differences.
The situation was so intolerable that in
802 the treasurer, Nicephorus, effected yet
another coup d'état ; Irene was seized in
the middle of the night, carried off to a
convent and forced to take the veil ; and
without further disturbance Nicephorus
(802–811) was accepted as emperor.

The new emperor enjoyed no personal
prestige ; he was known only as a
competent treasury official.   But recent
years had brought to the front no man of
distinguished talent, and the undistinguished but ambitious persons who tried to
supplant him were easily suppressed.   He
took the always unpopular but highly commendable course of maintaining a resolute
neutrality between iconodule and iconoclast ; and, though no soldier, he did his
best to restore the efficiency of the army.
But he failed to free himself from the
tribute to Haroun, and he fell in a

Bulgarian campaign, when the succession was secured by the incompetent Michael Rhangabe, his Greek son-in-law—the first of that race to wear the diadem.

### Frank Empire under Charles Martel

THE Frank empire, though without an official emperor, dominated the entire west of Europe. Charles Martel ruled the Franks for nine years after his triumph at Poitiers. In the course of them the shadow-king Theudebert died. Charles neither found a shadow-heir for him nor himself assumed the crown ; but he went on ruling as mayor of a non-existent palace or as ' duke ' of the Franks. The Moors made incursions from Spain and excursions from Narbonne, which they still held ; he fought them and beat them and penned them into a narrow area, though it was not till he was dead that they were finally cleared out and driven for ever beyond the Pyrenees. Aquitaine under Eudo's son Hunold was still semi-independent ; the Saxons on the north-east required chastisement, and the outlying provinces were restive ; but everywhere Charles left no room for doubt that he was master.

Boniface, now archbishop with several German bishoprics under him, was his vigorous friend and ally ; though the clergy complained bitterly of Charles' enforcement on them of due contributions to the coffers and to the military levies of the state. But in contrast to the Eastern emperors, he did not concern himself with properly ecclesiastical matters. He maintained friendly relations with both Liutprand and Gregory III in Italy, and when the pope chose to quarrel with the Lombard he declined to intervene in his favour.

In 741 Charles, though uncrowned, was undoubtedly the most powerful of living potentates, the equal at least of Leo

at Constantinople (who died in the same year), while the Ommiad dynasty was tottering. When he died, the Franks accepted the authority of his two legitimate sons, Pepin the Short and Carloman, as mayors of Neustria and Austrasia respectively. Pepin (741–768) ruled jointly and in perfect harmony with his brother till the latter elected to retire from the world to the religious life in 747. For four years he ruled alone as mayor, with the puppet Merwing king Childeric, whom he and Carloman had routed out and set on the throne in order to regularise their own position in 742. In 751, with universal approval and the express warrant of the pope Zacharias, he invited the acquiescent dummy to enter religion, and was himself crowned king of the Franks.

For seventeen years Pepin was consolidating and extending his power. Within the dominion he established his

**CARVEN STALLS OF LOMBARD KINGS**
Cividale del Friuli is rich in relics of the early Lombard kings, who were a constant menace to the Papacy—for example, these royal stalls in the cathedral. The final outcome of the quarrel between Liutprand (712–43) and Pope Gregory III was the absorption of the Lombard kingdom into the Frank monarchy.

**FOUNDER OF THE HOLY ROMAN EMPIRE**
Wearing the long mantle of the Franks and the royal crown, and bearing in one hand the sword and in the other the orb, this statue represents one of the Carolingian monarchs, most probably Charlemagne. As Frankish king and Roman Emperor he dominated Europe for more than forty years.
*Musée Carnavalet : photo, Archives photographiques*

authority over recalcitrant nobles and tribes, not without trouble ; punitory expeditions compelled the Saxons on the north-east to pay tribute ; he cleared the Moors out of Narbonne and drove the last of them across the Pyrenees ; and he did what no Frankish ruler had done before him—he made himself the arbiter of Italy by taking the field as the protector of the Papacy ; which no doubt was precisely what Zacharias desired when he commended Pepin to assume the crown.

Liutprand had quarrelled with Gregory, as we saw, and Charles had declined to intervene in arms on Gregory's behalf. But he imposed no harsh terms on Gregory's successor ; and Hildebrand and Ratchis, who followed him as kings of the Lombards, were at peace with the Papacy. But their reigns were brief. In 749 Ratchis entered religion, and his brother Aistulf again developed the spirit of active aggression. He finally ejected the imperial exarch from Ravenna, and then revealed his intention of reducing the Papacy to vassalage in respect of its temporal estates. The menace was much more real than it had ever been in the days of Liutprand, who never desired to deprive the pope of at least technical independence, in spite of the provocative attitude which Gregory III had so frequently chosen to adopt towards him. In the circumstances, for the image-worshipping pope to appeal to the iconoclastic fanatic at Constantinople would have been absurd ; and in 753 Pope Stephen, the successor of Zacharias, turned to a loyal son of the Church whom his predecessor had placed under an obligation, the newly-crowned king of the Franks.

Pepin responded handsomely. A campaign in 754 quickly reduced Aistulf to sue for terms. He did homage to Pepin as overlord, and promised to restore the cities he had seized. Pepin withdrew to avenge on the Frisians the martyrdom of Boniface, which had just taken place. Aistulf neglected to fulfil his promises, and in 755 marched on Rome. This brought down Pepin on him again ; and this time he was forced to hand over to the pope practically the whole of what had been the exarchate of Ravenna and thenceforth became the States of the Church. When Aistulf died, the new king of the Lombards, Desiderius, did not again challenge the old king of the Franks.

Charles Martel had, as a matter of course, left his realm divided between his two sons ; so also did Pepin, on his death in 768, in accordance with the immemorial custom of the Frank monarchy. Between those two, Charles and Carloman, there was no love lost. Civil war would almost certainly have rent the double kingdom, as in Merovingian days, if Carloman had not died in 771, leaving his elder brother king of all the Franks, not three years after the joint accession. The whole reign of Charles covered forty-six years (768–814) ; for the last fourteen of them he was not merely king of the Franks but Roman Emperor of the West. In those years he changed the basis of the whole European system by the double process of conquest and organization.

### Charlemagne begins his Victorious Reign

It is unnecessary to devote a great amount of space to the process of conquest. Aquitaine had made its last futile effort to break away before Carloman was dead. In 772 Charles, now sole king of the Franks, made his first move towards the subjection of Saxony, which gave him constant occupation for thirteen years and at intervals for nineteen years more. He had already imposed on the Saxons generally a formal submission when a quarrel between Pope Hadrian and the Lombard king Desiderius as to the right to certain cities provided him with an excuse for interfering in Italy in answer to the pope's personal appeal.

Charles crossed the Alps, not as an arbiter but actually as a partisan, for the elements of a serious quarrel with Desiderius were already there ; since the Frank had married the Lombard's daughter and then repudiated her within the year, and the Lombard was giving asylum to the widow of Carloman and his young son. Charles ordered Desiderius to hand over the cities which the pope claimed as being part of the Ravenna exarchate ; Desiderius was defiant. In 773 Charles descended on Lombardy, shut Desiderius up in Pavia, and starved him into surrender next year, when he was sent to pass the rest of his life in a monastery. Instead of setting up a new Lombard vassal-king, Charles proclaimed himself king of the Franks and Lombards. The Lombard kingdom survived, but as an appanage of the Frank crown. The duchy of Benevento however, succeeded in maintaining practical independence.

Meanwhile Saxony revolted. A great campaign compelled it to temporary submission. Lombard dukes revolted, and required to be brought to book ; whereon Saxony again rushed to arms, in vain. In 777 Charles celebrated the incorporation of Saxony at a great diet held at Paderborn.

In 778 Charles invaded Spain, invited thither by Moors who were defying Abd er-Rahman at Cordova. He got temporary possession of Barcelona, but failed to capture Saragossa, and when he retired through the Pyrenees his rear-guard was cut up in the pass of Roncesvalles. There fell the valiant captain Roland, of whom practically nothing else is historically known, though he became the foremost figure in the later traditions which gathered about the Paladins of Charlemagne.

### Saxons submit to Frank Supremacy

He returned to Aquitaine to learn that the Saxons were up in arms again. By 780 he had them once more in apparent subjection. They were Christianised in thousands by baptism, and their Christianity was emphasised by merciless punishment for lapses. In despair they blazed out again in 782. As always when Charles appeared in person, they were crushed into submission ; they surrendered more than four thousand persons of rank who had incited them to rebellion ; and the prisoners were slaughtered in cold blood. Thereupon the whole Saxon folk flung themselves into a life-and-death struggle, the end of which was a foregone conclusion. In 785 Witikind, their most indomitable leader, came in upon promise of his life. Though there were sporadic insurrections for nearly twenty years more, this was the last great struggle against the Frank supremacy.

Meanwhile, the ineffectiveness of the Spanish raid in 778 had been demonstrated. The Moors had reverted to their allegiance to Abd er-Rahman. In 785 began the long Spanish war, the conduct of which was entrusted to the king's third

**SPIRITUAL AND TEMPORAL POWER**
On Christmas Day in the year 800 Charlemagne
was crowned in S. Peter's by Pope Leo III and
proclaimed Emperor of the Romans. The
momentous event is alluded to in this mosaic
depicting pope and emperor at S. Peter's feet.
*Piazza S. Giovanni, Rome ; photo, Anderson*

son, whom later ages know as Louis the
Pious or the Debonnaire, with William
of Toulouse to guide him. The task fell
upon Louis, because Charlemagne had
made him viceroy with the royal title in
Aquitaine. The second son, Pepin, held
a similar position in Lombardy, and the
eldest, Charles, in Neustria north of Aquitaine. The conquest of Catalonia was a
gradual process ; but by 812 the third
Cordovan emir, el-Hakim, was driven
to a formal cession of the territory
between the Pyrenees and the Ebro, which
the Saracens evacuated completely.

Beyond the Elbe and the German
borderland, Charles was able, with very
little fighting, to impose allegiance, obedience and tribute on the Slavonic tribes,
who also embraced Christianity with no
apparent reluctance ; the more northern
group by a campaign in 789, the Bohemians
in 806. The Mongolian Avars from Hungary and Pannonia chose to raid into
Bavaria, and the north-eastern corner of
Italy which was a part of the Lombard
kingdom in 788. After one successful
campaign in 790, from which he was

recalled by an insurrection in Saxony,
Charles left the subjugation of the Avars
to his son Pepin. A vast spoil, accumulated in the days of their past power, was
taken ; and in 805 they were reduced to
making complete submission. They were
left a cowed and tributary nation under
a vassal khan or chagan of their own
race ; such power as remained to them
vanished somewhat later under the onslaught of the Magyars.

The conquests of Charlemagne, however,
did not reach the Danes and Northmen,
of whose daring exploits not only on
the seas but far up the rivers we hear
first in his reign. The conqueror's
approach in Saxony alarmed Godred,
the king of Jutland ; he gave harbour-
age to the Saxon Witikind, fortified
the neck of the peninsula from the
Baltic to the North Sea against attack
by land, having no qualms about his
security by sea, and, feeling himself
satisfactorily out of reach, began in
808 to harry the Frisian coast and the
southern shores of the Baltic, almost
with impunity, for two years. Doubtless
he would have felt the full weight of
Charlemagne's hand had he not been slain
by his own folk in 810, when his successor
hastened to make peace. But the era of
the Vikings had opened. The long-ships
of the northern rovers had already found
their piratical way to the coasts of England, of Ireland and of Aquitaine, though
they were no subjects of Godred or any
other overlord, but free war-chiefs.

### Creation of the Holy Roman Empire

IT was not, however, simply as king
of the Franks, or of the Franks and
Lombards, that Charles the Great carried
through the conquests of his later years ;
or as Roman Patrician, a title he had
claimed, like Odoacer three centuries
before him, when he annexed the Lombard
crown. In 800 Pope Leo III fled from the
bitter enemies in Rome who had proved
too strong for him to Charlemagne in
Saxony. Charles sent him back to Rome
with an escort that none durst challenge,
and himself followed late in the year,
to inquire into the charges that had been
levelled by or against the pope.

M*

The result of the investigation was a complete vindication for Leo and the utter condemnation of his enemies. On Christmas day, at the conclusion of the service held in S. Peter's to celebrate the holy day, as the unconscious king knelt before the high altar, Leo, moved, as he declared, by a sudden inspiration, set a crown upon his head, and proclaimed him Augustus, Emperor of the Romans, crowned by God. The words were taken up with a universal shout. The Holy Roman Empire had sprung into being.

The character of Charlemagne's empire, for which he was responsible only in so far as he had extended its borders, and its organization, which was derived from the past but shaped by his genius, determined the medieval system or feudal monarchy. As Pepin the Short left the Frankish kingdom, it was in form an absolute monarchy. The king was aided by a council, the men on whom he chose to rely, for the most part lay or ecclesiastical governors of the districts into which the

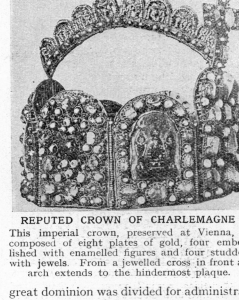

**REPUTED CROWN OF CHARLEMAGNE**
This imperial crown, preserved at Vienna, is composed of eight plates of gold, four embellished with enamelled figures and four studded with jewels. From a jewelled cross in front an arch extends to the hindermost plaque.

great dominion was divided for administrative purposes—dukes, counts, margraves of the marches or border districts, bishops, abbots. Occasionally, when some matter of supreme national concern was on hand, such as the change of dynasty which made Pepin king of the Franks, a general assembly was held to ensure the general approbation.

The counts and dukes were appointed or removed at the king's will ; but, as a matter of course, they were men of great estates which they enjoyed by hereditary right, so that in practice their official rank tended also to become hereditary, and to be claimed as of right. Especially this was the case in the outlying regions which had only recently ceased to be practically independent ; but such magnates were always liable to be dispossessed at the king's will, as in the case of the dukes of Aquitaine and Swabia. At the same time, by immemorial

**LOUIS LE DEBONNAIRE : A WEAKLING EMPEROR**
Charlemagne was succeeded in 812 by his only surviving son, Louis. His sobriquets ' the Debonnaire ' and ' the Pious ' indicate the weakness of character that brought nothing but trouble upon the Empire. This miniature portrays him in Roman ' chlamys ' and wearing the closed Byzantine crown.
*From a manuscript in the Bibliothèque Nationale*

Frank tradition, hereditary right descended not by primogeniture but by partition among the sons.

The germs of the later struggle between Papacy and Empire lay in the method of Charlemagne's coronation, though probably the possibility of it never entered his mind. As the champion of justice, he had used his power to reinstate Leo at Rome ; the pope had merely given expression to universal sentiment in the West when he took upon himself almost to force on his champion, the actual master of the West, the assumption of the title and authority of Roman Emperor. That did not give the pope an authority over him, which no pope had ever claimed over any Roman Emperor.

Nevertheless, it proved possible for later popes to claim that the spiritual head of Christendom had the right of conferring, and had in actual fact conferred the imperial authority upon the emperor of his choice. Neither before nor after

**CAROLINGIAN JEWEL OF THE NINTH CENTURY : THE 'CRYSTAL OF LOTHAIR'**

This remarkable crystal disk, engraved with episodes from the story of Susanna, may have been intended for the morse or clasp of a cope. The inscription over the central medallion records its having been made to the order of Lothair, King of the Franks, probably, therefore, the son of the emperor Lothair, and from 855 to 869 king of the district later known as Lorraine. After being in the possession of the Abbey of Waulsort on the Meuse for eight hundred years it disappeared, but was recovered from the bed of the Meuse in the nineteenth century.

*Bernal Collection, British Museum*

his coronation did Charles ever hesitate to interfere and dictate in matters ecclesiastical as seemed to him good ; he recognized that as emperor he had assumed even higher responsibilities than as king of the Franks ; but he never dreamed of regarding himself as responsible to the pope, though he regarded the pope as having become responsible to him, as he had not been to the king of the Franks. While Charles lived no one would have ventured to hint at the possibility of such a question being raised.

The great emperor died at Aachen, his favourite residence, in 814, the seventy-second year of his life and the forty-sixth of his reign. He was succeeded by his only surviving son, Louis, though his grandson Bernard the son of Pepin was already reigning with the royal title in Lombardy. Louis had shown a reasonable competence in his vice-royalty of Aquitaine and the Spanish march, but he was completely unfitted for the higher responsibilities that were now laid upon him. The most blameless and humble-minded of men, he was altogether in the hands of a scheming wife and of the priests whom his piety taught him to trust implicitly.

### Disastrous Weaknesses of Louis

THE results were disastrous. He sanctioned rather than committed the one conscious crime of his life when he put to death his nephew Bernard, who had come to him under a safe-conduct after taking up arms on learning that he was to be deprived of his Lombard kingdom ; and he was haunted for the rest of his life by this sin, for which he repented literally in sackcloth. But his morbid conscience caused him to repent with equal fervour the pettiest of peccadilloes. He dismissed his father's able ministers, who fell short of his moral standards, and reposed his undiscerning confidence only where it was utterly misplaced. He was a fond and foolishly forgiving father to sons who repaid him with brutal humiliations ; and he reserved his warmest affections for the child of his second marriage, so that his many projects on the boy's behalf ended by shattering the loyalty of his most loyal supporters.

**CHARLES THE BALD**
Tunic and chlamys of Roman fashion were items of Carolingian costume as shown in the Bible of Charles the Bald and other illuminated books of the period. Military dress resembled that of the Roman Praetorian Guard.
*Bibliothèque Nationale*

Louis began by crowning himself with his own hands, and was then feeble enough to submit dutifully to re-coronation at the hands of a new pope who had been elected without the imperial sanction. Then in accordance with precedent he provided his three sons with kingdoms ; for the eldest, Lothair, whom he associated with himself as emperor, Lombardy ; for Pepin, Aquitaine ; for Lewis, known in consequence as 'the German,' Bavaria and the eastern marches. Lothair was also to succeed to the rest. The partition led directly to the revolt and death of his nephew Bernard ; the actual penalty imposed on the rebel was not death but blinding, but the bungling infliction of it killed him.

Then the emperor's wife died, and very much against his own will he married again. In 822, most unfortunately, was born to him the son known as Charles the Bald, whence sprang endless troubles. For the doting father was bent on providing the youngest son with a kingdom, which could only be done at the expense of one or more of his half-brothers, none of whom would listen to any such scheme.

Degrading public exhibitions of penitential self-humiliation dictated by a morbid conscience only convinced men that the pious devotee was quite unfit for his imperial responsibilities. Every proposed partition for the provision of a kingdom for the child Charles produced a revolt of his brothers and a humiliating compromise, followed after an interval by a fresh partition and a fresh revolt. In

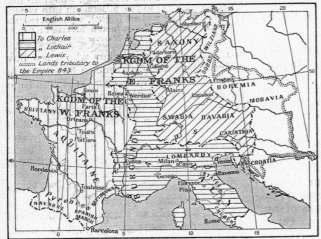

THE PARTITION OF VERDUN

By the Treaty of Verdun, made in 843 by the three sons of Louis I. Germany east of the Rhine went to Lewis, Neustria and Aquitaine to Charles the Bald, and the buffer territory between, together with Lombard Italy, to Lothair. France and Germany then for the first time came definitely into being.

the first of these civil wars Louis found himself with the rebels at his mercy, and forgave them without taking any security against a repetition of the offence. In the second, when the odds were all in his favour, he chose to negotiate ; the negotiations were prolonged while the princes sowed treason among his followers, till the unhappy father found himself deserted and helpless—men called the scene of this shameful performance Lügenfeld, the ' field of lies ' (833). Louis was deposed ; but his outrageous treatment brought reaction, and he was restored.

Fresh partitions only brought fresh revolts. The last of them was collapsing when Louis died in 840. On this occasion the rebels were Lewis the German and Pepin of Aquitaine, the nephew of the

three surviving brothers ; Lothair had for once taken sides with his father and his youngest brother. He was now emperor, and immediately drove the still youthful Charles into the arms of Lewis, though he succeeded in attaching Pepin to his own side. The crash of conflict came next year when Lothair was decisively beaten at the bloody battle of Fontenay. Lewis and Charles made a solemn compact, which they actually kept—the Oath of Strasburg, still more notable because they took it in two languages, the German of the east and the Roman which was on the way to become French of the west. The immediate outcome was the treaty of Verdun (843).

By the Partition of Verdun the unlatinised German east went to Lewis, the thoroughly Latin Neustria and Aquitaine (the greater part of modern France) to Charles, Italy and the whole wide intervening belt of territory from the Rhône basin to the Belgian coast to the emperor Lothair, including the original Austrasia, Burgundy and Provence, where Latin and German were not so much blended as inextricably entangled. And in this middle kingdom lay both the Frank capital, Aachen, and the capital of the Empire, Rome. The brothers ignored the nephew in Aquitaine, who remained a thorn in the side of Charles, whose kingdom was not yet known as France.

For ten years the brothers kept the peace with each other. Then Charles and Lewis started fighting, Lewis sending support to an insurrection in Aquitaine. In 855 Lothair died and was succeeded by his son the emperor Lewis II, whom he had already made king of Lombardy. But Lewis was fully occupied with the defence of Italy against the Mediterranean power of the Saracens ; his brother Lothair took possession of the northern division of his kingdom beyond the Alps, whence it received the name of Lotharingia (Lorraine), the southern half going to his other brother, Charles. The rising in Aquitaine collapsed ; but there ensued a chaos of struggles between brothers, uncles, sons and fathers to snatch territory from each other which it is not worth while to disentangle. (See genealogy in page 364.)

And meanwhile, from the beginning of the civil wars in 829, the Northmen in ever-increasing numbers had been taking advantage of the eternal discord to raid the coasts and sail or row up the rivers, looting or sacking the defenceless towns, and even for a time occupying Bordeaux, though their normal custom was to sail off with their spoils.

ENGLAND, meanwhile, was making progress towards unification. In the middle of the eighth century the preeminence of Northumbria, apart from her monasteries, her Bedes and her Alcuins, was on the wane ; the political ascendancy passed to Mercia under the rule of Offa, who compelled most of the other kings to recognize his overlordship, and curbed Welsh raiders by constructing Offa's dyke. Charlemagne had learnt from his fathers to respect England as the nursery of Willibrord and Boniface, as well as of his own friend Alcuin ; and, having no cause to quarrel with Offa, treated with him as a potentate of the first rank.

It was to the court of Charlemagne that young Egbert of Kent betook himself when he failed to secure the succession in Wessex to which he had some claim ; and doubtless it was there that he learnt much of the kingcraft of which he made good use when he returned to Wessex unopposed in

**COINS OF OFFA AND OF EGBERT**

From Northumbria predominance in England passed to Mercia under Offa (left), who ruled that kingdom from 757 to 796. Mercia in turn yielded to Wessex under Egbert (right), who secured the throne in 802 and conquered Mercia in 829.
*British Museum*

802. He was a wise man who knew how to bide his time. It came in 825 when he broke the Mercian power at Ellandune. By 829 every kingdom south of the Humber—for the most part willingly—had acknowledged him as Bretwalda, high king of the English ; and from his time dates the claim of the Wessex house of Cerdic to be the royal house of England even to the present day.

Vikings from Norway had already made for themselves a permanent footing in Ireland, but only an occasional raid visited the English coast while Egbert lived. When raiders did come he dealt with them effectively. On his death in 839 the whole land was at peace, and the accession of his pious but not very competent son Ethelwulf was accepted without demur. He was a devoted son of the Church, on which he lavished so much of the crown estates that a mistaken tradition has attributed to him the institution of tithes. The defence of the country against the now multiplying attacks of the Danes was mainly the work of the fighting bishop of Sherborne, Eahlstan. They suffered a great defeat at Aclea (Ockley ?) in 851 ; nevertheless, either in that year or in 855 they wintered for the first time in the Isle of Thanet or of Sheppey, though for some time their further activities were suspended. The great struggle began in the reign of Ethelwulf's second son, Ethelbert, 860–866, and lasted through the reigns of two more brothers in succession, Ethelred and Alfred the Great.

In the far north also unification was brought nearer when in 844 the two Celtic

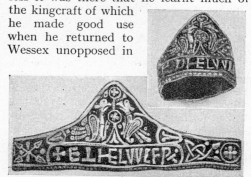

**KING ETHELWULF'S GOLD RING**

Son of Egbert and father of King Alfred the Great, Ethelwulf was king of Wessex 839–58. His noted piety is indicated by the early Christian design of two peacocks above the inscription Ethelvvlf Rex on his ring, found at Laverstock.
*British Museum*

kingdoms of the Picts and the Scots were joined because the young king of Scots, Kenneth McAlpine, was also unexpectedly left the legitimate heir of the Pictish crown under the Pict law of succession

### Dissensions in Empire and Khalifate

AT Constantinople, Nicephorus, as we have seen, was succeeded by the incapable Michael Rhangabe, who in 812 acknowledged the new Roman emperor of the West. Not his crimes but his incapacity led to his deposition in 813 by the soldier Leo V, ' the Armenian.' Leo's six years of rule did much to counteract the unhappy effects of Irene's reign, which that of Nicephorus had only in a small degree remedied ; and the Bulgars were firmly checked. More still would have been done if the emperor had been able to keep clear of the iconoclastic controversy, in which, like most soldiers, he was on the otherwise unpopular side of the iconoclasts. But, having thus made himself unpopular, he was assassinated in 820. The accession of another soldier, Michael II, 'the Amorian,' nicknamed the Stammerer, was attended by outbreaks of rebellion, and his nine years' reign was mainly memorable for the capture of Crete and the invasion of Sicily (attached to the Eastern, not the Western, Empire) by the Saracen fleets. Two years after the accession of his son Theophilus (829–842) war was renewed for thirty years between the Empire and the Khalifate.

The reign of Haroun, for all its picturesque splendours, its development of material wealth and its intellectual activities, did not in fact mean that the Khalifate was growing in strength. Even before his death in 809 the Aglabid dynasty had established its independence at Tunis. The Saracen fleets that dominated the Mediterranean were not his fleets ; they issued from the ports of Africa or Spain. He left his empire divided between three sons, who were soon fighting for supremacy ; in 813 the eldest, Emin, was killed, and the second, Mamun, became khalif (813–833).

Heresies and orthodoxies shaped political parties in the Mahomedan as in the Byzantine Empire, and the domestic distractions in both prevented each from attacking the other till the end of Mamun's reign, when Theophilus had already succeeded Michael the Amorian at Constantinople. It was the Corsairs that reft Crete from Michael ; it was the Aglabids that overran Sicily ; it was both Corsairs and Aglabids that were soon threatening Italy itself, like the Vandals in the fifth century.

### Sicily overrun by the Saracens

THE Aglabids were incited to their invasion of Sicily by the traitor Euphemius, a disgraced official who hoped by their aid to be made master of the island. From 827 to 831 successes and defeats alternated ; but in that year Mamun invaded Cappadocia, and Theophilus was forced to concentrate all his military efforts on the war with the Khalifate—a war in which it proved, in thirty years of fighting, that neither side could gain any permanent advantage over the other. Theophilus had provoked the attack by harbouring refugees from the khalif's religious persecution. The consequence was that he could no longer send aid to his Sicilian subjects, and, in spite of a prolonged and stubborn defence, the Saracen conquest of Sicily was practically completed with the fall of Enna in 859. Command of the Strait had already been won in 842 by the capture of Messina.

Before Messina fell the Saracens were in Italy. No king of the Lombards, whether Lombard or Frank, except Liutprand, had succeeded in bringing the Lombard dukes of Benevento under control; least of all Lothair, who was always preoccupied by quarrels with his father or his brothers. Naples and Calabria were still in the Byzantine allegiance. In 840 rivals were fighting for the Benevento dukedom. One invited help from the conquering Saracens in Sicily, the other from the Corsairs of Crete. As a matter of course, the Saracens turned the position to their own account, fought for their own hand in collusion with each other, and were very soon overrunning and more or less garrisoning all South Italy.

The saviours of Italy were Lewis the son of Lothair and Pope Leo IV. Lewis was made king of Italy and emperor designate in 845, following the Verdun partition ; incidentally, on the election of Pope Leo in 847, he reasserted the imperial claim to confirm it. In 849 a great Saracen fleet was completely shattered, partly by storms and partly by the fleet which Leo had made ready, and Rome was delivered from the menace which had threatened her. Lewis imposed a reconciliation and a partition of the duchy of Benevento on the rival dukes, and then devoted himself whole-heartedly to the struggle with the Corsair chief Mofareg, who was well on the way to establishing his own supremacy in the south. Though Lewis became emperor in 855, his preoccupation with Italy never allowed him to intervene in the dynastic quarrels which racked the rest of the Empire.

In the east Theophilus fought with Mamun and Mamun's successor Mutassem (833–841) with varying success. On his death in 842 the government passed into the hands of a council of regency on behalf of his infant son, afterwards unhappily known as Michael the Drunkard (842–867). A feeble government at Bagdad, a feeble government at Constantinople, and generals usually inefficient on both sides, kept the war dragging on indecisively.

### Warring of the Abbasid Dynasty

At Bagdad the Abbasid Khalifate was by this time markedly on the downward path. Mamun had in a high degree both the faults and the merits which distinguished his house, and was no unworthy successor to Haroun. But periods of great intellectual activity are apt to have a disintegrating side, and the antagonisms between old beliefs and novel speculations multiplied political dissensions. The uneasiness of the khalif's position was manifested by the necessity under which Mutassem found himself of large increases in the army of mercenaries, while provincial governors, especially in Khorassan, were year by year growing more independent. Wathek (824–847) and Mutawakkil (847–861), the successors of Mutassem, were men of little capacity and less character, and the way was being made ready for disruption.

At Constantinople the regency was directed by the young mother of the infant emperor, who was only four years old in 842. Theodora, the empress-dowager, was a fervent image worshipper for whom the religious question dominated all others ; she reversed her husband's policy and persecuted the iconoclasts. Administration generally went to pieces. At eighteen, Michael in 856 set his mother aside and ruled for ten years with his disreputable uncle Bardas, first as counsellor, then as colleague, always as boon companion. Then he had him put out of the way, and set in his place as Caesar another boon companion but a very hard-headed one, his ex-groom Basil the Macedonian. A twelvemonth later Basil had Michael murdered after a carouse (867), and, being already Caesar, assumed the diadem without opposition ; thus inaugurating the Macedonian dynasty, which reigned at Constantinople for nearly two centuries.

### Final Partition of the Churches

In the last year of Michael, the Synod of Constantinople formulated the pronouncement which marked the irrevocable parting of the Church in the East from the Church in the West. It denounced as damnable heresies the Roman doctrines of the Procession of the Holy Spirit from the Father and the Son, and of clerical celibacy. In the view of the Western Church, both were fundamental truths. Neither then nor since has success attended any efforts to bridge that impassable chasm. But the pronouncement itself was the outcome of the long-standing quarrel between Rome and Constantinople on the question of authority, which had reached a climax. In 858 Michael had of his own authority deposed the austere patriarch Ignatius and set in his place the more amenable Photius. The popes Benedict III and his successor, Nicholas I, had both proclaimed the invalidity of the action and denounced both Photius and the emperor in unmeasured terms ; and Nicholas, of his own authority, excommunicated the Byzantine patriarch. The Synod gave the imperial reply to papal arrogance, and in doing so made the cleavage permanent.

867 Accession of Basil I, the Macedonian.
England : Danish conquest of Northumbria.
869 Lothair II d. Partition of Middle Kingdom.
871 England : 'Year of Battles.' Alfred king.
872 Harold Fairhair founds Norwegian kingdom.
Norsemen colonise Iceland.
875 Lewis II d. Charles the Bald emperor.
876 Lewis the German d. His sons share Germany.
Basil II takes up Saracen war in South Italy.
877 Charles the Bald d. Louis II king of France.
878 Alfred defeats Danes at Ethandune : Danelaw
established by Treaty of Wedmore.
Saracens take Syracuse, completing conquest of
Sicily.
879 Louis III and Carloman kings of France.
Charles the Fat, of Swabia, k. of Italy.
880 Boso independent k. of Arles (Burgundy).
882 Charles the Fat sole German k. and emperor.
Carloman sole king of France.
Saracens in Campania.
885 Charles the Fat k. of ' All the Franks ' but Arles.
886 Northmen besiege Paris ; Charles buys them off.
Leo VI, the Wise, succeeds Basil I.
887 Arnulf elected German king. Charles abdicates.
888 Charles d. Odo count of Paris elected French k.
Permanent separation of France from Empire.
Rudolf independent k. of Upper Burgundy.
891 Wido of Spoleto emperor.
896 Arnulf crowned emperor.
898 Odo d. Charles the Simple k. of France.
899 Magyar incursion into Italy.
Arnulf d. Lewis the Child German king.
900 or 901 Alfred d. Edward the Elder k. of English.
901 Berengar of Friuli k. of Italy.
901-5 Contest of Berengar with Lewis of Arles, who is
crowned emperor.
905 Berengar expels Lewis.
905-925 Sancho I founds kingdom of Navarre.
909 Fatimid khalifate proclaimed at Kairwan.
910 Foundation of Abbey of Cluny.
Magyars defeat Lewis the Child.
911 Lewis d. Conrad I of Franconia elected German k.
Lorraine joins the Carolingian kingdom of France.
Treaty of St. Clair-sur-Epte ; Rollo duke of Normandy.
912 Abd er-Rahman III emir of Cordova.
Constantine VII Porphyrogenitus succeeds Leo VI.
915 Saracens in Campania crushed ; Berengar emperor.
918 Conrad I d. Henry I the Fowler of Saxony German
king.
919 Romanus I co-emperor with the boy Constantine.
923 Charles the Simple deposed ; Rudolf of Burgundy k.
of France. Lorraine reverts to Germany.
924 Henry I makes nine years' truce with Magyars.
925 Athelstan king of England.
928 Abd er-Rahman III assumes Khalifate of the West.
933 Egypt independent under the Ikshidis.
Henry I wars successfully with Magyars.
936 Rudolf d. Louis IV d'Outremer recalled and made
k. of France by Hugh the Great, count of Paris.
Henry I d. His son Otto I German king.
937 Athelstan shatters a northern coalition at Brunan-
burh.
942 Otto I reconciled with his brother Henry, who is made
duke of Bavaria.
945 Romanus I deposed ; Constantine sole emperor.
Bouids establish supremacy at Bagdad, while
maintaining Abbasid khalifs, for a century.
948 Ludolf son of Otto I made duke of Swabia.
950 Advance of Leon and Castile against Saracens.
951 Otto I annexes Italy.
952 Rebellion of Ludolf and Conrad of Lorraine.
954 Lothair succeeds Louis IV.
955 Otto I reconciled with German rebels. Decisive
defeat of Magyars at Lechfeld.
956 Hugh the Great, duke of France, succeeded by Hugh
Capet.
958 Edgar the Peaceful k. of England. Dunstan minister.
959 Constantine VII d. Romanus II emperor.
961 Romanus recovers Crete from Saracens ; Syrian
campaign.
Otto I goes to Italy to restore order.
962 Otto crowned emperor at Rome.
963 Otto deposes Pope John XII ; makes Leo VIII pope.
Romanus II d. Nicephorus Phocas emperor, with
the children Basil II and Constantine VIII.
965 Nicephorus recovers Cyprus from Saracens.
968 Nicephorus recovers Antioch.
969 Fatimid khalifate established in Egypt.
John Zimisces murders Nicephorus and becomes
co-emperor. Russians under Sviatoslav invade
Bulgaria and Thrace.

971 Zimisces defeats Russians ; Russian treaty.
972 Marriage of Theophano and Otto II.
973 Otto I d. Otto II succeeds.
975 Sancho the Great succeeds to Navarre, which he
makes the leading Christian power in Spain.
Syrian campaign of John Zimisces.
976 Zimisces d. Basil II reigns till 1025.
978 Otto II demonstrates in France.
979 Ethelred the Redeless (' Unready') king of England.
980 Lothair surrenders all claims in Lorraine.
982 Otto II's campaigns and defeat in Calabria.
983 Otto II d. Theophano regent for Otto III.
986 Lothair d. Louis V, last Carolingian.
987 Louis V. d. Hugh Capet elected king of France.
Beginning of Capet dynasty.
991 Olaf Trygvessen raids England.
992 Samuel k. of Bulgaria, begins Bulgarian war.
Boleslav duke of Poland ; founds Polish kingdom.
994 Olaf and Sweyn Fork-beard raid England.
995 Robert II succeeds Hugh as king of France.
Otto III in Italy ; makes Gregory V (Bruno) pope,
997 Stephen (Saint) king of Hungary.
998 Mahmud of Ghazni succeeds Sabuktagin.
999 Sylvester II (Gerbert) pope. Reforming activity.
1000 Leif the Norseman discovers Labrador.
1001 Mahmud's first invasion of Punjab.
1002 Massacre of Danes in England on S. Brice's day.
Otto III d. Henry II (of Bavaria) German king.
1003 Sweyn Fork-beard of Denmark invades England.
1013 Sweyn king of Denmark and England.
1014 Canute king of Denmark and England.
Henry II crowned emperor at Rome.
Basil II destroys the Bulgar army ; he is named
Bulgaroctonus, ' the Bulgar-slayer.'
1017 Norman adventurers in Italy take part against the
Byzantines in the south.
1018 End of first Bulgar kingdom.
1022 Armenian campaigns of Basil II.
1024 Henry II d. Conrad II ' the Salic ' German king.
(Salian line of emperors.)
1025 Basil d. Constantine VIII sole emperor.
1028 Canute adds Norway to his Scandinavian empire.
Constantine d. Zoe with Romanus II succeeds.
1030 Mahmud of Ghazni d. His dominion breaks up.
1031 Henry I king of France.
1033 Burgundy (Arles) incorporated with Germany.
1034 Romanus III d. Zoe with Michael IV.
1035 Sancho the Great d.
Canute d. Partition of his empire.
William the Conqueror (aged eight) duke of Normandy.
1039 Conrad II d. Henry III German king.
1042 Michael IV d. Zoe with Constantine IX.
Edward the Confessor king of England.
1045 Three rival popes. Rome appeals to emperor.
1046 Henry deposes all three popes ; names Clement II.
1048 Henry nominates Bruno to Papacy ; Bruno, having
made canonical election a condition of acceptance, becomes Leo IX. Very active reform
inaugurated.
1052 Hungarian independence acknowledged.
1053 Normans in alliance with Papacy after defeating
Leo at Civitate.
1054 Theodora empress at Constantinople.
1055 Victor II pope.
1056 Henry III d. Henry IV German king. Regency.
1057 Isaac Comnenus Eastern emperor.
1058 Malcolm III, having overthrown Macbeth, establishes the royal line of Scotland.
1059 Nicholas II pope. Lateran Council establishes
College of Cardinals as papal electors.
Isaac Comnenus retires : Constantine X Ducas.
Seljuk Turks under Tughril master Bagdad as
protectors of Abbasid khalif. Fall of Bouids.
1060 Philip I king of France.
Nicholas makes Robert Guiscard duke of Apulia.
First invasion of Sicily by Roger.
Tughril invades Armenia.
1061 Alexander II pope, without reference to Henry.
German bishops elect antipope Honorius.
1063 Alp Arslan succeeds Tughril as Great Sultan.
1066 Hastings. William of Normandy k. of England.
1067 Romanus IV co-emperor with Michael VII.
1071 Norman conquest of England completed.
Normans in Italy take Bari, ending Byzantine
occupation.
Romanus defeated at Manzikert by Alp Arslan, who
is succeeded as Seljuk sultan by Malik Shah.
1073 Sulayman takes Nicaea. Hildebrand elected pope as
Gregory VII.

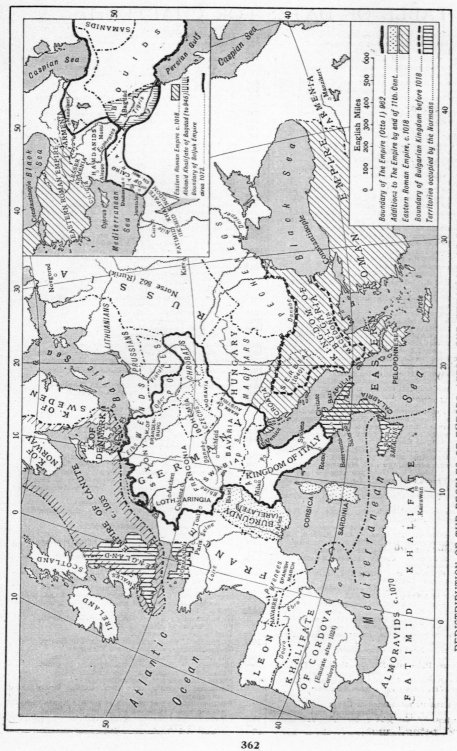

REDISTRIBUTION OF THE PEOPLES OF EUROPE AFTER THE BREAK-UP OF THE CAROLINGIAN EMPIRE

Geographical as well as racial facts largely determined the resettlement of western Europe after the disintegration of the Empire of Charlemagne. In the west was Gallic France, separated by the Rhine from Teutonic Germany and by the Pyrenees from the Iberian Peninsula now under Mahomedan dominion. The Danube provided the northern boundary of the Eastern Roman Empire, in which the Serbian and Bulgarian kingdoms had been absorbed. Northmen from Scandinavia reached France, there to become the Normans who gave England her kings and founded the Norman kingdom of Sicily.

362

# CHAPTER 17

# THE NATIONS IN BEING:
# 867–1073

NTIL the year 867 Christendom was at least in theory one. Now, however, two articles of the creed which the West regarded as fundamental were condemned by the East as essentially heretical ; and the breach thus made could in no wise be healed. Yet the full significance of the event was not immediately apparent. The prominent fact in the second half of the ninth century was not that the separation between East and West was a little more marked, but that the Western Empire of Charlemagne was in process of disintegration, and that the process was being hastened by the attacks of sea-going powers, Saracen or Scandinavian.

Now the Western Empire—excluding, that is, the subjugated but not incorporated Slavs and Avars on the east—was clearly a combination of three distinct groups : the Italian which was Latin with no more than a vein of German running through it ; the Gallic, also Latin with a difference, but with a distinct tincture of German ; and the German with the merest tincture of Latin. Moreover, these groups correspond to genuine geographical areas. The Italian is separated from both the others by the barrier of the Alpine mountain passes. North of the Alps there is no equivalent barrier between the Gallic or French group on the west and the German group on the east, though the Rhine may be regarded as providing a line of demarcation.

## Source of innumerable Wars

ONSEQUENTLY, between German and Gallic lay a broad belt from the Alps to the North Sea which belonged definitely to neither group, but had affinities with both. In the first stage of disintegration, this belt appears as a fourth division artificially attached to the Italian. But that is a connexion which cannot be preserved because of the geographical barrier ; there is no natural unity in the group

itself ; it breaks up, and the sections tend to absorption in either the Gallic or the German group—a process which was to be a main source of innumerable wars.

We saw that by agreement between the three surviving sons of Louis the Pious the Middle Kingdom with Italy and the imperial dignity went to the eldest, Lothair, and his heirs, the east to Lewis the German and the west to Charles the Bald ; and that on Lothair's death in 855 his realm was at once cloven in three between his sons, the eldest, the emperor Lewis II, taking Italy. That realm was never reunited, for Lewis was fully occupied in Italy till his death (without male issue) in 875 ; his youngest brother was already dead and his kingdom of Provence had been annexed (in 863) by Charles the Bald ; and on the death of the third brother, Lothair II, in 869, his northern kingdom of Lotharingia became a bone of contention between the uncles Charles the Bald and Lewis the German. In 875 the male line of the senior branch of the Carolingians or Karlings, the house of Lothair I, has already come to an end.

## Endless Partitions of the Empire

T this point Charles the Bald annexes the title of emperor and the kingdom of Italy. Next year (876) Lewis the German dies, and his German kingdom is divided between his three legitimate sons. Next year (877) dies Charles, the last of the sons of Louis the Pious, leaving his whole realm to his one son, Louis II of France, who dies in 879, leaving two sons, Louis III and Carloman ; a third (known as Charles the Simple) was born soon after his death.

There is a rapid succession of deaths, until in 884 the legitimate king of France is the child Charles the Simple ; Provence has set up as a separate kingdom under Boso, who claimed it in right of his wife, the daughter of the emperor Lewis II ; of the sons of Lewis the German, only one is surviving, Charles the Fat. who is now king of Germany, king of Italy, and emperor. Charles the Fat and Charles the Simple are the only legitimate Karlings in the male line left. Rather than face the dangers of a regency, France offers her crown to Charles the Fat, who thus for three unhappy years becomes the last sole king of all the Franks.

In 887 Charles the Fat died, immediately after surrendering his German crown to his nephew Arnulf, duke of Carinthia, the illegitimate son of his dead elder brother. Charles the Simple, now eight years old, was the sole legitimate Karling in the male line ; but, besides the illegitimate Arnulf, there were three princes whose mothers were Karlings—Lewis who at this moment succeeded his father Boso as king of Provence, Berengar duke of Friuli, whose mother was a sister of Charles the Bald,

in 911. Berengar won the Italian crown in 901 and the imperial title in 915, but died without an heir in 924. So vanished all who could even pretend to the name of Karling, save the uncertain occupant of the French throne ; and for seven years after the death of Charles, the reigning king of France was not his son but Rudolf of Burgundy.

An aimless, wearisome, meaningless welter ! But it is the inevitable outcome of that utterly destructive principle of divided inheritance from which the Frank tradition could not shake itself free. Germany has worked back to its own peculiar principle of an elective

FAMILY COMPLICATIONS OF THE CAROLINGIAN IMPERIAL HOUSE

and Wido (Guido) duke of Spoleto, whose mother was sister of the emperor Lewis II. All the four and also Lambert the son of Wido were at one time crowned emperors.

But the actual immediate result of the death of Charles the Fat was that the one legitimate Karling fled to England, the French nobles electing as their king one of their own number, Odo count of Paris ; the Germans got, what they much needed, a vigorous and capable king in Arnulf ; Wido and Berengar fought for the Italian crown ; and a Burgundian count, Rudolf, set up a little independent kingdom of Upper Burgundy on the upper Rhône. One or another of the princes might enjoy the title of emperor ; but disintegration was complete.

Charles the Simple was restored in 899 and reigned at intervals for the next thirty years ; the lines of Spoleto and Provence ended in 899 and 905 ; Arnulf died in 899, his only heir Lewis the Child

monarchy which still recognizes preferential hereditary claims, France to the principle of a hereditary monarchy which may under extreme pressure give place to election ; while in both the power of the monarch is closely circumscribed by a powerful nobility, consisting of territorial magnates, which has become hereditary.

But there was another effect of the welter. It allowed not a conquest but a penetration of France by the Northmen which materially influenced her future development by transmuting Vikings into Normans ; and at a later stage this Norman development in France had an immense influence on the development of England, of Italy and of Western civilization.

On the other hand, during the half-century under immediate consideration, from 867 to 918, the Northman had not yet become a Norman ; he was one of the barbaric forces which were increasing the welter. By the end of the half-century he had established his footing in France, where alone he was to be transformed into a Norman ; he had established his footing in England ; he had been beaten off in Germany ; and he was establishing himself on the border of the Eastern Empire as the Varangian or Russian, the name which was later to be transferred to the Slavonic or Mongolian tribes whom he was now dominating.

### Effect of the Northmen's Raids

MOST noteworthy, however, is an effect of the raids, as distinguished from the settlement, of the Northmen. The various kings of the house of the Carolingians were so much occupied in snatching territory from each other that they never concentrated their energies on meeting the peril from the marauders ; the worst offender being Charles the Bald, who, in order to go fighting elsewhere, deliberately bought them off when he had them almost at his mercy—a very effective method of inviting them to return. Consequently the local nobles were left to protect their lands and their dependants as best they could. The 'hosts' of the Northmen fought as a highly mobile mounted infantry, planting palisaded camps from which the raiders issued and to which they retreated. The nobles countered with troops of heavy cavalry, while they developed their own headquarters into strongholds impregnable to assault. Hence the noble's house became literally a castle, and he himself became the permanent captain of a troop of heavy cavalry.

Reunion of the France which developed from the Neustria of the Franks with the Germany which was the expansion of Austrasia was out of the question. When Charles the Fat died, a strong chief was an absolute necessity, and she elected not Charles' illegitimate German successor, but the valiant warrior who had saved Paris from the Northmen, Odo or Eudes the count of Paris, from whose brother descended the line which ultimately took the place of the Karlings.

Odo held the crown till his death, but he had to fight hard for it in his latter years, which demonstrated the insecurity of the title by election. The great nobles would not submit to a king who was only one of themselves with no ancestral claim to superiority. They made a figure-head of the young Carolingian Charles, the posthumous son of Charles the Bald, to whom they restored the crown but not the authority when Odo died on New Year's eve, 898, since Odo's brother Robert did not choose to contest the succession. It was therefore Charles the Simple who in 911 made terms with the Viking Rollo or Rolf and, under the treaty of S. Clair-sur-Epte, settled him with his followers in Normandy, there to become well-nigh the mightiest of all the feudatory nobles.

In the same year died Arnulf's son, Lewis the Child. Germany had to revert to election and chose Conrad of Franconia, while Lotharingia, clinging to the idea of a Karling, gave its allegiance to Charles the Simple. Since the death of Arnulf there had been no leadership ; the Slavs were surging into German lands, and a new group of eastern barbarians, the Magyars, who had overrun the Avars, were threatening Bavaria.

Throughout the nominal reign of Lewis the Child (899–911) and that of Conrad (911–918) the German nobles were fighting each other for their own hand, or singly and unsupported against the barbarian invaders. But on Conrad's death the Franconian house was public-spirited enough to withdraw its own claim to the succession and give its support to its rival, Saxony ; and Henry the Fowler, duke of Saxony, became king of the Germans (918–936). The task which he discharged was that of making ready for the revival of the Holy Roman Empire under the German kings by his son Otto the Great.

### Danish Invasions of England

DURING this half-century Harold Fairhair was steadily overcoming all his many rivals and building up a monarchy in Norway. During the same period the Vikings who raided the coasts and estuaries of France and penetrated into the Mediterranean went not by command of either the Norse or the Danish king, but very largely to escape from the yoke which those kings were endeavouring to lay upon them. So it was also with the Danes, who in 866 were taking the first step in their great invasion of England.

Ethelred of Wessex, third of the sons of the pious Ethelwulf, had just succeeded to the overkingship of England. The Danish hosts directed their opening attack not on Wessex but on the sub-kingdoms of East Anglia and Northumbria. In 867 they mastered Northumbria; after a pause they overran East Anglia and slew the king, S. Edmund, in 870. Then they fell upon Wessex. The year 871 is known as the Year of Battles; on the whole the Danes would seem to have had rather the worse of the fighting. There was a truce and they fell back from Wessex, though not without a handsome subsidy.

Alfred, the fourth brother, had succeeded Ethelred during the year, and had more than enough to do in organizing recuperation from the desperate struggle. The Danes, too, had more than enough in making good their conquest of the north and extending it into Mercia. In 876 began the decisive struggle which after alternating vicissitudes was ended by Alfred's victory at Ethandune and the Treaty of Wedmore in 878 confirmed in 884 by 'Guthrum's Fryth' (see the map in page 344), of which the treaty of St. Clair-sur-Epte was to be the French counterpart.

By the treaty the Danes held what they had conquered—roughly the lands east and north of the great road called Watling Street, from the River Lea in the southeast to the River Dee in the north-west, known thereafter as the Danelaw, while they became officially Christians and in some sort acknowledged the overlordship of Wessex. After that the land enjoyed comparative peace, since the Danish colony for the most part declined to help their countrymen in attacks on Wessex, and Wessex itself was so organized by its extremely sagacious and far-sighted king that it could hold its own securely both by sea and land against any attack that

could be brought against it; though Alfred's very able son Edward the Elder and his sons after him did not find it an easy matter to convert their shadowy overlordship into definite sovereignty.

Alfred was an extremely practical statesman, who created a fleet which beat the sea-rovers on their own element, codified the laws so as to harmonise

**LONDON PENNY OF ALFRED THE GREAT**

Succeeding his brother Ethelred as king of Wessex in 871, Alfred (849–901) was saddled with the task of quelling the Danes. By 878 he had forced on them the treaty of Wedmore, and by 885 had captured London, where this penny was struck bearing the monogram 'Londinia' on the reverse.

*British Museum*

diversities of custom, modified them so as to bring them into conformity with the most advanced ideas of justice, fostered education with a judicious zeal and set the highest standards of public and private morality; an idealist who could face adversity and apparent failure indomitably and victoriously, yet had the courage to recognize practical limitations instead of shutting his eyes to them. When he died in 900 he left his England at a height of prosperity and security such as no other land enjoyed; not yet unified, indeed, but much nearer to unity than it had ever been before, or than any contemporary kingdom. That is a record which fully justifies the title of 'The Great,' bestowed on him alone among English monarchs out of the love of his people.

Though the Northmen were already raiding the Mediterranean shores, the Saracen was still the main menace in the south. In the west, Charles Martel had stopped the onrush; Pepin had driven it back over the Pyrenees; Charlemagne had pressed it across the Ebro, while the stubborn invincibles of the old population, Gothic, Roman and Iberian, held out defiantly in Asturias, the north-west corner. The Spanish March was still nominally a province of the Frank dominion, but was on the way to become the independent Christian kingdom of Aragon.

In the ninth century, however, there was little co-operation between the Frankish governors of the March and the Gothic princes of the west. The leaders who were step by step forcing the Saracens southward, making the Douro a boundary corresponding to the Ebro, were the Alfonsos (Gothic Hildefuns) of Asturias and the Gascon Sancho, who among them were creating Leon, Castile and Navarre when the ninth century closed. The factions among the Mahomedans paralysed the emir at Córdova for effective resistance to the slowly creeping tide : though in 928 Abd er-Rahman III assumed officially the title of khalif. The Aglabids were firmly established in Sicily. Their advance in South Italy, when it threatened to become an effective conquest, was held up by the emperor Lewis II in spite of the difficulties in which he was involved by the Lombard dukes of Salerno and Benevento. But their expulsion was still unaccomplished when he died prematurely in 875. The task, however, was taken up by Basil the Macedonian, emperor of the East, the titular emperors and kings in the West being otherwise occupied.

### Eastern Empire and the Saracens

BASIL'S fleets drove the Corsairs off the seas ; his armies swept the Saracens out of Calabria ; but in Sicily he failed altogether, and he too died in 886, before he could expel them from Campania ; nor was there anyone left to carry on the work when he was gone. There the Saracens remained ; and if Italy was not conquered, it was mainly because they were satisfied with robbery and loot and were at no pains to organize a dominion. The Papacy, which in conjunction with Lewis had played no small part in the battle, was now falling upon evil days, successive popes proving themselves nothing more than most unspiritual faction leaders or agents. It was not

till 916 that Berengar, emperor at last, made common cause with the dukes of Spoleto and Benevento and blotted out the Saracen hornets' nest in Campania.

Basil had made himself emperor by murdering the man who had raised him to power while his victim lay in a drunken sleep ; a piece of villainy which proved highly profitable to the Empire. He reorganized the finances ; he directed the administration with vigour and substantial justice ; he recovered territories, long lost in the east, from the tottering Khalifate ; he rescued South Italy from the Saracens ; his fleets recaptured the mastery of the Mediterranean ; he so rehabilitated the government that its machinery again worked with automatic success through the long reigns of princes who took little interest in their duties.

Basil's son Leo the Wise (886–912) justified his title by writing a manual on tactics and making himself, like that monarch who was described seven centuries later as ' the wisest fool in Christendom,' an authority on witchcraft. But the Empire prospered. Constantine Porphyrogenitus (912–959) became emperor at the age of five, and was officially or unofficially set aside or reinstated at intervals ; commerce and the arts of peace flourished, and still the Empire enjoyed an inglorious prosperity ; for its machinery was adequate to hold the European barbarians on its borders in check, and the power of Bagdad had lapsed into a woeful decrepitude. Neither in the East nor in Europe was there any serious onslaught to be combated.

Deferring, then, the story of Mahomedan disintegration, we turn back to that of the reintegration of the Germanic Holy Roman Empire.

### The Germanic Holy Roman Empire

THE complete disappearance of the Karling line in Germany compelled either the dissolution of the German kingdom into its component parts or the election of a new head. Germany was in five great divisions or dukedoms : Saxony on the north, Franconia and Lotharingia on the west, Swabia on the south-west, Bavaria on the south-east, corresponding to fairly marked racial distinctions, Franconia and

Lotharingia being mainly Frankish. But Lotharingia was disposed to hold by the western Carolingian rather than depart from the Carolingian tradition. For the time it joined itself to France, though its stronger German affinities pulled it back to the German kingdom before long. The Franks, however, had an historic claim to hegemony among the Germans. The fact was recognized in the election of Conrad duke of Franconia as German king.

The Frank prestige, however, proved from the beginning an insufficient basis for the authority over the other dukes necessary to a strong monarchy. Conrad on his death-bed pointed out the man best fitted to discharge the supreme office, and it was Conrad's own brother and heir who in 918 nominated that man, Henry of Saxony, as Conrad's successor, and stood by him with unfailing loyalty.

The election was justified by the event. The new king was fully aware that premature attempts to enforce an unestablished authority conferred on him not as a right, but by the doubtful acquiescence of three magnates, each of whom was otherwise as powerful as himself, would merely plunge Germany into a prolonged civil war, the issue of which would be extremely doubtful. He had himself defied Conrad's dictation, and both Swabia and Bavaria would certainly defy dictation from him. He left them in practical independence, though formally they were in his allegiance, till his personal achievements had manifestly warranted his title. Happily for him, and much to the credit of the Franconian nobles, he could count securely upon them in his primary task, the defence of the North German marches against Slavs and Magyars; while the Danes found other occupation than attacks on Saxony, which had already proved a harder nut than they could crack.

### Magyar inroads into Bavaria

THE Magyars were of a Mongolian—that is, a non-Aryan—stock. They had made their way to South Russia, and thence, pushed westward by the pressure of the Petcheneg Turks, had driven their way into the old land of the Avars, which became their permanent home—the famous Bulgar king, Simeon, having very effec-tively stopped their movement over the Danube—at the close of the ninth century, led by their own national hero Arpad ; they had broken into Italy in 899 ; and from the first years of the tenth century they had turned their devastating attention mainly on Bavaria. While Lewis the Child was German king they inflicted a heavy defeat on the Bavarian duke, and another on the forces led by the boy-king himself a year before his death. In the days of Conrad the quarrels of the Bavarian and Swabian dukes with the elected king left South Germany almost undefended, and the squadrons of the Magyar horsemen pene-trated as far as Coblenz and even Basel.

It was not until 924 that the Magyars made the first onslaught on North Germany, to find that Henry the Fowler was their match. He did not indeed beat them decisively, but they were glad to make a nine years' truce on terms of a tribute being paid to them ; which suited Henry for the time because of trouble with Gorm the Old, king of Denmark, and with the Wends between the Elbe and the Oder

### The Mark of Brandenburg

HAVING thus temporarily disposed of the Magyars, Henry completed a settlement with Gorm, who had to pay him tribute, and proceeded to the subjugation of the Wends. It was perhaps in the organization of the new march which he annexed, the 'Mark of Brandenburg,' that Henry rendered his most valuable defensive service to Germany. All over the new districts he planted his Saxons and Franks on the soil, the centre of each colony being a new walled town within which a tenth of the colonists resided to form a standing garrison, the other colonists being responsible for the maintenance of the garrison's farms ; while quarters were provided in the towns to which the farmers could retreat when necessary. Henry, who married his son Otto to an English princess, may have derived the idea from the garrison towns planted in England by Alfred, which became the local centres of trade without the artificial encouragements that the German king was at pains to add. For the trading centres were an object secondary only to the provision of garrisons.

The garrison towns proved as effective a discouragement to the Magyar raids, when they were renewed on the conclusion of the truce and the refusal of the tribute, as Alfred's and Edward's in their conflict with the Danes. Henry's frontiers were so strengthened that he was able to make his authority more decisively felt in the southern and western duchies— for Lotharingia had reverted to Germany when the western kingdom set Rudolf of Burgundy on its throne; but caution still forbade him to challenge needless antagonism on the part of the dukes. It was left to his son to complete the establishment of the central authority.

### Accession of Otto the Great

**H**ENRY never claimed the imperial title, though he stands in the list of the emperors as Henry I. At his death in 936 he nominated as his successor his eldest legitimate son, Otto I the Great (936– 973), born shortly before his father's election to the royal dignity. An elder illegitimate son, Thankmar, was passed over, and Otto was preferred to his younger brother Henry, for whom it was possible to claim priority of title on the ground that he was born ' in the purple,' the son of a reigning king, not of a mere duke. Consequently the first years of Otto's reign were spent in fighting for his crown against the rebellious brothers, while his bold assertion of the supreme authority, over which his father had been so cautious, carried strong antagonistic elements to the side of the rebels.

Otto was a zealous and pious churchman, but of the type of Charlemagne, not of Louis the Pious. That is, he never dreamed of subordinating his own to ecclesiastical authority. The prelates were the natural allies of the crown against the pretensions of the hereditary lay lords, who were as jealous of their privileges as of royal encroachments. Otto was strong enough and self-confident enough to give all possible ecclesiastical pomp and ceremony to his coronation at Aachen; though his cautious sire had firmly declined to do so lest it should be claimed that the crown had been bestowed on him by the Church. Otto would have made short work of any such suggestion.

The rebellion of Otto's brothers was the outcome of the irritation of the dukes at Otto's uncompromising assertion of the royal authority, and of Saxon displeasure at his pan-German attitude. He declined to be a Saxon ruling over Franks and Bavarians, as his father had been; he chose to be the German head of a German nation without distinction between its component peoples. The brothers headed the revolt which broke out in Saxony in 938, and were soon joined by the dukes of Franconia, Bavaria and Lotharingia. Thankmar soon died, but the struggle was maintained with varying fortunes till 941, when Henry made final submission and was generously enough received into the king's favour.

In the course of the contest three of the dukes had fallen; the victorious Otto appropriated Franconia, made his pardoned brother Henry duke of Bavaria, bestowed Lotharingia on his own son-in-law, the Frank Conrad the Red, and made his own eldest but still very youthful son Ludolf duke of Swabia, Henry and Ludolf each marrying the daughter or sister of his predecessor in the dukedom. But, though all the dukes were members of the royal family, they were without the privileges of which Henry the Fowler had not ventured to deprive the earlier dukes, and in each duchy there was a count palatine, an officer appointed by the crown to safeguard its own interests. Otto was very unmistakably king of the Germans.

### Magyar Menace disposed of

**N**EVERTHELESS, though much more under control than before, the new dukes were still not very far removed from being independent sovereigns, and resented the curtailment of their powers. The rival ambitions of Henry and young Ludolf in Italy led to the intervention of Otto; Otto's intervention, to the detriment of Ludolf's plans, spurred Ludolf to revolt against his father in a coalition with Conrad of Lotharingia and the archbishop of Mainz; a civil war raged during 953; and though the rebels made submission, the Magyars seized the opportunity to develop an invasion of Germany in force. It was their last. In the face of the common menace, the Germans united; and Otto shattered the Magyar army at the decisive battle of Lechfeld (955). As in the north among the Wends, a new march was organized, the Ostmark—Austria. Lechfeld stayed the Magyar menace once for all.

In Italy, whither the quarrel of Ludolf and Henry had drawn him, Otto had rescued a princess in distress and taken her to be his second wife. The lady was Adelaide of Burgundy, the fair widow of Lothair of Provence, who had died while fighting with Berengar of Ivrea, the grandson of the emperor Berengar, for the crown of Italy. Berengar took her prisoner ; she appealed to the dukes of Bavaria and Swabia ; both came to her aid, but as rivals, not as colleagues, each intent on winning the Italian crown for himself. Otto, having no mind to let a German duke become king of Italy, intervened himself, released Adelaide and married her, gave the crown to Berengar as his vassal and a border district of Friuli to Henry of Bavaria (951), and very soon after, as we have seen, found himself at war with his own disappointed son.

The battle with the Magyars effected a general reconciliation. But in Otto's absence quarrels arose between Berengar and Pope John XII. John appealed to Otto, and Otto, having already decided that he must have the Papacy at his disposal for his own ecclesiastical ends in Germany, seized his opportunity. Berengar retreated, Otto entered Rome, and John discovered that he had called to his aid not a servant but a master.

### Imperial Mastery over the Papacy

JOHN, as a matter of course, acceded to Otto's demand that he should be crowned emperor (962) ; the emperor Otto proceeded to confirm the Papacy in possession of all the lands that had been conveyed or secured to it, known as the Patrimony of S. Peter, but with reservation of the imperial supremacy, and with a further declaration that no papal election was valid till the candidate had taken the oath of allegiance to the emperor. Also he demanded and received John's sanction for certain ecclesiastical measures to which most of the German bishops were

**OTTO II AND THEOPHANO**
Constant warfare troubled the reign of Otto II (955–983), who succeeded his father, Otto the Great, as German king and emperor in 973. This ivory diptych shows him with his Byzantine wife Theophano, daughter of Romanus II.
*Cluny Museum ; photo, Giraudon*

vehemently opposed. Then Otto marched against Berengar, with whom John began at once to intrigue against his new oppressor. Otto returned to Rome, deposed John on a variety of well-founded criminal charges, and set up a new pope, Leo VIII. As soon as Otto's back was turned, John reappeared in Rome, ejected Leo, and died. But the successor elected by John's party made abject submission and was promptly banished, while Otto's pope, Leo, was reinstated. Before Otto left Italy he had the young son (Otto II) whom Adelaide had borne to him crowned emperor also (967), Ludolf having died ten years earlier.

Otto at the end of his long and strenuous reign was a potentate far more powerful than any known since Charlemagne. He had mastered the dukes ; he had mastered

**OTTO III : IMPERIAL MYSTIC AND DREAMER**

This miniature from a copy of the Gospels at Munich belonging to Otto III (980–1002) depicts that emperor enthroned with priests and knights beside him and suggests his devotional character. An idealist who tried to revive the old conception of the Roman Empire, he proved inadequate to his position.

*From Schlumberger, ' L'épopée byzantine ' (Hachette)*

which the Bavarian house hoped to dominate. Henry was beaten and took refuge in Bohemia, while half his duchy was parted into margravates (march counties). Having established his authority in Germany, Otto made a demonstration in France at the head of a large army, mainly to frighten the young king Lothair, who had presumed to claim Lotharingia with its traditional affection for the Carolingian house, which had been restored in France on the death of Rudolf of Burgundy, who had reigned there from 929 to 936. Then Otto II turned to Italy (980), where the Crescenti were seeking to dominate the Papacy.

Otto suppressed the Crescenti, and then set about the conquest of South Italy, in one part of which the Greek towns were showing no disposition to accept their transfer from the Eastern to the Western Empire, while in another the Saracens were still in possession. In 981 and 982 he achieved a series of successes till he was ambushed and most of his force cut to pieces in Calabria. He himself made an adventurous escape, and the disaster only roused him, and the Italians and Germans alike, to a fresh united effort in what was now regarded as a sacred war. Only Venice caused delay by declining to provide the necessary ships, having profitable commercial relations with the Saracens ; and Otto died suddenly in 983, at the age of twenty-eight, before the preparations for the great campaign were completed. The infant Otto III (983–1002) had already been solemnly elected to the succession.

the Papacy. He had extended and organized the marches of the Empire under counts owing no allegiance to the dukes but directly responsible to the crown. He had finally disposed of the Magyar menace and the Slavs beyond the borders paid him tribute. In his very last days he procured as bride for his son a princess of the Eastern Empire, Theophano, who brought as her dower the Italian lands that had hitherto remained in Byzantine allegiance.

In 973 Otto the Great died in Germany, by no means an old man. The son who succeeded him, Otto II (973–983), was only eighteen, and his capacities were unproved. Naturally his cousin, the second Henry (' the Quarrelsome ') of Bavaria, was in rebellion before long because another Otto, the son of Ludolf, was placed in the vacant dukedom of Swabia,

THE regency was placed with the widow Theophano. The emperor's death prevented the prosecution of the Saracen war ; Henry the Quarrelsome reappeared ; bishops dominated the situation, and though very far from being in accord with each other they did succeed in effecting an uneasy pacification till the young emperor came of age and proceeded to Rome for his official coronation by the pope in 996.

Otto, half German and half Greek, bred under the tutelage of Bishop Bernard of Hildesheim, a scholar and a fervent Cluniac, was a born idealist with a vivid imagination, an active and receptive brain and the unmeasured enthusiasm of sixteen for his ideals. He was accompanied on his Italian journey by his dearest friend, an idealist as ardent as himself, and not much older, his cousin Bruno. While they were on the way the pope died. On Otto's nomination Bruno was forthwith elected pope as Gregory V. Gregory crowned Otto emperor, and the youthful pair started confidently to set the world to rights in accordance with their somewhat visionary ideals.

Three years later Gregory died, but Otto had ready to take his place Gerbert of Aurillac, a reformer no less ardent, but already advanced in years and long reputed to be so abnormally learned that he was suspected of being a wizard. So Gregory V was succeeded by Sylvester II. The emperor and the pope were thenceforth to rule the world in perfect harmony as God's vice-gerents, of course with the Holy and Imperial City as its centre. Kings would bow before them in acknowledgement of their divine mission and authority.

They did not reform the world. Otto died at two-and-twenty in 1002 ; Sylvester followed him to the grave next year. The emperor's Roman ideals were wholly incompatible with the needs of the German kingdom. The Papacy relapsed into the hands of the counts of Tusculum, as before it had relapsed into the hands

of the Crescenti. The next German king, Henry of Bavaria, the son of the 'Quarrelsome Duke,' was crowned as Emperor Henry II (1002–1024) ; but he belonged to the German kingdom and his relations with Italy were merely perfunctory. Otto had followed Otto till the dynasty had acquired the authority of hereditary prestige, but now there were no descendants of the first Otto in the male line ; any new dynasty had to make a fresh start. The imperial title might help the Bavarian in Germany, but not if he tried, like the last Otto, to be an Italian instead of a German.

Henry was competent and imperturbable, just and tenacious, pious enough to earn the title of 'the Saint.' He

**HENRY II, THE SAINTLY 'KING OF THE ROMANS'**

Henry II (973–1024), 'The Saint,' was elected German king in 1002. This miniature from a manuscript at Munich shows him and his consort, Cunegonde, being presented to Christ by SS. Peter and Paul with, below them, Germany between Rome and Gaul. In 1014 Henry was crowned emperor.

*From Schlumberger, ' L'épopée byzantine ' (Hachette)*

strengthened his borders and stabilised the government, preserving the peace and maintaining his authority—in Germany. But he left Italy alone ; and he did not found a dynasty. His reign exemplified the uses of unimaginative efficiency ; but it was undeniably commonplace.

The old divisional Five Nations of Germany still survived, but not as the old Five Dukedoms, each of which had been to some extent, at least, broken up ; while throughout the last century the crown, without falling under clerical domination, had strengthened the prelates as against the lay magnates. On Henry's death there was no one with an outstanding claim to the succession, and it was, in effect, the bishops of the anti-Cluniac party who gave the crown to the Swabian Conrad II ' the Salic ' (1024–1039) in preference to his cousin, Conrad of Carinthia, while it was largely the loyalty of the latter that enabled Conrad II to found a dynasty.

### Conrad founds a Dynasty

CONRAD made it his primary object to weaken the group, still a small one, of the greater nobles, by attaching the minor nobles directly to the crown, making the latter the ' king's men,' barons or vassals, over-riding or abolishing claims to their obedience on the part of the intermediary overlord, duke or count, to whom they were for the most part bound by the practice of ' commendation,' a mutual contract of protection and service. The method to which Conrad resorted was the application to the lesser barons of that principle of heredity on which the greater were laying such stress for themselves. Incidentally, the magnification of the theory of hereditary right fitted in with his own determination to make the kingship hereditary in his family. To that end he procured the coronation of his son, Henry, while still a boy.

The principal event of the reign was the inclusion in the Empire of the Arelate, Provence or Lower Burgundy, by contract with its last king, Rudolf III. The Arelate, most romantic of lands, was for centuries to be associated with neither France nor Italy, but Germany, and to be a buffer between the two Latin countries.

Conrad was thoroughly unpopular, and almost invariably successful. He proved himself master in Germany and Italy, and he compelled the Magyars in Hungary, the Czechs in Bohemia and the rising power of the Poles to acknowledge his sovereignty. When he died in 1039 he left to carry on his work a son young but carefully trained in both war and statecraft. Conrad's practical success was demonstrated when Henry III (1039-1056) assumed the reins of power unopposed and unchallenged.

In the seventeen years of his rule Henry the Black raised the Empire to the utmost height of power it ever attained. Poles, Czechs and Hungarians were subjected to a much more definite suzerainty, the first with little trouble, the other two not without hard work. The rapid and convincing subjugation of the east left the emperor free to deal with the problems of Germany and Italy. A man so strong as Henry could afford to be conciliatory where mildness in a weaker man would certainly have been misconstrued ; the moral atmosphere, so to speak, was made healthier by the emperor's personality. He created public spirit by the sincerity of his own public spirit, immensely to the welfare of the whole community. No one suspected his magnanimity of being a cloak either for fear or for craft.

### Henry's Italian and Papal policy

MOST notable, however, were his dealings with Italy and the Papacy. Otto I had suppressed the Crescenti popes. Otto III had gone further and set two idealists, one a German, the other a Frenchman, in the chair of S. Peter ; but relapse had followed the death of both emperors. The counts of Tusculum had taken the place of the Crescenti, and before the German king turned his attention to Italy the scandal had reached such a pitch that there were three rivals at once, each of them claiming to be the legitimate pope.

In 1046 Henry answered the appeal of a synod held in Rome. He came to Italy, took matters in hand himself, summoned two successive synods, at which all the three popes were deposed, and set the German bishop of Bamberg on the papal throne as Clement II, the first of that series which culminated with the election of Gregory VII in 1073. Clement died the next year, and his successor, Damasus, a few months later ; and then a second Bruno—a cousin of the emperor, as the first had been—became pope as Leo IX (1048). Each pope was Henry's nominee and a German. And each was a man of marked ability, of high character, and imbued with a lofty conception of his spiritual responsibilities.

The great Henry died prematurely in 1056, not yet in his fortieth year. Once again the undisputed successor was a child of six, Henry IV. The loss was irreparable. No regency could carry the power and authority of the dead man. Lacking that strong controlling force and personal example, nobles and prelates fell to wrangling for power, especially prelates. The boy's mother, an admirable consort for a strong king, was quite incompetent to direct affairs.

Archbishop Anno of Cologne superseded her, Anno was superseded by Adalbert bishop of Bremen, Adalbert was again superseded by Anno, and Anno once more by Adalbert, while young Henry was tossed like a shuttlecock from one to the other, and grew up untrained, hot-headed and self-willed, and full of resentment against everyone who had exercised control over him. Before he was twenty desultory rebellions were breaking out. He did not, in fact, become free from tutelage till Adalbert's death in 1072, and by that time Germany was in a state of confusion, to remedy which would have taxed to the utmost a prince of far stronger character than Henry IV.

### Norman Adventurers in Italy

NOR was the condition of Italy any better. The last chance of consolidating a strong Lombard kingdom disappeared when the emperor Berengar died in 924. South Italy had been a cockpit for the rivalries of Lombard lords, Saracen chiefs and Greek governors. Otto the Great himself had failed to establish his authority. Otto II had been technically sovereign of all Italy, not only Lombard but also Greek, in virtue of his marriage with Theophano, the Saracens having no

recognizable status ; but his first attempt to make his position good failed, and the second was strangled by his premature death. Otto III died before he had time to attempt giving practical effect to his ideals ; Henry II ignored Italy ; Italy almost ignored Conrad ; and the energies of Henry III in the peninsula were limited to his drastic dealing with the papal problem. Further, since the second decade of the eleventh century the South Italian problem had taken a new aspect, due to the adventurers from Normandy.

The achievements of the Norman house of Hauteville in Italy, and in Sicily, where the Saracens had been at this time in full possession for nearly a century, defying all attempts to eject them, were beginning to loom large. They were engaged in carving out a dominion for themselves, with Greeks or Lombard nobles as allies, rivals or victims, according to circumstances, when their activities brought them into conflict with the third of Henry III's popes, Leo IX, the emperor having just conferred the duchy of Benevento on the Papacy. The Italians rallied to the papal standard for the crushing of the predatory aliens, who in 1053 shattered their army at Civitate.

### The Normans and the Reforming Papacy

BUT the Norman had a genius for colouring successful rapacity with piety. He desired not the hostility but the blessing of the Church ; and instead of pressing his victory by force of arms, he sought and obtained a reconciliation by which both the Normans and the Papacy profited mightily. The Normans became the champions of the pope against all comers, and they could reckon in return upon the papal countenance for their own ambitious projects, though at first there was no formal pact.

Leo died next year (1054), but the alliance between the Normans and the reforming Papacy remained the central fact of Italian politics. And it was a fact which did not fit in with the claims of a supreme central authority having its seat in Germany ; though this was not apparent while the popes were men selected by an emperor who was in entire sympathy with their reforming activities. The alliance may be said to have been sealed in 959, three years after the death of Henry III, when Pope Nicholas II conferred the duchy of Apulia and (by anticipation) of Sicily on Robert Guiscard as the pope's liegeman. The death of Henry prepared the way for a development of papal claims which would have been incredible while he was living.

Leo, when Henry drew him from his bishopric of Toul to make him pope, had accepted the high office on condition that he was elected canonically, not only on the emperor's authority. He indeed magnified his office, and crowded an enormous and pervading activity into the six years of his reign, but without collision between his aims and Henry's. The imperial authority was in practical abeyance when Gerard of Florence became Nicholas II in 1058, in defiance of an attempt on the part of the Crescenti to recover control of the election. Nicholas reigned for only three years, but in that time he held the Lateran Council which permanently placed papal elections in the hands of the College of Cardinals, claimed the power of appointing the duke of Apulia and Sicily, and vigorously extended the Cluniac discipline which the old school of ecclesiastics detested.

His successor, Alexander II, was a Cluniac who was elected, without any reference at all to the imperial authority, in 1061, so that the German bishops claimed to set up an antipope, Honorius, though he could obtain little recognition outside Germany. And behind Alexander was Archdeacon Hildebrand, the inspiring genius of the theocratic movement, to whom both he and Nicholas owed their election. Not till Hildebrand succeeded in 1073 was the significance of that movement apparent.

**DUNSTAN, SAINT AND STATESMAN**
After his appointment to the archbishopric of Canterbury in 961 Dunstan became the most powerful man in England. He is figured (bottom left) in this eleventh century manuscript in pallium and mitre, with two other ecclesiastics at the feet of an enthroned archbishop—S. Gregory or S. Benedict.
*British Museum ; Cotton MSS. Claudius A iii*

THE final separation of Neustria from Austrasia, of the old Frankish dominion of France from the Empire which was to be in essence German, was accomplished when the West Franks elected king a western noble, Odo count of Paris, on the death of Charles the Fat. The only legitimate Carolingian left, Charles the Simple, was reinstated on Odo's death, but deposed by Odo's brother Robert and Rudolf of Burgundy in 923. Rudolf reigned till his death in 936, when Robert's son, Hugh the Great, who might have claimed the succession, chose instead to recall Louis IV

EPISODES IN THE NORMAN CONQUEST AS DEPICTED IN THE BAYEUX TAPESTRY

Executed to the order of William the Conqueror's half-brother, Odo, bishop of Bayeux, for his cathedral, the so-called Bayeux Tapestry is contemporary with the Norman Conquest of England and the primary authority on the Norman case. It comprises seventy-two scenes and supplies some unique evidence concerning the events illustrated. Here from left to right are (above) Edward enthroned, Harold taking an oath upon a reliquary to support the claims of William to the English throne, and the death of Edward; and (below) Harold crowned at Westminster with Archbishop Stigand beside him, and the death of Harold, pierced through the eye by an arrow, at the battle of Hastings.

(d'Outremer, ' from over the sea ' in England), the son of Charles, and set him on the throne, while himself retaining the real power as duke of France.

For fifty years Louis (936–954) and his son Lothair (954–986) made restive attempts to free themselves from the domination of Hugh the Great (who died in 956) and his son Hugh Capet, but found their astute and mighty vassals too strong. Lothair was succeeded by his son Louis V, who died next year. No man of the great house remained ; a new king from a new house must be elected ; Hugh was conspicuously the first among the nobles, and as a matter of course was elected—the first king of the Capet dynasty which reigned without a break in the male line until the fall of the monarchy in the Revolution ; though his grandfather had reigned for a few months and his great-uncle for a few years.

Hugh at last became king because no other king was possible ; he was in no sense a usurper ; but his crown had no traditional halo. The new French monarchy was weak, not because the princes were weak men but because they were not so exceptionally strong that they could overcome the inherent weakness of their position among feudatories who could on occasion command greater resources than their own. For the power which raised the house of Capet to the throne was derived from that development of feudalism which most restricted its power when it was on the throne.

### England and the Danish Conquest

**I**N the British Isles the development of feudalism was much less marked than in France, Germany or Italy. The stress of the struggle with the Danes in England enabled Alfred to create a strong central government, and his son and grandsons to make it effective from the Channel to the Tyne. There were no mighty terri-

**BRONZE SEAL OF AELFRIC THE TRAITOR**
This seal is identified as being that of Aelfric, the corrupt Mercian ealdorman who on two occasions whilst commander of the forces of Ethelred—in 992 at London and again in 1003—by his treachery saved the Danish host from annihilation. Ethelred's reliance upon unreliable ministers largely caused the final triumph of the Danes.
*British Museum*

torial nobles to challenge the authority of kings who were the incarnation of the national idea, whose military prowess was convincing and whose care for just administration was scarcely less marked. Edward the Elder, Athelstan and his brothers, were fighting men because the need for fighting had not passed ; but they did not neglect organization. Thus England was at the height of prosperity in the reign of Edgar the Peaceful (959–975), when the administration was in the hands of the great prelate Dunstan, who was also a zealous ecclesiastical reformer of the Cluniac school.

But with Ethelred the Redeless (or Unready) came disaster born of criminal folly and incompetence. The north lands were still sending forth adventurers. England had been an unprofitable objective for them for a hundred years past, when Olaf Trygvessen and Sweyn Fork-beard, the prince of Denmark, who was at odds with his father Harold Blue-tooth, began once more to harry the English coast. Having extorted from Ethelred a heavy ransom, they naturally returned ; presently Ethelred excited them to the highest pitch of wrath by a massacre of the Danes then in England ; and Sweyn, having succeeded to the Danish throne, set about the conquest of England. There was no heart in the resistance. Ethelred fled to Normandy ; England was annexed to the

Danish crown (1013) ; next year Sweyn died, and Canute, his son, became king of Denmark, England and (later) more or less of Norway.

For a time it seemed that a great Scandinavian empire might be formed ; but the elements of it were too disconnected, and it went to pieces when Canute died, wrecked by the ineradicable tradition of division among the sons. In 1042 England recalled Ethelred's pious son, Edward (the Confessor), from Normandy, which his soul loved. He returned with a train of Norman favourites, mostly ecclesiastics, and left the administration in the hands of the great earls who were Canute's disastrous legacy to England.

For Canute, himself a strong and very able ruler, had adopted the system which under such a ruler served admirably, of appointing district rulers responsible to himself, with the Anglo-Danish title of

**GREAT SEAL OF THE CONFESSOR**

Edward, son of Ethelred by Emma, and half-brother of Harthacnut (Hardicanute), her son by Canute, was chosen King of England in 1042. At heart a Norman and a monk he largely prepared the way for the Norman conquest.

*British Museum*

**ENGLAND'S DANISH KING CANUTE**

Notwithstanding his fierce Viking nature, Canute was an earnest Christian. He is pictured in this page from the Register of New Minster or Hyde Abbey with his wife ' Aelgifu '—Ethelred's widow Emma—placing a cross upon the altar.

*British Museum, Stowe MSS.*

earl, corresponding to the counts and margraves of Charlemagne and Otto. But when an incompetent or feeble successor took the great king's place, the earls stood to the crown as the great feudatories stood to the crown on the Continent, and as jealous rivals for power with each other. Under Edward the effective power in the state passed to the great Earl Godwin, and then to his son Harold. When Edward died in the first week of 1066, the only ' ætheling ' (prince of the royal house) was a child, and the times imperatively demanded a man on the throne. The Witan, the national council, reverted to the constitutional custom of election and Harold son of Godwin was crowned king.

ᛒUT William duke of Normandy chose to consider that promises made to him by Edward and by Harold entitled him to the succession, to which he obviously had no other claim. On the other hand, Harold Hardraada of Norway saw a prize to be snatched. Both the Norseman and the Norman invaded England. The Norseman landed first ; Harold Godwinson met him and slew him at Stamford Bridge, and flew south to meet the Norman and to perish in the desperately fought battle

**INTRIGUE OF AN EASTERN EMPRESS**

After the death of Romanus II his widow Theophano married Nicephorus Phocas, but tiring of him conspired with her Armenian lover, John Zimisces, to effect his assassination. This miniature in the manuscript History of Skylitzes at Madrid shows Zimisces about to clamber from a boat upon the Bosporus to the balcony where his mistress awaits him.

*Photo, G. Millet, Hautes Etudes, Sorbonne*

We need not trace in detail the story of the middle-European states that were growing into comparatively definite shape on the east of the German kingdom during the period covered by this chapter. The northern Slavs, in less immediate contact with the Germans, were beginning to consolidate into the kingdom of Poland ; its real founder was Boleslav (992–1025), whose power was a serious threat to Bohemia, but was followed by a relapse. The Czechs of Moravia and Bohemia under the Premyslid dynasty were in constant contact with the German kings ; they had long been Christianised, and though not actually absorbed into the Western Empire they were for the most part tributary, and their ecclesiastical system was a branch of the German.

The Magyars in Hungary, after their westward rush was stayed by Otto I, made great progress, politically and culturally, under Stephen I (997–1038), whose vigour and ability were tempered by a piety which caused him to be canonised fifty years after his death. Magyars and Poles as well as Czechs attached themselves to the Western, not the Eastern, church.

On the east of these three nationalities, two of which were Slavonic, Swedish captains, the ' Ros,' set up the Slavonic dominion which took their name and became known as Russia ; a dominion extending from the Baltic to the Black Sea, with its centres at Kiev and Novgorod. The original hero of the Russians was the more or less mythical Rurik. The second of their heroes, Sviatoslav or Svêtoslav, we shall meet in the account of the Eastern Empire, to which we now turn.

of Hastings. The other earls had failed him in the hour of England's need.

William marched on London. The Witan, or what passed for the Witan, recognized the accomplished fact and elected the Conqueror king of England. On Christmas day 1066 he was crowned. The lands of the ' rebels ' who had taken the field against him were distributed among the motley host which had joined his standard to overthrow the perjured king—who had been crowned by an uncanonical archbishop owning allegiance to the antipope Honorius, whereas William's banners had been explicitly blessed by Alexander.

England did not submit altogether tamely to its new master. During the next five years there were sundry revolts ; but the patriots had no common policy ; all the risings were crushed with an iron hand, and each provided new excuses for further distribution of forfeited estates. After 1071, indeed, the only rebels to be found in England were Norman barons. The Norman Conquest, with all that it meant for England, was completed.

A few years before the Norman invasion, Malcolm Canmore in Scotland had overthrown the usurper (or legitimate monarch) Macbeth, and established the royal line of Scotland.

THE Greek Empire, as we saw, continued on its placid and inglorious way through the lives of the son and grandson of Basil the Macedonian. It was not seriously menaced by any foreign foe, nor with internal disruption by hereditary military magnates in command of independent forces; the imperial authority, however feebly exercised, was not challenged; the army was the army of the state, and the administration was in the hands of a trained professional bureaucracy which worked mechanically but adequately. For a great part of Constantine's long reign the imperial title was shared and the imperial office discharged by a soldier of some distinction, Romanus I, whose name was given to Constantine's own son, who succeeded him in 959.

The reign of Romanus II was active but brief, inaugurating a period of military energy. The khalif at Bagdad was now the puppet of the Persian Bouid family; another family, the Hamdanids, had set up virtually independent emirates on the Greek borders at Aleppo and Mosul; a descendant of Ali, having proclaimed himself khalif at Khairwan, had absorbed the Aglabid kingdom and annexed Egypt, with part of Syria, where the Fatimid khalifate was now established. In the west there was a third khalif, since the Ommiad Abd er-Rahman III had so proclaimed himself in 928. Khorassan was rapidly falling under the sway of Turkish tribal chiefs, while the best of the Bagdad soldiery and captains were drawn from the same source. The

Bouids themselves, like most Persians, were Shiahs, though they preferred calling themselves the ministers of a Sunni khalif to acknowledging the Fatimid in Egypt. So that the time was favourable for an attack on the Saracens.

The emperor's general, Nicephorus Phocas, opened the attack in 960. Crete was recaptured, Cilicia was invaded. Romanus died in 963, leaving two infants, Basil II and Constantine VIII, to share the imperial crown, with their young mother Theophano as regent. The victorious general returned, married the widow, and associated himself on the throne with the infants, after the precedent of Romanus I. He recovered Cyprus, and his armies overran half Syria. But he was extremely unpopular with the clergy and at court; Theophano repented her marriage; she entered on a conspiracy with one of Nicephorus' captains, John Zimisces; John murdered the rather terrible emperor while he slept, and proclaimed himself—without opposition—the associate of the two children. Instead of marrying their mother, he shut her up in a convent (969).

Then, like Basil the Macedonian, he atoned for his crime. He treated the boys, his colleagues, with all the respect due to their position. One of their sisters he

**THEOPHANO SENT INTO EXILE BY HER PARAMOUR JOHN ZIMISCES**

Nicephorus Phocas was not popular as emperor and his assassination by John Zimisces was generally condoned. But Zimisces secured his own coronation only by repudiating Theophano, who had instigated the crime—a step he was not unwilling to take in view of her infidelity and treachery—and despite her frantic denunciation of his ingratitude he dismissed her with ignominy from the palace to the seclusion of a convent. The incident is thus illustrated in the History of John Skylitzes.

*Photo, G. Millet, Hautes Etudes, Sorbonne (Schlumberger-Hachette)*

SVIATOSLAV'S RUSSIAN TROOPS ROUTED BY BYZANTINE CAVALRY

Russians made their first appearance in Bulgaria in 967, when Nicephorus Phocas, then engaged in conflict with the Bulgarians, enlisted their assistance. Under John Zimisces Byzantine policy changed, and in 971 that emperor co-operated with Boris II in expelling the Russians who were overrunning Bulgaria under their prince Sviatoslav. Zimisces defeated them in two pitched battles, and thereafter concluded a treaty whereby the Russian became the ally of the Byzantine power.

*From the MS. History of John Skylitzes ; photo, G. Millet, Hautes Etudes, Sorbonne*

married himself ; the other became the bride of Otto II ; with his own wealth he was lavish in pious charity. The Russian Sviatoslav was overrunning Bulgaria ; in 971 John marched against him, defeated him in two desperate battles, and then struck a treaty, which converted the Russian power into an ally and the Russian people into Christians of the Orthodox Church. Then he went campaigning in Syria where the Saracens had been recovering ground. But his career of victory was cut short by his sudden death in 976.

Basil II, now twenty years old, admitted no new colleague to share the imperial power and dignity with his brother Constantine and himself. For nearly fifty years—till 1025—he reigned virtually alone. A new trouble had arisen in the increasing independence of territorial magnates in Asia Minor. Possibly it would have been better for the Empire had he sought to convert them into barons of the marches ; but the more obvious course, which he adopted with ultimate success, was to suppress them.

But while he was thus engaged, Bulgaria, profiting by the expulsion of the Russians, was again becoming powerful and troublesome under her king Samuel. Dominating the Serbs in the north-west, Samuel's raiders poured year by year over Macedonia. The first campaigns against them were ineffective. In 996 they harried

the Peloponnese but suffered a disastrous defeat while retiring. In 1002 Basil set about the work of conquest in earnest ; but it was not completed until in 1014 he won an overwhelming victory, taking 15,000 captives. He blinded those captives, all but a hundred and fifty, who were left an eye apiece to guide the rest home. The horror of the thing killed Samuel, while Basil won the grim honour of his distinctive name Bulgaroctonus, Basil the Bulgar-slayer. The Bulgars still held out till the last resistance was crushed in 1018. So ended the first Bulgar kingdom.

Basil, now an old man, next turned his arms against Armenia—a mistake, since thereby he destroyed an effective buffer between the Empire and the Mahomedan powers. With his death in 1025 passed the revived strength and energy of the Eastern Empire. Constantine was the last prince of the Macedonian house. He followed his brother to the grave in 1028. For the next twenty-six years the emperors were the successive husbands of his daughter Zoe ; during this period the last of the Greeks were being ejected from south Italy by the Norman Hautevilles, and the Eastern Empire was in effect without a ruler. For three brief years Zoe's sister, Theodora (1054–1057), did what she could to check the process of decay. In vain ; for she died at the moment when the Mahomedan world was falling to the Seljuk Turks.

WE saw in previous chapters that the Ommiads stood for the old Arabian party of the aristocracy of Islam and Arab supremacy within Islam. The Abbasids turned out the Ommiads, as the representatives of the party of equality among the peoples who joined the Faith, in association with the Shiahs, the mystics of Islam ; who as mystics were especially strong among the Persians, and as Fatimids had adherents in all parts. But from the middle of the ninth century the Abbasids had preferred the Old Believers to the Persians, and were at the same time growing increasingly dependent on the mercenary troops, drawn mainly from the Turkish tribes beyond the Oxus, the most materialistic of races ; to whom the Koran as literally interpreted appealed strongly, in contrast with mystic interpretations.

Further, the later Abbasids were without the personal ability of the first rulers. Hence the break-up in the tenth century, and the curious spectacle of a Sunni khalif at Bagdad, in the hands of the Shiah Bouids, yet surrounded by a Sunni Turkish soldiery with whom the Bouids did not dare to quarrel ; while his spiritual authority as khalif scarcely extended beyond Syria, and his temporal power was limited to a small area of which Bagdad was the centre. Already Turkish commanders had for short periods turned governorships in Egypt and Syria into independent lordships ; an actual Turkish domination had not been set up, for the simple reason that the adventurers had not a nation, a tribe, or even a company of sworn followers at their backs.

Even on their own ground, in the Trans-Oxus, the Turks were not a nation, though their tribes were beginning to work in

**BASIL II 'SLAYER OF BULGARIANS'**

Basil II (c. 958–1025), known as Bulgaroctonus from the atrocities that attended his extinction of the Bulgarian kingdom, was a ruthless man but a capable ruler, under whom the Eastern Empire rose to great power. This miniature from a contemporary psalter depicts him in imperial costume with obsequious officials on their knees before him.

*S. Mark's, Venice ; from Schlumberger, 'L'épopée byzantine'*

concert, sometimes against the Chinese and sometimes within the Mahomedan dominion, of which they could not be called subjects, though they formed a part of it in so far as they had adopted Islam. During this same period the Khitai Tatars were penetrating North China.

Towards the close of the tenth century, however, an actual Turkish dominion was in course of establishing itself, as champion of Mahomedanism in its most fanatical form, in the farthest lands of what had once been the empire of Alexander the Great. Its centre was at Ghazni, in the modern Afghanistan ; its founder was the Turk governor Sabuktagin, nominally an officer of the khalif ; its great figure was his son Mahmud of Ghazni (998–1030), mighty in war, destroyer of idols, and hardly less famous as an enlightened patron of learning. Sabuktagin, as lord of Ghazni, made himself an independent prince in fact if not in name ; Mahmud was a conqueror who once more broke through the mountain barrier of India and prepared the way for the coming Mahomedan supremacy, though he did not himself organize his own conquests. Ten several times or more he led his fiercely fanatical troops through the mountain passes, into the Land of the Five Rivers—the Punjab —which Alexander had conquered, and on to the Ganges basin or down the Indus to Gujarat, whence he bore away the famous gates of Somnath, the great Hindu shrine ; laying waste the temples, overthrowing the images of the gods and carrying off vast spoils. Famous poets and men of learning gathered at the court of Ghazni. Half Persia owned his sway, while he held off the swarms of the Turkish tribes, as Rollo or the Danes of the Danelaw held off their Viking kinsfolk.

Yet Mahmud did not create an empire. Soon after his death the Seljuk Turks broke in ; the Ghaznavid dynasty did not disappear, but it was reduced by the invaders to no more than a petty principality. It was the Seljuks who became the masters of the Mahomedan world. First they made themselves masters of Khorassan. Then they advanced upon Bagdad, led by their chief Tughril, not as rebels but to deliver the khalif from the hands of the heretical Persians. But the hands of the orthodox Turks were not more tender. The khalif was the spiritual head, whose authority it was Tughril's mission to retore, but the wielder of the sword retained the temporal power. The Bouids passed, but Tughril was the Great Sultan (1055).

### Asia Minor lost to the Seljuk Turks

In 1057, Theodora died, the last of the Macedonian family. She, had nominated a successor whose incompetence at once became obvious. He was deposed in favour of the soldier Isaac Comnenus, but Isaac, afflicted with a sore disease, retired to a monastery. He was succeeded by Constantine X Ducas, an experienced politician who was neither a soldier nor a statesman (1059).

In 1060 Alp Arslan, Tughril's successor, flung himself on Armenia. The Empire gave no effective aid to the country whose power Basil II had destroyed. The Seljuks overran Armenia, and then flooded into Asia Minor. At last a new emperor, Romanus IV Diogenes, took up the neglected task and attacked the invader. Alp Arslan inveigled him into the mountains, fought him in a great pitched battle at Manzikert (1071), took him prisoner and cut his army to pieces. The Seljuks swept on, and Michael, the young colleague of Romanus, was soon after reduced to buying a respite by the cession of virtually the whole of Asia Minor.

**EMPRESS ZOE TENDERING THANKS TO THE PEOPLE OF CONSTANTINOPLE**
As successive husbands of Zoe, daughter of Constantine II, Romanus Argyrus and the Paphlagonian Michael IV wielded the sceptre between 1028 and 1041. Zoe then adopted Michael Calaphates, who repaid her with imprisonment. She was released at the clamour of the populace, who cherished loyalty to her family. This illustration in the History of Skylitzes shows her leaving S. Sophia and entering the palace to thank the people. Zoe's last husband was Constantine Monomachus.
*From Schlumberger, ' L'épopée byzantine,' Hachette*

# TABLE OF DATES FOR CHAPTER 18

1073 Hildebrand elected pope as Gregory VII.
Henry IV occupied with the Saxons.
Sulayman captures Nicaea.

1075 Henry IV defeats the Saxons.
Gregory issues decree against lay investiture.
Henry declares Gregory deposed. Gregory excommunicates Henry and declares him deposed.

1076 Seljuk Turks seize Jerusalem.
German nobles and prelates turn against Henry.

1077 Canossa ; submission and humiliation of Henry.
Election of Rudolf of Swabia, followed by German reaction in Henry's favour.
Sultanate of Roum established at Nicaea by Sulayman.

1078 Nicephorus II deposes Michael VII Ducas.
1079 Gregory again excommunicates Henry.
1080 Death of Rudolf breaks up the German rebellion though Saxons elect Herman of Luxemburg.
Henry sets up antipope Clement III.

1081 Alexius I Comnenus deposes Nicephorus. Comneni rule for a century.
Robert Guiscard besieges Durazzo and defeats Byzantines.
Henry IV invades Italy and besieges Gregory in Rome.

1082 Henry occupies the Leonine City at Rome.
1083 Henry occupies Rome ; Gregory holds out in the castle of S. Angelo.
1084 Henry IV is crowned at Rome by Clement. Robert Guiscard returns from Macedonia, raises the siege of S. Angelo, sacks Rome, and retires. Gregory follows him to Salerno.
1085 Death of Gregory (May) and of Guiscard (June).
Robert succeeded as duke of Apulia by his son Roger ; Bohemund count of Otranto withdraws Normans to Italy.
Alfonso VI of Castile captures Toledo.
England : the Domesday Survey.
1086 Victor III pope.
Alfonso is defeated at Zallaca by the Almoravid Yussuf ; who establishes the Almoravid ascendancy in S. Spain (1086–98).
1087 England : William Rufus succeeds the Conqueror.
1088 Urban II pope.
1092 Sultan Malik Shah dies. Wars of succession.
1093 Rebellion of Henry's elder son Conrad.
1095 Alexius appeals to Urban at Council of Piacenza (March). The First Crusade proclaimed at Council of Clermont (November).
1096 Crusaders assemble at Constantinople (Dec.).
1097 Crusaders invade Asia Minor, take Nicaea, drive Kilij Arslan to Iconium, which becomes the capital of Roum, cross the Taurus, secure Edessa and besiege Antioch.
1098 Crusaders take Antioch. Fatimids recapture Jerusalem from Seljuks.
1099 Crusaders capture Jerusalem (July). Beginning of the 'Latin Kingdom' under Godfrey of Bouillon with title Advocate of Jerusalem.
Death of Ruy Diaz (Cid Campeador).
Henry IV has his second son Henry V crowned.
Death of Urban. Paschal II pope.
1100 Baldwin I succeeds his brother Godfrey at Jerusalem, with title of king. Organization of the Latin Kingdom of Jerusalem with feudatory princes at Edessa, Antioch and Tripolis ; the typical feudal state.
England : accession of Henry I (to 1135).
Death of antipope Clement ends schism.
1101 Deaths of Conrad and Roger I (count) of Sicily.
1104 Revolt of Henry V against Henry IV.
1106 Death of Henry IV. Henry V maintains quarrel with Paschal.
Henry I of England secures Normandy by defeating his elder brother Duke Robert at Tenchebrai.

1107 English settlement of investiture question.
1108 France : accession of Louis VI the Fat.
Hungarian war of Henry V.
1111 Henry V in Italy. Paschal resigns temporalities and then other claims ; crowns Henry V.
Death of Roger of Apulia ; William succeeds.
1112 Paschal repudiates his pledges. Series of revolts (1112–18) in Germany.
1118 Death of Paschal II.
1119 Sanjar Seljuk sultan (to 1159).
Calixtus II pope.
Alfonso I of Aragon wins Saragossa.
John II succeeds Alexius at Constantinople.
Baldwin II (cousin) succeeds Baldwin I.
1122 Concordat of Worms ends investiture dispute.
1124 Calixtus dies ; Honorius II pope.
Scotland ; accession of David I (to 1153).
1125 Death of Henry V. Lothair of Saxony elected emperor. Rivalry of Welf and Weiblingen.
1127 Roger II of Sicily succeeds William of Apulia and extends dominion over South Italy.
The Turk Zanghi made 'atabeg' of Mosul.
Institution of the Order of Knights Templars.
1129 Matilda (Empress Maud) d. of Henry I of England m. Geoffrey of Anjou.
1130 Fulk of Anjou (son-in-law) succeeds Baldwin II.
Election of rival popes Anacletus II and Innocent II. Papal schism to 1138.
1131 Bernard of Clairvaux and emperor Lothair support Innocent.
1132 Lothair campaigns against Roger II in Apulia.
1134 Lothair reconciled with Hohenstaufen. Anacletus recognizes Roger as 'king' of Sicily.
1135 England : accession of Stephen of Blois ; succession claimed by Empress Maud ; eighteen years of civil war and feudal anarchy.
1137 Quarrel of Lothair and Innocent. Death of Lothair (December).
Accession of Louis VII after marriage with Elinor of Aquitaine.
1138 Conrad III (Hohenstaufen) elected emperor.
Innocent attacks and is taken prisoner by Roger, who extorts recognition as king of Sicily, officially 'held of the pope.'
1139 Henry the Proud (Welf) deprived of Saxony and Bavaria.
Alfonso Henriques, count of Porto Cale, defeats Moors at Ouriques, and is first king of Portugal.
1141 Defeat of Sultan Sanjar by Kara-Khitais.
1142 Henry the Lion (Welf) restored in Saxony. Albert the Bear established in Mark of Brandenburg.
1143 Manuel I succeeds John II at Constantinople.
1144 Baldwin III (minor) succeeds Fulk at Jerusalem.
Zanghi of Mosul takes Edessa.
1145-49 Struggle in Spain between Almoravids and Almohades who win the supremacy.
1146 Zanghi succeeded at Mosul by Nour ed-Din.
Bernard of Clairvaux preaches a new Crusade.
Louis VII and Conrad III take the Cross (the 'Second Crusade').
1147 Conrad and Louis in Asia Minor.
1148 Collapse of the Second Crusade.
1149 Advance of Sancho IX of Castile in central Spain, signalised by the establishment of a Cistercian monastery at Calatrava.
1150 Union of Catalonia with Aragon through the marriage of Count Raymond Berengar of Barcelona to Petronilla the heiress of Aragon.
1151 Dissolution of marriage between Louis VII and Elinor of Aquitaine.
1152 Marriage of Elinor to Henry Plantagenet of Anjou and Normandy, son of Empress Maud.
Conrad III dies. Election of Frederick I Barbarossa of Swabia and Hohenstaufen.

# Fifth Era

# THE CRUSADING ERA

## 1073–1303

---

Chapter 18
### THE CLASH OF EAST AND WEST, 1073—1152

Chapter 19
### EAST AND WEST: CONFLICT AND INTERCOURSE, 1152—1216

Chapter 20
### THE AGE OF EASTERN IMPERIALISM, 1216—1303

---

ALTHOUGH the Byzantine state, under Greek or 'Latin' emperors, lingered until its destruction by the Ottoman Turks in 1453, what really gave it its death-blow was the loss of Asia Minor to the Seljuks at the battle of Manzikert in 1071 ; and it was these Seljuks who, by reversing the normal Mahomedan principle of toleration to Christian pilgrims in the Holy Land, made it possible for the Byzantine emperor to enlist the sympathy of the Western nations and set them crusading. Again, it was the election of Hildebrand as Pope Gregory VII in 1073, two years after Manzikert, that marked the rise of the Papacy to the greatest height of power and prestige ever attained by it, a prestige that enabled Pope Urban to organize the First Crusade in 1095 as the outward expression of an apparently united Christendom. Again, it was the crusaders who in the event gave its second death-blow, so to speak, to Byzantinism when the so-called Fourth Crusade captured Constantinople in 1204 and established the short-lived Latin Empire. And finally the Crusades, by promoting a renewed contact between East and West, had an economic and cultural significance that far outweighed their apparent political futility.

Events of world importance which it would be hard to link up with this nexus of facts took place in India and China throughout the period, but the foregoing is the justification for fixing 1073 as the date at which to terminate The Byzantine Era, and choosing The Crusading Era as the title of the one that here ensues. It extends to 1303, in which year the capture of Boniface at Anagni marked the end of papal pretensions, the last Christian fortress in Syria having fallen to the Saracens in 1291.

### CHAPTER 18

# THE CLASH OF EAST AND WEST:
## 1073–1152

**J**N the third quarter of the eleventh century two features presented themselves ·which are of first-rate importance in the history of the coming age. In Asia, Islam fell under the military domination of the Turks; and in Europe the Papacy, under the guidance of Archdeacon Hildebrand, was making ready to assert the supremacy of the spiritual over the temporal power in the Christian world.

Of these, the second inaugurated a prolonged conflict between a single authority claiming to · be universally absolute and the several authorities, imperial or royal, which claimed to be territorially absolute, affecting the development of every state in Europe ; and the first was the immediate cause of the renewed clash between the Oriental and the Western worlds which is characterized by the organization of the Crusades.

### The Seljuk Turks in Syria

**N**ow for three centuries and a half, since the triumphs of Leo the Iconoclast and Charles Martel, Mahomedanism had made no progress against Christianity; and Saracens had made no progress against Europeans, save for occasional thrusts into Asia Minor when the Eastern Empire was in a particularly demoralised state, the Aglabid conquest of Sicily, and the piratical occupation of territory in South Italy that technically pertained to Byzantium ; they had already been cleared out of Italy, were in process of being cleared out of Sicily, and were being continuously pressed farther south in Spain. The boundaries of the Eastern Empire were still intact, when the Turks broke into Asia Minor and established themselves there by the victory of Manzikert .

The sultan Alp Arslan was assassinated in 1072. The new Seljuk sultan, Malik Shah, left Asia Minor to his general, Sulayman, who captured Nicaea in 1073 and made it the capital of an independent kingdom of Roum (i.e. Rome), to be obviously the centre of a permanent menace to Constantinople ; though according to Turkish custom there was no attempt to supply the conquered territory with a political organization. The sultan's attention being mainly fixed on the Farther East, other Seljuk generals were engaged in bringing Syria, which had long ignored Bagdad, into the Seljuk obedience. In 1076 Seljuk troops captured Jerusalem.

### Reasons for the First Crusade

**T**HE Holy Land had passed into the hands of successive Mahomedan factions, Egyptian or Syrian, many times since its first conquest by the second khalif, Omar. Those vicissitudes had occasioned no change in Christian sentiment. The Mahomedans with rare exceptions had respected the Christian feeling for the holy places and given protection to the pious pilgrims from the West who came to pay their devotions. But the Turks had no such reverence for the piety of the infidel. In the few years during which they lorded it in Palestine the pilgrims were subjected to perils and their faith to insults such as they had never experienced from the Arabs.

Malik Shah died in 1092 ; the Seljuk chiefs were immediately involved in a prolonged faction fight between claimants to the succession ; but before the Egyptian Fatimids seized their opportunity to recover possession of Jerusalem in 1098 the mischief was done. The astute emperor at Constantinople had been provided with that exciting appeal to religious sentiment which was just what he wanted to sting the West into activity. The astute pope—no aspersion on his sincerity is implied—standing forth as the champion of the Cross, would become by the mere fact the undisputed leader of Christendom in a fashion impossible for any lay potentate then living.

The result was the First Crusade, and from the first the rest followed. The tales of the pilgrims who had seen and suffered under the Turkish regime gave life to the idea that the Saracen was the enemy of the Cross, and that it was the duty of good Christians to redeem from his sway the soil made sacred by the footprints of the Redeemer ; and the tales of the pilgrims were very thoroughly exploited not only by sincere religious enthusiasts, but by all who hoped to turn religious enthusiasm to account for the furtherance of their own interests or their own ambitions.

But before proceeding with the story of the Crusade we must review the developments taking place in western Europe and at Constantinople between the battle of Manzikert and the congress at Clermont, where the Crusade was inaugurated.

**W**HEN Pope Alexander II died in 1073, the duke of Normandy was undisputed king of England. The last English revolt against the alien dynasty had been suppressed. Beside him stood the able statesman-archbishop Lanfranc, and those two saw always eye to eye. The Church in England was being brought under the new ecclesiastical discipline ; the king gave Lanfranc a very free hand and very large powers, knowing that he was far too wise to use them to the detriment of the crown's prerogative.

The Church was ruled mainly by Norman bishops and abbots, the country by Norman barons. But the barons were not the lords of provinces ; their estates were dispersed over widely separate districts, and their vassals were the king's vassals ; and they, with the great ecclesiastics, formed the Great Council of the realm which the king consulted when he thought fit. William could with perfect safety pass much more of his time in his Norman duchy than in his English kingdom. The duchy, when he died (1087), was to pass to his eldest son, Robert, the kingdom to the second son, William Rufus.

In France, William's overlord was the young king Philip ' the Gross,' dissolute, lethargic, crafty ; having little enough control over his feudatories, but an immense capacity for turning their feuds to the advantage of the crown. For practically he was only one—to whom the rest owed a very dubious allegiance— among several princes ruling their own principalities, each of whom was individually as powerful as he : hereditary dukes or counts of Normandy, Blois, Champagne, Toulouse, Brittany, Flanders, whose vassals would follow their banners against the king himself. And he had not that

**LANFRANC'S SIGNATURE APPENDED TO A STATE DOCUMENT OF THE CONQUEROR**
William's ablest partner was Lanfranc, whom he made archbishop of Canterbury ; he was as successful in bringing the Church under Norman discipline as William on the civil side. At the foot of a document granting the primacy of England to the see of Canterbury his signature appears, first in the left-hand column beneath the crosses of the king and queen ; compare his neat calligraphy with the more antiquated hand of Wulfstan, Saxon archbishop of Worcester, last in the same column.
*By permission of Dr. Samuel Bickersteth, Chapter Library, Canterbury*

piety, genuine or assumed, which alone might have condoned his immoralities in the eyes of the clergy and brought them into alliance with him ; for the French monasteries were the nurseries of the most zealous of the reforming churchmen. Philip's cunning might prepare the way for his successors to assert the power of the crown, but he was not the man to do it himself.

In Spain the Córdova khalifate had fallen early in the century. Moorish Spain was split into a number of emirates ; Christian Spain, united for a time under Sancho the Great of Navarre, fell asunder on his death in 1035 into the four separate kingdoms of Navarre, Castile, Leon and Aragon on the upper Ebro, and the county of Barcelona (the Spanish March) between the Pyrenees and the lower Ebro. Christians warred with Moors, emirs with emirs, kings with kings, Saracen and Spaniard in occasional temporary combinations, till in 1072 Leon and Castile were again united under Alfonso VI. To the ensuing period belong most of the exploits of that somewhat dubious 'national hero,' Ruy Diaz, the Cid Campeador ; who was quite ready to fight for the emir of Saragossa against the king of Aragon, or to tear Valencia from another emir and hold it himself. But Alfonso of Castile established himself at Madrid, and in the year 1085 captured Toledo.

Meanwhile, across the strait the Almoravids, a sect composed mainly of Berber desert tribesmen, were establishing their supremacy among the African Moors. To their chief, Yussuf, the alarmed emirs in Spain appealed for aid. Yussuf came, inflicted an overwhelming defeat on Alfonso of Castile at Zallaca in 1086, and

**A GERMAN KING**

An eleventh-century panel of walrus ivory shows us the garb of a German king at the moment when the Empire was entering on its long and bitter struggle with the Papacy.
*British Museum*

instead of returning to Africa established himself as emir of Andalusia. The disaster of Zallaca failed of its full effect, because the Moors fell to fighting among themselves ; while Yussuf was mastering the other emirs, the Cid captured Valencia (1096), and Alfonso renewed his advance. The Cid died in 1099, and soon afterwards Valencia was recaptured. Saragossa had not yet been taken, the Almoravids were supreme in the south and were threatening to overwhelm Alfonso, when Yussuf died in 1106 and Alfonso two years later. Yussuf's death had saved him.

In Germany the long minority of Henry IV had dissolved most of the work done by his father in strengthening the imperial authority. That authority the self-willed and hot-tempered Henry intended to recover. All his confidence was given to his own Swabian countrymen, to the intense disgust of the North Germans and more especially of the Saxons, who regarded themselves as entitled to the hegemony of the German 'nations,' though at the time they were without a duke. In 1073 Henry found himself involved in a contest with the rebellious Saxons, in which he came very near defeat before he succeeded in forcing them to submission in 1075.

Now, when Pope Alexander died in 1073 the Roman populace acclaimed Archdeacon Hildebrand his successor. That highly irregular election was confirmed by the College of Cardinals, and the emperor was duly invited to give the ratification which he formally granted. The courtesies had been observed, and his own attention was fixed not upon Italy but upon Saxony. That election, however, was pregnant with revolution. In the old days vigorous popes had defied the emperor at Constantinople on questions of orthodoxy and ecclesiastical discipline ; but since the time of Charlemagne and down to the death of Henry III in 1056 every pope of distinction had been indebted for much of his power to the active support of a sympathetic emperor, who would nevertheless have made very short work of any attempt to control him in the exercise of any functions which he regarded as within his own sphere. If Nicholas II and Alexander II had set their claims higher, it was at a time when the emperor was a child.

But now Gregory VII was about to assert the unprecedented claim that the temporal authority was subordinate to the spiritual, the emperor to the pope. His courage was infinite, his sincerity beyond all possible dispute. He was too single-hearted, too uncompromising, to be a diplomatist ; he was as sure of his own mission as an Elijah or a Samuel ; and he

identified that mission, the regeneration of the Church and of the world, with the supreme office to which he had now himself been called. No impulse towards regeneration could be looked for from the princes whom he saw around him.

For five-and-twenty years pope after pope, generally with Hildebrand beside him, had striven to reform the besetting sins of the churchmen—self-seeking, worldliness, laxity. Early in 1075 Gregory at a synod in Rome issued, as they had issued, decrees against simony and clerical marriages, formally forbidden but habitually practised ; but to these was added a decree uncompromisingly forbidding lay investiture and denouncing penalties on all who should accept or convey such investiture. Protest against the practice, as an encroachment on the spiritual functions, was no new thing, but had been ignored by the princes. Bishops and abbots were holders of great territorial lordships ; no prince could afford to let their appointment pass out of his own control, and the appointment carried with it, as a matter of course, investiture with the symbols of authority, spiritual as well as temporal. But Gregory's denunciation was not a mere protest ; it was a declaration of war.

**HENRY IV ABASED AT CANOSSA**

In 1076 the Papacy for a brief moment triumphed over the Empire, when Henry IV abased himself before Gregory VII at Canossa. Canossa was in the domains of the countess Matilda, one of the pope's most ardent supporters, and this MS. shows the emperor kneeling before her.

*Vatican Library, MS. Lat. 4922 ; photo Giraudon*

Henry IV, fresh from the victory which brought the Saxons to submission, took up the challenge. There was no lack of simoniacal prelates to support this view in Germany, and of his own authority he invested a new archbishop of Milan. In January, 1076, supported by a synod of German bishops at Worms, he answered Gregory's denunciations by declaring that he was no longer pope, and ordered him to 'Come down.' Gregory responded with a synod at the Vatican in February, and a decree excommunicating and deposing Henry and releasing his subjects from obedience to him. The battle was joined.

But for Henry it was not merely a battle between Church and State. It was a fight for his own authority over his own lay vassals, who were fiercely suspicious of his aims and bent on yielding him no obedience which it was in their power to refuse. At a diet of the Empire in October the nobles and prelates not only refused him their support but required him to make submission and seek absolution from the pope before they would return to their obedience. The immediate result was the bitter humiliation of Canossa.

## Papal Triumph at Canossa

In the depth of winter Henry slipped away with his wife and child from Speier, where he was almost a prisoner, through Burgundy to Lombardy, where the nobles, unlike the Germans, were ready to give him vigorous support. But he had persuaded himself that submission would restore the lost loyalty of the Germans, and he dared not face the issue of war. Gregory was at the mountain stronghold of Canossa, in the northern Apennines, expecting an attack by the Lombards, and surrounded by an august company of eminent churchmen. Thither the despairing emperor betook himself almost unattended, to throw himself on the mercy of his great antagonist. For four days he remained outside the gates in the snow, a suppliant clad in the scanty garb of the penitent. Gregory would give pardon only on terms of complete and abject submission. Even so, Henry was to be restored to his imperial dignity only after the pope had inquired into and passed judgement on the charges levelled against him by his German subjects ; and if he were then restored he must obey the pope in all ecclesiastical matters.

The Lombards were disgusted by his craven submission ; the Germans were so far from being conciliated that their diet, to which Gregory sent his legates instead of attending and presiding himself, repeated the charges, and without giving any opportunity of defence proceeded to elect a new emperor, Rudolf duke of Swabia.

They had gone too far. Henry hastened back to Germany, to find there a vigorous reaction in his favour. It was one thing

to overturn him ; it was quite another to set up Rudolf. In the civil war which raged for two years, Rudolf's only whole-hearted supporters were the Saxons. Gregory declined to intervene actively. However, seeing that Henry reverted to the practice of lay investitures, Gregory in 1080, when Henry had met with a severe defeat, again declared him excommunicate and deposed, and recognized Rudolf, in terms asserting the power of the Church to bind and to loose, to raise up and to cast down kings and emperors.

Once more Gregory's confidence of victory had carried him too far, bringing Henry a host of new supporters. An assembly of German and Lombard bishops and nobles proclaimed the deposition of Gregory, and elected an anti-pope, who took the name of Clement III. Rudolf was killed in a great battle near Lützen before the year was over, and without haste or enthusiasm his partisans elected Hermann of Luxemburg as rival emperor to Henry. Manifestly now the serious enemy was the pope.

## Reaction in Favour of the Emperor

Into Italy, therefore, Henry carried the war. Rome with Gregory at the Vatican defied attack, though no external help was forthcoming even from the Normans, since Guiscard was more congenially occupied in invading Illyria. In 1081 and again the next year Henry failed to effect an entry. In 1083 he forced his way into the city. Gregory in the castle of S. Angelo still defied him, still demanded the unqualified submission of the enemy at his gate. Next year the emperor, after an expedition to Apulia, where the Normans were moving, returned with Clement to Rome, where the latter was enthroned as pope and crowned him emperor.

But the castle still held out ; Robert Guiscard, at last fully alive to the danger to himself if Henry won a complete triumph, recrossed the Adriatic and marched on Rome at the head of a very miscellaneous force. Henry retreated ; Robert forced his way into Rome, sacked it, working much havoc, and withdrew to the south. Gregory followed him from the desolated city, to which Clement

**NICEPHORUS III THE USURPER**

Nicephorus III Botaniates usurped the throne of the Eastern
Empire from Michael Ducas in 1078. His efforts to expel the
Turks from Asia Minor, with the help of his general Alexius
Comnenus, were ineffectual ; and in private he had a reputa-
tion for debauchery. He is here seen with his empress Maria.

*MS. of Homilies of S. John Chrysostom, Bibliothèque Nationale, Paris*

subjects and stirring up his
eldest son, Conrad, against
him ; remaining for the most
part in the south, where he
was secure of the good will—
on terms, at least—of the
Norman duke of Apulia,
Roger, younger son of Robert
Guiscard who had died a
month after Gregory, and
nephew of the other Roger,
now fully established as count
of Sicily.

North Italy remained a
cockpit in which Henry alternately won and lost the
mastery and Conrad disputed
with him the crown of Lombardy, while Clement's partisans dominated Rome from
the castle of S. Angelo and
the antipope himself remained
in the security of Ravenna.
It was not till 1094–5 that
Henry was so hard pressed
that Urban could set forth
on that northern progress
which culminated in the Congress of Clermont, the real
climax of Urban's career. Not
from Italy but from another
quarter had come the great
opportunity which he seized.

returned, though he, too, retired ere long
to Ravenna. The great pope, indomitable
to the last, died soon after (May, 1085) ;
defeated, as it seemed to the world.
He knew that he had actually accomplished nothing, but that was not the thing
that mattered : ' I have loved righteousness and hated iniquity, therefore I die
in exile—and therefore my hope is great.'

For three years there was a chaos of
faction fighting in Rome. The cardinals
elected a new pope, Victor III, who hid
himself in a monastery, where his life
flickered out after a year. And then
in March, 1088, the cardinals found the
man who was to carry Gregory's work
forward, the Frenchman Urban II.

It was not, however, in direct conflict
with Henry that Urban won his triumph.
The pope preferred to content himself
with fostering rebellion among Henry's

SINCE Manzikert the Greek Empire had
been in very low water. After the
death of Romanus, the feeble young emperor Michael Ducas was compelled to concede to the Turkish general Sulayman the
' governorship ' of all those provinces of
which he was in actual possession—in other
words, all but an insignificant portion of
Asia Minor ; which Sulayman, with the
assent of Malik Shah, very soon converted into the practically independent
sultanate of Roum. A few years later
Michael was deposed, but the usurper
Nicephorus III proved almost as incompetent and in other respects far worse
than Michael. Government went from
bad to worse, till in 1081 the able general
Alexius Comnenus removed Nicephorus
and assumed the diadem, which remained
in his family for a century.

Alexius was a skilful soldier, a capable administrator and an astute diplomatist, who had to make the best of bad materials. The best troops in his service were the Varangian guard, mostly composed of Swedes, Russians and miscellaneous Viking adventurers, and recently recruited from Englishmen who preferred the wages of the emperor to subjection to the Norman. The old Isaurian recruiting ground had passed under the sway of the Turk. The population over which he ruled was inert. Nicaea, the capital of Roum, was ominously near to the Bosporus. And the moment of his accession was also the moment chosen by the ambitious and restless duke of Apulia for his attack on Dyrrhachium (Durazzo), which he captured after a victory won by and against precisely the same tactics as Duke William's victory at Hastings, the Varangians playing the heroic but futile part of Harold's household troops. To the Norman, a zealous papalist, the heretic empire was a tempting and legitimate prey.

Robert and his elder son, Bohemund, were soon in Macedonia, where the latter remained when his father hurried back to Italy to the rescue of Gregory in 1084. But Alexius saved himself from disaster by a crafty and competent strategy ; Bohemund, too, returned to Italy on his father's death to secure himself in the possession at least of his county of Otranto ; and for the time Alexius was relieved from the Norman peril.

### Alexius appeals for Help to Urban

THERE was work enough for him in the recovery of effective control in his own dominions, but his ambition was to recover it also in the lost provinces of the Empire, which there was no hope of doing without aid from the West, and he set himself to procure that aid. He had already found Gregory not averse from the idea of a Holy War but dangerously disposed to make ecclesiastical submission to Rome a necessary condition. At first he had been inspired rather by fear of the Seljuks than by ambition, but his hopes rose with the disintegration of the Seljuk power on the death of Malik Shah in 1092. Still relying on the emotional

aspects of Turkish misrule in the Holy Land, he renewed his appeal to Pope Urban in 1095.

Urban had gathered at Piacenza a great assembly of which the first business was to denounce the sins of Henry and once more to proclaim the disciplinary decrees against simony and marriage of clerics. There was an emotional atmosphere in which the words of Alexius' envoys took deep effect ; but Urban did not yet give himself rein. He moved north to Burgundy, and meanwhile the seeds were being sown.

### Urban launches the First Crusade

URBAN was in the heart of the country which was the cradle of the Cluniac ideals. There in November a vast concourse was gathered at Clermont. For once we may with absolute rightness use a much-abused phrase and say that Urban had found, had indeed almost created, the psychological moment. To that concourse he issued his passionate appeal to Christian men to lay aside their private quarrels and discords and unite for the redemption of the Holy Sepulchre from the hands of the infidels ; the multitude was swept away on the torrent of irresistible emotion, and answered with one universal cry, ' It is the will of God.' Urban had launched the First Crusade.

Essentially the appeal was not to political interests but to religious emotion ; necessarily it sought and found its response not from governments and rulers as such, but from voluntary individual action. Leadership in such a movement was entirely impossible for the excommunicate emperor Henry, who was popularly regarded as a monster of iniquity, the excommunicate king of France, or the tyrant William Rufus who was ruling in England. No monarch as yet took part in organizing the movement whose impulse proceeded quite definitely from the pope, was most zealously fostered by the clergy, and permeated all social ranks.

Crusaders were, no doubt, stirred in many cases by various motives other than religious enthusiasm. For the ambitious new principalities might be attainable, for everyone there was at least the chance of winning the military

**CHURCH OF THE HOLY SEPULCHRE**
As long as the Mahomedans allowed access to the holy places
in Palestine, such as the Church of the Holy Sepulchre at
Jerusalem, there was no incentive to a crusade. This they did
until the rise of the Turks, whose repressive measures gave
Alexius the argument he needed to move Pope Urban II.

necessary funds—dull of wit
but a mighty man of his hands;
Raymond of Toulouse ; Godfrey, duke of Lower Lorraine
and Bouillon, commonly but
erroneously known as count
of Boulogne ; Bohemund of
Otranto and others, men of
mark and practised in war.
While they were making
efficient preparation, the ill
directed zeal of Peter the
Hermit and a knight known
as Walter the Penniless led a
rabble of enthusiasts on a wild
expedition which got itself
across the Bosporus and was
dissipated, cut to pieces or
carried into slavery by Kilij
Arslan, the sultan of Roum.

A year after the Congress
of Clermont the real crusading
host was swarming to its
appointed meeting-place, Constantinople. Alexius had overreached himself. Hoping to
raise in the West a force of
warriors whose services would
enable him to recover Asia
Minor, he had called in a
mighty host which cared not
at all for his empire and
seemed not unlikely to begin
its operations by dismembering what was left of it. But
his diplomatic skill was equal
to the occasion. In the spring
of 1097 he had passed them

renown which medieval knighthood
coveted above all other prizes. If religious
ardour were itself lacking, it was still worth
while to get the credit for displaying it.
In the last account with Heaven, to have
fallen in battle with the infidel would outweigh a multitude of sins. Merely as an
adventure, crusading offered no small
attraction. But in a great number of
instances the primary motive at least was
a genuine religious zeal.

The small men joined the standards of
the great nobles who took the Cross :
Robert of Normandy, who trustfully
mortgaged his dukedom to his royal
brother of England in order to raise the

all safely over the Bosporus, with no
intention of facilitating their return, their
leaders pledged to fealty while within the
theoretical borders of the Empire, of
which the provinces, when reconquered,
were to be restored to him.

The crusaders laid siege to Nicaea,
which surrendered in June. A great victory
at Dorylaeum drove Kilij Arslan east in a
skilful retreat in which he cleared the
country of provisions before the invaders.
But he could not stem their advance.
Asia Minor was won. The crusaders made
their way through the Taurus. Baldwin,
the brother of Godfrey, hastened to the aid
of Edessa, in upper Mesopotamia, which

was held by Christian Armenians, and established himself there as its prince. In October the main army laid siege to Antioch, which stubbornly defied their attack till the following June. Even then it was only treachery within the walls that gave Bohemund the entry, which was turned to account by a savage massacre.

### Fall of Jerusalem to the Crusaders

**D**ISSENSIONS were already raging among the Christians. They were also raging among the Saracens. Some months earlier the Egyptian Fatimids had set about the recovery of Palestine from the Turks, and had offered alliance, with promises to restore the old tolerant regime which had so long sufficed to satisfy Western sentiment in the past. A month after the fall of Antioch the Fatimids captured Jerusalem. But the Holy City itself was the crusaders' goal; it was to be delivered from the infidel, tolerant or intolerant, Fatimid or Turk.

It was not till the next spring, however, that the main army advanced on Jerusalem, leaving Bohemund in possession at Antioch (1099). In July, in a grand assault, Jerusalem was taken by storm, the capture being accompanied by a terrible massacre. Once more the banner of the Cross floated over the Holy City.

In effect what had been accomplished was the recovery of a large part of Asia Minor, but by no means the whole of it, for the Greek Empire; and of Syria from the Taurus to Jaffa, with a section of north Mesopotamia, by and for a group of adventurers under no single chief, whose leaders were great feudal nobles at home, but owed allegiance to no man in respect of the lands they had conquered. The adventurers, that is, were in military occupation of a wide area in which they could never be anything more than a garrison, since there was no prospect of attracting to it a great body of permanent European colonists, and their

conquest could be retained only by force of arms against attacks which would become exceedingly formidable if those enemies whose mutual antagonisms had made the conquest possible should unite.

For the garrisons the adventurers themselves could provide only a nucleus; for the rest they must rely on the irregular stream of temporary volunteers from the West. Such a stream was more or less insured by the exceptional character of the motive that had inspired the conquest; the adventurers won it and held it, so to speak, in trust for Christendom. At intervals, and for special reasons, the normal stream swelled to abnormal dimensions; the expedition which was on the largest scale is by general consent entitled the Third Crusade, but no principle can be laid down for the numbering of those which came after it.

Such then was the basis on which the conquerors had to organize their conquest when completed. Orthodox feudal theory required an official monarch for the kingdom of Jerusalem, to whom the rest would owe allegiance much as Robert or Raymond owed allegiance to their royal suzerain Philip. Godfrey was the first king, though he refused the royal title, since he would not wear the golden circle where the Saviour had worn the crown of thorns. He would only call himself

**ARMOUR SUCH AS THE CRUSADERS WORE**
The equipment of twelfth-century warriors, such as those who streamed to and fro between Europe and Palestine after the capture of Jerusalem in 1099 and the formation of the Latin Kingdom of Jerusalem, is well shown in this illustration of a siege, where the attackers are setting fire to the houses.
*MS. of Herrade de Landsberg; photo, Hachette*

count. Bohemund remained prince of Antioch, Baldwin count of Edessa; the conquest of Tripolis between Antioch and Palestine provided another county for Raymond; each county had its baronies. When Godfrey died in 1100, Baldwin succeeded him and was the first titular king of Jerusalem.

The 'Latin Kingdom' thus covered the whole of what had been known in ancient days as Palestine and Phoenicia, with Antioch, extending north across the Euphrates to Edessa. The kingdom had not grown up, but was deliberately modelled on the theory and practice of feudalism as understood in western Europe and consequently provided the most typical example of the feudal policy or constitution, as regards both its organization and its methods.

**FIRST OF THE PLANTAGENETS**
Geoffrey of Anjou, known as Plantagenet from his habit of wearing broom (planta genista) in his cap, was father of Henry II of England (1133–89).
*Le Mans Museum*

The whole Latin Kingdom, though its length from Edessa to Jaffa and Askelon was great, was none the less but a narrow strip from which no substantial eastward advance was made. Its Mediterranean ports were acquired only by degrees, and by the aid of the maritime cities of Italy which sought and found a rich commerical harvest by establishing their communities therein. Venice and Genoa in particular had their special quarters from which intercourse with the merchants of the East radiated, and on which it converged.

The organization of the kingdom was mainly the work of Baldwin I (1100–1118), who left his cousin, afterwards Baldwin II, at Edessa. Elected to the succession on the death of Baldwin I, the second Baldwin (1118–1130) carried on the work of his predecessor. Both were men of ability, but neither was able materially

to enlarge the kingdom, though the capture of Sidon fell in the reign of the first, and of Tyre in that of the second. Baldwin II was succeeded by his son-in-law Fulk of Anjou (1131–1143), whose eldest son, Geoffrey, was the father of Henry II of England. Fulk's reign was vigorous and successful; but when he died and his French county went to Geoffrey, the crown of Jerusalem passed to his very youthful half-brother, Baldwin III; and then disaster began.

We saw that on the death of Malik Shah the Seljuk power disintegrated. The great sultan's attention was concentrated on Persia and the East; the enemies against whom the crusading hosts had to fight their way were the minor sultans of Roum and Mosul, and the Egyptian Fatimids in Palestine itself. Now, in 1127 the Turk Zangi became lord or atabeg of Mosul. In the next few years Zangi's sway was extended over Mahomedan Syria and Mesopotamia. In 1142 he turned his arms against Edessa, where he was vigorously checked by Joscelyn of Courtenay on whom Baldwin II, when he became king, had bestowed the county. But Joscelyn and Fulk died almost at the same moment; the second Joscelyn was a poor creature; the kingdom of Jerusalem was out of action; and in 1144 Zangi captured the great northern fortress. The massacre at Jerusalem was requited in kind—and in full measure. Two years later Zangi died and was succeeded by the very able Nour ed-Din. The fall of Edessa was the first great shock to the Latin Kingdom.

Meanwhile in the West the struggle between Papacy and Empire, temporal and spiritual authority, Church and State, had passed through its first phase. Urban died a fortnight after the fall of Jerusalem, the triumphant climax of the crusade which he had launched, himself unquestionably the supreme figure in Christendom. His successor, Paschal II (1099–1118), was resolute to maintain the ascendancy that Urban had won. He would make no concessions to the unfortunate Henry, who was now eager for reconciliation on almost any terms ; his son Conrad was in arms against him, and it was quite impossible for him to bring either Germany or Italy under control so long as he lay under the papal anathema, which provided an unfailing excuse or pretext for rebellion.

### Relations of Henry V with Pope Paschal

**H**ENRY disinherited Conrad in favour of the younger son Henry, who was crowned as Henry V on condition that he would exercise no regal rights during his father's life. This indeed was of little moment while Conrad was still in arms. Conrad, however, died in 1101 ; but Paschal remained deaf to Henry's overtures, and in 1104 the younger Henry, who never allowed scruples of honour or generosity to stand in the way of what he took to be his interests, broke faith and called the ever rebellious Saxony to arms against his father. The emperor lost hope and spirit and threw himself on the mercy of the young king, who was not ashamed to entreat his forgiveness and then shut him up and compel him to abdicate. Henry IV escaped, but died in 1106, denied the papal absolution to the last.

But if Henry V (1106–1125) had turned the dispute with the pope to his own account in the quarrel with Henry IV it was with no intention of surrendering any imperial claims. For some time he was occupied with Hungarian and Bohemian wars, but in 1110 he was free to take that matter in hand, and descended on Italy with an army behind him. Paschal discovered that there was no quarter from which he could count upon armed support, and, in effect, surrendered. The Church would yield her temporal estates but not her exclusive right of ecclesiastical appointment and investiture.

The offer to sacrifice temporalities for spiritual freedom would have been magnificent if it had not been dictated by fear ; but it was correctly interpreted as an act of sheer pusillanimity. It was accepted as a matter of course by Henry, to whom it gave far more than he could ever have attempted to demand ; but when he presented himself for coronation as emperor at S. Peter's the ceremony was stopped by a scene of furious tumult. Henry retired with the pope a prisoner in his hands ; Paschal gave way altogether, conceding even the investitures ; the mob was not given a second chance, and the coronation was carried through (1111).

Paschal might give way, but he could not take the churchmen with him ; they unanimously repudiated the compact, and would have repudiated his authority altogether had he not, as soon as the emperor's back was turned, discovered that the pledge was invalid as having been extorted under duress. Moreover, all the forces that had operated against Henry IV in the same quarrel were now brought to bear against Henry V, while the clergy were solid instead of being divided. The Empire was in a ferment of plots and revolts. In 1118 Paschal died ; a new pope was elected ; Henry set up an antipope of his own ; the new pope died, and the cardinals elected a Burgundian prelate experienced in statecraft, Calixtus II (1119).

### Solutions of the Investiture Question

**I**N England a practical solution of the investiture problem had been reached some years before by the wisdom of the saintly archbishop Anselm and the shrewdness of the particularly hardheaded king, the Conqueror's youngest son, Henry I. The crown could propose a candidate for ecclesiastical office and veto an unsuitable candidate, but otherwise the election was to be free ; on the other hand, the elected candidate must do homage for his temporalities like any lay baron, but must not be invested with the spiritual office and its symbols by a layman. The Church could not force a candidate on the crown nor the crown on the Church, and neither the spiritual nor the temporal power encroached on the functions of the other.

Calixtus, like Anselm, wanted not war but peace ; he resolved to seek a compromise on the obviously reasonable lines ; and that end he achieved, not without the many difficulties which attend any policy of compromise between hot antagonists, by the Concordat of Worms (1122), virtually a repetition of the English settlement. Within three years both pope and emperor were dead ; at Worms the investiture conflict was buried. But it had been only one phase of a wider one, which was by no means ended.

## Struggle for Reform within the Church

THE conflict between the spiritual and temporal power was, in fact, the political aspect of what was in its initiation a religious movement as zealously supported by the greatest princes from Otto the Great to Henry III as by the great churchmen. The reform of the Church itself, the development of its influence in Christianising a world professedly Christian but very far from Christian in its normal activities, was the aim of the Cluniac reformers and of the popes from Leo IX to Alexander II. That motive was no less strong in Hildebrand, but with him it led to the conclusion that the kingdom of God would never be established on earth by laymen dominating the Church but only by the Church dominating the laymen.

To dominate the laymen the actual possesion of the temporal power was necessary, and hence developed the conflict between Church and State. At the same time the striving for temporal power was itself a de-spiritualising influence upon those who took a leading part in the conflict. But the pure religious enthusiasm was constantly finding expression in movements of the same type as that of Cluny, the founding and development of religious orders bound to an ideal rule of life. If Cluny itself had somewhat fallen away, its place as a spiritual power was more than taken by the recently founded Cistercian order and, above all, by the monastery of Clairvaux and its great abbot Bernard.

To the same impulse was due the foundation of those military orders of knights bound by the monastic vows of celibacy, poverty and obedience, the Knights Templars and Knights Hospitallers or Knights of S. John, who played so large a part in the eastern wars ; and of the Austin Canons or Canons Regular,ordained to combine the functions of the monk, who was bound to a rule ('regula'), with the ministry of the secular diocesan or parish clergy, who were under no special rule.

### The Papacy and Roger of Sicily

CALIXTUS, a pope whose all too brief reign had shown how much could yet be done by a man who was both strong and wise, was followed by Honorius II, whose legal acumen had been invaluable in the work of shaping the Concordat of Worms but did not suffice to make him a competent leader. His main difficulties were with the third of the Rogers, Roger II of Sicily, who had actually succeeded his father, Roger I, when a baby, in 1101. Roger of Apulia, the son of Guiscard, died in 1111 ; his line was extinguished a few years later, and Roger of Sicily resolved to unite his own county with Apulia.

Both Apulia and Sicily had originally been granted to Robert Guiscard as fiefs held from the pope by Nicholas II. Roger effected his object (1127), and with very small regard for his suzerain proceeded to absorb the remaining minor principalities of South Italy. Honorius strove vainly to form a league against him, but was compelled to recognize Roger's claims.

On the death of Honorius in 1130 his successor, regularly elected, was Anacletus, a candidate so offensive to the advanced party that they elected Innocent II in opposition. Innocent won the support of Bernard of Clairvaux, which was of even more importance than that of the emperor, which was also given to him ; but the contest between pope and antipope continued for eight years, during which Anacletus bought Roger's support by the title of 'king' of Sicily, which Innocent— the ultimate victor in the strife—was finally forced to recognize.

The death of Henry V without a direct heir in 1125 may be regarded as the beginning of another rivalry, between two great German houses, which was fraught with future strife. The Bavarian house of Welf had been commonly at odds with a succession of emperors and had habitually sided with the Papacy. The dukedom of Swabia had passed to Frederick, of Hohenstaufen and Weiblingen, whose wife was the sister and his sons the nephews of Henry V. Those sons, Frederick and Conrad, were now respectively dukes of Swabia and Franconia. Henry had destined one or other of his nephews to be his successor, but the combination of Bavaria with Saxony gave the imperial crown to the old and able duke of Saxony, Lothair II (1125–37).

### Origin of Guelphs and Ghibellines

THE matrimonial complications are not without interest. Henry the Black of Bavaria, who died next year, was the father-in-law of Frederick, but his son, Henry the Proud, became the son-in-law of Lothair. Ultimately the son of that marriage, the Welf Henry the Lion, became duke of both Bavaria and Saxony, when his cousin, the offspring of the other marriage, Frederick of Hohenstaufen or Weiblingen, was seated on the imperial throne as Frederick I. From the names Welf and Weiblingen derive the Guelph and Ghibelline, which later became the party labels of Italian factions, originating as Welf papalists and Hohenstaufen or Weiblingen imperialists.

Lothair's seizure of some of Frederick's lands brought on a civil war, in which Conrad of Franconia was set up as a rival German king ; but in 1135 the Hohenstaufen gave way and general peace was established, the old emperor—who was then past seventy—being too politic to be vindictive. Lothair did, in fact, devote himself mainly to the cause of peace, greatly to the benefit of the Empire, especially by his missionary zeal on the still pagan and barbarian north-eastern marches. Instigated by Bernard of Clairvaux, he went to Italy to support Innocent II against Anacletus and his ally Roger, and to be officially crowned emperor by the pope ; but the final effect of his interposition was a serious quarrel, which only

his own death (1137) prevented from developing into open hostilities.

Henry the Proud, duke of Bavaria and of Saxony in right of his wife, and lord of great possessions in Tuscany, aspired to the succession ; but his power as a prince was, in the eyes of other German princes, a very good reason for not making him emperor. A diet attended by neither Saxons nor Bavarians elected Conrad of Franconia, the first Hohenstaufen emperor. As was to be expected, the immediate result was civil war, which was not ended by Henry's death in 1139, his duchies having been officially forfeited while refusing to acknowledge their new dukes. A peace, however, was presently patched up by the reinstatement of the boy Henry (the Lion) in the Saxon duchy and of his mother and stepfather, the count of the Palatinate (for she promptly married again), in Bavaria. The peace had not long been established when the West was startled by the ominous news of the fall of Edessa, the outer bulwark of Christendom in Asia.

### England and Scotland in Norman Times

ENGLAND during the first half of the twelfth century was passing through the best and also the worst periods of the Norman rule. William I had reigned in the capacity of a conqueror who had to establish his domination over the conquered English and also over the new baronage, Norman, French, Breton or Fleming, with whom he had to share the spoil. William II, a soldier hardly inferior to his father, reigned as a tyrant by the might of his arm. Henry I (1100–1135) won the name of the Lion of Justice not because he cared in the least for justice in the abstract, but because he saw the way to power in enforcing stern justice whenever it did not collide with his own interest, and it paid him better to rule a well ordered than an orderless state.

But when Henry died, leaving a daughter, who was married to Geoffrey of Anjou (her first husband had been the emperor Henry V), but no son, his nephew Stephen of Blois captured the crown, and there followed a period of appalling misrule or no-rule while his

**DAVID I OF SCOTLAND**

The charter of Malcolm IV of Scotland to Kelso Abbey shows him (right) and his father, David I, its founder. David's sister had married Henry I of England, thus perpetuating the Saxon royal line; while he married Henry's sister.

adherents and those of his cousin the 'Empress Maud' fought each other up and down the country, robbing and pillaging; so that men cried out that 'Christ and his saints slept,' and the only power which sought to uphold some standard of justice and decency was the Church.

The period, on the other hand, was one of very marked progress in the northern kingdom of Scotland. Malcolm III, after ridding himself of Macbeth, had established himself on the throne with no rival. He kept or broke the peace with the Normans as occasion suggested, and found it advisable to pay some sort of homage to both the Williams; but whether it was for his crown or only for estates held by him in the north of England is a question quite impossible of certain solution. Assuredly, however, no Scots king after him, except his son Edgar, ever admitted an English king's title to overlordship.

More than any of his predecessors, however, he did deliberately Anglicise the Lowlands under the influence of his wife Margaret, a princess of the old English royal family ; from which two results followed : the Latin Church finally predominated over the Celtic Church in Scotland as well as in England, and, through the marriage of his daughter to Henry I of England, the blood of the house of Alfred has flowed in the veins of every king or queen regnant thereafter in England or Scotland until this day.

Malcolm was killed on an English foray in 1093, when his brother Donalbane usurped the throne, to be ejected later by Malcolm's sons, three of whom reigned in succession. The third, David I (1124–1153), played an active part in England as a feudatory in respect of English earldoms, and on behalf of his niece the Empress Maud. His reign confirmed what might be called a perpetual alliance between the crown and the Church in Scotland as against the feudal nobility, but it also gave the nobility its special brand of feudalism by the bestowal of many fiefs upon Normans who were also feudatories of the king of England.

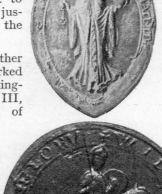

**SEALS OF RUFUS AND MAUD**

Lower : seal of William II 'Rufus' (1087-1100). Top: that of Maud or Matilda, the 'Empress' (she had first married the emperor Henry V), whose struggles with Stephen (1125-35) rent the kingdom.

*British Museum*

In France the power of the monarchy grew under the successors of Philip I. They followed a policy of patient and cautious persistence that bore steady fruit. Louis VI 'the Fat' (1108–1137) allied the crown with the Church by being always ready to pose or act as the champion of the oppressed, especially of oppressed clerics, against tyrannical barons ; he chose men as his counsellors not because they were powerful but because they were useful, herein following the example of his shrewd and troublesome vassal

Henry I of Normandy and England ; he skilfully fostered the feuds of the vassals themselves, and not infrequently reaped material profit thereby ; and when he died his son Louis VII (1137–1180) continued the same policy of alliance with the Church and the undermining of the power of the nobles.

But one most promising step which Louis VII took proved in the end to be most disastrous. While he was crown prince, he married Eleanor, the youthful heiress of Aquitaine, who brought with her wider territories than were under the sway of any other French feudatory ; but within a short time they quarrelled so seriously that the marriage was dissolved, on the ground of consanguinity, and the insulted Eleanor was promptly united to Henry count of Anjou, duke of Normandy and heir to the throne of England ; who thereby became duke of Aquitaine also, and lord of more than another quarter of France.

**STANDARD OF BATTLE**

In 1138 the Scots were defeated near Northallerton by the English border militia at the Battle of the Standard, so called from the crucifix that led them to victory.

*Corpus Christi College, Cambridge*

Palestine considered that campaigning in Spain en route was a partial fulfilment at least of their crusading vows. Saracens were the enemies of the Cross, whether in Spain or in Syria.

We saw (page 388) that Alfonso VI of Castile made a great advance, which was checked by the appearance of the Almoravid Yussuf, who was threatening to reverse the position when he died in 1106. For the next few years internal dissensions among Christians on one side and Saracens on the other prevented any material advance of either. But in 1118 Alfonso I of Aragon captured Saragossa, which had hitherto defied the efforts of the Spanish princes, thereafter dealt repeated blows to the Moors in Valencia, and before his death in 1134 raised Aragon

**W**HILE the Latin Kingdom was holding its own in Syria, the Christian states were again advancing in Spain, where the conflict was taking increasingly the character of a war of religion. Such would, in any case, have been the inevitable effect of the crusades in the East, which had stirred the spirit of fanaticism in Christians and Moslems alike, as it had not been stirred in the earlier conflicts. But to this was added the fact that the Berber Almoravids were very much more intolerant than the long-established Moors of Spain, and their harsh treatment of their 'Mozarabic' (i.e. Christian) subjects affected popular sentiment much as had the violence of the Turks in Palestine. The Spaniards were looked upon and regarded themselves as crusaders, and other crusaders bound for

**JOHN II COMNENUS AND HIS SON**

John II succeeded Alexius Comnenus at Constantinople in 1118 and proved as able a ruler as his astutely diplomatic father. This illumination from a manuscript dated 1128 shows him and his son Alexis crowned by Christ.

*From G. Millet, Hautes Etudes, Sorbonne*

to a foremost place among the kingdoms, which it had not hitherto achieved.

His work in the east of the peninsula was carried on by Raymond Berengar, count of Barcelona, who later united Aragon with Catalonia by marrying Alfonso's daughter Petronilla. On the western side Alfonso count of Portugal converted his little county into the kingdom of Portugal, between 1139 and 1148, by conquering the country as far as Lisbon ; and in 1149 Sancho IX of Castile signalised the capture of Calatrava by setting up there a Cistercian monastery. This great advance was facilitated by the rise in Morocco of a new and still more fanatical Berber sect which, having there won the mastery, invaded Spain in 1145. The four years during which the Almohades were overturning the Almoravids were the opportunity of the Spaniards.

### Events in the Eastern Empire

MEANWHILE there had been no co-operation between the Eastern Empire and the Latin crusaders. From their first appearance at Constantinople, Alexius had realized that he had very little to hope and much to fear from them ; he had done far more to thwart than to help them ; and after his death in 1118 his successor John had seen no reason to change an attitude which was fully recipro-cated by the Latins, or ' Franks,' as the East called them and calls the Euro-peans to this day. Even in Palestine itself the Franks distinguished between their ' Catholic ' and their ' Orthodox ' subjects, taxing the latter but not the former.

John (1118–1143) was an able and just ruler who gave to the Empire peace at home and was usually successful in such wars as he found it necessary to wage abroad, but he sought no reconciliation with the Franks. There was at least one respect in which the Empire had suffered from the establishment of the Latin Kingdom : the Levantine ports had robbed Constantinople of its trade, which had passed into the hands of the Genoese and Venetians ; and the loss had not been made good by the trading concessions in Con-stantinople itself granted by Alexius to the great maritime republic on the Adriatic.

### Fate of the Second Crusade

THE fall of Edessa startled the West and raised to white heat the crusading ardour of Bernard of Clairvaux, whose appeals for a new crusade rang through Christendom. Several expeditions on a considerable scale had set forth since the First Crusade, but all such had collapsed with varying degrees of ignominy. A mighty effort was now called for. Louis VII of France, already bent on taking the Cross to expiate a catastrophe for which he felt that he had been responsible, answered the appeal. With less en-thusiasm the emperor Conrad III was persuaded to follow Louis' example.

Yet the fate of that so-called Second Crusade was the fate of its predecessors. It was headed by two of the three most powerful monarchs of the West (for Roger of Sicily had in hand the separate business of conquering Saracens in Africa). It met with nothing but disaster. Conrad was first in the field. With a pretence of aid from his brother-emperor Manuel (1143–1180), John's successor at Constantinople, he passed into Asia Minor in 1146 with a mighty host ; Louis followed next year, but was joined at Nicaea by Conrad with only the remnant of his army, which had been cut to pieces. The crusaders tried a new route to the south coast ; of those who reached it only a few were able to embark for Syria ; the rest perished miserably. The small band remaining flung itself on Damascus, and would seem to have been on the point of taking it, when the leaders were tricked by treasonable counsels into changing their plan of attack, whereby failure became inevitable ; and first Conrad and then Louis went home with the followers that were left to them (1149).

In 1152 Conrad died ; and the choice of the imperial electors fell upon his nephew Frederick Barbarossa.

# TABLE OF DATES FOR CHAPTER 19

**1152** Frederick I Barbarossa elected German and Italian king.

**1153** English anarchy ended by treaty of Wallingford. Death of Bernard of Clairvaux. Henry the Lion of Saxony restored in Bavaria. Sanjar, last Seljuk sultan, defeated by the Ghuzz.

**1154** Frederick in North Italy. Accession of Henry II Plantagenet in England, Pope Adrian IV (Nicholas Breakspear), and William the Bad in Sicily.

**1155** Frederick leaves Italy after coronation in Rome by Nicholas, who makes terms with Roman commune, Normans and Lombard cities.

**1156** Frederick marries Beatrice of Arles.

**1157** Duchy of Austria instituted. Diet of Besançon, widening breach between Adrian and Frederick. Death of Sanjar ends Seljuk sultanate.

**1158** Frederick crowned king of Arles. Frederick invades Italy; beginning of war with Milanese League (to 1162).

**1159** Alexander III pope; Victor IV antipope (imperialist).

**1162** Fall and punishment of Milan. Frederick leaves Italy.

**1163** Veronese League (anti-imperialist). Almeric (Amalric) king of Jerusalem.

**1164-9** Struggle for domination in Egypt between Nour ed-Din's general Shirkuh and Almeric; Saladin wins distinction.

**1166** Frederick returns to Italy; marches on Rome.

**1167** Frederick takes Rome; Alexander escapes to Normans; plague breaks up Frederick's army.

**1168** Frederick withdraws from Italy.

**1169** Almeric leaves Egypt. Shirkuh secures wazirate in which Saladin succeeds him.

**1170** Murder of Archbishop Becket.

**1171** Henry II annexes Ireland. Saladin ends Fatimid khalifate in Egypt, ruling as Nour ed-Din's lieutenant.

**1173** Ghiyas ud-Din of Ghor, having overthrown Ghaznavids in Afghanistan and Punjab, sets his brother Shahab ud-Din (Mohammed Ghori) over his Indian conquests.

**1174** William the Lion of Scotland, taken prisoner at Alnwick, does homage for his crown; the treaty of Falaise. Frederick's fifth invasion of Italy. Baldwin IV the Leper succeeds Almeric. Death of Nour ed-Din; succession troubles.

**1175** Temujin, aged thirteen, succeeds his father as chief of Mongol tribes in Central Asia.

**1176** Frederick decisively defeated by Lombard League at Legnano. Saladin, dominating Syria, assumes title of sultan.

**1177** Truce with Lombard League. Frederick makes submission to Alexander, at Venice.

**1180** France; accession of Philip II Augustus. Henry the Lion deprived of Bavaria, which passes to the house of Wittelsbach. Death of Emperor Manuel. Alexius II Comnenus.

**1181** Henry the Lion deprived of Saxony, but retains Brunswick; is banished. E. Saxony goes to Brandenburg (house of Albert the Bear). Alexander III dies. Lucius III pope.

**1183** Definitive Treaty of Constance with Lombard League establishes free city states. Saladin completes his mastery of Syria. Usurpation of Andronicus Comnenus.

**1184** Frederick again in Italy.

**1185** Baldwin V king of Jerusalem. Andronicus killed: Isaac Angelus emperor.

**1186** Baldwin dies; his step-father Guy of Lusignan king; war of Guy and Raymond of Tripoli. Henry (VI) son of Frederick marries Constance of Sicily.

**1187** Saladin defeats Guy at Hattin or Tiberias (June); captures Jerusalem (Oct.) and other fortresses. Shahab ud-Din master of Punjab and Sindh.

**1188** European princes take the Cross.

**1189** Start of Frederick's Crusade ('Third'). Henry II dies. Richard I Coeur-de-Lion and Philip of France prepare for Crusade. Richard abrogates Treaty of Falaise.

**1190** Frederick drowned in Cilicia; his army breaks up. Tancred elected king of Sicily. Western crusaders winter in Sicily.

**1191** Richard conquers Cyprus; siege and capture of Acre; dissensions of crusaders; Philip and others return home; Henry of Champagne made titular king of Jerusalem; Richard gives Cyprus to Guy of Lusignan. Henry VI crowned emperor in Rome.

**1192** Treaty of Richard and Saladin ends Crusade. Richard on his return is captured by Leopold of Austria and held prisoner by Henry VI. Shahab ud-Din shatters a great Hindu confederacy at second battle of Tarain.

**1193** Death of Saladin; disintegration of his dominion.

**1193-1206** Conquest of the whole Ganges basin by Shahab ud-Din's slave-general Kutb ud-Din.

**1194** Richard released on doing homage to Henry VI. Death of Tancred; Henry takes crown of Sicily.

**1195** Henry the Lion dies. Guelphs hold Brunswick. Henry VI plans a 'crusade.' Alexius III Angelus deposes Isaac.

**1196** Philip repudiates Ingeborg, m. Agnes of Meran.

**1197** Henry VI dies; his crusade disperses.

**1198** Innocent III pope (to 1216). Sicily under the infant Frederick (II) separated from the Empire. Constance dies, leaving guardianship of the child and kingdom to Innocent. Gradual expulsion of Germans. Philip II (of Swabia) and Otto IV (of Brunswick) elected rival German kings.

**1199** King John succeeds Richard I.

**1200** Innocent lays France under interdict.

**1201** Innocent declares Otto emperor. Partial reconciliation of Innocent and Philip of France.

**1202-5** War of Philip and John, in which Philip wins Normandy, Anjou, Maine and Brittany.

**1202** Aladil brother of Saladin sultan (Eyubid dyn.). 'Fourth Crusade' assembling at Venice, diverted against Greek Empire.

**1203** First capture of Constantinople; Isaac 'restored.'

**1204** Second capture and sack of Constantinople; crusaders divide the spoils. Venice taking the lion's share. Baldwin of Flanders emp. Temujin conquers the Kerait Tatars. Peter of Aragon makes his kingdom a papal fief. Ottocar (Premislav) duke of Bohemia confirmed as king by Innocent.

**1205** Baldwin killed in Bulgarian war; Henry of Flanders succeeds. Independence of Bulgaria under Asen dynasty.

**1206** Temujin assumes title of 'Jenghiz Khan.' Shahab ud-Din dies. Kutb ud-Din first (Slave) sultan of Delhi. Theodore Lascaris Greek emperor at Nicaea.

**1207** Quarrel of King John and Innocent III.

**1208** England laid under interdict. Albigensian 'crusade' begins. Emperor Philip murdered; Otto sole emperor. Francis of Assisi founds Franciscan Friars.

**1209** Innocent crowns Otto emperor.

**1210** Otto attacks Sicily; excommunicated.

**1211** Death of Kutb ud-Din. Jenghiz Khan attacks China.

**1212** Frederick II elected; war with Otto IV. Innocent appoints Philip of France to depose King John, with English support. United Spaniards defeat Moors at Las Navas de Tolosa. Altamsh sultan at Delhi.

**1213** John makes submission to Innocent from whom he receives the crown as a vassal of Papacy. Accession of James I of Aragon (to 1276).

**1214** Ruinous defeat of Otto and his allies by Philip of France at Bouvines. Accession of Ferdinand III of Castile (to 1252).

**1215** Magna Carta extorted from John by barons. Fourth Lateran Council forbids trial by ordeal. Order of Dominican Friars instituted. Frederick II crowned at Aix.

**1216** Franciscan Order formally instituted. Death of Innocent III; Honorius III pope. Henry III succeeds John. Jenghiz Khan turns his arms westward.

### CHAPTER 19

# EAST AND WEST: CONFLICT AND INTERCOURSE. 1152–1216

THE brief period of sixty-four years covered by the present chapter is crowded with striking figures and dramatic events. It opens with the accession of perhaps the noblest, though not the most successful, in the long line of the Western emperors. Frederick I Barbarossa was the son of Conrad III's elder brother, whom he had succeeded as duke of Swabia. His mother was a Welf, sister of Henry the Proud and aunt of Henry the Lion, the young duke of Saxony ; there were high hopes that the union in his person of the houses of Hohenstaufen and Welf would end the division of Germany into partisans of one or the other family.

He had taken part in his uncle's crusade and had won high distinction therein ; and he had played a very creditable part in the strifes which had followed Conrad's return to Germany. If any man could have translated into actual fact the idea of the emperor as the accepted head of a united Christendom, Frederick Barbarossa would have done it. His failure was a final demonstration that the ideal—which he pursued all his life—was unattainable.

### Qualities of Frederick Barbarossa

YET the outset of his reign seemed to promise that it was practicable. Frederick's known qualities had made the election almost unanimous ; there was an unwonted disposition towards loyalty, markedly displayed by his cousin of Saxony, who was rewarded by reinstatement in the Bavarian duchy also. In two years confidence in Frederick and the stability of his position in Germany were almost confirmed, and he could turn to his other kingdom of Italy, where the German king's authority was seldom effective when his back was turned. But the premature move had the usual result ; disturbances broke out in Germany, and before a twelvemonth was out the em-peror had to hasten north again to quell them. And the Italian expedition had prepared a fresh crop of troubles.

Many of the cities of Lombardy and Tuscany had latterly acquired a great degree of autonomy. Broadly, they had first escaped from lay to episcopal overlordships, and then extracted practical self-government from the reluctant bishops. They now saw their self-government endangered by the appearance of a king with the loftiest idea of royal responsibilities, but also of royal authority ; their attitude was already that of sullen mistrust, very obvious in the case of Milan ; and this was intensified—though they gave their allegiance—by the drastic methods of Frederick in dealing with signs of recalcitrance.

### Rome infected by Revolution

MOREOVER, Frederick alienated Rome as well as the Lombard cities. A succession of weak popes had followed the death of Innocent II in 1143. In that year the people of Rome, moved by the example of Lombardy, had set up a commune, rejecting the suzerainty of their bishop the pope. The popes—one of whom, Lucius II, lost his life in attempting to suppress the revolution—were forced to give way, while the revolutionaries were led by the ardent ecclesiastical and political reformer Arnold of Brescia, whom Innocent had condemned as a heretic. The popes had abated none of their theoretical claims, but their temporal authority had fallen to a very low ebb, and was practically ignored by their nominal vassal, King Roger of Sicily and South Italy.

Then in 1154 (which happened also to be the year of Henry of Anjou's accession in England) Roger died, leaving as his heir William, called 'The Bad.' Frederick crossed the Alps to assert his authority in Lombardy, and the only Englishman in

**FREDERICK I, BARBAROSSA**

Frederick I (c. 1124–90) became German king
in 1152 and emperor in 1155. Despite his marked
ability his reign was not fortunate for the
Empire. He is figured in this relief in the cloister
of S. Zeno, at Reichenhall in Bavaria.

the entire list of the popes, Nicholas
Breakspear, became Pope Adrian IV.

Adrian was a strong man, resolute,
fearless, utterly convinced of the Gregorian
theory of the papal supremacy. He faced
the commune boldly, and frightened the
Romans into expelling Arnold by laying
the city under an interdict. At his call
Frederick, who desired formal coronation
as emperor in S. Peter's, came to his
aid ; for the Normans in the south were
threatening (1155). The first meeting of
the pope and the emperor almost wrecked
the accord, since Adrian required Frederick to alight and hold his horse's bridle
while he dismounted. Frederick first
refused, then gave way ; but the event
was ominous. Frederick was crowned,
but it was hard to say whether the Roman

populace was more hostile to the pope or
the emperor ; and at this juncture the
latter found that the call for his return
to Germany was imperative. He left
Adrian to make what he could by himself
of a very critical situation and recrossed
the Alps.

By his timely return to Germany
Frederick effected a new pacification. The
main troubles had been caused by the
count palatine of the Rhine, and by Henry
of Babenburg, who had been dispossessed
in Bavaria by the restoration of Henry
the Lion. Frederick now severed the
East Mark—Austria—from Bavaria and
erected it into a hereditary duchy for the
Babenburg ; Saxony retained the Middle
Mark ; while Albert the Bear, when
forced to resign Saxony on the earlier
restoration of Henry, had been placated
with the Northern Mark of Brandenburg,
which in the course of centuries was to
develop into the kingdom of Prussia.
Frederick also greatly strengthened his
own position by marrying the heiress of
Burgundy, which was thus attached to
the possessions of the imperial house.
But it was only by making politic concessions to the greater nobles that he was
able to collect the great force with which
he proposed in 1158 to impose his authority
on Italy once for all.

### Imperial Designs upon Italy

FOR Adrian had the full courage of his
convictions. He had no intention of
standing to the emperor only in such
a relation as that of earlier popes to
an Otto or a Henry III. Obviously his
Hildebrandine ideals were incompatible
with the imperial ideals of Barbarossa,
and to face that main issue minor issues
must be sacrificed. While Frederick was
establishing a long unparalleled supremacy
in Germany, Adrian was providing himself with allies, making terms with the
Normans, with the Roman commune,
with the communes of the north which
were preparing to defy the common enemy
of their independence, the German emperor. When Frederick in the plenitude
of his success in Germany was holding
a splendid diet at Besançon, Adrian's
emissary propounded ecclesiastical griev-

ances in terms which he intended as a claim to the over-riding authority of the pope.

In 1158, then, Frederick entered Italy at the head of a great army ; without as yet an open breach with Adrian, but with manifestly strained relations, ostensibly for the purpose of reducing the defiant cities, Milan and her supporters, to submission. Milan had formed and headed a league ; jealousy of Milan had brought about the formation of an opposition league, which saw its profit in supporting the emperor and claiming the reward of loyalty. So stubborn, however, was the resistance that Milan itself was only taken after a three years' siege, paying a proportionate penalty. For in each city Frederick appointed an official of his own, an alien governor called a ' podestà,' which meant the total disappearance of autonomy ; and the inevitable ejection of the podestàs was an act of open rebellion. The fall of Milan seemed to signalise the decisive triumph of the e m p e r o r. In 1162 Frederick returned to Germany.

His troubles were not at their end but at their b e g i n n i n g. When Adrian died, in 1159, the cardinals elected an anti-imperial champion in Alexander III. The imperialist opposition elected an anti-pope, Victor IV. Driven from Rome and hardly able to hold his ground in Italy, but formally acknowledged by the kings of France and England, Alexander, in 1162, took refuge in France ; and on his side was the whole weight of the great monastic orders in which lay the main strength of the Church.

As in the older quarrels, G e r m a n loyalty to the em-

peror was not wholly proof against the influence of the Church, though the fact did not at once manifest itself. The settlement of Italy, however, was far too superficial to last. A new league, encouraged by Venice, was formed by Verona, in 1164 ; the leaguers expelled their podestàs ; Alexander returned to Rome (1165) and excommunicated the emperor—generally a sure means of fomenting disloyalty. Once more, at the end of 1166, Frederick descended upon Italy at the head of a great host.

By taking the Mont Cenis route he turned the flank of the defence and marched straight on Rome, which fell, after a hard siege, in the late summer, Alexander making his escape to the Normans. But in the hour of victory a great pestilence smote the armies of the ' enemy of the Church,' shattered the conquering host, and encouraged the league to fresh energy. It only remained for Frederick to extract himself and what was left of his forces from Italy as best he could at the beginning of 1168.

Six years passed during which the emperor was striving to pacify the growing uneasiness in Germany, where the power of Henry the Lion, like the power of Henry, duke of Aquitaine and king of England, in France, was growing greater than beseemed a vassal, and the preponderance of the papal party among the churchmen was constantly increasing. In Italy the rivalries of the cities were crumbling in face of the imperial menace to their common liberties ; one after another joined the L o m b a r d  l e a g u e, pledged to mutual defence of those liberties. In 1174 Frederick could wait no longer ; for the

**HENRY THE LION AND HIS CONSORT**
Ambition distinguished Henry the Lion (1129–95), duke of Saxony and Bavaria, but he died in eclipse at Brunswick, where he is buried with his second wife, Matilda, daughter of Henry II of England.
*S. Blasius Cathedral, Brunswick*

fifth time he led an army into Lombardy, though a far smaller one. Two years later he met with a decisive defeat at Legnano, due mainly to the stubborn burgher infantry.

Frederick had learnt his lesson. Perhaps the real greatness of his character was most conclusively displayed in his recognition of the defeat as a proof that he had been in the wrong, and his courage in acting upon that very unpalatable conviction. He sought his peace with the pope, for he was not yet prepared to accept defeat at the hands of the rebel cities. But Alexander would not desert the cause and the alliances to which he was pledged. Frederick gave way. In effect he conceded all. For the second time an emperor threw himself at the feet of a pope and besought his pardon with tears. But Gregory had not been above inflicting degrading humiliation on Henry at Canossa; if at Venice (1177) Frederick humbled himself, Alexander, too, was great enough to know his adversary's greatness in defeat. On both sides the reconciliation was genuine; and it remained unbroken till Alexander's death, in 1181.

### Substance of the Treaty of Constance

THE details of the Italian settlement involved long negotiation and were finally completed by the treaty of Constance in 1183. Practically it established the cities as free self-governing states owing little more than a nominal allegiance to the emperor. When they were released from the fear of him, they returned to their old rivalries and dissensions. When Frederick returned to Italy in 1184 it was to find among his old enemies friends and among his old friends enemies; but there was on his part no revival of his old policy. The chief outcome of that last visit was the marriage of his own son and heir, Henry, to Constance, the heiress of the Sicilian crown. The union of Norman and Hohenstaufen was to bear unexpected fruit.

At the moment, however, a crisis was arriving in the East which absorbed the emperor's closing years. In 1187 the Sultan Saladin captured Jerusalem. Before turning to the 'Third Crusade,' the other movements in East and West during the period of Frederick's struggle with Adrian and Alexander demand our attention.

Frederick had started on his career with the definite design of realizing the theoretical idea of the emperor as the responsible but indisputable head of Christendom, in conjunction with but not in subordination to the supreme spiritual authority, the pope. Because the line between spiritual and temporal was impossible to define, the contest between Empire and Papacy had been renewed; and in the conflict between Frederick and Alexander the pope had been unmistakably the victor.

### Frederick crushes Henry the Lion

IN Germany, however, Frederick met with a much greater measure of success. How real was his power there may be seen from the career of his mightiest feudatory Henry the Lion, a prince whose dominions stretched from the North Sea to the Adriatic. It would hardly be fair to say that Henry became disloyal; but his interest in the consolidation and extension of his own dominion made him withdraw from the active support which he had at first given to Frederick's imperial policy in Italy.

Like Albert the Bear in Brandenburg, Henry pushed his power eastward over the Slavonic peoples beyond the imperial border. Tribes which had resisted for centuries were brought under his sway; he founded cities, built churches and planted German colonies even in Hungary; his power grew so that he sought to make himself absolute in his duchies; he took to wife the daughter of a king, Henry II of England. His activities and his growing power excited hostility among his own vassals and anxiety in his suzerain, as well as the jealousy of other princes lay and ecclesiastical. But only after Frederick's defeat at Legnano and his submission to the pope did the emperor come into direct collision with his mighty vassal.

Nevertheless the result was the decisive victory of the emperor. Henry was deprived of his duchies and banished, though he was allowed to retain lands in Brunswick and elsewhere (1180). Bavaria passed from the house of Welf to the house of

Wittelsbach, Saxony between the Elbe and the Weser to the son of Albert the Bear, and the more western lands were attached to the archbishopric of Cologne— recent events having forced Frederick actively to seek ecclesiastical support— as the duchy of Westphalia. And although Henry did afterwards make an attempt to recover his position, it failed completely.

Thus when the news of the fall of Jerusalem came from the east in 1187, Frederick had done something towards the retrieval of his defeat in Italy by his new alliance with Sicily, and his power in Germany was at its height. The Papacy had passed into the feeble hands of short-lived popes since the death of Alexander ; and by himself taking the Cross as the leader of a new crusade and the champion of Christendom against the infidel, Frederick seemed to have assumed once more the highest function of the imperial ideal, the function which Urban had once so effectively assumed for the Papacy.

### Growing Autonomy of the Cities

A FEATURE of the whole period common to all the Western powers was one which we have already remarked in Italy, the development of self-government in the commercial cities. Primarily this meant their release from the overlordship—which often meant the tyranny—of magnates lay or ecclesiastical, though the willingness of the churchmen to concede large powers of self-government to the cities under their jurisdiction so far simplified the process. Lay lords too were often not unwilling to make concessions at a price. Every monarch, moreover, was ready to weaken the personal resources of a turbulent baronage and to lend a favourable ear to complaints or demands which would make the crown the immediate overlord.

Frederick in Italy tried hard to resist the movement as rendering the cities too independent, but elsewhere the independent city might be regarded as practically a certain ally of the crown in aiming at reducing the power of the feudatories ; and a sovereign in want of money could on occasion—as when Richard wanted to equip his crusade—make a bargain out of the concession of chartered privileges.

In Germany, France and England alike it was the primary aim of statesmanship to strengthen the central government, and the primary difficulty of so doing lay in the power of the individual magnates, who could call their own feudal forces out to resist the central authority. Therefore, except when the temporal was in direct collision with the spiritual authority, or when cities claimed immunities incompatible with the authority of the crown, the regular tendency was for the crown to combine with the churchmen and to foster and multiply free municipalities, as a counterpoise to the territorial magnates. Italy provided precisely the two exceptions ; there the opposition to the crown arose not nearly so much from the nobles as from the Church and from the cities. There, moreover, the Church and the cities defeated the crown ; and the result was that there the free cities virtually developed into free states.

Both in France and in England the power of the crown progressed. In England sheer exhaustion brought the anarchy to an end when in 1153 Stephen came to terms with Henry ' Fitz-Empress.' Next year Stephen died, and Henry, the newly made husband of the ex-queen of France, a vassal of the French king in virtue of his lordship over a full half of the lands of France, became Henry II, king of England. His aim was no doubt the extension of his domains in France, but his main business was the organization of his English kingdom. The whole country was so utterly sick of anarchy that the nobles themselves welcomed a strong ruler and backed him in stamping out disorder and asserting the royal authority and the supremacy of the law.

### Henry's Conflict with Thomas Becket

UNTIL Henry's sons grew up and defied restraint, no rebellious feudatory stood a chance against him, and he carried out, and indeed carried much farther, that systematisation of the methods of government which his grandfather Henry I had inaugurated. His most serious difficulties at home arose from his endeavour to combat the pretension of his archbishop, Thomas Becket, that the clergy were subject only to the law of the Church and exempt from lay jurisdiction. Even in that quarrel he would have won—for the baronage was with him—but for the murder of the archbishop. Though he quarrelled with the archbishop he re-fused to quarrel with either Adrian or Alex-ander, both of whom had more than sufficient reason for desiring to remain on good terms both with him and with Louis VII. And he not only organized the government of England, but added to his do-minion the lordship of Ireland — without, as must be admitted, taking steps to make that lord-ship effective. Also he was the only king of England who succeeded in compelling a king of Scots to acknowledge his suzerainty, in the treaty of Falaise (1175) when he held William ' the Lion ' a prisoner. That treaty, however, was abrogated fourteen years later by his son and suc-cessor Richard I Coeur-de-Lion.

It was characteristic of Henry that, like some of the strongest rulers in the past, such as Charle-magne and Alfred the Great, he made constant use of the council of magnates, not on the theory that their assent to his reforms was neces-sary, but partly to test public feeling, and partly because, their formal approval of his proposals once pronounced, they were practically debarred from offering subsequent opposition. The practice, however, helped later to give warrant to the doctrine that the council was con-sulted ' of right,' not merely ' of the king's grace.' But of more immediate impor-

**VESTMENTS OF S. THOMAS**

Thomas Becket was canonised in 1173, but from the moment of his murder he was venerated as a saint and martyr. Memorials of him were eagerly sought and preserved as sacred relics.

*Sens Museum ; photo, Paul Robert*

tance at the time was the fact that Henry's methods of establishing the royal authority fixed more firmly than before in the English political mind the fundamental principle of the supremacy of the law, which was presently to be formu-lated in the Great Charter extorted from his son John, and under-lies in England far more than in any other country the whole his-tory of her constitutional development.

But Henry, king of England, was at the same time in France the most powerful feudatory and rival of the crown, a still more serious menace to the central authority than his son-in-law Henry the Lion to that of Germany. In fact he spent more of his time in France than in England, endeavouring to extend and consoli-date his power there by the absorption of pro-vinces to which his wife could exhibit a technical claim. To a great ex-tent he was successful. Louis found in Henry the grand obstacle to his insidious policy of strengthening the crown, which was none too strong, by fostering dis-sensions among the greater feudatories. It was left to Louis's able and unscrupulous son Philip to carry that policy to a triumphant issue after Henry had long been dead.

In the contest between Henry and his suzerain, diplomatic more than directly military, nothing helped Louis so much as the perpetual discords between Henry, his wife and his sons, who were apt to make common cause with Louis and his son after him—Louis died in 1180—to free themselves from their father's control. The contest between father and sons was not yet at an end when the unlooked-for thunder-clap, the news of the fall of Jerusalem, reverberated over Europe, calling a disunited Christendom to arms in one sacred cause.

After the fall of Edessa there had been no immediate advance of the Crescent against the Cross. Islam, as usual, suffered from its divisions, and the Seljuk sultanate at Bagdad was ended in disastrous collision with the eastern Turks in 1159; its power was never brought into play against the Latin kingdom, whose active adversaries were always the western sultans or governors in Syria, or the wazirs who dominated the Fatimid khalifate in Egypt.

At Jerusalem Baldwin III, the boy who succeeded Fulk as king, grew up to be an exceedingly capable and popular prince. The most dangerous of his enemies was Zanghi's successor at Mosul, Nour ed-Din, who was, however, more seriously concerned with extending his power over Moslem rivals than with attacking the Christian kingdom, for which a real expansion, based only on its own resources, was practically out of the question, though in the collisions which took place the honours perhaps rested rather with the 'Franks.' Baldwin died when still a young man in 1163, and was followed by his brother Almeric or Amalric.

Now, at this time the ruling wazir in Egypt was ejected: he bethought himself of appealing to Nour ed-Din, supreme in Syria since he had brought Damascus under his sway. Nour ed-Din sent an army under his general Shirkuh, who restored the wazir Shawer. Shawer took alarm at the power of his restorer, broke with him, and invited aid from the king of Jerusalem. Shirkuh, having captured

**MARTYRDOM OF S. THOMAS OF CANTERBURY**
His resistance to what he regarded as encroachments upon the legal privileges of the clergy led to Thomas Becket incurring hostility from Henry II which culminated in his assassination in Canterbury cathedral, December 29, 1170. The tragedy is vividly portrayed in this early 13th century manuscript.

*British Museum, Harleian MSS., 5102*

Pelusium, was besieged there by Shawer and Almeric. The outcome of the very confused campaigning which went on in Egypt and Syria between 1164 and 1169, in which Shirkuh's nephew Sala ed-Din Yusuf Ibn Eyub won brilliant distinction, was the withdrawal of Almeric (who died shortly afterwards) from Egypt, the immediate establishment there of Shirkuh himself as wazir of the Fatimid khalif, and, on his death, the succession to that office of Sala ed-Din, the great 'Saladin.'

Like all Turks, Saladin was a Sunni. As wazir of the Fatimid he was practically master of Egypt, and in 1171 he set aside the khalif and resumed the long-lost allegiance of Egypt to the orthodox khalif,

O

**THE CRUSADERS' GREATEST ANTAGONIST**

According to tradition this portrait—manifestly from life—is of Saladin. He wears the green turban of the Prophet and a dark red robe with a very large pattern, invariably an indication of exalted rank. The work dates from about 1180 and is the oldest extant Arabian portrait of the Khalifate period.

*From Martin, 'Miniature Painting of Persia, India and Turkey'*

the tyrannical Andronicus, who was killed in a rising of the Byzantine mob (1185), which set in his place the perfectly worthless Isaac Angelus : a prince without principles, in whose eyes duplicity was the essence of statecraft.

Such, then, was the position when the hosts of Saladin poured down on Palestine in 1187. At the battle of Hattin or Tiberias, in June, King Guy met him and suffered an overwhelming defeat, being himself taken prisoner. Saladin swept on, and in October captured Jerusalem. Very soon all that remained of the Latin kingdom was isolated cities and fortresses which stubbornly held Saladin at bay.

Western Europe felt the call not less potent than in the days of Urban. The new pope, Gregory VIII, took up the cause with zeal ; zealous, too, was his successor, Clement III, whom his death next year set on the papal throne. The great princes—the emperor, young Philip of France, Henry II of England, his son Richard, who was now independent duke of Aquitaine—did not leave the nobles to take the lead, as in the First Crusade ; they hastened themselves to take the Cross. The popes and the clergy urged

under the direct suzerainty of Nour ed-Din. When that great ruler died in 1174, Saladin before long made himself master of Syria, as well as Egypt, and turned to his grand project of expelling the Christian power from the East.

The Latin kingdom fell upon evil days. Almeric died in 1174. The boy who succeeded him, Baldwin IV, was a leper, Raymond of Tripoli acting as regent. Baldwin IV died in 1185, his nephew Baldwin V next year, and the succession was disputed between Raymond and Guy of Lusignan, as husband of Sibyl, the sister of Baldwin IV and mother by a previous husband of Baldwin V. The war of succession gave Guy the crown, but completed the disintegration of the Latin kingdom.

Meanwhile, the house of the Comneni at Constantinople had fallen. Manuel, John's successor, had been a brilliant but erratic person of the Coeur-de-Lion type, but the Empire needed something more than a recklessly daring knight-errant or a captain who won startling victories against heavy odds. The son Alexius II, who succeeded him in 1180, was a minor whose throne was usurped by his cousin,

**BALDWIN III ON CAMPAIGN**

Baldwin III (1130–63) succeeded his father, Fulk, as king of Jerusalem in 1143, but did not assume power until 1152. His ten years' personal reign was almost entirely occupied in warfare, chiefly with Nour ed-Din of Mosul.

*From ' De Passagiis in Terram Sanctam '.*

all Christian men to lay aside their personal feuds and join in the Holy War. Conspicuously, Frederick, despite his age, set himself at the head of the movement, gathered a great force, left his son King Henry in charge at home, and was 'on the march for Palestine by the old route through Asia Minor, crossing the Bosporus early in 1190, before the western monarchs were ready to take the field, or rather the sea, since it was by sea that they were to advance.

They were not ready because they could not lay aside their dissensions. Henry was actually at war with Richard leagued with Philip when he died in 1189, and Richard became king of England as well as lord of Aquitaine. The two kings were at this time theoretically warm allies, but even so it was not till the late summer of 1190 that their host embarked for Sicily en route for Syria.

Meanwhile Barbarossa's adventure had been wrecked. Both Isaac Angelus and Kilij Arslan at Iconium (Konia) did their best to thwart his progress without venturing on open opposition; but these difficulties were overcome and all seemed to be going well when Frederick was drowned in attempting to swim across a swift-flowing river. Among his followers, when they had lost their leader, a strange demoralisation

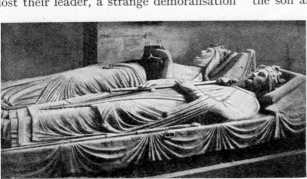

**PLANTAGENET TOMBS AT FONTEVRAULT**

Henry II died at Chinon, July 6, 1189, and is buried in Fontevrault Abbey. By his side sleeps Isabella, wife of his youngest son John, afterwards king of England. It was the discovery of John's intrigue against him that broke the heart of King Henry, whose domestic history had been tragical throughout.

*Photo, Daveau, Rouen*

set in; many of them deserted and went home; plague broke out, more than decimating the remainder; and only a remnant found its way to join the army which was besieging Acre—it had long since fallen to the Saracens—and was itself being besieged by Saladin.

There Philip arrived in April (1191), Richard in June. Already the rivalries and jealousies which were to wreck the 'Third Crusade' were in stormy operation. In Sicily Richard, with singular lack of policy but not without excuse, had quarrelled with Tancred, an illegitimate grandson of Roger, who had been made king in disregard of the legitimate claim of Constance and her husband Henry VI, the son and successor of Barbarossa. On his way from Sicily he had turned aside to eject the independent prince or self-styled emperor of Cyprus, Alexius Comnenus, who was certainly in collusion with the enemy. The capture might have proved of great value, but it had the appearance of a piece of brigandage for personal aggrandisement.

Philip had already learned to detest and dread his former ally Richard; who, in spite of his passion for mere feats of arms, was incomparably the ablest of the captains but was a perfectly impossible

**KING RICHARD I AND HIS MOTHER**

Although a brave and accomplished man, Richard I (1157–99) was not the 'perfect knight' that he was represented by troubadours. Notwithstanding his constant unfilial conduct it was by his own desire that he was buried in Fontevrault at his father's feet and beside his mother, Eleanor of Aquitaine.

*Photo, Daveau, Rouen*

**TOMB OF SALADIN AT DAMASCUS**

Saladin (1138–93) became sultan of Egypt and Syria in 1175. In 1187 he proclaimed a Holy War against all Christians, swept through Palestine and captured Jerusalem. The Third Crusade followed, ending in the suppression of the Latin Kingdom and the union of the Mahomedan East.

*Photo, Bonfils*

colleague by reason of his intolerable arrogance. To Richard the fall of Acre in July was undoubtedly due ; but it also gave the finishing touch which ensured the failure of the crusade. Guy had become king only because he was the husband of Sibyl who was now dead ; Conrad of Montferrat was the husband of her younger sister Isabella, and claimed to have a better title to the crown (which had ceased to have a kingdom) than Guy ; the crusaders became partisans of one or the other, and although the quarrel was temporarily patched up the cracks were only ' papered over.' Philip found that his presence was urgently needed in France, and withdrew, followed by most of the French cruaders.

The war with Saladin degenerated into a series of desultory engagements, brilliant enough as personal encounters but of no real military value. Conrad of Montferrat was murdered, his widow married Henry of Champagne, to whose claim Guy was obliged to give way, and Richard compensated Guy by presenting him with Cyprus. But all hope of unity had long passed away ; enthusiasm was dead ; instead of receiving reinforcements, the ranks of the crusaders were being constantly depleted by withdrawals. In bitter wrath and with genuine grief Richard realized in 1192 that nothing more could be accomplished, and signed with his magnanimous adversary the treaty which left the Holy Land in the possession of the Mahomedan power, with only certain ports in the hands of the Christians, from which free access for pilgrims to Jerusalem was guaranteed. The Latin kingdom of Jerusalem was no more, though the titular hereditary kingship survived for generations.

### Saladin's Influence on Histor

A YEAR later Saladin died. Under him Egypt and Syria had once more been joined in a single dominion, and he had once for all deprived the Christians of any foothold in Asia which could be made a base for military aggression, though a part of Asia Minor still appertained to the Greek Empire. Saladin's own sultanate was destined to break up ; in all such developments the only security for continuity lay in an established hereditary succession in a family which produced capable rulers in each generation. Division among Saladin's sons led as usual to years of strife, though by 1200 his brother Aladil had brought the bulk of the dominion into one sultanate. The name Eyubid (or Ayyubid according to another spelling) is given to the dynasty, from Eyub, the father of Saladin and Aladil.

From a Western point of view Saladin's great achievement was the suppression of the Latin kingdom ; from that of the Mahomedan world, the suppression of the Fatimid khalifate in Egypt was perhaps of no less importance. Thenceforth Islam in the West was orthodox, i.e. Sunni, though the Shiah doctrine never lost its hold in Persia, where it was presently to attain a decisive supremacy.

The Third Crusade ended the era in which the idea of ' chivalry ' was very largely intertwined with picturesque feats of arms in Palestine. Armed pilgrims continued to visit the Holy Land, expeditions were headed by nobles and even by monarchs, but there was never again anything that had so much as the semblance of being an effort of united Christendom, though pope after pope endeavoured to revive the crusading spirit. The romance of crusading departed with the disappearance of the two great romantic figures, Saladin and Coeur-de-Lion, and the commercial and peaceful communication between East and West was probably increased by the fall of the Latin kingdom.

THE brief eight years' reign of the emperor Henry VI (1190–97), the son of Barbarossa, was fraught with great possibilities, which were brought to naught by his premature death at the age of thirty-three. Lacking his father's nobility of character, his brain was keener and his ambitions even wider in their scope. He aimed once more at uniting Germany and Italy under the supreme sway of the emperor, and, when that was accomplished, at making the world empire not merely a theory but a fact. Able as he undoubtedly was, it does not seem probable that his genius, or, indeed, the genius of any man, was equal to a project so stupendous ; but his life was cut short before he had done more than carry through its first stages.

In Germany, Henry of Hohenstaufen had once more to deal with the Welf Henry the Lion. In the south, Sicily and South Italy had set aside his own and his wife's claims in favour of Tancred, being hotly antagonistic to German domination. He succeeded in winning over the Welf ; he did not succeed in ousting the Norman, with whom he had to be content with a compromise, till Tancred's death enabled him to establish his

own title in very drastic fashion over subjects who were seething with wrath at the arbitrary tyranny of the German rulers he imposed on them—very little to the liking of his wife, who was not a German but a Sicilian. Accident, too, had enabled him to get into his hands the king of England on his return from Palestine, and to extract from him, as a condition of release, homage for his kingdom which became for the moment technically a fief of the Empire.

He was embarking a mighty armament for the East, when he was smitten with a fatal illness ; the mighty armament made haste to disperse ; and the whole fabric of his imperial vision melted into thin air. For his heir was a two-year-old babe. And at this precise moment the death of the old pope, Celestin III,

**RICHARD'S CAPTIVITY AND DEATH**
Returning from the Holy Land in 1192, Richard was seized by Leopold of Austria and imprisoned in the castle of Durenstein on the Rhine. This event (left), and also his death in April, 1199, at an archer's hands while besieging the castle of Chaluz, is illustrated in this early French manuscript.
*British Museum ; Cotton MSS., Vitellius A.xiii*

made way for the election of the mightiest figure in the whole list of the popes, Innocent III.

The baby Frederick, later known as 'Stupor Mundi, ' the World's Wonder,' was king of Naples and Sicily ; there was little chance of his being accepted as German king, and inevitably the German and Italian divisions of Henry's Empire fell apart at once. Constance set about ejecting the Germans, renewed the old allegiance of the crown to the Papacy, and, dying next year, left the guardianship of king and kingdom to Pope Innocent. Henry's brother, Philip of Swabia, hastened to Germany in the interest of his nephew for the German election.

But the old Welf-Weiblingen rivalry was alive again. Henry the Lion was dead, and his eldest son, Henry of Brunswick, was away ; but Richard of England, now a prince of the Empire, put up the second son, Otto, his own favourite nephew, as a candidate. The election fell on Philip himself ; the Welf faction elected Otto independently ; there was practically continuous civil war till Philip was assassinated in 1208 ; and even then it promptly took on a new form, only to be finally ended by Otto's death in 1218,

which once more left a Hohenstaufen —the young Frederick II—sole and undisputed emperor. But for that prolonged struggle it would probably have been impossible for Innocent to achieve for the Papacy the unprecedented supremacy which it held in Europe at his death in the year 1216.

INNOCENT, a scion of the noble Italian house of Conti, was not yet forty when he became pope. Not Gregory nor Urban nor Alexander had a loftier conception of the authority of S. Peter's successor than he. Quite definitely and from the outset he claimed that the pope was above all temporal princes, each of whom was nothing more than lord of his own land ; the pope was God's vice-gerent over all Christendom, whereof they were all members, and consequently his subjects. By his authority emperors and kings could be made and unmade. In actual fact, when he died four European monarchs held their crowns as his liegemen, and he could claim that he had made two emperors and unmade two.

In 1198 Innocent became the guardian of the infant Frederick, king of Sicily, and the champion of the Italians against the Germans who had been set over them. He discharged that office faithfully, though it was not till 1208 that the Sicily of the mainland, otherwise called Naples, was fully delivered from the German tyrants. Very soon he was called upon by both sides to arbitrate in the conflict between the rival German kings, Philip of Swabia and Otto of Brunswick. Philip stood for the imperial ideas of the Hohenstaufen, and was, moreover, in alliance with his namesake, Philip II of France, who was the object of Innocent's sternest censure on account of his repudiation of his lawful wife, Ingeborg of Denmark ; Otto was in alliance with his uncle King John of England (who had succeeded his brother

**CHAMPION OF THE PAPAL TEMPORAL POWER**
His effective assertion of the papal supremacy in temporal affairs the world over is the outstanding fact in the pontificate of Innocent III, 1198-1215. All the European monarchs felt and bowed to his power in turn, while in the Church itself his authority exceeded that of any of his predecessors.
*Church of S. Speco, Subiaco ; photo, Moscioni*

Richard in 1199), now the most dangerous adversary of the French king, and as yet on amicable terms with the Papacy.

In 1201 Innocent gave his decision in favour of Otto. As a matter of course, Philip of Swabia rejected the decision which had gone against him ; the struggle went on, favourably to Philip ; but in 1208 he was assassinated by Otto of Wittelsbach on account of a purely personal grudge, and Innocent's candidate was accepted and indeed formally re-elected as German king. In 1209 Otto was crowned emperor

**WORST OF THE ENGLISH KINGS**

Succeeding his brother Richard in 1199, John lost Normandy and Anjou to Philip of France, under duress surrendered England and Ireland to the supremacy of the pope, and finally entered upon civil war with the English barons. He died at Newark, October 19, 1216, and is buried in Worcester Cathedral.

*Photo, E. J. Horner*

in Rome. The papal power had assumed alarming proportions. Sicily had always been nominally a papal fief ; the first king of Portugal, Alfonso Henriques, had secured his title by receiving it as from the pope of the day, and the reigning king, Sancho, failed in attempting to repudiate the papal suzerainty. Peter of Aragon deliberately made himself the vassal of Innocent in 1204. Philip of France had been forced to acknowledge Ingeborg as his wife, though in his original repudiation of her he could claim to have acted on the authority of the French clergy. Otto, while he was fighting Philip of Swabia, had conceded practically all Innocent's claims to secure his support, and had confirmed his concessions before his coronation at Rome. John of England was now in the thick of a conflict with Innocent over the appointment to the primacy in England, in which the prospect pointed to the king's defeat—which was completed in 1213, when John surrendered his crown to the pope and received it back as his vassal.

NEVERTHELESS, when Otto found himself emperor he also found himself attracted to the Hohenstaufen imperial policy ; having been crowned as a papalist, he became as anti-papal as his predecessors. The decisive step was his revival of the imperial claim to Sicily. Innocent's young ward Frederick, born of a Sicilian mother and bred a Sicilian despite his Hohen-

staufen ancestry, was now the representative of the Italian, the Welf emperor Otto IV of the German claim ; the union of Sicily with the Empire was the last thing a pope could approve ; and Innocent appealed to all the interests, foreign or domestic, which were antagonistic to Otto, whom incidentally he excommunicated.

The result was not quite what Innocent would have desired. The German opposition united on Frederick as their candidate (1212), and Innocent was forced to accept him, though only on condition of his doing homage again for Sicily. His own quarrel with John drove him into the arms of his former antagonist, Philip of France, whereby he was greatly embarrassed when John made his submission without withdrawing his support from his nephew. It was, in fact, Philip who won the victory, and the main fruits of it, by shattering the forces of Otto and his allies in the decisive battle of Bouvines (1214), though Otto still maintained a desultory resistance till his death in 1218. Bouvines made Frederick emperor ; it also made Philip of France the most powerful monarch in Europe.

Philip's ancestors had been kings of France in unbroken succession for two centuries, but it was he who in fact created the power of the French monarchy. When he came to the throne in 1180 at the age of fifteen, the domains of the crown were less than those of at least one great feudatory who was almost the equal

—apart from his English kingdom—of all the rest put together.

Most of his reign was spent in the conflicts with Richard and then with John which transferred to the French crown some half of the Plantagenet possessions in France, including Normandy and Anjou ; a process which ultimately proved of much benefit to England because it Anglicised the Norman baronage there

and gradually consolidated English nationalism, always hitherto in danger of being overridden by the interests of both king and barons in their French dominions. Also it consolidated France by the immensely increased strength it gave to the central government. The result, as we shall presently see, was that both France and England by the end of the thirteenth century reached a pitch of power and prosperity to which neither could otherwise have attained.

Philip, bold, astute, determined and perfectly unscrupulous, overcame all his enemies ; and, being like Henry II of England a born organizer, he — again like Henry—used his power when he won it to develop the organization of France. England owed not a little to the reigns of both Richard and John ; but, paradoxically, owed

### MAGNA CARTA : THE PALLADIUM OF ENGLISH LIBERTIES

Magna Carta was at once a grant of liberties made by the king and a treaty between king and subjects. It declared the fundamental principles of government in accordance with established law and custom, bound all parties to observe those laws, and sanctioned armed resistance to any attempt to override or change them without consent. Above is a facsimile of some of the articles, together with (top) a fragment of the original document sealed by King John at Runnymede, June 15, 1215.

*British Museum*

it not to the remarkable abilities possessed by both, but to Richard's happy preference for absenting himself from his kingdom and leaving it in the charge of capable and public-spirited lieutenants (justiciars), and to the personal vices and failures of his brother, which drove the baronage, the Church and the commons to recognize the community of their interests to an unprecedented degree and to extort from the would-be tyrant in 1215 the Great Charter —Magna Carta—which was not in itself a piece of revolutionary legislation, but embodied the basic principle of English political progress, that neither king, barons, churchmen nor commons may override or ignore the law of the land.

### Enlightened Reforms of Innocent III

INNOCENT by no means neglected the spiritual aspect of his office in his zeal to assert the universality of its supremacy. He denounced unsparingly the vices of monarchs, when a more complaisant diplomacy would have made them into useful allies, both Philip and John being cases in point. The decrees of the famous Fourth Lateran Council (1215) were rather an expression of ideals than a code of effective legislation, but their enlightenment is illustrated by their prohibition of trial by ordeal, especially of ordeal by battle. Innocent gave his countenance to the two most remarkable reformers of spiritual standards in the Middle Ages—not excepting even Bernard of Clairvaux—S. Francis and S. Dominic, sanctioning the rule and the orders of which they were the founders almost as his last acts.

He strove hard, too, and failed, to bring about a new crusade, though that project seemed on the verge of completion at the moment of his death. Certainly in Spain he helped to revive that spirit, which gained the one great success of his time in the conflict with Islam, the decisive victory of the united Spanish arms over the Moors at the battle of Las Navas de Tolosa in 1212. Less creditable, if no less sincere, was the development of a crusade against not heathens but heretics, the Albigenses of southern France, whose tenets are not easy to elucidate, but were represented as being not only unorthodox but desperately anti-social. However that may be, they were certainly subjected to a persecution of the most virulent type.

### Iniquity of the 'Fourth Crusade'

BUT for the most monstrous perversion of the crusading idea Innocent was not personally responsible. This was the piece of unqualified brigandage which is more or less ironically known as the Fourth Crusade, of which the object was in plain terms the dismemberment of the Greek Empire for the benefit of Western adventurers and the profit of the Venetian Republic. The obstinate heresy of the Greeks and the treasonable intrigues of the reigning house of the Angeli were the excuse for the diversion of the arms of the Cross against a Christian power which, whatever its shortcomings, had for centuries bridled the advance of Islam against eastern Europe.

The crusade began very much on the lines of the First Crusade, as concerned the leading nobles who took part in it. The houses of Blois, Champagne and Flanders were prominently represented, but no monarchs. But the plan of attack was new ; Egypt was to be the first objective. It was not till the crusaders were beginning to gather at Venice that the objective was again changed.

Isaac Angelus had incurred the wrath of Barbarossa in the first days of the Third Crusade by his obvious duplicity and bad faith. That emperor had reigned for some ten disastrous years, during which Bulgaria, after a long quiescence, had broken into rebellion and then practically established its independence. In 1195 Alexius III Angelus usurped his brother's throne, bringing no improvement. Anarchy prevailed at Constantinople and elsewhere. The Empire offered, in fact, an easy prey, when the Venetians, who were to provide the transport for the crusaders, very much to their own profit, suggested the attractive change of programme : a business proposition by which the men of war of the one part and the shipmen of the other part were to share the profits.

O*

The unholy compact was successful so far as the breaking up of the Greek Empire was concerned. The Greeks were driven out in 1204, after a pretence of ' restoring ' Isaac and his son, two self-styled Greek emperors setting themselves up at Nicaea and Trebizond respectively. The brigands proceeded to the division of the spoil after sacking Constantinople as ruthlessly as the Vandals of old had sacked Rome. Baldwin of Flanders was officially elected emperor of a feudal state modelled on the former Latin kingdom ; but the feudatories were seeking only personal advancement. The astute Venetians secured whatever was of most value for their own share. The Western feudalism was wholly alien to the population accustomed for centuries to Eastern bureaucracy ; the Franks despised the Greeks and the Greeks loathed the Franks ; among themselves the Franks snatched and quarrelled. In due course and in no long time the Latin Empire of Romania perished as it deserved.

### Dawn of a New Era in India

DURING this period the history of India was entering on a new stage. There had been no imperial power there since the Ghaznavid dominion of Mahmud was broken up by the advance of the Seljuks in the eleventh century. Mahomedan chiefs remained supreme in Afghanistan and the Ghaznavids had still a certain ascendancy in the Punjab, when in the latter half of the twelfth century a new era of Mahomedan conquest opened.

A blood feud having arisen between Bahram of Ghazni and Ala ud-Din, a Turk or Afghan chief, of Ghor in Afghanistan, the latter attacked and sacked Ghazni in 1150. The power of Ghor grew ; in 1173 the sultan of Ghor annexed Ghazni and Kabul, and handed them over to his brother, who is variously known as Shahab ud-Din or Mohammed Ghori. Shahab ud-Din set out on a career of conquest. By 1187 he had obliterated the Ghaznavids and was master of the Punjab and Sindh, though he had been heavily repulsed in an invasion of Gujarat. Advancing eastward in 1191 he was again heavily defeated at Tarain, west of the Jumna, by a great Hindu confederacy, but the verdict was reversed by the second battle of Tarain next year.

The command of his armies was then entrusted to his general, Kutb ud-Din, a slave captured in Turkistan who had risen to favour. In the next few years Kutb ud-Din and his subordinate, Mohammed Khilji, captured Delhi and conquered almost the whole Ganges basin, establishing the Mahomedan supremacy in the drastic fashion characteristic of the Turkish champions of Islam, but also organizing the dominion thus won.

On the death of Shahab ud-Din in 1206 the sultanate of the Indian conquests was assumed by the victorious Kutb ud-Din, first sultan of Delhi—thenceforth the centre of Mahomedan empires—and founder of the Slave dynasty. He died in 1211. The Mahomedan historians record with equal enthusiasm the might of his sword, the magnificence of his generosity and the vast multitudes of unbelievers whom he put to the slaughter. Within a few months of his death the son-in-law commonly called Altamsh had displaced his son and heir.

### Storm Clouds gathering in Asia

EUROPE knew nothing and India knew nothing of the terrific storm-cloud which was gathering in the heart of Asia. About the time when Shahab ud-Din was beginning his conquests, a boy of thirteen named Temujin succeeded his father as chief of a tribe or confederation of tribes of the Mongols in the regions lying between the river Amur and the Great Wall of China. After a prolonged struggle with many rivals, Temujin consolidated a great power ; in 1204 he crushed the strong confederacy of the Keraits, who became his subjects. Year by year he extended his sway over other Mongol or Turkish hordes, assuming in 1206 the title by which he is best known, Jenghiz Khan. The Mongols had long been subject to a tribute payable to the Chinese emperor ; in 1211 Jenghiz Khan refused the tribute and began a series of raids into China, which may be taken as the opening of the flood-gates. The new Mongol deluge had burst its banks, fraught with destruction.

# TABLE OF DATES FOR CHAPTER 20

**1216** Deaths of Innocent III, King John, Emperor Henry (of Flanders); acc. of Honorius III, Henry III, Peter of Courtenay.

**1217** Crusade of Andrew of Hungary.

**1219** John of Brienne captures Damietta. Aladil d. Jenghiz Khan invades Transoxiana.

**1220** Frederick's son Henry k. of the Romans. Frederick crowned emperor.

**1221** Damietta recaptured by Al Kamil. Emp. Peter d.

**1222** John III Ducas emperor of Nicaea. Mongol incursion into S. Europe.

**1223** Death of Philip Augustus; acc. Louis VIII.

**1226** Louis VIII d.; acc. Louis IX; Blanche of Castile regent to 1235. Frederick II m. Iolande of Brienne and Jerusalem.

**1227** Gregory IX pope. Frederick embarks on Crusade, but returns. Gregory excommunicates him. Jenghiz Khan d. Ogdai succeeds as Great Khan, but does not extend western conquests.

**1228** Frederick sails on Crusade and negotiates peace with Al Kamil, recovering Holy Places.

**1229** Frederick crowns himself king at Jerusalem, and returns to Europe. John of Brienne joint emperor at Constantinople with Baldwin II (of Courtenay).

**1230** Reconciliation of Gregory and Frederick; Treaty of San Germano. Union of Leon and Castile under Ferdinand III.

**1231** Frederick II issues 'Statute in Favour of Princes' for Germany.

**1231-5** James I 'the Conqueror,' of Aragon, conquers the Balearic Isles from the Saracens. Henry king of the Romans makes trouble in Germany, in opposition to Frederick.

**1235** Frederick deposes and exiles Henry. Louis IX's personal rule begins.

**1236** Ferdinand III of Castile captures Cordova.

**1237** Frederick defeats the revived Lombard League at Cortenuova; Conrad made king of the Romans. Advance of John Ducas in Thrace. John of Brienne d.

**1238** James of Aragon conquers Valencia. Ferdinand of Castile enters Seville. Al Kamil d. Succession rivalries among Eyubids.

**1239** Gregory IX, as protector of Lombard League, again excommunicates Frederick.

**1241** Great Mongol invasion under Batu. They devastate Russia and Poland; checked by Germans at Leignitz and Bohemians at Olmutz, they devastate Hungary; but on tidings of the death of Ogdai the Great Khan, Batu retires, S. Russia remaining subject. Mangu succeeds as Great Khan, Hulagu in western Asia (Ilkhan dyn.). Gregory IX dies while Frederick marches on Rome.

**1242** Es-Saleh Eyubid sultan in Egypt. Mameluke corps organized.

**1243** Henry III of England surrenders claims in Poitou. Innocent IV pope; takes up quarrel with Frederick.

**1244** Mongol bands fall on Jerusalem.

**1245** Mongols rout and massacre Christian forces. Innocent pronounces deposition of Frederick in Germany and Sicily.

**1246** John Ducas takes Thessalonica.

**1248** Louis IX heads a Crusade.

**1249** Louis captures Damietta. Scotland: acc. Alexander III.

**1250** Louis taken prisoner and his force destroyed by Es-Saleh's Mamelukes at Mansourah. Frederick II d.; Conrad IV and William of Holland rival kings of the Romans. Ferdinand of Castile captures Cadiz and Xeres.

**1252** Alfonso X the Wise acc. in Castile. Moorish dominion confined to Granada.

**1254** Conrad IV d.; Manfred holds Sicily for Conradin. Louis IX returns to France. Alexander IV pope.

**1255** Edmund of England papal candidate for Sicily.

**1256** William of Holland d.; 'Great Interregnum,' to 1273. Hulagu suppresses the Assassins.

**1257** Alfonso X and Richard of Cornwall elected rival kings of the Romans. Kutuz first Mameluke sultan of Egypt.

**1258** Hulagu sacks Bagdad and ends Abbasid Khalifate. Manfred assumes crown of Sicily.

**1259** Eccelin da Romano d.; ascendancy of Manfred. Territorial settlement by Louis and Henry III.

**1260** Ghibelline victory at Montaperto. Kublai succeeds Mangu as Great Khan. Hulagu defeated at Ain Gelat by Kutuz and Baibars; who kills Kutuz and seizes sultanate.

**1261** Michael VIII Palaeologus captures Constantinople, restoring Greek and ending Latin Empire. Urban IV pope.

**1262** Peter, prince of Aragon, m. Manfred's dr. Constance.

**1263** Alexander III of Scotland defeats Haakon of Norway at Largs and annexes the Hebrides.

**1265** Montfort's parliament; his fall at Evesham. Urban offers Sicilian crown to Charles of Anjou (brother of Louis IX), who accepts. Birth of Dante.

**1266** Charles defeats and kills Manfred at Grandella. Balban sultan of Delhi to 1286.

**1267** Conradin son of Conrad IV claims Sicilian crown.

**1268** Conradin, last of the Hohenstaufen, is defeated at Tagliacozzo, captured and beheaded. Charles I king of Naples and Sicily.

**1269** Baibars captures Jaffa and Antioch.

**1270** Louis IX's second crusade and death; Philip III.

**1271** Edward, English crown prince, in Palestine. Toulouse lapses to French crown. Gregory X pope.

**1272** England: acc. Edward I on death of Henry III.

**1273** Rudolf of Hapsburg elected king of the Romans. End of the Great Interregnum.

**1275** Pact of Gregory X and Rudolf.

**1276** Peter III succeeds James I of Aragon. Gregory X d. Kublai Khan completes conquest of China.

**1277** Rudolf at war with Ottocar of Bohemia. Baibars d.

**1278** Rudolf defeats and kills Ottocar at Marchfeld, recovering Austria, etc., which are appropriated to the Hapsburgs. Wenzel II succeeds Ottocar in Bohemia.

**1281** Japanese destroy Kublai's Armada.

**1282** Sicilian Vespers: Sicily revolts against Angevin rule and offers crown to Peter of Aragon. Ejection of French from Sicily.

**1282-1302** Struggle between Angevins and Aragonese for Sicily and Naples, which remain parted. Angevins keep Naples, Aragonese Sicily.

**1283** Edward I completes conquest of Wales.

**1284** Philip the Fair m. Joan of Navarre. Alfonso X d.; acc. Sancho IV.

**1285** Philip III succeeded by Philip IV the Fair. Charles I of Naples succeeded by Charles II. Peter III succeeded by Alfonso in Aragon and by his younger son James in Sicily.

**1286** Alexander III of Scotland d.; regency for his granddaughter Margaret the 'Maid of Norway.'

**1288** Ottoman Turks in Asia Minor under Othman.

**1289** Margaret d.; disputed Scottish succession. Mamelukes capture Tripolis.

**1291** Mamelukes capture Acre, last Christian fortress. League of Forest Cantons; Swiss confederation. James II succeeds Alfonso in Aragon; Sicilian claim taken up by his brother Frederick.

**1292** John Balliol king of Scots, as vassal of Edward. Adolf of Nassau succeeds Rudolf as k. of Romans.

**1294** Boniface VIII elected pope. Philip IV and Edward I at war. Kublai Khan d.

**1295** Franco-Scottish alliance begins. Edward I summons the Model Parliament. Ghazan becomes western Khan and adopts Islam.

**1296** Edward deposes Balliol and seizes Scots crown. Boniface issues bull 'Clericis Laicos.' Philip and Edward defy him successfully. Ala ud-Din Khilji seizes Delhi sultanate.

**1297** Scots War of Liberation begins.

**1298** Wallace defeated at Falkirk by English archery. Albert of Austria defeats and kills Adolf; is elected king of the Romans.

**1301** Boniface vainly claims Scotland as papal fief. Hungary: last Arpad king d.; crown becomes elective.

**1302** First decisive defeat of mail-clad cavalry by pikemen at Courtrai, in Flanders. Philip IV summons States General in France to denounce Boniface's extreme claims. Settlement between Frederick k. of Sicily and Charles II k. of Naples.

**1303** Philip takes Boniface prisoner at Anagni. Boniface d.; death-blow to Hildebrandine theory of papal sovereignty.

419

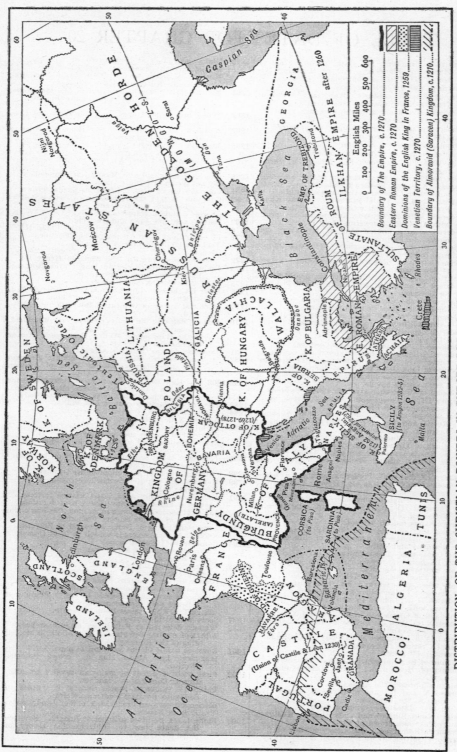

DISTRIBUTION OF THE CHRISTIAN POWERS IN EUROPE DURING THE PERIOD OF MONGOL RULE IN ASIA

While the Mongols were securing control of all Asia and eliminating the Christians as a power in the East, in Europe the Saracen power was being reduced until it was confined to Granada, one result being the emergence of Spain as a European power. Simultaneously France was acquiring cohesion and absorbing the English possessions there. South Italy became the Angevin kingdom of Naples, separated by the papal dominions from the congeries of city states in North Italy; and in Germany the imperial authority was being encroached upon by the princes of loosely confederated states.

### CHAPTER 20

# THE AGE OF EASTERN IMPERIALISM : 1216–1303

**W**HEN Jenghiz Khan assumed his title in 1206 and presently turned his arms against the immemorial Eastern Empire, north China had long been under the rule of the Kin Tatars. Having conquered the Kins, laid waste their cities and occupied their capital in the neighbourhood of the modern Peking, he left an army behind him and turned to complete the conquest of central Asia and thence to sweep on westward.

After the fall of the sultan Sanjar and the Seljuk sultanate, the supremacy and the protectorship of the Abbasid khalif at Bagdad had passed to the powerful rulers of Khiva in Transoxiana. On Mohammed of Khiva devolved the task of holding up the Mongol onslaught. In that task he signally failed, meeting with a crushing defeat at the hands of Jenghiz Khan in 1219. The attack had actually been invited by the khalif himself, Nasir, who found himself on the point of being crushed by his nominal protector. During the next six years Mohammed and after him his son Jelal ud-Din were hunted from pillar to post ; the whole of their dominion from Khiva to Georgia, Khorassan and half Persia, was ravaged, and the Mongol hordes began to pour into south Russia.

## Horrors of the Mongol Invasion

**W**HEREVER resistance was offered the conqueror smote without mercy, slaughtering by thousands and tens of thousands ; instant submission was rewarded with practical immunity. There was no attack on Bagdad, which had thrown down no challenge. Meanwhile, the Great Khan's lieutenants were making good the conquest in China. Two years later, in 1227, the great conqueror died, on an expedition to punish a rebel chief in Mongolia ; lord of an empire more vast than had ever owned the sway of a single master. That empire he divided between his four sons, naming one of them, Ogdai, as Great Khan.

For some fifteen years Ogdai ruled as Great Khan. During those years he and his brother Tuli were personally occupied mainly with the eastward expansion ; but the Mongol power was also exacting submission from the western Seljuk sultanates, flooding into Europe and razing to the ground the nascent civilization of Russia. Towards the end of Ogdai's reign the flood became a deluge which threatened, as Attila had once threatened, to submerge Western civilization altogether. The West was too much absorbed in its own internal quarrels to awake to the danger till it was at the very gates ; a hastily gathered force gave slight check to the storm at Leignitz, when it had already devastated Poland, in 1241, and more effectively it was turned aside from Bohemia to Hungary by the Czechs ; there it was pursuing its career when news came of the death of Ogdai.

### Ebb of Mongol Flood in the West

**T**HE tide was not rolled back, but without other apparent reason it ebbed as suddenly as it had risen—never to return. Its chief, Batu, a grandson of the mighty Jenghiz, established his own khanate in the regions of the Caspian. The Russian civilization had perished, and for centuries the Russian Slavs lay under the Tatar supremacy, their progress strangled.

The Great Khanate passed into the hands of the sons not of Ogdai but of Tuli : Mangu and after him the great Kublai. Both of them, like Ogdai, were concerned mainly with the Farther East ; the Nearer East, Mahomedan Asia excluding India, fell under the rule of the third brother, Hulagu. Mangu in due course crushed the last stronghold of the Kins in Honan and was engaged in subjugating the Chinese Sungs of the south when his death in 1260 gave the succession in the Great Khanate to Kublai (1260–1294), whose splendours were celebrated by the European traveller

Marco Polo. How Kublai's brother Hulagu advanced in the West and how his advance was stayed we shall presently see ; for we must now turn to the more familiar fields with which the last two chapters have been concerned.

For more than thirty years after the death of Innocent III the central figure in the West was the 'World's Wonder,' the emperor Frederick II. To this day, as in his own, a perplexed aston-ishment is the most definite feeling aroused by the study of his career. His audacious originality, his versatility, the universality of his interests, remind us of the most remarkable personality in the list of the great Roman emperors, Hadrian. He discarded the intellectual shackles of medievalism ; his brilliancy and his amazing modernity give him an intoxi-cating attraction ; and his accomplish-ment was to undo the best work of his grandfather, who was almost as far his inferior intellectually as he was his superior in stability and in character.

When Innocent died, Frederick was already emperor in consequence of his solemn engagement to devote himself to the new crusade on which the great pope's heart was set, and to maintain in permanence the separation of the Sicilian kingdom from the Empire. Innocent's successor, Honorius, was less masterful and more patient, readier to trust insincere assurances, easier to deceive. For ten years Frederick played with him, evading or breaking his own promises. He was always going on the promised crusade, but he did not go. He got his young son Henry crowned as successor both to the Empire and to the Sicilian kingdom, while he left Germany to the able administration of Archbishop Engelbert and concen-trated on the establishment of an absolute monarchy in the Sicilies ; and he was obviously on the point of reviving the old imperial claims in Lombardy when Honorius died in 1227, although he had apparently been at last making serious preparation for the long-promised crusade. The new pope, Gregory IX, was an old

**ASIATIC DOMINIONS OF JENGHIZ KHAN AND HIS IMMEDIATE SUCCESSORS**

At the time of the death of Jenghiz Khan the Mongol Empire extended right across Asia from the China to the Caspian and Black Seas. Later the Mongol invasion expanded westwards into Europe as far as the Dnieper, to ebb after Ogdai's death, and over the Near East as far as Ain Gelat under Hulagu. Kublai Khan absorbed China, but allowed the rest of the territory of the Great Khan to become distributed among the Chaghatai, Ilkhan and Golden Horde group of Mongols.

man, but of a temper as fiery and an energy as ardent as if he had been a young one.   In September Frederick's crusade put to sea and promptly put back again.   With equal promptitude, Gregory excommunicated the emperor. Frederick, however, had recently married Iolande of Brienne, who on her mother's death became titular queen of Jerusalem, whereby there had been aroused in him a new interest in the East, and ideas of his own as to the purpose of crusading.

In spite of a flood of papal anathemas, he sailed for the East in 1228 ; and next year—forty-two years after Saladin's capture of the Holy City— without having struck a blow, by reliance not on hard fighting but on diplomacy with an army behind it, he obtained from Al Kamil, successor of Aladil (see page 412), the treaty which once more, though for no very long time, restored to the Latins Jerusalem (reserving the Mosque of Omar) and the holy places around it.   In the Church of the Holy Sepulchre, with his own hands (since the ecclesiastics would have nothing to say to him) he set on his own head the crown of Jerusalem.

When the king of Jerusalem returned to Europe his practical interest in the East was apparently exhausted.   There was no military reorganization.   The kingdom's most effective defenders in the past, the great orders of the Temple and of S. John, were more likely to fight each other than to co-operate against the infidel ;   no effective control could be exercised by a king, away in Italy, who was at perpetual feud with the spiritual head of Christendom ;   and the Venetians, Genoese and Pisans in the ports, absorbed in purely commercial interests, were in deadly rivalry with each other.   Recovery, in fact, had become a sheer impossibility, though

**JENGHIZ KHAN**

Jenghiz Khan (1162–1227), Mongol and Tatar emperor, ranks with Alexander, Caesar and Napoleon as conqueror and empire builder.   This portrait is in the possession of one of his descendants.

*From H. Lamb, ' Genghiz Khan '*

a few enthusiasts in the West might and did still refuse to believe it.

YET for the time Islam was hardly in better plight.   In Asia it was overshadowed by the Mongols, whose lordship the northern Seljuk sultanates preferred to the extermination which attended resistance.   They had not as yet attacked the Eyubid power, but that power sped to dissolution when Al Kamil died in 1238.   In the fighting between rivals in Syria which followed his death, one party was rash enough to call in the aid of Mongol soldiery, bands of whom descended on Syria ;   and, being entirely impartial in matters of religion, they massacred Mahomedans and Christians alike when they came to Jerusalem.

The destruction of a force of crusaders which brought them to battle at Gaza in the year 1244 was practically the coup de grâce of the moribund Latin kingdom, though the onslaught had been a mere raid and was not followed by occupation.   Ogdai had only very recently died, and, though one of his nephews, as we saw, had been devastating eastern Europe, the main Mongol power had been too much preoccupied with central Asia and China (since Jenghiz Khan's death) to extend its dominion in western Asia.   Twelve years passed before Hulagu set about further conquest in that quarter, and in the meantime Jerusalem reverted to the Turks. The Mongols were to be brought to a standstill in 1260, but at the hands of neither Eyubid nor crusader.   That was to be the work of the great military caste which the Eyubid es-Saleh was even at this moment building up in Egypt.   In fact, Damascus was challenging Cairo, and it was only with great difficulty that es-Saleh kept possession of Palestine.   For the development of his own military power he organized an already existing force of slave soldiery, captives or the offspring of captives taken in war, who were known as Mamelukes. Such a force, composed of picked men, was capable of being trained to a very high standard of efficiency, and was invaluable so long as it was loyal to the sultan ; and its efficiency was very soon put to the proof.

The fall of Jerusalem did not, as in the past, bring into the field a host which could pretend to regard itself as the army of Christendom, but it did enable Louis IX of France—by no means the cleverest but assuredly the most admirable prince of his time—to lead a great expedition to the East for the redemption of the Holy Sepulchre. That the conquest of Palestine should be made through Egypt was coming to be recognized. Egypt was its objective ; in 1249 it arrived before Damietta, which was at once evacuated without attempting defence. But the campaign in the Delta which followed was on the same disastrous lines as that of 1221 ; the army was forced to retreat at Mansourah, and Louis, fighting a valiant rearguard action, was completely defeated and himself taken prisoner by the Mamelukes with many others. The crusade was over ; Louis and the rest of the captives were released only at the price of a huge ransom and the evacuation of Damietta.

Es-Saleh died while the campaign was in progress. Five years later the Egyptian Eyubids had been practically wiped out, and the lordship of Egypt had passed into the hands of the first of the Mameluke sultans, Kutuz, whose successors held sway for nearly three centuries. About the time when the Mameluke commander was seizing the throne of Egypt,

Hulagu, the lord of the western half of the Mongol empire, was becoming active. The whole East had long been tormented by the activities of the terrible sect or secret society known to the West as the Assassins. Yet no one had dared attempt to root them out till Hulagu called upon atabegs and emirs to unite for their extirpation in 1256. They were duly extirpated. But the Abbasid khalif of Bagdad declined to take part in the enterprise, thereby providing the Mongol with a sufficient excuse for falling on Bagdad, putting the khalif to death, giving the city with all its inestimable treasures to a forty days' sack, massacring or enslaving the inhabitants and leaving the Mahomedan world without any khalif at all (1258).

**CONTEMPORARY PORTRAIT OF KUBLAI KHAN**

Kublai Khan (1214–94) was a generous benefactor of the Confucian temple at Chu-Fou, in Shantung, and there this thirteenth-century portrait of him is preserved. It is especially valuable because early Chinese portraiture is remarkable for its successful combination of interpretation of character with representation of form and feature.

*From Arthur Waley, ' An Introduction to the Study of Chinese Painting,' Ernest Benn, Ltd.*

Then Hulagu set himself to complete the Mongol conquest of the west, and turned upon Syria. The princes of the north were already his submissive vassals, but the Mameluke sultan of Egypt, like his predecessors, claimed Syria for his own. In 1260 Kutuz and his lieutenant Baibars met him at the great battle of Ain Gelat in Palestine, and shattered his army. Beyond the Euphrates the Mongol 'Ilkhan' dynasty ruled where Seljuk or Abbasid had ruled. In the next generation the ilkhans turned Mahomedan. But the Mameluke had set the bounds to their advance westward, at the precise moment when the greatest of Mongol rulers, Kublai, succeeded Mangu as Great Khan.

EANWHILE, the Latin Empire at Constantinople had fallen to pieces. It never possessed more than an extremely unconvincing semblance of unity ; and the only purpose it served was to make finally impossible the consolidation of a really strong European power at the eastern gate of Europe. Henry of Flanders (1205–1216) made the best of an impossible situation, protecting his Greek subjects and keeping some control over his Latin vassals. His successor, Peter of Courtenay, was taken prisoner while on the way to assume the imperial crown, and died in captivity. His son Robert was a minor at his accession. During

**IMAGE OF FREDERICK II**
Frederick II, born December 26, 1194, was crowned German king in 1215 and emperor in 1220. His conflict with the Papacy ended with the Empire in collapse, and he died, a broken-spirited man, December 13, 1250.
*British Museum*

his ten years' reign, an Angelus—Theodore—who had already established himself in Epirus, got possession of Thessalonica, which was nominally a vassal kingdom.

Robert died in 1228 and was followed by his boy-brother Baldwin, whose guardians called in John of Brienne, the ex-king of Jerusalem. John did what he could as joint emperor till his death in 1237. Meanwhile, the Greek John III Ducas had succeeded Theodore Lascaris at Nicaea. He ejected Angelus from Thessalonica, but Constantinople was still impregnable. An infant succeeded him in 1254 at Nicaea ; but five years later the capable soldier Michael VIII Palaeologus, who had been acting as guardian, usurped the imperial crown, and in 1261 captured Constantinople by a surprise. The Latin Empire, born in infamy, perished thus

**NAVAL ATTACK ON THE TOWER OF DAMIETTA**
In the thirteenth century Damietta, near the mouth of the eastern branch of the Nile, was important as a bulwark of Egypt and was attacked several times by the crusaders. Probably drawn by Matthew Paris this picture represents an attack in 1218 during an eighteen months' siege; note the flail.
*Corpus Christi College, Cambridge, MS. 16*

ignominiously after fifty-six years of futility. The Greek Empire rose once more from its ashes, to struggle on dolorously as best it might for nearly two hundred weary years to an heroic end, its one last hour of glory.

THE excommunicate emperor and king of Jerusalem returned from the East to Europe in 1229 to find his Italian territories overrun by John of Brienne in the service of the pope, his inveterate enemy. He very soon cleared the papal forces out of Apulia ; Gregory found himself in dangerous plight, and in 1230, through the mediation of Hermann of Salza, Grand Master of the Teutonic Knights, pope and emperor discovered that their differences had been due entirely to a misunderstanding, which having been cleared up left them the best of friends— till one or other should find a favourable opportunity for dropping the mask. Their new amity was proclaimed to the world by the treaty of San Germano.

Frederick's real personal interest was concentrated on Italy, where he desired to establish his own complete absolutism. Feudalism, free cities and the Papacy were the obstacles. To fight his battle in Italy he wanted the support of the German feudatories and at any rate could not afford to alienate them. Trouble in Germany had repeatedly paralysed the imperial policy in Italy in the past. To avoid trouble in Germany he pursued in that country a course which was in exact contrast to his methods in Sicily and Italy. For the past ten years he had left the government to Germans, and had sent his son Henry, ' king of the Romans,' to take charge. Now he found that the young man was causing trouble, and dictated to him the policy embodied in what might be called the Charter of the Princes, which confirmed the greater nobles as almost independent territorial princes enjoying sovereign rights in their own lordships.

Instead of fostering the lesser nobles and the free towns as a counterpoise to the princes, he strengthened the great nobles to the utmost extent of his power, seeking thereby to reduce the privileges of the free towns, and actually diminishing those of the minor barons—not indeed from any active ill will to these lesser folk, but because he wished to ingratiate himself with the greater folk, in order to be free from German embarrassments in carrying through his Italian policy. In actual fact, however, the ' Statute in favour of the Princes ' (1231) did away with such possibility as had hitherto existed of establishing the supremacy of the imperial authority in Germany, so that for more than six hundred years she remained no more than a collection of loosely confederated independent states associated under an imperial president.

Frederick never hesitated to secure temporary support by making promises which he had every intention of breaking whenever it might suit him to do so. In that spirit he had promised Innocent to maintain the separation of the Sicilian and imperial crowns, and had broken that promise as soon as Innocent was safely out of the way. So now he gave the German princes their charter because he wanted

**BAGDAD'S GATE OF THE TALISMAN**
Brick walls with towers and noble gates formerly enclosed Bagdad, but repeated sieges and inundations have played havoc with them all. The Gate of the Talisman dates from 1220, nearly forty years before Hulagu sacked Bagdad ; it has been bricked up since 1638, when Murad IV captured the city.
*From Glück and Diez, ' Die Kunst des Islam '*

their support in the coming conflict with Gregory ; presumably confident that when he had won that battle he would be able to turn on them and reduce the powers conferred. Meanwhile, with the princes at his back, no serious challenge was likely to come from that quarter.

Nevertheless Germany continued for a while to offer distraction. Young Henry set himself not to carrying out a definite policy of his own, but to thwarting his father to the best of his ability by combining the lesser nobles and the cities against him. But the lesser nobles were too weak and the cities too shrewd to form an effective opposition under a leader so incompetent. The result was that in 1235

**SIEGE OF BAGDAD BY HULAGU**

This illustration in Rashid ed-Din's History of the Mongols depicts incidents on February 2, 1258, the last day of the siege of Bagdad by Hulagu. Mongol artillery are discharging their last bullets at the walls and the Commander of the Faithful is leaving his palace to surrender to his Mongol conqueror.

*From Blochet, ' Manuscrits orientaux de la Bibliothèque Nationale '*

Frederick deposed his son, exiled him to Apulia, where he presently became tired of life and rode his horse over a precipice (1242), and confirmed the princes in their recently acquired powers. In 1237 he had his younger son Conrad, the boy born nine years before to Iolande of Brienne, elected king of the Romans (the title which implied succession to the Empire). From this time it may be reckoned that the right of electing the emperor or more commonly the king of the Romans was vested in the small group of magnates who acquired the title of ' electors '—three archbishops and three lay princes, with whom was presently associated for that purpose the king of Bohemia.

An ascendancy similar to that of the magnates in Germany had been established by Eccelin da Romano at Verona while the old city leagues of Italy were reconstituting themselves and making alliance with Frederick's troublesome son Henry. So when Frederick returned to Italy after his settlement of German affairs in 1237, he turned to the suppression of the Lombard cities with Eccelin very much at his service. In the same year he won a decisive victory at Cortenuova, which brought about the immediate submission of all but the most stubborn, Milan and a few others, who were expecting once more active support from the now very aged but still amazingly energetic Gregory. In 1239 the pope again excommunicated and deposed Frederick.

The emperor's German policy bore the intended fruit. Germany declined to revolt at the pope's bidding. Gregory found himself without adequate military support, and only escaped falling into Frederick's hands by dying (1241). Pope and emperor were both devoting their entire energy to this vendetta at the precise moment when Batu and his Mongols, whom they completely ignored, were storming irresistibly through Hungary. The Mongols stopped and surged back thither whence they had come, but the temporal and spiritual heads of Christendom had no hand in their somewhat inexplicable retirement.

Gregory's death suspended the conflict. His immediate successor was already a dying man ; after him the papal throne remained vacant for nearly two years ; but when Innocent IV was elected, in 1243, the strife was renewed. Frederick drove the pope out of Italy, but Innocent was able to take refuge in the Arelate, though it was a part of Frederick's own dominions, and fulminated therefrom. Louis of France, eager for a general crusade, strove in vain to effect a reconciliation. Innocent again pronounced the emperor's deposition, but it was no easy matter to find a willing rival, though the war with the emperor was proclaimed a crusade.

At last William count of Holland was elected king of the Romans by the papalists, and for a long time maintained an indecisive contest with the young Conrad. Germany fell into feudal chaos, and in Italy Guelph and Ghibelline cities and factions in the cities fought and cut each other's throats with small apparent prospect of a decision being reached, victories and defeats alternating. The reckless struggle was still at its height when Frederick died in 1250.

### Sicilian Crown in Market Overt

**Ib**IS death brought no abatement. Conrad and William went on fighting for the imperial crown in Germany, while Conrad's illegitimate brother Manfred took over the government of the kingdom of Sicily on his behalf, and Innocent tried to find someone else on whom to confer its crown. Conrad, making no headway, left Germany to his supporters, and joined Manfred in the south, but died in 1254. His heir was the two-year-old infant Conradin in his German nursery. At the end of the year Innocent died, but his successor, Alexander IV, kept up the struggle.

The new pope offered the crown of Sicily to Edmund, the younger son of Henry III of England. In 1256 William died, and there was a split among the German papalists, one group electing Richard of Cornwall, Henry III's brother, and the other choosing Alfonso X the Wise, king of Castile, both of whom claimed the imperial title without seriously attempting to make the claim good.

Manfred accepted the Sicilian crown for himself from the Sicilian magnates in 1258, and established his authority throughout the kingdom. Eccelin, the Ghibelline tyrant in the north, met his death next year, and Manfred was left the one effective, if illegitimate, representative in Italy of the mighty house of Hohenstaufen. A Ghibelline victory over the Guelph Florentines at Montaperto in 1260 gave him a general ascendancy in Tuscany and Lombardy.

### End of the Hohenstaufen Dynasty

**O**N Alexander's death in 1261 his successor, Urban IV, offered the Sicilian crown to Charles of Anjou and Provence, who accepted it, much to the dissatisfaction of his brother, Louis IX. The terms of the appointment were ratified in 1265, when Clement IV had succeeded Urban. In 1266 Charles was crowned king in Rome, and invaded Manfred's dominions. In 1267 Manfred's army was shattered and he himself was slain at the decisive battle of Grandella.

The victor emphasised the completeness of his victory by a policy of rigorous terrorism. A reaction set in ; young Conradin, now fifteen, resolved to claim the crown which was his by inheritance. Though only a few Germans accompanied him, his appearance in Lombardy rallied supporters to his cause ; but in 1268 the Ghibelline forces were utterly routed at Tagliacozzo. Conradin was betrayed into Charles' hands, and the last of the Hohenstaufen was beheaded by his merciless captor. The medieval conception of the Empire was blotted out for ever. But the methods employed, latterly at least, by the Papacy in blotting it out had sealed the doom of the medieval conception of the Papacy as well.

Since the days of Otto the Great, the German king or emperor had been without question the greatest lay potentate in Europe. When William of Holland died in 1256, there was no longer any German king, though there were two foreign claimants to the empty title of king of the Romans. It was not till 1273 that the period known as the Great Interregnum was ended by the election of Rudolf of Hapsburg, a noble of minor rank, to the imperial dignity. The old primacy had passed; and when Louis IX died on his second crusade in 1270, no one would have refused him the name of the first monarch in Europe.

His grandfather Philip had organized the kingdom and centralised the government; his father Louis VIII (1223–6) had carried Philip's work a little farther; during his own minority his mother Blanche of Castile had saved that work from imminent wreckage; and his personal rule, which began in 1235, had done the rest. No one would dream of calling him a genius; he was incapable of practising the craft so characteristic of his grandfather; his statesmanship was not particularly perspicacious; but by force of an exceptionally pure and lofty character he achieved a moral ascendancy over his contemporaries and over his subjects which it would be hard to parallel.

The consolidation of France and ultimately of England also in the thirteenth century was primarily the result of that struggle between Philip and John of which the story has already been told (page **416**). It transferred to the French crown as immediate overlord all those fiefs in France which the Angevin kings of England had held as feudatories, except Gascony and Guienne; so that there was no longer any feudatory in France whose possessions were comparable in extent to those of the crown, though it became the royal policy to distribute the greater fiefs

**BLANCHE OF CASTILE**

As regent for her son Louis IX, during his minority and absence on Crusade, Blanche of Castile proved herself an adroit administrator.

*From Larousse, Histoire de France*

as appanages among the king's sons, not without disastrous results. But the Albigensian crusade was also turned to similar account in the south by the destruction of the power of the house of Toulouse which supported the heretics; of which the ultimate result was that in the reign of Louis IX Toulouse passed to his brother Alfonse, while another brother, Charles, on whom Anjou had been conferred, made Provence French, though not yet technically a part of France, by marrying its heiress. In his time, too, claims still maintained in Poitou by the king of England were finally disposed of.

The strength gained for the crown by Philip's policy, continued by his son and grandson, was fortified by the administrative system created by Philip and by the close alliance with the Church maintained by all three kings. The mere fact that a foreign queen-mother ruling as regent during the nine years of her son's minority was able to hold her own against the resentful nobles is convincing proof of the efficacy of the work accomplished by Philip and Louis VIII.

Evil, however, was to come in the future, though the danger was not immediately apparent, out of the transfer of the great fiefs from the crown to the royal princes. For this the responsibility lies on Louis VIII, and on Louis IX only in so far as he confirmed to his brothers the elevation destined for them by their father. A new nobility of the blood royal was thus created which later proved as hostile to the royal supremacy as the old feudatory nobility had been in the past. We may further note in passing that from this time the names Anjou and Angevin belong not to Plantagenets but to Louis IX's brother Charles and his descendants—that brother whom we have seen completing the downfall of the Hohenstaufen as papalist claimant to the Sicilian crown.

Twenty years after the crusade which had proved so signally disastrous, Louis repeated the adventure, which this time was ended by his death in Africa so far as concerned the French. Edward, the crown prince of England, attempted to carry on the crusade, which was the last that can be dignified by that name.   But he soon found that the task was hopeless.  Jerusalem was held by the Mameluke sultan Baibars, the mighty warrior who had shared with Kutuz the triumph of Ain Gelat and had then slain his chief and assumed the sultanate, setting the precedent habitually followed thereafter by the Mamelukes. The Christians of Syria preferred making an accommodation with Baibars to supporting the English prince and his small following.  Edward returned home.  Despite the efforts of Gregory X Europe would rouse itself to no fresh effort and before the century was ended the West had lost its last foothold in Syria ; only Cyprus under the Lusignans and Rhodes under the Knights Hospitallers remained of all that had been won by the crusaders.

**W**HILE the Christians were being as a political power finally eliminated in western Asia, the Saracens in Europe were being pressed back into that corner of Spain where alone they were still to maintain their hold for two centuries.  James I of Aragon (1213–76) when he came to man's estate drove them out of the Balearic isles (1232) and finally expelled them from Valencia in 1238.  Ferdinand III of Castile before his death in 1252 captured the old seat of the Moorish khalifate at Córdova in 1236, Seville in 1244, Jaen two years later, Cadiz and Xeres in 1250.  His successor, Alfonso X, helped by James of Aragon, completed the conquest of Murcia, which gave Castile access to the Medi-

terranean, and all that remained to the Moors was the small kingdom of Gránada. The union of Castile with Leon had been finally effected by Ferdinand, so that she was considerably the largest of the Spanish kingdoms, though Aragon's sea power set her on an equality with her bigger neighbour.

But this decisive advance of the Christian powers in Spain carried with it a change in the preoccupations of the Spanish monarchs and in their relations with the rest of Europe. At no earlier date is the offer of the imperial crown to a Spanish prince imaginable ; and at no earlier time could a Spanish prince have dreamed of laying claim

**TOMB OF A GREAT MAMELUKE SULTAN**
Baibars murdered Kutuz in 1260 and seized the sovereignty, proving himself one of the ablest of the Bahri Mamelukes. He re-established the Abbasid khalifate at Cairo and established his own authority all over Syria and Arabia.  He died July 1, 1277, and was buried at Cairo, where his tomb still stands.
*Photo, E.N.A.*

**HISTORIC STREET IN RHODES**
Rhodes was captured from the Saracens by the Knights
Hospitallers of S. John of Jerusalem in 1309 and held by them
until 1522. Eight Christian countries were represented in the
order, and the armorial bearings of these and their crusaders
are carved on many of the houses in this Street of the Knights.

*Photo, E.N.A.*

had been prepared by the
Anglicising of the dominant
Norman baronage owing to the
separation from Normandy,
and by the 'Barons' Wars'
with a king who sought to
govern through foreign favourites and foreign prelates nominated by the pope instead of
through English magnates.
The leadership of the opposition to the crown by Simon
de Montfort had given to it
a popular shape as incompatible with baronial as with
monarchical tyranny, and had
taught the crown prince Edward, the conqueror of Simon,
the principles upon which the
future constitutional development of the English government was to be based, by
conferring a really effective
power of direction upon the
'commons,' the lesser barons
and burgesses, and by confirming the doctrine embodied
in the Great Charter that
neither crown nor barons great
or small might with impunity
override the law.

IN the long contest between
Papacy and Empire the
Papacy had brought down the
Hohenstaufen, but only at
the cost of its own moral
ascendancy. The fall of the
Hohenstaufen had the practical though
not the technical effect of ending that
union not of Germany and Italy but
of the separate crowns of Germany and
Italy which had done so much to
prevent the consolidation of each of those
countries. But the severance came so late
that a genuine consolidation had become a
practical impossibility for either. What
had been the Italian kingdom in the
north resolved itself into a congeries of
a few powerful city states, each holding
in subjection to itself a group of states
which had once been its rivals—Venice,
Milan, Florence, Genoa. East and south of
it lay the papal dominion stretching from

to any other crown than that which he had
inherited. Yet now we find Alfonso X a
rival emperor to an English prince ; we are
on the point of finding the Sicilian crown
not only claimed but worn by a branch of
the royal house of Aragon ; and before
long we shall see English and French
taking sides in purely Spanish quarrels.
And we have reached the stage at which
the same Alfonso can direct a main part
of his energies to the consolidation of
his Castilian kingdom, at the same time
that Edward I was accomplishing a similar
work in England, following upon that
of the great Capetian kings in France.
The way for the English consolidation

the Adriatic to the Mediterranean. South Italy eventually became the kingdom of Naples under the Angevin dynasty of Charles, severed from the island kingdom of Sicily under an Aragonese dynasty; and if a union of Italy under papal hegemony had ever been possible, the possibility disappeared when the Papacy transferred its headquarters from Rome to Avignon, early in the fourteenth century.

When in 1273 the diplomacy of Frederick of Hohenzollern procured the election to the German throne of a minor Swabian noble, Rudolf of Hapsburg, by a few of the princes, the intention was obvious. The emperor was to be a figurehead without practical power to depress the princes, and with no prospect of founding a dynasty. The scheme was in some degree frustrated by the abilities of Rudolf, who succeeded in acquiring substantial territories for his family and raising it to a leading position, though he failed to secure the succession for his son. His main actual achievement was the recovery and appropriation to the house of Hapsburg of the territories on the 'east-mark,' Austria, Carinthia and Carniola, of which Ottocar of Bohemia had possessed himself during the Interregnum; and the war with Ottocar had forced him to conciliate possible allies of the king by formally acknowledging the papal claims in Italy and Sicily and Charles of Anjou's claim (by marriage) in the county of Provence, hitherto a fief of the Empire.

Rudolf was succeeded in 1292 not by his son Albert but by Adolf of Nassau, chosen by the electors—as Rudolf had himself been chosen—because he too was only a minor noble. Adolf tried hard to strengthen the central government against the princes by extending the privileges of the free towns whose only overlord was the German king and by alliance with the small barons, the 'knights' who also held their lands as the crown's immediate vassals. But the princes took alarm; Adolf was overthrown and slain by Rudolf's son Albert

**GRANADA THE LAST FOOTHOLD OF MOORISH POWER IN SPAIN**

Iberians, Romans and Vandals had all been dominant in Gránada before the Saracens established themselves there in the eighth century and made the city a splendid capital of the Moorish kingdom of Gránada. As such it flourished, outlasting all the other Moorish states in Spain until 1492, when Boabdil was forced by the Christians under Ferdinand and Isabella to sign away his kingdom. The city is superbly situated on the north-western slope of the Sierra Nevada, overlooking a fertile plain.

*From Hielscher, ' Picturesque Spain,' Fisher Unwin Ltd.*

of Austria (1298), and the electors found themselves unable to avoid his election to the German crown. This second Hapsburg is the Austrian tyrant of the Swiss legend of William Tell.

Louis IX's son Philip III the Rash was personally of no importance, but during his reign (1270–85) the French crown was accidentally strengthened by the reversion of Toulouse with the marquisate of Provence (not the county, which had gone to Charles of Anjou) on the death of the king's uncle Alfonse.

In the three years 1284–6 several monarchs died who were either themselves notable persons, or whose disappearance had notable results : Alfonso the Wise of Castile, then Charles (I of Naples) of Anjou, Peter III (the successor of James I) of Aragon, Philip III of France, and finally Alexander III of Scotland. The last named had been an able ruler, during whose reign the last pretensions of the kings of Norway, long maintained, to the lordship of the north of Scotland and the Hebrides, had been obliterated at

**A BATTLE IN THE THIRTEENTH CENTURY**

Public discontent with the misgovernment of Henry III culminated in 1264 in the Barons' War, in which the battles of Lewes and Evesham were the principal engagements. The strenuous hand-to-hand fighting of the period is depicted in this illustration by Matthew Paris in his *Vita Duorum Offarum*.
*British Museum*

the battle of Largs (1263). His death, followed by that of his daughter 'the Maid of Norway,' gave rise to a disputed succession, of which Edward I took advantage to claim first the suzerainty and then the crown of Scotland itself. The voluntary incorporation of Scotland with England would have been of untold benefit to both countries, but conquest was another matter, and the ultimately successful struggle for liberation meant two and a half centuries of constant hostility between the two.

THE career of Charles of Anjou had been one of unfailing success till shortly before his death. His overthrow of the Hohenstaufen left him undisputed master of the two Sicilies in 1268. As the pope's nominee and professed vassal, he was the obvious head of Guelph Italy, and there was every probability that the suzerain would very soon be the dependant of the vassal. His administrative ability had been thoroughly tested in Anjou and the county of Provence. But there was no question that his Sicilian kingdom had been won by the sword, from the rule of a very able and popular prince ; his new subjects submitted to him perforce and from the start detested him as an alien ; and his French officers and garrisons very soon taught them to detest him, as they had detested Henry VI with his Germans, as a hard and cruel tyrant.

**SIMON DE MONTFORT'S SEAL**

Simon de Montfort (c. 1200–1265) was the dominant figure in the opposition to Henry III and, in virtue of the Assembly he convened in 1265, the founder of the English parliamentary system. He was killed at Evesham.
*British Museum*

On an evening in 1282 the population of Palermo, without warning or premeditation, broke out in a blaze of fury and massacred the French garrison—the ghastly event known as the Sicilian Vespers ; the outbreak was followed by a universal rebellion against the Angevin rule ; and the Sicilians called upon Manfred's son-in-law Peter of Aragon to assume the crown and expel the tyrant. The Aragonese fleet was able entirely to prevent the transport of troops to the island from the peninsula, and the Angevins never recovered a footing in Sicily itself, though they kept their hold on the kingdom of Naples or South Italy.

No effect on the struggle was produced by papal anathemas launched on behalf of Charles. When Charles and Peter both died in 1285, Peter's younger son James continued the conflict with Charles II ; and when James resigned his pretensions on succeeding his elder brother in Aragon in 1291, the invitation of the Sicilians to take his place was accepted by his younger brother Frederick. The strife was at last brought to a close by a peace (1302) which left Sicily to Frederick and Naples to Charles, while the terms by which Sicily was ultimately to revert to the Angevins were never carried out.

In France Philip IV the Fair (1285–1314) continued, by very unscrupulous methods, the policy of bringing into his own hands fiefs large and small at the expense of the greater feudatories, including Edward I of England, the latter being constantly hampered by his conflict with the Scots, whose alliance with

**A MEDIEVAL KNIGHT**
This bronze ewer representing a knight on horseback was found in the river Tyne. It is of English make and dates from about 1300. Ewers in the form of a mounted man were common in the 13th and 14th centuries.
*British Museum*

France at this time became a fixed feature of Scottish history. Actually for France the permanent results of the reign are to be sought in Philip's further development of the centralised administrative system. But its most notable event belongs to the contest with the Papacy, in which both Edward and Philip were involved by the unwise aggression of Boniface VIII.

AFTER the fall of the Hohenstaufen and the rise of Charles of Anjou, Gregory X (1271–6) in the five years of his pontificate displayed qualities which in happier circumstances and a longer reign might have gone far to restore the moral prestige of the Papacy. In the next twenty years there followed a succession of five popes whose chief preoccupation was the elevation of one or another of the rival baronial houses of Savelli,

**HENRY III KING OF ENGLAND**
Henry III died in 1272 and lies in Edward the Confessor's Chapel in Westminster Abbey. His altar tomb rests on a pedestal and is surmounted by a gilt bronze effigy of the king in coronation robes with a simple crown. The now empty hands probably once held the sceptre and the dove.
*From Royal Commission on Historical Monuments in London*

**EDWARD I IN THE HOUSE OF LORDS**
Legislation, establishment of effective adminstration and the subjection of Wales were the principal concern of Edward I in the first fifteen years of his reign. He is here depicted presiding over a session of the House of Lords, Llewelyn of Wales assisting, and also Alexander III, king of Scotland.
*From Pinkerton, 'Iconographia Scotia'*

with Edward, which might have brought him the support of Philip's enemy, by declaring that Scotland (which at the moment was defying the English king) was a papal fief ; to which the reply was given by Edward's newly constituted parliament, nobles and commons, that the pope had nothing to do with the question at issue. Philip, perhaps taking example by Edward, summoned a 'states general' or assembly of the three estates, clergy, nobles and commons, which denounced the papal claims (1302). But he went further. French troops appeared at Anagni where Boniface was at the moment residing ; his person was seized ; and he was so brutally handled that he died a few days later. And no hand was raised to punish the outrage, which rang down the curtain on the age-long struggle for mastery between the spiritual and temporal powers (October, 1303).

Another event in Philip's career, before this terminal date of our chapter, must be recorded. He had found opportunity to dispossess Count Guy of Flanders. The government he set up enraged the burghers of the great Flemish cities ; they burst into revolt ; and when Philip in 1302 sought to crush them, the burgher infantry at Courtrai inflicted a crushing defeat on the chivalry of France arrayed against them. It was the first time, unless Legnano can claim to have been a precedent, that the power of heavy infantry to defeat the onset of the mail-clad horsemen had been demonstrated in medieval warfare.

Here we leave the European record and turn again to Asia and the east.

Orsini or Colonna, until the election of Boniface VIII (1294–1303), who once more endeavoured to assert the authority of Rome over the secular princes of Europe.

In the quite appropriate character of pacificator he offered arbitration between the two powerful kings of France and England, who were fighting over disputed claims in Gascony and Guienne. The kings rejected his arbitration ; whereupon he issued the famous bull ' Clericis Laicos ' forbidding the clergy to pay taxes to their temporal sovereigns without consent of the pope. The kings retorted, Philip by forbidding the export of gold and silver, so that no money from France could reach the papal treasury, Edward by outlawing the clergy till they should make submission. The kings won ; the clergy had to submit, and the pope had to explain the bull away.

But Boniface was not satisfied. He destroyed the chance of a reconciliation

ῖῂULAGU had met with his decisive check at Ain Gelat. He died in 1265. The power of the Mamelukes advanced under the great Sultan Baibars, penetrated to the sultanate of Iconium, extended south to the Sudan, and after his death finally ejected the Christians as a power from Syria. The might of the ilkhans waned, partly from the standing cause, disputed successions ; though at the close of the century a distinguished ruler arose in the person of Ghazan, who adopted Islam and not only produced but enforced a code of laws which did something to restore the prosperity which the Mongol devastations and wars had almost destroyed. It is significant, however, that during the Mongol period literature and poetry continued to flourish both in Farsistan, the heart of Persia, and in Roum.

**SEAL OF PHILIP THE FAIR**

Philip IV (1268–1314) succeeded to the throne of France in 1285 and ranks as one of the greatest of her kings. He died at Fontainebleau, November 29, 1314.

*British Museum*

one half of the produce of the land.

Finally we glance at the Mongol power in its highest manifestation under the greatest of its khans, Kublai, who extended over the whole of China a sway which may fairly be called both beneficent and enlightened. The great ruler's one failure was in his attempt to extend his empire across the sea to Japan, which had been developing in all but complete isolation from the Asiatic continent. For the invading fleets of the Great Khan were twice annihilated by the ships of the islanders or by the elements, and Japan continued to preserve her isolation. The greatness of the Mongol dynasty did not long survive his death, which occurred in 1294.

But during these latter years of the thirteenth century fresh hordes not of Mongols but of Turks were flowing in. The first of their leaders was Suleiman ; the second, Ertogrul, carried them to Asia Minor ; the third, Othman (1288–1326), who gave his name to the whole group, the ' Ottomans,' was even now preparing the way for creating, with Roum as its centre, the coming domination of the Ottoman power.

ℐN India the new Mahomedan empire under the Slave dynasty had the good fortune to escape the attentions of Jenghiz Khan and his successors, from which so many rulers had suffered. Its history is for the most part a bloodstained record of wars, feuds and slaughters of the infidels, highly applauded by the orthodox chroniclers ; and its most notable figure is the grim one of Balban, who 'never laughed,' a slave general under several rulers, who ultimately ascended the throne himself (1266–86). The dynasty was ended in 1290 by the murder of Kaikobad and the accession of Jalal ud-Din Khilji, an old man who was murdered and succeeded by his nephew and son-in-law Ala ud-Din (1294–1316), a ferocious ruler who made a point of oppressing the Hindus, whom he taxed at

**EDWARD I DEFYING THE POPE**

In 1296 Pope Boniface VIII issued the bull 'Clericis Laicos,' prohibiting the imposition of taxes on the clergy. This contemporary drawing depicts the reception of the bull by Edward I, who flatly refused to comply with it.

*British Museum, Cotton MSS., Vitellius A.xiii*

# *Sixth Era*

## TWO CENTURIES OF RENASCENCE

### 1303–1492

---

Chapter 21
### THE PASSING OF THE MIDDLE AGES, 1303—1396

Chapter 22
### BIRTH OF THE RENAISSANCE, 1396—1492

---

THE era now before us is the age of transition from the dying medieval conceptions to the modern expanding outlook upon a world suddenly and vastly enlarged. Medievalism fell with the humiliation of the Church ; the modern world began with the discovery of the New World. The era is one of spiritual degeneration, in which the old ideals have decayed ; the age of the Avignon Papacy, of the Great Schism and of the failure of the Council of Constance to effect a true reformation. It is an age of political turmoil. Hapsburgs and Luxemburgs fail to create an adequate organization for the Empire. England tries twice and fails twice to conquer France. Italy remains a stage of city-state rivalries and internal faction feuds, leading nowhither. Spain thrusts the Moorish power into a corner and, finally, unifying herself, ends it ; but in the east of Europe what still remains of the ancient Roman Empire is obliterated by the Ottoman. In Asia the might of the Mongol collapses after one last terrific eruption. It is an age, nevertheless, of material progress and commercial development. And, in the history of progress generally, it is above all the age of the intellectual revival and the renewed joy in beauty, beginning in Italy and spreading over Europe, which we call the Renaissance. Therefore, we take as our starting point the overthrow of Pope Boniface, and as our terminal point the discovery of the New World by Christopher Columbus.

# TABLE OF DATES FOR CHAPTER 21

1303 Boniface VIII taken prisoner by Philip IV of France.
His death ends the independence of the Papacy.
Andronicus II takes into his service the Grand Company of the Catalans, released from Sicily by the recognition of the Aragonese dynasty.
India : Conquests of Ala ud-Din Khilji in Deccan.

1305 Clement V (French) elected pope ; he remains in France. Beginning of 'Babylonish Captivity.'
Wenzel II, last of the Premislavs of Bohemia, dies without an heir.
William Wallace is captured and killed.

1306 The emperor Albert of Hapsburg procures the Bohemian crown for his son Rudolf.
Robert I Bruce is crowned King of Scots, and heads Scottish revolt against English supremacy.

1307 Edward I dies on Scottish border. Edward II acc.
Henry of Carinthia acc. in Bohemia.
Break up of Seljuk dominion in Asia Minor on death of Ala ud-Din III.
Philip of France attacks the Order of the Knights Templars.

1308 Albert I assassinated ; Henry VII (Luxemburg) emp.

1309 The Angevin Carobert elected king of Hungary.
Pope Clement establishes the Papacy at Avignon.
Naples : Robert, uncle of Carobert, acc.

1310 John of Luxemburg acc. in Bohemia.
Henry VII goes to Italy.

1312 Total suppression of the Templars.
Othman sultan in Asia Minor ; 'Ottoman' power.

1313 Henry VII d.

1314 Two rival emperors elected, Lewis the Bavarian and Frederick of Hapsburg.
Philip IV d. Louis X acc.
Clement V d.
Scotland's independence won at Bannockburn.

1315 Swiss defeat Hapsburgs at Morgarten.

1316 John XXII pope.
Louis X d. His daughter Joan is heiress of Navarre. His brother Philip V succeeds him in France by the recognition of the 'Salic Law.'

1320 India : Khilji dynasty of Delhi overthrown by Ghiyas ud-Din Tughlak.

1322 Galeazzo Visconti acc. at Milan.

1323 Emperor Lewis and Pope John XXII quarrel.

1324 James of Aragon recovers Sardinia.

1325 India : Mohammed Tughlak acc. at Delhi.

1326 Orkhan succeeds Othman.
India : Mohammed transplants Delhi population to Daulatabad.

1327 Edward III acc. Regency of Isabella and Mortimer.

1328 Treaty of Northampton recognizes Scottish independence.
Charles IV d. ; Philip VI of Valois succeeds under the Salic Law. Protest entered on behalf of Edward III of England.
Andronicus II d. Andronicus III acc.

1329 Robert Bruce d. Acc. of David II ; Randolph regent.

1330 Frederick of Hapsburg d. ; Lewis sole emperor.
Edward III suppresses regency in England.

1331 China : Acc. of Shun-Ti, last emperor of the Yuan or Mongol dynasty.
Stephen Dusan acc. as king of Serbia.

1333 Edward III makes Edward Balliol king of Scotland.
Poland : Acc. of Casimir III the Great.

1334 Benedict XII pope.

1337 Edward III asserts claim to the French crown.

1338 India : Mohammed Tughlak sends an expedition to China which fails disastrously.
Edward allies with Flemings as their lawful suzerain.
Meeting of Rhense and Diet of Frankfort repudiate papal intervention in imperial elections.

1339 Edward III invades Picardy. First campaign of the Hundred Years' War.
India : Bengal becomes independent of Delhi.

1340 Naval battle of Sluys ; England mistress of Channel.
Waldemar III in Denmark.

1341 Andronicus III d. ; John V acc.

1342 Hungary : Lewis the Great succeeds Carobert.
Naples : Joanna I succeeds Robert.
Clement VI pope.

1346 Charles (IV) son of John of Bohemia elected king of the Romans. John is killed at battle of Crécy, fighting as ally of France.

1347 India : Rise of Hindu kingdom of Vijayanagar and Bahmani sultanate in Deccan.
Rise and fall of Rienzi in Rome.
Edward III captures Calais.

1347 Lewis the Bavarian d. ; Charles IV of Bohemia and Luxemburg emperor.
John Cantacuzenus joint emperor at Constantinople.

1348 The Black Death devastates Europe.
Charles IV founds Prague University in Bohemia.

1349 Dauphiné annexed to France.
Charles the Bad acc. in Navarre.

1350 John the Good acc. in France.
Pedro the Cruel acc. in Castile.

1351 India : Firoz Shah succeeds Mohammed at Delhi.

1352 Innocent VI pope.

1353 Bern joins the Swiss Confederation.

1354 Cantacuzenus abdicates ; John V sole Greek emperor.
Turks occupy Gallipoli, establishing permanent footing in Europe.

1355 Coronation of Charles IV in Rome.
Stephen Dusan king of Serbia d.

1356 English victory over French at Poitiers ; King John taken prisoner.
Charles IV issues the Golden Bull.

1358 French peasant insurrection (the 'Jacquerie') which is mercilessly stamped out.

1359 Orkhan d. Murad I (Amurath) acc.

1360 Treaty of Brétigny ; height of English power in France.

1361 King John gives duchy of Burgundy to his younger son Philip the Bold ; nucleus of the later Burgundian dominion.
War between Denmark and the Hanseatic League.
Turks capture Adrianople, which becomes their capital.

1362 Urban V pope.

1364 John of France d. ; Charles V the Wise acc.

1366 Pedro the Cruel appeals to the Black Prince for aid against Henry of Trastamara, who is helped by the Breton captain Bertrand du Guesclin.

1367 Black Prince wins battle of Najaro or Navarrete.

1368 Hanseatic fleet takes Copenhagen.
China : Yuan dynasty expelled by Hung Wu, founder of the (native) Ming dynasty.

1369 Henry of Trastamara kills Pedro ; becomes Henry II of Castile.
Renewal of Anglo-French war ; French gradually recover territory.
Tamerlane (Timur) becomes king of Samarkand.

1370 Hanseatic fleet predominant in northern seas.
Casimir III of Poland d., succeeded by Lewis the Great, Angevin king of Hungary.

1371 David II of Scotland d. ; Robert I Stewart acc.

1376 Wenzel, son of the emperor, elected k. of Romans.

1377 Edward III d. ; Richard II acc. ; regency.

1378 Gregory XI dies at Rome where Urban VI is elected. French elect Clement VII. Great Schism begins.
Charles IV d. ; Wenzel acc.

1380 France : Charles VI acc. ; regency.
Lewis the Great d. ; his daughter Mary succeeds in Hungary, Hedwig in Poland.
Decisive defeat of Genoa by Venice.

1381 Naples : Charles III of Durazzo acc.

1382 Albizzi oligarchy set up in Florence.
Mary of Hungary m. Wenzel's brother Sigismund.

1383 Philip of Burgundy through his wife succeeds to most of Netherlands, d.

1385 Growing power of Milan under Gian Galeazzo Visconti.
Charles III of Naples claims Hungarian crown.
Portuguese independence secured at Aljubarotta.

1386 Union of Poland and Lithuania by marriage of Hedwig to Duke Jagellon (k. Ladislas V).
Swiss rout Hapsburg troops at Sempach.
Charles III assassinated. Disputed succession in Naples and Hungary.

1387 Sigismund secures Hungarian crown.
German 'town war.'

1388 India : Firoz Shah d. ; break up of Tughlak dominion.

1389 Hapsburgs recognize Swiss independence.
Turks defeat Slavs at Kossovo. Bajazet I acc.
Boniface IX Roman pope.

1390 Castile : Henry III acc.

1391 Constantinople : Manuel II acc.

1392 Beginning of rivalry in France between Louis of Orléans (Charles' brother) and Burgundy.

1394 Benedict XIII Avignon pope.
Tamerlane breaks up the Tatar Golden Horde.

1395 Wenzel makes Gian Galeazzo duke of Milan.

1396 Bajazet defeats Sigismund at Nicopolis.

### CHAPTER 21

# THE PASSING OF THE MIDDLE AGES: 1303–1396

THE Middle Ages reached their culmination in the thirteenth century. The zenith of the medieval idea of the Papacy was the reign of Innocent III. From the death of Innocent to the middle of the century the most brilliant, intellectually, of the whole line of emperors was reigning ; he was not indeed a typical representative of the medieval idea of the Empire, being a modern born before his time ; but with his death the medieval idea passed away for ever. All that was loveliest in the conceptions of Christianity was embodied in Francis of Assisi. The loftiest ideals of the ages were concentrated in the person not of pope or emperor but in the austere grandeur of Dante, born before two-thirds of the century had passed. In Louis IX chivalry gave its perfected type.

### Renascence after Decadence

IN the two following centuries medievalism has lost its ideals. It is passing. Something remains of its glamour, more of its glitter, hardly anything of its intensity ; but something else is being born or reborn, incompatible with that which is dying. Upon the Crusading Era follow the two centuries of renascence, an age of fermenting diversities, of individual developments, from which are being evolved the new state system, the new political organization, the new social structure, the new outlook moral and intellectual, which, with the new geographical horizons, differentiate the modern from the medieval world.

We cannot, then, as heretofore distinguish the steps in a stage-by-stage movement as it progresses in Europe or in the East ; we divide this era into two chapters, practically corresponding to the fourteenth and fifteenth centuries, as a matter of convenience merely. The Era has a definite starting point and a definite closing point ; but throughout there are no dominating ideas and no dominating personalities whose appearance or disappearance provide a marked line of division. Moreover the chronicler for a time has not two or three main streams to follow to which the rest are subsidiary ; he has only a number of minor streams— the progress of individual states—variously interlacing.

### The Far East: Conditions in Japan

FOR the first time our last chapter brought within our purview a Far Eastern nation, growing up in an isolation practically unbroken in the past and broken only occasionally for centuries to come. Seeds gathered from China had been sown among the Japanese, but in most respects their development had been to all appearance almost completely indigenous. For an unknown number of centuries Japan had been ruled by the royal house of the 'mikados' which is on the throne at the present day, a house far older than any in Europe. Both Confucian and Buddhist doctrines had found their way to Japan, and she had done battle with China for Korea.

Like the Chinese her people had been divided into four classes, military, mercantile, agricultural and artisan. She had entered probably upon a feudal stage at about the same time as western Europe, when great territorial houses became rivals for ascendancy, more or less dominating the mikado, the official head of the state ; the chief bearing the title of 'shogun,' and being in effect the ruler of the country.

In the twelfth century Yoritomo, of the Minamoto clan, had established a supremacy which enabled him to carry out an immense reorganization ; then the Minamoto were superseded by the Hojo, who broke up an attempt of the mikado to recover power, relegated the shogun as well as the mikado to the position of a puppet, and assumed the title of 'shikkén'

**FOUNDER OF THE SHOGUNATE**

Yoritomo (1147–1199) was head of the Minamoto family. In 1192 he was invested with the title of Sei-i-Tai Shogun (barbarian-subduing generalissimo) and instituted a system of government based on military administration which, exercising its power from Kamakura, remained effective for centuries.

or regent, under which they ruled. It was the Hojo Tokimune who organized the defence of Japan against Kublai Khan. But with his death, three years after the great triumph, degeneracy set in. In 1333 the Hojo power was destroyed in a civil war by the mikado Go-Daigo, but he did not succeed in restoring the power of the crown. The regency disappeared but the Shogunate was revived by the Ashikaga who had helped Go-Daigo to victory. Their ascendancy as shoguns lasted for more than two hundred years, but they were centuries of perpetual civil strife, though a notably brilliant period of Japanese art and literature.

In China the Mongol or—to give it its Chinese name—Yuan dynasty survived the death of Kublai for some three-quarters of a century. Kublai, great ruler though he was, never became popular ; the Mongol was an alien, and whatever the merits of his government might be, however tolerant and beneficial, it was the government of an alien. That it was beneficial there is no manner of doubt, but it remained unacceptable. His successors lacked his ability ; thirty years after his death the fourth of them was

murdered ; nine years covered the next three reigns ; and though the eighth and last— called Shun-Ti by the Chinese —was not actually deposed till thirty-five years later, the dynasty was obviously moribund before the beginning of his reign, which was full of disasters and rebellions.

The man who overthrew the foreign dynasty was Chu Yüan-chang, who deserted a Buddhist monastery to join an insurgent leader on the Yang-tse, and, being a born captain and organizer, became first his right-hand man and then his successor in the chieftain-ship in 1355. His power extended rapidly ; he captured Nanking ; the imperial forces were continually defeated ; and in 1368 he marched on the capital, Peking. The fall of Peking ended the Mongol supremacy. The victor was proclaimed emperor with the imperial name of Hung Wu, and once more a native dynasty, the Ming, was established. Shun-Ti escaped to Mongolia, but died in 1370.

The conqueror reigned for thirty years, during which he restored the Hanlin College and the educational system, made a new codification of the laws, and did what one man could do to cleanse the corrupt administration of justice. Doubt-less he would have done still more if the attempts of the Mongols to recover their lost power had not forced upon him con-tinuous warfare during the latter years of his reign, which ended in 1398.

### Mongol meets Mameluke

ALTHOUGH Kublai, as Great Khan, had been technically lord of the entire dominion wherein the Mongols held sway from the China seas to the Black Sea, his concentration on China had limited his real rule to that sufficiently vast country, while his brother Hulagu and Hulagu's successors ruled the west in practical independence. The expansion had reached its limit when it met its unexpected check at the hands of the Mamelukes in 1260 ; from that time the 'ilkhans' lost much ground, gained none, and found their grip on what they held continuously weakening. Syria went to the Egyptians—Baibars discovered and set up a dummy khalif of the Abbasid house who had escaped the massacre at Bagdad—and while Asia Minor was between the Mongol hammer and the Mameluke anvil, the Ottoman Turks under Ertogrul, and then Osman, displaced the old Seljuk lordship and made themselves its masters, defeating the efforts of the Palaeologi at Constantinople to recover some of the old Greek Empire. In the fourteenth century, after the death of Ghazan, the Mongol empire in the West was in dissolution as palpably as in the Far East, central Asia breaking up into independent principalities after the time-honoured fashion.

The Mahomedan empire or sultanate of Delhi, created at the beginning of the thirteenth century by Shahab ud-Din of Ghor, was continuous, in the sense

that an unbroken succession of sultans reigned at Delhi for some three hundred years without being displaced by new conquerors from beyond the mountains or overturned by rival Indian powers. But no dynasty was continuous ; that is, no family held the sultanate for many generations. In the thirteenth century very few of the so-called Slave dynasty ruled with any pretence to a hereditary title. The three sultans who next reigned from 1290 to 1318 are known as the Khilji dynasty, the three from 1320 to 1388 as the Tughlaks. Under one or another of the more powerful of the Slaves, Khiljis or Tughlaks the Delhi empire extended to huge dimensions, but by the middle of the fourteenth century it was breaking up, and before the century was ended Delhi was no more than one among many Mohamedan principalities.

One feature was common to the entire series of sultans ; they slaughtered Hindus without compunction on any pretext which had some colour of plausibility, and

**ENFORCED FLIGHT OF A MIKADO AS DEPICTED BY A JAPANESE ARTIST**

In the middle of the twelfth century a dispute concerning the succession to the imperial throne of Japan brought about a prolonged conflict between the great military families the Taira and the Minamoto, which affords a curious parallel to the Wars of the Roses in England. One of the puppet mikados around whom this quarrel raged was Go-Shirakawa ; in 1159 he was abducted and consigned to exile—an episode illustrated in this picture by a thirteenth-century Japanese artist.

*British Museum*

P

**GATE IN DELHI BUILT BY ALA UD-DIN**

Ala ud-Din Khilji, most famous and most ruthless of the Mahomedan conquerors of India, secured the throne of Delhi in 1294 and forthwith set about an invasion of the Deccan which, as well as Gujarat, Rajputana and Madura, he subjected to Islam. He died at Delhi in 1316.

*Photo, F. Deaville Walker*

and in 1320 an able soldier of Turkish descent, Ghiyas ud-Din Tughlak, was raised to the sultanate by election. Five years later Tughlak Shah's death was compassed by his son Mohammed.

From 1325 to 1351 Mohammed's reign presented an unparalleled example of the monstrosities which may be achieved by absolute power wielded by a man wholly unbalanced but yet endowed with brilliant intellectual qualities and an unfettered imagination. He chose to set up a new capital which he called Daulatabad, in the Deccan, and ordered the inhabitants of Delhi to clear out of that vast city in three days, and transfer themselves to this new abode. He punished all offences indiscriminately with death, often in the most repulsive forms. He extended his sovereignty southward to Mysore and Calicut ; but he sent to conquer Khorassan a vast army of which only fragments returned, and another through Nepal and the Himalayas to conquer China, which met a like fate.

taxed them to the utmost limit of their capacity. To the Hindu the Mahomedan was below caste ; but practically the Mahomedans formed one ruling caste which was not the lowest but the highest. Of all the sultans none was perhaps quite so systematic and thorough in his persecution of the Hindus as Ala ud-Din Khilji, who was on the Delhi throne at the beginning of the fourteenth century. His theory was quite simply avowed; they were to work for the benefit of the ruling race, but were themselves to derive no profit from their toil ; all was to be torn from them except the bare margin on which they could maintain life.

Ala ud-Din annexed Gujarat, and his armies ravaged far into the Deccan. A famous episode of his reign was the fall of the Rajput stronghold of Chitor, where the Rajputs held out to the last gasp, until further resistance was manifestly hopeless ; when all their women were gathered together to perish in a vast holocaust and, the fires having been kindled, the men sallied forth and fought till all were slain. After his death in 1316, most of his kindred were extirpated,

### Decline of the Delhi Sultanate

THE Mahomedan governor of Bengal revolted and achieved independence. When the spirit moved him Mohammed devastated his own territories. His taxation reduced his subjects to abject poverty, while he lavished the fruit of his exactions upon hospitals and upon men of learning. In his private life he was rigid in following the precepts of the Koran, and considered it necessary to procure from the Mamelukes' puppet khalif in Egypt the formal recognition of his sultanate. Apparently he was quite satisfied that as sultan he was but setting an admirable example as a model ruler, while we are told that the approaches to his court were stacked with the unburied corpses of the victims of his ' justice.'

Mohammed died in 1351—not, strangely enough, by the dagger of an assassin, but of a fever. He was succeeded by his cousin Firoz Shah. Long before his death the vast empire of the Delhi sultans was breaking up. Bengal had broken away comparatively early. By the middle of his reign—the dates are uncertain—the Hindus of the southern Deccan gave check to the Mahomedan advance and were establishing a great Hindu monarchy at Vijayanagar. About 1347 one of the sultan's generals in the northern Deccan, Zafar Khan, declared his independence, took the title of Ala ud-Din, and established what is known as the Bahmani dynasty (Mahomedan) in that quarter ; where for the rest of the century he and his successors waged savage wars with the Hindu princes of the Deccan. For two hundred years the whole of southern India was lost to the Delhi empire, though it remained a continuous battlefield between Mahomedan and Hindu powers.

Firoz Shah (1351–88) was a ruler of a very different type from Mohammed ; but the dead tyrant had so utterly sapped the foundations of the empire that a succession of Firoz Shahs could hardly have saved it ; though the finishing blow was not dealt till ten years after his death by the invasion of Timur the Destroyer —the Tamerlane of western literature— the Barlas Turk who is commonly called Tatar or Mongol. But Timur's career belongs mainly to the next chapter.

During his long sultanate Firoz strove to restore sound government, to remedy the economic ruin, and even to recover some of the already lost dominions. His wars were perfunctory, and if they escaped actual discredit they did nothing to strengthen the empire. But he was earnest in the pursuit of justice ; his rule, though not lacking in firmness, was notably mild, and exceptionally so towards the Hindus, though he could be intolerant enough to Shiah heretics. Incidentally, by remitting the poll-tax on Hindus to all who should become converts to Islam, he appreciably increased the Mahomedan population.

He was neither a hero nor a genius, but save in respect of military prowess it would be hard to name one of his predecessors more deserving of praise. When the old man died, there was no strong man to take up the responsibilities which he had himself assumed with extreme reluctance, and the still great realm went rapidly to pieces. For some time to come the most vigorous powers in India were not the northern sultans but the rival principalities in the Deccan.

### Rival Powers in the Near East

OUR scene shifts then to Asia Minor and the Balkan peninsula. The revived Greek Empire was in fact nothing more than a minor kingdom important merely because it held the almost impregnable fortress which was the gateway between Asia and Europe. Otherwise it controlled only a fragment of territory on each continent, while the larger islands were in the hands of the Venetians or the Knights of S. John ; the Venetians or independent dukes ruled in the Morea (the Peloponnese) ; and the Genoese, who had been repaid for their services to the Palaeologi by the concession of large privileges, fought with their Venetian rivals for ascendancy in the eastern trade and eastern waters. In the Balkans and on the Danube, Bulgaria and Serbia held independent sway, but the definite ascendancy was passing from the

**WAR-SCARRED FORTRESS OF DAULATABAD**
Crowning an isolated rock the hill-fortress of Daulatabad is an imposing memorial of Mahomedan rule in India. Constructed in the thirteenth century, it was captured by Ala ud-Din in 1294 and made the capital of the empire by Mohammed Tughlak. Later it passed to the Bahmani and Mogul dynasties.
*Photo, E.N.A.*

former to the latter, whose successive monarchs all bore the name of Stephen. Michael VIII at Constantinople was succeeded by his son Andronicus II (1282–1328), well-meaning but inefficient.

There was a moment when Andronicus had the opportunity of making at least a serious bid for the reconquest of Asia Minor, when the Seljuk power was breaking up and the Ottomans were not yet established in their place. In 1303 the troops from Catalonia, by whose aid Frederick of Sicily had just secured his crown, were seeking lucrative employment, and the 'Grand Company of the Catalans' took service with Andronicus. But he failed to make due use of them—he had in effect no army of his own worthy the name. They were sent across the Bosporus, but, getting neither military support nor pay, they broke with the emperor and lived at ease on the country, until it suited their convenience to transfer their services to another sovereign. From 1321 to 1328 the Empire was given up to civil war between the emperor and his grandson, who finally defeated and deposed him, and assumed the purple as Andronicus III (1328–41).

### Rapid Growth of Ottoman power

In 1307, on the death of the Seljuk sultan Ala ud-Din, Othman had appropriated the title and established a general supremacy in Asia Minor, the more easily since the Catalans had departed. Just before Othman's death in 1326 he had taken Brusa, which was made the Ottoman capital, and under his son Orkhan the Ottoman power advanced rapidly. In 1330 he captured Nicaea, and within a few years all that remained to Andronicus III in Asia was a strip of coast. More notable, however, even than his conquests was Orkhan's ingenious and extremely successful plan for providing himself with a new army and a new staff of administrators.

The standing condition upon which Christians under Turkish rule were allowed the exercise of their religion was the payment of tribute ; Orkhan instituted a tribute of children. Those children were brought up as Mahomedans and then drafted either into an imperial guard, the famous Janissaries, or into a sort of civil service, a sphere for which the Turk showed an unfailing incapacity. By this system the sultan held under his immediate control the best troops in his service and a trained body of non-Turkish administrators entirely dependent on his personal favour.

Andronicus III died in 1341. He left a so-called empire smaller even than it had been on his accession ; for while the Ottomans were extending their territories at his expense in Asia, the most vigorous of Serbian kings, Stephen Dusan (1333–55), was tearing from him his Balkan lands. Both processes continued unremittingly in the following years. He himself had been thoroughly incompetent ; he was succeeded by an infant, John V, while the government remained in the hands of his minister John Cantacuzenus, who shared the throne with the boy-emperor till his own deposition, from 1347 to 1354.

### Turks obtain a Footing in Europe

CONSTANTINOPLE only escaped capture by Stephen Dusan because of the city's impregnable strength ; the intrigues and bargainings of the domestic factions with the external enemies present a nauseous picture ; and in 1354 Orkhan established for the first time what proved to be a permanent footing in Europe by capturing and occupying Gallipoli, while Genoese and Venetians were fighting not the Turks but each other for the mastery of the sea. In 1361 Orkhan's successor, Murad (Amurath) I, captured Adrianople, which remained the Turkish capital in Europe till the fall of Constantinople in 1453. John V, failing to obtain aid from the West, acknowledged himself the vassal, and in 1381 the tributary, of the Ottoman.

In fact the resistance to the Turks in Europe was maintained not by the Empire but by the Slavonic states ; and Murad before his assassination in 1379 (when he was succeeded by Bajazet) shattered the armies of a great coalition which had formed against him at Kossovo. As a result Serbia was brought into Bajazet's obedience, he annexed Bulgaria, and beyond the Danube Wallachia became his tributary. Probably Constantinople itself would have fallen but for the devastating advance of Tamerlane, whose story is more conveniently postponed to the next Chronicle, though the growth of his power is commonly dated from 1369 when he established his sovereignty in Samarkand.

### Beginning of the ' Babylonish Captivity '

WE left the West at the point where the long struggle of the Papacy to subordinate the secular powers to its supremacy received its death-blow at the hands of Philip the Fair. Boniface's successor, Benedict XI, could not venture an attempt to reside in Rome, where the Colonna faction, the enemies of the dead pope, were dominant ; within a year he too was dead. Some months later, in 1305, by a compromise between the Italian and French parties, the archbishop of Bordeaux, who was supposed to be an adherent of Edward I and therefore an enemy of Philip, was elected to the Papacy as Clement V ; but the papal coronation took place at Lyons—not yet annexed to France—and in 1309 Clement took up his residence at Avignon, which continued to be the abode of the popes for nearly seventy years ; a period known as the Babylonish Captivity.

For though Avignon was not in France but in Provence, which belonged to the Angevin house of Naples, the Papacy while it resided there was necessarily dominated by French influences ; and all Europe regarded it—in spite of its occasional restiveness—as the virtual dependent of France. Even its spiritual authority sank very low, though not so low as in the years which followed, the disastrous years of the period which is known as the Great Schism.

There too is told the final tragedy of the great Order of the Knights of the Temple. Of the three Orders the Teutonic Knights had already devoted themselves to the battle with paganism and barbarism in the Baltic lands ; the Knights of S. John remained as an outpost to uphold the Cross against the Crescent in the eastern Mediterranean, keeping a precarious hold for long centuries ; the Templars might perhaps have embarked on a new career as the Papacy's fleshly arm, since they had discarded their several

political nationalities and owed allegiance to no secular sovereign. But they had an ill reputation, vast wealth, no friends and many enemies ; and it was not long before Philip gave the finishing touch to his overthrow of the papal power by exterminating the order and appropriating much of its wealth, two years before his own death in 1314.

Before the close of his reign Philip had done much to strengthen France and the French monarchy. He had indeed failed to establish the mastery of Flanders which had been one of his main aims, and he had gained little by his wars with his great feudatory in Aquitaine, Edward I of England ; but Edward's death and the accession of his incompetent son Edward II in 1307 enabled him to make further encroachments in that region, and the preoccupation with Italian schemes of the emperor Henry VII allowed him to effect the annexation of Lyons in 1312.

But much more important than the territorial acquisitions which he owed to accident rather than skill was his development of the legal machinery which transferred much of the fiscal and judicial administration from the nobles to the hands of trained lawyers. Of the legal bodies or corporations thus created the

### GREAT SEAL OF EDWARD I

Edward I (1239–1307) ranks as one of England's greatest kings. He systematised the English laws, gave the English parliamentary system its definite form and defied the Papacy's pretensions to secular supremacy.

*British Museum*

most famous was the 'parlement' of Paris which acquired an extraordinary constitutional authority. It had, however, no resemblance to the English parliament which had just received its permanent shape at the hands of Edward I, being a body of professional lawyers, not of the people's representatives, and having no powers of legislation or taxation.

When Philip became king of France, son had followed father on the French throne in unbroken succession for three hundred years. Philip had three sons and several daughters; but all his grandsons, save one who died in infancy, were the children of his daughters. For the first time therefore a question of the right of succession to the French throne was obviously impending. There was no law generally recognized in Europe. Custom had varied in different kingdoms. Everyone accepted the view that a son had prior rights over a daughter,

**HIGH COURT JUDGES**

One notable legal reform in the reign of Edward I was the formation of a professional class of trained lawyers, not ecclesiastics, from whom a small number of royal justices was appointed.

*British Museum, Royal MS. 6, E.vii*

a brother over a sister; but in the absence of male offspring would a daughter or a daughter's son have priority over a brother, or over a cousin whose descent in the male line from the common royal ancestor was unbroken ?

When the question became acute, France answered it for herself by declaring that the right of succession lay in the unbroken male line, giving it, after Philip's own sons, to his nephew Philip (VI) of Valois; and in due course his daughter's son, Edward III of England, challenged that nephew's right. The result was the prolonged struggle known as the Hundred Years' War. That war, which ended in the complete expulsion of the English from all France except the Calais Pale, had an immense effect on the commercial and political development of both countries.

Edward I died seven years before Philip. Like the latter in France he had greatly advanced the consolidation of his kingdom. He had finally united Wales to England and all but effected the annexation of Scotland, though his death postponed the union of the English and Scottish crowns for three hundred years. The attempt is a classic example of a policy sound in itself pursued by aggressive methods which made it utterly abortive, to the serious detriment of both England and Scotland. When the issue was made one not of voluntary union but of forcible subjection, the Scots preferred liberty to material prosperity, and won it against heavy odds on the field of Bannockburn in 1314, when

**HARLECH CASTLE IN MERIONETHSHIRE**

With the execution of David in 1283 following the death of his brother Llewelyn in 1282, Welsh independence was completely suppressed. To keep North Wales in permanent subjection, Edward I built Conway, Carnarvon, Criccieth and Harlech castles, this last on the site of an earlier Roman fortress.

*Photo, Great Western Railway*

for the second time, as at Courtrai, the phalanx of spearmen utterly shattered the charging squadrons of mailed knights. How they might have fared had the old king been living to lead the English army is another question.

As with Philip IV, however, Edward I's greatness lay not in his military achievements, which give him high rank as a captain, but in his practical application of ideas of government, which saved England alike from feudal anarchy and from despotism. That the effects which he produced were those which he had in view is more than doubtful. In giving to the national assembly or parliament a permanent shape which was primarily intended to counterbalance the power of the great barons, he was obliged also to acknowledge very reluctantly limitations to the powers of the crown, which made it dependent on the good will of the commons whenever it might be in need of more than the restricted supplies recognized as customary. When neither new taxes could be raised nor new laws made without the assent of an elected body which was quite capable of withholding assent on occasion, and the administration of justice was very largely in the hands of trained lawyers who had nothing to fear and no inducement to show favour, England was provided with checks on monarchical and feudal tyranny such as no other country enjoyed.

The work thus accomplished by the great

**EFFIGY OF EDWARD II**

Edward II (b. 1284), a weak and worthless king, was deposed, and murdered at Berkeley Castle, September 21, 1327. His tomb in Gloucester Cathedral is a masterpiece of Gothic art.

*From Stothard, ' Monumental Effigies '*

Edward survived the incapacity of his son and the factions among the barons. In Edward II's reign Scotland won in 1314 the independence which was confirmed by the treaty of Northampton in 1328, the year after the deposition and murder of the feeble king in favour of his young son Edward III. In the same year the third of Philip IV's sons died and Philip VI of Valois became king of France, though not without the entering of a formal protest on the part of Edward, who nevertheless did homage for his French possessions.

The young English king strove unsuccessfully to recover the suzerainty of Scotland, when her great king Robert was dead and a child, David II, wore his crown, by lending aid to a rival claimant, Edward Balliol. But though Scotland was distracted, to subjugate her had proved a task too hard for his grandfather, and the English king's eyes were soon turned in a more promising direction. He resented his position as a feudatory instead of an independent prince in Aquitaine ; English trade with the great Flemish cities was throttled by the connexion of Flanders with the French crown ; the Flemings would back him in a claim that he, not Philip of Valois, was their lawful suzerain. His own claim to the French crown might be flimsy enough, but in the circumstances it was a card worth playing, not so much for the sovereignty of France as for that of Aquitaine and

**DAVID II AND EDWARD III**

David II of Scotland (left), 1324–71, spent eleven years in Edward III's hands after his defeat at Nevile's Cross in 1346. The proposed union of the two kingdoms under Edward had David's assent, but was rejected by Scotland.

*British Museum, Cotton MSS., Nero D.vi*

glamour and pageantry been more picturesquely set forth than in the pages of its chronicler Froissart. Victories snatched by small forces brilliantly led against overwhelming numbers, chivalry shown to a conquered foe, indomitable courage and endurance, heroic self-sacrifice—a glittering picture, not without a real splendour ; and, on the other side of it, the 'mirror of knightly chivalry,' the Black Prince, massacring the helpless civilians of Limoges and leading his armies to fight for the unspeakable Pedro the Cruel of Castile.

In 1340, really the first year of the war, the English naval supremacy in the narrow seas was established by a decisive victory in the harbour of Sluys. The repeated victories of the English by land over apparently superior forces during the next twenty years were mainly due to their development of the longbow, an arm of which they had a complete monopoly, giving them the same sort of advantage as would be enjoyed by troops armed with magazine rifles fighting against troops equipped with arms no more deadly than muzzle-loading muskets. Of these English victories the classic examples are those of Crécy (1346), Poitiers (1356) and, in a much later phase of the war, Agincourt (1415).

Flanders. In 1338 he propounded that claim, and in 1339 the first campaign of the Hundred Years' War opened.

Rarely has the ultimate futility of war been more decisively displayed than in that long struggle, and never have its

**ENGLAND'S KING DOING HOMAGE FOR HIS FRENCH POSSESSIONS**

On the death of Philip IV's youngest son, Charles IV, in 1328, the senior male line of the Capet became extinct, and by a decision of the French peers—to which, much later, the term Salic Law was attached—the succession was given to Philip of Valois. Edward III, as son of Philip IV's daughter, Isabella, disputed this decision, but ultimately consented to do homage to Philip VI for his possessions in Guienne. The incident is thus illustrated in a fourteenth-century French chronicle.

*British Museum, Royal MS. 20 C.vii*

In actual contact with the enemy Edward III and his eldest son, the Black Prince, were superb commanders, though they presently found a rival in the Breton captain, Bertrand du Guesclin. But their triumphs were merely brilliant episodes redounding to their fame and the prestige of the English arms, battles fought to extract themselves from the very tight places into which they had blundered. The one really important capture was that of Calais—starved into surrender because the French failed to come to its relief (1347)—which remained a gateway for the invasion of France for two hundred years and a base for the development of English trade on the Continent.

The result, however, of the twenty years of fighting was that England was able to extort from France the treaty of Brétigny (so-called) in 1360, which if its terms had been loyally carried out would have left the king of England possessor in free sovereignty of all Aquitaine, the Calais Pale and the Channel Islands. But both sides found in the actions of the other warrant for breaking away from the understandings, and in 1370 the war was renewed.

**RELICS OF EDWARD THE BLACK PRINCE**

The tomb of Edward the Black Prince (1330–1376), eldest son of Edward III, with a remarkably fine portrait effigy (right), is in the Trinity Chapel of Canterbury cathedral. Above it hang his surcoat, his helmet and wooden shield with leather covering (left), gauntlets and scabbard.

*From Vetusta Monumenta and Stothard, 'Monumental Effigies'*

### Diminution of England's Glory

ᴅURING the ten years' truce a young and very able king had come to the French throne; on the other hand, Edward was prematurely senile, and the Black Prince had ruined his own health and the finances of Aquitaine, of which his father had made him prince, by a campaign in Spain on behalf of Pedro the Cruel of Castile; mainly because the French were supporting the rival claimant to the throne, Henry of Trastamara; of which the only fruit was a brilliant victory (Navarrete), which secured to Pedro a happily brief tenure of his crown. The Black Prince returned to England to die; his brother, John of Gaunt, was a hopeless failure as a commander; an English fleet suffered at the hands of a Spanish fleet a disaster which for a time broke the English naval ascendancy; and when Edward died in 1377 he held, Calais excepted, less in France than forty years earlier. Though not technically ended, the war was in effect suspended for nearly forty years.

In the early days of the war not the combatants only but all Europe had been devastated by the appalling visitation known as the Black Death, an epidemic of what we now call bubonic plague. To its effects upon the rural populations

P*

**HOW ENGLAND SECURED THE MASTERY OF THE SEA AT THE BATTLE OF SLUYS**

In 1340, when Edward III claimed the throne of France and thereby opened the Hundred Years' War, he claimed also the Sovereignty of the Narrow Sea. He made that claim good the same year when, on June 24, he destroyed the French navy at the Battle of Sluys. Edward in person led the English fleet of 200 sail into the roadstead where the French fleet, 190 strong, lay at anchor, and in a long succession of hand-to-hand conflicts carried ship after ship with terrific slaughter. Of the entire French fleet only 24 ships got away. This drawing of the naval victory dates from c. 1350, only ten years later.

*British Museum, Royal MS. 20 D1*

must be mainly attributed the desperate rising of the French peasantry known as the Jacquerie (1358) and the later English peasant revolt called Wat Tyler's (1381) ; but contributory causes were the demoralisation of the English of all classes wrought by the war, and the intensification of the miseries of the French peasantry in whose midst the war was carried on. The result in England was merely a temporary check in the continuous economic movement towards emancipation from serfdom, the substitution of free for forced labour ; but in France it riveted the chains of serfdom more tightly than before.

### Economic Effects of the French Wars

IN other respects, too, the war had directly contrary effects in England and France. The boldest and most adventurous of England's sons were away fighting on foreign soil, but the country was not devastated by the tramp of soldiery ; she held the seas and her communications with Flanders and Aquitaine were practically uninterrupted. Edward had been very largely actuated by the commercial motive in starting the war, and he made the most of it for commercial purposes, having realized, like his grandfather, that the prosperity of his subjects was a source of strength to the crown; so that it may be said that England's commercial prosperity dates from his reign and was almost nursed into life by his encouragement. Whereas the war, carried on upon French soil, with the Black Death on the top of it, was utterly ruinous to France's industrial development.

Again, the foundations of parliamentary power were strengthened in England by the heavy demands of the crown for supplies for military purposes, obtainable only with the good will of both commons and lords. Edward's attempts to override the law were frus-

trated by parliament's control of the purse strings. In France the States-General attempted to acquire corresponding powers and did for a moment gain actual control of the government; but it drove the crown and the nobles to coalesce, while its conduct of the war showed no improvement ; the lead taken by Paris under the provost of the merchants, Etienne Marcel, was resented outside the capital ; the revolutionary government was overthrown ; and the promise of a parliament for France on the English model was throttled at birth (1358).

In fact, Charles V the Wise (1364–80), first as crown prince while his father, John, was a prisoner in England, and then as king, was able to increase the power of the monarchy, though at the same time future dangers were being multiplied by the extension of the practice of bestowing great appanages on members of the royal family, a practice most unhappily copied by the king of England. Dauphiné, a province of the old Arelate, was bequeathed to Philip VI just before his death in 1350, and became the appanage of the crown prince, known henceforth

**CAVALRY IN ACTION AT POITIERS**

At Poitiers, in 1356, an attack by the French mounted vanguard was repelled in confusion by the English archers. The Black Prince's cavalry then charged, and another body of cavalry, taking the French in flank, routed the French host. This illustration is from a nearly contemporary French manuscript.

*British Museum, Sloane MS. 2433*

as the dauphin. At the end of John's reign the duchy of Burgundy, already a French fief, lapsed to the crown through failure of heirs, and was bestowed on his youngest son, Philip the Bold, whose possessions were further immensely increased by his marriage to the heiress of the county of Burgundy (Franche Comté) and of Artois, which were not under French suzerainty. As a consequence, the dukes of Burgundy for the next century and a half were virtually independent princes who were a constant menace to their cousins on the French throne.

Edward died in 1377, leaving his throne to the young son of the Black Prince, Richard II, while earldoms were accumulating in the hands of the young king's uncles. Charles V died in 1380, leaving his throne to a son, Charles VI, who had long fits of insanity. Both countries were plunged into endless faction troubles

headed by princes of the royal family, of which it is unnecessary here to say more than that the active continuance of the struggle between England and France was thereby postponed for more than a generation.

### Unrest and Confusion in Germany

THE only chance for the consolidation of Germany was to be looked for in the accession of a continuous dynasty of able rulers ; which was precisely the last thing desired by the German princes. They had elected Rudolf of Hapsburg because he was a noble of only second or third rank. He raised the house of Hapsburg to the first rank, so they chose Adolf of Nassau as his successor instead of his son Albert. Albert was strong enough to overthrow Adolf and impose himself on the electors. For ten years (1 98-1308) he strove with considerable success to carry

**BURGHERS OF CALAIS SURRENDERING TO EDWARD III**

His capture of Calais in 1347 was Edward III's most important achievement in the first twenty years of the war with France. This picture from an illuminated fifteenth-century manuscript of the St. Albans Chronicle, now in Lambeth Library, depicts the well-known incident of the arrival of the burghers of Calais in shirts and with halters round their necks to make submission to Edward III, who was only induced to spare their lives by the entreaty of his consort, Philippa of Hainault.

*Lambeth Palace Library*

out his predecessor's policy of freeing the great towns and expanding his own family's possessions ; but assassination cut short his career, and the electors chose Henry VII (of Luxemburg). Henry, reviving the old dream of Italy as the true centre of the Empire, deserted Germany in pursuit of that dream, and died in the fifth year of his reign (1313). One group of electors then chose Frederick of Hapsburg, while the opposition group chose Lewis, duke of Upper Bavaria. A desultory war between the rivals occupied the next nine years. In 1322 Frederick was taken prisoner.

Since Henry's death the Avignon popes Clement V and John XXII had striven to revive, through their ally the Angevin king of Naples (Robert, son of Charles II), the ' Guelph ' domination of North Italy ; and now John XXII thought fit to revive the old papal-imperial conflict by claiming that the rivals for the imperial crown should submit the case to his judgement, and by excommunicating Lewis when he ignored the demand. The thunders of Avignon no longer inspired the awe of the Vatican thunders. Nevertheless, Lewis alternated between defying them till his own victory was in sight, and then quailing under them.

Within the Church the Franciscan order maintained doctrines which brought them into direct collision with the popes (who found their most zealous supporters in the rival Order of Dominicans) and made them champions of the imperial against the papal pretensions ; and the new conflict was entirely despoiled of its original aspect as a contest between the spiritual and the temporal authority. It led to nothing, beyond its effect in intensifying Lewis's natural irresolution. It failed entirely to create in Germany, as it had always

CORONATION OF CHARLES V OF FRANCE
Charles V (1337–80) became the real ruler of France in 1356, when his father, John II, was taken prisoner to England after the battle of Poitiers, but he did not actually succeed to the throne until 1364. His coronation at Reims is thus depicted in one of the manuscripts of Froissart's Chronicles.
*Bibliothèque Nationale, Paris, MS. 2643 ; from De Witt, ' Froissart '*

created before, a strong clerical opposition to the emperor, since it was felt as a French even more than a papal interference in German affairs. Such was the result of the blow that Philip IV of France had dealt to the Papacy in 1303. Yet when Lewis died in 1347 it was the papal candidate, Charles IV, of Luxemburg and Bohemia, who succeeded him.

Had Lewis known how to make use of his advantages, he might well have won a great triumph. The national sentiment which united Germany in defying foreign intervention might have been turned to the consolidation of Germany under a national leader. But he threw away his chances. He wasted his energies on the old Italian will-o'-the-wisp ; he cringed for absolution when victory was in his hands ; and he alienated his own supporters by his greed in snatching territories for the magnification of the house of Wittelsbach. In 1338 he had the almost unanimous backing of the princes, who solemnly pronounced at Rense and Frankfort that the election of an emperor by the German electors was final, needing no papal ratification, and even denounced forfeiture against nobles who should take arms against the emperor or refuse to obey his summons to arms ; yet in 1346 five electors declared him deposed, and nominated Charles IV as king of the Romans in his place ; though the succession did not take effect till the death of Lewis in 1347.

Charles was the grandson of the Luxemburg emperor Henry VII ; and he was king of Bohemia. Before proceeding with the story of his reign as emperor, we must turn back to that of the lands which lay on the eastern marches of Germany itself, of which hitherto there has only been incidental mention.

When Ottocar of Bohemia was defeated and killed by Rudolf of Hapsburg, he was

**RICHARD II OF ENGLAND**

This panel of a diptych at Wilton House represents Richard II kneeling before his patron saints, S. Edmund, Edward the Confessor and John the Baptist. It was painted, perhaps, by an English artist, soon after Richard's accession in 1377.
*Courtesy of the Earl of Pembroke*

succeeded on the throne by his son Wenzel II, who died in 1306. The murder of his son Wenzel III next year ended the Premyslav dynasty of Bohemia. In 1301 died Andrew III, the last of the Arpad dynasty in Hungary. Both countries had to find new rulers, and for a while there were rival candidates for both crowns; but in 1309 Charles Robert, commonly called Carobert, of Anjou, grandson of Charles II of Naples and of a Hungarian princess, was definitely recognized as king of Hungary, while in the same year his uncle Robert secured the succession in Naples ; and in 1310 the Bohemian nobles gave their crown to John, the young son of the emperor Henry VII.

**PARISIANS SUBMITTING TO CHARLES VI**

Internal discontent troubled the early years of the reign of Charles VI (1380–1422). In 1382 Paris rose in revolt, with some temporary success, but in 1383 Charles reduced the insurgents to submission and executed a terrible vengeance on the city by fines and executions and suppression of its privileges.
*Bibliothèque Nationale, Paris, MS. 2644 ; from De Witt, Chroniques de Froissar'*

John was too young to be a candidate for the imperial crown when his father died ; but as king of Bohemia, apart from his county of Luxemburg, he was an elector of the Empire, the most irreconcilable enemy of Lewis the Bavarian, and by consequence the ally of the pope and of France. He was a picturesque person of the prevalent adventurous chivalric type ; though he had lost his eyesight fighting the pagans in Prussia, he was killed at Crécy, fighting quite superfluously for the French. It was owing to his blindness that the German opposition put up his son instead of himself as king of the Romans in 1346. John had already fallen, and Charles was actually king of Bohemia when the death of Lewis and the lack of a strong opposition candidate made him emperor.

The Magyar kingdom of Hungary under the rule of its Angevin monarchs Carobert (1309–1342) and Lewis the

**HENRY VII HOLDING COURT IN ITALY**
After his recognition as German king in 1308, Henry VII sought to restore the imperial authority in Italy and crossed the Alps in 1310. He assumed the Lombard crown in 1311 and then marched to Rome, where he was crowned emperor in 1312. Henry died near Siena, August 24, 1313.
*Codex Balduineus ; from Irmer, 'Die Romfahrt Heinrich's VII'*

Great (1342–82) became much more closely assimilated to the western peoples than heretofore ; Lewis's title was not undeserved, and his kingdom acquired an unprecedented prestige among the nations of Europe, the more no doubt because his ambitions were not those of a conqueror, but of an enlightened administrator. Towards the close of his reign he acquired the crown of Poland in addition to that of Hungary, not by war but in virtue of a long-standing agreement with its king Casimir, whom he succeeded on the throne in 1370. The crowns, however, were not associated for long. He engaged successfully in wars with Venice ; and the confusion as to the succession to the crown of Naples which followed the death of his great-uncle Robert caused him to assert his own claims (for he was the grandson of Robert's elder brother). But after some successful campaigning he was prudent enough to withdraw them, and leave other disputants to settle the affair as best they might.

**A GREAT HAPSBURG PRINCE**
In the confusion that prevailed in Germany in the 13th century, Rudolf I of Hapsburg (1218–91) emerged as a dominant figure. This equestrian portrait of him on the façade of Strassburg Cathedral dates from the year of his death.
*Courtesy of Chapter of Strassburg Cathedral*

At the moment of the death of the emperor Lewis of Bavaria, his rival's chances of making his own claim good seemed meagre enough. It was by no means to his advantage that Charles was universally regarded as the papal and French candidate. Most of the princes were definitely hostile, and those who

**AN ENLIGHTENED PRINCE**

Robert of Anjou (1275–1343) succeeded to the
throne of Naples in 1309, in which year his
nephew Carobert became king of Hungary.
This portrait of Robert is contained in an
illuminated address dated c. 1335–40.

*British Museum, Royal MS. 6 E.ix*

inclined to support him were not disposed
to make sacrifices on his behalf. Lewis's
policy had in one respect not been half-
hearted; his territorial acquisitions had
vastly aggrandised the various branches of
the house of Wittelsbach, who among them
held all Bavaria, the Palatinate, Tyrol
and Brandenburg: also the free cities
were on his side because of the favour
he had shown them.

Nevertheless, Charles's diplomatic skill
was equal to the difficult conditions,
aided as he was by the opposition's
difficulty in finding a willing candidate on
whom they could agree. Their mutual
jealousies and rivalries enabled him to
win over supporters by judicious conciliation of one or another—in other words
by political or territorial bribery. The rival
who was at last elected died within the

year; and in 1350 his title was no longer
disputed.

The actual base of Charles's power was
in Bohemia. Probably he intended to
make that kingdom the centre of an
empire of which his conception differed
fundamentally from those of predecessors.
The dynasty must, of course, be established—that was common ground; he
secured for his family a second electoral
vote by acquiring in the course of his
reign Brandenburg as well as Bohemia;
and he procured the election during his
own lifetime of his eldest son Wenzel
as king of the Romans, which no emperor
had succeeded in doing for more than a
hundred years past. But more significant

**SPIRITUAL POWER IN GERMANY**

Henry VII of Luxemburg, Lewis of Bavaria
and John of Bohemia were all crowned by Peter
of Aspelt, archbishop of Mainz. The fact is
recorded pictorially and in Leonine verse on
the archbishop's tomb in Mainz Cathedral.

*Courtesy of Mainz Museum*

**AUTHOR OF THE GOLDEN BULL**
Charles IV (1316–78) is remembered as the promulgator, in 1356, of the Golden Bull, which regulated the election of the German king. He is portrayed on this transcript of it with his son Wenzel, king of the Romans.
*From O. Jäger, ' Weltgeschichte '*

of the difference of his aims were the magnification of Bohemia, and the diplomatic betrothal of his second son Sigismund to the daughter and heiress of Lewis the Great of Hungary and Poland. The eastward expansion of the Empire was to take the place of its visionary basis in Italy, where Charles procured his own coronation as Italian king at Milan and as emperor in Rome merely as a useful constitutional form.

Charles's scheme was not destined to fulfilment. Poland was never added to the Empire, nor Hungary attached to it till more than a century had passed after his death, at a time when the imperial succession had passed back to the Hapsburgs, who entered upon the greater part of the Luxemburg inheritance. But his reconstruction in Ger-

many was lasting. This was effected by the decree known as the Golden Bull.

That decree established and defined the position of the seven electors, the archbishops of Mainz, Trier and Cologne, and the electors of Saxony, Brandenburg and the Palatinate with the king of Bohemia. The succession in the lay electorships was permanently fixed, while the two most powerful territorial princes, Bavaria and Austria, were excluded from their number. Not expressly but implicitly the whole papal claim to a voice in the question was wiped out. The electors formed a single group ranking above all other princes and limiting the power of the crown, but with a common interest in maintaining a degree of unity in an empire constantly threatened with disruption. Under this system concentration of power in the hands of the monarch, the aim of the English and French kings, was out of reach ; but at least it gave security against the utter disintegration that had overtaken Italy.

It is possible but doubtful that Charles's constitution might have been made the basis of a more efficient concentration of authority if he had been succeeded by strong and able sons and grandsons ;

**PRINCELY ELECTORS IN PLENARY SESSION**
This miniature in the chronicle of Baldwin, archbishop of Trier (Trèves), depicts the election of his brother, Henry VII, as emperor. From left to right the seven electors are the archbishops of Cologne, Mainz and Trier, the elector palatine of Bavaria (not yet excluded by the Golden Bull), the duke of Saxony, the margrave of Brandenburg and the king of Bohemia.
*Codex Balduineus ; from O. Jäger, ' Weltgeschichte '*

in that case he would not have been condemned as he has been by the general consensus of historians. For Bohemia he was the best ruler she had ever known ; under him she prospered as never before ; the new university he created at Prague rapidly rose to a foremost position in Europe ; and his administration is entitled to unqualified praise.

### Inauguration of the Great Schism

BEFORE his death in 1378 Charles was witness to the beginning of a new stage in the troublous story of the Papacy. It had always been his desire to end the ' Babylonish Captivity ' and bring back the seat of the popes from Avignon to Rome. More than one of the Avignon popes had visited Rome with that hope, but none had ventured to stay there. Gregory IX tried in 1377, but was on the point of departure when he died in March 1378. The election had to be held in Rome, and consequently the choice fell for the first time since seventy years on an Italian, Urban VI, whose attitude towards the French cardinals was such that they proceeded to the election of a French antipope, Clement VII, who again took up his residence at Avignon.

Thus the Great Schism was inaugurated, with one pope supported or recognized by France and the friends of France, and the other by the rest of Europe, the latter having obviously the more legitimate title. The Schism, which sank the credit of the Papacy to its lowest depth, lasted till the Council of Constance (1414–18), which was convened in order to terminate the scandal. At the close of the Schism's opening year Charles died. The failure of his schemes was made the more certain by his own act. Perhaps because he recognized Wenzel's incapacity, he did not leave the consolidated territories he had acquired to his imperial successor, Brandenburg going to the second son, Sigismund, and Moravia to a nephew who proved to be a thorn in Wenzel's side.

Wenzel, a self-indulgent drunkard, controlled neither himself nor anyone else. He had not the vigour or the intelligence, even if he had the power, to prevent a confused civil war, the ' war of the towns,' in which nobles and knights (that is, the small military tenants-in-chief who had no overlord but the emperor) were engaged in suppressing, with very limited success, the leagues of towns which, not content with asserting immunities, were threatening to curtail what the nobles regarded as their own indisputable rights. Central government virtually ceased.

In 1380 Lewis of Hungary died, without a son. Hungary accepted the succession of his elder daughter Maria, the princess betrothed to Sigismund. Poland chose her sister Hedwig, and insisted on her marrying Jagellon, the prince of the still heathen Lithuania, who, however, adopted Christianity—wherein his subjects followed his lead—and founded in the united kingdom of Poland and Lithuania a dynasty under which it became one of the recognized European powers. Sigismund was disappointed of the expectation of receiving the Polish crown with his bride, and only won the bride herself with the Hungarian crown after long dispute with her mother, who preferred another candidate for her hand, and the Hungarian nobles, who preferred another candidate for the throne. This, with the threatening pressure of the Turks on the Danube, prevented him from intervening effectively on Wenzel's behalf against the aggressive intrigues of their cousin Jobst of Moravia, to whom he had himself pawned part of Brandenburg to raise troops for his Hungarian quarrel. It was owing to the Ottoman advance under Bajazet that in 1396 he gathered a great army, which was cut to pieces by Bajazet's Janissaries in the battle of Nicopolis whence Sigismund himself hardly escaped with his life.

### Development in Europe's minor States

THOUGH a lively interest attaches to the history of many minor states at this period, it is impossible to give a detailed account of them ; we can here only enumerate baldly certain points necessary to the understanding of future events.

In the north the Teutonic Knights had conquered, Christianised and to a great extent Germanised pagan and Slavonic Prussia on the south-west of the Baltic ;

but the raison d'être of that crusading order disappeared with Lithuania's conversion from paganism under Jagellon, and the military state thus created was destined to early absorption. Denmark under her king Waldemar III made a great bid for the complete domination of the Baltic Sea which brought her into collision with the German cities of the Hansa or Hanseatic League ; while the three Scandinavian kingdoms were now, at the end of the fourteenth century, on the point of being combined under one crown by the Union of Kalmar.

In southern Germany the League of the Forest Cantons had gradually expanded into a wider Swiss confederation which had shaken off the old Hapsburg overlordship and now recognized no suzerain save the emperor. At Morgarten in 1315 the Alpine peasants and townsmen had routed the Hapsburg men-at-arms, but the real decision was achieved at Sempach (1386) and was confirmed by a definite treaty, after another Swiss victory at Näfels, in 1389, from which date the Switzers form a distinct political body .

### Events in France, Spain and Italy

IN the west the crown of Navarre had for a moment been united to that of France by the marriage of Philip IV to its heiress Joan. But on the death of Philip's eldest son, Louis X, in 1316, the French crown went to his brother Philip V, and that of Navarre, where female succession was recognized, to his daughter, whose son Charles the Bad played an always uncertain and usually treacherous part in the Anglo-French struggle. In Castile we have seen French and English intervening in a struggle for the crown between the egregious but legitimate Pedro the Cruel and his illegitimate half-brother Henry of Trastamara. Peter won the crown, but his unique career of crime was closed by his brother's dagger in 1369. Henry ascended the throne, but his house was not firmly established till the accession of his grandson, Henry III, in 1390.

In Italy there remained no semblance of unity. At the end of the fourteenth century Venice had broken the power of Genoa ; the democratic republic of

**SOVEREIGN DUKE OF MILAN**

Gian Galeazzo Visconti (1347–1402) greatly increased the territories and prestige of Milan. This relief on his tomb at the Certosa di Pavia commemorates his creation as independent duke of Milan by the emperor Wenzel in 1395.

*Photo, Brogi*

Florence was the leading state of Tuscany ; the Visconti had established a despotism in Milan, where Gian Galeazzo Visconti had at last brought almost the whole of Lombardy under his sway, and the marriage of his daughter Valentina to a French prince, Louis of Orléans, was pregnant with troubles in a still distant future. Rome in 1347 had witnessed the meteoric rise and fall of the 'tribune' Rienzi. In the kingdom of Naples on the death of the much-married Joanna, grand-daughter of the old king Robert, the crown was secured by her cousin Charles of Durazzo and his heirs ; but the heir she herself had chosen, another Louis, a brother of the French king, got possession of Provence and clung to the empty title of king of Naples ; his claim was revived a century later by a French king, with momentous results.

Finally, at the moment when our chapter closes, Tamerlane's hosts were deluging central Asia, and the threatening of the terrific storm about to burst on western Asia was giving unexpected pause to the Ottoman advance after Nicopolis. In spite of that great disaster, Europe was given a moment's respite.

# TABLE OF DATES FOR CHAPTER 22

1396 Turks defeat Sigismund at Nicopolis.
1397 Union of Kalmar combines Scandinavian crowns.
1398 Tamerlane invades India and sacks Delhi.
1399 Ladislas secures crown of Naples.
     Henry IV (Lancaster) deposes Richard II.
1400 Rupert III elected rival k. of Romans to Wenzel.
1402 Gian Galeazzo d. Gian Maria in Milan.
     Tamerlane overthrows Bajazet at battle of Angora.
1404 John the Fearless becomes duke of Burgundy.
     Innocent VII pope.
1405 Tamerlane d. on his way to conquer China. Break up of his empire.
1406 Henry III of Castile d. ; acc. John II.
1407 Louis of Orléans assassinated by John of Burgundy.
1409 Council of Pisa ; demands resignation of both popes and elects a third, Alexander V.
     Sicily reverts to Martin I of Aragon.
1410 Civil war of Burgundians and Armagnacs in France.
     Alexander V d. ; John XXIII elected pope.
     Rupert III d. ; Wenzel sole king of the Romans.
1411 Sigismund elected joint king of the Romans.
1412 Filippo Maria Visconti acc. in Milan.
     Ferdinand I acc. in Aragon and Sicily.
     Mohammed I restores Ottoman power in Asia Minor.
1414 Ladislas of Naples d. ; acc. Joanna II.
     Council of Constance meets.
1415 Martyrdom of John Huss in spite of Sigismund's safe-conduct. Deposition of John XXIII.
     Frederick of Hohenzollern receives Brandenburg.
     Henry V renews Hundred Years' War ; capture of Harfleur and battle of Agincourt.
1416 Alfonso V acc. in Aragon and Sicily.
1417 Martin V elected pope at Constance ; Councils to be held at intervals. End of Great Schism.
     Henry V again invades Normandy.
1418 Council of Constance dissolved.
     Strife of Burgundians and Armagnacs prevents relief of Rouen, besieged by Henry V.
1419 John of Burgundy assassinated. His son Philip ' the Good ' allies with Henry.
     Wenzel d. ; Sigismund emperor, but Bohemia rejects him as the betrayer of Huss.
1420 Hussite wars begin ; Ziska the Hussite general.
     Treaty of Troyes ; Henry V to succeed Charles VI. Dauphin Charles and Armagnacs reject it.
1421 Mohammed I d. ; Murad II acc.
1422 Henry V and Charles VI d. ; Bedford French regent for Henry VI ; Charles VII recognized in south of France. Henry VI in north.
1424 Ziska d. ; succeeded by Prokop.
1425 Greek emperor Manuel II d. ; acc. John VI.
1427 Continued successes of Hussites.
1429 Joan of Arc relieves Orléans ; Charles VII crowned at Reims.
1430 Prince Henry the Navigator organizes exploration.
1431 Council of Basel meets. Eugenius IV pope.
     Joan of Arc tried and burnt at Rouen.
1432 Basel Council and Eugenius quarrel.
1433 John II acc. in Portugal ; supports Prince Henry.
     Basel Council comes to agreement with Hussites.
     Cosimo de' Medici exiled from Florence.
1434 Conflict of Calixtines and Taborites in Bohemia. Defeat of Taborites and death of Prokop.
1435 Philip of Burgundy reconciled with Charles VII ; English lose ground continuously after this.
     Naples : Joanna II d. ; succession disputed between Alfonso V of Aragon and René of Provence.
1436 Sigismund accepted and crowned king of Bohemia.
1437 Sigismund d. ; Albert of Austria acc.
1438 Albert II elected king of the Romans. From this time Hapsburgs are continuously elected.
     Council of Ferrara and Florence.
1439 Beginning of a royal army in France.
1440 Albert II d. His son Ladislas Postumus acknowledged in Hungary ; Bohemia elects Ladislas III of Poland. Frederick III of Styria k. of Romans.
1441 Portuguese round Cape Blanco.
1442 Naples : Alfonso secures the crown.
1443 Printing press (approximate date).
     Scanderbeg heads Albanian defiance of Turks.
1444 Ladislas III killed in great defeat by Turks at Varna. The child Ladislas Postumus k. of Bohemia and Hungary. Regencies under George Podiebrad and Janos Hunyadi.
1446 Portuguese round Cape Verde.

1447 Nicholas V pope.
     Filippo Maria Visconti d. ; Milanese republic.
1448 John VI d. ; Constantine last Greek emperor.
     Sweden under Karl Knudsen separates from Denmark.
1449 Council of Basel dissolved.
1450 Francesco Sforza at Milan.
     Jack Cade's insurrection in England.
     India : rise of Lodi dynasty at Delhi.
1451 Murad II d. ; acc. Mohammed II the Conqueror.
1452 Frederick III crowned emperor in Rome.
1453 Fall of Constantinople ; end of the old Empire.
     Hundred Years' War ends ; English expelled from France except Calais and Calais Pale.
1454 Mohammed grants terms to Venice.
1455 Calixtus III pope.
     Wars of the Roses begin in England.
1456 Siege of Belgrade raised by Janos Hunyadi, who dies the same year.
1457 Christian I of Denmark again unites the three Scandinavian crowns.
     Ladislas Postumus d. ; Austria goes to Hapsburgs.
1458 Hungary elects Matthias Corvinus, son of Hunyadi ; Bohemia elects George Podiebrad.
     Alfonso V d. His brother John II succeeds him in Aragon and Sicily, his son Ferrante in Naples.
     Pius II (Aeneas Sylvius) pope.
1460 Pius issues bull Execrabilis, denouncing appeals to councils ; end of conciliar movement.
     Henry the Navigator d.
1461 Louis XI acc.
1463 Turco-Venetian war begins.
1464 Paul II pope. Cosimo de' Medici d.
1465 War of the Public Weal in France.
1466 Francesco Sforza d.
     Treaty of Thorn ; Teutonic Knights retain East Prussia only, as fief of Poland.
1467 Scanderbeg d. Albanian resistance breaks up.
     Philip of Burgundy d. ; acc. Charles the Rash.
1469 Lorenzo de' Medici rules Florence.
     Isabella, sister of Henry IV of Castile, m. Ferdinand, crown prince of Aragon.
1470 War of Louis XI and Charles the Rash.
1471 Edward IV crushes Lancastrians at Tewkesbury.
     George Podiebrad d. ; acc. Ladislas IV (Jagellon).
     Sixtus IV pope.
1474 Charles the Rash begins Swiss War.
     Henry IV of Castile d. ; acc. Isabella.
1476 Charles defeated at Granson and Morat.
     India : Bahlol Lodi annexes Jaunpur (Oudh).
1477 Charles defeated and killed at Nancy.
     Louis XI seizes Burgundy and Artois.
     Mary, dr. of Charles, m. Maximilian, son of emperor.
1479 John II of Aragon d. ; acc. Ferdinand. Union of the crowns of Castile and Aragon.
     Turco-Venetian war ends.
1480 Turks invade Italy and take Otranto.
     René of Anjou d. ; leaves Provence to Louis XI.
     Bahmani sultanate of Deccan begins to break up.
1481 Anjou and Maine revert to French crown.
     Mohammed II d. ; acc. Bajazet II. Turks evacuate Otranto. Turkish advance suspended.
1482 The infant Archduke Philip succeeds in Burgundy, to exclusion of his father Maximilian.
1483 Edward IV d. ; acc. Richard III.
     Louis XI d. ; acc. Charles VIII. Regency of Anne of Beaujeu.
     Italian league against Venice.
1484 Innocent VIII pope.
     War of Matthias Corvinus and Frederick III.
1485 England : Henry VII establishes Tudor dynasty.
     Naples : Nobles revolt against Ferrante.
1486 Bartholomew Diaz rounds Cape of Good Hope.
     Frederick III procures election of his son Maximilian as king of the Romans.
1490 Matthias Corvinus d. ; Ladislas IV. of Bohemia elected king of Hungary.
1491 Maximilian recovers territories lost to Matthias.
     Charles VIII m. Anne of Brittany, which becomes part of the French royal domain.
     Savonarola preaches in Florence.
1492 Conquest of Moorish kingdom of Granada.
     Alexander VI pope.
     Lorenzo de' Medici d. ; Piero de' Medici acc.
     Christopher Columbus discovers the New World.

CHAPTER 22

# THE BIRTH OF THE RENAISSANCE: 1396–1492

THE key-note of the fourteenth century was the persistent disintegration of the old order. Before the close of the fifteenth, the bases of a new order have emerged ; but, until more than half of it has passed, disintegration remains the obvious feature ; in the political world the new forces are working, so to speak, still under cover ; it is only towards the end that they come suddenly into the open. The chronicler is still in the stage of entanglements, apparently isolated happenings, with a story which seems to have no plot. At the very outset we are faced with a volcanic eruption, wholly destructive, the shattering career of Tamerlane.

### Tamerlane's Conquest of Central Asia

THE great Mongol empire created by Jenghiz Khan had ceased to exist a century after the mighty conqueror's death ; in the west the sway of the ilkhans dwindled ; in the far east the power of the Yuan dynasty, founded and built up by Mangu and Kublai in China, collapsed ; all central Asia was given up to the feuds and rivalries of Turk or Tatar tribal chiefs, when in 1369 Timur or Tamerlane established himself as king of Samarkand. For five and twenty years he waged war perpetually, first with the eastern Chipchac Tatars, then with their western kinsfolk called the Golden Horde. His supremacy was not established indisputably till 1395, when his age was little less than sixty. The Chipchacs, however, were only the most active and vigorous of the enemies whom Tamerlane chastised (merely as a moral duty or in self-defence, though the chastisement was apt to be somewhat drastic). In fact, he had extended his conquests over Persia and Georgia, wiping out the remnant of the ilkhan monarchy.

In various respects Tamerlane differed from the Mongol conquerors. Both as a matter of course massacred without discrimination all who ventured to resist them. Both professed to spare those who made prompt and humble submission. But the practice of the Mongols was in general accord with their profession, whereas Tamerlane was habitually the victim of circumstances which prevented him from giving effect to his magnanimous intentions. Jenghiz Khan had destroyed ; Tamerlane obliterated. At Ispahan he raised a pyramid of 70,000 skulls.

A second point of difference is that the pagan Mongols were entirely careless of their subjects' religion ; whereas Tamerlane was not only a zealous Mahomedan, but a declared partisan of the Ali succession in the Khalifate, therein departing from the common Sunni fanaticism of the Turks, but deriving from it justification for smiting heretics as well as infidels.

### Western Asia in Tamerlane's hands

BEFORE completing the conquest of western Asia, Tamerlane turned aside to the conquest of India, where he stormed irresistibly through the Punjab, put to utter rout the armies which endeavoured to oppose him, and, having entered Delhi with the promise that it should be spared, gave it over to a five days' sack and massacre (1398), shortly after which he retired. Before trying conclusions with the Ottomans in Asia Minor, he took Syria in hand ; when he had done with Syria and laid Damascus in ruins, it was the turn of Bajazet, who, since Nicopolis, had been continuing his Danubian conquests, but now found it necessary to concentrate all his energies on meeting the invader.

The decisive battle was fought at Angora (1402), where the Ottoman army was shattered and the Ottoman sultan taken prisoner—to die shortly after, still in captivity. The fall of Constantinople was postponed for fifty years. However, Tamerlane elected to make China his next objective instead of Europe, and died on his way thither in 1405, at the age of seventy.

461

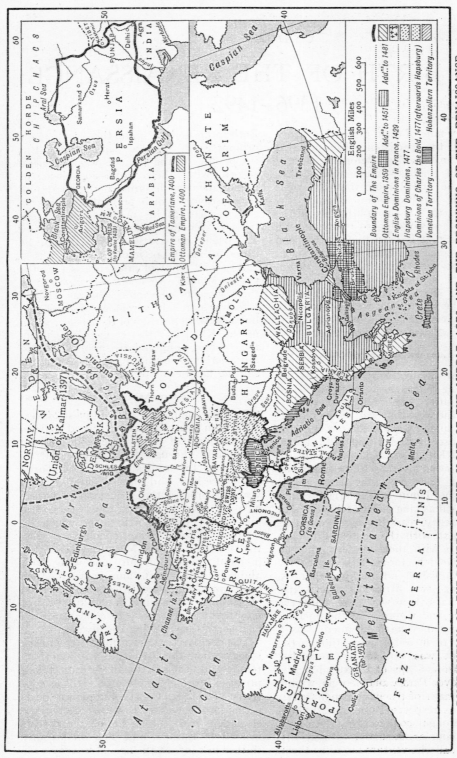

DISTRIBUTION OF THE POWERS AT THE CLOSE OF THE MIDDLE AGES AND THE BEGINNING OF THE RENAISSANCE

Maps in pages 420 and 422 show the distribution of the Christian powers in Europe and of the Mongol empires in Asia in the period 1216–1303 covered by Chapter 20. The broad changes effected in the years between then and the end of the period covered in our present chapter are shown above. The notable points in Europe are the growing power of Hapsburgs and Hohenzollerns in the Empire, the fluctuation of the English dominions in France, the restriction of the Saracen power in Spain, the development of the Ottoman Empire and the extension of the Venetian territories. In the East the most notable fact was the destructive though short-lived career of Tamerlane.

As a destroyer Tamerlane has no peer ; even Jenghiz, who perhaps had hitherto held the record, lags behind him, besides having to his credit so much at least of reconstructive work that it was only in the fourth generation that the empire he created began to break up. Tamerlane's empire vanished with his own death, having nothing whatever to hold it together. His descendants reigned in Samarkand or elsewhere, but as little more than minor chiefs, though one of them was the founder, a hundred years later, of the Mogul dynasty in India. Tamerlane's own deeds were written in the oceans of blood that he spilt, and the blood that he spilt is his sole monument.

China escaped the visitation, thanks to the death of the destroyer. The Ming dynasty had been securely established on the throne by its able founder Chu Yüan-chang or Hung Wu, who died in 1399 ; but with the exception of Yung Lo (1403–25), an efficient administrator, his successors were undistinguished alike in peace and in the wars with which the north was harassed by the Tatars or Mongols on its borders. One of the emperors, Cheng Tung, was captured in 1449 and held prisoner by these foes for eight years. Otherwise he is chiefly remarkable for abolishing the practice introduced by the first Mings of sacrificing slaves at the imperial funeral.

### Wreck of the Mahomedan Delhi Empire

INDIA, however, as we have seen, did not escape. Tamerlane's devastating incursion, the sacking of Delhi and the terrific slaughter by which it was accompanied, wrecked the little that was left of the Mahomedan Delhi empire, which was reduced to the position of a minor principality till the crown was seized in 1450 by an Afghan noble, Bahlol Lodi, under whom, and his successors, the lost power began to be revived.

Still, Tamerlane's devastation hardly extended east or south of Delhi and Agra. In the fifteenth century Bengal was already established as an independent kingdom ; Jaunpur, roughly corresponding to Oudh, was virtually independent till its recovery by the Lodis ; so were Kashmir on the north-west and Malwa, between the rivers Chambal and Nerbada ; and since the middle of the fourteenth century no part of the Deccan had paid any sort of allegiance to Delhi. Throughout the fifteenth it was divided mainly between the two great kingdoms, that of the Bahmani dynasty and the Hindu dynasty of Vijayanagar, all but the last of the kingdoms named being under Mahomedan rule. Their annals, chiefly of wars which had no particular consequences, do not demand attention ; but it is to be noted that at the close of our era the Bahmani kingdom was rapidly dissolving into five separate sultanates.

### Recovery of the Ottoman Power

FROM the Chinese marches to the Mediterranean all the khanates, kingdoms and sultanates of Asia were laid in ruins by Tamerlane's irruption. The Ottoman power was the first to recover. Within twelve years of the great overthrow at Angora, one of Bajazet's sons, Mohammed I, established his ascendancy over the rest. Manuel II at Constantinople made prompt submission, and Mohammed was engaged till his death in 1321 in bringing into subjection the various princelings of Asia Minor who indulged vain hopes of escaping from the Ottoman supremacy. Manuel rashly challenged his successor Murad (Amurath) II by encouraging a rival. Murad slew the rival and laid siege to Constantinople, where he was repulsed and had to retire in order to deal with another rival ; but on his return in 1424 Manuel again made submission, renewing and increasing the tribute which Bajazet had extorted from his father.

Next year John VI (1425–48) succeeded Manuel. John's contribution to the defence of Europe was a treaty with the Western ecclesiastical council of Ferrara (1439) for the union of the Greek and Latin churches which he was quite unable to impose on his own subjects. Throughout his reign Murad simply ignored Constantinople, having more serious antagonists than the feeble John to deal with—the Slavonic peoples on both sides of the Danube, in conjunction with Hungary and from 1440 with Poland. How the crowns of Poland and Hungary

came at this time to be united we shall
see in a different connexion.

Serbia, Bosnia and Wallachia had all
been made tributary by Bajazet ; they
combined to defy Murad, and purchased
the aid of Sigismund (who had suffered
the disastrous defeat by the Turk at
Nicopolis in 1396—see page 458) by
ceding to him the great fortress of
Belgrade. Until 1440 the war went constantly in favour of Murad. In that
year Ladislas III of Poland accepted the
Hungarian crown ; and during the next
three years the allies were constantly led
to victory by the great Hungarian captain
Janos Hunyadi (whose actual nationality
is doubtful). In 1444 they forced upon
Murad the peace of Szegedin, by which
he surrendered his claims on the three
Slavonic states. But before the year was
out Ladislas broke the treaty, crossed the
Danube and marched on Varna, where
he met with a shattering defeat and was
himself slain. Hunyadi, who had been
made regent of Hungary, attempting to

**MOHAMMED II THE CONQUEROR**
Apart from his military activities which terrorised
all Christendom Mohammed II (1430–81) organized the Ottoman system of administration
and was an enlightened patron of learning. This
portrait was painted by Gentile Bellini.
*National Gallery, London*

renew the war in 1448, was again defeated
at Kossovo. The coalition was broken up.

Since Varna the Turkish forces and the
sultan's son Mohammed had been dealing
very unsuccessfully with a new and
indomitable foe, the Albanian George
Castriot, better known as Scanderbeg
(Iskander, i.e. Alexander, Bey), who
preferred the rôle of patriot to that of a
commander in the sultan's service. Carried
off by the Turks as a child, he had been
brought up as a Mahomedan, attracted
the notice of Murad, and won high
distinction as an officer. But in 1443 he
deserted with a chosen company of
Albanian soldiers, seized the fortress of
Croya by a stratagem, discarded Islam for
the Christianity of his early childhood,
and proclaimed defiance of the Turk.

The Albanians rose to his call ; in the
passes his troops cut to pieces Turkish
forces of thrice their numbers. After
Kossovo, Murad advanced against him
in person in 1449, but his army, laying
siege to Croya, was so roughly handled
that he raised the siege and retired in
disgust. For some twenty years, till his
death in 1467, Scanderbeg broke in pieces
every expedition that was sent against

**SCANDERBEG'S HELMET**
Albania's national hero is George Castriot
(1403–1467), universally known as Scanderbeg,
in complimentary reference to Alexander the
Great. For twenty-five years this 'Dragon of
Albania' resisted Turkish aggression.
*Kunsthistorisches Museum, Vienna*

him, only once suffering defeat, fighting his battle unsupported from without ; and the immediate collapse of Albania when he died testifies to the genius with which he had carried on the struggle.

But when Murad died in 1451, Scanderbeg did not deflect his successor Mohammed II the Conqueror from his larger projects. At once he set about his preparations for the grand attack on Constantinople. John was dead ; the emperor now was his brother Constantine XI. As a last despairing effort to procure aid from western Europe, he again proclaimed the union of the Eastern and Western churches. The only effect was the alienation of his own subjects, who were at best lethargic before. The Slavs were broken ; succession troubles paralysed Hungary ; the West generally was exhausted, and absorbed by internal dissensions ; from no quarter was aid forthcoming, except the Venetians,

Genoese and Catalans, to whose commerce the fall of Constantinople would be a menace or worse ; and it was to these allies that Constantine was compelled to entrust not merely maritime defence but the actual garrisoning of the hitherto impregnable fortress on the Bosporus.

In 1452 Mohammed completed his preparations unhindered. Early next year the siege began. A Genoese squadron carrying supplies forced its way into the harbour, and an attack in force on the walls was stoutly repulsed ; but the scanty defenders of the vast fortifications girdled by a huge enemy host could have had little enough hope of maintaining their resistance for any length of time. No hint of help came. By advice of his astrologers, Mohammed waited for the fortunate day (May 29, 1453), when the grand assault was delivered on all sides simultaneously, by sea and by land.

The small garrison offered a desperate resistance to the swarming foe, but when once a footing was gained on the ramparts they were overwhelmed, fighting heroically to the last, led by Constantine in person. Buried among the heaps of slain, the body of the last of the Greek emperors was never recovered. There was no general massacre, but the great city was very thoroughly sacked, its literary treasures were dispersed or destroyed, and 60,000 of the population were sold into slavery.

In that same year, 1453, the so-called Hundred Years' War between France and England came to its inglorious end with the total expulsion of the English from French soil, except that of Calais and the Calais Pale, which they had held for a hundred years and were to hold for a hundred more.

At the close of the fourteenth century the fighting in France had become so desultory that a thirty years' truce was struck, leaving England in

**CONSTANTINOPLE BEFORE ITS FALL**

This plan of Constantinople was drawn for a work entitled Liber Insularum Archipelagi, published in Florence in 1422, thirty years before it fell to the Turks, and is the oldest in existence. The top left legend indicates the weakest spot where the Turks usually delivered their fiercest attacks.

possession of little more than Guienne and Calais. Both countries were, in fact, too much absorbed with domestic dissensions for the pursuit of an energetic foreign policy. In England the young king Richard II, long held in resentful tutelage by his uncles, was aiming at breaking the power of his kinsmen and their allies among the greater nobles, and establishing his own autocratic supremacy. In 1399 his cousin Henry of Lancaster returned from exile, headed a successful revolt, compelled Richard to abdicate, and usurped the

## A KING'S TRAGEDY AND A KING'S ACHIEVEMENT

In 1399 Henry of Lancaster, taking advantage of Richard II's absence in Ireland, landed in England and made a bid for the crown. On August 19 Richard surrendered to Henry at Flint and was taken to London by his rival (top). On September 30 he signed a deed of abdication, whereupon Parliament deposed him (bottom) and installed Henry—shown here wearing a high cap—on the throne.

*British Museum, Harleian MS.* 1319

**ENTRY OF ISABEL OF BAVARIA INTO PARIS AS BRIDE OF CHARLES VI**

Charles VI of France married Isabel, daughter of the duke of Bavaria, in 1385, and the arrival of the bride in Paris is thus depicted in an illuminated manuscript of Froissart's Chronicle. Notwithstanding the feebleness of intellect of the king, which culminated in actual insanity, she bore him a numerous progeny before separating from him in 1404. Queen Isabel several times acted as regent of France, and in the vexed politics of the time generally favoured the Burgundian party.

*Bibliothèque Nationale, Paris*

crown, which the parliament pronounced to be his by right of lawful succession, ignoring the prior claim of a very youthful cousin, the great-grandson of his father's elder brother (whose legitimate title thereto passed ultimately to his sister and her son, Richard of York).

Henry's own title, won by armed rebellion, sanctioned by the authority of peers and commons in parliament, and confirmed by the murder of the fallen king, rested so palpably and so precariously on popular support that his reign (1399–1413) was troubled by repeated rebellions, and his parliaments were able to exercise an amount of authority which was both premature and unprecedented.

Somewhat differently, but not less

**HENRY OF MONMOUTH**

By his successful conduct of a popular war, of which the victory of Agincourt was the crowning triumph, by his manly character and strong personality, Henry V (1387–1422) established his reputation as one of England's national heroes.

*National Portrait Gallery, London*

seriously, France, too, was now suffering from the power and the rivalries of the nobles of the blood royal. Charles VI was feeble-minded when not actually insane. His mighty uncle Philip of Burgundy was ruler of dukedoms and counties not only in France but also outside the French king's sovereignty. He virtually controlled the crown in despite of the king's younger brother Louis of Orléans and his partisans, among whom was presently numbered Charles's wife, Isabel of Bavaria. When Philip died, the rivalry continued between his son John the Fearless and Louis till John assassinated Louis in 1407. The anti-Burgundian or Orleanist party were then headed by Bernard of Armagnac, and became known as the Armagnacs ; and between them France was torn in pieces, while both sides intrigued to purchase the support of the king of England, whose alliance might prove particularly valuable to the Burgundian overlord of more than half the Netherlands.

In these dissensions Henry V (1413–22), the ambitious son of Henry IV, found his opportunity for reviving the English claim to the French crown, a claim very much weaker than his great-grandfather's, which had been weak enough. For his father's title by birth to the English throne could be maintained only by repudiating female succession, reversing the theory on which Edward had rested such claim as he had to the French throne. The temptation, however, was more than Henry could resist, his conscience being salved by the solid support of the clergy, while policy pointed to military glory as the most effective antidote to domestic disaffection.

The policy was popular in England, which plumed itself upon the martial exploits of Edward III and the Black Prince, and thirsted to avenge the ignominious failures in the second stage of the war, without troubling to weigh the right and wrong of the quarrel. Henry could have obtained immense concessions from either or both of the French parties without striking a blow, but concessions merely whetted his appetite.

In the summer of 1415 the English expedition was ready. Even at the moment of sailing, the weakness in the domestic position, which was one of the motives of the war, was manifested by the discovery of a plot, foreshadowing the War of the Roses, against the king's life in favour of the cousin, Edmund Mortimer, whose claim had been brushed aside on the accession of Henry IV, and was to be re-asserted forty years later by his nephew.

Henry's immediate aim was to establish in Normandy a strategic base more effective than Calais. After a sharp siege he captured Harfleur, while Burgundians and Armagnacs failed to reconcile their differences sufficiently to send a relieving force. There the campaign should have ended ; but Henry elected to risk with some six thousand men, for the most part archers, what ought to have been a quite impossible march from Harfleur to Calais ; on which, instead of being annihilated, he repeated at Agincourt Edward III's triumph at Crécy—thanks to the infinite incapacity of the French commanders.

The strategic results were nil, but the moral effect was enormous.

The second campaign was postponed for two years. This time Henry aimed at and achieved nothing less than the conquest of Normandy, the serious business of reducing one by one every fortress in the duchy. In the first campaign John of Burgundy had held aloof ; in the second he could not help making a show of patriotism ; but the actual result was his assassination, at a conference for conciliation, by Charles, the third of the king's sons to inherit the title of dauphin and the leadership of the Armagnacs.

The murder drove into Henry's arms John's son Philip, now duke of Burgundy, and all the Burgundians, who were for other reasons joined by the queen (who detested her youngest son). The crazy king was in their hands ; and so in 1420 the treaty of Troyes was struck with Henry, recognizing him as heir to Charles on his death and regent during his life. The treaty was of course repudiated by the Armagnacs and the disinherited dauphin, while it was upheld by Burgundy, who for the next fifteen years remained the ally of England.

Broadly, the north and east of the country was dominated by the English and Burgundians, the south, centre and west by the Armagnacs. The occupation of Paris did not mean the possession of France. For England, annexation would entail the piecemeal conquest of the whole country with garrisons established from end to end of it, for which her resources were totally inadequate. In 1422 Henry V died, leaving his brothers to carry on the war on behalf of his infant son Henry VI, who was proclaimed king of France on the death of Charles VI some weeks later, while the crown was of course claimed by the dauphin as Charles VII.

The English arms continued to make slow progress under the duke of Bedford, who was constantly embarrassed by the strife of factions in England, and had much ado in preserving amicable relations with Philip of Burgundy, whose good will was absolutely essential. But in fact the coolness between England and her Burgundian ally grew till Bedford's

### FAMOUS SIEGES DURING ENGLAND'S OCCUPATION OF NORTH FRANCE

The French war of 1415–53 was largely a war of sieges, two of which are thus depicted in the fifteenth-century Life of the Earl of Warwick by John Rouse.   On the left Henry V is seen conducting the siege of Rouen, which succumbed on January 19, 1419, after a heroic resistance.   On the right is a scene at the siege of Calais by Philip duke of Burgundy (after his alliance with England was at an end) in 1436, when the duke of Gloucester and the earls of Warwick and Stafford routed the besiegers.

*British Museum, Cotton MSS., Julius E.iv*

death in 1435 put an end to the alliance ; England became the prey of party factions, and from that time ground in France was continuously lost, though it was not till 1453 that the last foothold in the south finally disappeared, and Calais alone was left.

To the years 1429–31 belong one of the most amazing episodes that history records, the glorious tragedy of S. Joan, infinitely noble, infinitely pitiful, infinitely shameful. A farmer's daughter from Picardy, she persuaded persons in high authority that she was acting under divine direction. She was given the command of a

### A TREACHEROUS MURDER

At a meeting held on the Bridge of Montereau, September 10, 1419, to effect reconciliation with the dauphin, John the Fearless was felled with an axe by Tanneguy du Chastel, one of Charles's escort, as seen in this Froissart miniature.

*Bibliothèque Nationale ; from Larousse, 'Histoire de France'*

### JOHN THE FEARLESS

John, duke of Burgundy (1371–1419), won his surname ' the Fearless ' in battle against the Turks at Nicopolis in 1396. This early 15th century portrait by an unknown Flemish artist is one of the treasures of the Antwerp collection.

*Musée des Beaux Arts, Antwerp*

troop of soldiers, relieved Orléans, which the English were besieging, raised the siege, escorted the dauphin through hostile country to Reims, where he was at last crowned, and would then have retired, her ' mission ' accomplished, but was not allowed to do so.

Such miracles, according to the accepted beliefs of all classes, from archbishops to peasants, could have been wrought only by either divine or infernal agency ; and the enemy, whose knees became as water when her presence in the field was known, had no doubt that her inspiration was of the Devil. Also its manifestations were in very unorthodox form. She went on winning miraculous victories till she was taken prisoner by a band of Burgundians, delivered for trial to a court of French and Burgundian ecclesiastics, condemned by them for heresy and witchcraft and handed over to the secular arm—the English authorities, who burnt her in the marketplace of Rouen. More than five and a half centuries later she was canonised by the church which then condemned her.

The whole episode, however, demands our closer attention, because it sheds a flood of light on the medieval attitude of mind. The whole world believed not vaguely but intensely in the perpetual intervention of supernatural powers in mundane affairs ; Joan declared that she herself held converse with actual God-sent beings whom she was bound to obey. To the other side, either she was simply a lying impostor or the beings who misled her were not God-sent but Devil-sent. Her examination made the first theory incredible ; therefore the second must be true. If it was true, there was no escape from the logical conclusion that she must die as a heretic who held traffic with the arch-enemy of mankind.

The judges for the most part were high-minded men who were convinced that they had no alternative. Bedford, not a judge but the executioner, stands out among his contemporaries as a man of conspicuously fine character ; yet in this matter he had no qualms. That is the unspeakably pitiful side of the story. The glory and the beauty of the Maid need no words. The indelible shame is for those who, unheeding or incredulous of her inspiration, whether of God or the Devil, either sought her destruction because she stood in their way, or raised no finger on her behalf when she could no longer be of use to them.

The war, carried on always upon foreign soil, had singularly little effect on the prosperity of England ; the Burgundian alliance kept her trade with the Netherlands open, and even when that alliance was dissolved Philip did not bring his possessions outside France into the war. The recovery in the numbers of the rural population, depleted by the Black Death, restored the economic tendency, checked by that great visitation, towards the substitution of rent and paid labour for forced labour ; so that rural serfdom practically disappeared, and was not the

cause but merely one of the pretexts for Jack Cade's rebellion in 1450, which was in fact a popular protest against general misgovernment or failure of government due to factions in high places.

England, moreover, was developing rapidly a cloth-making industry which competed profitably in foreign markets with that of the Flemings ; and it was growing up not so much in the old boroughs as in rising towns where there was no trade-guild control. The problem of a surplus labouring population was at hand, but had not yet arrived. Even the mismanagement of the government was felt mainly as mismanagement of the war. It did not develop into the faction War of the Roses till the French war was ended.

In France, on the other hand, it is not impossible to understand how such a man as Henry V could actually persuade

**CHARLES VII ' THE WELL-SERVED '**
Crowned king of France in 1429 as a result of the efforts of Joan of Arc, Charles VII (1403–61) was a mental and physical weakling who contributed little to the deliverance of France from the English. Nervousness and melancholy characterise this portrait of him by Jean Fouquet, painted about 1444.
*The Louvre*

himself that it was for France's sake that he resolved to conquer her. A mad king, a wicked queen and a nobility who were so devoid of patriotism that even when the foreign foe was within their gates they fought by choice not against him but with each other—under such conditions government went to pieces altogether. But Charles VII, despite his despicable failure to defend the Maid, not so much from the English as from his own partisans, actually did much towards a reorganization after his reconciliation with Philip of Burgundy, who was more intent upon consolidating his own dominion than on controlling the government of France.

Charles found able ministers ; the main credit for what was effected is doubtless

**' THE ROYAL SAINT '**

Gentle, studious and pious, Henry VI (1421–71) was the hapless victim of the party strife that culminated in the Wars of the Roses and his own imprisonment and death. Eton and King's College, Cambridge, are his abiding monuments.

*National Portrait Gallery, London*

**BEDFORD PRAYING TO S. GEORGE**

John, duke of Bedford (1389–1435), acted as regent and English commander in France after the death of his brother Henry V. This picture, from the Bedford Missal written for him about 1430, is an obvious portrait of the man.

*British Museum : Additional MS. 18,850*

due not to the king, but to the men who counselled and served him. But this, at least, belongs to him : that he took their counsel and allowed them to serve him and the state. The nobles were no more disposed than of yore to lose any of their privileges, yet in spite of them an ordinance in 1439 created a standing army wholly under royal control, maintained by an unlimited tax leviable by the royal authority, called the ' taille,' in lieu of the taxes hitherto levied by the nobles themselves nominally or actually for the maintenance of troops under their own control. The ' free companies ' which had varied their fighting services by unrestrained plundering of the population were either suppressed or absorbed into the new army which was kept under strict discipline.

England had more or less solved the problem of strengthening the central government without creating an absolute monarchy by vesting the power of the purse in the parliament and mainly in the Commons ; lacking a parliament, France could achieve the strengthening of the central government only by making the crown absolute. In neither country was the disintegrating force of feudalism broken without a further struggle; but the lines of the development into parliament's supremacy in England and the crown's supremacy in France were already laid down.

THE history of Castile during this period is that of the brief but beneficial reign of Henry III (1390–1406) and the long but inefficient one of John II (1406–54), which has no features of general interest. Nor is it necessary to follow in detail the story of Aragon, beyond observing that in 1409 the crown of Sicily, held for a century by the younger branch of the house of Aragon, reverted to the Spanish branch, and that Alfonso V (1416–58) also acquired the crown of Naples, as the adopted heir of the last ruler of the old Neapolitan house of Anjou, Joanna II, who died in 1435. The crowns, however, were again separated on his death without legitimate issue in 1458, when

Aragon and Sicily went to his brother John, but Naples to the illegitimate son Ferrante or Ferdinand, whom he had nominated as his heir. The definitive union of the 'Two Sicilies' and Aragon was left to be accomplished by another Ferdinand in 1504.

Portugal, near the close of the fourteenth century, was saved from absorption by her big neighbour Castile by winning the crushing victory of Aljubarotta over her in 1485. The reign of John I (1385–1433), though consistently peaceful save for Moorish wars after her independence was securely established, is one of those which can fairly be called 'epoch-making,' because in the course of it began the activities of his younger son—whom the world knows as Henry the Navigator—which owed not a little to the far-sighted sympathy of John himself.

From about 1418 till his death in 1460 Henry devoted himself to equipping the

**THE MAID OF ORLÉANS BEFORE THE DAUPHIN AT CHINON**

As early as 1424 Joan of Arc (1411–31) first heard the angelic voices calling her to free France from the English. Not until 1429, however, did she secure the audience with the dauphin at Chinon illustrated in this fifteenth-century Flemish manuscript, in which she persuaded him of her divine commission. Then armed with a falchion—what is supposed to be the identical weapon (left) was found at Domrémy and is now at Nice—she led her army forth on her victorious campaign.

*Right, British Museum, Royal MS. 20 D.viii*

Q

ships, training the mariners and organizing the expeditions which gradually crept along the hitherto unexplored West African coasts and seas, rounded Cape Verde in 1446, and reached Sierra Leone before he died. Prince Henry was the first states-man to realize that the sea was not a limit to man's activities but a highway for his trade ; and it was through his genius and pertinacity that the little state of Portugal, out of her own resources, more than half a century before any of her more powerful neighbours, led the way in the oceanic exploration which opened out the entire globe to the European peoples who had hitherto been accustomed to regard less than one-eighth part of it as the whole. Portugal was too small to hold for long the lead she took in the fourteenth century, but the fact rather increases than detracts from the honour due to her and to Prince Henry.

## Union of the Scandinavian Kingdoms

THE three Scandinavian kingdoms, Den-mark, Norway and Sweden, stood outside the Empire, but in close relation, for commercial reasons, with the commer-cial cities that were largely or mainly concerned with the Baltic trade. Their story therefore was in the fourteenth century very intimately bound up with that of the Hanseatic League. In 1397 the three crowns, but not the constitutions, were joined together under a very able queen, Margaret, by the Union of Kalmar. Unfortunately, when heirs failed, the three kingdoms persistently elected differ-ent successors to the joint crown, which became a sort of shuttlecock—disputed successions were the rule rather than the exception all over Europe throughout the fifteenth century—but in 1457 all the three countries were induced or com-pelled to acknowledge Christian I, of Oldenberg, as their common sovereign, while he also held within the Empire the duchies of Schleswig (Slesvig) and Hol-stein. Sweden nevertheless remained practically independent under the rule of the noble house of Sture. And in Den-mark Christian's accession had been conditioned by terms which greatly re-stricted the power of the crown as against the nobility.

No less turmoil, confusion and diversity mark the history of the Empire, of Italy and of the Church. In the last years of the fourteenth century Wenzel was actual king of Bohemia and nominal king of the Romans, since he had not been crowned emperor. His brother Sigismund was king but not as yet master of Hungary, and their cousin Jobst of Moravia was scheming to acquire the imperial crown for himself. Rival popes, Benedict XIII and Boniface IX, were anathematising each other from Avignon and Rome with very dubious support from their respective patrons, the kings of France and of the Romans ; of whom one was crazed and the other a drunkard. The despot Gian Galeazzo Visconti had been formally recognized as duke of Milan by Wenzel (see page 459) and was mastering all Lombardy, while Genoa had sought security from him by submitting herself to the protection of France. Ladislas, the son of Charles of Durazzo, had secured the crown of Naples against the rival claim of Louis of Anjou who remained in possession of Provence ; and he was now ambitious of gaining the effective if not the formal domination of Italy.

### Two Kings of the Romans and three Popes

SUCH was the position in the year 1400. In that year the three ecclesiastical electors joined the elector palatine, Rupert, in declaring the deposition of Wenzel and the election of Rupert himself. Had Rupert been a commander of even moderate ability he would doubtless have crushed his incompetent rival ; but the actual result of the brief and desultory civil war which followed was that after 1402 the two ' kings of the Romans ' tacitly left each other alone, Rupert exer-cising the sovereignty, such as it was, in the west and Wenzel in the east, till Rupert's death in 1410.

In so far as concerned the increasing urgency of the papal problem, the schism was destroying all respect for the papal authority, and men's minds were inclining to the doctrine that the ultimate authority rested not in the pope but in the councils of the Church Catholic ; with the logical corollary that it was within the capacity of councils to depose or appoint popes as a last resort. The only possible way out of the existing dilemma was the simultaneous resignation or deposition of both popes and the unanimous election of another. Benedict remained at Avignon ; Boniface was succeeded at Rome by Innocent VII and Innocent by Gregory XII ; but throughout the changes it was obvious that whatever professions or overtures might be made on one side or the other, neither really meant to give way. At last cardinals on both sides united to summon, on their own responsibility, a council at Pisa in 1409 which proceeded to depose both Gregory and Benedict, and to elect Alexander V. Neither of the deposed popes would admit the authority of the council which had deposed them. So there were three popes at once. Alexander died within a year, and the council could find to replace him no better candidate than a notorious man of war whom they elected as John XXIII (1410).

A̲T this moment the death of Rupert revived the question of the imperial crown. The only possible candidates were the three princes of the house of Luxemburg, Wenzel, Sigismund and Jobst of Moravia. Wenzel had never admitted the legality of his own deposition, and he had all the time been more or less in possession though his incompetence was palpable. Sigismund by his rule in Hungary had of recent years acquired a reputation which on the merits made him the most desirable choice. Jobst was a thoroughly unprincipled but crafty and skilful politician who preferred the future security of a judicious bargain with Wenzel to precipitate action in the present. Reckoning that it would pay him better to wait, he gave his support to Wenzel, who was to be recognized as emperor while Jobst was to be the king of the Romans and, of course, Wenzel's successor. Sigismund claimed to be de jure and Jobst to be de facto elector of Brandenburg, and thus each was elected by different groups of electors at different times.

**THE EMPEROR SIGISMUND**

Already king of Hungary, Sigismund (1368–1437) was elected German king and Roman emperor in 1411. He succeeded to the throne of Bohemia in 1419, but owing to Hussite resistance did not secure effective power there until 1436.

*Painting by Albrecht Dürer, German Museum, Nuremberg*

So there were three kings of the Romans as well as three popes, when Jobst happily died in 1411. A new bargain between the brothers on practically the same lines as Wenzel's previous bargain with Jobst provided a comparatively simple adjustment. Wenzel was content to keep Bohemia with Moravia and the imperial title, while for all practical purposes Sigismund became emperor. Before long the difficulties in which John XXIII found himself involved with the ambitious king Ladislas of Naples led him to appeal to Sigismund for support, which he would give only on condition that John should summon a general council to meet on German soil. John was obliged reluctantly to yield, and the council met at Constance—three months after the unexpected death of Ladislas—at the end of 1414.

The proceedings of that momentous council need only to be summarised here. It had two main problems to deal with. The scandal of the schism must be terminated and the unity of Christendom restored ; but to this recent events had added, as of pressing importance, the reformation of the Church itself. The council dealt with the first, which successfully claimed priority ; with the second it failed.

It deposed the three popes, Benedict, Gregory and John, and appointed in their place a man of ability, character and weight, Martin V, after providing for the summoning of a series of councils to deal with reforms ; but Martin made haste to affirm uncompromisingly the unchallengeable authority of the pope himself.

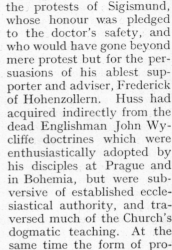

**COIN OF EUGENIUS IV**

Eugenius IV was pope from 1431–47. His effective resistance to the conciliar movement did much to restore the Papacy to the position it had held before the Great Schism.
*Coin Cabinet, State Museum, Berlin*

And before the deposition of John XXIII it had brought to the bar on a charge of heresy the Bohemian doctor John Huss, whom it condemned to death in spite of the protests of Sigismund, whose honour was pledged to the doctor's safety, and who would have gone beyond mere protest but for the persuasions of his ablest supporter and adviser, Frederick of Hohenzollern. Huss had acquired indirectly from the dead Englishman John Wycliffe doctrines which were enthusiastically adopted by his disciples at Prague and in Bohemia, but were subversive of established ecclesiastical authority, and traversed much of the Church's dogmatic teaching. At the same time the form of procedure adopted by the council, of representation by 'nations,' substantially if unintentionally strengthened the growing conception of national churches with a separate individuality of their own. In 1418 the council was dissolved.

The Hussite wars were the immediate aftermath of the Council of Constance. During its proceedings Wenzel had remained torpid in Bohemia. His death without children in 1419 left Sigismund

**INVESTITURE OF FREDERICK AS ELECTOR OF BRANDENBURG**

Frederick of Hohenzollern was appointed Sigismund's representative in Brandenburg in 1411 and was invested with the electorate by the emperor at Constance in April, 1417. The investiture is depicted in this wood engraving published at Augsburg by Anton Sorg in 1483. Frederick, holding the banner blazoned with the Red Eagle of Brandenburg with which he has just been presented, kneels before the emperor who sits with sword of state, while trumpets and trombones sound a fanfare.

*British Museum*

sole king of the Romans and natural claimant to the Bohemian crown. But Bohemia, seething with wrath at his betrayal of Huss, refused to submit either to him or to the council's decrees against the reformer's heresies. For some fifteen years war raged over central Europe, the Hussites winning repeated victories under their brilliant captain John Ziska, till his death, which occurred in 1424, when his place was taken by the only less brilliant Prokop. The last ' crusade ' dispatched against the heretics, with the blessing of Pope Martin, fled ignominiously on the Hussite leader's approach (1431).

At this moment a new council met at Basel, pope Martin died, and the council, eager for peace, invited the Hussites to send a delegation. A compromise was reached, sanctioning some but not all of the reformers' demands; it satisfied the moderates or Calixtines, but not the extremists or Taborites, who predominated in the Hussite armies. The result was a split between the council and the new pope, Eugenius IV, and between the Taborites and Calixtines who, united by no foreign foe, set about fighting each other.

The Calixtines had learnt the art of war from Ziska and Prokop himself; they crushed the Taborites and killed Prokop at the battle of Lipan (1434). Unlike the Taborites, the Calixtines were not unwilling to admit Sigismund provided that their religious liberties were secured, and in 1436 he entered the Bohemian capital as acknowledged king. Bohemia was formally pacified, and the extension of the war of religion to the rest of Europe was averted.

### Sigismund's Failure as Emperor

Sigismund had procured the assembly of the Council of Constance as the champion of reform, with every prospect of gaining immense prestige as the leader of Europe who had restored the peace of the Church. He owed it to his own vacillation and lack of steady resolution that, in spite of his spasmodic energy, those hopes were disappointed. No one could place any confidence in him, or trust him to pursue to-morrow the scheme on which his heart was apparently set to-day. When he made

### SEAL OF LADISLAS III

Ladislas III (1424–44), king of Poland and Hungary, covered himself with glory by his victorious campaign against the Turks in 1443. Violating the treaty of Szegen, he resumed the war and was killed at Varna, Nov. 10, 1444.

*State Archives, Berlin*

friends he could not keep them, and quarrelled quite unnecessarily with his most loyal supporters. He let his hold on the Council of Constance slip through his fingers. The ablest of the German statesmen, Frederick of Hohenzollern, aimed at concentrating power in the emperor's hands, but—after he had acquired from Sigismund the electorate of Brandenburg —abandoned the project in despair. Germany was no nearer to union at the end of his reign than at its beginning.

The male line of the house of Luxemburg ended with Sigismund's death in 1437. His heir, so far as he had an heir, was his son-in-law, the Hapsburg Albert of Austria, who actually succeeded him as king of the Romans, of Hungary and of Bohemia, but died in 1439, before the birth of his child Ladislas ' Postumus.' Bohemia accepted the infant; Hungary offered her crown to Ladislas of Poland, who accepted it; the German electors pitched upon another Hapsburg, the very incompetent Frederick (III) of Styria, for king of the Romans, to whose descendants the imperial crown remained—not indeed in form but in actual practice—hereditary till the Holy Roman Empire came to an end in the nineteenth century.

Ladislas of Poland was the still youthful son of that Duke Jagellon of Lithuania whose marriage to Sigismund's sister-in-law Hedwig had incorporated his duchy with the Polish kingdom. When Ladislas was killed in battle with the Turks at Varna in 1444, he was shortly succeeded in Poland by his brother Casimir, but Hungary acknowledged Ladislas Postumus, so that the Bohemian and Hungarian crowns were again temporarily united.

The Council of Basel was the second that had been summoned since the dissolution of the Council of Constance. It was vigorously anti-papal, that is, bent on curtailing the personal power and authority of the pope, as compared with that of councils. Antagonism between Eugenius and the council hardened year by year, and with it the tendency for the church-men within the several European states to make their demands from a national and individual point of view.

The intrigues and intricacies of the contest which went on throughout the life of Eugenius cannot be traced here. It was so acute that in 1438 Eugenius declared the council dissolved and called a counter-council at Ferrara ; whereupon the Basel council deposed Eugenius and set up the duke of Savoy as antipope (Felix V). Mainly by the skilful but most unscrupulous diplomacy of Aeneas Sylvius —afterwards Pope Pius II—the lay rulers of Europe were drawn to the side of the pope, having hitherto preserved a general neutrality. The bargains were almost completed when Eugenius died in 1447, and were endorsed next year by his successor Nicholas V. In 1449 Felix resigned, and the Council of Basel, which could no longer hold its own, was dissolved. The Papacy entered on a new phase. It had successfully broken the ' conciliar ' movement and scotched reform, and it was this success that made the Reformation inevitable.

### Rivalry between Milan and Venice

IN North Italy the domination of the Visconti was for a time broken up by the death of Gian Galeazzo in 1402. His elder son Gian Maria had all his father's vices in an exaggerated degree, with none of his ability. When Gian Maria was murdered in 1412, his younger brother Filippo Maria set about the recovery of what had been lost by employing the services of brilliant condottieri (captains of mercenaries) with much success ; but Venice took advantage of the position first to strengthen herself, and then under the guidance of the Foscari to embark upon a career of aggrandisement on land, also by the employment of condottieri, in which she too achieved considerable success. Hence, by the middle of the century the rival powers of Milan and Venice shared the domination of the north.

The death of Filippo Maria in 1447 without male issue seemed to promise the establishment of a republic in place of the despotism at Milan, and a great opportunity for the extension of the power of Venice. But two events combined to remove that prospect. The condottiere Francesco Sforza, who had commanded Filippo Maria's armies and married his daughter, made himself master and duke

**FRANCESCO SFORZA OF MILAN**

By venal military genius and political acumen Francesco Sforza (1401–66) rose to be a dominant factor in medieval Italy. Established as duke of Milan in 1450, he was rivalled in splendour and power only by the Medici of Tuscany.

*Relief by Romano in Florence Museum : photo, Anderson*

of Milan in 1450, and the Turks captured Constantinople in 1453. Venice patched up the peace of Lodi with Sforza and terms with Mohammed, but, after an interval, she devoted herself to a heroic sixteen years' struggle with the Turks in which she fought practically single-handed.

In Tuscany, on the other hand, Florence developed her ascendancy. At the close of the last century control of the government had, by manipulation of the democratic machinery, been secured by the Albizzi, who extended the Florentine dominion over their Tuscan neighbours, in spite of Milan, against which they procured the alliance of Venice. They procured also the exile of the enormously wealthy Medici family, who were regarded as the leaders of the democratic opposition. But their power waned. In 1434 there was a revolution which enabled Cosimo de' Medici to return and exiled the Albizzi.

From this time Cosimo employed his great wealth and abilities in establishing a virtual despotism under democratic forms and a far-reaching diplomatic influence. His attitude helped at least to turn the scale in favour of Sforza's despotism, because he meant to preserve the balance of power in the north between Milan and Venice, the latter having now become the more dangerous of the two. He thus inaugurated the policy of alliance between Florence, Milan and Naples that was a marked feature of the rule of his grandson Lorenzo (1469–92), who, without assuming any titles, established the Medici family among the princely houses of Europe, himself an uncrowned king who reigned like Augustus merely as the Florentine republic's first citizen.

Mohammed II continued his career of conquest after he had captured Constanti-

COSIMO DE' MEDICI, ' PATER PATRIAE '

The Medici family had long been prominent in the Florentine Republic as merchants and bankers, and Cosimo de' Medici ' the Elder' (1389–1464) skilfully employed his vast wealth to secure the despotism of Florence. He figures in Botticelli's Adoration of the Magi, kneeling before the infant Jesus.

*National Gallery, London ; photo, Anderson*

nople. Before his death in 1481 he had subjected the whole Balkan peninsula south of the Danube and the Save, as well as Wallachia on the north of the great river. The resistance of Albania broke down after the death of the invincible Scanderbeg in 1467. He consolidated the Ottoman power in Asia Minor, and he mastered most of the islands of the Aegean. But the Turkish advance on the Danube was brought to a standstill for generations by the heroic defence of Belgrade in 1456 —the crowning exploit of Janos Hunyadi who died immediately after his last and greatest triumph ; and the Knights of S. John maintained their grip on Rhodes.

At the end of the war with Venice (1463–79), the republic retained her hold

**LORENZO THE MAGNIFICENT**
By able diplomacy and lavish use of his great riches Lorenzo de' Medici (1448–92) raised Florence to the pinnacle of its greatness and was the pre-eminent figure of his age. From the panel by Vasari.
*Uffizi Gallery, Florence ; photo, Alinari*

in the Morea, but only at the price of a heavy tribute, and lost everything else except the trading quarter in Constantinople, which Mohammed's sagacity had conceded to her when he first took the city. The conqueror's last and, to the West, most alarming project was his invasion of Apulia and occupation of Otranto in 1480 ; but his death and a disputed succession next year caused its evacuation by the Turks. Bajazet II who succeeded lacked the ability of his predecessors, and the menace was not renewed.

When on the death of Ladislas of Poland at Varna the child Ladislas Postumus became king of Hungary as well as Bohemia, the regency of the latter country was in the hands of George Podiebrad, and Hunyadi became regent of the former. The boy was the ward of his father's cousin, the emperor Frederick III, but all intervention on his guardian's part was rejected in both kingdoms. When Hunyadi died, Ladislas—then in his eighteenth year—whose jealousy of both the regents had been aroused, began to assert himself in sinister fashion, finding an

excuse for putting Hunyadi's elder son to death ; but in the next year, 1458, he was carried off by the plague, not without unwarranted suspicions of poison. Austria went to the Hapsburgs ; but to the two crowns there was no hereditary title. Bohemia chose to crown her very able regent George Podiebrad, while the Hungarians elected Matthias Corvinus, the second and worthy son of her dead hero Hunyadi.

It seemed probable that there would be close alliance between these two national monarchs, but they fell out because the orthodox Matthias was invited by Pius II (Aeneas Sylvius) to be the papal champion against the Hussite George, whose daughter he had married, and whom he hoped to succeed on the Bohemian throne ; and the result of the quarrel was that when Podiebrad died in 1471 he was succeeded by Ladislas, son of Casimir of Poland. When Matthias himself died in 1490, without an heir, Hungary offered her crown also to Ladislas, mainly perhaps to prevent it from passing to the Hapsburgs again.

Frederick III endeavoured at every opportunity to assert Hapsburg claims both in Bohemia and in Hungary, but was invariably unsuccessful, since his guiding principle, whenever a serious difficulty had to be faced, was either to do nothing or to run away and leave the difficulty to solve itself. Inertia, coupled with a buoyant confidence in something turning up, carried him through, and the difficulties did solve themselves, not without ignominy but without irreparable disaster. He did not rule the Empire, but he succeeded in evading technical deprivation of imperial rights ; fortune gathered into his hands nearly all the divided inheritance of the various branches of the house of Hapsburg ; and he secured the imperial succession to his son Maximilian by procuring his election as king of the Romans in 1486, seven years before his own death, after a reign of more than fifty years, in 1493. And already Maximilian, by his marriage in 1477 to Mary the heiress of Burgundy, had immensely widened the basis for the impending Hapsburg ascendancy.

Moscow as the centre, he brought under his own sway first the neighbouring lordships and then the free republic of Novgorod, advanced to the Ural Mountains and the Arctic Sea, and in 1480 repudiated and successfully defied the Tatar sovereignty. There was little enough intercourse with the West ; but before his death in 1505 he had succeeded in consolidating a Russian or Muscovite tsardom.

Immediately after the evacuation of France, England was plunged into the succession wars of ' the Roses,' or rival houses of York and Lancaster, which proved to be the death-blow of feudalism. The contest was ended by the fall of Richard III and the accession of the astute Henry VII (Tudor) in 1485. Lack of funds and the slenderness of his title

### RICHARD III OF ENGLAND
Unscrupulous yet intellectual and courageous, Richard III (1452–85) tried to maintain by terrorism the throne he had secured by crime. Disaffection bred rebellion, culminating in his death at Bosworth Field, August 22, 1485.
*National Portrait Gallery, London*

Meanwhile on the east of the Empire the power so long maintained by the Teutonic Knights went to pieces. The dominion of a military order whose members were vowed to celibacy and depended for recruitment on voluntary accessions to their numbers, while they differed in race from the mass of the population, could have no national or permanent character. They could hold their own against their Prussian subjects, but when these appealed to their Slavonic kinsmen of Poland the end could not be far off. Though the Knights fought with their backs to the wall, they were beaten. By the treaty of Thorn in 1466 West Prussia was absorbed into Poland, and the Knights were left in East Prussia, but held it only as a fief of the Polish crown.

Thus the power of Poland waxed ; and while it did so a new power, essentially barbarian, came to birth on her east. For some time past the grand dukes of Moscow had been the most powerful vassals of the Tatar khan. In 1462 Ivan III the Great became grand duke. With

### FOUNDER OF THE TUDOR LINE
The diplomatic astuteness and strength of character whereby Henry VII (1457–1509) established the Tudor dynasty are revealed in this fine bust, attributed to the Italian Torrigiano who visited England in the early 16th century.
*Victoria and Albert Museum*

made him for many years very dependent on his parliaments ; the first he remedied largely by the substitution of crushing fines and confiscations for the accustomed drastic penalties of treason (whereby incidentally he completed the fall of the great baronial families), and the second by marrying the representative of the rival house ; while the diplomatic astuteness in which Ferdinand of Aragon was both his partner and rival restored England's lost position as a European power.

Charles VII of France died in 1461, Philip of Burgundy in 1467. Charles had created a machinery for the concentration of power in the hands of the crown, but his son Louis XI had a long struggle, in which there were failures as well as successes, before he achieved that decisive supremacy which was the aim of his life. As dauphin he had joined or headed the rebellion of the great nobles against the royal curtailments of their power ; as king it was his policy to break their power. His instruments were drawn from the

**LOUIS XI OF FRANCE**

By subtlety, personal courage and administrative ability, Louis XI (1423–83) broke the power of the nobles, averted the menace of an English invasion, and thus was the consolidator of modern France. This portrait was painted by Jean Fouquet.
*Bibliothèque Nationale, MS. francais* 19,819

**A 'PRINCE OF THE LILIES'**

Hostility to France dominated Charles the Rash of Burgundy (1433–77). His extravagant ambitions being frustrated in France, he challenged the independence of the Swiss, by whom he was finally defeated, and slain, at Nancy, June 5, 1477.
*Dijon Museum ; photo, Neurdein*

bourgeois class, or at best from the minor nobility ; his most dangerous adversaries were the dukes of Burgundy, Bourbon and Brittany. Intrigue and a profound capacity for gauging men's characters were his weapons, since soldiering was not his craft. He evaded direct collision with Philip, at whose court he had found asylum in his rebellious days ; but the duke in his old age allowed his hot-headed and ambitious son Charles an increasingly free hand ; and from 1465 to 1477 Louis was constantly engaged, openly or covertly, in a duel with Charles the Rash.

As a vassal of France, Charles desired to diminish the power of his suzerain ; as an independent potentate, he meant to revive the old Middle Kingdom of Burgundy from the mouth of the Rhine to the mouth of the Rhône. But between the Burgundies and the Netherlands intervened Champagne and Lorraine, and southward it was not easy to establish a title to Switzerland and Provence. On the other hand, there was always promise of reviving effective alliance with England against Louis.

**A ROYAL BETROTHAL**

Maximilian, afterwards emperor, married Mary, daughter of Charles the Rash of Burgundy, in August, 1477, seven months after the death of her father. This contemporary drawing shows the young couple during their engagement.

*German Museum, Nuremberg*

In 1465 a combination of the ' princes of the lilies,' i.e. of the blood royal, called the ' League of the Public Weal,' was formed against the royal usurpations. Louis must have been altogether crushed but for the royal army created by his father. As it was, he was forced to make great concessions to the dukes ; but the coalition was soon broken up by jealousies and rivalries among themselves, fostered and turned to his own account by the king, who so managed matters that Champagne, which Charles expected to pass under his own control, eventually fell into Louis' own hands. The duke, finding himself without trustworthy allies in France, set about the development of his ambitions on the other side of the Rhine, where Louis was comfortably satisfied to stir up enemies without taking an open part ; and Charles finally met his death in a great defeat at Nancy, at the hands of the Switzers over whom he claimed sovereignty in virtue of a bargain with the Hapsburg Sigismund of Tyrol, whereby the Swiss Confederation secured final recognition of its independence.

Charles had been completely baulked of his extravagant ambitions. He left no son, and he had married his daughter Mary to Maximilian, not yet Roman king, in the vain hope of being rewarded with the title of king by the emperor Frederick. With the exception of the duchy of Burgundy, which Louis succeeded in annexing, all Charles' possessions went to Mary, including the trans-Rhenish county of Burgundy, so that the name of Burgundy still attached to the dominions generally. When Mary died they passed not to her husband but to their infant son, the ' archduke ' Philip, whose son in the next generation became the head of the house of Hapsburg.

When Louis died in 1483, his supremacy in France was thoroughly established and the royal domains had been immensely extended. He left an infant heir, Charles VIII, with the regency in the capable hands of his elder daughter Anne of Beaujeu ; and the young king's marriage to the heiress of Brittany in 1491 brought almost the last of the great duchies into the king's own control.

### Union of Aragon and Castile

THE Spanish kingdoms, like France and England, were at last in process of consolidation through the marriage of the sovereigns of Castile and Aragon, Isabella and Ferdinand. In 1474 Isabella succeeded her half-brother Henry IV on the throne of Castile, in priority to his reputed daughter, of whom the world declined to believe that he was the real father. She secured her crown, not without difficulty, though her title to the succession had been formally recognized six years earlier, immediately before her marriage to the crown prince of Aragon, who succeeded his father, John II, on the throne in 1479. Ferdinand in Castile was only king-consort, and Isabella queen-consort in Aragon.

The two kingdoms remained separate with separate constitutions and institutions, like the Scandinavian kingdoms, or like England and Scotland in the seventeenth century. But the two very able monarchs worked always in perfect harmony, as though they had been one. In relation to foreign countries there was a single Spanish kingdom. But in each kingdom there was the same need for establishing the supremacy of the central authority: Castilians and Aragonese were too jealous of each other to unite against the monarchs, who could call in the Castilians against their Aragonese subjects and vice versa in case of necessity ; their measures were as a rule conspicuously to the general advantage however opposed to particular established interests ; and thus under Ferdinand and Isabella Spain definitely emerged as a great power.

Half of their joint reign and two-thirds of Ferdinand's belong to the next chapter, but the first period has features of vital importance. The establishment of the

**DISCOVERY OF NEW WORLD**
This woodcut is an illustration to a pamphlet printed at Basel in 1494, describing ' the islands lately discovered in the Indian sea.' It depicts Columbus landing on the island of Hispaniola.

Inquisition with a power and latitude of action elsewhere unknown gave to Spain her peculiar character as the champion of religious persecution and intolerance in its most extreme form. The expulsion of the Jews exemplified the same spirit, and later brought its economic nemesis.

The conquest of the Moorish kingdom in the south (Nov., 1491), completed by the fall of Granada in the next year, ended the Mahomedan power which had maintained itself in Spain for nearly eight hundred years and rounded off the new Spanish kingdom, leaving Portugal the sole independent state in the Peninsula, since Navarre had practically ceased to reckon as Spanish. And the fall of Granada left the monarchs free to dispatch a Genoese explorer on what was the most momentous voyage in the world's history, though the question had in fact come to be only—who should be the first to face the great adventure ?

For the work of Henry the Navigator was on the point of attaining its full fruition. In 1486 the Portuguese Bartholomew Diaz rounded the Cape of Good Hope, sailed on the waters of the Indian Ocean, and opened the new highway between the West and the immemorial East. It was an accident, the short-sightedness indeed of Henry VII of England, that gave the patronage of Christopher Columbus with all its tremendous consequences to the Spanish monarchs.

There were a hundred and twenty men, all told, on the three ships with which Columbus set sail on August 3, 1492, to seek the Indies by voyaging not east but west. Exactly ten weeks later land was sighted. Columbus had not reached the Indies, as he always believed ; but he had found a New World.

**CHRISTOPHER COLUMBUS**
Painted by the Venetian artist Lorenzo Lotto, this is reputed the best portrait of Christopher Columbus. It was on October 12, 1492, that Columbus set foot in the Bahamas and opened a new volume of world history.
*Musée du Marine, Madrid ; photo, Laurent*

# Seventh Era

# THE WORLD ENLARGED

### 1492–1660

---

### Chapter 23
## THE EPOCH OF THE REFORMATION, 1492—1555

### Chapter 24
## THE AGE OF PHILIP II, 1555—1598

### Chapter 25
## THE AGE OF THE THIRTY YEARS' WAR, 1598—1660

---

WITH the close of our Sixth Era we reach the point at which, by general consent, ' Modern History ' opens : the moment when the two halves of the world, hitherto unaware of each other, became suddenly conscious of each other's existence ; when the hitherto pathless ocean became for the first time a highway and a battlefield, because the adventurous peoples of the West had discovered at once new outlets for expansion and new fields of rivalry, even at the moment when new intellectual and moral horizons were revealing themselves, and Europe politically was organizing itself upon the Great Powers basis. The Seventh Era is the first phase of the new order. In it the most prominent feature is the struggle which vainly hurled nations against each other and divided them against themselves for the mastery of one or the other of two rival religious ideals, only to learn that neither could be mastered by the other ; while the oceanic expansion was less conspicuously shaping the lines on which future rivalries were to develop.

# TABLE OF DATES FOR CHAPTER 23

1492 Acc. Pope Alexander VI (Borgia).
Lorenzo de' Medici d.
Conquest of Granada by Ferdinand and Isabella ends Moorish dominion in Spain.
Christopher Columbus discovers West Indies.

1493 Frederick III (emperor) d.; Maximilian succeeds, but is never crowned by pope.
Pope Alexander issues bull granting to Spain all territories discovered west of a line drawn down the Atlantic, all east of it to Portugal.

1494 Treaty of Tordesillas completes partition of the New World between Spain and Portugal.
Asia: acc. Babar in Ferghana.
Charles VIII of France invades Italy.

1495 Charles occupies Naples, but withdraws and has to fight his way back to France.

1496 French expelled from Naples.
Archduke Philip of Burgundy, son of Maximilian, m. Joanna, dr. of Ferdinand and Isabella.

1497 The Cabots discover Labrador and Newfoundland.

1498 Vasco da Gama lands at Calicut in India.
France: acc. Louis XII (duke of Orléans).
Savonarola burned at Florence.

1499 Louis XII claims and takes Milan.

1500 India: the Sikh brotherhood founded by Nanuk.
Voyage of Amerigo Vespucci; S. American coast-line explored.
Treaty of Granada between Louis XII and Ferdinand of Aragon.

1501 Louis and Ferdinand seize Naples.
Cesare Borgia in Romagna.

1502 Disagreements between Louis and Ferdinand.

1503 Alexander III d.; Julius II pope. Fall of Cesare.
War between Louis and Ferdinand; Gonsalvo de Córdova, the 'Great Captain,' wins battle of Garigliano.
James IV of Scotland m. Margaret Tudor; origin of the Stuart succession in England.

1504 Ferdinand secures Naples permanently. Isabella d.; Joanna proclaimed queen of Castile, and her husband Philip king.
Asia: Babar makes himself king of Kabul.

1505 Ivan III of Moscow d.

1506 Philip of Castile d.; Ferdinand regent for Joanna and her son Charles.

1507 Portuguese seize Ormuz (Persian Gulf).

1508 League of Cambrai for dismemberment of Venice.

1509 Henry VIII acc.; m. Katharine of Aragon.
D'Albuquerque viceroy of the Indies.

1510 Portuguese establish themselves at Goa.

1511 The Holy League formed against France.

1512 Rise of Wolsey in England.
Medici family return to Florence.
Gaston de Foix killed at battle of Ravenna; expulsion of French from Italy.
Ferdinand annexes Navarre s. of Pyrenees to Aragon. N. Navarre remains independent.
Ottomans: Selim I deposes his father Bajazet II and massacres most of his kinsmen.

1513 Julius II d.; acc. pope Leo X (Medici).
James IV of Scotland killed at Flodden.
Balboa discovers the Pacific from Darien.

1514 Selim routs Persians and drives them behind the Tigris.

1515 Acc. Francis I in France. He captures Milan, after winning battle of Marignano.
D'Albuquerque d.

1516 Ferdinand of Aragon d.; his grandson Charles of Castile and the Netherlands, inheriting Aragon and the Sicilies, becomes Carlos I of Spain.
Selim I overthrows the Mamelukes in Syria.

1517 Martin Luther at Wittenberg denounces indulgences.
Selim conquers Egypt, deposes and deports the khalif to Constantinople, and assumes the Khalifate, to be retained by the Ottoman sultans for four centuries.

1519 Maximilian I d.; his grandson Carlos I of Spain succeeds to the Austrian inheritance, and is elected Emperor Charles V.
Magellan sails on first voyage of circumnavigation.
Cortés begins conquest of Mexico.
Babar makes an exploratory raid on Punjab.

1520 Selim I d. while besieging Rhodes; acc. Suleiman the Magnificent.
Field of the Cloth of Gold.
Christian II of Denmark massacres Swedish nobles at 'blood-bath of Stockholm.'
War begins between Charles V and Francis I.
Luther burns Leo X's bull of excommunication.

1521 Diet of Worms begins battle of Reformation.
Charles transfers Austrian inheritance to his brother Ferdinand.
Suleiman captures Belgrade.
Adrian VI (Burgundian) pope.
Zwingli at Zurich.

1522 Suleiman takes Rhodes.

1523 Gustavus Vasa elected king of Sweden.
Knights' War in Germany.
Clement VII (Medici) pope.

1524 Peasant revolt in Germany.
India: Babar invades Punjab, but retires.

1525 Albert of Hohenzollern, last grand master of Teutonic Knights, made duke of Prussia.
Francis I defeated and taken prisoner at Pavia.

1526 Diet of Speier recognizes religious authority of princes—' cujus regio ejus religio.'
Lewis of Hungary and Bohemia killed at Turkish victory of Mohacs. His brother-in-law Ferdinand of Austria succeeds to both crowns.
Babar destroys Lodi empire of Delhi at Panipat.

1527 Rome sacked by imperialist troops.
Babar defeats the Rajputs.

1529 Protest of Speier follows reactionary diet.
First unsuccessful siege of Vienna by Turks.
Henry VIII resolves to discard papal authority.
Fall of Wolsey.
Peace of Cambrai between Charles and Francis.

1530 Diet and Confession of Augsburg.
Charles V crowned by pope. Ferdinand k. of Romans.
Babar d.; acc. Humayun at Delhi.

1531 League of Schmalkalde. Peace of Cappel (Swiss).

1533 Pizarro conquers Peru. End of Inca empire.

1534 Paul III (Farnese) pope. Final repudiation of papal authority in England.

1535 Charles V's Tunis expedition.
Jacques Cartier on the S. Lawrence.

1536 Calvin's Institutes.

1538-9 Dissolution of English monasteries.

1540 Paul III institutes Jesuit order.
Sher Shah expels Humayun from India.

1541 Calvin permanently established at Geneva.
Disastrous Algerian expedition of Charles.
Religious compromise of Ratisbon.

1542 James V of Scotland d.; infant Mary queen.
War of Charles and Henry with Francis.
Portuguese ships visit Japan.

1544 Peace of Crespy.

1545 Council of Trent opens.
Sher Shah d.

1546 Luther d. Outbreak of Schmalkaldic war.

1547 Henry VIII and Francis I d.; acc. Edward VI and Henry II.
Defeat of Schmalkaldic League at Mühlberg.
Council of Trent, sitting at Bologna, adjourns.
Moscow: acc. Ivan IV the Terrible.

1548 Mary q. of Scots sent to France. Mary of Lorraine regent in Scotland.
Charles V issues Interim of Augsburg.

1550 Acc. Pope Julius III.

1551 Council of Trent reassembled by Julius.

1552 Maurice of Saxony, in agreement with France, rises against Charles and drives him out of Germany. Henry occupies Metz, Toul and Verdun. Charles is compelled to accept Pacification of Passau.

1553 Maurice d. England: acc. Mary.

1554 Mary of England m. Philip, crown prince of Spain.
Begins persecution of Protestants.

1555 Settlement of the religious question in Germany by the peace of Augsburg.
Acc. Pope Paul IV (Caraffa).
Charles resigns Netherlands and Italy to Philip.
India: Humayun returns and retakes Delhi.

1556 Charles abdicates; acc. Philip II (Spain) and Ferdinand (Empire).
India: Humayun d.; acc. Akbar.

# THE EPOCH OF THE REFORMATION
## 1492–1555

THE practically simultaneous discoveries, a few years before the fifteenth century closed, of the ocean routes from Europe to the East and to a vast unknown continent beyond the western ocean are taken, so far as any date can be taken, to mark the dividing line between the medieval and the modern worlds. Both discoveries resulted indeed inevitably from the oceanic activity inaugurated early in the century by Henry the Navigator, and could not have been long deferred after the impulse given by him ; but without it they might have been postponed for centuries. Hitherto the whole 'world of which Europe had any consciousness was contained within the compass of the northern half of one hemisphere. By this double discovery the existence of the other three-quarters of the globe was at one stroke revealed ; and the event was sufficient in itself to inaugurate a vast revolution among the nations of the known world. That is what gives it its unique character among the events and movements which differentiate the medieval from the modern world.

### Effect of the Maritime Discoveries

THE printing press facilitated the diffusion of knowledge ; the fall of Constantinople gave an accidental impulse to humanism by the attendant dispersion of Greek books ; the conquest of Granada and Charles VIII's invasion of Italy were significant of the new stage of national consolidation arriving in western Europe ; Luther's denunciation of indulgences gave the Reformation movement the character of a direct challenge to the Papacy : but all these were merely notable incidents in the course of a group of movements which in combination amounted to a political and intellectual revolution, and a long interval of time separated the first of them from the last. None of them had the individual significance or the unexpectedness of the double maritime discovery.

The effect, however, did not immediately make itself felt in the European situation. Portugal for the time monopolised the advantages to which she was fully entitled in the east, and Spain in the far west. An English expedition, under the Genoese or Venetian captains John and Sebastian Cabot, was the first actually to reach the American mainland, but the discovery was not followed up, since the region, Labrador, seemed not to be worth exploiting. The Portuguese Cabral, carried west when he meant to go east, discovered and annexed Brazil, which fell to Portugal under the bull of partition issued in 1493 by Pope Alexander VI ; otherwise Spain had the New World to herself until her exclusive rights were challenged by the Elizabethan seamen. How she dealt with the civilizations which she found established there before her we shall see in the course of this chapter.

### 'Balance of Power' in Europe

HENCE there is no apparent convulsion in European politics ; yet in actual fact a revolution has already been accomplished in the European system. Four 'great powers have come into being, and the relations between them, primarily between three of them—Spain, France, the Hapsburgs—are the determining factor ; England is comparatively, but only comparatively, detached from the rest because she no longer has direct territorial interests on the Continent ; but various portions of Italy and Burgundy never cease to provide bones of contention among the other three. For a long time to come England's main concern is to prevent either France or Spain from gaining such a preponderance over the other as to create a menace to herself ; a new formula is taking shape—the 'balance of power.'

It is important, however, to remark that the division into great powers is not so much national as dynastic. For French and English, dynasty and nation

Imperator Cæfar Diuus Maximilianus
Pius Felix Augustus

**A VERSATILE EMPEROR**

Maximilian I (1459-1519)—see also page 483—
became emperor in 1493. A versatile man, he
included the writing of books in his activities,
employing among others for their illustration
Albrecht Dürer, who drew this portrait of him.
*British Museum*

are indistinguishable or very nearly so ;
but Spain definitely includes, dynastically
but not nationally, the island of Sicily,
and there is no Hapsburg nation. The
Hapsburg power is not the German
nation, for there is no German nation ;
it is the lordship of two German groups
(at the close of the fifteenth century)—
the eastern conveniently labelled Austria
and the western labelled Burgundy—
since the young archduke of Austria is
heir to the headship of the house of
Hapsburg, and, accompanying these lordships, to the hegemony of the German
principalities expressed in the title of
' emperor,' to which it has no actual
hereditary right. And, further, the
Italian and Burgundian territories for
which the three continental powers are
going to contend have no national connexion with any one of them ; their
titles to possession are purely dynastic.

The point is emphasised when, within
a few years, the heir apparent of the

Hapsburgs is also the heir presumptive
of the Spanish kingdoms ; when the two
powers are for a time united under one
Hapsburg prince ; and when, at the
close of this chapter, they remain linked
together though no longer actually united,
as the Spanish Hapsburg power which
retains Burgundy, and the Austrian
imperial Hapsburg power, which has
attached to itself Czech Bohemia and
Magyar Hungary.

Our present chapter falls into two
definitely distinct divisions, marked by
the accession of Charles V as emperor
in 1519 at the moment when the Papacy
was taking up the challenge which had
just been flung down to it by Martin
Luther. The first division corresponds
with the imperial reign of Maximilian,
who succeeded Frederick III in 1493,
the second with that of his grandson who
abdicated in 1556. It was Maximilian's
death that combined Spain, Burgundy
and Austria under the Hapsburg, and it
was the abdication of Charles that again
divided the Hapsburgs into eastern and
western. It was Luther's challenge that
suddenly created a new line of cleavage
in Europe, neither national nor dynastic,
but religious, of which there had been no
symptom while Maximilian lived—a line
vague at first, but just reaching definition
when Charles abdicated.

### International Importance of Dynasties

HAVING reached the point at which four
dynastic powers have developed, we
have come also to the point at which
dynastic rights of succession, whether
domestic or in relation to claims to
external territory, acquire international
importance, and genealogies cannot be
neglected. In our first period Maximilian's
son Philip has inherited Burgundy, not
from his father, but from his mother.
But he is also his father's heir. By his
marriage to Joanna, the daughter and
heiress of both Ferdinand of Aragon and
Isabella of Castile—kingdoms still separable—his son Charles becomes heir presumptive to both in addition to his
Hapsburg inheritance. Philip dies before
Maximilian, and thus it is Charles who in
1519 succeeds to the whole Hapsburg

and Spanish heritage (though he makes over Austria to his brother Ferdinand), a vast assortment of heterogeneous territories and nationalities with no territorial continuity and no common traditions.

Henry VII of England marries his daughter to the king of Scots ; with the result, due to the matrimonial eccentricities of his son Henry VIII, that where our chapter ends the young queen of Scots is in one view the legitimate heiress-presumptive to the English throne, to which at the beginning of the next century her son actually succeeds. The kings of France and Aragon both lay claim to the crown of Naples, the former as representing the house of Anjou, which had reigned there till the accession of Alfonso of Aragon, the latter as the legitimate heir of Alfonso himself, who had left it to his own illegitimate offspring. And Louis XII of France claims the duchy of Milan as grandson of Valentina, the legitimate sister of the last Visconti duke, Filippo Maria, whereas the reigning

**' FATHER OF HIS PEOPLE '**
Like Charles VIII, whom he succeeded in 1498, Louis XII occupied himself disadvantageously with Italian affairs, although in France his rule was popular. This miniature in a French manuscript depicts his entry into Genoa in 1507.
*Bibliothèque Nationale ; from Larousse, ' Histoire de France '*

Sforza family are the children or grandchildren of his illegitimate daughter Bianca.

Italy, at the very height, during our first period, of her intellectual brilliance, matching that of the Greeks of the fifth century before the Christian era, is also the main stage of the political drama ; but her political history is even literally poisonous. Italian patriotism and even the conception of Italian unity have no place in it. The one statesman who was possessed with that idea, Niccolo Machiavelli the Florentine, could see no hope of its realization except in the appearance of a despot who would shrink from no crime that would help to make his power irresistible. There was no lack of candidates with this necessary moral qualification, but something else was needed in which they were wanting, and they never achieved irresistible power. How they might have used it is another question. In fact, only one of them, Cesare Borgia,

**CHARLES VIII OF FRANCE**
Charles VIII (1470–98) succeeded his father, Louis XI, in 1483, and until 1491 his sister, Anne of Beaujeu, ruled France. Against her advice Charles then embarked upon his Italian schemes, which brought him small credit.
*Uffizi Gallery, Florence ; photo, Alinari*

**A POLITICAL GAME OF CARDS IN 1500**

This French caricature—perhaps the earliest example of a political cartoon—shows Louis XII playing cards with the Swiss and Venetian rulers, anxiously watched by his ally, Pope Alexander VI. The emperor stands by with a fresh pack and Henry VII of England converses aside with Ferdinand of Spain.

*From Jaime, ' Musée de la Caricature '*

came near to achieving eminence, and his fall was as sudden as his rise had been rapid. His father, Roderigo Borgia— Pope Alexander VI, 1492–1503—was disqualified by his office, not by his character.

The fighting in Italy was actually started by the misrule of the reigning dynasts of Naples, King Ferrante (Ferdinand) and his son who succeeded him as Alfonso II in 1494. The nobles resolved to offer the crown to a prince with a legitimate title, and they fixed upon Charles VIII of France. He accepted the offer as the lawful representative of the house of Anjou, in which capacity he was already in possession of Provence to the exclusion of his cousin René of Lorraine, who had been disinherited by his father, the last really Angevin king of Provence. In 1494 Charles crossed the Alps at the head of a French army, meeting no effective opposition, but rather welcomed in north Italy. Alfonso ran away, and early next year Charles was master of the kingdom.

The rapidity of his success alarmed the north into form-

ing a league against him. He marched thither, leaving the government of his new kingdom in French hands, and found that he had to fight his way back to France. He did nothing more in Italy, died in 1498, and was succeeded on the throne by his cousin Louis XII (of Orléans). Meanwhile, the French made themselves so unpopular in Naples that Ferdinand II, son of Alfonso, recovered the crown there with little difficulty, but, dying next year, passed it to his uncle Frederick.

Louis as duke of Orléans had already attempted unsuccessfully to assert his shadowy claim to Milan. His domestic administration in France not undeservedly won him the name of the father of his people, but unhappily he could not resist the lure of Italy, where misfortune awaited him. He evicted Lodovico Sforza from Milan and then turned to Naples, but found that Ferdinand of Aragon was now disposed to assert his own claim there. The pair thereupon made an unholy bargain for the partition of the kingdom by the treaty of Granada (1500), and Frederick, seeing that resistance was hopeless, surrendered Naples to Louis. Here the French king's successes ended. Friction with the Spaniards developed into war.

**' BEHOLD, I WILL BRING A SWORD UPON YOU '**

While preaching one of his Advent sermons at Florence, in 1492, Savonarola beheld a vision of the sword of the Lord descending towards the earth while voices promised vengeance to the wicked and mercy to the faithful. The vision is recorded on a contemporary medal of the school of Niccolo Fiorentino.

*British Museum*

The young Spanish commander, Gonsalvo de Córdova, whose brilliance won him the name of the Great Captain, gained repeated victories against heavy odds, the French were ejected, and the whole kingdom of Naples was annexed (1503) to Aragon.

Meanwhile, Savonarola in Florence and the Borgias in central Italy had run their tragic courses. Lorenzo de' Medici died in 1492. His younger son was made a cardinal, and became Pope Leo X in 1513 ; the elder son, Piero, succeeded to Lorenzo's position, but made himself so unpopular that the Medici were expelled from Florence. The Dominican Savonarola, who .had acquired immense influence as a reformer of morals, unhappily assumed the character of a political leader ; his political sagacity was not equal to his moral enthusiasm ; he found himself in collision with Pope Alexander ; the hot fit of emotional fervour which he had aroused among the Florentines cooled down ; in 1498 he was condemned as a heretic and executed as a traitor. Fourteen years later the Medici were restored in Florence.

**' DESPOT UNDER THE FORMS OF LAW '**

Subtlety of intellect and strength of will were principal characteristics of Henry VIII (1490–1547) and both are suggested in this portrait of him attributed to Holbein. In his intervention in European affairs and also in his breach with Rome, he was largely influenced by zeal for the greatness of England.

*National Portrait Gallery, London*

Alexander (Roderigo Borgia) was the nephew of a previous pope, Calixtus III, who had set an evil example by raising him to the cardinalate in spite of notorious vices—so completely had the Council of Constance failed, in restoring the Papacy, to restore its spiritual character. He was the father of sundry illegitimate but acknowledged children, among them Cesare and Lucrezia, who enjoys a lamentable and probably quite undeserved fame as an expert in the use of poison for political or sentimental purposes. Nevertheless, intrigue brought him the tiara on the death of Innocent VIII in 1492. His primary object was to convert the numerous principalities of the Romagna (once the Ravenna exarchate), actually independent but nominally under papal sovereignty, into a solid principality for Cesare, whose successful methods in pursuing that object filled Machiavelli with admiration and hopes which were disappointed. For he was planning to add Tuscany to the Romagna when, in 1503, he and his father—as it was universally believed—drank of the wine they intended for an adversary. Alexander died ; Cesare recovered ; but in the meantime another adversary secured his own succession to the papal throne as Julius II. The Borgias were Spaniards ; Cesare fell into

GASTON FOXIVS

**GASTON DE FOIX, DUKE OF NEMOURS**
Gaston de Foix (1489–1512), scion of a historic
family and nephew of Louis XII, ranks almost
with Bayard as a French national hero. His
death in the moment of victory at Ravenna
was an irreparable loss to France.
*Uffizi Gallery, Florence ; photo, Alinari*

the hands of Julius' ally Ferdinand of
Aragon, and disappeared into Spain, where
he was killed in a skirmish a few years
later. Julius appropriated the Romagna
as a papal domain.

The reign of Julius (1503–13) was
mainly devoted to the attempt to make the
pope the leading secular prince in Italy.
Ferdinand, after Isabella's death in 1504,
was much occupied with securing his own
control over Castile, where he was not king,
as regent for his daughter Joanna and
her son Charles ; but he, Louis XII,
Maximilian and the Venetian republic,
as well as the pope, all had diverse interests in the Italian question. The result
was the League of Cambrai (1508), a
league of the other four powers against
Venice, with intent to a partition between
them of her subject territories. But when
she had been duly stripped the league
broke up. Julius wanted to turn the French
out of Italy ; and in 1511 the Holy League
between Julius, Ferdinand and Venice set
about that project, Ferdinand, according

to his custom, throwing the burden of
the work upon his allies. The young
king of England, Henry VIII (1509–47),
and Maximilian were both drawn into the
league, that they might effect a diversion
by attacking French Flanders and Guienne.

The French at first won brilliant victories
under a young captain of genius, Gaston
de Foix. But with his death in 1512 the
tide turned. The French were driven
out ; the Sforza and the anti-French
Medici were restored in Milan and Florence ;
the Switzers, whose infantry hardly knew
what it meant to be defeated, and had
rendered invaluable service, were rewarded with control over the principal
Alpine passes ; and Ferdinand incidentally
annexed the Spanish portion of the kingdom of Navarre. The former subjects
of Venice were restored to her. When
Julius died in 1513 he had established the
Papal State, but the foreigner was as firmly
planted in Italy as ever.

Two years later the French were back in
Milan. The coalition against them dissolved when the fighting pope died and
the various members had no common
object in view. Louis died at the very
beginning of 1515 and, leaving no male
heir of his body though thrice married, was
succeeded by his cousin Francis I (of
Angoulême). Francis forthwith set about
the recovery of Milan, invaded Italy, and
at the stubbornly contested battle of
Marignano (September, 1515) for the first
time defeated, though he could not rout,
the hitherto invincible Swiss who were
fighting for the duke, Maximilian Sforza.
Milan opened its gates, and Milan, together with Parma and Piacenza, passed
again into French possession. At the same
time Francis came to an agreement with
Pope Leo whereby certain rights surrendered by earlier popes to the French
church were transferred to the crown ;
with the later result that all the higher
ecclesiastical appointments became a preserve for the French noblesse.

### King of Spain becomes Emperor Charles V

FERDINAND had kept his hold on the
regency of Castile n spite of the
efforts first of his son-in-law the archduke
Philip and then, on the death of Philip,

of his father, Maximilian. Ferdinand died in 1516 ; Joanna was insane ; and the boy Charles, already lord of Burgundy, succeeded to the kingdoms of Castile, Aragon, Sicily and Naples. Three years later the death of Maximilian gave him at the age of nineteen the rest of the heritage of the Hapsburgs. No other German prince was willing to be a candidate for the imperial crown ; the kings of France and England offered themselves ; but Germany preferred an untried boy who was a Hapsburg to a Valois or a Tudor ; and Charles (Carlos I of Spain) became the emperor Charles V.

A GENERAL council had restored the Papacy, and the restored Papacy had scotched the 'conciliar' movement (see page 475), and with it all prospect of that systematic reformation of which the Church was in crying need. Since the earnest efforts of Pius II to awaken once more the ancient crusading spirit had failed, the popes had one and all been dead to their spiritual functions even when they were not notoriously evil livers. But they had fostered the intellectual movement in Italy which made the period one of the most brilliant in history ; and so far as that movement was directed to religion it was preparing a revolution.

**FRANCIS I IN ROYAL SPLENDOUR**
Superficially Francis I (1494–1547), who succeeded Louis XII in 1515, was a very kingly king, with a splendid air, brave, witty and courteous. His real frivolity appeared in his addiction to gallantry and dress. This portrait was painted by Jean Clouet, shortly before the king's disaster at Pavia in 1525.
*The Louvre, Paris ; photo. Archives photographiques*

The fact was not immediately apparent. The scholars such as Erasmus and Thomas More conceived that ignorance was at the bottom of the trouble, and that the

**FRANCIS I LEADING A CHARGE AT THE BATTLE OF MARIGNANO**
Immediately after his accession Francis I prepared for his Italian campaign and early in September, 1515, reached Marignano, ten miles from Milan, where he was confronted by the Swiss mercenaries in the service of Sforza. Battle was joined on September 13, and during the day Francis in person led his men-at-arms in a tremendous charge upon the Swiss—the incident recorded in this bas-relief on his tomb at St. Denis. Resumed at dawn on September 14, the battle ended in a French triumph.
*Photo, Giraudon*

**LUTHER THE CHALLENGER OF ROME**

Born at Eisleben, Martin Luther (1483–1546) was educated at Erfurt. He studied for the Church, but became a vigorous assailant of its abuses and finally the leader of the Reformation. He upheld the doctrine of justification by faith with courage and determination.

*Pinakothek, Munich : photo, Hanfstängl*

way to reform was through education. Stereotyped misinterpretations of the Scriptures, crude distortions of pure doctrine, and cheap superstitions would perish under the shafts of enlightened ridicule and the illuminating exposition made possible by the study of the New Testament in the original Greek, and orthodoxy would be unimpaired by the disappearance of these alien excrescences. And the scholars were gaining ground rapidly, many of the higher clergy being notable educationists.

What they might have effected if matters had been left in their hands for a few years longer, and a spiritually-minded pope had been raised to the pontificate, is an interesting and highly debatable question ; but the fighting Julius II was followed by the cultured pagan Leo X, who was quite unaware that moral issues were at stake. And the intellectuals were thrust on one side by the explosive energy of a man for whom

nothing counted except the moral issues, whose emergence from the obscurity of a professorship at Wittenberg rent Europe into hostile religious camps for a century and a half. The final line of cleavage was laid down by the Council of Trent, which closed its sittings in 1563—acceptance or rejection of the unqualified spiritual supremacy of Rome and of the validity of all dogmas affirmed by Rome. No name can be applied to either party without offending some school of religious opinion ; but Romanist for those who maintained, and Protestant for those in protest against, the claim of Rome seem to be the labels least open to objection.

The immediate occasion, which brought Luther conspicuously to the front was the official sale, on an unprecedented scale, of indulgences ; the object being the replenishment of the papal treasury. According to the popular belief, which the distributors of the indulgences were at no pains to dispel, the purchase of an indulgence carried with it absolution for the sins of the purchaser. This was in 1517. Martin Luther denounced indulgences as implying that the pope had the power, possessed by none but God, to forgive sins, and he persuaded the elector of Saxony to forbid the sale in his duchy. He was denounced as a heretic, and retorted by a vigorous and uncompromising propaganda against other current doctrines and papal claims, one point in which appealed strongly to secular princes —that the customary contributions to the papal treasury were unjustifiable. There matters stood at the moment when Charles V was elected emperor in 1519.

### Selim the Ottoman conquers Egypt

IN the east and in the far west, the same chronological line of division between the two periods may be accepted. For thirty years after the death of Mohammed the Conqueror, the Ottomans under the inactive Bajazet II made no advance either in Europe or in Asia. The Turks grew restive and the troops mutinous, until in 1512 Bajazet's energetic son Selim I took matters into his own hands, deposed his father, put all his inconveniently near relations to death, and opened a new era of conquest. He quickly brought to subjection the petty princes of Asia Minor who did not acknowledge the Ottoman sovereignty, and in 1516 flung himself upon Syria, where the Mameluke sultans of Egypt still held sway. The issue was decided by the defeat and fall of the sultan Kansuh in the fierce battle of Marg Dabik.

Selim swept on to Egypt, where the Mamelukes made a desperate stand and met with utter overthrow close to Cairo (1517). Egypt was annexed to the Ottoman dominion, though it was left practically as a tributary state in the hands of the Mamelukes. But Selim seized the opportunity to end the puppet Abbasid Khalifate which the Mamelukes had revived and kept in being, carried off the last of the line to Constantinople, and himself assumed the office and the title, which remained with the ' Grand Turk ' until the twentieth century. Selim's further projects of empire were cut off by his death in 1520, but they were developed mightily under his son Suleiman the Magnificent.

### The Far East and the Far West

**J**N India the Bahmani power in the Deccan during this period broke up into five independent states under Mahomedan rulers, the last established being Golconda in 1518. The Lodi sultans at Delhi extended their dominion over the greater part of the Ganges basin though Bengal remained independent. But beyond the north-western passes the most picturesque and attractive of Oriental conquerors, Babar, the founder of the Mogul dynasty, fifth in descent from Tamerlane and descended also through his mother from the Mongol Jenghiz Khan, was preparing for the great adventure which was to crown an abnormally adventurous career, the conquest of northern India. In the Indian Ocean the Portuguese were occupied in establishing a maritime empire, not seeking to conquer territory, but occupying naval stations as bases for the control of the seas.

Similarly, in the far west Spaniards discovered one after another of the West Indian islands, and the South American

coast line ; a Florentine merchant, Amerigo Vespucci, sailing on a Spanish ship, gave his name to the new continents ; Pope Alexander VI, on the hypothesis that heathen lands were in the pope's gift, drew the line from north to south, bestowing all lands that had been or might be discovered to the west of it on Spain, and all to the east on Portugal ; English expeditions, followed by Frenchmen, away in the inhospitable north, discovered Labrador and Newfoundland, and the estuary of the St. Lawrence. In 1513 Balboa, from the neck of land that joins the north and south continents, discovered the ocean that lies between them and Asia. When Maximilian died in 1519,

**SULTAN SELIM I**

Bigotry, cruelty and ambition stamped Selim I (1465–1520), the conqueror of Persia, Syria and Egypt and first Ottoman khalif. This portrait of him is attributed to Haidar Bey, a sixteenth-century artist highly esteemed by the Turks.

*Bibliothèque Nationale, Paris*

Hernando Cortés was already heading the adventure which before the year was out was to achieve the conquest of Mexico. And also before the year was out Ferdinand Magellan set sail on the first voyage of circumnavigation.

Magellan, a Portuguese who had taken service with Charles, found and penetrated the strait that bears his name, between the continent and Tierra del Fuego, which for long was supposed to be another vast continent, crossed the Pacific and died among the Philippine Islands, whence his ships made their way southward round Africa, and reached Spain, having sailed completely round the globe. The strait was not yet regarded as a practicable route ; but the voyage finally demonstrated that the earth was a globe, and that a vast ocean lay between America and the real Indies, though the American tribes remained 'Indians' in the established popular parlance.

The Spaniards had planted themselves on the Isthmus of Darien but not elsewhere on the mainland, when Velasquez, the governor of Cuba, with a view to the conquest of Yucatan, sent an exploring expedition which traced the coast of the

Exma S.D. Fernando Cortés Conquistador de Mexico Gobernador y capitan

**CONQUEROR OF MEXICO**

Daring and determination enabled Hernando Cortés (1485–1547) to win for Spain the vast Aztec Empire in Mexico. His immense services to his country were repaid with rank ingratitude and he died a disappointed man.

*Municipal Palace, Mexico ; from Maudslay, 'Conquest of New Spain,' Hakluyt Society*

Gulf of Mexico in 1517. Next year he set Cortés in command of another expedition. In February, 1519, Cortés sailed, disregarding his orders, with some four hundred Europeans, half as many natives and less than a score of horses and guns. In Yucatan he learnt of the existence of the Aztec empire of Mexico, for which the outlying tribes had no affection. He actually burnt his boats, informed the Aztec emperor Montezuma (Motecuzoma) that he was about to visit him as the envoy of a mighty king from over the sea, and then proceeded to pay his exceedingly unwelcome visit. The strangers having accordingly been admitted, Montezuma offered submission and tribute, but declined to worship strange gods ; the emperor was, in fact, a virtual prisoner, while the

**CORTES' VICTORY AT MICHUACAN**

One of the fiercest battles fought by Cortés in Mexico was with the natives of Michuacan, near the Pacific seaboard, in which he was assisted by the Tlaxcalans with their war dogs. Native treachery led to the engagement, typified, in this old Mexican painting of the battle, by the Indian hanged in the background.

Spaniards assumed the government in his name. Velasquez sent an expedition to recall Cortés, who went out to meet it, leaving behind a garrison in the capital, and ended by attaching most of it to his own force.

Meanwhile, the garrison, seeing that the great city and its immense population were in a state of ferment, and fearing an organized rising, struck first, attacking a great gathering held for a religious celebration. Thereby they brought on the very thing they had feared, and found themselves in danger of being overwhelmed by an apparently countless foe. Cortés with difficulty forced his way back. When the garrison produced their prisoner, Montezuma, and he attempted to pacify his people, they turned their wrath upon him, and he was so roughly handled that he died. The Spaniards barely succeeded in cutting their way out and escaping to friendly territory ; so small a band could not afford the losses involved in fighting swarms which seemed to be increased instead of diminished by massacre. But Cortés received some reinforcements, collected native auxiliaries, and when he returned found a resistance which, though at first stubborn, could not long be maintained. In 1521 he had recovered the capital, and could set about a reconstruction of the government and the persistent extension of the Spanish dominion. Mexico became the centre from which it expanded on the north of Darien.

### Spanish Conquest of the Incas

MEANWHILE the existence of a second large and civilized empire in the western equatorial area was sufficiently confirmed to excite the adventurous and acquisitive spirit of Francisco Pizarro. Having obtained the necessary authority and funds, he started on his expedition by sea from Panamá in 1530, made his base at Tumbez, near the westernmost point of the continent, and, having learnt that there was civil war between the Inca brothers Huascar and Atahualpa, marched to the conquest of the Inca Empire at the head of one hundred and sixty-eight men. The advance of so tiny a force did not seriously alarm Atahualpa, who had usurped the

throne ; but Pizarro found him waiting near Cajamarca with some forty thousand men, and quite disposed to be friendly. The Spaniard invited the Inca to a conference at which he was surprised and kidnapped ; the army which attempted to rescue him was routed with great slaughter, being from a European point of view no better than an undisciplined and unarmed mob.

After the Mexican precedent Pizarro proceeded to act ' under the authority ' of his prisoner, who only excited the cupidity of his captors by offering a vast ransom for liberty. Atahualpa, having good reason to fear intrigues between the Spaniards and his deposed brother, gave secret orders for the execution of Huascar, but by so doing he only gave Pizarro an excuse for treating him as a traitor and usurper. Atahualpa was put to death and a puppet set in his place for a short time ; but even the pretence that the Spaniards were acting under any other authority than their rights as conquerors was very soon dropped. Few though the Spaniards were, they had the natives completely at

**CONQUEROR OF PERU**

Francisco Pizarro (born c. 1475) embarked in 1530 upon the conquest of Peru, which he had been planning for some years. Treachery and brutality stained the conqueror's career, which was ended by his own assassination in 1541.

*After a painting in Lima Museum*

their mercy, and Lima, which the conquerors made their headquarters, became the centre from which their easy conquests were further extended.

Independently, other expeditions established the Spaniards in the south-east of South America on the Rio de la Plata. Everywhere the vast mineral wealth of the land attracted settlers from Spain. All conquered territories were won and held as private estates of the king of Spain, and very soon annual treasure ships were transporting vast quantities of the precious metals across the Atlantic to the Spanish ports for the royal exchequer. Also Europe was flooded with tales of a great city of fabulous wealth wherein was reported to dwell the Man of Gold, El Dorado; so that the discovery of 'El Dorado' became the fantastic dream and the irresistible magnet of innumerable adventurers. No one, however, as yet challenged Spain's title to keep the new world to herself, though she paid no heed to what went on north of Florida ; where there were no precious metals, but the cod banks of Newfoundland and the search for a north-west passage to Asia were providing for English and French mariners a stormy school of seamanship which was soon to make them infinitely the superiors of the Spaniards.

In the Far East the Portuguese came into touch with China and even for a moment with the Japanese, to whom they introduced the use and manufacture of firearms. Japan was still in the stage of what is described as the Ashikaga anarchy. The effect of the contact with China was so unsatisfactory, owing mainly to the misconduct of the Portuguese, that China shut her doors to the Europeans, and the great missionary François Xavier the Apostle of the Indies, who had prosecuted his labours in Japan for more than two years, was refused admission. The great feature of Oriental history while the emperor Charles V was reigning in the west was the founding of the Mogul empire in India.

### Babar founds the Mogul Empire

AT the close of the fifteenth century central Asia was broken up into many principalities, several being in the hands of descendants of Tamerlane. In 1494, in his twelfth year, Babar succeeded his father as king of Ferghana. By the time he was twenty he had twice won and twice lost Samarkand, the recovery of which was the unfulfilled dream of his life. He had the Mongol blood of Jenghiz Khan in his veins from his mother, and hence, although he loathed that race, he bore the name Mughal or Mongol, or Mogul in its most familiar form ; but in his own eyes he was the heir of Tamerlane the Turk. Driven out of Transoxiana by the Tatar

INCA WARRIORS OF THE TYPE THAT PIZARRO OVERCAME

Pachacutec, meaning ' he who changes the world,' was the name conferred upon the Inca Yupanqui who in the fifteenth century converted the Cuzco kingdom into the vast Inca empire extending to the Pacific which Pizarro found established when he first reached Peru in 1527. Government administration was elaborately organized and the army was efficient and well equipped. An old Peruvian vase-painting includes these figures of Inca warriors of the period shortly before the Spanish conquest.

*From Stübel and Reis, ' Das Todtenfeld von Anco in Peru'*

conquerer Shaibani, the young adventurer made his way with many hairbreadth escapes to Afghanistan, where a cousin had been deposed by a usurper, collected a few daring adherents and made himself king at Kabul and master of most of Afghanistan. He still could not resist the lure of Samarkand, but, though he reached it in a hurricane campaign and held the city and the throne for a few months, he had to fly for his life again (1512), and when he got back to Kabul he finally abandoned his earlier ambitions and made up his mind that what he really wanted was to be emperor of India.

In 1519 he made his first expedition across the Indus with a force of some two thousand men, laying claim to the Punjab as being a part of the heritage of Tamerlane. Nothing came of this. For the next five years he was mainly occupied in consolidating his position in Afghanistan, though he found time for two raiding expeditions. But in 1524 he found his opportunity in a double appeal from an exiled prince of the house of Lodi and from the governor of the Punjab, who was in revolt against Ibrahim, the reigning sovereign at Delhi.

The defection, however, of his Indian allies after he started caused some delay, and it was not until the end of 1525 that he made his invasion in force—that is, at the head of twelve thousand men, Turks, Afghans and Mongols. He got some reinforcements from rebels against Ibrahim, whose army he shattered at Panipat, the field of several decisive engagements in Indian history, in 1526. That made him master of Delhi and of enormous wealth, which he gave away lavishly. His men wanted to go home with their huge spoils, but he would be content with nothing short of the conquest of Hindustan, i.e. northern India. If he celebrated his

**AN AMIABLE MOGUL EMPEROR**

Humayun (1508–1556) succeeded his father Babar as Mogul emperor of Delhi in 1530. Though gallant and amiable he had a certain weakness of character well suggested in this portrait painted by Bhagvati, an Indian artist of the sixteenth century, depicting him listening to two Hajjis reciting the scriptures.

*British Museum*

victories in the merciless fashion of the Tamerlane tradition, he could also display a most lordly generosity which brought him adherents ; the mutinous spirit subsided, and by the end of 1530 he was practically master of the land from Kabul to the Bay of Bengal. Then he died—as he and everyone about him believed by a magnificent act of self-sacrifice ; for his best-beloved son and heir, Humayun, was apparently on the point of death, and the father prayed that his own life might be taken in the place of his son's. In the plenitude of his powers, at the age of forty-eight, the great conqueror fell ill and died, but Humayun was restored to health.

Babar was no mere devastator like his terrible ancestors, Turk or Mongol. But in five years he had conquered an empire, without having attempted to organize it,

ROYAL POMP AND PAGEANTRY AT THE FIELD OF THE CLOTH OF GOLD

This picture representing Henry VIII on his way to meet Francis I at the Field of the Cloth of Gold in June, 1520, was painted, probably by John Crust, shortly after the event it commemorates, and reproduces actual details with minute accuracy. On the left in the English procession is King Henry on a white horse, Wolsey beside him and the marquis of Dorset in front bearing the sword of state. On the right is the temporary palace erected for Henry's reception, with two fountains spouting wine in front of it, and behind are the lists, kitchen tent and some of the 2,800 tents erected for the kings' retinues.

*Engraving after the painting in Hampton Court Palace*

and the princes and nobles who had submitted to him were by no means ready to submit to his gallant and amiable but not very able son. Humayun was driven out again within ten years by an Afghan adventurer of great ability, Sher Shah, who established himself in Bihar and proved himself, in a reign of no more than five years, to be a ruler and administrator, as well as a soldier, of a very high order. Humayun, at the end of fifteen years of exile, in the course of which he experienced every vicissitude of fortune, was able to return and renew the fight for the empire of India in 1555. Sher Shah was dead, his successors lacked his ability, and Humayun recaptured Delhi. But seven months later, in January, 1556, he was killed by an accidental fall, and the loyalty of his soldier minister Bairam secured the accession to his thirteen-year-old son, the famous Akbar, the builder of the Mogul empire.

### Problems confronting Charles V

CHARLES V was elected emperor in the year of Babar's first Indian expedition ; he resigned Burgundy to his son Philip II three months before Akbar's accession at Delhi. The period, of which he was throughout one of the principal figures, is one of the most momentous in European history. Nor was there any man who had a task before him more complicated than his. He had to consolidate Spain, not yet accustomed to unity ; to attempt once more to establish the supremacy of the central authority in an empire intensely opposed to centralisation ; to rule at the same time over Burgundy, traditionally, racially and geographically separated from and antagonistic to the rest of his dominions ; to face in Burgundy and in Italy the rivalry of the most highly centralised monarchy in Europe ; and on the top of all this to control a quite unprecedented religious revolution which, except in Spain itself, intensified each one of his other difficulties. And still there was lurking in the background the growing menace of the Ottoman power on the Mediterranean waters and on the eastern flank of the Empire.

The French rivalry was what he felt as his most immediate concern. Wolsey

**VICTIM OF OVERWEENING AMBITION**
' In the time of his authority and power the haughtiest man that then lived ' was his loyal servant George Cavendish's verdict upon Thomas Wolsey (c. 1475–1530). It is endorsed in this portrait of the cardinal by an unknown artist.
*National Portrait Gallery, London*

in England was eager for the rôle of arbiter of Europe, holding the balance between the Hapsburg and the Valois, but suffered from the fact that his most skilfully laid plans might be thwarted by the capricious impulses of a master whom he dared not cross. Charles and Francis each of them desired active support from England, or, failing that, her neutrality ; but neither would be deterred from fighting by her opposition. In Italy both Pope Leo and Venice were more afraid of French than of imperial aggression ; and, in spite of the splendid extravagances of the famous meeting between the two kings known as the Field of the Cloth of Gold (1520), the emperor drew England into an anti-French league.

The war proved disastrous to Francis, though England's share in it was never more than half-hearted. The real arena

**CAPTURE OF FRANCIS I AT PAVIA**

Francis I's defeat and capture at the battle of Pavia, February 25, 1525, are thus depicted in a copper engraving by Matthew Merian, the seventeenth-century Swiss engraver, based upon an earlier original and contributed to Gottfried's Historical Chronicle—a work brought down to the year 1618.

*British Museum*

was in Italy, where in 1525 Francis met with a crushing defeat at Pavia and was taken prisoner. To procure his release he had to submit to humiliating terms, and even in accepting them declared that he would not be bound by them, for they included the surrender of all claims in respect of Milan, Naples and Flanders. The unlooked-for completeness of Charles' success alarmed his allies, who now entered on a new league for the expulsion of the emperor from Italy ; but his successes continued ; in 1527 his troops stormed and sacked Rome itself, and he was able to dictate a peace by which Francis had to confirm the promises made after Pavia, and Pope Clement VII, cousin and second successor of Leo X, found himself almost a puppet in the emperor's hands.

Meanwhile, however, the religious revolution had been very thoroughly inaugurated. Luther had burnt his boats. Made uneasy by the vigour of his propaganda, Leo X, in 1520, excommunicated the Wittenberg professor, who re-

plied by publicly burning the bull of excommunication. The pope could inflict no further penalty directly, but a diet of the empire was about to be held, and the young emperor was willing to oblige ; so Martin Luther was summoned to defend himself before it.

He appeared at the Diet of Worms under a safe-conduct, like Huss at Constance, but also under the protection of the elector of Saxony, who had no mind to allow him to suffer the fate of Huss ; and he had powerful support from other lay princes of the empire, from practically the whole body of the knights, and from widespread public opinion. Luther refused to recant unless convinced of error. Being, on the contrary, convinced that his denounced doctrines were true, it followed that those who denounced them were in error. Popes and councils, therefore, were not infallible ; the one infallible authority was Holy Scripture,

**FREDERICK III, ' THE WISE '**

Succeeding his father as elector of Saxony in 1486, Frederick III (1463–1525) was an enlightened statesman and intellectual man. In 1502 he founded the university of Wittenberg, where he appointed Luther and Melanchthon professors, and thereafter remained Luther's steadfast champion.

*Pinakothek, Munich*

of which, by the grace of God, it was in the individual's power to find the true interpretation.

The diet had other work before it. Luther, taking his departure, was kidnapped for his safety by his friend the Saxon elector, and hidden away in the Wartburg, in Thuringia. When the diet had begun to disperse, and some of Luther's supporters had left, the other party carried a decree putting him to the ban of the empire, but no one was prepared to start a civil war in order to execute it. Charles was too deeply involved in his war with Francis to risk the stirring up of trouble in Germany. Pope Leo died at the end of the year ; Charles procured the election of the Burgundian Adrian VI ; Adrian died in 1523 and was succeeded by the Medici Clement VII.

The German knights, mainly supporters of Luther, headed by Ulrich von Hutten and Franz von Sickingen, raised what was intended to be a national revolt against the political domination of the princes and foreign influences generally ; but they got no encouragement from Luther and they were crushed in the same year. Fanatical reformers, who, as so often happens, associated the destruction of the existing social order with their religious doctrines, stirred up a great revolt of the German peasantry,

**CHAMPION OF THE OPPRESSED**

A wealthy German knight with a congenital love of fighting, Franz von Sickingen (1481–1523) engaged in many feuds, usually on behalf of the oppressed. His militant championship of the early Reformers was discouraged by Luther.
*From Bechstein, ' Deutsche Männer '*

who suffered under a crushing serfdom, and that revolt, too, was trampled out in blood (1525), while Luther vainly denounced the revolutionists. Nevertheless, the wild doctrines of the extremists were attributed to the spirit of defiance aroused by Luther, and the scholars who before his rise had been the active reformers became prominent in the reaction.

On the other hand, just at this stage the accord between pope and emperor was broken. Confident that his attitude would now be anti-papal, the imperial diet at Speier in 1526 in Charles' absence decreed in effect that each prince should control the religion of his own subjects in his own territory, with the result that electoral Saxony, Hesse, Brandenburg and other principalities adopted the Lutheran principles, thus inaugurating the religious division of Germany.

At the beginning of 1529, however, Charles and Clement had come to terms, and another diet at Speier, under the imperial influence, revoked the decree and returned to that of Worms ; while a number of Lutheran princes and cities united to sign the protest from which the

**POPE ADRIAN VI**

Adrian Dedel (1459–1523) had a distinguished career at Louvain university and in 1507 became tutor to Charles V, who later appointed him inquisitor-general of Aragon. His election to the Papacy in 1522 was largely due to Charles.
*Uffizi Gallery, Florence ; photo, Alinari*

reforming movement took the name of Protestant. At the Diet of Augsburg next year, when Charles presided in person, the Protestants produced the Augsburg confession of faith, and made it clear that they would abide by it, and that coercion would mean civil war. At the end of the year (1530) they formed the defensive league of Schmalkalde. Charles could not take that risk. He was master in Italy, but the Turks were advancing on Vienna, and must be met. For a time there was a truce in Germany, but it was an armed truce which might at any moment become war.

In Switzerland, nominally within the Empire but practically outside it, the reforming movement was led by Zwingli of Zürich, quite independently of Luther, from whose views his own differed materially, though they were no less irreconcilable with papal theories. There the religious question was complicated by a political question, for Zwingli wished to equalise the votes of the cantons in the diet of the

**GENEVA'S DISCIPLINARIAN**

John Calvin (1509-1564), theologian and reformer, was more definite and methodical than Luther. Rigidly moral, he purified life at Geneva, and is renowned as author of the Institutes of the Christian Religion.

*Contemporary engraving*

confederation, while the four forest cantons were determined not to lose the predominance they enjoyed under the existing system. A struggle ensued which ended with the fall of Zwingli in the battle of Cappel in 1531 ; but the treaty which followed secured the control of religion to the congregations in the individual cantons. The Swiss and Lutheran schools of Protestantism continued to be hardly less hotly antagonistic to each other than both were to Rome.

### Henry VIII breaks with Rome

IN France and in England the governments gave no countenance to the new theology ; but in both, the kings were influenced primarily by personal or political considerations. Both began to realize that by cultivating friendly relations with the German Protestants they could add to the emperor's embarrassments ; and from 1529 onwards Henry had reasons of his own for defying and repudiating the authority of the pope, who had his own reasons for evading the English king's desire to be released from his marriage with Katharine of Aragon, the aunt of the emperor.

When Henry had made up his mind to a decisive breach with Rome, the weight of England was necessarily cast on the side of Protestantism. And the French government, while it repressed Protestantism in France, was always ready for alliance with Protestants outside France, in order to embarrass Charles.

In Germany the North German princes tended to the Protestant side, the South Germans to the papal side. Consequently Protestant influences prevailed also in the Scandinavian countries, which were undergoing revolutions. In 1520 the crowns of all the three kingdoms—Danish, Swedish and Norwegian—were worn by Christian II, who was determined to rule as well as to reign in all of them. In that year he crushed the independence of the Swedish nobles, following up his victory by a massacre known as the 'blood-bath of Stockholm.' His savagery caused a reaction. Gustavus Vasa, who had escaped the massacre, raised a revolt against the hated Danish domination, and at the same time the Danish nobles

**CHRISTIAN II IN 1517**

Succeeding to the thrones of Denmark and Norway in 1513 Christian II (1481–1559) also recovered the crown of Sweden by force of arms, but his ruthless autocracy alienated all his subjects and in 1523 he was driven out.

*Royal Gallery, Copenhagen*

rose and expelled Christian from Denmark. The Swedes elected Gustavus king, and the Danes elected Frederick of Slesvig-Holstein. The two crowns were separated permanently by the treaty of Calmoe (1524), though Norway and the southern province of Skania went with Denmark.

Frederick introduced without enforcing the Lutheran teaching, and Lutheranism became the established religion of Denmark in the reign of his son Christian III. Gustavus, in dire need of money to be expended in setting Sweden on her feet again, resolved, like Henry VIII in England, that the Church must disgorge her wealth, adherence to the new doctrines being the inevitable corollary. The opposition seemed too strong to be overcome till he declared the alternative—his own resignation of the crown. That, as everyone knew, would mean anarchy; and the opposition collapsed (1527). Lutheranism soon became the national religion of Sweden. When Gustavus died in 1560, he had revived the national prosperity, consolidated the kingdom, and

firmly established the power of the crown, which was made hereditary in 1544.

In 1521 Charles handed over his Austrian heritage to his brother the archduke Ferdinand, who married the sister of Lewis, the Jagellon king of Bohemia and Hungary. Suleiman, later to be known as 'the Magnificent,' succeeded his father, Selim I, as Grand Turk in 1520. He at once set out on a career of aggression. He forced the Knights of S. John to abandon the Christian outpost at Rhodes and fall back to Malta; his fleets swept the eastern Mediterranean under the great corsair captain Khair ed-Din Barbarossa. In 1521 he captured Belgrade, hitherto the bulwark of Hungary; and Lewis of Hungary, advancing against him, was overwhelmed and slain at the battle of Mohacz in 1526.

On the death of Lewis, his brother-in-law Ferdinand advanced and made good his claim to the succession in Bohemia and Hungary; but the latter country had always been restive under Hapsburg

**LIBERATOR OF SWEDEN**

After the Blood Bath of Stockholm in 1520, Gustavus Eriksson Vasa (1496–1560) roused the Swedes to revolt, expelled the Danes and in 1523 was himself crowned king, first of the Vasa dynasty. This portrait was painted in 1542.

*University Library, Upsala*

R

sovereigns, and a portion of it now adhered to a Magyar noble, John Zapolya, who did not scruple to accept Turkish support against his rival. Nor did the Turk scruple to keep a large part of the disputed territory in his own hands, so that Hungary was divided under three sovereigns. But from this time the Ottoman advance was an ever-present menace, though it served to postpone open civil war in the Empire.

For some years then Germany continued in a state of uneasy tension, while Charles and Francis pursued the course of

their rivalry by devious methods and with varying fortunes, diversified by conflicts on the part of Charles, and alliances on that of Francis, with Suleiman. Henry VIII in England was following a course of his own which made it convenient to be friendly sometimes with one and sometimes with the other. Both Francis and Henry made overtures to the German Protestants of the League of Schmalkalde, which looked askance at both. For Francis, though eager for alliance with heretics or even Mahomedans abroad, with political ends in view, was the 'Most Christian King' who persecuted Protestants zealously in his own dominions ; and Henry, having flatly repudiated the papal authority, and being engaged on despoiling the Church, was nevertheless the prince on whom in earlier days Leo had bestowed the title of 'Defender of the Faith,' and who still prided himself on his theological attainments and his rigid orthodoxy.

The Mediterranean was infested with corsairs from the African ports, encouraged by Khair ed-Din, who seized Tunis from its independent ruler and held it himself as from the sultan. In 1535 Charles attacked and defeated Khair ed-Din in a great sea fight, and restored the former prince as his own vassal. Francis found an excuse for repudiating the last treaty, renewing his claim on Milan, and scandalising Christendom by an alliance with Suleiman against the emperor. Charles invaded Provence, where he was starved out by the French commander Montmorency, and had to retire with diminished prestige.

In 1538 a ten years' truce was arranged by Pope Clement's successor, Paul III. Charles utilised the interval for the suppression of the still inconveniently powerful national assembly or Cortes of Castile, and, with Francis' concurrence,

### SIXTEENTH-CENTURY RHODES

Rhodes fell to the Turks in 1522. Its strength is shown in these woodcuts, published a few years earlier, of the unsuccessful Turkish assault of 1480 on the harbour and (above) on the walls.

*From Caorsini, 'Stabilimenta Rhodiorum Militium,' 1496*

of revolts in the Netherlands ; but the hostility of Francis was revived by his repudiation of the half-promises he had given. In 1541 Charles sailed with a great fleet to root out the Algerian pirates, but most of his fleet went to the bottom in a terrific storm. Francis renewed his alliance with Suleiman, and again found an excuse for declaring war in 1542. In the campaigning fortune on the whole favoured Charles, but in 1544 he offered peace (the Treaty of Crespy) on unexpectedly favourable terms. In 1547 Henry VIII and Francis died, and Charles alone was left of the three princes who had swayed Europe since 1519.

ATTACK ON ALGIERS, THE PIRATES' LAIR

Algiers became the chief seat of the Barbary pirates about 1530 and so remained for three hundred years. In October, 1541, Charles V attempted to capture the town, but his fleet was destroyed by storm and his army by the Algerians. A German broadsheet of 1542 contains this woodcut of the attack.

*From O. Jäger, ' Weltgeschichte,' Velhagen & Klasing*

MEANWHILE, other developments were in progress which vitally affected the course of the Reformation. The motives at work were exceedingly mixed. The genuine desire to arrive at a convincing body of religious truth was wide-spread. Dissatisfaction with a system under which the teachers of religion were manifestly absorbed more often in the pursuit of political than of spiritual aims, the very unspiritual character of so many successive popes, the glaring examples of moral depravity among the higher clergy reflected in their lower ranks, the frequent abuse for debased and debasing purposes of doctrines and practices in themselves defensible, the tendency to maintain ecclesiastical authority by checking inquiry and criticism—all these things were reprobated by the most orthodox, and cried aloud for reform ; reform desired no less zealously by those who believed it to be attainable without repudiation of the papal authority in things spiritual than by those who were as firmly convinced of the contrary.

On the other hand, they aroused an anti-clerical spirit ; the laity at all times resented the wealth of the Church, of which the expropriation offered a tempting bait to impecunious princes and nobles ;

and from time immemorial princes had fought against the division of clerical allegiance between the secular ruler and the foreign head of an international organization ; though not a few dreaded that rejection of the recognized spiritual authority would be only the preliminary to the defiance of all constituted authority whatever, a view to which the German peasant revolt gave some colour. That revolt had been suppressed, though the fanatical extremists, under the name of Anabaptists, still found adherents, mainly among the down-trodden. But two serious movements began to make themselves felt, one among the Protestants in revolt from Rome, the other among the most earnest opponents of the new doctrines. The Zürich reformers had never been in harmony with the Lutherans ; but under the leadership of a French refugee, John Calvin, a new school grew up at Geneva whose tenets were even more irreconcilable than Zwingli's with those of Rome and of Luther alike. The special characteristics of the Calvinistic theology do not here concern us ; they turned mainly on his peculiar doctrine regarding predestination ; but Calvin laid down and published in 1536 the scheme of church government known to us as Presbyterianism, which dispensed with bishops, and was so democratic in structure— though its effect in Geneva was to make Calvin himself a dictator—that it was difficult for any lay prince to reconcile himself with it. And it was to Calvin, not to Luther, that the reformers turned in France (where they were known as Huguenots), in Scotland, in the Netherlands and in parts of Germany.

### Order of Jesus constituted

ON the other side a missionary brotherhood was formed at about the same time—destined to play an immense part in the religious struggles of the next hundred and fifty years—by the visionary enthusiasm of the Spaniard Ignatius Loyola. His conception was that of a company formed on the military model, which was to fight for the Church, but with the arm of the spirit, not of the flesh. The first company was formed in 1534 of a band of seven enthusiasts, to one of whom at least, François Xavier, the title of Saint is entirely appropriate ; it increased, and in 1540 the ' Society of Jesus,' popularly known as the Jesuits, was formally constituted with the recognition of the pope, Paul III, by the bull *Regimini militantis ecclesiae*, September 27.

Christendom did not yet recognize that it was split into irreconcilable parties which must either agree to live side by side or fight for the complete supremacy, which neither would concede to the other. There was a general desire, except on the part of the pope, for a general council whose authoritative decrees should be final binding pronouncements on all questions in dispute. But everyone wished to ensure that his own views should predominate, especially Charles, whose understanding of the religious sentiments involved was limited, while his desire was to dictate a compromise acceptable to no one. Consequently it was not till 1545 that a council was summoned at Trent. Even then it had hardly met when Paul and Charles quarrelled, since the pope was as much afraid of an imperial supremacy as he was

hostile to the Protestants. Charles, having just freed himself from the French war, was about to embark on the Schmalkaldic war against the German Protestant league, and the vicissitudes of that struggle materially affected the proceedings of the council during the reigns of Paul and his successor, Julius III (1550–55).

### 'The Interim' and its Consequences

LUTHER, whose influence had always been strongly cast against a settlement by force, died at the beginning of 1546. Charles was bent on uniting Germany—a most laudable object—by enforcing a religious compromise, and on establishing at last the imperial supremacy ; and he believed that the suppression of the League of Schmalkalde would remove the most serious obstacle to both projects. He declared war on the League, shattered its forces at Mühlberg (1547), capturing its leaders, whom he treated with inexcusable severity, and apparently had the ball at his feet. But he overrated his triumph. He concocted on his own responsibility and manoeuvred through the diet at Augsburg (1548) a religious compromise known as the Interim, which accentuated antagonisms instead of allaying them ; and he imposed upon the paralysed diet a reconstruction of the imperial constitution which practically placed the whole executive power in the control of the emperor.

But this was the last result desired by the princes who had supported him, or by Maurice of Saxony, to whom he owed his victory at Mühlberg. Maurice promptly and secretly organized revolt, allying himself with Henry II, who had succeeded Francis on the French throne. In return for Henry's assistance against the emperor, the administration of certain important cities in Lorraine was to be conferred on him as imperial vicar. While Charles still supposed Maurice to be engaged in suppressing resistance to the Interim, in 1552 he suddenly marched his troops on Innsbruck, from which the hitherto unsuspecting emperor barely had time to escape. Maurice brought down Charles' edifice of power like a house of cards. Charles was reduced to entrusting his brother Ferdinand, whom he had offended by attempting to oust him from the imperial succession, with the task of making the best terms he could at the treaty of Passau. And meanwhile French troops had occupied the promised cities, and being there could by no means be ejected. Metz, Toul, Verdun and Cambrai had virtually become a part of France.

Maurice's success caused the hasty adjournment of the Council of Trent, which so far had accomplished nothing towards a pacification. The Protestants who attended found themselves treated rather as prisoners at the bar than colleagues on the bench ; and it had already become evident that the validity of its decisions as a general council of the Church would never be admitted by the Protestant minority.

Charles was beaten, though Maurice was killed in the disturbed fighting which followed on the breakdown of the imperial authority. A general pacification of Germany was effected by the diet held at Augsburg (1555), under the guidance of Ferdinand It confirmed the treaty of Passau ; it confirmed to the princes the right of controlling religion within their own territories ; it reinstated in the imperial council the Lutherans whom Charles in the hour of his triumph had excluded. But it made no mention of Calvinists and it retained what was called the ' ecclesiastical reservation,' which required Catholic ecclesiastical princes to resign their sees if they changed their religion—with disastrous results in the future.

Charles had failed to secure German support for his desire to be succeeded in the imperial dignity by his son Philip, who in German eyes was a Spaniard. Towards the end of 1555 he handed over the Netherlands and Italy to

Philip and at the beginning of 1556 announced his abdication of the imperial crown, recommending as his successor his brother Ferdinand of Austria who had already long been king of the Romans.

In 1555 also Cardinal Caraffa, the organizer and head of the Inquisition in Italy, was elected pope as Paul IV. His accession, with the Pacification of Augsburg and the abdication of Charles V, together provide a definite landmark in the European chronicle.

**PICTURE OF CARE-WORN MAJESTY**

This portrait of Charles V was painted by Titian in 1548, the year the emperor issued the unsatisfactory ' Interim ' and attempted an abortive reconstruction of the imperial constitution. The tired face and sad eyes in the picture reflect the weariness and disillusionment which presently confirmed the emperor in his intention to abdicate.

*Pinakothek, Munich*

# TABLE OF DATES FOR CHAPTER 24

1555   Treaty of Augsburg lays down a modus vivendi for the antagonistic religions within the Empire.

1556   Charles V abdicates. Philip II succeeds him in Spain, Italy and the Netherlands. Ferdinand I (of Austria) elected emperor.
India : Humayun d. ; acc. Akbar. Decisive victory of Akbar and Bairam at Panipat.

1557   Philip at war with France ; England under his wife Mary Tudor is drawn into the war.
Portugal : Acc. Sebastian.

1558   Francis of Guise captures Calais ; loss of England's only foothold in Europe.
Mary Stuart m. dauphin Francis.
Mary Tudor d. ; acc. Elizabeth.
India : Akbar takes Rajput stronghold of Chitor.

1559   Peace of Cateau-Cambrésis.
Acc. Pope Pius IV.
Henry II d. ; acc. Francis II.
English religious settlement under Act of Uniformity.

1560   Francis II d. ; acc. Charles IX. Queen mother Catherine de' Medici regent ; the Guises are out of favour.
Scotland : Mary of Lorraine d. Treaty of Leith ends the old French alliance and establishes the Reformation.
Sweden : Gustavus Vasa d. ; acc. Eric XIV.
India : Akbar dismisses Bairam.
Japan : War of Nobunaga and Iyeyasu.

1561   Japan : Alliance of Nobunaga and Iyeyasu.
Scotland : return of Mary queen of Scots from France.

1562   Third session of Council of Trent, in which no Protestants take part.
Massacre of Vassy opens French wars of religion.

1563   Council of Trent lays down permanent definitions of (Roman) Catholic doctrine.
Murder of Francis of Guise. First War of Religion ended by peace of Amboise.
India : Akbar conquers Gujarat.

1564   Ferdinand I d. ; Maximilian II emperor.
Birth of Galileo and Shakespeare.

1565   Conference in Spain between Catherine de' Medici and Alva creates Protestant alarm.

1566   Suleiman the Magnificent d. ; acc. Selim II.
Acc. Pope Pius V.

1567   Second French War of Religion.
Alva sent to the Netherlands ; reign of terror.
Scotland : murder of Darnley.

1568   Peace of Longjumeau, followed by outbreak of Third War of Religion.
Revolt of Netherlands headed by Lewis of Nassau. Execution of Egmont and Hoorne.
Mary q. of Scots takes flight to England, where she is held prisoner for eighteen years.
Eric of Sweden deposed by his brother John III.

1569   Huguenots defeated at Jarnac and Montcontour.

1570   Pacification of St. Germain. Increasing influence of Coligny.
Pius V issues bull deposing Elizabeth.

1571   Turks capture Cyprus from Venice, but are heavily defeated by Don John ' of Austria ' in great sea-fight of Lepanto.
Ridolfi plot to set Mary on English throne.

1572   Capture of Brille by Netherlands ' Sea Beggars ' begins the great War of Independence.
Acc. Pope Gregory XIII.
Henry of Navarre m. Marguerite of Valois ; Huguenots assembled in Paris are slaughtered in massacre of S. Bartholomew.
Camoens publishes the Lusiads.

1573   Japan : Nobunaga ends Ashikaga Shogunate.
Requesens takes Alva's place in Netherlands and seeks to reconcile Catholic provinces.
French pacification by July Edict.

1573-82   Japan : Nobunaga with Hideyoshi and Iyeyasu suppresses feudal independence.

1574   Tasso's ' Jerusalem Delivered.'
Siege of Leyden.
Charles IX d. ; acc. Henry III. Ascendancy of the Politiques.
Selim II d. ; Murad III acc.

1576   Requesens d. The ' Spanish Fury ' reconciles the provinces in the pacification of Ghent.
Don John takes Requesens' place.

1576   Acc. Rudolf II emperor.
Stephen Bathori k. of Transylvania.
India : Akbar conquers Bengal.

1577   Don John issues Perpetual Edict which again dissolves unity of the provinces.
France : Seven years' pacification by Edict of Bergerac.
Drake starts on voyage of circumnavigation.

1578   Don John d. ; Alexander of Parma takes his place.
Sebastian of Portugal d. in Morocco.

1579   Protestant Netherlands unite in Union of Utrecht, ultimately forming Dutch Republic, and seek French (failing English) support. The south remains in Philip's allegiance.

1580   Philip claims (through his mother) Portuguese crown, ignoring title of house of Braganza.
Great Jesuit campaign in England.

1581   Francis of Anjou, heir presumptive of French throne, goes to United Provinces.

1582   Gregory XIII introduces Gregorian Calendar.
India : Akbar sets up a new religion.
Japan : Nobunaga d. ; ascendancy of Hideyoshi.

1583   Treason and flight of Francis of Anjou.

1584   Francis d. leaving Henry of Navarre heir presumptive under Salic Law. Guises form Catholic League to prevent a Huguenot succession.
Assassination of William the Silent. The Union appoints his son Maurice of Nassau captain-general.
Ivan the Terrible d. ; acc. Feodor (Fedor, Theodore), last tsar of the house of Rurik.

1585   Acc. Pope Sixtus V.
Spain and England declare war. Leicester goes to Netherlands ; Drake sails to Cartagena.
French ' War of the three Henrys ' (Henry III, Henry of Guise and Henry of Navarre).
Raleigh's first Virginia colony.

1586   Babington's plot ; trial and condemnation of Mary q. of Scots.

1587   Mary beheaded. Drake destroys Spanish shipping in Cadiz harbour.
Sigismund, crown-prince of Sweden, k. of Poland.
Japan : Hideyoshi's supremacy established ; expulsion of Jesuits.

1588   Henry III assassinates Guise and joins Henry of Navarre. League headed by Guise's brother Mayenne.
Spanish Armada sails (July), and is broken up in battle of Gravelines ; its remnants are shattered by storms.

1589   Henry III assassinated. The League allies with Philip to exclude Henry IV.

1590   Henry IV wins battle of Ivry ; his progress checked by Parma's invasion from Netherlands, where Maurice of Nassau makes progress in his absence.
Japan : Hideyoshi plans conquest of China.

1591   Archduke Charles of Styria succeeded by his son Ferdinand, a zealous Catholic.
India : Akbar annexes Orissa.

1592   Sweden : John III d. ; acc. Sigismund (k. of Poland) whose papalist designs are opposed by his uncle Charles.
Parma d. Continuous progress of Maurice.
Clement IX pope.
Japan : Hideyoshi's first invasion of Korea.

1593   Henry IV declares his conversion to Catholicism. Break up of the League.

1594   Henry declares war on Philip.

1595   Pope Clement recognizes Henry as k. of France.
India : Akbar annexes Kandahar.

1596   English raid on Cadiz.
India : Akbar annexes Berar.

1597   Japan : Hideyoshi expels Catholic missionaries.

1598   Japan : Hideyoshi d. after capturing Seoul. His policy of expansion is dropped.
Sweden : Sigismund retires to Poland, leaving Charles governor.
Russia : Tsar Feodor d. ; Boris Godunov tsar.
Henry IV makes peace of Vervins with Philip ; issues Edict of Nantes, securing Huguenot liberties. Sully in charge of finances.
Philip II d. ; acc. Philip III.

### CHAPTER 24

# THE AGE OF PHILIP II : 1555–1598

THE abdication of Charles V, begun in 1555 and completed in 1556, marks the close of the first stage of the Reformation, both in its political and in its religious aspect. The states of Europe had definitely taken the colour which they were to retain from that day, and the last hope of reconciling Protestant and Romanist had disappeared. Religion had not, up to that time, provided a motive for international contests, though it had caused civil war in Germany, which was on the point of finding its counterpart in France.

At the moment, in England, a Romanist reaction on the part of the government was in full swing; but it had no chance of surviving the impending accession of the reigning Queen Mary's sister Elizabeth, who, whatever her theological views might be, was debarred from Romanism politically by the fact that no Romanist from the pope down could admit the legitimacy of her birth. In Scotland a Romanist regency was still fighting a Protestant nobility backed by Protestant popular sentiment, which were sure of victory if once support from England were forthcoming. The Scandinavian countries were definitely Protestant, Spain and Italy definitely Romanist. In Germany Protestant and Romanist principalities were intermingled, Romanists preponderating in the south, Protestants in the north. In France the Huguenots were in a minority, but were headed by some of the most powerful nobles, while the royal family was for the most part fanatically orthodox, as was the capital, the strength of the Huguenots lying in the south.

## Hapsburg Inheritance divided

THE abdication of Charles gave Spain, the Sicilies, the Netherlands and the New World to his son Philip II, but transferred the imperial succession to the Austrian branch of the Hapsburgs. Ferdinand, Charles's brother, who now became emperor, aimed at maintaining in the Empire the compromise between the religions which he had been mainly instrumental in effecting at Passau and Augsburg. Philip, on the other hand, looked on himself as the instrument chosen for the stamping out of heresy not only in his own dominions but elsewhere also ; a theory which for the time made close association impossible between the two branches of the Hapsburgs. All through his reign he was the dominant figure in western Europe, because his power and ambitions were a constant menace both to France and to England.

## Looseness of the Spanish Empire

PHILIP's weakness lay primarily in the fact that neither territorially nor politically was his gigantic dominion consolidated. None of its four divisions could communicate with another except by sea, without the leave and good will of intervening potentates. By sea, the Mediterranean between Spain and Italy or Sicily was comparatively secure, but the Netherlands could be reached only by way of the narrow seas between England and France, so that open hostility with either of those countries made the passage extremely precarious ; while the ocean route to the New World was open to the predatory attacks of lawless adventurers of all nations, as well as of the naval squadrons of enemy states.

Politically, the work of Charles V had made it comparatively easy for his son to establish his autocracy in Spain and the Sicilies, but in the Netherlands the king of Spain was a foreigner ruling arbitrarily through alien ministers supported by alien troops in complete disregard of traditional liberties which none of his Burgundian predecessors had ventured to ignore. The result was that the Netherlands were goaded into revolt early in Philip's reign, and the attempt to suppress them kept his best troops and his ablest officers ceaselessly occupied till the end of it, when the independence of the Dutch republic was in sight.

At the moment of Philip's accession England was no more than a minor power, whose queen was actually the wife of the new king of Spain—the result of the mis-government which had followed the death of Henry VIII. The country was in need of recuperation and reorganization before it could again take its place as a first-class power. The heiress designate of the crown had not, according to the Roman view, been born in wedlock, and from that point of view the legitimate heiress was the young queen of Scots, whose mother, Mary of Guise, was regent in Scotland while she herself was in France and on the point of marrying the French dauphin.

**TREZZO'S MEDAL OF MARY TUDOR**

Jacopo da Trezzo, Milanese goldsmith, made this medal about 1554. On the obverse is a fine portrait of the queen. The reverse depicts her as Peace burning the implements of war and restoring sight to the blind.

*British Museum*

**A CHAMPION OF CHRISTENDOM**

Philip II (1527–98) became king of Spain on the abdication of his father, the emperor Charles V, in 1556, two years after his marriage to Mary I, queen of England. This portrait was painted by Titian in 1552.

*National Museum, Naples ; photo, Anderson*

Should the succession be disputed, France stood to gain by the success of Mary queen of Scots, which for that very reason would not at all suit Philip, who took for granted that Elizabeth would feel herself to be his dependant ; whereas what Elizabeth saw, when she did succeed in 1558, was that Philip could not afford to en-danger her tenure of the English throne. Hence she was able to proceed on her own devious way with a more or less polite disregard of Philip's efforts to frighten her into going his, until England was strong enough to make further politeness

**MARY QUEEN OF SCOTS**

Throughout her dramatic and passionate life Mary queen of Scots (1542–87) was the storm centre of political and religious intrigue. This portrait was painted by François Clouet, in 1559, the year after her marriage to Francis II.

*Bibliothèque Nationale ; photo, Giraudon*

superfluous, and Mary was prisoner in England instead of queen in Scotland.

In France, on the other hand, the antagonism between Huguenots and Catholics was growing continuously more acute. The most powerful among the nobles were the brothers of the house of Guise, a junior branch of the old house of Anjou, of which the senior branch were now dukes of Lorraine ; and they were zealous Catholics. The official leader of the Huguenots was Antony of Bourbon, the husband of the queen of Navarre and father of the future Henry IV. When the reigning king Henry II died in 1559 he left four sons, of whom the eldest, Francis, was sixteen. After them, Antony of Bourbon was next heir.

Francis and his newly married wife, Mary of Scotland, became king and queen of France and Scotland, but on his death next year Mary returned to Scotland, and the queen-mother, Catherine de' Medici, secured the regency and was practically

the ruler of France almost throughout the successive reigns of her second and third sons, none of whom had offspring. She, in fact, favoured the Catholics but feared the Guises ; her primary aim was to prevent either Catholics or Huguenots from winning such a domination as would threaten her own ascendancy ; so for forty years France was without a settled policy, and was repeatedly plunged in civil war with religious politics as motive.

THE second session of the Council of Trent was broken up by the successes of Maurice of Saxony in 1552 ; nearly ten years passed before it met again under Pius IV (1559–65). Meanwhile, the Papacy had begun to set its own house in order. Paul IV (1555–59) was a zealous reformer of morals and discipline, and set his successors a much needed example by abolishing the nepotism which his predecessors had practised habitually for a hundred years past. The man who had organized the Roman Inquisition after

**MARY OF GUISE**

Mary of Guise (1515–60) married James V as her second husband in 1538, and as regent of Scotland during the minority of her daughter, Mary queen of Scots, showed great political astuteness. Sir Antonio Moro did this portrait.

*Collection of Leopold Hirsch*

R*

the Spanish model was rigid in the suppression of heresy, with which he would have no compromise, but was no less an enemy of laxity, and the popes who followed him took the same line under the stress of a public opinion which was much more favourable to fanaticism than to carelessness.

Thus when the Council was once more summoned for its third and last session in 1562, L u t h e r a n s, Calvinists and Anglicans were unrepresented ; and the decrees promulgated on its dissolution in 1563 were, in the main, the authoritative exposition of the dogmas of what Rome recognized as the Catholic faith and of the papal claims to authority. The latter, however, were not all admitted by the monarchs and governments that remained within the dogmatic pale. The Gallican church in particular declined to subscribe to them, as contravening the independence it had always claimed ; and Philip personally always regarded the pope as a colleague rather than a superior.

Paradoxically enough, Philip was hardly seated on the Spanish throne when he found himself forced into war with Paul IV, who wanted to turn the Hapsburgs out of Italy, and appealed to France for aid. Philip drew Queen Mary's govern-

**BOURBONS, CATHOLIC AND HUGUENOT**

Francis II (right) was born in 1544 and in 1559 became king of France, but died in 1560 without issue. After his brothers, of whom two became king as Charles IX and Henry III, the heir presumptive was Antony of Bourbon (left), the father, by the queen of Navarre, of Henry IV.

*Drawings by Francois Clouet, Bibliothèque Nationale ; photos, Giraudon*

ment in England into the strife, though the administration there had gone so entirely to pieces that plunging into war was the wildest folly. The result was that the duke of Guise captured Calais, and England lost the foothold in France which she had held for two centuries (January, 1558). Otherwise the military successes were preponderantly Spanish ; but religious scruples made Philip and Alva, his general in Italy, more anxious to recover the pope's favour than to take full advantage of his defeat. The treaty of Cateau-Cambrésis, that ended the war in 1559, reconciled Spain with the Papacy, and, Calais apart, practically restored the pre-war conditions.

Elizabeth was already seated on the English throne. The deaths of Henry II of France in the same year and of his Guise-ridden son Francis II in 1560 gave the crown to the boy Charles IX and the regency to Catherine de' Medici. Elizabeth's intervention in Scotland and the death of the regent Mary of Guise or Lorraine in 1560 gave the control in that country to the reforming party, who were intensely hostile to French influences hitherto prevalent ;

**CATEAU-CAMBRESIS PEACE TREATY MEDAL**

This silver medal, by Giampaolo Poggini, commemorates the Peace of Cateau-Cambrésis, signed April 2, 1559, which terminated the Franco-Spanish war. Obverse: bust of Philip II ; reverse: Peace burning arms before the closed temple of Janus and the legend 'Peace established on land and sea, 1559.'

*British Museum*

and in 1561 the widowed Mary Stuart, not yet nineteen, embarked on that stormy career in Scotland which ended with her flight to England in 1568.

The English queen sought religious peace at home by requiring outward conformity to formulae which permitted such wide diversity of doctrine and ceremonial as satisfied the great majority of her subjects. In France no such solution of the religious antagonisms was possible ; there the one way to pacification was not comprehensiveness but toleration ; no compromise could bring Catholics and Huguenots into one fold, and the two parties were organized up to such a point that the suppression of one by the other could only be effected by decisive victory in the field. Political unity required that they should agree to differ and to live and let live, so far as religion was concerned, and this was the aim of the small group of politicians with whom the queen-mother associated herself, since her dread of the Guises prevented her from definitely attaching herself to the party of which they were the acknowledged leaders.

### France torn by Religious Strife

𝔘NDER these influences an edict issued early in 1562 relaxed the penalties which Guise influence had imposed on the Huguenots and in some degree sanctioned the Huguenot worship ; to the extreme indignation of the Guises and the Catholics generally. A league was formed, which Antony was bribed into joining by specious promises. There was a collision at Vassy between some of Francis of Guise's troops and a congregation of unarmed Huguenots, in which some scores of the latter were killed and many more were wounded, and the duke on his arrival in Paris after the ' Massacre of Vassy ' was greeted as a hero by the fanatical city. The Huguenots, headed by Antony's brother Condé and Admiral Coligny (whose title did not mean that he was in fact a sailor), took up arms. Antony, commanding government troops, was killed ; a pitched battle was fought at Dreux, in which the commanders on both sides, Condé and the constable Montmorency, were taken prisoners, and both sides claimed the victory. Guise was

assassinated by a Huguenot fanatic, and the Peace of Amboise (1563) was arranged by which further though still very restricted concessions were made to the Huguenots.

The Guises had been able to pose as the royal government, having Catherine and the young king in their hands, and the world at large credited her with favouring persecution. That belief, and the mistrust of her, were intensified when in 1565 she visited her daughter (whom Philip had married when Mary Tudor died and Elizabeth declined his hand) in Spain, and interviewed Alva, whose ideas on the subject were notorious and were about to be savagely expressed in the Netherlands. But in fact she still dreaded the League, though the new duke of Guise, Henry, was a boy hardly older than Antony's son, the young Henry of Navarre, whose mother was bringing him up as a Calvinist ; Catherine's wish was to hold the balance between the two parties.

**CHARLES IX, KING OF FRANCE**

Charles IX (1550–74) succeeded Francis II in 1560. His acquiescence in the massacre of S. Bartholomew in 1572 is the darkest blot upon his reign, throughout which he was a puppet in the hands of Catherine de' Medici.
*The Louvre ; photo. Archives photographiques*

She refused then to sanction persecution, but the mistrust grew as Alva developed his policy in the Netherlands. Huguenots suspected that she was merely biding her time to strike when Alva and his troops should be within call. In 1567 they planned a coup de main to seize the king's person and compel further concessions and securities. The plot miscarried ; Catherine was violently alienated, but the old constable Montmorency was killed at an indecisive engagement at St. Denis, and a truce was patched up which confirmed the Amboise treaty (March 1568). But the moderates gave place to Guise partisans in the council,

**ADMIRAL COLIGNY**

Gaspard de Coligny (1519–72) became the active leader of the Protestant party in France about 1557 and, after Condé's death in 1569, sole commander of the Huguenot army.

*Francois Clouet ; photo, Giraudon*

the pope, Pius V, absolved Catherine from her promises, a decree was issued forbidding Huguenot worship on pain of death, and before the year was out the third of the wars of religion was in full operation.

Condé was defeated and killed at Jarnac in March. Coligny's skill was crippled by lack of funds, and he too was defeated in October, 1569 ; but Catherine again drew back. Henry of Guise and his uncles were in high favour with Philip of Spain, who was obviously hoping through them to obtain control of the French government ; the independence not only of Catherine but of France herself was threatened. In the

**MASSACRE OF VASSY THAT BEGAN THE WARS OF RELIGION**

On March 1, 1562, the duke and the cardinal of Guise, passing through Vassy in Champagne, came upon a number of Huguenots assembled for service in a barn. In a preliminary altercation the duke was struck by a stone, whereupon his troops fell upon the unarmed congregation and killed twenty-three and wounded more than a hundred. In this contemporary picture of the incident the duke is shown upright with drawn sword, the cardinal leaning over a wall on the extreme left.

*Tortorel and Perrisson Collection ; from Larousse, 'Histoire de France illustrée'*

summer of 1570 the war was brought to an end by the treaty of St. Germain, which confirmed once more the previous rights of the Huguenots, and placed in their hands four towns. The possession of the port of La Rochelle gave them a stronghold that was of the utmost value to them for sixty years to come.

It appeared that the outcome of a war which had gone decidedly against the Huguenots was to be the victory of their cause. The nobles returned to court and to favour. Henry of Navarre, not yet twenty, was betrothed to the king's youngest sister Margaret. Coligny acquired a strong personal influence over King Charles, whom he inspired with his own patriotic hostility to foreign influences and especially to Philip, and encouraged in his desire to take the reins of government from his mother's hands into his own. The marriage of Henry and Margaret was to be celebrated in Paris in August, 1572, and the triumphant Huguenots flocked to the capital for the occasion in vast numbers.

**LA ROCHELLE, THE HUGUENOTS' STRONGHOLD**
This fifteenth-century plan shows the fortifications which enabled La Rochelle to withstand more than one determined siege. The two towers, built in 1375 and 1384, defending the harbour and the lantern tower of 1445 at the south-west angle (top right) are preserved in Vauban's exisiting fortifications.
*British Museum*

ℬUT the reaction had filled Henry of Guise and Henry of Anjou, the king's next brother, with rage and Catherine with panic when she saw her own hitherto supreme influence with the king giving way to Coligny's. The marriage had already taken place (August 18) when the three agreed that Coligny must be removed. The attempt to assassinate him failed (August 22) and Paris was flung into wild excitement. Then the three came to their desperate resolve, and coerced Charles into giving his miserable consent. The horror was skilfully planned, and on the morning of S. Bartholomew's day (August 24) the gutters of Paris were running with the blood of the Huguenots who had been massacred before dawn. Other towns made haste to follow the example set by the capital, computations of the slaughter ranging from ten to fifty thousand or even more. Among the victims was Coligny ; Henry of Navarre and his young cousin of Condé escaped the murder but were required to renounce their faith, and were held in practical captivity for some years.

ℳEANWHILE the Netherlands were passing through the preliminary stages leading up to their revolt and the long and ultimately successful struggle of the northern provinces for religious freedom and political independence. The Netherlands, though technically the ' Burgundian Circle ' of the Empire, were not under the jurisdiction of the emperor or the diets. They consisted of a number of provinces with diverse institutions and traditions, which marriages and diplomacy had accumulated in the hands of the dukes of

**CATHERINE DE' MEDICI**

This portrait, painted late in life, reveals the strong character of Catherine de' Medici (1519–89), who as queen consort and queen mother dominated France for half a century.

*The Louvre ; photo, Archives photographiques*

Burgundy, and so had formed part of the inheritance of Charles V. Charles himself, born and for the most part bred in the

Netherlands, had gone as far as he could venture in the direction of centralising the government and repressing heresy ; but his ministers were Netherlanders, and both Lutheranism and Calvinism had held their ground in spite of his efforts, mainly in the northern provinces and in Brabant.

Philip, on the other hand, was a Spaniard who cared nothing for his northern subjects, had no sort of sympathy with or understanding of them, and was in their eyes an alien. When his French war was ended by the treaty of Cateau-Cambrésis he left the country never to return to it in person ; and instead of entrusting the governorship to one of the native nobles, he appointed his half-sister, Margaret duchess of Parma, with a council of three ; whose authority overrode that of the council of state, hitherto the chief governing body consisting mainly of the nobles, whereas the new body commanded no confidence. Protestantism was to be severely repressed, and the ecclesiastical organization of the province was to be reconstructed on lines which were resented as much by Catholics as by Protestants.

**FANATICISM'S HIDEOUS CRIME : THE MASSACRE OF S. BARTHOLOMEW**

This picture of the massacre of Huguenots that began on S. Bartholomew's Day, 1572, was painted by François Dubois who, born at Amiens in 1529, was an eye-witness of its horrors, but made his escape to Geneva, where he died in 1584. Although executed from memory the oil painting was probably based upon hurried sketches made at the time, and thus is historical evidence for such details as the duke of Guise's complacent contemplation of Coligny's corpse, just flung from a window.

*Courtesy of the Musée des Beaux-Arts, Lausanne*

**MARGARET DUCHESS OF PARMA**

Philip II's appointment of Margaret duchess of
Parma as regent of the Netherlands in 1559 was
a wise one, for she was familiar with the people
and conditions ; but her authority was over-
ridden and she retired in 1567.

*Painting by A. S. Coello, Royal Museum, Brussels*

The leaders of the native nobility were
Count Egmont, who was a distinguished
soldier and a loyal Catholic, and William
prince of Orange and Nassau, who was
not yet a declared Protestant and had
been in high favour with Charles V. The
moving spirit of the government was
Granvella, archbishop of Mechlin. In
1563, Egmont, Orange and Admiral
Hoorne petitioned Philip for the removal of Granvella. He was removed,
but Philip continued to act on his advice.
In 1565 Egmont, with Margaret's approval, was sent to Spain to urge the
series of reforms needed if the loyalty of
the Netherlands was to be saved. Philip
wanted not loyalty but subjection ; and
after some months of delay he flatly
rejected the reforms and ordered the
decrees against the Protestants to be
rigorously enforced, in the Edict of Segovia.

So far matters had been left to the
nobles. Their failure drove the minor
nobles and others to form a new and more
defiant league against the government,
headed by William's brother Lewis of
Nassau. Another petition of protest

was forwarded to Philip, who replied by
promising some minor concessions which
he had no intention of carrying out. The
dissatisfied confederates presented a new
petition to the regent, who received it
coldly, and the confederates—from whom
the greater nobles still held aloof—prepared to offer armed resistance. But at this
moment there was a sudden outbreak,
entirely popular in character, of Protestant fanaticism, which injured their
cause, the political leaders being bound
to stand by the law.

The outbreak was sharply repressed ;
but Philip had now made up his slow-
moving mind to crush all opposition
mercilessly. William, seeing no hope of
successful resistance, retired to Nassau,
beyond Philip's jurisdiction ; Egmont
remained, not to fight but to struggle
desperately for conciliation ; but Philip
dispatched Alva to the Netherlands, first
as captain-general and then as governor
in place of the more conciliatory Margaret.
And Alva's conception of government was
a military reign of terror (1567). Egmont
and Hoorne, who had done their best to

**THE COUNT OF EGMONT**

Lamoral, count of Egmont (1522–68), ranks as
one of the martyrs of Flemish freedom. As
governor of Flanders he was at once conciliatory
and firm, but patriotism, conflicting with loyalty
to Philip II of Spain, brought him to the scaffold.

*Engraving in Cabinet des Estampes, Brussels*

**SCOURGE OF THE NETHERLANDS**

Haughtiest pride and relentless cruelty were the dominant qualities of Fernando Alvarez de Toledo, duke of Alva (1508–83). They are manifest in this portrait of him painted by Sir Antonio Moro. In practice they found their most terrible expression in his presidency of the informal and infamous Council of Blood.

*Royal Museum, Brussels ; photo, Mansell*

which the hitherto prosperous country was entirely dependent. Flaying was the one political operation that Alva was qualified to carry out, and even he began to understand that merely to ruin the wealthiest portion of his master's dominions was not desirable, and to urge his own recall. But before a successor could take his place, desperation had reached the limit. Many fugitives had taken to the sea and to piracy ; and in April, 1572, a band of the ' Sea Beggars ' as they were called seized the port of Brille.

THE capture of Brille began the war which ended only with the independence of Holland ; within a few weeks, ports and cities were everywhere, but especially in the north, declaring for William. Coligny was at the height of his influence with the French king, and was urging him to war with Philip ; French help might almost be counted upon ; Elizabeth in England was angling for a French alliance, and had only for form's sake ceased to harbour the Sea Beggars in her ports. Lewis seized Mons, and when Spanish troops laid siege to it, a French force advanced to its relief. William, whom several northern provinces had nominated as their ' stadtholder ' or civil head, advanced over the Rhine. And then the whole situation was suddenly and violently changed by the massacre of S. Bartholomew, which wiped France off the board.

act as moderators, were arrested as leaders of sedition. An arbitrary Spanish tribunal was set up, with Flemish assessors who had no voice in its decisions, which sent men to death actually by hundreds. The Protestant Flemings fled the country by thousands, to be received with open arms in England and elsewhere. Lewis of Nassau collected a very miscellaneous force, with which he defeated Alva's troops at Heiligerlee (1568), and Alva retaliated by executing Egmont and Hoorne, both of whom were Catholics, and defeating Lewis at Jemmingen.

Then Alva proceeded to flay the unhappy Netherlanders by imposing taxation which was not merely grinding but utterly destructive of the industry on

THE relations of England with Spain, France and the Netherlands are perhaps easier for us to unravel than they were for contemporaries, for the reason that it was Elizabeth's primary aim to keep everyone, including her own ministers, thoroughly befogged as to her own intentions and policy. In the country, hostility to Spain and a fervent desire to help Protestants who were fighting for their religion abroad had been growing for fourteen years ; while the queen herself was determined on no account to be dragged into war or to give open countenance to subjects in rebellion against their rulers.

She knew that however Philip might threaten, he would not go to war with her if he were not in effect forced to do so ; both she and Philip carried provocative action and provocative argument to the utmost limit, but officially the peace continued to be preserved, while year after year it was only by exhausting all the arts of prevarication that Elizabeth succeeded in keeping England and, above all, the English mariners from flying at the throats of the Spaniards. By keeping

France in constant expectation of a matrimonial alliance which she never had any intention of consummating, she also kept Philip in constant fear of such a coalition. In short, what she wanted was to gain time and more time for the development of the national strength and resources, while reducing both Spain and France to inaction from their uncertainty as to what her next move would be.

It so happened, however, that the Paris massacre and the revolt of the Netherlands took place at the moment when the imprisonment of the queen of Scots in England and a singularly impolitic bull issued by Pius V combined to warrant or impose on the English government a much more rigorous Protestant and anti-Romanist attitude than heretofore. The bull instructed all good Catholics that it

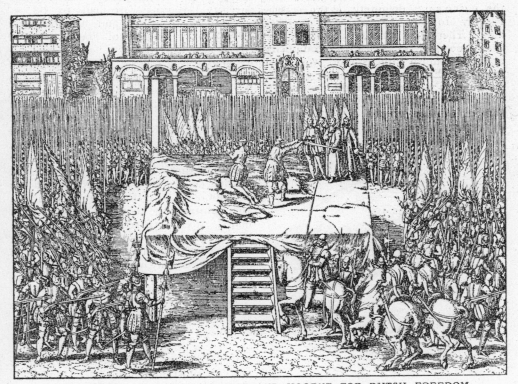

**MARTYRDOM OF COUNTS EGMONT AND HOORNE FOR DUTCH FREEDOM**

William of Orange and the counts of Egmont and Hoorne led the patriotic party that resisted Philip II's intention to convert the Netherlands into a Spanish dependency and to introduce the Inquisition there. Soon after Alva's arrival in 1567 to enforce both the despotism and the persecution Egmont and Hoorne were seized and after a farcical trial condemned to death for high treason by the Council of Blood. Next day, June 5, 1568, they were beheaded in front of Brussels Town Hall.

*Engraving by Hogenberg, in the collection of Th. Hippert ; from Hymans, ' Bruxelles à travers les ages '*

was their duty to aid in the removal of the heretic queen, but that they were justified in maintaining the appearance of unqualified loyalty to her. It followed that to be a Romanist was to be suspect of treason, and to preach Roman doctrines almost amounted to overt treason. That treason would inevitably centre in the person of the captive queen, whose accession in England Philip would no longer regard with the old-time reluctance, since her French connexion was with the Guises and therefore with the group definitely friendly to the Spanish king. There had already

**BADGE OF THE GUEUX**

'Gueux'—beggars—was the nickname adopted in 1566 by the patriotic party in the Netherlands. It is indicated in the reverse (above) of the badge they all wore by two gentlemen carrying wallets.

*British Museum*

been one plot in which the complicity of the Spanish ambassador was past question. Elizabeth's ministers and her parliaments were emphatically Protestant, much more so than the queen herself, and popular opinion viewed Romanism with increasing dislike and suspicion.

The Paris massacre for the time made any sort of co-operation between

France and Protestants anywhere an impossibility; and although it was hailed with enthusiasm by Pope Gregory XIII, the inaugurator of the reformed or Gregorian Calendar, and by Philip himself, it did not pave the way for alliance, and in fact it disquieted many of the Catholics. The Huguenots were made only the more stubborn in their refusal to be crushed, and Catholics headed the new party of the 'Politiques' who called for toleration. The suppressive edicts issued immediately after the massacre had to be recalled and a substantial degree of liberty restored by a new edict in 1573.

Next spring Charles IX died and was succeeded by his brother Henry III, one of the instigators of the massacre, a fanatic who easily fell under the influence of the fanatical group ; but his younger brother Francis of Alençon, who became duke of Anjou after Henry became king, and is referred to sometimes by one title and sometimes by the other, associated himself, as did Henry of Navarre and the young Condé, with the Politiques. Though the fighting was renewed, the war was ended, after a fresh treaty and a fresh outbreak, by the treaty of Bergerac in 1577, which again placed several towns and fortresses in the hands of the Huguenots, and conceded liberty of private worship to the nobles. It seemed for a time that the religious pacification might be permanent.

William of Orange had regarded foreign aid as essential to a successful struggle, and the chance of foreign aid, at least in any very substantial form, had disappeared. But he was now a declared Protestant and determined to fight to the last gasp. Alva, not yet superseded, conducted the war till the close of 1573. On both sides it was carried on with ferocity. Zutphen fell, and the inhabitants were put to the

**PROTEST AGAINST OPPRESSION**

This satirical medal, struck in 1566, depicts the Belgic lion being squeezed by the duke of Alva, Cardinal Granvella and Margaret of Parma, and bears the legend, 'Why do ye press so hard ? What if the lion's noble ire should wake ? '

*British Museum*

sword. Haarlem, with a garrison of four thousand men, held out heroically for seven months against a besieging force of thirty thousand ; and though in the end it fell, too, its valiant resistance remained a permanent inspiration to the patriots ; when Alkmaar was besieged, it held out till the approach of a relieving force.

THE new governor Requesens discarded to the best of his power Alva's policy of terror, which had failed of its purpose and made the names of Alva and Spaniard a lasting horror to the Netherlands. But Philip would not let him follow his own disposition. Requesens himself thought that the religious opposition in the north would be removed by the offer of free pardon to all who returned to the Catholic fold ; but the time when any large number of Protestants might have been thus brought over had passed. The patriots suffered a heavy loss in the death of Lewis of Nassau in 1574, but it was followed by a striking triumph. Leyden was undergoing a prolonged siege, and its surrender was impending, when it resorted to the last desperate expedient and opened the dykes, letting in the sea over the land from fifteen miles away. The besieging Spaniards fled before the flood, Leyden was saved, and the event was commemorated by the founding of the celebrated University of Leyden.

An attempt had already been made to conciliate the south, but the demands put forward by the patriots went beyond what Requesens was empowered to grant. Negotiations were opened with William and the north, but the terms gave no security that the promises would not be shelved as soon as the north disarmed, and still offered only the alternatives of recantation or exile to Protestants. The negotiations broke down, having only hardened the defiance of the northern Protestantism into intolerance of Romanism—against the will of William, though the provincial estates enlarged the personal powers with which he was entrusted. Moreover, whereas loyalty to the crown had hitherto been professed, Holland and Zeeland now began to look for some foreign prince who would accept the sovereignty—an

offer which was politely declined both by the English queen and the French duke of Anjou who was credited with Huguenot sympathies.

The campaigning was renewed with the breakdown of the negotiations in 1575. The patriots met with considerable successes. But Requesens died suddenly, and, pending the appointment of his

### PORTRAITS OF QUEEN ELIZABETH

Of these two miniatures by Nicholas Hilliard the upper was painted in 1572, when the queen was thirty-nine. Elizabeth insisted on his painting the later, lower, one in the ' oppen light,' deeming that shadows were unflattering.

*National Portrait Gallery, London, and (above) courtesy of Christie, Manson and Woods, Ltd.*

successor, the conduct of affairs was in the hands of a council. The Spanish troops, already mutinous because their pay was heavily in arrear, broke out of hand, looted right and left, and sacked Antwerp for the three hideous days which became known as the 'Spanish Fury.' William seized his opportunity to win over the south where the religious question weighed rather in favour of the government, and all the provinces joined in the treaty called the Pacification of Ghent ; whose demand was for religious toleration, the withdrawal of Spanish troops, and (in effect though not actually in form) the governorship of William under Philip's sovereignty (1576).

### A WELL-MEANING OFFICIAL

Don Luis Requesens was appointed governor of the Netherlands in 1573. He did his best to counteract the harm done by Alva, but the task was impossible and he died, worn out, March 25, 1576. The engraving is contemporary.
*From Hymans, ' Bruxelles à travers les ages '*

At this stage a new governor arrived, the king's younger illegitimate half-brother Don John ' of Austria,' a young man who had achieved a brilliant reputation by the great naval victory won by the Spaniards over the Turks at Lepanto five years before. He was popular and ambitious, and Philip was desperately jealous and suspicious of him, as indeed he was of every great officer he employed. Don John found so solid a front presented to him in the Netherlands that concession was the only course possible ; and the concessions were promised in the Perpetual Edict of February, 1577. But promises without guarantees did not satisfy William and the northern provinces to whom religious liberty was vital.

It is probable that Don John himself had designs of setting himself on the throne of England by marrying either Elizabeth or her imprisoned rival. Though he fostered dissensions between the northern and southern leaders, he could gain the confidence of neither, and Philip's natural jealousy was being intensified by the intrigues of interested rivals in Spain. Philip openly showed his distrust of his brother, while the parties in the Netherlands united to call in a new champion by

### HENRY III OF FRANCE

The dissimulation and cruelty that characterised Henry III (1551–89) show in this contemporary portrait. His treacherous murder of his formidable rival, Henry of Guise—see page **530**— led to his own assassination in the following year.

*The Louvre ; photo, Giraudon*

offering the governorship to the Austrian archduke Matthias, who, in fact, proved a very poor reed to lean upon. Don John defeated him at Gemblours in 1578, but died before the year was out.

His successor was Alexander of Parma, the son of the former regent Margaret, a soldier of the highest ability and a skilled diplomatist, who had not yet excited his uncle Philip's jealousy and at once set himself, with great success, to conciliate the south and foster the growing rupture with the north, while it seemed likely that Francis of Anjou would take the place vacated by Matthias. France had found temporary pacification in the Bergerac compromise, and a dominating position in the Netherlands was extremely desirable for her though extremely embarrassing for Elizabeth. Parma's diplomacy, however, brought about the separation of the south from the north where a new Union of Utrecht drew the Protestant provinces into a combination more solid than that of Ghent (1579), while the Catholic south attached itself to Parma. Two more years passed, however, before the Union definitely repudiated the sovereignty of the king of Spain.

The thing was Philip's own doing. Under the mistaken impression that he could frighten William personally into submission, he set a price on his head. William responded by publishing a bitter indictment of Philip and entering on closer relations with Anjou, not because he trusted that degenerate prince or his brother's and mother's government in France, but rather in the hope of forcing the hand of the queen of England, whose subjects would have hailed her active intervention with joy. While Parma moved forward, not with violence but with a quiet, grinding persistence, a bargain was struck with Anjou which would have made him little more than a figure-head.

**EYE WITNESS'S IMPRESSION OF 'THE SPANISH FURY'**

In June 1576 mutiny broke out among the Spanish and Walloon troops in the Netherlands to whom long arrears of pay were due. The mutineers established themselves at Alost in Brabant, but in November they marched on Antwerp and for three days—November 3 to 5—sacked the town, massacring 6,000 citizens, burning down 800 houses and doing damage estimated at over £2,000,000. This hideous atrocity, known as the Spanish Fury, is thus illustrated in a contemporary engraving.

*Engraving by Franz Hogenberg ; from Michael Aitsinger, ' De Leone Belgico '*

**DON JOHN OF AUSTRIA**

Don John of Austria (1545–78) was appointed governor-general of the Netherlands in 1576. Though politically out-manoeuvred by William of Orange, he defeated the patriot army, but the jealousy of Philip II robbed his work of fruition.

*Prado Museum, Madrid*

Unfortunately, when he arrived he was not content to occupy that position, plunged in intrigues, attempted in 1583 a coup d'état by means of his French troops, failed ignominiously, and vanished to die ignominiously in the following year.

In 1584 also William ' the Silent ' was assassinated—a method of dealing with political obstacles which Philip habitually practised more or less indirectly—but his work was done. Nothing now would shake the stubborn resolve of the northern Union never to yield to Spanish domination, cost what it might. The Dutch fought on, and before long found in William's young son Maurice a leader who added military genius to his father's indomitability.

Ｔ HE disgrace of Anjou ended the French connexion. His death produced a new political situation ; for it left Henry of Navarre, a Huguenot, heir presumptive to the French throne, which, according to the Catholic doctrine, no heretic could legitimately occupy. Next to him was his uncle Charles, a cardinal. The house of Guise descended, though not in unbroken male line, from the first Valois kings and hoped, with Philip's alliance, to secure the ultimate succession for itself. In 1585 the Guises formed the Catholic League to exclude Henry of Navarre and all heretics from the succession.

Much as Henry III detested Henry of Navarre, he detested Henry of Guise hardly less. But he submitted to the dictation of the League (which had incidentally offered Navarre and Béarn, not even under French sovereignty, to Philip as a bribe). The three Henrys took the field with three independently acting armies ; a miscellaneous foreign force under the German Count Dohna entered France to support the Huguenots. The king himself went to meet the Germans, whom he persuaded to retire, while his main army was being defeated by Navarre at Coutras ; Guise arrived in time to attack the withdrawing Germans and return to Paris as a victor where the king had been afraid to fight, and Henry had to flee in haste from his own capital. Finding himself a mere puppet in Guise's hands, he tried to relieve himself from his immediate difficulties by having the duke assassinated (December, 1588). A fortnight later Catherine de' Medici died.

Mayenne, the murdered duke's brother, now headed the League, in open war against Henry III, who, deserted by the Catholics, came to terms with Navarre. Together they were marching on Paris, when a fanatical monk avenged Henry of Guise by stabbing Henry III. Save for the disqualification of heresy and the fact that more than half his subjects refused to recognize him, Navarre was indisputably Henry IV, king of France, engaged in a desperate struggle for his crown with a League which chose to recognize his elderly uncle Charles, the cardinal of Bourbon, as the legitimate king, though he was actually in his nephew's hands (August, 1589).

Had William the Silent fallen at an earlier stage of the contest, the blow might well have been fatal to the cause of which he had made himself the champion. Even as matters stood, it was some time before the United Provinces found efficient leadership. They actually tried the offer of their sovereignty to Henry III before the war of the three Henrys had fully developed; and when Henry after hesitation declined, they turned to England.

Elizabeth had always steered her perilous course with a determination never to commit herself so deeply to any one or any thing that she could not find an excuse for evasion, and to postpone to the last possible moment the conflict with Philip which was bound to come sooner or later. She did not mean that Philip should conquer the Netherlands; she did not mean that France should be their liberator and reap the fruits of their liberation; and she did not mean to spend a penny more than was absolutely necessary, or before it was so. Philip, on the other hand, was no less convinced that time was on his side. When he had crushed the Netherlands, it would be Elizabeth's turn, and when the time came he had no doubt of the result; but meanwhile each desired to inflict as much damage as possible on the other, and both allowed their subjects the utmost latitude in unofficial breaches of the peace, of which the English mariners in particular took full advantage.

Elizabeth then declined for herself the sovereignty offered by the United Provinces, but she promised help, on terms. Drake sailed to Vigo a few hours before the

**DESTRUCTION OF THE TURKISH FLEET AT THE BATTLE OF LEPANTO**
Alarmed by the Turks' conquest of Cyprus in 1571 Spain and Venice entered into alliance to combat the Ottoman menace to the Mediterranean and gave the command of the combined fleet to Don John of Austria. With 208 galleys, six galleasses and many smaller vessels he encountered the much larger Turkish fleet at Lepanto on October 1, 1571, and completely annihilated it, the Turkish losses being 190 galleys captured, 30,000 men killed and 10,000 prisoners. The allies lost 7,500 killed.
*Painting (part) by Vicentino, Ducal Palace, Venice ; photo, Anderson*

**ALEXANDER, DUKE OF PARMA**

Alexander Farnese, duke of Parma (1545–92)
succeeded Don John of Austria as governor-
general of the Netherlands in 1578. Although
success attended his arms and his diplomacy
he received small encouragement from Philip.
*Engraving by J. Wierix, 1591*

Spanish complicity therein, had just been
exposed, and England was clamouring for
her execution. With the assent of Elizabeth—which she tried to repudiate when
it was too late—Mary was beheaded in
February, 1587, and in April Drake sailed
into Cadiz and destroyed all the shipping
in the harbour.

The great Armada was postponed for a
year by this 'singeing of the king of
Spain's beard.' It sailed in 1588, and was
annihilated by superior seamanship and
superior gunnery, and finally by the winds,
the waves and the rocks. Spain might and
did build fleets to retrieve the disaster,
but her effective power on the seas was
gone for ever, and the English and Dutch
entered upon the inheritance. The immediate effect of the defeat of the Spanish
Armada was the closure of the sea-
route between Spain and the Netherlands,
and the serious hampering of Parma's
activities, at a time when Philip had
become almost as mistrustful of him as he
had previously been of Don John.

Parma's loyalty was in fact above

fully expected arrival of counter-orders
from the queen, and thence to Cartagena
in the West Indies, from which he returned
with vast booty ; and Leicester was sent
to the Low Countries with an army which
was kept as inactive as possible. Parma
mastered the central provinces and captured Antwerp after a memorable siege,
but got little profit thereby because the
Union kept its hold of Flushing, which,
commanding the entry of the Scheldt,
paralysed Antwerp, whose commerce
passed very largely to Amsterdam. Elizabeth undoubtedly entered on secret
negotiations with Parma which she never
intended to have any material result ;
her conduct and Leicester's excited
intense distrust and suspicion ; and the
expedition was in part withdrawn in 1587.

But Philip had already resolved on the
step which was to prove his ruin. Instead
of waiting till he had crushed the Netherlands he would put an end to Elizabeth at
once, and for that purpose a great fleet
of convoys was in active preparation at
Cadiz at the close of 1586. The last plot
on behalf of the captive Queen Mary, and

**WILLIAM THE SILENT**

From 1572 until his assassination, William,
Prince of Orange (1533–84), was leader of the
revolt in the Netherlands against the tyranny of
Alva. This portrait of him in late life was
painted by J. Van Mierevelt.

*Rijks Museum, Amsterdam ; photo, Mansell*

reproach, and he was the best of living generals and a hardly less expert diplomatist ; but though he remained in supreme command till his death in 1592, he was almost paralysed by Philip's interference with his plans and by the suspicions which always kept him short of supplies. And when Parma was gone, the Union armies were under the command of a military genius, young Maurice of Nassau, William's second son, who had already had time to prove that he was a match even for Parma.

**MEMORIAL OF A POLITICAL CRIME**

This medal commemorates the murder of William the Silent, July 10, 1584. It shows on the obverse Balthazar Gerard, instigated by Philip II, firing at William, and on the reverse the Spanish wolf flying at the Dutch shepherd. The legend promises vengeance for the atrocious crime and preaches mistrust of Spain.

*British Museum*

The withdrawal of Leicester had not involved the complete retirement of the English, and the Dutch had helped in the destruction of the Armada by their blockade of the ports that were in Parma's hands ; but there was more of jealousy than of active co-operation between the two, and much disunion between the Provinces themselves. Parma advanced continuously, while his politic lenience had the best effect. But the war between Henry IV and the League distracted Philip towards France.

In March, 1590, Henry, at the risk of total annihilation, fought and won the battle of Ivry. The victorious Huguenots marched on Paris, when Parma received peremptory orders to effect a diversion from the Netherlands. Paris was on the point of being actually starved out when Parma's approach compelled Henry to raise the siege. Parma having accomplished his purpose withdrew ; but his absence from the Netherlands gave Maurice the chance of proving his own skill and the merits of the forces he had been reorganizing. He recaptured one after another of the towns held by the Spaniards, and when Parma returned and again took the field against him in person, the young general out-manoeuvred his elder, who had to retire (1591).

Meanwhile, Henry, though he had been baulked at Paris, was making steady progress. Again by the king's order Parma had to leave the Netherlands to save Rouen from Henry. Again he succeeded in the immediate object, and withdrew ; but this time he was already a dying man unfit to cope with his young rival, who had almost completed the ejection of the

**HENRY DUKE OF GUISE**

The militant champion of Catholicism in France, Henry, third duke of Guise (1550-88), captured the people by his charm of manner and his spectacular valour. This portrait by François Clouet shows him in the prime of manhood.

*Palais Bourbon ; from Jäger ' Weltgeschichte'*

Spaniards from the last towns they still held in the north. Before the year was out, Parma was dead.

So long as Henry was a professed heretic, the Catholics in France would not acknowledge him ; but his uncle the cardinal was dead. There was no one else left in the male line of succession. The Huguenots could hardly hope to conquer the Catholics, and the Catholics could not expect to conquer the Huguenots without aid from Spain. If at this juncture Philip had intervened in support of the Guise succession Henry's chances would probably have been small. But Philip proposed his own daughter (whom he married to his nephew the Austrian archduke Ernest), her mother having been a sister of Henry III. A Spanish queen and

**ASSASSINATION OF THE DUKE OF GUISE**

Alarmed at the immense popularity of the duke of Guise and his aspirations to secure the crown, Henry III arranged for his assassination, and on December 25, 1588, the duke was stabbed at a meeting of the royal council, in presence of the king, who actually spurned the corpse with his own foot.

*Bibliothèque Nationale, Paris ; photo, Hachette*

a German king, who would be the creatures of the king of Spain, were more than any but the most fanatical Catholics could accept.

Henry himself was a political Huguenot with no particular religious convictions, but a very clear secular conviction that in toleration of both the creeds lay the only hope of restoring France. Also, the crown of France was ' worth a mass.' If he could not give toleration as a Huguenot, he would give it as a Catholic, and as the champion of France against foreign intervention. In 1593 he announced his conversion to the Catholic faith.

Though the extreme section of the League, led by Mayenne, still held out, while the archduke Ernest betook himself as governor to the Netherlands, where his arrival proved of no advantage to Philip, the moderate Catholics came over, some at once, others more slowly, the young duke of Guise being among them. The Leaguers obviously depended on continued unofficial support from Philip. In 1595 Henry, who had now been crowned, declared war on Spain. The League, in alliance with Philip, was exposed as an anti-national conspiracy. There was still hard fighting to be done, however, and in this Henry was less successful than in the diplomacy which gained over Pope

**A GREAT QUEEN'S FAVOURITE**

Although an inefficient statesman and indifferent soldier, Robert Dudley, earl of Leicester (1532–88), was long the most powerful man in England as the favourite of Elizabeth. This portrait, by an unknown artist, shows him in his prime.

*National Portrait Gallery, London*

Clement VIII and one after another of the remaining League leaders—to their very great profit, and the lively annoyance of the Huguenots.

In 1597 the League had practically ceased to exist, and all but the last strongholds were captured. Philip agreed to a truce. Early in 1598 the last resistance was extinguished. In April Henry issued the Edict of Nantes which was the charter of the Huguenots, and in May the war between France and Spain was ended by the treaty of Vervins ; in which, however, neither England nor the United Provinces which were still fighting for independence was included. Henry was free to set about the reorganization of France, with the Edict of Nantes as his starting-point.

### Spanish Sea Power lost to England

PHILIP'S preoccupation with France had enabled Maurice, with the less difficulty, to establish practically the independence of the United Provinces which Philip still declined to acknowledge ; but the continuation of the war in that quarter belongs to our next chapter. The Dutch and the English were both in nominal alliance with Henry, but the former were almost entirely engaged in the Netherlands, and the English in the maritime war which Elizabeth's government directed, not to the destruction of the Spanish power (which Elizabeth meant to cripple but still to preserve as a counterpoise to that of France), but mainly to the raiding of Spanish sea-borne commerce ; greatly to the profit of English mariners who preyed upon Spanish treasure galleons and fleets, and had no desire for the ending of a war so conducted.

The Dutch were soon to share with England the ocean supremacy held by Portugal and Spain for a century and definitely lost by them when Philip's Armada suffered its annihilating defeat. Portugal, too small a country to maintain her magnificent effort, had disappeared as a separate power when the death of her childless king Sebastian on a chimerical crusade in Morocco, and of his aged uncle two years later, enabled Philip to claim the succession for himself (through his mother) and secure the crown in spite of the better title of his cousins and subjects of the house of Braganza.

Four months after the peace of Vervins Philip II died, still unconscious that instead of making Spain the dictator of Europe he had made her domination for ever impossible, and instead of extirpating heresy had created in the Netherlands the most obstinately Protestant state in Europe, intensified the Protestantism of

**A TRAGIC QUEEN**

This portrait of Mary Queen of Scots—now at Hardwicke Hall—was painted in 1578, when the queen was in captivity in Sheffield Castle. It was the tenth year of her captivity, and she was still only thirty-six.

*Photo, Annan*

England, and established on the French throne the champion of toleration and the uncompromising foe of the Hapsburgs.

The Empire took no part for or against Philip or the forces of Protestantism, though Ferdinand, and after him his son Maximilian II, offered occasional remonstrances. Both Ferdinand and Maximilian (1564–76) were committed to the principle of toleration as adopted at the pacification of Passau (the right of each prince to control religion in his own territories), and Maximilian personally was suspected of Lutheran leanings. He succeeded his father in Austria, Hungary and Bohemia, and also as emperor, while Styria went to his brother Charles. No further division was made on his death, when his eldest son Rudolf II succeeded him.

The Hapsburgs in this third generation became more definitely anti-Protestant ; Rudolf made unsuccessful attempts to turn the tide, and his young cousin Ferdinand of Styria, under Jesuit influ-ences, was zealous in the suppression of heresy in his own dominions. Lutheranism, however, and still more the Calvinism which had found no recognition in the pacification, spread in the north, where, in many sees in which vacancies occurred, and Protestantism was dominant, lay administrators were appointed who claimed the right to discharge the political functions of the bishop in a Protestant sense ; while between Lutherans and Calvinists there was no love lost, the former being at best half-hearted in backing up Calvinist claims ; and the Catholics denounced the legality of the claims of both.

### Events in Hungary, Poland and Russia

In Hungary, of which a great part had become a Turkish province, while the Hapsburgs were compelled to pay tribute for the portion in which they exercised sovereignty, Transylvania asserted its independence in 1571 under Stephen Bathori, who, five years later, was elected king of Poland, the old line of Jagellon being exhausted. On Stephen's death in 1586 that crown was given to Sigismund, the crown prince of Sweden, grandson of Gustavus Vasa, who had died in 1560. The king now reigning in Sweden was his second son John III, who had become an ardent Catholic, and was endeavouring unsuccessfully to restore that religion. Sigismund, an equally ardent Catholic, himself became king in 1592, but after a visit to Sweden returned to Poland, leaving the charge of the kingdom to his Protestant uncle Charles.

For Poland was now in collision with the rising power of Russia. Ivan IV the Terrible, grandson of Ivan III the creator of the Muscovite monarchy, succeeded his father Vasili at a very early age in 1533. He first assumed the title of tsar. He estab-

**HERO OF THE SPANISH MAIN**
Sir Francis Drake (1545–95) was trained for his wonderful career by his kinsman, Sir John Hawkins. He fought the Spaniards in the West Indies, and was the first Englishman to sail round the world. He was knighted by Queen Elizabeth on board the Golden Hind at Deptford.
*Engraving by Hondius*

lished a merciless despotism by methods which won him his name ; he extended the power of Moscow as far as the Caspian. But Russia was so completely cut off from the western world that English sailors who found their adventurous way there in Queen Mary's reign by the White Sea and were well received by the tsar spoke of the ' discovery of Muscovy ' ; it became the established craving of the tsars from Ivan's time to force their way to the Baltic and to intercourse with the west by sea ; and Poland blocked the way. Ivan died in 1584, but the long era of Russian rivalry with Poland had commenced.

The Ottoman power, growing ever stronger and more menacing to Europe in spite of the tremendous naval defeat at Lepanto in 1571, was nevertheless not expanding in Asia. As early as the days of Bajazet II the unenterprising, the Shiah Ismail el-Safi, founder of the Safid or ' Sofy ' dynasty, had established an unorthodox principality in Persia where the Shiah doctrine always prevailed. He had pushed into Irak, but had been heavily defeated and driven back by Selim II in 1515, as a preliminary to the conquest of Syria and Egypt. Suleiman's European ambitions gave him no time for the conquest of Persia and the Safid power was left to grow gradually, till under Shah Abbas (1586–1629) the ' Persian Sofy ' and his fabulous wealth began to dazzle western imaginations in rivalry with the Great Mogul himself.

𝕱OR those were the days of the greatest of all the Moguls. Akbar's father Humayun had returned from his wanderings and recaptured Delhi as the heir of Babar (see page 501), only to meet his death from an accidental fall while his thirteen-year old son was away in the

**DEATH MASK OF QUEEN ELIZABETH**

Queen Elizabeth died March 24, 1603, and in accordance with precedent a death mask was made from her face in wax. From this the lead reproduction shown above was made by the cire perdue process and used, it is believed, as the model for the recumbent marble effigy on her tomb in Westminster Abbey.
*Courtesy of Messrs. Spink & Son, Ltd.*

Punjab with Bairam dealing with one of the three other claimants to the Empire of Hindustan. Bairam proclaimed Akbar ; another claimant marched on Delhi from Gwalior, and took it, and had to be crushed in another battle at Panipat (1556). Bairam established Akbar's authority from Peshawar to Allahabad before his own death in 1561, and in 1562 Akbar's real personal reign began.

He was a deliberately aggressive and successful conqueror who attacked and annexed every independent principality he could reach. Gondwana, Malwa and Rajputana were brought under his direct rule or his sovereignty by 1569 ; in 1573 he gained access to the sea by the conquest of Gujarat. Bengal was annexed in 1576. After his capture of Kabul in 1581, his supremacy and his personal ascendancy north of the Nerbada were never

**PHILIP II AS SEPTUAGENARIAN**
This portrait depicts Philip II of Spain at the
age of 71.  It was painted by Sir Antonio Moro
shortly before the king's death, September 13,
1598, and is preserved in the library of the
Escurial, where his death occurred.
*Photo, Mansell*

challenged without immediate disaster to
the challenger; but he did not succeed
in extending effective conquest into the
Deccan, and his last years were troubled
by the ill-doings of his sons.

Akbar's conquests would have made
him a man of mark if he had had no
other title to fame.  His organization and
administration of the vast empire he
subjugated would have secured his place
among the greatest of Oriental rulers,
though his father's rival Sher Shah was the
real originator of some of his most effective
measures, while others owed as much or
more to the ministers of his choice than to
himself.  His liberality in matters of
religion was in strong contrast with the
uncompromising intolerance prevalent in
Europe, and was perhaps born of his own
extreme unorthodoxy which, by Mahomedans, is scarcely accounted to him for
righteousness.  He was eager in his
encouragement of learning, admitted
foreigners freely, and suffered them in his

presence to hold high debate with each
other and with the pundits of his own
people.  But of all his many claims to
greatness the highest is the fact that he
was the first to break with the old tradition
of Moslem domination, to treat the Hindu
and Moslem populations as though all the
peoples of his empire were one—to dream,
it might almost be said, of creating an
Indian nationality ; Rajput princes and
Brahman advisers being among the most
trusted of his generals and counsellors.

In China the Ming dynasty was nearing
its end, but the onslaught under which it
perished did not come till the next century.  At the moment, however, where this
chapter closes, the power which seemed
to threaten it was not that of the Manchus
who afterwards overthrew it, but that of
Japan.  For the long feudal anarchy under
the Ashikaga shoguns was brought to an
end, a masterful central government was
set up, and it appeared that, under a man
of genius, the island power was embarking
on a career of expansion.

**FIRST TSAR OF RUSSIA**
Ivan IV (1530–84), known for his tyranny and
cruelty as ' The Terrible,' had himself crowned
as tsar of All Russia in 1547—being the first to
assume that title.  This is an authentic portrait.
*Contemporary woodcut at Vienna*

When Bairam was establishing Akbar on the throne of Delhi, Nobunaga, the baron of Owari, was at war with his neighbour Tokugawa Iyeyasu ; and the skill of his defence so impressed the latter that the two became allies instead of rivals, gradually dominated their neighbours, and in 1573 overturned the feeble Shogunate. That office had for centuries been the recognized monopoly of the Minamoto clan. It fell into abeyance for a few years. Nobunaga, ruling under another title, continued to reduce obstinate nobles to submission, largely through the services of his ever-loyal henchman Hideyoshi, who had risen to be a particularly distinguished general. Nobunaga in 1582 died by his own hand when a treacherous attack was made upon him ; but Hideyoshi was prompt to smite the traitor, became the practical head of his dead master's faction, and ruled Japan gloriously from 1584 till his death in 1598 —an amazing feat in itself for a man of very humble birth in a land of feudal aristocrats.

Theoretically there was no revolution ; Hideyoshi was the minister of the mikado, as the shoguns had been before him and were to be after him. But he compelled the nobles to submit to the central authority, though it was not till 1590 that

**GREATEST MOGUL EMPEROR**

Akbar the Great (1542–1605) was the real builder of the splendid and prosperous Mogul Empire. This pencil sketch was drawn— almost certainly from life—by one of the painters attached to the court of the Grand Moguls.

*From Laurence Binyon, ' Court Painters of the Grand Moguls '*

his sway was undisputed throughout Hondo (Honshu) and Kioshiu, with Iyeyasu as practically his viceroy in the north.

Unfortunately for Christianity, which the Jesuits had been spreading, he grasped the idea that the missionaries were only the heralds of attempted political domination, expelled them from the country, and closed its gates to them. The last years of his life were spent in conquering Korea from the Chinese, with the Chinese empire itself as his next objective ; and with every prospect of success, till in 1598 death cut him off at the age of sixty - two. The Japanese government abandoned the attempt which without Hideyoshi's genius to direct it was impossible, and withdrew from Korea. But he left behind him a restored Japan.

**SOLDIER AND STATESMAN**

Notwithstanding his peasant origin Hideyoshi (1538–98) rose by his great military capacity to supreme power in Japan. To his wise statesmanship and good government as regent from 1584 to 1598, after the death of his colleague Nobunaga, the country's restoration to prosperity was due.

# TABLE OF DATES FOR CHAPTER 25

1598 Peace of Vervins ; Edict of Nantes.
Philip II d. ; acc. Philip III.
1599 India : Akbar in the Deccan.
1600 Henry IV. m. Marie de' Medici.
Charter of London East India Company.
1603 Elizabeth d. ; acc. James I (and VI). Union of English and Scottish crowns.
Spinola in command of Spaniards in Netherlands.
Japan : Iyeyasu shogun ; founding of the Takugawa Shogunate.
16^4 Sweden : Sigismund deposed ; Charles IX crowned.
Peace between England and Spain.
1605 India : Akbar d. ; acc. Jehangir.
Don Quixote published.
1608 Rudolf transfers Hungary and Austria to Matthias.
America : English settlement under Virginia charter ; Champlain at Quebec.
1609 Netherlands : Dutch and Spaniards make twelve years' truce ; Dutch independence de facto, but still unacknowledged.
Cleves succession question ; German Protestant Union ; Henry IV's league.
Bohemia extorts Charter of Majesty from Rudolf.
1610 Henry IV assassinated ; acc. Louis XIII ; regency of Marie de' Medici ; renewed factions, and revival of the Huguenot conflicts.
Henry IV's league dissolved. Maximilian of Bavaria forms German Catholic League to counteract the Protestant Union.
1611 Englishmen favoured in Japan (Will Adams).
Sweden : Charles IX d. ; acc. Gustavus Adolphus.
1612 Rudolf II d. ; acc. Matthias.
1613 Russian ' interregnum ' ended by election of Michael Romanov, founding Romanov dynasty.
Elizabeth, dr. of James I, m. Frederick, elector palatine.
1614 France : States-General called ; not again summoned for 175 years.
Japan : Iyeyasu expels (Catholic) Christians.
1615 India : English embassy of Sir T. Roe to Jehangir.
1616 China : the Manchus having mastered the north, Nurbachu proclaims himself emperor ; official beginning of Manchu dynasty.
Japan : Iyeyasu d. ; Hidetada shogun.
1617 Bohemian diet acknowledges succession of Ferdinand of Carinthia, cousin and heir of Matthias.
1618 'Defenestration' of Ferdinand's ministers at Prague ; begins the Thirty Years' War.
The elector of Brandenburg inherits Polish duchy of East Prussia.
1619 Matthias d. ; Ferdinand II elected emperor.
Frederick, elected k. of Bohemia, accepts the crown.
1620 Bohemian War, German Protestants standing aloof.
Maximilian brings in the League army, under Tilly's command ; defeat of Frederick at the White Mountain.
Voyage of the Mayflower ; the ' Pilgrim Fathers.'
1621 Philip III d. ; acc. Philip IV.
Protestantism stamped out in Bohemia.
Spaniards from Netherlands in Lower Palatinate.
Dutch War renewed on expiry of truce.
1622 Maximilian in Upper Palatinate. Mansfeld and Christian of Brunswick (or Halberstadt) command for Frederick.
Japan : Shogunate of Iyemitsu.
1623 Palatinate and electorship conferred on Maximilian. Breach between England and Spain.
1624 Richelieu at head of Louis XIII's ministry.
James I negotiates with France, Sweden and Denmark for intervention.
1625 Futile English expedition to Netherlands. James I d. ; acc. Charles I.
Christian IV of Denmark heads Protestant coalition ; Saxony and Brandenburg standing aside.
Maurice of Nassau d. ; Frederick Henry stadtholder.
Gustavus and Sigismund at war.
1626 Wallenstein raises an independent army for the emperor. Mansfeld d. Christian IV defeated by Tilly at Lutter.
1627 Continued progress of imperialists.
Richelieu lays siege to Huguenots in La Rochelle ; futile relief expedition of Buckingham.
India : Shah Jehan succeeds Jehangir.
1628 Fall of La Rochelle ; Buckingham assassinated.
Wallenstein fails to take Stralsund.
China : Acc. Chung Cheng, last Ming emperor.

1629 Denmark retires ; Peace of Lübeck ; Ferdinand, urged by Maximilian, issues edict of Restitution, in spite of Wallenstein's protests.
Richelieu ends Huguenot conflict by treaty of Alais, and helps to negotiate treaty of Altmark between Poland and Sweden.
England takes no further part in the war.
1630 Landing of Gustavus at Usedom ; dismissal of Wallenstein ; neutrality of Brandenburg and Saxony.
1631 Fall and sack of Magdeburg ; Saxony and Brandenburg join Gustavus, who defeats Tilly at Breitenfeld. His triumphant progress necessitates recall of Wallenstein.
1632 Lützen ; d. of Gustavus, retreat of Wallenstein ; Christina q. of Sweden ; Oxenstierna rules.
1633 League of Heilbronn, led by Bernard of Saxe-Weimar.
1634 Wallenstein assassinated ; defeat of Bernard at Nördlingen.
1635 Ferdinand II d. ; Ferdinand III acc. Peace of Prague. Saxony and Brandenburg join imperialists. France declares war on Spain.
Japan : Iyemitsu, having completed constitutional reforms, closes Japan to Europeans.
1638 Louis XIV b. Bernard conquers Alsace.
1639 Bernard d. France retains Alsace.
Fort St. George (Madras) granted to E.I.C.
1640 Frederick William, the 'Great Elector,' succeeds George William in Brandenburg. He makes peace with Swedes and begins reconstruction.
England : the Long Parliament meets.
Portugal revolts from Spain, proclaiming John of Braganza king. War of independence.
1642 Richelieu d.
English Civil War begins.
Galileo d. Isaac Newton b.
1643 Louis XIII d. ; acc. Louis XIV. Anne of Austria regent ; Mazarin first minister.
1644 China : Chung Cheng, the last Ming, d. Manchu or Ching dynasty established.
Christina assumes control in Sweden.
Descartes' Principia.
1645 War of Candia (Turkey and Venice) begins.
Russia : Michael Romanov d. ; acc. Alexis.
England : decisive defeat of Royalists at Naseby.
1647 Turenne in Bavaria.
1648 Treaty of Munster ; Dutch independence.
Treaties of Westphalia end Thirty Years' War.
Franco-Spanish war continues.
Civil war of the Fronde begins in France.
Masaniello's revolt at Naples.
William II of Orange stadtholder.
Denmark : Acc. Frederick III.
1649 England : Commonwealth ; Charles I beheaded.
Poland : Acc. John Casimir.
1650 William II d. William III and Marlborough b.
1652 Two years' naval war between England and Holland.
1653 End of the Fronde. Mazarin supreme in France.
Cromwell Lord Protector in England.
1654 Sweden : Christina abdicates ; acc. Charles X.
Holland : John de Witt Grand Pensionary. House of Orange excluded from stadtholdership.
1655 Cromwell attacks Spain in West Indies.
1656 Mohammed Kiuprili grand wazir ; vigorous Turkish reorganization for aggression.
Pascal's Lettres Provinciales.
1657 Brandenburg acquires Prussia in full sovereignty.
Ferdinand III d. ; acc. Leopold I.
Anglo-French alliance.
Charles X invades Denmark.
1658 Cromwell's troops with Turenne in Netherlands.
Cromwell d. Break up of Commonwealth government.
Truce between Sweden and Denmark.
India : Aurangzib deposes Shah Jehan. Rise of the Maratha leader Sivaji.
1659 Peace of the Pyrenees ends Franco-Spanish war.
1660 Charles X d. ; acc. Charles XI. Sweden under control of an oligarchy. Frederick III establishes absolutism in Denmark.
Treaties of Oliva and Copenhagen end Baltic war.
Mazarin retires ; Louis XIV m. Maria Teresa (Spanish infanta) and assumes personal control of French government.
England recalls Charles II ; the Restoration.

### CHAPTER 25

# THE AGE OF THE THIRTY YEARS' WAR : 1598–1660

FOR forty-two years the sombre figure of Philip II of Spain had over-shadowed Europe. From the beginning of his reign to the end of it there was no prince who could claim to rival his power on the Continent, at least after the death of Henry II of France ; and for thirty years no one outside England supposed that any power, unless it were that of the Turk, could successfully challenge Spain's supremacy on the seas, while the Turkish fleet itself had been shattered at Lepanto before half that time had passed.

He came to the throne ambitious to dominate an enfeebled and divided Europe and to wipe out heresy ; he had at his disposal vast fleets, the armies of Spain, the wealth of the Netherlands, the riches of America, the commerce (after his annexation of the Portuguese crown) of the East Indies. He was enormously self-confident, infinitely laborious, hampered by no inconvenient scruples of honour, generosity or even natural affection. But he died with every one of his ambitions defeated, the might of Spain hopelessly sapped, her fleets at the mercy of the northern maritime powers, her trade monopolies collapsing, the United Provinces of the Netherlands irretrievably lost, though their independence was not yet acknowledged, and Protestantism, wherever it had taken root, more firmly established than before. When Philip died, Spain was no longer the dominant power. The part she was to play in the future was, at best, secondary.

## Decline of Spain and Rise of France

IN the sixty-two years which are covered in this chapter it was only the shrewdest of statesmen that realized that the menace of a European domination centred not in Madrid but in a Hapsburg consolidation with its focus at Vienna. The progressive weakening of Spain, the failure of the Austrian Hapsburgs to unify the Empire, and the rise of France to the position of the premier power, together with the establishment of the Dutch and English maritime supremacy, are the features of the period in relation to the dominant international problem of Europe, the ' balance of power.' Superficially, the Thirty Years' War, which occupied half the period and generally gives it its title, was a war of religion ; but its effect on the religious question was only to show, at a hideous cost, that religion was not in truth an international issue and could not be decided by international conflicts. Its fundamental importance lay in the fact that it decisively prevented the unification of Germany, and enabled France to achieve that ascendancy which for the next century and a half she dreamed of transforming into a universal domination.

## An Era of great Men

OUR main interest, then, will be concentrated upon France and Germany, with Germany as the stage, but with Sweden intervening in a very remarkable episode during which her king became the central figure of the European drama. Great Britain was for the most part too deeply engaged on a drama of her own to intervene with effect in Continental affairs. It is an era in which great figures stand out : Henry IV and Richelieu, Gustavus Adolphus and Wallenstein, and in the twelve last years Oliver Cromwell ; but Henry disappears in 1610, Richelieu is on the stage only between 1625 and 1642, Gustavus and Wallenstein for less than ten years, all falling within the Richelieu period ; bigger men all of them than Philip, but none of them pivotal, as he had been. And none save Henry's pupil, Richelieu, achieved the aim with which he had set out.

It is Great Britain, however, that demands our first attention, because her development at this period, though im-

**FIRST KING OF ENGLAND AND SCOTLAND**

The accession to the throne of England in 1603 of James of Scotland united the two countries under one crown. The full-length portrait in the royal collection, after which this was engraved by J. Smith, was painted by Van Dyck during his visit to England, 1620–1621, when the king was about 55.

*British Museum*

The accession in England of the king of Scots had a further powerful effect on the constitutional development of both countries, though another century was to pass before the incorporating union. The Scots parliament possessed no such powers as the English parliament, and the Scots king wholly misunderstood the relations between the latter and his Tudor predecessors. Since he claimed that the English parliament enjoyed such powers and privileges as it possessed entirely by the king's grace, friction arose, especially as to the royal rights of taxation and control of religion. Also, both king and country still believed in the power of Spain, but to the king she was a power to be conciliated, to the country she was an irreconcilable foe to England and to Protestantism, to be fought at every available opportunity.

The antagonism between crown and parliament only became more acute when in 1625 the easily-frightened James was succeeded by his obstinate son, Charles I. Neither side would abate its claims; the king, unable to obtain supplies from parliament, could take no part in foreign complications when he tried to rule without calling a parliament (1629–40). In 1642 the great civil war broke out. After three years Charles was decisively defeated; in 1648 the army which had defeated him resolved that he must die, and in the following January he was beheaded. What remained, by leave of the army, of the parliament which had been sitting since 1642 put down rebellions against its authority and reorganized the navy; but when it attempted to convert itself into a permanent oligarchy, Cromwell, with the army behind him, ejected it and became in effect a military dictator for five years (1653–58).

mediately it distracted her from European politics, vitally affected her future influence. The death of the great Queen Elizabeth in 1603 called to the throne of England the Scots king, James VI, in virtue of his descent from the elder daughter of Henry VII, who had married James IV of Scotland just one hundred years before. The crowns of two kingdoms which had been intermittently hostile and never on terms of solid friendship for centuries were united, never again to be separated, though for some time their separation was a possibility in the background. The two countries remained separate kingdoms with separate legislatures and administrations, but while they remained under one crown they could not go to war with each other, nor take opposite sides in foreign wars, nor make antagonistic treaties.

The chaos that followed his death was ended only by the restoration of Charles II in 1660 on terms which definitely fixed the income of the crown at a figure very far short of the amount required for the government's normal peace expenditure. All additional expenditure must be met by taxation, which could only be imposed with the express consent of parliament.

**F**OR twelve years after the making of peace with Spain at the treaty of Vervins and of the religious peace in France by the Edict of Nantes, Henry IV, the first of the Bourbon kings, was reorganizing the government of France on the lines which were to make his grandson Louis XIV the most absolute of monarchs and France herself the leader of Europe. By the Edict, France remained a Catholic state but gave toleration to the Huguenots. They enjoyed freedom of worship, and equal freedom with the Catholics for employment in the public services ; certain cities and fortresses

**DEATH MASK OF CHARLES I**
This plaster cast of the face of Charles I was taken from the original cast made from his head after the execution in 1649. A small number of these casts were distributed among his intimate personal friends.
*London Museum*

**EXECUTION OF KING CHARLES I AT WHITEHALL**
This nearly contemporary engraving by Sebastian Furck depicts the decapitation of Charles I in front of the Banqueting Hall, Whitehall, January 30, 1649. Bishop Juxon attended the king, and upon the scaffold besides the executioner and his assistant were Colonels Hacker and Tomlinson. ' The blow I saw given,' Philip Henry, an eye-witness, wrote, ' at the instant whereof there was such a grone by the Thousands present as I never heard before and desire I may never hear again.'
*British Museum*

were under Huguenot control and were garrisoned by Huguenots, so that a turn of the wheel could not bring them under Catholic domination ; and Henry's principal minister, Sully, was himself a Huguenot. And though the national religion was Catholic, France had taken exception to certain of the decrees of the Council of Trent, so that the Gallican church still claimed a degree of independence of the papal authority, coupled with dependence on the crown.

The French settlement was unique because the position of the two religions in France was unique. Almost everywhere else princes and kings had been able to persuade or compel their subjects to adhere to the form of religion laid down by the ruler, except where Protestantism had taken so strong and general a hold that it

### GREAT FRENCH MINISTER

Sully (1560–1641), appointed superintendent of finances of France in 1597, was Henry IV's principal adviser. He reformed financial abuses, lightened taxes, maintained the country's defences and fostered agriculture.

*Drawing by Moustier, the Louvre ; photo Giraudon*

won complete victory in spite of the ruler, as in the northern Netherlands and in Scotland. In France its grip was only on a minority, but was so strong that it defied suppression, and the country had long been divided into two armed and hostile factions, neither of which could crush the other. Both must live and let live if the internecine conflict was to end. But the Huguenots were so much the fewer that their security required the material guarantees they received under the Edict. The guarantees, however, themselves generated a new danger, which did not make itself felt as long as the disposition of the government was evidently friendly to the Huguenots ; they were able to form a highly organized political community which could be brought into play for purposes quite other than the defence of religious liberty, while their leaders included some of the most powerful of the nobility.

After such a long period of something like chronic civil war, a king who had been obliged to fight hard for the crown which was legitimately his necessarily made it a first object to gather power into his own hands. Like the ablest of his predecessors, Henry employed in administrative offices, wherever possible, not powerful nobles but

### A TOLERANT MONARCH

Henry IV, first of the Bourbon line in France, granted toleration to the Huguenots by the Edict of Nantes (1598). He began the reorganization of the French government and the anti-Hapsburg policy later pursued by Richelieu.

*Painting by Pourbus, the Louvre ; photo, Giraudon*

**PRINCE CHARLES AT THE GRINDSTONE**
This broadside of 1651 satirises the conditions exacted from young Prince Charles by the Scottish Presbyterians, before they offered him the crown in 1650. Presbyterianism, so strong a force in Scotland, is personified holding the young king's nose to the grindstone, while ' Jockie ' turns the handle.

middle-class officials with a professional training whose interest was to serve him faithfully and win his favour and confidence. In England the obstacle to the concentration of power in the hands of the king lay in the claims of the commons to control supply ; in France it lay in the privileges of the higher nobility. By employing commoners, Henry placed no powers in the hands of the commons as a body, while he withdrew power from the nobles as individual magnates with common class interests.

The second need—the religious question being settled—was for financial reorganization, with the double object of developing the national wealth and refilling a treasury depleted by the drain of the recent wars and by continuous maladministration. This was mainly the work of Sully, who was Henry's right-hand man. He found himself faced at the outset with a huge debt, a huge annual expenditure, a crushing burden of taxation from which the nobles were exempt, borne exclusively by the wealth-producing classes, and a very scanty revenue because most of what was collected disappeared on its way to the treasury. A rigid economy, a rigorous supervision, a strict selection of agents who could be trusted and realized that

dishonesty would be dangerous, the development of industries and the partial removal of the tolls which fettered internal trade, enabled Sully to pay off the debt in twelve years and, in spite of diminished taxation, to raise an annual revenue exceeding the annual expenditure in normal times.

Henry was probably the one statesman of the day who realized the actual weakness of Spain and the potential power of a Germany united under the Austrian Hapsburgs and allied with the Spanish Hapsburg. If such a combination should be brought about, France, facing Germany on the east and Spain on the south, would be between the upper and the nether millstones. A primary condition, however, of such a Hapsburg consolidation would be the suppression of German Protestantism.

**PURITAN SQUIRE WHO MADE HISTORY**
This portrait of Oliver Cromwell, frequently considered to be the best likeness, was painted by Samuel Cooper and the original is at Sidney Sussex College, Cambridge. He emerged during the Civil War as a great leader and organizer.
*Photo, Stearn and Sons*

Ferdinand I and Maximilian II had maintained a steady toleration in their own principalities and strict imperial neutrality in matters of religion ; but Rudolf II and his nephew Ferdinand of Carinthia, who was expected in course of time to enter on the whole Hapsburg inheritance, both displayed a marked inclination to come out as zealous Catholics.

It was therefore Henry's policy to foster, in German Protestant states particularly, a fear of the revival of aggressive Hapsburg Catholicism, and to persuade them to look to Catholic but tolerant France as the champion of toleration. A league of Protestant powers with Catholic France at its head could not be aggressively Protestant, and would be a guarantee of European peace—besides being very useful to France as a check on the Hapsburgs and as increasing her own international influence.

Henry's diplomacy was working to bring about the league of his vision when Rudolf helped him by a palpable attempt to get the succession to Juliers, Cleves and other western principalities into his own hands. It was just such an opportunity as Henry wanted ; his plans were formed, and he was on the very verge of armed intervention when he was assassinated by the fanatic Ravaillac (1610). The whole scheme collapsed, the newly formed confederacy crumbled, and France was left to the regency of his queen, Marie de' Medici, the mother of the new nine-year-old king, Louis XIII.

For the next fifteen years France counted in Europe no more than England under the ' Scottish Solomon,' who suffered from an ineradicable conviction that his neighbours would listen to reason when they had arms in their hands and he had none. The promptitude of a Catholic faction, supported by the Paris Parlement, secured the French regency to the queen mother, Henry having made no arrangements to ensure the continuity of his policy when he should not be there to direct it. Marie was a Catholic partisan in the hands of

ASSASSINATION IN PARIS OF HENRY IV BY FRANCOIS RAVAILLAC
On May 14, 1610, Henry IV of France set out in an open coach to visit Sully at the Arsenal. In the rue de la Ferronnerie the coach was brought to a stop by an obstructing hay wagon, and François Ravaillac, a visionary fanatic, seized the opportunity to spring at the king, who was reading a letter, and stab him just above the heart, severing the aorta. The assassination, which excited profound grief throughout France, is graphically depicted in this contemporary print.
*Bibliothèque Nationale, Paris ; from ' Histoire de France,' Hachette*

**LOUIS XIII IN BOYHOOD**

From a spoiled child Louis XIII of France
(1601–43) developed into a weak, though not
uncourageous man. He was a puppet in the
hands of his mother during her regency, and in
later years was eclipsed by Richelieu.

*Uffizi Gallery, Florence ; photo, Alinari*

Richelieu's part. He had no concern with
factions ; his policy was the policy of
Henry—to suppress factions, establish
toleration, strengthen the crown and make
France the first power in Europe. To
that end he had joined the de facto
government of Marie, and to that end
he remained in the new de facto government of the king. But effective intervention in Europe, plunged by this time
into the Thirty Years' War, was impossible
until the domestic troubles of France
should be brought under control.

SPAIN'S maritime war with England
continued after the death of Philip II,
mainly in the form of the raids of English
adventurers on Spanish commerce, until
the accession of James I in England, when
peace was made ; the new king making it
his business to conciliate the power which
he still dreaded. The United Provinces
continued their struggle for independence
under the leadership of William the Silent's
son Maurice of Nassau, whose brilliant
abilities were taxed to the uttermost by

Catholic partisans ; Sully in despair retired from public life ; Protestant alliances
were the last thing desired by the regent,
for whom Henry's conception of the Hapsburg menace meant nothing, and France
was once more the prey of factions. The
protests of the Paris Parlement, the guardian of the constitution, were ignored ; the
States-General were called in 1614, only to
be dismissed after accomplishing nothing,
and not to meet again till 1789.

As the young king grew up he tried to
get the reins out of his mother's hands
into his own ; it was not till 1622 that he
succeeded, and in taking over the government took over also the services of the
mighty minister Richelieu, the bishop of
Luçon, who had very recently joined the
queen. This was not a desertion on

**MARIE DE' MEDICI**

Rubens painted this portrait of Marie de'
Medici, who became regent for her son, Louis
XIII, in 1610. She reversed her husband's anti-
Hapsburg policy and arranged a marriage for
Louis XIII with Anne of Austria.

*Prado, Madrid ; photo, Anderson*

the skill of the Spanish general Spinola. The southern provinces of the Netherlands did not make common cause with the Protestant provinces of the north ; but the Netherlands were now practically cut off from Spain, and in 1609 Philip III (1598–1621) made with the United Provinces a truce for eleven years. Although their independence was not therein formally recognized, and after the truce lapsed the attempt at reconquest was renewed, yet the Dutch Republic was from that time a sovereign state, ruled by Maurice as ' stadtholder ' till his death in 1625, when he was succeeded in that office by his brother Frederick Henry (1625–47).

During these years Sweden, Poland and Russia were engaged in constant conflicts.

Sigismund, king of Poland and Sweden, having vainly tried to recover Sweden for Catholicism, had in 1598 to leave the country in the hands of his uncle, who seized the Swedish crown as Charles IX in 1604, having the nation behind him. Charles was succeeded by Gustavus Adolphus (1611–32), the ' Lion of the North,' Sigismund also dying in 1632. In Russia the last ruler of the house of Rurik, Feodor, the son of Ivan the Terrible, had died in 1598, when the crown was seized by his brother-in-law Boris Godunov. Sigismund, hoping to gain ascendancy in Russia, had supported a pretender to the Russian throne, Dmitri, who by his aid overturned Boris in 1605. Next year a rival pretender displaced Dmitri by the

### THE STATES-GENERAL OF FRANCE IN PLENARY SESSION

Marie de' Medici summoned the States-General in 1614. It held its meetings in the great hall of the Hôtel du Petit-Bourbon, as shown in this contemporary print, the opening session taking place on October 14. The convocation was barren of results, for although the clergy were reasonably accommodating, the differences between the nobility and the third estate proved irreconcilable. The three estates presented their memorials to the king on February 23, 1615, and the Assembly was dismissed.

*Bibliothèque Nationale, Paris ; from Larousse ' Histoire de France illustrée '*

aid of Charles of Sweden, who had no mind to see Sigismund dominating Russia. In 1610 he in turn was displaced, and Sigismund made his own son tsar, while Charles put up his own younger son as a rival candidate. Then Charles died, his successor Gustavus was involved in a war with Denmark, and the Russian nobles, sick of foreign claimants, elected Michael I, the first tsar of the house of Romanov (1613), though it was only by making considerable territorial concessions both to Sweden and to Poland that he was able to procure his own recognition, and peace with both countries, in 1617.

Since Sigismund still regarded Gustavus as a usurper, war again broke out between the two in 1620 for the possession of Esthonia and Livonia, continuing till Richelieu's diplomacy brought it to an end by the treaty of Altmark in 1629, which released Gustavus to play his brilliant and brief part in the Thirty Years' War.

Here also we may note an event the importance of which was not immediately obvious. Prussia had until 1525 been in possession of the Order of Teutonic Knights. In that year the last grand master, Albert of Hohenzollern, received the duchy of East Prussia as a fief held of the Polish monarchy ; his son succeeded him as duke and lived till 1618 ; he had no male issue, but his eldest daughter was the wife of the head of the house of Hohenzollern, John Sigismund, elector of Brandenburg ; and the Polish duchy of East Prussia, lying outside the Empire altogether, passed to the Brandenburg electors, who took the title of king of Prussia in 1701.

The actual storm centre of Europe was the Empire, which had been only on the fringe of the main political movements among the western powers since the death

**ARCHITECT OF THE FRENCH MONARCHY**
The main aim of Cardinal Richelieu (1585–1642), here painted by Philippe de Champaigne, was the aggrandisement of France. His diplomacy was successful in crushing the nobles and Huguenots who threatened the monarchy, and he intervened with effect on the Protestant side in the Thirty Years' War.
*The Louvre ; photo, Mansell*

of Charles V. The pacification of Passau and the treaty of Augsburg (1555) had provided a modus vivendi for the still hostile religions, and the emperors had abstained from aggressive attempts to gather increased authority into their own hands. The many princes, lay or ecclesiastical, were practically independent rulers in their own lands, raising their own troops and levying their own taxes. For administrative purposes the principalities were grouped in 'circles,' but the common affairs of the Empire were decided in the imperial diets, practically by the 'chamber of princes,' though the imperial elections were in the hands of the 'chamber of electors' — Saxony, Brandenburg, the

S*

**' THE LION OF THE NORTH '**
This portrait is from the original painting by
Van Dyck of Gustavus Adolphus (1594–1632) of
Sweden, Protestant leader in the Thirty Years'
War. One of the greatest captains of history, he
died in the hour of victory at Lützen.
*Pinakothek, Munich ; photo, Brückmann A.G.*

Palatine elector and the archbishops of
Cologne, Mainz and Trier, with the king
of Bohemia, whether the last was or was
not the emperor himself ; for three successive generations, however, the emperors
had worn the Bohemian crown. The
third chamber, of 'free cities,' had no
effective voice in the decisions of the diet.
On the other hand, the emperors had
developed the practice of referring disputes between the princes to the arbitration of a sort of privy council whose
members were appointed by the emperor,
known as the Aulic Council.

The pacification held as a modus
vivendi, because Protestants and Catholics
were fairly equal in the chamber of princes,
and apart from Bohemia there were three
Protestant lay electors and three Catholic
ecclesiastical electors. But the balance
would obviously be upset by changes of
religion among the princes. The Catholics
had a safeguard in the terms which required an ecclesiastical prince to resign if
he went over to Protestantism ; but the
Protestants claimed that when this took
place a Protestant lay bishop or administrator might be appointed, who was

entitled to the privileges of the prince.
A diet predominantly Protestant would
admit such administrators, one predominantly Catholic would not. The Protestant
position was further weakened by the
antagonism between Lutherans and Calvinists, whose rights were not recognized in
the terms of the pacification. One thing
was perfectly clear : if the Hapsburgs
deserted the attitude of neutrality and
became partisans on either side, trouble
was certain to ensue.

### Antecedents of the Thirty Years' War

Now, when the seventeenth century
opened, the emperor Rudolf and his
nephew Ferdinand of Carinthia both very
clearly intended to repress Protestantism
within their own dominions. The emperor's brother Matthias, on the other hand,
as yet stood for the former Hapsburg
policy of toleration. Ferdinand was successful ; Rudolf failed both in Hungary
and Bohemia, which were outside the Empire and did not come under the pacification. The Bohemians were the descendants
of the Hussites, and Protestantism had
taken strong root in Hungary. In 1606
Hungary revolted against Rudolf, Matthias
associated himself with the rebels, and in
1608 Rudolf had to make over Hungary to
his brother, who established complete
toleration. At the same time the Bohemian
estates took the opportunity of Rudolf's
embarrassments to extort from him the
' Charter of Majesty ' which secured freedom of worship, and at the same time
forbade the erection of new churches or
religious establishments without leave of
the local magnate. Rudolf proving restive,
Matthias was crowned in his place. Next
year (1612) Rudolf died, and Matthias was
elected emperor. It appeared that there
would be an imperial reversion to the
policy of toleration.

The Hungarian and Bohemian troubles
had arisen at the moment when Rudolf
had involved himself in complications in
the western parts of the Empire. In 1608
Christian of Anhalt had drawn together
the union of the Rhineland Protestants,
mostly Calvinist, headed by the elector
palatine, primarily for defence against
aggression, which there was reason enough
to anticipate, on the part of Rudolf and

the zealous Catholic Maximilian of Bavaria, who countered by drawing together a Catholic League for the protection of Catholic rights, in 1610. Meanwhile the succession to Cleves and Juliers was contested between the Protestant houses of Brandenburg and Neuburg; and Rudolf's intervention with the obvious intention of getting those principalities under Catholic control enabled Henry IV to form that wide Protestant league under his own leadership, whose armies he was on the point of heading when he was struck down by Ravaillac, with the

**MAXIMILIAN OF BAVARIA**

Maximilian I (1573–1651), elector and duke of Bavaria, played an important part in the foundation of the Catholic League in 1610. This portrait is from an engraving by Wolfgang Kilian dated 1620, showing him at the age of 47.

results we have already seen. Ultimately Juliers went to Neuburg, who turned Catholic, and Cleves to John Sigismund of Brandenburg, who passed from Lutheranism to Calvinism.

In 1612, then, Matthias was king of Bohemia, king of Hungary (though Transylvania was ruled independently by the Calvinist Bethlen Gabor, and half the country owned the sovereignty not of the Hapsburg but of the Turk), and emperor. He had, as we have seen, a record as a tolerationist, and he did not openly depart from it. But he was advanced in years, he and

**EMPEROR RUDOLF II CEDING THE CROWN OF HUNGARY TO MATTHIAS**

Protestantism had taken strong root in Hungary and dissatisfaction with the emperor Rudolf II's anti-Protestant policy led to his more tolerant brother Matthias taking over the control of affairs there in 1605. His general policy was displeasing to the emperor, but Matthias secured the support of the national party, gathered an army, and in 1608 compelled Rudolf to cede the crown of Hungary to him. Its ceremonial transfer is thus depicted in Gottfried's Historical Chronicle, 1657.

*British Museum*

his surviving brothers were childless, and he desired the entire Hapsburg inheritance to pass intact to the one representative of the house in the next generation, his nephew Ferdinand. As concerned the German provinces, the agreement of his brothers was easily secured. Hungary acquiescently elected Ferdinand.

The difficulty was in Bohemia. Matthias himself was accused of evading the Charter of Majesty ; the rigour with which Ferdinand had suppressed Protestantism in his own dominions was notorious. Left to themselves, the Bohemians would certainly claim the right of electing Matthias' successor, and would elect not the aggressive Catholic Ferdinand but someone definitely Protestant, possibly the young elector palatine Frederick, whose wife was the lovely daughter of the king of England. So the emperor's agents startled the Hungarian diet in 1617 by announcing that the Bohemian succession was not elective but hereditary ; Matthias himself had succeeded without formal election. The diet, having no answer ready for this unlooked-for proposition, was tricked or coerced into assenting, and Ferdinand as the hereditary successor of the reigning king was at once acknowledged and crowned.

Ferdinand swore to observe the Charter, but left the administration in the hands of a regency. When it was too late, the opposition nobles, headed by Count Thurn, protested against the whole of the proceedings. Matthias ignored the protest, and on May 23, 1618, Thurn and his friends entered Prague in arms, hunted out the regents, and pitched them out of a top-storey window into the dry moat seventy feet below. One of them cried out to the Virgin. ' Now,' quoth the murderer, ' let his Virgin save him. . . . By God, she has ! ' The victims were alive and were crawling away.

CRIME THAT PRECIPITATED WAR : THE 'DEFENESTRATION OF PRAGUE'

War between Bohemia and the emperor Matthias in 1618 was precipitated by the incident depicted in this almost contemporary engraving by M. Merian in Gottfried's Historical Chronicle. Indignant with the emperor's increasingly ultramontane policy the Bohemian Protestant leaders, headed by Count Thurn, proceeded to the Hradčany palace at Prague, and on May 23 denounced the emperor's most trusted councillors Martinic and Slavata, and hurled them out of the window.

**FERDINAND II**

This illustration from an engraving by Wolfgang Kilian shows Ferdinand II in state robes. He is wearing the reputed crown of Charlemagne, illustrated in page 354, and the cope of the Holy Roman Empire.

*British Museum*

On the face of it, the outrage and the success or punishment of its perpetrators were the affair of the king who had been defied and the subjects who, with or without justification, had defied him. The Switzers and the Netherlanders had delivered themselves from the Hapsburg yoke when the promise of success had been far less. But they had been carried through by an indomitable spirit of heroic self-sacrifice for the cause. If the Bohemian nobles and people had faced Ferdinand in that spirit, the few half-hearted troops ready to take the field in the king's service could have done little enough against them ; but they had no plans, no organization and no inclination for self-sacrifice. They would have collapsed if they had not been reinforced by troops under the adventurer Count Mansfeld, released from his service by Charles Emmanuel of Savoy, who hoped to deal a blow to the Haps-

burgs without himself taking the stage. Mansfeld was supposed to be in the service of the elector palatine, to whom the Bohemian nobles were about to offer their crown. Frederick, however, promised the rebels the support of the Protestant Union if Bavaria or other princes should come to the support of Ferdinand.

No one else moved. John George of Saxony would not countenance war, at least so long as the terms of the pacification were not manifestly trampled upon. George William of Brandenburg, who succeeded John Sigismund in 1619, was only anxious to keep clear of trouble ; after all, Bohemia was not the concern of Germany. Maximilian of Bavaria meant to intervene if necessary, but at his own time and on his own terms. But Frederick's ambitions were aroused by the prospect of gaining the Bohemian crown, which was offered to him by the rebels. The idea was repugnant to the Lutheran princes, for it would raise a Calvinist to the position of the most powerful among them, with a double vote in the electoral chamber. Acceptance might be regarded as a breach of the

**GENERALISSIMO OF THE IMPERIAL ARMIES**

This portrait of Albrecht von Wallenstein (1583–1634) was painted by Van Dyck. At the outbreak of the Thirty Years' War, in 1618, he joined the emperor Ferdinand II, and in 1626 held the supreme command. Jealousy and intrigue led to his assassination in 1634.

*Pinakothek, Munich*

imperial constitution. His father-in-law in England had nothing but condemnation for the project.

In March, 1619, Matthias died. No alternative candidate could be agreed upon, and on August 28 Ferdinand was unanimously elected emperor. The day before, Frederick had been formally elected king of Bohemia. A month later he accepted the election and in November was crowned in state at Prague. No one would move in his support. Bethlen Gabor, of Transylvania, who had at first joined himself with the Bohemians, found that he could extract more satisfactory terms from Ferdinand than from his allies, and made his peace. Just twelve months after his coronation, the ' Winter King's' forces were shattered by the imperial general Tilly at the White Hill close to Prague, and Frederick and his wife were seeking an asylum with Maurice of Nassau at The Hague.

### Maximilian of Bavaria intervenes

WHEN Frederick accepted the Bohemian crown and took up arms against the emperor, the war became not merely a Bohemian but an imperial war. It was time for Maximilian of Bavaria to intervene. He brought the forces of his Catholic League into action ; Tilly was the League's officer, and the troops at the White Hill were mainly the League's troops. The Protestant Union armed itself, but otherwise it awaited events. Frederick's rash action drove the zealous constitutionalist John George to the emperor's side ; Frederick, as King James also held, was manifestly in the wrong. Spain, however, had already joined with Ferdinand, and Spanish troops from the Netherlands were overrunning the Lower or Rhenish Palatinate, which was separated widely from the Upper Palatinate bordering on Bavaria. Maximilian meant to have the Upper Palatinate for himself, with the electoral honours transferred from the Palatinate to Bavaria.

Frederick was put to the ' ban of the empire,' in other words, outlawed for treason. Maximilian occupied the Palatinate, while the Bohemian rebels were relentlessly crushed, their estates forfeited, and their leaders put to death. The eleven years' truce between Spain and the Dutch lapsed, and the renewal of the Dutch war withdrew Spanish troops to the Netherlands. The cause of Frederick was defended only by the adventurers Ernst, Count von Mansfeld, and Christian of Halberstadt, with their mercenaries, who maintained themselves by plundering friends as ruthlessly as foes.

The imperialists then were sweeping the board, and their success was alarming, going far beyond the legitimate suppression of the Bohemian revolt and the adequate penalisation of Frederick. When Maximilian in 1623 was formally given the electoral dignity and the administration of the Palatinate, the German balance was entirely upset. Protestant onlookers outside Germany became nervous, and King James set about forming a league, which might have been most effective if he had possessed efficient ministers and money. Having broken with Spain, he got the promise of support from France, where Richelieu was just beginning to exercise the supreme influence. His offers to Gustavus were not sufficiently attractive ; but he brought in Christian of Denmark, who, as duke of Holstein, was a prince of the Empire, as well as some of the Lutherans of North Germany—Saxony and Brandenburg still refused to budge.

### Emergence of Wallenstein

THE French intervention was never intended to be active, and the English intervention was a mere fiasco. James died at the beginning of 1625, and Charles I was immediately involved in a paralysing conflict with a parliament which was willing enough for a Spanish war, but took no interest in the restoration of the king's brother-in-law in the Palatinate, and would vote no supplies so long as Charles's favourite Buckingham remained in power. France was too deeply engaged with domestic troubles for a militant foreign policy. Christian of Denmark put up a fairly creditable fight for two years. But the determining factor was the appearance of Wallenstein.

Albrecht von Wallenstein was a Bohemian noble who had fought on the imperial side in the Bohemian war. He had acquired vast wealth by marriage. He offered to raise a volunteer army under his own command, and that offer Ferdinand accepted. His volunteer army was an army of mercenaries who were ready to sell their swords to any captain and any cause, to serve with entire fidelity according to the established mercenary code of honour, and to change sides without compunction the instant that the agreed period of service was at an end. The method of pay was unprecedented ; Wallenstein must have the imperial authority to exact contributions, instead of letting his mercenaries live at free quarters on the population. Such an army, organized and led by such a general, was an instrument of war more formidable in the field and hardly less desolating in its movements than any which had yet made its appearance.

In 1627 Christian was driven off the field ; next year Wallenstein made his one serious failure before Stralsund, which could not be blockaded on the sea side and defied storming on the land side. In 1629 this phase of the war ended with the treaty of Lübeck, which appeared to satisfy the claims of those Lutherans and Calvinists who had abstained from active hostilities. Yet even at the moment when the peace was made its whole value was shattered by a colossal blunder on the part of Ferdinand, who, at the instigation of Maximilian, issued the fatal Edict of Restitution, requiring the restoration to the Church of all lands secularised since 1552, when the previous secularisations had been confirmed by the Passau pacification. A fresh outbreak was inevitable ; no one was ready to surrender secularised lands.

In fact, the real question of the moment in Germany was whether Maximilian and

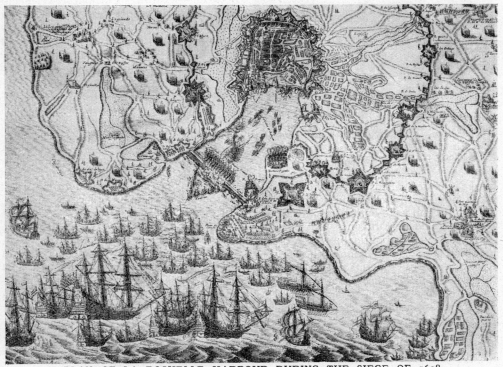

**PLAN OF LA ROCHELLE HARBOUR DURING THE SIEGE OF 1628**
This is a portion of an engraving published in Paris in 1649 illustrating the siege of La Rochelle by Cardinal Richelieu in 1628.    The city held out for a year, but despite some assistance from English troops under Buckingham and the vigour of the mayor Guiton, starvation eventually drove the people to surrender. It is interesting to compare this view of La Rochelle harbour with the fifteenth-century plan of the fortifications contained in page 517.
*From Valdor, ' Ludovici justi XIII monumenta '*

**LOUIS XIII IN HIS PRIME**

This fine bronze statue by Simon Guillain presents all the more attractive qualities of Louis XIII. Physically he was an active man, fond of field sports and violent exercises, and played a soldierly part in the siege of La Rochelle.

*The Louvre ; photo, Giraudon*

his League or Wallenstein was to hold the ascendancy with Ferdinand. Maximilian and Ferdinand were both bent on the suppression of Protestantism. Wallenstein's aim was purely political ; he was indifferent on the religions—there were almost as many Protestants as Catholics in his armies—but he meant to create a supreme army owing allegiance to no one but the emperor and the emperor's general and right-hand man, Albert of Wallenstein. Thus would the central imperial authority be firmly established, but only on the basis of toleration, not on the domination of one group. What the next stage might be was another matter.

The League could not possibly reconcile itself to his aims, which meant the subordination of the princes to the emperor and

the abandonment of their own primary aim. Ferdinand had to choose between the imperial project and the religious project ; he could not get both, and when he followed the lead of Maximilian he definitely alienated Wallenstein. A year after Lübeck, Wallenstein was dismissed, to await the day when the emperor should be forced to recall him. A month before his dismissal Gustavus of Sweden landed at Usedom on the Baltic.

### Influence of Cardinal Richelieu

THE intervention of Gustavus as the Protestant hero of the day was largely the work of a statesman who certainly was not a Protestant hero, Cardinal Richelieu. Since 1624 he had been all-powerful with King Louis. In one of its aspects, the faction fighting in France of the previous years had resolved itself into a conflict between the always Catholic government and the Huguenot nobles, the latter striving not so much for religious liberty as for political independence. Their defeat in 1623 deprived them of certain of the fortresses which the Nantes Edict had placed in their hands. Nevertheless they were in arms again in 1625, when they were again defeated, and once more in 1627. The centre of their resistance to the government forces was La Rochelle, which heroically endured a long siege, but was at last starved into surrender by the completeness of the blockade, in contrast to the failure of Wallenstein before Stralsund in the same year (October, 1628). The Huguenots continued the struggle in the south, but it had now become hopeless. They surrendered in the following year. But Richelieu's policy was the policy of Henry IV. The terms of the treaty of Alais (1629) deprived them of their fortresses, and therewith of the temptation to armed rebellion, but otherwise in effect confirmed the rights and privileges conferred on them by the Edict of Nantes. The Huguenots as Huguenots ceased to be a danger to the royal government.

But when the Huguenots were not taking the stage, there were ceaseless intrigues among the other nobles, eager to recover the ancient feudal independence which was incompatible with a strong central government, against the influence of Richelieu, which was directed to the strengthening of the crown. Louis stood loyally by the great minister, not because he loved but because he trusted him. It was still long, however, before Richelieu had mastered his enemies, and long therefore before he could throw France fully into the European struggle.

But Richelieu all through had a definite policy—to keep Germany from consolidation, to extend France to her ' natural ' boundary, the Rhine, at the expense of Spain and of the Empire, and to establish a footing in North Italy. He had encouraged the entry of Denmark into the war in 1624. He recognized the menace in Wallenstein's imperial policy, and his agents worked hard and successfully for the great man's dismissal in 1630 ; but he did not intend Maximilian's policy to attain success, and when Christian of Denmark was beaten he set about substituting Gustavus for him as leader of the Protestants. Working always by diplomacy, it was he more than anyone else who brought about the pacification with Sigismund which set the Swedish king free for his task in Germany. He would have wished to make Gustavus his own tool, but such hopes were doomed to disappointment, and Gustavus took up his work entirely his own master. French help might be desirable, but it must be given only on his own terms.

Now, it was only quite a small section of Protestant Germany that had hitherto taken active part in the conflict. The Lutherans had always tried to persuade themselves that if they maintained a strictly constitutional attitude their rights would be respected. Even now they hoped that they would be able to get the Edict of Restitution withdrawn, and they showed no readiness to be rescued by a foreign champion. On the other hand, the dismissal of Wallenstein and the disbanding of most of his army paralysed the action of the imperialists. Gustavus organized his position in Pomerania, and struck his bargain with Richelieu. Magdeburg openly revolted, and called for aid, which he could not give, because Brandenburg, stubbornly inert, lay between ; and no German princes joined him.

### The Sack of Magdeburg

IN March, 1631, Tilly opened an attack which was foiled, and fell back to lay siege to Magdeburg. Still Brandenburg and Saxony blocked the way, and in May Magdeburg fell and was put to the sack with an accompaniment of rapine, lust and cruelty which has become proverbial. Thereupon John George was ordered to dismiss the forces held in readiness in case of accidents ; he refused, and Tilly invaded Saxony. That ended the neutrality of both Saxony and Brandenburg. With his new allies Gustavus marched

### VICTORIOUS ENTRY OF GUSTAVUS ADOLPHUS INTO MUNICH

After wintering at Mainz, Gustavus Adolphus at the head of his Swedish-Saxon army pursued Tilly through Bavaria to Ingolstadt, where Tilly died of wounds, garrisoned Augsburg and Ulm, and on May 16, 1632, arrived before Munich. On May 18, as recorded in the contemporary broadsheet containing this illustration, the citizens surrendered the keys to him and he made a triumphal entry into the town, followed by the king of Bohemia, the elector of Saxony and other princes.

*From O. Jäger, ' Weltgeschichte,' Velhagen & Klasing*

**POWERFUL SWEDISH STATESMAN**

The organizing genius of his chancellor, Count
Oxenstierna, was an important factor in the
success of Gustavus Adolphus in the Thirty
Years' War. This is an engraving after a painting
of the count by Michiel van Miereveld.

against Tilly and shattered his army at
Breitenfeld in September.

For fourteen months triumph followed
triumph. His progress virtually resolved
itself into a continuous chain of successes.
By marching on the Rhine he secured
all North Germany, which no longer
held back from joining him. He rejected
overtures from Wallenstein—one or the
other might head a united or a Protestant Germany, but to share the headship
was impossible. From the west he
turned to Nuremburg ; thence he advanced on Munich, defeating and killing
Tilly on the way. Ferdinand found no
hope, save in recalling Wallenstein on his
own terms. The disbanded army sprang
to life again. Wallenstein marched on
Nuremburg ; Gustavus tried in vain to
storm his entrenchments and then to
entice him into a pitched battle by a
withdrawal. Wallenstein, instead of pursuing him, threw himself on Saxony ;
Gustavus pursued him, caught him up
before he had formed his entrenched camp,
and won at Lützen what would have been

the decisive battle had he not been
himself slain in the hour of victory.

The death of Gustavus again changed
the whole character of the war, as his
entry had changed it. Without him, it had
neither lofty purpose nor an inspiring
personality. Whatever Wallenstein's intentions might be, they did not include a
second retirement or the occupation of
any secondary place. Thenceforth everyone concerned was striving to win whatever
could be snatched out of the welter. The
Lutherans had committed themselves at
last, and must fight out their own salvation. The League could by no possibility
compromise with Wallenstein ; Ferdinand
could hardly hope that Wallenstein's
victory would leave to himself anything
more than a shadow of power. The
Swedish government, now under the
youthful Queen Christina, was guided by
Gustavus' very able minister Oxenstierna,
who intended to have at least the whole of
the provinces on the Baltic ; he drew together the western Germans, who were
bound to support him, in the League of
Heilbronn under the captaincy of Bernard
of Saxe-Weimar.

### Richelieu's Position strengthened

**W**ALLENSTEIN then was playing his
own hand in his own way. In
1634 Ferdinand took the decisive step of
again dismissing him. Wallenstein ignored
the order, and marched to hold a conference with Bernard, when he was
assassinated by a band of his own mercenaries who had made up their minds
that their faith was pledged not to him
but to the emperor. Six months later
Bernard and the Swedish general Horn
were heavily defeated at Nördlingen ;
but the effect was to drive the Heilbronn
League into the arms of Richelieu, who
had now so completely mastered the
opposition in France that he was ready
to take a more direct part in the war.
Also he had been strengthening his position in the Rhineland and in Italy,
where he had secured an entry through
Savoy and blocked communication with
Germany through the Valtelline.

So in 1635 Ferdinand made with
John George, who had refused to join

the Heilbronn league, the peace of Prague, which brought Saxony and Brandenburg to his side, practically returning to the peace of Lübeck without the Restitution Edict. The Heilbronn league would have been forced to submit but for its foreign allies, France and Sweden— and, immediately preceding the peace of Prague, France declared war on Ferdinand's ally, Spain. France, Sweden and the Heilbronn league maintained the struggle, which, on the part of France and Sweden, was simply for territorial gain.

France brought four armies into the field, at first with little enough success. But in 1637 Ferdinand II was succeeded by Ferdinand III, a much feebler personality ; next year Bernard practically made himself master of Alsace. His death in 1639 averted the serious quarrel between him and Richelieu which was imminent, and the conquered province was held for France. In 1640 Catalonia revolted against Spain, and Portugal followed suit, proclaiming John of Braganza king, the legitimate claim of his house having been simply pushed aside when Philip II usurped the Portuguese throne in 1580. Saxony had so far been on the imperial side, embarrassing the Swedes and suffering at their hands ; but in 1640 George William of Brandenburg died, and the new elector, Frederick William, at once sought an accommodation with the Swedes, and retired from the war, an example followed three years later by John George.

When Richelieu died in 1642 his aims were all but attained. He had crushed the disintegrating forces in France ; he had secured Alsace ; he had secured Roussillon, a secular bone of contention with Spain, to which it gave the entry. Savoy was under a friendly regent, the mother of the young duke, who owed her position to France ; the Valtelline was held by friendly Switzers. The Wallenstein scheme for a consolidated military German empire was past resuscitation till it materialised again in the days of Bismarck.

Louis died six months after Richelieu. His son and successor, Louis XIV, was four years old, and the regency was secured by the parlement for the queen mother, Anne of Austria, who chose for her minister the supple Italian cardinal, Mazarin. Troublous times were in store ; but the position was stabilised by the young Condé's dramatic victory over the Spaniards at Rocroy. The interest of the continued fighting is purely military, Condé achieving an immense reputation, while Turenne was proving himself to be one of the greatest soldiers the world has known. Germany was utterly exhausted, and fought on only to escape the surrender of German soil to Swedes or French, who

**MURDER OF WALLENSTEIN AND HIS ASSOCIATES BY MERCENARIES**

These engravings by Matthew Merian show the scenes that took place on the night of February 25, 1634, at Eger.   Left : A band of mercenaries broke into the house whither Wallenstein's supporters had been treacherously decoyed, and murdered them.   Right : They then went to the house where Wallenstein was staying and pursued him to his bedroom, where he was slain by a thrust from Captain Devereux's partisan.   The crime was generally understood to have the emperor's approval.

*From Winter, ' Geschichte des Dreiszigjährigen Krieges '*

**DISCIPLE OF RICHELIEU**

Cardinal Mazarin (1602–61), chosen by Richelieu as his successor, continued his patron's policy of centralising monarchical power. His Italian gift for intrigue procured his triumph in the Fronde Wars and peace with Spain in 1659.

*Painting by Mignard, Musée de Chantilly ; photo, Giraudon*

fought on because each wanted to snatch more. The final battle was fought at Zusmarshausen in 1648 (May).

Negotiations had long been floating on all sides. In October the long-drawn-out agony was eventually brought to an end by the peace of Westphalia, largely because the young queen of Sweden, Christina, who had a very strong will of her own, insisted on moderating the demands of her ministers. France retained Alsace, except Strassburg, which remained a free city of the Empire. Pomerania was divided between Sweden and Brandenburg. The Lower or Rhenish Palatinate, with the old electoral dignity, was restored to the eldest son of Frederick, who was a Catholic ; Bavaria kept the Upper Palatinate and her new electoral dignity, so that there were now eight electors. Also, the treaty for the first time recognized both Holland and Switzerland as independent sovereign states. But the war between France and Spain, begun in 1635, was not affected by the treaty, and dragged on for

**ANNE OF AUSTRIA PRESIDING OVER THE PARIS PARLEMENT**

Louis XIV was not five years old when he became king of France on May 14, 1643. By the terms of Louis XIII's will, Anne of Austria was nominated regent, and four days after her son's accession she summoned the Parlement of Paris and secured their ratification of her appointment. This contemporary engraving shows the Parlement in session, with the boy-king seated under a canopy of state and the queen-regent, wearing widow's weeds, beside him.

*From Larousse, ' Histoire de France illustrée '*

**FRONDEURS AND MAZARINS IN THE BATTLE OF S. ANTOINE**

This old print illustrates a particularly dramatic engagement in the Fronde. Condé marching on Paris was overtaken on July 2, 1652, by the royal troops under Turenne and hemmed in in the Faubourg S. Antoine with the Porte S. Antoine closed at his back. The Frondeurs were on the point of being annihilated when the duchess of Montpensier persuaded the citizens to open the gate and admit them, and herself turned the guns of the Bastille upon Turenne's forces and routed them.

*Cabinet des Estampes, Paris; from Larousse, 'Histoire de France illustrée'*

eleven years longer. In Germany the independence of every prince, Lutheran or Calvinist, in matters of religion was recognized. The wars of religion, in the international sense, were over.

At the moment when the Thirty Years' War was ending, the Paris Parlement was attempting to assert constitutional rights bearing a close resemblance to those which the English parliament had claimed for centuries. The absolutism established by Richelieu was being exercised by a Spanish regent and an Italian minister; and this body of lawyers sought to bring some check on it, in the absence of any other body endowed with legal powers. Some of the nobles associated themselves with the movement, with the object of strengthening not the lawyers but their own licence of action. The party became known as the Fronde; and what had started as a constitutional movement degenerated into a struggle between the court party and the nobles of the Fronde, who were headed by Condé.

This civil war of the Fronde went on with startling changes of fortune till

**GREAT FRENCH MARSHAL**

This pastel portrait of Turenne, marshal of France, is one of the masterpieces of Robert Nanteuil, and was painted in 1665 when the great general was 54. Turenne was a prominent figure in the Thirty Years' War.

*The Louvre; photo, Giraudon*

Turenne finally joined the court party, suppressed the Frondeurs, and drove Condé to exile in Spain, which was glad enough to employ his military talents against his own countrymen, in 1652. The Spanish war had been in progress all the time, but, fortunately for France, the revolts of Catalonia and Portugal, diversified by a democratic revolt in Naples under a leader known as Masaniello, had prevented Spain from making adequate use of her opportunity, though she had gained ground in what were to be known as the Spanish Netherlands. Condé had turned the patriotic tide against himself in France by associating himself with the national enemy.

### Attitude of the Commonwealth

MEANWHILE England had beheaded her king three months after Westphalia; Charles II was an exile ; the Commonwealth had crushed revolt in Ireland and subjugated Scotland, had embarked on a naval war with the Dutch, and was on the point of passing under the rule of Cromwell's military dictatorship. The Dutch Republic was under the rule of an oligarchy headed by John de Witt, the infant William of Orange being held under close tutelage. Both Spain and France were soon considering the possibility of attracting England to an alliance ; while Cromwell's ideas on foreign policy were those of an Elizabethan Protestant who still regarded Protestantism as at stake and Spain as presumably the enemy. In no case would he ally with a power which he counted hostile to Protestantism. He was still suspicious of France—though he closed down the Dutch war readily in 1654—when he opened an attack on Spain in the West Indies in 1655.

So far nothing decisive had taken place in the Franco-Spanish war ; but next year Mazarin satisfied Cromwell by intervening in Savoy to stop the persecution of the Protestant Vaudois, and in 1657 Cromwell sent his Ironsides to join Turenne's army in the Netherlands, with decisive effect on the campaign in that quarter. The scale having once turned thoroughly in favour of France, it was convenient for Mazarin that Cromwell died (Sept., 1658) and chaos again beset the government in England, so that Mazarin was able to end the Spanish war by the peace of the Pyrenees in 1659, unhampered by English

#### CHARLES II LANDING AT DOVER AT THE RESTORATION

This animated print corroborates Samuel Pepys' well known account of the enthusiastic scenes at Dover when, on May 26, 1660, King Charles II set foot on English soil after his long exile. ' Infinite the crowd of people and the horsemen, citizens, and noblemen of all sorts. . . . He talked awhile with General Monk and others, and so into a stately coach there set for him, and so away through the town towards Canterbury. . . . The shouting and joy expressed by all is past imagination.'

*British Museum*

demands. France, besides all that she held at the peace of Westphalia, had secured a right of way through Lorraine, a foothold in the Netherlands, and beyond the Rhine a group of practically dependent German principalities and the assured friendship of the Dutch Republic.

In 1660 Mazarin retired, surrendering the reins of government not to a new minister, but into the hands of the young king Louis XIV himself, at the moment when his cousin Charles II was recalled to England amid the rejoicings of the entire population. Two years earlier the still younger Leopold I succeeded Ferdinand III as emperor, and king of Bohemia and Hungary. The marriages of Louis in 1660 and Leopold in 1665, each a son of a sister of Philip IV of Spain, to Philip's elder and younger daughters respectively (see page 583), were fraught with grave consequences to the future peace of Europe.

**FREDERICK WILLIAM, THE GREAT ELECTOR**

Succeeding his father as elector of Brandenburg in 1640, Frederick William (1620–88) greatly extended his dominions, founded the Brandenburg-Prussian army and the Prussian navy, and established Prussia as an independent duchy. This engraving is after the painting by Govaert Flinck, c. 1660.
*British Museum*

We turn now to the three Baltic kingdoms, Poland, Sweden and Denmark, to which must be added Brandenburg, since its acquisition of eastern Pomerania with a Baltic seaboard at the treaty of Westphalia. The exceedingly competent Frederick William, known as the Great Elector, took the place of his inefficient father, George William, in 1640, and devoted his first years to the recuperation of which his dominion stood in sore need. It became his ambition and his business to raise Brandenburg to the position of the strongest state in North Germany, and the leader of the Protestants. She was at last in possession of a seaboard on the Baltic, but he wanted not half but the whole of Pomerania. She had her outpost in the west, in Cleves ; and she had her duchy of East Prussia as a fief of the Polish crown, but between East Prussia and Pomerania lay West Prussia ; to consolidate his

dominion and make it territorially continuous, he wanted West Prussia also, and he wanted both in independent sovereignty, not as a noble of Poland.

Queen Christina in Sweden enjoyed a brief and brilliant reign. But the daughter of Gustavus turned Catholic ; she had no doubt that the ruler of Sweden ought to be a Lutheran ; and in 1654, at the age of twenty-eight, she abdicated in favour of her cousin, Charles X. John Casimir of Poland, whose father Sigismund had once been king of Sweden, refused to recognize Charles's title. Charles, a brilliant soldier, like so many others of the house of Vasa, flung himself on Poland, marching through East Pomerania, where he extorted a free passage from Frederick William, routed John Casimir, and then, doubting the elector's fidelity, marched into East Prussia and required him to acknowledge his own suzerainty in place of John Casimir's.

But Poland was not conquered ; Denmark, alarmed by his successes, was threatening an attack ; and he had to return to Sweden, thinking that he had secured Brandenburg by ceding East Prussia in full sovereignty.

But in 1657 he was fighting the Danes, and Frederick William went over to John Casimir, who bought him by confirming on his own account the cession made by Charles. Charles completely defeated Frederick III of Denmark in an amazing winter campaign, marching his forces over the frozen sea, extorted from him the treaty of Roeskilde, and, not content with that, renewed the war in 1659, thereby bringing both Holland and Brandenburg to the aid of Denmark. His death in February, 1660, ended the war ; and the treaties of Oliva and Copenhagen, the counterpart in the north of the treaties of Westphalia and the Pyrenees, retained for Sweden what she had actually won from Denmark, and left Frederick William his East Prussian duchy in full sovereignty, while John Casimir abandoned his claim to the Swedish crown, now worn by the infant Charles XI.

CHARLES GUSTAVUS X
Charles X of Sweden (1622–60) was cousin to Queen Christina and their marriage was strongly urged by Oxenstierna. Christina, however, disliking masculine control, appointed him her successor and he was crowned on her abdication.
*British Museum*

QUEEN CHRISTINA OF SWEDEN
Christina (1626–89) succeeded Gustavus Adolphus on the throne of Sweden in 1632 and assumed power in 1644. She was an exceptionally brilliant woman, but extravagant and impulsive, and in the year 1654 she abdicated.
*Portrait by Sebastian Bourdon, Versailles Gallery*

OMINOUS for the West was the revival of aggressive energy in the Turkish empire at this time under the great wazir Mohammed Kiuprili. Since the death of Suleiman the Magnificent and the battle of Lepanto, the Turks had sunk into torpor, till in 1645 Sultan Ibrahim roused himself to attack the Venetians in Crete. Venice, however, more than held her own under the captaincy of Mocenigo, till the sultan was deposed and the mother of the new sultan, Mohammed III, appointed wazir Kiuprili—an Albanian—old but energetic. He at once set about a vigorous and drastic reorganization, defeated and killed Mocenigo, laid resolute siege to Candia, and turned to make the sovereign power of the Porte felt in Transylvania, where at the moment of his death in 1661 the party of independence was led by Kemenyi, who had just appealed to the emperor Leopold for support.

In the Far West during this century English colonists had established themselves in two groups of colonies, the planters in the south and the farmers and traders of New England in the north, along the North American seaboard, while Frenchmen were pioneering and planting themselves in the basin of the St. Lawrence, the Dutch occupied on the Hudson a wedge between the two English groups, and all three were occupying West Indian islands not in actual occupation by Spaniards.   From the Spaniards themselves Cromwell appropriated the great island of Jamaica, which was captured and held in 1655.

To turn from the Far West to the Far East.  India was ruled by Jehangir and Shah Jehan, the son and grandson of Akbar, till the latter was finally deposed in 1658 by his son Aurangzib.  This was the most splendid and prosperous period of the Mogul empire, during which, incidentally, the London East India Com-

**GREATEST OF JAPAN'S SHOGUNS**

Tokugawa Iyeyasu (1542–1616) belonged to the Minamoto family and in 1603, mainly through the agency of Hideyoshi, obtained the title of shogun, which remained in his family until the abolition of the Shogunate in 1868.

pany was allowed to establish depots known as factories at Surat, at Madras

**MAP OF NEW FRANCE, WITH NEWFOUNDLAND AND LABRADOR**

Following Cabot's discovery of Newfoundland, Jacques Cartier in 1534 sailed down the straits of Belle Isle, already known to Breton fishermen, explored the Gulf of St. Lawrence, and secured a large tract of land thereabouts for France.    Above is part of Jacomo di Gastaldi's map of the region, dating from c. 1550.  Terra Nuova and the islands south of it together represent Newfoundland ; the serpentine line is a sand bank, the then agreed limit of fishing.

*From Winsor, ' Narrative and Critical History of America'*

and on the Hooghli, the remote beginnings of the British Indian Empire.

China saw the overthrow of the Ming dynasty, by the hosts of the Manchus, whose dynasty was still reigning in the twentieth century. At the same time Japan entered on a new phase. Nobunaga (see page 535) had re-created a central government; the genius of Hideyoshi, despite his humble birth, had established it, and under his dictatorship Japan had seemed on the point of a great imperial expansion at the expense of China, whose collapse before the Manchus suggests that his ambitions, for such a man, were well within reason, though out of range for anyone smaller than he. Moreover, on his death in 1598 there was no one on whom his mantle could fall with a double portion of his spirit, and his son was still a child.

The conduct of the government was vested in councils, who prudently and promptly withdrew from the Korean adventure. The Octavian for this Julius was Hideyoshi's old colleague Tokugawa Iyeyasu, who was no longer a young man. By 1603 he had overcome his most serious rivals and procured from the mikado his official appointment as shogun, an office which he made hereditary by initiating the practice of appointing his son to the Shogunate during his own lifetime while keeping the actual control in his own hands—as western emperors procured the election of their sons as king of the Romans.

IYEYASU admitted English and Dutch traders and shipwrights, and at first Jesuits, Dominicans and Franciscans; but, coming to the conclusion, not without evidence, that the latter must be regarded as agents for an aggressive king of Spain, he closed the gates of Japan to all Roman Catholic priests. Christianity, or at least the Catholic Christianity of the missionaries, was, it appeared, politically subversive, and under Iyeyasu's successors in the Shogunate it was penalised out of existence. Even the English and Dutch traders, towards whom the government showed no direct enmity, were discouraged by hampering regulations, since it seemed that where Europeans came to trade the traders were apt to be precursors of cannon. Europe in the throes of the Thirty Years' War did not strike Japanese observers as a happy model for imitation.

The system now established in Japan provided a strong centralised government, with checks upon the nominal ruler, the mikado, on one side and on the military organization of the daimyo—the greater nobles — on the other, which gave security against either absolutism or a return to feudal anarchy. The English traders had shut down their factories. In 1636 the shogun Iyemitsu made a decree forbidding any Japanese to leave the islands, and in 1641 all Europeans were excluded; except the Dutch, who were allowed to remain on a tiny island, and to send no more than ten ships annually to the port of Nagasaki. Deliberately Japan isolated herself from the rest of the world, and persisted in her isolation for two hundred years.

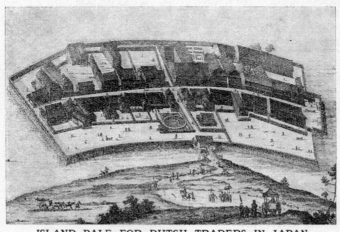

**ISLAND PALE FOR DUTCH TRADERS IN JAPAN**
Japanese suspicion of Christianity and of Western methods generally led in 1641 to the exclusion of all foreigners. The only exception made was in favour of the Dutch traders, and they were confined to this small island of Deshima off Nagasaki, and only permitted to send ten ships annually to that port.

# Eighth Era

## THE PRIMACY OF FRANCE

### 1660–1815

---

Chapter 26
THE AGE OF LOUIS XIV, 1660—1713

Chapter 27
DEVELOPMENT OF THE GREAT POWERS, 1713—1789

Chapter 28
THE FRENCH REVOLUTION & THE NAPOLEONIC AGE, 1789—1815

---

D URING the century and a half preceding the moment at which this era opens, the main troubles of the European states, international and internal, arose from religious animosities. That phase has passed. In the new era, beginning with the personal autocracy of Louis XIV and ending with the downfall of Napoleon, continental politics revolve round French ambitions ; while all Europe is dominated in thought, art, literature and manners by France. But it is also the era in which Great Britain establishes her supremacy on the seas and eliminates French rivalry in India and America, though paying a heavy price in the loss of her American colonies ; the era in which first the Ottoman power is broken, then the Russian empire is created by a barbarian of genius, and then Prussia thrusts her way into the front rank of the European powers. And it ends as the period of the great social and political upheaval of the French Revolution, and of the first stage of the no less momentous economic revolution wrought by the invention of power-driven machinery.

# TABLE OF DATES FOR CHAPTER 26

**1660** Louis XIV m. Maria Teresa ; takes control on Mazarin's retirement.
Restoration of Charles II in England.
Treaties of Oliva and Copenhagen.

**1661** Ahmed Kiuprili grand wazir.
England acquires Bombay from Portugal.

**1662** Colbert's financial, maritime and colonial policy inaugurated in France.

**1664** Turkish defeat at St. Gothard-on-Raab. Austro-Turkish truce of Vasvár.
French East India Company established.

**1665** Second Anglo-Dutch war.
Portuguese independence established.
Leopold I m. Margaret Teresa of Spain.
Philip IV d. ; acc. Carlos II of Spain.

**1667** Anglo-Dutch Treaty of Breda.
Louis invades Netherlands ; Devolution War.
Milton's Paradise Lost.

**1668** Secret Treaty of Louis and Leopold. Triple Alliance of England, Holland and Sweden.
Louis accepts Peace of Aix-la-Chapelle.

**1669** Fall of Candia ends Turco-Venetian war.
Poland : John Casimir, the last Jagellon, abdicates. Michael Wiesnowiecki elected k.

**1670** Secret Treaty of Dover (Louis and Charles II).

**1671** Rise of Louvois, superseding Colbert's influence.

**1672** Louis and Charles declare war on Dutch ; murder of the De Witts. William III declared stadtholder and captain-general. French advance checked by opening the dykes.
Turks, at war with Poland, checked by John Sobieski.

**1673** Dutch form defence league with German states.
Molière d.

**1674** John Sobieski king of Poland.
England withdraws from Dutch war.
Turenne's campaign in Alsace. French seize Franche Comté.

**1675** Tököli's insurrection in Transylvania.
Turenne killed at Saltzbach.
The Great Elector, Frederick William, defeats superior Swedish force at Fehrbellin.

**1676** Kara Mustafa succeeds Ahmed Kiuprili as grand wazir.
India : Aurangzib revives poll-tax on Hindus.

**1677** Spinoza d.

**1678** Treaty of Nimwegen (Nimeguen), marking the height and the limit of Louis' power.

**1679** Treaty of St. Germain-en-Laye deprives the Great Elector of the fruits of his victory over the Swedes at Fehrbellin.
Louis sets up the Chambers of Reunion to enforce French interpretation of disputed questions in the Rhineland.

**1680** India : Sivaji founder of the Maratha power d.

**1681** Breach between Louis and the pope. Louis begins persecution of Huguenots.
Louis occupies Strassburg.

**1682** Russia : Acc. Ivan V and Peter (the Great) ; the government in the hands of Sophia.

**1683** Kara Mustafa lays siege to Vienna ; John Sobieski comes to the rescue, joins Charles of Lorraine, and shatters Turkish army. Imperial troops continue the war.
Colbert d.

**1684** Corneille d.

**1685** Revocation of Edict of Nantes ; great emigration of fugitive Huguenots.
England : Charles II d. ; acc. James II.

**1686** League of Augsburg among German princes.
Venetians reconquer Morea.

**1687** Parthenon at Athens accidentally destroyed.
Publication of Isaac Newton's Principia.
Charles of Lorraine defeats Turks at Mohacz.

**1688** English statesmen of all parties invite intervention of William of Orange.
Louis attacks not Holland but Palatinate by advice of Louvois. William lands in Torbay ; James flees to France leaving throne vacant.
Great Elector d. ; acc. Frederick.
Mustafa Kiuprili grand wazir.

**1689** William III and Mary II proclaimed king and queen in England and Scotland, where Jacobite resistance collapses after Killiecrankie.

**1689** Ireland : siege of Derry by Jacobites.
League of Augsburg develops into Grand Alliance.
Imperialists take Belgrade from Turks.
Russia : Peter displaces Sophia.

**1690** William defeats Irish Jacobites on the Boyne.
French defeat English fleet off Beachy Head.

**1691** Capitulation of Limerick.
Louvois d.

**1692** Decisive English naval victory of La Hogue.

**1694** Turks recapture Belgrade.
Voltaire b.

**1696** Peter the Great takes Azov from the Turks.
Allies recapture Namur.

**1697** Treaty of Ryswick (a set-back for Louis).
Eugène's victory over Turks at Zenta.
Peter the Great's journey in western Europe.
Charles XI of Sweden d. ; acc. Charles XII.

**1698** First Spanish Partition Treaty between Louis and William ; electoral prince of Bavaria the principal heir.
Augustus of Saxony elected king of Poland.

**1699** Treaty of Carlowitz between Austria, Russia and Turkey.
Northern league against Charles of Sweden.
Racine d.
Electoral prince d.

**1700** Second Partition Treaty by Louis and William.
Carlos II d. leaving the whole Spanish inheritance to Philip ; Louis accepts.
Charles XII routs Russians at Narva.

**1701** Louis takes possession in Spain, Netherlands and Italy ; William draws together new Grand Alliance. Austrians open Italian campaign.
Frederick of Brandenburg crowned first k. of Prussia.

**1702** Allies declare war. William d. ; acc. Anne.
Marlborough captain-general of British and Dutch in Netherlands ; Eugène commands for the allies in Italy.
Charles XII invades Poland.

**1703** Marlborough pushes France back in Netherlands.
French campaign on the Danube spoilt by attempt to master Tyrol ; but Vendôme forces Eugène back to the Alps from Italy.
Portugal joins the Allies who claim Spain for Archduke Charles.
John Wesley b.

**1704** Marlborough concerts Blenheim campaign with Eugène. While the French armies are massing on the Danube, he throws himself by a surprise march between them and Vienna and wins decisive battle of Blenheim.
Rooke captures Gibraltar.
Charles XII enforces election of Stanislaus Lecszinski in Poland.

**1705** Leopold I d. ; acc. Joseph I.

**1706** Marlborough wins Ramillies ; Eugène drives French out of N. Italy by victory of Turin.
Charles XII imposes treaty of Altranstadt on Augustus of Saxony.

**1706-7** Incorporating union of England and Scotland.

**1707** French under Berwick win Almanza against English under (Huguenot) Ruvigny earl of Galway.
India : Aurangzib d. Disintegration of Mogul Empire sets in.

**1708** Marlborough wins Oudenarde. British under Stanhope capture Minorca.
Charles XII invades Russia.

**1709** Marlborough's last victory at Malplaquet.
Charles XII, defeated at Pultava, escapes to Turkish territory, where he remains.
Augustus of Saxony recovers Polish crown ; renewed attack on Swedish territories.

**1710** Turks declare war on Peter.
Conference at Gertruydenburg fails.
Victories of Vendôme in Spain.

**1711** Fall of Whigs and recall of Marlborough.
Joseph I d. ; acc. Charles VI.
Peter, trapped on the Pruth, is granted peace by the Turks, and joins in dismembering Sweden.

**1712** Virtual suspension of hostilities.

**1713** Peace of Utrecht.
Frederick I of Prussia d. ; acc. Frederick William I

CHAPTER 26

# THE AGE OF LOUIS XIV: 1660–1713

IN 1660 Louis XIV, being twenty-one years of age, took over into his own hands the control of France from Mazarin, and married the eldest daughter of the king of Spain. For the next fifty years his ambitions dominated all the international relations of Europe ; and, apart from political rivalries, France became, during his rule, the dictator or the model of all Europe in thought, in art, in literature and in manners. Mazarin had completed the work of Richelieu. France was consolidated and her government centralised as it had never been before. Her armies were led by the two greatest captains of the age ; her frontiers had been extended and strengthened ; she held the passage to Italy, the passage to Spain and the entry to Germany ; her diplomatists were unequalled ; she had no rivals who could contemplate aggression against her.

### France safe from Foreign Aggression

AN enfeebled Spain had lost her hold on Portugal, and was ruled by an elderly king who was soon to be succeeded by a half-imbecile boy ; Germany was depopulated, bled almost white by the Thirty Years' War, with no more unity than was given by the official presidency of an emperor over a crowd of princes each of whom was practically an absolute ruler in his own territories ; and the emperor himself was threatened by Magyar insurrections and Turkish aggression in his Hungarian kingdom. Sweden was remote and reckoned among great powers only when her king happened to be a great captain— and at the moment her king was a child of four. England had just restored a king who was the French king's cousin and could not afford to quarrel with him. The last thing to be anticipated was an attack on France by any foreign power, or any development of power which could be a menace to France. There was no existing excuse for France to turn her own power to aggressive purposes. Nevertheless this position did not satisfy the inordinate egotism of Louis XIV.

From the outset he was determined to make good the old French claim on Franche Comté and the new French demand for the 'natural' boundary on the Lower Rhine, in other words the possession of the Spanish Netherlands, to which France had no pretence of a title. Beyond that was the determination to dominate Europe, making Holland and the western German principalities into dependencies of France. All these ambitions he had apparently formulated when Mazarin resigned. At this stage the final ambition to make Spain a Bourbon instead of a Hapsburg monarchy can hardly have presented itself even as a dream.

### Colbert's financial Reforms

ACTIVE aggression, however, demands at least something which the aggressor can put forward as a pretext with some appearance of plausibility. Awaiting such a pretext, Louis' immediate concern was the further internal consolidation and development of France herself. The man for the work was Colbert. Louis, wholly lacking in originality himself, had a genius for finding men with ideas which he could up to a certain point appreciate, and to whom, so far, he gave a free hand.

Henry IV and Sully had reorganized French administration and finance. Richelieu and Mazarin had preserved the basic idea of their administration—that it should be in the hands not of powerful nobles but of professionals from the bourgeoisie or the minor nobility, directly responsible to the crown. But Sully's rigid economy and strict supervision had disappeared with his retirement, and the old evils had revived. The restoration of the national finances was Colbert's first task. Strict supervision was once more the order of the day, and a development of industries much more vigorous than under Sully, who suffered from the prevalent conviction that the only form of wealth production which really mattered was agriculture.

But Colbert was the first and almost the only French financial minister to realize

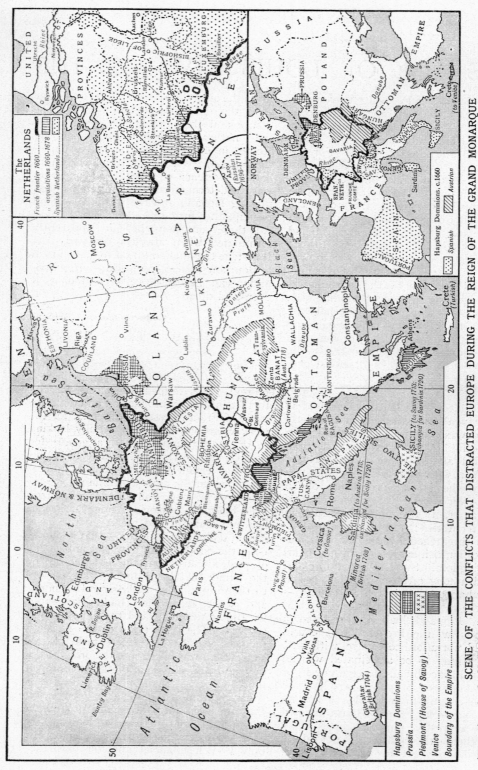

**SCENE OF THE CONFLICTS THAT DISTRACTED EUROPE DURING THE REIGN OF THE GRAND MONARQUE**

Aggressions in the Netherlands occupied Louis XIV from 1660–78, and the shifting of the frontier effected in that period is shown in the upper inset. Further ambitions involved him in the war of the Spanish Succession, ending in his abasement by the Treaty of Utrecht (1713). In central Europe a dominant incident was the westward expansion of Turkey as far as Vienna from which the Empire was delivered by Sobieski of Poland. In the north-east there was conflict between Russia and Sweden, Peter the Great defeating Charles XII at Pultava in 1709. The period also witnessed the foundation of Prussian power by the Elector of Brandenburg.

that the wealth of England and Holland was derived from their maritime expansion; and he entered upon a rivalry with them in the field of oceanic, colonial and naval development with a success which was the more remarkable because its vitality depended entirely on his personal energy. While he was allowed his own way, the wealth of France increased rapidly —though it was presently to be dissipated on his master's grandiose schemes. Two things no man could do: redistribute the burden of taxation with any approximation to justice, because the classes that were prac-

**ABSOLUTE MONARCHY**

Louis XIV was born September 5, 1638, and became king in 1643. This portrait by Nicolas Mignard was painted in 1663, when the king was in the twenty-fifth year of his age.

*Engraving by Kühner*

tically immune, the nobles and the clergy, were too strongly entrenched to yield up their privileges; and break down the barriers to internal trade which local short-sightedness persisted in maintaining—though here a real advance was made by the development of groups of communities adopting free trade between themselves, greatly to their advantage.

Louis' marriage with the Spanish Infanta, Maria Teresa, was a stroke of policy on the part of Mazarin which provided the king with a starting point for his ambitions. The heir to the Spanish throne was

**NUPTIALS OF LOUIS XIV AND THE INFANTA MARIA TERESA**

An essential clause in the Peace Treaty of the Pyrenees, 1659, stipulated for the marriage of Louis XIV to Maria Teresa, eldest daughter of Philip IV of Spain, the bride renouncing all rights of inheritance from her father in consideration of payment of a large dowry. Mazarin's idea was that the renunciation would be invalidated by default of the money payment, with consequent advantages to the French party to the contract. The marriage was celebrated at St. Jean-de-Luz, June 9, 1660.

*Engraving after painting by Charles Le Brun*

**PHILIP IV OF SPAIN**

Philip IV (1605–65) became king of Spain in 1621, but delegated the administration to Olivarez and other favourites, devoting himself to sport, pleasure and dilettantism. He was a patron of Velasquez, who painted this portrait of him.

*The Louvre ; photo, Giraudon*

a sickly little boy, the son of Philip's second wife. Maria Teresa was the daughter of his first wife. There were no brothers. But in certain provinces of the Netherlands succession went to the children of the first wife, whether boys or girls, in priority to any children of a second marriage. On this principle Louis chose to argue that when Philip died the succession in the Netherlands would go, of right, to his wife, not to the boy Carlos, though in Spain the right of the latter was of course indisputable.

King Philip died in 1665, having just married his second daughter, Margaret Teresa, to the emperor Leopold. If the boy king should die without issue she, not Maria Teresa, would be his heir, because the latter's resignation of all right of

succession in Spain had been a condition of her marriage to Louis. Still, there was a possibility that some ground for asserting her claim might be forthcoming. This, however, was as yet a contingency too uncertain to affect practical politics.

But Philip's death gave Louis his opportunity for putting forward his claim in the Netherlands. Until now he had been content to foster antagonisms between his neighbours which might weaken them. He had encouraged a renewal of the war between English and Dutch which Cromwell had stopped in 1654—the more Dutch and English fleets hammered each other, the better for Colbert's schemes— and had helped Portugal to establish her independent monarchy under the house of Braganza, an aim finally achieved by the Portuguese victory at Villa Viciosa in 1665.

Louis at once pressed his claim. Diplomacy naturally failed. In 1667, at the moment when Dutch and English, tired of obstinate and indecisive fighting, were coming to terms, Louis dropped diplomacy and sent Turenne to take forcible possession of the Netherlands in what is known as the War of Devolution. Turenne's

**LEOPOLD I**

The reign of Leopold I (1640–1705), German king and emperor, was spent in continual resistance to the aggressions of Louis XIV. He was father of the Austrian and grandfather of the Bavarian claimants to the Spanish succession.

*Engraving by Bartholomäus Kilian*

**MURDER OF THE BROTHERS DE WITT**

In August 1672 the Grand Pensionary, John De Witt, and his brother Cornelius, leaders of the anti-Orange party, were seized by an Orange mob and savagely murdered. This silver medal shows their busts on the obverse, and on the reverse an allegory of madness rending them in pieces.

*British Museum ; photo, Oxford University Press*

projects of his own which he could only carry out by his cousin's financial aid, and was quite ready for a bargain, though its terms could not be confided to his ministers. The bargain was duly struck, and in 1672 France and England declared war on the Dutch Republic.

Unfortunately for the scheme, an internal revolution overturned and murdered the De Witts and made William stadtholder and captain-general. Instead of securing a dependant, Louis by attacking Holland had raised up the implacable foe who wrecked his ambitions. Whatever the odds, William never faltered in the intensity of his resolve to devote his life to fighting against Louis. The English fought the Dutch by sea ; neither could decisively beat the other, and Charles took the earliest opportunity to extricate himself from the conflict. The French fought the Dutch by land, and

success was so rapid and complete that England, Holland and Sweden took alarm, and formed a Triple Alliance to induce Louis by force, if diplomatic pressure failed, to make peace with Spain on reasonable terms. Louis meanwhile had taken his own measures. A surprise invasion of Franche Comté gave him complete mastery there ; he had secured the neutrality of the German princes, and made a secret compact with Leopold as to an ultimate partition of the Spanish dominions. So with a fine display of magnanimity he acceded to the demands of the Triple Alliance, restoring Franche Comté, but retaining in the Netherlands an almost impregnable chain of fortresses stretching from Dunkirk to Charleroi.

The next step was to be the domination of Holland. There the republican government of De Witt had held the house of Orange in depression for twenty years ; its restoration to power in the person of the young William would place the country practically at the disposal of his restorer, the king of France. The English fleet would be useful ; William was the English king's nephew ; Charles had domestic

**LOUIS XIV CROSSING THE RHINE**

This picture by Joseph Parrocel shows Louis XIV fording the Rhine at Tolhuis, June 12, 1672, on his way to join Condé's forces in the Dutch campaign. Although in Napoleon's estimation a fourth-rate military operation, this incident provided the subject for numerous poems and paintings.

*The Louvre ; photo, Archives photographiques*

**ONE OF COLBERT'S BATTLESHIPS**

In the French navy as reorganized by Colbert, the principal type of vessel was the three-masted line-of-battle ship. They were divided into five classes, ranging from 192 feet in length with 49 feet beam to 114 feet in length with 26 feet beam, and armament ranging from 100 to 30 guns.

*Musée de la Marine, Paris*

William turned the sea itself upon them by opening the dykes.

Moreover, Louis' aggressive aims were now so thoroughly unmasked that Frederick William of Brandenburg took alarm—he, not Louis, ought to have the leadership of West Germany—and drew together a coalition to resist France, whose only ally was Sweden. From 1673 to 1678 France was fighting almost single-handed against a circle of foes, who, happily for her, had no unity of plan and no generals in any way comparable with Turenne. She won victory after victory even after Turenne was killed in 1675 ; the fleet Colbert had created even beat the Dutch ; but against such odds the victories could mean no more than that she was holding her own with a small

**RATIFICATION OF THE TREATY OF NIMWEGEN BY LOUIS 'THE GREAT'**

With the conclusion of the Dutch War in 1678 Louis XIV was definitely arbiter of the destinies of Europe. Peace was made with the United Provinces by the Treaty of Nimwegen (Nimeguen), signed August 10, 1678, a historical event commemorated in this painting by Charles Le Brun. A second treaty was signed with Spain, Sept. 17, 1678 ; and on Feb. 5, 1679, Leopold accepted Louis' terms. The pacification was completed by supplementary treaties with Brandenburg, Denmark and Sweden.

*Musée des Beaux-Arts, Budapest ; photo, Hanfstängl*

margin of advantage. Both sides became exhausted ; William and William alone was set upon a fight to a finish, and in Holland itself his popularity was waning under the tremendous strain. One after another of the belligerents dropped out, making their separate terms, Holland first, then Spain, then Leopold, whose belligerency, owing to Turkish and Hungarian embarrassments, had always been half-hearted. The group of treaties which terminated the war are known as the Peace of Nimwegen, or Nimeguen (1678).

Frederick William of Brandenburg had made use of the war mainly for the decisive defeat of Sweden ; but he was not allowed to profit thereby, since Louis would not desert his ally. France alone had achieved solid gains, which were mainly at the expense of Spain. She took Franche Comté and added to the number of her fortresses in the Spanish Netherlands. She had proved the adequacy of her military organization to face odds which ought to have overwhelmed her. In the hour of his triumph the monarch on entering his capital was enthusiastically hailed as Louis the Great. Had he died then, posterity might have endorsed the title.

### Louis at the Zenith of his Career

BUT Louis was not satisfied with his achievement ; as concerned Holland at least, he had created not a dependency but an irreconcilable enemy, and that enemy had just married the heiress presumptive to the throne of England. Colbert's influence had waned and that of the great militarist minister of war, Louvois, was in the ascendant. Colbert the economist detested wars of aggression except for the depression of a commercial rival ; for Louvois, the only use for economy was to provide means for wars of aggression. For a time, however, while Louvois was training a great standing army and raising its organization to an unprecedented perfection, Louis abstained from further military adventures, effecting his aggressions by pacific methods.

The successive treaties had brought into Louis' hands various towns and districts ' with their dependencies '—a highly disputable term, which he inter-

**FAMOUS FRENCH STATESMAN**
This engraving by Lubin shows Jean Baptiste Colbert (1619–1683), whose persistent endeavours to effect financial reform in France were nullified by the heavy national expenditure which his sovereign's ambitions incurred.
*Photo, W. F. Mansell*

preted as covering Strassburg, Luxemburg and much else that had hitherto belonged to various West German princes. Louis settled these questions to his own satisfaction by setting up French courts called ' chambers of reunion ' to decide the points in dispute ; what the French courts decided to be French territory he forthwith treated as French ; and as yet there was no one who durst say him nay. There were protests, but they were silenced by the ingenious proposal, confirmed by a diet at Ratisbon, that the discussion of the legality of Louis' action should be postponed for twenty years. Colbert's son Seignelai was allowed to maintain the navy in a state of high efficiency, against the time when it might have to serve against the Dutch. France, in fact, was constantly and increasingly prepared for war as no other country was prepared —as a guarantee not against attack but against resistance when next she should assert aggressive claims.

Now, the old policy of Henry IV and Richelieu in the rivalry to the Hapsburg

### REVOCATION OF THE EDICT OF NANTES
The wise policy of religious toleration inaugurated by Henry IV
of France was reversed by Louis XIV, and after 1681 repressive
measures were enforced against the Protestants culminating
in the revocation of the Edict of Nantes, October 17, 1685.
Above is the preamble of the decree signed by Louis XIV.
*Archives Nationales*

power had been to unite the forces of
Protestantism with a France posing as
the champion of toleration, in opposition
to the aggressively Catholic Hapsburgs.
The Hapsburgs were no longer aggressive
Catholics ; the religious question had
ceased to be an international cause of
quarrel ; but Louis went out of his way
to revive it by the religious policy he
pursued in France—making himself appear
as the zealous enemy of Protestantism
while the Hapsburgs could assume the
tolerationist rôle. In so far as regards the
religious policy that he saw fit to adopt, it
is sufficient to remark here that it opens
upon a conflict with the Papacy, on
the question of authority in the Gallican church, which conflict in Louis'
eyes imposed upon him the necessity
of simultaneously demonstrat-
ing the rigidity of his own
orthodoxy.

No better proof of it could
be given than the severe repression of heresy, though
Richelieu had transformed the
Huguenots into the most loyal
and financially valuable element of the population. Louis
attacked the Huguenots, first
by excluding them from the
public services, then by further
penalising measures, especially
the 'dragonnades,' beside
which the almost contemporary persecution of the Scottish

Covenanters was anaemic, and
finally by revoking the Edict
of Nantes altogether (1685).
These measures had no
countenance from the Pa-
pacy ; they did not draw
Catholic princes to the side
of the king of France ; but
they did excite extreme alarm
and hostility in every Protestant state. The small West
German principalities, once
the protégés of Richelieu, set
about forming a secret defensive league, which was presently to develop into the
European League of Augsburg.

IN the same year died Charles II, the
'Merry Monarch.' The Stuart restoration meant in the result the restoration
at once of the prestige of the crown and
the authority of parliament. For twenty
years Charles, masking consummate political astuteness by an apparently reckless
frivolity, strove to recover the effective
power of the crown, and did actually in
the end recover it for himself, but only
on a basis in which there could be no
permanence—his own French pension, the
purchase price of his overt or covert
support of Louis' designs. But the king's
power to levy taxes had gone for ever,
the parliament's claim to control expenditure as well as taxation was secured, and
no future minister charged with misconduct could hope to find shelter from

### TRIUMPH OF FIERCE INTOLERANCE
Savage satire distinguishes this Dutch medal commemorating
the revocation of the Edict of Nantes. The obverse shows
the pope riding a monster that devours a man, woman and
child, and supported by a Jesuit and a dragoon. On the reverse
a woman swings from a gibbet and others are being maltreated.
*British Museum ; photo, Oxford University Press*

punishment by pleading the king's orders.

Charles was succeeded by his brother, James II, an avowed Romanist, whose intention of restoring Romanism in England was very soon manifesting itself. James's heiress was his Protestant daughter Mary, the wife of William of Orange, who was also his nephew and stood next to her and her sister Anne in the line of the English succession. To William England would certainly turn if James carried his Romanist policy too far—since the late king's illegitimate son Monmouth, William's only possible rival, perished on the scaffold after an abortive rebellion before James had been six months on the throne. With a modicum of tact James could have procured a considerable extension of tolera-

**ENGLAND'S 'MERRY MONARCH'**
The Stuart line was restored to the English throne in 1660 in the person of the amorous, intriguing Charles II. His sardonic features are cleverly reproduced in this bust by Honoré Pellé dated 1684, the year before the king's death.
*Victoria and Albert Museum*

tion for Romanists and a secure position as a constitutional monarch; he flung his chances away by reverting to arbitrary methods and alienating the stoutest of the crown's traditional supporters, the high Anglicans, lay and clerical. If James persisted in alienating his subjects it was in the interest both of James and of Louis that William should be too thoroughly occupied elsewhere to answer any appeal for intervention in England— an appeal which was at once made, on the unexpected birth of a son to King James in 1688: half England believed that the thing was a shameless fraud for the provision of a Roman Catholic heir.

So Louis reckoned that the time had come for him to strike before the League of Augsburg, with its wide ramifications and complicated interests, was ready; for nearly all the powers great or small

**JAMES II OF ENGLAND**
It was the firm determination of James II, a zealous Roman Catholic who succeeded in 1685, to secure toleration for his co-religionists and to catholicise the government. His scheme failed, and he fled the country in 1688.
*Painting by J. Riley, National Portrait Gallery*

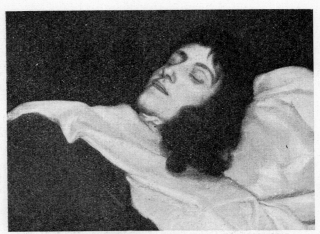

**REBEL CLAIMANT TO THE ENGLISH THRONE**

James duke of Monmouth, illegitimate son of Charles II,
sought to succeed his father on the throne in 1685; but
being defeated by superior forces at the battle of Sedgmoor he
was captured and executed at the order of James II. This
portrait of him after death was painted by Sir G. Kneller.

*National Portrait Gallery, London*

needed him but to him was of
no use for any other purpose ;
he realized that for the avoidance of political deadlocks,
ministers must be appointed
who were in harmony with
the parliamentary majority.
Party government was inaugurated, though not established till the next reign. Incidentally the annual meeting
of parliament for the voting
of supplies and the continuance of the small standing
army, the independence of
the judges, and the new system of national finance, the
national debt and the Bank of
England, all acquired during
his reign a permanent place
in the law and practice of
the constitution. Louis had
brought England into the war
on the top of all his other enemies : to
the English the 'War of the League
of Augsburg' had become the 'War of
the English Succession.'

For three years William was engaged in
establishing himself in his new kingdom.
The Jacobites (James's supporters) rose in
Scotland under 'Bonnie Dundee,' but after

had by this time joined it. But James
had offended him by refusing the terms
on which Louis offered his help against
William. To give his cousin a fright and
teach him a lesson, Louis opened his
attack not on Holland but on the Palatinate, avowedly in order to maintain the
claim of his own favoured candidate for
the archbishopric of Cologne
against the candidate favoured by Leopold and nominated by the pope.

Holland was secure for the
moment. William sailed for
England ; James, finding his
supporters deserting him, took
flight to Paris, an ignominious
collapse which Louis had not
anticipated ; and both England and Scotland offered
their crowns to William and
Mary. The offer was ac-
cepted (February, 1689) on
the terms—the 'Declaration
of Right '—which thenceforth
became the statutory text-
book of British constitutional
principles. William required
a free hand for his foreign
policy as the condition of remaining in a country which

**JAMES II'S FLIGHT TO FRANCE**

Romeyn de Hooghe's engraving shows James II escaping from
the land that had wearied of his arbitrary methods and called
in William of Orange in his stead. The embarcation here
depicted represents the king's second, and successful, attempt
at flight to the Continent, which was connived at by William.

his fall in the hour of victory at Killiecrankie (1689) the rebellion broke down completely. Ireland was for the most part in arms for James, but the Ulster Protestants stood out. James came over in person, but after the defeat of his forces at the battle of the Boyne went back to France. His supporters held out heroically in the south, but with the capitulation of Limerick (1691), upon

**WILLIAM OF ORANGE LANDING AT BRIXHAM AT THE REVOLUTION**

Growing detestation of James II led to some influential noblemen dispatching an invitation to William of Orange to ' bring over an army and secure the infringed liberties of England,' and on November 5, 1688, he landed at Brixham in Torbay. An inscription on the picture (part shown here) by an unknown artist in Hampton Court Palace gives the date of the event incorrectly, but otherwise the details are accurate as far as can be judged and the painting is a valuable document.

*By permission of the Lord Chamberlain*

terms which the victorious government soon afterwards broke shamelessly, resistance collapsed and was made impossible for the future by the penal laws which rendered the Catholic population helpless.

In that year William was able to return to Holland; in 1692 he was again in command of the Dutch armies. Hitherto the French fleet had more than held its own against the British, on which it had inflicted a minor defeat off Bantry Bay and a very heavy one off Beachy Head; but in 1692 it suffered itself a still heavier defeat in the battle of La Hogue, after which no attempt was made to restore it, and the English and Dutch fleets held complete command of the seas.

THE attack on the Palatinate had set William free for the English adventure, because it at once brought upon Louis the attack of the entire circle of his enemies, which included Spain, the emperor, Savoy, the West German princes and Sweden, as well as Holland. France was without a single ally; with her troops engaged on every frontier, she was actually on the defensive from the outset. Her fortresses had been made virtually impregnable by the great engineer Vauban, but between her and Holland lay another chain of fortresses which had been made equally impregnable by Cohörne. The French generals, Luxembourg in the north and Catinat in Italy, won brilliant

**SCENE IN WESTMINSTER ABBEY AT THE CORONATION OF WILLIAM AND MARY**

The skill of the distinguished Dutch artist Romeyn de Hooghe in grouping the figures present at a large assembly is well exemplified in his etching of the coronation ceremony of William and Mary in 1689. This is a portion of a larger etching showing various scenes on the wedding day. There had been much controversy as to whether William or Mary should be supreme monarch, but a satisfactory compromise was finally reached by their being crowned joint sovereigns.

victories in the field but could turn them to no further account. The Palatinate was mercilessly ravaged in the first year of the war, but the struggle was thereby embittered without anything being gained.

After Seignelai's death in 1690 the artificial navy of France began to be neglected and did not survive the defeat of La Hogue. Louvois died in 1691, leaving to Louis the purely military policy which no successor could carry on with equal efficiency. After William's return to the front the struggle went on drearily, but with little enough prospect of decisive success on either side—a war of sieges and of battles fought for the relief of sieges, one fortress or another occasionally changing hands. Both sides were becoming exhausted and weary of indecisive battling ; and the war was brought to a conclusion by the Peace of Ryswick in 1697.

THE peace definitely meant the defeat of Louis. He had to give up all that had come into his hands since Nimwegen except Strassburg, and also the Italian frontier fortress of Pinerolo, which he had held before ; he had to allow the Dutch to garrison a chain of frontier fortresses within the Netherlands ; and he had lost his control in Lorraine. Also he had to withdraw his support from the exiled Stuarts (James II and his son James),

**BONNIE DUNDEE**
John Graham of Claverhouse (c. 1649–89) was created Viscount Dundee by James II in 1688. An enthusiastic Jacobite, he died for his cause at the battle of Killiecrankie. This miniature of him in pen and ink is by David Paton.
*Scottish National Portrait Gallery ; photo, Annan*

and to recognize William as king of England and the succession as laid down in England, which excluded the claims of all Roman Catholics.

He had fought Europe single-handed and had been not by any means crushed but quite definitely beaten. And he was

**DESTRUCTION OF THE FRENCH FLEET AT THE BATTLE OF LA HOGUE**
The annihilating defeat of the French fleet at La Hogue in 1692 by the British navy under Admiral Russell dealt a severe blow to the hopes of the Jacobites and effectively crushed France's erstwhile endeavours to become a great naval power. This contemporary engraving by Romeyn de Hooghe represents the final destruction of Tourville's fleet at the end of a struggle which had lasted for six days. Admiral Russell's squadron can be seen on the horizon (right).
*British Museum*

T*

**GREAT FRENCH ENGINEER**
Sebastien Le Prestre de Vauban (1633–1707)
attained fame in the wars of Louis XIV by
his genius in supervising the defences of the
French fortresses, having more than 160 under
his charge.   This painting is by Largillière.
*Musée de Versailles ; photo, Giraudon*

also in a worse position for future conflicts
than he had been at the beginning of the
war, because the fleet which had then been
a match for the English had since been
virtually wiped off the seas.   But unhappily he himself saw in his defeat
nothing more than a check, to be retrieved
at the first opportunity.   The biggest of
the wars for which his ambition was
responsible was still to come.

### Events in Northern and Eastern Europe

THE battle with Louis, however, had
not been the only concern of Europe
during the thirty-seven years since the
Treaty of Oliva (see page 562).   Turkish
aggression had been as menacing in the
East as French aggression in the West ;
and modifications of great importance for
the future had been taking place in the
position of the Baltic states.

Throughout these years the ' Great
Elector ' Frederick William was laying
the foundations of the power of the future
kingdom of Prussia, until his death on the
eve of the War of the League of Augsburg,
in 1688.   Before the treaty of Oliva he

had reorganized and centralised his rule
over Brandenburg itself and the scattered
provinces attached to it, developing its
resources by encouraging commerce and
industry.   In this latter object he was
materially aided, in the closing years of
his life, by the great Huguenot emigration
of fugitives from the French persecution,
who were welcomed in Brandenburg as a
century earlier the Flemings, fleeing from
Alva, had been welcomed in England.
After the treaty of Oliva he established
his autocracy in his Prussian duchy, by
methods more astute than just.

The troops from Brandenburg had
played no distinguished part in the Thirty
Years' War ; Frederick William organized
and trained a small but highly efficient
army, which displayed its quality in the
war with Sweden by routing a Swedish
force twice its size—the Swedes had never
before been defeated by inferior numbers
—at Fehrbellin (1675), the starting point
of Brandenburg-Prussia's military reputation.   He did not thereby add to his
territory, because he was robbed of the
fruits of his victory by the interposition
of Louis and the acquiescence therein of
Leopold, following upon the peace of
Nimwegen—one of the grievances against
the Hapsburgs for which they were to pay
dearly at a later day.   But before his death
he had made Brandenburg the best
ordered state in Germany.   In the War
of the League of Augsburg his son
and successor, Frederick, played his part
respectably but without distinction.
Thirteen years after the Great Elector's
death Frederick achieved his great ambition and was allowed to assume the title
of king of Prussia (1701).

Sweden, on the death of Charles X, had
fallen under the sway of a few powerful
self-seeking magnates.   She joined the
Triple Alliance of 1668, but was as ready
as Charles II of England to sell herself to
Louis ; paying the penalty in her conflict
with Brandenburg, but reaping the inglorious fruits when the treaty of St.
Germain-en-Laye followed that of Nimwegen, in 1679.   By this time, however,
Charles XI had grown up.   Denmark,
which had now sunk to insignificance, had
seized her opportunity during the war to

attack Sweden, but was defeated—and owed her defeat to the unexpected energy of the young king. Charles, however, had the wisdom to perceive that what Sweden needed was not martial exploits but sound government, to which end the first necessity was the suppression of the self-seeking oligarchy. When this was accomplished, he devoted the remaining years of his reign, till his death in 1697, to the development of industry and commerce. The boy who succeeded him on the throne, Charles XII, was of an altogether different type.

In Poland John Casimir, the antagonist of Charles X, abdicated in 1669. There was no successor of his house ; the Polish crown was theoretically elective, and from this time the 'Polish succession' was an endless bone of contention, European powers backing this or the other candidate for the crown, in pursuance of their own interests. On this occasion the choice of the Polish nobles fell upon one of their own number, Michael Wiesnowiecki, not so

much because he was supported by Leopold as because his rival candidate was supported by France. Five years later he was succeeded by John Sobieski (1674–97).

The great reviver of Turkish aggression, the wazir Mohammed Kiuprili, died in 1661, and was succeeded in office by his son Ahmed, at the time when he was aiming at the subjection of Transylvania, and the Transylvanian patriots were appealing to Leopold for support. In 1664 Ahmed was heavily defeated by Leopold's general Montecuculi at the battle of St. Gothard (on the Raab) ; but the peace of Vasvár which followed was a diplomatic triumph for the defeated commander. Turks and imperialists alike were to evacuate Transylvania, which was to be autonomous under its own prince but was to continue paying tribute to the Turk. There was to be peace for twenty years.

Ahmed, temporarily checked in Hungary, next set about the completion of the reduction of Crete, which the fall of Candia

**FREDERICK OF BRANDENBURG ENTHRONED AS FIRST KING OF PRUSSIA**

As a reward for military service rendered to the emperor Leopold, Frederick III, elector of Brandenburg, was elevated to royal rank and, on January 18, 1701, crowned himself at Königsberg as Frederick I of Prussia. This engraving by Johann Wolffgang shows the king enthroned with his queen
consort Sophie Charlotte. This lady was his second wife and one of the most cultured princesses of
the age. She was a sister of the English king George I and the mother of Frederick William I.

*From ' Der Königlich-Preussischen Crönung hochfeierliche Solemnitäten, 1717*

in 1669 transferred from Venice to the
Ottoman empire. This being accomplished,
Poland, where Michael had just been
elected, was the Turk's next objective.
Here he was occupied till his death in
1676 in fighting with John Sobieski, first
as Michael's general and then as king
of Poland. The war ended just before
Ahmed's death with the peace of Zuravno,
which John was forced to accept—his
brilliant feats of arms being more than
counterbalanced by the enormously greater
forces at the disposal of the Turks.

Meanwhile Leopold had been engaged
in a contest of his own in Hungary,
seeking to establish his effective autocracy
in defiance of the traditional liberties and
rights of the Magyar aristocracy, and at
the same time zealously persecuting the
Hungarian Protestants. But he was
simultaneously involved in that conflict
in the west which was to be suspended by
the peace of Nimwegen. Unable to concentrate on either quarter, he failed to
bring the Hungarian insurgents under
Tököli to subjection ; and when the peace
came he found that he had already driven
Tököli into the arms of the Turk.

**UNFORTUNATE TURKISH WAZIR**

Mohammed IV's grand wazir, Kara Mustafa,
had more ambition than capacity. His grandiose
scheme to form a Moslem empire in the west was
frustrated by his defeat by Sobieski at Vienna,
and he was beheaded at Belgrade in 1683.

*Engraving by J. Cole*

Ahmed Kiuprili had been succeeded by
his kinsman Kara Mustafa, whose ambition
aimed at nothing less than Vienna. The
conflict with Poland had delivered the
Cossacks of the Ukraine to Turkey ; the
Cossacks revolted and appealed to Russia ;
and Kara Mustafa had not been able
immediately to escape from this entanglement. But in 1681 a peace was patched
up, and he was free. He had made his
bargain with Tököli ; Leopold would get
no help from France ; Sobieski, it was
believed, would not act against France's
wishes. The peace of Vasvár was on the
point of lapsing, and proposals were put
forward by Kara Mustafa for its renewal,
which amounted to a declaration of war.

The pope, Venice and sundry German
states did what they could to send aid to
Leopold, whose position was more than
precarious. In the spring of 1683 a vast
Turkish host was assembled on the Drave.
In July Vienna was invested. The garrison
held out valiantly, but the field army
under Charles of Lorraine could not
engage the enormously superior forces of
Mustafa. The rescue came from Poland.

**TERROR OF THE TURKS**

The relief of Vienna, invested by a vast Turkish
host, was accomplished by the brilliant generalship of John Sobieski, king of Poland, in 1683.
He was a son of the castellan of Cracow.

*From Erdmannsdörffer , ' Deutsche Geschichte '*

John Sobieski, whose name was held in terror by the Turks, declining to be a tool of Louis, effected a junction with Charles of Lorraine, and on September 12 fell upon the besieging army and put it utterly to rout. Vienna was saved. The fall of Vienna would have compelled the West to unite in a desperate struggle against the triumphant Ottomans, and to do so under the leadership of France ; and the victory of the West would have meant the universal empire of Louis. But there was no fear of a universal empire under the Polish saviour of Europe.

The delivery of Vienna was the turning of the tide. Kara Mustafa paid for his failure with his life. Some years passed before the Turks again came under the capable direction of another Kiuprili, Mustafa. They were continuously pressed back on the Danube by the imperial troops under the command of Charles of Lorraine or Lewis of Baden, while the Venetians under the leadership of Morosini, who had maintained the defence of Candia for so many years, reconquered the Morea and captured Athens (at the woeful cost of the destruction of the Parthenon), though their hold there could not be kept for long. Imperial Hungary withdrew its resistance on terms, and recognized the hereditary title of the Hapsburgs to the crown ; Transylvania acknowledged the Hapsburg suzerainty, and the Turkish power was broken in Turkish Hungary at another battle of Mohacs.

In 1689 Mustafa Kiuprili became wazir, and Louis in the west had opened battle with the League of Augsburg. Again Leopold and the German princes were distracted between the needs of the war in the east and of the war in the west.

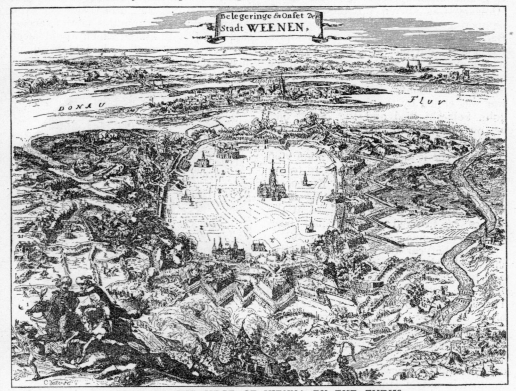

### PLAN OF THE SIEGE OF VIENNA BY THE TURKS
This plan, engraved by C. Decker and published in Amsterdam in 1683, shows the siege of Vienna in progress. Contingents of Turks are attacking on all sides and there are strong Turkish entrenchments on the banks of the Danube shown in the background of the picture. Batteries to left and right of the walls were erected by Rudiger von Starhemberg, whose gallant defence enabled the besieged to hold out until the arrival of the Poles and Germans under John Sobieski.

**EXPLOSION THAT SHATTERED THE PARTHENON**

In 1687 the Venetians, under Morosini, laid siege to Athens, which had been in Turkish possession since 1458. One of the besiegers' shells fell among a Turkish powder supply stored in the Parthenon and caused the explosion here depicted. The middle of the temple and its side columns were destroyed.

*From Fanelli, ' Atene Attica '*

Belgrade was captured and lost again. Hungary was stirred up anew, gravely hampering the operations of Lewis of Baden. Then, on the one side Kiuprili was killed, and on the other Lewis was withdrawn to the western war, his place being taken by the young Augustus ' the Strong ' of Saxony. In 1697 the western war was ended by the peace of Ryswick, John Sobieski died and the Polish diet bestowed the crown upon Augustus the Strong ; and the Turkish war was carried on under the leadership of a captain who was now emerging from the second to the first rank, the landless Prince Eugène of Savoy (of a junior branch of the ducal house), who had placed his sword at the service of Leopold after it had been declined by Louis.

Before the year was out Eugène utterly shattered the Turkish forces at the decisive battle of Zenta, and in January, 1699, the Treaty of Carlowitz ended the Turkish war, though not without possibility of renewal. Its actual concluding stage was postponed for sixteen years. The Ottomans still held Belgrade and the neighbouring province called the Banat of Temesvar ; otherwise they were driven completely out of Hungary, the whole of which now acknowledged Leopold. Venice held the Morea, and Azov was ceded to the young Russian tsar who had captured it while the war was in progress—Peter the

Great. At last Russia had come on the field as a European power. The last great Ottoman expansive effort had been maintained for fifty years ; it had broken down and Ottoman aggression was never again a serious menace.

EUROPE was now face to face with a long impending problem. King Carlos of Spain was childless and sickly, very much in the hands of his immediate entourage. His life could not last much longer. Who, then, was to inherit the great Spanish Dominion, which included Sicily, the greater part of Italy, and the Netherlands, besides half the world on the other side of the Atlantic ? No indisputable law of succession could be produced which would meet the case : even if there had been an indisputable law, half the states in Europe

**PRINCE EUGENE OF SAVOY**

Possessing a genius for the art of war, Prince Eugène of Savoy (1663–1736) had a glorious military career. His name is closely linked with that of Marlborough, with whom he co-operated during the War of the Spanish Succession.

*Engraved by J. Smith after D. Richter*

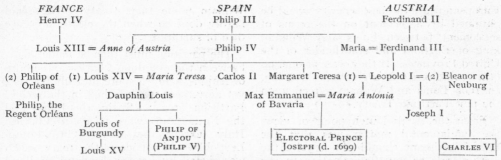

| FRANCE | | SPAIN | | AUSTRIA |
| --- | --- | --- | --- | --- |
| Henry IV | | Philip III | | Ferdinand II |

GENEALOGICAL TABLE SHOWING CLAIMANTS TO THE SPANISH THRONE

This table explains the genealogical relationships on which the French, Austrian and Bavarian aspirants to the Spanish throne based their claims. The names of the princesses who resigned their rights to it upon marriage are given in italics, while those of the three claimants appear in capitals. Attempts at a partition were defeated by Louis XIV's acceptance of the Spanish king's will leaving the entire inheritance to Philip of Anjou ; and the War of the Spanish Succession ensued.

were so deeply concerned that the law would inevitably have been challenged.

The king's sisters had been married to the reigning king of France and the reigning emperor respectively. His father's sisters—there were no brothers in either generation—had been the mothers of those two monarchs respectively. The two French queens had formally resigned their rights of succession, the two empresses (both younger sisters) had not ; while in other respects the terms of Maria Teresa's marriage had not been carried out, and Margaret Teresa's daughter had been required to resign the rights descending to her on her marriage to Max Emmanuel, the elector of Bavaria. On the other hand, no bar could be raised (save these questionable prior claims) to the claim of the emperor Leopold himself and his sons by a later marriage.

Such was the problem as a question of law. As a question of public expediency Europe could not afford to allow that whole vast dominion to be added to the dominions of either the Hapsburg emperor or the Bourbon king, or even to pass to a Hapsburg or a Bourbon cadet. Public expediency and the dubious answer to the question of law both called for compromise and partition—the partition which would be least disturbing to the European balance of power. But a partition was precisely the thing to which the Spanish monarchy itself would not consent.

It was Louis who had the wisdom to take the initiative in seeking a settlement

by consent before the crisis—the death of Carlos—should actually arrive. Leopold, Louis and their heirs apparent being obviously out of the question from a European point of view, any partition would have to be arranged between three claimants—the infant son of the elector of Bavaria, the younger son of Leopold (the archduke Charles) and the younger grandson of Louis (Philip duke of Anjou). For

CARLOS II OF SPAIN

The extreme delicacy of Carlos II (1661–1700), king of Spain, is apparent in this portrait by Coello Claudio. His childlessness made the Spanish succession a question of intense interest to the monarchs of contemporary Europe.

*Prado, Madrid ; photo, Anderson*

European peace the best security would be obtained by agreement on the terms of settlement between Louis and William, king of England and stadtholder of the United Provinces. If they were at one, no other could resist their combined decision. In 1698 Louis and William agreed upon the first Partition Treaty.

From the Anglo-Dutch point of view, the fundamental matter was that the French claimant should not acquire the Netherlands or naval domination in the Mediterranean. From the European point of view, the balance of power would be least disturbed if the electoral prince of Bavaria acquired the bulk of the inheritance. On these lines Louis and

William made their treaty. They had hardly done so when the electoral prince died of smallpox.

The partition must then be made anew, between the archduke Charles and Philip of Anjou—a much more difficult matter ; yet agreement was reached in the second Partition Treaty. Spain, the Indies and the Netherlands were to go to Charles, Italy (except the Milanese) to Philip. Leopold would not accept the treaty, which was signed by France, England, Holland and some minor states. Carlos would not hear of any partition, made a will leaving everything to Philip, or to the Archduke Charles if Philip refused the whole, and died (1700). Louis tore up the treaty and accepted the whole inheritance on behalf of his grandson Philip.

The Spaniards were with Louis. French troops occupied the Netherlands and reinforced those in Spain and Italy. England was out of temper with her Dutch king ; no one except Leopold was ready to challenge the accomplished fact or to support Leopold so long as he claimed the whole inheritance. But throughout 1701 William's diplomacy was negotiating a league to enforce a partition which would give the Netherlands and the Sicilies at least to Charles ; while Leopold started fighting in Italy on his own account.

William succeeded ; Leopold, seeing that no league would support his larger claims, came in ; England was converted by finding that Louis had no thought of opening commerce with the Spanish dominions, and by his theatrical declaration of his intention of restoring the son of the dying James II to the throne of his fathers. Once more the great fight with France was to be renewed. William became

'LE ROI SOLEIL' AT THE AGE OF 63

This portrait of Louis XIV in 1701 by Rigaud is in the Louvre. It shows the 'Grand Monarque' when the zenith of his power was past. His inordinate ambition and aggressions had raised up enemies on every side and in the War of the Spanish Succession they combined to defeat and humiliate him.

actually popular for the first time since his accession. Even at that moment he died and Anne became queen of England (March, 1702) ; but a man abler than William himself was there to carry on William's policy, John Churchill, earl (soon to be duke) of Marlborough.

In Louis' previous wars France had always fought single-handed (except for a temporary alliance with Sweden) against coalitions of varying magnitude. In the War of the Spanish Succession France and Spain were united, with the Spanish resources under French control, and with a valuable ally in the elector of Bavaria, as well as the duke of Savoy at the start. On the side of the Grand Alliance which William had built up Austria was at last free from the incubus of the Turkish war and the Hungarian troubles, while from the outset the maritime powers, England— or Great Britain as the island power became at an early stage of the war—and Holland held complete command of the sea ; and the allies possessed in Marlborough and Eugène generals of a far higher quality than any who had appeared since Turenne. Their generalship, however, was discounted by limitations on their freedom of action ; Marlborough because he was captain-general for the Dutch, who could never look farther afield than their own frontiers ; Eugène because of the very inadequate organization of the Austrian or imperial armies, and by the impossibility of relying upon energetic co-operation from the duke of Savoy, the nominal ally (after he changed sides in 1703), who held the strategic control of the gateway between France and Italy.

### Campaigns of the War of Spanish Succession

EUGENE had already opened the war by a clever campaign in North Italy in 1701–2 ; but he was too heavily outnumbered and was gradually pushed out. Lewis of Baden, who had won a high reputation in the Turkish war, kept watch on the French armies in Alsace. Marlborough on the Netherlands frontier, prevented from fighting a pitched battle by the Dutch ' field-deputies ' who accompanied him, nevertheless by skilful manoeuvring pushed the French back till

**ANNE, QUEEN OF GREAT BRITAIN**
Anne (1665–1714), younger daughter of James II, succeeded William III in 1702. This portrait by Michael Duhl shows her at the age of thirty, with her son William, duke of Gloucester, who died when ten years old.
*National Portrait Gallery, London*

he had cleared the lower Rhine as far as the town of Coblenz.

In 1703 Eugène was in difficulties in Italy and Leopold was again being distracted by an insurrection in Hungary. The French command planned a junction with the Bavarian forces on the upper Danube, and a march on Vienna. But Max Emmanuel insisted on first effecting the annexation of Tyrol, which refused to be annexed, and the opportunity was lost. Also at this moment Savoy went over to the allies, and the French commander Vendôme's operations against Eugène were paralysed ; while Portugal, hitherto neutral, also joined the alliance and inspired it with an unfortunate hope of ejecting Philip from Spain, where he had been welcomed with open arms, and setting up Charles as ' Carlos III,' although this had been no part of its original programme.

In the next year, 1704, came the great crisis of the war. France was to strike the blow which the unexpected resistance of Tyrol had postponed in 1703. Troops poured into the Netherlands, to pin Marlborough the more firmly to that

PANORAMIC VIEW OF THE BATTLE OF BLENHEIM, MARLBOROUGH'S GREAT VICTORY

This engraving by J. van Huchtenburgh, chosen by William III to record Marlborough's battles, gives a bird's eye view of the field of Blenheim about the moment of Marlborough's delivery of the winning blow. His army is in the centre of the picture with the village of Blenheim in the left foreground. The Austrians, under Eugene of Savoy, are at the extreme right. By a cavalry charge Marlborough pierced the Franco-Bavarian line, advanced upon Blenheim and cut off the retreat of the large French garrison. Marshal Tallard was taken prisoner and is here shown in Marlborough's carriage.

region ; the French force was increased in Bavaria under Marsin, to be joined later by Tallard from Alsace. Between Vienna and the accumulated army in Bavaria there was no force which could hold it up, and when Vienna should fall Louis could dictate his own terms to the allies. But the programme was wrecked by the genius of Marlborough and the brilliant co-operation of Eugène, who had been forced out of Italy. Marlborough's plan was a lightning march across Germany which would place him between the Bavarian army and Vienna. To effect it, he must not only have Eugène with him, but must hoodwink the French commanders and the English and Dutch governments as to the objective of his movements.

There was to be a grand campaign on the Moselle. Marlborough moved up the Rhine to Mainz in May to concert measures with Lewis of Baden and Eugène at Stolhofen, and the world had hardly realized that the Moselle campaign was a mere blind when he was storming the lines of Schellenberg (July 2) and capturing Donauworth, blocking the way to Vienna and threatening Bavaria. South of the Danube, Tallard was racing to join Marsin and the elector ; north of it Eugène was hurrying to join Marlborough.

### Marlborough's Victory at Blenheim

Six weeks later (August 13) the armies faced each other at Blenheim and the decisive battle was fought. While the main attack was being apparently developed against the Franco-Bavarian left by Eugène, and a secondary English attack on their right at Blenheim, the real blow was being prepared against the weakened centre by making passable the marshy ground which was supposed to be adequate cover for its front. On that point then the cavalry crashed suddenly, pierced it, and rolled up the lines to right and to left. The army which was to have won the war at a stroke was virtually annihilated. Bavaria lay at the mercy of the allies, and the French were barred behind the Rhine for the rest of the war.

A few days earlier it had occurred to Admiral Rooke, commanding an Anglo-Dutch squadron, to capture Gibraltar ;

**THE DUKE OF MARLBOROUGH**
This miniature by Thomas Forster, dated 1712, shows John Churchill, duke of Marlborough (1650–1722), the great soldier and diplomatist. He won a series of brilliant victories for the allies in the War of the Spanish Succession.
*Victoria and Albert Museum*

which did not again pass out of British possession, and served with Minorca, captured four years later, to furnish a permanent British naval base at the gate of the Mediterranean.

The next year, however, saw no material advance. Marlborough in the Netherlands continued to be hampered by the Dutch field-deputies, and Eugène, back in Italy, by the studied inertness of Savoy. The allies, moreover, were frittering away their energies on the futile effort to conquer Spain, of which the only portion friendly to them was Catalonia, which had never reconciled itself to the monarchy of united Spain. But 1706 brought two great successes : Marlborough won at Ramillies a battle, tactically perhaps more brilliant even than Blenheim, the effect of which was to sweep the French back from the Netherlands to the line of fortresses on the frontier of France itself ; while Eugène, by another brilliant campaign in North Italy, shattered the French forces before Turin, raising the siege of the duke of Savoy's Piedmontese capital. The French were practically cleared out of North Italy, and in the south an insurrection at Naples enabled Austrian troops to occupy the city and proclaim King Charles. The general situation had hardly been affected by the death of Leopold in 1705 and the accession of his elder son, Joseph I.

### Last Battles and the Treaty of Utrecht

AFTER Ramillies and Turin, Louis was ready to treat for peace, but the triumphant allies would listen to no terms. In 1707 hostilities were partly suspended by the threatened intervention of Charles XII of Sweden, who had just blazed upon a startled world with a series of amazing military exploits, of which more anon. Charles, however, was persuaded to turn his arms against Russia. In 1708 there were general revolts of the French-speaking populations in the Netherlands against the Dutch government set over them after Ramillies ; and the French were gaining ground rapidly till they again suffered a disastrous defeat at the hands of Marlborough—who was joined by Eugène in person, though without an army—at Oudenarde. Marlborough would have marched on Paris, but even to Eugène the risk seemed too gigantic. Instead, he laid siege to Lille, which fell in December.

Louis again opened negotiations, but the only terms to which the allies would listen were that he should help them to drive his grandson out of Spain, where the cause of the allies had not been prospering, apart from the British capture of Minorca. The result was a magnificent rally of French patriotism, leading up to the last great engagement of the war and the last of Marlborough's victories, the battle of Malplaquet (1709), in which the French were driven off the field but not out of their lines at La Bassée, and the losses of the allies were much the heavier.

The only common object which the allies now had in view was the humiliation of France ; their idea of the profits which were to accrue to themselves respectively differed fundamentally. Intriguing took the place of fighting. The most successful wire-pullers were the astute politicians at the head of the Tory party in England,

who procured the recall and downfall of Marlborough, made their own bargain behind the backs of their allies, and finally shaped the Treaty of Utrecht which ended the war in 1713.

By that treaty the Bourbons retained much in the surrender of which they would have acquiesced after Ramillies or Oudenarde, and to which William would have acquiesced in 1701. The Bourbon king Philip was established on the Spanish throne, with a formal renunciation of any possible claim that might arise to the succession in France. Savoy got Sicily—afterwards exchanged for Sardinia—with the regal title. Charles got the Netherlands, Sardinia, Naples and Milan (he was now the emperor Charles VI, his brother Joseph having died two years before). Holland got a chain of ' barrier fortresses ' in the Netherlands. Frederick I, son of the Great Elector, was recognized as king of Prussia by all the powers. Great Britain —the incorporating Union of England and Scotland had received the assent of both countries in 1706–7—retained Gibraltar and Minorca, acquired Acadia or Nova Scotia from France and certain trading rights known as the ' asiento ' in the South Seas from Spain, and (for what it was worth) obtained the guaranteed recognition of the Protestant succession to the throne when the reigning Queen Anne should die. And in addition she had emerged from the war with an unprecedented military reputation and a navy which not even Holland could rival.

### Incorporating Union of England and Scotland

IN the half-century we have been describing, Great Britain had attained an entirely unprecedented position as a European power ; at the same time she had practically completed her own constitutional revolution, and transformed the union of the crowns of England and Scotland into an incorporating union.

England and Scotland were still two independent kingdoms when Anne succeeded William in 1702, though their union under one crown was a guarantee against actual armed conflict between them. For Scotland's commercial prosperity, a commercial union with her neighbour was a necessity which England had no disposition to concede. England, however, had repudiated the succession of the next legitimate heir to the throne ; Scotland was free to recognize it on Anne's demise. That climax England could not afford to risk ; the price she had to pay for security was an incorporating union ; and that measure was carried by the parliaments of both countries, not without hot opposition in Scotland, in 1706, taking effect in 1707 ; conveying to the electress Sophia of Hanover and her heirs the succession to the crown of Great Britain, while Ireland remained a dependency with a subordinate parliament in the control of the Protestant minority.

### Contemporary Events in Russia

ONLY casual reference has been made hitherto to the story of Russia since the accession of the house of Romanov to its throne in 1613, or to Sweden, Poland and Turkey since 1697 (the year of the peace of Ryswick), the battle of Zenta, and the peace of Carlowitz in 1699.

In Russia the first Romanov, Michael, had been succeeded by his son Alexis in 1645. Alexis was followed by Feodor, 1676–82, on whose death his two young brothers Ivan and Peter were recognized as joint tsars, but the reins of government were actually grasped by their extremely energetic elder sister Sophia. In 1688 Sophia was removed by a coup d'état ; Ivan was imbecile, and Peter began his reign at the age of sixteen, still under the tutelage of the men who had deposed his sister. Russia joined in the war in which the Turks were being beaten back by the imperial forces, and the young tsar took an active part in the siege and capture of Azov in 1696, an acquisition which Russia retained at the treaty of Carlowitz. The Azov campaign opened the effective autocracy of Peter the Great, the founder of the Russian power.

Russia was in effect a barbarian country, more oriental than European, as yet scarcely penetrated by European ideas ; amorphous and disjointed, with large portions of its population still leading a virtually nomadic existence. Peter's immediate predecessors had begun to borrow

**PETER THE GREAT IN EARLY MANHOOD**
Admiration for Western culture led Peter the Great (1672–1725), the semi-barbarous tsar of Russia, to reorganize his realm after European models. His ambition for territorial expansion brought him into conflict with the Swedes.
*Painting by J. M. Nattier*

ideas from the West and to carry them out by means of agents also borrowed from the West. Peter, realizing that Europe was far in advance of Russia, conceived the daring notion of remodelling Russia upon Western lines. The Turkish war was no sooner off his hands than he set out on a journey of investigation, saw with his own eyes and practised with his own hands the methods which had given the European nations their mastery, and returned to Russia in 1698 intent on filling the old bottles with the new wine—and most particularly convinced that Russia wanted a fleet on the Black Sea, a fleet on the Baltic and that access to the Baltic from which she was barred by provinces under the sway of the kings of Poland, Sweden and (after 1701) Prussia.

As a matter of course, the tsar must be an unqualified autocrat ; and the first step was the suppression of the imperial guard, the Streltsi—the equivalent of the Janissaries of the Turk or the Praetorians of the old Roman Empire. Peter also set about revolutionising social habits, religious customs and political traditions in a characteristically drastic way. But almost immediately opportunity arose for the territorial aggrandisement which was no less dear to his ambitions.

Charles XI of Sweden died in 1697, having laboriously reconstructed the power of the crown. Charles XII was a boy of sixteen, already a mighty hunter, but unversed in affairs of state. There was a new king of Poland who was also elector of Saxony ; the king of Denmark wanted the duchy of Holstein, which belonged to Charles's brother-in-law ; Peter wanted Esthonia, Livonia, anything that could be snatched to give him his Baltic sea-board. Livonia itself wanted to be rid of the Swedish sovereignty. The exiled Livonian patriot Patkul easily drew Frederick of Denmark, Augustus of Poland and Peter of Russia into a common plot for the redistribution among themselves of Sweden's Baltic provinces. Next year (1700) the triple attack was opened—by Denmark on Holstein, by Augustus on Riga, by Peter on Narva.

They had reckoned without their host. Charles had all the warrior instincts of his

**SWEDISH WARRIOR KING**
This engraving after a portrait by Kraft shows Charles XII (1682–1718), the energetic and war-loving Swedish king. He utterly defeated the forces of Peter the Great at Narva in 1700, and was himself beaten at Pultava in 1709.
*Engraving by Pieter Tanje*

house concentrated in his own person. He was a born fighter and a born leader who inspired his followers with his own reckless courage. The Swedes had a mighty reputation, won under Gustavus and Charles X, to retrieve. Charles and his Swedes flung themselves at Copenhagen ; Frederick, saved from destruction by the diplomatic intervention of England and Holland, was allowed to back out of the war ignominiously. Augustus retreated from Riga. Charles with 8,000 men crossed the Baltic and routed 60,000 Russians at Narva. Peter did not shine on the occasion, but his comment was characteristic : ' The Swedes will beat us—but they will teach us how to beat them.' Peter's genius was of the kind which knows how to learn from failure the way to success. But for the moment Russia was off the board.

### Achievements of Charles XII of Sweden

WHEN Charles had reduced Livonia and Courland to obedience, he devoted himself to the punishment of Augustus of Poland and Saxony. The Poles would not fight for a Saxon king whose manifest intention had been to make himself an absolute monarch. City after city was captured, and in 1705 the Polish diet deposed Augustus and elected Stanislaus Lecszinski, the nominee of Charles, much against its own will. Still the fighting in Poland went on, till Charles invaded Saxony. Augustus, in spite of various discreditable shifts, had to resign the crown of Poland to Lecszinski and break off the alliance he had renewed with Russia (1706). It was at this point, just after Ramillies, that a quarrel with the emperor almost induced Charles to join in alliance with Louis ; but Marlborough's diplomacy persuaded him that he would be better employed in punishing the tsar.

So, like a greater than he in 1812, Charles in 1708 marched for Moscow. Peter had learned his lesson too well to seek him in a pitched battle, but harassed his rear and his line of march, cutting off supplies. Charles turned aside to the Ukraine where he expected help from the Cossack Mazeppa, but got none. There he had to pass the winter, getting very insufficient supplies as best he could. In the spring (1709) he marched on Pultava and laid siege to it, though his troops were insufficient and he had neither supplies nor a siege train. Peter's time had come. In June he fell upon the exhausted Swedes with an immensely superior force and annihilated them. Charles, with a wounded foot, barely escaped, and crossed the Turkish frontier, where he remained for the next five years, while Augustus (restored in Poland) and Peter worked their will on the Baltic provinces.

Even if Peter instead of Charles had been shattered at Pultava, the political conquest of Russia was no more feasible in 1709 than in 1812 or 1915 ; and Charles had no resources except a small if efficient army and a genius for winning pitched battles against heavy odds and inferior generals—an insufficient equipment for a successful conqueror. How he would have fared against a Marlborough or a Eugène is hardly a matter of doubt.

Charles without an army was powerless ; he succeeded, however, in persuading the Turkish wazir to declare war on Peter in 1710. Peter came through that conflict with better fortune than he deserved ; for he fell into a trap, campaigning on the Pruth, where he found himself at the mercy of the Turkish army, but was allowed to conclude a peace (1711) on no harder terms than the cession of Azov and the razing of Russian forts on Turkish soil. The further adventures of Charles and Peter belong to our next chapter.

### Developments in America and South Africa

BEYOND the oceans developments were in progress during the reign of Louis XIV, of which the profound importance was not yet fully manifest. In North America the English settlements multiplied ; the first of Charles II's Dutch wars transferred the Dutch settlement on the Hudson—to be known thenceforth as New York—from the Dutch to the English, giving the latter the entire coast line between the French Acadia on the north and Florida on the south. The French colony on the St. Lawrence expanded to the Great Lakes, in rear of the northern British colonies ; but the treaty of Utrecht gave Acadia to the British and recognized the British ownership of Newfoundland, as well as of sundry West Indian islands whose history at this time belongs to the story of the buccaneers.

In South Africa, the Dutch had started the Cape Colony under the regime of the De Witts ; and the revocation of the Edict of Nantes supplemented the Calvinistic Dutch population there with a considerable number of co-religionists, fugitive Huguenots from France.

### Contemporary Events in the East

IN India the last really powerful Mogul, the emperor Aurangzib, reigned from 1658 to 1707 ; expanding his sovereignty over the entire peninsula, but in the process ensuring disintegration. The expansion itself made the empire uncontrollably unwieldy, and drove the Mogul to appoint satraps over vast provinces, who were quite certain sooner or later to aim at establishing independent dynasties. Moreover, Aurangzib departed from the policy of the three princes who had ruled for a hundred years before him, and reverted to that of the old Delhi emperors, by depressing the Hindus and treating Mahomedans, whatever their origin, as of a dominant, conquering race, reviving the old-time hostility between the two religions which his fathers had sought at least to reduce to a minimum. A result was the vigorous development of the Hindu Maratha tribes in the western Deccan, whom Aurangzib's lieutenants failed to crush, and of a reformed Hindu sect, united as a brotherhood half religious and half military, the Sikhs, for the most part in the Punjab and Sirhind.

But at the same time the French, under Colbert's influence, entered upon the competition, mainly with the English, for the trade with India, which in the middle of the eighteenth century was to issue in a hard-fought duel, ultimately though not immediately for sovereignty. The rivalry was there, but the battle had not yet opened ; for the British and French companies judiciously agreed that their relations should not be affected by European wars.

1713 Treaty of Utrecht ends War of Spanish Succession. Duke of Savoy becomes k. of Sicily. Bourbon dynasty established in Spain.
Prussia : Frederick I d. ; acc. Frederick William 1.

1714 Philip V of Spain m. Elizabeth Farnese. Alberoni becomes first minister.
Treaty of Rastadt complementing Utrecht.
Turco-Venetian War.
Charles XII quits Turkey, reaches Stralsund.
Queen Anne d. ; acc. George I of Hanover.

1715 Northern League against Sweden.
Jacobite rising (the ' Fifteen ') ; Sheriffmuir.
Louis XIV. d. ; acc. Louis XV (his great-grandson). Philip of Orléans becomes regent and heir-presumptive, Philip V having abjured the succession. Rapprochement between French and British governments to maintain the Hanoverian and Orleanist successions.

1716 Charles XII attacks Norway.
Eugène's victory over Turks at Peterwardein.
Leibniz d.

1717 Eugène's decisive victory of Belgrade.
Triple alliance of Great Britain, France and Holland.
Spanish forces occupy Sardinia, where they are welcomed.

1718 Charles XII killed at Fredrikshald.
Peter the Great puts his son Alexis to death.
Treaty of Passarowitz marks end of Turkish aggression westwards.
Spaniards occupy Sicily, but their new fleet is destroyed at Cape Passaro.

1719 Collapse of Alberoni's projects ; his fall.
Sweden : Acc. Ulrica Eleanor and Frederick of Hesse. Oligarchical rule established.

1720 Austria exchanges Sardinia for Sicily, the house of Savoy becoming kings of Sardinia with Savoy and Piedmont.
' Northern War ' concluded by treaty of Stockholm.
Charles VI issues Pragmatic Sanction to secure Austrian succession to his daughter.

1721 Walpole's ministry begins in England.
Sweden concludes treaty of Nystadt ceding Baltic provinces to Russia.

1722 Peter the Great attacks Persia through Caucasus.
1723 Louis XV comes of age ; end of Orléans regency.
1724 Immanuel Kant b.
1725 Louis XV m. Maria Lecszinska ; causing a breach with Spain.
Treaty of Vienna between Spain and Austria. Opposition league of Hanover between Great Britain and France joined by Prussia and minor powers. Spain guarantees Pragmatic Sanction.
Peter the Great d. ; acc. Catherine I.

1726 Fleury becomes Louis' minister.
1727 George I d. ; acc. George II. Walpole retains power.
Catherine I d. ; acc. Peter II.
Isaac Newton d.

1729 French dauphin b., excluding probability of a disputed succession in France.
Treaty of Seville between France, Spain and Great Britain.
Lessing b.
John Wesley starts Methodist Society at Oxford.

1730 Russia : Peter II d. ; acc. Anne (Ivanovna) of Courland who recovers supremacy of the crown.

1731 Carlos (younger son of Philip V) established in duchy of Parma.

1733-38 War of the Polish Succession.
1733 Secret (Bourbon) family compact between France and Spain against Austria and England.
Augustus of Poland and Saxony d. ; Stanislaus Lecszinski, supported by France and Spain, is again elected but expelled in favour of Augustus III maintained by Russia and Austria. War of Polish Succession begins.

1734 Carlos of Parma captures Naples.
1735 Carlos retains Naples and Sicily but has to surrender Parma. Augustus retains Poland ; Stanislaus is given Lorraine with reversion to France, and Francis of Lorraine gets Tuscany and the hand of Charles VI's dr. Maria Teresa ; but hostilities drag on.

1736 War between Russia and Turkey.

1737 Austria joins Russia in Turkish war.
1738 Polish Succession War ends with treaty of Vienna, confirming the arrangements of 1735. France guarantees Pragmatic Sanction.

1739 Nadir Shah the Persian sacks Delhi but retires, having ended the Mogul's effective authority, which survives in legal theory.
War (of Jenkins' Ear) between England and Spain.
Austria deserts Russia by separate treaty of Belgrade with Turkey : Russia has to accept the Turkish terms.

1740-48 War of the Austrian Succession.
1740 Anne of Russia d. ; acc. Ivan VI (a child).
Charles VI d. ; acc. Maria Teresa, principal counter-claimant being Charles Albert of Bavaria.
Frederick William I d. ; acc. Frederick II.
Frederick marches into Silesia and demands its cession as the price of his support of the claims of Maria Teresa. She refuses. The 'Silesian War ' begins the war of the Austrian Succession.
India : Dupleix at Pondicherry plans the ejection of the British.

1741 Ivan VI deposed ; Elizabeth tsaritsa.
Frederick wins battle of Mollwitz, establishing reputation of Prussian army.
The war becomes general, France and Spain siding with Bavaria, England with Maria Teresa, as 'auxiliaries.'
Maria Teresa appeals to Hungarians, who respond with enthusiasm. Frederick makes agreement of Klein-Schnellendorf and withdraws (Oct.), but re-enters in Dec. French take Prague.

1742 Charles Albert of Bavaria emperor as Charles VII ; the only breach in the Hapsburg continuity after Frederick III.
Austrians overrun Bavaria ; Frederick's Moravian campaign fails but he defeats Austrians at Chotusitz, obtains treaty of Breslau, and again retires. Austrians recover Prague.

1743 British squadron imposes neutrality on Carlos at Naples. Battle of Dettingen. Alliances revised by treaties of Worms and Fontainebleau and the auxiliaries become principals.

1744 Frederick re-enters the war.
1745-6 The ' Forty-Five.'
1745 Charles VII d. ; acc. (Bavaria) Max Joseph, (Empire) Francis I of Tuscany. Prussia and Bavaria both retire permanently from the war. French successes (Fontenoy).
Jacobite rising ; Prince Charles Edward lands at Moidart, captures Edinburgh, marches to Derby, and then retreats.

1746 Jacobitism finally crushed at Culloden (April).
Philip V d. ; acc. Ferdinand VI. Spain retires.
India : La Bourdonnais captures Madras.

1747 Orange stadtholdership restored in Holland.
1748 War ended by Treaty of Aix-la-Chapelle ; Prussia retains Silesia.

1749 Goethe b.
1750 Rise of Kaunitz, who plans ' Diplomatic Revolution.'
India : renewal of Anglo-French hostilities, on pretext of supporting rival claimants to native thrones. French gains.

1751 Capture and defence of Arcot by Clive.
1754 Dupleix recalled ; hostilities suspended.
1755 Hostilities in America ; Braddock's disaster. Great earthquake at Lisbon.

1756-63 Seven Years' War.
1756 Anglo-Prussian Treaty of Westminster.
Kaunitz completes circle of alliances for the crushing of Prussia, including France, Russia and Saxony.
India : Tragedy of the Black Hole of Calcutta.
French squadron captures Minorca : first action of the Seven Years' War.
Frederick invades Saxony ; takes Dresden.

1757 Frederick invades Bohemia ; wins battle of Prague but is defeated at Kolin.
William Pitt the elder heads British ministry.
India : Clive overthrows nawab of Bengal at Plassey and becomes master of Bengal.
Command in western Germany given to Ferdinand of Brunswick.
Frederick defeats French at Rossbach and Austrians at Leuthen.

**1758** Ministry of Choiseul in France.
Development of British naval attacks on French ports.
Frederick defeats Russians at Zorndorf, and effectually checks Austrian advance in spite of a reverse at Hochkirch.
India : Lally commands French in the south, and takes Fort St. David but fails at Madras.

**1759** Frederick defeated by Russians at Künersdorf ; French defeated and driven behind Rhine at Minden by Ferdinand ; French Toulon fleet broken up by Boscawen off Lagos (August).
Wolfe takes Quebec (Sept.).
Hawke shatters French fleet at Quiberon Bay ; Prussian force capitulates at Maxen (Nov.).
Ferdinand VI d. ; Carlos of Naples acc. as Carlos III. His younger son Ferdinand succeeds at Naples.
Pombal suppresses Jesuits in Portugal and sets about vigorous reforms.
James Watt begins experiments in steam power.
Robert Burns b.

**1760** India : Decisive defeat of Lally by Eyre Coote at Wandewash.
Frederick checks Austrians at Liegnitz and Torgau (last pitched battle).
George II d. ; acc. George III.

**1761** Pitt resigns ; Frederick's subsidies withdrawn.
Ahmad Shah from Afghanistan invades Upper India and shatters Maratha armies at Panipat.
British take Pondicherry.
Second Bourbon Family Compact.

**1762** War declared between Great Britain and Spain.
Tsaritsa Elizabeth d. ; acc. Peter III who reverses her policy and allies with Frederick, but is deposed and put to death by his wife Catherine II, who assumes neutrality. Frederick holds his own against Austria.
Publication of Rousseau's Contrat Social.

**1763** Seven Years' War ended by Treaties of Paris between Great Britain, France and Spain, and Hubertusburg between Austria and Prussia. France cedes Canada and is excluded from rivalry in India ; Frederick retains Silesia.
Polish crown vacated by d. of Augustus III.

**1764** Catherine secures Polish succession for her favourite Stanislaus Poniatowski.
Suppression of Jesuits in France.
Hargreaves invents spinning jenny.
India : British ascendancy in Bengal finally established by battle of Baksar.

**1765** Francis I d. ; Joseph II elected emperor, his brother Leopold taking Tuscany. Maria Teresa retains her crowns and supremacy.
Grenville's Stamp Act opens quarrel between Great Britain and her American colonies.
Clive obtains from the Mogul for the East India Company the Diwani or official financial control of Bengal, placing the British position on a legalised footing.

**1766** Lecszinski d. ; Lorraine passes to France.
Chatham's second ministry formed, known as the Grafton ministry ; his health breaks down.

**1767** Carlos III suppresses Jesuits in Spain.
Charles Townshend imposes tea and other minor import taxes on American colonies.

**1768** Turkey as liberator of Poland declares war on Russia in support of Polish insurgents.
France acquires Corsica from Genoa.

**1769** Napoleon Bonaparte b. in Corsica.
Frederick II and Joseph II in conference.
James Watt's steam-engine patented.

**1770** Choiseul having restored French navy is dismissed.
North's ministry of ' King's Friends ' ; George holds ascendancy in parliament till 1782.
Frederick initiates conspiracy with Catherine and Joseph for partition of Poland.
Beethoven b.

**1771** Maupeou's ministry ; suppression of ' parlements.'
Acc. Gustavus III in Sweden.

**1772** First partition of Poland between Russia, Prussia and Austria, a remnant remaining as Kingdom of Poland.
Gustavus III restores absolutism in Sweden.

**1773** Pope Clement XIV suppresses Jesuit Order. It nevertheless survives.
' Boston tea-party.'
North's Regulating Acts for controlling Indian administration of East India Company ; the first experiment of the kind since Rome.

**1774** Canada Act establishing Roman Catholicism in Canada.
Boston Port Act and other penal acts to bring American colonies to submission ; colonists call a general ' Continental Congress.'
Warren Hastings first governor-general over British presidencies in India ; with a council which can and does outvote him.
Russian treaty of Kuchuk Kainarji with Turkey.
Louis XV d. ; acc. Louis XVI. Maurepas' ministry. Parlements recalled. Turgot finance minister.

**1775-83** War of American Independence.

**1775** Turgot's reforms.
American war opened by skirmish at Lexington. George Washington in command. B. of Bunker Hill. Unsuccessful invasion of Canada.

**1776** Turgot dismissed ; Necker finance minister.
American Declaration of Independence. British evacuate Boston and occupy New York.
Adam Smith's Wealth of Nations published.

**1777** Joseph II claims Bavarian succession, arousing Frederick's antagonism.
British force surrenders at Saratoga ; France resolves to enter the American War.

**1778** French treaty with Americans ; French fleet dominant in western seas.
Voltaire d.

**1779** Spain comes into the war ; opens three years' siege of Gibraltar. Indecisive military operations.
Bavarian question settled by treaty of Teschen.

**1780** Haider (Hyder) Ali of Mysore invades the Carnatic.
Maria Teresa d. ; Joseph II rules alone.
Armed neutrality of North Sea powers ; war declared between Great Britain and Holland.

**1781** Dutch fleet disabled by battle of Dogger Bank.
Cornwallis, blockaded by Washington and the French fleet at Yorktown, surrenders ; ensuring American independence.
Joseph II allies with Catherine.
Resignation of Necker.
Kant's Critique published.

**1782** Rodney's victory of The Saints over de Grasse restores British naval ascendancy. Spain takes Minorca ; Gibraltar is relieved.
Fall of North's ministry ends George's supremacy in parliament. ' Grattan's Parliament ' set up in Ireland.
Mysore treaty. Haider Ali d. ; acc. Tippu Sahib.

**1783** Treaty of Versailles ends war. American independence recognized. Migration of loyalists to Canada and New Brunswick.
Turkey cedes Crimea to Russia.
Seventeen years' ministry of William Pitt the younger begins.
Calonne's ministry in France.

**1784** Pitt's India Act sets up dual control of British administration in India (ends 1858).

**1785** Joseph's schemes of Hapsburg aggrandisement checked by French guarantee of the closed Scheldt to the Dutch, and by Frederick's League of Princes (' Fürstenbund ').

**1786** Cornwallis first governor-general under new Indian system.
Frederick II d. ; acc. Frederick William II.

**1787** Assembly of Notables ; fall of Calonne ; ministry of Brienne.

**1788** Joseph joins Catherine in Turkish war ; the campaigning goes favourably for Turks against Joseph, unfavourably against Russia.
Necker recalled ; Parlement demands summoning of States-General for the first time since 1614.
India : Cornwallis begins administrative reconstruction.
Great Britain annexes Australia ; first convict settlement.

**1789** George Washington first president of the United States of America.
French States-General assembles May 5.

THE OATH OF FEALTY: MARIA TERESA AS ARCHDUCHESS OF AUSTRIA RECEIVES HER PEOPLE'S HOMAGE

On November 22, 1740, the orders of Lower Austria took an oath of fealty to Maria Teresa, queen of Hungary and Bohemia. This picture shows part of the procession on its way to the Cathedral of S. Stephen, with the city guards of Vienna drawn up on two sides of the Trinity Column which Leopold I had erected in 1682 in gratitude for deliverance from the plague. Maria Teresa is carried in a sedan chair, preceded by public officials and members of the nobility. The captain of the imperial horse guards, Count von Daun, and Count von Cardana, captain of the life guards, follow the royal chair.

*From Georg Christoph Kriegl, 'Erb-Huldigung welche Mariae-Theresiae als Ertz-Herzogin zu Oesterreich abgeleget worden,' Vienna, 1740*

# DEVELOPMENT OF THE GREAT POWERS: 1713–1789

FOR nearly fifty years out of the long reign of Louis XIV, the politics of Europe were dominated by the French king's ambitions. After the Treaty of Utrecht it was not till France herself had overturned everything in France which was most characteristic of the Grand Monarque, his ideas and his system, that Europe was again seriously threatened with a French dictatorship. Utrecht, in fact, marked the decisive defeat of his schemes. It is true that it set a Bourbon on the throne of Spain, but for twenty years the fact was the cause of discord between the French and Spanish governments ; and afterwards, though a hostile Spain might have been a source of danger, her alliance could be of little positive value.

In no other respect was the power of France greater at the setting of her ' Sun King ' than it had been at his rising, though she was still actually the most powerful state on the Continent, with no rival save Austria—as we may thenceforth conveniently name the heterogeneous dominion of the house of Hapsburg, since the unity of the Holy Roman Empire was purely fictitious.

## Great Britain's Supremacy at Sea

ON the other hand, Great Britain had definitely emerged from the struggle as a European great power, whenever she chose or might be forced to play an active part in European affairs. She had definitely won her place as mistress of the seas—a position which she could lose only by reckless mismanagement. In quality her fleets might be matched by the Dutch, but Holland was too small to maintain a competition on equal terms ; and France, with the constant drain of her armies, never attempted a sustained maritime rivalry, though there was no comparison between the military forces available for the two nations. Moreover, during the last half century the British mercantile marine had not only overtaken the Dutch but gained a great lead, and the country was rapidly increasing that wealth which was to provide her allies with the sinews of war.

It was difficult always for Austria to be dangerously aggressive, constantly hampered as she was by the doubtful loyalty of Hungary and the problem of maintaining communications with Italy and the Netherlands, now hers but offering a standing invitation to France for attack.

Two other powers, however, had come into being, though not yet fully developed. In Russia there was manifestly a power potentially of the first magnitude, though still only in the making. The second was the new kingdom of Prussia, whose capacities were so far undeveloped and unsuspected. Turkey as an aggressive power was on the point of receiving her coup de grâce at the hands of Prince Eugène, though, like Poland, she was to be a source of plentiful contention among her neighbours in the future. Sweden without Charles XII was negligible—but Charles himself was incalculable.

## European Situation after Utrecht

THE immediate position, however, after Utrecht, was curious. Philip V of Spain and the emperor Charles VI each considered that he had been robbed for the benefit of the other, and was waiting to snatch back something of what he regarded as his own. The old king of France was near his end—actually he died in 1715— his heir was his infant great-grandson, and, till that infant should be grown up, a ' French succession ' problem might at any moment become acute ; since it was unlikely that Philip of Spain would hold himself bound by the renunciation of title which had been forced upon him, while his cousin Philip of Orléans was by the European treaty recognized as the heir presumptive. Great Britain had fixed her

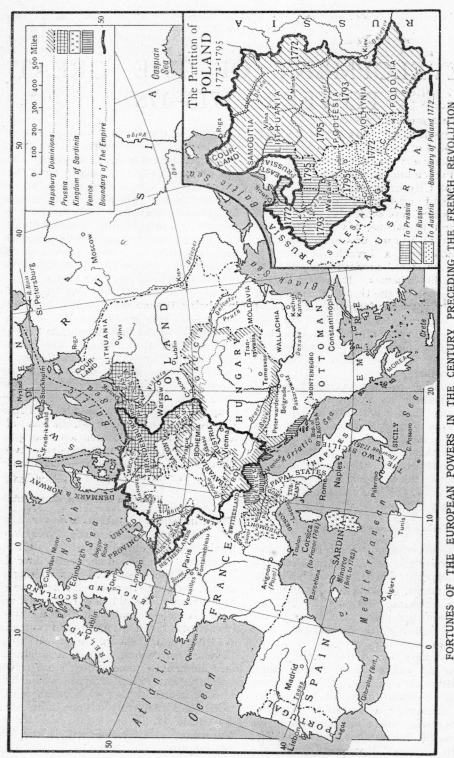

**FORTUNES OF THE EUROPEAN POWERS IN THE CENTURY PRECEDING THE FRENCH REVOLUTION**

In the period under review in this chapter France gradually receded from her predominant position in Europe, and Russia and Prussia emerged as first-class powers. Austria was occupied in resisting disintegration after the death of Charles VI. The Ottoman power was cleared out of Hungary. Sweden ceased to count as a serious factor after the death of Charles XII. The sea power of Spain was destroyed, and Poland suffered the first of her partitions, all three of which are shown with dates in the inset map. Meantime, the sea power and wealth of Great Britain were increasing steadily.

**PHILIP OF ORLEANS REGENT**

Nephew and son-in-law of Louis XIV, Philip duke of Orléans was regent of France from 1715 until his death in 1723. His engaging personality is apparent in this portrait by J. B. Santerre, engraved by F. Chéreau.

Hanover succeeded to the British throne a year after Utrecht. Next year a Jacobite rising was suppressed without difficulty. For thirty years more, any foreign power hostile to Britain could provide her with a menace of civil war by fostering Jacobite intrigues—a menace which did not finally disappear till the desperate attempt of Prince Charles in 1745 had been crushed at Culloden. But the material prosperity of the country counted for more than the sentiment of loyalty to the exiled dynasty, the people at large could never be roused to an active hostility to the house of Hanover, and Jacobitism, till its final suppression, was a source of constant uneasiness rather than of actual danger.

Louis died in 1715 ; Philip of Orléans, the heir presumptive of the child Louis XV, became regent. His dynastic interests and the dynastic interests of George I in England bound the two governments close together, while in each country there was a legitimist party zealous in the one for recognition of Philip V of Spain's title to the succession, in the other for a Stuart restoration.

own succession, when Queen Anne should die, on George of Hanover, whose title was similarly recognized by the treaty, but would always be open to challenge by the exiled princes of the house of Stuart.

When Louis XIV died Philip of Orléans became regent for the infant Louis XV, and George I was already on the British throne ; but it was so obviously in the interest of both George and Philip that the successions as laid down in the Treaty of Utrecht should be maintained at all costs, that the French and British governments entered upon a close alliance. And to this it had to be added that, the elector of Hanover, a prince of the Empire, being also king of Great Britain, neither of those two governments could disregard the interests of the other, if either or both should be involved in any European complications. On the other hand, it was not yet apparent either to the French or to the British government that the antagonistic interests of the two nations in America and India foreboded a duel for oversea empire.

In spite of Jacobite intrigues, George of

**KING GEORGE I OF ENGLAND**

George of Hanover (1660–1727), son of the electress Sophia, succeeded Queen Anne in 1714 by virtue of the Act of Settlement of 1701. This portrait of him as king of Great Britain was painted by Sir Godfrey Kneller.

*Guildhall, London*

**ECCLESIASTIC AND DIPLOMAT**
Giulio Alberoni (1664–1752) rose from humble
beginnings to be as prime minister and cardinal
a principal agent of Elizabeth Farnese in her
Spanish-Italian policy. G. B. Busch engraved
this ' true and not false ' portrait of him.
*From Oncken, ' Friedrichs des Grossen '*

Meanwhile, Philip V had taken for his
second wife Elizabeth Farnese, an ambitious lady who was determined that in
course of time her husband should be
king of France, and that her own children,
whose chance of succession to the Spanish
crown was remote, should succeed to
the duchies of Parma and Tuscany—and
of course that the Sicilies
should come back to Spain.
At the moment, it must be
remembered, Naples and Sardinia had gone to the emperor
while the duke of Savoy had
become king of Sicily. Incidentally, the marriage raised
the Italian (cardinal) Alberoni
to the position of chief minister
and actual director in Spain.

Simultaneously the Turks
were embarking on their last
attempt to reverse the decisions which had been reached
by the treaty of Carlowitz.
Hitherto they had refrained
from challenging the Western
powers ; but they had doubtless derived encouragement

from the war in which they had recovered
Azov from Tsar Peter ; in 1714 they
picked a quarrel with Venice and promptly
reconquered the Morea which the treaty
of Carlowitz had given to the Venetians.
Venice appealed to her old ally Austria to
maintain the treaty ; Austria answered the
appeal ; war was declared, and Eugène
took command of the Austrian armies.

In 1716 a great Turkish force was
besieging Peterwardein in Hungary. On
August 5 that army was shattered by
Eugène, who then besieged and captured
the only fortress remaining to them in
Hungary, Temesvar. In the next spring
Eugène laid siege to Belgrade, and on
August 16, 1717, shattered the Turkish
army advancing to its relief, Belgrade
surrendering on the next day. In 1718
the treaty of Passarowitz confirmed
Austria in her possession of Temesvar and
Belgrade. It did not restore the Morea
to Venice, but it cleared the Ottoman
permanently out of Hungary. And it
again set Austria free to safeguard her
interests against Western aggressors.

Those aggressors had been active ; for
Spanish ambitions required in every
direction the reversal of the Utrecht
settlements, and the foresight which was
not lacking in Alberoni's schemes was
traversed by the impatient temper of the
king and queen. He was forced to open
his attack, which was not itself unprovoked,

**AUSTRIAN CAVALRY IN ACTION**
Several times during the eighteenth century Austria was
involved in war with Turkey. This engraving by G. C.
Bodenehr, from an original drawing by G. Phil. Rugendas the
elder, a contemporary South German artist, depicts a cavalry
engagement in the Turco-Austrian war of 1738–9.
*From Erdmannsdörffer, ' Deutsche Geschichte, 1648–1740 '*

**ADMIRAL BYNG'S VICTORY OVER THE SPANIARDS OFF CAPE PASSARO**

In furtherance of Queen Elizabeth Farnese's ambition to recover Sardinia and Sicily, Cardinal Alberoni reorganized and revived the Spanish navy, and in 1718 dispatched a large fleet to Palermo. On August 11, Admiral Byng engaged the Spaniards off Cape Passaro, completely defeating them and compelling their withdrawal from the invasion of Sicily. This picture of the battle was painted by Richard Paton. To Admiral Byng is due the final destruction of the naval power of Spain.

*Greenwich Hospital; by permission of the Lord Commissioners of the Admiralty*

before he was ready, by invading Sardinia in 1717. As the population preferred the old Spanish to the new Austrian connexion, the conquest of the island was completed in a few weeks. Spanish enthusiasm was aroused ; unable to resist it, Alberoni threw all his energies into preparation for the coming struggle ; while Austria, engaged in her settlement with the Turks, appealed to the 'Triple Alliance' which had been formed by Great Britain, France and Holland, to maintain the Treaty of Utrecht.

The Triple Alliance proposed terms to the emperor, who accepted them, and the Triple became the Quadruple Alliance. But meanwhile Alberoni's energy had recreated a large though untrained fleet which sailed for Palermo, and landed a large Spanish force, to which the Sicilians submitted as readily as the Sardinians. An English squadron was dispatched to the Mediterranean to watch the fleet. There had been no declaration of war, but the English admiral, Byng, found an excuse for engaging the Spanish fleet, and wiped it out off Cape Passaro, practically without loss. Alberoni had been intriguing on every side—for a

French rebellion, a Jacobite rebellion and Swedish co-operation under Charles XII. All the schemes broke down. Charles was killed at Fredrikshald, French troops entered Spain, Austrian troops entered Sicily.

**ENGLAND'S FIRST 'PRIME MINISTER'**

Sir Robert Walpole (1676–1745) was head of the government from 1721–42, being generally regarded as the first 'prime minister.' This picture of him while premier conversing with Speaker Onslow in the House of Commons was painted by William Hogarth and Sir James Thornhill.

*Engraved by A. Fogg*

**CARDINAL DE FLEURY**
André Hercule de Fleury (1653–1743) became
chief minister to Louis XV in 1726. His administration was economical, but his pacifist foreign
policy was over-ruled and he died a disappointed
man. This portrait is by Hyacinthe Rigaud.
*From Seidlitz, ' Porträtwerk.' Brückmann A.G.*

At the beginning of 1720 Philip made
his peace with the allies, having dismissed
Alberoni two months before. He accepted
the terms on which the Quadruple Alliance had agreed. By the new treaty,
Victor Amadeus of Savoy became king of
Sardinia instead of Sicily, which went
to Austria in exchange ; the emperor
Charles renounced all claims on the
dominions which Utrecht had allotted to
Philip, and the reversion of Parma and
Tuscany was secured to Carlos, the eldest
son of Philip's second marriage. Superficially the European harmony was restored. In the following year began the
twenty years' ascendancy in England of a
minister, Walpole, whose aim was to
develop the material wealth of Great
Britain to the utmost extent possible, and,
with that end in view, to keep her at
peace with the rest of the world at all costs.

The regency of Orléans ended in 1723
with the official coming of age of Louis XV.
Orléans died and the Orleanist interests
ceased to dominate French policy ; for
three years the government was in the

**LOUIS XV AND HIS CONSORT MARIA LECSZINSKA**
Problems of paramount international importance were involved in the selection of a consort for
Louis XV, whose health in boyhood was precarious. Plans for his marriage to the little infanta
Maria of Spain had been maturing for some time, but in 1725 the duke of Bourbon opened negotiations
with other European courts and the choice finally fell upon Maria Lecszinska, daughter of Stanislaus
Lecszinski, ex-king of Poland, and the nuptials were solemnised at Fontainebleau, September 4, 1725.
*Portraits by Jean-Baptiste Vanloo (Musée de Versailles ; photo, Neurdein) and, right, Charles Van Loo (the Louvre ; photo, Alinari)*

**JENKINS' EAR : A POPULAR SATIRE ON PACIFISM IN HIGH PLACES**

Walpole's and Fleury's pacifist policy is satirised in this contemporary caricature. Walpole 'in place' is waving aside Captain Robert Jenkins, who, in proof of the Spanish ill treatment of British mariners, produces the ear severed from his head by a Spanish naval officer in 1731. A servant ejects another merchant complainant, and in front of the table Fleury's emissary offers French mediation. This incident of Jenkins' ear was a contributory cause of the Anglo-Spanish war in 1739.

hands of the duke of Bourbon, who in 1725 married Louis to Maria Lecszinska, daughter of the ex-king of Poland. In 1726 Bourbon was dismissed, and Louis' old tutor Cardinal Fleury became first minister ; but it was not till a son was born to the king in 1729 that the prospect of a possible Spanish claim to the French succession disappeared from the complications of international politics, and a secret rapprochement between the two Bourbon monarchies took its place.

Yet there were two other dynastic complications already threatening. When the emperor Joseph of Austria had died in 1711, he had been succeeded, having no sons, by his brother, Charles VI ; but he left two daughters. By 1720 Charles also had two daughters ; the chance that he would ever have a son was remote ; and in that year he issued a decree known as the Pragmatic Sanction, declaring that the Austrian succession lay in his own daughters and only after them in the daughters of his elder brother.

**EMPEROR CHARLES VI**

Charles VI (1685–1740) is chiefly remembered as the author of the Pragmatic Sanction—a decree (1720) securing the Austrian succession for his daughter that proved a fertile cause of European dissension. The portrait above is by Auerbach.

*National Gallery, Vienna ; photo, Kunstverlag Wolfrum*

U

Whatever renunciations might be formally made, it was certain that the husbands of the latter—they married respectively Charles Albert of Bavaria and Augustus the younger of Saxony—would denounce and resist the Pragmatic Sanction ; and it became the ruling desire of Charles VI to have his decree guaranteed by all available powers against such opposition. Consequently the guaranteeing of the Pragmatic Sanction figured in all diplomatic bargaining between Charles and other European governments. The decree of course concerned not the imperial but only the Austrian succession, though that included the crowns of Bohemia and Hungary ; in respect of which there lurked always in the background the time-

**A SHUTTLECOCK KING**

In the vicissitudes of the Polish monarchy in the eighteenth century Stanislaus I played an undignified part, and was finally dispossessed of the crown in 1739. He retained the empty title of king and was given the duchy of Lorraine.

*Painting by L. M. Van Loo, Versailles ; photo, Giraudon*

**KING GEORGE II**

George II (1683–1760) became king of Great Britain and Ireland in 1727. His sympathies were strongly German, but he had the sense to recognize the power of the popular will and acted consistently as a constitutional sovereign.

*Painting by R. E. Pine*

honoured doctrine that those crowns were not hereditary but elective. The remaining dynastic problem was that of Poland ; where the crown was indubitably elective, but the de facto king, Augustus of Saxony, was bent on making it hereditary.

Fleury, who was already past seventy when he became his former pupil's first minister, shared Walpole's desire to keep the peace, and the two worked harmoniously as pacificators. But Fleury was embarrassed, as Walpole was not, by European ambitions, as a result of which he found himself forced into wars, while Walpole was strong enough to prevent George II (who succeeded his father in 1727) from plunging into the fray. Actually Fleury's secret project took shape in a secret treaty with Spain, known as the Family Compact (1733) ; its aim was the disintegration of Austria, which (having been accomplished through England's failure to come to her assistance under Walpole's pacific regime) would alienate her from England, and would establish in Europe a United Bourbon supremacy in which it would be easy to force Walpole to acquiesce. In actual fact, the attempt to break up Austria failed ; the accord between Britain and Austria survived ; and Walpole himself discovered, to his extreme chagrin, in 1739 that when the English fell into a war fever, with or without reason, the British government would be forced to fight willy nilly.

### War of the Polish Succession

FLEURY, however, must be acquitted of having organized or initiated the attack upon Austria. The European conflagration from which Walpole succeeded in holding aloof is known as the War of the Polish Succession. Augustus wanted his son to be elected as his successor ; the rival candidate was his own former rival Stanislaus Lecszinski, the father of the queen of France. The Polish question affected both Russia and Prussia, who did not wish French influence to dominate Poland, and would have set up another foreign candidate. Charles VI did not want the French candidate but tried in vain to persuade Augustus to recognize the Pragmatic Sanction as the price of his support. The Poles were tired of foreign kings and wanted Lecszinski—in the lack of a stronger candidate.

The question was still unsettled when Augustus the Strong died in February, 1733. His son, another Augustus, gave Charles his price, thereby becoming the Austrian candidate ; but the Poles elected Stanislaus. Russia under a new tsaritsa, Anne, supported Augustus. French public opinion forced Fleury to send Stanislaus support, but what he sent was very inadequate. The Russians and Saxons drove Stanislaus in flight from the country to Prussia, and the Poles—having no option—recognized Augustus III. The king of Prussia, Frederick William, gave Stanislaus his protection, but declined otherwise to intervene on his behalf.

France and Austria, however, had both committed themselves to the war, and France struck at Austria by sending armies not to Poland but to Italy. The annexation of Austrian provinces in Italy was eminently attractive both to the king

of Sardinia and to Carlos, that son of the king and queen of Spain to whom Parma and the succession in Tuscany—not yet vacant—had been assigned. Spain and Sardinia joined with France. The War of the Polish Succession became a war for the expulsion of the Hapsburgs from Italy.

That object was not achieved. The war was extraordinarily devoid of interest, and was carried on without energy or skill on either side. The Spaniards practically conquered Naples and Sicily much as they had before conquered Sardinia and Sicily in the days of Alberoni, and the Austrians were almost driven out of Lombardy ; but Fleury was in constant fear of the British intervention for which King George in his loyalty to the emperor was eager. Diplomacy took the place of fighting, and when peace terms were arranged in 1735 Italy was very thoroughly redistributed, but Austria was very far from being ejected. Lombardy was restored to her. Carlos got Naples and Sicily, but gave up Parma, which went to the Hapsburgs, and the reversion of Tuscany, which went to Charles' prospective son-in-law,

**AUGUSTUS THE STRONG**

Augustus of Saxony (1670–1733), shown in this engraving by Wortmann after the portrait by Louis de Silvestre, was elected king of Poland in 1697. Compelled by Charles XII of Sweden to give up his crown in 1702, he regained it in 1709.

*From Seidlitz, ' Porträtwerk,' Bruckmann A.G.*

Francis of Lorraine, who resigned Lorraine to Stanislaus, who resigned the Polish crown to the de facto king of Poland, Augustus. But France had made one invaluable acquisition : Lorraine, long coveted, was to go to her on the death of Stanislaus, whose daughter was the queen of France. Walpole and Frederick William I had successfully kept Britain, Hanover and Prussia out of the embroilment which had been bleeding all their neighbours in men and money.

### Consequences of the Pragmatic Sanction

THE war was practically ended in 1735, though the peace terms were not fully ratified till four years later. In the course of the negotiations Charles had collected various additional paper guarantees of the Pragmatic Sanction, but had very completely alienated Prussia by the consistent duplicity of his dealings with her extremely narrow-minded, dull-witted and honest monarch Frederick William I. He had also joined the tsaritsa Anne in a very ill-conducted war with the Turks which again lost him Belgrade. In 1739 the endless quarrel between the Spanish government and the British people over trading rights and wrongs in the South Seas reached such a pitch of blind hostility that Walpole, very much against his will, was forced by the popular excitement to declare war on Spain, with every prospect that France would join forces with the Spanish Bourbon.

In 1740 the tsaritsa Anne died and it was not till some years had passed that Russia had a government which could play an active part in western politics. Frederick William died and was succeeded by his son Frederick, who was as unscrupulous as his father had been honest, and as astute as his father had been stupid. Charles VI died, and under the Pragmatic Sanction his daughter Maria Teresa, not long married to Francis of Tuscany, succeeded to the Austrian inheritance. Out of the next twenty-three years fifteen were filled with the War of the Austrian Succession and the Seven Years' War ; Prussia took her place as a military power second to none ; and France and Great Britain fought their duel for supremacy in

North America and India. Before entering on that story, we must review the development of Prussia under Frederick William and of the tsardom under Peter the Great and his successors.

### Decline of the Swedish Power

IN 1713 Frederick William I succeeded his father Frederick I as the second king of Prussia. In that year Charles XII of Sweden was still a very unwelcome guest in Turkey, engaged in fruitless efforts to persuade the sultan to renew the war with Russia which had been brought to an end by the treaty of Pruth in 1711. Peter, having thereby obtained a fortunate release from the Turkish imbroglio, had devoted himself anew to the recovery or capture from Sweden of the provinces on the east of the Baltic, while Augustus II of Saxony and Frederick IV of Denmark were engaged in a similar process on the south and west, and Frederick William was soon persuaded to join them for the recovery of Pomerania.

In 1714 Charles, who had hitherto resisted all attempts to eject him from Turkey, suddenly resolved to return to Sweden, now all but stripped of her trans-Baltic possessions, raced with one companion across Europe to Stralsund, which was being besieged, threw himself into the town, and carried on the struggle with desperate energy. But Sweden, single-handed against encircling foes, had no real chance. Charles had to evacuate Stralsund. His minister, Gortz, however, struck a bargain with Peter, and Charles was already invading Norway when he was slain, probably by the bullet of a traitor, before Fredrikshald in 1718.

His heir was a nephew, son of his elder sister ; but the depressed nobles found their opportunity, and raised his younger sister Ulrica Eleanor to the throne upon terms which practically divested the crown of all power. Ulrica herself abdicated in favour of her husband, Frederick of Hesse-Cassel. Largely through the friendly mediation of England the series of treaties known as the Peace of Nystadt (1721) ended the ' Northern War.' Peter kept his provinces ; Frederick William got Danzig with access to the Baltic ; Frederick of Denmark kept

Slesvig. But Peter's hope of acquiring Mecklenburg and with it a status as a prince of the Empire was foiled. With the death of Charles XII Sweden ceased to be a serious factor in European politics.

### Achievements of Peter the Great

THE figure of Peter the Great is an extraordinary one. Physically and intellectually the man was a giant, a personality of overwhelming forcefulness: an outer barbarian dwelling among barbarians on the outskirts of an extremely sophisticated civilization, yet of a genius that could realize the effective superiority which that civilization gave to the nations of the West. He never became civilized himself, but he was entirely resolved that his people should be compelled to discard their own traditions and imitate that civilization so far as he understood it. utterly alien though it was. What he imposed upon them was not assimilation—that was impossible, for he could not in fact assimilate it himself—but imitation: and he effected his purpose. He revolutionised the Russian social and political system on Western lines; but he did it without transforming the Russian into a Western. And what he did could have been accomplished by no man with a less torrential will overriding all opposition, or with a less capacity for learning from defeat the way to victory, and from his own errors the way to success.

Peter was sufficiently thorough-going in his work of political and social reconstruction. How he extended his dominion to the Baltic (where he planted his new imperial capital on the Neva) we have already seen. The remainder of his reign, which ended with his death in 1725, was largely occupied in extending his dominion eastward by wars with Persia.

What Peter had wrought mainly through the force of his own personality was not destroyed by his death ; but it was gravely imperilled by the character of his successors and the difficulties they had to face. The succession itself was a serious problem. He had himself put to death, in circumstances of great brutality, the son Alexis whom his first wife had borne to him, and Peter (afterwards Peter II) the son of Alexis was an infant. He had taken as his second wife his low-born but very able mistress Catherine, who actually did succeed him with the support of Menschikov, the minister who had been his right-hand man in carrying through the reforms. By her Peter had two daughters, of whom the elder, Anne, was married to the duke of Holstein, whose son later became Peter III, on the death of the younger, Elizabeth, who succeeded

**FREDERICK WILLIAM I OF PRUSSIA**
Rigid economy characterised the administration of Frederick William I (1688–1740), who became king of Prussia in 1713. His passion for military life led him to develop a highly efficient army, but he guarded its perfection by avoiding wars. This engraving by Wolffgang is from the painting by Antoine Pesne.
*From Seidlitz, ' Porträtwerk,' Bruckmann A.G.*

**RECRUITING PRUSSIAN INFANTRY**

These figures form part of an eighteenth-century poster seeking the enrolment of soldiers in Prince Anhalt-Zerbst's infantry regiment. The rigorous training of its creator made this regiment notable in the service of Frederick William I.

*From Erdmannsdörffer, ' Deutsche Geschichte, 1648-1740 '*

before him.  But besides Peter's own descendants, there were the daughters of his own elder brother Ivan, Catherine of Mecklenburg, whose grandson became Ivan VI, and Anne of Courland, who was Ivan's predecessor on the throne.

The actual order of succession was : Catherine I, widow of Peter the Great, 1725 ;  Peter II, his grandson, 1727 ; Anne of Courland, 1730 ;  Ivan VI, 1740 ; Elizabeth, Peter's own daughter, 1741 ; Peter III, his grandson, 1762.  Peter III married a German princess, Catherine of Anhalt, who promptly superseded him, and reigned as the great tsaritsa Catherine II, 1762–1796.

Catherine I carried on her husband's policy for two years ;  on her death, the reactionaries got the upper hand.  When the boy Peter II died after three years, the same party set Anne of Courland on the throne ;  they had hardly done so when she recovered the supremacy by a coup d'état, reverted to the policy of

Peter to the best of her not very conspicuous ability, and fought with no great success against the Turks.  Her infant great-nephew, Ivan I, was only a phantom, who was deposed in 1741 by a palace revolution which set the great Peter's daughter Elizabeth on the throne.

### Organization of the Prussian Army

FREDERICK WILLIAM of Prussia was not a man of genius like Peter the Great ; but he was a man of one idea, which he pursued with such concentration that he made Prussia into a first-class power. That one idea was the organization of an invincible military machine.  He created it, but he had no use for it ;  it was an end in itself.  He made no wars ;  but he felt that he was surrounded by cleverer men than himself, and that his one security against being robbed by them was an army which they would encounter at their peril.  He did not save himself from being robbed, but he left to his son an instrument of vengeance and reprisal of which Frederick II made full and effective use.

He had no sense for any of the amenities of life, whether for himself, for his family or for his subjects ;  art, music and letters had for him no meaning ;  commerce and indeed all foreign intercourse were to be shunned.  Industry was to be encouraged so far as it provided the necessaries of life ;  Prussia must be made self-sufficing, wholly independent of foreign supplies, as she must be made irresistibly secure against foreign attack.  The superfluities would do her more harm than good ;  she must neither purchase them nor produce them ;  and all things were superfluous which did not fit in with a more than Spartan rigidity of discipline. All virtues were summed up in unquestioning obedience.  So he built up his fighting machine, the perfecting of which was the absorbing passion of his life, without any desire to put its perfection to the proof.

It did not save him from being duped, as his father had been duped before him, by Austrian craft.  Charles got promises out of him—the guarantee of the Pragmatic Sanction for one—knowing that he would keep them, by himself making promises which he neither kept nor intended to keep ; but, unfortunately for Austria, Frederick William's son was entirely free from those conscientious scruples on which Charles reckoned in his dealings with the father, and Leopold before him in dealing with the grandfather. There were certain heritages which had been promised to one or the other and then disposed of otherwise. And Frederick meant to have them. His chance came when in 1740 he succeeded his father in Prussia and Maria Teresa at the end of the year claimed the succession to her father in Austria.

### European Rivalries in East and West

IT was not only in Europe, however, that the coming collision was to take effect. In fact, the first actual outbreak of hostilities was occasioned by the failure of the treaty of Utrecht to satisfy British trading demands in Spanish America. Moreover, British and French commercial rivalry in India had reached a pitch that set the East India Companies fighting as soon as open war was declared between the two nations in the west ; and the British and French colonial expansions in North America had so converged that neither could make further advance save at the expense of the other's claims.

Of these three causes of quarrel, the first had been active for nearly two centuries. It had begun when English mariners enforced at the sword's point what they claimed as their ' right ' to trade with the Spanish colonies in defiance of the Spanish government. In the seventeenth century it had degenerated into the piracy of the buccaneers ; the refusal of Louis XIV, when he accepted the Spanish crown for his grandson, to relax the Spanish policy of exclusion had been a potent factor in swinging English public opinion over to the support of William's policy when he organized the Grand Alliance of 1701. Some trading concessions had been secured by the treaty of Utrecht which from the English point of view proved very inadequate ; English ships evaded the treaty regulations, and Spanish officials exercised their powers with intolerable arrogance and severity. Both sides lost their tempers and refused to listen to reason, and both countries went wild with joy when their governments yielded to popular clamour and declared war in 1739.

### Status of Europeans in India

THE Indian position was the outcome of the disintegration of the Mogul Empire. When Aurangzib died in 1705, the vast dominion theoretically recognized the supremacy of the Mogul ; practically the governors of its great provinces were already independent princes, each one bent on establishing a dynasty, while he was nominally no more than an official holding office during the Mogul's pleasure. The Europeans in India were merely a few traders established in some half dozen ' factories ' on the coast by grace of the native rulers, with some scores of soldiers who might perhaps have seen some service in European wars. The companies' servants were allowed to defend themselves —always on the understanding at home that they must not involve their respective national governments in military adventures. All the territory either of them owned was a few square miles. Among the Indian powers, they had neither political nor military status ; they were upon Indian soil merely on sufferance.

No French and no British government dreamed of conquest, though local ' governors ' had dreamed of acquiring influence at native courts that would further the interests of their companies. This was the dream that was brought nearer by the disruption of the empire and the feebleness of the central authority ; and what remained of that central authority received a shattering blow in 1739 when the Persian Nadir Shah swept through the north-western passes, swept through the Punjab, swept upon Delhi, put the capital once more to the sack, and bore away with him its vast treasures, including the famous Peacock Throne. At that disastrous moment in the history of the Moguls, the governorship of the French Company at Pondicherry passed into the hands of François Dupleix, of whose imperialist visions the British were destined to reap the fruits.

Finally, in North America the French colony on the St. Lawrence, small in numbers but highly centralised and with a military organization, had extended past the Great Lakes blocking the westward expansion of the northern British colonies ; away in the south on the Mexican Gulf they had planted the colony of New Orleans ; they had traced the course of the Mississippi, claimed the whole of its basin for their own, and were now claiming the basin of its great tributary the Ohio. If that claim were admitted, the British would be shut in for ever between the Ohio, the Mississippi and the Atlantic. Canada was under a single government ; the British colonies between the St. Lawrence and Florida, now thirteen in number, were very much the more populous, but they were under thirteen separate governments without any common authority or machinery for joint or military organization. If a collision should come, it was by no means a foregone conclusion that the British would have the best of it. The decision would turn upon the amount of active support which French or British received from Europe.

England, it may be remarked, had at this time sunk, under Walpole's extremely materialistic regime, to an abnormally low state of spiritual and moral lethargy. This year, 1739, was curiously also the birth-year of a movement which revived in the masses that sense of things spiritual which seemed moribund ; for in it the brothers John and Charles Wesley and George Whitefield may be said to have opened the first campaign in that evangelising mission of Methodism which infused new and stronger life into Nonconformity generally.

### War of the Austrian Succession begins

ℐN 1740 British and Spanish were fighting each other, with no great credit to either, in the West Indies ; both in full expectation that it would not be long before France intervened on the side of Spain. Before Charles VI died he had procured guarantees of his Pragmatic Sanction for the disposition of the Austrian inheritance from everyone except Spain, Charles Emmanuel of Sardinia and Charles Albert of Bavaria, the husband of Charles's niece, Maria Amelia, his elder brother's daughter. He had failed to procure any guarantee of the imperial succession for his daughter's husband Francis of Tuscany (formerly of Lorraine).

On his death Maria Teresa was proclaimed his heiress and queen of Hungary and Bohemia ; the male line of the house of Hapsburg had come to an end. Charles Albert claimed the whole inheritance ; Spain and Sardinia were eager to assert claims in Italy. But they were not strong enough to make those claims good on their own account in the face of the guaranteeing powers. An appeal to arms appeared, on the whole, improbable.

But the young king of Prussia had no qualms and no scruples. He marched his hitherto untried army into Silesia, announced his own claim to that and other provinces, and declared his readiness to support Maria Teresa in all her other

**MARIA TERESA OF AUSTRIA**
The empress Maria Teresa (1717–1780) was about twenty-three years of age when Martin Meytens painted this portrait of her. It represents her as queen of Hungary with one hand resting upon the crown of S. Stephen.
*Photo. Reiffenstein, Vienna*

claims if those provinces were ceded to him. The young queen repudiated the insolent offer with indignation ; an Austrian army marched to suppress the upstart ; and the upstart's troops shattered it at the battle of Mollwitz (April, 1741).

The aged Fleury was still at the head of the French government, but he was unable to make head against the ambitious Belle-Isle. The opportunity had arisen for dismembering the Austrian dominion and dividing Germany into independent principalities, none of which could make head against France. Prussia, after Mollwitz, must be taken into account ; before it, Frederick's proceedings had looked like midsummer madness. No one, doubtless, would give him anything but a very qualified support ; but he had a surprisingly efficient army and in Silesia he was actually in possession. Great Britain was committed to the Austrian side, but Walpole, the man of peace, was still at the head of her government. France could nullify her own guarantees of the Pragmatic Sanction by explanations ingenious if unconvincing.

### Results of Belle-Isle's Diplomacy

BELLE-ISLE'S diplomacy had a difficult task, but it was successful. Frederick, indeed, had no mind to be turned into a tool for carrying out Belle-Isle's plans : the cession of Silesia would have set him firmly on the side of Maria Teresa ; but her resolute refusal, in spite of pressure from Great Britain and Hanover, drove him to accept the French terms—with mental reservations. Charles Albert was to receive the bulk of the inheritance, including Bohemia, and was to be emperor ; Frederick was to surrender part of his claims to Augustus of Saxony and the elector palatine, and Sardinia and Spain were to share the spoils in Italy. France was to keep whatever she could take in the Netherlands. The compact being arranged, France entered the war not as a principal but as an ' auxiliary ' of Bavaria. Great Britain and Hanover did likewise, as auxiliaries of Maria Teresa ; the auxiliaries, technically, were not ' at war ' with each other.

Maria Teresa's prospects were black enough, for little effective aid could be looked for from the maritime powers, and the accession of Elizabeth in Russia removed the hope of help from that quarter. But she faced the circle of foes with undaunted courage and her bold appeal to her down-trodden Hungarian subjects was answered with an enthusiasm wholly unexpected. Also she yielded to her advisers and made offers to Frederick to detach him from his allies. It suited him to accept them—the allies were not making the rapid progress expected—and by the compact of Klein Schnellendorf the Austrian force in Silesia was released to defend the Austrian territories against the advancing foes, while Frederick sat still.

### Charles VII elected Emperor

FREDERICK was obviously playing a double game ; but the French were only roused to greater activity. Prague was captured. Frederick threw over his compact, which had never been made public, and at the imperial election in January, 1742, the elector of Bavaria became the emperor Charles VII. But if Maria Teresa's friends failed her, her own courage and energy were unshaken. Troops were hurried together from every quarter, and Passau, which had been occupied by the Bavarians, was recaptured on the day of Charles's election.

Frederick attacked Moravia, but in three months he had made up his mind that the game was not worth the candle ; there was no love lost between him and the allies, who naturally distrusted him utterly. He dropped the Moravian campaign. The war party in England was at this moment greatly strengthened by the retirement of Walpole ; but even his successor Carteret insisted that terms must be made with Frederick as the price of British activity ; Hanover could not afford to lay herself open to his attack. The terms proposed did not satisfy him, and he proceeded to rout an Austrian army at Czaslau, reckoning that this would bring Austria to reason. He left the Austrians to drive back the French, while he reopened negotiations before their successes should go too far. By midsummer

U*

he had got his terms practically accepted. In return for the cession of the greater part of Silesia in full sovereignty, he retired from the war. The treaty of Breslau was signed in June, 1742, and in September Saxony followed Frederick's example and assumed neutrality.

France, thus deserted, and with her troops in a very precarious position, made overtures for peace, but would not herself desert the emperor. Maria Teresa, now full of the hope of obtaining in other directions compensation for the territories she had ceded, refused the proffered terms ; but the campaigning continued to be indecisive, while Charles Emmanuel of Sardinia was engaged in extracting terms to his own advantage alternately from Austria and Spain, the two powers directly concerned in the redistribution of Italian territories. Carlos at Naples was put out of action by the British Mediterranean fleet, whose commander gave him an hour to decide whether he would engage to remain neutral or subject Naples to bombardment. He chose neutrality, but he did not forgive the indignity.

**MARSHAL SAXE THE COURAGEOUS**
This pastel portrait by La Tour shows Maurice of Saxony (1696–1750), marshal of France and one of the first generals of his age. Afflicted with dropsy, he was carried to Fontenoy in a wicker chariot and won a decisive victory (1745).
*The Louvre ; photo, Giraudon*

### Treaties of Worms and Fontainebleau

THE war dragged on, with varying fortunes which it would be superfluous to follow in detail, till a new treaty—' of Worms '—between Maria Teresa's supporters revived the never very quiescent fears of Frederick that if the allies were too successful his own acquisitions would be threatened. The treaty of Worms was countered by the treaty of Fontainebleau —a curious agreement by which France engaged to secure for Spain whatever she wanted, while she took her own chance of gaining something in the Netherlands. The fiction that most of the belligerents were merely the auxiliaries of someone else was dropped, France declaring war upon England and Hanover (1744).

Before the summer was over Frederick cast off his neutrality and invaded Bohemia. The French concentrated their efforts upon the Netherlands, where they gave the command of their armies to Maurice of Saxony—commonly referred to as Marshal Saxe—an illegitimate half-brother of Augustus of Saxony, who for

his part definitely attached himself to Austria out of his fear and jealousy of Prussia. Frederick was now posing as the champion of the imperial rights of which the emperor Charles VII was being deprived. Of course he made his bargain with that unlucky prince, who had already lost his own Bavaria to the Austrians.

Frederick's Bohemian campaign was foiled, partly because the French repaid his previous desertion by failing to help him, partly by the skill of the Austrian Traun. Then at the beginning of 1745 the emperor died. His son Maximilian Joseph had no imperial ambitions, though reluctant to resign his claims on the Austrian inheritance. That reluctance was removed by the rapid movement of Austrian forces. An Austro-Bavarian reconciliation in April, by incidentally ensuring the imperial succession to Maria Teresa's husband Francis, deprived Frederick of the pretext that he was the constitutional defender of the emperor's authority.

The French were fighting for their own hand in the Netherlands. The destruction of Frederick had become Maria Teresa's primary aim ; he was fighting for life now, and he got no help from France. But Traun was no longer directing the Austrian armies, and at Hohenfriedberg Frederick won a decisive victory. Maria Teresa's principal ally, England, had always refused to engage in hostilities with him, and now England was distracted with domestic alarms caused by the great Jacobite insurrection headed (July, 1745) by Charles Edward Stuart, the 'Bonnie Prince Charlie' of the Highland clans and the 'Young Pretender' of English and Scottish Whigs. Charles invaded England with a small army of his clansmen at his back, having routed such troops as had opposed him ; but the English Jacobites did not rise, and when he reached Derby (November) the momentous decision to retreat was taken. Advance

would probably have meant annihilation ; retreat meant inevitably the abandonment of the adventure—though it was not altogether abandoned till the clansmen had been cut to pieces at Culloden (April, 1746), and the prince was a fugitive. Thenceforth Jacobitism was not even a potential political force, but only a sentimental memory.

The rising, however, was only at its beginning when George II and Frederick came to terms in the Treaty of Hanover. From the British-Hanoverian point of view it was absolutely necessary to compromise the quarrel between Frederick and Maria Teresa, nor did this view involve any departure from the attitude taken from the outset by the British government. Maria Teresa must yield to their representations. She declined, however, and made a fresh compact with Saxony.

### Peace of Aix-La-Chapelle ends the War

THE French overran the Netherlands, from which British forces were withdrawn to deal with the Jacobites. While Austrians and Saxons were endeavouring with greatly superior forces to crush Frederick, the Spaniards were rapidly gaining ground in Italy. Frederick, instead of being crushed, not only defeated the Austrians but invaded Saxony and entered Dresden. With Saxony in Frederick's grip, and England refusing subsidies as long as the Prussian war continued, Maria Teresa was forced to give way, and in December the treaty of Dresden ended the Prussian war. Frederick, confirmed in possession of Silesia, retired for the third time and remained thenceforth a neutral.

Still the war dragged on for nearly three years. By the end of 1746 nearly the whole of the Netherlands was in possession of the French, who were without allies except the Spaniards. On the other side the Austrian campaign was mismanaged, and Sardinia was inactive. Maria Teresa wanted terms which France and Spain were not ready to concede ; and negotiations which her own allies Great Britain and Holland initiated broke down in 1747. English and French were fighting each other by this time both in America, where

**A PRINCE IN PETTICOATS**
This engraving by J. Williams shows the female disguise adopted by the Young Pretender, Charles Edward Stuart, when he fled from Scotland after his defeat at Culloden in 1746. Above: the prince's ' medusa head ' targe.
*Photo (below), W. F. Mansell*

**FREDERICK II IN YOUNG MANHOOD**
This engaging portrait was painted by Antoine Pesne in 1739, the year before Frederick ascended the throne. It shows the prince, then twenty-seven years of age, powdered and wearing the ribbon of the Order of the Black Eagle
*State Museum, Berlin*

robbed Austria of the greater part of Silesia. The one prince who had gained, and gained heavily, was—as concerned his relations with other powers—the most cynically unscrupulous of all, Frederick II. He had made his name and won his prize. But he had done it by methods which made it absolutely certain that sooner or later he would have to fight his hardest to keep it. For the rest, practically all conquests made during the war were restored as before the war began.

Frederick had a respite of eight years which he devoted to the recuperation and reconstruction of which Prussia was sorely in need. He had no friends on whom he could rely, because none could place reliance upon him ; he could only be sure that Hanover would not embroil herself

the British captured Louisbourg, and in India, where the French captured Madras. At last in 1748 England and Holland came privately to terms with France, and the pressure they brought to bear on Maria Teresa forced her to give way. The War of the Austrian Succession was brought to an end by the peace of Aix-la-Chapelle, signed by the various powers in October and November, 1748.

For eight years Europe had been expending a vast amount of blood and treasure. The results were singularly barren. Sardinia had absorbed a few more leaves of the Lombard artichoke, the price paid by Maria Teresa to Charles Emmanuel for his alliance. Austria had rather gained and France had definitely lost prestige. Neither Bourbon nor Hapsburg had gained territory, but Prussia had

**AUSTRIAN DIPLOMATIST**
An Austro-French alliance against Prussia was effected in 1756 by the skilful diplomacy of Wenzel Anton Dominik von Kaunitz (1711–94), minister to Maria Teresa for forty years. This portrait of him is by Steiner.
*National Gallery, Vienna ; photo, Kunstverlag Wolfrum*

with him, if she could possibly avoid doing so, and that he could count upon British support if he were attacked by France. No one else would move a finger to help him if he got into trouble unless his enemies happened to be their enemies as well. On the other hand his own and his army's military prestige was security enough against any attack unless by a coalition which he would have to face single-handed. The formation of such a coalition was at the same time the primary aim of the very able minister Kaunitz, who was beginning to take the leading place in the councils of Maria Teresa.

During the years of peace, while Kaunitz was weaving his diplomatic web, the contest between French and British in India was passing through its second phase. The first phase had begun with the declaration of war between France and England in 1744. It was initiated by the French governor at Pondicherry, Dupleix. His idea was to establish a dominant French influence at the courts of the two most powerful governors in southern India, the Nizam of the Deccan at

**ROBERT LORD CLIVE**

The chief founder of British Empire in India was Robert Clive (1725–1774), shown in this portion of a picture by Nathaniel Dance. His defence of Arcot (1751) and victory at Plassey (1757) are his most famous military exploits.

*National Portrait Gallery, London ; photo, Emery Walker*

Hyderabad and his subordinate lieutenant-governor, the ' nawab' of the Carnatic at Arcot. The British Company had three ' presidencies ' in India, at Bombay, at Fort William (Calcutta) on the Hugli (Hooghli), one of the mouths of the Ganges, and at Madras in the Carnatic. The French head-quarters were at Pondicherry, also in the Carnatic. Dupleix's plan was to eject the British under favour of the nawab. When the rival was disposed of, diplomacy would establish French influence at Arcot, then at Hyderabad, and then——

Dupleix sought and obtained the favour of Nawab Anwar ud-Din. He concerted his attack on the British with La Bourdonnais, the French admiral in command at the Isle of Mauritius, which lay on the flank of the sea route from the Cape to India. He got leave from Anwar ud-Din to attack Madras ; the squadron came up from Mauritius, there was no British squadron in Indian waters, and Madras fell. Dupleix intended to keep it. He had taken a leaf out of the Portuguese book in the past, and drilled some

**GOVERNOR OF FRENCH INDIA**

The territorial ambitions of Joseph François Dupleix (1697–1763), governor-general of French establishments in India, were frustrated by the genius of Clive and lack of support from officials in France. This drawing of him is by Sergent.

*Bibliothèque Nationale, Paris*

hundreds of natives under French officers in the European discipline. Anwar ud-Din proposed to take over Madras: Dupleix declined to hand it over. The nawab sent ten thousand men to wipe him out, and Dupleix's little force of sepoys put them to rout. The nawab, whose position was not too secure, did not renew the attempt, and the fame of Dupleix and the French was noised abroad.

To his disgust the Treaty of Aix-la-Chapelle compelled him to restore Madras to the British. His scheme took a new shape. The succession both to the nawabship and to the nizamship was in dispute. He could not now attack the British, since the two nations were at peace ; but he offered his support, which was joyfully accepted, to two of the claimants. If they secured the succession through him, his influence at both courts would be supreme and the British would be eliminated. The British offered their support to the rival pair of candidates.

It appeared that victory was going decisively in favour of Dupleix, when the governor of Madras allowed Robert Clive to march with five hundred sepoys against Arcot—the French nawab was engaged in besieging the British nawab far away at Trichinopoli. Clive captured Arcot ; a great force was marched up from Trichinopoli to recapture it. Clive held the place for seven weeks, repulsed a great attempt to storm it, then sallied out and scattered the besieging force, joined hands with the commander of a small force recruited from England, and marched to the relief of Trichinopoli. The French got their candidate on to the throne at Hyderabad, the British at Arcot, but the prestige had passed from the French to the British. The hostilities were stopped by the recall of Dupleix in 1754, and so ended the second phase.

In America, too, there were preliminary skirmishes during the Austrian Succession war, when a British colonial force captured Louisbourg, which was restored to the French by the peace treaty as on the other side of the world Madras was restored to the British. The skirmishing continued in desultory fashion during the peace. The French set up Fort Duquesne on the Ohio ; a small expedition sent under the English General Braddock to eject them was cut to pieces—an event which incidentally gave the colonists a very poor impression of the British regular troops and their officers. It was becoming manifest that a critical conflict between French and British both in America and in India could not long be deferred. It was not, but should have been, equally obvious that in their conflict sea power would be the decisive factor.

### Diplomatic Revolution and Seven Years' War

MEANWHILE the ' Diplomatic Revolution ' was taking place in Europe. Its master spirit was the Austrian Kaunitz, its aim the destruction of Frederick. But Austria's old ally Britain had also been persistently friendly to Prussia, would not help to destroy her, and was from the military point of view a valuable ally only against France or Spain, by reason of her navy, which could operate effectively against them. To destroy

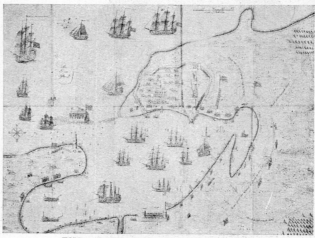

**THE ' DUNKIRK OF THE NORTH '**
Louisbourg was strongly fortified by the French in 1720. In 1745 it was invested by British land and sea forces and after a siege lasting forty-eight days surrendered to General Pepperrell. An account of the operations in which this plan was included was published in London the same year.
*From James Gibson, ' A Journal of the Late Siege '*

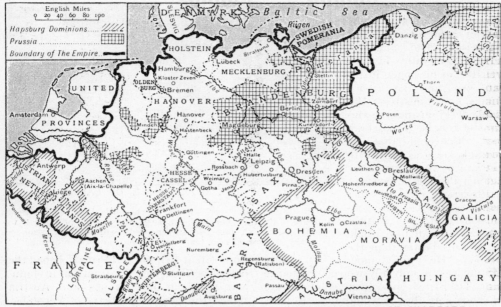

**COCKPIT OF CONTENDING DYNASTIES IN FIFTEEN YEARS OF WARFARE**

Prussian territorial ambitions and Bavarian claims to the Hapsburg succession consequent upon the death of Charles VI led in 1740 to the War of the Austrian Succession, in which Great Britain took sides with Austria and France with Prussia. In the event the war was barren of results, the principal territorial gainer being Prussia, which acquired the greater part of Silesia. The carnage of the Seven Years' War (1756–63) was hardly more productive of changes, the territorial distribution of Europe remaining much what it was before.

Prussia, Austria must have allies. She could make sure of Saxony's good will; the most promising quarter was Russia, where the tsaritsa, Elizabeth, was imbued with an intense personal hostility to Frederick, who had made caustic comments on her character. On the other hand, the Bourbons were Austria's traditional foes, who had quite recently been the allies of Prussia and might easily become so again.

Still, if France and Prussia combined, neither would have any real trust in the other. But suppose France could be induced to reverse her traditional policy, and join Austria ? The worst that could befall would be the intervention of Britain, which would hamper France but otherwise would be of no great consequence. British administration throughout the last war had been incompetent ; there was no British army to speak of ; the British navy was large but it had accomplished singularly little. Kaunitz resolved to abandon the British in favour of a French alliance.

**ADMIRAL BYNG AND HIS ACCUSERS**

Tried by court-martial for failing to save Minorca from the French in 1756, Admiral John Byng was sentenced to death and shot in March, 1757. In this bitter and unjust caricature, 'Cowardice Rewarded,' Justice hales him to execution while Neptune, Mars and the Devil point derisive fingers at him.

The procuring of that alliance was a brilliant diplomatic achievement. But Frederick had alienated France generally by the vagaries of his policy in the late war, and the French king's latest mistress, Madame de Pompadour, by his caustic tongue. Louis himself discovered that he might balance accounts with Heaven by crusading against Protestant powers.

Frederick, on the other hand, came to the conclusion that the British-Hanoverian alliance would serve him better than the French. He wanted money badly, and Britain was the only ally who could finance him. The British government was in a state of chaos, sure that it would have to fight France, but extremely anxious to quarrel neither with France nor with Prussia. While Kaunitz was pulling the last strings which brought France into the Austrian league, Frederick was overcoming British hesita-

SITE OF THE BLACK HOLE OF CALCUTTA
Within the railings shown in this picture is enclosed the site of the ghastly dungeon known as the ' Black Hole' at Fort William, Calcutta. On June 20, 1756, the nawab of Bengal, to whom the British fort had surrendered, confined 146 prisoners in this narrow space. Only 23 survived until the morning.

tion. Great Britain and Prussia signed the defensive Treaty of Westminster in January, 1756 ; in May France and Austria signed the defensive Treaty of Versailles. Both Prussia and Austria excluded the oversea quarrels of Great Britain and France from their bargains. And every one was arming hastily.

The first move was made by France against England ; in itself it involved none of the other powers. A French squadron sailed from Toulon for Minorca. The English admiral in the Mediterranean would not risk a decisive engagement, and Minorca fell to the French. Byng was tried for his blunder, condemned, and shot on his own quarter-deck. In America the French governor Montcalm attacked and captured two British forts. In India a native potentate, the nawab of Bengal, seized Fort William, shut his prisoners up in a small windowless chamber, and forgot them—most of them died that night in the famous ' Black Hole of Calcutta.' For Great Britain, 1756 was a year of disaster.

France had started a war of her own with Britain, where the government remained in a condition of utter confusion till the voice of the country irresistibly summoned William Pitt to the helm at the midsummer of 1757. Within six months of the first outbreak Frederick started the war on the Continent. He was thoroughly aware that Austria was only waiting to attack till the armies of

THE ELDER PITT
Richard Brompton's portrait shows William Pitt, earl of Chatham (1708–1778), a man of integrity in a corrupt age. His conduct of the Seven Years' War, in collaboration with Frederick the Great, restored Britain's foreign prestige.
*National Portrait Gallery, London*

Russia, France, Saxony and others were ready to act in concert, and he resolved to strike first. Bohemia was his objective, and the way to Bohemia lay through Saxony. In August he invaded Saxony and marched on Dresden. His sole excuse was the certainty that Saxony was in the league against him. The Saxons blocked his passage at Pirna. Relief from the Austrians came too late. They were starved into surrender ; Frederick occupied Dresden and impressed the Saxons into his own service. But they had held him up long enough to deprive his attack on Bohemia of surprise.

In the spring of 1757 the whole coalition was moving upon Frederick from every side ; the only cover he had was Hanover on his western flank. Austria, Russia and France, each of them had armies double the size of his own. His only chance was to attack them in detail with shattering blows, and so prevent their concentration. Saxony, at any rate, was off the board.

As soon as possible he flung himself on Bohemia and won a brilliant victory

**FRENCH FOREIGN MINISTER**

The duc de Choiseul (1719–85), shown in this portrait after Louis-Michel Van Loo, directed French foreign policy during the Seven Years' War. His efforts to revive the French fleet received a crushing blow at Quiberon Bay in 1759.

*Musée de Versailles*

before Prague in May. But Prague defied him ; a month later, attempting too much, he suffered a disastrous defeat at Kolin and had to retreat to Prussia. The slowness of the Austrian commander saved him from immediate destruction. The covering army of German auxiliaries on the Weser under Cumberland was defeated by the advancing French force at Hastenbeck, and was forced to capitulate at Kloster Zeven in September.

### Brilliant Victories of Frederick

A SECOND French army advanced upon Saxony ; but Frederick enticed it to a pitched battle at Rossbach in November, and won a brilliant victory against greatly superior numbers. Meanwhile, the Austrians were pouring over Silesia— the activities of the Russian army had been fortunately checked by a report that the tsaritsa was dying and that on her death the Russian policy would be reversed. A month after Rossbach Frederick won, over the Austrians in Silesia, a victory even more brilliant at Leuthen. The French first army had not turned its success to account, and the army on the Weser under a new commander, Ferdinand of Brunswick, was joined by a substantial British contingent. The news had not yet arrived of Clive's great victory in June over the nawab of Bengal at Plassey, which practically placed the rule of that great province in the hands of Clive himself.

Clive's victory did not affect the war in Europe ; Frederick's brilliant victories could do little more than relieve now on one front and now on another the pressure which would be renewed as soon as his back was turned. But in 1758 Pitt's methods at last came into full play. The fleet distracted France by perpetual descents upon the naval ports which, though they came to little enough, kept masses of French troops perpetually locked up. The tsaritsa had recovered, and the renewed Russian advance was checked by a hard-won victory at Zorndorf, while the Austrians were advancing into Saxony ; and when Frederick dashed back to oppose them he met with a defeat, and was again saved from disaster only

**BRITISH TRIUMPH IN AMERICA : THE CAPTURE OF QUEBEC**

The year 1759 witnessed a series of British victories of which the taking of Quebec was one of the most notable. This contemporary print shows the English ships advancing up the St. Lawrence to the spot where General Wolfe climbed the Heights of Abraham. The French forces, under Montcalm, were routed on the summit. Both Wolfe and Montcalm fell during the battle, but Wolfe rallied beneath his mortal wound long enough to know that the English were victorious.

by the excessive caution of their commander, Daun.

In 1759 the toils were tightening about Prussia, for to Frederick victories were only less exhausting than defeats, since his enemies had incalculably larger reserves to draw upon. France, however, was becoming practically absorbed in the duel with Great Britain, which in this year achieved a series of triumphs. She had a substantial share in the victory of Ferdinand of Brunswick at Minden (August) which drove the French permanently behind the Rhine ; in two engagements, off Lagos and in Quiberon Bay, she annihilated the French fleet, which the French minister, Choiseul, was zealously reviving ; and the hitherto indecisive campaigns in America were crowned by the capture of Quebec. In the second month of the next year, the French suffered their coup de grâce in India at Wandewash.

Frederick, however, met with a series of misfortunes. The Russians were again advancing ; he flung himself against them at Künersdorf ; not content with a hard-won victory, he tried to annihilate them ; they rallied, and the victory was turned into a complete rout. Again he

was saved by the expectation of a change of government in Russia. He had fallen into despair, but Russia's inaction revived his courage ; he failed, however,

**AN INDEPENDENT MONARCH**

Homely and blameless in private life, George III (1738–1820) was determined to direct policy, though he cannot be held responsible for all the misfortunes of his reign. This engraving by W. Holl is from the portrait by Sir T. Lawrence.

to prevent an Austrian advance into Saxony, which passed into their hands. But for his subsidies from England he could hardly have maintained the struggle ; as matters stood he was still able, though with difficulty, to hold his own and a little more against the Austrians alone through 1760 ; since the Russians did not move again and France was now wholly absorbed in the vain endeavour to strike at England.

No material change arose in the situation during the next year, apart from the facts that there was a new king in England, George III, that alarm was being taken in certain quarters at the country's enormous war expenditure, and that the retirement of the great war minister, Pitt, was clearly impending. On the Continent Russia was kept inert by the uncertainties of her domestic situation ; it was impossible for Frederick to strike with the old vigour, and Austria, which had never at any time known how to make use of any advantage she gained, was suffering from the lassitude of exhaustion.

### Futile Intervention of Spain

CHOISEUL, the French minister, was about to play his last card, by bringing Spain into the war. Ferdinand, the successor of Philip V, was a resolutely pacific monarch, bent not on aggression but on recuperation. Spain's ' vigorous ' foreign policy had ceased with his accession while the War of the Austrian Succession was still in progress, and Ferdinand remained deaf to every invitation to join leagues or embroil himself in the quarrels of his neighbours. But in 1759 Ferdinand died. The heir was his half-brother Carlos of Naples. A condition on which he had received his Italian kingdom was that the Spanish and Sicilian crowns should never be united. Succeeding in Spain as Carlos III, he resigned the Sicilies to his younger son Ferdinand.

Like his elder brother, Carlos cared more for wise administration than for aggression, but against England he cherished an ineradicable grudge. In 1762 Spain declared war against England. In fact, the sole result was to lay her own colonies at the mercy of the British fleet, which set about appropriating them one by one. Her intervention was not even an embarrassment. But Pitt had already resigned, and vigorous action on the part of the British government was no longer to be looked for.

### Russian Situation favours Frederick

OF very much greater importance was the death of Tsaritsa Elizabeth, which set on the throne her nephew Peter III of Holstein, who had made a hero out of his aunt's bugbear Frederick the Great. For the moment Russia became Frederick's active ally, just as the new government in England was persuading itself that it had no obligations to Prussia. The British subsidies were withdrawn, and Frederick was thereby transformed into a bitter enemy of the power without whose help in the past he must have been annihilated, but which was undoubtedly in a great degree indebted to him for the overwhelming character of her own triumphs. Six months after his accession, Peter was deposed and put to death by his wife, Catherine II ; but though she withdrew her support from Frederick she declined to renew the alliance with Austria ; and Frederick still proved himself more than a match for his inveterate enemy.

Great Britain, Prussia and Russia acting in concert could have prolonged the war to their own territorial advantage and with the certainty of success. The British government could have imposed almost any terms it chose upon France and Spain, and Austria isolated must have yielded to her pressure. But Russia did not mean to fight, and King George and his ministers were eager only for peace. By the terms of the treaties of Paris and Hubertusburg (February, 1763), Great Britain, enormous as were her spoils, restored much that she could legitimately have claimed from France or Spain by ' right of conquest ' ; but except by the British government itself her moderation was attributed not to magnanimity but to a pusillanimous economy. She left Frederick to take care of himself, and he remained in possession of precisely what he possessed when the war began ; the Saxon, Austrian and

Russian territories also remained as before. Prussia's position was completely established, Austria's position was unchanged.

Apart from the enormous wastage of the Seven Years' War, the one serious sufferer was France, who found herself shut out of both North America and India ; the one power which had made positive gains was Great Britain, left without a rival in North America or a European rival in India, where the East India Company was now definitely recognized as one among several territorial powers ; while by the treaty she recovered the one serious loss with which the war had opened —her Mediterranean naval station, Minorca.

Every one of the powers was suffering from exhaustion except Russia ; none was ready to enter upon a new armed conflict. Nearly thirty years passed before there was another general European conflagration, the outcome of the French Revolution. Yet, before that event took place, the British Empire had on the one hand been rent in twain, and on the other had established its footing, though not yet its irresistible ascendancy, in India ; and the intervention of France in the American quarrel had brought the Revolution itself appreciably nearer. During the same period the new application of power to machinery in England and Scotland was developing the industrial revolution which was to change the economic basis of the world.

### Problems occupying Great Britain

GREAT Britain after the Peace of Paris ceased to interest herself in the affairs of Europe at large. She was absorbed in two constitutional struggles ; one directly concerning the relations between the crown, parliament and the electorate, the other the relations between the mother country and her colonies ; while incidentally she was forced to make tentative efforts to deal with the new obligations imposed on her by the unprecedented situation in India. Her three problems, domestic, colonial and Indian, directly concerned no one but herself, though the two latter presently brought her into conflict with France, which saw in her troubles the opportunity at least of avenging, and possibly of recovering, her own lost position in the West and in the East, though bringing herself thereby to the verge of bankruptcy.

The industrial revolution was in effect a world revolution which had its birth in Britain at this time, because it was there that the inventions were made which multiplied production by the substitution of machinery, driven first by water power and then by steam power, for tools or instruments operated by hand, and the accompanying substitution of iron and steel for wood ; while there also the necessary iron could be produced in abundance, and in proximity to the great coalfields from which the fuel required for the new manufacturing processes could be procured. The British mercantile marine was already the world's carrier ; the new development of the machinery of which Britain had the practical monopoly turned the island into the world's workshop ; and the simultaneous development of Adam Smith's new economic doctrine of wealth, displacing the hitherto unchallenged mercantilist creed, rapidly enriched—though for a time at the expense of the welfare of the labouring classes—the country, which was

**A GREAT ECONOMIST : ADAM SMITH**
A portrait medallion by Tassie shows Adam Smith (1723–90) in profile. His reputation rests chiefly on his Wealth of Nations (1776), a powerful defence of free trade.
*Scottish National Portrait Gallery ; photo, Annan*

already much wealthier than its Continental rivals.

The domestic problem turned upon the attempt of George III, fore-shadowed by Charles II, to recover the supremacy of the crown, not by overriding parliament after the fashion of Charles I and James II, but by himself procuring that power of controlling parliamentary majorities which the great land-owning Whig families had been able to exercise for half a century. Within ten years of his accession, George had attained his object ; for some twelve years the king's ministers were the men of his own

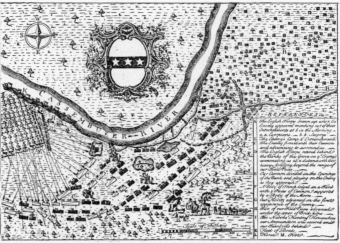

**PLAN OF THE BATTLE OF PLASSEY**

Robert Clive's brilliant victory over the nawab of Bengal, Surajah Dowlah, on June 23, 1757, at Plassey, made the British masters of Bengal. This plan gives the disposition of the opposing armies. The enemy's camp and entrenchments are on the right, while Clive's forces are drawn up on the outskirts of a grove on the left.

*Memorials of the Revolution in Bengal,* 1760

choice and were supported by unfailing parliamentary majorities ; then the system broke down because the ' king's friends ' proved intolerably incapable administra-

**FIRST GOVERNOR OF BRITISH INDIA**

The forceful policy pursued by Warren Hastings (1732–1818), first governor-general in British India, in a difficult situation, evoked criticism, a protracted trial and, finally, in 1795, acquittal. This portrait is by Sir T. Lawrence.

*National Portrait Gallery, London*

tors ; the king chose a minister who was never a figure-head and presently became a dictator, and the new royalist system went the way of the old Whig system. Both rested upon recognized methods of corruption which, effective in ordinary times, gave way in the face of intense public feeling ; the rights of free speech and free criticism having been established.

THE popular impression that Clive at the head of a handful of Englishmen overthrew a great empire and conquered India has not, perhaps, been wholly eradicated even now. In 1740 the Mogul empire was in a state of complete disinte-gration ; the great governorships had already become in effect independent kingdoms under Mahomedan rulers each of whom intended to establish his own dynasty, though none of them held his position by any kind of hereditary right. The Mogul had neither the power nor the will to control them, though they might occasionally appeal to his authority to provide a legal sanction for what they had done or intended to do.

British and French began to fight each other under the pretext of maintaining the lawful authority of rival claimants to governorships ; the result of the fighting was the elimination of French influence. The nawab of Arcot had become a puppet in the hands of the British at Madras ; their influence dominated the Nizam of Hyderabad. The crazy aggression of the half-mad nawab of Bengal had necessitated an armed expedition thither under Clive's leadership ; he had associated himself with a native conspiracy for the deposition of the nawab whose forces he routed at Plassey ; and he found that he had thereby made himself responsible for the preservation of law and order in that great province where he had in effect set up a new nawab. To retire was impossible, and to remain was profitable. He obtained legal sanction for the position of the East India Company as rulers of Bengal from the legal sovereign, the Mogul at Delhi, by negotiation. He and subordinate officers, Eyre Coote and Monro, established a reputation as invincible captains.

### British Government in India

Thus a company of traders in London found itself responsible for the administration of a huge province with a mixed population of millions of Hindus and Mahomedans, with laws, customs and diversities of religion for which Europe provided no parallel. A government had to be created, and the British government at home had an uneasy sense that it could not escape responsibility for the character of that government. The result was the enactment of the lame constitution of the ' Regulating Acts ' of 1773, under which Warren Hastings was made governor-general of the three British presidencies.

Clive had not conquered India. The British authority did not extend beyond Bengal, with the towns of Madras and Bombay and the immediately neighbouring districts. It did not extend even over Arcot. India was covered with potentates great and small, Hindu or Mahomedan. The Hindu Maratha confederacy was recovering from its disaster at the hands of Ahmad Shah, and was dominating central India and the Mogul himself at Delhi. Oudh under a nawab-wazir lay between Delhi itself and Bengal ; its

wazir had very soon made up his mind that the British were the rising power, and cultivated their friendship from fear of the Marathas. In the south, a Mahomedan adventurer, Haider Ali, was making himself master of the Hindu kingdom of Mysore. The Nizam, with the Marathas on two flanks and Mysore on another, also cultivated British friendship, for a similar reason, though not so whole-heartedly as the Oudh wazir. Over none of them had the British any authority. None of them wished to quarrel with the British ; but all looked at them askance as possibly useful allies but certainly dangerous rivals.

As for the British, neither the Madras government nor the Bombay government had the least compunction in traversing the policy of the governor-general and involving him in quite needless complications with the country powers ; his hands were tied by the Calcutta Council, nominated from London, who could and did habitually outvote him ; while he was obliged to raise from the country the necessary funds for administration, for maintaining the needful military establishment (mainly sepoys), and for

**HAIDER ALI KHAN**

The activities of Haider (or Hyder) Ali (c. 1722-82), a low-born adventurer who became the powerful sultan of Mysore, were an obstacle to British progress in India. This sketch of him was drawn by J. Leister in 1776.

**IN DEFENCE OF WARREN HASTINGS**

This satirical print by Gillray, published in 1786, represents Warren Hastings as the saviour of India repelling a violent assault made upon him by a gang of political banditti, Lord North, Burke and Fox. It satirises the impeachment of Hastings for the methods which he employed as governor.

providing a surplus out of which the Company might pay handsome dividends to its shareholders—besides working out the principles upon which administration must be organized. It is small wonder that he was driven occasionally to expedients excusable only on the grounds of sheer necessity : much more astonishing that he was able to create in Bengal a better government than it had known since the days of Akbar, to increase British prestige, to defeat the powers with which he was forced to fight, and to leave the British established as the ascendant power in India ; though he neither extended nor sought to extend the British territory. For which services he was duly impeached on his return to England in 1785. Pitt (the younger) had already passed the India Act, setting up the revised system of government that lasted till 1858.

Great Britain's first problem was merely a reactionary episode in the story of her constitutional development. The issue of her second problem was the European penetration of India. The issue of the third was the birth of a nation.

At the close of the seventeenth century the twelve British colonies in North America—Georgia had not yet come into being—were separate communities, each of them having a form of government modelled with diverse variations of detail on that of the English constitution at the accession of James I ; that is, before the developments which issued in the Revolution of 1688 ; with executives responsible not to the representative assemblies but to the governor who represented the crown. The assemblies taxed themselves for their own purposes ; but the royal prerogatives ran in the colonies as they ran in England.

The colonies held their privileges under charters granted by the crown, without detriment to the rights of the crown, which included that of regulating trade. Technically the charters implied that the ultimate inclusive rights of the English ' King in Parliament ' extended to the colonies ; but in practice it was assumed that the home government would no more claim to levy supplies—to tax for revenue—than the king in England could levy supplies by his own authority. The right of regulating trade, even when the regulation was avowedly intended to benefit English at the expense of colonial trade, was constantly practised, and its legality was never disputed, though it was resented as unjust and irksome. Ireland always, and Scotland until the Union of 1706–7, had a similar grievance, though England claimed to regulate trade not in, but only with, Scotland. The Revolution in England brought no change ; but the doctrines laid down at the Revolution were clearly incompatible with the right, never abrogated but never practised, to levy revenue otherwise than by consent of those from whom the taxes were levied, given by their representatives : the doctrines summed up in the phrase ' no taxation without representation.'

Not only technically then but actually the ' rights ' of the colonies remained after the Revolution as they had been before it ; whereas in England the powers of parliament as against the crown had very substantially advanced, however the

HISTORIC MEETING OF THE FRENCH STATES-GENERAL AT VERSAILLES IN 1789

The refusal of the Parlement of Paris to register fiscal edicts led to the convocation of the French States-General on May 5, 1789. The last States-General had been summoned in 1614 and the rarity of the event made the occasion especially notable. This engraving by Helman, after C. Monet, the court painter, shows the assembly of the three estates of nobles, clergy and commons before Louis XVI at Versailles. The first and all-absorbing question facing the members concerned procedure, and discussion arose as to the method of voting. It was finally agreed that the deputies should deliberate in a single chamber.

*Photo, W. F. Mansell*

parliamentarians might claim that the revolution settlement only gave statutory form to what had always been the law. The colonies had not acquired for themselves the liberties which the English parliament had acquired for itself in the struggle with the Stuarts ; and the fact was a constant source of irritation, somewhat mitigated by the deliberate abstention of the home government for fifty years from anything beyond the most perfunctory enforcement of its own regulations. Moreover, whatever irritation the colonists might feel, they also felt that their grievances were the price they paid for security under the British flag against the increasingly aggressive expansion of the French colonies on the St. Lawrence and the Mississippi. In the last resort they had behind them in that rivalry British troops and the British navy. The result was shown in the Seven Years' War. British troops and the British navy removed the Canadian menace—but by so doing they also removed the principal reason which had induced the colonies to submit to the grievances. Colonial loyalty to the empire now was certain to break down unless the grievances themselves were removed.

### Friction with the American Colonies

INSTEAD of removing the grievances, the British government, alarmed by the debts it had incurred through the war, and hunting for additional sources of revenue, began to enforce vigorously the trade regulations which in practice had become almost a dead letter. Then it put forward a novel though by no means unwarrantable demand that the colonies should make a voluntary contribution to the expenses of the war by which they had so greatly profited ; coupled with the unfortunate threat that if the voluntary contribution were insufficient a compulsory contribution would be levied. Then the compulsory contribution was levied by Grenville's Stamp Act, palpably and avowedly a tax to raise revenue for the British Treasury.

Pitt, now out of office, Burke the rising orator, and many others recognized the injustice or the folly, or both, of the government measures ; in America public opinion was, of course, solid, but unfortunately found expression in action actually illegal, or legal but palpably hostile. Grenville was forced to resign and a new ministry repealed the Stamp Act, but was immediately ejected. Pitt formed a new ministry, accepted the title of earl of Chatham, and forthwith became incapacitated for the conduct of the government by gout. The ministry was without leadership except such as it got from King George ; it went on to substitute for the Stamp Act a series of duties trivial in themselves, as, in fact, the Stamp Act had been, but open to the same criticism. Exasperation, agitation, retaliation, denunciation developed rapidly on both sides of the Atlantic ; the king was obstinate, the Americans became every day more hostile. Boston in particular set the law at defiance ; the British government retaliated by suspending the charter of Massachusetts and closing the port of Boston.

The colonies had no central government, but they created one for themselves. Representatives from nearly all of them

ADVOCATE OF THE COLONISTS

Sir Joshua Reynolds painted this portrait of Edmund Burke (1729–97), who consistently advised an indulgent colonial policy. His speeches urging the conciliation of the American colonies are considered his masterpiece.

*National Portrait Gallery, London*

assembled in a congress at Philadelphia ; it had no legal powers, but was at once treated almost universally as the sovereign authority, the only one which could be acknowledged in the existing emergency. The home government would certainly apply coercion and the colonies armed to resist coercion. Peace-makers endeavoured to make themselves heard on both sides, but their voices were drowned by the agitators and the reactionaries. The British government persisted in its belief that resistance would collapse in face of a small display of force. A troop of soldiers was sent by the governor of Massachusetts to destroy an arms depot at Concord ; on its return it was fired upon by colonial sharpshooters, who inflicted on it considerable loss without suffering any themselves. The skirmish of Lexington opened the War of American Independence (April, 1775).

**AMERICAN COMMANDER IN CHIEF**
At the outbreak of the American War of Independence George Washington (1732–99) was appointed to the chief command of the American forces, and his skilful generalship largely contributed to their success. In 1789 he became the first president of the United States.
*Painting by John Jenninbull*

The newly acquired colony of Canada showed no disposition to make common cause with the old British colonies. The population was mainly French, and under the new British rule it enjoyed practically all the liberties to which it was accustomed under the French system. Its religion was Roman Catholic, whereas the northern British Colonists were the descendants of the English Puritans. The English governor had not attempted to Anglicise its French institutions ; it had no traditions of parliamentary government ; it was, in consequence, not hostile to its British rulers, and had no sympathy with the motives which inspired the British colonies to rebellion, no desire to be assimilated to them—which would have been the inevitable result of union with them. When those colonies tried to win them over, the attempt recoiled on their own heads. So far as Canada entered into the war, it was as a military base for the British.

### The American War of Independence

AT the outset, public opinion in America was not yet determined upon separation, and a very substantial body of public opinion in England denounced the war and sympathised with the colonists. Being in arms against the government, they must be forced to give way—but to fight them at all was very much against the grain. No energy was thrown into the campaigning ; no large forces were raised to effect an immediate and decisive conquest. British regulars, supplemented by soldiery hired from Germany, or still more unhappily by Red Indian allies, would bring them to submission, since their own troops were merely civilian volunteers, without military discipline, called away from their normal avocations which they could not afford to desert for long, and commanded by amateurs. The amateur-in-chief appointed by the Congress was George Washington.

The resistance, however, did not collapse. With inexhaustible patience and infinite tact, Washington, loyally supported by the Congress, kept together the troops, which were elated by finding that they could hold their own against the regulars. Fifteen

### THE MARQUESS CORNWALLIS

Painted by Gainsborough, this portrait of Charles Cornwallis (1738–1805) shows a man of character and integrity. Leader of a British force in America, he was compelled to capitulate to the French and Americans at Yorktown.

*National Portrait Gallery, London*

alliance with the Americans, sent them troops, successfully challenged the supremacy of the British fleet in American waters, and thereby turned the scale decisively in their favour. One British force was shut up in New York, while a second under Cornwallis was endeavouring to conquer the south. As it was too small to plant garrisons, Cornwallis might win but could not hold what he had won. He retreated to Yorktown ; but a larger French squadron was there first. Cornwallis was blockaded on the land side by troops drawn from before New York, on the sea side by the French, and he was forced to surrender (October, 1781). As far as concerned American independence the fall of Yorktown was decisive.

But Britain was by this time fighting not so much for victory over the Americans as for her life, so completely had the situation changed since the days of Pitt's supremacy. She had no friends ; she had her old enemies ; she had incurred by her conduct at the end of the Seven Years' War the ill will of her former ally, Frederick. France, with a new navy, had opened her attack in 1778 ; Spain had followed suit in 1779, and was endeavouring

months after Lexington the Congress had made up its mind and issued the Declaration of Independence which definitely made separation the American goal. In 1777 came a decisive event. The British commander, Sir William Howe, had one plan of campaign which he carried out. The British government had another ; the attempt to carry out the latter while the former was in progress was a disastrous failure resulting in the surrender of a British force at Saratoga, which proved that bringing the colonists to submission would be a much more difficult matter than had been anticipated and deprived Howe's success of all its value.

But it did more ; it brought the Americans an ally. France had been watching the conflict with interest. Saratoga suggested that intervention on behalf of the colonists would almost certainly deal a deadly blow to the power of Great Britain. Choiseul had once again given France a powerful navy : the British navy was still powerful, but maladministration had seriously weakened it. France entered the war in 1778 in

### ADMIRAL SIR GEORGE RODNEY

The victory won by Sir George Rodney (1718–92) over the French fleet off Dominica in April, 1782, was the crowning achievement of a distinguished naval career. This portrait of him is by Sir Joshua Reynolds.

*National Portrait Gallery, London*

to recover Gibraltar and Minorca ; the enemy fleets in European waters were already larger than her own when the Dutch joined the circle of her foes in 1780, and the fleets of the other Baltic powers were threatening to come in.

The disaster of Yorktown, however, was followed by a naval recovery. The intended junction of the French and Spanish fleets was foiled by a decisive action off the Saints in the West Indies, in which Rodney broke up the French fleet (April, 1782) ; Gibraltar was relieved and the grand attack on it of the Spaniards was foiled in October ; the Dutch fleet had already been put out of action by its losses in a stubborn fight off the Dogger Bank in 1781. These victories came too late to affect the American situation, but they recovered for Great Britain the ascendancy on the seas which she had lost for a time, and was in danger of losing permanently. A new government in England was ready to acknowledge American independence. Peace preliminaries were signed with the Americans in November, 1782, and with France and Spain in February, 1783, the Treaty of Versailles following in the same year.

Minorca was lost to Spain, Senegal and Gorée in Africa, with the island of Tobago, to France. The British conquests from the Dutch in the East Indies were restored. Apart from the sundering of the British Empire there was little enough to show as the result of seven years' fighting. William Pitt the younger came into office and set about the restoration of the national finances with amazing success, while France sank deeper and deeper into the financial morass in which she had been immersed by her military policy ; of which her participation in the American War had been the last and perhaps the most fatal manifestation. Some five years after the Peace of Versailles—in 1788— Great Britain almost unconsciously began her next stage of colonial development by annexing the Australian continent, where hitherto no European settlement had been attempted.

### Events in Russia and Poland

IN 1762 Catherine II became tsaritsa. In 1765 the emperor Francis died and was succeeded by his eldest son, Joseph II, while the grand duchy of Tuscany went to his second son Leopold. The Hapsburg possessions remained under the rule of their mother, Maria Teresa, and her minister, Kaunitz, though formally she associated Joseph with herself. The actual

**RELIEF OF GIBRALTAR : ENGLISH FLEET BRAVES SPANISH BATTERIES**

Disastrous as was the issue of the War of American Independence to Great Britain, yet towards the end of the struggle some memorable victories restored her naval ascendancy. This illustration, which appeared in the European Magazine in 1782, depicts the relief of Gibraltar by the English fleet under Admiral Darby on April 12, 1781, and gives a perspective view. Stores for the starving garrison were landed amid a heavy bombardment, all the Spanish batteries having opened fire.

**WILLIAM PITT THE YOUNGER**

Thomas Gainsborough painted this portrait of the gifted William Pitt (1759–1806), who became prime minister at the age of 24. He was distinguished for his brilliant oratory and unfailing devotion to his country's interests.

*Iveagh Bequest; photo. Pullman*

rule did not pass to him till her death in 1780. Some vigour and vitality were restored to the Swedish kingdom by the accession in 1771 of Gustavus III, who effected a coup d'état whereby the power of the crown, in abeyance for the last half century, was recovered. Augustus III of Poland and Saxony died in 1763 ; the youth of his sons prevented their candidature for the Polish succession to which Stanislaus Lecszinski (who died in 1766) made no claim ; and the Polish crown was secured by Catherine of Russia for her creature and puppet, Stanislaus Poniatowski.

The main objects of Catherine's foreign policy were two—to establish Russian domination in Poland, and to expand the Russian power at the expense of Turkey. In both projects Austria had a lively interest, because Poland and trans-Danubian Turkey were buffers between her and Russia, which she did not wish to be removed. In Poland, Frederick II had a lively interest, because Polish Prussia, which he wanted for himself, lay between his own East Prussia and Brandenburg.

Polish Prussia under Russian control would always be a potential menace to the Prussian kingdom.

Poland herself was a menace to the general peace, not because of her strength, but because of her weakness. Theoretically she was a monarchy ; virtually she was an aristocratic republic, because the crown had no power. Her sovereign was the diet of nobles ; but Protestants and Orthodox ' Greeks ' were excluded from all public office ; and the power of the diet was limited by the ' liberum veto '— any legislation could be vetoed by a single vote. There was a constitutional party which wanted to reorganize the political system and make it practically workable. There was a ' dissident ' party which desired to enfranchise the non-Catholics. There was a party which wanted no change because any change would place some sort of limiting control over them.

Catherine wanted control in Poland, and being an Orthodox Greek she favoured the dissidents. Frederick wanted control, and as a Protestant he, too, favoured the dissidents. Neither favoured the con-

**JOSEPH THE BENEVOLENT**

This painting by Anton von Maron shows Joseph II of Austria (1741–90), eldest son of Maria Teresa, and her successor in 1780. He was industrious and beneficent, but his reforms for the people's welfare were not appreciated.

*Photo. Kunstverlag Wolfrum*

**FIRST PARTITION OF POLAND**

A contemporary engraving by Le Mire satirises
the partition of Poland between Russia, Austria
and Prussia in 1772, and shows Catherine II,
Maria Teresa, Joseph II and Frederick II
apportioning the spoils with the aid of a map.
*Bibliothèque Nationale ; photo, Giraudon*

stitutionalists, because Frederick wanted
Poland kept weak, and Catherine wanted
a government which she could control
either in person or through her nominee.
The third party could call themselves
' patriots,' because they were opposed to
foreign influences altogether. Catherine
had got Stanislaus on to the throne,
because he was connected with the leading
constitutionalists, who expected him to
give effect to their policy, which they
soon found that Catherine would by no
means permit.

The scheme Frederick had in mind was
an agreed partition of Poland, which
would, however, probably involve taking
Austria into the syndicate. Nobody else
would interfere, Great Britain and France
being preoccupied. From this point of
view Russian friendship was immediately
essential to Prussia, while an increase
of Russia's power would make Austria's
friendship still more essential, in spite of
Maria Teresa's life-long hostility, in case
the other friend should find occasion

to turn enemy. Catherine preferred
Frederick's partnership to his hostility,
and she did not want Austria to intervene
in her anti-Turkish schemes.

Stanislaus, with Catherine behind him,
found himself forced to support the dissidents. Constitutionalists, and patriots
when they began to grasp the situation,
revolted. Russian troops intervened,
and in so doing violated Turkish territory.
Making this a casus belli, Turkey —
instigated but not aided by France
—declared war on Russia in the rôle
of liberator of Poland (1768). Russian
troops overran Wallachia. Turkey appealed to Frederick and the emperor
Joseph. Frederick had already made
overtures to Joseph, who did not share
his mother's hostility. The two were
actually in conference at Neustadt when
the Turkish appeal reached them in
1770. Frederick opened negotiations with
Catherine ; Kaunitz overcame the scruples
of Maria Teresa. In 1772 the treaty of
partition was signed. Russia retired from
Wallachia and took the biggest share of
the spoil. Frederick took West Prussia,
Austria took Galicia, and Stanislaus was
allowed to keep what was left of the
kingdom of Poland.

In 1774 the Russians won a victory over
the Turks which enabled Catherine to
dictate the treaty of Kuchuk Kainarji.
She kept faith with her allies and retired
from Wallachia on the Turkish promise
of full toleration for the Christians ; but
she retained Azov, with the right of free
navigation in Turkish waters.

### Frederick and the Holy Roman Empire

THE accord between Frederick and Joseph
did not last long. Joseph was one
of those idealists who do most honestly
desire to set a crooked world straight,
and are convinced that that aim will be
immediately accomplished under their
own dictatorship. As emperor he was
very far from being a dictator. To
establish his effective ascendancy he
must strengthen Austria ; to strengthen
Austria he wanted Bavaria ; the distant
Austrian Netherlands were a source rather
of weakness than strength. The reigning
Bavarian line was exhausted : Bavaria

reverted to the Palatinate branch of the house of Wittelsbach, and Joseph wanted to exchange the Netherlands for Bavaria. But he began by putting forward an ancient Hapsburg claim to the Bavarian succession. Frederick, on the other hand, while anxious to strengthen Austria as against Russia, intended Prussia, not Austria, to be the effective head of Germany. At the same time there was an increasing rapprochement between Joseph, who wanted a free hand in Germany, and Catherine, who wanted a free hand against Turkey ; this, too, was by no means what Frederick wanted.

So when Joseph backed his claim to the Bavarian succession by force, Frederick declared himself the champion of the constitutional rights of the German princes, and Joseph had to withdraw (1779). Then Joseph tried to strengthen his position in the Netherlands, where there was no love for the Austrian rule, by ousting the Dutch from the ' barrier fortresses' and compelling them to open the navigation of the Scheldt, where they had treaty-right of control. But here he was faced, not only by the Dutch, but by both French and British protests ; and when the Anglo-French war ended France, Britain and Prussia united to guarantee the treaty rights of the Dutch in the Scheldt by the treaty of Fontainebleau (1784), which was torn up by the French republican government eight years later, with momentous consequences. But here, again, Joseph was foiled, though the barrier fortresses were evacuated.

Joseph's next move was to arrange, instead of enforcing, the exchange of the Netherlands for Bavaria ; again Frederick intervened as the constitutional champion and formed a league of the German princes, the ' Fürstenbund' (1785), to resist imperial aggression ; and again Joseph was foiled. Frederick had actually achieved for Prussia the hegemony within the Empire. But what he had achieved was not secure. Next year he died, and the nephew, Frederick William II, who succeeded him, was not the man to carry Frederick's ambitions to completion. Eighty years passed before the Prussian supremacy was established.

In the next year (1787) war again broke out between Russia and Turkey. Catherine the astute had no intention of arousing the antagonism of the other powers to her aggressions ; as in the case of Poland, she preferred to get what she wanted for herself, bribing them, if necessary, with a share of the spoils. Joseph swallowed the bait, and the Austrian declaration of war with Turkey followed the Russian. When the States-General met in France in 1789, Austria was engaged in a war in which her own armies were being beaten by the Turks, while the Turks were being beaten by the armies of the tsaritsa.

BEFORE tracing the course of events in France between the Peace of Paris and the meeting of the States-General we must deal briefly with those in the Spanish peninsula. In Spain, Carlos III succeeded his half-brother Ferdinand VI in 1759, resigning Sicily to his younger son. His hostility to England involved him in the last phase of the Seven Years' War, and again brought him, in the wake of France, into war with Great Britain (1779–82). The Peace of Paris left him still in

**FREDERICK THE GREAT**
This striking portrait is of Frederick the Great in later life, at about the time when he was forming the Fürstenbund or league of German princes. The facial expression reveals both the strength and the cynicism of the ambitious Prussian monarch.

possession of the conquests the British fleet had achieved while the peace negotiations were in progress, and the Peace of Versailles restored Minorca to Spain. Otherwise his reign, like his brother's, was mainly devoted—with considerable success —to administrative and financial reforms ; his death in 1788 left the crown to a son, Carlos IV, who unhappily proved wholly incapable of carrying on the father's useful work.

In Portugal a brilliant minister, Pombal, also carried out reforms, but of a character too drastic to last after his hand was withdrawn. But it was Pombal in Portugal who led the way in breaking down the political power of the Jesuit organization which had for so long exercised an immense influence, especially among the Latin peoples. The lead given by Pombal in Portugal was followed both in Spain and in France ; so that in 1773 Pope Clement XIV was induced to issue an official decree suppressing the order. The society in fact survived the decree, and recovered some of its influence, but never to the old extent.

**PORTUGUESE STATESMAN**
Chief minister of Joseph I of Portugal, the marquess of Pombal (1699–1782) carried out drastic internal reforms and successfully attacked the Jesuit organization in his country.
*From John Smith, ' Memoirs of Pombal '*

THE French Revolution, which was inaugurated by the meeting of the States-General on May 5, 1789, was the product of many causes—political, social, economic, speculative—some of long standing, some of recent development, and each contributing in its degree its respective quota ; here we are in the main concerned with the political outline from 1763 to 1789.

France in the Seven Years' War had suffered heavy losses ; her treasury was depleted ; the normal peace expenditure was greatly in excess of the normal peace revenue ; yet she laboured under a very heavy load of taxation, nearly all of which was borne by those who were least able

to bear it. Technically her peasants were not for the most part in a state of serfdom, but practically they were hardly less at the mercy of their seigneurs than if they had been, and they lived in a state of grinding poverty from which there was no escape. The first necessities for the country were the release of industry from its fetters, the relief of those who bore the burden of taxation by something approaching an equitable distribution of that burden, and the reduction of that burden by a rigid economy. The failure of successive governments to effect the necessary reforms made the Revolution inevitable : and in the meantime the empty treasury made a vigorous foreign policy wholly impracticable.

Choiseul, the minister who had risen to the chief control during the war, could do no more than tinker with the rotten financial system, while endeavouring to restore efficiency in the national services. In that particular reform he was so successful that the fleet of his creation was able, after he had been retired, to play a very effective part in the American War. But Frederick and Catherine could work out their plans in the east of Europe without fear of French intervention. Choiseul was dismissed in 1770 because he refused to bow down to the last and the most despicable of the king's mistresses. There was no one of equal capacity to take his place. The Paris Parlement, supported by the provincial parlements, tried to assert itself, but with the object not of tackling financial reform but of getting more political power into its own hands. There was no other check upon the crown's absolutism; and the result was the suppression of the parlements.

In 1774 Louis XV died. Louis XVI was a young man who would have meritoriously adorned any private station ; his intentions were excellent, and his moral virtues were unimpeachable ; but he was quite incapable of devising or of carrying out the solution of an enormously difficult political problem. His queen was the clever, self-willed sister of the emperor ; the marriage was the outcome of the Austrian alliance, which was never popular in France ; and Marie Antoinette's imperial brother was imbued with the most elevated ideas of divine right. The queen's sympathies were entirely monarchical and aristocratic, and Louis was very much under her sway.

Something was to be hoped for when Maurepas became the king's minister and the financial direction was placed in the hands of Turgot, who set about reforms more drastic than the privileged classes would tolerate. Turgot's economies were sound but they deprived aristocrats of their sinecures. His free-trade measures loosened the industrial fetters, but at the expense of vested interests. He held back the country from plunging into the American War, but against its will. When he began to tax the noblesse, it was too much. Maurepas dared not support him, and he was dismissed after eighteen months (1776). Against his advice, the ministry had already sought popularity by reinstating the parlements, which proved not a help but a hindrance. Necker took Turgot's place ; the British disaster at Saratoga made the war party irresistible,

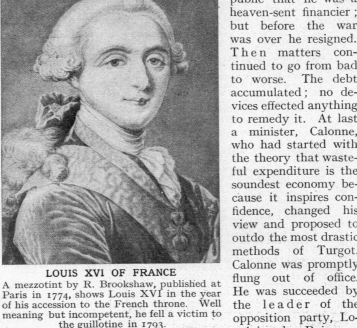

**LOUIS XVI OF FRANCE**

A mezzotint by R. Brookshaw, published at Paris in 1774, shows Louis XVI in the year of his accession to the French throne. Well meaning but incompetent, he fell a victim to the guillotine in 1793.

and for four years the debt piled up, while Parisian society lavished enthusiasm on the homespun-clad sons of liberty, the envoys from America. The name of liberty had not yet become ominous.

Necker had effected some economies, raised loans with surprising success, and produced an ingeniously misleading national balance sheet which convinced the public that he was a heaven-sent financier ; but before the war was over he resigned. Then matters continued to go from bad to worse. The debt accumulated ; no devices effected anything to remedy it. At last a minister, Calonne, who had started with the theory that wasteful expenditure is the soundest economy because it inspires confidence, changed his view and proposed to outdo the most drastic methods of Turgot. Calonne was promptly flung out of office. He was succeeded by the leader of the opposition party, Loménie de Brienne, though public opinion was already demanding the return of Necker. Brienne fared no better, for he had to propose new taxation which the Parlement refused to register ; and though it gave way under pressure, it met the next demand by itself demanding the summoning of the States-General—which had not met since 1614. The king yielded ; Brienne resigned ; Necker was recalled ; the instructions were issued for calling the Assembly of the Three Estates. On May 5, 1789, the curtain rang up for the drama of the Revolution.

# TABLE OF DATES FOR CHAPTER 28

**1789** George Washington first president of the United States of America.
May 5 : Meeting of the French States-General.
June 20 : the Tennis Court Oath.
,, 27 : Attempted coup d'état having failed, National (Constituent) Assembly is recognized, sitting as one chamber.
July 14 : Fall of the Bastille.
Aug. 4 : Abolition of feudal privileges and rights.
Oct. 5–6 : ' Insurrection of Women '; royal family moves from Versailles to Tuileries.

**1790** Joseph II d.; acc. Leopold II, whose second son Ferdinand succeeds in Tuscany. Leopold reverses his brother's policy, makes concessions in Hungary and Treaty of Reichenbach with Prussia.
The French Assembly attacks Church property and organization; celebration of new constitution on July 14.
India : Cornwallis at war with Mysore to 1792.

**1791** April 2 : Mirabeau d.
June 20 : Flight of Louis to Varennes, where he is stopped and brought back to Paris.
Aug. : Declaration of Pilnitz, regarded in France as threat of foreign intervention.
Sept. : Louis accepts new constitution.
Oct.: Constituent Assembly ends; Legislative Assembly begins.
Treaty of Sistowa (Turkey and Austria).
Canada separated into Upper and Lower.

**1792** Washington again president of U.S.A.
Cornwallis' Permanent Settlement (Bengal).
Jan. : Treaty of Jassy (Russia and Turkey).
March : Leopold d.; acc. Francis II, elected emperor July. Sweden : Gustavus III d.; acc. Gustavus IV.
April : France declares war on Austria.
July : Prussia declares war on France; Brunswick issues Coblenz manifesto.
Aug. 10 : Louis driven from Tuileries, where Swiss Guard die fighting; Assembly suspends monarchy and summons National Convention.
Aug. 23 : Prussians take Longwy.
Sep. 2–6 : ' September massacres ' in Paris.
,, 20 : Cannonade of Valmy; Prussians retire.
,, 21 : Convention meets; proclaims Republic.
Custine advances on the Rhine.
Nov. : Savoy and Nice annexed from Sardinia.
,, 6 : France decrees opening of Scheldt.
Dumouriez wins Jemappes and overruns Netherlands.
,, 15 : Decree to abolish all existing authorities where French armies are in occupation.
Dec. : Trial of Louis ' Capet.'
Godoy becomes Spanish minister.

**1793** Jan. 21 : Execution of Louis. Committee of Public Safety constituted.
Second Partition of Poland.
Feb. : War with England declared.
March : War with Spain declared.
Fall of Dumouriez. Revolutionary Tribunal created.
June : Arrest of Girondins. Committee of Public Safety reconstructed; Carnot ' organizer of victories.'
July : Marat assassinated by Charlotte Corday.
Sept. : Law of Suspects.
Oct. : Reign of Terror begins; execution of Marie Antoinette and Girondins. Fall and destruction of (royalist) Lyons.
Dec. : Fall of Toulon (Major Bonaparte).

**1794** Polish revolt of Kosciusco.
March 24 : Fall of Hébertists.
,, 30 : Arrest of Dantonists.
April 3 : Death of Danton. Robespierre supreme.
Ap.–July : Successes of Pichegru in the Netherlands. Prussia though subsidised by England remains inactive.
June 1 : Howe's naval victory; Vengeur legend.
,, 7 : Festival of the Supreme Being.
July 28 : Fall of Robespierre; ' Thermidorean reaction '; end of the Terror.
Oct. : Polish revolt crushed.
Dec. : Flight of Stadtholder William V to England. Pichegru's cavalry capture Dutch fleet.

**1795** Jan. : Third partition and end of Polish kingdom.
Feb. : Tuscany withdraws from coalition.
April : Treaty of Basel; Prussia withdraws.
May : Paris ' insurrection of Prairial' suppressed; Hoche in Brittany.
William V cedes Cape Colony to England for the period of the war. British occupation till 1802.
June : Dauphin (Louis XVII) d. Spain and Holland ally with France.
Oct. 5 : Insurrection and coup d'état of Vendémiaire. The Convention, having established the Directory, is dissolved.
Dec. : Failure of French campaign on Rhine, and of attempted invasion of Ireland.
Bonaparte appointed to Italian command.

**1796** Bonaparte in Italy.
April : Montenotte; Sardinia (Piedmont) retires.
May : Bridge of Lodi; gives Lombardy to French.
Bonaparte occupies Ferrara and Livorno.
Austrians are shut up in Mantua.
Oct. : French Danube campaign frustrated by Archduke Charles.
Nov. : Bonaparte defeats Austrians at Arcola.
Russia : Catherine II d.; acc. Paul I.
John Adams elected president U.S.A.

**1797** Jan. 15 : Bonaparte's decisive defeat of Austrians at Rivoli.
Feb. 2 : Capitulation of Mantua.
,, 14 : Spanish fleet broken up at St. Vincent.
Bonaparte forces treaty of Tolentino on pops.
Italian conquests formed into Cispadane and Cisalpine Republics.
Bonaparte defeats Archduke Charles at Tagliamento; advances to Leoben, where peace preliminaries with Austria are signed, April 18.
Sept. 4 : Coup d'état of Fructidor.
Oct. 6 : Dutch fleet defeated at Camperdown.
,, 14 : Treaty of Campo Formio; Great Britain isolated. Venice given to Austria.
Nov. : Congress set up at Rastadt.
Dec. : Frederick William II d.; acc. Frederick William III.

**1798** India : Mornington (Marquess Wellesley), governor-general (to 1805).
Roman and Helvetic Republics set up.
France annexes left bank of Rhine.
May : Bonaparte sails from Toulon, takes Malta and reaches Egypt (June), wins battle of Pyramids and enters Cairo (July 25).
June : Irish rising suppressed at Vinegar Hill.
Aug. 1 : Nelson finds and annihilates French fleet at Aboukir Bay (B. of the Nile). Isolation of Bonaparte in Egypt.
Nov. : Second coalition, joined by Austria, Russia, and Naples. French take Naples, Ferdinand securing himself in Sicily; and occupy Tuscany and Piedmont.

**1799** India, March–May : Mysore war and capture of Seringapatam.
March : French checked in North Italy.
Ap.–Aug. : Victories of Russians under Suvarov in Italy; Moreau conducts withdrawal. Break up of the Directory.
Sept. : Masséna defeats Korsakov at Zürich; Suvarov retreats through the Alps.
May–Oct. : Bonaparte foiled in Syria by failure to capture Acre. He deserts the army in Egypt, slips across the Mediterranean, and lands at Fréjus, Oct. 9.
Nov. 9 : Coup d'état of Brumaire; Sieyès' new constitution, remodelled, makes Bonaparte ' First Consul ' with autocratic powers under democratic forms.

**1800** Bonaparte crosses the St. Bernard and reconquers N. Italy by victory of Marengo (June 14). Tsar Paul makes secret agreement, but negotiations with Austria and Britain break down.
Sept. : British take Malta.
Dec. : Moreau defeats Austrians at Hohenlinden.
Ireland incorporated with Great Britain by Act of Union (June); first Parliament of the United Kingdom of Great Britain and Ireland meets next year.

# TABLE OF DATES (*continued*)

**1801** Feb. : Treaty of Lunéville strips Austria of territory and again leaves Britain isolated.
March : British expedition to Egypt. Resignation of Pitt (Catholic emancipation question). Revival of Armed Neutrality. Paul I murdered ; acc. Alexander I.
April : Battle of the Baltic.
May : Capitulation of French troops in Egypt.
Oct. : Peace preliminaries.
Holland becomes the Batavian Republic.
U.S.A. : Thomas Jefferson President.

**1802** Jan. : The Cisalpine becomes the Italian Republic, with Bonaparte president.
March : Peace of Amiens.
April : Bonaparte's concordat with pope.
Aug. : Napoleon declared Consul for life.
Sept. : Annexation of Piedmont and reorganization of Helvetic Republic. Diet of Ratisbon deals with German affairs.
Dec., India : treaty of Bassein with peshwa.

**1803** Jan. : Publication of Sebastiani's report on Egypt which alarms British government.
May : Declaration of war between France and England. Menace of invasion.
India : Maratha war ; battles of Assaye and Laswari.

**1804** Issue of Code Napoléon.
March : murder of duc d'Enghien.
May : Napoleon proclaimed emperor.
French occupy Hanover.
Pitt resumes office. Alexander seeks to form a new coalition.
Francis II assumes title ' Hereditary Emperor of Austria.'
Organization of Army of Invasion at Boulogne.
Napoleon crowns himself in presence of Pius VII.
Spain joins France.

**1805** April : Anglo-Russian league ; joined by Austria, Naples and Sweden.
Italian Republic makes Napoleon king.
March–July : Nelson's pursuit of Villeneuve.
Aug.: Completion of Coalition.
Sept. : Grand Army marches on Danube.
Oct. 20 : Capitulation of Ulm ; 21 : Trafalgar.
Nov. 13 : Vienna occupied.
Dec. 2 : Austerlitz ; 15 : Treaty of Schönbrunn with Prussia ; 26 : Treaty of Pressburg with Austria.

**1806** Jan. : Pitt d. British reoccupy Cape Colony.
Napoleon distributes kingdoms and principalities among his kinsfolk and marshals. Joseph k. of Naples, Louis k. of Holland, etc.
July : W. German states combined in Confederation of the Rhine, separated from Empire. End of Holy Roman Empire.
Oct. 9 : Prussia declares war ; 14 : Prussian army crushed at Jena and Auerstädt.
Nov. : Napoleon issues Berlin Decree for exclusion of British shipping and commerce from Europe (the ' Continental System ').

**1807** Britain retaliates with successive Orders in Council.
Russia supports Prussia ; Eylau (Feb.), Friedland (June).
April : British bombardment of Copenhagen.
July : Treaty of Tilsit ; humiliation of Prussia. Grand duchy of Warsaw set up.
Jerome Bonaparte k. of Westphalia.
Junot occupies Lisbon ; flight of Portuguese royal family to Brazil.

**1808** Napoleon makes Carlos IV and Ferdinand abdicate (Spain), giving crown to Joseph, whose place is taken at Naples by Murat.
Reforms of Stein (Prussia) and Stadion (Austria).
July : Spain revolts ; surrender of French force at Baylen. Great Britain intervenes in Portugal.
Aug : Vimeiro ; Convention of Cintra ; French evacuate Portugal. Peninsular war begun.
Oct. : Conference of Erfurt. Dismissal of Stein.
Napoleon's Spanish campaign. Moore attacks his communications (Dec.). Napoleon leaves Spain to Soult.
Russia takes Finland from Sweden.

**1809** Jan. : Moore's force embarked at Corunna ; Soult invades Portugal.
Austria declares war.
May : Confiscation of Papal States. Wellesley returns to Portugal ; expels Soult. Napoleon enters Vienna but is checked at Aspern.

**1809** July : Napoleon defeats Austrians at Wagram. Wellesley (Wellington) invades Spain ; wins Talavera but retreats to Portugal. Disastrous Walcheren expedition (British).
Oct. : Treaty of Vienna ; transfers of Austrian territory. Metternich's ascendancy begins.
Sweden : Gustavus IV deposed ; acc. Charles XIII.
U.S.A. : Madison president.

**1810** Louis k. of Holland deposed for admitting English commerce ; Holland annexed to France.
Napoleon divorces Josephine, m. Marie Louise of Austria.
Masséna in Peninsula ; takes Ciudad Rodrigo ; is checked at Busaco by Wellington, who falls back (Sept.) on Lines of Torres Vedras.
Bernadotte adopted as crown prince of Sweden.
British capture Isle of Mauritius.

**1811** Retreat of Masséna.
May : battles of Fuentes d'Oñoro and Albuera. Wellington again retires to Portugal.
Growing breach between Napoleon and Alexander, who breaks from the ' Continental System.'

**1812** Spanish provisional government at Cadiz draws up the ' Constitution of 1812.'
Wellington storms Ciudad Rodrigo and Badajoz.
Bernadotte as virtual ruler of Sweden joins Alexander.
June : French Grand Army invades Russian Poland.
July : Wellington defeats Marmont at Salamanca, but again has to retire.
Sept. : Retreating Russians make a stand at Borodino ; their defeat enables Napoleon to enter Moscow (14), which is set on fire.
Oct. 19 : Retreat from Moscow begins.
Nov. 27 : Battle of Bridge of Beresina.
Dec. 30 : Prussian commander Yorck makes convention of Tauroggen.
War between Great Britain and U.S.A., whose attempt to invade Canada is repulsed.

**1813** Feb. : Treaty of Kalisch between Russia and Prussia.
March : Prussia declares war.
May : Napoleon defeats allies at Gross Görschen and Bautzen.
June : Armistice of Poischwitz. Negotiations fail. Wellington wins decisive victory at Vittoria.
Aug. : Austria declares war ; Blücher's victory at Katzbach ; Napoleon's at Dresden.
Sept. : Allies renew agreement at Töplitz.
Oct. 16–18 : ' Battle of the Nations ' at Leipzig. Napoleon rejects peace terms.
India : Moira (marquess of Hastings) governor-general to 1822.

**1814** Wellington penetrates the Pyrenees.
Ferdinand VII, restored in Spain, abolishes the Constitution.
Allies invade France.
March 30 : Paris capitulates.
April 10 : Soult and Wellington at Toulouse.
11 : Napoleon abdicates ; is sent to Elba.
29 : Louis XVIII restored.
May 30 : Treaty of Paris ; French boundaries as in 1792 ; details referred to Vienna Congress.
June 2 : Louis issues the Charta.
Nov. : Vienna Congress meets. William of Orange made king of Holland and Belgium ; Norway transferred from Danish to Swedish crown ; Poland reconstituted as a kingdom for Alexander ; Sardinia reinstated ; Venice to Austria. Discord among the powers.
Dec. : Peace of Ghent ends Anglo-American war but leaves disputed questions unsettled.

**1814–16** India : Gurkha war.

**1815** March 1 : Napoleon escapes from Elba and lands at Cannes ; 13 : Vienna Congress declares him a public enemy ; 19 : Louis flies to Ghent : 30 : Napoleon at the Tuileries.
April and May : Napoleon rebuilds an army to strike before Austria and Russia can take the field ; Prussian army brought up under Blücher, Wellington in command of composite force in Belgium. Murat attacks Austrians in Italy unsuccessfully ; is expelled.
June 15 : Napoleon seizes Charleroi ; 16 : Strikes at Ligny, to split Wellington from Blücher, who is driven off the field but wheels to Wavre ; 18 : Attacks Wellington at Waterloo, but is held up through the day till Prussians arrive on his flank and his army is completely shattered.
July 15 : Napoleon surrenders, and is sent to St. Helena.

THE BATTLE OF AUSTERLITZ: NAPOLEON'S GREAT VICTORY OVER AUSTRIANS AND RUSSIANS

Napoleon's boast concerning the opposing forces at Austerlitz was no idle one. 'Avant demain au soir, cette armée est à moi,' he observed on December 1, 1805. On December 2 he overwhelmingly defeated the Austrians and Russians, killing or taking prisoner about 35,000 of their 83,000 troops, and capturing forty flags that were the standards of the Russian imperial guard. The result of this battle was to break up the anti-French coalition from which Pitt had hoped so much. The Russians withdrew and Austria signed the peace of Pressburg. This aquatint is by Duplessis-Bertaux.

### CHAPTER 28

# THE FRENCH REVOLUTION AND NAPOLEONIC AGE: 1789–1815

THE story of this chapter begins with the opening of the States-General at Versailles on May 5, 1789, and closes with the elimination of Napoleon as a factor in European politics at Waterloo on June 18, 1815. Throughout the whole period, as in the days of Louis XIV, the interest of European history is concentrated upon the activities of France; though at the same time in Asia India was passing under a Western ascendancy, and on the other side of the Atlantic a new nation was building itself up.

The immediate cause of the summoning of the States-General in 1788 was the necessity for dealing with a financial situation with which the king and his ministers had proved themselves unable to cope, in spite of the abilities with which Necker was credited. The Parlement demanded the States-General, on the theory that in view of the failure of ministers the country must deal with the problem. But it followed that the country must also deal with the problem of reforming the whole system of administration; and it was no less certain that the country, having been taken into consultation, would insist upon dealing not only with finance and administration, but with the grievance of the class privileges which were at the bottom of the trouble.

The appeal to the States-General, then, must be made an appeal not to one class or another, but to the nation. The chambers of the Three Estates—noblesse, clergy and commons—together represented the nation; but the first two represented each only a privileged class, forming together only a fraction of the nation, and that fraction which had hitherto foiled all attempts at reform. If the three chambers voted separately, those two would combine to resist any reform which touched their purses or their privileges and outvote the Third Estate, whose representation would be a farce, though its numbers equalled those of the other two together.

When the States-General was opened it was announced that the Three Estates would meet and vote separately. The Third Estate, led by Mirabeau, one of the few 'aristocrats' who had joined them, a man of battered moral reputation but great ability, at once joined battle, proclaiming that the three must sit and vote together. The Commons could then be sure of a general majority, as some of the minor clergy who had grievances of their own would vote with them, and also some few of the noblesse. They met to discuss not the prepared agenda but the present situation, the principle of political equality. They declared on June 17 that the one chamber was the National Assembly, whether the other two joined it or stayed away. Shut out from their hall on June 20, they nevertheless met and took the famous 'tennis-court oath' not to separate till they had won constitutional government. The king threatened to disperse them by force; they defied the threat, and he surrendered. Some of the clergy and of the aristocrats were already joining them. On June 27 Louis requested the other two chambers to join the National Assembly.

### Attack on the Old Regime in France

PARIS was seething with excitement; the troops were not to be trusted. German and Swiss troops were brought up. The excitement grew and came to a head on July 13, when the mob rose, marched on the Bastille (the great but feebly guarded prison-fortress which was the symbol of the old absolutism) and stormed it without difficulty. To Paris and to the world at large the fall of the Bastille seemed to signify the downfall of the 'ancien régime,' which rested upon the conviction that the force it could call into play was irresistible—but the Bastille had gone down like a house of cards.

The sober citizens of Paris organized in Paris a control to take the place of that which had collapsed—a commune, or

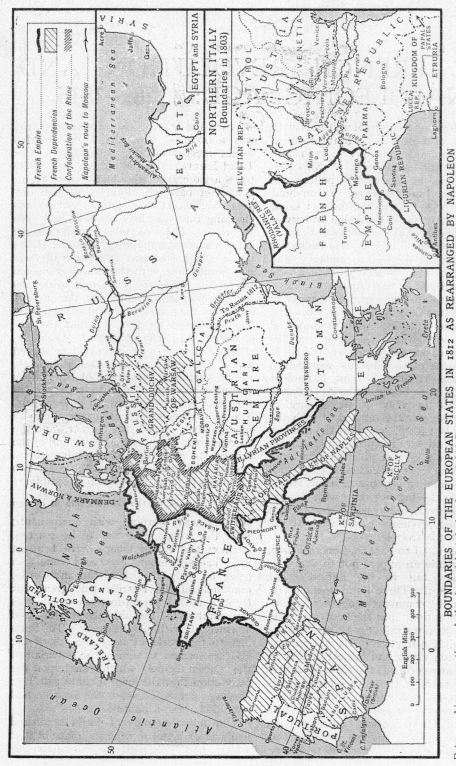

**BOUNDARIES OF THE EUROPEAN STATES IN 1812 AS REARRANGED BY NAPOLEON**

Between his assumption of the imperial style in 1804 and his Russian disaster in 1812, Napoleon extended French control in Europe over the area indicated here. The kingdom of Naples he bestowed on his brother-in-law Murat. Eugène Beauharnais acted as his viceroy in the kingdom of Italy, which had absorbed the northern Italian republics of Directory days, shown in the lower inset. The Grand Duchy of Warsaw absorbed part of Prussia. Although represented as a French dependency, because nominally ruled by Joseph Bonaparte, Spain from 1808 was in chronic revolt, only controlled by the presence of French armies engaged in the Peninsular War. Inability to wrest command of the sea from Britain defeated Napoleon's design to assimilate Egypt and Syria.

municipal government. The Commune enrolled a new national guard for the preservation of order, setting in command of it the popular young aristocrat Lafayette, champion of liberty, the French hero of the American War. And meanwhile the peasants in the country were rising against the seigneurs and burning their châteaux. There, too, national guards were being enrolled—but their sympathies were with the insurgents. The king's brothers and many of the aristocrats — the 'émigrés' of the next few years—fled from a dangerous country and were soon clamouring for foreign intervention. But

**FRENCH FINANCE MINISTER**
Appointed director-general of finances in 1788, Jacques Necker found the situation too difficult even for his undoubted abilities, and advocated the summoning of the States-General.
*Portrait by Duplessis; from Seidlitz, 'Porträtwerk'*

in Paris the Commune and its chiefs, the leaders of the Third Estate—reformers as yet, not conscious revolutionists—held control.

The National Assembly turned itself into the Constituent Assembly for the framing of a constitution and the abolition of grievances. On August 4, three weeks after the fall of the Bastille, it abolished all the privileges which had survived feudalism. It adopted Rousseau's doctrine of the Rights of Man as its fundamental principle, and went on to invent the ideal constitution, planned out with mathematical precision, taking the absolute separation of the

**PARIS MOB STORMS THE BASTILLE, SYMBOL OF ROYAL ABSOLUTISM**
On July 14, 1789, the populace of Paris rose, stormed the Bastille, and razed it to the ground.   To the frenzied mob this massive prison-fortress was the embodiment of royal autocracy and their own subjection, while its fall signified the collapse of the detested 'ancien régime.'   This drawing by Prieur (like that in page 644, an original drawing for one of his famous engravings) represents the chaotic scene in the smoke-shrouded courtyard during the attack.
*The Louvre; photo, Giraudon*

executive from the legislative as the basic law of sound government ; nevertheless, after a hot contest it was decided to allow the crown, the head of the executive, a suspensive veto on legislation.

Meanwhile the populace was clamouring not for an ideal constitution but for bread, of which there was a painful scarcity. On October 5 was witnessed the amazing procession of the women of Paris to the palace at Versailles ; the Commune could still keep male mobs in check but not a mob of women. The court had to remove from Versailles to the Tuileries, that its presence in Paris might be a guarantee that there should also be bread in Paris.

### Work of the Constituent Assembly

THE Assembly abolished the Parlement as being of no further use. It made a new division of the country into ' departments,' for administrative purposes, each being theoretically a self-governing area. Symmetry in form, uniformity in method, equality in numbers were the aims in view. Reform of the ecclesiastical system followed reform of the feudal system ; the Church was to be a department of the state, and the clergy its state officials ;

her lands were to be nationalised. Half the clergy refused the functions assigned to them and resigned, and the lower as well as the higher clergy were set in antagonism to what was manifestly revolution.

The privileges had gone ; but without consideration of the reasons which had brought them into being in days when they were not grievances but safeguards. With them had gone the whole of the old machinery of which they had formed a part ; a new and untried machinery had been set up, but it was not yet in working order. The disappearance of the privileges did not bring immediate relief of the popular discontents, and in fact probably intensified class hostility. The air was thick with suspicion and distrust. Mirabeau wanted to strengthen the executive— officially, the crown—while keeping it in touch with the legislature, the body representative of popular feeling with all its diversities ; but that meant that the king must be under the guidance of the strong man—Mirabeau. Actually the king was under the guidance of his reactionary court, who detested Mirabeau, while the extreme wing at least of the popular party suspected him of aristocratic leanings ;

FRENCH OATH OF LOYALTY AT THE FESTIVAL OF THE CHAMP DE MARS

At the suggestion of the municipality of Paris, the National Assembly decreed a general federation of all France to be held on the Champ de Mars on July 14, 1790, the anniversary of the fall of the Bastille. Deputations from all parts of the country attended and a vast assembly took the oath of fidelity to the constitution in the presence of the king and queen. This engraving by Helman is from the original drawing by Charles Monnet, painter to Louis XVI.

*Photo, W. F. Mansell*

**FLIGHT OF THE FRENCH ROYAL FUGITIVES ARRESTED AT VARENNES**

In June, 1791, Louis XVI, with his wife and children, attempted to escape in disguise from Paris, where they had been virtually held captive in the Tuileries. This contemporary aquatint represents the well known incident of the detection and arrest of the runaways at Varennes at eleven o'clock at night. A retired soldier recognized the king from his effigy on an assignat and stopped the progress of his carriage. The royal family were brought back to Paris the following day.

*Bibliothèque Nationale, Paris*

and the king himself, so long as he remained in Paris, was not a free agent.

In the summer of 1790 there was an enthusiastic display of harmony, when a vast concourse assembled on the Champ de Mars in the presence of royalty and all with acclamation took the oath of loyalty to the constitution. But beneath the surface the dissensions were growing more acute, fostered by the antagonistic political clubs, Cordeliers, Jacobins, Feuillants, and by the flood of pamphlets constantly issuing from the press. Still there was a moment when it seemed that an understanding between the queen and Mirabeau might effect a combination strong enough to control the situation; but the prospect, such as it was, vanished when Mirabeau suddenly broke under the terrific strain of his labours and died after a few days' illness, in April, 1791.

Less than three months had passed when the king took the fatal step of attempting flight. At Varennes, almost on the Netherlands border, he was recognized, stopped and taken back to Paris. The situation hardened. The flight from one point of view amounted to an abdication; from another it pointed to an appeal for foreign intervention; it was scarcely possible to reconcile it with loyalty to the new constitution. Extremists openly called for the establishment of a republic. But the 'Constituent' Assembly was constitutionalist, not republican; the moderates in it were the majority. It preserved order, and settled down to a revision of the constitution, which was formally accepted by Louis in September, arrangements having been made for the summoning of a new assembly.

The new body, distinguished as the 'Legislative Assembly,' was of a very different type. Expressly all the old members were excluded from it, though the old extremists found a field for themselves outside it, in the Paris Commune, which they dominated. But the most notable of the new members were the Girondists, the deputies from the Gironde, most of them filled with republican theories extracted from a somewhat perverted study of Roman history. But there was no present intention of subverting the revised constitution, which had further restricted the king's powers.

### European Reaction to the Revolution

UNHAPPILY, however, the new assembly came in at the moment when a spark had been struck which fired the train that kindled the great European conflagration, because it touched the inflammable material in France in a manner which had not been intended.

Europe had hitherto watched the progress of the revolution in France with varied feelings. In England it excited interest primarily as a commendable but undisciplined and uninstructed attempt to achieve for France at one stroke the constitutional government which England had achieved for herself in centuries of development. Advanced and ardent spirits were enthusiastic over the fall of the Bastille ; though before long Burke was denouncing the excesses of the revolutionists and prophesying troubles to come with a surprising insight, yet failing to arouse much alarm, since the sense of class antagonisms was less in England than in any continental state. The idea of intervention in the domestic affairs of France seemed absurd.

On the Continent, however, where almost every state had done its best to copy the despotic French system, the collapse of despotism in France was viewed by the despots as ominous. The

**WIFE OF LOUIS XVI**
Her Austrian origin, her extravagance and interference in politics all contributed to the unpopularity of Marie Antoinette, shown in this painting by Madame Vigée-Lebrun. Guillotined in 1793, she faced death with fine courage.
*Musée de Versailles*

sympathies of every despot were with the French monarchy. In Russia, indeed, Catherine viewed the revolution hopefully as something which did not concern herself directly, but might usefully keep the attention of Austria and Prussia fixed on the west rather than on her own activities in the east. Frederick William II again was more anxious about Poland than about Paris. Generally the key of the situation was to be found in the policy which the emperor might decide to adopt. The French queen was the emperor's sister, and in France the fear on one side and the hope on the other were constant that Austria would thereby be drawn into intervention.

Now, as recorded in the last chapter, Joseph II had thoroughly committed himself to the Russian alliance in 1788 and plunged into a war with Turkey, while Prussia, guided by the minister Hertzberg, stood aloof, purposing to intervene at the moment when intervention would bring most advantage to herself. The

**LEADER OF THE THIRD ESTATE**
Couderc's painting shows the comte de Mirabeau in 1789. His ideal was a strong constitutional government, but the suspicious attitude of the court estranged him. Elected president of the National Assembly in February, 1791, he died in April of that year.
*Musée de Versailles ; photo, Neurdein*

war went ill for Austria in that year and only less ill in the next ; but Russia was gaining ground. Hertzberg wished to break up the Austro-Russian combination, and the Austrian position became critical. Hertzberg was on the point of intervening on behalf of the Porte, when Joseph died at the beginning of 1790, and the accession of his brother Leopold II changed the whole situation.

Joseph had been an unlucky failure. He had sought power for himself, and extension of his dominions, with the benevolent intention of improving the lot of his subjects in his own way—a way which did not appeal to them. He acquired their hostility instead of gaining their affection, and his schemes for territorial concentration and aggrandisement had been consistently foiled. The Netherlands were in open revolt, and Hungary was on the verge of it. He had pursued his ideals with a persistent disregard of facts.

Leopold was an eminently practical statesman who had shown his quality by the excellence of his administration in his grand duchy of Tuscany. On his accession he reversed Joseph's policy. He dealt tactfully with the subjects whom Joseph had only succeeded in irritating. He had no sympathy with Joseph's grandiose schemes of expansion. Seeing no real advantage for Austria in continuing the Turkish war and much inconvenience in the hostility of Prussia and the moral support of Prussia's friends, he diplomatically invited Prussia's friendly mediation ; but when Prussia responded with proposals for the territorial exchanges for which Hertzberg hankered, Leopold uncompromisingly r e j e c t e d them. The proposals themselves were not to the taste of Frederick William's northern allies, England, Holland, Sweden and Poland ; and Leopold's skill effected the

treaty of Reichenbach with Prussia (July, 1790), and the peace of Jassy, between Austria and Russia on the one hand and Turkey on the other, in January, 1792.

Leopold was the last man to allow his judgement to be overruled by sentimentalism. But the flight of Louis to Varennes, his detention, and his return to Paris practically as a prisoner in June, 1791, stirred the émigrés to new clamours ; Leopold had established formally amicable relations with Frederick William ; and in conjunction with the latter he issued, in August, the famous Declaration of Pilnitz, the spark which fired the train.

$\mathfrak{I}$N fact the declaration missed its mark. Intervention for the restoration of the monarchy, it said, might be necessary, provided that the powers generally were

**FAMOUS VICTIM OF THE TERROR**

This oil painting, which shows the strong, scarred face of the revolutionary leader Georges Jacques Danton (1759–94), dates from the last years of his life. He discountenanced the fanaticism of the extreme Terrorists, and Robespierre secured his arrest. He was guillotined, April 5, 1794.

*Musée Carnavalet*

in agreement. As there was no prospect of the powers generally agreeing, it should have been correctly interpreted as a snub to the émigrés ; moreover, the monarchy was actually restored three weeks later, on Louis' acceptance of the new constitution ; but in Paris at least it was interpreted as a threat to France ; and France was very soon ablaze with indignation— very much as a century before England's wrath had blazed when Louis XIV presumed to recognize the exiled James II as her lawful king. Austria was already more than sufficiently unpopular, because the extremely unpopular Marie Antoinette was an Austrian princess. Whether Leopold himself could have allayed the storm may be doubted ; but in March, 1792, he was dead, succeeded by a young and inexperienced heir, Francis II. On April 20 the unfortunate Louis was compelled to come down to the Assembly and pronounce a formal declaration of war against his nephew the ' king of Bohemia and Hungary '—the imperial election not having yet taken place.

The French troops were already on the Netherlands front—the point of contact between France and the Austrian dominion ; but the men were under officers whom they distrusted as aristocrats ; their commander, Lafayette, enjoyed the confidence neither of the king nor of the ministry, though he wanted to be loyal to both. The first collisions with the Austrian troops were unfortunate ; the king and the Girondist ministers were at odds ; new but incompetent ministers were appointed from the moderate party, the Feuillants. The Paris mob broke into the Tuileries ; Prussia declared war in alliance with Austria ; Paris rang with the strains of the Marseillaise, the new war song of Revolutionary France ; in the popular belief the king and the moderates — including Lafayette — were traitors playing into the hands of the enemies of France ; and on July 27 the

INVASION OF THE TUILERIES BY INSURRECTIONARY PARISIANS

On June 20, 1792, an armed Parisian mob marched to the Tuileries with loud cries of ' Vive la nation ! Vive les sansculottes ! '    The crowd surged into the Assembly Hall and invaded the royal apartments.    Although in great peril, the king and queen faced the clamouring multitude with courage and dignity, and refused to make any promises.    The insurgents were finally dispersed by the intervention of Pétion, the popular mayor of Paris.    This drawing is by F. L. Prieur.

*The Louvre*

**SAVAGE SATIRE AGAINST THE JACOBINS**
A German aquatint of 1793 shows the Devil clutching his brood and rejoicing at its success in wrecking the French monarchy. His better half scorns his efforts as futile compared with the Jacobin whom she herself has hatched.
*Bibliothèque Nationale*

these conditions the elections for the new assembly, the ' Convention ' which was to take the place of the Legislative Assembly, were being carried on. On September 20 the new commander on the front, Dumouriez, engaged the Prussian troops at Valmy and was not defeated. The ' victory ' was hailed with wild enthusiasm ; once again the soldiers of France had proved that they were invincible. Military confidence was restored, and from that moment the French troops fought to win.

The Convention met on September 21. The Royalists had been wiped out, and the chiefs of the Commune, the Jacobins, extremists who had Prussian commander, the duke of Brunswick, confirmed the belief by a manifesto threatening Paris with divers penalties if any harm befell the royal family.

Then the Paris Commune, headed by Danton, took control, having with it the armed force of the city, the National Guard. The royal family (August 10) fled from the Tuileries—where the Swiss Guard, refusing submission, fought and fell to the last man—to the feeble ' protection ' of the Assembly. The Assembly could only obey the orders of the Commune, at whose dictation it appointed an arbitrary ' tribunal for the trial of suspects.' Lafayette would have marched on Paris to restore order ; but no one would follow him, and he fell instead into the hands of the Austrians, who held him prisoner. Prussian troops advanced and captured Longwy and then Verdun (September 2). The Commune had already arrested and flung into prison a huge number of suspects. On September 3 it organized a massacre of the prisoners in their prisons. The example was followed all over the country. Under

**TERRORIST WHOM THE TERROR SLEW**
This portrait shows the determined profile of Maximilien Marie Isidore Robespierre (1758–94), the revolutionary leader most responsible for the Reign of Terror. Nemesis finally overtook him and he was guillotined in July, 1794.
*Musée de Versailles ; photo, Alinari*

sat in the old Constituent Assembly, were back again. They formed an organized body, headed by Danton and Robespierre, which knew its own mind and had no scruples about the method of attaining its ends ; the party was known as the Mountain. The Girondists suffered from scrupulosity and indecision, though nominally the larger party ; they were the new moderates, what was left of the adherents of law and order. Between them and the Mountain floated the ' Plain,' attached to neither but not themselves forming a party. There was no delay in proclaiming the end of the monarchy.

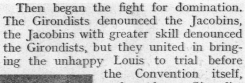

Then began the fight for domination. The Girondists denounced the Jacobins, the Jacobins with greater skill denounced the Girondists, but they united in bringing the unhappy Louis to trial before the Convention itself, and the Girondist leaders were among the bare majority which passed the death sentence. On January 21, 1793, the head of the deposed king fell under the guillotine — the ghastly challenge to the monarchies of Europe flung down by the French Republic ; but it was only the finishing touch.

For at the beginning of 1792 the Legislative Assembly had conceived

**FRENCH REVOLUTIONARIES TRIUMPHANTLY EXHIBIT THE HEAD OF LOUIS XVI**
Jacobins and Girondists combined in bringing Louis XVI to the trial before the Convention that led to his death by guillotine on January 21, 1793. This fine water colour drawing by an unknown but closely contemporary artist shows the scene of execution. Top, Ducreux's portrait, painted in the Temple three days before the execution, shows Louis XVI, well-meaning but weak, who paid with his life for the faults and follies of his predecessors as much as for his own.
*Musée Carnavalet (top)* ; *Bibliothèque Nationale (bottom)*

**'ORGANIZER OF VICTORY'**

Lazare Nicolas Marguerite Carnot (1753–1823) brilliantly reorganized the armies that won the Republican successes of 1794. This picture of him appeared among Bonneville's Portraits of Celebrated Characters of the Revolution.

*From Seidlitz, ' Porträtwerk,' Brückmann A.G.*

Rhenish principalities and in the Netherlands ; and thus at the beginning of 1793 the war became general.

On the part of the coalition it was conducted with extreme inefficiency, each of the allies having their own distinct objects in view, and their own view of the way in which those objects could be most conveniently attained. Only in England was there any enthusiasm, and British enthusiasm concerned itself only with naval operations, though British gold supported the armies of the allies. France, on the other hand, threw herself into the struggle with her whole soul. The allies were hide-bound by military conventions established in the Seven Years' War ; the French flung the old conventions to the winds, and only demanded of their captains that they should win battles—if they failed to win them their shrift was short. Any man who showed ability was given his chance ; if he failed then he was not given another, and an amazing amount of first-class talent came to the front, while in the armies of the allies no first-class talent appeared at all. Moreover, while

itself to be forced into war by the aggressive threat of interference in French affairs by foreign powers ; at the end of the same year the Convention had itself openly assumed the attitude of aggression, had declared its purpose of aiding the peoples to rid themselves of their rulers, had incidentally reasserted the right of France to acquire her own 'natural' boundaries, and, in connexion therewith, proclaimed her intention of tearing up the treaty of Fontainebleau and opening the Scheldt—to the extreme detriment of Holland and Holland's guarantor, England. In other words, she had declared herself to be the enemy of every existing government in Europe which was not in form republican. Even this might conceivably have been ignored by England, as not seriously concerning a country which prided itself upon being the land of liberty ; but the claim of France to tear up at her own choice treaties to which she had been an active party was incompatible with international ethics. French armies were already giving effect to the doctrine of republican aggression in the

**A PUPPET MONARCH**

This painting by Goya shows Carlos IV, incapable king of Spain from 1788 to 1808. The real rulers of the country were his queen (left) and her favourite, Godoy, who committed themselves to alliance with France.

*Prado, Madrid ; photo, Anderson*

the other states expected their standing military machines to work automatically, in France the military organization passed into and remained through successive changes under the direction of a man of supreme genius, Carnot. Consequently the French armies met with continuous success and the allied armies with repeated failure, though the British fleets commanded the seas.

The allies showed no energy, because even from the outset Prussia was more interested in Poland than in the French war, from which she could expect to derive no direct advantage. Austria, also mindful of Poland, expected the British for their own sakes to do most of the fighting in the Netherlands, and Spain had fallen under the feeble rule of Carlos IV. Prussia kept her armies in the field— away from the fighting front—only because she could do so at the expense of Great Britain. In 1795

**LAST HOURS OF MARIE ANTOINETTE**
On October 16, 1793, the guillotine claimed Marie Antoinette, whose last portrait, by Prieur, was painted in the Conciergerie a few days before the execution. Her calm on the tumbril is cruelly portrayed in Jacques-Louis David's sketch done as he stood among the crowd (top).
*Musée Carnavalet*

he made a separate peace and retired from the coalition, Spain following her example and improving upon it by joining France ; while the French overran the Netherlands, and in Holland the republican party drove the stadtholder William out of the country, proclaimed the 'Batavian Republic' and joined France. Thus in 1795 the 'coalition' meant Great Britain, Austria and the minor principalities in Germany and Italy which still adhered to it.

In that year Poland as an independent state disappeared from the map of Europe. Even at the moment when Frederick William was declaring war in 1792, Catherine was completing with him her bargain for the second partition ; they could afford at the moment to ignore Austria. Poland was powerless, and no one else would dream of interfering. Catherine annexed a substantial part and Prussia a smaller portion of the prey. The final partition of what still remained came in 1795. This time it was with Austria that Catherine struck her bargain, lest there should be trouble over her own designs against Turkey. She offered a substantial share of Poland as the price of acquiescence, while Prussia, however reluctantly, would have to be content with the remaining fraction. Poland disappeared into the maws of her three big neighbours.

**M**EANWHILE France, winning victories abroad, extending her borders and transforming hostile principalities into friendly or dependent republics, was passing through a long internal agony. The Jacobins gained ascendancy over the Girondists ; the Girondist Dumouriez, the hero of Valmy, tried and failed to organize a plot for a monarchist restoration ; the Girondists were branded as traitors and their leaders were thrown into prison by the triumphant Jacobins. In various quarters there were royalist

## BONAPARTE CRUSHES THE PARISIAN RISING OF VENDÉMIAIRE

The new constitution devised by the abbé Sieyès in 1794 did not meet with universal approval, and prompt action was necessary to quell the violence of its opponents. The government troops, under young General Bonaparte, were successful in crushing the rising of Vendémiaire (October), 1795, in Paris. Charles Monnet's famous picture, engraved by Helman, shows the struggle outside the church of S. Roch, Rue St. Honoré. The insurgents, ill equipped and ill led, were no match for regular troops.

*Photo, W. F. Mansell*

revolts, which were crushed, not without difficulty but without mercy. When the Girondists fell, the Jacobins had already pinned their faith to Robespierre, while Danton, the organizer of the 'September massacres,' was under suspicion as a 'moderate,' an 'indulgent.' The Convention bestowed absolute powers on a Committee of Public Safety (July, 1793) with Robespierre at its head, from which Danton was excluded.

In October the real Reign of Terror began. A 'revolutionary tribunal' sent the Girondist chiefs and Marie Antoinette to the guillotine, and after them a host of 'aristocrats.' Early in 1794 Robespierre turned upon the most repulsive group among his followers, the Hébertists, who were getting out of his control; a fortnight later he smote down the 'indulgent' Danton. The victims of the guillotine multiplied. But the agents of the Terror began to fear that they would become its victims; the orgy of bloodshed was followed by a revulsion; a plot was formed; Robespierre was suddenly arrested by order of the Convention in July—the month which the Republic had re-christened

Thermidor—and followed his victims to the guillotine. The mob applauded his death as it had applauded theirs; but it wanted no more. The Terror was over.

Freed from Robespierre, the Convention, with moderates in the ascendant, recovered its lost control; but the Commune and the Committee of Public Safety were reconstituted; almost as a matter of course a new constitution was devised by the indefatigable architect of symmetrical systems, the abbé Sieyès. The executive was to be in the hands of a directory of five, the legislature was to consist of two chambers in which members of the Convention itself were to predominate. The natural result was the rising of a hostile mob in Paris in October ('Vendémiaire'), 1795. Barras, the head of the Directory, entrusted the defence of the city to the young artillery officer Napoleon Bonaparte (who soon afterwards adopted this French spelling of his Corsican name); he brought up guns and cleared the streets; the rising was effectively suppressed and the Directory's authority established; and Bonaparte at the age of twenty-seven was rewarded with the command of the

French armies in Italy, where little progress had been made since the taking of Savoy itself from the king of Sardinia.

Italy, in fact, was held by the Sardinians or Piedmontese ; by the Austrians, and the Naples Bourbons within the coalition ; by the Papacy, which was hostile to the Republic that had secularised the Church ; and by Venice, which with Tuscany was a neutral.

### Victories of Bonaparte in Italy

THE appointment of Bonaparte to the command was immediately justified. He found three armies opposing him. He routed the central army at Montenotte, driving it to right and left upon Turin and Milan. He wheeled upon Turin, where the king of Sardinia could only submit to the terms he dictated—the surrender of fortresses, and Sardinia's withdrawal from the war. Then it was the turn of the Austrian Beaulieu, who tried to cover Milan. By an audaciously planned and brilliantly won victory at the Bridge of Lodi, Beaulieu was forced to fall back upon Mantua. Milan opened its gates to the victor. The contingent from Naples which had joined the Austrians retreated hastily to the south. Bonaparte seized Brescia in Venetia, the Tuscan port of Leghorn and Bologna in the papal territory—all neutral states. He drove the Austrians from Peschiera into Tyrol. Austrian reinforcements, released by a victory of the archduke Charles over Jourdan at Würtzburg, were pouring in to relieve the force at Mantua, to which he laid siege ; but he broke them up in detail at Arcola and Rivoli ; in February, 1797, Mantua was reduced to surrender, though with the honours of war. A fortnight later the pope was forced to sign the treaty of Tolentino, by which he surrendered Bologna and Ferrara. Bonaparte was master of all North Italy, which he had 'liberated' ; that is, he had imposed upon the conquered territories a system of self-government on the French model, for which they had to pay a heavy price in hard cash and art treasures. They were now united as the 'Cisalpine Republic,' under the protection of France, the mother of republics.

But Bonaparte was also his own master —not the Directory whose nominal servant he was. Two very brilliant soldiers, Hoche and Moreau, were now in command of the armies which the Austrian archduke had driven back, and he did not intend them to share the honours in bringing Austria to terms. The naval domination of Great Britain was in doubt ; she had, indeed, just won a decisive victory at Cape St. Vincent over the Spanish fleet which had gone over to France, but her sailors were becoming out of hand and mutinous, and the Dutch fleet would soon be available ; and Bonaparte, besides, was not alone in underrating the effectiveness of sea power, the only power the British were manifesting. The matter of immediate importance was to effect a settlement with Austria. On his own responsibility he advanced on Trieste, defeating the archduke on the way, and thence to Leoben. There he was met by Austrian envoys who were now ready enough to accept the terms he offered— the surrender of the Netherlands and the Milanese and the partition of Venice as the return for her uneasy neutrality. It was easy to find an excuse for attacking Venice and extracting the cession of the Ionian islands. The rest of Venice passed to Austria when the terms of Leoben (April) were confirmed by the treaty of Campo Formio in October. In the interval, the mutinies in the British fleet had been quelled, and the Dutch fleet put out of action at Camperdown.

### Bonaparte's Egyptian Expedition

BONAPARTE had conducted both his military and his political operations without any regard to instructions or prohibitions from Paris, and the French government had to accept the fait accompli. The Directory, in fact, was tottering ; three of its members (the 'triumvirate,' as they were called) were in constant opposition to the other two. Monarchical plots were in the air ; prominent generals were under suspicion. The triumvirate defeated their opponents, and expelled Carnot himself from the Directory and the country, mainly through the help Bonaparte chose to give them from a

### THE VICTOR OF TRAFALGAR

The genius of Admiral Horatio Nelson (1758–1805), whose features are here portrayed by L. F. Abbott, lay in his courage, knowledge and judgement. Daring and humane, he excelled as a commander and was beloved as well as obeyed.

*National Portrait Gallery, London*

in England and the minister Thugut in Austria were already planning a new coalition, in which they were to find a formidable ally in Tsar Paul, who had succeeded Catherine in 1796, and to whom the Revolution was anathema.

Nelson, in command in the Mediterranean, with sound instinct pursued the French towards Egypt, but was led off on a false scent. Bonaparte reached Alexandria, having captured Malta on the way, in June. Egypt was theoretically a province of the Turkish Empire ; he was coming to deliver it not from the sultan, with whom there was no war, but from the tyranny of the Mamelukes. By the end of July he had crushed the Mamelukes in the battle of the Pyramids, and was organizing his own rule ; but on August 1 Nelson at last tracked down the French fleet in Aboukir Bay, and annihilated it in the Battle of the Nile. Thenceforth the British fleet held undisputed control of the Mediterranean and Bonaparte's communications with Europe were completely severed.

### Coalition Successes and Bonaparte's Return

By this time the new coalition was on the point of striking ; the first and very unsuccessful move was made by the contemptible Ferdinand of Naples, who attacked the Roman Republic, was himself immediately ejected from Naples, and took flight to Sicily, where his safety was guaranteed by Nelson's victorious fleet. The Italian half of his kingdom was promptly organized as the Parthenopean Republic. But after that came disasters for the French in the first months of 1799. The archduke Charles defeated Jourdan at Stockach ; Masséna was isolated at Zürich ; Russian forces under Suvarov entered Italy, and his victory on the Trebbia prevented the junction of Macdonald's army from Naples with Moreau's in the north. Ferdinand was brought back to Naples, and with Nelson's aid inflicted savage punishment on the rebels who had ejected him.

The tale of disaster leaked through to Bonaparte, who had conquered Egypt and made it his base for the conquest of Syria, which in its turn was to be his

distance. When at last he returned in triumph to Paris he could have made himself master of the state there and then ; but he did not choose to do so yet. He was planning that Egyptian expedition the aims of which have been variously interpreted ; but had it not been for the British fleet it might quite possibly have made him master not only of Paris but of the world. The Directory, however, warmly approved a scheme which removed their dangerous servant to a safe distance.

When the expedition sailed in May, 1798, successfully evading the British squadron which was watching Toulon, France had already found means for ejecting the aged pope from the Papal States and turning them into the Roman Republic, and for adding the Helvetic Republic to the circle of dependencies. Also the Treaty of Campo Formio had left over the question of the treatment of other German principalities to a conference at Rastadt, which French diplomacy used to antagonise Austria and Prussia and to bring western Germany, and the Rhineland in particular, more decisively under French domination. Pitt

NELSON'S MASTERLY VICTORY OVER THE FRENCH AT THE BATTLE OF THE NILE

On August 1, 1798, Nelson, despite the numerical inferiority of the English fleet, inflicted on the French an overwhelming naval defeat in Aboukir Bay, from which time he became a national hero. As a result of this victory the British won command of the Mediterranean, and Bonaparte's communications with Europe were severed. The incident in the battle which this engraving, after the painting by De Loutherbourg, represents is the blowing up of the French flagship Orient.

base either for a conquest of Asia, including India, or of Europe from the east, while France held her in the west. He did not conquer Syria because he could not capture Acre without command of the sea, and while Acre stood his communications with Egypt were always liable to be cut. But the news from Europe decided him that it was time for him to return to Paris and take control. With a few comrades he took boat—leaving Kléber in command in Egypt—threaded his way undiscovered across the Mediterranean, and landed at Fréjus in October.

The military situation had been completely changed during the interval. Moreau had effected a masterly retirement from Italy, while Suvarov had been forbidden to move till a fresh force under Korsakov joined him. Masséna dealt summarily with Korsakov, who did not reach Italy. Suvarov, and his master Paul, considered that they had been betrayed by Austria, and Russia withdrew from the war in high dudgeon.

Bonaparte hastened to Paris, where moderates were now in the ascendant in the Directory itself and in one of the Chambers, but Chambers and Directory were in constant dissension. Sieyès, now at the head of the Directory, had another mathematically flawless constitution ready, but needed a general to institute it. The arrival of Napoleon left no choice as to the general who was to carry out the coup d'état—the coup d'état of Brumaire (November 9, 1799). It was duly carried out, not without some extremely critical moments ; and its product was not the constitution of Sieyès with its finished scheme of checks and balances which must have completely paralysed any action whatever, but one which, while preserving something of its outward form, placed the legislature in the control of the executive, and the executive in the hands of one man, the 'First Consul,' with two phantoms beside him who also bore the name of consul, with hardly even a semblance of authority. It was not long before the First Consul adopted the monarchical signature. Henceforth he is to be known as Napoleon, though more than four years were to pass before he assumed the title of emperor.

The new constitution was ratified by an overwhelming plébiscite. The Revolution had been born of popular grievances—the seigneurial rights and the aristocratic and clerical privileges which had actually been abolished before the fall of the monarchy. Their abolition had involved the destruction of the old system of government, for which it had been attempted to substitute democracy. The result had been not democracy but despotism exercised by a succession of small groups—first concentrating in Robespierre's Committee of Public Safety and then, very uncertainly, in the Directory. The culmination came with the despotism

of a successful general with a genius for administration, who chose to retain a semblance of democratic or republican forms, like Augustus in Rome eighteen centuries before him, and France was satisfied as Rome had been satisfied.

THE military situation was still critical, though Russia had retired. Masséna in Italy was isolated at Genoa, the Austrians being in greater strength. The First Consul made separate peace overtures to Austria and to Great Britain ; neither trusted him and neither would make terms without the other. The negotiations fell through, and in 1800 Napoleon invaded Italy while Moreau advanced into Germany. No relief was sent to Masséna, who was starved into surrender in June ; but a fortnight later Napoleon defeated the Austrians at Marengo. He procured thereby an armistice, which he employed in placating the tsar—in whose eyes he was now the representative not of Jacobinism but of autocracy—while he beguiled Spain with concessions which meant nothing. The British fleet captured Malta ; he had just promised it to the tsar, but it was retained by its captors.

Hostilities were renewed, and Moreau won a brilliant victory over the Austrians at Hohenlinden, which forced them to conclude a separate peace at Lunéville in February, 1801, on much the same terms as the earlier peace of Campo Formio. Great Britain was isolated, the tsar was on the point of turning upon her, and she was threatened by the 'armed neutrality' of the Baltic states, who resented her doctrines about the respective rights of neutrals and belligerents on the seas. However, she dispatched an expedition to Egypt which was completely successful ; her fleet broke up the armed neutrality by its attack upon the Danes in the Battle of

**BONAPARTE DISPERSES THE DIRECTORY**

Bonaparte's realization that the French executive government, in the hands of the Directory, was unpopular, led him to determine upon its overthrow. The bold scheme was carried out in the coup d'état of Brumaire (November) 1799, and François Bouchot's painting represents the disorderly scene which accompanied Bonaparte's dissolution of the government.

*The Louvre*

the Baltic ; Paul was assassinated, and his youthful successor, Alexander I, made haste to seek a reconciliation with Great Britain. There was no longer sufficient reason for refusing peace ; and the war ended—for the time—with the Peace of Amiens in March, 1802.

The treaty included definite pacts on both sides, and indefinite understandings. The pacts were not carried out, because each side refused to make the first move. Napoleon's own proceedings were in the British view gross violations of the under-standings. While he reinstated the pope, he reconstructed the Cisalpine and Ligurian Republics, accepting for himself the pre-sidency of both. The German questions were again to be settled, as after Campo Formio, by a conference at Regensburg, which again appeared to mean only that the French grip on western Germany was to be tightened ; British protests were denounced as being in violation of the treaty terms. In May, 1803, fourteen months after the treaty of Amiens, war was again declared between Great Britain and the French Republic. Diplomacy was not a strong point with the British, who invariably found themselves out-manoeuvred and put apparently in the wrong by that past master in the art whose services Napoleon enjoyed—Talleyrand.

For Great Britain the sea was the only possible field of warfare, and her fleet established an effective guard over the French ports, while Napoleon was organizing a great army of invasion, in the vain hope of finding or creating an opportunity for carrying it across the Channel unmolested, and stabilising his own posi-tion in France and in Europe. He reconciled himself with the Church by restoring the pope in Rome and declaring the old faith to be the official religion of the state. The royalists were welcome to return, whatever their past record might have

**TALLEYRAND THE DIPLOMATIST**
As foreign minister under the First Consul, Charles Maurice de Talleyrand (1754–1838) had wide scope for his remarkable diplomatic talents. Later, he headed the anti-Napoleonic faction. François Gérard painted this portrait.
*From Seidlitz, ' Porträtwerk,' Brückmann A.G.*

been, on condition only of loyalty to the new order. His taxation was heavy but even-handed, and the old leakages in the collection of revenue were very thoroughly stopped. Through his own nominees he con-trolled local administra-tion and the courts of justice. His expenditure was lavish and magnifi-cent, but in the main directed to economically profitable public works, and, of course, to military efficiency. And he ap-propriated and made his own two great concep-tions which he really owed to the reformers whose admirable work under the Convention had been overshadowed by the more dramatic and terrible aspects of

**THE DUC D'ENGHIEN**
Fear of Bourbon royalism in France led to the kidnapping of the duc d'Enghien, a prince of the blood, at Baden. After a mock court martial he was executed at Vincennes, March 21, 1804.
*Drawn from life in 1798, engr. by N. Bertrand*

**STEPSON OF NAPOLEON**

Appointed viceroy of Italy by Napoleon in 1805, Eugène de Beauharnais (1781–1824) ruled the kingdom well and exhibited great military talent. In 1807 he was created prince of Venice.

*Miniature by Isabey; Wallace Collection, London*

with Pitt, who had returned to the helm (after a brief retirement, owing to George III's refusal to concede Catholic emancipation in Ireland), set about organizing a new coalition.

Through 1805 the Coalition was taking shape on the one hand, and on the other Napoleon was endeavouring to obtain that temporary domination on the European seas without which the invasion of England could not even be attempted. Napoleon's grip on the dependent states was palpably tightening. The German provinces on the left bank of the Rhine had been annexed ; the Ligurian Republic had been absorbed ; the Cisalpine Republic, after conversion into the Italian Republic, converted itself into a monarchy and offered the historic Iron Crown of Lombardy to Napoleon, who accepted it and appointed his stepson, Eugène Beauharnais, viceroy. The assumption of the imperial title was almost a challenge to the Austrian emperor. Pitt and

its history—educational reconstruction and that codification and reform of the law which we know as the Code Napoléon, the penetration of which into the dependent republics and states, in fact, made the Revolution in them a permanent reality.

Napoleon, however, required for himself the form as well as the substance of royalty. Bourbon royalism in France was still, it seemed, a danger. In 1804 the duc d'Enghien, a prince of the blood, was kidnapped on German soil, carried over the border and, after a mock military trial, executed. Immediately afterwards Napoleon procured the plébiscite which put an end to the republican fiction and made him emperor. But the death of Enghien was in the eyes of the young tsar, Alexander I, a firm believer in the divinity that doth hedge princes as well as kings, an unforgivable crime ; and the tsar, in conjunction

**NAPOLEON AS EMPEROR OF THE FRENCH**

As a result of a plébiscite taken on the subject of the imperial title, Napoleon became emperor of the French on May 18, 1804. At the coronation ceremony, which took place in Notre Dame on December 2, 1804, Napoleon waved aside the pope and crowned himself. This portrait is by H. Lefèvre.

*Musée de Versailles; photo, Neurdein*

Alexander adjusted the differences in their respective views ; Austria was on the point of coming in, though the Spanish government was completely subservient to Napoleon. The armies were mobilising, when Napoleon made his move against the ' tyrant of the seas '—and failed.

The Coalition was still incomplete when, in March, 1805, the Toulon fleet under Villeneuve came out—not to fight Nelson, but to draw him away to the West Indies, leave him there, effect a junction with the Brest fleet, and clear the Channel for the army of invasion. Nelson went in pur-

suit ; Villeneuve evaded him and returned ; but the news reached England ; Villeneuve found a squadron on the watch, knew that there could now be no chance of bringing out the Brest fleet, and made for Corunna. Napoleon knew that his scheme had failed and launched the army of invasion not upon England but upon Austria.

The Austrian frontier force at Ulm was trapped and forced to capitulate (October); Napoleon marched on Vienna, and entered it on November 13. The Russians were already at hand ; from Vienna Napoleon marched to meet them, and shattered them at the brilliant victory of Austerlitz (December 3). Russia felt that Austria had failed her, and retired ; Prussia might have joined the Coalition but for Austerlitz—as matters stood, she swallowed the bait dangled before her by Napoleon, that Hanover should be handed over to her. Austria lay at the conqueror's mercy ; he was content to take from her by the treaty of Pressburg all her possessions in Italy and on the Adriatic.

Great Britain was again isolated, though Russia had not yet formally made peace.

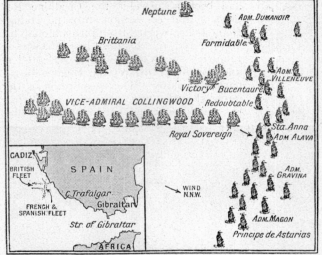

**BRILLIANT NAVAL VICTORY THAT MADE BRITAIN MISTRESS OF THE SEAS**

Nelson's annihilating defeat of the combined French and Spanish fleets at Trafalgar, on October 21, 1805, established British maritime supremacy. Reproduced for the first time in 1928, this sketch representing the battle was drawn by Admiral Spencer Smyth, who was himself there. Bearing down upon the enemy in two parallel lines (see plan and inset map above), Nelson and Collingwood broke the French line at two points, and nearly every enemy ship was captured or destroyed.

*Courtesy of ' The Daily Telegraph '*

But, six weeks before Austerlitz, Nelson had shattered the combined French and Spanish fleets at Trafalgar. No hostile fleet could again take the seas after that great victory. Napoleon professed to ignore it ; he believed that he had another way of bringing England to her knees—but it was a way that could not in fact succeed, so long as her fleets swept the seas unchallenged and she held an unqualified monopoly of the ocean trade routes and in the Mediterranean ; though his own supremacy on the continent might seem indisputable.

To that supremacy a challenge came from an unexpected quarter. There was a war party in Prussia which resented the pusillanimity of the government. Frederick William III—his father died in 1797—was feebly conscientious but timid, and very much in the hands of a minister who habitually overreached himself by the short-sighted cunning which he mistook for statecraft. The discovery that Hanover was not to be handed over after all gave the war party the upper hand. Prussia declared war.

Before she did so, Napoleon had turned Ferdinand out of Naples, set up his own brother Joseph as king, and made another kingdom for another brother, Louis, out of the Netherlands and the Batavian Republic. The western German principalities combined in the Confederation of the Rhine, with the military forces at the service of the French emperor ; and the German emperor Francis proclaimed himself 'Austrian' instead of 'Holy Roman' emperor, just over one thousand years having elapsed since Charlemagne's coronation at Rome on Christmas Day in 800.

In the two battles of Jena and Auerstädt, the Prussian armies were shattered on a single

**FREDERICK WILLIAM III OF PRUSSIA**
His subjects loved Frederick William III of Prussia (1770–1840) for his kind heart and simple ways. Yet his statecraft was marred by weakness and inconsistency, which left him largely at the mercy of stronger personalities.

**NELSON'S DEATH MASK**
A death mask of Lord Nelson was taken immediately after his death at Trafalgar. This cast is now preserved in the Portsmouth Dockyard Museum.
*Photo, Stephen Cribb*

day (October 14, 1806). A fortnight later Napoleon was in Berlin, with Prussia under his heel. Her king found an asylum with the tsar. Napoleon issued the Berlin decrees, followed next year by the Milan decrees, which were intended to bring Great Britain to her knees by closing all European ports to British commerce and declaring all British ports to be under blockade. The British replied by successive orders in council which declared all ports that refused to admit British shipping to be under blockade. The British had a fleet to enforce their blockade, and Napoleon had none—and the British made sure that he should continue to have none by attacking and seizing the neutral Danish fleet.

A brief Russian campaign convinced the tsar

that his allies were quite useless, and Napoleon that an agreement with the tsar was preferable to a duel. The tsar had no good will to England, but was benevolently disposed to Prussia. Napoleon found no serious difficulty in reaching an amicable arrangement with Alexander in a conference held on a raft in midstream on the Niemen, the issue of which was the treaty of· Tilsit (1807). In effect—the actual details are unknown—the tsar was to have a free hand in the East and Napoleon in the West. Russia was to maintain what Napoleon called the 'Continental System' of excluding British goods from the Continent (on the mistaken assumption that the Continent would or could do without them). Frederick William was to be reinstated in some half of his kingdom, virtually as Napoleon's vassal. Half of the rest was to provide a kingdom of Westphalia for the youngest Bonaparte, Jerome ; the other half—the 'Grand Duchy of Warsaw'—went to the king (hitherto elector) of Saxony, whom Napoleon expected to be useful. Once more Britain was isolated. But while the Con-

**FRENCH KING OF SWEDEN**

This painting by Kinson shows Jean Baptiste Bernadotte (1763–1844), who by his eminent military abilities rose to the rank of marshal in Napoleon's armies. Chosen as successor to the king of Sweden, he became Charles XIV in 1818.

*Musée de Versailles ; photo, Neurdein*

tinental System did gravely increase her difficulties, it strangled Europe, to which British or British-borne goods were a necessity—and Europe began to feel that it was Napoleon who was strangling her.

Denmark's hostility to England was now a matter of course. Sweden persisted in friendliness to her, but could be left to the tender mercies of Russia. Presently she took matters into her own hands, deposed Gustavus IV, set his uncle Charles XIII on the throne, and invited his adoption of the brilliant French marshal Bernadotte as his heir ; virtually Bernadotte became king of Sweden.

Spain was subservient, but Portugal still obstinately refused to enter the Continental System. A French army under Junot marched across Spain to Lisbon ; the Portuguese royal family, having no other course open, escaped to a British squadron in the harbour of Lisbon, and sailed for Brazil. Junot took over the administration. Napoleon wanted a more complete control in Spain, where Carlos IV and the crown prince Ferdinand were quarrelling. He enticed them over the

**JOSEPH BONAPARTE**

After his attainment of supreme power Napoleon made his eldest brother Joseph (1768–1844) king of Naples, and, in 1808, king of Spain, where his nominal authority lasted until Wellington's victory at Vittoria in 1813.

*Engraving after Mme. Kinson, British Museum*

border to Bayonne, where he prevailed on both to abdicate, while a complaisant gathering of nobles elected the king of Naples, Joseph Bonaparte, to the throne, and the vacated throne of Naples was passed on to Marshal Murat.

### Beginning of the Peninsular War

So matters stood in the summer of 1808, when the Spanish people, though without guidance, rose against the foreign usurper, and the British government resolved to intervene ; with the result that for the next five years a quarter of a million or more of Napoleon's troops and some of his best generals were constantly locked up in Spain, vainly endeavouring to crush the insurgents and to drive the British out of the base provided by Portugal ; whence year by year the British general Arthur Wellesley—presently viscount and finally duke of Wellington—delivered deadly thrusts against one or other of the French armies. The division of the French command in the Peninsula between generals whose jealousy of each other prevented them

from co-operating was doubtless invaluable to Wellington—but whether Napoleon in person would have succeeded in ' driving him into the sea ' is a question not easy to answer with confidence.

In Spain, then, King Joseph's forces suddenly discovered that they were masters of the ground they stood upon just as long as they were standing on it ; and a British force, landing on the north of Portugal, defeated Junot and forced him to evacuate Lisbon. Napoleon himself took charge for a brief interval, swept Spain from north to south, and was retiring in triumph when Sir John Moore from Portugal fell upon his communications. Napoleon left Soult to deal with him and departed from Spain, never to return ; Moore escaped, with Soult at his heels, to Corunna (January, 1809), where the troops were embarked, though he himself fell, after repulsing Soult's attack.

In April Wellesley arrived at Lisbon to take the command ; in May he surprised Soult at Oporto and flung him out of Portugal ; and in July he won at Talavera, in the centre of Spain, the victory which

**BRITISH GENERALS WHO DISTINGUISHED THEMSELVES IN THE PENINSULAR WAR**

In 1808 Lieutenant-General Sir John Moore (1761–1809) was in command of the British troops in Portugal ; he fell in a victorious rearguard action at Corunna in 1809. This great soldier, shown in Sir T. Lawrence's painting (right) did distinguished work in training the infantry. Left · Robert Home's portrait shows Arthur Wellesley (1769–1852) in 1806—he became duke of Wellington in 1814. His series of victories against Napoleon's armies culminated in Waterloo.

*National Portrait Gallery, London*

**GREAT PRUSSIAN STATESMAN**

Drastic reforms were effected in Prussia by the wise statesmanship of Carl Friedrich von Stein (1757–1831), shown in this lithograph by Heyne. He attained power after the Treaty of Tilsit, and initiated the reorganization of the army.

*From Seidlitz, ' Porträtwerk,' Brückmann A.G.*

spot. He could never, apparently, rid himself of the conviction that nothing but incompetence prevented successive generals of the highest repute from crushing the Spanish rebels and wiping out their British allies.

### Turn of Napoleon's Fortunes

AFFAIRS in Europe, after Tilsit, seemed at first to go smoothly. Napoleon permitted in Prussia the appointment of Stein as a minister from whom he looked for financial reforms by which he himself would ultimately profit. Stein set about a much wider reorganization, abolishing the restrictions which conduced to multiplied class divisions, developing municipal self-government, creating a council of ministers with collective responsibility, fostering a new sense of common citizenship and unity, and, by no means least, inaugurating a new system of army organization. Napoleon awoke to the danger and Stein had to flee ; but the work was carried on by Hardenberg and Scharnhorst. Still all seemed to be well when Napoleon was called from an ostentatiously friendly conference of the monarchs at Erfurt by the revolt of Spain in 1808. When he returned from Spain, all was not so well.

Austria, too, was reorganizing. Napoleon had taken Tyrol from her and presented it to his protégé the Bavarian elector. Austrian armies marched on Bavaria in April, 1809 ; the Tyrolese, ever loyal to the Hapsburgs, rose and flung out the Bavarians. Before the month was out Napoleon, marching on Vienna, inflicted a series of defeats, on successive days, on the archduke Charles. Before he could reach Vienna, however, he met with a serious reverse at Aspern-Essling ; but in July he won at Wagram a victory which was, but need not have been, decisive. His reward was the Treaty of Vienna (October) making Austria almost a dependency, which was supplemented next year by his marriage to the Austrian emperor's sister, Marie Louise—an alliance for the sake of which he divorced Josephine.

The Corsican adventurer had forced his way into the innermost circle of the royal families, but he could not keep British goods out of Europe. Even his brother

earned him his title. But two other armies were converging on him, and he had to fall back into Portugal. In the autumn an expedition, by no means ill conceived but grievously mismanaged, was sent to Walcheren for the reduction of Antwerp ; it failed disastrously. Wellington had perforce contented himself with the preparation of the impregnable ' lines of Torres Vedras,' covering Lisbon, where he held Masséna up through the winter of 1810–11 till the French were in effect starved into retreat. Marmont took Masséna's place, and was decisively defeated at Salamanca in 1812 ; and only in 1813, when Napoleon had already suffered his Moscow disaster, the battle was fought at Vittoria which drove the French armies in retreat across the Pyrenees.

Napoleon's plans went forward, irrespective of the war in the Peninsula which was sapping his power and setting to other European peoples the example of indomitable defiance—Spain being, like Russia, a country which has no organically vital

Louis, the king of Holland, was opening the gate to them. Louis was deposed and his kingdom annexed to France ; but the tsar was tiring of the deprivation of goods his people wanted, and he, too, began to admit them. Bernadotte in Sweden had no love for the emperor, and identified himself with the interests of his adoptive country ; he came to an understanding with the tsar. From 1810 the rift between the autocrats grew. In 1812 it had become a gulf, and Napoleon resolved to bring the tsar to reason.

As with Spain, so with Russia. Napoleon did not see that she was vitally invulnerable. He took Moscow for her heart ; he gathered the mightiest army he had yet commanded and launched it upon her. Prussia and Austria gave him their alliance but no active support. A month before Wellington's victory at Salamanca the Grand Army was over the Niemen (June). The Russian armies retreated continuously, enticing Napoleon farther and farther from his base, to Smolensk, giving battle only in rearguard actions. In September they halted and faced him at the Bridge of Borodino, whence after an exceptionally sanguinary struggle they were able to draw off and revert to their old methods, clearing the country of supplies and harassing his communications. A week after Borodino, Napoleon reached Moscow. On the same night half the city was in flames. Moscow might burn, but it was the occupying army that suffered, and there was no foe at whom Napoleon could strike.

After another month the Grand Army began its retreat (October 19). It could only march back over the old devastated ground, with the Russians harassing it on flank and rear, for its own numbers had already been hideously depleted, and the alternative route southwards was held in force by the Russians. Dwindling always, it struggled on its desperate way ; it was still on the march when the Russian winter

**SUFFERINGS OF THE FRENCH ARMY IN THE RETREAT FROM MOSCOW**

The impossibility of wintering in Moscow, ruined by fire and pillage, compelled Napoleon to begin the celebrated retreat in October, 1812. The troops of his Grand Army suffered terrible hardships and losses in the ensuing march, pursued by the enemy, and enduring the cold of a Russian winter. Atkinson's picture, published in 1813, conveys some idea of the appalling conditions under which the shivering, starving troops encamped for the night.

*Aquatint by M. Dubourg, British Museum*

fell and made still more complete what was already an irreparable disaster. It was only an infinitesimal remnant of the Grand Army that struggled back over the Prussian frontier in December. Napoleon had hastened ahead and was already working titanically to retrieve the catastrophe.

Prussia was an ally—but Yorck, the Prussian commander in the eastern district, threw over the government and declared for Russia. Frederick William tried to repudiate his action, but Prussia had been reborn in the last four years, and the king found himself unable to stem the tide of public opinion. He yielded to it, and in February transferred his alliance to Russia by the treaty of Kalisch  In March Prussia declared war on Napoleon.

The terrific power of the man Napoleon was never more tremendously manifested than during the next twelve months. He had lost an army of half a million men ; all Europe was now gathering against him, though Austria, guided now by Metternich, was holding aloof, reckoning that she could dictate the terms of her own alliance with either side. But Napoleon raised new

**PRINCE METTERNICH**

A diplomat of genius, Clemens Lothar Wenzel Metternich (1773–1859) became foreign minister of Austria in 1809, and, after Napoleon's fall in 1815, dominated European politics. Sir Thomas Lawrence painted this portrait of him.

*From Seidlitz, ' Porträtwerk,' Brückmann A.G.*

**LOUIS XVIII OF FRANCE**

This portrait by François Gerard, first painter to the king, shows Louis XVIII, in whose person the Bourbon monarchy was restored to France in 1814. Upon Napoleon's escape from Elba he fled the country but returned after Waterloo.

*From Seidlitz, ' Porträtwerk,' Brückmann A.G.*

armies, though he had to draw heavily on the army in Spain. The princes of the Rhenish confederation were hesitating. He rejected offers of mediation from Metternich ; he inflicted two defeats on the Prussians and Russians ; he rejected fresh terms offered by Metternich, and Austria, followed by Sweden, joined the new coalition. Wellington shattered the main French army in Spain at Vittoria (June) and drove it through the Pyrenees. Napoleon won another great victory over the allied forces at Dresden in August, but in October his foes were swarming round him ; after the ' battle of the nations ' at Leipzig, the struggle became desperate. He still struck hard at his enemies in detail, but if he checked them in one quarter they were still sweeping on towards Paris in another. Metternich won over the hesitating German princes—German nationalism had left them cold, but his promises of ' unreserved sovereignty ' appealed to them. Wellington was in France, though with Soult in front of him. Marmont at Paris capitulated on March 31.

In plain terms, Napoleon was overwhelmed ; his marshals saw it, and when they insisted on surrender, practically deserting him, resistance was no longer possible. He abdicated, unconditionally (April 11). The allies permitted him to retain the imperial title, but nothing else, and exiled him to the ' principality ' of the island of Elba in the Mediterranean.

NAPOLEON being out of the way, the victorious powers took charge of Europe. Between them they laid down the main lines for immediate settlement by the Treaty of Paris, postponing details to a congress, to be held at Vienna in winter. Royalist influences procured the restoration of the Bourbon monarchy in France in the person of Louis XVIII, brother of Louis XVI, who was required to accept a constitution : the French boundaries were to be as before the first hostilities broke out in 1792. The war had given many French and Dutch colonies to Great Britain ; for the most part she restored them, though she retained Cape Colony, which she had occupied in 1806 with the assent of the exiled stadtholder, in return for cash. In Italy, Austria retained Venetia, while Murat—who had

first joined and then deserted Napoleon in the last campaigning—remained in Naples.

The congress met at Vienna in November. The interests to be consulted were those not of populations but of princes. Hanover went back to George III, with the title of king. Holland went back to William of Orange, with the title of king, and with the Netherlands—Belgium—annexed to his kingdom. Victor Emmanuel was restored in Sardinia, Savoy and Piedmont. This was comparatively simple, but the claims or demands of Russia, Prussia and Austria in relation to Saxony, which had held by Napoleon, and to the grand duchy of Warsaw, were so difficult to reconcile that before long it seemed that Napoleon's conquerors would be fighting each other.

### Napoleon's Return and final Defeat

IT was Napoleon himself who compelled them to reconciliation. Encouraged by the dissensions of the powers and the disfavour with which France viewed the Bourbon restoration, he resolved to grasp at dominion once more. He slipped from Elba as before he had slipped from Egypt, landed at Cannes on March 1, called upon

**PLENIPOTENTIARIES OF THE GREAT POWERS AT THE CONGRESS OF VIENNA**
The astonishing return of Napoleon from Elba interrupted the deliberations of the congress which met at Vienna in 1814 to reorganize the political system of Europe after the upheaval it had undergone during the revolutionary and Napoleonic wars. Its agreements were signed, however, on June 9, 1815, by Austria, Prussia, Russia, Britain, France, Sweden, Spain and Portugal. This lithograph by Dorndorf after Jean Baptiste Isabey's picture shows a session of the Congress.

France to support him, appealed to the soldiers sent against him by the government, and to the marshals; of whom those who had not taken the new oath of allegiance, and Ney, who had done so, joined his standard. He marched on Paris at the head of a constantly increasing force, and Louis fled. The powers at Vienna proclaimed him the public enemy of Europe on March 13; on March 30 he proclaimed himself emperor in Paris. He made overtures for his recognition by Europe as a constitutional monarch; but that was a risk the powers would not take. The stake was to be all or nothing.

Russia and Austria were a long way off—their armies would not be ready for months; Prussia was comparatively ready to take the field, and the British army, always numerically small. Napoleon wrought again titanically to create an army which should shatter the

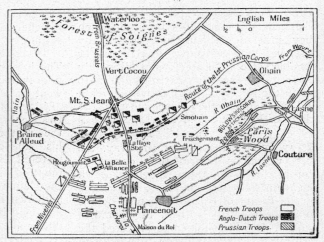

THE OPPOSING ARMIES AT WATERLOO

In this plan, showing the disposition of the opposing forces south of Waterloo, Wellington's army (top), with infantry in front and cavalry behind, faces the farm of La Haye Sainte and the château of Hougoumont. On the right is the road to Wavre, whence came Blücher's relieving contingent

Prussians and British first, and then advance to a new Austerlitz unless Russia and Austria should come to terms with him first. Wellington took the command, in Belgium, of a mixed force, half British, the other half North Germans, Belgians and Dutch, the two last being, at best, half-hearted in the cause. There was no half-heartedness about the Prussians who came up under Blücher. But Napoleon was swifter than his adversaries. He was ready to strike before Wellington and Blücher had completed their junction.

On June 15 he sprang on Charleroi, which the Prussians held; next day he flung himself on the Prussian position at Ligny—the blow which was to split the Prussians from the British and drive them back on Namur and Brussels respectively. He smote the Prussians but did not rout them; Blücher fell back, not on Namur, but on Wavre.

The British had held up Ney at Quatre Bras, preventing him from turning the Prussian flank at Ligny. Wellington, covering Brussels, concentrated on the Waterloo Ridge, where it was Blücher's aim to effect his junction. This he did—Grouchy, who had been dispatched in pursuit, having strayed on a false scent—in the late afternoon of June 18 when

FAMOUS PRUSSIAN GENERAL

The relentless energy characteristic of Gebhard Leberecht von Blücher (1742–1819) is well brought out in Groger's painting of him. His intervention with the Prussian army at Waterloo decided the day in favour of Wellington.

*From Seidlitz, ' Porträtwerk,' Brückmann A.G.*

**THE DERELICT CHATEAU OF HOUGOUMONT**
Fierce French attacks upon the château of Hougoumont, protecting Wellington's right at Waterloo, reduced it to this skeleton building shown in S. Wharton's sketch made after the battle. Jerome Bonaparte's efforts to storm the château were repulsed by the valour of a detachment of the Guards.
*From Wharton, 'Twelve Views of Waterloo,' 1816*

Wellington had been barely holding his ground for half a day against Napoleon's onslaught. The unexpected appearance of the Prussians on Napoleon's right flank, when he had supposed them to be in the grip of Grouchy's pursuing force, was decisive ; the British hurled back the last desperate attack of the Old Guard, on the French left, while the Prussians stormed in on their right ; the defeat became a rout, and the rout a headlong flight. Napoleon's army had ceased to exist. When the emperor reached Paris he found himself without supporters. For the second time he abdicated, and then, finding escape impossible, surrendered himself to the commander of the British frigate Bellerophon. The 'Revolutionary and Napoleonic Wars' were ended.

T HE era of those wars in Europe was also in England and Scotland the era which established the Industrial Revolution, which, having its beginning in the British Isles, revolutionised the economic conditions and in many respects the whole social structure of the world in the course of the nineteenth century. In its beginnings it substituted

manufacture for agriculture as the main industry of the islands, along with the commerce which led Napoleon to refer contemptuously to the English as a 'nation of shopkeepers.' It had already been inaugurated by the inventions which first developed water power and then applied steam power to the production of goods hitherto manufactured by hand. The steam-driven machinery and the enormous accompanying increase in the use of iron, of steel the product of iron, and of coal, deprived the agricultural population of the by-industries by which the yeoman and the cottager had hitherto supplemented their livelihood ; large-scale farming was proving itself infinitely more productive than small-scale farming ; and the yeoman practically disappeared, while the cottagers were driven from the countryside to seek, but by no means always to find, employment in the towns which grew up round the new machinery.

The numbers of the population increased rapidly ; machinery increased production tenfold with half the labour, while the market for the goods expanded,

**SATIRE ON THE IRISH UNION**
This print of 1799 shows Pitt driving the Union Coach with the Scottish members safely inside. On top of the coach a figure, apparently Melville, throws the shells of nuts to the Irish members seated precariously at the back. Catholic emancipation, promised as a condition of union, was not forthcoming.
*British Museum*

but not with equal rapidity since Europe was submerged in war ; and for the time there was no employment for half the displaced labour. But the new machinery was a British monopoly ; the raw materials for the new manufactures—coal, iron, cotton and wool—were available in far greater quantity than elsewhere ; and Britain secured a lead in manufacturing capacity which set her out of reach of competition for three-quarters of a century. At the close of our period, however, the second stage of the revolution, the stage which applied mechanical power to locomotion and transport, was still undeveloped though the first steam - boats had been built.

A reluctant Ireland was incorporated in the United Kingdom in 1801, but without the Catholic emancipation promised and demanded as a condition. It failed, largely for that reason, to effect such a genuine union as that which had resulted from the incorporation of England and Scotland as Great Britain a century earlier. On the other hand, Great Britain, immediately before the French Revolution, had annexed in the eastern ocean the continent of Australia, where there was only a very sparse population still in a state of the most primitive culture known to Western travellers. The new lands were occupied primarily for the deportation of criminals, but were soon found to offer promise for colonisation, though as yet they attracted few adventurers.

In India the development of a British ascendancy among the country powers between whom the Mogul empire was being redistributed can only be touched upon here. From time to time efforts were made under the French Republic to recover French influence at the courts of the greater potentates, which imposed upon British governors, the Marquess

Wellesley (Wellington's elder brother) and his successors, the necessity of military operations first against Tippu Sultan (Tippoo Sahib) of Mysore, and then against the Maratha confederacy, which in turn involved annexations of territory (failing which no native power regarded itself as having been defeated) that passed under direct British administration, and the assumption of something like sovereignty over the potentates themselves

'TIPPOO SAHIB' OF MYSORE

When the British entered Mysore in 1790 Tippu Sultan (1753–99), retaliated by a counter-invasion. He was killed during the storm of Seringapatam. Engraving after drawing by Mauraisse.

—the general control which had fallen away completely from the nominal sovereign, the Mogul at Delhi.

Meanwhile, on the other side of the Atlantic, changes had been brought about in Canada by the migration thither of the United Empire Loyalists from the former colonies which had separated themselves from the Empire. While Lower Canada remained mainly French in its institutions, this new population in Upper Canada was essentially British ; and Canada was divided into two separate governments, the Upper presently known as Ontario and the Lower as Quebec, while both were separate from the colony on the right bank of the St. Lawrence, New Brunswick, the Acadia of old times.

Both Central and South America still continued to be subject to the Spanish crown, and attempts to foster revolt from Spain during the war failed ignominiously. But the Creoles—the American-born Spaniards—during that period when Spain was unable to govern either herself or her colonies, had acquired a control denied to them by Spanish monarchs, and were ripe for revolt when any attempt should be made to revive the old system of administration by governors and officials sent from Spain.

The thirteen states, once British colonies, which had achieved their independence in 1783 were faced with the problem of transforming themselves into a united state. To begin with they were thirteen separate states, 'united' but not unified. In 1789 they provided themselves with a constitution as the United States of North America, and elected George Washington, the hero of the war, as their first president. The constitution provided them with a common central government, while leaving each state under its own state government; but it took three-quarters of a century to settle finally the relations between the central and the state governments. For the states had conflicting as well as common interests, and, as in ancient Hellas and in the Holy Roman Empire, each was very jealous of any curtailment of its individual rights. Broadly, however, it was the inevitable result of the conditions that the northern group tended to favour the strengthening of the central authority, the southern to resist it; the two groups being roughly distinguished as Federalist and anti-Federalist or Republican.

**THOMAS JEFFERSON**

Secretary of state under Washington in 1790, and president 1801-9, Thomas Jefferson (1743–1826) led the Democratic Republican party which upheld the sovereignty of the individual states.

Washington would associate himself with neither party; though he was himself a Southerner, a Virginian, the two chief ministers of his selection were the Northerner Alexander Hamilton and the Southerner Thomas Jefferson. Financial reconstruction was the first necessity. The debts of the several states were taken over by the Federal government, and a national bank was established on the analogy of the Bank of England—making the maintenance of the Federal or central government's stability a matter of first-rate importance to the moneyed interests.

Washington could not resist the practically universal insistence on his retaining the presidency for a second term of four

years, at the moment when France, at war with Great Britain, was urging the new nation, whose 'liberation' she had materially assisted, to renew the offensive alliance. Neutrality was the obvious interest of the States, and Jacobinism was hateful to Hamilton, though vindictiveness towards the old enemy and sympathy with the new republic made the South urgent on the other side. Washington was firm in declining the invitation; his position was only strengthened by the injudicious attempt of the French ambassador to appeal to the people against the president, and the States remained neutral. Washington could not be persuaded to enter on a third presidential term, and from

**FIRST AMERICAN PRESIDENT**

The skill of George Washington (1732–99), who became the first president of America in 1789, effected a compromise between the two antagonistic parties that divided the U.S.A. Gilbert Stuart painted this portrait in 1797.

1797 the presidential elections became a party question. John Adams, a Federalist, became president, but jealousies between him and Hamilton split the party, and the next president was the Republican Jefferson (1801). The change was accompanied by a redistribution of offices on the disastrous principle of ' the spoils to the victor.'

In 1803 Napoleon purchased American friendship by selling Louisiana, which he had acquired from Spain, to Jefferson —a transaction which implied the possession of powers by the Federal government incompatible with Republican doctrine.

**F**RICTION arose between the United States and the British over Great Britain's claim to prevent neutral trading with her enemies—a comfortable doctrine for the mistress of the seas, and one which she could not afford to discard. Napoleon's Berlin and Milan decrees in effect made a similar claim for France, but Napoleon's navy could not enforce his decrees, while the British navy could enforce the orders in council which were her reply to them. The friction became acute, and the Americans were roused against the power whose action did in actual fact interfere seriously with their commerce. The British also exercised irritating ' rights of search ' on the high seas. Other causes of friction developed. At last in 1812 the British offered concessions, but it was too late. In June of that year Jefferson's successor, President Madison, declared war.

To Great Britain the affair was merely a by-issue of the huge conflict in which she was engaged. For a year American privateers and stray American frigates were more than a match for the British frigates and shipping with which they came in conflict ; then the British got the upper hand ; but there were no fleet actions. The States troops invaded Canada, but instead of finding a response they found an extremely vigorous loyalty to the British flag, and were very thoroughly beaten off. In 1814, on Napoleon's first abdication, British troops were released from Europe ; a campaign in the north was disgraced by the destruction of Washington, and a campaign in the south was distinguished by the complete repulse of the Peninsular veterans before New Orleans by Andrew Jackson.

The war had been on both sides an affair not of reasoning but of ill temper. It was impossible that it should benefit either ; the northern states, for commercial reasons if for no other, were anxious for a renewal of amicable relations, and when the last wasteful fight took place at New Orleans the belligerents had in fact already come to terms in Europe and signed the Peace of Ghent (December 14, 1814), though the news had not reached the combatants in America. That peace did not remove the original pretexts for the quarrel ; it dealt with the question of the Anglo-American boundary on lines hotly resented by the Canadians, but so ambiguously that it was a guarantee that disputes would be renewed in the future, and it left a legacy of ill will which did not finally pass away until the third generation.

**FIGHT BETWEEN SHANNON AND CHESAPEAKE**
Friction between Britain and America over the former's commercial restrictions led to naval reprisals. On June 1, 1813, a battle took place in Boston Bay between the British frigate Shannon and the American frigate Chesapeake. This picture illustrates the British capture of the Chesapeake.
*Engraving after Whitcombe*

# *Ninth Era*

# THE WONDERFUL CENTURY

## 1815–1914

---

Chapter 29
## THE AFTERMATH OF REVOLUTION, 1815—1848

Chapter 30
## CONSOLIDATING OF THE GREAT POWERS, 1848—1878

Chapter 31
## THE WORLD DRIFT TO WAR, 1878—1914

---

DURING the century following the fall of Napoleon, the European states passed through three phases. In the first, all governments alike were anxious to avert international wars, while the absolutist governments were no less anxious to repress the ideas known as ' the revolution ' generated in the course of the struggle, democratic and nationalist—both of which were seething among the peoples. For a time the monarchs succeeded. Then arose conflicts, popular or nationalist, with the result that the German empire and the Italian kingdom were created and consolidated, though at the cost of international wars, while the democratic idea was making great advances in France and England, and the British Empire was developing into a commonwealth of nations. The United States had fought out their own battle of unification ; the South American states had become stabilised. The result was the third phase, that state of unstable equilibrium which was to issue in the Great War.

# TABLE OF DATES FOR CHAPTER 29

1815 Waterloo.
 Napoleon sent to St. Helena.
 Louis XVIII restored in France, where an army of occupation is to remain till a heavy indemnity has been paid.
 Holy Alliance of Christian Princes.
 Quadruple Alliance of Russia, Austria, Prussia and Great Britain; Second Treaty of Paris; Era of Congresses.
 England: The Corn Law of 1815.

1816 Germany: First Diet of German Confederation.
 Portugal: Maria I d; acc. John VI, who remains in Brazil; regency of Beresford.
 South American colonies in revolt; Morillo establishes royalist authority in north.

1817 U.S.A.: James Monroe president.
 S. America: Argentina establishes independence. Rise of Paez in Venezuela.

1818 Congress of Aix-la-Chapelle.
 Army of occupation withdrawn from France, which has paid the indemnity and joins Quadruple Alliance.
 India: Pindari and Maratha war.
 Charles XIII of Sweden and Norway d.; acc. Charles XIV (Bernadotte).

1819 Germany: Carlsbad Resolutions or decrees issued to suppress revolutionary propaganda.

1820 George III d.; acc. prince-regent George IV.
 Spain: Ferdinand VII forced to accept Constitution of 1812.
 France: Assassination of duc de Berri.
 Congress of Troppau, transferred to Laibach.

1821 Greek rising in Wallachia is suppressed but followed by revolt of the Morea and of Ali Pasha of Janina.
 Italy: Revolution in Piedmont suppressed with Austrian help; Victor Emmanuel abd.; acc. Charles Felix. Revolution in Sicilies suppressed by Austrians.
 Napoleon d. in St. Helena.
 U.S.A.: The Missouri Compromise.
 S. America: San Martín from Chile takes Lima. Royalists defeated in north; Colombia declared independent.

1822 Greece: Fall of Ali Pasha; massacre of Chios. Greek successes.
 Congress of Verona refuses support to Greeks.
 England: Castlereagh d; Canning Foreign minister.
 Portugal: John VI, on his return from Brazil, (1821), accepts a constitution.
 Brazilian Empire proclaimed under Pedro I, son of John VI of Portugal.

1823 Spain: Ferdinand delivered from the constitutionalists and despotic rule restored by French troops.
 President Monroe enunciates 'Monroe doctrine.'
 Santa Ana proclaims Mexican Republic.

1824 Louis XVIII d.; acc. Charles X.
 Canning recognizes independence of the Spanish American states.
 India: First Burmese war.

1825 Ibrahim, son of Mehemet Ali Pasha of Egypt, in southern Greece.
 Tsar Alexander I d.; acc. Nicholas I (brother).
 England: Repeal of combination laws; Stockton and Darlington railway.
 U.S.A.: John Quincey Adams president.
 S. America: Bolivar, from Colombia, takes Quito.

1826 Ibrahim takes Missolonghi; suppression and massacre of Janissaries by Sultan Mahmud II.
 John VI d.; acc. Maria da Gloria, dr. of Pedro of Brazil. Her uncle Miguel regent.

1827 England: Ministry of George Canning.
 Treaty of London (Great Britain, France and Russia) to impose peace on Turks.
 B. of Navarino. Egypt withdraws from Greece. Canning d. England neutralised.

1828 Russia declares war on Turkey.
 Miguel usurps Portuguese crown; constitutionalist resistance.
 India: Lord William Bentinck governor-general. Suppression of suttee; introduction of Western education; beginning of suppression of thuggee and dacoity.

1829 Russians take Adrianople; treaty of Adrianople.
 Greek independence under Capo d'Istria recognized.
 United Kingdom: Catholic emancipation.

1829 Germany: Prussia inaugurates the Customs Union or Zollverein, which gradually extends to all Germany except Austria.
 U.S.A.: Andrew Jackson president.

1830 George IV d.; acc. William IV. Grey's Reform ministry.
 France: Occupation of Algiers. The 'July Revolution'; flight of Charles X; acc. Louis Philippe of Orléans.
 Belgian rising against Dutch supremacy. London conference encourages Belgian claims.
 Polish revolt.
 Sicilies: Francis I. d.; acc. Ferdinand II (Bomba).
 S. America: Bolivar 'the Liberator' d. By this time Argentina, Chile, Uruguay and Paraguay are established as republics in the south, Colombia, Venezuela, Bolivia, Peru and Ecuador in the north.

1831 Charles Felix d.; acc. Charles Albert.
 Leopold of Saxe-Coburg accepts Belgian crown.
 Polish rising crushed.
 Risings in Papal States; Austrians occupy Bologna, to support Papacy.

1832 Otto of Bavaria made king of Greece.
 French troops occupy Ancona as a check on Austria in Italy.
 Poland made a Russian province.
 'Great Reform Bill' carried in England.
 Mehemet Ali conquers Syria.

1833 Mahmud II cedes Syrian pashalik to Mehemet, but makes treaty of Unkiar Skelessi with Russia, whose ascendancy is established at the Porte.
 Spain: Ferdinand d.; acc. Isabella II, with her mother Christina as regent; supported by the constitutionalists, while the crown is claimed by her uncle Carlos. Beginning of Carlist wars.
 Leopold I recognized as king of the Belgians.
 British Empire: Abolition of slavery. First English Factory Act.

1834 England: Poor Law Amendment Act.
 Portugal: Expulsion of Miguel by constitutionalists.

1835 Austria: Francis II d.; acc. Ferdinand I.

1836 Spain: Christina concedes 1812 constitution.
 Cape Colony: The Great Trek. Dutch farmers (Boers) emigrate over Orange River.

1837 William IV d.; acc. Queen Victoria. Separation of British from Hanoverian crown, to which the queen's uncle Ernest of Cumberland succeeds under Salic law.
 Canada: Papineau's rebellion in Lower Canada.
 U.S.A.: Van Buren president.

1838 England: The Chartist movement.
 Austrians and French leave Bologna and Ancona.
 First Atlantic crossing under steam only.
 S. Africa: Boer victory over Zulus (Dingaan's day).

1839 Mehemet Ali again attacks sultan. Mahmud d.; acc. Abdul Meiid.
 India: First Afghan expedition deposes Dost Mahomed. Ranjit Singh of Lahore d.
 First China War begins.
 Definitive treaty between Holland and Belgium.
 Carlos expelled from Spain.

1840 Mehemet Ali checkmated by action of Palmerston. He surrenders Syria, retaining Egypt as hereditary pashalik. Ascendancy of Great Britain at Constantinople.
 Canada: Durham report produces Act of Reunion.
 New Zealand: Treaty of Waitangi with Maori.
 Prussia: Frederick William III d.; acc. Frederick William IV

1841 India: The Kabul disaster.
 U.S.A.: John Tyler president.

1842 Second Afghan expedition restores Dost Mahomed.
 Treaty of Nanking ends China war.
 Ashburton Treaty (Great Britain and U.S.A.).
 British annex Natal; Boers withdraw to Transvaal.

1843 British annexation of Sindh.

1844 Sweden: Charles XIV d.; acc. Oscar I.

1845 U.S.A.: Polk president; annexation of California.
 India: First Sikh war.

1846 Affair of the Spanish marriages.
 Pius IX elected pope; begins reforms.
 U.S.A. and Great Britain: Oregon Boundary dispute settled.
 U.S.A.: Mexican war.

1847 Canada: Elgin introduces responsible government.

1848 Sicilies: Constitution forced on Ferdinand II.
 France: The February Revolution.

### CHAPTER 29

# THE AFTERMATH OF REVOLUTION: 1815–1848

THE French Revolution and the consequent wars had turned Europe upside down, and Europe required to have its equilibrium restored. The restoration was the business before the Vienna Congress, which had been rudely disturbed by the last episode of the 'Hundred Days.' Palpably it could be attained only by the common consent and continuous co-operation of the great powers —the four before whom Napoleon had gone down—together with their minor allies, and France herself; but primarily the four, Great Britain, Russia, Austria and Prussia. France must undergo a period of probation before she could count fully with the others.

### Reaction after the Revolution

THEY reconstructed the map of Europe, primarily in their own interests. France retained her territory, as laid down in the peace of Paris, though an army of occupation was to remain for some years within her borders. Austria retained the Italian dominions she had acquired during the wars; what had been the Austrian Netherlands, henceforth to be known as Belgium, she resigned to William, the restored stadtholder of Holland and now king of 'the Netherlands.' Prussia resigned her claim to the grand duchy of Warsaw, acquired in the partitions of Poland and taken from her after Jena; she was compensated by acquiring the German provinces on the Rhine which had been annexed by Napoleon. The grand duchy became once more the kingdom of Poland—not annexed to Russia, but with the tsar as king. Great Britain retained the Ionian Islands and Malta.

The king of Sardinia was reinstated in Savoy and Piedmont, with Genoa added to his dominion; the States of the Church were restored to the pope; Ferdinand was reinstated in Naples, whence Murat, who had declared for Napoleon, was ejected. He tried to restore himself, but was captured and shot. The Spanish Ferdinand, the son of Carlos IV, was reinstated in Spain; in Portugal the administration, in the name of Queen Maria, was placed in the hands of the English chief of the army, Field-Marshal Beresford, the royal family remaining in Brazil. In the north, Norway was transferred from Denmark (in accordance with a previous compact between the tsar and Bernadotte) to Sweden—not an incorporating union, but a union of crowns—by way of compensation for her loss of Finland to Russia.

In Germany the absorption of innumerable minor principalities by their bigger neighbours was accepted; the Holy Roman Empire had disappeared, and the surviving states including Austria were joined together in the German Confederation, with the Austrian emperor as its president. The close accord between Prussia and Austria, so long as both were really directed by the Austrian minister Metternich, prevented the rivalry between them for ascendancy in Germany from coming to a head as yet. Metternich was the guiding spirit in both governments for another generation. In the reconstruction of the map, it occurred to no one to consider any but dynastic interests; populations were transferred from one dynast to another without consulting their wishes. The autocrats were determined to 'make the world safe for autocracy'— that was their answer to the Revolution which had declared war on autocracy.

### Holy Alliance of Christian Princes

THE dynasts were restored unconditionally; but Tsar Alexander was an idealist, whose conviction that princes were rulers by divine authority and responsible to none but the Almighty was qualified only by an intense sense not of the claims of his subjects upon him but of his own duty towards them as a Christian prince; though he, of course, was the sole judge of what that duty might be. He was a great

**TERRITORIAL DISTRIBUTION OF EUROPE AFTER THE CONGRESS OF VIENNA**

The settlement of Europe effected at the Congress of Vienna was dictated almost entirely by dynastic considerations ; but beneath the surface was a craving for national independence from alien dominion that manifested itself in the revolutionary movements of the succeeding era. In 1831 Belgium achieved her independence of Holland and by the same year Greece, having defied her Turkish over-lords, had become autonomous. By 1848 Italy still remained a 'geographical expression.'

admirer of liberty, but of the liberty which the benevolent father concedes to his children, to be withdrawn if abused, and

**FOUNDER OF THE HOLY ALLIANCE**

The subject of this engraving of a portrait by Pierre Michel Bourdon is Alexander I (1777–1825), idealist tsar of Russia. The so-called Holy Alliance of Christian Princes was his creation.

*From Seidlitz, ' Porträtwerk,' Brückmann A.G.*

certainly not to be claimed as a right. He credited other despots with a similar idealism, and promulgated a Holy Alliance of Christian Princes, all pledged to pursue the ideal—which for the time included the granting of (revocable) constitutions to their peoples—and all pledged to support each other in the spirit of Christian brother-hood. All, except for obvious reasons the sultan, were invited to join ; practically all did join, except the pope, who regarded the tsar as a heretic, and the king of England, who had become hopelessly insane, while the prince regent was con-veniently precluded from joining by the Constitution. Nor was there a single one among them whose subsequent course of action was affected by a hair's breadth.

The Holy Alliance was a dead letter from the beginning, because it rested on the assumption that princes in their own dominions were accountable to no one except the Almighty, from whom they had received their authority—not even to other princes. On the other hand, the great powers agreed together, not as individual princes but as the powers in whose hands the peace of Europe was reposed, to hold periodical congresses for the settlement of international questions and agreement upon joint action when required.

ɪɴ restoring the Bourbon monarchy in France the powers had insisted upon the provision of a constitution, a course to which Louis XVIII was agreeable, though his brother Charles of Artois and not a few of the émigrés were not. Louis was perfectly aware that what the ultra-royalists wanted was a restoration of the pre-revolution class privileges, and also vindictive action, which, as he knew, would inevitably bring about another revolution ; even with a constitution it was difficult enough to keep the ' ultras ' under control, and the government in the hands of moderates. There were German states in which the princes took a similar view ; and Alexander gave the Poles a constitution. Elsewhere, however, such constitutions as the rulers chose to grant conveyed no real power to the assemblies, and the princes were as despotic as ever. The Diet of the German Confederation was itself a diet of princes ready to encourage each other's despotism, all dreading ' the Revolution,' none of them with a German national as opposed to a state consciousness, and all dominated by Metternich, the arch-enemy of popular power and of national consolidation.

But the French Revolution had created everywhere a demand for popular liberties, and the national revolts of Spain and then of Prussia against a foreign domination had developed the sentiment of nationalism among peoples on many of whom the Vienna settlement had riveted the domination of foreign rulers more firmly than before. The Sicilies detested the Bourbon

dynasty ; Hungary, Lombardy and Venetia detested the Austrians, Poland the Russians, Belgium the Dutch, and the Greeks their slavery to the Turks. Neither nationalism nor popular liberties were compatible in fact with the absolutist theories of Alexander the idealist or Metternich the materialist ; whereas both appealed strongly alike to French and to British sentiment, although both in France and in Great Britain there was still a widespread and lively dread of ' Jacobinism ' at home.

It must be remarked, however, that the demands of nationalism—the spirit of

**REACTIONARY EUROPEAN RULERS**
The spirit of national liberty that flourished widely in post-Revolutionary Europe was ruthlessly suppressed by despots like Ferdinand II, whose rule over the Two Sicilies has been described as the ' negation of God.' Goya's painting (right) shows Ferdinand VII of Spain, another monarch who repressed popular liberties.

national liberty and national unity—were not always immediately reconcilable with the democratic demand for popular and civic rights and liberties. In Germany, for example, the only organ of national unity was the monarchist Diet of the Confederation ; and to strengthen its central control would strengthen the control of the several princes over their subjects, diminishing the subjects' chances of extracting popular concessions from their rulers. German ' liberalism ' was nationalist in the abstract, but in the concrete it was apt to concentrate upon the demand for popular liberties ; though at the same time a real unification with a real central control was still, as ever, the last thing desired by the dynasts.

Y*

The reaction then was everywhere predominant. The two Ferdinands in Spain and in the Sicilies and Victor Emmanuel in Piedmont suppressed the popular liberties. The Spaniards during the Peninsular War—when they refused to recognize the king set over them by Napoleon—had set up the 'Constitution of 1812,' which Ferdinand on his return accepted and then promptly overturned. The country at large had, in fact, been quite ready to accept Ferdinand ; but he set himself to restore all the worst features of the old system, to persecute everyone who had been concerned with the 1812 constitution, and to establish an unqualified tyranny. Ferdinand of Naples followed a similar course, less aggressively and more gradually. In neither country was there any pretence of a tolerable government, in which the benevolent despot had a thought for the welfare of his subjects. In both countries the tyranny begot active revolutionary movements, with the result that both monarchs in 1820 were compelled by military insurgents to accept the Spanish 'Constitution of 1812,' while Ferdinand of Naples appealed to Austria.

Even in England the dread of Jacobinism led to severe restrictions on rights of assembly, free speech and free criticism. In France, however, after the first outbreak of vindictiveness on the part of his brother Charles and the royalist ultras, Louis procured an assembly in which the majority supported the 'moderate' ministers of his own choice, under whose regime stability was reached so rapidly that in 1818 a congress at Aix-la-Chapelle withdrew the army of occupation and admitted France to the Quadruple Alliance —mainly owing to the insistence of the tsar and of Wellington on behalf of Great Britain. But the increasing strength of the 'liberals' in the Chambers, and the assassination of the king's nephew the duc de Berri, alarmed the moderates and gave the reactionaries the upper hand, which, by a change in the electoral law and a renewed repression of free speech, they were able to retain for a decade.

### Diverse Views on Intervention

THE French government, but not the French people, deserted the attitude of resolute non-intervention in the troubles of other states which Castlereagh, and after his death in 1822 George Canning, maintained steadily. The main difference between those two British ministers was that Canning more emphatically insisted that there was a right of intervention to prevent intervention—that if other powers intervened on one side, Great Britain would have warrant to intervene on the other.

Alexander, who had begun with an enthusiasm for liberal movements emanating from the autocrat, regarded them with horror when they emanated from the people, and became in effect no less a champion of the reaction than Metternich ; while Frederick William followed Metternich's lead with no less docility than his nominal master, Francis II.

Within Germany during the five years after Waterloo liberal movements had been repressed, and their repression had been effected through pressure exercised by Austria and Prussia, notably by the Carlsbad decrees repressing free speech and comment. England and Russia recognized that those two powers were so directly affected that their intervention in the affairs of the states of the German

**VISCOUNT CASTLEREAGH**
After the Treaty of Vienna in 1815, Viscount Castlereagh (1769–1822), the British foreign secretary, pursued a policy of non-intervention. His brain gave way under intensive hard work and unpopularity, and he died by his own hand.
*Painting by Sir T. Lawrence; National Portrait Gallery, London*

Confederation was warranted, without compromising the principle of non-intervention by ' the powers ' in the domestic affairs of particular states.

Portugal was in a somewhat peculiar position. The royal family had taken refuge in Brazil, not from revolutionary subjects but from Napoleon's intrusion. Practically Portugal itself was under British protection during the war, and when it was over the British field-marshal, Beresford, became regent, while King John, who succeeded to the throne in 1816, remained in Brazil. In 1820 the Portuguese insisted on their king's return. He came (leaving the crown prince Pedro in Brazil), to find himself faced with a constitution which he accepted without demur ; while Pedro, in Brazil, was preparing for a declaration of Brazilian independence as the ' Empire of Brazil,' which took effect two years later—a separation that was inevitable ; for Brazil, after being the seat of royalty, would not return to dependence on the government in Lisbon, and Portugal would not accept the position of an appanage to her own colony. These, however, were matters in which foreign intervention was obviously out of the question.

Finally, the restoration of the Spanish monarchy had brought to a head the disaffection of the Spanish colonies in South and Central America, where revolts became general ; Spain was obviously incapable of coping with her transatlantic revolutionists ; and Ferdinand was eager to appeal for European support.

### Interventions in Italy and Spain

Such, then, was the situation in 1820, when the tsar rejected Metternich's proposal that Russia and Austria should take the Spanish and Italian questions into their own hands, and the Congress of Troppau, presently transferred to Laibach, was called to deal with them. The tsar had come definitely over to the view that it was the business of the powers to suppress ' the Revolution ' wherever it raised its head. France was already inclining in that direction. Castlereagh rejected the doctrine, but admitted Austria's right as an Italian power to intervene in Italy.

**BRITISH REGENT OF PORTUGAL**
William Carr Beresford, who entered the British army in 1785, was distinguished for his military valour. He did good service in the Peninsular War by reorganizing the Portuguese armies, and later became regent of Portugal.
*Painting by Rothwell ; National Portrait Gallery, London*

Austria restored Ferdinand in Naples, where he gave full rein to his vindictiveness. Then Piedmont rose ; the king yielded, accepted a constitution, and abdicated. His brother, Charles Felix, who succeeded him, was an uncompromising reactionist ; for a moment his cousin and heir-presumptive, Charles Albert, seemed likely to head the revolutionists, but preferred to follow second thoughts, and the insurgents were crushed by Austrian troops (1821). Austria virtually dominated Italy.

The tsar wished to intervene in Spain ; Metternich did not want Russian forces in the west. France put in a claim to be the agent of the powers in Spain in virtue of her own Spanish interests ; but the proposal met with emphatic protest from England, which also had Spanish interests. Another congress met at Verona in 1822, the insurrectionary movement having now developed in the Balkan peninsula. The powers, in spite of the British protest, demanded a modification of the Spanish constitution in favour of the crown ; the Spanish ministry declined ; the French troops which had already massed on the border entered Spain (1823) and restored Ferdinand, who had been virtually held a prisoner. The savage vindictiveness with which he exercised his restored powers excited the protest of the French themselves. Canning, now the controller of British policy, retorted by acknowledging the revolutionary governments in South America as the de facto sovereigns.

In Portugal the reactionaries, headed by the queen and by King John's second son Miguel, procured the fall of the constitution and the restoration of absolutism. The king, who preferred constitutionalism, found himself powerless in the hands of his wife and son, from whom he escaped on a British ship. Here it was in fact the ultras who were attacking the reigning monarch with the people on his side. John was restored without difficulty and with a constitution, and Miguel, though pardoned, was banished—for the time.

ꟿEANWHILE, however, Greece was becoming the storm centre. The Turk in the Ottoman Empire was the military master of subject Christian populations— those of his subjects who had embraced

TSAR NICHOLAS I

Brother of the visionary Alexander I, Nicholas I (1796–1855) succeeded to the Russian throne in 1825. As sternly autocratic as he appears in Krüger's painting of him, he concentrated on advancing Russian interests by practical means.
*From Seidlitz, ' Porträtwerk,' Brückmann A.G.*

BYRON AS GREEK LIBERATOR

The courageous struggle of Greece for independence from Turkish rule aroused great sympathy among lovers of liberty in Europe. Byron was among the volunteers in the cause of Greek freedom and died at Missolonghi in 1824.
*Engraving after sketch made in Greece*

Islam being alone on an equal footing. The Turkish idea of government scarcely went beyond that of extracting for the masters as much as possible from the subjects. The sultan, theoretically the master of all, was in practice very much in the hands of the imperial guard, the Janissaries. The Turk, having no conception of administration, employed Christians as administrators. Serbs, Bulgars, Rumanians, Albanians, Greeks and Macedonians were the heterogeneous mass of his subjects in Europe.

The Greeks, among whom some sense of the traditional glories of their race had recently been spreading, began a revolt in 1821, under the impression that the tsar would come to their aid ; but Metternich, who did not want to see Russia in control of Turkey, persuaded him that the Greek insurrection was merely another manifestation of the Revolution. The Albanian Ali Pasha of Janina revolted ; the Greeks, a maritime people, won successes at sea ; the Turks retaliated by massacres of the Christians who were in their power, and the Greeks retorted in kind. Janina fell and Ali Pasha was killed ; but although the Greeks were fighting without any common organization, and the massacres and atrocities committed by the Turks were on a bigger scale, the successes on the whole were on the side of the Greeks. The Congress of Verona declined to intervene, though in England and France there was a vast amount of sympathy with the Greeks, whom Canning officially recognized as belligerents.

In 1825 the sultan invited the co-operation of his great vassal, the pasha of Egypt, Mehemet Ali. The Egyptian troops, under Mehemet's son Ibrahim, and the Egyptian fleet turned the scale ; in two years it was evident that without intervention the Greeks would be hopelessly crushed, in spite of the help they received from British and French volunteers.

And meanwhile Alexander I died ; his next brother and heir, Constantine, flatly refused the crown, which the third brother, Nicholas, was obliged to assume. Nicholas was the incarnation of rigid autocracy, in whose eyes resistance was the worst of crimes ; but he was no visionary like Alexander ; he concentrated whole-heartedly upon the advancement of Russia and Russian interests. Intervention in the Balkans would advance Russian interests, and the sultan did not count as a Christian autocrat ruling by divine right. Before long it became evident that he would intervene.

By this time there was not much remaining of the idea of unity among the powers. Metternich, with Prussia in his wake, was opposed to anything in the shape of Russian intervention in Turkey, whereas Nicholas was bent on intervening. Canning, whose sympathies were entirely with the Greeks, as were those of France, hesitated to break through the principle of non-intervention, but could not leave Russia to intervene by herself. The result was an agreement between Russia, France and Great Britain to bring joint pressure to bear for the acceptance of agreed terms ; and then, when the sultan rejected their proposals, to enforce an armistice. The French and British fleets entered the bay of Navarino where Mehemet Ali's fleet was lying, a shot was fired which the British admiral interpreted as an attack, and the Egyptian fleet was promptly sunk (1827).

Some weeks earlier Canning had died ; Wellington, now at the head of the British government, was above all things anxious to avoid war ; but to resent action on the part of Nicholas after this incident was obviously impossible. Mehemet Ali, seeing that there was nothing to be gained by fighting, readily withdrew ; Russian troops invaded both European and Asiatic Turkey, with varying success ; diplomacy was endeavouring to arrange for a Greek principality, autonomous but tributary, when in 1829 the Russian general Diebitsch settled matters by capturing Adrianople with a small force, which he represented as the advance guard of a quite imaginary main army—and the Porte submitted.

The treaty of Adrianople (September, 1829) was in effect a Russian triumph. It created an autonomous Greek republic— under the presidency of Count Capo

**KING GEORGE IV**
After acting as regent during his father's insanity, George IV (1762–1830) became king of England in 1820. He had the vices of his age and his rule was neither successful nor popular.

**DESTRUCTION OF THE TURCO-EGYPTIAN FLEET IN NAVARINO BAY**

By their decisive victory over the Turks in the naval battle fought at Navarino on October 20, 1827, the Allied powers (Britain, France and Russia) secured for the Greeks the autonomy they sought. The Ottoman fleet, supported by an Egyptian squadron, was destroyed in the space of two hours. In the centre of this print illustrating the action is Vice-Admiral Sir Edward Codrington's flagship Asia engaged with the Egyptian flagship (right) and the Turkish flagship (left).

*Macpherson Collection*

d'Istria, once a minister of Tsar Alexander —till the powers should succeed in providing it with a prince, under Turkish sovereignty; it opened the Dardanelles and the Bosporus to merchant shipping, and it gave autonomy to the trans-Danube provinces, Wallachia and Moldavia, but under Russian protection. The effect was to give Russia a predominant influence within the Turkish empire, precisely what both Metternich and Canning had wished to avoid. But in 1831 Capo d'Istria was assassinated—his bureaucratic methods, though well intentioned, had been very unpopular; Louis Philippe, the 'citizen king,' was on the French throne; Palmerston, Canning's disciple, was at the British foreign office; Metternich had always held that sovereign independence for Greece, from the Austrian point of view, was an alternative undesirable in itself but preferable to a tributary autonomy which made her look to Russia as her protector; the Porte had no objection to a bargain; and Prince Otto of Bavaria became king of Greece in 1832 with a

ready-made constitution provided for him. This time it was Russia that had been out-manoeuvred. Nicholas' attention had been distracted by affairs in Poland.

ALEXANDER I, until he was mastered by his dread of the Revolution, was ever anxious to propagate liberal ideas and practices. In Russia he had endeavoured to mitigate the system of rural serfdom, which had come into being under the earlier Romanovs, by inducing the nobles to emancipate their serfs; but the emancipation was attended by educational and disciplinary regulations the novelty of which caused them to be hardly less resented than the serfdom. In Poland he intended to create a constitutional Utopia, and when its success was demonstrated to restore again to Poland the districts his grandmother had annexed to Russia. The Poles' idea of liberty was anarchical rather than Utopian, and the Russians did not want their tsar's other kingdom to develop into a powerful and highly organized neighbour. As early as 1820

Alexander found himself obliged to tighten the grip of the autocrat upon the Constitutional Diet of Poland; with the result that repression bred disorders; more repression, more disorders—so that Nicholas on his accession found on his hands not a Utopia but a country ripe, but quite unorganized, for revolt against any restraining authority, but immediately and above all against Russian rule. His elder brother, Constantine, who had refused the tsardom, was placed in command at Warsaw, while Nicholas made preparations to deal with the rebellion he anticipated.

The rebellion came. In 1830—a few months after the successful ' July Revolution ' in France—it broke out in Warsaw, from which Constantine beat a hasty retreat. The moderates tried to direct the Warsaw revolution, while Nicholas marched a Russian army against the rebels. Its approach wrecked the moderates and brought in the extremists, who proclaimed the deposition of the Romanov king. The two powers, France and Great Britain, which had maintained the doctrine of non-intervention on behalf of an autocrat when his subjects were in rebellion, could not claim a right of intervention on behalf of revolutionists, though they might enter mild protests. The

PROMINENT BRITISH STATESMEN OF THE NINETEENTH CENTURY

George Canning (top), oratorically posed in this portrait by Lawrence, became foreign secretary in 1822, and premier in 1827. He maintained Castlereagh's policy of non-intervention but favoured the Greek cause against the Turks. The duke of Wellington (left), portrayed by Count d'Orsay, became premier in 1828, and deprecated Canning's Greek policy. Lord Palmerston (1784–1865) vigorously supported liberalist movements against reaction and repression. J. Partridge painted this portrait of him.

*National Portrait Gallery, London*

**OTTO KING OF GREECE ENTERS NAUPLIA**

In 1832 the Convention of London declared Greece to be an independent kingdom under the protection of Great Britain, France and Russia, and Prince Otto, son of Louis I of Bavaria, became its king. His rule was not popular, for his ideals were despotic and his advisers Bavarian. A painting by Peter Hess gives an impressive idea of Otto's entry into Nauplia in 1833. Nauplia, then the seat of the administration, was superseded by Athens as capital of Greece in 1834.

*Pinakothek, Munich*

**CHARLES X OF FRANCE**

The count of Artois, younger brother of Louis XVI and Louis XVIII, succeeded to the French throne in 1824 as Charles X. His determined attempts to restore the old absolutism met with failure and he abdicated in 1830.

*British Museum*

Polish revolutionary government had many leaders but no leadership; it went to pieces, and for the same reason its army did likewise. When the Russians arrived at Warsaw a desperate resistance was maintained for three days, and then the end came. The Poles by thousands were deported to Siberian or Caucasian regions or fled into exile, while those who were left cherished a burning hatred for the Russians; and Poland became a province of Russia, in the year when Greece became an independent kingdom.

IN France we have seen that the judicious moderation of Louis XVIII could not prevent the royalist reaction which followed the assassination of the duke of Berri in 1820. Hence the intervention of France in Spain in 1823 and the reinstatement of Ferdinand as an autocrat, proceedings which would have found no favour with a ministry of moderates. When Louis died in 1824 and was succeeded by his brother Charles (of Artois) X, there was no longer any doubt that the crown intended to get rid of the constitution and recover its old-time unqualified absolutism, although on the

Greek question the government was disposed to act with England, where, we may observe, the liberal movement was travelling along a different course. There the reaction was at its height in the first years after Waterloo, but as the Jacobin bugbear faded the movement towards constitutional reform, which had been rudely checked by the French Revolution, revived, and gained ground during Canning's ministry. While the French government was growing increasingly repressive, the British government was relaxing restrictions, restoring the liberties which had been suspended, and tending to further reforms broadening the basis of popular representation in parliament.

But in France the reaction was preparing its own downfall. Its first ministerial chief was Richelieu, who had for some time been the chief of the moderates. Richelieu was still too much of a moderate for the party, and was succeeded by Villèle. When Charles X succeeded his brother, Villèle, under pressure from the extremists and the king, pressed forward measures for additional compensations to the returned émigrés, and for gagging the press, which in Paris grew increasingly critical of the government. When the gagging measure was rejected by the Chambers, the desired effect was attained by a royal ordinance. Outside Paris, the

**ENGLAND'S 'SAILOR KING'**

William IV, who succeeded George IV in 1830 and reigned until 1837, was deeply attached to the navy in which he served. In 1832 he sought to obstruct the first Reform Bill, although he was a Whig before his accession.

*Engraving by J. Cochran after Henry Dawe*

country was not excited by domestic politics; the measures adopted under the moderate regime had made it prosperous, and it was pleased by the ' vigorous ' foreign policy of intervention in Greece ; the government began to pin its faith to the achievement of popularity

**NOTABLE FRENCH MINISTERS UNDER LOUIS XVIII AND CHARLES X**

The duc de Richelieu (left, after Lawrence) was too moderate long to retain the position of first minister under the ultra-royalist monarchy of Louis XVIII. He was displaced by the extremist Villèle (centre), a minister after the heart of Charles X, but whose unpopularity forced him to retire in 1828 in favour of the more moderate Martignac. In 1829 Martignac was superseded by the reactionary Jules de Polignac (right), under whose unpopular ministry the Bourbon regime came to an end.

**LOUIS PHILIPPE RIDING WITH HIS SONS**
The 'Citizen King' Louis Philippe (1773–1850) was raised to
the French throne by the bourgeois constitutionalists in 1830.
His position was extremely difficult and, failing to please all
parties, he fled the country in 1848.   Horace Vernet painted
this equestrian portrait of the king and his sons.
*Musée de Versailles; photo, Alinari*

deal with a counter-revolution.
In less than a week, Paris had
deposed Charles and declared
his cousin, Louis Philippe of
Orléans, king in his place.
Charles found himself powerless, abdicated in favour of
his legitimate grandson and
heir, the young comte de
Chambord (whose claim was
ignored by the French provisional government), and
retired to England ; and for
eighteen years after this bloodless ' July revolution,' which
was placidly accepted by
the country, France enjoyed
a constitutional monarchy,
the 'Orléans monarchy,' the
triumph of the bourgeoisie.

There was a moment when
the rising in Paris threatened to
take on a Jacobin character ;
but in fact the revolution
was simply the defeat of the
absolutist reaction by the
middle-class constitutionalism
to which Jacobinism was no less abhorrent.
So long as the Bourbons should prove
loyal to constitutionalism France had
been ready to keep them. When their
loyalty failed, they gave place to that
branch of the family, the house of
Orléans, which had taken the popular
side in the great Revolution. When
Louis Philippe later showed a tendency
towards reaction, coupling therewith
an unpardonable dullness, the house of
Orléans followed the senior branch of
the Bourbons into exile. But when that
time came it owed its exile to ennui more
than to passion.

in this direction.  But in the Chambers
the opposition grew stronger instead of
weaker.  Villèle retired.  For a moment
prudence prevailed, and the king chose
the moderate Martignac as the head of a
new ministry ; but it was not long before
Martignac was displaced by the advanced
reactionary Polignac (1829).

Polignac had a scheme for the absorption of Belgium, which detested its subordination to the Dutch under the system
which had transferred it to the kingdom
of Holland.  Polignac's scheme, however,
was promptly vetoed by Prussia.  The
country was insufficiently soothed by the
success of an expedition sent to quell
the arrogance of the Dey of Algiers.  The
Chambers grew more restive.  The king
found that he must either yield to them
or break them.  He tried to break them
by royal ordinances renewing the press-
gagging law, and so changing the electoral
law as to secure subservient Chambers
(July 26, 1830).  The ordinances were in
flagrant violation of the Constitution ;
they meant in fact an absolutist revolution.
But no preparations had been made to

THE ' July revolution ' encouraged the
reform movement in England, the
movement which transferred parliamentary predominance from the landed
interest to the professional and commercial classes.  The lurid vision of
Jacobinism had been losing its terrors
only by slow degrees ; but the ease and
orderliness with which France effected her
second revolution went far to dissipate
middle-class fears.  Two years after the

ejection of Charles X the British parliament passed what was known for the next half-century as the Great Reform Bill—under the impression that with it democracy had reached its limit.

In 1833 nationalism and constitutionalism had won the day jointly in Greece ; in Germany both had been depressed ; in Italy both had been defeated, though the July revolution had encouraged an unsuccessful attempt at constitutional emancipation in the Papal States which were under the temporal dominion of the pope. There the revolution was put down by the intervention of Austria, while French troops occupied Ancona more as a precaution against the development of an Austrian protectorate than with intent to actual counter-intervention. Constitutional reform in Great Britain, constitutional monarchy in France, both seemed to be successfully established as against absolutism on one side and a proletariat democracy on the other. But both Spain and Portugal were in the throes of a constitutional conflict.

In Portugal the death of King John in 1826 left his elder son Pedro I, the emperor of Brazil, his heir. Barred by the Brazilian constitution from holding both crowns, Pedro transferred his rights in Portugal to his little daughter Maria da Gloria. Meanwhile, his brother Miguel was to act as regent, and was presently to become king by marrying the child when she was old enough. Miguel did not choose to wait ; he seized the crown ; Pedro came to Europe to protect his daughter's interests. Neither party could master the other till the support of Palmerston began to turn the scale on the legitimist and the constitutionalist side ; and even then a definite decision seemed remote.

In Spain, Ferdinand had proved himself a reactionary and a clerical of the worst type. His heir presumptive was his brother Carlos—another of the same type. But Ferdinand, thrice a childless widower,

**A MOMENTOUS JOURNEY : LOUIS PHILIPPE SETS OUT FOR THE HOTEL DE VILLE**

The July Revolution of 1830 which overturned the reactionary monarchy of Charles X was the opportunity of Louis Philippe, duke of Orléans. Elected lieutenant-general of the realm, he decided to test popular opinion of his acceptance of the office by going through Paris from the Palais Royal to the Hôtel de Ville, the headquarters of the Republican government. Vernet's painting shows the beginning of his perilous journey which, despite ominous signs, was successfully accomplished.

*Musée de Versailles ; photo, Neurdein*

married a fourth time, and had a daughter Isabella. Setting aside the recent constitutional enactment which had adopted the 'Salic' law of succession, he issued a 'pragmatic sanction' declaring that his daughter, not his brother, was heir. To Carlos this was an unwarrantable invasion of his own rights. Ferdinand died in 1833; Isabella was proclaimed queen with her mother the queen-dowager Christina as regent, with the support of the constitutionalists, to whom the idea of Carlos was intolerable ; and as a matter of course the two uncle-pretenders in Spain and Portugal made common cause against the two little queens who were their respective nieces.

**A SPANISH CLAIMANT**

On the death of his brother Ferdinand VII, king of Spain, in 1833, Don Carlos claimed the throne, but a decree of the late king named the infanta Isabella as queen. Don Carlos took the field but lost his cause.

Actually, however, when the two official governments also made common cause, with the moral support of France and Great Britain, in 1834, Miguel abandoned the struggle ; though it was not till 1839 that Carlos followed his example, and the Carlists were finally suppressed in 1840.

In yet another quarter the example of the July revolution had produced its effect. Belgium, the 'Netherlands' of the eighteenth century, resented its subordination to the Dutch in the 'Kingdom of the Netherlands' which the Vienna Congress bestowed on the house of Orange. Its absorption by France was not to be thought of, from either a British or a Prussian point of

**INTERNATIONAL CONGRESS OF INFANT ROYALTIES**

This satirical print was published in 1833 when constitutional conflict was disturbing several countries whose sovereigns were of tender age. Isabella of Spain (right) was only three when her proclamation as queen led to the first Carlist war. In Portugal, Dom Miguel claimed the crown of Maria II, aged fourteen. Otto (left), shown as a boy of twelve, was king of a newly independent Greece ; and the imperial crown of Brazil overweights the head of Pedro II, five years old. (Two of the cartoonist's ages are inaccurate : Otto was eighteen and Pedro, five at his accession, was eight at the date of the print).

*British Museum*

view. But, failing to gain constitutional equality, the Belgian constitutionalists asserted their national independence. To the tsar, any departure from the Vienna settlement was intolerable ; all the powers were bound by it. But it had been made over Belgium's head, and at least two powers, France and Great Britain, could not ignore that fact. To forbid Belgium her independence would be a monstrous tyranny. France declared that if Prussia, another champion of the Vienna settlement, intervened on behalf of the king she would intervene on the other side.

The moment was inconvenient for Nicholas, owing to affairs in Poland. Metternich's preoccupation was with Italy. A conference was sitting to deal with the Greek question, in London, where France and Great Britain made joint proposals for the settlement of the Belgian question. The first terms put forward were rejected by the Belgians, but they accepted amended terms. The essential point was that Belgium was to be an independent monarchy, a king having been found for her in the person of Leopold of Saxe-Coburg. She had offered the crown to a French prince, but that was inevitably vetoed. William rejected the proposed terms ; Dutch troops invaded Belgium, Leopold appealed to France, French troops entered Belgium, and the Dutch retired ; but it was not till the British fleet moved that they evacuated Antwerp (1832). Nobody wanted to fight, but it was not actually until 1839 that Holland was induced to sign the peace, to which France, Prussia and Great Britain were parties, which guaranteed the borders and the neutrality of the Belgian kingdom. Great Britain, with France and Prussia, had for the first time broken through the fetish of cast-iron permanence in the Vienna settlement which had been an axiom of the tsars and of Metternich.

### Problems in the Near East

MEANWHILE, the Near Eastern problem was passing through another phase. The sultan Mahmud, who had been forced to concede Greek independence, was not popular with his Mahomedan subjects.

**FIRST KING OF THE BELGIANS**
Belgium was established as an independent state with a constitutional and hereditary monarchy in 1831. The crown was offered to Prince Leopold of Saxe-Coburg, and on June 4, 1832, he was proclaimed as Leopold I, king of the Belgians.
*Engraving by T. Blood*

He had surrendered territory to the infidel, and he was a reformer ; reform meant, among other things, bridling corruption. He had removed one source of imperial weakness in 1826 by the suppression of the Janissaries, who were as dangerous to the sultan as the Praetorian Guard had been to so many Roman emperors ; but he had not created an equivalent military organization under his own control. And he had irritated the most powerful of his viceroys, Mehemet Ali of Egypt, by refusing to convey Syria to him—the reward he was to have received for the subjection of the rebellious Greeks, which he had failed to effect. In 1832 Mehemet, after the fashion of English medieval barons, marched an army into Syria merely in order to deliver his honoured suzerain from the evil counsellors who were leading him astray.

Mahmud's troops fled before Mehemet's redoubtable son, Ibrahim. Mahmud appealed to the powers. The powers, Russia excepted, had more pressing engagements. Russia offered her benevolent aid. Mahmud hesitated ; Ibrahim advanced. Mahmud accepted Russian aid ; Russian troops advanced. Britain and France woke up and sent fleets to the Dardanelles, urging Mahmud to make concessions. Mehemet would be satisfied by the cession of the Syrian pashaliks. So for the moment the problem was solved. But Russia had proved herself the friend in need, and with Russia Mahmud concluded the treaty of Unkiar Skelessi (1833), which virtually made Turkey a Russian protectorate.

Now there were four powers interested in the near east : Austria for the single reason that Russian domination in the Turkish Empire would be a menace to herself in Europe. Russian domination there had been the dream of every tsar from the days of Peter the Great. France, since Bonaparte's Egyptian adventure, had hankered for Egypt, whether for itself or as a stepping stone to India. Great Britain did not want France in Egypt ; she did not want Russia to develop a great Mediterranean fleet ; she had learnt to suspect Russia of ulterior designs upon India ; and Russia was the one power to whose armies, as distinguished from fleets, India might prove accessible. To Great Britain, even more than to Austria or to France, Russian control of the Dardanelles and Russian domination in western Asia were

to be resisted at all costs ; and still more because Russian domination was creeping over central Asia, submerging Turkistan and threatening to swamp the buffer states of Persia and Afghanistan. The persistent rise of the Russian tide in Asia, drawing ever nearer to the British borders, was from this time onwards for the rest of the century the factor which made an accord between Britain and Russia impossible, and forced upon Britain the conviction that the Turkish Empire must be preserved not only from conquest but from domination by Russia.

In 1833 all the diplomatic gains in the Near East went to Russia ; the supreme influence at the Porte was undoubtedly hers. But in 1838 Mehemet again challenged Mahmud by withholding the Egyptian tribute. Mahmud had been reorganizing his army ; he took up the challenge, denounced Mehemet as a rebel, dispatched a force to invade Syria—and died, leaving a sixteen-year-old heir, Abdul Mejid. He was hardly dead when Ibrahim routed the Turkish troops, and the Turkish admiral, with the Turkish fleet, declared for Mehemet. All the powers wished to stay the advance of Mehemet ; France wished him to be recognized as independent sovereign of Egypt and Syria ; Nicholas at this stage, reckoning his own ascendancy in Turkey

## PROMINENT PERSONALITIES IN THE DRAMA OF THE NEAR EAST

The strife between the Turkish sultan Mahmud II (centre) and his ambitious viceroy Mehemet Ali of Egypt (left) was of interest to Europe in view of Mahmud's appeal for Russian intervention on his behalf, since the westward advance of Russia was regarded with growing concern by the European powers. In 1839 Mahmud was succeeded by his sixteen-year-old son Abdul Mejid (right, engraving by W. J. Edwards), in whose reign the great powers intervened to protect Turkey against Mehemet Ali.

secure, wished the Turkish empire to be preserved in its integrity—and he wished to break the always uneasy alliance of the French and British governments. Great Britain and Austria, too, wanted to preserve Turkey. On the initiative of Nicholas, the three powers, with the Porte, jointly offered generous terms to Ibrahim ; he rejected them. The British fleet settled the business without waiting : it seized Acre ; the Syrians rose against Mehemet —and he submitted, surrendering all claims upon Syria, while his position as hereditary pasha of Egypt was confirmed. France was included with the other powers in the final Treaty of London, in 1841. But palpably it was Great Britain this time, as in 1833 it had been palpably Russia, to whom the Porte was indebted for the defeat of Mehemet's designs, and British instead of Russian influence became predominant at the Porte.

Ɉɴ the British Isles the industrial revolution had now reached its second stage, the rapid development of steam transport both on land and on sea. The parliamentary Reform Bill of 1832, which transferred to the commercial, manufacturing and professional classes the preponderating political influence hitherto enjoyed by the aristocracy and the landed gentry, had been immediately preceded by the opening of the first passenger-carrying railway ; it was followed by a period of active industrial legislation restricting the hours of labour for women and children and reorganizing the methods of poor relief, and, in the next decade, by the development of free trade on the principle that the sole legitimate purpose of taxation was the provision of revenue—a doctrine which

**QUEEN VICTORIA IN CORONATION ROBES**

Born May 24, 1819, daughter of the duke of Kent, Alexandrina Victoria became heir presumptive to the crown of Great Britain and Ireland in 1830 and ascended the throne June 20, 1837. This portrait painted by Sir George Hayter presents her in the dalmatic robes worn at her coronation, June 28, 1838.

*National Portrait Gallery, London*

was soon found to be convincing in a country whose manufacturers could defy competition. Otherwise the political event of the most profound importance was the accession of the young Queen Victoria in 1837. For the next heir, her uncle the duke of Cumberland, was a reactionary of the most pronounced type, whose accession might even have been fatal to the monarchy ; and at the same time the crowns of Great Britain and Hanover ceased to be united, that of Hanover passing to the male heir. Cumberland's departure from England removed all

**FREDERICK WILLIAM IV**
The liberal party in Prussia eagerly welcomed in 1840 the accession of Frederick William IV, here shown as crown prince in a lithograph by Krüger; but he disappointed their hopes of reform. In 1857 he became insane and died in 1861.

serious risk of a democratic revolution in England, though he signalised his arrival in Hanover by abolishing the constitution enjoyed by that kingdom under his predecessors.

GERMANY generally enjoyed a material prosperity, while political agitation, whether of nationalists who dreamed of German national consolidation, or of liberals who craved for constitutional governments, was gagged by the official suppression of free speech and comment, which was resented chiefly by the educated middle classes. In Germany, as in the British Isles, there were angry undercurrents of dissatisfaction, but no widespread revolutionary fervour.

The prosperity of North Germany was largely due to the development of the Prussian Zollverein or Customs Union, removing the trade barriers between the states which were members thereof ; and the Zollverein at the same time tended to produce among these states a closer union under the hegemony of Prussia, a more definite consciousness of community of interests, which gave Prussia a clientèle of her own in the Confederation. The fact was not conspicuous so long as Prussia did

not enter upon a conscious rivalry with Austria—and neither Prussia nor Austria was desirous of a German consolidation ; but it was to prove of no little importance after the death of the old king Frederick William III in 1840, and the accession of his elder son Frederick William IV— though not immediately even then. The hopes of the liberals were also excited by the new king's accession and his promise of a new Prussian constitution, until on its promulgation in 1846 it appeared that actually it was to be ignored at the monarch's convenience.

Motives to revolution were strongest in the Austrian empire and in Italy, which was almost an Austrian protectorate ; but all the organization was in the hands of the governments, while there was nothing to co-ordinate the diverse aims of the diverse revolutionary groups. Austria proper was German ; the imperial government was a German government which was imposed upon Czechs in the north, Magyars in the centre, Slavs in the south and Italians in Venetia and Lombardy. If each one of these fundamentally different nationalities resented the German domination, they were only a shade less antagonistic to each other. Metternich held them all in his grip, and continued to do so after the death of the old emperor Francis II and the accession of his son Ferdinand I in 1835.

### Austria's Mailed Hand on Italy

IN Italy, Charles Felix of Sardinia and his successor, Charles Albert, in Piedmont, were comparatively free from Austrian domination and made no tyrannical use of their despotic power. But Austrian bayonets had established the pope's authority in the Papal States. Ferdinand II at Naples was scarcely an improvement upon his father Francis, and his strength rested upon the knowledge that he too had Austria to lean upon. From end to end of Italy Austria was the force behind the despotisms and the force which was supremely interested in prolonging the disunion of an Italy that had never known unity—and in the unification of Italy lay the sole hope of expelling the Austrian. And the idealist prophet of a united Italy, Giuseppe Mazzini, driven from Piedmont, from Switzerland, from France, was issuing his propaganda from a garret in London. Only a gleam of light seemed to have appeared when Pius IX, elected to the Papacy in 1846, alarmed and shocked Metternich by inaugurating liberal reforms in the Papal States. Yet—a liberal movement headed by the Papacy was almost a contradiction in terms.

France had attained a constitutional monarchy, a bourgeois monarchy, under her citizen-king Louis Philippe, the son of Philippe 'Egalité' of Orléans, who had voted for the execution of Louis XVI. The government was of a drab respectability, playing for safety. It had been able to congratulate itself on the restoration of French prestige by its share in the establishment of Belgian independence. It had been cold-shouldered by the powers in the settlement of the Eastern question in 1840. It had preserved a superficial entente with Great Britain, but in a fashion which France generally interpreted as perpetual surrender to Palmerston. It had found a base for developing an African empire in Algiers, but enthusiasm on that head was somewhat forced. It had intrigued in Spain and in Switzerland, with besmirched credit in one case, and nothing gained in the other. And, on the other hand, French imagination had been fired by the skilful revival of the Napoleonic legend, the tale of France's glories under the great conqueror's leadership. France was being bored to extinction by the Orléans monarchy and ministries, while the monarch and the ministers remained placidly self-satisfied and unconscious. And below the boredom, in the industrial population created by the Industrial Revolution, Jacobinism had come to life again, though no one yet suspected that Paris was to be the starting point of a new revolutionary convulsion.

## The World outside Europe

THE history of Europe as we have traced it in this chapter is the account of the aftermath of the great upheaval of the preceding six and twenty years, which had consciously unsettled the foundations of the entire political and social structure among the peoples of Europe and unconsciously revolutionised its economic bases. The history of the world outside Europe during the same period is upon different lines, for it is very largely the story of the birth, infancy and adolescence of new communities, new states, under conditions differing widely from those of Europe.

In Asia the British were creating an empire of a kind for which there had been no precedent since the Roman expansion ceased—the whole process was one which now, since the exclusion of the French, was taking place more or less in isolation, a change which, however important, touched the history of the outside world at very few points. Russia was expanding there also, but with a difference, thrusting her way southward between the Caspian and the Aral Seas, and establishing a footing that dominated Khiva on the Amu Darya, as well as on the Sir Darya—the Oxus and Jaxartes of the Greeks ; and a new contact was beginning to be established between Europe and the farthest East.

**CONSTITUTIONALIST MONARCH**
The wise reign of Charles Albert greatly strengthened his kingdom of Sardinia, which he ruled from 1831 until his abdication in 1849, after being defeated by Austria. In 1848 he granted his people a liberal constitution.
*Painting by Vernet ; Pinakothek, Turin*

Japan still remained in the isolation she had chosen for herself, behind the gates which were barred and bolted against the admission of Europeans. China was less successful in maintaining her exclusiveness. The European demand for a commercial entry was not to be gainsaid. In 1793 the emperor Ch'ien Lung received with extreme politeness a British embassy intent on procuring a commercial treaty ; but he conceded nothing. Emperor and provincial governors were ready enough to call in the aid of British warships for the suppression of the pirate fleets that infested the China seas, but remained resolutely deaf to all invitations to facilitate commercial intercourse, until in 1839 they provoked an actual collision followed by reciprocal demands for compensation that could have only one issue. In 1842 the Chinese government gave way and signed the Treaty of Nanking, which, besides conceding substantial damages, ceded Hong Kong to the British. The door was not flung open, but it was ajar. Nor was it only the British who now set themselves to widen the opening.

### South America wins Independence

IN South America we have seen that Brazil formally separated herself from her European parent state, Portugal, in 1822, retaining the prospective head of the royal house as her own emperor, while in due course his daughter succeeded to the Portuguese crown. The rest of South America and Central America broke away from the Spanish connexion, but only after a prolonged struggle, and in the form not of one but of several states— not of course hereditary monarchies, but nominal republics which were in fact controlled, so far as they were controlled at all, by military dictators who for the next half century only held power until they were dismissed or eliminated by the next military pronunciamento.

The movement which culminated in the total loss of America to Spain in fact had its rise when Napoleon dispossessed the legitimate monarchy in Spain and set up his brother Joseph as king. The Spaniards in America declined to recognize the new authority and claimed to set up their own governments in place of the existing system, generally professing loyalty to the legitimate but dispossessed dynasty. The struggle went on over four areas—the Mexican and, in South America, the northern, southern and western. It was only in Mexico that there was anything in the nature of a racial conflict between Spaniards and the indigenous population ; elsewhere it was between American Spaniards and Spanish Spaniards. The demand for independence developed only when Ferdinand VII was restored in Spain, abrogated the constitution, and set about reviving the old despotism. The Creoles had no chance of having their claims recognized ; the crown obviously intended to re-establish the old system, and the

### LIBERATORS OF SOUTH AMERICA FROM SPANISH DOMINATION

Simon Bolivar (1783–1830)—left—led Venezuela's fight for independence and in 1822 became first president of the republic of Colombia, in which Venezuela was incorporated. José de San Martin (1778–1850)—centre—freed Chile from Spanish rule in 1818, and then secured that of Peru with the aid of Bolivar as dictator. Antonio López de Santa Ana (1795–1876)—right—was a principal agent in the liberation of Mexico in 1833 and served several terms as president of that republic.

**AUTHOR OF THE MONROE DOCTRINE**
James Monroe (1758–1831) fought in the American War of Independence, served in France and Britain as American minister, and from 1817–1825 was president of the United States. The Monroe Doctrine is his international monument.
*Engraving by J. Vanderlyn*

struggle was soon translated into one between royalists and republicans. There were leaders who proposed to create constitutional monarchies under nominated European princes (the plan first adopted in Europe for Greece and Belgium), but those schemes did not materialise.

Argentina in the south was the first to organize a government before Ferdinand's restoration, and the first (1815) to declare its independence when the restored monarchy showed its reactionary character. In that quarter royalism had no chance, though Argentina failed to incorporate Uruguay and Paraguay. In the northern quarter the ' liberator ' Bolívar was defeated by the arrival of Spanish troops under Morillo, a capable leader who in 1816 seemed to have established his authority. Royalism was strong in the west, but forces from Argentina under San Martin helped Chile to release itself without completely freeing Peru (1817–1820). In the north again the insurgents found a successful leader in the peasant Paez—thereby preventing Morillo from intervening in the west. The successes of Paez brought Bolívar into the field again ; and the retirement of Morillo

virtually ensured the independence of Colombia (1821).

The resources of Spain were in fact wholly unequal to the attempt to restore the Spanish supremacy ; and when it appeared likely that the European autocrats might intervene on behalf of Ferdinand, the action of President Monroe in America and of Canning in England, insisting upon the principle of non-intervention, was decisive. America was left to fight out its own salvation. San Martin in Chile left Bolívar to complete from Colombia the overthrow of the royalists in Peru. But the northern provinces refused to amalgamate ; and by 1830 South America had resolved itself into a collection of independent states—the Brazilian Empire, the several republics of Argentina, Uruguay and Paraguay in the south, of Chile and Peru in the west, and of Colombia, Ecuador, Bolivia and Venezuela in the north. Mexico had followed a separate course. After prolonged struggles between rival faction leaders, it had declared itself an independent republic in 1823 under the dictatorship of Santa Ana, with a paper constitution modelled on that of the United States, but with additional clauses, one of which made Roman Catholicism the state religion.

### Developments in the United States

THE story of the United States during the period has two main aspects—their relations with Europe, the European powers, and especially with the British Empire in America, and their internal development and expansion from the Alleghanies and the Mississippi basin to the Pacific. Their unhappy conflict with the British had terminated in 1814 during Madison's presidency ; the eight years' presidency of his successor James Monroe (1817–25) was notable primarily for the promulgation in 1823 of the ' Monroe Doctrine,' the doctrine that European powers as such have no concern with America. Spain's right to fight for her possessions in America could not of course be called in question, but the right of other powers to intervene was emphatically repudiated—following upon the recognition by the United States themselves of the independence of the South American states in 1822. Any such intervention then or in the future would be regarded by the United States as an ' unfriendly act ' which would be resented, if necessary, by force. The actual pronouncement came at the moment when Santa Ana had established his own dictatorship in Mexico.

The doctrine having once been established and practically recognized in Europe, questions of foreign policy in the United States were in effect only such as arose between them and Mexico on the south or Great Britain on the north. These again were mainly concerned with boundary disputes, begotten of the inadequate definitions of earlier treaties. These came to a head during the ministry of Peel in England, when Palmerston was for a time displaced from the Foreign Office ; and they resulted first in the Ashburton Treaty of 1842 which practically conceded all the American claims, to the intense annoyance of the British colonists whose rights or supposed rights were shelved by the home government. But three years later the westward expansion of the United States led to the Oregon boundary dispute which, in the exigencies of a presidential election, threatened to issue in an armed collision, but actually resulted in a partial settlement more accordant with the British than with the American claims, continuing the 49th parallel of latitude as the line of demarcation from the Rocky Mountains to the coast facing Vancouver Island. About the same time the whole of Texas and California was absorbed by the United States (1848) as the result of a conflict with Mexico.

### Antagonism of North and South

THE two internal questions which rent the great republic were those of state rights as against the powers of the federal government, and, intimately associated therewith, the question of slavery. The southern semi-tropical ' plantation ' states were dependent upon negro slave labour ; the northern industrial and agricultural states were not. Consequently the South was firmly convinced of the moral justifi-

cation of slavery, while the North was not. The North, eager for its own industrial development, favoured the exclusion of foreign goods. The South, producing raw materials, wished to buy its manufactured goods in the cheapest market. Thus there was a double antagonism of interests between the northern and the southern states. The northern were the more numerous and therefore the more powerful in the federal government ; the South was in constant fear that its own interests would be over-ridden by the federal government in favour of those of the North.

### State Rights and Slavery

IT followed that the South was zealous first to assert state rights and secondly to multiply ' southern ' states in the westward expansion and to resist the multiplication of ' northern ' states. The North accepted the view that there should be no interference with slavery in the states where it was already established, but whether the establishment of slavery in new states should be permitted was another matter. As the expansion went westward, and the newly settled districts attained a population standard which warranted their recognition as separate states, the question whether they should be slave or non-slave states became vital. The class questions which agitated Europe had no place in America ; there were no swarms of operatives dependent upon capitalist employers, no peasantry dependent upon landlords, and no body of men enjoying hereditary privileges.

The most serious question was disposed of for a time by the Missouri Compromise of 1821, which fixed the line drawn westward from the southern boundary of the State of Missouri as the boundary between slave and non-slave states, Missouri itself being acknowledged as a slave state.

Meanwhile, the three areas in which the British were pushing forward their colonial development, in North America, in South Africa and in Australasia, were progressing not indeed upon identical lines, but unconsciously towards an identical goal. In the course of less than a century the Second British Empire was to become a commonwealth of nations.

# TABLE OF DATES FOR CHAPTER 30

**1848** Jan. : Revolt in Sicily, then in Naples ; Ferdinand concedes a constitution.

Feb. : ' February Revolution ' in France ; flight of Louis Philippe ; Second Republic proclaimed. Dalhousie governor-general (India).

March : Revolutions in nearly all German states. Flight of Metternich ; Frederick William takes popular side. Revolt of Slesvig. Charles Albert and Pius IX grant constitutions ; Charles Albert declares war on Austria. Revolts in Lombardy and Venetia ; Radetzky retires to the Quadrilateral.

April : Chartist demonstration and collapse (England).

Hungarian independence acknowledged.

May : Emp. Ferdinand withdraws to Innsbruck. Meeting of German ' Frankfort parliament.' Successes of Italian troops.

June : Windischgrätz masters Prague. Radetzky advances in Italy.

July : Radetzky's victory at Custozza. South Slavs (Jellachich) support crown.

Aug. : Italian armistice.

Oct. : Windischgrätz and Jellachich master Vienna.

Nov. : Murder of Rossi and flight of Pius IX. Schwartzenberg minister at Vienna.

Dec. : Roman and Florentine republics proclaimed. Ferdinand II abd. ; acc. Franz-Joseph. Louis Napoleon elected president (France).

**1848** India : Second Sikh War.

**1849** India : Sikhs defeated ; annexation of Punjab. Revolt of Hungary ; renewal of war in Italy. Charles Albert, defeated at Novara, abd. ; acc. Victor Emmanuel. Peace, Austrian troops remaining in Piedmont.

Savage suppression of Sicilian revolt (Bomba). Hungarians crushed by Russian armies. Frederick William IV refuses imperial crown of Germany and drops popular rôle.

U.S.A. : Fillmore president.

**1850** U.S.A. : Fugitive Slave law. Frederick William surrenders to Austria in the convention of Olmütz.

**1851** Australian gold fields discovered.

Dec. : Napoleon's coup d'état makes him president for ten years.

**1852** Cavour minister in Piedmont. Slesvig-Holstein settlement by Treaty of London. U.S.A. : Publication of Uncle Tom's Cabin. India : Dalhousie's annexations by lapse. Transvaal republic recognized by Sand River Convention. Napoleon III emperor of the French (Nov.).

**1853** Russo-Turkish War begins. Turkish fleet sunk at Sinope.

**1854** March : France and England join Turkey.

Sept. : Anglo-French expedition to Crimea. Siege of Sevastopol begun after battle of Alma. Battles of Balaclava and Inkerman. Florence Nightingale at Scutari (Nov.). Orange Free State recognized by Bloemfontein convention. Responsible government in Australasian colonies.

**1855** Sardinia joins allies in Crimean War.

March : Nicholas I d. ; acc. Alexander II.

Sept. : Fall of Sevastopol ; peace negotiations.

**1856** Peace of Paris, Sardinia participating. Anglo-Persian War withdraws Indian troops. China war, arising from ' Arrow incident.' Canning succeeds Dalhousie ; Oudh annexed.

**1857** William prince of Prussia regent.

U.S.A. : Buchanan president.

India : Meerut mutiny ; Mogul proclaimed at Delhi (May). Cawnpore massacre ; siege of Lucknow Residency begins (June). Storming of Delhi and first relief of Lucknow (Sept.). Final relief of Lucknow (Nov.).

**1858** Oudh and central Indian campaigns ; fall of Jhansi (June) ; gradual suppression of local resistance. End of East India Company. Plombières interview (Cavour and Napoleon).

**1859** Italian liberation war, Napoleon intervening ; battles of Magenta and Solferino ; peace of Villafranca ; cession of Savoy and Nice to France ; incorporation of N. Italian states in ' Kingdom of North Italy ' by plébiscite. Darwin's Origin of Species published.

**1860** Garibaldi's Sicilian expedition (May) ; invasion of mainland (Aug.) ; he enters Naples (Sept.) as dictator ; meets Victor Emmanuel, ' King of Italy ' (Oct.) ; siege of Gaeta.

U.S.A. : Abraham Lincoln elected president (Nov.) ; S. Carolina announces secession (Dec.).

**1861** United kingdom of Italy proclaimed (excluding Rome and Venetia) after fall of Gaeta (Feb.). Cavour d.

Abdul Mejid d. ; acc. Abdul Aziz.

Frederick William IV d. ; acc. William I. Constitutional struggle, Bismarck becoming king's chief minister.

Napoleon's Mexican adventure begun.

Alexander II emancipates the Russian serfs.

U.S.A. : Outbreak of Secession war ; first heavy engagement at battle of Bull Run (July).

**1862** U.S.A. : Confederates' successes ; blockade of their ports.

Slesvig-Holstein question reopened by accession of Christian IX .

Garibaldi, attempting to capture Rome, is defeated by royal troops at Aspromonte.

**1863** Greece : acc. George I (of Denmark). Prussia and Austria invade Denmark. Polish revolt.

U.S.A. : Slave emancipation proclamation. South gradually overwhelmed by growing N. armies.

**1864** Denmark submits to Treaty of Vienna. Polish revolt crushed. Geneva convention ; birth of ' Red Cross.' Ulysses Grant made Federal commander-in-chief.

**1865** Convention of Gastein between Austria and Prussia. Surrender of Confederate forces ; end of American war. Murder of Abraham Lincoln.

**1866** Bismarck prepares for Austrian war ; league with Italy. War declared, June 15 ; Prussia occupies Saxony, Hanover and Hesse-Cassel ; crushes Austrians at Königgratz, July 3 ; Italians defeated at Custozza ; armistice of Nikolsburg ends ' Seven Weeks' War.' Austria, permanently excluded from German Confederation, cedes Venetia to Italy.

Garibaldi attacking Rome defeated at Mentana.

**1867** N. German confederation established under Prussian presidency. Dual monarchy (Austrian and Hungarian) in Austrian empire.

Federation of Dominion of Canada under British North America Act.

Withdrawal of French troops from Mexico. Death of ' Emperor ' Maximilian.

**1868** Isabella II expelled from Spain ; search for a foreign prince to succeed.

**1869** Decree of Papal Infallibility.

**1870** Leopold of Hohenzollern withdraws from Spanish candidature.

The Ems Telegram (July). Franco-Prussian War.

Battles of Wörth, Mars-la-Tour and Gravelotte (Aug.). Fall of Sedan (Sept.).

Sept. : End of Second Empire ; proclamation of Third Republic ; siege of Paris begins.

Rome occupied by Royalists becomes Italian capital ; pope ' prisoner of the Vatican.'

**1871** Jan. : William I proclaimed German emperor at Versailles ; capitulation of Paris. May : Treaty of Frankfort. Aug. : Thiers president.

Treaty of London, revising Black Sea Treaty.

**1872** League of the three emperors (Dreikaiserbund).

**1874** Spain : Acc. Alfonso XII.

**1875** Insurrection of Bosnia and Herzegovina. Suez Canal shares purchased by Disraeli.

**1876** Rejection of Berlin Memorandum by England. Revolt of Bulgaria ; Bulgarian atrocities. Acc. Abdul Hamid ; abortive conference of Constantinople.

**1877** Queen Victoria proclaimed Kaisar-i-Hind. Russia declares war on Turkey, Rumania joining. July and Sept. : Russian repulses at Plevna. Nov. : Fall of Plevna and of Kars.

**1878** Jan. : Schipka Pass won ; Russians at Adrianople ; March : Treaty of San Stefano.

June : Berlin Congress meets under presidency of Bismarck ; private agreements between Russia and Austria, Russia and England, England and Turkey. Austria gets Bosnian protectorate ; Bulgaria a small principality ; Rumania and Serbia independent ; England gets Cyprus.

Rift between Germany and Russia.

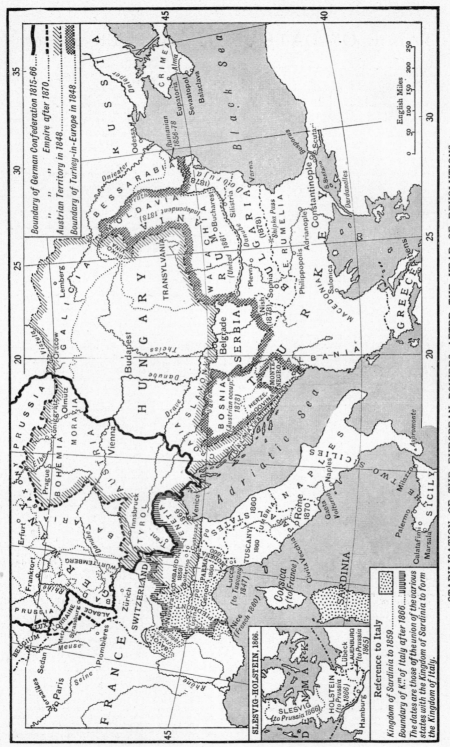

**STABILISATION OF THE EUROPEAN POWERS AFTER THE YEAR OF REVOLUTIONS**

The currents tending towards national unity manifest among the European states in the first half of the nineteenth century steadily gathered volume and eventuated in a flood of violence that caused the year 1848 to be called the Year of Revolutions. Geographical changes resulting from the earlier tentative movements are shown in the map in page 672. The state of more or less stable equilibrium achieved between 1848 and 1878 is shown in the map above, France attaining stability after 1870 under the Third Republic. In these years the unification of Italy and Germany was accomplished.

### CHAPTER 30

# THE CONSOLIDATING OF THE GREAT POWERS: 1848-1878

A T the opening of the year 1848, the 'Year of Revolutions,' the surface in Europe was calm. Between the powers there were no hostilities threatening. All the western and Scandinavian states were under constitutional monarchies. All the states of the German Confederation were ruled by dynasts restricted by no constitutional fetters, but with no disposition to carry oppression beyond the repression of democratic propaganda, or to develop a closer nationalist unity which would limit their individual authority. The Austrian imperial government held its subject populations in an apparently irresistible military grip ; in the dominions of the tsar any attempt at revolution was almost unthinkable ; and, while Austria held her position in Italy, Ferdinand at Naples and the pope in the States of the Church could play havoc with any popular insurrections.

## Undercurrents of Discontent

B ELOW the surface, indeed, there were seething currents of discontent, varying in motive and intensity, often incompatible in their aims, unorganized for the most part, powerless against organized governments with organized military forces. The Vienna settlement had at least so far accomplished its aims that for more than thirty years there had been no international wars, and that despotism had decisively held its own except where established constitutionalism had held its own ; while Greece and Belgium alone had provided examples of successful nationalist movement in the direction either of liberation or of consolidation.

Nevertheless, before six months had passed, revolution, either nationalist or democratic, had not only raised its head but appeared to be on the verge of triumphing, if it had not actually triumphed, in France, where the first blow was struck, in Germany, throughout the Austrian empire and in Italy. Only

in England, where the democratic movement was represented by Chartism, it had already collapsed harmlessly, while the nationalist movement in Ireland never had a chance. Yet before another eighteen months were over it appeared that everywhere it had been decisively beaten.

## Governmental Changes in France

T HE third French Revolution, which created the Second Republic and led up to the Second Napoleonic Empire, was carried through its first stages almost as rapidly as and with no more resistance than the second, which had substituted the constitutionalist Orléans monarchy for that of the reactionary Bourbons. Paris and the Parisians were the stage and the actors. The king and his minister Guizot held a majority in parliament, where, however, there was also a vigorous opposition ; and the Paris press was with the opposition, mainly constitutionalist in its doctrines, but demanding wider franchise, a change of government and a more vigorous foreign policy. There was a republican wing, in which the extremists had adopted the title of socialist, though not as yet the economic formulae of twentieth-century socialism. The Paris proletariat was swelled by great numbers of the unemployed, the offspring mainly of the expanding industrial revolution—clamouring of the 'right to work,' that is, of the right to have work and wages provided for them ; meanwhile, hungry.

The opposition organized a vast public banquet, to be held on February 23. The government vetoed it ; Paris seethed. The organizers announced that the banquet would not be held ; Paris seethed none the less. The king took fright, announced a change of ministry, and dismissed Guizot on February 23. But mobs paraded the streets and the National Guard could not be relied on. On February 24 Louis Philippe abdicated in favour of his grandson, who was proclaimed king by the Chambers. The mob swamped them, and proclaimed a republic ; the leaders formed a ' provisional government.' Meanwhile another provisional government was being formed elsewhere. The two combined and summoned a national convention, to be elected by universal suffrage, while the king and the royal family faded across the Channel to England, the natural home of refugees.

The socialists dominated the Parisian provisional government ; they did not dominate the new national convention. In June the Paris mob rose, and there was a raging struggle in the streets for three days between them and the National Guard, who were with the government. The government troops under Cavaignac were completely victorious. In the next few months the new constitution was formulated. In December was held the election of the president, who was to be at the head of the executive ; and three-fourths of the votes cast were given to Louis Napoleon Bonaparte, the son of the great emperor's brother Louis, some-time king of Holland—for no reason except that he was Napoleon's nephew and claimed to be the incarnation of the Napoleonic idea.

This third French Revolution could scarcely be called the product of a ' movement.' It was republican, not because France was fervently republican but because the Orléans monarchy was incurably self-satisfied and incurably dull. It was democratic, but the extreme democrats were unsupported outside Paris ; the only fighting was that between them and the troops of the new government. The revolution was not in fact completed till the first president had imitated his mighty uncle and proclaimed himself emperor of the French.

𝕭UT the immediate success of the February revolution, the bloodless collapse of the Orléans monarchy, gave the needed touch to set all the revolutionaries in Europe in motion. Even in England the agitation of the extreme democrats for the ' People's Charter ' created a brief alarm ; but the great bulk even of the Chartists preferred constitutional to revolutionary

methods, and before the end of April it became manifest that there was no danger of the agitation developing into an armed insurrection. In Ireland the same attitude predominated among the advocates of the repeal of the legislative union with Great Britain ; and, though a handful of the patriots under the name of Young Ireland did actually take the field in arms in July, a few days sufficed to disperse or arrest them. The duchies of Slesvig and Holstein, within the old German empire but attached, much against their will, to the crown of Denmark, attempted to break away, though with no prospect of success unless the German Confederation should intervene on their behalf. Intervention was in fact attempted, but in the end came to naught. Elsewhere, however, the initial movements of the revolutionaries seemed to promise success.

### Progress of Liberalism in Germany

𝕴N Germany and among Germans, including those in the Austrian empire, what statesmen of the Metternich type called ' the Revolution ' was not advanced democracy but what at that time was

**FRANÇOIS GUIZOT, FRENCH PREMIER**
Opposed to the reactionary policy of Charles X, François Guizot (1787–1874) came into office on the accession of Louis Philippe. In 1847 his refusal as premier to grant various popular demands precipitated the revolution of 1848.
*Painting by Jacquand, Musée de Versailles ; photo, Giraudon*

**THE PATRIOT KOSSUTH**

Fierce enthusiasm for Hungarian autonomy led Louis Kossuth to head a national revolt against Austrian domination in 1848. The rising failed and he abdicated in 1849. Tietze's engraving is from a daguerreotype made two years later.

generally known as liberalism ; and of German liberalism there were two aspects : constitutionalism which demanded limitations upon arbitrary power and extension of popular control over the government, and nationalism which demanded at least advance towards the consolidation and unification of the German peoples who were included in the German Confederation. For reasons already explained those two aims were not always easily reconcilable ; the existing union being a union of princes. The liberal ideal was a constitution not only in each of the states but for the Confederation as a whole. Metternich's ideal was a collection of despotic principalities dominated by Austria. In Germany, therefore, there was much alarm but nothing in the nature of armed revolt ; but within a month of Louis Philippe's abdication the erratic king of Prussia had assumed the rôle of popular leader with a programme which included a new constitution for Prussia, and the calling of a pan-German parliament—to which the alarmed Diet (of Princes) yielded immediate assent—to

**ARRIVAL OF FRENCH ROYAL REFUGEES SEEKING SHELTER IN ENGLAND**

The French revolution of 1848 overthrew the constitutional monarchy which the rule of Louis Philippe had failed to popularise, and the king, in face of a powerful opposition, abdicated. With the connivance of the British consul at Havre, he and his queen escaped from France as ' Mr. and Mrs. Smith,' and in Pingret's painting the fugitives are seen arriving at New Cross Station. Louis Philippe died at Claremont, Surrey, which Queen Victoria placed at his disposal, on August 26, 1850.
*Aquatint by Cuvillier and Bayot*

devise a constitution for the Confederation. The parliament met at Frankfort in May.

BEFORE Frederick William moved, the Revolution had started in every quarter of the Austrian empire, with the rest of Italy. In Austria proper, which was German, the demand was for a constitution. Elsewhere the motive was nationalist; Czechs, Magyars and South Slavs each demanded a constitution of their own, free from Teutonic domination but still subject to a very limited imperial sovereignty. The Italians went farther; they knew that there was no hope for Italy till the Austrians should be completely ejected.

Louis Philippe abdicated in the last week of February; in the first week of March, Louis Kossuth in the Hungarian diet called upon Hungary to lead the way in demanding autonomy and release from German domination for each of the peoples in the Empire. In Vienna the constitutionalists rose; by March 13 they were masters of the city. Metternich was in full flight for England, and the government was in the hands of self-constituted committees which controlled the new ministry set up by the panic-stricken emperor Ferdinand; Prague was in the hands of the Young Czechs. A few days later the Hungarian diet had formulated the 'March Laws,' its demands for a constitution. By the end of the month the imperial government had conceded all the demands, virtually making Hungary an independent state linked to the empire

**MARSHAL RADETZKY**

The Italian revolt of 1848 was crushed by the energy of the Austrian commander-in-chief Josef Radetzky (1766–1858), victorious over the insurgents at Custozza (1848) and Novara (1849).

*From Dayot, 'Raffet et son oeuvre'*

only by the crown. In another week the Czech demands, too, had been conceded. Only the South Slavs failed to draw a favourable response from Vienna, because their claims were incompatible with those of Vienna herself on one side and of Magyar Hungary on the other.

Meanwhile Italy was up in arms. Charles Albert of Sardinia had very recently granted the oft-demanded constitution in his own kingdom. His sympathies were liberal and nationalist. Though he was politically a timid person, it was only under his leadership that a common centre could be provided for an Italian attack upon the Austrian domination, though Pius IX had not yet shed his liberal professions. Charles marched into Lombardy, all Lombardy and Venetia rose, troops came up from the Papal States and even from Naples; and the Austrian Marshal Radetzky, grim and imperturbably confident, was driven within the strategic group of fortresses known as the Quadrilateral.

The Italian success was short-lived. Charles was inert, doing nothing. Mistrust of the leader and dissensions as to aims and methods developed. Republicanism was a passionate faith with the most ardent of the patriots, not easily to be reconciled to the leadership of an apparently half-hearted monarch. Radetzky, who understood his business thoroughly, waited just long enough and then struck, inflicting a heavy defeat on the Italians at Custozza in July, which made

**JOSEPH JELLACHICH**

The clever policy of Joseph Jellachich (1801–59), appointed governor of Croatia in 1848, of supporting the Croatian nationalist demand for independence of Hungary proved successful in preserving the Slav kingdoms for Austria.

*Engraving by T. L. Raab*

him again master of Lombardy and Venetia. It was only to avert the risk of French or British intervention that he consented to an armistice. Hostilities were suspended, and during the rest of the year the Italians were growing more disunited, Radetzky was gathering strength and Pius IX, terrified by the assassination of his liberal secretary Rossi, shook off the dust of liberalism from his feet and took refuge at the court of Naples—where Ferdinand had taken heart of grace and cancelled the constitution which he had recently been frightened into granting. Meanwhile the imperial government at Vienna had issued a new imperial constitution which satisfied no one and raised a new storm in the capital. The emperor retired hastily and secretly to the security of Innsbruck, and Vienna set up for itself a committee of public safety (May).

### Democratic Movement fails in Austria

By this time the pan-German parliament had met at Frankfort, and proposed to include Bohemia among the German states. The great Czech majority in Bohemia was again threatened with absorption under German domination. Prague countered by calling a pan-Slav conference, and proclaimed the separation of the Bohemian from the Austrian government. Ferdinand at Innsbruck acquiesced, but Vienna was irrevocably antagonised. The German and Czech factions in Prague rose against each other; whereupon Prince Windischgrätz, commanding the imperial troops, took matters into his own hands, brought cannon and bayonets to bear, promptly overwhelmed resistance, and established himself as master of Prague in the emperor's name. Bohemian autonomy had gone for good (June).

Hungary had won virtual independence, but the South Slavs in Hungary detested the dominant Magyars even more than the Germans. The new Hungarian government, nevertheless, ventured to appoint the Croat Jellachich governor of Croatia, and Jellachich made no delay in defying the authority of the government which had appointed him. But by his ingenious assumption of loyalty to the imperial as against the Magyar authority, the former was easily brought to support him, desiring nothing more earnestly than the humiliation of the Magyars, to whom it owed its own humiliation.

The tide in the Austrian empire had thus definitely turned by the end of July. Windischgrätz was master of Bohemia, Radetzky had fought and won at Custozza, Vienna's brief amity with the nationalist movement had dwindled on the discovery that it would involve the loss of the German ascendancy, Croatia and the South Slavs had declared against Hungary. Ferdinand returned to Vienna. The Magyars obviously would fight to keep what they had won and were now threatened with losing—but the Magyars were alone, save for their sympathisers among the Vienna democrats, and in September the risk of the revolutionary movement reaching the peasantry was removed by the general abolition of peasant services.

In September, Jellachich was marching on Pesth, the Hungarian capital; and the imperial commander in Pesth was murdered by the mob. In October, Jellachich was appointed to the general command, the mob rose in Vienna, and again Ferdinand took flight, to Olmütz. Windischgrätz, marching from Prague, treated Vienna as he had before treated Prague. Ferdinand, having appointed a new ministry under Schwartzenberg, who had no scruples and knew his own mind, abdicated in favour of his young nephew Francis Joseph (December) ; Hungary was completely isolated, while Radetzky in Italy, where the armistice was still in force, had the situation thoroughly in hand. It was announced that a new constitution for the whole empire was to be promulgated. Hungary replied by refusing to acknowledge the new 'king of Hungary' till he had sworn to the Hungarian constitution.

### Course of the Revolution in Germany

MEANWHILE the 'Revolution' was collapsing in Germany. The parliament at Frankfort was absorbed in working out a theoretically perfect constitution. It created an executive, wholly separate, of course, from the legislature, headed by an elected regent—and the regent elected was not the king of Prussia but the Austrian archduke John, whose appointment was confirmed by the Diet of Princes as of its own authority. The parliament had instructed Frederick William as its mandatory to intervene on behalf of Slesvig and Holstein ; the Prussian troops had done so, for the moment effectively. But this had brought in emphatic protests from Palmerston on one side and from Nicholas, the unqualified champion of the Vienna settlement, on the other. Prussian popular sentiment was all on the side of intervention, but the Prussian government quailed before the Anglo-Russian threat.

Frederick William then concluded with Denmark the Convention of Malmö, which in effect recognized her claims, deserting the pan-German cause. Austria had no sympathy with that cause. Without the support of either Frederick William or the archduke-regent, the Frankfort parliament could talk and send sympathetic delegations to its friends in Vienna or elsewhere, but it could not act. It proclaimed the incorporation of German Austria in the German nation, and almost at the same moment the Slavs of the Austrian empire were declaring for the imperial unity which was wholly incompatible with Germanism. Windischgrätz crushed the Vienna liberals ; Frederick William's accord with the Prussian liberals was worn out, and he dissolved the Prussian diet and set up a reactionary Prussian ministry in December. At the close of the 'Year of Revolutions' the victory of the reaction, all over Europe save in France, was already almost a foregone conclusion. At the close of the next year, 1849, it was apparently an accomplished fact.

### Failure of the Rising in Italy

THE Italian question was the first to be settled. Ferdinand of the Sicilies had already recovered his ascendancy, and in the first months of the new year he crushed the Sicilian rebels with a vindictive savagery which won him his nickname 'Bomba,' and caused the Bourbon rule in the south to be more bitterly execrated than ever. Rome, deserted by the pope, declared itself a republic in February ; Tuscany followed suit, deposing the grand duke ; but the divergence between the monarchists of Piedmont and the republicans became the more emphasised.

**FRANCIS JOSEPH OF AUSTRIA**
Nephew of the imbecile Ferdinand of Austria, Francis Joseph (1830–1916) succeeded his uncle in 1848. His long reign was filled with vicissitudes and tragedy, culminating in the murder of his nephew, Archduke Ferdinand, in June, 1914.
*Engraving from a photograph about* 1868

**AT THE SIEGE OF ROME**

In 1849 France undertook to reinstate the pope in Rome whence he had been driven by the Italian revolution of 1848. Despite Garibaldi's defence, the city fell and papal power was restored. These soldiers are French artillerymen.

*From Dayot, ' Raffet et son oeuvre'*

Though Charles Albert, as the leader of the Italian cause, dared to denounce the armistice and again challenge Austria, he met with a crushing defeat at Novara. For him, it was equally impossible to carry on the struggle or to accept the humiliating terms offered by the victor. He abdicated in favour of his son, Victor Emmanuel, to die shortly afterwards in exile. The Austrians offered the young king alternative terms : the prolonged occupation of Piedmont by the Austrian troops, with the payment of a crushing indemnity, or the abrogation of the constitution his father had given, involving the elimination of the Sardinian kingdom as a factor in the liberation of Italy ; a course full of danger and bitterness, or a course of inglorious ease. Victor Emmanuel chose the former, and eleven years later he had his reward.

Rome and Vienna still held out. Rome would have no reconciliation with the papal renegade to the cause of liberty. Austria would certainly reinstate Pius by force, but was for the moment tied up by the successes of the Hungarians. The president of the French republic reckoned on strengthening his own position by again asserting French as against Austrian interests in Italy, but also by winning the support of the Church. French forces appeared at Civita Vecchia. But it appeared that their intention was to reinstate the pope under guarantees. Rome refused to admit them ; but though they were defeated in an engagement with Garibaldi they laid siege to the city, which had to admit them in July, and the papal government was restored—without guarantees. Being restored, it ruled in the old fashion, setting aside the constitution granted by Pius IX on his accession, while the French could only protest. In August Venice was once more under the heel of the Austrians, whose troops had been relieved from the Hungarian imbroglio by the intervention of Nicholas.

THE chances of the Hungarians when they refused submission to the new imperial government in December had seemed desperate ; the Rumanian population in Transylvania had risen against their domination, which the German colony there also repudiated. But they found a brilliant guerrilla leader in Görgei. The advance of Jellachich on one flank and Windischgrätz on the other, and dissensions between Görgei and the political chief, Louis Kossuth, threatened the Hungarians with immediate destruction ; nevertheless Görgei and a second guerrilla captain, Bem, achieved such a series of military successes that the imperial government was reduced to imploring the aid of Nicholas. In June the Russian armies were pouring over the border ; in August the Hungarian resistance was overwhelmed by sheer weight of numbers. When further armed resistance had become impossible, Nicholas withdrew unconditionally ; having done what he conceived to be his duty in restoring despotism, he left the imperial government to enjoy an orgy of vengeance, in which it indulged itself to the full.

In Germany the movement was going to pieces. Pan-German national unity required an entirely German confederation including German Austria and excluding the non-German divisions of the Austrian empire. Austria could assent neither to her own exclusion from a unified German confederation nor to her inclusion without the rest of her empire ; pan-German unity and the unity of the Hapsburg empire were incompatible. That was the rock that wrecked the whole scheme. Actually, the condition of German unification was the exclusion of Austria, to which neither Austria herself nor the greater German princes were prepared to assent, however Frederick William might hanker irresolutely for a Prussian hegemony. When the Frankfort parliament actually propounded that scheme, offering to Frederick William the imperial crown of a confederated Germany without Austria, but with a constitution, in April, he rejected the offer.

The parliament had no means of enforcing its authority ; one after another the princes withdrew their representatives. Frederick William, with a quite futile plan of his own, collected another dubious

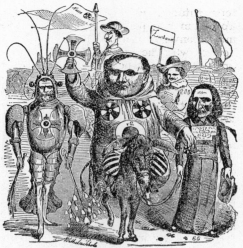

**FRANKFORT CONFERENCE SATIRISED**
A contemporary drawing by Wilhelm Scholz caricatures members of the Frankfort Conference who offered to Frederick William IV the crown of a confederated Germany, which he refused.
Left to right: Bismarck, Gerlach and Stahl.
*From ' Kladderadatsch,' 1849*

league which produced nothing more than a general admission that the old confederation was still in being and the old diet still the supreme lawful authority, and the calling of another futile federal parliament to meet at Erfurt next year. The Erfurt parliament when it met could accomplish nothing ; Frederick William's efforts to maintain an opposition to the dominant princes came to nothing ; Austria's attempt to reorganize the diet on lines which would practically have made her supreme within it came to nothing ; and in May, 1851, the confederation constituted as it had been before the revolutions began was again definitely established. The unification of Germany had to await the rise of Bismarck.

$\mathcal{J}$N France affairs moved along very different lines. A republic had taken the place of the constitutional monarchy, with an elected president in place of a constitutional king ; in actual fact a president whose character and abilities had been under no test, an adventurer who had carried the votes of the democracy by his name and nothing else, except his own restless ambition to follow in his uncle's footsteps. He had posed as

**LOUIS NAPOLEON AS PRESIDENT**
Sebastien Cornu's painting, engraved by Pichard, portrays Louis Napoleon (1808–73), nephew of Napoleon I, in 1849, the year after he was elected president of France. In 1852 he ascended the imperial throne as Napoleon III.
*From Flathe, ' Restauration und Revolution'*

representative of the Napoleonic idea. To retain the position he had won, he must convince the French people that he was what he professed to be, the representative of stable and popular government at home and of glory abroad ; convince them at least sufficiently to secure the retention of his power when his three-years' term of office should end.

He had come in upon the tide of the victory of the party of order over the new Jacobinism or socialism, and the Assembly and the ministry were perforce somewhat conservative. But the first Napoleon had proclaimed his own personal supremacy as the consummation of the Revolution, and that was a fiction which the new Napoleon must maintain. He could never be a Caesar without getting credit on one side and discredit on the other by the arts of the demagogue and by elaborate intrigue ; and he had not behind him an army adoring him as a captain of proved invincibility.

### The Second Empire established in France

THE success of the intervention in Italy was a qualified one. In attempting to bring the Church to his side he had displeased the popular sympathy with the republicans ; in his protests against the use made of its recovered power by the papal government he had shaken the confidence of the clericals. In 1850 he reconstructed his ministry, but the conservative Assembly changed the electoral law by restricting the franchise. The president posed as advocate of popular rights against a reactionary and unrepresentative assembly, thereby gaining popularity, but antagonising the Assembly itself. But legally a renewal of his presidency could be obtained only if authorised by a three-to-one majority of the Assembly. Failing that, a coup d'état—in strict accordance with Napoleonic precedent—was the only chance.

Openly, he intended to invite the Assembly's authorisation ; secretly, he prepared the coup d'état, to fall back on if the Assembly failed him when the time came, in July, 1851. It did fail him ; the majority was large, but not large enough. Palpably, then, the vote of a minority in a reactionary Assembly had flouted the ' manifest will of the people.'

The sands were running out fast when in November the president invited the reactionary Assembly to revise the electoral law and restore universal suffrage. It declined. The war minister, the chief of police and the commander of the troops in Paris were in the president's plot, while an active agitation had been carried on in the country. On the morning of December 2 Paris woke up to find the streets placarded with proclamations and patrolled by soldiers, while during the night the leaders of the opposition had been arrested. There was active but unorganized resistance which was crushed in a couple of days, not without superfluous violence and bloodshed. Republican extremists and other ' dangerous ' persons were imprisoned or exiled in batches ; the ' saviour of society ' appealed triumphantly to the people to confirm his re-election as ' prince president,' and a year later another overwhelming plébiscite proclaimed Napoleon III emperor of the French. For, as Louis XVIII had reckoned the short-lived son of Louis XVI as Louis XVII, so Louis Napoleon counted his uncle's dead son by Marie Louise as Napoleon II in the imperial dynasty.

### Friction between France and Russia

SINCE Waterloo there had been in Europe not a little fighting, but no armed conflicts between sovereign states except Russia and Turkey, and in 1848-9 between Austria and Sardinia ; that much at least stood to the credit of the Vienna settlement. The twenty years following Louis Napoleon's coup d'état witnessed a series of such wars, of which all but the first were the offspring of the nationalist movement ; and their issue was the consolidation of a new German empire and a new kingdom of Italy, the fall of the French Second Empire and the birth of the French Third Republic. But the first war was a quarrel begotten of international rivalries and personal ambitions.

France was by tradition the protector of the Latin or Catholic Christians in the Turkish empire, Russia of the Greek or Orthodox Church. France for a century had neglected her protégés, while Russia had sedulously fostered hers. The result was that sundry privileges in relation to the Holy Places had passed from the Latins to the Greeks. Napoleon saw a double opportunity of strengthening his popularity in France by championing the Catholic Church and asserting himself against the tsar. He demanded from the Porte the restitution of the old Latin privileges. Nicholas claimed the right to veto the transfer, under the treaty of Kainarji. If Napoleon wanted to fight, he was ready. Neither would abate his pretensions.

Palmerston was not at the British foreign office ; the British ministry was pacific and not over-friendly to Napoleon. Austria's dislike of Russian ascendancy in the Balkans told one way ; her dislike of French influence in Italy told the other way. Her very recent debt to Russia in the Hungarian affair made her more resentful than grateful. To gain British support, Nicholas revived an earlier suggestion for a partition of the moribund Turkish empire between Russia and Great Britain. He failed to realize that British public opinion was entirely convinced that Russia wanted Constantinople as a stepping-stone to India ; the effect of his proposal was precisely the opposite of what he had intended. Yet Nicholas still refused to believe that either England or Austria would act against him. The Porte was equally confident that both would do so.

In June, 1853, Russian forces crossed the Pruth ; their right to enter the trans-Danube principalities under the treaty of Kainarji could hardly be questioned. Diplomatic notes passed between the five powers concerned ; the

Porte would not concede the Russian demands ; the tsar refused to evacuate the principalities, while declaring that he would not take the offensive—but on November 30 a Russian squadron sank the Turkish fleet in the harbour of Sinope, Turkey having in actual fact declared war. French and British naval squadrons entered the Black Sea in January, 1854 ; in March both the powers declared war as allies of the Turks. Austria gathered troops on the frontier, but merely as a precaution.

The Russian army did not roll irresistibly on to Constantinople. It was held up on the Danube by the indomitable valour of the Turks at Silistria, while the Black Sea fleet was shut up in its ports, and a British fleet dispatched to the Baltic could make no impression on the defences of Kronstadt. French and British troops

**ALLIED GENERALS IN THE CRIMEAN WAR**
Severe censure from press and public was heaped upon the conduct of the Crimean War by the British commander-in-chief, Lord Raglan (1788–1855), seen (right) in a portrait by Sir Francis Grant. Left: His French colleague, Marshal St. Arnaud (1801–54), who died a few days after the allied victory at the battle of the Alma.
*From Dayot, ' Raffet et son oeuvre ' and (right) Army and Navy Club*

**SEVASTOPOL HARBOUR FROM ABOVE TELEGRAPH BATTERY**

The English, French and Turkish forces in the Crimea were levelled against the capture of Sevastopol, whose harbour sheltered the main forces of the Russian fleet. The allies began their bombardment in October, 1854, the year in which Col. Beek made the sketches from which, with the aid of a Russian government survey, this view was drawn; and the town sustained a siege of eleven months, being evacuated by the Russians in September, 1855, after the French capture of Malakoff fort.

reinforced the Turks in June, with their headquarters at Varna, where cholera was soon raging. In July the siege of Silistria was raised, the Russian forces fell back over the Pruth, and Austrian troops entered the principalities. Russia could hardly have rejected terms which were not positively humiliating.

### Outbreak of the Crimean War

ḄUT the war fever was high in France, whose troops so far had done nothing in particular, and in England, which had persuaded itself that the bombardment at Sinope had been an act of gross treachery, demanding condign punishment. The two governments concerted or instructed their generals, St. Arnaud and Raglan, to concert a joint attack upon Russia in the Crimea. In September a large Franco-British force was carried across the Black Sea to Eupatoria, routed a Russian force at the battle of the Alma, and, after a delay which gave the Russians time to strengthen materially the fortifications of the great arsenal of Sevastopol, laid siege to it, without being able to make the investment complete, while the Russian field army fell back. The harbour they

found blocked by ships that had been sunk for that purpose.

The British held the right of the besieging lines, with their supply base at the port of Balaclava. The Russian field force attempted to cut their communications but were foiled in the battle of Balaclava, famed in British annals for the two cavalry charges of the Light Brigade and of Scarlett's Heavy Brigade, the one a magnificent but useless blunder, the other a not less magnificent but successful operation of war (October 25). A few days later the massed attack of the Russians was again beaten off in the battle of Inkerman (November 5), fought in a heavy fog in which any common direction was impossible, and won by sheer disciplined valour. Then the siege settled down, the men holding on grimly through the terrible Crimean winter, perishing from the lack of necessary supplies, till a change of government at home with Palmerston as the new prime minister reorganized the utterly inefficient methods of the ministry which had plunged into the campaign, and the heroic Florence Nightingale with her band of nurses arrived at the hospital base at Scutari to inaugurate the hither-to undreamed-of activi-ties out of which arose the Red Cross.

In February, 1855, Sardinia joined the allies, not because she had any eastern interests at stake, but because the political perspicacity of Victor Emmanuel's great minister Cavour per-ceived that by doing so she would compel her recognition as a power with a right to make her voice heard; and all the more because the attitude assumed by Austria at this moment was in the eyes of France and England tantamount to a desertion.

In March, Nicholas died—a tragic, almost an heroic figure who had striven all his life after a strange ideal all but unin-telligible to Western minds; utterly con-vinced that salvation lay in the irresistible autocracy of princes, and that all that the West means by liberty is incompatible with the order which is Heaven's first

**ALEXANDER II OF RUSSIA**

Resembling his visionary uncle Alex-ander I, Alexander II (1818–81) suc-ceeded to the Russian throne in 1855. His most notable achievement was the emancipation of Russian serfs in 1861.

*Almanack de Gotha, 1856*

law ; a supremely honest man who appeared to the world which misunder-stood him to be the incarnation of perfidy. The son who succeeded him, Alexander II, should have been the offspring of the visionary Alexander I, for he, too, was a visionary who dreamed of Utopias. But the son's visions were scarcely more im-possible of attainment than the father's ideals.

On Alexander's acces-sion peace negotiations were opened, but broke down. In September, however, the capture of the Malakoff fort by the

French made Sevastopol no longer tenable, and its fall, which the French could claim as their own victory, gave the emperor some of that prestige in France which was so neces-sary to the maintenance of the Napoleonic legend. Diplomacy set to work again, and the war was ended by the treaty of Paris in March, 1856, Sardinia having secured her position as a member of the peace

**THE CONGRESS AT PARIS THAT ENDED THE CRIMEAN WAR**

The terms of peace that concluded the Crimean War in 1856 were arranged by a congress at Paris of the seven powers concerned—Great Britain, France, Russia, Turkey, Austria, Prussia and Sardinia—two plenipotentiaries being present from each, as shown in this engraving after Dubufe. Turkey's position as a European power was guaranteed, the neutrality of the Black Sea recognized and the Danube declared free for navigation.

*Musée de Versailles*

**FAMOUS FIGURES IN THE DRAMA OF ITALY'S FIGHT FOR FREEDOM**

By his stirring writings, the patriot Joseph Mazzini (left) inspired the Italian people, crushed beneath a foreign yoke, with his own idealistic zeal for the liberation of their country. It was he who founded the influential movement of ' Young Italy.' The brilliant diplomacy of the Italian statesman Count Cavour (right), who arranged alliances with France and England, contributed vitally to the success of the Risorgimento. Born 1810, he died in the year of the unification of Italy.

*Right, engraving after portrait by Metzmacher*

conference. All warships of all nations were to be excluded from the Black Sea, while it was made free to all merchantmen. Turkey, pledged to administrative reforms which in fact never materialised, was guaranteed her position as a European power with full sovereignty in her own dominions, and the Russian protectorates were annulled. All that England had fought for was secured—on paper.

### Sardinian Schemes for Italian Unity

THE Italian war of 1848–9 had made it certain that the liberation and unification of Italy could never be achieved except under the leadership of the Sardinian monarchy. Victor Emmanuel and Cavour recognized that the ejection of Austria needed the assistance of France as well as the recognition of the status of Sardinia by the powers. French assistance would not be given against the pope or for the establishment of a powerful Italian kingdom. Mazzini and his followers, the idealists whose inspiration alone had created among the Italians the moral enthusiasm which was the life of the Italian movement, detested the policy which would make Italy owe her liberty to foreign aid, above all to the aid of the ' man of the coup d'état ' ; yet Cavour could not do without their co-operation, while Napoleon's aid would not be forthcoming except at the price of material advantages to France at Italy's expense. But the fact remained that the victory could not be won without him. England under Palmerston might be trusted to keep the ring and prevent external intervention on the Austrian side, but she would not herself intervene actively on the Sardinian side. Cavour's problem was intricate and difficult.

A great step had been taken when Sardinia ensured moral support and recognition from France and England by joining them in the Crimean War when Austria was holding aloof. Her position was again greatly strengthened when she turned the peace conference to account by emphasising the grievances under which Italy suffered. Napoleon, too, felt that the aspirations of France for military glory had not been satisfied by the Crimean War or the Crimean peace. In 1858 the French emperor and the Sardinian minister met unofficially at Plombières, and came to terms. France's intervention was to be rewarded by the cession of Savoy and Nice ; and Austria was to be ejected to make way not for an Italian kingdom but for an Italian confederation under the pope's presidency. But France could not act unless Austria should appear as the ostensible aggressor.

### Cavour and Garibaldi in Italy

At the beginning of 1859 Piedmont was obviously arming. So was Austria. Each was earnestly protesting that her own action was being forced on her by the other. England at the moment was under a ministry not too sympathetic to Italy. From Russia came a proposal that the Italian question should be submitted to a congress ; Austria demanded Sardinia's exclusion from the congress, and then ruined her own case by an ultimatum to Sardinia demanding her immediate disarmament. Napoleon could no longer hold back ; a week later France declared war and Austrian troops entered Piedmont (April 20). The Papal States revolted, Tuscany joined Piedmont, volunteers poured in ; within six weeks the Austrians had met with a series of reverses, which culminated in the Franco-Italian victory of Solferino (June 24). Napoleon took alarm ; the Italian triumph would mean the thing that he did not want—Italian consolidation under Victor Emmanuel. At Villafranca, on July 11, he arranged the betrayal with Francis Joseph. Sardinia could only bow to the inevitable. She accepted the terms by the Treaty of Zürich (November). Lombardy, but not Venetia, was to be ceded to France, which was to pass it on to Sardinia.

But Victor Emmanuel's acceptance left the central Italian states free. They had turned out their rulers ; if they declined to reinstate those rulers there was nothing to prevent them from voluntarily joining

**CHAMPION OF ITALIAN LIBERTY**

Inestimable service was rendered to the cause of Italian liberty by its energetic devotee Giuseppe Garibaldi (1807–82), leader of the victorious ' Thousand.' The photograph from which W. Holl made this engraving was taken about 1860.

themselves to Sardinia ; that right Napoleon dared not veto. His own career had committed him irrevocably to the doctrine of the sanctity of plébiscites. He wanted, and he had not got, Savoy ; from a congress he would never get it. The British government proposed that central Italy should decide its own fate by plébiscite. That solution was adopted, and the central Italian states voted themselves into the Sardinian kingdom, while Cavour could not escape from his old pledge at Plombières to cede Savoy and Nice, to the resentment of Garibaldi and other fiery patriots (March, 1860). The first parliament of the expanded kingdom was held at Turin in April. But Venetia was still in Austria's grip, Bomba's son Francis still misruled the Sicilies, and the pope, secure in the protection of France, still reigned over Rome.

The next episode was supremely dramatic. Sicily once more broke into revolt against the Bourbon tyranny. Sardinia had no excuse for interference ; but Cavour could shut his eyes while Garibaldi collected a band of enthusiastic volunteers, seized a couple of ships, sailed with his 'Thousand,' the Red Shirts, for Sicily, and landed at Marsala on May 11, having escaped the ostentatious vigilance of the Sardinian fleet. Within a week he had routed the government forces at Calata-fimi; Palermo proved too strong for assault until he enticed the greater part of the garrison to pursue him into the hills while a picked troop effected an entry on May 30. Another victory a month later at Milazzo established him as undisputed 'dictator in Victor Emmanuel's name,' though without authority or official countenance from the king. In August he was over the strait, marching for Naples.

Cavour was anxious. If Garibaldi cleared the Bourbon out of Naples, would he be persuaded by the republicans to proclaim a Sicilian republic under his own dictatorship ? Would he advance on Rome and bring down foreign interven-tion, fatal to the cause ? It was more than likely. On the other hand, his possible defeat would be disastrous. Francis meant to fight for his crown, but Garibaldi's progress in the south was a sort of triumphal reception. The dis-loyalty of the troops in Naples was so manifest that on September 6 Francis beat a retreat from the capital, which Garibaldi entered next day.

Cavour made a bold move. He discovered that the foreign troops in the pope's pay were a menace to Italy, and demanded their dismissal. The demand was ignored and Piedmontese troops entered Umbria. Napoleon protested but sat still ; he more than suspected that the papal government was fostering plotters for a Bourbon restoration in France. The papal troops were routed, but Rome and the Roman territory—the ' patrimony of S. Peter '—were kept inviolate. By plébiscite, the rest of the territory joined the northern kingdom. On October 4 the Turin parlia-ment ratified the incorporation.

### Birth of the new Italian Kingdom

MEANWHILE, Francis was making a stand on the Volturno. Driven thence, his troops held out in Gaeta. On October 13, Victor Emmanuel and the Piedmontese forces were over the Nea-politan border, pushing towards Gaeta—all that was still in the hands of the Bourbon. Plébiscites were taken in each of the Sicilies ; both declared for annexa-tion. Would Garibaldi the conqueror and his devoted followers accept the verdict ? No one knew. On October 25 the king and the dictator, with their armies at their backs, came face to face, and Garibaldi hailed Victor Emmanuel as king of Italy. The cause was won.

Gaeta, covered by a French squadron, remained defiant. In January, 1861, the French squadron was withdrawn and Gaeta was occupied by the victors. The parliament of Italy met at Turin in February, and on March 17 the new kingdom of Italy was formally pro-claimed ; there remained outside it only Venetia and Rome. They were still outside when Cavour died, but their inclusion was not long postponed ; though

**VICTOR EMMANUEL II**

Courageous and popular, Victor Emmanuel II (1820–78), who succeeded Charles Albert on the throne of Sardinia in 1849, was declared king of a united Italy in 1861. He showed great wisdom in his appointment of Cavour as premier in 1852.

*From a photograph*

a desperate attempt by Garibaldi to capture Rome in defiance of the Turin government in 1862 had to be foiled at Aspromonte by the Italian government itself.

THE extrusion of Austria from Italy was the condition precedent of Italian unification ; her extrusion from Germany was no less the condition of German unification, because German Austria could not be at the same time an integral portion of a German nation and an integral portion of an Austrian empire three-fourths of which was not German at all. When, after the Year of Revolutions, the old German and Austrian systems were both re-established, the prospect of German unity seemed as remote as ever. In the decade which followed, however, the power of Austria was weakened by the vacillations in the Turkish war which alienated her from both Russia and France, and by her defeat in the Italian struggle which made Victor Emmanuel king of Italy. On the other hand, Prussia and Prussian influence in Germany had been strengthened by Austria's failure to procure her inclusion in the Prussian customs union or Zollverein which gave free trade within Germany to all the rest of the German states while maintaining tariffs against the foreigner, and by the accession to the Prussian throne—though at first only as regent—of Frederick William's brother, William I, the king's health having broken down irrecoverably in 1857, though he did not die till 1861.

William was not an acute statesman ; but he had the courage of his convictions, and on certain points his convictions were strong. Also he had the capacity for fixing upon abler men than himself whom he could trust and backing them up with an unfailing loyalty, provided always that his own conscience was satisfied. His primary conviction was that of the need for a military reorganization which should give the Prussian army the position in Europe which it had held in the days of Frederick the Great, and the men he chose to carry out the work were Von Roon and Moltke. But the scheme was costly and unpopular, demanding heavy taxation which the crown could not legally levy

**FIRST GERMAN EMPEROR**
William I (1797–1888) became king of Prussia in 1861 after acting as regent for his brother, Frederick William IV, since 1858. After the successes of the Franco-Prussian war he was proclaimed German emperor on January 18, 1871.
*Painting by Winterhalter,* 1854

without the consent of the Assembly. It must be forced on the country in the teeth of an opposition which had the law behind it ; and the man he found, with the audacity and the iron resolution to carry that policy through at the risk of revolution, was Otto von Bismarck. The scheme and the taxes were enforced, over-riding the law. There was no revolution against the government ; but the absolute authority of the crown was irresistibly established, and the new military machine was in full working order in 1864. And meanwhile Bismarck had also established an accord with Russia by supporting her, despite unavailing protests from France and England, in the crushing suppression of a Polish revolt, which left the unhappy Poles more helplessly at the mercy of the Russian government than ever.

Meanwhile also Austria's defeat in Italy had taught her that a reform in the administration of the empire was a necessity ; but the changes she instituted still did not go far enough to satisfy her subjects. Moreover, in 1863 she propounded a new scheme for a German federal constitution. Bismarck was now strong enough to induce William to reject it, while at the same time he attracted popular favour by declaring for a freely elected federal parliament. The German princes generally wanted not to be dominated by either Austria or Prussia, but to hold the balance, and they did not want a democratic parliament, though their subjects did.

At this moment the Slesvig-Holstein question again became acute. The duchies desired separation from the Danish crown, which had set at naught the treaty conditions under which the powers had confirmed it in the succession. The duchies desired incorporation in the German Confederation, under the rival claimant, the duke of Augustenburg. This would suit neither Prussia nor Austria ; Bismarck induced Austria to intervene jointly with Prussia to demand of the new Danish king, Christian, the fulfilment of his treaty obligations. Danish public opinion practically forced Christian to refuse. In February, 1864, the Prussian and Austrian troops invaded Denmark, which had no chance against them. A conference of the powers came to nothing, because they could arrive at no agreement. Prussia and Austria were left to dictate to Denmark their own terms, which she was not in a position to resist. Prussia was to take over the administration of Slesvig, Austria that of Holstein ; an arrangement by no means to the taste of the Confederation Diet, which the two powers agreed to ignore by a convention of their own at Gastein, in the following year.

### Bismarck outwits Napoleon III

BUT Bismarck, now that the efficiency of the new military system had been tested, was ready for the fight which it was now his business to bring about—as soon as he could make Austria the ostensible aggressor. His main difficulties were to persuade the king, who had a conscience, that conscience demanded the war, and to make Napoleon believe that the battle between Austria and Prussia would be to his own advantage. In both cases he was completely successful. The sphinx-like impenetrability with which the world at that time credited Napoleon III was as an open book to the apparently guileless German statesman by whom he was entirely duped at an informal conference at Biarritz. Austria was thoroughly isolated as concerned foreign powers, but one finishing touch was desirable. Italy was craving for Venetia ; an Italian flank attack at the convenient moment would be useful. By April, 1866, Bismarck had removed Victor Emmanuel's first suspicions, while Austria had rejected an Italian offer for the purchase of the coveted territory. The pact was completed. If Austria and Prussia declared war within three months, Italy would strike as Prussia's ally, and Venetia was to be her reward.

### Prussia victorious over Austria

THERE was one other necessary preliminary — the manipulation of Prussia's relations with Austria so that the act of aggression should come from her. The Austrian government in Holstein was, it seemed, encouraging the view favoured by the German Diet that Augustenburg should be recognized in the duchies, to the resentment of the Prussian governor in Slesvig. In January, 1866, Austria, in spite of her compact with Prussia, was committing herself to that view. Clearly, the coming meeting of the Diet would be stormy. Then Napoleon proposed a congress and the cession of Venetia to Italy. Austria made the offer, which Italy found unsatisfactory, and also proposals with regard to the congress which would have rendered it futile. Napoleon reckoned that the war was coming, and that in due time—his own time—he would step in as arbiter.

The Diet met in June. Austria referred the Slesvig-Holstein question to it. Bismarck replied that the Confederation could have no voice in the matter till the reform of its own constitution was settled, and to that end he propounded his own scheme, which included a federal parliament and the exclusion of Austria. Prussian troops entered Holstein. Austria called upon the Confederation to assert its authority in arms, and when the Diet carried the Austrian motion Prussia withdrew from it. (June 14).

The princes were with Austria ; but in a fortnight the Prussian troops had effectively paralysed North Germany and the Hanoverian army had surrendered (June 28). Meanwhile, the Italians, carrying out their programme, were defeated at Custozza (June 25). But on July 2 the Austrian and Bavarian forces were smashed by the Prussians at Königgratz (Sadowa). It was all over before Napoleon could stir. The Prussian troops occupied the South German principalities. On July 22 an armistice was declared, and on July 26 the peace preliminaries were signed, seven weeks after the explosion in the Diet. The actual Peace of Prague was signed four weeks later.

It was no part of Bismarck's policy to humiliate Austria—her friendship would be useful later on. Venetia must go to Italy, as promised, but not the Trentino, which had not been promised ; and Austria must be excluded from the German system, because that was necessary to the Prussian hegemony of Germany. Napoleon's demand for ' compensation' on the Rhine was a mere futility which alarmed and antagonised the South German princes, making them feel their own dependence on Prussian protection. Russian uneasiness at the completeness of the Prussian triumph was placated by a hint that her expansion in Asia commanded Prussian approval and sympathy. So much for foreign relations. These were subservient to the main purpose—the creation of the Prusso-German Empire. First came the consolidation of North Germany by absorption into or dependence on Prussia, through a new North German Confederation and the Prussian annexation of Hanover and Hesse, completing the Prussian territorial continuity. The absorption of South Germany must be voluntary, not compulsory—a favour

granted to the South Germans in due time. Such was the outcome of the Seven Weeks' War and the treaty of Prague.

Bismarck did not intend to precipitate the next issue that he contemplated until he should be so thoroughly ready that rapid victory would be assured. France would have to be fought and very soundly beaten—and France must be the aggressor. For France would certainly do her utmost to prevent the consolidation of Germany—that had been an unfailing feature of her policy since the days of Richelieu—and the Rhine frontier must be rectified so as to render her powerless

**GENERAL PRIM ON HORSEBACK**
The Spanish statesman Juan Prim (1814–70) joined with Francisco Serrano in 1868 to overthrow the unpopular government of Queen Isabella, who was strongly under Jesuit influence. The revolution was successful, but Prim fell a victim to assassins in 1870. Henri Regnault painted this portrait of him.
*Musée de Louvre ; photo, Alinari*

for aggression. And before forcing the decisive conflict Bismarck wanted a solid Germany at his back. The Austrian war had made him a national hero for Prussia, instead of the bugbear of the German liberals, whose hostility vanished when he adopted the rôle of a constitutionalist who had only been reluctantly compelled by the urgent necessities of state to override the law for the time being—though with the happiest effect. Bismarck was quite ready to work through constitutional forms so long as his aims were not hampered thereby.

By a similar show of judicious concession he secured in his new North German Confederation an effective dictatorship for Prussia in the guise of a constitution with an assembly elected by manhood suffrage and a federal council representative of the several autonomous governments under the presidency of the king of Prussia represented by his chancellor. That Otto von Bismarck would know how to manage the council and that for practical purposes the sovereignty of the Confederation was vested therein, he had no manner of doubt.

**LEOPOLD OF HOHENZOLLERN**
William I of Prussia did not encourage the candidature of his relative Leopold of Hohenzollern for the vacant throne of Spain in 1870, and, in spite of Bismarck's approval of the project, Leopold declined to accept it.

The inclusion in it of the South German states whose commercial interests were bound up with the Zollverein, of which they were already members, would be merely a matter of time.

### Origins of the Franco-Prussian War

IN 1870, just three years after the establishment of the constitution, the crisis arose which enabled the chancellor to shatter France.

Spain was the occasion of the quarrel. The unhappy plight of that country under Queen Isabella has not demanded our close attention hitherto ; it is enough here to say that it had been so unhappy that in 1868 General Prim headed a revolution, the queen fled from the country, and the general set up a provisional government which decided to offer the crown to a foreign prince, its own royal family having become impossible. After the consideration and rejection of various candidatures, the crown was ultimately accepted in 1870 by Victor Emmanuel's younger son, the duke of Aosta, who had already declined it once. But one of the princes whose candidature had been tentatively invited was Leopold of Hohenzollern-Sigmaringen, a kinsman of the king of Prussia. William I did not countenance,

**OTTO VON BISMARCK**
The foundation of the German Empire under William I of Prussia was achieved by the genius of Otto von Bismarck (1815–98), following the French defeat at Sedan. His dominating personality is apparent in this photograph.

but quite unmistakably discouraged the candidature ; Bismarck secretly encouraged it ; France's hostility to it was not disguised. Bismarck was defeated. Leopold definitely refused the offer (July 12, 1870), but William had not definitely vetoed it. For a moment Bismarck believed that his own public career was at an end. But on July 14 he had the game in his hands.

Napoleon's position in France was critical. His successes, such as they were, in Italy and the Crimea could hardly be regarded as brilliant. He had been palpably out-manoeuvred by Bismarck in 1866 ; he had intervened in troubles in Mexico (see page 718), and his intervention had been a disastrous failure. The palpable clerical influence in his counsels was a weakness rather than a strength in France and had driven him to maintain the Papacy in Rome, while the sympathies of the country were with the republicans. In a very recent Roman rising Garibaldi had been defeated at Mentana by the ' chassepots ' of the French troops. He had lived on the Napoleonic idea, and the idea would be exploded unless he did something worthy of his mighty uncle's name. An overwhelming diplomatic success or a triumphant war had become almost a necessity. France believed fervently that the French army could repeat its triumphs under the first Napoleon, whereas he knew that the army organization was honeycombed with corruption ; but there was a gambler's chance of success, and the probable alternative was the collapse of the Third Empire. He did not want war, but he dared not exercise the necessary restraining influence. Yet the announcement of Leopold's refusal of the Spanish crown was, on the face of it, an immense diplomatic victory.

### Incident of the Ems Telegram

**H**IS minister, Grammont, threw the victory away. The French ambassador was instructed on July 13 to demand from William, who was at Ems, a pledge that he would in no circumstances support Leopold's candidature. William replied with perfect truth that he never had supported it, that the refusal was final, but that to give pledges was out of the

question. There, he supposed, the matter was ended, and he telegraphed a report of the interview to Bismarck at Berlin. Late that night the telegram appeared in a condensed form in the Norddeutsche Zeitung. The condensed telegram conveyed to all Germany the impression that an outrageous demand had been answered with firmness but without discourtesy ; to all France that an entirely justifiable demand had been met with insolent

**NAPOLEON III AS EMPEROR**
The force of the Napoleonic legend and his own ambition raised Louis Napoleon from French president to emperor in 1852. His attempts to satisfy the national desire for military glory ended in failure. Painting by Flandrin.
*Musée de Versailles ; photo, Neurdein*

**COUNT VON MOLTKE**

The German army that defeated France in 1870 was prepared by the genius of the Prussian field-marshal Helmuth von Moltke (1800–91), a master of military organization and strategy. His fine character won him universal admiration.
*From a photograph*

defiance. Twenty-four hours later Napoleon declared war, and the French armies began to mass on the German frontier.

The war was a plain duel between France and Prussia—but Prussia meant a solid Germany. On the face of things, it was quite impossible to claim that Prussia was the aggressor ; though Germany might not have been solid and the French war fever would not have been so uncontrollable if the Ems telegram had not been ' condensed.' The South German states were under no obligation to take part in a Prussian quarrel with which they did not sympathise, but the telegram as published ensured their lively sympathy, and added fuel to the fire in France. And France's blunder had given to Bismarck and to the Prussian army precisely the chance Bismarck wanted, as Austria's blunder had given him his chance four years before. But he had been able to count on the first blunder ; the second was a gratuitous gift. Russia could be relied on to keep Austria neutral, and British neutrality would be broken only if the guaranteed Belgian neutrality were violated, a blunder which Bismarck was too shrewd to commit. Since 1866 Moltke and Von Roon had brought the general German army organization up to the Prussian standard. France—not Napoleon

**FRENCH CABINET COUNCIL WHICH DECLARED WAR ON PRUSSIA**

The publication of the Ems telegram with its implied insult to France had exactly the result that Bismarck intended. The declaration of war that followed came from France, and in the ensuing hostilities Prussia achieved a signal triumph over her enemy. The group of ministers surrounding Napoleon III in this photograph, taken in 1870, comprises the cabinet council which reached the momentous decision to face ' trial by battle ' with the Prussian foe.

*[handwritten letter in French, signed Napoleon, dated "Sedan le 1 Sept. 1870"]*

## NAPOLEON III SURRENDERS HIS SWORD

After a desperate fight the army of the Emperor Napoleon III surrendered to the Prussians at Sedan on September 1, 1870. Napoleon's letter, written to King William I on the same day, expresses his regret that he did not perish with his fallen troops.
*From Oncken, ' Zeitalter des Kaiser Wilhelm '*

—believed that her own armies would march to Berlin ; Bismarck knew that his would march to Paris.

The first collision was at Saarbrücken on August 2, where the Germans were forced to evacuate an advanced post they had occupied. But in the course of the month a succession of German victories at Wörth (August 6), Colombières (14), Mars-la-Tour and Gravelotte (16 and 17) shut up Bazaine in Metz with 170,000 men, and drove Macmahon to join the emperor at Sedan, where, after a hot resistance, Napoleon was forced to surrender with his whole force on September 1.

The emperor would perforce have accepted any terms ; but the Empire ended at Sedan. His ministry had already been swept away ; the bubble had burst, and Paris for the third

time proclaimed the French Republic, with a ' government of national defence ' under General Trochu, Jules Favre and Léon Gambetta. The empress with her son had taken flight to England, where she was ultimately joined by her husband. The Republic was willing for peace, but not at Bismarck's price, which included the cession of Alsace and Lorraine with Metz and Strassburg. On September 19 the Prussian crown prince's army was at the gates of Paris, which stood defiant and prepared itself as best it might for a long siege.

On September 27 Strassburg fell. The government shut up in Paris could do nothing outside the city ; on October 7 Gambetta escaped in a balloon to Tours, where he became in effect the French

## COMMANDER OF THE FRENCH

Distinguished for his services in Italian campaigns, Marshal Macmahon (1808–93) held high command in the Franco-Prussian war. In August, 1870, he was defeated at Wörth and, in September, wounded and captured at Sedan. Elected president of the French Republic in 1873, he resigned in 1879.
*Painting by R. Princeteau*

government and the inspiration of the French defiance. He raised new armies in the provinces, but on October 27 Bazaine and his great host in Metz surrendered. Gambetta proclaimed a levée en masse. The raw troops fought with heroic devotion, but the desperate successes they won were counterbalanced by far more crushing defeats ; while Paris held out grimly till sheer starvation forced her to capitulate on January 28, 1871.

The Germans dictated their own terms to the French government, to the head of which was called the veteran Thiers, who had been a constitutionalist leader in the revolutions

**LEON GAMBETTA**

Prompt to proclaim the third French Republic in 1870, Léon Gambetta (1838–82) became minister of the interior in the Government of National Defence, and president of the Chamber of Deputies in 1879.

of 1830 and 1848. The terms were crushing. The preliminaries were signed on February 26, and the definitive Treaty of Frankfort on May 10. Alsace and most of Lorraine, with Metz and Strassburg, were ceded ; an enormous indemnity was to be paid, German troops remaining in partial occupation till the process should be completed.

Bismarck's grand object was achieved. He had created a German Empire with the king of Prussia as hereditary emperor. While the war was in progress, one after another of the South German states had been admitted to the Confederation ;

**A SORTIE FROM PARIS DURING ITS SIEGE BY THE GERMANS IN 1870**

Great fortitude was displayed by the heroic defenders of the French capital from the attacks of the opposing army in 1870. Much damage was done to property during the siege and the Arc de Triomphe, shown in this sketch sent by balloon post to an English newspaper, was protected against the heavy fire, while defence works were erected in the streets. Sorties were made at intervals in the hope of dislodging the invaders, but starvation at length enforced surrender.

Bismarck had gradually overcome the opposition of the monarchs, including William himself, to the imperial project ; and on January 18, ten days before the capitulation of Paris, William I had been acclaimed German emperor by the assembled princes in the Hall of Mirrors at Versailles.

Incidentally the withdrawal of the French troops from Rome, necessitated by the war, enabled Victor Emmanuel, immediately after Sedan, to capture and incorporate Rome with the Italian kingdom, and make it the national capital, while the pope remained in the Vatican deprived of all temporal power ; also Russia, supported by Bismarck, was able to procure the virtual abrogation of the Black Sea Treaty of 1856 by the Treaty of London of 1871. The results of the Crimean War were washed out. A burning hostility to Germany had been implanted in the soul of every Frenchman, and England was more convinced than ever that her own Indian empire was Russia's objective.

### French Intervention in Mexico

ℑN the period during which Italy and Germany were each achieving the unification which in the one had never been known since the days of the Roman Caesars and in the other had never been attained before, the great trans-Atlantic republic was working out a corresponding process under very different conditions, and was at the same time coming into line with the white peoples of the old world in the attitude they had so recently adopted towards the institution of negro slavery ; an institution reconcilable with democratic doctrines only on the hypothesis that these apply to white races alone. In America the two questions were inextricably intertwined, because the maintenance of the institution was in fact incompatible with unification.

We turn then to the American developments that were contemporary with the European developments which have hitherto been the subject of the present chapter ; giving precedence, however, to Mexico, because it was more directly connected with European affairs, and was, moreover, among the subsidiary causes

**LOUIS ADOLPHE THIERS**

In the critical days of French humiliation and defeat after Sedan Louis Adolphe Thiers (1797–1877) secured acceptance for the terms of peace dictated by the Germans, and faced the hard task of reconstruction under the new Republic.

*Painting by Bonnat ; the Louvre*

that contributed to the downfall of Napoleon.

Santa Ana's last dictatorship (see page 691) was overthrown in 1855. After further faction struggles the anti-clerical Benito Juarez secured the presidency in 1860. Next year he met the financial difficulties in which the government was involved by secularising ecclesiastical estates and suspending the payment of Mexico's debts to her European creditors. Napoleon saw an opportunity for intervention, since the United States were at that moment entering upon a domestic struggle which must absorb all their energies for a long time, so that effective opposition from them, based on the Monroe doctrine, to European intervention in the western hemisphere was precluded. He proposed, with the support of the clericals in Mexico, to end the anarchy by giving her a constitutional monarch from Europe (who would owe his throne to France). Success would be at once a French and a clerical triumph, greatly increasing the stability of his own position at home.

Austria would be conciliated by the nomination of the archduke Maximilian to the Mexican crown. Spain would co-operate, and perhaps England, which had financial interests in Mexico, though she would not go beyond what might seem necessary to procure the payment of the debts.

A joint ' demonstration ' was arranged at the end of 1861—to insist upon the restoration of order and the payment of debts. But the Spanish commander Prim (who afterwards effected the expulsion of Queen Isabella) soon realized that he was intended to be Napoleon's catspaw, a position he had no intention of accepting, and the British were satisfied by the Mexican president's offers. Napoleon could not afford to stop, and France went on alone. The French and the clericals took Mexico city, but Juarez and Porfirio Diaz maintained the struggle year by year. Maximilian arrived in person in 1864, but

decisive victory remained remote ; Napoleon's resources were severely strained ; no glory had been or seemed likely to be won ; in 1865, the war in the United States reached a decisive conclusion and their intervention was imminent. In 1866 Napoleon left Maximilian to his fate. The success of the Republicans was now assured, but the ' Emperor ' of Mexico would not desert his supporters, and in the next year he was captured and shot. Juarez was once more established in the dictatorship, in which he was succeeded five years later by Diaz.

### Causes of the American Civil War

THERE were no serious questions pending between the United States and European powers in 1848. But their recent difference with Mexico on one side caused the fall of Santa Ana, and on the other the acquisition of California ; and this soon brought about a new crisis in

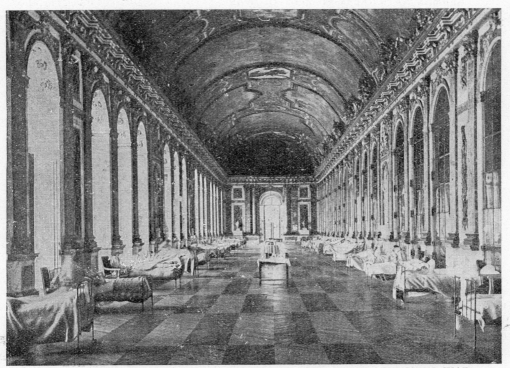

**NOVEL USE FOR THE HALL OF MIRRORS IN THE FRANCO-PRUSSIAN WAR**
Many historic scenes have been enacted in the famous Hall of Mirrors at Versailles, which this photograph shows during its temporary conversion into a German hospital at the time of the Franco-Prussian war. Here, on January 18, 1871, King William I of Prussia was proclaimed German Emperor, and within these walls was signed, on June 28, 1919, the treaty that ended the Great War.

**GERMAN NATIONAL MONUMENT OF WAR**
In commemoration of the German military triumphs of 1870–1, the Emperor William I unveiled this commanding statue of Germania on the crest of the Niederwald in 1883. The bronze figure, designed by Joannes Schilling, is thirty-three feet high. Allegorical figures and portraits decorate the statue's base.
*Photo, Neuen Photographische Gesellschaft*

body of definitely abolitionist opinion was growing in the North, inflamed by the publication of almost the only work of fiction which has directly influenced the course of political events, Uncle Tom's Cabin — a lurid picture of the conditions of negro slavery which is open to criticism—and the enforcement of the 'fugitive-slave law' in the free territories was not only resented but openly resisted.

The atmosphere of acquiescence was not long preserved. More territory was occupied, reviving the question in 1854; local option was again proposed, though the whole Kansas-Nebraska area was north of the Missouri line. The abolitionists were up in arms, though there was no real doubt that local option would keep the whole area 'free.' Then a judgement of the supreme court laid it down that slave

the 'slave' or 'free' state question. New states must be created, and the Northern and Southern immigrants, swarming into the new territory in which gold had been discovered, were in hot opposition to each other. The new territories were partly north and partly south of the Missouri line, while the line itself could not be continued as a line of demarcation between new states. If the question, slave or free, was to be decided by local option—by each state for itself—the Northerners, being generally in a majority, would carry the day everywhere, and the preponderance of the North in the central government would be substantially increased.

The moderates on both sides desired a compromise ; the extremists in the South were determined not to be swamped, those in the North were bent on swamping them. A compromise was, in fact, adopted (1850) introducing the principle of local option, accompanied by the 'fugitive-slave law,' which entitled slave owners to recover slaves who had escaped into free territory. But at the same time the

**MAXIMILIAN I OF MEXICO**
The Austrian archduke Maximilian (1832–67), victim of Napoleon III's America scheme, was declared emperor of Mexico in 1863. In time of need, French support was withdrawn and he was shot by the republicans in 1867.
*Engraving by Metzmacher*

owners could retain their property in their slaves on free territory.

To most of the North the recognition of slavery at all upon free territory was a moral abomination, though only the abolitionist minority were ready to demand its suppression where it was already legally established. But the South, which regarded the institution not only as an economic necessity but as ordained by Scripture, felt that, with a great Northern predominance in the central government, abolition would be only a question of time. If the South was to be saved,

state rights as against the central government must be asserted even to the point of acting upon what it claimed as its legal right of secession from the Union. The crisis arrived with the presidential election at the close of 1860, when from the splitting of votes among four sectional candidates the lot fell upon Abraham Lincoln. Lincoln loathed slavery without being an abolitionist—abolition was still wholly impracticable as an avowed policy; but the South saw in his victory the certain presage of the gradual if not the immediate submerging of the Southern economic interests by those of the North. Secession was the only course left open.

Carolina led the way with an ordinance dissolving the Union in December. In February, 1861, six more of the Southern states drew up a constitution for ' the Confederated States of America,' (the term confederate implying a union from which any member is free to separate itself, while the term Federal, adopted by the North, implies an indissoluble union) ; soon nearly all the slave states had joined the Confederates, and elected Jefferson Davis their president ; while Lincoln in his inaugural presidential address declared his intention of enforcing the laws of the Union in all the states. On April 14 the Confederates seized and occupied the arsenal-fortress of Fort Sumter, and next day Lincoln issued a proclamation calling for 75,000 volunteers.

The issue to be fought out was definitely the right of secession, not the retention or abolition of slavery, though the latter was indirectly involved in the former. Were there to be two American nations with conflicting interests, or was the American nation to be one ? European

**PRESIDENT ABRAHAM LINCOLN**

Abraham Lincoln (1809–65) was elected president of the United States in 1860 and entered office in March, 1861, a month before the Civil War broke out. This photograph was taken in the war years, throughout which the onus of carrying affairs to a successful conclusion fell mainly upon him.

*Robert Coster Collection*

## FEDERAL AND CONFEDERATED STATES OF AMERICA

Originating in the question of the abolition of slavery—passionately advocated in the North—or its retention—deemed necessary to the economic existence of the South—the American Civil War was definitely fought to decide the right of individual states to secede from the Union. In December, 1860, Carolina declared for secession, and in the following February the other slave states except Missouri and Kentucky joined the Confederate States of America in opposition to the Federal states of the North.

sympathies were divided on the question, the rights of minorities appealing on one side, the principle of unification on the other.

Bull Run, the first big battle of the war, was notable, apart from its results, as the first historic occasion on which the possession of a railway junction was the strategic objective of the opposing armies ; and the victory was won by the Confederates through their successful use of the railway. It inspired the South with confidence and roused the North to a fuller consciousness of the magnitude of the struggle before it. In the autumn occurred an incident which nearly forced Great Britain into war with the North. On the standing principle of non-intervention in the domestic quarrels of foreign states, Great Britain refused to take either side, though recognizing the Confederates as belligerents—an attitude much resented by both, since each was firmly convinced that the justice of its own cause was so manifest that to refuse it support was inexcusable. Commissioners from the South for England who had

### JEFFERSON DAVIS

Elected president of the Confederates in 1861, and re-elected in 1862, Jefferson Davis (1808–89) showed considerable skill in organizing the armies of the South, but he lacked the genius of his opponent, Lincoln, for managing men.

*From Wilson: 'History of the American People'*

taken passage on a British ship, the Trent, were forcibly removed from her by a Federal warship ; war was only averted with extreme difficulty.

In the next year (1862) the area of the fighting was widely extended, and the naval superiority of the Federals enabled them to establish a blockade of all the Southern ports—a very serious matter for the South, which was dependent for its supplies upon imports and for money upon its exports. Incidentally, it produced a 'cotton famine' in England ; where, nevertheless, the sympathy of the cotton operatives for the slaves in what now became definitely a war of emancipation was too strong to be overridden by the sufferings brought on themselves by the stoppage of employment.

The military operations of the year were indecisive ; but in September Lincoln proclaimed that all slaves in all states which should be in arms against the Federal government at the close of the year would then be declared free. The emancipation proclamation was duly issued on January 1, 1863, and the South found itself not only threatened by the North but in danger of negro risings within its own gates. Yet for still another year the Confederate forces continued to hold their own in the field against forces often greatly superior to their own in number.

### Victory of the North over the South

THE South, however, had almost no reserves of men to draw upon as their numbers became depleted, the slave labour hitherto employed in essential production could no longer be relied upon, and the blockade cut them off from imports ; whereas in the North increasing numbers of volunteers could still pour in to fill up the military gaps without a dangerous depletion of productive power. The turn of the tide was marked by the check to the advance of the Confederate General Lee— against much larger forces—in the three days' struggle at Gettysburg at midsummer, 1863. From that time the Southerners were fighting with their backs to the wall against overwhelming odds.

In May, 1864, the supreme command of the Federal armies was given to Ulysses Grant ; still, through desperate fighting, Lee held his own in Virginia, but no more. At the end of the year Lincoln was re-elected to the presidency. A second Federal army under Sherman worked its way to the south, ending up with the famous march to the sea, and in January began the northward march which the Confederate commander Johnston could only check at intervals. In April Lee was completely enveloped by Grant's overwhelming numbers, and had to choose between annihilation and surrender at Appomattox Court House ; and his surrender (April 9, 1865) was the surrender of the South. Five days later Abraham Lincoln was shot by a crazed assassin.

The battle had been fought to a finish. Slavery was no more, and the political unity of the American nation was at last an established fact, though it was still long before the South could reconcile itself to

**SITE OF TWO SOUTHERN VICTORIES**

In the neighbourhood of Bull Run, in West Virginia, the Confederate troops were twice victorious. In July, 1861, it was Johnston who put the Federals to flight and in August, 1862, Lee himself was in command. This engraving after a photograph of the latter year shows Confederate fortifications at Manassas junction.

*From Johnson and Buel, ' Battles and Leaders of the Civil War '*

**GENERAL ROBERT LEE**

A great general and a benevolent man, Robert Lee (1807–70) commanded the Confederate forces in the American Civil War. His courage and tenacity were finally overcome by the numerical superiority of Grant's army.
*After a photograph*

the new order. And, though slavery was gone, the negro problem remained.

ℑN the British Empire during these years all the greater colonies, after the Canadian precedent, were endowed with a very large degree of autonomy, with parliamentary constitutions varying according to their individual choice, and in full possession of responsible government as concerned their domestic affairs ; and in North America all the colonies, with the exception of Newfoundland, were federated, under one government, in the Dominion of Canada by the British North America Act of 1867. A very considerable impulse was given to Australian colonisation by the gold rush caused by the

discovery of gold in large quantities in 1851. Hitherto the country had attracted mainly agriculturists ; but now many industrials, who went out for gold, remained permanently, and with the presence of skilled artisans began the development of manufactures. In India the work of beneficent administration progressed, but not without difficulty. At home the trade unions, a characteristically British creation, were on the point of receiving recognition as a legal and even a privileged form of industrial organization, at the moment when the Parliamentary Reform Act of 1867 was transferring the preponderant voting power from the ' middle classes' to the artisans.

ℑN the Far East revolution was in progress. Until the middle of the nineteenth century, when China was involved in her first war with the British as related in the last chapter, she had successfully maintained the barriers excluding European penetration. That war gave to the British not an open door but a chink ; and other powers were soon pressing for corresponding privileges, France and the United States leading. Another collision with the British, known as the Arrow Incident, in 1856, brought on another

**BROADWAY LANDING, APPOMATTOX RIVER**

When the fall of Richmond became inevitable in April, 1865, General Lee retreated upon Lynchburg, but was intercepted by Sheridan at Appomattox Court House and compelled to surrender. Broadway Landing was one of several points at which the winding Appomattox river had to be crossed in the course of these operations.
*Contemporary photograph*

war, in which France, having grievances of her own, joined the British. The advance of the allies upon Peking induced the Chinese government to make concessions formulated in the treaty of 1858 ; but its failure to give the concessions effect caused the war to be renewed in 1860. Again the allies marched on Peking, captured it, and imposed upon it the permanent presence of official 'residents,' representing the European governments. The Peking government was the more amenable, because it was in danger of being overwhelmed by the long-growing Taiping rebellion, for the suppression of which in 1864 it was mainly indebted to American and European officers.

### Japan Opened to Western Influence

IN 1641 the Tokugawa Shogunate in Japan had finally chosen its policy of isolation from all European influences, having already discarded Hideyoshi's schemes of imperial development on the Asiatic continent. All that Japan knew of the outside world was through her very slight intercourse with China and with the Dutch merchants to whom she conceded a very limited admission. She was not menaced with foreign attack, and until the middle of the nineteenth century there had been no urgent pressure to force commerce upon her.

For more than two centuries the hereditary shoguns had ruled her in peace and prosperity, unchallenged theoretically as the ministers of the semi-divine mikados, who in effect never sought to exercise the control which no one questioned their right to resume. But now the time had come when Japan had to face the European and American expansion which, as we have seen, began in the 'forties, to bring the West into collision with China. In so far as regards the awakening of Japan to the situation as it existed, we must here summarise the movement which suddenly ended her isolation and brought her into the circle of the world states.

About 1846 the menace on the hitherto peaceful horizon began to obtrude itself. If Japan was to maintain her exclusiveness, she must be prepared to resist Western pressure. Not only the shogun but also the new mikado Komei awoke to the fact. The shogun was aware that Japan lacked the resources for suddenly bringing her defences up to the necessary standard. The mikado and the great majority of the nobles had no such fears and were bent on increasing the rigidity of exclusion ; while there was a small but able and well informed minority who were convinced that exclusion was a fundamental error and that knowledge of, and

### CAPTURE OF THE NORTH FORT, PEIHO

Treacherous breach by the Chinese of the treaty concluded with Lord Elgin at Tientsin in 1858 led to a second expedition being dispatched in 1860. French forces took part in this campaign and in August the allies again went up the Peiho en route to Peking. This drawing after a sketch by an artist with the expedition records the storming and capture of the Peiho forts on August 21, after which the allies marched to the capital where the Chinese opened negotiations and ratified the treaty of 1858.

**COMMODORE MATTHEW PERRY**

Matthew Calbraith Perry (1794–1858) crowned a distinguished naval career by his negotiation of the treaty, signed March 31, 1854, between the United States and Japan which reopened Japan to Western influence after 250 years' isolation.

*From a photograph*

intercourse with, the West should be scientifically turned to advantage.

The shogun could not afford to associate his policy with this third group. If he set himself in opposition to the mikado, the titular sovereign would become the active sovereign, with the country behind him, the Shogunate would go—having no divine sanction behind it, like the Mikado-ship—and Japan would be plunged into a struggle with the Western powers which could end only in utter disaster. He must appear to be carrying out the popular policy and yet manage to evade the foreigner's wrath.

The appearance of the American naval commander Perry, in 1853 and 1854, with demands for an open door, brought matters to a head. The shogun, whom the West conceived to be the actual emperor, dared not refuse concessions, including the admission of an American consul. The popular resentment grew. Two years later the European allies were ominously hammering Peking. The consul demanded, and got, more concessions in 1858. There was a new and youthful shogun; the Shogunate policy was in the hands of the old shogun's right-hand man, Kamon no

Kami, and in 1860 he was slain by a band of Samurai, the military caste of the 'patriot' party. A series of attacks was made on foreigners, official or otherwise. British warships appeared; there was a collision between them and the forts of the baron of Satsuma. The shogun was compelled to order vigorous action against the foreigners; the baron of Choshiu fired upon shipping passing through the Strait of Shimonoseki. His forts were bombarded, and he was forced to pay a heavy indemnity (1863).

The mikado and his party realized their blunder in forcing action, but threw the blame on the shogun and Choshiu. The shogun reconciled himself with the mikado, but Choshiu, arguing that he had acted under orders, revolted, demanding the removal of the mikado's evil counsellors. The shogun took counter-measures which deprived him of the mikado's support. Civil war was imminent. Then (1866–7) mikado and shogun both died. The new shogun was Kokei, his predecessor's minister and cousin; the new emperor was a boy, Mutsuhito. Events had coerced the Shogunate—including Kokei—to commit itself to a policy which

**MUTSUHITO, EMPEROR OF JAPAN**

Mutsuhito (1852–1912) succeeded his father in 1867 and did much to forward the establishment of Western civilization in Japan. His reign was signalised by victorious wars with China and Russia, and alliance with Great Britain.

*Almanack de Gotha, 1877*

was not its own ; the policy which it would fain have followed from the beginning had become that of its original opponents, the party of the mikado. Kokei, moreover, could not be a party to the reinstatement of Choshiu, to which the mikado was committed. The Shogunate had become incompatible with an active Mikadoship ; in 1867 Kokei solved the problem by a voluntary resignation, and Mutsuhito became emperor in fact as well as in name.

IN 1871, then, a new power, though one not yet recognized as such, had been created in the Far East. In the Far West unification had triumphed over the forces of disruption. In Europe, Italy was for the first time since the days of the Roman Empire united under a constitutional monarchy. The Austrian Empire still had its problem of reconciling a central control with the divergent interests of the Germans, North Slavs, South Slavs and Magyars, for which it had found a partial solution satisfactory to Hungary, in the establishment of the Dual Monarchy.

In the Turkish Empire diverse Christian populations were still under the Ottoman sovereignty. Germany had for the first time in her history become united, and united with her own assent, under an irresistibly organized central government, which controlled an army incomparably the most powerful in Europe. France, shorn of her Rhine provinces and exhausted by a crushing war, had for the third time set up, though she had not yet established, a republic ; she had still a crowd of difficulties to surmount before her old power could be restored— and it was the interest of her victorious neighbour to foster those difficulties.

Bismarck had no desire for a German expansion. What he did want was to secure the friendship of Austria, now that she could no longer be Prussia's rival in Germany, and to avoid the hostility of Russia, which would set an enemy on either flank of the new empire. When in 1872 he had established the un-written ' League of the Three Emperors,' there was nothing to be immediately feared. But the danger point for the per-manence of the new league lay in the Balkans, to which the eyes of Austria, now shut out from Germany, were more persistently turned. Austro-Russian rivalry for ascendancy in the Balkans might produce a breach, and Germany might be reduced to the painful necessity of taking a side. If she were, she would take Austria's—but such a con-tingency must not arise if it could be prevented. Russia must be encouraged to find in

**EARL OF BEACONSFIELD**

Benjamin Disraeli (1804–81), created earl of Beaconsfield in 1876, entered parliament in 1837 and after 1842 was the recog-nized Tory leader. As prime minister, 1874–80, he adopted an anti-Russian policy in the Eastern question. This statuette was modelled by Lord Ronald Sutherland Gower about 1878.

*National Portrait Gallery, London : photo, Emery Walker*

Asia the field for the development of her ambitions. If that brought her into collision with the British, Germany would lose nothing. From this point of view Russia's progress in Turkistan during the last decade was quite promising. But the Balkans were uncontrollable.

Serbia, Rumania and Montenegro had all attained a tributary autonomy. But in 1875 the peasants of Herzegovina revolted against their Moslem masters. All their Slavonic neighbours actively sympathised. Both Russia and Austria had some title to pose as the natural protectors of the Slavs, Orthodox and Catholic respectively. The insurgents appealed not to one or the other, but to the powers generally. The Porte had given effect to none of its promised reforms ; it was reasonable that the powers should insist upon them—the insurgents demanded no more, but they would remain in arms till they got something more substantial than promises on paper. The Porte had no sort of objection to making any number of promises, but an ineradicable objection to fulfilling them.

### The Near Eastern Question

ꞮN May, 1876, the three emperors issued a memorandum to which they invited the assent of the other three powers. Disraeli, the British prime minister, declined ; Turkey was not to be coerced—if the Turkish sovereignty were allowed to go, Russian ascendancy would take its place, and that was a thing Great Britain could in no wise permit. The memorandum programme was strangled at birth. At the same time the Bulgarians rose, and the atrocities with which the suppression of the revolt was accompanied stirred up a fiery anti-Turkish political campaign in England, though in parliament Disraeli's ascendancy was complete. The new sultan, Abdul Hamid, who succeeded in June, was defiant. In July, Serbia and Montenegro declared war on Turkey.

If a frank and cordial understanding between Russia and Great Britain had been possible, the Eastern Question might conceivably have been settled. Mutual mistrust made it quite impossible. The Beaconsfield cabinet (it was at this time

**DEFENDER OF PLEVNA**

Distinguished for military service in the Crimea and in Crete, the Turkish marshal Osman Pasha (c. 1835–1900) won highest renown for his gallant defence of Plevna for over four months against a heavy Russian bombardment in 1877.

*After a photograph*

that Disraeli took his earldom) was divided on the question of armed intervention on behalf of Turkey. When Great Britain herself demanded from Turkey an armistice and a conference of the powers to be held at Constantinople in December, Abdul Hamid dared not refuse. But when the conference met he laid before it a full-blown scheme of reforms which he proposed to carry out—as a sovereign who would submit to no external control over his actions. The meaning of which was obvious. Diplomacy failed to find a way out of the deadlock ; and in April Russian forces, having been granted free passage through Rumania, crossed the Pruth.

Austria had made a private compact of neutrality ; Germany had no motive for intervention ; Great Britain was satisfied to wait and watch. Three months passed before the Russians could effect their passage of the Danube ; for the next month they advanced rapidly ; then suddenly they found themselves held up by the Turks under Osman, who had seized and entrenched a flanking position at Plevna, whence the most desperate efforts, culminating in a grand attack on September 11, failed to dislodge him. But assault was abandoned for investment ; three months later, after a desperate attempt to cut his way out, Osman was compelled to surrender (December 10). In the east, too, the Russian advance through the Caucasus had been held up in the first months, but there, too, the tide had turned decisively before December. After the fall of Plevna the Turkish resistance began to crumble ; on January 20, 1878, Russian forces were in Adrianople, where on January 31 peace preliminaries were signed. On March 3 the Adrianople Convention became the Treaty of San Stefano.

Meanwhile, however, the fall of Plevna had set the governments of the other powers in motion. A sweeping triumph might enable Russia to dictate terms destructive both of Austrian and of British interests—regardless of the conditions upon which those powers had observed neutrality. Neither Russia nor Britain wanted war, but the British government felt it necessary to demonstrate its readiness for that alternative, and through the first months of the year the tension was extreme. Austria proposed a conference, which ultimately took shape as the Berlin Congress, since the terms of the Treaty of San Stefano

intensified instead of allaying the perturbation of Austria as well as of England. The fundamental disagreement between the powers was on the question, how far had Russia the right to dictate her own terms, and how far had the powers concerned in the previous treaties the right to insist upon their own modifications ?

The congress met in June at Berlin under the presidency of Bismarck as Germany's representative, in the character of the sincere friend of all parties, having no interests of his own at stake and desiring only to induce them all to accept equitable adjustments of their divergent or antagonistic interests. The result was the Treaty of Berlin, generally regarded as a triumph for Beaconsfield's diplomacy, since at the end of it very little was left of the San Stefano Treaty ; while it was accompanied by independent pacts on the one hand between Great Britain and Turkey and on the other between Austria and Russia, which left the whole Eastern Question on a footing new but scarcely more harmonious than before. The treaty was in fact, the opening of a new phase rather than the closing of an old one, so that its provisions will form the starting point of our next chapter.

**EUROPEAN PLENIPOTENTIARIES AT THE BERLIN CONGRESS IN 1878**

The terms of the San Stefano treaty (March, 1878) concluding the Russo-Turkish war aroused so much dissatisfaction in Europe that Lord Beaconsfield secured the convocation of a congress of the powers at Berlin for the treaty's revision. In this painting of a session of the congress by Anton von Werner, Bismarck, who presided, is seen shaking hands with Count Shuvalov, and on the left Prince Gortchakov (seated) is engaged in apparently amiable conversation with Lord Beaconsfield.

# TABLE OF DATES FOR CHAPTER 31

1878    Victor Emmanuel d. ; acc. Humbert I.
Pius IX d. ; acc. Leo XIII.
Berlin Congress and treaties. Complete independence of Serbia, Montenegro and Rumania ; Bulgaria much reduced from the Russian plan ; Bosnia a temporary Austrian protectorate ; Russia takes Bessarabia, giving Rumania Dobruja ; British protectorate in Cyprus.

1879    Macmahon resigns French Presidency ; Bonapartism perishes with the death of the Prince Imperial in the British Zulu war ; permanence of the French Republic gradually assured.
Alexander of Battenberg accepts principality of Bulgaria as the tsar's protégé.
Afghanistan : British legation at Kabul cut to pieces, beginning Afghan war.

1880    Afghan campaigns. After decisive victories the British retire, leaving Abd er-Rahman to establish himself as amir.
Gladstone ministry ; Lord Ripon Indian viceroy.
U.S.A. : President Garfield assassinated.

1881    France, encouraged by Bismarck, occupies Tunis, causing friction with Italy.
Transvaal war ; Transvaal retroceded to Boers.
Bulgaria : Prince Alexander's coup d'état.
Alexander II murdered by nihilists ; acc. Alexander III.

1882    Italy joins in Triple Alliance with Germany and Austria.
Bombardment of Alexandria and overthrow of Arabi Pasha. Tewfik's government restored under British protectorate and control. Mahdi appears in Sudan.

1883    Alexander restores Bulgarian constitution and dismisses Russian advisers.

1884    India : Racial feeling aroused by Ilbert Bill. Lord Dufferin succeeds Ripon as viceroy.
General Gordon sent to the Sudan.
U.S.A. : Grover Cleveland elected president (1).

1885    Union of Rumelia with Bulgaria under Prince Alexander ; Serbia declares war on Bulgaria, and is heavily defeated at Slivnitza.
Alfonso XII of Spain d. ; acc. Alfonso XIII ; regency of Maria Christina.
Penjdeh incident (collision of Russian and Afghan troops) smoothed over.
France acquires protectorate in Annam and Madagascar.
Fall of Gordon at Khartum ; temporary abandonment of Sudan.

1886    Alexander of Bulgaria is kidnapped, and resigns. Bulgar government maintained under Stambulov.

1887    Agreed delimitation of Afghan, Indian and Russian frontiers. Annexation of Burma. First meeting of Indian ' National Congress.'
Bulgaria : Acc. Ferdinand of Saxe-Coburg.

1888    William I d. ; acc. Frederick I, then William II.
U.S.A. : Benjamin Harrison president.
India : Lord Lansdowne viceroy.

1889    William II pays first state visit to the Sultan.

1890    William II dismisses Bismarck.
Anglo-German treaty delimiting spheres of influence in Africa.

1892    U.S.A. : Cleveland president (2).

1893    Serbia : Fall of Obrenovitch dynasty ; acc. Peter Karageorgevitch.

1894    Alexander III d. ; acc. Nicholas II.
France : Murder of President Sadi Carnot.
Bulgaria : Fall of Stambulov ; Ferdinand takes control into his own hands.
India : Lord Elgin viceroy.
Chino-Japanese war ; defeat of China. Treaty of Shimonoseki. The powers intervene to scramble for Chinese concessions.

1894-6   Turkey : Armenian massacres and insurrections.

1895    Franco-Russian agreement, developing into Dual Alliance, balancing central Triple Alliance.
S. Africa : the Jameson Raid.

1896    Final Armenian massacres ; the Kaiser compliments Abdul Hamid.
U.S.A. : Venezuelan-British boundary dispute submitted to American arbitration. McKinley elected president.

1897    First German naval programme.
Cretan revolt helped by Greeks ; stopped by the powers (Germany and Austria abstaining) who guarantee Cretan autonomy. Greek invasion of Thessaly totally defeated by Turks.
The European powers demand and obtain concessions in China, where hostility to foreigners raises the Boxer rebellion.

1898    China : Empress-dowager usurps power, deposing the emperor.
The tsar assembles first Hague Conference.
American-Spanish war ; complete defeat of Spain ; U.S.A. annex Philippines.
Re-conquest of Sudan. The Fashoda incident ; irritation in France against England.
India : Lord Curzon viceroy.

1899    S. Africa : Boers invade Natal ; beginning of South African war (Oct.).

1900    China : European legations in Peking besieged by Chinese ' rebels.'
Germany : Great development of naval programme.

1901    Commonwealth of Australia established.
Queen Victoria d. ; acc. Edward VII.
China : International forces march on Peking and relieve the legations ; submission of the Chinese government.
U.S.A. : Murder of President McKinley ; Theodore Roosevelt succeeds to the presidency.

1902    Germany obtains Bagdad railway concession from Turkey.
Anglo-Japanese treaty of alliance.
End of South African war.

1903    Tariff reform agitation in England intensifies German suspicions of British hostility.

1904    Japan declares war on Russia (Feb.) ; Yalu battle and siege of Port Arthur (Ap.) ; Russians driven back on Mukden ; Russian fleet destroyed (Aug.); Russian defeat on Sha-ho (Nov.).
Anglo-French entente adjusting outstanding causes of friction.
U.S.A. : Roosevelt president (2).
India : Lord Minto viceroy.

1905    Japan : Port Arthur surrenders (Jan.) ; Russians driven from Mukden (Feb.) ; new Russian squadron annihilated (May) ; war ended by treaty of Portsmouth (Aug.).

1906    Responsible government restored in Transvaal and Orange River Colony.
Germany submits a dispute with France supported by England (Morocco) to Algeciras conference.

1907    Anglo-Russian adjustment ; the Triple Entente.

1908    The ' Young Turks ' compel Abdul Hamid to concede a constitution. Ferdinand proclaims independence of Bulgaria and assumes title of tsar. Austria, supported by Germany, announces annexation of Bosnia ; Russia has to acquiesce.
U.S.A. : Election of President Taft.

1909    Indian Councils Act.
Abdul Hamid deposed by Young Turks ; acc. Mohammed V (Mehmed Reshed).

1910    Union of South Africa established.
Edward VII d. ; acc. George V.
India : Lord Hardinge viceroy.

1911    The king-emperor George V visits India ; Delhi reinstated as capital of the Indian Empire.
Italy demands protectorate of Tripoli ; Turco-Italian war. Italy annexes Tripoli.
Agadir incident ; immediate threat of war averted.

1912    Venizelos organizes the Balkan League. Albanian revolt. War declared between League states and Turkey (Sept.) ; Turkish débâcle ; armistice (Nov.).
Chinese imperial dynasty ends ; Chinese republic.
U.S.A. : Woodrow Wilson elected president.

1913    Balkan war renewed ; stopped by powers. Treaty of London (May) ; Bulgaria attacks Serbia (June) and is totally defeated. Treaty of Bukarest (Aug.).

1914    Irish crisis.
June 28 : Francis Ferdinand murdered at Serajevo.
July 23 : Austrian ultimatum to Serbia ; 28 : War declared on Serbia ; 31 : Austria and Russia mobilise.
Aug. 1 : Germany declares war on Russia ; 3 : Germany declares war on France ; 4 : Great Britain declares war on Germany.

### CHAPTER 31

# THE WORLD DRIFT TO WAR: 1878–1914

THE ostensible effect of the Turco-Russian War, followed by the San Stefano treaty and the Berlin Congress, was the establishment or the strengthening of sundry independent principalities in the Balkan peninsula, and the reassertion of the principle that the 'Concert of Europe,' not the particular interests of a successful military power, must have the deciding voice in material redistributions of European territory, which necessarily have their repercussions upon Europe generally. For thirty years to come the Concert of Europe was the background of international politics.

### Rift in the 'Dreikaiserbund'

BUT in actual fact the episode had another effect quite as far-reaching though not so superficially obvious. It had brought about the thing which the most powerful statesman in Europe was most anxious to avert, a rupture in the relations subsisting between Germany, Austria and Russia. For in Bismarck's view there were three European powers which counted for Germany, since England's non-intervention could generally be ensured, though definitely to alienate her would be inadvisable: Russia, Austria and France. French hostility to Germany was a matter of course. Austrian hostility had melted away under tactful management; Austrian and Prussian interests no longer clashed, since Germany had identified itself with Prussia; Austrian friendship was the best security available for Germany. But Russia remained.

Germany had a hostile France, which might again become powerful, on one flank. A hostile Russia on the other flank would be a serious menace, especially in conjunction with a recovered France. It was therefore essential for Germany to preserve friendly relations with Russia, only in less degree than with Austria. If Germany should ever be forced to choose between Russia and Austria, she must choose Austria. Since the French war it had been a main object with Bismarck to maintain the friendliness of the three powers—the 'Dreikaiserbund'—and to avert any complications which would drive Germany into siding with one against the other. But the antagonistic interests of Russia and Austria in the Balkans had been too much even for Bismarck. However skilfully he might pose as the 'honest broker,' the fundamental fact remained that by the Berlin Congress the ambitions of Russia in the Balkans suffered a setback, those of Austria were advanced, and Germany had done nothing to forward Russian interests, though it was at the hands of England that Russia had most conspicuously suffered diplomatic defeat.

There was no open breach between Germany and Russia; but the rift was there. Bismarck suffered from no illusions on that point. It became of the utmost importance to prevent the rift from developing into a breach, but also to find a means of strengthening the two Central powers, in case of accidents; of drawing still closer the bond between those two powers; of keeping France and Russia apart, and of discouraging any rapprochement between either of them and England.

### Franco-Russian Rapprochement

NEVERTHELESS, the trouble that Bismarck had been so anxious to guard against developed by degrees. The rift between Russia and the Central empires widened. France, already convalescent, grew stronger as the years passed. The gulf between the despotic tsardom in the east and the democratic republic in the west proved not to be an insuperable barrier. The perpetual sources of friction between England and France on the one hand and Russia on the other proved capable of accommodation. So that at last all Germany convinced itself that those three powers were joint conspirators whose common aim was her own destruction.

And the outcome of that conviction was—Armageddon. These developments, however, were not immediate. For a quarter of a century the British Empire remained in 'splendid isolation,' and France hardly less than Great Britain, though after a long interval the beginnings of amity sprang up between her and Russia; while the effect of the Berlin treaties was at first to intensify the established antagonism between Russia and Great Britain.

Russia's intention had been to create what may be called a Greater Bulgaria, which would be very much the largest of the Balkan states, would dominate Constantinople and control the Aegean coast, and would be Russia's henchman. The revised partition under the Berlin treaties

**SATIRE ON THE CYPRUS CONVENTION**
While the Berlin Congress was in session in June, 1878, Britain and Turkey came to a separate agreement by which the former guaranteed the latter's Asiatic dominions and was allowed, in return, to occupy Cyprus. The Punch cartoon, A Blaze of Triumph, represents Lord Beaconsfield carrying a smiling Turk.
*By permission of the proprietors of 'Punch'*

reduced Bulgaria to about one third of the size proposed by Russia; another third, as Eastern Rumelia, was to be autonomous but under Turkish suzerainty, while Macedonia and the Aegean coast were to be left in Turkish hands but under joint supervision by the powers. The independence of the new Bulgaria, and of Serbia and Montenegro, was to be complete. Austria was to occupy and administer Bosnia. Rumania had to be content with Dobruja instead of Bessarabia, which was annexed to Russia.

Each of the Balkan states was left sorely aggrieved, because each held that it was itself entitled to territories awarded to another; Serbia, Greece and Bulgaria were each convinced that Macedonia belonged of right to her; both Bulgaria and Serbia were denied effective access to the sea; while Rumania was particularly sore because Russia had rewarded her extremely valuable services by appropriating Bessarabia herself.

Great Britain had made a private bargain with the Porte guaranteeing the Asiatic possessions of the Turks—other than those ceded to Russia under the treaties—conditionally upon the carrying out of reforms, and upon the British occupation and administration of the island of Cyprus; which would provide her with a naval station of considerable value in the eastern Mediterranean.

Nor was Russian policy in Bulgaria successful in furthering her own projects. The prince nominated for Bulgaria was the tsar's nephew, Alexander of Battenberg. At the outset, Russian influences predominated, arousing patriotic antagonism to foreign control. But the prince established his own despotic authority by a coup d'état setting aside the theoretically admirable but practically paralytic constitu-

**FIRST KING OF BULGARIA**

Nephew of the Russian tsar, Alexander of Battenberg was elected first prince of Bulgaria in 1879. His acceptance of the sovereignty of Eastern Rumelia in 1885 aroused Russian indignation and he was forced to abdicate in 1886.

tion which had been bestowed on the principality. Russia applauded, but when he turned his powers to account, assumed the championship of Bulgarian independence, and dismissed the Russian counsellors, Russia was wroth. He could and did gain popularity by restoring the constitution (1883), without loss of authority.

In 1885 Eastern Rumelia ejected its Turkish governors and proclaimed its own union with Bulgaria. Alexander hastened to assume the proffered sovereignty. Serbia took alarm—she must be compensated for this Bulgarian expansion. Compensation was not forthcoming, so she declared war, and was badly beaten at Slivnitza. Austria intervened and stopped the fighting. The Porte saved its face by appointing Alexander governor of Rumelia, a practical acceptance of the fact that he had got it and meant to keep it. Only a threatened blockade by a British squadron restrained Greece from attempting to snatch ' compensation ' for herself.

But Alexander's triumph wrought his fall. The tsar's indignation was high ; Russian conspirators kidnapped the Bulgarian king, forced him to sign his abdication and carried him over the border. But the national government carried on under his indomitable minister Stambulov ; Alexander, less indomitable, threw up the struggle in the face of the tsar's implacable hostility, and resigned the crown which the Bulgarians would have restored. Stambulov, fervidly anti-Russian, remained dictator until in 1887 a new prince was found—ready to take the risks and play a waiting game—in Ferdinand of Saxe-Coburg. Meantime, Stambulov remained at the helm in Bulgaria, while the Balkan states continued to seethe.

As concerned the Balkans, then, the actual outcome was that Russia lost ground, since she succeeded in alienating both Rumania and Bulgaria without definitely attracting Serbia or Greece under her influence. Austria had gained by establishing herself in Bosnia and giving to that region an administration infinitely better than it had ever known before. England had acquired a dominating influence at the Porte, though she was too unsympathetic to Turkish methods

**' THE BISMARCK OF THE BALKANS '**

Stepan Nikolov Stambulov (1854–95), the strongminded Bulgarian minister of Alexander, headed a council of regency upon that prince's abdication. In 1887 he became premier and dominated Balkan politics for eight years.

for the satisfaction of the Turkish government ; which continued in its old ways, but with a much smaller Christian population under its rule than of yore. And between the several Balkan states there was no love to lose, while none of them was gratefully conscious of a deep debt to any European power for disinterested services rendered.

### France's Colonial Ambitions

ʙISMARCK'S position as the dominating factor in international politics was unchanged. From France in isolation there could be nothing to fear for a long time to come, and to keep her isolated was no very difficult task. A republic which could set up no administration of tolerably convincing stability could hardly be attracted by or attractive to the iron despotism of Russia. Between her and Great Britain Egypt provided a constant source of friction ; and an opportunity occurred for providing another source of

**THE PRINCE IMPERIAL**
Eugène Louis Jean Joseph Napoléon (1856–79), the only son of Napoleon III and the Empress Eugénie, was known as the Prince Imperial. Until his death in a British expedition to Zululand, he was the centre of Bonapartist hopes.

friction between her and Italy, incidentally attracting the latter to the Central powers.

France had effected an amazing economic recovery since the war, but in 1878 it was still uncertain whether monarchism might yet take the place of the republic. The resignation of Macmahon marked the turning point ; Bonapartism disappeared with the death of the Prince Imperial in Zululand, in 1879 ; the legitimism which clung to the house of Bourbon was paralysed in the country by the firmness or obstinacy with which the Bourbon princes, like the exiled Stuarts, clung to their religious and political convictions or prejudices ; no glamour attached to the house of Orléans. From that time monarchism was merely a pious opinion, and the continuity of the republic grew continuously more secure.

It was at this time that France found herself encouraged to develop her aspirations in Africa by taking possession of Tunis, for which she found a pretext in 1881. England had no objection, as it might make her less irritable on the subject of Egypt. Germany had no objection, having no African interests and a perception that Tunis might bring to France more trouble than profit ; for Italy, with her own eyes on Tunis, would certainly regard the annexation of Tunis by France as an unfriendly act towards herself. She did ; and her annoyance made it comparatively easy for Bismarck to draw her into a somewhat non-committal alliance in 1882 with Germany and her former bête noire, Austria. If trouble with France should arise, Italy would be on Germany's side.

France's acquisition of Tunis did nothing to mitigate her jealousy of British influence in Egypt, which she had never ceased to covet since the days of the first Napoleon. In the successive complications of the Eastern Question, she had kept that objective before her throughout the Bourbon and Orleanist monarchies ; while Palmerston, with preservation of the ' integrity of the Turkish Empire ' as a fundamental aim of his policy, had been a constant obstacle. But the maintenance of French influence there had remained a constant aim, furthered by the construction of the Suez Canal, a

## AN INTERESTING STAGE IN THE HISTORY OF THE SUEZ CANAL

Disraeli's politic purchase of Suez Canal shares from the impoverished khedive of Egypt, in 1875, ensured British control of this important waterway. In 1869 the future King Edward VII was conducted over the canal's then unfinished works by the French engineer de Lesseps, as seen in this contemporary wood engraving. The royal visitor performed the ceremony of opening the sluices of the dam that admitted Mediterranean waters into the first section of the canal.

French project in which Palmerston had no share, though Disraeli had more than made up for the oversight by his dramatic purchase from Khedive Ismail of the bulk of the company's shares in 1875, virtu-ally placing control of the canal in the hands of the British government.

At the same time the khedive's ex-travagance, and his huge debts to British and French financiers, had forced him to

## FOUNDER OF THE 'DUAL CONTROL' AND ITS OPPONENT

The extravagance of Ismail Pasha (1830–95), who became khedive of Egypt in 1867, led to his appeal for financial assistance to France and Britain, which occasioned the 'dual control' of his country by these two powers. Under Ismail's feeble successor, Tewfik, the discontent felt by Egyptians with their government and with European interference manifested itself in an agitation nominally headed by Arabi Pasha (right), whose revolt was crushed, and who was himself deported.

*Left, photo, Elliott & Fry*

place the Egyptian finances in the hands of a dual board of control, British and French, with the inevitable result—illustrated in Indian history by the British assumption of the Diwani in Bengal—that the board became in effect, though not in form, largely responsible for the government ; a state of things by no means to the liking of the officials, drawn for the most part from other parts of the Turkish empire, who had hitherto battened according to custom upon the khedive's helpless subjects and the revenues, of which only a fraction reached the treasury.

### British Occupation of Egypt

IT was not difficult, in the circumstances, to raise the cry of ' Egypt for the Egyptians,' or to draw an army colonel, Arabi Pasha, into the rôle of patriot leader and champion of the anti-foreign sentiment. Ismail's successor, Tewfik, found himself powerless ; the anti-foreign agitation became a grave danger to the very considerable European population in Alexandria and elsewhere. The Porte (the suzerain) would not and the khedive could not do anything. The French and British governments offered Tewfik their support at the beginning of 1882, and sent naval squadrons ; the only effect was to produce riots. A European conference was called to deal judicially with the problem ; but the position at Alexandria and the menace to the Europeans there from Arabi's troops were too critical for delay. The British admiral took the responsibility, which the French admiral declined to share, of sending an ultimatum to Arabi and, when it was ignored, of opening a bombardment and occupying Alexandria, while the French retired.

The force at the admiral's disposal was obviously inadequate for the restoration of order and security. With due notification to the sultan, troops were dispatched to Egypt from England and India. Arabi's army was shattered in a brief and decisive campaign, and he himself was deported. But the whole situation had been changed. The khedive's government—anything that could be called a government—could be restored only by the British. In the public interest the British on their own sole responsibility had taken upon themselves to do the thing that was admittedly necessary but which no one else had been ready or willing to undertake either alone or in conjunction with them ; the French had had the opportunity but had deliberately rejected it. The British had therefore done the thing single-handed, and it was recognized that they were entitled to a perfectly free hand in the necessary reconstruction on their own terms.

But just as in India they had repeatedly refrained from annexation or had restricted annexation to the lowest practical limit, so now they did not annex Egypt, though it would have been more than difficult to deny their right to do so. Reconstruction required at the least an army of occupation to maintain order during the process, and effective control of the entire administration. They ' occupied ' Egypt as the Austrians occupied Bosnia, on the theory that they would evacuate it as soon as a government had been established which could stand securely upon its own feet. And in the meanwhile the government continued to be the khedive's, the Egyptian government, not the British ; though the army of occupation was British, the reorganization of an Egyptian army was in the hands of British officers, and the administration was in the hands of British officials in the service of the khedive. There was no room for French ambitions in Egypt, and though France was thoroughly conscious that she had no one but herself to thank for the fact, that made her none the less resentful.

### Unrest in Italy, Spain and Russia

ITALY had attained her unity under Victor Emmanuel, but half the country had not yet been accustomed to the idea that governments exist for some other purpose than the oppression of the people. Economic stability was still distant, and, if she ranked as a great power, it was still only by courtesy, eager though she was to assert herself. The almost simultaneous deaths of Victor Emmanuel and Pius IX did not heal the breach between the crown and the Papacy.

Spain on the other hand was entering upon an era of recuperation after her prolonged sufferings. The king, Amadeo of Savoy, who had accepted her crown when it was refused by Leopold of Hohenzollern, resigned it again in disgust in 1873 ; but after a year of dictatorship in the guise of a republic she recalled Alfonso XII, the son of the formerly expelled queen Isabella. There was a brief struggle before the old Carlist party was finally broken up ; the young king set himself seriously to the task of government ; and when he died prematurely in 1885 his widow, Maria Christina, discharged with tact and discretion the duties of regent on behalf of the infant Alfonso XIII, until he reached man's estate.

Russia as we saw lost ground in Europe. Within the tsardom, Alexander II had striven or rather groped after ideals, while lacking the resolution and the insight without which it was impossible to bring them to realization. He had liberated the serfs without restoring to them what they regarded as their own rights in the soil. He had encouraged Western education, but it had fallen upon ground in which it was only the seed of passionate revolt, and government terrorism was faced by the black spectre of Nihilism. The tsar himself was no enemy of reform ; but even at the moment when an effort was being made in that direction the world was shocked by his murder at the hands of the nihilists (1882). All thought of reforms vanished, and under the dead tsar's son, Alexander III, the tyranny became if possible more rigid and more merciless than before.

Foiled in the Balkans, Russia as usual became more active in Asia, pushing constantly and in British eyes alarmingly in the direction of India. But the collision, in 1885, between Russian and Afghan troops known as the ' Penjdeh incident,' which threatened to be the beginning of an Anglo-Russian war, actually prepared the way for an adjustment—thanks in no small measure to the hard-headed shrewdness of the Afghan amir Abd er-Rahman— and an agreed delimitation of frontiers in 1887. For Russia was changing her Asiatic objective, aiming at the Farthest East and

**A WISE AFGHAN AMIR**

Abd er-Rahman (1830–1901), proclaimed amir of Afghanistan by the British in 1880, proved himself a strong ruler. His shrewd handling of the situation at the time of the Penjdeh incident prevented imminent Anglo-Russian hostilities.
*Photo, E.N.A.*

the Pacific ; as yet no more conscious than the rest of the world that a power had arisen, and was consolidating itself in that quarter, with which she would have to try conclusions before her aims could be accomplished.

### Colonial Expansion in Africa

THERE was at this period a general European movement towards expansion. France had turned her eyes once more to the East ; if India was unattainable, there were still lands beyond India where a footing might be established ; though it was not without many troubles that she acquired from China the protectorate of Annam by the Treaty of Tientsin in 1885. Her activities in Indo-China were probably the real though not the ostensible warrant for the British annexation of Upper Burma in 1887. European interests in the Farthest East were developing. But it was the scramble for Africa that set in most vigorously in the years immediately following the Berlin Congress.

Expansion manifestly could take place only in lands—whether densely or sparsely populated—where the civilization in general and the community organization in particular were on a lower plane than those of Europe. America was already occupied by Europeans ; so was most of

**SCENE OF A BOER VICTORY OVER THE BRITISH**

On the night of February 26, 1881, Sir George Colley, governor of Natal and commander-in-chief of the British forces in South Africa, seized and occupied Majuba Hill. Driven from this position early next morning, the British forces suffered heavy losses, to the great detriment of British prestige, Colley himself being among the fallen.

*Photo, E.N.A.*

Australasia and the islands of the Pacific. Western Asia was not an open field ; northern and central Asia were out of reach except for Russia. In the farthest east of Asia there were perhaps possibilities, but there was the Chinese empire to be reckoned with. But the whole African interior was an almost unknown region, scarcely penetrated except by an occasional adventurous missionary, peopled by negro races whose culture was primitive and barbaric. The coastal districts on the Mediterranean were provinces in which such governments as existed might fairly be classed as barbaric. The Atlantic sea-board was dotted with European 'colonies' which were little more than very unhealthy trading depots. The south was occupied by the British, the Boers and the Portuguese. Farther north, on the east, Zanzibar and Abyssinia, like Morocco on the northwest coast, and to some extent the island of Madagascar, claimed a doubtful recognition as independent states. But the rest of Africa was open to any Europeans who could take effective possession.

The British then, as we have seen, established a 'temporary' protectorate in Egypt, to which other powers could hardly refuse assent ; France established her own protectorate in Tunis, not only with assent but with positive encouragement from Great Britain and Germany, though very much to the annoyance of Italy, who could only hope to find compensation on the north of Abyssinia and ultimately in Tripoli. France without European intervention set up (1885) a protectorate in Madagascar which was later transformed into annexation. But all the European powers, including Germany, who had hitherto felt no call to colonial expansion, had suddenly realized that Africa was the only division of the earth's surface still open to appropriation, and that the British, with a northern base in Egypt, a southern base in Cape Colony and sundry starting points on the western and eastern coasts, would by mere force of circumstances absorb the interior and leave nothing for anyone else to appropriate unless they made haste to anticipate her.

The precedents of the eighteenth century, when France and Great Britain had fought each other to a finish for America and India on the hypothesis that there was not room there for both, were not promising. In Africa after all there was room for everyone ; and so between 1880 and 1890 a series of treaties or compacts was entered upon, partitioning the Dark Continent into protectorates or 'spheres of influence' appropriated to one or another of the European states, though not without leaving occasions for acute controversy in the future.

AT the same time events were taking place which were of moment to the future expansion of the British in Africa. First in the south, in 1879, they came into collision with the military power of the Zulus, which led to the annexation of Zululand. Immediately preceding this, they had resumed the control which they had abrogated in 1852 over the Boers in the Transvaal, who without British protection were in danger of being wiped out by the Zulus. Freed from that menace by the Zulu war, the Transvaalers demanded the retrocession of their virtual independence, rose in arms, and at Majuba Hill (1881) cut up the British regiments which had been sent out to restore the British authority, though the British government had already resolved to concede the demand of the Boers. On the hypothesis that the justice of that demand was not affected by Majuba, the government stopped the hostilities and carried out the retrocession, practically claiming to retain control over the foreign relations of the Boers ; who, on the other hand, were firmly convinced that they had extorted their rights by force of arms from a government which had neither the power nor the energy to maintain its own claims —whereof the consequences were manifested in the South African War, which broke out before twenty years had passed.

Meanwhile in Egypt trouble was brewing. The effective rule of Egypt had

**EMPEROR FREDERICK I**
Prince Frederick William succeeded to the German imperial throne as Emperor Frederick I in March, 1888. His tragic death in June of the same year from cancer of the throat crushed the hopes of the Liberal party whose views he shared.
*Engraving by D. J. Pound*

never extended above the lower cataracts of the Nile, though she had habitually claimed lordship over the Upper Nile and the desert tribes of the Sudan ; among whom there arose at this time a ' Mahdi ' claiming to be the successor of the Prophet of Islam who was to overthrow the Khalifate and establish the supremacy of the Faith. Before long he was exercising a despotic authority over the Sudanese ; the Egyptian garrisons in the Sudan were powerless, and Egypt herself was threatened by his fanatical hordes. The British government had taken up the task of providing Egypt with a healthy government ; it was not prepared to take upon itself also the business of restoring the Egyptian authority in the Sudan ; the abandonment of which was the only alternative, involving the withdrawal of the garrisons.

It appointed for the execution of that task General Gordon, soldier and mystic, with virtually a free hand, subject to the instruction that withdrawal and nothing more was to be attempted, and the warning that no great military expedition would be sanctioned, though it was known to be Gordon's own conviction that the ' smashing ' of the Mahdi was imperative ; while he was a man who would certainly

**GENERAL GORDON**
The heroic endeavour of Charles George Gordon (1833–85), renowned for his almost uncanny influence over half-civilized peoples, to ' smash the Mahdi ' in the Sudan ended in tragedy. The expedition to his relief in Khartum was too late.

**' DROPPING THE PILOT '**

Dissension soon arose between the Emperor William II, who ascended the German imperial throne in 1888, and Bismarck. Sir John Tenniel's well known cartoon affords a poignant illustration of the latter's dismissal on March 20, 1890.
*By permission of the proprietors of ' Punch '*

not allow his own conviction of a sacred duty to be overridden by the expediencies of politicians. Tragedy followed. Gordon, in the Sudan, found himself shut up in Khartum by the Mahdist hordes, and when at last a long-delayed expedition was dispatched up the Nile to rescue him it reached Khartum only to find that the place had been stormed two days before its arrival, and Gordon had fallen in the defence. There was nothing more to be done, and the Sudan was abandoned till the time should be ripe for its conquest after the lapse of thirteen years.

IN 1888 the emperor William I died at the age of ninety ; three months later his son Frederick I followed him, and his grandson William II became the German

kaiser. The German Empire had been achieved through the never-failing loyalty of the old man and his great chancellor to each other. What might have befallen if Frederick had not been already a dying man when he succeeded to the imperial crown none can say, for it was notorious that there were many points on which emperor and chancellor did not see eye to eye ; but during those months there was no breach between them. On Frederick's death it seemed at first that Bismarck's ascendancy would be unimpaired, but the new kaiser believed implicitly in himself ; he had ideas of his own which were not Bismarck's, and in 1890 William ' dropped the pilot ' and took the management of affairs into his own hands. The world did not know what to make of Germany's new master and his passion for unexpected activities and startling pronouncements, which were occasionally somewhat nerve-racking ; but it was, on the whole, inclined to regard them as temperamental eccentricities which must not be taken too seriously. How far the chancellor's fall had actually changed the European situation was a matter of much uncertainty.

### Alliance between France and Russia

ONE thing, however, was clear. Bismarck had striven to the last to placate Russia and prevent any rapprochement between her and France. That a rapprochement was taking place became more apparent every day. In 1891 the French channel fleet visited Kronstadt, where it received an ovation ; two years later a Russian squadron paid a return visit to Toulon, where its reception was even more enthusiastic. Alexander III died in 1894, when he was succeeded by the third of the tsar-idealists, Nicholas II ; next year an alliance between France and Russia became an accomplished though not a published fact, the existence of which was acknowledged and even emphasised by somewhat ostentatious displays of mutual good will in the two following years. Germany can hardly be reproached if the conviction was implanted, and grew ever stronger, that hostility to her was the bond between the two powers, otherwise so inappropriately yoked together, which lay on her western and eastern marches.

There could be no question about the solidarity of the interests of the two Central powers. If they broke with each other, neither would be secure against attack by one or, more probably, two hostile powers ; while they stood together, holding strategetically the 'interior lines,' the risk of attacking them would be too great to be undertaken lightly. And at the same time they had no clashing interests, and no material divergences of political sentiment such as those which made a firmly rooted friendship so difficult between a typically despotic and a typically democratic state. By attaching Italy to themselves they had gained an additional security in relation at least to France. On the other hand, concord between Russia and France gave to each security against aggression by the Central powers. An equilibrium was established simply because the issue of an armed conflict would be too doubtful—the more because no one was able to gauge the real efficiency of Russia's strength.

### Britain's 'Splendid Isolation'

**A**T the same time the isolation of Great Britain was complete, nor had she any desire that it should be otherwise. She was in possession or occupation of the greater and better part of so much of the world as had not been occupied by Europeans before the middle of the eighteenth century, a position from which no one could hope to oust her while her fleets commanded the ocean highways ; those fleets were an impassable bulwark except where their place was taken by the all but impassable mountains of the Indian frontier, or where her only neighbour was the American republic. She was hardly conscious of a challenge to her commercial and manufacturing supremacy, which she had learnt to regard as a matter of course. So long as she kept her navy up to standard she had nothing to fear from powers whose resources were under the perpetual strain of maintaining huge armies, while she could content herself with one comparatively insignificant in size.

She could see no cause of quarrel with any of her neighbours save Russia, except what she felt to be their rather unreasonable jealousy ; she had no sense of hostility to any of them—with the same exception, Russia. Consequently she had no desire for alliances which might prove embarrassing, but if she should incline to one scale or other in the European balances it would fairly certainly not be the Russian scale. Though French and English had fought each other often enough in the past, they had also occasionally fought side by side, and towards France England had no sort of ill will ; France might persist in her annoyance about Egypt, but common sense would forbid her to manufacture a casus belli ; while if at times the British relations with Austria and Prussia had not been over cordial, they had not fought each other for more than a century, nor was there any apparent reason why they should wish to fight each other now. If the other powers chose to quarrel with each other, the less the British Empire allowed itself to be implicated in their differences the better, though it would be always in her interest that peace should be preserved.

NICHOLAS II OF RUSSIA

Nicholas II succeeded his father as tsar of Russia in 1894 and shortly afterwards married Princess Alix of Hesse, this photograph being taken in the same year. He was assassinated in 1918.

**THE MARQUESS OF SALISBURY**
The British public had great confidence in the conservative and pacific Lord Salisbury (1830–1903) both as premier and foreign secretary. His cession of Heligoland to Germany in 1890, however, was not universally approved.

She was hardly alive, however, to the fact that jealousy was growing in Germany, who had embarked on an active career of trade expansion, was pushing her way into markets which the British had hitherto monopolised, and was very ill satisfied with the bargains struck over the partitions of Africa—though the British expansionists were no less displeased by the ' graceful concessions ' of Lord Salisbury's diplomacy. The German commercial community felt more and more that British rivalry and British intrigues were barricading her out of her rightful ' place in the sun.' On the other hand, the kaiser had realized the fundamental fact that ' peaceful penetration ' was the only useful weapon that could be employed until there was a German navy which could hold its own against the British navy.

But an equilibrium depending simply on equality of armament between two groups of powers filled with suspicion and mistrust of each other could only mean that each group would strive ceaselessly to raise its own standard of armament above that of the other group ; and so the exhausting race went on year by year—touching Great

Britain less than anyone else, because as concerned armies she saw no need to enter the race, and as concerned navies she already held a lead which kept her above immediate competition. None of the powers wanted a conflagration, however, and so long as that was the case it was to the interest of all that the status quo should be maintained at least within Europe.

No one then was disposed to interfere in the troubles of minor states or nationalities. No one was concerned if Norway wanted the separation from Sweden which she achieved, by strictly constitutional methods, at the opening of the twentieth century. The depression of the Poles by Russia might demand sympathy, but certainly not intervention. The absorption of Finland into the Russian system disturbed no one but the Swedes. The subordination of the Slavs within the Austrian Empire to Austrian or Magyar domination made Slavs everywhere look to Slavonic Russia, developing the race hostility between Slav and Teuton ; but

**ABDUL HAMID, SULTAN OF TURKEY**
Considerable diplomatic talent was shown by Abdul Hamid II in his dealings with the European powers, and German influence in Turkey throve under his encouragement. He was sultan from 1876 until 1909, when he was deposed.
*Photo, W. & D. Downey*

the time was not ripe for a duel—and the astute sultan was very well aware that all the powers would fight shy of active interference with his doings, lest they should thereby be brought into active collision with each other. The inflammability of the Balkan peninsula was the standing menace to that general peace which the ' Concert of Europe ' was most anxious to preserve, while that same desire paralysed the Concert itself for drastic action. Incidentally, since Germany had no territorial interests of her own in the Turkish Empire, Abdul Hamid, having nothing to fear from her ' friendship ' and possibly much to gain, was ready enough to cultivate it, while the kaiser was thoroughly alive to the advantages that might accrue therefrom.

### Friction between the Balkans and Turkey

In the Balkan storm centre, Serbia was too much torn by domestic troubles to endanger the peace of her neighbours, though a period of reconstruction was promised by the fall of the Obrenovitch dynasty and the accession of a prince of the former rival house of Karageorgevitch in 1903 ; though the consequent development of pan-Slav doctrines was ominous from the Austrian point of view.

In Bulgaria, Ferdinand watched and waited while Stambulov ruled, till the chance came in 1894 for accepting the minister's resignation—much to the surprise of Stambulov himself, who was assassinated not long afterwards. Ferdinand was far too wary to commit himself to provocative action in any direction, while he was especially careful to cultivate the good will of the Porte on one side and Germany on the other. With a Hohenzollern reigning in Rumania and a Coburg in Bulgaria—both states which declined to regard themselves as Slavonic, and both having very definite grudges against Russia—the gravitation of both towards the Central empires was inevitable.

When definite trouble arose, it was within the Turkish dominions. It appeared in 1894 that there was a revolutionary movement in Armenia which needed repressing. The Turk repressed it, finding himself under the unhappy neces-sity of massacring some fifty thousand of the population before the European Concert was in tune for intervention, though, as a matter of course, he then accepted the paper scheme of reforms submitted by the powers, which as usual failed to materialise. Next came the revolt of Crete, bent on escaping from the Moslem sovereignty and on joining herself to the Greek kingdom. Greece answered the call of Crete and sent a force to the island. The Concert intervened ; when a joint squadron arrived at Canea, bringing peremptory orders that the fighting was to stop, that the Greeks were to withdraw and no more Turkish troops were to be landed, the orders were perforce obeyed. But the Greeks lost their heads and invaded Thessaly, whence they were decisively ejected by the Turkish troops.

To deny the right of the Turks, in the circumstances, to demand rectifications of the Thessaly frontier was impossible ; but the powers—without Germany and Austria, who refused to co-operate—required from Turkey autonomy for Crete under their joint supervision, with the second of the Greek princes as governor. In Crete, Greek patriotism centred in the future minister, Venizelos. But with Abdul Hamid German influence was supreme, though a ' Young Turk ' party, a Turkish nationalist party, was now coming into being with a programme of its own which was not favourable to the khalif, who in the last twenty years had lost for Islam effective sovereignty in Cyprus, Egypt, Rumelia, Bosnia and finally Crete. Its existence, however, was as yet unsuspected. The accord of Germany and the Porte bore significant fruit in 1902, in the authorisation of a German railway to Basra and Bagdad, which would give the Germans their first foothold in the Middle East. For in the Far East the scramble for penetration bases in China had already begun.

### Development and Expansion of Japan

In her astonishingly swift emergence from feudal obscurity to the rank of a first - class power, Japan had remodelled herself upon Western lines, somewhat as, long ago, Peter the Great had sought to remodel Russia. But her aim was not to Westernise herself, but to hold her own among the Westerns by learning and adapting scientifically to her own use all that a critical study of Western methods could teach her. She reorganized her government, her army, her navy and her policy. She turned her eyes to the continent of Asia, as she had done long ago in the days of Hideyoshi. Organization, not aggression, was her immediate object ; but the king of Korea forced war upon her, rather as Burmese monarchs had forced war upon the British in India ; and the position which she then took up in Korea displeased China, who claimed there a

Japan certain, unless Japan should give way to Russia. Germany, whatever her ultimate aim may have been, ranged herself along with Russia and France, and England could not encourage Japan to defy that combination. Japan submitted with dignity, and bided her time.

China, however, did not love the 'foreign devils.' A year later (1897) two German missionaries were murdered. Germany demanded compensation, and got it in Kiao-chau. France and Russia demanded equivalents for the concessions to Germany, and got them ; on the same principle, Weihaiwei was leased to Great Britain. The concessions intensified the popular Chinese hostility to the foreigners,

**FORMER BRITISH NAVAL AND COALING STATION AT WEIHAIWEI, CHINA**
The British leased Weihaiwei, a Chinese naval station on the north-east coast of the Shantung peninsula, from China in 1898, and retained possession of it until, at the Washington Conference of 1921, it was agreed that it should be restored to China. The territory consists of all the islands in Weihaiwei bay, the island of Liukung and a strip, ten miles wide, along the coast, in all 285 square miles.
*Photo, B. R. Muddett*

shadowy suzerainty. In 1894 China proposed to submerge her, with the result that after a few months' fighting China was very thoroughly ejected from Korea, and Japan proposed to reap the natural fruits of her victory by the treaty of Shimonoseki.

Great Britain was the only European power which had recognized the status of Japan as a civilized, not a merely semi-civilized, nation. Europe intervened and forbade her to reap the fruits, and the powers were duly rewarded by China for their intervention ; Russia in concessions for the railway she was carrying across Siberia to Vladivostok, France in the neighbourhood of Tonkin, Germany at Tientsin—arrangements which made an ultimate collision between Russia and

and to the emperor Kuang Hsü, who was deposed next year by the dowager-empress, Tzu Hsi, the incarnation of the anti-foreign reaction ; while North China was seething with the ' Boxer ' rebellion.

All the foreign powers had ' legations ' at Peking, and in 1900 came the news that the legations were either in the hands of the Peking mob or were on the point of falling into them. All the powers, Japan and the United States included, took joint action, and dispatched to China contingents which marched on Peking, where they found that the legations had, after all, held out successfully. The Chinese government submitted, with professions that it had done its best but had been unable to control the rebels. The allies refrained from demanding further concessions, though insisting on effective guarantees for security in the future; and in the following years it appeared that the progressive or Westernising element predominated in the Chinese government, though Tzu Hsi continued to reign.

The conduct of Japan throughout had more than established her right to recognition on an equal footing with the Western powers, which was sealed by a treaty of alliance with Great Britain in 1902. The treaty meant that, if and when Russia and Japan should come into armed collision, Great Britain would not join Japan against Russia by herself, but would intervene if anyone else joined Russia against Japan.

The collision was not long postponed. Russia wanted both Manchuria, where she had established herself, and Korea, where Japan had established herself. Japan proposed mutual accommodations ; Russia

**KUROPATKIN AT MUKDEN**
In March, 1905, after much strenuous fighting, the Japanese under Oyama defeated the Russians at Mukden, in China. Kuropatkin, the Russian commander, is here seen in Mukden imperial cemetery with the Chinese authorities.

claimed that the compromises should not be reciprocal. Japan proposed control for Russia in Manchuria and for Japan in Korea. Russia returned no answer, and in February, 1904, Japan declared war. She had only the resources of her own islands to draw upon, while Russia's resources in men at least were incalculably greater. But she could bring her whole force to bear at once ; of Russia's naval squadrons one was ice-bound at Vladivostok, while she could reinforce her armies in Manchuria only by way of the single-line trans-Siberian railway, which was still far short of completion.

On February 9 Japan broke up the second Russian fleet from Port Arthur,

**JAPAN'S GREAT ADMIRAL**
The destruction of the Russian fleet at Port Arthur in February, 1904, was one of the most celebrated exploits performed by the Japanese naval commander-in-chief, Heihachiro Togo, here seen heading a procession in Vyeno Park, Tokyo.
*Photo, E.N.A.*

PART OF THE SUNKEN RUSSIAN FLEET IN PORT ARTHUR HARBOUR BEFORE THE SURRENDER TO THE JAPANESE

Leased by Russia from China in 1898, the fortified seaport of Port Arthur, in Manchuria, became the chief base for the Russian eastern fleet. Its harbour was blockaded by the Japanese from the beginning of the Russo-Japanese war, and after a siege of eleven months General Stoessel surrendered to the besiegers on January 1, 1905. This view of the harbour shows the submerged Russian battleship, Retvizan, sunk by gunfire on December 8.

*From a photograph by General A. M. Stoessel*

whither she drove it back and which she proceeded to blockade. A little later she was able to invest it on the land side also, while the Russian commander Kuropatkin was endeavouring not to overwhelm but to hold back her main army on the Yalu till he should be adequately reinforced. Port Arthur held out stubbornly, and in spite of heavy fighting the Japanese commander could make no impression until a desperate effort was put forth at the end of the year in order to anticipate the expected arrival of a new Russian fleet, the Port Arthur squadron having sallied forth in August, only to be annihilated by Admiral Togo.

### Progress of the Russo-Japanese War

KUROPATKIN had been pushed back from the Yalu in May ; he was again pushed back upon Mukden in August, as the result of the nine days' battle of Liao-yang, in which the Japanese actually suffered more heavily than the Russians. Being at last reinforced in October, he resumed the offensive, but was again compelled to retire upon Mukden after a fifteen days' battle on the Sha-ho, which left both armies so exhausted that neither could take the offensive. Port Arthur, however, was so hard pressed by Nogi's final onslaught that it was forced to surrender on January 1, 1905.

Nogi was thus released to reinforce the main army, after which another prolonged and exhausting struggle drove Kuropatkin from Mukden at the end of February back to the lines which he was able to hold for the remainder of the war, since there was no more heavy fighting on land. The sea, however, provided one more episode. Rhozhdestvenski's fleet arrived in May, only to be obliterated by Togo in the battle of Tsushima. Japan could not hope to add to her gains ; Russia could not hope to recover ground ; both had suffered enormous losses, and both were thoroughly exhausted. The war was ended by the treaty of Portsmouth, U.S.A., in August, 1905 ; Russia evacuating Manchuria, while Japan retained Korea with the Liau-tung peninsula.

The Russo-Japanese war had upon Russia's position among the powers the same sort of effect that the defeat of the Armada had upon Spain at the end of the sixteenth century. She ceased to be a bogy credited with incalculable power. Her navy had shown itself almost grotesquely inefficient, and her armies, without being outnumbered, had left the Japanese masters of the field after each of the prolonged and stubbornly contested engagements. To strike effectively at Russia would always be as desperately difficult as Napoleon had found it, but holding her at bay would present no insuperable difficulties.

As concerned Europe, no change in the isolation of Great Britain had taken place when the twentieth century opened. It was a moment when every country on the Continent was sympathising not with her but with her stubborn antagonists in the South African War, under the curious conviction that all the dominions of the British Empire were craving to be free from a bondage which had no existence. As late as the middle of the nineteenth century it had been the commonly accepted doctrine that colonies break away from the mother country as soon as their own security is not endangered by doing so; the cleavage of the British Empire in the

**GENERAL COUNT NOGI**

Count Maresuke Nogi (1849–1912), the victorious Japanese commander at Port Arthur in the Russo-Japanese War, showed his devotion to an old tradition of his country by committing harakiri on the death of his emperor Mutsuhito.

*Photo, Swaine*

**A DAMP JOURNEY : JAPANESE INFANTRY ADVANCING ON LIAO-YANG**

Furious fighting took place in the nine days' battle of Liao-yang, whence the Japanese drove the Russians in 1904. Although the result of the battle was favourable to the Japanese, they were not successful in cutting off the retreat of the Russians, under their commander, Kuropatkin, on Mukden, and the value of the victory was modified by the terrible losses suffered by the Japanese troops.

*Photo, F. A. Mackenzie*

last quarter of the eighteenth century being regarded as a typical instance of a general law.

In actual fact, for fifty years past Great Britain had consistently fostered autonomy in her colonies, which were aware of no bondage except when the exigencies of international relations made the imperial government actually or apparently neglectful of the interests of particular colonies. Regarding themselves and being regarded as partners in the Empire, not subordinates, they had no desire for separation, however jealous they might be in regard to their own rights and privileges ; and the sense of imperial solidarity was growing, not diminishing. South Africa was on a different footing from the rest, for the simple reason that the Dutch element

**THE PORTSMOUTH PEACEMAKERS**
President Roosevelt stands in the centre of this group of statesmen who arranged the Treaty of Portsmouth (U.S.A.), which ended the Russo-Japanese war in 1905, by excluding Russia from Manchuria and giving Korea to Japan. On his right are Witte and Rosen ; on his left. Komura and Takahira.
*Photo, Underwood and Underwood*

**KITCHENER OF KHARTUM**
In 1892 Sir Herbert Kitchener (1850–1916) was appointed Sirdar or commander-in-chief of the Egyptian army. He avenged Gordon's death by his crushing victory at Omdurman in 1898, and his capture of Khartum.

there declined to regard itself as British, looked upon the British as interlopers, and resented the British claim to sovereignty in territories which the Dutch, who had been there long before them, regarded as being rightfully their own. And that sentiment among the Boers had been intensified by the retrocession of the Transvaal's independence in 1881.

When this antagonism issued in the South African War in 1899, the popularity of Great Britain in Europe had not been increasing. Her prospective evacuation of Egypt seemed to grow more remote ; it could not come till the Egyptians could be trusted to govern themselves, and she was not teaching them the art of self-government. She was teaching them how the thing ought to be done, giving them stable rule, developing their resources, bringing to the fellaheen an unprecedented prosperity ; but the men who were doing it all, holding all the responsible posts, were not Egyptians but Britons—after the Indian precedent, and for the same reasons.

In 1896 she made the first open move towards the reconquest of the Sudan by pushing the Egyptian frontier defences up to Dongola. The business was done in the single campaign of 1898. The fanatical hordes of the Khalifa, the Mahdi's successor, were completely shattered at the battle of Omdurman. The Sudan became what it had been before in theory, but never in fact, a province of Egypt, and virtually a British protectorate. But the concentration of the Khalifa's forces against the British advance had enabled a small expeditionary party from the French Congo to reach Fashoda unharmed and hoist the French flag there; and French susceptibilities were painfully irritated when Sir Herbert Kitchener, the conqueror of the Khalifa, declined to recognize the validity of the French occupation. The French government acknowledged the British claim, but French sentiment cherished yet another grievance against what it regarded as British aggression.

The republics were annexed, to be administered temporarily as 'crown colonies,' but instead of exacting indemnities the victors provided large sums for the reinstatement of the farms which had suffered in the war.

All told, the casualties—mainly incurred not in the field but from enteric—in the two and a half years' fighting were to be repeatedly outnumbered in a single week, sometimes in a single day, in the Great War, of which it was in no sense a foretaste. There had certainly been on the Continent a strong inclination to intervene, but though the Kaiser's attitude in the preceding years had caused some resentment in England, during the war his influence was certainly exerted to discourage intervention. It may be that he realized the practical futility of attempting, as matters stood, to challenge the British fleet; for it was while the war was in progress that he developed an unprecedented naval programme for

Two years after the reconquest of the Sudan, the antagonism of the Dutch to the British in South Africa issued in the outbreak of the South African War, a struggle which, in its ultimate result, made possible at last, and with little delay, a united South Africa

In the first months the British troops met with a series of reverses, but by the following midsummer they were in occupation of the two capitals, Bloemfontein and Pretoria. In September the annexation of the Boer states was proclaimed. Nevertheless they refused to submit, maintaining a persistent guerilla warfare until so many of them had been rounded up that the remnant could no longer keep the field; and in May, 1902, the peace of Vereeniging terminated the war.

**TOMB OF THE MAHDI AFTER BRITISH BOMBARDMENT**
At Omdurman, chosen by the fanatical Mahdi as his capital in place of Khartum in 1885, this gigantic tomb was built upon his death in the same year. It was constructed by order of the Khalifa, the Mahdi's successor. After Kitchener's capture of Omdurman in 1898 the British destroyed the tomb, and only its ruins now remain.
*Photo, Captain E. A. Stanton*

**BRITISH TROOPS RETURN TO LADYSMITH AFTER THE DISASTER OF NICHOLSON'S NEK**

In the early stages of the South African War of 1899–1902, the superior artillery of the Boers forced Sir George White's troops to retreat on Ladysmith from the advance position which they held at Glencoe near Dundee. Battles were fought on the way at Talana Hill, Elandslaagte and Nicholson's Nek, where a stampede of mules carrying ammunition and guns rendered the British artillery useless. The troops in action being compelled to surrender on October 30, 1899, Sir George White withdrew the main body, whose entry into Ladysmith, thereafter invested for four months, is the subject of this photograph.

*Photo, Horace W. Nicholls*

Germany which was difficult to dissociate from the idea of rivalry with the leading maritime power.

THE South African War had not long been ended when new factors began to influence European relations. In Great Britain, where for half a century free trade had been the accepted theory and practice on all hands, a new propaganda was vigorously pushed and in some quarters enthusiastically adopted, of which the economic merits or demerits cannot here be discussed at due length ; but it had a political effect which could hardly have been anticipated ; it was interpreted in Germany as being malevolently directed against German commerce and German prosperity. That conception was unaffected by the defeat of the tariff reformers at the ensuing general election of 1906, and the conviction was thoroughly established in the popular mind that the British were saturated with jealousy of her commercial progress.

It befell, moreover, that at the moment when the propaganda was in full swing Great Britain and France discovered that their outstanding differences were capable of reasonable adjustment and that living on terms of mutual good will was much more satisfactory than the perpetuation of needless friction. The long reign of Queen Victoria had just ended ; the new king, Edward VII, had the gift of popularity, and a visit to France facilitated the development of the new spirit of friendliness. The position of the monarch in England is not readily grasped in other countries, and it was not difficult to imagine that a Machiavellian diplomacy was at work. Coupled with the supposed anti-German tariff agitation, the new accord between Great Britain and

France was doubly ominous and the belief in England's sinister designs gained ground.

Nor was this all. France had already established friendly relations with Russia, and the accommodation of interests between France and Great Britain was soon followed by a similar accommodation between Great Britain and Russia, made possible as it had never been before by the effects upon Russia of the disastrous Japanese war. It had been a fundamental part of Bismarck's policy to keep those three powers at arm's length from each other. There had been plenty of motives holding them apart ; there could be only one for their reconciliation—their common desire for the destruction of Germany. The development of this idea was at least a fundamental factor in the complicated

**KING EDWARD VII IN 1910**
Unfailing industry and an acute understanding of men characterised Edward VII (1841–1910), who succeeded Queen Victoria on the British throne in 1901. Throughout his reign he exerted his very great diplomatic gifts to maintain that world peace which was shattered so soon after his death.
*Photo, E. H. Mills*

## AN INTERNATIONAL CONFERENCE AT THE HAGUE DISCUSSING THE PROMOTION OF WORLD PEACE

At the suggestion of Nicholas II, tsar of Russia and a man with humanitarian ideals, the first international peace conference was convoked at The Hague in 1899. It was attended by representatives from European countries and the United States. The conference achieved the establishment of an international court known as the Hague Tribunal, but was unsuccessful in its endeavours to reach an agreement on the question of disarmament. The assembly, which held its meetings at the Huis ten Bosch (House in the Wood), is shown in a drawing from sketches by an artist who was present.

story of the ensuing years, and its catastrophic climax in August, 1914.

ʒT is curious to observe that the most idealistic if not the most successful efforts to design an organ for the preservation of the world's peace have emanated from Russian tsars, Alexander I and Nicholas II. Long ago, the first of these two dreamers had designed the Holy Alliance of Christian Princes, which under Metternich's manipulation was converted —so far as it operated at all—into an instrument for the suppression of popular liberties. But he had also dreamed the dream of Nicholas, the dream which held in it the germ of the League of Nations.

In the last thirty years of the nineteenth century international disputes had with increasing frequency been referred for decision to a neutral arbitrator, Great Britain and the United States having practically led the way by referring their own dispute over the Alabama claim to a neutral court of arbitration. The same course had been followed by the same nations in relation to Alaska, to Vancouver and to Venezuela (though in the last case the United States arbitrated in a dispute between Great Britain and Venezuela). Similarly the Penjdeh incident had been referred to arbitration.

In 1898 Nicholas invited the powers to send delegates to a conference to be held at The Hague to discuss ways and means for the reduction of armaments by consent, the common adoption of what may be called humanitarian regulations in warfare, and the establishment of a permanent court of international arbitration to which nations might, if so minded, refer their disputes. As a result the Hague Tribunal was actually set up. No agreements could be reached as to reduction of armaments,

because no scheme was in the German view compatible with Germany's security. Regulations were generally though not universally accepted later for the humanising of warfare which were loyally observed by the belligerents both in the South African and the Russo-Japanese wars; but in them there was the grave defect that no sanction existed for their enforcement if any belligerent chose to ignore them; just as it was open to any nation to refuse the appeal to arbitration.

ⅠbERE, however, we must revert to the progress of events in the western hemisphere. The South American states in general had at last attained a stability which was more than a temporary equilibrium with intervals of revolution. Brazil had turned itself into a republic, a change which had been carried through without violence and accepted with cheerfulness by the deposed emperor, Pedro II. In Mexico Diaz still ruled with a masterful hand. Great Britain had a boundary dispute with Venezuela in 1895, and when the United States threatened to intervene satisfied them by submitting

**SALVAGE MEN AT WORK ON THE MAINE**

The short war which took place in 1898 between Spain and America resulted from the latter's belief that the former was responsible for blowing up the American warship Maine in Havana harbour. The men employed in the salvage boats shown in this photograph found it an extremely difficult task to work upon the shattered vessel.

**CHAMPION OF THE MOSLEM**

A cartoon by Bernard Partridge which appeared in Punch in May, 1905, represents Kaiser William II theatrically posed in Moslem robes, thus satirising his attitude as the friend and protector of the Moslem peoples.

*By permission of the proprietors of ' Punch'*

the British case to investigation by an American commission, which confirmed the British claims on every point ; a diplomatic concession which went far towards setting the relations between the two great English-speaking nations on a more harmonious footing.

The improved sentiment was confirmed by a quarrel between the United States and Spain—the first armed collision between the western republic and a European state since the Anglo-American war of 1812–14. The island of Cuba was under the Spanish crown, and Spaniards governed or misgoverned it, though only a fraction of the population was Spanish. The Americans had considerable commercial interests in Cuba, where trade and production were brought almost to a standstill by repeated insurrections and attempts to suppress them by drastic but very unsuccessful methods. Should the United States intervene—by the same

warrant that the Concert periodically claimed to intervene in Turkey ?

American public opinion was divided as to the expediency of going beyond vigorous protest ; non-intervention seemed to have definitely carried the day in January, 1898 ; and then in February the American warship Maine, lying in the harbour of Havana, was blown up. The Spanish government inquired, and satisfied itself that the thing was a pure accident in which no Spaniard was concerned ; the American public was entirely convinced to the contrary.

### The Spanish-American War

ON April 22 war was declared. On August 12 peace was signed. At the outset an American squadron annihilated the Spanish squadron in the Philippines, where the Filipinos were in revolt. The Spanish West India squadron was annihilated in July a fortnight before the capture of Santiago. Porto Rico was practically, though not completely, conquered, and Manilla was on the eve of surrender when the peace terms were signed—it fell the next day, the news of the peace arriving later. Any disposition on the part of European powers to intervene was effectually damped by the certainty that such action would bring the British fleet into the picture.

The United States annexed Porto Rico and the Philippines—where, however, the Filipinos, who had risen against the Spaniards for their own independence, maintained a prolonged resistance to an equally alien if more enlightened domination. Cuba was made an independent republic, and, failing in the task of self-government, lost its independence a few years later. Europe and America were already in contact on the east of Asia. To be involved in the political complications of the Old World was still the last thing that America desired ; whether she would be able to preserve her isolation was already becoming doubtful.

A question was soon to arise in regard to which she could not wholly maintain her aloofness.

Great Britain and France reached their mutual understanding, their ' entente,' in

1904. Both powers had interests in Morocco, both had interests in Egypt; each recognized in effect that the other should have a free hand in the country where her interests were paramount. Their agreement, which was not an alliance, was laid before the Triple Alliance, and no objections to it were raised. But the kaiser had for some time been posing as the friend of Moslem peoples in general —both Russia and Great Britain had a vast number of Mahomedan subjects. In 1905 it became apparent to Germany that the interests of the sultan of Morocco as well as those of Germany in Morocco required protection from France's peaceful penetration. Incidentally, Russia was having a bad time in her struggle with Japan, and France could not count upon effective support from that quarter. Unless Great Britain supported her she would have to give way.

When it became apparent that Great Britain would stand loyal, Germany proposed that the question should be dealt with by a conference. The proposal was accepted, though it involved the resignation of the French foreign minister, Delcassé. The Conference of Algeciras was held in 1906, all the powers, including the United States, participating. Germany's demands were supported by Austria alone. It appeared, however, that she was satisfied with the result, while no one suggested that she had met with a rebuff, though for practical purposes the position of the French in Morocco was confirmed.

The conference was preluded by the sanctioning in Germany of a huge programme of naval construction; on the other hand, only a year later, the entente between Great Britain and France was supplemented by the entente between Great Britain and Russia, already the ally of France; while at the conference Italy had rather significantly affirmed the identity of her interests with those of England. It was not clear how far Italy regarded herself as committed to support the policy of her imperial allies.

Thus the grouping of the powers and their attitudes towards each other had

**REPRESENTATIVES OF THE POWERS MEET AT THE CONFERENCE OF ALGECIRAS**
Germany's objection to French action in Morocco secured the convocation of an international conference at Algeciras to discuss the regulation of Moroccan affairs. Lasting from January 16 to April 7, 1906, the conference, under the presidency of Spain, resulted in an agreement being signed that accorded France her privileged position in the country and provided for the sultan of Morocco's acceptance of France's proposed administrative reforms.
*Photo, Topical Press Agency*

**KING GEORGE V**
Born June 3, 1865, King George V succeeded
to the throne of Great Britain, May 6, 1910,
and was crowned June 22, 1911. This portrait
of his Majesty as admiral of the Fleet was taken
shortly before his coronation.
*Photo. Thomson & Co.*

changed materially in the four years
1903–7. At the beginning (as also at the
end) Germany and Austria were balanced
against France and Russia ; while the
security of the central alliance against
Franco-Russian aggression was guaranteed
by the actual adherence of Italy and by
the constant friction between the Dual
Alliance and Great Britain. At the end
Russian prestige and self-confidence had
suffered a shattering blow, in itself a
sufficient guarantee against aggressive
action on her part ; but the friction with
Great Britain had passed, while between
Great Britain and Germany friction had
undoubtedly set in. The expectation, little
short of certainty, that the maritime
power would operate against Franco-
Russian aggression had given place to the
still more confident expectation that it

would operate against Teutonic aggression,
while little but neutrality could be looked
for from Italy if the Central powers should
be the aggressors. That was the lesson of
the Algeciras episode.

If, then, each group suspected the other
of aggressive intent, the one security
against a general conflagration was the
consciousness on both sides of the doubtful-
ness of the issue ; whereof the corollary
was that one side at least was resolved to
ensure beforehand that the issue should
not be doubtful. At the same time, there
were in the Balkans uncontrollable factors
which might at any moment upset the
calculations of the most acute statesmen.

### Declaration of Bulgarian Independence

EUROPE, then, in 1908 was staging for
a new drama, in which the first act
was unexpectedly opened by the Young
Turks. Their organization had secured the
support of the army at Salonica ; in July
they suddenly demanded the long-promised
constitution which had never materialised.
The sultan promptly acceded. The powers
hopefully withdrew their supervisors from
Macedonia, to give the reformers free play.
Consequently, in October, Ferdinand of
Bulgaria judged that his time had come ;
he proclaimed the complete independence
of Bulgaria, and assumed the ancient title
of tsar. Two days later Austria announced
the annexation of her protectorate in
Bosnia, in defiance of the undertakings
under which the protectorate had been
established. This was very definitely the
concern of Russia. But beside Austria, in
the kaiser's significant phrase, stood
Germany ' in shining armour ' ; after brief
hesitation, Russia acquiesced.

If the Central powers had been checked
at Algeciras, they recovered now more than
they had lost then. But the price was the
intensification of Slavonic hostility to the
German-Magyar domination over the Slavs
in the Austrian empire. It was generally
believed that the Austrian heir-presumptive favoured a constitutional reconstruction which would have placed the three
races on an equal footing ; but the
ascendancy party was too strong to
allow such a solution to be attempted ;
the racial antipathy was fostered by

pan-Slavism within and without the Empire, and the fruit thereof was bitter.

For two years there was no further move. Each of the Entente powers had its own domestic troubles. England was in the thick of a prolonged constitutional crisis, in the course of which Edward VII died, and was succeeded by George V ; conflict raged round the powers of the House of Lords, arising from the unexpected exercise of their technical right to reject the financial proposals of the Liberal government, which were carried in the Commons by the support of the Irish parliamentary party. The strife was marked by exceptional bitterness, which increased in virulence when, after two general elections within twelve months, which proved the parties within Great Britain to be of all but equal strength, the Irish group obviously held the scale ; and the Liberals held that their pledge in 1905 to suspend their avowed Home Rule policy was no longer valid.

At the same time one section of the British press was crying aloud that the British navy was no match for the German navy, while another section was proclaiming with equal fervour that expenditure on naval construction was nothing short of blatant folly. Also in India the Morley-Minto scheme was introduced, admitting Indians to the enlarged provincial councils, exciting lively opposition among British officials and residents in India ; while it was accompanied by a highly seditious agitation in the vernacular press, which was treated by the Indian government with what was zealously denounced as pusillanimous leniency or intolerable tyranny according to the predilections of the critic.

Between factions at home and Indian unrest, it did not appear that any formidable intervention in European affairs on England's part was to be looked for, whatever her commitments to the other Entente powers might be. Russia's weakness had been manifested by the Bosnian affair. In 1911 Germany made the real testing move. France's paramount interest in Morocco had been recognized at Algeciras and later by separate agreements both with Spain and with Germany. But the sultan of Morocco was totally incapable of controlling his turbulent subjects ; anarchy in Morocco had its repercussions upon the tribesmen of Algeria ; and in the spring of that year France marched troops to the capital for the defence of the sultan and the restoration of order. On the assumption that this was merely a preliminary to the partition of Morocco between France and Spain, Germany dispatched the corvette Panther to Agadir (July), an unmistakable threat of war.

**GERMAN CRUISER AT AGADIR**
The dispatch of the German gunboat Panther to Agadir, Morocco, in 1911 was a minatory gesture that came near to evoking war. The Panther was shortly replaced by the German cruiser Berlin, which this photograph from a contemporary journal shows at anchor beneath the walls of the old fortress.
*Photo, André Morizet*

It appeared, however, very shortly that this was by no means what Germany intended. In the interval the minister in England, Lloyd George, who was at that time credited with being the most zealous of pacifists, made a speech which in the view of pacifists was almost truculent. Thereupon the Agadir incident was explained away. Germany was only anxious lest her commercial interests in Morocco should be prejudiced by the French domination, for which fears a portion of the French Congo territory would be adequate compensation. The agreement was duly signed in November, and harmony was officially restored.

MEANWHILE, however, war had broken out in another quarter—war with which neither the Central powers nor the Entente could claim to be directly concerned. When France occupied Tunis, Italy had been in some degree placated by the recognition of her own paramount interests in Tripoli. This, however, did not prevent peaceful penetration by German commerce and the development of German influence, which threatened to supersede that of Italy, which could only be saved by the declaration of a formal protectorate. The Young Turks, moreover, were doing their best to undermine all infidel influences. Italy demanded from the Porte, the nominal suzerain of Tripoli, the recognition of her own protectorate ; acquiescence was not immediately following, and she declared war on Turkey (September, 1911).

Twelve months of desultory maritime warfare followed. Italy occupied the Tripolitan coast towns, and seized islands in the Aegean whereby she annoyed the Greeks, in whose eyes Aegean islands were ' Hellas irredenta.' Austria would not allow her to seize territory on the Balkan mainland, the war was expensive and unprofitable, and in October, 1912, peace was made which left her in possession of

### A MOMENTOUS OCCASION IN THE BRITISH HOUSE OF COMMONS

General uneasiness was caused throughout Europe by Germany's action in the matter of the Agadir incident. On November 27, 1911, Sir Edward Grey, who was foreign secretary at the time, made a speech which demonstrated that the pacifist intentions of the government must not be misinterpreted as indicating invertebracy in regard to matters of principle. Occupants of the front bench, from left to right, are Winston Churchill, Lloyd George, Sir Edward Grey, H. H. Asquith and Sydney Buxton.

*Drawing by Cyrus Cuneo in ' Illustrated London News '*

**TERRITORIAL CHANGES EFFECTED IN THE BALKANS BETWEEN 1878 AND 1914**
The map on the left shows the distribution of the various Balkan States after the San Stefano treaty of 1878, when the independence of Rumania, Serbia and Montenegro was recognized and an autonomous Bulgaria, tributary to Turkey, was established.   The map on the right gives the reconstruction after the Balkan Wars of 1912–13, wherein Greece received Macedonia, Albania became independent, Serbia was enlarged and part of Thrace went to Bulgaria, who ceded much of Dobruja to Rumania.

Tripoli and her captures in the Aegean, while the doubtful bonds which held her to the Triple Alliance had been loosened.

Almost at the moment when Turkey and Italy were signing the peace, four Balkan states were declaring war on Turkey, where the Young Turks had thoroughly established their ascendancy, exiled Abdul Hamid and set in his place his feeble-minded brother Mohammed V, but had by no means dissolved the amity with Germany.   Their rule in Macedonia was no more to the liking of the independent Balkan states than that of Abdul Hamid.   The Cretan leader, Venizelos, had now become the trusted minister of the king of the Hellenes.   Mainly through his diplomacy, Greece, Bulgaria, Serbia and Montenegro reconciled their differences and united in the Balkan League with a view to the liberation and absorption of Macedonia upon agreed lines, as an alternative to its erection into an independent state ; the various negotiations between state and state having been conducted separately without any of the

powers being privy thereto.   This point was reached before midsummer in 1912.

At that moment the Albanians, whom no one, Mahomedan or Christian, had ever been able to rule except by sheer force of a dominating personality like Skanderbeg, revolted against the Turkish governors, whose troops mutinied and either joined the rebels or broke before them, and the Albanians began to invade Macedonia. At Constantinople the Young Turks, who were held responsible, were turned out of office.   In September the new League appealed to the powers to intervene ; the powers remonstrated, but forbade the League to move ; but by the middle of October war had been declared between Turkey and all the states of the League.

There followed, before the Concert could recover from its astonishment, an amazing débâcle.   The old Turkish army had been broken up, and a new one was in course of organization under German officers—but it was not yet organized. Each of the League states had its allotted task.   The Greek fleet swept the seas ; in the western area the Serbs routed the

Turks in one battle after another ; in the eastern the Bulgars were threatening Constantinople and investing Adrianople. Before the end of November the Greeks only just anticipated the Bulgars in capturing and occupying Salonica. Then the powers stepped in ; there was a brief armistice ; a conference in London was apparently on the point of achieving a settlement, when the Young Turks suddenly recovered control at Constantinople and rejected the peace terms. The fighting started again (February) ; J a n i n a , Adrianople, Scutari fell in

Eleutherios Venizelos

rapid succession. The powers stepped in again, the armistice was renewed, the London conference was reopened, and at the end of May, 1913, the Treaty of London was signed.

Much as after Japan's triumphant victory over China, the powers which had merely looked on and written notes arranged matters according to their own ideas, to the unmitigated dissatisfaction of every one of the states which had shared the triumphs of the war. But the most—and most justly —dissatisfied was Bulgaria, which had been allotted

Mohammed V of Turkey

George of Greece

Ferdinand of Bulgaria

Peter of Serbia

Nicholas of Montenegro

Carol of Rumania

## RULERS OF THE RESTLESS STATES INVOLVED IN THE BALKAN WARS

Liberation of Macedonia from Turkish rule was the primary object of the Balkan League formed in the summer of 1912. Bulgaria and Serbia first entered into a military convention against Turkey ; Montenegro adhered to Serbia and Greece joined the League later. After the victorious conclusion of the first Balkan War disagreements arose, and in January, 1913, the second Balkan War broke out, Bulgaria pitted against Serbia and Greece ; in July Rumania also intervened against Bulgaria.

*Photos, Boucas and Exclusive News Agency*

**TURKISH SOLDIERS ON THE MARCH NEAR ADRIANOPLE**

Adrianople, on the Sofia-Constantinople railway near the Bulgarian frontier, was Turkey's chief fortress in Europe and, barring as it did the road to Constantinople, was the first objective of Bulgarian attack in the Balkan war. It was held by a force of 60,000 Turks, and in October, 1912, was completely invested by the Bulgarians. The investment was maintained during the armistice, and siege operations were renewed in February, 1913. On March 26 the fortress succumbed to a combined assault by 100,000 Bulgarians and Serbians.

*Photo, T. J. Damon, Constantinople*

the hardest task, achieved the most striking victories and got next to nothing for her pains. In an evil hour Bulgaria resolved to remedy the injustice by a sudden attack (June 29) on Serbia, to which had been allotted portions of Macedonia that she regarded as rightfully her own. The Serbs defeated the Bulgars, the Greeks came in to the support of the Serbs, Rumania joined in on her own account, and the last state of Bulgaria was worse than the first.

In August she was compelled to accept the Treaty of Bukarest, whereby she lost territory to Rumania, to Serbia, to Greece and finally to Turkey. Before, if she had not the spoils she had at least the honours. Her tragic blunder had lost her the honours, and subjected her to actual spoliation; but it

**KING GEORGE OF GREECE IN SALONICA**

Hostilities between Greece and Bulgaria nearly broke out over the possession of Salonica. The Greeks occupied the town on the morning of November 9, 1912, and refused admission to the Bulgarians, who arrived in the afternoon. But, giving way to a threat of force, they yielded it to the Bulgarians next day.

*Photo, Illustrations Bureau*

Notwithstanding the veto of the great powers who had constituted Albania an autonomous state, King Nicholas of Montenegro ordered the investment of Scutari, which was defended by Essad Pasha with some 30,000 Turks and Albanians. On April 22, 1913, Essad Pasha capitulated and surrendered the key to Prince Danilo, who, a few days later, carried it to his father at Cettinje,

Janina in Epirus, near the Albanian frontier, was famous from 1788 to 1818 as the stronghold of Ali Pasha, the tyrannical 'Lion of Janina.' It remained a Turkish stronghold, and in the first Balkan War was held by a large garrison. A Greek division arrived before the place in November, 1912, and, reinforced by troops released by the capture of Salonica, invested the fortress, delivered a general assault on March 5, 1913, and captured the town the following day.

## SCUTARI AND JANINA FALL TO THE BALKAN LEAGUE

*Photos, Illustrations Bureau*

had done more. It had shattered the new accord among the Balkan states, and brought back the old atmosphere of brooding and vindictive suspicion.

The Central powers would have profited by Bulgaria's victory over the other members of the now shattered league, of which, on the other hand, the consolidation would have been particularly inconvenient for Austria. As matters stood, the state which gained most by the war was the one whose depression she most desired—Serbia. But Serbia had failed to gain access either to the Adriatic or the Aegean sea ; her want of a sea-board made it the easier to bring a strangling economic pressure to bear on her ; and she had been deprived of Monastir, which she had captured, and on the acquisition of which she and Greece and Bulgaria were all set. Monastir would be a bone of contention calculated to keep alive the mutual jealousies and suspicions of the Balkan states, which were all to Austria's advantage, since it had been her purpose to open for herself the way to the Aegean, which would be blocked to her as long as they remained even

**COLONEL ENVER BEY**

Enver Bey (1882–1922) was a foremost leader of the Young Turks. In July, 1913, he recovered Adrianople from the Bulgarians, to whom it had been ceded by the Treaty of London.

superficially united. And while Bulgaria, and possibly Greece, might be won over, Serbia was at once the main obstacle to

**CROWD OUTSIDE THE SUBLIME PORTE DURING THE YOUNG TURK COUP D'ETAT**

Reconstruction of the Turkish Empire and complete Turkification of its peoples were the objects of the political organization known as the Young Turks. Their secret Committee of Union and Progress was formed in 1905, Colonel Enver Bey holding the foremost place in it. In February, 1913, by a sudden coup d'état they overthrew the Kiamil cabinet nominally over the question of the surrender of Adrianople, and with but little unrest set up a Young Turk government in its place.

**GUN RUNNING IN IRELAND JUST BEFORE THE GREAT WAR**

Civil war in Ireland was imminent in the summer of 1914, and gun runners were boldly supplying the nationalists with arms and ammunition. One specially notable incident occurred on July 26, when some three thousand rifles were landed at the Hill of Howth, about eight miles from Dublin. The National Volunteers of Ireland, marching with their newly landed rifles to Dublin, were intercepted by a battalion of the King's Own Scottish Borderers, but resisted an attempt to disarm them.

*Photo, Sport & General Press Agency*

the Austrian expansion, and the external focus of Slavonic sentiment which was the most disintegrating influence within the heterogeneous Austrian empire.

THE motives which actuate governments and those which actuate their peoples at moments of crisis are not necessarily the same, though the peoples may be unconscious of the difference—the more in those countries where the governments do not derive their authority directly from the people. It is not difficult to believe in the genuine conviction of the German people that the Entente was a grand conspiracy, born of political vindictiveness and begotten of commercial jealousy, for the overthrow of Germany; that the organization of the nation for war was nothing more than necessary preparation for self-defence, and that when the Central powers flung down the challenge it was only because no other course was open to them. But it is not possible to credit the German government with the same belief, or to doubt that it chose its own moment under the impression that it would have only France and Russia to fight and would be able to wipe France off the board before Russia could come into action effectively. Nor is it easy to doubt that the kaiser and his

entourage, like Napoleon a century before, were deliberately aiming at a world domination, that Algeciras, Bosnia and Agadir were all moves intended to test the strength of the opposing combination, and that the mastery of the Near East was regarded as the key to the situation.

In the affairs of Algeciras and Agadir the British attitude had been disturbing; England, without acknowledging the existence of any formal alliance, had manifested a determination to stand by France if she were made the definite object of aggression. England had indeed professed her own warm desire for such a mutual understanding with Germany as she had already reached with France and Russia, her readiness to do her best to facilitate a similar understanding between the two empires and the other Entente powers, and even to pledge herself to neutrality should the latter take aggressive action against the Central powers; but she had firmly declined to pledge herself to neutrality should the Central powers be the aggressors.

But in 1914 a change had apparently befallen. England was paralysed. The Irish question had reached such a pitch of intensity that Ulster was proclaiming her right to resist in arms her subordination to an Irish national parliament and executive, half England was declaring that Ulster was in the right, and officers of high standing in the army were openly asserting that they would refuse to act against Ulster. Civil war was in the air. A Liberal government was in office, and it was the established belief of European chancelleries that Liberal governments were peace-at-any-price governments. All the circumstances being taken into consideration, the risk of England being drawn into a European war was small, and if she did come in, her army was small and apparently mutinous, her fleet, according to her own vociferous publicists, was inefficient, either Nationalist Ireland or Ulster would seize the opportunity to revolt—England was probably off the board altogether ; if she were not, she might give some trouble, but the risk was worth taking.

The hour, then, had come for striking. The Bismarck tradition required that an occasion should be manufactured, and that the occasion should have at least the appearance of being an unwarrantable aggression by the party that was in fact being attacked.

The occasion arose in June, 1914. The

**EMPEROR WILLIAM II**

From his accession as German emperor in 1888 until his abdication, November 9, 1918, William II was a restless and disturbing figure in Europe owing to his military preoccupations and ambitions. This photograph was taken in 1913.

*Photo, Voigt*

archduke Francis Ferdinand, heir presumptive to the Austrian imperial crown, the

**VICTIMS OF THE TRAGEDY THAT PRECIPITATED THE GREAT WAR**

Archduke Francis Ferdinand, heir to the Austrian imperial throne, accompanied by his wife, paid a visit to Serajevo, the chief town of Bosnia, on June 28, 1914. On their way to the Town Hall a bomb was thrown into their car ; this the archduke himself threw away on to the road, where it exploded. When they had left the Town Hall, only two or three minutes after this photograph was taken, a Bosnian high-school student fired two shots at the royal pair, instantly killing them both.

*Photo, Walter Tausch*

prince who was generally believed to be Slavophil, was assassinated in the streets of the Bosnian city of Serajevo. The assassins were Austrian subjects—but they were Serbs. The murder, then, must be a Serbian plot fostered by the Serbian government. It was indeed not difficult to suggest an entirely different origin for the crime, since it could in no conceivable manner further Serbian or Slavonic interests; but the Austrian government had no doubts about the matter. Even at the best, the intolerable Slavonic propaganda emanating from Serbia must be at the bottom of the outrage. After a brief interval, on July 23, Austria sent to the Serbian government a series of demands acceptance of which would be a complete abrogation of Serbia's sovereignty. Austria was to be at once the accuser, the investigator and the judge, exacting such penalties as she thought fit. Serbia pleaded for appeal to the Hague Tribunal; Austria would have none of it.

Serbia, by herself, lay at Austria's mercy. But Austria's action was a direct challenge to Russia. If Russia failed to

**LICHNOWSKY'S LAST DAYS IN LONDON**
Prince Charles Max Lichnowsky, appointed German Ambassador to the Court of St. James's in 1912, was consistently actuated by desire to improve Anglo-German relations. His dejection is reflected in this photograph of him leaving the Foreign Office the day before the ultimatum.

defend Serbia, that would be an end to the particular matter, but it would also be the end of Russian influence in the Balkans, and an intolerable humiliation in the sight of all the world. If she took up the challenge France could not withhold her support; Germany would uphold Austria as the aggrieved party. England, which was under no pledge, urged reference of the whole question to a European conference; Germany explained that in her view this was Austria's private affair. England offered mediation; Austria declined it. No one had a doubt that at a word from Germany Austria would waive her claim to be the sole arbiter, but the word was not forthcoming.

### Outbreak of the Great War

ON July 28 Austria declared war on Serbia. Russia, if she left Serbia to her doom, would cease to count as a European power. During the next two days Germany suggested that Britain should remain neutral if the outbreak of war should compel her to attack France via Belgium —whose neutrality all the powers were bound under the most solemn obligation to respect, as Bismarck had respected it in 1870. In the British view, however, those obligations were binding. On July 31 mobilisation orders were issued both in Austria and Russia. If, as it is possible to believe, there was still, as concerned Austria and Russia, some shadow of a chance of peace, it was obliterated by an ultimatum—on the same day—from Germany to Russia and to France. On the next day, August 1, she declared war on Russia. France, bound to take her stand by Russia, renewed her pledge to respect Belgium's neutrality, which Belgium declared her determination to maintain; Germany evaded the question—on which the British government resolved to stake its own action. On August 2 German troops entered Luxemburg and Germany declared war on France. On August 3 her troops entered Belgian territory. On that night the British ultimatum was sent to Germany. The violation of Belgium had welded the whole country into solid support of the government. On August 4 Great Britain declared war on Germany

# Tenth Era

## THE GREAT WAR AND AFTER

### SINCE 1914

---

Chapter 32
## THE GREAT WAR, 1914—1918

Chapter 33
## AFTERWARDS: SINCE 1918

---

THE Tenth Era of our record is that wherein we are still living, the era inaugurated by the greatest convulsion known in the history of mankind. The Great War raged for four years and a hundred days. It devastated a vast area of Europe beyond recognition ; it cost millions of lives on the battlefield ; it paralysed productive industry and destroyed sources of production ; it shattered political systems ; and it wrecked the entire nineteenth-century outlook upon life. It gave to old problems a new aspect, and created new problems for solution, involving complete reconstruction. The grand inclusive problem of reconstruction was that with which the world found itself faced, the problem with which it has been struggling, not we believe without some degree of success, in the ensuing years. But we can no longer feel even that degree of finality in our judgements with which we pronounce upon the past ; there can be no considered consensus. Consequently there can be no uniformity in the pronouncements upon the various aspects of the story of the years since 1914 such as we have been able to maintain heretofore in this work ; no ' judgements of history.' The tale is the tale of the beginnings of the grand attempt to lay the foundations of permanent world peace not only between nations but also between classes ; to substitute co-operation for rivalry, to dissipate jealousies and distrust. And as yet we seem to be only at the beginning.

# TABLE OF DATES FOR CHAPTER 32

1914 Aug. 3 : Germans invade Belgium.
    „  7 : Fall of Liége.
    „ 22 : British at Mons.
    „ 23 : Japan declares war. Battle of Mons. Fall of Namur. Retreat of British, and French left.
    Russian invasion of East Prussia ; successes, followed by disaster of Tannenberg. Russian invasion of Galicia.
    Aug. 26 : British stand at Le Cateau.
    „  28 : Fall of Longwy ; retreat continues.
    Serbians repulse Austrians and invade Bosnia.
    Sept. 5 : Retreat ends, still covering Paris.
    „  6 : French counter-offensive begins ; battle of Marne forcing German retirement, and developing (13) into battle of the Aisne. German line stabilised ; both lines extend north till the coast is reached.
    Russians capture Lemberg ; drive through Galicia.
    Oct. First German invasion of Poland held up on the Vistula.
    „ 10 : Fall of Antwerp and (16) of Ostend.
    „ 19 : Belgians at Nieuport. The opposing lines extend from Belfort to the sea.
    „ 20 : Battles of Arras and Ypres begin.
    Nov. 1 : Battle of Coronel.
    Britain declares war on Turkey.
    „ 18 : Last German attack at Ypres broken.
    Second German thrust in Poland held up on the Vistula.
    British force lands at head of Persian Gulf.
    Dec. 8 : Battle of Falkland Islands.
    S. African revolts of De Wet and Maritz ended.
    Russo-Turkish campaign begins in Caucasus.

1915 Jan. : Third German thrust in Poland held up.
    Russian victories in the Caucasus.
    Feb. : Fourth German thrust narrowly escapes disaster at Prasnytz.
    Turkish attack on Suez Canal shattered.
    British naval attack on Dardanelles opens.
    Germany announces submarine war on commerce.
    March : Russian advance in Galicia ; Przemysl taken.
    Failure of naval attack in Dardanelles.
    Battle of Neuve Chapelle.
    British declare naval blockade of Germany.
    April : Russians partly penetrate Carpathian passes.
    British victory at Shaiba (Mesopotamia).
    Second battle of Ypres. First use of poison gas.
    British troops force landing on Gallipoli.
    May : Mackensen opens German offensive in Galicia. Russian line driven back to Przemysl by the end of the month.
    Sinking of the Lusitania.
    French advance in front of Arras.
    Italy declares war on Austria.
    June : Conquest of German South-West Africa.
    Fall of Przemysl and Lemberg (Galicia).
    July : German advance in Poland, on Warsaw.
    Aug. : Russians abandon Warsaw.
    British landing at Suvla Bay ; surprise fails.
    Mesopotamia : British occupy Kut el-Amara.
    Germans take Kovno and Brest Litovsk.
    Sept. : Battle of Loos.
    German invasion of Russia checked on Vilna-Rovno line.
    Oct. : Bulgaria declares war on Serbia and attacks.
    French and British troops occupy Salonica.
    Nov. : Serbia overrun by Bulgars, Austrians and Germans.
    British advance on Bagdad abandoned.
    Dec. : British force isolated at Kut.
    British evacuate Gallipoli.

1916 Jan. : Russian advance in Caucasus.
    Feb. : Russians take Erzerum.
    „ 21 : First German blow at Verdun ; French lines driven in ; thrust stopped on 26th.
    March 2–14 : Second drive at Verdun.
    Great Britain adopts general conscription.
    April 9–12 : Third drive at Verdun.
    Relieving force fails to reach Kut ; surrender.
    Rebellion in Ireland fails.
    May 3–June 6 : Fourth battle of Verdun front.
    May : Austrian thrust in the Trentino.
    „ Battle of Jutland.
    June : Last German effort before Verdun fails.
    Russians open great offensive in Galicia ; Austria abandons Trentino adventure ; German and Austrian reinforcements called east.
    Arab revolt under Sherif of Hejaz declares Arabian independence.

1916 July : Allied offensive opens in the west ; British begin battle of the Somme. Russian successes in Galicia.
    Aug. : Rumania enters the war and drives through Carpathian passes into Transylvania. Russian progress in Galicia checked.
    Italians take Gorizia.
    Constant fighting and gradual gain of ground by Allies on the Somme.
    Sept. : Rumanians pushed back by German counter-offensive. Mackensen invades the Dobruja.
    First appearance of ' tanks ' ; considerable advance of Allies on the Somme front.
    Venizelists set up provisional Salonica government.
    Oct. : Allied push continues, very gradual advance on western front. German invasion of Rumania advances, but is stoutly resisted.
    Nov. : Western push suspended by weather conditions ; Mackensen forces Danube, compelling Rumanian retreat.
    Serbians and French capture Monastir.
    Dec. : Fall of Bukarest ; Rumanians confined to Moldavia.

1917 Jan. : Allies reject German peace overtures.
    Feb. : Turks cleared from Kut.
    Renewal of the Allied push in the west.
    March : British in Bagdad. Advance on Palestine from Egypt held up at Gaza.
    Western front approaches St. Quentin.
    Constitutional revolution in Russia ; Nicholas II abdicates (15) ; provisional government.
    April : United States declare war on Germany.
    Vimy Ridge stormed ; French gain footing on Chemin des Dames, but fail to master it.
    May : Continuous development of submarine campaign.
    Russian army undermined by Bolshevik teaching.
    June : Messines ridge blown up ; partial British advance.
    Constantine abd. ; Venizelist government.
    July : Brussilov with loyal troops opens desperate offensive in Galicia ; which is wrecked by disloyal troops. Russia ceases to count.
    Aug. : Desperate Rumanian stand against Mackensen.
    Obstinate but futile campaign in the mud of Flanders.
    French recover ground before Verdun.
    Sept. : German advance in Baltic provinces.
    Oct. : French master Chemin des Dames.
    Germans shatter Italian centre at Caporetto ; Italian retreat, pursued by Austrians, turns to bay on the Piave.
    British push to Passchendaele.
    Nov. : Lenin overthrows Kerensky government ; Bolshevik domination in Russia.
    Surprise British spring at Cambrai ; countered by heavy German reinforcements.
    Allenby captures Gaza.
    Dec. : Allenby occupies Jerusalem.

1918 Jan.–Feb. : Preparations for decisive struggle.
    March : Russo-German treaty of Brest Litovsk.
    German drive against British right on Somme. British stand on the Ancre, ' back to the wall.' Foch appointed commander of Allied armies.
    April : German thrust towards coast held up.
    American troops arriving.
    Zeebrugge wholly and Ostend partially sealed.
    May : German drive against French left, to Marne. American troops in fighting line.
    June : Failure of last Austrian offensive on Piave.
    July 15 : Final German thrust across the Marne.
    „ 18 : Foch opens victory offensive.
    German withdrawal begins.
    Aug. 9 : British join offensive on French left. Additional offensives develop continuously to left and right.
    Sept. British penetrate Hindenburg line ; Germans evacuate St. Mihiel, taken by Americans.
    „ 15 : Allied offensive against Bulgars.
    „ 30 : Armistice dictated to Bulgars.
    „ 19–21 : Battle of Megiddo ; Syria invaded.
    Oct. : Cambrai taken ; Lille and Douai evacuated.
    „ 23 : Rout of Austrians on Italian front.
    Decisive defeat and surrender of Turkish army in Mesopotamia. 30 : Armistice dictated.
    Nov. 3 : Austrians sue for armistice. Battle of Sambre. 7 : Americans enter Sedan. 9 : flight of Kaiser ; German provisional government.
    „ 11 : Mons entered ; Armistice.

### CHAPTER 32

# THE GREAT WAR:
## 1914–1918

THE Central powers entered upon the Great War with a confident expectation of rapid and decisive victory, for which there was no small warrant apart from certain miscalculations. In the first place, the presumption was that at least in the initial stages they would have to deal with only two powers that counted, France and Russia, one on the west and the other on the east, while on the north and on the south they were secure. Holding the interior lines, and provided with a network of strategic railways, they could mass troops on either front and transfer them from one to the other in overwhelming force as circumstances might demand; whereas the French and the Russians were each of them pinned to a single front.

In the second place their own military machine—or that of the Germans, at least—was in perfect working order; those of France and Russia were not. It was barely ten years since the weakness of the Russian system had been revealed in the Japanese war, and there had been very recent revelations of defects in the French military administration. It was almost certain that Russia would not be able to bring her full power into play for some months, which would give Germany time to clear France off the board.

It would give time because one section of her frontier, where it marched with Belgium, was very nearly defenceless, so that it could be swiftly penetrated by a march through Belgium, whose neutrality, guaranteed by treaty, had been faithfully observed in the war of 1870 by both sides —but while several powers, including Prussia, were then pledged to observe that neutrality, none were pledged to oppose its violation in arms. The invasion of France through Belgium was an integral though unavowed part of the German plan.

The German staff, however, had taken into consideration the possibility that Great Britain might, sooner or later, join with France and Russia. It was in itself improbable, since in the first place there was no treaty obligation binding her to give armed support (as there was between Russia and France) to the other members of the Entente; secondly, there was a Liberal government in power, and Liberal governments were notoriously averse from war; thirdly, the critical position in Ireland would greatly strengthen the peace party. And if, after all, the war party should predominate, England's military power was all but negligible; the German navy believed itself able to neutralise the naval power which a vociferous section of the British press had long been declaring to be totally inadequate for its task; and rebellion in Ireland, in South Africa and in India would tie her hands.

Finally, the German government was assured that in the east the Central powers would be supported by Turkey, while it was extremely unlikely that any of the other Balkan states would come to the aid of Serbia; and it was highly improbable that Italy would desert the Triple Alliance, though she might deny any obligation to give it armed support. It was not unreasonable, therefore, to anticipate that the war would be won for Germany before Christmas, possibly in the early autumn.

### Opposed Views on War Guilt

THE German government had a solid Germany behind it; a Germany convinced that she was embarking on a war imposed upon herself in self-defence by the machinations of enemies who were awaiting their opportunity to crush her. It is not easy to credit the imperial government itself with a similar belief, or that of Austria. To the Entente powers it appeared quite simply that German militarism had been consistently planning for years to force on them at the moment of its own selection a war that should lay Europe prostrate before it, and should

IB*

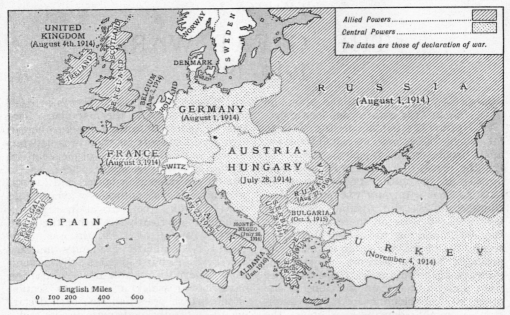

HOW EUROPE WAS DIVIDED AGAINST ITSELF IN THE GREAT WAR

This map of the belligerent European countries in the Great War of 1914–18 shows that, in spite of the imposing numerical array of nations actually or nominally at war with the Central powers, the territorial discrepancy, especially at the beginning, was inconsiderable. Furthermore, Germany held what are known as the 'interior lines,' and could transfer forces from front to front by a system of strategic railways. Hence she was not unjustified in counting on a speedy victory.

achieve for Germany what Napoleon I had attempted to achieve for himself.

The flaw in the German plan lay in its miscalculation of factors which were not obvious. It was reckoned that the French would fight brilliantly to win but would go to pieces in the face of defeat ; whereas when they were defeated they fought on as tenaciously as ever. It was reckoned that Russia would only come slowly into action, and would be fully engaged in meeting the Austrian offensive ; whereas before a month was over she was delivering an offensive on the east German front which, disastrously though it ended for her, was an invaluable diversion for her allies in the west. It was reckoned that Belgium, seeing the hopelessness of resistance, would give the German troops a free passage ; resistance was hopeless, but the free passage was not given and, though Belgium paid the penalty for her heroic sacrifice, she impeded the rush while the Allies were reinforcing that front. Most fatal, however, was the miscalculation of the part to be played by the British.

Down to the last moment the British cabinet was divided, one section of it being convinced that if the European war could not be averted, honour and interest alike demanded British intervention ; the other that there was no obligation of honour and that British interests would be best served by present neutrality. At the last moment the ranks were closed, not only in the cabinet but from end to end of the country, by the German invasion of Belgium. It was a breach of faith of a kind which, if it were tolerated, would render all treaties futile. Without that, Great Britain might and probably would have entered the war, but only in the face of a strong opposition at home from the Liberal and Labour benches and from the Irish ; by it Great Britain was rendered practically solid, and Ireland swung into line with Great Britain. Nor was it long before it was abundantly manifest that the Dominions of the Empire would play their part no less zealously, that in South Africa there remained only a fractional body of Boer intransigents, and that Indian loyalty was assured.

Nor was this all ; for the ' decadent ' fleet, providentially concentrated in home waters, had already been quietly stationed precisely where it was most wanted, so that from the first day of the war no German squadron or surface ship was able to appear upon the North Sea for any purpose except a hasty raid on the British coast, or an engagement with a British squadron from which it had to extricate itself and seek security in its own mine-defended ports before it should be annihilated by the arrival of an overwhelming naval force. Moreover, from the first week of the war this control of the seas outside the Dardanelles and the Baltic enabled the British to carry across the Channel, not indeed without risk but without appreciable loss, troops, munitions and other

accessories to military operations, to the full extent of the country's capacity for providing them ; while it established at headquarters a complete confidence that dreams of a German invasion were chimerical, so that practically all the fully trained fighting force was available to take its place in the French fighting line.

That force was numerically insignificant and was grievously lacking in the heavy-gun equipment required for the campaigning methods developed by the Germans ; but in other respects it was astonishingly efficient, as was the organization which placed it in the field on the other side of the Channel within three weeks of the declaration of war. Great Britain even now for a time persistently declined to envisage the compulsory training and service which the experts had warned her would be needed in a

ARRIVAL OF SIR JOHN FRENCH AND HIS STAFF AT BOULOGNE

The moment it became evident that British intervention in the war was inevitable Field Marshal Sir John French was selected for the command of the British Expeditionary Force to be despatched. On August 14, 1914, he landed with his staff at Boulogne—he can be identified behind the officer in the centre of this photograph of the occasion—and went to the French army headquarters. Next day he visited Paris, and on Monday, August 17, reached his own headquarters at Le Cateau.

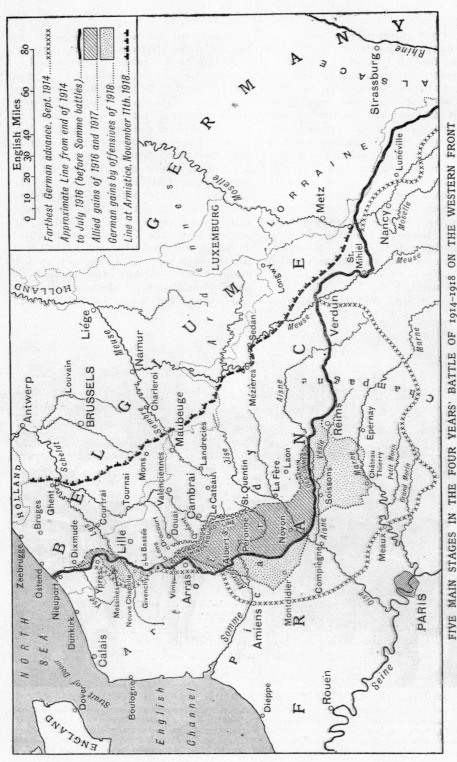

**FIVE MAIN STAGES IN THE FOUR YEARS' BATTLE OF 1914-1918 ON THE WESTERN FRONT**

From 1914 to 1918 most of the so-called 'battles' on the western front—really the whole campaign was a prolonged battle—resulted in gains and losses of territory, entirely disproportionate to the loss of life involved, that appear insignificant on a large-scale map. Hence the operations can be simplified into five broad phases. First there was the German maximum advance. This the battles of the Marne and the Aisne, followed by the outflanking race northwards, converted into the stabilised trench line from sea to Switzerland that remained substantially unaltered for more than a year. Next, there were the Allied gains of 1916-17; next, the German advance in the spring of 1918; and, last, the Allied advance that ended with the Armistice.

European conflict. But even as matters stood the ' expeditionary force ' was twice the size of any British force which had taken part in any previous war ; and the call to arms was answered by multitudes of volunteers, who were ready and fit to take the field in less than half the time that had been looked upon by the most optimistic as the minimum for producing even a moderate efficiency. Among these must be reckoned the recently organized and partly trained Territorial forces, whose terms of enrolment had exempted them from the service oversea for which almost without exception they now volunteered.

THE neutrality of the small state of Luxemburg, as well as that of Belgium, was guaranteed, and was ignored to maintain the continuity of the German line. The Franco-German frontier was protected by a powerful line of fortresses, from Belfort at the gap between the Vosges and Switzerland (whose neutrality was not to be challenged) to Longwy on the Belgium-Luxemburg frontier, by way of Nancy and Verdun. It was on this line that the attack was anticipated, and the French were in strength. North of this in Belgium lay the Ardennes, not a good country through which to deliver an attack in force, though the French line was as a matter of course tenuous. The real German attack, therefore, was to be delivered across the Meuse on the weak line between Lille and Maubeuge, turning the French left and clearing the way for a march on Paris, and taking the French army in rear ; the Allies being quite unconscious of the concentration upon this line.

The plan would almost certainly have been carried out successfully but for the unexpected resistance of Belgium, which compelled the Germans to account for Liége and Namur before they could cross the French border. No one outside

**FORT LONCIN, LIEGE, SHATTERED BY GERMAN SIEGE GUNS**
Brialmont designed and superintended the Belgian defences of the valley of the Meuse, completing the fortification of Antwerp, Liége and Namur in 1884–86. The principal feature was the cupola fort, carrying guns in domed turrets. The method is open to criticism on the grounds that it cannot be concealed, provides a fixed target, and is liable to have its machinery put out of gear ; a lesson enforced by this view of a fort after the German heavy guns had dealt with it on August 15, 1914.
*Photo, Imperial War Museum*

**GENERAL SHAW AND HIS STAFF AFTER THE BATTLE OF MONS**

The first encounter between the British and German infantry occurred when the latter made their sudden attack on the British position at Mons ; after heavy fighting, evacuation and retreat proved for the British the only alternative to envelopment. A photograph, taken while the Germans were actually firing into and over the barricade at the top of this street at Frameries, shows General Shaw discussing operations with his staff after the battle.

Germany had counted on the destructive effects of the German long-distance guns and high explosives upon the best of fortifications constructed on the old lines ; yet, though Liége itself fell on August 7, its satellite fortresses held the Germans up for another week. While the main Belgian forces were being pushed north upon Antwerp the main German column advanced on Namur ; though it was checked on the way, the bombardment opened on the 20th ; Namur fell on the 23rd, though satellite forts held out for three days more. All the defences had been blown to pieces, and of the Belgian southern army nothing was left. But by this time it was three weeks since the declaration of war, and the British army corps were already, on the 22nd, entrenching themselves on the French left, west and north-west of Charleroi through Mons. The Belgian resistance to the rush for turning the French flank had been crushed ; but it had been maintained just long enough to enable a new obstacle, the British expeditionary force, to take its place.

To overwhelm or envelop that force was now the immediate objective of the German command on the German right. While the British were entrenching themselves the Germans were uncovering their right by thrusting the French on the Ardennes front back over the Meuse and forcing the retirement of their extreme flank on the Somme, so that on the 23rd Von Kluck, with four army corps, was able to make a frontal attack on the whole British line, at the same time threatening to turn both its flanks. The frontal attack was actually held up, though Mons had to be evacuated, and it had become clear that retreat was the only alternative to envelopment. Next day (24th), therefore, the whole line fell back to a line running west from Maubeuge, fighting heavy but effective rearguard actions both on its right and left, and again on the 25th to Le Cateau ; where a desperate stand was made on the 26th which gave pause to the German onslaught, so that on the 28th the British were on a line from La Fère to Noyon. But for a second week the retreat was continued in conformity with the French retirement on the right, past the Marne, till the British force lay behind the Grand

Morin, with its left extended by a new French force covering Paris.

For the armies on the Belgian front from Longwy to Charleroi, though not definitely pierced, had been swung back, hingeing on Longwy ; and when Longwy fell on the 28th, Verdun became the hinge, the line falling back behind the Aisne and then the Marne until it lay from Paris on the west to the salient including Verdun on the east, from which point it remained unshaken south-eastward through Nancy to Belfort. The failure of the Germans either to outflank the left or to pierce the centre—though they had come very near to doing both—had saved the situation. The momentum of the attack was exhausted, and that fact was very possibly due to the strain on the eastern front imposed by the unexpected Russian diversion in East Prussia.

Now, however, at the end of the first month the French line was being reinforced by reserves. At the moment when Von Kluck was almost at the gates of Paris, the immediate fall of which was anticipated in some quarters, the French opened the counter-offensive (September 6) on the Marne. The result was that now it was the Germans who had to swing back on their hinge before Verdun, the envelopment of their right flank being threatened by the Anglo-French left, to say nothing of the penetration of their centre, which was also menaced.

On the 9th began the retreat of the German right, while Foch was delivering a smashing attack on the weakened right centre. On the 10th the whole line was in retreat, but it was an organized retreat covered by stubbornly fought rearguard actions. On the 13th the retirement from the Marne developed into the battle of the Aisne, which resulted immediately in the stabilising of the German line westward from the Verdun salient across the front of Reims and Soissons, leaving them still in occupation of two-thirds of the French territory over which they had advanced. This was followed by a continuous

**MEN OF THE BRITISH NAVAL EXPEDITION SENT TO RELIEVE ANTWERP**
The German thrust southward towards Paris had left the Belgian forces isolated in the north of their country, where they gradually concentrated on Antwerp. The condition of the town was already precarious—the outer fortifications and an inner fort having fallen—when, on October 4, the British Naval Division and a brigade of Marines were sent in by Winston Churchill for strategical reasons that have been questioned. This photograph shows a trench being dug at Vieux Dieu.
*Photo, Imperial War Museum*

**GENERAL VON KLUCK**

Alexander von Kluck, who commanded the German forces at the battle of the Marne, was born in 1846, and entered the Prussian army in 1865. He served in the Austro-Prussian and Franco-Prussian wars and retired in 1916.

*Photo, Record Press*

struggle for the extension of both lines northward, past the front of Amiens and Arras, primarily for the envelopment of the opposing flank—an end attained by neither—till both reached the North Sea, so that from Ostend and Dunkirk to Belfort each presented an unbroken front with no flank to be turned, while the

occupation of Ostend by the Germans gave them the whole Belgian coast line.

The hope of the Allies that they would carry their line up to Antwerp was foiled. The Belgian forces, penned in the north, had continued to hamper the German invasion of France by raids for which they were mercilessly penalised, and the doom of Antwerp was sealed. With the help of a gallant but half-trained British force and British ships the Belgian troops were enabled to evacuate Antwerp before its fall on October 10, and to take up their position on the extreme left of the Allies, their front soon protected by ground submerged by the old device of opening the dykes, while the British held the famous Ypres salient.

In the course of the extending movement there was much hard fighting. Antwerp had already fallen before the British left was in front of La Bassée, from which it failed to expel the Germans, who occupied Lille next day. On October 16 the Germans were in Ostend, and on the 19th the Allied line had been extended by French and Belgians up to Nieuport, covered from the sea by the guns of British monitors.

The last phase of this struggle was the first battle of Ypres and the battle of Arras. The German object in the latter was to snap the connexion between the French at Arras and the British to the

**GERMAN ARTILLERY IN THE COASTWISE PURSUIT OF THE BELGIAN ARMY**

On October 9 Antwerp was evacuated, and, apart from 18,000 who escaped into Holland, the Belgian army retreated down the coast, eventually to form the left wing of the Allied forces which had by now worked their way almost to the sea in an attempt to outflank the German right. The final move by which the Germans countered this attempt was their pursuit of the Belgians over the dunes, which by the 19th had given them the whole of the Belgian coast to the Yser.

north of them. It began on the 20th, but though Arras was smashed by the German bombardment the French line held, while at the end of a week's fighting the Germans still held their position on the almost impregnable Vimy ridge. The battle for Ypres began on the 20th ; its crisis came on the 31st when the Germans, making their greatest effort, were nevertheless repulsed at the end of a day during which the fray had rocked furiously backwards and forwards. In the next three weeks the assaults were thrice renewed and thrice repulsed, in spite of greatly superior numbers and artillery, and the stabilising of the two opposing lines from the North Sea to the Swiss frontier was completed. Until 1918 there was no advance of either line for more than a few miles upon a small sector.

On the western front, then, the first round of the great conflict was over before the end of November. The Central powers had delivered a very heavy blow, and remained in possession of a very substantial area of enemy territory, while their own soil was intact ; but their attempt to make that blow decisive had definitely failed. On the eastern front they had been less successful.

### Russian Advance in East Prussia

ACCORDING to plan, Germany was to concentrate upon her own great offensive in the west, while holding in the east her own strongly protected frontier with its elaborate support of strategic railways. Russia, it was assumed, would not be ready to move for some time to come.

Russian Poland formed a great salient with East Prussia on the north, Prussian Poland on the west and Austrian Poland or Galicia on the south. The whole was practically without frontier defence. Austria then was to invade Poland from Galicia, and at the same time to put Serbia out of action. But, as it happened, Russia had much stronger forces ready than was supposed, and some commanders of high ability ; whereas, at the moment, the German commander in East Prussia was incompetent and the Austrian command was extremely defective.

Consequently, while the Germans were trampling through Belgium the Russian northern army poured over the eastern borders of East Prussia, flinging the Germans back in rout to Königsberg, and creating something like a panic in Berlin. The German command was promptly transferred to Hindenburg, an old general, then of no great reputation, but one who knew the country thoroughly. The Russian left pushed forward into the Masurian lakes, losing touch with the centre, and there, in the last days of August, when the Anglo-French line was being rolled back towards Paris, was all but annihilated by Hindenburg, in the tremendous disaster of Tannenberg. East Prussia was saved, and the Russian main army had to fall back. It can hardly be doubted, however, that the critical moment in the east reacted upon the force of the German advance in the west.

### Serbians in Bosnia and Russians in Galicia

MEANWHILE the Serbians had dealt faithfully with the Austrian punitory expedition, ejecting it from Serbia before the end of August, and proceeding to the invasion of Bosnia ; here, however, they made no material advance, though there was some heavy fighting in September. But the Austrians had to be content with holding them up, since their own offensive in southern Poland was being more than cancelled by an unexpected Russian offensive in Galicia. Before the end of August the Russian armies were threatening its capital, Lemberg ; at the beginning of September they inflicted on the Austrians a rout only less overwhelming than the rout of Tannenberg, occupied Lemberg, almost cleared Poland of the invading Austrian force by the middle of the month, and were soon investing the powerful fortress of Przemysl, on the way to Cracow.

Hindenburg, on the other hand, after Tannenberg, which had established his reputation, attempted a counter-invasion not of Poland but of Russia from East Prussia, but was completely held up on the Niemen, and forced to retire across the Prussian frontier before the end of September. Apart from the actual check

SKELETON BUILDINGS OF THE BEAUTIFUL CATHEDRAL CITY OF YPRES AFTER THE GERMAN BOMBARDMENT OF 1915

While the Belgians, with the aid of British monitors, were holding up the German advance in the flooded region of the Yser, the British on their right were engaged in a fierce conflict, centred round Ypres but stretching south to La Bassée, whose result was to stabilise the line in Flanders. The town itself was not seriously affected until the second battle of Ypres, in April, 1915; the civil population were then evacuated and the town virtually destroyed. The ruins of the famous Cloth Hall appear almost in the centre of this photograph with the Cathedral of S. Martin beyond.

he had received, it had become imperative to relieve the pressure in the south. The fall of Cracow would be an incitement to all the northern Slavs to revolt against their Austrian masters, would threaten to turn the flank of Hungary whose Galician front was protected by the Carpathians, and might have on the Balkan states effects which it was not possible to calculate ; and already Russian troops were penetrating the Carpathian passes.

Early in October, then, Hindenburg had organized the invasion of West Poland, with Warsaw as his objective, expecting a Russian retirement. But the Russians prepared their stand along the line of the Vistula, and the Germans, when they tried to cross it, were not only held up in the centre, but found both their flanks threatened and were rolled back all along the line. In the first week of November Poland had been practically evacuated, and the fall of Cracow seemed imminent. But by this time the German command was satisfied that its own line in the west was established impregnably for defence from the North Sea to Switzerland, and had learnt in front of Ypres that the prospect of creating a flank in the Allied line was remote ; therefore an intensive onslaught on the eastern front was in preparation. Cracow did not fall.

VON HINDENBURG ON THE EASTERN FRONT

His outstanding military abilities and victories over the Russians early raised Paul von Hindenburg to the rank of German generalissimo on the eastern front, where he is here seen at headquarters with his staff. In 1916 he received the appointment of chief of the general staff of the field army.

*Photo, Central News*

About the same time the finishing touches were given to the British command of the sea. The Central powers had no battle fleet in the Mediterranean, where the French were in charge ; their main fleet was shut up in the North Sea ports, sheltered by their mine fields, whence only an occasional cruiser could emerge to make a dash for the English east coast, shell one or two watering places and race back to its own port before it could be overtaken by pursuers ; though loose mines and submarines made the movement of ships in the North Sea somewhat precarious. At the beginning of the war, however, there was a German squadron in Chinese waters, as well as some cruisers in the Mediterranean. The last escaped to the nominally neutral port of Constantinople, to help the Turks in their preparation for dropping the mask.

On the other hand, Japan took her place with the Allies and declared war on Germany in August, so that Von Spee's squadron, which could not hope to engage the Japanese fleet successfully, after detaching the Königsberg and the Emden retired from Tsingtau (the port of the leased territory of Kiao-chau) across the Pacific, to experience in the first place success, but in the long run disaster. The Japanese intervention was followed by the fall of Tsingtau, and the Japanese fleet rendered further service in patrolling

**ABOARD THE GOEBEN**

At the beginning of the war French command
of the Mediterranean drove the few German
cruisers into Turkish waters; among them the
Goeben, aboard which the Kaiser and Enver
Pasha are shown at Constantinople in 1918.

*Photo, Abrahams, Devonport*

the Pacific and convoying Australian and
Indian troops to the West, the latter taking
their place temporarily in the fighting
line immediately on their arrival.

The Porte, while proclaiming its neutrality, had made its secret treaty with
the Central powers at the moment of the
war's outbreak. The alliance was an
integral part of the scheme; it was designed
to place western Asia under German control, to turn the Russian flank and to
eject the British from Egypt and the Suez
Canal. Turkey openly entered the war at
the beginning of November.

THE last heavy attack before Ypres was
repulsed on November 11. A week
later Hindenburg was renewing the assault
on the Russian front in West Poland, and
Mackensen was driving its centre back,
only to find that his drive forward promised to result in his own envelopment;
and it was only with great difficulty and
heavy loss that he extricated himself from
his perilous position. The Russian wings,
however, fell back on a more secure line;

the threat to Cracow was relieved by the
threat to Warsaw. Another German drive
on the centre in January (1915) was held
up, renewed in February and again held
up, while the Russians were once more
threatening East Prussia. The Germans
concentrated on the northern flank; the
experiences of November were almost
repeated at the end of February; the
thrusting columns were first stayed and
then almost encircled at Prasnytz, only
escaping after a desperate struggle. The
onslaughts on the Russian centre and right
had both failed.

Meanwhile the Austrians were endeavouring to thrust the Russians back from
the Carpathian passes and to recover the
lost ground in Galicia. Though they met
with some successes, Przemysl fell before
the end of March. Its fall enabled the
Russians to renew the attack on the Carpathian passes; by the middle of April
they had made considerable progress.
But by this time a fresh drain on their
resources and an additional field of operations in the Caucasian region had been
forced upon them by Turkey's entry into
the war; and the Germans had resolved
to take the saving of the situation on the
Carpathian front into their own hands.
The attacks in Poland had indeed saved
Cracow, but had accomplished little or
nothing more. Now they were concentrating—though the design was not understood elsewhere—on the Russian flank in
Galicia. Mackensen, not the unsuccessful
Austrian general, was to be in charge.

### Fighting in the Colonial Areas

SINCE the beginning of the lull on the
western front neither side had down
to this point made definite progress in
spite of the heavy fighting in the east. In
the colonial areas, the British and Japanese
command of the seas made it an easy
matter to eject the Germans not only, as
we have seen, from China, but from the
islands they had occupied in the South
Seas, and from their colonies on the
northerly coast lands of West Africa.
Except where such conquests were a pre-
ventive against the stirring up of native
hostility, they were of no serious importance, as had been repeatedly demonstrated

in the Anglo-French and Spanish maritime wars for over two centuries past.

German West Africa in the south and German East Africa were another matter, because of their bearing upon the Anglo-Dutch Union of South Africa. Here the eviction of the Germans was postponed owing to the trouble caused by the remnant of Boer intransigents within the Union. The revolts, however, headed by Maritz and De Wet, were put down before the end of 1914 by Botha and Smuts—who with De Wet himself had been the most distinguished and indomitable of the Boer leaders in their war with the British ; while in East Africa the small balance of gains was rather in favour of the Germans. In the spring, however, Botha and Smuts were conducting a skilful campaign which cleared German South-West Africa in the course of the summer.

ON the other hand, the entry of the Turks was about to have momentous results. To begin with, it inaugurated a winter campaign against Russia in the Caucasus region where the Turkish frontier marched with that of Russia and with a corner of Persia which had already been for some time occupied by both Russian and Turkish troops. The Turks in Asia, not having as in Europe the benefits of German military directorship, were de-

feated in their offensive ; but the Russians, though they secured Tabriz, failed to reach Erzerum, while the diversion reacted upon their strength in Poland and Galicia. At the same time, however, the Turks were directly challenging the British by attacking the Suez Canal from Palestine. The attacks were repulsed ; but there was a further effect. Great Britain, with the assent of France and Russia, converted the occupation of Cyprus into annexation, and the occupation of Egypt—where the khedive threw in his lot with his Turkish suzerain—into a formal protectorate.

Moreover, it gave the British warrant for a counter-attack upon the Turkish flank in Mesopotamia, which offered a field of action for the Indian army better than the Belgian front, and for the bold design of seizing the Dardanelles. Granting the possibility of success, the advantages of this scheme were obvious. The capture of the Dardanelles and the fall of Constantinople would inevitably have placed the whole of the Balkan peoples at the disposal of the Allies, bringing Italy also in on their side, and Russia would no longer have been isolated. Even in her isolation it appeared in the winter and the early spring that she was at least able to hold her own against the utmost efforts of the Central powers—though the appearance was illusory. If she were reinforced from

## HEADQUARTERS OF SECOND AUSTRALIAN DIVISION GUARDING THE SUEZ CANAL

Turkey's entry into the war on the side of Germany was the result of a scheme to divert the attention of the Allies to fresh frontiers and to lessen their concentration in Europe. Defence of the Egyptian frontier and the Suez Canal necessitated the speedy despatch of troops to the East. Among the contingents sent to this area of the war were Australian troops, who built the floating bridge over the canal that this photograph shows being opened to allow a vessel to pass.

*Photo, Australian Commonwealth*

### ALLIED NAVAL ATTACK ON THE DARDANELLES
This sketch, made by a naval officer during operations in the Dardanelles in March, 1915, shows the British battleships Queen Elizabeth, Lord Nelson, Agamemnon and Inflexible opening up a long-range bombardment in the general attack on the Narrows on the 18th. This attempt to force the Narrows ended in failure and heavy losses for the Allies ; the Inflexible suffering serious damage from collision with a floating mine.

the Balkans, there would be little chance for Hungary and Austria, and Germany would be involved in a desperate struggle for life on both fronts.

The Allies, under a mistaken impression of the German strength on the western front, had designed a great offensive there in the spring. Concentration upon this object forbade the diversion of troops to the eastern front. In February the navy, with no army in support, though aid from Greece was in contemplation, began its attack on the Dardanelles, cleared the entrance, and was then, in March, brought up short by the Narrows, which were under the concentrated fire of land batteries in every direction, as well as torpedoes from the shore, while the waters were sown with floating mines. French and British battleships were sunk, nothing was achieved, and in the coming weeks the Turks, under German leadership, were busily engaged in making their land defences impregnable.

The Mesopotamian expedition from India reached the head of the Persian Gulf in November, captured Basra and Kurna, inflicted a heavy defeat on the Turks at Shaiba in April, and did not continue its advance until June.

And, in the meanwhile, the Germans, who had learnt the futility of attempting, for the time at least, to challenge battles with British naval squadrons, inaugurated the submarine campaign ; while the British, on their part, replied by declaring a blockade of all German ports, affirming the largest rights of search and detaining all goods destined for Germany, whether contraband or not. As in the case of Napoleon's Berlin Decrees and the British Orders in Council, the Americans for the time resented the British more than the German action, because the one interfered immediately and effectively with their commerce, while the other did not take unmistakable effect until a later stage, in spite of the terrible object lesson given by the sinking of the passenger liner Lusitania in May, with more than a thousand non-combatants on board.

### Allied Offensives of 1915

DURING the winter and spring fighting was continuous from end to end of the western front—murderous, costly, futile. Multitudes of volunteers from home or from overseas were training in England to pile up new armies, and to take their place in the fighting line as soon as they were trained and equipped; while the Germans were perfecting the trench system which was to hold up any possible onslaught. Then at the end of March the Allies began what was proclaimed as their grand offensive.

But the grand offensive was local and inadequately co-ordinated. The British began in the north with a thrust towards Lille at Neuve Chapelle, preceded by an intensive bombardment; it carried some three miles of front about a mile forward, with casualties on both sides—probably about equal—estimated as exceeding 25,000. The French made some progress in the south on both sides of the German salient at St. Mihiel between Verdun and Nancy; but, in fact, they hardly shook the German line, and in April the Germans retorted with an attack on Ypres, where they effected a temporary breach in the Franco-British line by the use of poison gas, which had been unanimously repudiated as a permissible instrument of war at the Hague Conference. The breach, however, was made good, before the Germans could thrust through, by the newly arrived Canadians, and Ypres was held, though the defensive line was shortened. In May the French a little farther south hurled themselves against the Vimy ridge, and made an advance more considerable than that of the British at Neuve Chapelle; but the ridge proved impregnable.

### The Dardanelles Campaign

THE futility of a purely naval attack on the Dardanelles had been demonstrated in March; at the end of April England began her military effort, though by this time the land defences had been scientifically strengthened. The real marvel of that glorious disaster was not that it failed, but that it so very nearly succeeded. The forces sent to Gallipoli were outnumbered by the defence, which was very thoroughly equipped, held all the commanding positions and was under very able conduct. The British troops detailed for the task were very largely the battalions of volunteers from Australia and New Zealand that had been detained in Egypt until it was clear that the Turkish menace to the Suez Canal was not likely to prove serious. Like the Canadians on the western front, the 'Anzacs,' as they were called, displayed magnificent qualities of dash and endurance, and it was precisely the quality of the troops which brought them within an ace of achieving the miracle.

### THE VILLAGE OF NEUVE CHAPELLE AFTER THE BATTLE

The 'grand offensive' planned by the Allies in March, 1915, began with Sir John French's determined attack on Neuve Chapelle, a village north of La Bassée, which had been in German hands since 1914. The British bombardment began on March 10, and, although the casualties were heavy, Neuve Chapelle was captured the same day. The battle wore on, without further ground being gained, until March 12. This photograph conveys some idea of the effect of the British artillery.

*Photo, Central News*

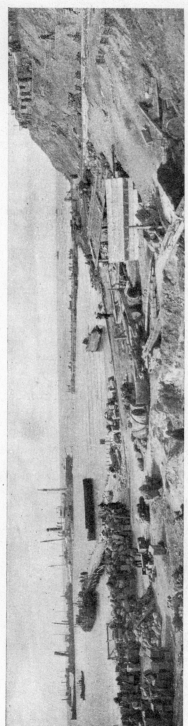

**SUVLA BAY, GALLIPOLI : SCENE OF A GREAT ALLIED ATTACK THAT FAILED**

During the Gallipoli operations, in August, 1915, a British force landed unexpectedly at Suvla Bay, with the object of gaining control of the central heights of the peninsula. The advantage gained by the surprise element of the attack was lost by ensuing delay in advance and the Turks had time to consolidate before an assault in force was made on their positions. Substantially the project was a failure for the Allied arms.

*Photo, Imperial War Museum*

A landing successfully effected at five different points, and four days of hard fighting, put the British in possession of a very precarious foothold on the extreme tip of the Gallipoli peninsula. For six weeks bombardment of the Turkish trenches, impetuous assaults that won positions impossible to retain, and counter-bombardments of the much more exposed positions actually held, continued ; while submarines took their toll among the covering battleships and, in effect, imposed their withdrawal. The assaults were repeated at intervals until the end of July, still without substantial progress towards the objective.

But a bigger effort was at hand ; reinforcements were at last arriving. On August 7, while three attacks on the usual points were engaging the attention of the Turks, a force had been landed at a new and wholly unexpected point farther north, Suvla Bay, on the comparatively unguarded side of the Turkish defences. But the attack did not develop until the 9th, when it had lost the invaluable element of surprise, and it was held up. Fresh and more experienced troops were added, and the attack was renewed on the 21st. It was too late ; the defences had been thoroughly organized, and, though a substantial amount of ground was secured, the last chance of carrying the peninsula had gone for good and all.

### Entry of Italy into the War

BOTH sides had been doing their best to draw Italy, Bulgaria, Rumania and Greece into the struggle. Italy was the first to depart from her neutrality. The temptations offered by Austria were not sufficiently strong ; there was a chance of getting the whole of ' Italia irredenta ' by alliance with the Allies, none by alliance with the Central powers, who were making to Bulgaria offers incompatible with Italian ambitions. The Entente was more sympathetic to the historical claims of Italy on the east of the Adriatic. At the end of April Italy made her treaty with the Allies, and in May declared war upon Austria. But it was to war with Austria on the Italian front that the whole of her attention was devoted ; which mattered

**THE COLLIER RIVER CLYDE BEACHED AT GALLIPOLI**

The naval attempt to force the Dardanelles having failed, the Allies sought to effect their object by capturing the Gallipoli peninsula, which forms the northern shore of the strait. The British steamer River Clyde, converted into a troop ship, was used in the famous landing at Beach V on April 25, 1915. Disembarkation was effected after nightfall and the Turkish positions stormed the next day. In the centre of the photograph may be seen the explosion of a Turkish shell.

*Photo, Imperial War Museum*

the less to Austria, because the Russian menace to her in the east was being dissipated by her German ally, and her Italian frontier was virtually impregnable, though her most advanced lines were driven in.

Neither Bulgaria nor Rumania intended to move till they saw something like a certainty of profit to themselves from their intervention ; while as yet they could be sure of nothing more than that Bulgaria would not get much out of the success of the Allies or Rumania from the success of the Central powers. The mind of Greece was painfully divided, since her leading statesman, Venizelos, was quite definitely on the side of the Allies, while her king, Constantine, primarily anxious to keep outside the quarrel, was alternatively

**A QUIET MOMENT AT ANZAC COVE, GALLIPOLI**

The term 'Anzac' popularly applied to troops from Australia and New Zealand was adopted for official use by the War Office in 1916. It is derived from the initial letters of the words Australian (and) New Zealand Army Corps. This cove north of Gaba Tepe, Gallipoli, was christened 'Anzac' by the troops who landed in April, 1915—the first occasion on which the use of the name is recorded.

*Photo, Imperial War Museum*

disposed in favour of the Central powers, all the more because Venizelos was endeavouring to coerce him. The Bulgarian and Greek crises arrived in October.

Success then had not attended the Allied offensive in any quarter except the head of the Persian Gulf, where its initial aims were not ambitious but were intended mainly to give security to the Persian Gulf itself and to worry the Turks by a threat to Bagdad. In June it had pushed up the Tigris to Amara. In August its advance troops occupied Kut. Without heavy reinforcement it was insufficient to undertake more than the holding of what had been won, but it was tempted to an effort to rush Bagdad. But the forces covering Bagdad at Ctesiphon made the odds so heavy that the attack had to be abandoned, and the troops were back at the beginning of December in Kut, where they were presently isolated by floods.

Iᴛ was far otherwise, however, with the concentration of the German offensive upon the Russian left flank. At the end of April, when a Russian offensive through the Carpathians was generally expected, Mackensen's hurricane burst upon Galicia with an artillery storm such that the Russians were wholly unable to meet it. They were rolled back staggering, but fighting hard, from the Dunajetz, over the San, out of Przemysl, out of Lemberg, which fell on June 22. That was far enough for the time. Meanwhile another army had been thrusting on the northern flank and the Russian line covering Warsaw had become an extended salient again. Mackensen turned his attack against its southern side, the second German army attacked the northern, and the Austrians in the centre pressed on the salient's apex.

The Russians were forced to fall back upon Warsaw, only holding the line until the city could be evacuated (August 4); then, behind it, fighting desperately as the shortened line straightened up. The weakened right, however, was now more seriously menaced than it had been by even the heaviest of Hindenburg's onslaughts. The fall of Kovno in the middle of August

**KUT PERILOUSLY ENVELOPED IN A BEND OF THE TREACHEROUS TIGRIS**
The geographical position of Kut, situated in a U-shaped bend of the Tigris, renders it liable to flooding and consequent isolation. This fate befell the British troops under Townshend in December, 1915, when the Turks invested the town. After a valiant defence, Townshend surrendered Kut in April, 1916, but operations were begun for its recapture in December of the same year. In February, 1917, Kut came again into the possession of the British, who reconstructed it after the war.
*Photo, Royal Air Force, Crown copyright*

After the Russian evacuation of Warsaw in August, 1915, the German troops, commanded by Prince Leopold of Bavaria, entered the Polish capital in triumph. This spectacular view represents the prince outside Warsaw's Russian church watching his regiments march past. The retreating Russians blew up the three bridges over the Vistula as they went.

The Russians laid siege to Przemysl, a Galician fortress city, in September, 1914, and in December of the same year Hindenburg began operations for its relief. The city surrendered to the Russians in March, 1915, but they were unable to hold it long, for a successful Austro-German campaign in Galicia enabled Mackensen to advance on Przemysl in May and to accomplish its recapture in June. The Austro-German troops are here seen entering the town.

REVERSES OF RUSSIAN FORTUNE IN POLAND AND GALICIA

**FLUCTUATING FORTUNES OF WAR UPON THE EASTERN FRONT**

It should be noted that the lines on this map of the operations in the eastern area do not in most instances represent continuous battle fronts. For one thing, the trench system was never so highly developed as in the west; for another, they are intended to show limits of advance or retreat that were not necessarily contemporaneous. For instance, the advance of the Russians in East Prussia in 1914 had been broken at Tannenberg before their maximum advance in Galicia was attained.

was followed by that of Brest Litovsk at the centre before the end of the month, and touch between the northern and southern Russian lines was severed by the Pripet marshes. By this time, however, the fury of the storm was abating, partly owing to the distance of the advance from the base, and the Russians in September were able to keep their hold on Vilna and the railway to Petrograd, and partly though not wholly on the rail from Vilna south to Rovno.

The defeat of the Russians cleared the way for the Central powers to carry out their programme in the Balkan peninsula. They had satisfied Ferdinand of Bulgaria that they were the winning side, and in October he mobilised against Serbia. A few French and British troops occupied Salonica at the invitation of Venizelos, who was determined to carry out Greece's treaty obligation to go to the help of Serbia if she were attacked by Bulgaria. But King Constantine dismissed the minister and repudiated the obligation. The Allied force at Salonica was too small to render effective aid, and Serbia, attacked on all si les, suffered her martyrdom, her people fleeing, while her armies fought a series of desperate rearguard actions to cover the retreat, to the coast and across the Adriatic ; and Bulgars, Austrians and Germans overwhelmed them. And before the year was over the British accepted their defeat on the Dardanelles, and effected without loss the evacuation of the Gallipoli peninsula— a feat of skill difficult if not impossible to parallel.

### The Battles round Verdun

THE Allied offensive, if it should still be so called, on the western front continued in the autumn and early winter on the same unproductive lines on the British front and in Artois and Champagne. That is to say, there were

**LAST ACT OF THE DARDANELLES TRAGEDY**

The terrible if magnificent blunder of the Gallipoli campaign ended with a brilliant military operation when the peninsula was evacuated gradually throughout December, 1915, without the knowledge of the Turks. This photograph shows preparations for firing stores with straw and petrol, which were set off by time fuses after the last man had embarked on January 9.

*Photo, Imperial War Museum*

fierce local attacks by which a few square miles distinguishable only on large-scale maps were left in occupation of the Allies instead of the Germans, and minor local attacks in which the losses and gains were balanced ; while the casualties, also probably balanced, were very heavy on both sides. But the Germans had concentrated on their eastern offensive, which had carried them to the limits of their possible advance against Russia, having ever in mind the warning of Napoleon's disastrous advance to Moscow ; they had established their own and their allies' predominance in the Balkan peninsula, though they had not yet won over Greece and Rumania, which were both still sitting on the fence ; and they could afford to concentrate again on the west. The feature of the first half of 1916 was the western offensive of the Central powers ; that of the second half was the Allies' counter-offensive.

While on the defensive, the Germans had virtually limited their expenditure of men and munitions to holding their

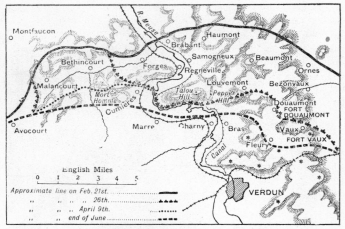

**THE GERMAN ATTACK ON VERDUN**

The German assault on Verdun during the first half of 1916 was divided into three main attacks, beginning on February 21, March 2 (with a subsidiary one on April 9) and May 3; all resulted in German advances, as shown in this simplified map, all failed in their ultimate object, and the last ended in a French recovery of ground.

comparatively large one, able to take over a longer section of the line than before, though it was only now that voluntary enlistment was superseded in Great Britain itself, though still not in the Dominions, by conscription.

The German grand attack was on Verdun, the salient thrusting out into the German line in the south ; threatening movements against the French at other points and against the British were also made, but these were primarily to prevent reinforcement at Verdun, since it was imperative for the Allies to prevent a German thrust to the coast, to Calais and Boulogne. The object of the northern demonstration was to mask the main attack, which burst on February 21.

Verdun, with its own fortifications, stood at the centre of a defensive arc having a

lines, so that in spite of the enormous demands on the Russian front they were able to accumulate both for the coming onslaught in the west. On the other hand, the Allies had greatly increased their own production of war materials, and the small British army had grown into a

**FORT VAUX TWO YEARS AFTER THE CESSATION OF HOSTILITIES**

What Ypres is to British sentiment Verdun is to French ; at few points on the western front was the fighting more bitter, the combined French and German losses there in 1916 being estimated at nearly 700,000. Most of the German advance was achieved in the first attack, which drove in the outer French defences to a line running from Vaux fort on the east to the Mort Homme ridge on the west. On the extreme French left the line in front of Béthincourt and Malancourt still held.

*Photo, Imperial War Museum*

radius of nine or ten miles—about one-third of a circle—facing north, the line continuing southward at each end. Between the outer circle and Verdun were two more lines of defence. If those lines were carried, so that the siege guns could be brought within effective range, Verdun would become untenable, and the moral effect of its fall would be tremendous, though it might not sever the French eastern and western forces.

The German attack drove in the centre of the outermost and weakest line on the first day, and the rest of the line had to fall back in conformity. On the centre and right the French continued to be

and gave them the actual fort of Douaumont, of which they remained for the most part in possession, but not, as they had imagined, the command of the ridge, which remained perpetually contested; while they had only flattened the centre without bulging it, and the shortened line was rather stronger than the longer one. Also, French reinforcements were more than filling the gaps.

The first great thrust had failed, after all. On March 2 began the second great thrust, this time against the French left, in the direction of Mort Homme. For a week the Germans were gaining ground; then the battle on the left was supple-

MEMORIAL TO FRENCH HEROISM ON THE SUMMIT OF MORT HOMME RIDGE

After the first attack on the Verdun sector the Germans only made material progress on the two flanks of the flattened Verdun salient; Vaux fort fell on June 6, and the Mort Homme ridge, after changing hands several times in May, was left with the attackers established precariously on it. Here was the most desperate fighting of the whole engagement, and in 1919 the memorial seen above was erected; but the terrain, as at Vaux fort, was left otherwise untouched.

*Photo, Imperial War Museum*

pushed back until they lay on the line from Vaux and Douaumont on the east, through Pepper Hill and Talou Hill in the centre, to Malancourt and Béthincourt on the west, as the result of four days' desperate fighting. Then Talou Hill had to be abandoned, and on February 25 the Germans launched the assault that was to shatter the defence. At nightfall they believed themselves to have achieved their object; next day they discovered their mistake. They had attacked the centre and right. In the centre they had carried Louvemont, but failed at Pepper Hill. On the French right they had concentrated great forces that carried them to the top of the Douaumont ridge

mented by an attempt to turn Douaumont ridge on the right; which failed, however, though they were getting nearer to Mort Homme, on which they gained a footing on March 14. By the end of the month they had almost, but not quite, turned its left. Another heavy attack along the left and left centre began on April 9, and developed into a three days' battle, at the end of which Mort Homme and Pepper Hill and the line between them still held, though here again the fray had rocked furiously forwards and backwards.

The struggle had been frightfully exhausting and costly for both sides, and there was a lull for three weeks. The storm burst again on the left on May 3,

**AUSTRIANS ON THE ITALIAN FRONT**

The early fighting on the Italian front saw slight Italian successes; but in May, 1916, the Austrians developed a successful offensive. These are troops of the Austrian Alpine Corps scaling a hill during the first Italian offensive on the Isonzo.

*Photo, Photo Press*

accompanied by another attempt upon Douaumont ridge. The Germans were bent on achieving their object this time, whatever the cost. By the end of the month they forced the French back to a straight line from Avocourt to the left bank of the Meuse, while on the right they had carried Douaumont, lost it, and carried it again, threatening Vaux, which held out till June 6. But they could get no farther. There was a pause for nearly a week, and then, though it was the Germans who renewed the attack, it was the French who recovered ground. And at the moment when the attack on Verdun was exhausted the British, on July 1, opened their offensive on the Somme.

It was at the end of May that the German fleet broke its inaction and put to sea to meet the British fleet in what was the only serious naval engagement during the whole course of the war—the battle of Jutland. Though it was a strategical defeat for the Germans, it may not unfairly be described as a tactical victory; for the German battle fleet escaped, having inflicted more dam-

age than it had suffered. But no portion of it issued from its ports again till the war was over. From the day of the battle of Jutland it was out of action—action, for the German navy, was confined to the submarine campaign.

While the Germans were carrying out their offensive against French and British the Austrians were conducting their own counter-offensive against Italy, which was not as yet technically at war with Germany; practically the entry of Italy into the war was a resuscitation of her immemorial feud with the Hapsburg power. Austria might well have contented herself with holding her own frontier, which was of immense strategic strength; but the temptation to penalise Italy was too strong for her, and the threat might induce some dispersion of French and British forces for the defence of their Italian ally, which would be convenient for her own German ally. So in May she developed an attack through the Trentino, directed towards Venice.

The advance began successfully enough, turning the flank of the Italian offensive on the Isonzo line, which was directed against Trieste. But at the end of a month the advance was checked by Italian reinforcements, and by a sudden advance of the Russians in the east. The defence of Galicia was much more important than a spectacular advance in Italy, and by the end of June the Austrians were falling back. That offensive, too, had failed.

### Renewed Activity of the Russians

ELSEWHERE the British had met with a reverse in Mesopotamia, where the Turks had been under German command since Ctesiphon. The advance force at Kut had been isolated, the attempts to relieve it were baulked by the Tigris floods, and it was forced to surrender at the end of April. On the other hand the Russians, though reduced to inaction in Europe, had conducted a very successful winter campaign in the Caucasus, whither the grand-duke Nicholas had been transferred from the chief command of the armies in Europe. Erzerum was captured in February, though it was not till April that the same fate befell Trebizond.

It was not the fault of the Russian troops or the Russian generals that they had been driven back to the last defensive lines in 1915. For that the ineptitude—or worse —of the Russian bureaucracy was responsible ; and the great Allied offensive of 1916 was opened not by the British on the Somme, but by the Russians in Galicia.

The Russians, after being swept back to the line running north and south from Vilna to Rovno, had held up the further attacks aimed at Riga in the north, while Mackensen had been withdrawn in the south to deal with Serbia. Later they had made tentative attacks at various points ; but it was at the beginning of June, when the Austrians were dissipating their forces in the Trentino adventure, that they opened a powerful offensive along their whole left front between the extremity of Galicia and the Pripet marshes ; the forces opposed to them being mainly Austrian, though in their right centre they were under a German commander, Bothmer.

For a fortnight from its beginning on June 3 the attack drove forward successfully, crumpling up the Austrian resistance, held up before Tarnopol by Bothmer, but turning his right and thrusting into Bukovina, the province marching with Rumania. In the next three weeks the Austrians were out of Bukovina, Bothmer

was finding it very difficult to cover Lemberg and Stanislau, and it appeared possible that from the north as well as the south of the Pripet marshes Russian armies might converge upon Brest Litovsk, while their left was sweeping through Galicia again. On the other hand, German troops—and commanders—had arrived and were still arriving at top speed from Verdun, and Austrians from the Trentino (where the Italians were rapidly recovering the ground previously lost).

The pressure was checked, not stopped. Concentrating on the Galician wing, the Russian advance on Bothmer's left and right in July compelled him to fall back, and early in August Stanislau was taken ; but by the end of the month Bothmer was able to hold his ground, though in the two following months the Russians seemed about to penetrate the Carpathians.

THE Russian successes ended Rumania's hesitation and brought her into the war in August—quite obviously for the purpose of joining to herself Transylvania, where the Magyars ruled over a mainly Rumanian population. As a matter of course, the Rumanian armies made Transylvania their objective, and swept triumphantly through the Carpathian passes on their frontier. But the result was unfortunate for the Allies and disastrous to

**SOLDIERS OF THE ITALIAN ARMY ADVANCING THROUGH ALPINE SNOWS**

The Austrian advance in Italy was a short-lived success ; for under a vigorous counter-stroke by General Cadorna, in June, 1916, and alarmed by the renewed Russian activity in Galicia, they retreated, not without loss, to the old frontier lines. Italy's entry into the war on the side of the Allies (May 23, 1915) had been strongly influenced by the consideration that only from their victory did she have a chance of obtaining the ' Italia irredenta ' under Austrian rule.

*Photo Imperial War Museum*

themselves. Russia, not without excuse, failed to give the support expected from her; and the Rumanians as they swung forward found themselves exposed to a German counter-offensive, the Germans having promptly taken the matter into their own hands on the top of the battle of the Somme and the defence of Galicia. In September Mackensen was invading the Dobruja and Falkenhayn was driving back through the Carpathian passes without any movement on his flank from the Russians. Even so it was not till November that the Rumanian resistance in Wallachia was broken and Bukarest fell on December 5. All that was left to her was the northern province of Moldavia.

### The First Battle of the Somme

$\mathfrak{I}$T was well for the Germans that the long struggle before Verdun had so exhausted the French for the time that their share in the Allied offensive in the west was less than it would otherwise have been; since masses of German troops and munitions were perforce withdrawn from the west to counter the Russian and then the Rumanian offensives in the east. The

result showed what warrant there had been for their confidence in the strength of their own lines in the west.

The growing British armies had been able to take over from the French a great part of the line on their own right, which now extended almost to the north bank of the Somme between Amiens and Péronne, considerably to the south of the previous offensive of 1915. It was here on a front running some dozen miles north of the river (British) and a like distance south of it (French) that the battle of the Somme opened on July 1, carrying that line forward during the following months to a depth of about seven miles. The German trenches were constructed in series far away to their rear, running deep underground, so that even when a trench line had been shelled and carried, it had itself been rendered almost untenable for the victors while the line behind was intact.

Without very large maps it is impossible to follow the details of the prolonged struggle at one point or another, the captures and recaptures, advances, retreats and recoveries; there was never anything like a break through, though that was what

**FIELD-MARSHAL VON MACKENSEN ENTERS BUKAREST IN TRIUMPH**

The Rumanian decision to espouse the Allied cause was based on hostility to the Hungarians who ruled over a large Rumanian population in Transylvania; while the temporary Russian successes of June–August, 1916, seemed to indicate the moment for intervention. After successfully piercing the Carpathians, however, the Rumanian army found itself fronted by Germans under Mackensen; and the autumn saw a complete débâcle that only ended with the fall of Bukarest in December.

*Photo, Imperial War Museum*

A feature of the Somme offensive was the tremendous artillery bombardment that preceded it, lasting for seven days. Yet it is acknowledged that the artillery preparations were insufficient : shells began to run short before three weeks, and there was a lack of heavy guns for counter-battery work. This is the 39th siege battery of 8-in. howitzers between Fricourt and Mametz in August.

The German Verdun offensive had forestalled a great Allied push designed for the summer of 1916 ; in order to relieve the French the latter was started early (July 1) before preparations were quite complete. The front stretched from Gommecourt in the north to Soyecourt, the French under Fayolle being responsible for the sector from Hardecourt southwards ; the whole operation is known as the first battle of the Somme. Supports are here moving up near Ginchy, September 25.

**SCENES NEAR THE FRONT DURING THE BATTLE OF THE SOMME**

*Photos, Imperial War Museum*

WHAT AN ATTACK DURING THE GREAT ARTILLERY BATTLES LOOKED LIKE : THE ADVANCE ON MAMETZ

The real innovation of the Somme battle was not the long preliminary bombardment, for that had been employed in 1915, but the creeping barrage, first introduced on a small scale by the French at Verdun. The infantry went forward behind an advancing wall of shells ; and under these conditions it is not in the initial stages that the heaviest losses occur, the attack offering the unspectacular sight of a line of men proceeding, over torn ground at a slow pace owing to weight of equipment. This photograph of the assault on Mametz on July 1 was taken just after the barrage lifted.

*Photo, Imperial War Museum*

**CONSTANTINE, KING OF GREECE**

In 1913 Constantine (1868–1923) became king of the Hellenes. His policy of maintaining Grecian neutrality in the Great War finally caused his deposition in 1917. Restored to the throne in 1920, he abdicated in 1922.

*Photo, Russell & Sons*

Galicia, gave no help to Rumania, though they were progressing in Asia Minor, and made no diversion for the benefit of the Allied offensive in the Balkans from the Salonica base ; for which things the responsibility lay not with the generals but with the political system. Austria was disintegrating, and the disintegration was hastened by the death of the aged emperor, Francis Joseph. Arabia was in revolt against Turkey and had declared its independence. In the Balkans the French, with the valiant remnant of the Serbian army, captured Monastir, but real progress was postponed for a long time, because Greece was divided against herself ; and if the war party was the more popular, King Constantine retained control of the government and was apparently doing his best to play into the hands of the Central powers, while at Salonica the Venizelists set up a provisional government for themselves. And the German submarine campaign was developing steadily.

the uninstructed public across the Channel were looking for, whatever the actual anticipations of the commanders on the spot may have been. The most marked successes attended the fighting in September, when the British for the first time brought ' tanks ' into play. It is probable, however, that the line that had been reached by the British and the French on their right by the end of November was short of what it had been hoped to attain in the first week of the Somme battle. Whether it had cost the Allies or the Germans the more in serious casualties is a highly disputable question. Meanwhile the Italians were making progress on the Isonzo front, having captured Gorizia in August ; but Rumania was being broken, and her conquered territories gave the Germans control of invaluable oil fields. The Russians had latterly made little advance in

**FRANCIS JOSEPH I, EMPEROR OF AUSTRIA**

After a long and tragic reign Francis Joseph I, who ascended the Austrian imperial throne in 1848, died on November 21, 1916. His very real endeavour to rule his heterogeneous empire had done much to retard its disintegration. He was succeeded by his grand-nephew Archduke Charles.

*After the painting by L. Horowitz*

## PERONNE WRECKED BY THE RETIRING GERMANS IN 1917

Throughout 1917 the initiative on the western front lay mainly with the Allies, who in the opening of the year began offensive operations with the old Somme front as the centre. Before them the Germans retreated methodically to the Hindenburg lines; Péronne beneath Mont St. Quentin fell to the British on March 18, but before evacuation the Germans wrecked it by fire and explosive.

## ENTRY OF THE U.S.A.: BRITISH AND AMERICANS FRATERNISE

The deciding factor in the war was the entry of the Americans (April, 1917); for without them, whichever side eventually won, the final issue must have been delayed for many bitter months, perhaps years. Their first troops arrived in France under General Pershing in June of the same year and started an intensive training behind the lines. This photograph shows American and British officers meeting for the first time. By July of the following year a million troops had arrived.

*Photos, Imperial War Museum*

On the face of things, then, at the close of 1916, the presumptions pointed to a stale-mate, though it was easy for each side to persuade itself that the presumptions were in its own favour, since neither could fully gauge its own capacity for endurance, still less that of the other. If either side won, it would be the one which could hold out longest. Each wished to end the war, but only on its own terms, which meant that the other side must definitely acknowledge itself the defeated party and original aggressor. The Germans invited the friendly interposition of the United States to negotiate a peace ; the Allies responded to the first overtures with a definite declaration of their own minimum requirements ; the German government implicitly repudiated the American president's own demands in respect of the submarine campaign ; the president finally came to the conclusion that Germany's ambitions were an intolerable menace to world progress, and that the cause of world progress demanded the armed intervention of America. In April the United States declared war on Germany (see pages 4733–34).

The American declaration of war and the Russian revolution were the two events of the spring of 1917 which wrought fundamental changes in the situation. The one meant that the Germans, if they were not to be beaten, must have the Allies decisively beaten before the American armies were ready to take the field in strength. The other, not at first so obviously, meant that Russia would cease to count. When Russia was off the board, Germany made her supreme effort in the spring of 1918, and when that effort reached its culmination the new armies from America were already taking their place in the fighting line.

### Allied Offensives of 1917

WHEN 1917 opened, however, the Allies were confident that they could win, and the Germans were confident that they could at any rate hold what they had already won, though on a slightly modified line more impregnable than that of which they were still in occupation. The British and French pressure began again in January along a front constantly extending both northwards and southwards, the Germans retreating gradually before it to the newly prepared line, since they had no intention of renewing a struggle for the devastated Somme battlefields ; but it

### VIMY RIDGE : PRIZE OF THE SECOND BATTLE OF ARRAS

When the Hindenburg lines proved impregnable the Allies endeavoured to outflank them by simultaneous attacks north and south. Both attempts failed in their ultimate object ; but while the French under Nivelle were repulsed before the Chemin des Dames, the British made substantial advances in the second battle of Arras (April), capturing the immensely important Vimy Ridge and entrenching in the plain beneath. These Canadians are digging reserve trenches on the ridge itself.

*Photo, Imperial War Museum*

**GENERAL MAUDE**

Sir Frederick Stanley Maude (1864–1917) was in command of the 13th Division in Gallipoli, Egypt and Mesopotamia in 1915. In 1916 he was appointed to the chief command in the Kut area, and entered Bagdad in March, 1917.

*Photo, Swaine*

was an organized, if reluctant, retreat in which they fought for every inch of ground, but no longer than was necessary to prevent the retirement from being inconveniently hustled. The stolid repetition of the announcement after each withdrawal that it had been successfully executed ' according to plan ' had more than an element of truth in it, though it excited the sarcastic comments of the Allied press. And the mangled territory they left behind them was itself a protection to that section of their front; which enabled them to concentrate forces upon the wings where the main struggle was bound to take place.

In March, then, the Somme advance at the centre, where the French and British armies joined, was pushed almost up to St. Quentin, running north to the southern point of the old 1915 sector in front of Arras and facing the Vimy ridge, and southward to the north-east of Soissons. On April 9, four days after the American declaration of war, the British began the second battle of Arras. In two days the Vimy ridge had been

captured, and within the week the line south of it had been carried forward four or five miles so as to threaten the flank of the new ' Hindenburg ' lines. But Nivelle's attack at the southern extremity on the Chemin des Dames was not equally successful ; ground was won, but the Germans were not driven out, and the general effect of the second battle of the Aisne on the French was as depressing as that of Arras was encouraging to the British.

In the ' side-shows,' however, in Africa and Asia, which were mainly the concern of the British Empire on the one side and of Germany and Turkey on the other, the British were winning in every quarter. The South African Union and troops from India had at last cleared the Germans out of German East Africa, and their forces were now being added to the other Dominion troops in Europe. In the Mesopotamian area the new commander, General Maude, by a series of skilful operations, cleared the Turks from Kut in February and occupied Bagdad in March. The Turkish troops escaped from the trap in which they had almost been caught, but by the end of April, when climatic conditions suspended campaigning, Bagdad was eighty miles behind the British front. An offensive from Egypt had been hitherto ˙ prevented by the disturbances among the desert tribes ; but these had now been quelled, and an advance on Palestine had opened.

### Final Collapse of Russia

**B**UT the collapse of Russia was the factor for which the change of front in America was the much-needed compensation. In its initial stage the revolution looked as if it was likely to prove very much to the advantage of the Allies, since it seemed to be only the victory of the Russian constitutionalists over the poisonously corrupt bureaucracy, which was more than suspected of treason to the Allied cause. But the control of it rapidly slipped out of the hands of the constitutionalists into those of the socialist moderates, and from them to a fanatic of genius, Lenin, and his colleagues, the champions of a movement begotten and born of anti-Semite pogroms and the 'nihilism' that had first been created and then apparently crushed by the unspeakable tyrannies of the bureaucratic regime, having as its aim the total subversion of the existing social and political order, not only in Russia, but everywhere ; something much more destructive than had been dreamed of by the most reckless of the French revolutionaries at the end of the eighteenth century.

At the beginning of March there were disturbances in the capital ; troops there mutinied, and some of them shot their officers. The Duma—what passed for a parliament—set up a provisional government, of which the socialist moderate Kerensky became the leader, and on March 15 the tsar abdicated. But the effective power was in the hands of the council of delegates called the Soviet, in which the extremists, who were known first as Maximalists and then as Bolsheviks, very soon predominated. In May the provisional government, which was still acting under the leadership of Kerensky, was reconstructed on a more extreme basis. In the meantime Kerensky used every possible effort to revive patriotic zeal in the conduct of the war, but the multiplying soviets organized by the extremists were zealous only for the social revolution which they had been preaching among the soldiery, whose discipline had gone to pieces.

With the most trustworthy of the troops Brussilov, at the beginning of July, opened a desperate offensive towards Lemberg, winning at first astonishing successes, reminiscent of the French revolutionary armies at the end of 1792. But he had no reserves ; when the Germans delivered the inevitable counter-offensive on the 19th half the Russian troops refused to fight and fled in complete rout.

The last chance of a successful stand was gone. Lenin in Petrograd had raised an insurrection and the government was tottering. In August the Rumanians, deserted by the Russian government and the Russian troops, made a heroic stand against the onslaught of Mackensen which gave the shattered south Russian armies breathing space but did not prevent the Germans in the north from advancing upon Riga, though they were as anxious as Lenin himself to end the war on the eastern front and leave the Russian revolution to pursue its disintegrating and destructive career. In November Kerensky's government collapsed altogether, and the only government left was that of the Bolsheviks headed by Lenin and Trotsky, whose first aim was to negotiate the withdrawal of Russia from the war.

### British Offensives in Flanders

IN the west, the scheme of the great Allied 'push' all along the line broke down with Nivelle's failure to carry and hold the Chemin des Dames in April. The further efforts of the French and British were not concerted. Progress

**NICHOLAS II AND BRUSSILOV**

The Russian tsar Nicholas II (left) was compelled by the revolution to abdicate on March 15, 1917. Under General Brussilov, here seen beside the tsar, the Russian troops met first with some success, but finally with failure.

*Photo, Central News*

1C*

**MARSHAL PETAIN**

Born at Cauchy-à-la-Tour in 1856, Henry Philippe Pétain held a succession of distinguished commands in the French army, 1914–18. In March, 1918, he became commander-in-chief of all the French armies.

*Photo, E.N.A.*

German control of the Belgian coast—the base of that submarine campaign which was the one effective offensive weapon of the Germans against Great Britain, the islands being so greatly dependent upon food supplies from overseas. For the air raids, though exasperating, did no great amount of military damage.

Hence the month of June witnessed the most resounding and nearly the most spectacular stroke of the war. On the way towards Ypres lay the Messines ridge ; it had been the stage of much hard fighting which, as at Vimy until the Canadians stormed it, had failed to dislodge the Germans. Subterranean engineering operations had been in progress undetected for some time past. The whole of the surface defences were subjected to a terrific bombardment during the first week of the month, and on the 7th the simultaneous explosion of nineteen mines blew what was left to pieces in one vast eruption. The practical effect was to force on the Germans a retirement which left Ypres a salient no longer. But the success was not followed up for some weeks, during which the new German line was consolidated, with the advantages accruing from the shortening of it. No more effective advance was attempted

at the centre against the Hindenburg line offered less promise than a northward extension of the British advance before Arras, with a view to diminishing the

**SPOIL OF WAR ON THE CAPTURED WYTSCHAETE RIDGE**

The operations known as the battle of Messines were a continuation of the British 1917 offensives, but directed rather to the coast than to the outflanking of the Hindenburg line. They involved the Messines ridge itself, where the attack was opened by the explosion of nineteen enormous mines (June 7), and, in addition, the Wytschaete ridge, its extension dominating the Ypres salient. Both were captured ; and this is a German field gun being hauled off near Wytschaete on June 10.

*Photo, Imperial War Museum*

till the end of July, when, simultaneously, the weather broke and the Flanders flats were converted into an ocean of mud on which movement was almost impossible.

The British armies got no nearer to the Belgian coast. Still, however, they hammered on in Flanders, despite the adverse conditions, checked here and gaining some ground there, with little enough to show. In November there were some brilliant days when, without the warning of artillery preparation, an attack was launched by their right against Cambrai, where the Germans were taken by surprise. If the British success had been complete another withdrawal would have been imposed on them ; but just in time masses of reinforcements were rushed up from elsewhere, the attack was held up, being inadequately supported, before its objective was reached, and in the end the ground that had to be abandoned was more than what was won.

The French autumn campaign, Nivelle's place having been taken by Pétain, was not ruined like that in Flanders by climatic conditions, was less ambitious in its scope, less critical from the German point of view, and proportionately more successful in its achievement, and it did much to restore French confidence. Most of the ground won by the Germans in the attack on Verdun was recovered during August, and in October they were at last forced definitely to abandon the Chemin des Dames.

𝕵N the east, King Constantine's pretence of neutrality became so meagre that his authority could no longer be tolerated and the arrival of Allied warships in June forced him to abdicate in favour of his second son, who was a minor ; for practical purposes the government became a regency

**DRAMATIC SURRENDER OF JERUSALEM**
General Allenby entered Jerusalem on December 11, 1917, an event that resounded throughout the Christian and Mahomedan worlds. The town had surrendered two days earlier to a small British advanced post in command of a sergeant, the mayor (seen with walking stick) coming out under the white flag.
*Photo, Imperial War Museum*

under Venizelos. But the collapse of Russia paralysed the advance projected on the Salonica front, besides releasing masses of German and Austrian troops for recuperation or for reinforcement of the west, and of Turkish troops for resistance to the British advance in Mesopotamia and on Palestine.

In this last quarter, however, was achieved a triumph of military skill which also made an intense appeal to all western sentiment. The advance on Palestine from Egypt had begun prematurely and with insufficient forces in the spring, when it was held up before Gaza. It was not till the end of October that Allenby suddenly opened his offensive. In the first week of November he had turned both flanks of the fortress and entered it. On

December 11 he was in Jerusalem, over which the flag of Islam had flown since the day when it was captured by Saladin. Nor was the triumph any shock to the orthodox Moslems of Arabia, who had already repudiated both the spiritual and temporal supremacy of the unorthodox Ottoman.

Victories in Asia, however, could exercise little immediate influence on the war in the west, where the German high command was well aware that if Germany was to win the war the thing must be done before the arrival in force of the Americans, and Ludendorff was preparing to win it. Probably it was with the primary purpose of compelling the diversion of French and British troops to Italy that in October the Germans struck hard on the Italian front, where hitherto they had not shown themselves.

SINCE the summer of 1916 the Austrians, absorbed at first by the great Russian offensive, and then in part by threatening disintegration within the empire, had contented themselves with maintaining their own frontiers, while the Italians

**GENERAL LUDENDORFF**

Erich von Ludendorff, born in 1865, shared supreme command of the German army with Hindenburg in 1916, and organized the extensive use of surprise attack and gas in 1917. He was dismissed in October, 1918.

*Photo, E.N.A.*

had concentrated all their energies on a single objective, the capture of Trieste. They had captured Gorizia and bitten their way a little closer, but still the impregnable bastions stood between them and the prize on which their hearts were set. They had accomplished brilliant feats of daring and skill, but the odds of position even more than of numbers were overwhelmingly against them. Also parts of the population—and, more ominously, of the army—were seething with disaffection, the fruits of the new Russian propaganda, and were ready to follow the example of the Bolshevised Russian soldiery which had wrought such havoc with Brussilov's last desperate offensive. Some of those disaffected troops were stationed about Caporetto at the centre of the Italian line—and the Germans had found it out.

It was at this point that they launched their surprise attack on October 24. The Italian centre was pulverised; only swift retreat screened by the most stubborn rearguard actions could save the wings

**GENERAL ALLENBY**

Edmund Henry Hynman, first Viscount Allenby, born in 1861, commanded the Egyptian expeditionary force in 1917-18 and directed the operations in Palestine that defeated the Turks. He became a field marshal in 1919.

*Photo, H. Walter Barnett*

from annihilation. They got across the Tagliamento, which rose behind them in a torrent, swollen by a fortunate break in the weather, and gave them some breathing space to reach the Piave, where they made their stand, covering the way to Venice. The German blow had done its work. Without extraneous support the Italians could not hope to hold out long against the Austrians, and British troops, which were soon to be badly wanted on the British front itself, as well as French, were dispatched to the Piave. They might hold out as long as they chose ; from the German point of view the important thing was that they should be bottled up in Italy, not fighting in France or Flanders. The Germans left the rest of the Italian campaign to the Austrians.

Russia was already off the board ; though her peace negotiations did not finally issue in the ignominious treaty of Brest Litovsk until the beginning of March, there was no need for the Central powers to retain large armies on the eastern front when Russian loyalist generals were struggling in vain to make head against the Bolshevik domination, and the main desire of the Bolsheviks themselves was to be free from the German imbroglio.

As the winter advanced to the spring of 1918 it became quite certain that Germany was preparing for the decisive effort. France believed with entire conviction that the storm would burst upon the French armies, and that the imperative necessity was the strengthening of the lines south of the Somme. The fact was palpable that all the Allied offensives had been robbed of effectiveness by the lack of that co-ordination of effort which characterised all the German movements, because all the German operations were directed as parts of a single plan controlled by a single command—just as in the wars between Napoleon and the coalitions. To counteract that disadvantage was an urgent need ; France had for some time been calling for a unified command under a French generalissimo. But it was even more essential that the generalissimo should be the right man, a man equal to the enormous task, a man in whom the British chiefs would have confidence—and that man had not yet been found.

When Ludendorff struck, the French and British views of the military situation were not in complete accord, and the British, though calling for reinforcements which did not come, were reluctantly lengthening southward and weakening

GUARDS BRIGADE RUSHED TO THE DEFENCE OF ARRAS, MARCH 26, 1918

Ludendorff's whole scheme of attack in 1918 is known as the second battle of the Somme, or as the battle of St. Quentin, from the sector where the first smashing blow was delivered on March 21. But the Arras-Vimy area was also involved in the assault, and here the defence held firm, largely owing to the heroism of the Guards in the third defence system before Arras. The Second Brigade is here seen moving up the Arras road by motor lorry.

*Photo, Imperial War Museum*

their line, in order to shorten and strengthen that of the French. Both the French and British commands were more anxious about the strength of their defences south-ward and northward re-spectively than about the centre on the Somme. This, however, was precisely the point chosen by Ludendorff for the blow which was to sever the French and British armies.

On March 21, taking example by Byng's spring at Cambrai in November, with no warning prepara-tion by the customary bombardment, the picked

**FRENCH DEFENDERS OF AMIENS**

Montdidier, a key position protecting Amiens on the south, is here being defended by French and British troops near Nesle, on March 25, occupying hastily dug pits more like the defences of 1914 than of 1918. The town fell on the 28th, but further advance was stayed.

*Photo, Imperial War Museum*

**MARSHAL FOCH**

Ferdinand Foch (1851–1929) magnificently justi-fied his appointment to the belated post of generalissimo of the Allied forces on the western front in the great crisis of March, 1918. On August 6 he became marshal of France

*Photo, Imperial War Museum*

German troops sprang upon the extreme British right. The Germans had saved Cambrai by whirling up huge reinforce-ments, but there were no reserves, British or French, to whirl up to the British line. The surprise—aided by fog which con-cealed the German movement—was com-plete. The British were flung back reeling, fighting desperately, wherever a stand could be made, for a week across the old battlefields, French or British, while the force on their left was compelled to swing back to keep in touch, and the French also, on their right, succeeded in keeping touch ; back to the Ancre line running just in front of Arras and Albert and Amiens.

At more than one point there had been a rift, at still more points the line had been so strung out that it could scarcely have checked a rush ; but the drive was impeded by the devastated country ; it never thrust clean through ; and when the halt in the retreat was called before Amiens, the German attack was vigorously repulsed, though there was another week's hard fighting before it was certain that the attempted penetration was held up. The Germans had achieved a striking success—but they had not attained their objective, though the effort was the biggest that had yet been made. Also, before the fighting was finished, the much needed generalissimo had been found —on March 25 Foch was appointed to the supreme command.

If the British right had been saved after the first shattering blow, it was by a serious weakening of the extreme left. A German thrust to Calais would in fact be less serious than a break through elsewhere, but it was in that quarter that Ludendorff directed his next effort, though on a much smaller scale, when the British resistance at the centre had been stabilised. The attack was delivered in accustomed style north of La Bassée ; but though it drove heavily forward the British right held at Givenchy. A great bulge was made in the line, but more troops were now crossing the Channel, some French reinforcements also arrived, the Belgians fought manfully, and practically nothing more was gained.

By the end of April the prospect of another heavy offensive against the British front had faded ; and during that month the first great contingent arrived from America to finish its training in France. Twelve months had passed since the American declaration of war ; when the stream began to flow it was soon swelling into a flood ; but the creation of an army five times the size of the British army at the beginning of the war, out of a civilian population which had never been concerned with so much as the prospect of a big war except in one fratricidal conflict, had been a gigantic task.

Germany then must either acknowledge defeat or attempt to achieve a decisive triumph before that stream became a flood ; the crash forward in the last week of March, the recovery in a few days of so much ground which the Allies had only won by months of furious fighting at enormous cost, appealed to the popular imagination—not only in Germany—far more than the fact of its actual failure ; and Ludendorff staked everything on a last throw.

It was perhaps almost as much for the reassurance of English public opinion as for its effects upon the German submarine campaign that a British squadron at the end of April achieved the spectacular but

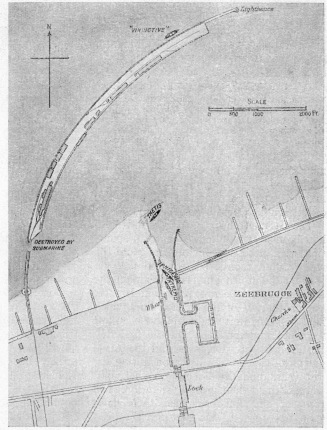

**PLAN OF ZEEBRUGGE AFTER THE RAID**
Zeebrugge had been left intact when evacuated by the British navy in 1914, and formed a submarine base for the Germans. On April 23, 1918, an expedition under Vice-Admiral R. Keyes sealed up the harbour with block ships (see photograph in following page). The light-shaded portion of this plan represents foreshore.
*Imperial War Museum*

AIR VIEW OF THE BLOCK-SHIPS SUNK ACROSS ZEEBRUGGE HARBOUR

Spectacular in its heroism, the Zeebrugge raid was also successful, both in practical results and in its effect on public 'moral.' While Vindictive, with the ferry boats Daffodil and Iris, covered by Warwick and destroyers, created a diversion by landing a party on the mole (which the explosion of a submarine under a viaduct had isolated from the land), Thetis, Iphigenia and Intrepid crept in. The first grounded prematurely, but the two last (seen above) were neatly sunk sealing the harbour.

*Photo, Imperial War Museum*

none the less magnificently heroic feat of sealing up the powerfully defended submarine bases at Zeebrugge and less completely at Ostend.

The German effort in March and April had been a tremendous strain ; preparation was necessary before it could be renewed. A month passed, and then on May 27 the storm burst, not again on the British, as had been expected in France, but on the left of the French line, which held positions that ought to have been but were not impregnable. On the first day the French were driven behind the Aisne out of all that Pétain had won during the last year ; and the British on their left, who had held their ground, were forced to conform and fall back lest their flank should be turned. On the 30th the head of the German thrust had reached the Marne. Then they set about widening the thrust to right and left. On their left they were held up before Reims ; on their right they were successful for a considerable distance to a point where they were again held up—this time by the first section of the American contingent brought into the fighting line.

The Marne ' pocket ' between the Vesle and the Marne was the way to Paris—or to destruction. The weeks passed. Minor attacks, which may have been intended only to draw troops elsewhere, came to nothing, while they drained Ludendorff's resources ; and still the Marne flowed between the Germans and Paris. Foch's well concealed preparations were complete when the last German onslaught was launched on July 15 not only in the pocket but on the line to the east of Reims. There it failed completely. In the pocket it crossed the Marne ; but Foch's hour had come. On the 17th French counter-attacks began ; on the 18th the German troops in the pocket found themselves fighting to cover retreat.

From that day all the German fighting was in the nature of rearguard actions as the line swung back and back until the final catastrophe in November. For there were half a million Americans in France now with thrice the number to follow, and unlimited reserves to swing up to any point where they might be wanted; and the German reserves were exhausted. The coming of the Americans was the arrival of Blücher's Prussians on the field of Waterloo. They won the war precisely in the sense that Blücher, not Wellington, was the conqueror of Napoleon.

At this turning-point of the war the Italian campaign had already degenerated into a merely subsidiary operation for which in itself there was no prospect of Austrian success. The last Austrian offensive on the Piave in June had failed disastrously; the ' ramshackle empire ' itself was on the verge of dissolution; and Italian troops could even be spared to play a part in Foch's operations—a sounder course than endeavouring to hasten the Austrian collapse by a precarious offensive. On the Italian front, in the Balkans and in Asia matters continued to be quiescent—that is, no conspicuous military movement took place—until September.

WHEN Foch opened his victory offensive on July 18, its import was guessed by few and its full import was known perhaps only to himself. There was no indication at the moment that he was doing more than successfully repelling an attack that had once more exhausted itself before reaching its objective ; as the old drive on Verdun, the two drives into Italy and the recent drive on the centre towards Amiens had been arrested. On that day Mangin delivered an attack west of the Marne pocket that threatened to turn the pocket itself into a trap from which it required no little skill on the part of the Germans to extricate themselves. They did so ; in the course of a fortnight the whole salient had been flattened out again, not without heavy losses but without anything verging on a rout at any point. Men were asking not ' What will be Foch's next stroke ? ' but ' Where will Ludendorff launch the next drive ? '

There was no next drive. The French left continued to press the Germans back little by little for a few days ; then

GERMANY'S FINAL EFFORT : TROOPS ON THE CAPTURED CHEMIN DES DAMES
Chemin des Dames, the road that gives its name to the summit of the Craonne plateau in the heights of the Aisne, for the conquest of which the French shed so much blood throughout the summer of 1917, was recaptured by the Germans in their last great ' push ' of May, 1918. Here a column of German reinforcements is seen moving up the famous road in the early days of June, to their advanced trenches which by then were over the Aisne and up to the Marne.
*Photo, Imperial War Museum*

suddenly on August 9 the British right before Amiens sprang forward, towards St. Quentin, its southern flank covered by French troops, against what was perhaps the strongest section of the German line. In a week they had made a material advance, capturing many prisoners and guns. On the 21st the British section on the left of the advance, north of the Ancre, swung forward, while there was no relaxation of the pressure by the British right and the whole French left. Thus the movement continued without pause, the pressure never ceasing along the whole line which had once come into action, but constantly extending to a new sector either on the right or the left. The Germans could never concentrate at any point for a counter-offensive, because to do so would involve weakening at the risk of snapping the line at some other point. By the middle of September the Germans were back on the lines they had held in March, and at points these had been penetrated.

The Americans in action had hitherto been brigaded with French or British troops ; now they entered the line as a third national army on the right of the French, compelling the retirement of the Germans on the line south of Verdun which no French attacks had shaken throughout the war. The Americans' capture of the St. Mihiel salient was followed by peace overtures from the other side, but only of a kind that had no possible chance of acceptance from the Allies. The German retreat was no longer, as before, a planned withdrawal to a stronger defensive line ; it was a retirement all along the line imposed by the enemy, which would not end until they were expelled from French and Belgian soil or surrendered.

DURING the two concluding months of the war, while the Germans were being forced back mile by mile across the devastated lands, stubbornly contesting every

AMERICAN TROOPS MARCH BACK AFTER CRUSHING THE ST. MIHIEL SALIENT

Long before the Americans were in the line they had helped to solve the pressing problem of reserves ; next they fought brigaded with other Allied troops ; and finally they took the field independently in the St. Mihiel sector, where they succeeded in capturing the salient on September 12–13, 1918, as part of Foch's general scheme of advance. Here a body of them is seen passing through the French village of Nonsard, flags flying, on return from the victory.

*Photo, Imperial War Museum*

**FOUR YEARS AFTERWARDS : MONS RECAPTURED BY THE CANADIANS**

The Belgian town where the British troops first saw action in 1914 was also the farthest advanced point occupied by them in the pursuit of 1918 when the Armistice came into force at 11 o'clock on the eleventh day of the eleventh month. On the 10th the Canadian Division had reached Mons, which was fairly strongly held, but an enveloping movement followed by an attack from two sides ensured its fall, and on the following morning they entered behind the pipes of the Canadian Scottish.

step, their allies in every quarter were crumpling up. Even the Bolsheviks found a new enemy in the host of Czecho-Slovaks who had fought reluctantly in the Austrian ranks, had become Russian prisoners of war by thousands in the numerous Austrian defeats, and had then enthusiastically taken up arms on the side of their captors for the overthrow of the Austrian tyrant. They had held fast to their new loyalty (rooted in their immemorial hostility to the Teuton) when the Bolshevised Russian troops mutinied and fled, and now they attached themselves to the independent loyalist government which was seeking to establish itself in Siberia. They did not in fact crumple up the Bolsheviks—who were a useful bulwark to the Germans but not their official allies—but did add to their difficulties.

The Balkans went first. Since the abdication of King Constantine Greece had been unequivocally Venizelist. Nevertheless, no effective moves had been made until on September 15 the Serbs and the French, supported on their right by the British, launched their attack on the Bulgars. No effective help

**LILLE AT LAST RESTORED TO FRANCE**

It was a blow to France when Lille, the manufacturing centre, fell in the early days of the war. The town was recaptured on October 18 (this photograph shows the arrival of President Poincaré, welcomed by General Birdwood), but its prosperity had been temporarily ruined by destruction of factory plant.

came from the Austrians. The Bulgar defences were pierced, their whole front collapsed, and on the 30th the French commander was able to dictate an armistice on his own terms. Bulgaria being lost, the Austrian hold on the Balkans was lost. The Turks were left alone.

The Turks were not yet gone, but they were going ; Allenby in southern Palestine had bided his time to deal an absolutely decisive blow. By a surprise attack consummately planned and consummately carried out he practically annihilated the entire Turkish force in Palestine in the three days' fighting (September 19 to 21) comprehensively known as the battle of Megiddo, and proceeded to the conquest of Syria. Damascus fell on the 30th, then Beirut, and then Aleppo (October 26). Meanwhile the Mesopotamian army had been pushed up the Tigris ; and after a battle which lasted for a week the Turkish army on the Tigris surrendered and an armistice was signed (October 30) which put the Allies in possession of the Dardanelles and the Bosporus.

Austria remained. She had been hustled out of the Balkan peninsula, the South Slavs were joining Serbia, the Czecho-Slavs were threatening her, Hungary was exhausted ; but through September and for three weeks of October the

**WHERE THE ARMISTICE WAS SIGNED**

The clearing in the forest of Compiègne where the trains bearing Marshal Foch and the German plenipotentiaries met to sign the Armistice was long marked by this simple notice, only replaced by permanent memorials in 1922.

Italian front was stationary. If Italy was to reap, across the Adriatic, any of the coveted fruits of the imminent Austrian collapse she must precipitate it by her own action. Italians and British opened the attack on October 23, Italians and French almost simultaneously, and on the 27th the Austrians were in flight. On November 3 they signed an armistice dictated by the Italian commander. Germany stood absolutely alone, and she was fast in the toils.

### Final Operations of the War

THE advance of the Allied line had been continuous. The Germans had exhausted their reserves in the last offensive, at the moment when the available forces of the Allies were doubled. The British had penetrated the Drocourt-Quéant line early in September ; at the end of the month they were through the Hindenburg line, the Belgians were in Dixmude, and the French were on the point of entering St. Quentin. By the middle of October the whole German line farther south had been pushed back on the Meuse by the northward thrust of the Americans and over the Aisne by the French, and Cambrai had fallen to the British with American support. In the northernmost sector the attack of Belgians, French and British compelled the abandonment of the Belgian coast, and the evacuation of Lille and Douai on the 17th.

Ludendorff's resignation on October 26 was significant. In the first week of November the American push northward down the Meuse was greatly accelerated ; on the 7th they were in Sedan. The French were pressing hard on the centre ; on the left the British captured Valenciennes on the 2nd and then drove forward in the decisive battle of the Sambre. On the 9th they were over the Scheldt. The fleet at Kiel was in mutiny, revolution was breaking out in Berlin, the Kaiser was safe on neutral territory, and a socialist provisional government was set up. In the early morning of November 11 the Canadians broke into Mons as the Germans were submitting to the crushing armistice terms dictated by the Allies. The last shot had been fired. In the military sense, the Great War was ended.

# TABLE OF DATES FOR CHAPTER 33

**1918** Nov.: Germany submits to armistice terms dictated by Allies (11th). Yugo-Slav constitutional monarchy and Austrian, Czecho-Slovakian and Hungarian republics proclaimed. William II abdicates. Bulgaria: Ferdinand abd.; acc. Boris. Great Britain: Lloyd George's coalition ministry returned to power.

**1919** Jan.: Peace Conference in Paris opened.
Feb.: Ebert elected president of German Republic.
March: Communists seize Hungarian government.
April: Peace Conference adopts League of Nations Covenant.
June: Treaty of Versailles signed.
Aug.: Rumanians occupy Budapest. Anglo-Persian and Anglo-Afghan agreements.
Sept.: D'Annunzio seizes Fiume. Peace treaty of St. Germain-en-Laye with Austria.
Nov.: Peace treaty of Neuilly with Bulgaria.
Dec.: Government of India Act passed.

**1920** Jan.: Mustapha Kemal in Anatolia; 'National Pact' of Angora.
First meeting of League of Nations Council.
Feb.: War between Poland and Soviet Russia.
March: German troops enter the Ruhr to suppress communist disorders.
April: French troops occupy Frankfort and Darmstadt.
Conference of San Remo allots mandates.
June: Greek advances against Turks in Asia Minor. Peace Treaty of the Trianon with Hungary.
July: Spa conference on reparations.
Aug.: Treaty between Czecho-Slovakia and Yugo-Slavia.
Treaty of Sèvres with Turkey (unratified).
Oct.: Russo-Polish armistice; Polish troops take Vilna.
Nov.: Treaty of Rapallo (Italy and Yugo-Slavia) to settle Fiume question.
U.S.A.: Election of President Harding.
Dec.: Irish Government Act becomes law.

**1921** Jan.: Conferences in Paris and London.
March: Russo-Polish peace of Riga; alliance of Poland and Rumania; Anglo-Russian trade agreement.
Germany declares to incredulous Allies that she cannot pay. Sanctions put in force.
June: Little Entente linked up. British Imperial Conference.
Aug.: Silesian question referred to the League. U.S.A. issues invitations to the Washington Conference on reduction of naval armaments.
Nov.: Washington Conference opened. Albanian republic recognized.
Dec.: Four Powers Treaty takes the place of Anglo-Japanese alliance. Treaty of Washington.

**1922** Jan.: Cannes conference.
Feb.: Court of International Justice opened.
Great Britain declares Egypt independent, with reservations for security.
April: Genoa conference; German-Soviet treaty of Rapallo; temporary non-aggression pact.
Aug.: Greek rout at Kalahissar.
Sept.: Turks burn Smyrna and march on Straits. Constantine, King of Greece, abd.; acc. George.
Oct.: Neutrality of Straits preserved; armistice of Mudania. Fascist ministry in Italy under Mussolini. Bonar Law ministry in England. Angora government abolishes Sultanate.
Nov.: Flight of Sultan; Abdul Mejid made khalif. Conference of Lausanne opens for settlement of Turkish question.

**1923** Jan.: Germans declared in default with reparations; Ruhr occupied by French and Belgian troops. Germany issues passive resistance order; fall of the mark. Turks reject the draft treaty of Lausanne.
Feb.: China denounces treaties with Japan. Vilna recognized as Polish territory.
May: German proposals rejected. First Baldwin ministry.
July: Turkey accepts amended Lausanne treaty. Entente relations strained by Ruhr question.
Aug.: Stresemann ministry takes office in Germany.
Sept.: Death of President Harding; Calvin Coolidge succeeds him.
Greek-Italian question of Corfu settled.
Spain: Dictatorship of Primo de Rivera.
Oct.: Mustapha Kemal, Turkish president.
Dec.: Two committees of experts appointed to examine German reparations question. Greek republic proclaimed.

**1924** Jan.: Adriatic treaty (Italy and Yugo-Slavia). MacDonald ministry in England.
Feb.: Turkish government abolishes Khalifate.
March: Adoption of Dawes Reparations Report.
July: London Conference; U.S.A. agree to take part in Reparations Commission.
Aug.: French begin evacuation of Ruhr.
Oct.: England and Turkey accept League settlement of Irak boundary. Publication of Zinoviev letter; second Baldwin ministry. The League adopts Geneva protocol, which is rejected by England in favour of regional pacts (Nov.).
Nov.: President Coolidge re-elected.
Dec.: Sun Yat-sen's government recognized.

**1925** Feb.: Germany suggests a security pact relating to the Rhineland.
April: Hindenburg elected German president.
May: Anti-foreign (especially against British and Japanese) riots in China.
Oct.: Locarno Conference meets, with Germany on the same footing as the other powers.
Rhineland pact adopted, with a series of arbitration conventions.
Demirkapu incident; frontier collision of Greek and Bulgar forces; war averted by intervention of the League.
Dec.: Ratification of Locarno treaties; British begin evacuation of Cologne. Deposition of shah of Persia; Rhiza Khan elected shah.

**1926** March: Germany's admission to the League suspended by action of Spain and Brazil.
England: Long coal and short general strike.
Aug.: French operations against Abd el-Krim in Morocco.
Sept.: Germany enters the League of Nations.
Nov.: British Imperial conference adumbrates without defining the meaning of 'Dominion status.'

**1927** Feb.: Disorders at Hankow and Shanghai; British troops landed.
March: Heavy floods in the valley of the Mississippi.
May: Parliament House at Canberra opened by the Duke of York.
June: Conference at Geneva on the limitation of naval armaments; no result.

**1928** June: Chang Tso-lin d.; Kuomintang established at Peking. Chiang Kai-shek president (Oct.).
Aug.: Acceptance of Kellogg Pact by fifteen 'nations,' followed by others.
Nov.: H. C. Hoover elected president of the U.S.A.
Dec.: Albanian republic elects Ahmed Beg Zogu as king.
Afghan revolt against Amanullah.

**1929** Jan.: U.S.A. ratify Kellogg Pact.
Absolutist revolution in Yugo-Slavia.
Feb.: Vatican treaty with Italy restoring temporal sovereignty to the Papacy.
May: General election in Great Britain.
June: Second Labour ministry formed under J. Ramsay MacDonald.

**1930** Jan.: Conference on Reparations at the Hague; Young Plan accepted by Germany.
Oct.: Airship R 101 destroyed in France.

**1931** April: Rising in Spain; King Alphonso leaves the country, which becomes a republic.
June: Moratorium of a year proposed by President Hoover and accepted by the Powers.
Aug.: Political crisis in Great Britain; National Government formed.
Sept.: Great Britain goes off the gold standard.
Oct.: General election ends in victory for the National Government; Free Trade policy abandoned by Great Britain.

**1932** March: Eamon de Valera succeeds W. T. Cosgrave as president of the Irish Free State.
June: Conference at Lausanne reaches agreement about reparations.
July: £2,000,000,000 of 5 per cent. war loan converted.
Imperial Conference meets at Ottawa.
Nov.: Franklin D. Roosevelt elected president of the U.S.A.
United States refuses to agree to request made by Great Britain and France for an extension of the moratorium.

### CHAPTER 33

# AFTERWARDS: SINCE 1918

FOR four years and a hundred days all Europe and much of the world outside Europe had been whirling in the maelstrom of the Great War without time or thought to spare for anything but the war in some of its many aspects. The war had wrecked the foundations of the entire pre-war fabric—international, industrial, constitutional, social, religious. All the greater historic states and peoples, with the exception only of Spain, the Dutch, the Swiss and the Scandinavians, had been involved in it as active or at least nominal belligerents ; among the active belligerents, determination to win at whatever cost had overshadowed every other consideration.

When it ended, the Austrian, Russian and Turkish empires had ceased to exist, though Austria, Russia and Turkey survived ; the German empire in Europe was intact save for Alsace, but was no longer focussed in the person of an emperor. Half a dozen nationalities, or groups, had separated themselves from the broken empires and were clamouring for recognition as independent states, apart from the territorial claims upon one or another of them of other already established states. The territorial chaos was incomparably greater than it had been when Napoleon was interned in St. Helena.

## Chaotic State of the Post-war World

NOT less was the industrial chaos. For the industrial world had been drained of its young manhood to fight instead of training itself in industry ; millions of these had perished, and millions more were physically wrecked or at least partially incapacitated, and industrial employment during those years had been restricted to the production of the bare necessities of life or of munitions of war in some form —not wealth, but the machinery for destroying wealth ; machinery which had been appallingly successful in effecting the purpose for which it had been created, while it perished simultaneously itself. Again, on all sides governments were

tottering, if they had not already fallen ; the governing capacity of the governing classes, if not of all governments, was in the crucible ; they were responsible for the war, the mismanagement of the war, and all the havoc that it had wrought. In the more democratically ruled countries hostility to the old order was less virulent : most virulent in those which had been most despotically ruled in the interests of particular sections of the community. But in all was the virus.

Ethically the disappearance of regulated discipline at home among the young, coupled with the reaction of their elders against the rigid discipline of battle service to which they had willingly or unwillingly submitted themselves, told heavily against moral restraints of every kind ; while the fearful devastation and suffering caused men, when they turned their thoughts to religion, to feel as they had felt in the days of the Norman King Stephen when they cried out that ' Christ and His saints slept.' The world, to put the thing in its simplest terms, had to recover balance, and for years after the war was over it was still rocking.

### Objects of the Peace Makers

WITH the cessation of hostilities, the first necessity of the moment was to ensure against their present recrudescence, which, from the point of view of the victors, meant to paralyse Germany for hostile action. That was practically effected by the terms of the armistice, which imposed on her immediate disarmament and surrender to the victors of military stores and material. The next step was to formulate such a general settlement as should provide the strongest possible guarantee for the future against the resort to arms for the adjustment of international differences. Theoretically, the Vienna Congress of 1814–15 had the same object in view ; but it failed to attain it, though it had prevented international wars for nearly forty years.

Precedent demanded the immediate adjustment of inter - state boundaries, transfers of territory, recognition of new states, indemnities which the victors were entitled to claim from the vanquished in the great conflict. But much more than this was required if the peace was to end not only the war which had just been fought to a finish, but the menace of wars greater and even more destructive in the future. The matter was taken in hand by the 'big five' who had been mainly instrumental in winning the war—France, Great Britain representing the British Empire, the United States of America, Italy and Japan; in consultation with the minor states but clearly with the intention that what the 'big five' agreed upon must prevail; though with the serious difficulty in the background that America might—as she ultimately did—refuse to ratify the decisions of her representative, President Woodrow Wilson.

This however was a point which did not affect the drafting of the peace treaty, in which the American president took a very leading part, since it was largely based upon the 'fourteen points' which he had enumerated as essential, and it was he who most unhesitatingly insisted on the inclusion of the Covenant of the League of Nations as a fundamental portion of the treaty itself—something vitally different from the 'Holy Alliance,' not of peoples but of princes, with which Alexander I, having the same object in view, had sought so ineffectually to supplement the Treaty of Vienna in 1815.

THE treaty, then, was to be a treaty of peace between the victors and Germany to which all the signatories would be pledged; to be supplemented by further treaties with Germany's allies. The enormous task of shaping and drafting it was carried through in the first months of 1919 by the representatives of the big five—though Japan took active part in it only when it dealt with matters in which she was concerned,—with the assistance of the delegates of the other states in relation to matters with which they were directly concerned. Germany's share in it was confined to ineffectual protests against terms which were imposed upon her, having as the only alternative the advance of the Allied armies into the territories which she was no longer in a position to defend. On May 7 the German delegates met the delegates of the 'Allied and Associated' powers, who were already in possession of the treaty terms. They were given some six weeks to accept or reject them; but it was not till June 28, when they had been threatened with an immediate advance of the Allied troops, that the Treaty of Versailles was actually signed by the assembled delegates in the same Hall of Mirrors where, in 1871, William I had been proclaimed German emperor.

**THE GERMAN FLEET SURRENDERS IN 1918**

The terms of the armistice imposed by the Allies included the surrender of all German submarines and the internment of many of their warships. Of the German surface ships which came to Rosyth for internment on November 21, 1918, the majority was sunk by their crews at Scapa on June 21, 1919.

*Photo, Royal Air Force, Official Crown copyright*

## THE SIGNING OF THE PEACE AT VERSAILLES IN 1919

The international peace treaty that concluded the Great War was signed in the historic Hall of Mirrors at Versailles on June 28, 1919, and its signature is the subject of this fine painting by Sir William Orpen. Seated, from left to right, are General Tasker Bliss, Colonel House, Henry White, Robert Lansing, Wilson, Clemenceau, Lloyd George, Bonar Law, Arthur Balfour, Viscount Milner, G. N. Barnes and Marquis Saionzi; signing, the German delegate, Dr. Johannes Bell.

The treaty opened with the Covenant of the League of Nations, to which the 'High Contracting Parties' declared their agreement, and then proceeded to the reconstruction of the map of Europe in relation to Germany and the conditions, penal or otherwise, to be exacted from her. As a matter of course Alsace-Lorraine—the provinces taken from France in 1871—were restored to France. East Prussia remained attached to Germany, subject to local plébiscites, which proved to be decisively in favour of that course ; but she was deprived of the trans-Niemen territory, which was subsequently allotted to the new state of Lithuania. Poland was restored as an independent state, with a corridor to the port of Danzig, which was to be an independent free city under the protection of the League of Nations. Czecho - Slovakia, comprising what had been the northern Slavonic provinces of the Austrian empire, excepting those which were again attached to Poland, was also recognized as an independent state. The question whether certain Germanised portions of these lands should remain German or be included in Poland was left to later settlement, preferably by local plébiscite. Denmark's claim to Slesvig, of which Prussia had deprived her in 1864, was to be decided by plébiscites, which ultimately gave one portion of it to Denmark and another to Prussia. There were adjustments with regard to Belgian territory and a highly complicated arrangement with regard to the German Rhineland on the French frontier, which for ten years to come was to prove a fruitful source of friction.

The territorial arrangements of the Treaty of Versailles were theoretically completed by the supplementary treaties with Germany's former allies. The Austrian treaty of St. Germain-en-Laye opened with the 'Covenant.' It divided what had been the Austrian empire into the separate states of Austria, Hungary and Czecho-Slovakia, while it transferred Galicia to Poland, Bukovina and part of Transylvania to Rumania, and the South Slav districts to Serbia, and gave to Italy not only all the Italian-speaking districts, but also the German-speaking districts of South Tirol. The most serious difficulties here were in the adjustment of the rival claims of Italy and Serbia or Yugo-Slavia. The treaty of the Trianon with Hungary, the other member of the former official Dual Monarchy, of which various portions had been assigned to Czecho-Slovakia, Yugo-Slavia or Rumania, leaving Hungary about half its former size, was not completed until June, 1920. Bulgaria, by the treaty of Neuilly (November), lost her coast line on the Aegean, but was secured ' economic outlets ' thereto. The Treaty of Sèvres with Turkey was never signed by the sultan, so that it passed into oblivion. The United States having declined to commit themselves to the League Covenant, that power was not a party to any of the treaties, but made its own separate terms with each of the states with whom it had itself been at war.

Other independent states appeared in the new map of Europe, on the Baltic. Soviet Russia had so far committed itself to doctrines of ' self-determination,' the principle on which the powers had endeavoured to base their treaties, that it could raise no objection when these provinces separated themselves from her.

**REPRESENTATIVES OF THE 'BIG FOUR'**

Of the ' big five ' mainly concerned in arranging the terms of the peace treaty that ended the Great War, Japan only took active part in so far as she was herself affected. Representatives of the other four powers, Britain, Italy, France and America, are (left to right) Lloyd George, Orlando, Clemenceau and Woodrow Wilson.

At the head of the Baltic came Finland, then Esthonia, then Latvia and finally Lithuania, which had been united with Poland under one crown since her Duke Jagellon (see page 458) acquired the Polish crown, an association which was now terminated.

The rearrangement made by the Treaty of Vienna a century earlier, after the Napoleonic wars, had been based wholly upon monarchist doctrines of dynastic legitimism, entirely ignoring ideas of nationality or affinity, and the claims of peoples—as distinguished from the dynasts—to a voice in their own disposal. Now, ' sceptre and crown had tumbled down ' in the defeated states ; there was no thought of restoring them ; Romanovs, Hapsburgs and Hohenzollerns had fallen, and with them all the lesser dynasties of the German Empire. In the new settlement, dynastic claims counted for nothing ; the purpose in view was to give to national affinities the first claim to consideration and, so far as was practicable, to minor groups which did not desire or could not be accorded independence the right of self-determination ; that is, of choosing for themselves by plébiscite the recognized state to which they should be attached. But in many areas the populations were compounded of diverse or positively antagonistic elements, so that any attempted solution must fail to be satisfactory to all. That dissatisfaction would rise to angry and even perilous heights was hardly to be doubted ; but no settlement could conceivably have been made which would not have involved that risk.

### Settlement Outside Europe : the ' Mandate '

GERMANY was the only one among the defeated powers which had possessed dominions over sea. From them she had been completely ejected in the course of the war, and by the peace treaty she resigned all claims to them. They were not annexed to any power, but were dealt with by ' mandate ' under the terms of the League Covenant, which entrusted their administration for the most part to Great Britain, to be ruled in the interests of their respective populations. Mandatory powers were to be in effect trustees for the League. Arabia remained under the chief who had been proclaimed sultan of the Hejaz ; in 1920 the mandate for the administration of Syria was given to France, and for Mesopotamia and Palestine to Great Britain. For the time the Porte retained almost nothing in Europe except Constantinople, the terms of the armistice with Turkey remaining in force as the Treaty of Sèvres was unsigned.

### Difficulties of European Reconstruction

IN the reconstruction of the map of Europe the treaties dealt with a subject bristling with difficulties, conflicting interests and sources of friction not only between victors and vanquished but also among the victors themselves ; but by dint of creating the League of Nations it was earnestly hoped that they had at the same time provided an instrument by means of which defects in the treaties might be subsequently compensated, since it was morally certain that defects would be found. But besides the territorial arrangements and the creation of the League, they had to deal with another extremely thorny subject—the reparations and indemnities which the victors severally might justly claim from the vanquished for the sufferings and losses inflicted by a war for which in the view of the former the whole responsibility lay upon the latter ; who, as they held, had also conducted it with an unprecedented disregard of the recognized ethics of warfare between civilized states. And as against those claims they had to calculate the effective capacity for making them good. And in addition they had to provide security against any attempted repetition of the offence of which in their view those powers had been guilty.

The fear of renewed German military aggression in the future was in the nature of things much more prominent for France and Belgium than for anyone else ; on the question of the share of compensation due to itself and to others every state had its own views, and those views were divergent ; and on the question of capacity to pay there were not and could not be adequate data, while there was everywhere a strong popular disposition to exact the uttermost farthing rather than to consider the general economic effect of so doing.

The problematic character of the whole situation was further complicated by the fact that Russia was an unknown and incalculable quantity. The powers found themselves quite unable to recognize the Soviet government as one which could be relied upon to keep faith and carry out its engagements ; since its agents were notoriously and avowedly employed abroad in a propaganda which aimed at the overthrow of all existing governments, its activities within Russia itself were condemned by all civilized opinion, and it had already repudiated all obligation to carry out engagements undertaken by the Russian government in the past. The powers desired to revive a settled order ; Russia desired to destroy settled order ; the two aims being obviously incompatible, there was no possibility of arriving at agreement as to the means. The powers wanted security, and Soviet Russia was a standing menace to all security.

**O**N what we have called the third question, then, there were two aspects of the problem for settlement : compensations, and guarantees for Germany's neighbours against future aggression. The latter was concerned with Germany's effective disarmament, the demilitarising of the German frontier territory facing France and the present occupation thereof by the Allies. The indemnities imposed were far short of what was considered adequate compensation, but, on the other hand, according to the Germans far in excess of anything they could possibly pay. If they were compelled to make promises, the promises were accompanied by warnings that it was in fact quite impossible to execute them.

At the same time the withdrawal of the Allied forces from the frontier provinces was made conditional upon their execution ; and it continued by no means easy for the Allies, and above all for France, to believe in the honesty either of the German protests or of professions of complete disarmament. Napoleon had disarmed Prussia drastically enough after Jena, but the result had not been what he

**PRESIDENT WILSON**

Thomas Woodrow Wilson was elected president of the United States in 1912. At first an advocate of peace, he finally countenanced America's entry into the Great War. This photograph was taken during the electoral campaign.

*Photo, E.N.A.*

had intended. The Allies were in no mood to rely upon German good faith without the most convincing material guarantees ; the Germans were resentful both of the charges brought against them and of the penalties exacted, so that the tone they adopted was not calculated to allay distrust. If the British were disposed to be more lenient than the French, with their devastated lands under their eyes, it was only because it was easier for them to be so. The rival parties to a dispute can hardly be expected to form an unbiassed judgement on the issues, and in the nature of the case one of the parties was here unequivocally the judge as well.

The natural result was that the terms were drastic, and did not tend to early reconciliation. There was a prospect of at least modifying the nervousness of France in the proposal, to which both President Wilson and the British government assented, that America and Great

Britain should jointly guarantee the security of France against German aggression ; but it came to nothing, because it was essential that the guarantee should be a joint one, whereas, as with the League of Nations, in the devising of which the president had played so large a part, America refused her ratification. France remained with no more security than she could derive from the Treaty of Versailles. Inevitably therefore she was resolved to let go nothing that she could logically claim under its terms. She would take no risks—and Germany as victor in 1871 had acted strictly upon the same doctrine.

### Diplomacy by Conference

THE series of treaties between the ' Allied and Associated Powers ' on one side and the defeated powers on the other was left incomplete, inasmuch as the Treaty of Sèvres with the Turks remained unratified. Nor did they cover the agreements which it was necessary for the major and minor powers to arrive at among themselves before a permanent atmosphere of amity could be attained. The powers, however anxious they might be, were by no means ready to submit their rights of private judgement to the control of the new international instrument they had brought into being—the League of Nations—at least until that instrument should be tested and perfected. The League was indeed set in immediate operation ; but the method adopted for dealing with the biggest questions was ' diplomacy by conference.'

It was a method, departing from the ordinary practice of diplomacy, initiated in the years immediately following the Napoleonic wars, when congresses had been summoned at short intervals ; since then it had been employed on certain notable occasions, such as the Berlin Congress, the Hague Conferences and finally the Conference of Paris which drafted the Versailles treaty ; and now during these critical years it was developed and repeatedly brought into full play. Conferences meant not that, as in the ordinary course, each government communicated with each other government through its ambassador at this or

that capital, but that the heads of the respective governments or their foreign ministers met together in conclave at San Remo or Lausanne or Locarno or elsewhere for the joint solution of the intricate problems of divergent interests which required to be dealt with ; the governments being normally those of the great powers with whom the last word would necessarily lie.

### The New States on the Baltic

THE new Baltic states that came into being at this time had been separated from Soviet Russia by the Treaty of Brest Litovsk at a moment when Germany conceived that they would as a matter of course become client states of her own, her troops being in fact in effective occupation. The independence of the Ukraine had been at the same time recognized by the Russians and the Central powers. The authority then acquired by Germany passed to the Allied powers with the Treaty of Versailles, and with it the responsibility not for enforcing but for procuring such a settlement between them—and Poland with them—as should command their common assent, while precluding the association of any of them with Germany. Between Poland and Russia there had been no settlement beyond the tsar's earlier promise of liberation for Poland ; and the soviets had announced that they were not bound by any engagements entered upon by the fallen tsardom. Before long, Poland and Russia were at war, and there were also acute differences between Poland and Lithuania.

Finland was prompt to declare herself an independent republic. She had an immediate dispute with Sweden on the question of sovereignty over the Aaland Islands, once in possession of Sweden. The matter was complicated, but the two states were persuaded to submit it to the League of Nations, and both loyally accepted its pronouncements thereon, which were embodied in a Convention signed in October, 1921. Notable in connexion therewith was the League's declaration that the general principle of self-determination did not confer upon every community the right to transfer itself from one sovereign state to another ; the Aaland islanders having expressed a preference for the sovereignty of Sweden. A boundary dispute between Finland and Russia concerning the title of the former to an ice-free port on the White Sea was settled in Finland's favour in the peace treaty of Dorpat (October, 1920) between these two states, which till then had been technically in a ' state of war,' the Finnish government having much ado to repress in Finland the Bolshevik activities emanating from Russia.

Esthonia, too, had her initial difficulties, because her government, like all governments, was anti-Bolshevik, for the simple reason that everywhere the Bolshevik propaganda was directed against every government not itself Bolshevik. Consequently some of the anti-Bolshevik Russians tried to make Esthonia their own base for hostilities against the Bolshevik government of Russia, which was hardly more agreeable to Esthonia, because the anti-Bolshevik Russians avowedly did not admit the right of the Baltic provinces to separate themselves from the legitimate Russian Empire. The collapse of the Russian monarchist efforts, however, at the end of 1919 led to the settlement of the Esthonian question to Esthonia's satisfaction by another Treaty of Dorpat in February, 1920, between Esthonia and the Russian Soviet government.

The experiences of Latvia were similar to those of her neighbour. Her independence was in like manner recognized by a Russian treaty in August, 1920 ; but the relations of these two little states with Russia must remain uneasy so long as she is, and they are not, Bolshevik. Even in conjunction it would be difficult for them to resist aggressive activities on the part of their big neighbour, though for defensive purposes the League of Nations stands behind them.

Between Lithuania, Poland and Russia the relations were complicated. The Russian government had accepted the separation from Russia of Lithuania, as

**ZELIGOWSKI'S TROOPS ASSEMBLED IN VILNA AFTER ITS SEIZURE**

The possession of Vilna, in which the Lithuanian provisional government was originally set up, became a subject of dispute between Lithuania, Poland and Russia. Ignoring the armistice procured by the League of Nations after its seizure by the Russians in 1920, the Polish general Zeligowski made his unauthorised march upon the town and effected its recapture. So successful was this coup d'état that Vilna later received European recognition as belonging to Poland.

*Courtesy of Polish Press Bureau*

distinct from Poland, at the Treaty of Brest Litovsk, with the corollary that Lithuania was intended, in effect, to become a German protectorate. In theory she would be an independent state, as she became when the Versailles treaty washed out the protectorate design. Before the war was over the Lithuanian provisional government was set up at Vilna, but on the German retirement the Russians again took forcible possession of Vilna in January, 1919. Meanwhile, the Poles had established their own provisional government. In their eyes Vilna was Polish, and in April they ejected the Bolsheviks from Vilna.

### Settlement of the Vilna Imbroglio

LITHUANIA declined Poland's proposals for the reunion of Poland and Lithuania. The Poles, in spite of Lithuanian resentment, kept their grip on Vilna, which they had won back after Lithuania lost it to the Russians ; but in 1920 the Russians renewed the attack and recovered Vilna. They did not stop at Vilna ; they marched on Warsaw, the Polish capital, only to meet with very unexpected and altogether decisive defeat on the Vistula. The intervention of the League of Nations brought about an armistice ; but a Polish general, on his own responsibility, ignored the armistice, marched on Vilna, seized it, and entirely refused to retire, though, at least officially, he was acting in defiance of his own government. The League, after divers experimental moves which proved ineffectual, left Poland and Lithuania to settle their claims by negotiations between themselves. But the Poles were in effective possession ; a majority of the inhabitants of the Vilna district apparently preferred to be attached to Poland, and presently Europe recognized Vilna as being within the Polish sovereignty. Russia withdrew her own claims by the Treaty of Riga (March, 1921) with Poland.

Vilna as part of Poland links up Poland with Latvia, and so with the North Baltic states, but severs Lithuania from Russia. As part of Lithuania, it would be a Lithuanian gateway to Russia and would sever Poland from Latvia. Incidentally, Lithuania is an easier channel of communication between Germany and Russia than Poland provides, since Lithuania has not the same historic causes as Poland for antipathy to Prussia. It was perhaps inevitable that western distrust of Germany and of Bolshevik Russia should foster, in France especially, the feeling that Poland must be, so to speak, a watch-dog and custodian in the east.

### Friction between Italy and Yugo-Slavia

OF the big five who had taken part in the war and taken on themselves the peace settlement, America had repudiated responsibility for European affairs, from which Japan also stood apart. Whatever differences there might be among the others and their fallen antagonists, armed conflict among them was out of the question. The public danger lay in the fact that the sense of responsibility weighed less heavily upon the minor states, whom it might be difficult to restrain from appealing to arms for the settlement of their disagreements—and bitter experience had shown that small fires may develop into great conflagrations. The east, therefore, with its great congeries of minor states was a constant source of anxiety ; and between Yugo-Slavia—the new, expanded ' Greater Serbia '—and one of the great powers there were standing sources of friction ; the territorial claims of Italy and Serbia on the Eastern Adriatic being incompatible.

These last, however, proved themselves capable of adjustment by the good sense of the Italian and Serbian governments. The most notable instance was the case of Fiume. France and England had made engagements with Italy on her entry into the war which they were prepared to keep, but they were not prepared to extend them at the expense of the unified South Slavs. They would not support her later-asserted claim to the port of Fiume, which it was extremely difficult to assign to any one nationality. Fiume, like Danzig, was to be an independent free port. The Italian government reluctantly acquiesced ; not so the fervent Italian nationalist and poet d'Annunzio, who in Garibaldian fashion raised a troop of his own and seized Fiume. So popular, however, was the action of the poet that it was not till the end of 1920 that the Italian government ventured to conclude with Yugo-Slavia the treaty of Rapallo to enforce d'Annunzio's withdrawal. Fiume was declared independent, but even then the position proved to be so impracticable that finally in 1924 Italy and Yugo-Slavia achieved a pact which gave Fiume itself to Italy but secured to Yugo-Slavia privileges in connexion with the port which met her most pressing requirements.

### Hungary and the Balkan States

ANOTHER of the threatening storm centres in the near eastern lands was Hungary. The Magyars, always resentful of subordination to the Teuton in the empire under which they were combined, had always been no less insistent on the subordination of the Slav to the Magyar in Hungary. Of recent years they had enjoyed a status of equality with the Teuton while retaining domination over the Slav. Now, in the break-up of the empire, Teuton and Magyar were definitely separated, and so far as disentanglement was possible the Slavs had broken free from the domination of both. But further, the Slavs, while they had no fears of an Austrian attempt to recover ascendancy over them, felt no such security in regard to the Magyars. The same applied to the 'Roumanes' of Transylvania, now transferred to Rumania. Hungary had taken her stand with the Central powers, shared in their humiliation, and resented as an injustice when meted out to herself the treatment in which she had seen no injustice when meted out by herself to subject peoples.

Hungary, moreover, early became a source of trouble, because in March, 1919, her government was seized by the communist or Bolshevik faction, which presented itself as a menace to Rumania, who in her turn had special grudges against Hungary, born in the recent war. Rumania invaded Hungary ; conciliatory missions from the west failed. The communist government fell, but the Rumanian troops did not withdraw till they had exacted severe indemnities from Hungary. There followed some disastrous attempts to restore the Hapsburg monarchy in Hungary, which to Hungary's neighbours was as disturbing as the plunge into communism. It was not surprising, therefore, that Yugo-Slavia, Czecho-Slovakia and Rumania made a treaty of alliance among themselves, which united them in what was known as the 'Little Entente' for the defence of the common interests for which the western powers did not appear to offer

### GABRIELE D'ANNUNZIO AT FIUME

Dissatisfied with the attitude of the Peace Conference towards the fate of Fiume, Gabriele d'Annunzio, the Italian poet and patriot, decided to seize the port. He raised a band of enthusiastic troops to assist him in the raid, and annexed Fiume on Italy's behalf in September, 1919. He is here seen addressing his legionaries.

*Photo, E.N.A.*

them adequate safeguards ; interests which appeared to be threatened by Bolshevism on one side, possibly by Italy on the other side, and by Hungary at the centre. Nor is it surprising that from another point of view the safeguarding of those interests meant the depression of Hungary.

It would indeed be a sound general statement to say that conditions gave strong though by no means absolute security against the rekindling of war in the west, but that as regions lay farther and farther from the armies of the western powers the security for peace diminished. The great powers, including Germany, would leave no stone unturned to avoid collision among themselves ; but necessarily it was to this end that their attention and energies were most continuously directed, and their control eastwards was comparatively sporadic, and spasmodic, in proportion as their alertness to the course of events waxed and waned. It was in, and in connexion with, what had been the Turkish Empire that the menace of a serious conflagration suddenly made itself most acutely felt.

### Troubles of the Turkish Empire

THE Turkish Empire had matched the Austrian Empire in the completeness of its collapse. The sultan, for four centuries khalif and official head of the Sunni Mahomedan world, though not so recognized in the Shiah regions, still officially reigned at Constantinople, but his temporal dominion in Europe was reduced to the city itself and outside Europe was woefully shrunken. Egypt had gone, Syria and Palestine had gone, Arabia had gone, Irak (the revived name for Mesopotamia) had gone, Armenia had gone. How those populations, formerly under Turkish sovereignty, wholly without the experience or even the remote tradition of self-government other than the irresistible authority of a local despot, were to be governed now was a sufficiently difficult problem for settlement by the powers who had broken down the military tyranny of the Turk ; and how what remained of Turkey was to be made to serve instead of disturbing the welfare of the rest of the

world was another ; but Turkey's own revival was the last thing to be expected.

The sultan's government was permitted to remain in Constantinople mainly for two reasons—the difficulty of placing anyone else in possession (except the Americans, who firmly declined), and the reluctance to inflict on the Khalifate a humiliation which might have a disastrous repercussion upon the Mahomedan world. Meanwhile a considerable area about the straits was demilitarised and Allied troops under British command occupied Constantinople. The responsibility for Turkey's final collapse had lain with the Young Turks and their leader Enver. In his place Mustapha Kemal, who had displayed marked qualities both of soldiership and statesmanship, was sent to the Turkish headquarters in Anatolia.

### Kemal's Reorganization at Angora

WHILE the government at Constantinople was negotiating the Treaty of Sèvres, Mustapha Kemal, with very different views, was organizing a government in Anatolia, while Enver vanished into more obscure regions in the east, and Greece, almost unresisted, was by force of arms making good her classical but dubious claims to Smyrna and other coastal districts in Asia Minor. Mustapha called a congress at Sivas and formulated the policy embodied in what came to be called the National Pact, which Constantinople ignored. Mustapha consequently ignored Constantinople and set up a national government at Angora in 1920. The Angora government, repudiating the Sèvres peace terms, failed to extract the concessions it demanded from the Conference of London in 1921 ; while the Greek forces were continuing to advance, apparently with the intention of sharing the Turkish Black Sea provinces with Armenia, till they were checked a long way from their base by Angora troops on the Sakaria.

The Constantinople government was a phantom ; that of Angora was a reality which commanded the loyalty of the Turks in Asia and was inspired by a leader of genius. It had ignored but not officially repudiated Constantinople. It struck a treaty of its own with the Russian Soviet government. The French and British governments had announced their neutrality in the Graeco-Turkish war, in which the Greeks were conspicuously the aggressors. Without departing from neutrality, but recognizing the facts of the situation, France virtually recognized the Angora government by concluding with it a convention regarding the Turco-Syrian boundaries in October, 1921. Attempted mediation by the powers between the belligerents failed ; when the Greeks in the following July proposed to occupy Constantinople the powers, whose troops were in actual occupation, refused to admit them.

### Greeks Defeated in Asia Minor

AND then in August Mustapha Kemal, who had bided his time, shattered the Greek army, whose retreat soon became an unequivocal rout, while the Turkish army was engaged partly in keeping them on the run, partly in marching towards the straits, on the way to Thrace. The very considerable Greek population in the districts which the Turks were now over-running fled headlong to the coast, where it was taken off by neutral as well as by Greek ships. King Constantine, who had been restored, abdicated for the second time, in favour of his son, George II.

If the Angora troops approaching the straits entered the demilitarised zones on the east of the straits, that would be an act of war. Would the Allies resist it ? If they did not, their acquiescence might have on the Mahomedan world an effect which Great Britain was not disposed to risk. With or without support from the Allies she was resolved to maintain the freedom of the zones and the straits. France and Italy declined to support her, and withdrew their troops. The strained relations between the Allies were relieved by their agreement on a joint note inviting Greece and Turkey to a peace conference, and the situation was saved by the combined tact and energy of the British commander, General Harington, and Mustapha Kemal's wisdom and controlling influence over forces flushed with victory and far outnumbering the British at the moment. Some Turkish troops actually crossed the boundary, but were withdrawn in time to avoid a collision. There was no act of war. Mustapha held a conference with the British commander, and agreed to open negotiations with the Greeks. The armistice was signed on October 11.

Three weeks later the Angora government proclaimed the abolition of the Sultanate ; the sultan, who had never been more than a puppet, fled to security on a British ship, and Turkey became a republic. A new khalif—not sultan— was appointed, but a year later (February, 1924) the government abolished the Khalifate itself—an event which did not have upon Mahomedans at large the disturbing effect anticipated ; since it could not be attributed to Christian hostility to Islam. The final peace terms, taking the place of the still-born Treaty of Sèvres, were arranged at the Conference of Lausanne (1922–23), which was followed by the abdication of George II—the

**MUSTAPHA KEMAL PASHA**

Mustapha Kemal Pasha, born 1882, set up the Angora government in 1920 and became president of the Turkish republic in 1923. His Westernising policy is brought out by this photograph of him dancing with his adopted daughter at the ball given to celebrate her marriage.

*Photo, General Photographic Agency*

ID

ANGORA : THE ANATOLIAN TOWN THAT REPLACED CONSTANTINOPLE AS CAPITAL OF TURKEY

The rapid growth of Angora since it became the Turkish capital in 1923 was promoted by Mustapha Kemal, who turned a backward country town into a modern city. New buildings and roads replace former unhealthy quarters and narrow streets. The old town, still surrounded by its medieval walls, is seen on the hill at the back, while the new town is spread along the valley below.

*Photo, E.N.A.*

Greek monarchy could not survive its disastrous failure—and Greece became one more among the new republics.

The Treaty of Lausanne (July, 1923) was the last in the series of treaties, beginning with that of Versailles, establishing peace between the group of victorious powers and the several defeated powers in the Great War, the relations with Turkey having hitherto been controlled by the armistice, not by a definitive peace. It gave to Turkey substantially better terms than she could have obtained under the Treaty of Sèvres, mainly at the expense of Greece, whose aggressive activity had brought that fate upon her. A substantial portion of Thrace was given back to what may be called the new Turkey, as well as Adrianople, the bulwark of Constantinople. The delimitation of the Turkey-Irak boundary was left to the Turks and the British as 'mandatories' for Irak, with the League of Nations as referee.

### Shortcomings of the Settlement

IT will have been clear enough in the course of this chapter that the post-war settlement lacked one very vital desideratum. It was not, because it could not be, a settlement by consent in which the interests of all parties concerned were judicially adjusted and all were treated on an equality. It was a case in which one party was in a position to dictate its own terms which the other could only accept, or rather submit to, under protest, nursing its own conviction that they were dictated not by justice, but by vindictiveness, and that it was morally entitled to evade them to the best of its power. Security for the victors against renewed aggression by the vanquished, even in a remote future, was for them the first essential, meaning that renewed aggression must be placed—permanently if possible —out of the power of the vanquished. In the eyes of the victors the vanquished had been guilty of gratuitous and criminal aggression developed by criminal methods which, apart from security, deserved salutary punishment which the victors were entitled to exact. The defeated powers had inflicted damage for which the victors claimed the fullest compensation.

But it was also inevitable that the victors themselves should not see eye to eye as to the methods by which security should be obtained, the extent and the distribution of the compensations available, and the limits beyond which the depression of the vanquished would react to the detriment of the victors themselves. The fact that ultimate security against war could only be achieved by the substitution of good will and mutual confidence for traditional ments at Paris. The Versailles treaty itself was the work of the Paris Conference which formally terminated in January, 1920, when the ratifications of the treaty were completed. A fresh conference met in London in February, which dealt less drastically than had been expected with the question of the ' war criminals,' since the chief of them was on neutral Dutch territory where he could not be seized and whence the Dutch government

**' DIPLOMACY BY CONFERENCE ' AT SAN REMO IN 1920**

After the Great War the Allied leaders adopted the conference system as the best method of handling the numerous questions demanding settlement. This photograph shows members of the supreme council assembled at the Villa Devachan, where the San Remo Conference met in April 1920, its main concern being German disarmament. The French premier, Millerand, is seated on the extreme left ; Nitti, Italian premier, is in the centre, while Lloyd George and Lord Curzon are on the right.

*Photo, Topical Press Agency.*

hostility and suspicion was indeed recognized by the creation of the League of Nations ; but that was admittedly a tentative experiment which might have incalculably beneficial results but might prove entirely futile. Time alone would show. Meanwhile, an atmosphere of good will was not one of the realities of the situation ; and the fundamental necessity was the agreed action of the Allies, whose unanimous will no one else could resist. Hence, the method of ' diplomacy by conference ' was substituted for the traditional ambassadorial diplomacy as at once more rapid in action and keeping the Allied governments in closer touch with each other.

The execution of the treaty terms was carried out under the supervision of the Conference of Ambassadors — the accredited agents of the respective govern-

declined imperturbably to eject him. It gave up the attempt to settle the question of Fiume, which it left to Italy and Yugo-Slavia, and it decided that the Turk should be permitted to remain in Constantinople. A third conference met in April at San Remo. It agreed upon the ' internationalisation ' of the Dardanelles and the Bosporus, left Armenia to carry on as best it might, and was chiefly occupied with the thorny question of German disarmament.

German troops had been marched into the Ruhr district, officially to suppress communistic disturbances there. This looked very much like a move of the German military party ; it disclosed the fact that the Germans still had under arms a much larger number of regular troops than should have been the case ; and the entry of German troops at all into the demilitarised area was a breach of the peace terms. The French at once took alarm, and replied by occupying Frankfort and Darmstadt. In doing so on her own responsibility France was within her technical rights, though in some quarters her action was felt to be needlessly aggressive, while in others it seemed to be more than warranted, not only by Germany's failure to reduce her army, but by her demands that the period allowed for her disarmament should be extended and the extent of the disarmament itself reduced. A reasonable harmony, however, was restored, and the conference rejected the German demands. The German troops were withdrawn, and the French followed suit. But the Germans were also for the first time invited to meet the Allies in conference for the better execution of the peace terms. Before this conference met at Spa, in July, there were several minor conferences, mainly for the adjustment of French and British points of view, and to consider the financial position in Germany.

### Conferences at Spa, London and Genoa

THE aim of the Germans at Spa was to obtain very substantial remissions of their treaty indebtedness on the ground that it was not practically possible to make the stipulated payments. They failed to satisfy the Allies of the genuineness of their plea, though the latter repudiated any intention of victimising them. The chasm, however, between the views presented by the Germans and those maintained by the Allies was not appreciably diminished.

Nor did the situation become more promising with the London Conference of February, 1921. The Germans declared that the scheme of reparation payment submitted by the Allies was impossible of fulfilment, and propounded a counter scheme so inadequate (from the Allied point of view) that its uncompromising rejection was accompanied by the threat of the application of ' sanctions ' if the Germans maintained what was regarded as a wilful refusal to carry out their treaty obligations. The sanctions were applied ; and, by another London conference of

the Allies alone, the Germans were given a week to accept somewhat modified terms. A new but far from stable German government submitted. But it soon became obvious that they would again default. A Paris conference in August failed entirely to agree on the settlement of another problem, the partition of Upper Silesia between Germany and Poland, which was finally handed over to the League of Nations.

A conference at Cannes early in 1922 was abortive and was followed by a conference at Genoa, in April, which was productive of more discord than harmony. For so far as France took part in it, it was only to emphasise the fact that her own policy was fixed ; Germany was, in effect, declaring herself bankrupt ; Bolshevik delegates had been invited to attend, and their contributions to debate only served to intensify the distrust with which they were regarded, and the general sense of the utter impracticability of any co-operation with them ; and the German delegates took the opportunity to strike with them at Rapallo a treaty of ' recognition and commerce ' which the Allies could only interpret as a deliberate defiance, while the French premier—in France, not at Genoa—virtually announced the intention of taking such measures as were necessary to the due fulfilment of the terms of the Treaty of Versailles, preferably with the co-operation of the other powers ; but, if that were not forthcoming, without it. In spite of the astonishing attitude of the Russian delegates, Great Britain and Italy endeavoured to procure a convention with Russia, which should at least pave the way for admitting her to the European comity, but failed, since neither France nor Belgium, nor finally the Soviet government itself, would adopt it.

### The Need for Economic Revival

THE reign of good will seemed farther off than ever, and the conference powers even took the precaution of making a temporary pact of non - aggression among themselves, Germany and Russia included. But one point of actually hopeful omen was emerging : the powers were beginning to realize that the sickness of Europe could not be cured until her economic conditions were restored on a healthy basis. Economic revival was beginning to be recognized not as a minor but as a primary necessity.

Meanwhile, however, another separate conference had been at work at Washington, with much more progressive effect ; a conference called not by the treaty powers, but by the United States of America, who took at most a watching part in the European conferences. Europe was indeed concerning itself with disarmament, but in the imagination of Europe that was mainly visualised as the compulsory disarmament of Germany. To America, as to the League of Nations, it meant the discovery of a basis for the persistent universal agreed reduction of armaments to what might be called a police level—the standard of controlled force necessary to the guardianship of the public peace. To a conference with this object, the limitation of armaments, in view, America invited the four treaty powers, Great Britain, France, Italy and Japan, to which were added China and the three minor European states which were concerned with Pacific and Far Eastern questions. The conference met on Armistice day, 1921, concluding its sessions on February 6 following.

### Washington Conference & 'Four Power Treaty'

THE five great powers dealt with the problem of naval disarmament, since it became immediately evident that military disarmament could not as yet be profitably discussed ; the nine with the other group of questions which touched them all. The German navy having ceased to exist, only the five were directly touched by the naval question. America proposed that, subject to equivalent action on the part of Britain and Japan, she should abandon her existing programme of capital-ship construction, and scrap a number of existing battleships, the powers agreeing to limitations on future naval construction. Here agreement was comparatively easy ; but on the question of ' auxiliary ' craft it was soon found that no common term was possible, the special needs of the several states being controlled by diverse and divergent conditions. The total abolition of submarines was mooted by Great Britain, but found no favour with those of the powers which regarded them as essential to their own defence, and the conference contented itself with denouncing their use as commerce destroyers, a denunciation which from the British point of view appeared entirely impossible to enforce.

The agreement as to capital ships, however, was a very material advance, as also was the ' Four Power Treaty ' between America, France, Great Britain and Japan, which took the place of the standing Anglo-Japanese treaty of alliance, in which America detected a possibility of developments hostile to herself, since there had been considerable friction between her and Japan in the past. With no possibility of German or Russian fleet activities in the Pacific, the continuance of the standing treaty was viewed with suspicion ; but when it was translated into the Four Power Treaty it became an instrument of common accord. The new treaty was not technically the work of the Washington conference, but was accessory to it. Similarly the conference conduced to but did not in itself effect a treaty between Japan and China, which was made at the same time, regarding the vexed question of Shantung, from which the Germans had been expelled by the Japanese during the war, while China claimed its reversion to herself. The conciliatory action of Japan in this matter was capped by the British restitution of Weihaiwei to China, and the resignation by other powers of sundry concessions that had been made to them.

### Lausanne and the Ruhr Invasion

IT was not long after the dispersal of the Genoa conference that Greece suffered her crushing defeat at the hands of Mustapha Kemal. It has already been told how the advance of the Turks led up to the conference of Lausanne, of which the main concern was the settlement of the Turkish question, and the other main feature was the avoidance of the breach which was threatening between the Western powers. It may be noted that at this moment the British coalition ministry fell and Lloyd

George, who was not on the most sympathetic terms with the French premier, was succeeded by the Unionist leader Bonar Law, while the coalition foreign minister, Lord Curzon, remained in office, and almost simultaneously Mussolini became Italian prime minister.

The Lausanne conference was prolonged; it did not actually conclude until after midsummer in 1923, and there were critical moments during its course; but the most anxious moments of that anxious year were not concerned with the Lausanne negotiations; for it opened with the declaration by the ' Reparation Commission,' which was in charge of the matter, that Germany was in wilful default in the discharge of the payments due from her, and more particularly in the delivery of coal. Two days later, on January 11, French troops in concert with Belgium marched into the Ruhr district and occupied it; as, at least in their own view, which it was more than difficult to controvert, they were entitled to do in the circumstances under the Versailles treaty. But, with the exception of Belgium, the action of France was without support from her allies. Their active opposition was out of the question.

The German government did not—probably in the state of German public opinion it dared not—acquiesce. Since active resistance was impossible, there was only one way left—passive resistance. The coal deliveries ceased, work

## MEMBERS OF LLOYD GEORGE'S COALITION MINISTRY

The fine war-time service rendered to the British nation by David Lloyd George (lower left) secured him the premiership in 1916. His coalition ministry was returned in 1918 and held office until his resignation in October, 1922. Top : Lord Curzon (1859-1925) succeeded Balfour as foreign secretary in 1919, resigning in 1924. Andrew Bonar Law (1858-1923), who for some time shared the coalition leadership with Lloyd George, later helped to destroy it, and succeeded as Unionist premier, 1922-23.

*Photos, Russell, Vandyk and Elliott & Fry*

## THE TWO LEADERS OF THE NATIONAL GOVERNMENT

James Ramsay MacDonald, the first Labour prime minister of Great Britain, held that office for ten months in 1924 and returned to it in June, 1929, remaining premier after the national ministry was formed in August, 1931. Stanley Baldwin, having been head of a Unionist government May 1923 to January 1924 and again October 1924 to June 1929, joined MacDonald in August 1931 in forming the national ministry, of which he became deputy leader

*Photos, Lafayette*

ceased, all payments were refused. But it was on the working population of the Ruhr and in Germany at large that the burden of the consequent suffering fell. France, relatively, was merely inconvenienced. In Germany the mark dropped to a fabulously low level. British public opinion generally, but by no means universally, disapproved if it did not openly resent the French action. The relations between the two governments, without whose co-operation the restoration of European stability was unattainable, were strained almost to breaking-point—but not quite.

Matters in Germany went from bad to worse. In May she made proposals that were regarded as too futile to be seriously discussed. The French government would not contemplate the evacuation of the Ruhr until the passive resistance ceased. For that reason it rejected a second German offer in July. British 'notes' to France were met by polite but uncompromising replies—including rejection of the suggestion, which looked like a reflection upon the Reparation Commission, that

Germany's capacity to pay should be referred to a commission of impartial experts. It appeared possible that in the impasse which had been reached the British government was contemplating independent action. Germany was only encouraged to maintain the passive resistance by the prospect of a complete breach between France and England—but for that England herself was not prepared. If she had contemplated independent action, she abstained from taking it. The sword remained suspended, even if it was by no more than a hair.

The strain of the fatal passive resistance policy upon Germany was already more than she could bear. She was threatened not only with complete economic ruin, but with political disintegration by a separatist movement in the Rhineland, mainly traceable to the French occupation of the Ruhr and the revolutionary fever born of hunger ; a movement not for union with France, but for an independent republic. France remained immovable. But Germany had at last acquired a ministry whose chiefs had the courage

831

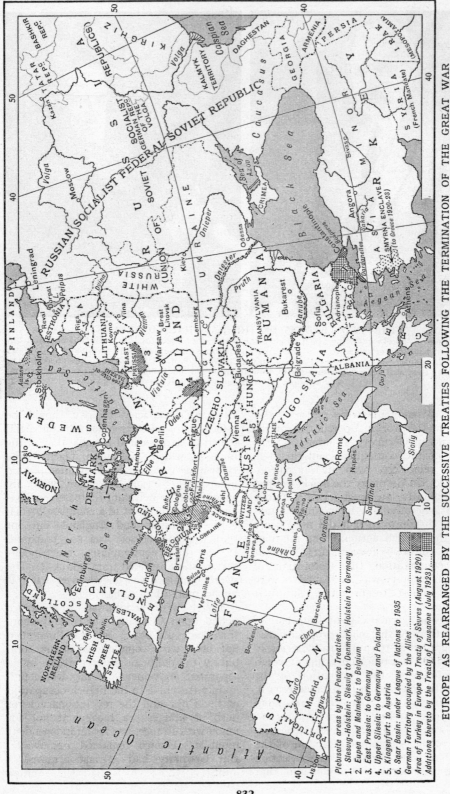

**EUROPE AS REARRANGED BY THE SUCCESSIVE TREATIES FOLLOWING THE TERMINATION OF THE GREAT WAR**

Whereas after Waterloo the policy on which the redistribution of Europe was effected was governed by dynastic considerations, the basic principle of its redistribution by the Treaty of Versailles in 1919 was the satisfaction of national aspirations and recognition of the right of the smaller nations to self-determination. In this map the main divisions of the new Europe are shown with shaded portions indicating areas where the ultimate settlement was left to plébiscite, also the areas in German territory occupied by the Allies pending fulfilment by the Central powers of obligations imposed upon them by the Treaty.

*Plebiscite areas by the Peace Treaties......*
1. *Slesvig–Holstein: Slesvig to Denmark, Holstein to Germany*
2. *Eupen and Malmédy: to Belgium*
3. *East Prussia: to Germany*
4. *Upper Silesia: to Germany and Poland*
5. *Klagenfurt: to Austria*
6. *Saar Basin: under League of Nations to 1935*
*German Territory occupied by the Allies*
*Area of Turkey in Europe by Treaty of Sèvres (August 1920)*
*Additions thereto by the Treaty of Lausanne (July 1923)*

to face facts, the insight and the patriotic faith to deal with them unflinchingly. At the end of September the new government withdrew its predecessor's passive-resistance decrees—and the German army instead of breaking into a militarist revolt stood loyally by the government.

Only a few days before, Baldwin, who had succeeded Bonar Law as head of the British government, had a meeting with Poincaré which, without affecting the latter's firmness, did much to relieve the tension. The action of the German government did still more, for France had carried her fundamental point that the cessation of passive resistance must precede any relaxation of the French grip. In November the Reparation Commission itself—with a French chairman—appointed two independent expert commissions of inquiry, the precise point on which the British government had been most urgent, of which the issue was the 'Dawes report' (March, 1924). The French remained in the Ruhr, but 'with the passing of resistance their activities there became less obtrusive, and the new British premier, MacDonald, approved himself a most judicious diplomatist. Poincaré was succeeded by the conciliatory Herriot.

### Recommendations of the Dawes Report

A LONDON conference was opened in July, which was attended by American delegates. The recommendations of the Dawes report were substantially approved, and greatly strengthened by the unexpected discovery that America was ready to co-operate actively by sending delegates to the Reparation Commission, whereby the prospect of raising a loan to help Germany on to her feet would be immensely improved. The vital advance was in the recognition of the economic fact that Germany would continue to default, whether wilfully or not, until she was able as well as willing to make the necessary effort. Till that was recognized she would be neither able nor willing. The hesitation of France to adopt and of Germany to accept the offer which was formulated on the basis of the Dawes report was overcome ; and the conference concluded the agreement, which was not in the form of a treaty, under which the Dawes scheme was brought into operation. The conference had taken the first real step towards reconstruction.

The adoption, however, of the Dawes report was not merely a material step towards financial reconstruction ; it was the first significant omen of an improving atmosphere, of diminishing hostility and suspicion, of relaxing antagonisms. References to 'war guilt' had hitherto been an unfailing irritant ; at the London conference they had been tactfully dispensed with. It was much to the credit of the Allies that they had persuaded themselves —without withdrawing their claims—to moderate the form of their demands and to add thereto offers of assistance ; it was no less to Germany's credit, and particularly to that of the small group of statesmen, headed by the president, Ebert, who were piloting her through very difficult waters, that she accepted the offer in a corresponding spirit and played up to it.

### Beginning of German Rehabilitation

THE armed occupation of the Rhine districts was due, under the Versailles treaty, to be withdrawn by degrees, beginning with the evacuation of Cologne in January, 1925, but only if Germany had duly discharged her obligations by that date ; she had not done so, and the occupation continued. The French evacuation of the Ruhr was not completed until after midsummer ; but Germany had dropped her attitude of sullen inertia, and was seriously setting about her own economic revival and showing a marked disposition to endeavour at least to carry out her treaty obligations instead of evading them. Sundry efforts of the League of Nations to evolve a treaty giving a real security against the appeal to arms in the future had broken down or were breaking down, when in February, 1925, Germany herself submitted a tentative proposal to the French government, the essence of which was a security pact guaranteeing the present territorial status on the Rhine, the result of her own defeat.

It was perhaps as well that this notable effort did not attract too much of the public attention, which is apt to produce heated and recriminating controversy in the press, while the responsible ministers of France, Great Britain and other countries were exchanging views on the various knotty points arising from the suggestion, the practical possibility or impossibility of security pacts not only for the Rhineland but in other regions where boundary questions were international sources of friction ; matters upon which there were many divergences, which did not, however, wreck the keen desire for concord.

## Work of the Conference at Locarno

THE outcome was the momentous Conference of Locarno which met in October ; momentous not so much for what it actually accomplished as because it marked and emphasised the attainment of a new plane of discussion in which not antagonisms but community of interests held the first place. The value of the Locarno pact was indeed very great ; but it was exceeded by that of the new ' Locarno spirit.' The past could not be blotted out, but it could be left behind. To revive old controversies on the rights and wrongs of which men had long made up their minds once for all could benefit no one ; as subjects of discussion they were dead and buried, and their ghosts must not be allowed to walk. The ghosts were not as a matter of fact completely laid—they reappear when tempers become provocative ; but they were quiescent at Locarno.

It was the first time that Germany had come into conference unequivocally on an equal footing with her former foes and as a promoter of peace—actually the prime promoter of the conference itself, since it was clearly traceable to her initiative in the preceding February.

The conference met on October 3 ; its invaluable work was completed in a fortnight. The work was done in an atmosphere of unprecedented good will, not penetrated by controversial comment from irresponsible quarters, and facilitated by the freedom from formalities in its procedure. The agreements arrived at, when ratified by the respective governments, were embodied in the Treaties of London, commonly referred to as the ' Locarno

Pact,' in December. All the conference powers guaranteed the French-German-Belgian frontiers and the conditions applied to the demilitarised zone under the Versailles treaty. Germany and France and Germany and Belgium pledged themselves not to resort to war against each other except in defence against an act of flagrant aggression ; to refer disputes, where they could not agree between themselves, to some form of judicial decision, and at once to report any violation of the terms to the League of Nations ; all the signatory powers pledging immediate support to the aggrieved party if the League confirmed the charge.

Besides accessory guarantees, there were added arbitration conventions between Germany on the one hand and France and Belgium severally on the other. A more elaborate German-Polish and German-Czecho-Slovakian arbitration agreement left open the possibility of future frontier modifications by mutual agreement between those powers. Two complementary treaties were made, mutually guaranteeing frontiers, by France with Poland and Czecho-Slovakia, to which the other powers were not parties, since Great Britain and Italy, while ready to give guarantees in the west, could not extend that readiness to the east. But the vital fact remained. Germany and her former foes had at last persuaded themselves at least to shake hands.

## Germany Admitted to League of Nations

THE note of Locarno was the note of reconciliation ; confirmed next year by the termination of Germany's semi-outlawry, an outlawry which had been at once an inevitable corollary of her defeat in the war and an insuperable obstacle to European recuperation and reconstruction. It ended with her admission to the League of Nations in 1926, with the status of a great power therein. She had accepted the conditions which could convert her into a colleague instead of an antagonist. We need not here deal at length with the story and the effects of that change, nor need we dwell upon the continued abstention of the United States from joining the League, and the persistent hostility of Soviet Russia to everything for which the

League stands. The fundamental point of the change that had taken place was not that reconciliation was complete and suspicion and distrust had vanished, for they still lurked beneath the surface and still occasionally broke loose, but that from this time the note of reconciliation was definitely predominant.

Some reference, however, must here be made to minor episodes illustrative of some of the difficulties of preserving peace and evolving goodwill in a Europe whose nerves had been torn to rags by the strain and the sufferings of the war. Such was the unhappy incident of the murder of some Italian officers upon Greek soil in August, 1923, the consequent high-handed seizure of Corfu by the Italian government, and the compromise under which the League abstained from insistence on its own authority to deal with the matter when Italy chose to acknowledge in its place that of the Council of Ambassadors, whose award probably did not differ substantially from that which would have been made by the League. Such, again, was the sudden menace of armed collision

**ALEXANDER OF YUGO-SLAVIA**
Alexander, second son of Peter of Serbia, did notable service in the Balkan wars of 1912–13. Proclaimed first king of Yugo-Slavia in 1921, his reply to divisional discord was the establishment in 1929 of a royal dictatorship.
*Photo, Vandyk*

between Greece and Bulgaria in October, 1925, which was stopped by the instant intervention of the League and the self-restraint of the two governments concerned in the face of intense popular excitement.

$\mathfrak{T}$HE aim of the statesmen of the Versailles treaty was a settlement which should be in fact a reversal of all that was most dear to the hearts of the statesmen of the Vienna settlement of 1815. They had shaped the map of Europe on the basis of nationalism, regardless of dynastic claims ; only one monarchy, the Bulgarian, survived where the defeated powers had ruled ; the new states were all republics save for Yugo-Slavia, which was new only in the sense that the old Serbian kingdom now embraced populations which had before been denied union with it—and Yugo-Slavia was a constitutional monarchy with parliamentary institutions. The American president had declared that the peace was to make the world safe for democracy. In short, the settlement

**PRIMO DE RIVERA**
Under the leadership of the Spanish soldier and statesman Miguel Primo de Rivera, born in 1870, his country's constitution was suspended in 1923. In 1925 he became premier in the civilian administration which he introduced
*Photo, Kâulak, Madrid (E.N.A.)*

was in theory the triumph of what had been known of old as ' the Revolution.'

Nevertheless, neither nationalist groupings nor democratic political systems proved to be simple propositions ; the first, because within each of the larger groups were minority groups of diverse nationality which did not immediately amalgamate ; the second, because democracy presupposes a certain standard of educated intelligence, and of what may be called the co-operative spirit. Democracy found its enemy not as of yore in hereditary privilege, but in communism. In general, democracy (including

**TWO PRESIDENTS OF THE UNITED STATES**
Neither of President Wilson's successors, Warren Gamaliel Harding (left), nor Calvin Coolidge (right), carried on his policy of assuming American leadership in European affairs. Harding became the Republican president in 1920, and Coolidge, who was his vice-president, succeeded him on his death in 1923.
*Photo, Topical Press Agency*

**MUSSOLINI IN FASCIST COSTUME**
The organizing genius of Benito Mussolini, born of humble parents in Romagna province in 1883, developed the Italian Fascist movement as a weapon against Bolshevism. Becoming premier in 1922, he undertook his country's reconstruction.
*Ministry of Foreign Affairs, Rome; photo, Henry Manuel*

' constitutionalism ') was strong enough to cope with communism ; but in Russia communism had democracy by the throat ; while it is a somewhat ironic commentary on the whole situation that at the end of 1928 Spain, Italy, Yugo-Slavia and Turkey had in fact passed under the control of unqualified autocrats, and to these may be added Albania.

There was indeed nothing surprising in the fact that the president of the Turkish republic gained such a personal ascendancy that he became an autocrat under republican forms, except that his power arrived without the normal accompaniments of bloodshed, almost as a thing of course. It was equally natural that Albania, which had never in the whole course of her history submitted to any rule save that of some chief endowed with an irresistible personality, such as Skanderbeg, acquiesced in the assumption of the crown by a president who would seem to possess the traditional qualifications. Rivalries and jealousies between the newly united divisions of Yugo-Slavia drove its king to a coup d'état establishing his own autocracy as the only effective means to the enforcement of law and order. For Turks, Serbs and Albanians the ' strong man ' had always been necessary to political salvation.

The two Latin kingdoms, however, having very different historic antecedents,

**ABD EL-KRIM AFTER HIS SURRENDER**
The strife which broke out in 1925 in Morocco between the forces of the rebellious tribal leader Abd el-Krim and the French was brought to a sudden conclusion by the surrender of the former in May, 1926. He is seen (fourth from the left) in this group with his attendants and some French officers.
*Photo, Chusseau-Flaviens*

The system is one which would have rejoiced the heart of Machiavelli. It is the negation of what the 'Nordic' peoples understand by 'liberty.' The people, being a congeries of factions, is incapable of directing an efficient government ; for its own good it must have an efficient government, and one that is irresistible and has absolutely unlimited power and right of control ; as against the government, the people have no rights. The state is incorporated in the government, and the government is incarnate in the person of its chief. The law as laid down by the government is supreme ; only the government itself is above the law, and of it no adverse criticism may be tolerated. That would seem to be the theory of Fascism ; and its efficiency in the hands of the Duce is so convincing that it is easy to overlook the fact that it is bound up with the personality of the Duce himself.

present a different development. Spain, for considerably more than a century, had been struggling to build up a strong government on constitutional lines, for the most part under painfully adverse conditions. The reigning king, his mother and his father, had been more successful than their predecessors, but the governing power was still inefficient ; and it was the sense of inefficiency, and perhaps the example that was being set by Italy, that brought about the sudden establishment of a dictatorship still under the crown, in 1923, and the suspension of constitutional rule. This, however, was not a departure from precedent in the theory of government, whatever the developments in store may be ; emergencies have produced dictatorships as their only available immediate solution, from time immemorial—successfully or otherwise according to the abilities of the dictator.

Italy, on the other hand, made a new departure. Parliamentary government had brought her neither political nor economic stability, when at the end of 1922 Signor Mussolini became her prime minister and began to lay the foundations of the Fascist state, hardly veiled by the retention of the hereditary monarchy.

THE League, the economic problems of Europe after the war, the story of Bolshevik Russia and its influences upon Europe, all essential parts of the history of the post-war period, cannot here be dealt with in any detail, but their culmination in the financial crisis of 1930-32 will engage our attention in later pages. Europe, to which, with Turkey, our attention has hitherto been confined, is not the only field which has to pass under review. While America—in the sense of the United States — interested herself actively in European and extra-European affairs, she rejected the rôle of leader laid down for her by President Wilson, and under his successors, Presidents Harding and Coolidge, declined to share the direct responsibilities of the European powers ; an attitude regretted by the latter, and not easily intelligible to the mind of western Europe, exciting at times adverse comment which was not always according to knowledge.

IN Africa the most obvious product of the war was the elimination of German influences, with the substitution of the influence of one or another European power in the areas where they had predominated. But in relation to Mahomedan Africa, Africa from Egypt to Morocco, it had earlier become evident that German influences could not be established without a sharp conflict with France or Spain or both, if not with Great Britain as well ; while on the remaining section of the Mediterranean littoral her ' peaceful penetration ' had been checked by Italy's declaration of the Tripoli protectorate. Subject to a reasonable security for her own commercial interests, and a free hand in Egypt, England regarded the expansion of the three Latin powers with a friendly eye, and their relations with each other had shown themselves capable of amicable adjustment.

The African populations, however, were not equally amenable. In Morocco the inland tribes, led by Abd el-Krim, were so successful in their resistance to the Spanish efforts at domination that in 1925 they took occasion to challenge the French also, since the latter were encroaching on what they regarded as their own preserves ; and it was only at the cost of severe campaigning that the two European powers were able in combination to compel the submission of the Moroccan champion in 1926. Of the three Latin powers, France was the most successful both in conciliating the tribesmen and in developing the commercial possibilities of the area over which she extended her administrative sway ; but the immemorial tribal organization is not of a kind to acquiesce readily in European conceptions of government, or indeed in any alien domination.

In those portions of western Asia where the authority of western ' mandatory powers ' took the place of the old Turkish regime, the ' autonomy ' which materialised was extremely tenuous. The first king of the Hejaz was displaced by the chief of the puritan Wahabi sect ; his son was made ' king ' of Irak, but such authority as he had was derived entirely from the British ; Syria resented the French regime, which was of a more military character than that of the British in the neighbouring areas. Palestine was judiciously organized largely for the benefit of the Jews, but in such a manner as to develop the prosperity of the non-Jewish populations. In fact, in all these areas the general security was much greater than before, but the new wine of misunderstood Western ideas was fermenting in old bottles. Tact and sympathy were very necessary to insure against disaster.

In fact, the secular problem of the irreconcilable divergences between Orientalism and Occidentalism had come to life again. In Japan the antagonism was least in evidence, because her Orientalism was a thing apart, and she had started on the line of an essentially critical but wholly practical assimilation not of Westernism but of selected Western materials. Something of the kind was being attempted

**THE LATIN ALPHABET COMES TO TURKEY**

Kemal Pasha's determination to abolish the old Arabic signs in Turkey led to the declaration, on December 1, 1928, that the Latin alphabet should be compulsory. In Constantinople the governor compelled a mobilisation of all between the ages of fourteen and forty to learn the new Latinised Turkish.

RIZA SHAH OF PERSIA

Risen from the ranks of the Persian army, Riza Khan engineered the deposition of Persia's reigning ruler, and, being elected shah, crowned himself at Teheran in April, 1926, with a crown specially made for the occasion.

*Photo, Pacific & Atlantic, Ltd.*

in Turkey under the inspiration of its president and presiding genius Mustapha Kemal, though the problem had for him the additional complication of Islam, and of resistance to Occidental domination with which Japan was not threatened. Turkey's future was trammelled, as Japan's was not, by her past. But all over Asia—during more than the last half-century, by political and commercial penetration more than by military conquest—the tentacles of European domination had been making themselves increasingly felt, while at the same time Asia was increasingly conscious that it was only by learning from Europe how to do it that she could release herself from the European pressure. Now Asia was much disposed to turn to Bolshevik Russia, still more Oriental than Western at bottom,

for the teachers whom Bolshevik Russia was glad to supply. Her own turn would come when the ascendancy of the 'bourgeois' powers had been broken—perhaps.

Turkey had set the example. Persia followed it under the astute leadership of Riza Khan, who successfully engineered the deposition of the dynasty (which had not appropriated Western ideas, but had submitted itself and the country to Western domination) and procured his own recognition as shah. Like Mustapha, he reversed the policy, adopting Western methods while rejecting Western ascendancy. In 1926 Turkey and Persia, the new Turkey and the new Persia, formed an alliance. Some time earlier, a new amir in Afghanistan, Amanullah, had declared that British ascendancy there must end. As the British had no desire to exercise any more control in Afghanistan than would secure her against being used as a cat's-paw by Russia, British acquiescence was readily forthcoming—though the amir's methods had been aggressive enough to enforce a brief but decisive campaign as a preliminary. The subsequent relations were entirely amicable. But it may be noted that the Angora, Persian and Afghan governments all signed treaties with Russia at Moscow in 1921. Amanullah, however, was no less zealous to impose Western practices on his people than to resist Western dictation, so that at the end of 1928 his zeal brought about a revolution and his own expulsion from the kingdom. It is not difficult to see why at that time Bolshevik Russia eagerly propagated and England's enemies eagerly swallowed the curious fiction that the fall of Amanullah was to be attributed to British machinations.

### Changes in the British Empire

THE relations between the several portions of that 'commonwealth of nations,' the British Empire, had been materially affected by the war, though it had by no means weakened the bonds, whether of sentiment or of interest, which held together that great exemplar of unity in diversity. But it had ceased to be possible to apply the old terminology of 'colonies' and 'possessions' which belonged to a bygone age. The change was marked not so much by legislative acts as by the adoption of unprecedented practices as though they were normal developments from the practices of the past.

The ' Dominions ' severally, with India, were admitted to membership of the League of Nations, without actual definition of their status. No formal right was bestowed upon them of sharing in the actual direction of imperial policy, but the sense that they had acquired that right was a pervading one—though not yet absolutely as a matter of course. They did not desire complete independence in the control of their foreign relations, but it was tolerably manifest that they would not hold themselves bound by agreements to which their assent had not been given, though it would be given as a matter of course if they had no strong reasons to the contrary. Apart from foreign affairs their autonomy was unqualified. ' Dominion status ' in short was a condition without rigid definition,

but as to which misunderstandings in practice were not likely to arise, or likely to prove difficult of adjustment if they did arise.

Not in the Dominions themselves— though there appeared still to be a few intransigents in South Africa—but in other quarters, demands for separation from the Empire were heard. The scheme for Irish home rule, which had been so much in evidence before the war, broke down as a scheme when the war was over ; the old ' Nationalists,' whose loyalty had been so conspicuously displayed in the great crisis, lost control of the movement, which was now guided by the fanatics of separatism, the Sinn Fein party ; all the old smouldering passions and hostilities blazed up as fiercely as ever, and Ireland became the unhappy stage of insurrection, outrages and reprisals, until the British government arrived at a compromise with the less fanatical Sinn Fein leaders. They surrendered the demand for an independent Irish republic, the major

**AT THE AFGHAN COURT ON THE EVE OF AMANULLAH'S ABDICATION**

Although Amanullah, amir of Afghanistan, opposed Western rule in his dominions, he was extremely zealous in introducing Western customs. A revolution broke out among the Afghan people, unappreciative of his reforms, and he fled from his kingdom in January, 1929. Amanullah, wearing morning dress, is seen in the centre of this group of courtiers also dressed in Western fashion at the last meeting of his court before he abdicated. His brother, Inayatullah, in a light summer suit, is on the left.

*Photo, Fox Photos*

portion of Ulster was allowed to separate itself from the rest and remain attached to Great Britain, and the rest of Ireland became the autonomous Irish Free State with ' Dominion status ' within the Empire and membership in the League of Nations. Within the Free State the new Free State government was left with entire responsibility for the preservation of order and the maintenance of law without British interference. The new constitution became law in December, 1923.

Egypt had been formally separated from the Turkish empire and transformed into a British protectorate at an early stage of the war without being actually annexed. From the beginning, however, in 1882, Great Britain had declared her assumption of control to be in intention temporary. When the war was over the old agitation for the complete independence of Egypt revived. Nationalism was so much to the fore in the European settlement that it was difficult to ignore its claims in dealing with Orientals who declined to accept the theory, of which the truth is so obvious to the Western mind, that the arguments

for the autonomy of European communities do not apply to other peoples. In 1922 the British government, not without misgiving, made up its mind to end the protectorate and leave Egypt to govern herself—or to find out for herself how to do so. But though she was to be in theory a sovereign state, Great Britain had too many interests of her own, and too many responsibilities at stake, to concede absolutely without qualification this independence, which was granted with reservation of certain subjects. These included the protection of foreigners in Egypt, her defence, and the control of the Sudan, which had never been an effective Egyptian possession and had, as a matter of actual fact, been brought under control not by Egypt but by the British. That control the British were to retain, with due respect for Egyptian interests.

Egypt was presented with a constitutional monarchy under King Fuad, who had figured as sultan during the protectorate. But the agitation, by no means favoured by the king, for the total withdrawal of all British controlling influences, continued ;

AN EPISODE IN THE IRISH SINN FEIN MOVEMENT IN 1921

The rebellion, boycott and bloodshed which came to characterise the Sinn Fein movement originated in the strongly nationalist desire of its supporters for Irish independence. The Irish republican army organized under Sinn Fein auspices was responsible for the guerilla warfare which inaugurated the series of mutual outrages and reprisals of 1920–21. In May, 1921, the Customs House at Dublin was fired by Sinn Feiners and street fighting occurred. A Sinn Feiner lies dead in the foreground.

*Photo, Central News.*

with an accompaniment of occasional assassinations and 'student' outbreaks somewhat embarrassing to a party whose business it should have been to demonstrate its own administrative efficiency. That the limit of concession had been reached was made clear when a sympathetic Labour government in England proved as inflexible as its predecessor.

THE Asiatic problem — as affected by the war—was no less prominent in India. The loyalty then displayed had given India a right to claim her reward, though whether what her agitators were demanding would be a reward was another matter. A great administrative experiment was at once inaugurated, extending in British India the amount of responsible control to be entrusted to Indians and to Indian elective bodies—the system to which the name of dyarchy was given. It did not touch the autonomous Indian principalities—not under British administration at all—which form approximately one third of the Indian Empire, a very important fact not always realized either in England or elsewhere. To the princes the unity of India meant the union of diverse states, of which they were the chiefs, in an empire by no means homogeneous, focussed in the person of the king-emperor, for which unity the only imaginable guarantee is the British imperial sovereignty. In the nature of the case they do not sympathise with movements in British India which tend to weaken that authority, however anxious they may be, individually or as a group, for an increased influence in the imperial counsels.

It was to British India then that dyarchy was to apply ; and dyarchy may be described as provincial autonomy carried as nearly as possible to the safety limit, based on bodies of elected representatives, on the model — mutatis mutandis — of English representative institutions ; the

**A GANDHIST PROCESSION IN DELHI**
Imprisonment of the Indian nationalist leader, M. K. Gandhi, in March, 1922, did not stop the non-co-operation movement. 'Gandhi Day' was devoted each month in Delhi to anti-British demonstrations ; the spinning wheel paraded in this procession proclaims the boycott of foreign cloth.
*Photo, Topical Press Agency*

supreme government reserving to itself the control of certain specific subjects, a general overriding authority to be brought into play only if necessary, and sundry guarantees. The whole thing was avowedly experimental ; it did not and was not intended to convey any promise of full parliamentary institutions, still less of even an ultimate withdrawal of the overriding British authority.

Nevertheless, the British supremacy in India is faced—in certain sections of the community within British India—by that anti-European sentiment which we have noted as prevalent in Asia, and which in India, and elsewhere, is curiously misrepresented, by its most fervent and voiceful propagators, as Indian 'nationalism.' Dyarchy, therefore, is the reverse of satisfactory to the extremists of Indian nationalism, whose desire is nothing less than the extrusion of the European, which it brings no nearer ; so that the disaffected faction have directed their energies mainly to the attempt to make the whole reform abortive by withholding co-operation. But in India, as elsewhere, it is to be noted that the anti-Europeans pin their faith, for the defeat of Europe, to methods and theories which are themselves the product not of Orientalism but of Western political and natural science.

### China's new Republican Regime

CHINA presented at once the most emphatic and to Western eyes the most chaotic example of this revolt of the East against the West. Very shortly before the war the Manchu dynasty had been abolished, and under the guidance of the idealist Sun Yat-sen the empire had been transformed into what purported to be a democratic republic. Perhaps we may say that the ideal of which the new leaders were in pursuit was that which Japan had so amazingly achieved for herself in her revolution towards the close of the nineteenth century, when she remodelled herself on the basis of a scientific study of Western methods scientifically adapted to her own conditions by the patriotic co-operation of the political thinkers and the military caste, without foreign interference. But in China the political thinkers were befogged quite as much as they were aided by groping among Western ideas ; they had no patriotic feudal aristocracy to strengthen their

**CHIANG KAI-SHEK AT HANKOW**
The Cantonese nationalist leader Chiang Kaishek became president of China in October, 1928. He supported the Bolshevik agent at the public demonstration which fomented anti-foreign feeling at Hankow in 1927.
*Photo, Topical Press Agency*

hands ; and the Europeans were always in the way. Also from their point of view it might be said that the Japanese counted not as Orientals but as ultra-Europeans. And on the top of this there came the Bolshevik propaganda, fundamentally anti-European—while beneath lay the normally inert masses who were always ready to attribute whatsoever evils befell them to the doings of the foreign devils, more particularly British and Japanese.

South China was dominated by the new progressive nationalists, North China by the old reactionaries ; agreeing in their hostility to the foreigners and in nothing else ; while naturally it was the south, not the north, that was disposed to put its trust in Bolshevik agents.

Though the foreigners had acceded at Washington to many modifications in the treaty rights they had acquired previously, they still retained rights which were galling. Trouble then broke out in 1925 in the form of anti-foreign riots at Shanghai, spreading to Canton, Hankow and elsewhere. The government, whether willing or not, was no more able than it had been in the past to give the foreigners the security for which they had to make provision themselves ; and their doing so, as always, inflamed the popular Chinese hostility, while Bolshevik agents poured oil on the flames.

The Chinese republic had never succeeded in establishing a strong central government, even under the leadership of the highly respected begetter of the New Nationalism, Sun Yat-sen, who died in 1925. The Nationalist organization at Canton, whose military head was Chiang Kai-shek, did not recognize the military dictator Chang Tso-lin at Peking ; there had already been active hostilities between the two parties, sundry generals intervening, each of them playing for his own hand with a tendency to kaleidoscopic permutations. The Europeans, finding nothing that they could definitely treat as the sovereign authority to deal with, sought to observe a strict neutrality while making such arrangements for security as were possible with any de facto authority which seemed likely to carry out its engagements, and supplementing them by the presence of sufficient naval and military forces for taking action in the last resort.

The civil war seemed in 1926 to be going—with fluctuations—in favour of the Nationalists, whose avowed programme included the demand for the disappearance of all those foreign privileges which, it must be admitted, no European state would have tolerated in its own territories. To those claims Great Britain was much disposed to give full recognition, as soon as there should be a sovereign government in China. But there was no diminution of the anti-British agitation ; though the British went to unprecedented lengths of conciliation in the hope of convincing the Canton or Hankow government of their own good faith ; while the carefully limited strength of their military precautions was denounced as proof to the contrary, and the Kuomintang (the Nationalist government), with which the influence of Bolshevik agents was at its zenith, showed no power of controlling the excesses of its followers.

Its troops captured Nanking (March, 1927), but met with a sharp reverse at the hands of Chang Tso-lin when they advanced on Peking. The Kuomintang was apparently falling to pieces : Chiang Kai-shek tried to absorb its authority into his own hands, and lost his own authority instead in August ; only to be recalled in November as the one man who might succeed in restoring unity. This proved at any rate so far successful that by midsummer the Nationalists were in possession of Peking, the northern resistance was practically broken, and it was reasonably possible to claim that there was once more a supreme government—that of the Kuomintang—in China. Chiang Kai-shek became president in October ; the Kuomintang was shaking itself free from the sinister toils of its Bolshevik advisers ; an efficient government in China was of more value to the

**CHIANG KAI-SHEK'S ARMY MARCHES NORTH**

Under the able leadership of General Chiang Kai-shek the Chinese Nationalist army advanced on Peking in 1928. His troops were ejected from Tsinan-fu, where they clashed with the Japanese, but Peking was nevertheless occupied at midsummer. This Southern detachment is seen entering Tsinan-fu.

*Photo, Sport and General Press Agency*

Europeans than concessions extorted from one that was thoroughly unstable ; and the year ended with at least a reasonable prospect—though as yet by no means a certainty — of materially improved relations in the near future.

WE return then from the Far East to the West. It is to be noted that on the death of the first German president in 1925 the election to the Presidency fell upon the most respected if not the most brilliant of the German war chiefs, Marshal Hindenburg. Some perturbation was caused by the suspicion that this was a victory of the militarist faction, but this was finally removed by his acceptance of the Locarno Pact. When a soldier so distinguished and so loyal had faced the facts and set himself, without shedding a fraction of his patriotism, definitely on the side of European reconciliation, it was easier for Germany both to trust and to be trusted. The entry of Germany into the League followed Locarno in 1926 ; in 1927 began the withdrawal of the military occupation ; and in spite of the fact that her claim to have completely fulfilled her obligations to disarmament was in some respects disallowed, the further supervision of her disarmament was transferred to a League commission of control, which replaced the inter-Allied military commission.

Disarmament had now become perhaps the leading international question. The cause was unfortunately little enough furthered by another naval conference, in which France and Italy did not join, while America, Japan and Great Britain failed to arrive at an agreed scheme, and more misunderstandings than understandings were developed. There was a still more curious sequel ; for in 1928, with a presidential election pending, it appeared that the security of the United States demanded not reduction but an extended programme of naval construction.

At the same time, however, there came from the same quarter a remarkable proposal not for disarmament but for an international pact renouncing war as an instrument of national policy. This was in reply to a less sweeping proposal from France for a Franco-American pact of perpetual friendship. France suggested that the operation of the pact should be limited to ' wars of aggression.' Nevertheless, a draft declaration was drawn up and submitted for consideration to the greater powers as a basis for discussion. Great Britain led the way in expressing lively interest in the proposal and approving the principle, but urging the elucidation of details—primarily so that it might not be interpreted as an abrogation of the right of self-defence, or as overriding obligations incurred under the Covenant of the League of Nations. From the ensuing discussions it resulted that in July the British Empire generally and its member states severally declared their readiness to sign the pact. In August the Kellogg Pact was actually signed by the representatives of fifteen ' nations ' including Germany ; while no fewer than fifty declared their adherence to it, though its final ratification by the United States was deferred till January, 1929, when H. C. Hoover, the Republican candidate for the presidency, had just defeated Alfred E. Smith, the Democrat, by an enormous majority.

### Conferences on Disarmament

THE first decade after the Great War ended on a note of promise and hope, but four years later the world was further than ever from the Utopia of assured peace and steady prosperity that was so eagerly desired. In the purely political sphere a little progress was made. Conferences met from time to time to deal with the questions of Disarmament and Reparations. In January 1930 one assembled in London to discuss naval disarmament. General agreement was not reached as France and Italy found themselves unable to come to terms, but the other three Powers—Great Britain, the United States, and Japan— signed in April a treaty by which they undertook to reduce the number of their battleships by not carrying out the rebuilding programmes arranged at Washington in 1921–22 and fixed a maximum tonnage for their cruisers, destroyers and submarines. A general disarmament conference met at Geneva early in 1932, but, in

**GERMANY SIGNS THE KELLOGG PEACE PACT**

There were fifteen signatories, of whom seven represented the British Empire, to the pact renouncing war which was proposed by the U.S. Secretary, F. B. Kellogg, in July, 1928, and accepted by the Senate of the United States in January, 1929. Herr Stresemann, the German delegate, was the first to sign.

*Photo, Photopress*

the face of Germany's refusal to attend unless her claim to equality in armaments was granted, no results had been achieved by the autumn. However, the conference remained in being and its members reassembled in November. France put forward an elaborate plan, which included the establishment of an international air force under the control of the League of Nations, and Great Britain one which provided for the abolition of submarines and tanks and reductions of other armaments.

### Reparations and the Moratorium

THE other prime questions of international politics were reparations and war debts. These were discussed at two conferences held at the Hague, and at both Great Britain succeeded in securing better terms from her creditors. The second conference, held early in 1930, put the payment of reparations by Austria on a more satisfactory footing. Germany, although now in the grip of a trade and financial depression, accepted the scheme known as the Young Plan, but it was soon evident that a breakdown was in sight. Her position grew steadily worse until relieved by the proposal, put forward on June 19, 1931, by President Hoover, for a moratorium of a year for all war debts and reparations. The idea was accepted, quickly by Britain, less quickly by France, and by the additional aid of other measures Germany's financial collapse was averted.

The moratorium of 1931 was not a settlement, only a breathing space. Germany's statesmen declared quite clearly that their country could not continue to pay reparations and Great Britain took the lead in seeking a lasting settlement. In June, 1932, after one false start, a conference met at Lausanne under the presidency of Mr. MacDonald. After much discussion it was decided, subject to certain contingencies, not least the co-operation of the United States, that the payment of reparations should cease. In return Germany undertook to contribute the sum of £150,000,000 towards the reconstruction of Europe, and a world economic conference was arranged for 1933. Europe's payments to the United States again became due at the end of 1932, but just after the presidential election in November, Great Britain, France and Belgium asked separately for an extension of the moratorium.

### The Economic Blizzard

EARLY in 1929 there were signs that all was not well in the financial and economic spheres, but until the autumn very little attention was paid to them, and they offered only the most transient interruption to the onrush of speculative activity. In September the failure of the companies controlled by C. G. Hatry disturbed financial circles in London, and in October a sudden panic swept the New York stock exchange, but no one, least of all the bankers and economists, had any idea of the disastrous period to come.

During the three years 1930–32 the whole world was involved in an economic blizzard to which history affords no parallel. Roughly speaking, the sequence of events was as follows. The wholesale prices of commodities, especially the primary ones, such as wheat, fell heavily ; in some cases they became cheaper than they were before the World War. Rubber fell from 10d. a lb. in 1929, by no means a year of high prices, to under $2\frac{1}{2}$d. a lb. in 1931. In October, 1932, it was stated that the price of wheat was lower than it had been since Shakespeare's time. These and other falls equally calamitous meant that the producers of these commodities and also the holders of their stocks could not, in many cases, meet their liabilities, still less were they in a position to incur fresh ones. There was an enormous fall in the volume of orders sent to the manufacturers and the number of the unemployed rose by leaps and bounds. This meant a further reduction of purchasing power and so the process continued, until it is hardly an exaggeration to say that the world's income, in terms of money, had been reduced by one half. Concurrently the prices of almost all securities, especially industrials, fell heavily, and soon many of them stood at only a fraction of their value in 1928–29. Probably the world's capital, like its income, had been reduced, again in terms of money, by fully one half.

In Great Britain the banking system stood the strain well, but the storm found weak points in the finance of companies created only for fair weather, and there were a number of large failures, in some of which deliberate dishonesty played a part. None of the British frauds, however, attained the colossal proportions of the one engineered by the Swede, Ivar Kreuger, who committed suicide in March, 1932. In the United States and elsewhere bank failures were numerous and widespread, and investors suffered enormous losses. In Germany, as already stated, there was, towards the middle of 1931, something very like a complete breakdown of the mechanism of finance. In varying degrees every country from China to Peru felt the effects of the storm.

### Nature and Causes of the Crisis

THE economic crisis of 1930–32 was a new phenomenon in the world's history. Want and unemployment have, unfortunately, been common enough in the past, and financial collapses have been by no means unknown, but they have usually been associated with some failure of the crops, or other great catastrophe, such as a devastating war ; their progenitors have been " plague, pestilence and famine." This crisis was accompanied, not by want but by abundance—super-abundance—of all that man needs.

The bulging corn bins of Mr. Lloyd George's imagination really existed in Canada, the United States and the Argentine. Tin and oil, the supplies of which, we were told a few years ago, were soon to fail, were produced in such quantity that drastic restriction of output was forced upon the industries. Coffee was burned in Brazil, and in Australia and New Zealand there was a smaller loss in driving the sheep to death than in selling them for food. In the United States proposals were made to plough in part of the unwanted cotton crop. Coal, like oil, glutted the markets. Vast quantities of livestock could not find buyers even at the ruinous prices that prevailed, and a similar story could be told of other commodities. Even gold, which occupies a unique place in the world's economy, was being produced in greater quantities than ever before. If the theories of Richard Cobden had held good the world, with everything cheap and plentiful, would have been a perfect paradise.

Other features of the situation were almost equally remarkable. The blizzard was alike devastating to the countries of the New World that had been untouched by the Great War and to those of the Old World that had been invaded by hostile armies. It visited equally Germany and Austria, the vanquished, and France and Rumania, the victors. It made no distinction between Great Britain with its free trade policy and the United States with its tariffs.

Perhaps the most tragic result was the creation, or rather the augmentation, of the great army of willing but unwanted workers. Great Britain had become used to a standing army of unemployed numbering some 2,000,000, but in 1932 the figure rose to nearly 3,000,000, one-sixth of the working population. In the United States, with its abounding natural resources, unemployment was worse. In 1926 the present writer was engaged on editorial work in New York. Dealing with the subject of unemployment, he was told that he need add nothing about unemployment in the United States as there it did not exist. Five years later it was stated that there were 12,000,000, about one quarter of the workers, unemployed in that country. Germany's highly efficient industrial system did not prevent the unemployed there from being counted in millions, and from France, Italy and elsewhere came much the same story.

### The Failure of the Expert

JUST as the financiers and economists had failed to give the world any reasoned warning of the coming catastrophe, so they were equally unable, when it came, to agree upon its causes or to suggest an adequate remedy. Almost each practitioner diagnosed the complaint differently. One attributed it to reparations and war debts and declared that until payment of these was abolished, or at least radically reduced, there was no hope of improvement ; another said it was due to tariffs, which hindered the flow of international trade, and a third blamed the restriction of credit by the banks. One authority saw a remedy in the greater use of silver as currency—a form of bi-metallism—and another saw it in the distribution of the hoarded stocks of gold. Inflation was advocated by one, denounced by another, and disguised as reflation by a third. Some urged the issue of great loans to finance public works, while others regarded this remedy as but an aggrava-tion of the disease. The relative merits of spending and saving as solvents of unemployment were freely discussed. To some the crisis proved that the capitalist system was breaking down ; it could produce on a scale of unprecedented magnitude, but it had wholly failed to solve the complementary problem of distribution. A return to barter was seriously discussed and in a few cases transactions of this kind were arranged.

### The Ordinary Man and the Crisis

To the plain man the problem, though not its solution, was clear. Owing to doles and the like we were not literally " starving in the midst of plenty," but the statement nevertheless throws a flash of light on the position. Almost everything that man can want, not only the neces-sities of life such as wheat and beef, leather and wool, but the luxuries such as motor cars and gramophones, were produced in abundance, and yet the vast majority of the world's population was living in poverty. Even in countries such as Britain, France and America, which were, relatively speaking, wealthy, the bulk of the people, though vastly better off than a century or less before, lived amid surroundings that certainly conveyed no suggestion of wealth and little even of comfort.

The less thoughtful attributed the malaise to over-production or to an excess of population, but these views will not stand examination. Over-production is but another name for under-consumption, and, as Sir Arthur Salter has said, it is absurd to talk about it until " the last Hottentot dies a millionaire." Those who saw the remedy in a decline of popula-tion forgot that every individual, however poor, is a consumer and if the number of consumers is reduced the demand for commodities will follow suit. Indeed it might be argued that a considerable increase in population would, by consum-ing the surplus commodities, set in full motion again the wheels of trade. To the more thoughtful the problem was first and last a financial one. The com-modities, raw and finished, the capital and the workers, the buyers and the sellers, all existed ; only the mechanism of exchange was wanting. To provide this was the task of the financiers and econo-mists, and they stood before a waiting world unable or unwilling to supply it.

### National Finances

The general contraction of business soon showed itself in the finances of the various nations, most of which, including Great Britain, had hitherto proceeded on the comfortable assumption that there was no limit to the capacity of the taxpayer to pay. The first signs of ill-health came from Australia, but with great com-placency the financiers regarded the inability of the Commonwealth to balance its budget as quite an exceptional event ; they were soon to learn that it was the rule rather than the exception. By heroic efforts, and after a period of grave un-certainty, Australia succeeded in avoiding default on her loans, and in bringing about an equilibrium between revenue and expenditure. In Germany, France, the United States and Japan the national accounts showed a marked excess of expenditure over revenue. The smaller countries, unable to sell their products, were in an even worse position, and in 1931–32 Brazil, Austria, Greece and other states found it impossible to meet the interest on their foreign loans, some of them raised under the auspices of the League of Nations. This meant further losses to investors, many of whom were in Great Britain. In 1931 nation after nation followed Great Britain in abandon-ing the gold standard, until it was retained only in the United States, France, Switzer-land, Belgium and the Netherlands.

### Affairs in Great Britain

In Great Britain the crisis in the nation's finances came in the summer of 1931. In 1929 the Unionist ministry of Mr. Baldwin had been replaced by a

Labour one under Mr. Ramsay Mac-
Donald and the work of spending had gone
merrily on. The bankers, wrong as
usual, continued to utter their annual
platitudes to the effect that they saw
signs of improvement, and the politicians
were equally ignorant or, as some thought,
worse.

But in July, 1931, there was a sudden
change of tone. Mr. Philip Snowden,
then chancellor of the exchequer, spoke
of the possibility of an unbalanced
budget, and a committee under Sir George
May reported that a deficit of £120,000,000
on the year's accounts was in sight.
Events then moved rapidly. Early in
August there was a sudden fall in British
credit abroad. Funds were withdrawn
from London on a large scale, and the
Bank of England, having secured credits
to the extent of £50,000,000 from France
and the United States, appealed to the
Government for help.

Mr. MacDonald and his colleagues replied by declaring that the Budget must
be balanced, and a plan to do this was
prepared. The majority of the Labour
party, backed by the trade union congress,
refused to agree to the proposed economies,
and on August 24th the ministry resigned.
Before this the leaders of the Unionist and
Liberal parties had been in consultation
with the King and the Premier, and with
their aid a National Ministry was formed,
Mr. MacDonald retaining the position of
Premier. Of his leading colleagues only
Mr. Thomas, Mr. Snowden and Lord
Sankey stood by him; the vacant places
were filled by Mr. Baldwin, Sir Austen
Chamberlain, Mr. Neville Chamberlain,
Sir Herbert Samuel, Lord Reading, and
other Unionists and Liberals.

### The National Ministry

THE programme of the new ministry
was to balance the Budget and then to
submit its case to the electors. Parliament
was called together on September 8th, and
two days later Mr. Snowden introduced a
supplementary budget. Economies were
made in the public services, these including
cuts in the salaries of cabinet ministers,
judges, teachers and others, and in the
payments to the unemployed, and taxation was increased.

But the crisis was not yet over. Funds
were still being withdrawn from London,
and on September 20th it was stated that
the credit of £50,000,000 was nearly
exhausted. On September 21st, therefore,
an Act was passed through Parliament
relieving the Bank of England from the
obligation to sell gold at a fixed price.
Britain thus went off the gold standard, to
which she had returned, prematurely as
many thought, in 1925.

The general election took place on
October 29th and resulted in a sweeping
victory for the National Government,
which now had 558 supporters in a House
of 615 members. Mr. Arthur Henderson,
who had succeeded Mr. MacDonald as
leader of the Labour party, lost his seat,
as did most of his colleagues. His place in
the House of Commons was taken by Mr.
Lansbury, who had 51 followers, a gigantic
force compared with the three returned to
support Mr. Lloyd George. Mr. MacDonald
had asked the electors for " a doctor's
mandate," and before setting about his
healing task he reconstructed the ministry.
The most important recruits to the
Cabinet were Sir John Simon as Foreign
Secretary, and Mr. Walter Runciman as
President of the Board of Trade. Mr.
Neville Chamberlain succeeded Mr. Snowden as Chancellor of the Exchequer.

### Tariffs and the Ottawa Conference

THE first great task of the new ministry
was to introduce some kind of protection for British industry, all parties being
now convinced that tariffs in one form or
other were essential. Heavy, but temporary, duties were imposed on certain
classes of goods, pottery and woollens
among them, which were entering the
country in " abnormal " quantities, and a
little later the same medicine was applied
to horticultural imports. In 1932 a general
tariff of 10 per cent. was imposed on all
goods coming from foreign countries,
certain foodstuffs and raw materials being
the only exceptions. The tariff policy
adopted provided for the establishment of
a committee, under Sir George May, the
functions of which were to review the
duties imposed in 1931 and to impose
others in cases where the condition of an
industry required it.

All these changes had been made with the knowledge that a conference was to meet in the summer at Ottawa to deal with the whole question of imperial trade, and for the first time Great Britain's representatives went to such a gathering with unbound hands. They were no longer tied to the obsolete doctrine of free trade —more correctly " free imports without free trade." Seven Cabinet ministers crossed the ocean from London, and when they returned trade agreements had been made with all the Dominions, India included, save only the Irish Free State, and also with the protectorates and crown colonies represented by the Secretary of State for the Colonies.

The conclusions of the conference led to the resignation from the ministry of Sir Herbert Samuel and a few of his Liberal colleagues. The imposition of a general tariff early in the year had made Sir Herbert uneasy, and an " agreement to differ " on this matter had been reached, but this did not, so he thought, cover the arrangements made at Ottawa. His withdrawal was the necessary sequel, but fortunately, as two such leading Liberals as Sir John Simon and Mr. Runciman remained with the ministry, its national character was in no way impaired.

Before these ministers resigned the Government had won an unqualified success in the department of finance. Its term of office had been marked by a steady improvement in British credit, and in the summer of 1932 good use was made of the plethora of cheap money. The 5 per cent. war loan, amounting to £2,000,000,000, was converted into a 3½ per cent. one, and a little later there was a further conversion of £300,000,000 of debt. The saving was estimated at £38,000,000 a year.

### Ireland and India

THE Cabinet's occupations included the steady pursuance of a non-party policy in India and the handling of a sudden crisis in the Irish Free State. To take the latter incident first. For ten years, power had been in the hands of Mr. Cosgrave and his party, who had loyally carried out the terms of the treaty of 1921. But in 1932 a general election ended unfavourably for Mr. Cosgrave, and his opponents, under

Mr. de Valera, took office. The new president proceeded to carry out his avowed policy of separation from Great Britain. He took steps to abolish the oath of allegiance, and a little later refused to pay to Great Britain the interest on the money borrowed in order that the farmers might buy their land. The British Government at once shouldered this liability, as its guarantee required, and levied duties on Irish imports in order to provide the necessary funds. Mr. de Valera's reply was to impose duties on British goods entering the Free State.

During the year there were several attempts at a settlement, meetings of ministers taking place both in Dublin and in London. Arbitration was proposed, but the British Government adhered to its condition—unacceptable to Mr. de Valera —that membership of the proposed court should be confined to the Empire. The deadlock, therefore, continued, and the Free State, although represented, secured no advantages from the conference at Ottawa. The British Government occupied an unusually strong position when it confronted Mr. de Valera with the plain alternative. The Free State could not, at one and the same time, enjoy the benefits of the imperial connexion and evade its obligations and responsibilities.

In 1927, a royal commission, with Sir John Simon as chairman, had been appointed to report on the future government of India. Its report was issued in two parts in June, 1930, at a time when the country was seething with discontent. A powerful party had declared for independence, and Mr. Gandhi, for heading a movement of disobedience to the law, had been arrested. Business was paralysed in Bombay, where 23,000 persons were put in prison, and there were outbreaks at Peshawar and Sholapur. Economic depression was partly responsible for the unrest, and British trade suffered heavily from a boycott. Nevertheless, the British Government moved on its appointed path. Conferences were held both in England and in India, Mr. Gandhi visiting London for one of these, but on the main issue, the rival claims of Hindus and Moslems for representation, no agreement was reached. The Government therefore issued in 1932 an award fixing the membership of the provincial legislatures. After this the position improved somewhat and the conference that met in London in November 1932 seemed to have a better chance of success, but the agitation on behalf of the depressed classes continued to disturb the country.

## Germany

IN Germany, more than in most other countries, the economic crisis led to a serious political unrest. This was heralded by the appearance of a new party. Its members were called National Socialists—in short Nazis—and were led by an Austrian named Adolf Hitler. In 1930 they secured over 6,000,000 votes at the general election and became the second strongest party in the Reichstag. They were not, however, yet strong enough to overthrow the ministry under Dr. Brüning, the chancellor, who took office in March, but during his term of power their activities were a constant source of anxiety.

In 1932 there were several trials of strength between the new party and the old order. When the presidential election came round von Hindenburg was again elected, but Hitler secured several million votes, sufficient to make a second ballot necessary. In July, after the general election, the Nazis became the strongest party in the state, and a constitutional crisis took place. Acting by virtue of the extraordinary powers given to him under the constitution, the president ignored the parties in the Reichstag and made Franz von Papen, who had no following therein, chancellor, the government being carried on by decrees. By one of these the ministry in Prussia was dismissed and von Papen was entrusted with the control of affairs there, actions which were only partly upheld by the supreme court at Leipzig. This ministry of national concentration continued, however, to function without any pretence that it was supported by the electorate until November when, the Reichstag having been dissolved, there was another election. In this the Nazis again polled the largest number of votes, although 2,000,000 fewer than in June. The next strongest parties were the Socialists and the Communists. As a result von Papen resigned, his successor being General von Schleicher.

## The Ends of the Earth

IN 1931 a rising in Spain, differing little save in its results from many earlier ones, forced King Alphonso to leave the country and a republic was proclaimed. Under the president, Señor Zamora, autonomy was given to Catalonia and the Church and the large landholders lost their estates.

Almost at the other side of the globe a new state, Manchukuo, or Manchuria, was created, largely by the action of Japan. Just previously the League of Nations had sent out a commission under the earl of Lytton to report on the position there, and its conclusions raised questions of some gravity, for the new state remained in theory part of the republic of China.

Another event was the recognition of Irak as an independent state. In 1931 it ceased to be controlled by Great Britain under mandate, and was elected a member of the League of Nations. A brief revolution converted Siam from an absolute into a constitutional monarchy, but in Turkey Mustapha Kemal became more a dictator than ever. In Russia there was evidence that the elaborate plans of the Soviet authorities were not working smoothly, but there were industrial developments of considerable magnitude. The sweated products of the Russian workers were an unsettling influence on world markets and a menace to world stability South America did not escape the prevailing unrest. There were risings in Brazil and Chile during 1932. In the latter country a socialist regime was established and the great nitrate combine, known as "Cosach," was attacked as the prime cause of the country's troubles. On the other hand, as evidence of some continuity in human affairs, there were rejoicings in Italy in October to mark the completion of ten years of Fascist rule, and in Russia to celebrate the survival of fifteen years of a regime still more hostile to liberty.

In the United States three years of depression produced a remarkable result at the presidential election of November, 1932. The Democrats, who since the Civil War had only two presidents, won a striking victory when Franklin D. Roosevelt was elected by a majority of 6,700,000 over H. C. Hoover.

# INDEX

Figures in *italic* signify illustrations.